CONTEMPLATIVE LITERATURE

CONTEMPLATIVE LITERATURE

A Comparative Sourcebook on
Meditation and Contemplative Prayer

Edited by

Louis Komjathy

BL
625
.C663
2015

Cover Image: Labyrinth (dat. 13th c.) in Cathédrale Notre-Dame de Chartres (Chartres Cathedral) in Chartres, France. Photograph by Jeff Saward (Labyrinthos). Used with permission.

Published by State University of New York Press, Albany

© 2015 State University of New York

All rights reserved

Printed in the United States of America

No part of this book may be used or reproduced in any manner whatsoever without written permission. No part of this book may be stored in a retrieval system or transmitted in any form or by any means including electronic, electrostatic, magnetic tape, mechanical, photocopying, recording, or otherwise without the prior permission in writing of the publisher.

For information, contact State University of New York Press, Albany, NY
www.sunypress.edu

Production, Ryan Morris
Marketing, Michael Campochiaro

Library of Congress Cataloging-in-Publication Data

Contemplative literature : a comparative sourcebook on meditation and contemplative prayer / edited by Louis Komjathy.
    pages cm
Includes bibliographical references and index.
ISBN 978-1-4384-5705-5 (hardcover : alk. paper)
ISBN 978-1-4384-5706-2 (pbk : alk. paper)
ISBN 978-1-4384-5707-9 (e-book)
1. Contemplation.   2. Meditation.   3. Religions.   I. Komjathy, Louis, 1971– editor.

BL625.C663 2015
204'.3—dc23   2014031752

10 9 8 7 6 5 4 3 2 1

Contents

Illustrations — vii

Preface — xi

Acknowledgments — xiii

Abbreviations — xv

Part I
Approaching Contemplative Practive

Chapter 1. Approaching Contemplative Practice — 3
   Louis Komjathy

Chapter 2. Contemplative Traditions — 53
   Louis Komjathy

Part II
Contemplative Traditions

Chapter 3. Daoist Apophatic Meditation: Selections from the Classical Daoist Textual Corpus — 89
   Harold D. Roth

Chapter 4. Quaker Silent Prayer: *A Guide to True Peace* — 145
   Michael Birkel

Chapter 5. Jewish Kabbalah: Hayyim Vital's *Shaarei Kedusha* — 197
   Shaul Magid

Chapter 6. Southern Buddhist Meditation: The *Ānāpānasati Sutta* — 265
   Sarah Shaw

Chapter 7. Sufi Contemplation: 'Abdullah Shah's *Suluk-i Mujaddidiyya* — 307
   Arthur F. Buehler

Chapter 8. Eastern Orthodox Prayer: The *Rasskaz strannika*   359
    John Anthony McGuckin

Chapter 9. Mahāyāna Buddhist Visualization: The *Guan wuliang shoufo jing*   407
    Kenneth K. Tanaka

Chapter 10. Hindu Classical Yoga: Patañjali's *Yoga Sūtras*   457
    Edwin F. Bryant

Chapter 11. Roman Catholic Prayer: The *Novem modi orandi sancti Dominici*   503
    Paul Philibert

Chapter 12. Daoist Internal Alchemy: Liu Huayang's *Huiming jing*   547
    Louis Komjathy

Chapter 13. Therapeutic Meditation: Herbert Benson's *The Relaxation Response*   593
    Louis Komjathy

Chapter 14. Techniqueless Meditation: J. Krishnamurti's *This Light in Oneself*   645
    Constance A. Jones

Part III
Reapproaching Contemplative Practice

Chapter 15. Comparative Reflections   705
    Louis Komjathy

Appendix: Toward a Technical Glossary of Contemplative Studies   737

About the Contributors   753

Index   757

Illustrations

1.1.	Major Types of Contemplative Practice	6
1.2.	Roland Fischer's Cartography of Meditative and Mystical States	8
1.3.	Some Major Contemplative Practices with Global Distribution in the Modern World	8
1.4.	Contemplative Studies as Interdisciplinary Field	12
1.5.	Four Aspects of the Study of Religion	18
1.6.	Autonomic Nervous System	27
1.7.	Human Brain Anatomy	27
1.8.	Brain Regions and Associated Functions	29
1.9.	Rorschach Inkblot (Card V)	29
1.10.	fMRI of Carmelite Nuns	31
1.11.	Dimensions of (Religious) Praxis	38
2.1.	Interior of Korean Son (Zen) Buddhist Meditation Hall	56
2.2.	*Sema* of the Mevlevi Sufi Lineage	59
2.3.	Dimensions of (Religious) Praxis	61
2.4.	Comparative Chart of Contents of *Contemplative Literature*	76
3.1.	Western Han Statue of *Se*-zither Player	96
3.2.	Summary of Inner Cultivation	101
3.3.	Selections from the Classical Daoist Textual Corpus	102
4.1.	Quaker Meeting House of Brigflatts	155
4.2.	Interior of Brigflatts Meeting House	155
4.3.	Sections of *A Guide to True Peace*	159
5.1.	*Etz Hayyim* (Tree of Life)	207
5.2.	Categories and Associations of the Ten *Sephirot*	209
5.3.	Sections of the Received *Shaarei Kedusha*	212

5.4.	Letters of the Hebrew Alphabet	215
5.5.	Chart of Kabbalah Letter Permutations	264
6.1.	Statue of Seated Buddha	266
6.2.	Wall Mural Depicting the "Sermon at Deer Park"	270
6.3.	Some Key Dimensions of Southern Buddhist Meditation	276
7.1.	Mujaddidi Cosmology	316
7.2.	Subtle Centers and Associated Colors Utilized in Mujaddidi Visualization	317
7.3.	The Mujaddidi Path	320
7.4.	Sections of the *Suluk-i Mujaddidiyya*	321
8.1.	Nineteenth-Century Map of Russian Cities Where Pilgrims Purchased "Pilgrims' Booklets"	362
8.2.	Redaction Chart of the Received *Rasskaz strannika*	363
9.1.	Taima (Tall Hemp) Mandala	417
9.2.	Sixteen Visualizations according to the *Guanjing*	418
10.1.	Harappan Seal	459
10.2.	Classical Sāṃkhya and Yoga Psychology	464
10.3.	Yogic Consciousness	466
10.4.	Sections of the *Yoga Sūtras*	469
11.1.	Side Panel Depicting Saint Dominic	504
11.2.	Nine Ways of Praying according to the *Novem modi orandi sancti Dominici*	515
11.3.	First Way of Praying: Bowing	532
11.4.	Second Way of Praying: Full-Body Prostration	533
11.5.	Third Way of Praying: Self-Flagellation	534
11.6.	Fourth Way of Praying: Repeated Kneeling	535
11.7.	Fifth Way of Praying: Standing with Gestures of the Hands	537
11.8.	Sixth Way of Praying: Standing with Outstretched Arms	538
11.9.	Seventh Way of Praying: Standing with Upraised Body and Hands	540
11.10.	Eighth Way of Praying: Sitting and Reading	542
11.11.	Ninth Way of Praying: On a Journey	544
12.1.	Sections of the Received *Huiming jing*	563
12.2.	Eight Stages of Alchemical Transformation according to the *Huiming jing*	564
12.3.	Stage 1 of Alchemical Transformation: Cessation of Outflow	578

12.4.	Stage 2 of Alchemical Transformation: Six Phases of the Dharma Wheel	582
12.5.	Stage 3 of Alchemical Transformation: Governing and Conception Vessels	584
12.6.	Stage 4 of Alchemical Transformation: Embryo of the Dao	586
12.7.	Stage 5 of Alchemical Transformation: Sending Out the Fetus	588
12.8.	Stage 6 of Alchemical Transformation: Transformation Body	590
12.9.	Stage 7 of Alchemical Transformation: Facing the Wall	591
12.10.	Stage 8 of Alchemical Transformation: Disappearance into the Void	592
13.1.	Herbert Benson, circa 1996	596
13.2.	Sections of *The Relaxation Response*	614
13.3.	Lockhart Building	618
14.1.	J. Krishnamurti, circa 1924	649
14.2.	J. Krishnamurti, 1968	652
14.3.	Sections of *This Light in Oneself*	658
14.4.	J. Krishnamurti Speaking at Brockwood Park School	667
15.1.	Cruciform Posture	709
15.2.	United States Military Sniper	718
15.3.	Contemplative Studies as Interdisciplinary Field	724
15.4.	Labyrinth in Chartres Cathedral	727

Preface

This edited volume is the first theoretically informed and historically accurate comparative anthology of primary texts on contemplative practice. Written by international experts on the respective texts and corresponding traditions, *Contemplative Literature: A Comparative Sourcebook on Meditation and Contemplative Prayer* provides introductions to and primary sources on contemplative practice from various religious traditions. The book begins with two introductory chapters on interpretive issues in the emerging interdisciplinary field of contemplative studies, which involves research and education on contemplative practice and contemplative experience, and on contemplative traditions, the strains of religious traditions that emphasize contemplative practice. This is followed by the twelve chapters that form the core of the book. These chapters cover classical Daoist apophatic meditation, Quaker silent prayer, Jewish Kabbalah, Southern Buddhist meditation, Sufi contemplation, Eastern Orthodox prayer, Pure Land Buddhist visualization, Hindu classical Yoga, Dominican Catholic prayer, Daoist internal alchemy, modern therapeutic meditation, and techniqueless meditation. Each chapter follows a standardized six-part format that covers biographical and historical context; associated religious tradition and textual corpus; religious and soteriological system, including the distinctive method of contemplative practice; textual survey of primary text; legacy and influence; as well as interpretive issues related to the comparative study of contemplative practice and contemplative experience. Each introduction is followed by annotated translations and selections from the associated texts on contemplative practice. Readers will thus gain not only a nuanced understanding of important works of contemplative literature but also resources for understanding contemplative practice and contemplative experience from a comparative and cross-cultural perspective.

Acknowledgments

The authors gratefully acknowledge the following individuals and publishers for permission to reprint illustrations and primary texts in this book. Acknowledgments are also included in each chapter. When permissions are not noted, figures and translations are either original work or within the public domain.

Illustrations

Cover and figure 15.4, Labyrinth in Chartres Cathedral. Photography by Jeff Saward, Labyrinthos.

Figure 1.2, Roland Fischer's Cartography of Meditative and Mystical States, in Roland Fischer, "A Cartography of the Ecstatic and Meditative States," *Science* 174.4012 (1971): 879–904, courtesy of the American Association for the Advancement of Science.

Figure 1.5, Four Aspects of the Study of Religion, from Jensine Andresen and Robert K. C. Forman, eds., *Cognitive Models and Spiritual Maps: Interdisciplinary Explorations of Religious Experience* (Bowling Green: Imprint Academic, 2000), courtesy of Imprint Academic.

Figure 1.7, Human Brain Anatomy, from Marlene Oscar-Berman and Ksenija Marinkovic, "Alcoholism and the Brain: An Overview," National Institute of Alcohol Abuse and Alcoholism, http://pubs.niaaa.nih.gov/publications/arh27-2/125-133.htm, courtesy of Marlene Oscar-Berman.

Figure 1.10, fMRI of Carmelite Nuns, from Mario Beauregard and Vincent Paquette, "Neural Correlates of a Mystical Experience in Carmelite Nuns," *Neuroscience Letters* 405 (2006): 186–90.

Figure 2.1, Interior of Korean Son (Zen) Buddhist Meditation Hall, courtesy of the Jogye Order of Korean Buddhism.

Figure 2.2, *Sema* of Mevlevi Sufi Lineage, courtesy of the International Mevlana Foundation.

Figure 3.1, Western Han Statue of *Se*-zither Player, courtesy of Fitzwilliam Museum Images.

Figures 4.1 and 4.2, Quaker Meeting House of Brigflatts and Interior of Brigflatts Meeting House, courtesy of Warden, Brigflatts FMH.

Figure 6.1, Statue of Seated Buddha, Gal Vihara, Polonnaruwa, Sri Lanka, photo by Bernard Gagnon, Wikimedia Commons.

Figure 6.2, Wall Mural Depicting the "Sermon at Deer Park," Dambulla cave temple, Sri Lanka, photo by Bernard Gagnon, Wikimedia Commons.

Figure 7.3, The Mujaddidi Path, by and courtesy of Shamin Homayun.

Figure 8.1, Nineteenth-Century Map of Russian Cities Where Pilgrims Purchased "Pilgrims' Booklets," *Soobshcheniia Imperatorskago Pravoslavnago Palestinskago Obshchestva* 12 (1902). Courtesy of Slavonic Library, University of Helsinki.

Figure 9.1, Taima (Tall Hemp) Mandala, late Kamakura period (1185–1333), hanging scroll consisting of ink, color, and gold on silk, courtesy of Metropolitan Museum of Art, New York, NY.

Figure 10.1, Harappan Seal, copyright J. M. Kenoyer/Harappa.com, courtesy Department of Archaeology and Museums, Government of Pakistan.

Figure 10.2, Classical Sāṁkhya and Yoga Psychology, from Gerald James Larson, *Classical Sāṁkhya* (Delhi: Motilal Banarsidass, 1979), courtesy of Motilal Banarsidass.

Figure 11.1, Side Panel Depicting Saint Dominic, courtesy of Galleria Nazionale dell'Umbria, Perugia.

Figures 11.3–11.11, Nine Ways of Praying according to the *Novem modi orandi sancti Dominici*, reproduced by permission of Biblioteca Apostolica Vaticana, with all rights reserved.

Figure 13.1, Herbert Benson, circa 1996, courtesy of Margaret Kois Photography.

Figures 14.2 and 14.4, J. Krishnamurti, 1968 and J. Krishnamurti Speaking at Brockwood Park School, 1972, by Mark Edwards, copyright Krishnamurti Foundation Trust. Figure 14.1 is in the public domain.

Figure 15.2, United States Military Sniper, photographer unknown, courtesy of StockFreeImages.com.

Primary Texts

Chapter 3, translations from the *Neiye* (Inward Training) and *Huainanzi* (Book of the Huainan Masters) appear with permission from Columbia University Press: Harold D. Roth, *Original Tao*, copyright 1999 Columbia University Press; John S. Major, Sarah A. Queen, Andrew Seth Meyer, and Harold D. Roth, *The Huainanzi*, copyright 2010 Columbia University Press.

Chapter 9, translation of the *Guan wuliang shoufo jing* originally appeared in Hisao Inagaki, *The Three Pure Land Sutras* (Berkeley: Numata Center for Buddhist Translation and Research, 1995) and is used with the permission of the Bukkyō Dendō Kyōkai (Society for the Promotion of Buddhism; BDK) and the Numata Center for Buddhist Translation and Research.

Chapter 10, "Translation of Sutras" originally appeared in Edwin F. Bryant, *The Yoga Sūtras of Patañjali: A New Edition, Translation and Commentary* (New York: North Point Press, 2009) and is reprinted with permission of North Point Press, a division of Farrar, Straus and Giroux, LLC.

Chapter 13, excerpts from *The Relaxation Response*, by Herbert Benson, MD, with Miriam Z. Klipper (New York: William Morrow and Company, 1975) are reprinted with permission of HarperCollins Publishers.

Chapter 14, selections from J. Krishnamurti, *This Light in Oneself: True Meditation*, copyright 1996 by Krishnamurti Foundation Trust, Ltd., are reprinted by arrangement with The Permissions Company, Inc., on behalf of Shambhala Publications, Boston, Massachusetts.

Abbreviations

abbr.	abbreviated
Ar.	Arabic
BCE	Before the Common Era
bk.	book
c.	century
ca.	circa
CE	Common Era
ch.	chapter
Chn.	Chinese
dat.	dated
disc.	discovered
d.u.	dates unknown
fl.	flourished
Fr.	French
Grk.	Greek
Heb.	Hebrew
Jpn.	Japanese
j.	*juan*
Kor.	Korean
Lat.	Latin
lit.	literally
no.	number
p.	page
par.	paragraph
Per.	Persian
pers. comm.	personal communication
pl.	plural
r.	reigned
Rus.	Russian
sec.	section
sing.	singular
Skt.	Sanskrit
Viet.	Vietnamese
vol.	volume

Part I

Approaching Contemplative Practice

Chapter 1

Approaching Contemplative Practice

Louis Komjathy

Contemplative practice refers to various approaches, disciplines, and methods for developing attentiveness, awareness, compassion, concentration, presence, wisdom, and the like. Often the purview of ascetics and monastics, contemplative practice in a modern context has become embraced by people of every possible persuasion and social location. There are now contemplatives and contemplative communities that are both rooted in and independent of more encompassing religious traditions. Informed by the academic study of religion, with particular attention to contemplative practice and contemplative experience, this book is a comparative sourcebook on meditation and contemplative prayer. In using these categories, the volume draws attention, albeit somewhat obliquely, to the diverse tradition-specific technical terms approximated by "contemplative practice." In the pages that follow, we explore and expound the nuances of tradition-based and religiously-committed contemplative practice. By engaging contemplative literature, the technical writings on contemplative practice, and by understanding contemplative traditions, the contemplative strains or dimensions of religious traditions, we encounter important insights into not only the transformative effects of dedicated and prolonged practice but also lived religiosity as expressed in contemplative ways of life. One might, in turn, reflect on the characteristics of a "contemplative approach" to being and aliveness.

There are a variety of ways to approach contemplative practice and contemplative experience. In this chapter, I provide a representative overview of theoretical and methodological issues in the emerging, interdisciplinary field of contemplative studies, especially from the perspective of the comparative, cross-cultural, and multidisciplinary study of religion. In the next chapter, I examine some tradition-based issues and perspectives. This chapter in turn covers "contemplative practice" as a comparative category and contemplative studies as an emerging interdisciplinary academic field. With respect to the latter, I give particular attention to a Contextualist approach as well as reflect on the contributions and limitations of empirical approaches, especially concerning the relative merits of neuroscience and neuroimaging technologies. Finally, I identify and discuss key issues in the study and practice of religiously-committed and tradition-based contemplative practice and contemplative experience.

Contemplative Practice

"Contemplative practice" is a more-encompassing comparative category, with some rough equivalence to "meditation."[1] However, unlike "meditation," which sometimes implies seated postures and which is often reduced to Buddhist meditation, "contemplative practice" functions as a larger umbrella category. In terms of religious traditions, it encompasses meditation and contemplative prayer. As such, it challenges one to investigate religious practice from a nuanced and comprehensive perspective; it also requires reflection on the heuristic value and relationship among "meditation," "prayer," and "ritual," among other comparative categories. Moreover, as Jensine Andresen asks, "Heuristically, is it more useful to distinguish categories such as 'meditation' and 'prayer' in terms of method, or in terms of goal?" (2000, 20). At the same time, there are "secular" forms of contemplative practice, and interdisciplinary academic programs are being formed that include art, dance, movement awareness, music, photography, theater, and so forth. Possible connective strands or family resemblances include attentiveness, awareness, interiority, presence, silence, transformation, and a deepened sense of meaning and purpose (cf. Roth 2006, 1789, 1793). From my perspective, definitional parameters should be explored and discussed rather than rigidly defined.

"Contemplative practice" thus encompasses meditation and certain forms of prayer. Here some confusion may arise because "prayer" is often equated with petitionary or penitential forms and because the meaning of "meditation" and "contemplation" differs according to context (see also Underwood 2005). It is important to recognize that there are many forms of prayer, including petition, invocation, thanksgiving (praise or adoration), dedication, supplication, intercession, confession, penitence, and benediction (Gill 2005, 7367–68; see also Heiler 1932; Phillips 1965). Although fluid definitionally as a comparative category, "prayer" may be defined in terms of its devotional, relational, and communicative characteristics. However, these may also be present in contemplative practice, so prayer may become meditation and meditation may become prayer. As one member of a local Seattle mosque told me concerning Islamic prayer, "If Salat does not involve inner silence and awareness of Allah's presence, it is not true Salat." However, in other forms of contemplative practice, subject-object distinctions are not utilized or disappear. For example, in Daoist apophatic meditation and Sōtō Zen meditation, the practitioner is that which might be worshipped or given devotion in dualistic prayer.

In religious studies, "meditation" serves as a comparative category, usually without a strict definition; in the Roman Catholic and Eastern Orthodox churches, "meditation" and "contemplation" have more technical meanings. Etymologically speaking, "meditation" and "contemplation" relate to the Latin *meditatio* (to think over or to consider) and *contemplatio* (to look at or to observe), respectively. In Catholic monastic contexts and Catholic-influenced forms of contemplative practice, the terms most often relate to types of prayer, with prayer having four aspects or stages: (1) prayerful or holy reading (*lectio divina*); (2) meditation or reflection on specific topics (*meditatio*); (3) an inward, silent, or vocal response to God's message or presence (*oratio*); and (4) maintaining silent awareness of God (*contemplatio*). Christian "contemplative prayer" is thus roughly synonymous with "meditation" as utilized as a comparative category. "Contemplative practice" thus includes meditation and contemplative prayer more strictly defined.[2]

In terms of the comparative study of religion and the scientific study of meditation,[3] various attempts have been made to define meditation, especially through reflection on Buddhist practices. Some theoretically informed, comparative, and nuanced definitions include the following:

> Using attentional mechanisms as the basis for the definition, we may state that *meditation refers to a family of techniques which have in common a conscious attempt to focus attention in a nonanalytical way and an attempt not to dwell on discursive, ruminating thought.* (Shapiro and Walsh 1984, 6; italics in original)

> Meditation may be conceptualized as a process of attentional restructuring wherein the mind can be trained both in concentration, the ability to rest undisturbed on a single object, and in mindfulness, the ability to observe its own moment-to-moment nature, to pay attention undistractedly to a series of changing objects. This perceptual retraining allows a finely honed investigation of the rapidly changing self-concepts that perpetuate the sense of self. (Epstein and Lieff 1986, 58)

> Perhaps, then, it is not too bold to claim that in its broadest sense, meditation is associated with the process of increasing self-awareness. . . . A caveat should be raised, however. Although research on meditation may necessitate a working definition of sorts, attempts to craft a precise definition of meditation threaten to limit the phenomena artificially and to obscure the subtlest nuances of its practice. . . . According to the discursive/non-discursive schema [advocated in this chapter], the crucial difference between meditation and prayer is that the former is non-discursive while the latter is discursive. (Andresen 2000, 21)

Reservations concerning the relative merit of definitions have also been expressed:

> In the experimental [quantitative scientific] literature, meditation has many meanings. It has been defined in terms of certain physiological variables, for example, as a certain meditation pattern, measured by EEG; by certain changes in arousal; by more specific autonomic variables; and by a certain pattern of muscular tensions/relaxation. Others have defined meditation more in terms of attention deployment, related cognitive control mechanisms, or ego control mechanisms. Still others have defined meditation more as a process of therapy, with resultant significant changes in affective and trait variables.
>
> There is little agreement on: how to define meditation, what should be measured, and what the most useful measuring instruments may be. Research on meditation is still in an embryonic state. No doubt, the slow process of data accretion will advance our knowledge of meditation so that we may better know what sort of data to collect. Yet, the present state of meditation research is largely wasteful; some consensual criteria must be used to establish which kinds of data are most useful to collect. The two most fundamental questions in meditation research should be: (a) What are the most important variables of meditation and how may they be operationally defined and

measured? (b) How are these variables related to each other? (Brown 1977, 236–37; cf. Murphy et al. 1999, 2)

Each of these definitions provides some insight into the defining characteristics of "meditation" as a comparative category. They are also informed by concentration on specific religious traditions and methods: Southern Buddhist Vipassanā in the case of Shapiro and Tibetan Buddhist meditation in the case of Andresen. One notices some general agreement, specifically with respect to developing attention and awareness. However, the theoretical move to emphasize "nonanalytical" or "nondiscursive" forms of consciousness seems problematic. If one adheres to a more inclusive and comprehensive approach to the study of contemplative practice, then certain methods appear to develop attention and awareness through analytical and discursive faculties. Some examples include Hindu mantric practices, the Ignatian spiritual exercises and Examen, as well as early Pure Land visualization (see ch. 2 herein).

There is thus diversity within religious traditions and within the academic study of meditation in establishing definitional parameters for prayer, meditation, and contemplative practice. As mentioned, my own approach attempts to be more phenomenological and inclusive. It aims to identify types of practices with strong family resemblances. The latter include seated postures, attentiveness, awareness, interiority, presence, silence, transformation, and a deepened sense of meaning and purpose. In terms of religious studies, one might also include theological and soteriological concerns, which are discussed later.

With respect to understanding the apparent diversity of contemplative practice, an interpretive framework based on cartographies and typologies may be helpful. Based on my own comparative research and teaching, I would identify at least the following types of contemplative practices.[4] Alchemical methods, which include certain Tantric and Yogic practices, are complex physiological techniques, usually involving stage-based training aimed at self-transformation and/or divinization.

1. Alchemical	13. Mantic
2. Apophatic	14. Mantric
3. Attentional	15. Mediumistic
4. Communal	16. Mystical
5. Concentrative	17. Quietistic
6. Devotional	18. Respiratory
7. Dualistic	19. Secular
8. Ecstatic	20. Solitary
9. Enstatic	21. Therapeutic
10. Ergotropic	22. Trophotropic
11. Kataphatic	23. Unitive
12. Kinesthetic	24. Visualization[6]

Figure 1.1. Major Types of Contemplative Practice

Apophatic techniques emphasize nonconceptual and contentless states of consciousness, often with an implied skepticism concerning linguistic and intellectual categories. Attentional (mindfulness) methods emphasize open awareness or observation of phenomena without discrimination. Communal techniques are those practiced by a group or community within a communal framework. Concentrative practices emphasize focused consciousness; they may be "with support" (objects as aides) or "without support" (objectless). Devotional techniques involve affective adoration of or focus on a specific person or object. Dualistic practices emphasize an unbridgeable distinction between the adherent and the sacred; they tend to conceptualize practice in terms of relationships. Ecstatic techniques are those through which practitioners go beyond or outside of themselves; this usually involves higher levels of physiological activity (ergotropic) and assumes a transcendent view of the sacred. In contrast, enstatic methods are those through which practitioners go inward and gain an expanded sense of interior space; this usually involves lower levels of physiological activity (trophotropic) and assumes an immanent view of the sacred.[5] Ergotropic methods involve hyper-arousal; these are techniques characterized by high levels of physiological activity, with different senses activated in different types of ergotropic contemplative practices. Kataphatic practices emphasize conceptual and content-based states of consciousness, which usually include optimism concerning linguistic and intellectual categories. Kinesthetic methods involve physical movement. Mantic techniques are characterized by a divinational, magical, or prophetic dimension; they may involve invocations and ritual. Mantric practices utilize a sound, syllable, or phrase that are usually considered sacred or efficacious. Some *mantra*-based techniques consider the sacred as vibratory in nature, and mantric methods may be invocational, concentrative, petitional, reverential, and so forth. Mediumistic techniques are those through which adherents enter altered states wherein a god or spirit takes possession of them (voluntary possession); they involve divine communication or channeling. Mystical practices emphasize mystical experience, or experience of the sacred as defined by the individual practitioner or community. Quietistic techniques are characterized by nonconceptual, contentless awareness, with silence, stillness, and emptiness being primary. Respiratory methods focus on inhalation and exhalation or utilize breath-control techniques; there is awareness of respiration or conscious patterning of the breath. Secular forms are nonreligious practices, which are usually appropriated from religious traditions, purged of religious content, and reconceptualized according to modern materialistic, medicalized, and/or psychologized worldviews (secularized and domesticated). They are often framed in terms of a "science"/"religion" distinction, with efficacy defined in terms of quantitative and technological measurements. Solitary techniques are practiced by an individual in solitude or isolation. Therapeutic methods emphasize health benefits, and they may involve health maintenance or recovery. The latter are remedial; they are meant to heal or alleviate discomfort. Trophotropic practices involve hyperquiescence/hypoarousal; these are techniques characterized by low levels of physiological activity, with a strong deemphasis on sensory, emotional, and intellectual engagement. Unitive practices emphasize a distinction between the adherent and the sacred that may be transcended or overcome through practice; the culmination is complete identification or union of the practitioner with the sacred. Finally, visualization methods are imaginative exercises involving complex visual content. The perceptive reader will note that these typologies are not cognates. Some emphasize psychological dimensions, while others emphasize conceptual, physiological, or social ones. The point is to map contemplative practice and contemplative experience in as comprehensive, nuanced, and inclusive way as possible.

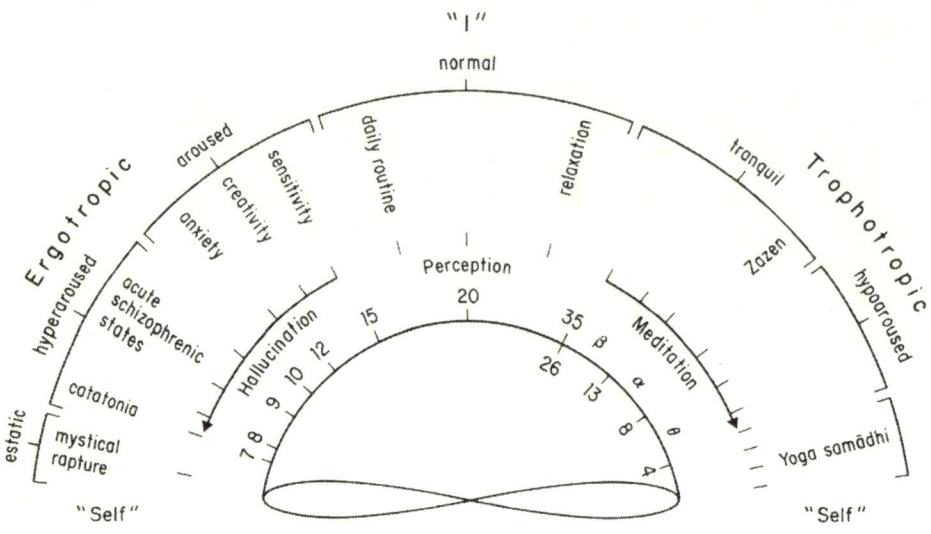

Figure 1.2. Roland Fischer's Cartography of Meditative and Mystical States[6]
Source: Fischer 1971.

Some of these interpretive categories also form dyads or pairs: apophatic/kataphatic, communal/solitary, ecstatic/enstatic, ergotropic/trophotropic, and so forth. However, many fully developed contemplative systems may alternate between apparently exclusive or antithetical tendencies. There is also overlap among categories. For example, devotional practices tend to be dualistic, ergotropic, and kataphatic, while apophatic techniques tend to be quietistic, trophotropic, and unitive.

Centering Prayer (Christianity)	Quaker prayer (Christianity)
Deity yoga (Buddhism)	Relaxation Response (Mind-Body Medicine)
Ignatian prayer (Christianity)	Remembrance (Islam)
Internal alchemy (Daoism)	Teresian prayer (Christianity)
Kirtan (Hinduism)	Transcendental Meditation™ (TM™) (Hinduism)
Kriya Yoga (Hinduism)	Vipassanā (Buddhism)
Mindfulness-Based Stress Reduction (MBSR) (Mind-Body Medicine)	Zazen (Buddhism)

Figure 1.3. Some Major Contemplative Practices with Global Distribution in the Modern World

We may, in turn, consider some specific examples. In Sōtō Zen practice, most frequently referred to as "silent illumination" (Chn.: *mozhao*) or "just sitting" (Jpn.: *shikan taza*), the practitioner aims to enter a state of silence and emptiness. This practice is nonconceptual and contentless. In terms of the aforementioned categories, it is apophatic, quietistic, trophotropic, and possibly unitive. It may be solitary and/or communal. In contrast, Dominican prayer, as expressed in the *Novem modi orandi sancti Dominici* (Nine Ways of Prayer of Saint Dominic; see ch. 11 herein), involves various exercises during which the contemplative identifies with Jesus Christ. It is devotional, dualistic, ergotropic, kinesthetic, and kataphatic. Finally, the Relaxation Response (see ch. 13 herein), a secularized and medicalized version of Transcendental Meditation™ (TM™), involves focusing one's attention on a chosen word or phrase. It is attentional, concentrative, mantric, secular, and therapeutic.

As this cartography indicates, there is often overlap between "contemplative practice" and "contemplative experience" (see ch. 2 herein). Strictly speaking, we may define the latter as types of experiences that occur during contemplative practice, especially experiences deemed relevant, significant, or efficacious by the practitioner or community. In the case of contemplative practice, there is often a strong emphasis on associated experiences. For example, if one practices apophatic meditation, one should presumably enter a trophotropic state. Moreover, here one finds a potential overlap with other forms of "religious experience," especially mystical experience. As discussed later and in the next chapter, the relationship between contemplative practices and mystical experience is a complex one, and one that varies depending on specific practitioners, communities, and traditions. Some emphasize the importance of mystical experience, at least as byproducts and/or indicators of successful training, while others dismiss any concern for "extraordinary experiences" as distraction.

Contemplative Studies

Contemplative studies is an emerging interdisciplinary field. It is closely associated with other fields of inquiry such as consciousness studies, mysticism studies, neuroscience, psychology, religious studies, and so forth. Contemplative studies provides a framework for the investigation of contemplative practice and contemplative experience,[7] considered inclusively and comprehensively, as well as for the application of contemplative practice to academic life and university culture. The latter includes the possible contribution of "contemplative pedagogy" to teaching and learning.

The field of contemplative studies is in an embryonic or formative phase, and its parameters are still being established. One approach emphasizes the development of awareness or mindfulness in each and every area of inquiry, including teaching and learning within an academic community. From this perspective, contemplative practice might contain art, dance, literature, movement awareness, music, theater, and so forth.[8] A more narrowly focused and religious studies–oriented approach seeks to map the entire breadth and depth of contemplative practice and contemplative experience as documented within and transmitted by religious adherents and communities. In either case, contemplative studies recognizes the importance of both third-person and critical first-person approaches; it makes space for direct personal experience with specific forms of practice. In this way, it challenges the denial of embodied experience within academic discourse and brings the issue of religious adherence in religious studies into high relief. Can one fully understand contemplative practice without practicing? Can one fully understand Hindu contemplative practice without being rooted in a Hindu worldview?

As an emerging field, contemplative studies, specifically expressed as a lived commitment to contemplative practice and its application to daily life, began with a series of interreligious conferences.[9] Some of these events included Traditional Modes of Contemplation and Action (Rothko Chapel; February 27, 1971; Ibish and Marculescu 1977), The Gethsemani Encounter (Abbey of Gethsemani; July 22–26, 1996; Mitchell and Wiseman 2003), and Purity of Heart and Contemplation Symposium (Camaldoli Hermitage; June 25–July 1, 2000; Barnhart and Wong 2001). These gatherings brought adherents together to explore contemplative practice from a religiously-committed and lived perspective. At the same time, more scientifically inclined and quantitative researchers began exploring meditation in terms of physiology, psychology, and eventually consciousness studies and neuroscience. Much of that early research focused on Vipassanā and Transcendental Meditation (TM), while more contemporary research privileges Tibetan Buddhism. The latter is partially the result of the Dalai Lama's support and participation. This type of research and the application of contemplative practice to contemporary social problems led to the establishment of various independent organizations, including the Fetzer Institute (1962), Mind and Life Institute (MLI; 1990), Center for Contemplative Mind in Society (CMind; 1991)—including its Association for Contemplative Mind in Higher Education (ACMHE)—and Santa Barbara Institute for Consciousness Studies (SBICS; 2003), among others.[10] These organizations frequently sponsor independent conferences on meditation and consciousness as well as the relevance of such research to contemporary social problems. Interestingly, there has also been a more recent movement to introduce contemplative practice into university education, to develop a contemplative pedagogy, and to institute contemplative studies programs. Among the latter, Brown University, California Institute of Integral Studies, Emory University, Naropa University, Rice University, University of Michigan, University of Redlands, and University of Virginia are most prominent. The growing subfield of contemplative pedagogy has been particularly well documented in a variety of recent publications: "Contemplative Studies: Prospects for a New Field" (Roth 2006), *The Heart of Learning* (Glazer 1999), *Contemplative Teaching and Learning* (*New Directions for Community Colleges* 151 [Fall 2010]), *Meditation and the Classroom: Contemplative Pedagogy in Religious Studies* (Simmer-Brown and Grace 2011), *Contemplative Studies in Higher Education* (*New Directions for Teaching and Learning* 134 [Summer 2013]), and the special issue of *Buddhist-Christian Studies* 33 (2013).[11]

Returning to contemplative studies as a field, Harold Roth, Director of the interdisciplinary Contemplative Studies Initiative at Brown University, describes it as follows:

> A new field of academic endeavor devoted to the critical study of contemplative states of experience is developing in North America. It focuses on the many ways human beings have found, across cultures and across time, to concentrate, broaden and deepen conscious awareness. Contemplative studies is the rubric under which this research and teaching can be organized. In the field of contemplative studies we attempt to:
>
> 1. *Identify the varieties of contemplative experiences of which human beings are capable;*
>
> 2. *Find meaningful scientific explanations for them;*

3. Cultivate first-person knowledge of them;

4. Critically access their nature and significance.

That is, we study the underlying philosophy, psychology and phenomenology of human contemplative experience through a combination of traditional third-person approaches and more innovative, critical first-person approaches. In other words, we study contemplative experience from the following perspectives:

1. Science, particularly psychology, neuroscience, cognitive science and clinical medicine;

2. The humanities, exploring the contemplative dimensions of literature, philosophy and religion;

3. The creative arts, focusing on the study of the role of contemplation in both the creation and the appreciation of the visual and fine arts, creative writing and in the various performing arts of dance, drama and music. (Roth 2008, 19–20, italics in original; see also Roth 2006, especially 1794)

Here one notices a number of distinctive parameters. First, Roth emphasizes "contemplative experience" over "contemplative practice." Perhaps the former presupposes the latter, but there is an interpretive issue here, which parallels earlier academic studies of mysticism. The emphasis on contemplative experience might simply suggest that it involves an experiential understanding and internal investigation of contemplative practice. Second, Roth, like others in contemplative studies (see, e.g., De Wit 1991; Varela and Shear 1999; Ferrer and Sherman 2008; Thompson 2010), includes "critical first-person approaches." This means that disciplined subjective experience, based in systematic investigation and reflectivity, is legitimate. Such a theoretical stance challenges the "taboo of subjectivity" at work in much of academic discourse (see Wallace 2000)[12] and potentially makes space for autobiographical accounts as primary source material and evidential support. The latter has also played a primary role in recent studies of mystical experience (see, e.g., Forman 1999, 20; Paper 2004, 1–3). However, Roth, like many in religious studies, hesitates to include what I would call "critical adherent perspectives" (Roth's "committed first-person perspectives" [2006, 1793]).[13] This carryover from Enlightenment sensibilities and positivistic science, including the problematic notion of the disinterested and "objective" observer, is challenged not only by religious adherence but also by postmodernism and postcolonialism. Let me be clear: I do not advocate and do not support apologetics, confessionalism, dogmatism, evangelism, indoctrination, or proselytization in academia. Rather, what I am suggesting is that the tendency to objectify "the other" should be inhibited (cf. Roth 2008). The idea that religious adherents cannot be committed, reflective, and open is outdated and does not hold up to critical scrutiny. I am not advocating privileging the adherent either. My perspective is that the contemporary American—and arguably global—context of religious pluralism and multiculturalism requires the serious researcher of religion to include adherent voices in the study, teaching, and learning of religious traditions. To do otherwise is to become a dogmatist oneself, most likely under the implied hegemony of secular materialism and scientific reductionism.[14]

These comments of course express and evidence a specific social and institutional locatedness. As a professor at a church-affiliated ("sectarian") university, I can make space for theological and adherent perspectives without, presumably, jeopardizing my power, authority, or livelihood. This is not the case for others involved in religious studies, especially those at secular liberal arts and public research universities. In any case, contemplative studies involves interdisciplinary, cross-cultural, and multiperspectval commitments. While neuroscience, sometimes under the guise of "contemplative science," is currently being privileged, contemplative studies actually encompasses various theoretical and methodological approaches. In this way, it might parallel other subfields of religious studies. Again, this is not to reduce contemplative practice to religiously-committed forms. At the same time and as discussed later, it challenges those of us in religious studies to investigate the ways in which contemplative practice expresses and is located in specific religious communities and traditions.

Concerning the present volume and the study of religiously-committed forms of contemplative practice, we may identify a variety of interpretive approaches, namely, anthropological, comparative, experiential/experimental, historical, textual, philosophical, theological, as well as psychological and neuroscientific (cf. McGinn 1991, 265–343; Komjathy 2012). The most developed of these include comparative, historical, textual, and neuroscientific approaches, and there is, of course, overlap. On the most basic level, a comparative approach investigates the similarities and differences among contemplative practices. It also includes developing more comprehensive interpretive frameworks, like the cartography presented earlier (see fig. 1.1). From my perspective, this approach utilizes

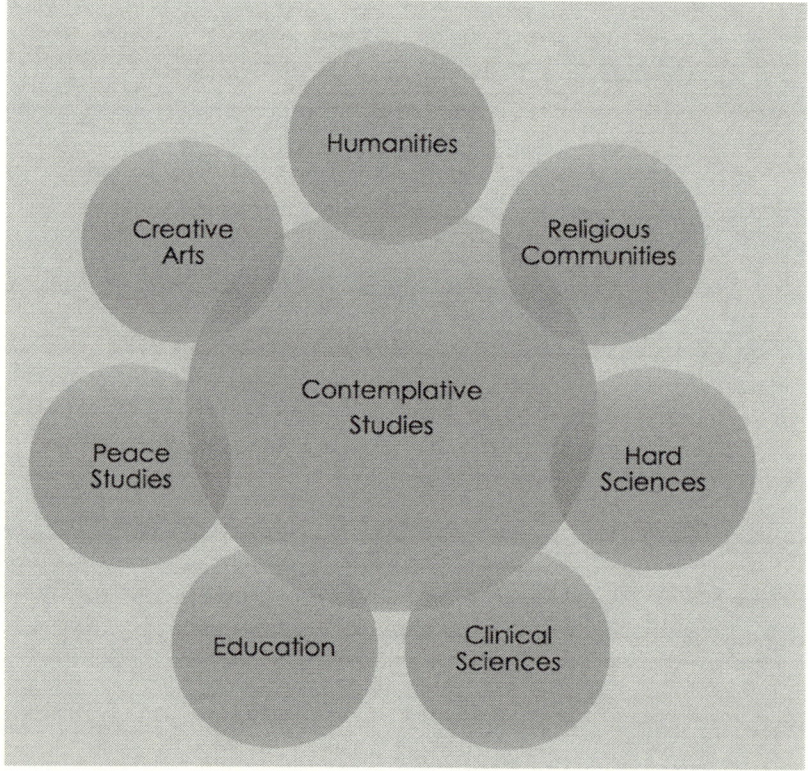

Figure 1.4. Contemplative Studies as Interdisciplinary Field

theoretical and methodological insights derived from and applicable to religious studies. Historical approaches emphasize cultural, historical, religious, and social contexts. An example would be to locate the *Novem modi orandi sancti Dominici* (Nine Ways of Prayer of Saint Dominic) within medieval Spain, Roman Catholicism, and the emerging Order of Preachers. This would include biographical information on Domingo de Guzmán Garcés (St. Dominic, 1170–1221), the founder of the Order of Preachers (Dominicans). A textual approach employs close textual analysis to reconstruct and interpret contemplative practice. At the most advanced levels, it involves annotated translation of primary sources. The present volume primarily utilizes a combination of comparative, historical, and textual approaches.

Neuroscientific approaches most frequently utilize modern neuroimaging technology to map the human brain and corresponding states of consciousness. In a parallel fashion, psychological approaches frame the study of contemplative practice in terms of emotional, intellectual, and, at times, spiritual development. Humanistic and transpersonal psychologies have been especially interested in meditation. One can imagine a multitude of anthropological approaches. More conventionally, fieldwork could be conducted on specific contemplatives and contemplative communities; here there is overlap with the study of asceticism and monasticism. One might also engage in participant-observation, wherein one would live and practice within a specific contemplative context. In this way, it might overlap with an experiential approach, in which one gains direct experience of the contemplative practice under consideration. A philosophical approach would identify and debate major issues related to contemplative practice and contemplative experience; this type of approach might parallel concerns over epistemology expressed in earlier studies of mysticism. It might fall into the category of the "philosophy of religion," specifically the "philosophy of religious practice" (see, e.g., Schilbrack 2004). Given the emergence of neuroscience as an academic discipline, psychological and philosophical positions could be evaluated through certain empirical and experimental studies. Finally, a theological approach would seek to understand the ways in which contemplative practice might inform and clarify communion with the sacred. In this way, one might see a connection between contemplative studies and spirituality as an academic discipline. From a religiously-committed perspective, one could argue that theology informs contemplative practice and contemplative practice embodies theology. Perhaps contemplation is applied theology and theology is theoretical contemplation.[15]

In the following pages, I provide specific details on comparative, historical, textual, psychological, and neuroscientific approaches to contemplative studies. I also discuss major interpretive issues in contemplative studies, in the interdisciplinary study of contemplative practice and contemplative experience, as I understand them.

Context and Locatedness

One might begin thinking about contemplative practice by shifting the frame slightly toward the study of mysticism. I offer this perspective neither to equate contemplative practice with mystical experience nor to suggest any necessary connection between the phenomena (see further on).[16] Rather, it is because one often finds a similar naïveté in contemplative studies as was expressed in early studies of mysticism, and because few writers on contemplative practice seem familiar with parallel debates and resulting insights from research on mysticism.

Early studies of and philosophical views concerning mystical experience evidence various underlying unquestioned assumptions and biased perspectives. Among these, one of the most prominent and influential was a commitment to Perennial Philosophy, or the belief that the diversity of religions simply represents different interpretations of the same, ultimate reality. Major early proponents of Perennial Philosophy include Aldous Huxley (1894–1963), Huston Smith (b. 1919), and Frithjof Schuon (1907–1998). This view remains central outside of elite academic discourse communities, especially among popular writers, nonspecialists, and the larger public. One may summarize Perennial Philosophy as follows: the "divine" is unitary in nature (monotheism or monism); consciousness is unmediated; and mystical experience is the experience of the same reality with different *interpretations* superimposed onto that reality. These views have been challenged from various theoretical positions, including consciousness studies, historicism, literary studies, neuroscience, philosophy, psychology, and theology (see, e.g., Katz 1978a, 1983a; Paper 2005). With respect to the latter, advocates of Perennial Philosophy most often express, knowingly or unknowingly, a normative monistic theology, or the belief that there is one impersonal reality beyond human comprehension and conceptualization. While Perennial Philosophy may be theologically convincing, experientially valid, or socially agreeable to many, it simply does not hold up to critical scrutiny. Careful study of religious traditions, including the diversity of contemplative practice, mystical experience, and theological discourse, reveals equally convincing, mutually exclusive accounts of "reality." Especially in terms of mystical experiences, and as expressed in the writings of mystics themselves, it would seem that there are many "realities." That is, theologically speaking the academic study of religion seems to provide more support for a normative polytheistic theology, or at least a normative pluralistic stance. In any case, totalizing interpretations, like Perennial Philosophy, involve colonialism and domestication.

It is not my intention to review the entirety of this debate here, even though there are many parallel, interpretive issues, especially concerning the nature of consciousness and human ways of experiencing (see later discussion). However, the emergence of a Contextualist approach to mysticism, and contemplative practice by extension, deserves consideration. Contextualism was partially formulated as a challenge to Perennialism, with its naïve view of human consciousness and experience, often superficial and selective reading of primary texts (in translation), and unquestioned belief in a single divine source that exists beyond the confines of religious beliefs and characterizations.

As the name implies, Contextualism emphasizes the importance of context for understanding any mystic or mystical system. In its nascent form, a Contextualist approach to mysticism was advocated by Gershom Scholem in his *Major Trends in Jewish Mysticism* (1995 [1941]):

> The point I should like to make is this—that there is no such thing as mysticism in the abstract, that is to say, a phenomenon or experience which has no particular relation to other religious phenomena. There is no mysticism as such, there is only the mysticism of a particular religious system, Christian, Islamic, Jewish mysticism and so on. . . . History rather shows that the great mystics were faithful adherents of the great religions. (5–6)

Experiences and phenomena defined as "mystical" do not occur and cannot be understood outside of a given religious tradition and/or sociocultural context. Even in the case of modern, "trans-tradition" forms of mystical experience, a worldview and informing system are still involved. As Scholem's pioneering and still standard account of Jewish mysticism reveals, there are complex doctrinal and historical factors that, at least partially, determine a given mystic's experiences as well as the recognized significance of such events.

The Contextualist approach became more fully developed by Steven Katz and his colleagues and is most well known through two volumes edited by Katz (1978a, 1983a; see also Berger and Luckmann 1966; Berger 1990). Throughout these volumes, emphasis is placed on the sociocultural and religio-historical aspects of mystical experiences, specifically the diverse and alterior forms of mysticism as expressions of *different religious traditions with different conceptions of the sacred*. In addition, Contextualist theorists of mysticism often emphasize the relationship between "experience" and "interpretation," both within and beyond the originary event itself:

> When I speak of "interpretation" here I mean to refer to the standard accounts of the subject which attempt to investigate what the mystic had to say *about* his experience. This interpretative enterprise is, of course, carried on at several different removes and in several different ways. Among these are: (a) the first-person report of the mystic; (b) the mystic's "interpretation" of his own experience at some later, more reflective, and mediated, stage; (c) the "interpretation" of third persons within the same tradition (Christians on Christian mysticism); (d) the process of interpretation by third persons in other traditions (Buddhists on Christianity); and so on. (Katz 1978b, 23; see also Smart 1965; Sharf 1998; Komjathy 2012)

It is important to consider both the ways in which "experience" is, at least partially, determined by one's worldview and social location as well as subsequent interpretations by diverse discourse communities and contexts of reception. At least on some level, interpretation may be involved throughout the entire process of *experiencing*, particularly with respect to anticipated outcomes (see later discussion).

Because of the apparently overdetermined characteristics of "experience," Contextualism, which is also referred to as Constructivism due to this point, *assumes* a very specific view of human consciousness:

> *There are* NO *pure (i.e. unmediated) experiences.* Neither mystical experience nor more ordinary forms of experience give any indication, or any grounds for believing, that they are unmediated. That is to say, *all* experience is processed through, organized by, and makes itself available to us in extremely complex epistemological ways. The notion of unmediated experience seems, if not self-contradictory, at best empty. . . . The significance of these considerations is that forms of consciousness which the mystic brings to experience set structured and limiting parameters on what the experience will be, i.e. on what will be experienced, and rule out in advance what is 'inexperienceable' in the particular given, concrete, context. (Katz 1978b, 26–27, italics in original; see also Gimello 1983; Gill 1984)

Claiming parallelism between ordinary human consciousness and mystical forms of consciousness, Katz argues that *every* experience is conditioned and determined by both the limited nature of the human mind and enculturation into a given religious tradition. Human consciousness, whether mystical or not, is mediated by epistemological categories and enculturated beliefs, which are at work before, during, and after the experience (27). From a Contextualist perspective, this is so much the case that deconditioning (e.g., the Daoist emphasis on forgetting and emptying) is really only reconditioning (57; cf. Evans 1989, 54).

While the Constructivist view of consciousness is problematic and has been challenged from a variety of perspectives (see, e.g., Komjathy 2007 and later discussion in this chapter),[17] few serious and conscientious researchers of mysticism would take issue with the Contextualist "plea for the recognition of differences" (Katz 1978b, 25) and the importance of being attentive to relevant historical, cultural, and religious factors, the lifeworld of a given mystic if you will. This includes recognizing the ways in which consciousness and experience are conditioned: from social and religious enculturation to interpersonal relationships and personal habituation. It also involves identifying various elements of any worldview, such as the way in which metaphor conditions perception (see Lakoff and Johnson 1980). A Contextualist approach could, of course, move in many directions: from an analysis of the larger socioeconomic and political context to a narrower focus on the religious tradition. Both involve attentiveness to historical issues.

The intellectual naïveté and interpretive waywardness of early studies of mystical experience, which were challenged and clarified by more sophisticated research, seem to have migrated to engagement with meditation. One of the most ubiquitous of these assumptions relates to Perennial Philosophy. For example, in his foreword to the recent *The Experience of Meditation* (2006), Ken Wilber, a prominent representative of transpersonal psychology, claims,

> There is little question that meditative or contemplative practice has been at the heart of virtually all of the great wisdom traditions [*sic*], East and West, North and South. And while the myths and dogmas [*sic*] of these religions vary enormously—and categorically disagree with each other on virtually every major issue—the contemplative practices in each of these traditions tend to have an astonishingly similar outlook. (xii)

Here one may simply note the excessive degree of qualification in Wilber's comments. In a parallel manner, though with slightly more nuance, Jonathan Shear, the volume's editor, suggests,

> There is also wide agreement about the nature of many of the experiences of the deepest levels of inner awareness. In particular they [meditation traditions] all emphasize that successful meditation can enable the mind to leave behind all of its ordinary activities of thinking and perceiving . . . and settle so deeply within its own nature that it reaches its own source in a state of *absolute, pure silence*. This state is quite unique. For it has no content in it at all . . . not even, indeed, any time or space in which such things could be located. (Shear 2006, xviii, italics in original; see also xviii–xix; cf. xvi)[18]

Shear's construction of contemplative practice and contemplative experience parallels that of Robert Forman with respect to mystical experience. In fact, Shear seems to be equating the "deepest levels of inner awareness" with Forman's notion of a Pure Consciousness Event (PCE) (see Forman 1990), also referred to variously as Absolute Unitary Being (AUB; D'Aquili and Newberg 1999,

198–203) and Ultimate Pure Being (UPB; Austin 2006, 7, 10, 393). Such claims evidence a specific philosophical, and arguably theological, commitment. They are not phenomenological. In previous work, I have suggested that Forman's reduction of "mystical experience" to trophotropic (i.e., hypoaroused/hyperquiescent) types unjustifiably privileges specific traditions over others (see Komjathy 2007). Interestingly, the exclusions involve some of the most well-known and influential mystical experiences in the Roman Catholic tradition. In a parallel ordering of consciousness and experience, neuroscientists (the "hard side" of consciousness studies) frequently identify one form of mystical consciousness as the pinnacle of human consciousness. This too is not phenomenological, as it is based on specific constructions. A more nuanced understanding of the entire spectrum of contemplative practice would recognize that there are various ergotropic forms, including corresponding experiences with high degrees of visual and/or auditory content. As is discussed later, neuroimaging of contemplative practice and mystical experience should not arbitrarily limit the "data set." The spectrum of contemplative practice also reveals radically different psychologies and views of consciousness, which should be considered in neuroscientific studies and interpretations.

Given the theoretical sophistication and heuristic viability of Contextualism, especially its requirement of close textual analysis and systematic comprehension, one may say that it is *absolutely essential* to locate religiously-committed forms of contemplative practice in their given religious traditions and soteriological systems.[19] For present purposes, we may say that contemplative practice, like mystical experience, is socially located. Every type of contemplative practice is informed by specific worldviews and larger frameworks. As discussed later, this is equally true of modern "secular" or "nonreligious" forms of contemplative practice. Considering contemplative practice related to religious traditions, it is essential to understand those traditions, including the informing worldviews and soteriological systems. In this respect, Andresen and Forman's map of different aspects of religious traditions and corresponding research trajectories may be utilized to develop a more comprehensive interpretative framework for understanding contemplative practice.

As we can see from figure 1.5 on page 18, a more comprehensive and sophisticated understanding of contemplative practice and contemplative experience would be attentive to subjective experience, doctrinal analysis, scientific research, and social expression. Transcending the limitations and problematic privileging of a "scientific approach" in this model, we may work toward developing an interdisciplinary and/or multidisciplinary approach that recognizes and investigates informing worldviews, social dimensions, subjective experience, as well as biological, physiological, and neuroscientific dimensions (see also ch. 2 herein). It is essential to locate contemplative practices within their larger frameworks. Careful study of contemplative practice reveals diversity and complexity, both practically and theologically.

In terms of religious studies, what I am advocating is understanding and studying contemplative practice in a comprehensive and integrated way. As expressed in the present volume, this involves close textual reading and historical contextualization, including an attempt to understand the given contemplative practice in terms of its informing worldviews, associated religious tradition, and soteriological system. Though experiential understanding and contemporary adherent perspectives may have a place,[20] the methodology is, first and foremost, historical reconstruction and textual analysis. On a more general interpretive level, one may ask how the contemplative practice embodies the corresponding religious tradition and soteriological system. That is, the contemplative practices presented herein are simultaneously informed by

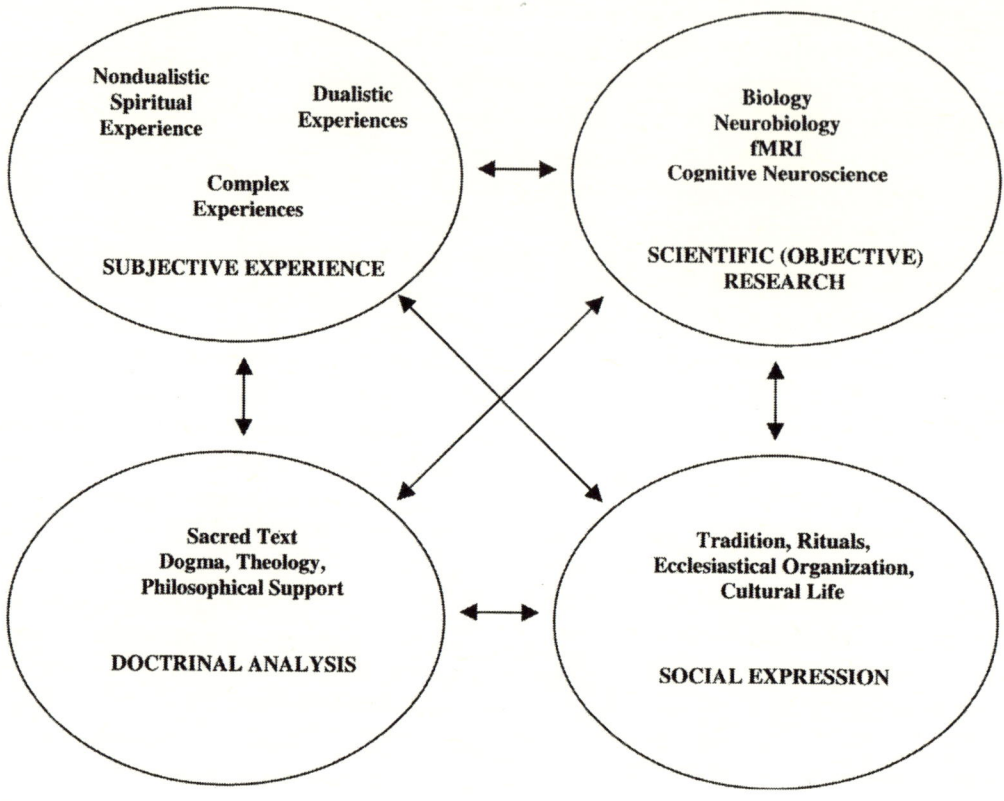

Figure 1.5. Four Aspects of the Study of Religion
Source: Andresen and Forman 2000.

and expressions of a larger framework. One might, in turn, consider other dimensions related to contemplative practice, namely, architecture, art, asceticism, community, diet, ethics, material culture, monasticism, mystical experience, place, ritual, scripture, and so forth (see ch. 2 herein).

Let us briefly examine the ways in which a Contextualist approach would account for contemplative practice by examining one specific example. Eihei Dōgen (1200–1253), the founder of Sōtō Zen (Chn.: Caodong Chan) in Japan, advocated a form of contemplative practice known as "just sitting" (*shikan taza*), which refined the earlier Chan meditation practice of "silent illumination" (*mozhao*). Both practices evidence influence from classical Daoist apophatic meditation, especially as expressed in the *Daode jing* (Scripture on the Dao and Inner Power) and *Zhuangzi* (Book of Master Zhuang). Conventionally speaking, *shikan taza* practice involves emptying and stilling the mind of excess intellectual and emotional activity. As expressed in Dōgen's "Zazen-gi" (Rules for Zazen), "Sit solidly in samādhi and think not-thinking. How do you think not-thinking? Non-thinking. This is the art of zazen" (Tanahashi 1985, 30). In studying this practice, a Contextualist approach might first examine Dōgen's life, his biographical background.

One finds that Dōgen was ordained as a Tendai monk, studied under Eisai (founder of Rinzai Zen) in Japan, and traveled to China with Myozen, one of Eisai's senior disciples. During his visit to China, Dōgen met and received Dharma transmission from Rujing (Jpn.: Nyojo; 1163–1228), an ordained monk of the Caodong lineage of Chan Buddhism. From these biographical and historical details, one could seek to understand the ways in which Dōgen was located in Chan Buddhism in general and in the Caodong lineage in particular. Moreover, from Dōgen's extant writings, especially his *Shobogenzo* (Treasury of the True Dharma-Eye), we know that he lived and taught at a variety of Japanese Zen mountain monasteries throughout his life. That is, his contemplative practice was informed by and benefited from living in secluded and natural landscapes, which Dōgen saw as supporting and expressing the condition of enlightenment. He also wrote some famous essays on monastic life, including "Tenzo kyōkun" (Instructions for the Cook) and "Jūundō-shiki" (Regulations for the Auxiliary Cloud Hall). These and other writings reveal that, for Dōgen and early members of Sōtō Zen, *shikan taza* was a solitary and communal monastic practice. It was informed by daily monastic discipline, including conduct guidelines and work assignments, as well as applied to various duties. Moreover, Dōgen's contemplative practice was located in and expressed a Zen Buddhist soteriology, which identified spiritual realization as the ultimate purpose of human existence. A thorough understanding of this soteriology would have to address Dōgen's views on karma and reincarnation as well as potential Daoist and Shinto influences. For example, in his "Sansui-kyō" (Mountains and Waters Sutra), Dōgen seems to express a perspective informed by a panenhenic mystical experience, wherein he has dissolved into Nature and the local landscape. These and other context-specific details lead to larger interpretive questions. In order to attain the "practice-realization" that Dōgen envisions, does one need to become a monastic? Is a secluded, natural place necessary? What role do the monastic community, monastic regulations, and monastic life play in this contemplative practice? Does one need a master, and should one study the teachings and writings of Zen masters? Taking a more sociopolitical position, one might even ask if "just sitting" was a way for Dōgen to escape the politics of his time, both in the Tendai order and the larger Kamakura (1185–1333) society. Some sources also indicate that Dōgen may have fallen into despair late in life; corresponding to his quasi-exile in Echizen Province (present-day Fukui prefecture) in 1243, "he fell into a depression that had been building up through the external pressures and animosities of the dark times he was going through. The year that he spent in Kippō-ji [Yoshimine-dera] marked a low point of his life" (Dumoulin 1990, 62).[21] If this was indeed the case, was *shikan taza* a psychological coping mechanism? Does Buddhist meditation lead to a dissociative state? That is, a Contextualist approach could be informed by historical, psychological and sociological perspectives.

While some individuals (e.g., Michael Murphy, Ken Wilber) would like to extract contemplative practices from their informing soteriological systems and religious traditions in order to create a universal form of spirituality or wisdom philosophy, others (e.g., Thich Nhat Hanh, Thomas Keating) understand these and additional dimensions, such as community and place, as essential and interdependent. Of course many in the former camp would characterize the latter as "sectarians," "dogmatists," or "ideologues," as limiting "human potential" and "human spiritual evolution." But these individuals could just as easily respond with labels such as "spiritual colonialists" and "New Age capitalists." As discussed in more detail later in this chapter, there are contributions and limitations of community and tradition, whether religious or other. But the point of the present section is to highlight the ways in which contemplative practice is always socially located. For example, in the course of my life I have met a variety of Daoist contemplatives and hermits, both in mainland China and in North America. These Daoist practitioners usually have a variety of parallel characteristics: rejection of the dominant social order (mundane reality); acceptance of Daoist eremitic religious models; and a larger conception of community, which encompasses actual Daoist communities and simultaneously transcends notions of temporality and physicality. The latter suggests that the "Daoist body," the community of Daoists, is not limited by geographical proximity, historical contemporaneity, or physical embodiment. In fact, many of these Daoists claim to have had encounters with immortals, spirit beings, and disembodied teachers. Thinking about social location, there is an underlying exchange with both the larger society and an invisible network of participation. At the same time, their physical seclusion is informed by religious precedents and models as well as by influential scriptures. Often this involves loose affiliations with a temple or monastic community, including veneration by the latter.

Individuals advocating modern secularized, spiritualized, or therapeutic forms of contemplative practice more often than not present them as transcending the limitations of "institutionalized religion," as being free of this and similar "problems."[22] However, as mentioned, every contemplative practice utilizes a specific worldview and locates the practitioner in a larger system. Prominent, "nondenominational" contemplative practices include Focusing (Eugene Gendlin), Integrative Restoration (iRest; Richard Miller), Mindfulness-Based Stress Reduction (MBSR; Jon Kabat-Zinn), Relaxation Response (Herbert Benson), and so forth. One interesting detail is that most of these methods derive from religiously-committed and tradition-based contemplative practices: iRest from Hindu Yoga Nidra; MBSR from Theravāda Buddhist Vipassanā; and the Relaxation Response from Transcendental Meditation (TM), itself a modified Hindu practice. The "originators" of the modern modifications do not seem to see a problem with their own increase in power, wealth, and cultural capital. There are, however, ethical and political issues involved, including the question of ownership and distribution of benefit, as, for instance, in Bikram Choudhury's (b. 1946) trademarking of a series of Hatha Yoga postures into so-called Bikram Yoga©™ (Hot Yoga; now the Bikram Yoga Franchise).

In any case, here we are primarily concerned with analyzing such practices from a Contextualist perspective. One example will suffice. In *The Relaxation Response* (1975), Herbert Benson (b. 1935), the eventual founder of the Mind/Body Medical Institute and now the director emeritus of the Benson-Henry Institute for Mind Body Medicine at Massachusetts General Hospital, discusses his discovery of the "relaxation response" (see ch. 13 herein). This is both a specific method developed by Benson as well as a corresponding physiological state. As a stress-reduction and self-care technique, the Relaxation Response is a secularized and medicalized Hindu *mantra* practice that was modified from Transcendental Meditation. Benson and his colleagues developed the particular Relaxation Response method, which conventionally involves constant repetition of a self-selected word or phrase. In one section of the book Benson recommends "ONE" (130).[23] However, according to Benson,

> It is important to remember that there is not a single method that is unique in eliciting the Relaxation Response. . . . we believe it is not necessary to use the specific method and specific *secret*, personal sound taught by Transcendental Meditation. *Tests at the Thorndike Memorial Laboratory of Harvard have shown that a similar technique used*

with any sound or phrase or prayer or mantra brings forth the same physiologic changes noted during Transcendental Meditation. (128, italics in original)

So, the Relaxation Response as a method is "trans-religious." Whether religious, spiritual, or "nonreligious," individuals may apparently benefit from the practice. The primary purpose of meditation practice in Benson's view is to elicit the physiological condition known as the "relaxation response." This is a hypometabolic (trophotropic), or restful, state, in which there is decreased activity of the sympathetic nervous system; the relaxation response is the opposite of the so-called fight-or-flight response. There are, in turn, various "scientifically proven" medical benefits. Throughout *The Relaxation Response*, Benson also repeatedly emphasizes the scientific nature of his approach as well as the various scientific studies that validate it.

With this background in place, we may now locate the Relaxation Response in its larger sociohistorical, "religious," and "soteriological" context. First, as a cardiologist (MD) and as someone working within an allopathic (Western biomedical) paradigm, Benson seeks to justify the efficacy of the Relaxation Response through empirical and experimental data. This is partially due to the resistance and conservative nature of the American allopathic medical establishment, especially in the 1970s and 1980s before the emergence of so-called traditional, alternative, and complementary medicine. That is, Benson, like Jon Kabat-Zinn, was attempting to establish a new branch of medicine, eventually called "Mind-Body Medicine." Second, the publication of *The Relaxation Response* emerged during a time of both interest in and criticism of Maharishi Mahesh (1918–2008) and his Transcendental Meditation movement. This included various attempts by Maharishi to provide scientific validation through TM-sponsored research on the practice. In that context, representatives were claiming that TM had special benefits that might justify the exorbitant fees charged by Maharishi and the TM organization. Contrasting the Relaxation Response with the so-called fight-or-flight response also locates Benson and practitioners of RR in a Darwinian evolutionary struggle for survival of the fittest. More pertinent to the present volume is the informing worldview and system of the Relaxation Response itself. Practitioners of the Relaxation Response technique are located in an allopathic medical and science-based framework. In particular, meditation practice is framed in terms of the corresponding physiological response, namely, the Relaxation Response. Here the worldview of Mind-Body Medicine suggests that states of consciousness have specific physiological characteristics, and that health and disease also have physiological correlates. In particular, stress causes various forms of disease. By practicing the Relaxation Response method, one can decrease stress and avoid disease. Utilizing an implied materialistic view of self, namely, self as biological organism, the Relaxation Response defines human existence in terms of medical health and the avoidance of disease. Simultaneously, it reduces both contemplative practice and contemplative experience to physiology. As long as one remains in this framework, within an allopathic and secular materialist framework, the Relaxation Response makes sense. However, if one believes that human experience and existence cannot be reduced to physiology, and that scientific validation is neither necessary nor sufficient, then one discovers various deficiencies. What if the chosen sound is not simply sound but also invocation? What role does community play in "wellness"? What if direct personal experience is privileged over scientific measurement and technological certification?[24] As discussed in more detail later, there are contributions and limitations to a psychobiological and neuroscientific approach to contemplative studies.

To summarize, contemplative practice always occurs within a specific context. There is always an informing worldview and discourse community involved. In the case of religiously-committed forms of contemplative practice, adherents practice prescribed methods within the parameters of a religious tradition and soteriological system. The corresponding system includes distinctive views of self, religious concerns, theological commitments, and additional forms of religiosity. The more-encompassing training regimen may involve such undertakings as asceticism, dietetics, ethics, monasticism, ritual, and so forth. To locate contemplative practice in this way, to approach contemplative practice in a comprehensive and nuanced way, in an interdisciplinary way, inhibits the tendency to isolate contemplative practice and/or to reduce contemplative practice to mere technique or experience. It also requires one not to privilege any particular interpretive approach (e.g., neuroscience).

Psychology, Consciousness Studies, and Neuroscience

In the previous section of this chapter, I emphasized some potential trajectories for an interdisciplinary approach to contemplative practice and contemplative studies, especially one rooted in religious studies. Such an approach would apply theory and method derived from anthropology, history, literature, philosophy, theology, as well as psychology and neuroscience to the study of contemplative practice and contemplative experience. An interdisciplinary approach would, of course, also have to be informed by the careful study and nuanced understanding of religiously-committed and tradition-based forms of meditation and contemplative prayer. That is, it should not simply superimpose theory onto "data"; the voices of contemplatives and religious communities also should be included.

As mentioned, modern research on contemplative practice, or "meditation," has been dominated by psychological and neuroscientific approaches, particularly through empirical and experimental ("objective") studies. Given the prominence of these approaches, we should consider the contributions and limitations of psychology, consciousness studies, and neuroscience to contemplative studies. Although some members of these disciplines might object, I would suggest that the associative grouping is justified. Each area overlaps with the others, and each one investigates dimensions of human consciousness, mental life, and behavior on some level.

The modern field of psychology is diverse and vast. For present purposes, we are most interested in those areas that have examined contemplative practice and that are most clearly applicable to contemplative studies. This is, of course, open to interpretation. From my perspective, there are two relatively accepted approaches and two emerging and less familiar ones. The former include humanistic and transpersonal psychology,[25] while the latter consist of tradition-specific and contemplative psychology.[26] There is overlap among humanistic, transpersonal, and contemplative psychology, and between contemplative and tradition-specific psychology. These psychological approaches tend to relate to both existentialism and developmental psychology, with "human development" being framed to include "spiritual dimensions." Partly as a critique of the emphasis on pathology in conventional psychology, especially in the forms of psychoanalysis and behaviorism and partly as a response to the existentialist search for meaning and purpose, humanistic psychology emerged in the 1950s.[27] Two prominent early representatives include Carl Rogers (1902–1987) and Abraham Maslow (1908–1970). The influence of phenomenology and existentialism is obvious in various book titles: *Toward a Psychology of Being* (Maslow), *The Farther Reaches of Human Nature* (Maslow), *On Becoming a Person* (Rogers), *A Way of Being* (Rogers), *The Art of Being* (Fromm), *To Have or To Be* (Fromm), and so forth. Utilizing a "high anthropology,"[28] humanistic psychology emphasizes the possibility of becoming fully human, with special attention to self-fulfillment and self-actualization. Rogers refers to this as development into a "fully functioning person" with "unconditional positive regard" for both self and other (1961), while Maslow speaks of "Being-cognition" (B-cognition) in contrast to "Deficiency-cognition" (D-cognition) (1999). One finds similar humanistic views in Erich Fromm's (1900–1980) emphasis on a "being-mode" versus a "having-mode" (2002) and Arthur Deikman's distinction between a "receptive mode" and "object mode" (1982).[29] Although each view has its nuances, there is general agreement on the human potential for psychological wellness and aliveness. At the higher levels of "full functioning" or "self-actualization,"[30] people are less bound to a desire-based and object-oriented perspective; they begin to develop the ability to see situations beyond the limitations of their own psychoses and egocentrism. In the being and receptive mode, humans experience life closer to its immediacy, to things as they are in their own being. Simultaneously, such individuals focus on the present as sufficient and on meaning and purpose beyond future-directed goals. This often involves choiceless awareness. In developing such consciousness, including the place of contemplative practice and mystical experience in one's life, Deikman (1982) emphasizes a process of "deautomatization," while Forman (1990, 1999) speaks of "deconditioning." Both approaches suggest that one may overcome habituated tendencies, tendencies formed through social conditioning, familial obligations, and personal reactivity. Maslow, in particular, connects Being-cognition with "peak experiences" (1964), which parallels Csikszentmihalyi's notions of "optimal experience" and "flow" (1988, 1990). That is, there are experiences that indicate and manifest self-actualization. As one can see from this brief description, specific types of contemplative practice apparently support self-actualization. They may facilitate and strengthen higher degrees of aliveness and states of consciousness often defined as "higher" or "advanced" (see ch. 2 herein).

Partially as a response to the individualistic and anthropocentric limitations of humanistic psychology, and as a further expansion of developmental psychology, transpersonal psychology seeks to include "trans-human" and "spiritual" aspects of existence. Transpersonal psychology makes space for "altered states of consciousness," "paranormal abilities," and "anomalous experiences" (see Cardeña et al. 2000) in the study of higher modes of being. In this way, there is some overlap with consciousness studies. Some key early figures in transpersonal psychology include Michael Murphy (b. 1930; Esalen Institute), Stanislav Grof (b. 1931), Charles Tart (b. 1937), Ken Wilber (b. 1949; Integral Institute), and Roger Walsh (d.u.). Transpersonal psychology tends to be comparative and cross-cultural, meaning that it brings tradition-based "spiritual technologies" and philosophy into psychological views of human potential.[31] At its farthest reaches, as in the work of Grof, it includes the use of psychotropic and psychedelic drugs (entheogens, or God-spawning substances) in the expansion of consciousness. In any case, transpersonal psychology locates human meaning and purpose both within and beyond the individual; it includes "metaphysical" or "theological dimensions" in the search for aliveness, actualization, and authenticity. Transpersonal psychologists also place a fairly consistent emphasis on "transformation" and "extraordinariness." With respect to contemplative practice, one of the clearest and most comprehensive accounts appears in Michael Murphy's *The Future of the Body* (1992). Emphasizing the human capacity for transformation through embodied practice, Murphy examines somatic disciplines, adventure and sport, martial arts, as well as more distinctively religious practices. In the final section of the book, he then moves on to discuss a larger conception of "transformative practice" with an aim toward "integral practices" (cf. Wilber et al. 1986; Wilber et al. 2008). According to Murphy,

> In establishing transformative practices, we depend upon inherited bodily processes. We can cultivate somatic awareness and control, for example, because nerve cells that evolved from analogous structures in the earliest vertebrates are deployed throughout our bodies. Relaxation exercises are effective because we possess a parasympathetic system that developed during the long course of mammalian evolution. We can become creatively absorbed in work, perhaps, because we have inherited capacities for catalepsy, analgesia, and selective amnesia that facilitate escape and hunting. In short, self-regulation skills, regenerative relaxation, and performance trance, like other kinds of creative functioning, are based on capacities that developed among our animal forebears. And while transformative practices draw upon our animal inheritance, they also employ uniquely human activities. The imagination we use to enjoy books can be cultivated to induce metanormal cognitions or to facilitate extraordinary skills. The self-reflection we sometimes practice when confronted by difficulty can be deepened by means of sustained meditation. Transformative disciplines use both inherited and socially acquired attributes to improve many kinds of functioning. (1992, 543)

And,

> Transformative disciplines, then, rely on inherited, socially acquired, and ego-transcending activities, and these all play roles in the psychophysical alterations in this book. Here I will emphasize some that are especially important for integral development. I will refer to their deliberate employment as *transformative moves* or *modalities*. (544, italics in original)

Murphy correlates his proposed integral practices with the corresponding transformative modality, including practice outcomes related to twelve attributes of higher human functioning (567–75). Applied to contemplative practice, Murphy's insights suggest that certain forms of meditation and contemplative prayer may facilitate human growth and transformation, especially with respect to extraordinary existential and ontological conditions.[32] The latter might involve the activation and enhancement of other human capacities, commonly referred to as *siddhi*, "supernatural powers" or numinous abilities, in Indian religious traditions. Such paranormal capacities include clairaudience, clairvoyance, knowledge of previous incarnations, multilocation, multivocality, self-directed reincarnation, and so forth.

The other two relevant psychological approaches, namely, tradition-specific psychology and contemplative psychology, are less developed. Tradition-specific psychology, or psychological views and insights derived from and utilized within religious traditions, is only just beginning to be explored systematically. More often than not, there is interest among professional Western psychologists in "Buddhist psychology" as a corrective to the perceived deficiencies of received paradigms, especially an abnormal or pathology-based model.[33] Although Buddhism is, no doubt, the *belle de jour*, one can find sophisticated psychological views within many of the major religions, including Hinduism and Daoism. There seems to be general agreement among these traditions concerning causes of suffering and vexation in the human condition. Simply stated, the primary source of suffering is oneself.[34] As a subject, one encounters the phenomenal world, the world of "objects," as a source of desire-fulfillment or frustration. This is due to a particular psychological pattern, namely, the activation of one's perceptual system in relation to the phenomenal world with corresponding thoughts, desires, emotions, and residual memories. In this ordinary and habitual or conditioned relational pattern, one becomes agitated and disturbed by various events and experiences. However, in the "psychology of realization" and corresponding religious discipline (see ch. 2 herein), one severs ties to the phenomenal world as habitually perceived, disrupts ordinary perceptual patterning, and decreases intellectual and emotional activity. One enters a state of stillness or interior silence in which consciousness becomes purified of psychological agitation and confusion.[35] This brief discussion is simply meant to provide a glimpse into what tradition-based psychology might look like. In fact, more systematic research is required, especially with respect to the *specific* psychological qualities of various moments in contemplative practice. It should also be mentioned that one finds fairly developed tradition-based psychology in pastoral psychology and spiritual direction, most often in their Christian expressions. These applied approaches contain an explicit engaged and theological dimension.

Contemplative psychology has certain parallels with tradition-based psychology, but the latter is located *within* religious traditions and in the perspectives of adherents. Contemplative psychology, on the other hand, draws insights from religious traditions in an effort to create an integrated psychological system focusing on spiritual development (cf. Wilber 2000). In this way, contemplative psychology tends to be comparative, interreligious, and syncretistic. Han de Wit is the primary advocate of contemplative psychology, especially as expressed in his book by that name (De Wit 1991; see also Roth 2006; Ferrer and Sherman 2008). As stated by De Wit, "In using the term *contemplative psychology*, we are referring to the *psychological* insights, knowledge and methods that we find *within contemplative traditions* themselves" (1, italics in original).[36] Moreover, "The term *contemplative psychology* refers rather to the psychological insights and beliefs that are often implicitly present in the vision of religions, and that become concretized in the authentic religious practices of individuals" (12, italics in original). And

> This brings us to the main purpose of this introductory study in contemplative psychology: to make explicit and clarify the nature and position of the psychological *know-how* that contemplative traditions contain. . . . The clarification of the psychological aspects of contemplative traditions may also contribute to *a general understanding of the value of contemplative traditions and their psychological perspectives*, both from a practical and from a scientific psychological or methodological point of view. (14, italics in original)

For De Wit, contemplative practice utilizes and activates a special set of psychological states or conditions. It involves a specific type of knowing (contemplative epistemology), which includes first-person experience (31–32). However, this is not uncritical adherent discourse, that is, the discourse of apologetics and dogmatics; rather, it is a more systematic investigation of one's life through experiences within contemplative practice. The goal, ideally, is to become more conscious, integrated, and, from one perspective, realized. De Wit identifies this as a path to that which religious traditions identify as enlightenment, liberation, fulfillment, emancipation, salvation, and so on (18). This recalls my earlier points about contemplative practice as located in soteriological systems. For De Wit, an existential and psychological shift occurs through contemplative practice. Such shifts are documented in the psychological views of religious traditions. Contemplative psychology in turn attempts to map the "higher" levels of human functioning.

Consciousness studies may be located in relation to both psychology and cognitive science. In its philosophical expressions, consciousness studies parallels humanistic and transpersonal psychology in its search for more authentic and enlivening forms of being and relating. It includes perspectives drawn from religious adherents, contemplatives, mystics, philosophers, and theologians. It could and often does proceed along the lines of comparative philosophy and comparative religious studies, specifically concerning various views of "mind" and "consciousness" (see, e.g., Andresen and Forman 2000).

In its more "scientific" or quantitative expressions, it becomes neuroscience. Neuroscientific accounts of meditation have their roots in earlier experimental studies. The neuroscientific approach, increasingly referred to as "contemplative science," is quickly becoming the dominant voice in contemplative studies. It relies on ever-increasingly complex technologies and has a high degree of mediation (see Andresen 2000), including an apparent distrust of subjective experience. The neuroscientific study of meditation thus utilizes contemporary brain research, specifically with respect to the nervous system, neuro-regions, and brain functions. Here I attempt to provide a concise overview of neurobiology related to the study of contemplative practice.[37] Generally speaking, neuroscience understands human beings from an evolutionary perspective, with the autonomic nervous system being "more primitive" and the cerebral cortex allowing "higher-order functioning." Briefly stated, the human nervous system is divided into the central and peripheral nervous systems. The central nervous system (CNS) consists of the brain and spinal cord and plays a key role in controlling behavior. The peripheral nervous system (PNS) is made up of all the neurons in the body outside of the central nervous system and is further subdivided into the somatic and autonomic nervous systems. The somatic nervous system (SNS) is made up of afferent neurons that convey sensory information from the sense organs to the brain and spinal cord and efferent neurons that carry motor instructions to the muscles.[38] The autonomic nervous system (ANS) is responsible, in conjunction with the rest of the brain, for maintaining baseline body functions. The ANS is, in turn, divided into two subsystems, namely, the sympathetic nervous system (SNS) and parasympathetic nervous system (PNS) (see Guyton and Hall 2006, 5–6, 555–76).

The SNS is responsible for the so-called fight-or-flight response, which is the physiological basis of human adaptive strategies either to noxious stimuli or to highly desirable stimuli in an environment. The PNS is responsible for maintaining homeostasis. This involves the conservation of body energy and the maintenance of baseline metabolism. As we have seen, certain forms of contemplative practice, including the Relaxation Response, decrease physiological activity; they are trophotropic and lead to deeper states of relaxation. They thus involve decreased activity in the sympathetic nervous system and may help to initiate more enduring states of homeostasis.

Moving to the next level of cognitive functioning, the human brain is a highly organized and complex system, and this system is still being explored and charted. While popular and conventional perspectives divide the brain into the so-called right hemisphere and left hemisphere, which are associated with intuitive/holistic and logical/analytical functions, respectively, modern

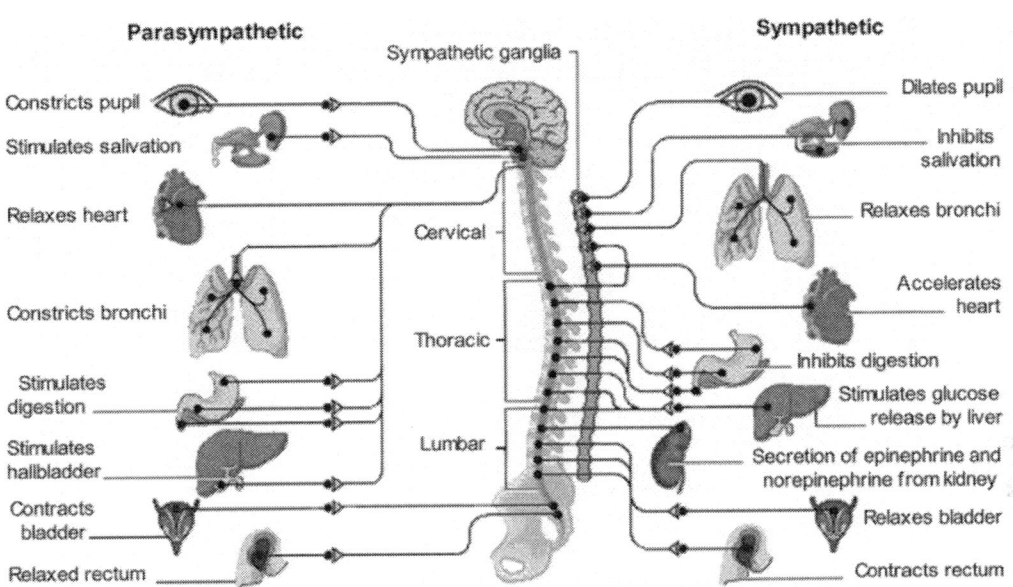

Figure 1.6. Autonomic Nervous System

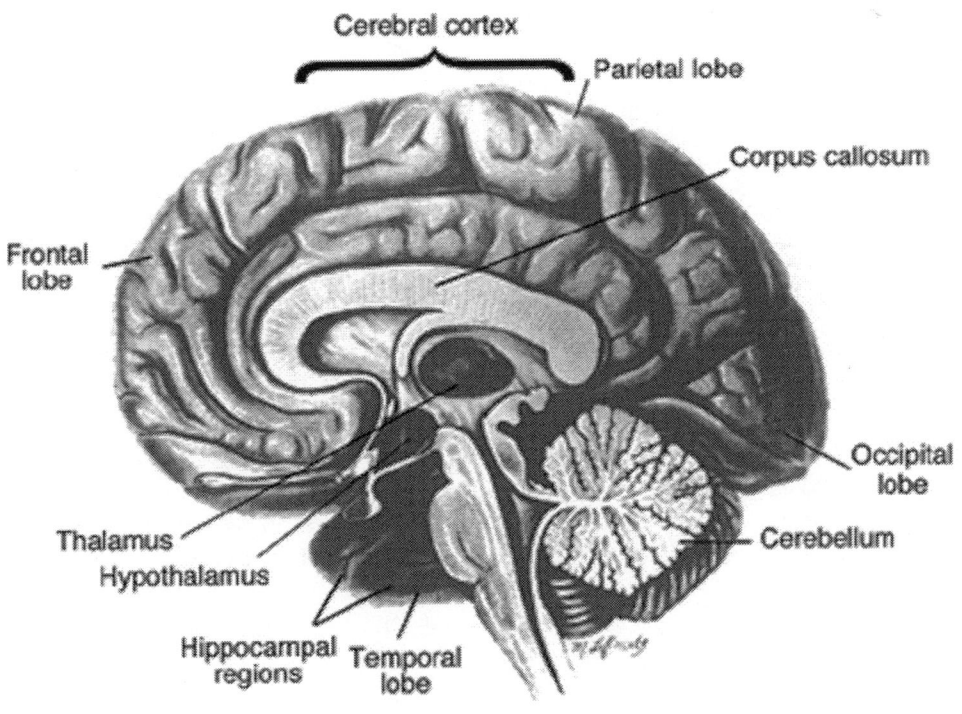

Figure 1.7. Human Brain Anatomy
Source: Marlene Oscar-Berman, Boston University School of Medicine.

neuroscience generally rejects this simplistic account. On the most basic level, the cerebral cortex is the outer layer of gray matter that covers both of the cerebral hemispheres. It is known that the cerebral cortex likely underlies the development of complex thought, language, religion, art, and culture. The brain is further divided into various "regions" with corresponding, complex, and often overlapping functions (Lutz et al. 2007, 527). In terms of higher cognitive, sensory, and emotional functioning, there are four areas that integrate neuronal activity from various other areas of the brain. These include the posterior superior parietal lobule (PSPL), the inferior temporal lobe (ITL), the inferior parietal lobule (IPL), and the prefrontal cortex (PRC). The PSPL is heavily involved in the analysis and integration of higher-order sensory information. The ITL neurons scan the entire visual field so as to alert the organism to objects of interest or motivational importance. The IPL is located at the confluence of the temporal, parietal, and occipital lobes. It is generally regarded as responsible for the generation of abstract concepts and relating them to words. The PRC is involved in mediating concepts via its interconnections with the inferior parietal lobe. In addition to the cerebral cortex, there are a group of structures near the base of the brain that are sometimes referred to as the "limbic system," though contemporary neuroscience largely problematizes this characterization. These structures are associated with the more complex aspects of emotions and involved with assigning emotional feelings to various objects and experiences and directing these emotions outward via behavior. Central aspects include the hypothalamus, amygdala, and hippocampus. The amygdala is preeminent in the control and modulation of higher-order emotional functions, particularly those related to arousal or fear. In addition, the amygdala is involved in attention, learning, and memory. The hippocampus plays a major role in information processing, including memory, new learning, cognitive mapping of the environment, and focusing attention (D'Aquili and Newberg 1999, 21–44; Austin 1998, 149–290; Ward 2009, 17–31). While there are still other dimensions of the brain, this general overview suggests that specific contemplative practices would engage and disengage different brain regions and functions. Although such research is only just beginning, especially with respect to neuroimaging techniques (see later discussion), one would presume that devotional visualization practices, for example, would activate the sensory and emotional regions of the brain.

As mentioned, contemporary neuroscientific research on contemplative practice and mystical experience has its roots in earlier quantitative and experimental studies. From the late 1950s to the present, the United States has witnessed increasing interest in meditation, especially as practiced in Hinduism and Buddhism. Some of the earliest and most prolific studies focused on Transcendental Meditation (TM), Vipassanā, and the Relaxation Response.[40] With respect to TM, various studies were critiqued on methodological grounds, especially given the fact that Maharishi Mahesh's organization and associates funded much of the research and that the research was often conducted by TM adherents. In addition, some researchers challenged TM's claims concerning uniqueness and expressed concerns regarding scientific reproducibility by non-TM researchers, as the organization refuses to disclose TM's characteristics and specific methods (secret *mantras*) (see ch. 13 herein). In any case, early studies suggested that trophotropic forms of meditation *in general* resulted in specific health benefits. These included relief of hypertension and stress (identified as a cause of disease) and reduction of heart rate, blood pressure, and physiological arousal. These effects fall under the general category of "relaxation." Other research examined meditation using electroencephalography (EEG) machines as well as Rorschach tests.[41] The latter, now largely out

Brain Region	Associated Function
Frontal lobe	Higher-level cognition, language formation, motor skills, planning, problem solving, reasoning. Also emotion
Occipital lobe	Vision
Parietal lobe	Processing tactile sensory information such as pressure, touch, and pain
Temporal lobe	Emotion, language comprehension, memory, speech recognition

Figure 1.8. Brain Regions and Associated Functions[39]

of favor, is a psychological test in which subjects' perceptions of inkblots are recorded and then analyzed using psychological interpretation.

In one especially fascinating study, Daniel Brown and Jack Engler (1984) administrated a Rorschach test to a variety of practitioners of Mindfulness meditation, with the intention of establishing patterns of perception and cognition correlated to different stages. Interestingly, the only practitioner identified by members of the Buddhist tradition as a "master" provided a

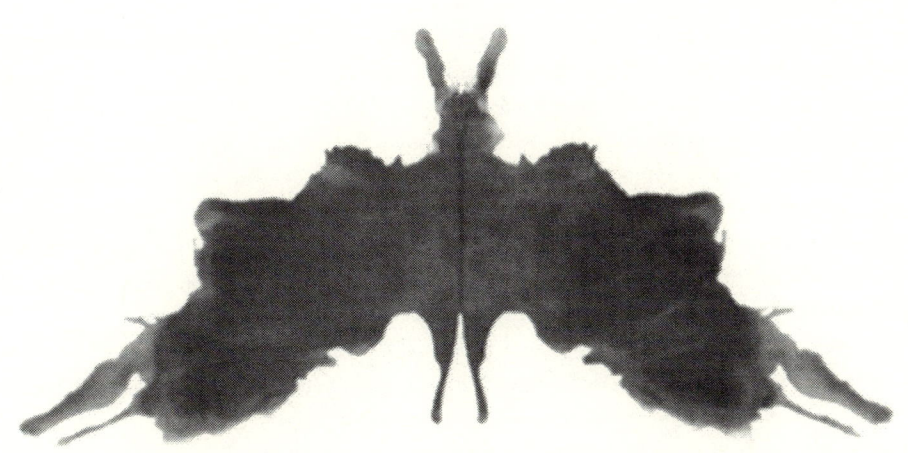

Figure 1.9. Rorschach Inkblot (Card V)
Source: Psychodiagnostik (Psychodiagnostics) (1921), by Hermann Rorschach (1884–1924).

comprehensive and integrated interpretation rooted in Buddhist doctrine (249). From a Buddhist perspective, this expresses a higher level of consciousness or enlightenment. For Brown and Engler, this may indicate both a pedagogical approach rooted in compassion for the listener and a radical, enduring reorganization of one's intrapsychic structure (260). Alternatively, it might indicate complete and seamless indoctrination, although Brown and Engler suggest otherwise (259).

As a more neuroscientific approach, EEGs record electrical activity along the scalp produced by the firing of neurons within the brain; the technology utilizes electrodes placed on the scalp. With respect to meditation, EEGs have been used to measure brain amplitude changes and electrical coherence in the brain (see Andresen 2000, 32–42). EEG is precise with regard to time but imprecise with regard to spatial resolution compared to other, more recently developed neuroimaging technologies. Generally, the chosen methodology depends on one's primary research agenda and area of investigation (e.g., fast perceptual processing requires using EEG) (Evan Thompson, pers. comm.).

More recently, new neuroimaging technologies have been developed. These include functional magnetic resonance imaging (fMRI), positron emission tomography (PET), and single photon emission computed tomography (SPECT), all of which provide fairly sophisticated images of brain activity. As explained by Antoine Lutz, John Dunne, and Richard Davidson (2007, 540), PET measures emissions from radioactively labeled chemicals that have been injected into the blood system and uses the data to produce two- or three-dimensional images of the distribution of the chemicals throughout the brain and body. Using different tracers, PET can reveal blood flow, oxygen and glucose metabolism, and neurotransmitter concentrations in the tissues of the working brain. SPECT is similar to but less sophisticated than PET, and it produces images of neurochemical function that have less spatial resolution than PET. MRI uses magnetic fields and radio waves to produce high-quality two- or three-dimensional images of brain structures without injecting radioactive tracers. Using MRI, scientists can see both surface and deep brain structures with a high degree of anatomical detail; MRI techniques can also be used to image the brain as it functions. Finally, fMRI relies on magnetic properties of the blood to enable the researcher to measure the blood flow in the brain as it changes in real time. This technology enables researchers to make maps of changes in brain activity as participants perform various tasks or are exposed to various stimuli. Thus, the neuroscientific understanding of the "meditative mind" is directly connected with specific technology and the challenges, albeit rarely mentioned, of interpretive analysis. Hypothetically speaking, this means that neuroscientists could produce neuroimages or brain maps of various types of contemplative practice. In contemporary American society, the majority of attention is being given to Buddhist, especially Tibetan and Zen Buddhist, meditation (see Austin 1998, 2006; Davidson and Harrington 2002; Wallace 2007), but a neuroscientific approach could be applied to the cross-cultural and comparative study of contemplative practice.

As a possibly relevant correlate, Beauregard and Paquette have attempted to map the "neural correlates of mystical experience" in Carmelite nuns (2006) utilizing fMRI technology (cf. Newberg et al. 2003). The resultant fMRI shows areas of activity during specific experiences identified as "God's presence" by Carmelite nuns (see fig. 1.10). In a more skeptical approach, Michael Persinger of Laurentian University has developed the so-called God Helmet.[42] This research continues the long-standing fascination with the temporal lobe, a region of the cerebral cortex associated with auditory processing.[43] The God Helmet, originally a modified snowmobile helmet, stimulates people's temporal lobes artificially with a weak magnetic field in order to

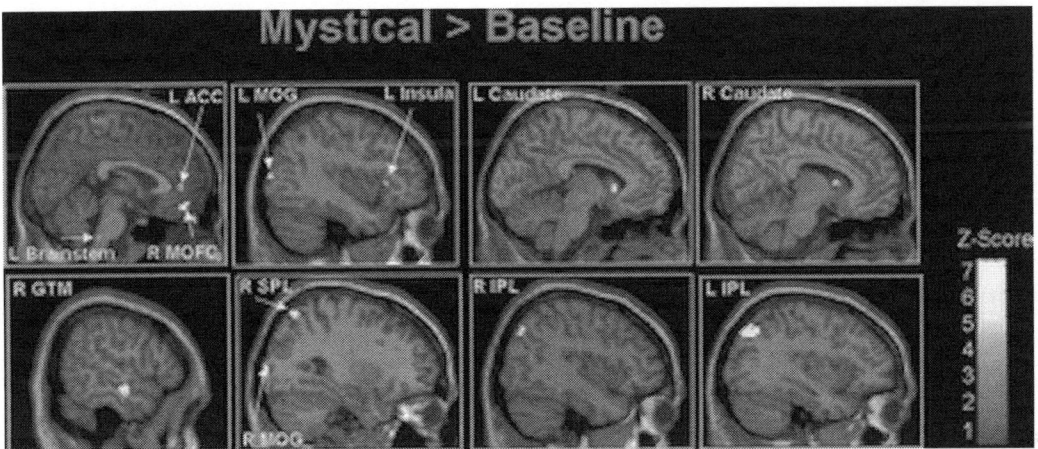

Figure 1.10. fMRI of Carmelite Nuns
Source: Beauregard and Paquette 2006.

elicit a "spiritual experience." Specifically, Persinger claims that people experience a "sensed presence" that is variously interpreted religiously. For Persinger, like other secular materialists and neuroscientific reductionists, such experiments supposedly support the "God delusion," or the mistaken identification of neurochemical changes as experiences of the divine.[44] On a different track, B. Alan Wallace of the Santa Barbara Institute for Consciousness Studies and Clifford Saron of the Center for Mind and Brain (University of California, Davis) have initiated a meditation training program that utilizes neuroscientific measurements before, during, and after the training.[45] The Shamatha Project represents a collaborative research project and parallels many interdisciplinary approaches in the emerging field of contemplative studies. In its most thoughtful and careful expressions, neuroscience has the potential to provide a window into contemplative practice. Specifically, it would be fascinating to have brain maps of the effects of specific methods that could be compared.

As mentioned, the neuroscientific approach to contemplative practice ("contemplative science") has become the dominant paradigm in contemplative studies. However, there are various limitations that deserve further reflection. Considering neuroscience and neuroimaging technology on their own terms, there are complex methodological issues. These include a required recognition of the diversity of methods, technique-specific effects and results, experience levels, and stages of practice (see also Andresen 2000; Lutz et al. 2007). As discussed in the next chapter, many religious systems identify stages of practice and levels of attainment. An increase in the level of complexity of neuroscientific research agendas and experiments will prove challenging with respect to evidential support and conclusive results. In addition, the following question needs to be addressed: What are neuroscientists really studying? Although there is a claim to understand human consciousness and experience, it is equally plausible that neuroscience is studying its own technological interaction with the brain, or at least its ability to understand consciousness as technologically measurable. Second, neuroscience can too easily degenerate into "neuroscientific reductionism," or the reduction of every dimension of human existence, including contemplative practice and contemplative experience, into neurological activity. This often involves an idea that humans are "hardwired" (neurobiologically determined) to think and act in the ways that they do. In examining contemplative practice and related experience, neuroscience may, as is often the case in the study of mysticism, simply see "experience" in terms of physiology. So, if one can demonstrate, as the Good Friday Experiment and God Helmet appear to, that the same neurological shift, the same physiological pattern, appears, then such individuals appear to have the "same experiences." However, this fails to locate human life and experience in context. In the case of contemplative experience, one might identify four primary dimensions: the trigger (source), the actual experience (not reducible to physiology), its interpretation, and the context (Komjathy 2012). The trigger is also not reducible to techniques. There may be other factors influencing certain experiences. For example, one might have the same neurophysiological change and even the same interpretation of that change, but the source of the experience may be completely different. Of course, this challenges secular materialist and atheistic assumptions. The latter often assumes a quasi-Cartesian dualism between "mind" (psychical) and "body" (material) because physiology is defined, *ipso facto*, as biological, not theological, in origin. However, if physiology itself is a *hierophany*, to use Eliade's phrase, then one of the dominant neuroscientific paradigms breaks down.[46] This is clearly the case in Daoist internal alchemy practice (see ch. 12 herein). We should thus avoid the problematic Eurocentric view of neuroscientific reductionism. Third, tradition-based contemplative practice, specifically contemplative practice rooted in community and place, emphasizes the importance of direct, first-person experience. The use of technology is a third-person methodology that, arguably, includes an implicit skepticism concerning the reliability of personal experience.[47] As complementary to contemplative practice and contemplative experience itself, neuroscience may have an important, but not privileged, place in contemplative studies. However, perhaps contemplative practice represents a challenge to and remedy for the ubiquitous presence of technology and machinery in contemporary human life. That is, technological mediation may, in fact, contradict basic commitments of various contemplatives. Perhaps contemplative practice is best understood as embodied indwelling, as an entry into interior silence beyond human constructions, including "research agendas," and beyond systems of fabricated meaning. It may reveal that the production and utilization of various technologies is detrimental to human flourishing.[48]

As an additional point of reflection, there are a variety of exciting and promising collaborative projects currently being conducted. Some of these are under the auspices of the organizations mentioned earlier. As one might expect, the Fourteenth Dalai Lama (Tenzin Gyatso; b. 1935) and Tibetan Buddhism are focal points. For present purposes, what stands out is the recent attempt to overcome Eurocentric cultural biases, biases often implicit in "scientific approaches to meditation." That is, there are alternative discourse communities involved. In the case of *Visions of Compassion* (2002), various prominent neuroscientists, who are also Tibetan Buddhist adherents or sympathizers, conducted neuroscientific fieldwork studies with and on Tibetan monks living near Bhagsu Mountain, located close to Dharamsala, Himachal Pradesh (northern India). As Houshmand and his colleagues explain, "For the first time, highly accomplished yogis were being invited to become involved, not just as subjects, but as collaborators in research" (4). And,

> Although they welcomed the scientists warmly and were very interested in discussing the project, most were reluctant to participate in the testing. They questioned the scientists' goals and motives. They had doubts, very candidly expressed, about the

premises of the research. And they were worried about the personal risks involved. (10; see also Andresen 2000, 48–53)

This research is noteworthy, like recent intermonastic conferences, for its willingness to include the voices of adherents in the academic study of religion, for its resistance to the ubiquitous tendency to objectify and marginalize members of religious traditions (see also Orsi 2002, 2005). At the same time, it too deserves some reflection, given the fact that researchers seem to reduce contemplative practice to techniques and corresponding physiology, especially "beneficial physiological changes." Paralleling earlier TM research, there is also a privileging of the Tibetan Buddhist tradition itself, as many of the volume's contributors begin with the assumption that (Tibetan Buddhist) compassion is a "higher form of consciousness." One would also do well to consider potential political motivations on the part of the Dalai Lama and Tibetan diaspora community (see, e.g., Lopez 1999), including the relevance of "scientific validation" (cf. TM in the 1950s and 1960s). For instance, why is similar research not being conducted on Christian Centering Prayer with the participation of prominent figures like Thomas Keating (b. 1923) and William Meninger (d.u.) of Saint Benedict's Monastery (Snowmass, CO)? If certain practitioners and communities are resistant to such research, this merits documentation, reflection, and discussion. Rather than simply presupposing a set of neuroscientific agendas and self-justifying narratives, we would do well to consider alternative approaches and perspectives. Finally, the researchers fail to locate Tibetan Buddhist practice within its larger context. Is it possible that living in the Himalayas with other monastics is as significant as consistent practice of the methods? Of course, this, in combination with Shamanic and ritual dimensions of the tradition, would make it much more difficult to export and disseminate Tibetan Buddhism to the West, let alone to reconceptualize it as a "therapeutic technique" for psychological and social well-being.

A final point regarding neuroscientific approaches to contemplative studies involves the recent emergence of "neurophenomenology" (see, e.g., Varela 1996; Lutz and Thompson 2003; Thompson 2010). Basically, this approach includes *both* subjective descriptions of contemplative experience *and* neuroimaging of the associated experience. Neurophenomenology attempts to determine the degree to which there is congruence. Preliminary findings suggest that subjective accounts by committed and advanced practitioners do, in fact, correspond to the brain maps. That is, certain accounts of subjective experience may be accurate and reliable. Paralleling the research of Richard Davidson, B. Alan Wallace, and others, neurophenomenology thus represents one emerging and fruitful model of collaboration between contemplatives and neuroscientists.

Interpretive Issues in Contemplative Studies

As one moves forward into the primary texts in this volume, various interpretive issues arise. Careful study of contemplative practice and contemplative literature inspires philosophical reflection, and philosophical reflection is required for deep understanding of contemplative practice and contemplative literature. Here I briefly introduce some interpretive issues derived from and applicable to the types of contemplative practice presented in this volume.

There are a variety of discourse communities involved in the study of contemplative practice, including adherents, contemplatives, and academic researchers. The latter group is complex, as it consists of adherents (scholar-practitioners), sympathizers, and skeptics. It also includes individuals with diverse interpretive interests and methodological approaches. In approaching contemplative practice, we may consider the concerns, values, and questions that inform each of these. There clearly are debates within religious communities that academic researchers identify as irrelevant. The same is true in the opposite direction. As the Tibetan Buddhists mentioned in Houshmand et al.'s work indicate, many practitioners would explicitly challenge, both philosophically and existentially, the relevance of neuroimaging. What are the central commitments and concerns of each sector of contemplative studies? Is it possible that, to use the philosopher W. V. Quine's phrase, there is an "indeterminacy of translation" between the different discourse communities? We need to identify and consider debates within, between, and outside of religious communities. For example, what types of conversations occur during intermonastic gatherings? How do these differ from those at academic conferences? Could a comprehensive approach to contemplative studies make space for all of these?

As mentioned, contemplative studies as an emerging interdisciplinary field utilizes both third-person and critical first-person approaches (De Wit 1991, 31–32; also Varela and Shear 1999; Roth 2006; Frohlich 2007; Ferrer and Sherman 2008). The former involves studying contemplative practice from the position of observer and outsider while the latter from that of participant and insider. There are various issues here. First, does participant-observation, direct personal experience with contemplative practice, cross a necessary line? What happens when one allows students in university courses to practice specific methods and analyze their own experience? "Critical first-person discourse" frames the inquiry as investigation of one's own psychosomatic experience and of the relationship between practice and experience. "Critical" or "disciplined" would seem to inhibit the tendency to privilege one particular perspective, to take one's own beliefs and experience as normative. Can one facilitate such inquiry and, simultaneously, help students appreciate diversity? Contemplative practice, and religious studies for that matter, necessarily entails and inspires such questions. Contemplative studies includes theology on some level, and this will make many scholars of religion uncomfortable. At the same time, and this is noteworthy, such an approach would appear to meet students' interest in exploring their own beliefs (see Walvoord 2007). The introduction of contemplative practice into university education clearly crosses the divide between theory and practice.[49] It has the potential to assist students in maintaining habits of wellness and in becoming more embodied and engaged. Another point to consider is the degree to which one becomes a "participant" and "insider" by practicing specific methods. For example, in his Theory and Practice of Buddhist Meditation course, Harold Roth of Brown University has his students participate in a variety of "labs," during which they learn, practice, and gain experience with a multitude of methods. This is a "buffet-style" or "wine-tasting" model. One finds a similar approach in a variety of other humanities courses that advocate applying contemplative practice to issues related to peace and social justice. In combination with "scientific studies," this is one of the few ways to receive funding for contemplative studies. However, one can legitimately question such appropriative agendas, including the associated tendency of decontextualization and reconceptualization, with respect to origins and context. This directly relates to notions of "experience," including the degree to which one is actually practicing a given method. Arguably, the informing worldview and social location of contemplative practice are as important as the actual technique itself. That is, "Buddhist meditation" practiced without an informing Buddhist worldview and outside of a Buddhist community is not Buddhist.[50] The alternative would seem to be to enculturate students into Buddhism, which of course is highly problematic. How does one understand contemplative practice and related experience within context? What is the informing worldview and social location of contemplative studies programs at private liberal arts colleges and public research universities? That is, institutional locatedness exerts some influence on the way that the discourse and learning outcomes are framed. Other course designs are possible, and one might also include guest speakers from or site visits to the associated tradition. Once again one encounters the complex issue of lived religiosity in religious studies. This brings me to my third point about first-person discourse. Why does such an approach only include supposedly objective or neutral investigators? Why must the voices and contributions of "critical adherents" be excluded? I would suggest that adherents and religious leaders can be as reflective and analytical about their traditions as scholars. We can and should make space for them in contemplative studies. In fact, they are already among us, holding many of the most prominent endowed chairs in religious studies. There are two final points. The first relates to autobiography. If first-person discourse is included in contemplative studies, then it would follow that autobiography becomes a viable genre of academic research. As is the case in the study of mysticism (see Forman 1999; Kripal 2001; Paper 2004), one can imagine scholars utilizing direct first-person experience as evidential support for certain dimensions of research. Finally, the "third-person"/"first-person" framework fails to include interpersonal, or "second-person," dimensions of contemplative practice (see Thompson 2001). Where does dialogue *between* contemplatives and practitioners of contemplative methods fit into contemplative studies? Are there other possible subjects (e.g., animals) for interrelational dialogue? This would again place emphasis on the communal, rather than solitary, dimension of contemplative practice.

We should also reflect on the contributions and limitations of community and tradition, including the influence of place. As we have seen, there is a tendency among secular humanists, empirical researchers, as well as hybrid spiritualists and transpersonal psychologists to extract religious practices from their religious contexts and traditions. This involves reframing the relevance and importance of specific methods, often without an awareness of the ethical and political dimensions of such activities. Is appropriation and redefinition, especially by those without adherence and affiliation to the associated tradition, ethical? What happens to the individual and social lives of the representatives of the traditions, traditions that have been marginalized and repackaged? In all of this, there are some implicit and often explicit critiques of tradition-based contemplative practice: religious commitment is based on indoctrination and dogmatism; institutionalized religion (and perhaps institutions in general) inhibit human potential and human flourishing; religious traditions only have a partial view of "reality" and often rigidly cling to their own truth-claims; religious traditions are patriarchal and oppress women; religious traditions tend to favor preservation and conservatism over innovation and creativity; religious adherence tends to lead to opposition and even violence toward others, rather than acceptance and peace. Such views of course contain some important insights into the limitations of community and tradition, but they focus on very specific dimensions of religiosity. Moreover, they have their own assumptions and ingrained opinions, such as the belief that there is a single, trans-religious reality (monistic theology). If one focuses on contemplative strains of religious traditions, specifically contemplatives and contemplative communities, one finds deep philosophical and theological systems, sophisticated psychological and soteriological insights, as well as comprehensive training regimens aimed at "higher" ontological conditions and cosmological integration. Although meditation has become part of the larger American counterculture and even mainstream, deep contemplative practice, practice that is integrated, holistic, consistent, and prolonged—in short, practice that is an all-pervasive existential and soteriological commitment—is most often undertaken by clerical and monastic elites. It requires long periods of training and a life oriented toward the sacred. I am not suggesting that only religious elites can engage in contemplative practice, but rather that they tend to be the individuals who completely embrace such a way of life. For example, there are many self-identified academic contemplatives, but certain aspects of academic life (concern for reputation, attachment to power and position, committee work, politicized decision-making, etc.) are clearly antithetical to contemplative commitments. Returning to the contributions of community and tradition, I would suggest that religious participation, in its most beneficial, transformative, and life-affirming moments, deepens one's understanding and practice. I am of course talking about authentic and committed religious life with an emphasis on contemplative practice. Contemplative practice itself may be the corrective to many of the problems of religious disorientation. As discussed in the next chapter, participation in religious community and tradition may clarify the deeper dimensions of contemplative practice. For example, one could practice a specific method with an antithetical worldview; one would, in turn, be unlikely to receive the intended benefits or spiritual insights of the method. Assuming that community elders express and embody certain commitments, social participation and spiritual direction may also inhibit tendencies toward self-delusion, especially concerning spiritual advancement. Community and tradition may inhibit the pitfalls of autodidacticism and correct the perils of spiritual athleticism, exhibitionism, and materialism (see the technical glossary in this volume).

Another interpretive issue focuses on the place of method or technique in contemplative practice. There is a tendency to reduce contemplative practice to mere technique. If I practice mindfulness as described by S. N. Goenka, then apparently I am practicing Vipassanā and located in Buddhism. This is clearly not the case. For Vipassanā, an early form of Buddhist meditation, to be a Buddhist method, one must also understand and locate oneself in a Buddhist worldview, especially concerning the three characteristics of existence, namely, suffering (*dukkha*), impermanence (*anicca*), and no-self (*anatta*), as well as the Five Aggregates that reveal the illusion of "self" conventionally conceived. One might argue that practicing Vipassanā correctly as a method will lead to this type of spiritual awareness, but that "spiritual awareness" is itself Buddhist. In any case, contemplative practice is more complex and sophisticated than the practice of technique. It cannot be reduced to method. As I have suggested earlier, religiously-committed and tradition-based contemplative practice locates one in a specific worldview, soteriology, and theology. Integrated and holistic contemplative practice tends to be multidimensional. It often includes asceticism, ethics, monasticism, ritual, scripture study, spiritual direction, and so forth. We should reflect on the relative importance of method in contemplative practice and religious traditions. Moreover, what is the origin and purpose of the method? Do specific techniques express specific religious commitments? Think back to the Rorschach study on Buddhist meditators mentioned earlier in the chapter.

At the same time, one should consider the actual variety of tradition-based methods that might be categorized as "contemplative." As we have seen, there is a tendency in the emerging field of contemplative studies to privilege apophatic, attentional, and trophotropic methods, including medicalized, psychologized, and nontheistic types. Thus, one encounters a strong interest in Vipassanā, Zen, and Tibetan methods emphasizing "wisdom and compassion." In the previous section of this chapter, I have emphasized the way in which this parallels the construction of "mystical experience" as synonymous with contentless, hypoaroused unitive experiences, with an assumed monistic theology. However, one could just as easily privilege the opposite. In the case of religiously-committed and tradition-based contemplative techniques, we should adopt a comprehensive and inclusive approach. This would involve studying methods that make some secular humanist scholars of religions uncomfortable, such as devotional, dualistic, petitionary, and theistic methods. If one wishes to suggest that contemplative practice involves increasing attention, awareness, interiority, presence, silence, and transformation, and perhaps even a sense of sacrality, then the question may be asked of less easily domesticated methods. We need to take religious traditions seriously on their own terms, including the ways in which such concerns may challenge our conceptualization. For example, do Hindu *mantra*-based techniques lead to a state of interior silence and union? Does Salat (Islamic prayer) require interior silence to be performed well? In a related way, how do different traditions understand "silence," both as an ontological/theological concept and its purpose in human existence? Moreover, rather than overemphasize "consciousness," attention also needs to be given to physical embodiment and posture, to the psychosomatic dimensions of contemplative practice (see Komjathy 2007). What types of postures (body-configurations) are used? Are those postures seen as essential? Do the postures and associated methods provide a clear window into the larger informing framework?

It is also important to reflect upon the heuristic value of "prayer," "meditation," "ritual," as well as other comparative categories. This connects with the question of religious training regimens and ways of life considered more comprehensively. As mentioned, "prayer" is conventionally understood in terms of devotion, petition, and penance. "Meditation" frequently implies seated postures and is assumed to be synonymous with Buddhist meditation; as such, "meditation" comes to refer to a specific type of practice centering of emptiness, nondiscrimination, silence, and stillness. Finally, "ritual" is often equated with external performances and theatrical movement patterns undertaken in a communal context (Grimes 1995; Bell 1997). The Catholic high Mass might be taken as representative. Even if one accepts such conventional views, tradition-based contemplative practice frequently includes all three. Take Zen Buddhist meditation for example. Could not the commitment to sit silently be understood as a petition and invocation for enlightenment, perhaps even devotion to Śākyamuni Buddha? Of course, Zen conventionally tells one, "If you see the Buddha on the road, kill him." That is, one should recognize that one *is* the Buddha; there are no distinctions. So, "devotion to the Buddha" is "devotion to oneself," although that "self" is empty of own-being. Moreover, in tradition-based Zen practice, there is a great deal of bowing and chanting. Meditation, prayer, and ritual intersect. Extended beyond these three categories, contemplative practice parallels soteriological training regimens. That is, outside of the modern world, meditation and contemplative prayer are multidimensional and only provisionally efficacious. Integrated and holistic religious training includes ethics, scripture study, ritual, and perhaps even ascetic or monastic life. Should such training regimens be understood as "contemplative practice" itself, or does "contemplative practice" refer to particular dimensions? Can scripture study or precept study and application be "contemplative practices"? Perhaps "meditation" as a distinct category of practice, as a separate "tradition," only exists in the modern world.

Much has also been made about meditation as a method to facilitate mystical experience. From one perspective, meditation and mysticism have a necessary connection. This is a complex issue because of the relative importance of both contemplative practice and mystical experience in specific traditions (see Gimello 1978). For present purposes, we can define mystical experience as experience of that which a given individual or community identifies as sacred (e.g., Allah in Islam). From the perspective of mystics, mystical experience involves direct experience of a trans-human reality, an interaction between an individual and/or communal subject and a sacred dimension. The latter may include the denial or transcendence of subject/object dichotomies. There is, in turn, a broad spectrum of mystical experiences and informing theologies; not all mystical experiences are the same, and different mystical experiences suggest mutually exclusive, equally convincing accounts of "reality." In terms of the relationship between contemplative practice and mystical experience, one must investigate specific practices and specific experiences, if the latter occur. If the method is correlated with specific stages and experiences, how does the tradition identify, define, and locate such experiences in religious training? As discussed in more detail in the next chapter, there is a general tendency in religious traditions to understand mystical experience in a variety of ways, including as a *by-product* of spiritual practice and/or as confirmation of progress.[51] However, the search for "extraordinary" experiences can also be a source of distraction and become dangerous. Insanity is an ever-present possibility in undisciplined and disoriented contemplative practice (see, e.g., Grof and Grof 1989), and even within tradition-based, community-directed practice (e.g., Tantra and Daoist internal alchemy). This issue requires careful study of both mystical experience and contemplative practice. Where is mystical experience located in contemplative practice? While the overall relationship between contemplative practice and mystical experience is open to debate, requiring careful study of individual contemplatives and communities, there can be no doubt that the two dimensions of religious life frequently overlap. Many well-known contemplatives were also mystics (e.g., Teresa of Ávila). Moreover, many contemplative practices anticipate or facilitate mystical experiences. In addition to considering this and similar patterns, do we need to make a distinction among different types of experiences, such as "ordinary experience," "contemplative experience," "mystical experience," and so forth (see, e.g., Cardeña et al. 2000)?

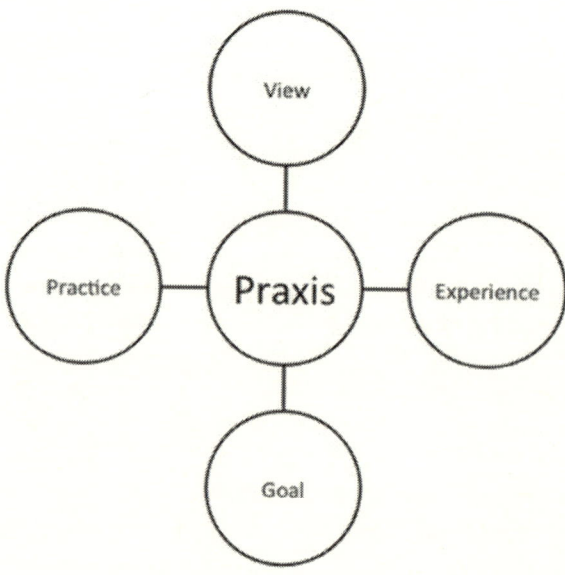

Figure 1.11. Dimensions of (Religious) Praxis

Another issue briefly touched upon involves informing worldviews. As I have previously suggested (Komjathy 2007), there is a complex relationship among worldview, practice, and experience. Each informs the other in complex ways. If one analyzes contemplative practice with attention to this framework, one inquires into the ways in which specific methods express and confirm specific worldviews and lead to specific types of experiences, the ways in which specific worldviews inform specific practices and lead to specific types of experience, and the ways in which specific types of experiences confirm specific worldviews and the efficacy of specific methods. Each facet of religious praxis, and human life more generally, has multiple dimensions. For example, "practice" could include asceticism, ethics, meditation, prayer, ritual, scripture study, and so forth. "Worldview" could include cosmology, epistemology, ontology, psychology, soteriology, theology, and views of self. Here I would suggest that attention to cosmology and theology is especially important. That is, how does a given tradition conceptualize the structure and underlying principles of the cosmos and the nature and characteristics of the sacred? For example, the traditional and foundational Indian worldview identifies the cosmos as samsaric and based on karma, the universal law of moral cause and effect. How does such a cosmology inform Hindu, Jain, or Buddhist contemplative practice? As a comparative category, "theology" refers to discourse on or theories about the "sacred," with "sacred" being another comparative category used to identify the ultimate concern and its defining characteristics within the context of distinct religious traditions. The latter should not be *assumed* to be singular in nature. Tradition-specific conceptions of the sacred would include YHWH in Judaism, Brahman in Hinduism, and Dao in Daoism. That is, as a comparative category, "theology" can neither be reduced to Christian theology nor to theistic conceptions of the sacred. Broadly understood, beyond tradition-specific theologies, we may identify the following types of theology: animistic (nature populated by spirits), atheistic (no gods), monistic (one impersonal reality), monotheistic (one personal god), panenhenic (Nature as sacred), pantheistic (sacred immanent in the world), panentheistic (sacred in and beyond the world), and polytheistic (multiple gods). Many of these may be theistic (personal) or nontheistic (impersonal). Most tend to be relational, or based on subject/object dichotomies. However, some theologies make space for apotheosis (elevation to godhood), self-divinization, and divine incarnation (sacred manifest as physical beings). That is, there is a spectrum of theological views on a transcendence-immanence spectrum: the sacred as outside of space and time and wholly different from the world (most transcendent); humans as containing the sacred (more immanent); the world as the sacred (most immanent). There are also transpersonal and nondualistic perspectives that challenge conventional subject/object dichotomies. Viewed from this perspective, different tradition-based contemplative practices utilize different theologies; their informing communities and traditions identify different sacreds with different characteristics. In short, careful study of religious traditions reveals mutually exclusive, equally convincing accounts of "reality." These accounts inform tradition-based contemplative practice, and such practice embodies, quite literally, those accounts.

As a final point concerning tradition-based contemplative practice and contemplative experience, careful study and sophisticated interpretation requires us to "think through" the associated system. This involves both "familiarization" and "defamiliarization"; we must endeavor to see the unfamiliar as familiar and the familiar as unfamiliar (see also Smith 1982, xiii; Smith 2004, 383). Assuming encounter with "unfamiliar others," through an act of generosity and sympathy, of creativity and imagination, we may locate ourselves, to a certain extent, in a new landscape. The "symbol system," to use Geertz's concept, makes perfect sense on its own terms.

To recognize this, of course, requires that one identifies one's own assumptions and ingrained opinions. Every worldview has its "seams," the places where enough pressure splits it apart and renders it fragmentary and discardable. However, to comprehend the texts in the present volume, I suggest that we endeavor to undertake a sympathetic and generous reading first. Taken seriously, the texts in the present volume contain unexpected and profound insights into human existence. In addition to providing a window into the associated traditions, they may challenge and clarify one's perspective.

There are of course many other issues that could be identified, but these are some of the most interesting from my perspective. They are also directly applicable to the texts contained in this anthology. They are relevant as much to researchers in contemplative studies as they are to individuals approaching contemplative practice from a critical first-person perspective, and perhaps even from an adherent perspective.

Notes

The present chapter has benefited from the comments of Willoughby Britton (Brown University), Jorge Ferrer (California Institute of Integral Studies), Andrew Fort (Texas Christian University), Fran Grace (University of Redlands), Jeffrey Kripal (Rice University), Kevin Schilbrack (Appalachian State University), Evan Thompson (University of British Columbia), and the volume's contributors. I am also grateful for grant support from the Wabash Center and the University of San Diego.

Some of the information in the first and second sections in this chapter has benefited from the contributions of members of the Contemplative Studies Group of the American Academy of Religion, especially Thomas Coburn, Fran Grace, Anne Klein, Harold Roth, and Judith Simmer-Brown.

My gratitude notwithstanding, all views and interpretations are my own.

1. The history of the terms "meditation," "contemplative practice," and the like has yet to be written. Preliminary insights may be found in Engel 1997a; Underwood 2005; Baier 2009.

2. For a discussion of tradition-specific technical terms related to contemplative practice, see chapter 2 and the technical glossary in this volume.

3. This is not the place to provide a critical discussion of the categories "religion," "religions," and "religious." Suffice it to say that my perspective and the conception of the present volume have benefited from the insights of Mircea Eliade, Clifford Geertz, William James, Ninian Smart, J. Z. Smith, and Paul Tillich, among others. For a more detailed presentation of Daoism in terms of religious studies, see my *The Daoist Tradition* (Komjathy 2013).

4. As discussed later here and in the next chapter, I utilize "praxis," and occasionally "practice," as a more encompassing technical category. "Methods," "practices," and "techniques" are basically synonymous. They refer to the specific disciplines that make up the whole of praxis, with the latter often understood in terms of integrated and holistic embodied being-in-the-world. From this perspective, "contemplative practice" would be only one type of praxis. It also would indicate a specific "way of being."

5. The categories of "ergotropic" and "trophotropic" derive from Fischer 1971 and 1980. See also Forman 1990; Komjathy 2007.

6.

Varieties of conscious states mapped on a perception-hallucination continuum of increasing ergotropic arousal (left) and a perception-meditation of increasing trophotropic arousal (right). These levels of hyper- and hypoarousal are interpreted by man [sic] as normal, creative, psychotic, and ecstatic states (left) and Zazen and samādhi (right). The loop connecting ecstasy and samādhi represents the rebound from ecstasy to samādhi, which is observed in response to intense ergotropic excitation. The numbers 35 to 7 on the perception-hallucination continuum are Goldstein's coefficient of variation, specifying the decrease in variability of the EEG amplitude with increasing ergotropic arousal. The numbers 26 to 4 on the perception-meditation continuum, on the other hand, refer to those beta, alpha, and theta EEG waves (measured in hertz) that predominate during, but are not specific to, these states (Fischer 1971, 898).

See also Forman 1990, 6. Regardless of what one thinks of the specifics of Fischer's chart, it is helpful for bringing our attention to the spectrum of physiological activity related to different types of contemplative practice and contemplative experience.

7. Both "contemplative practice" and "contemplative experience" may lead to interpretive problems. "Contemplative practice" may create a tendency to reduce contemplation to method or technique. "Contemplative experience" may create a tendency to privilege experience over practice.

8. From my perspective, some noteworthy examples include Mark Rothko's (1903–1970) paintings contained in the Rothko Chapel (Houston, TX); the experimental composer and music theorist John Cage's (1912–1992) *4'33"*; the Zen Buddhist photography of John Daido Loori (1931–2009); the modern dance performances and choreography of Philippina "Pina" Bausch (1940–2009); as well as *The Artist Is Present* (2010) by the modern performance artist Marina Abramović (b. 1946).

9. The history of contemplative studies as an emerging field is complex and open to debate; different scholars would construct the field in different ways. Some would flatly reject the association with "interreligious dialogue." They would prefer to construct it "scientifically" and "objectively," that is, through quantitative and "objective" research and through the exclusion of religious practitioners and the voice of "professional contemplatives."

10. For a comprehensive and inclusive overview of organizations and programs related to contemplative studies, see the Contemplative Studies website maintained by Louis Komjathy (University of San Diego).

11. For a concise FAQ sheet on contemplative pedagogy, see Coburn et al. 2011. For a CMind perspective, which is interdisciplinary and relatively secular and addresses issues of implementation, see Barbezat and Bush 2014.

12. Many teacher-scholars working in university education also find the schism between personal identity and professional persona limiting and debasing. For some critical insights into vocation in teaching, see Palmer 2007. For a recent study of student interests in religious studies courses, specifically for existential clarification, see Walvoord 2007. This approach is often framed as "spirituality in education" or "transformative education."

13. In order for Roth's formulation to work, we would have to make the following amendment: religiously-committed first-person perspectives. Every first-person perspective is "committed" to something, no matter how "objective" or "neutral" it aims to be. One could, moreover, argue that secular materialism and scientific reductionism have become the new dogmas (cf. McCutcheon 2001). In the context of contemplative studies, one would also have to add technological optimism and trans-tradition spirituality.

14. There are, of course, complex political and economic issues involved. Based on the supposed "separation of church and state," publicly funded universities and their faculty must be careful not to cross the imagined line. There is also justifiable uneasiness about the place of religious beliefs in university education. However, one must acknowledge that while separation of church and state may be legally possible, separation of religion and politics is not.

15. In the present volume, "theology" refers to that which a given individual or community identifies as "sacred" or ultimately real. From this perspective, there are "nontheistic" types of theology. See Komjathy 2012, 2013.

16. Here "mystical experience" refers to experiences of that which a given individual or community identifies as sacred or ultimately real. From the perspective of mystics, mystical experience involves a direct

experience of a trans-human reality, an interaction between an individual and/or communal subject and a sacred dimension. See Komjathy 2007, 2012.

17. One of the more influential counterpositions has been advocated by Robert K. C. Forman and his colleagues (see Forman 1990), which emphasizes the possibility of Pure Consciousness Events (PCEs), especially through various methods of deconditioning, forgetting, and so forth. Advocates of this position have labeled it "Decontextualism" and "Perennial Psychology." The latter is relevant in the present volume, especially with respect to consciousness, psychology, and neuroscience, as it suggests a shared humanity and universal substrate of consciousness.

18. *The Experience of Meditation* is also problematic in other ways. Most notably, one should reflect on the relative importance of the presented methods, specifically on their degree of representativeness with respect to the associated tradition. The book clearly has a modernist bias; there is an emphasis on more contemporary methods that are often informed by the worldviews for which they purportedly provide evidential support. Moreover, the book includes a mistaken identification of Qigong as a form of "Daoist meditation." This comes from both misunderstanding about the Daoist religious tradition (see Komjathy 2013) and the self-promotional nature of the authors' presentation. It may also derive from Shear's own long-term commitment to the practice of Taiji quan (Great Ultimate [Yin-yang] Boxing) (270), a Chinese "internal martial art" that is often misidentified as Daoist (Komjathy 2013). As a side note, Daoist traditions of meditation are quite diverse and include apophatic meditation, ingestion, inner observation, internal alchemy, respiratory methods, visualization, and so forth (see Komjathy 2013). Technically speaking, modern forms of Qigong, which may or may not be Daoist, fall more clearly under the category of "health and longevity techniques," or Daoyin (guided stretching) and Yangsheng (nourishing life) in indigenous terms. This is not to say that they do not have contemplative dimensions, but rather that they are not forms of "Daoist meditation."

19. In the present volume, "soteriology" is used as a comparative category to refer to actualization, liberation, perfection, realization, salvation, or however an individual or community defines the ultimate purpose of human existence. See the technical glossary in this volume.

20. I make this qualification because of the influence of interreligious cross-pollination, ubiquity of theological domestication, and tendency toward apologetics in contemporary America. That is, there is a tendency among certain practitioners to gloss over, polish away, or dilute religious differences in the name of peace and harmony. Individuals taking tradition-specific perspectives, which involve commitments to a more-encompassing soteriological framework, are likely to be seen as "not going with the program." They are "sectarians," "fundamentalists," or "dogmatists" who are inhibiting "unity." However, such is the unity of monoculture, not of wilderness.

21. In this respect one also thinks of the Carmelite Catholic friar and mystic Juan de la Cruz's (John of the Cross; 1542–1591) discussion of the "dark night."

22. Although many of these perspectives express humanistic and transpersonal psychologies, they seem to remain rooted in earlier psychological views that pathologize religious adherence. Here one thinks of Sigmund Freud (1856–1939) in particular. To this dominant, modern psychological viewpoint we may juxtapose a slightly modified version of William James (1842–1910), who makes a distinction that roughly corresponds to "religion of the sick-minded" and "religion of the healthy-minded" (see James 1999). This perspective encourages one to investigate the ways in which religious commitments contribute to or undermine human and "nonhuman" flourishing.

23. During my interview with Benson (see ch. 13 herein), he mentioned that various people, both sympathizers and detractors, have infused this word with metaphysical significance. However, in the original formulation, the word was simply the number one. This too is significant with respect to its elementary nature.

24. Benson has since modified his views to take on more religious dimensions ("the faith factor") (see ch. 13 herein).

25. It should be recognized that humanistic and transpersonal psychology has largely been marginalized from academic departments of psychology, which, generally speaking, have embraced a scientific paradigm as well as the empirical and quantitative research model. That is, many academic psychologists would object to this presentation. The situation is more complex on the clinical and applied side.

26. Of course, like "theology," one can take issue with the use of "psychology" as a comparative category. From a historical perspective, "psychology" refers to a Western discipline with a particular history and social location, including specific cultural influences. However, as a comparative category, "psychology" may be used in a larger and inclusive sense of discourse on or theories about consciousness (*psyche*).

27. Humanistic psychology is often referred to as the "third force" in psychology, following behaviorism and psychoanalysis.

28. While "anthropology" is most often used to designate the social scientific discipline that studies human culture, the term is also employed in theological contexts to refer to discourse on and theories of human personhood, especially in relation to the sacred.

29. Deikman explicitly discusses the place of meditation in his "mystical psychology" (1982, 135–52).

30. Maslow is well known for postulating a "hierarchy of needs," in which basic needs such as material sustenance, safety and security, belongingness and love, respect, and self-esteem must be met before one can attain Being-cognition. That is, Maslow's views include a sociopolitical dimension.

31. It should be noted, however, that there tends to be an anti-religion bias in most transpersonal psychologies; religious communities and traditions, as aspects of "institutionalized religion," are defined as limiting human potential or as resources for a "spiritual" or "nonsectarian" approach.

32. In fact, Murphy has an explicit critique of tradition-based contemplative practice (1992, 543–44, 555–57). While Murphy's account provides some important insights into potential deficiencies of certain approaches to transformative practice, it also generally neglects the benefits of community-centered, tradition-based practice or privileges one approach over another without recognizing the theological commitments embedded in his analysis. As I have suggested, contemplative practice is located in a larger soteriological system, and this is equally true of Murphy's transpersonal program. As discussed later, we, of course, need to provide a balanced analysis of the contributions and limitations of religiously-committed contemplative practice. This includes the potential dangers of autodidactic and unsupervised practice. Egocentrism and self-delusion too easily emerge from modern appropriative agendas, including those of humanistic and transpersonal psychology.

33. This, of course, raises the question of what qualifies as "ordinary" and "normal." From a contemplative perspective, "ordinary" human consciousness, characterized by habituation and agitation, may be abnormal, that is, conventional psychological views of human being focus on lower levels of consciousness.

34. This is not to suggest that there are not forms of suffering, such as economic exploitation, political oppression, social injustice, and actual enslavement, beyond an individual's control. Rather, it brings our attention to the ways in which much suffering is psychological and related to particular states of consciousness.

35. There are, of course, potential dangers to such an approach, including dissociation, the loss of self in a negative sense, and implicit perpetuation of social injustice and exploitation. That is, one may come to see the world simply as "samsaric," as something to "escape" and "transcend."

36. In contrast to some humanistic and transpersonal psychologists, De Wit uses the phrase "contemplative traditions" in explicit connection with religion, specifically adherents and communities committed to contemplative practice and spiritual development. In premodern religious practice, this would be the purview of the religious elite, often ascetics, clerics, and monastics. See chapter 2 herein.

37. The present overview is primarily a distillation of d'Aquili and Newberg 1999, 21–44. See also Austin 1998; Andresen 2000; Lutz et al. 2007.

38. That is, the "mind" is literally in the "body."

39. This illustration represents my attempt to provide a relatively straightforward map of brain regions and associated functions. However, it is a simplification and deserves qualification. Specifically, "It has been

hypothesized that the neural activity crucial for consciousness most probably involves the transient and continual orchestration of scattered mosaics of functionally specialized brain regions, rather than any single, highly localized brain process or structure," and "A common theoretical proposal is that each moment of conscious awareness involves the transient selection of a distributed neural population that is both integrated or coherent, and differentiated or flexible, and whose members are connected by reciprocal and transient dynamic links" (Lutz et al. 2007, 527).

40. For some helpful overviews of scientific research on meditation, see Engel 1997a, 1997b; Murphy et al. 1999; Andresen 2000; UAEBPC 2007; Lutz et al. 2007; Baier 2009.

41. Biofeedback has also been utilized. This process involves measuring a subject's specific and quantifiable bodily functions such as blood pressure, heart rate, skin temperature, sweat gland activity, and muscle tension in order to convey the information to the patient in real time. This raises the person's awareness and therefore the possibility of conscious control of those functions. In terms of the present volume, one in turn wonders if biofeedback could be identified as a modern form of contemplative practice ("technological meditation").

42. See, for example, www.shaktitechnology.com. Compare the Marsh Chapel Experiment (a.k.a. Good Friday Experiment) conducted by Walter Pahnke in 1962.

43. Some researchers have suggested a direct correlation between temporal lobe epilepsy and certain types of mystical experiences. In a similar "pathologization" of mystical experience, specific mystics have been identified as "schizophrenics" or "chronic migraine sufferers." See, for example, Sacks 1992, 299–301.

44. This research approach is often identified as "neurotheology," which can be misleading. As utilized among secular researchers, that term suggests that every theological belief is reducible to neurological activity. That is, "religious experience" is simply shifts in brain activity that is *interpreted* as religious. However, it is equally plausible to imagine "neurotheology" as a branch of contemporary theology that employs neuroscience to clarify certain cognitive dimensions of religious experiences, especially theologically committed ones.

45. For a description, see www.sbinstitute.com/research_shamatha.html.

46. One might, in turn, reflect on the "theology of the body."

47. On the category of "experience" in religious studies, see Proudfoot 1985; Sharf 1995; Komjathy 2007; Martin and McCutcheon 2012. This discussion also continues in chapter 2 herein.

48. This insight, of course, challenges certain movements in contemplative studies toward "contemplative science" and "contemplative technologies." It is little surprise then that Buddhism, which tends to be more mind-based and apparently less theistic than other religious traditions, is so central here. The prominence of neuroscience in turn brings issues of economics, power, and interpretive authority in contemplative studies into high relief. In a context dominated by "scientism" (science as religion), it appears that one needs quantifiable data and support for subjective claims, especially with respect to cultural capital and sociopolitical access.

49. As indicated by the diversity of proposals for Contemplative Practice Fellowships through the Center for Contemplative Mind in Society (formerly in association with the American Council of Learned Societies), there are many possible approaches to introducing contemplative practice into university education. See www.contemplativemind.org/programs/academic/fellowships.html.

50. Harold Roth, one of the pioneers and key theorists in contemplative studies, of course recognizes this (pers. comm.). Here I am presenting Roth's course, including its use of "labs" in an elite, secular private research university, as an opportunity for reflection. See also Komjathy 2014.

51. Mystical experience also is frequently the trigger for conversion and entry into the priesthood or monastic orders. Many individuals had mystical experiences as "signs" and "inspiration," but these often depart as soon as one fully commits to a religious path. Based on extant literature, and the frequent lamentation for such "loss," it appears that many adherents do not recognize the eventual irrelevance of mystical experience. Moreover, according to some religious traditions, and some mystical experiences themselves indicate this, it is possible to enter a more enduring and permanent state of "mystical being and mystical experiencing" beyond the momentariness of "mystical experiences" (see Komjathy 2007).

Works Cited and Further Reading

AAR Contemplative Studies Group. 2011. "Select Bibliography of Contemplative Studies." http://www.sandiego.edu/cas/contemplativestudies/resources/publications.php. Accessed on June 1, 2014.

Andresen, Jensine. 2000. "Meditation Meets Behavioral Meditation." In *Cognitive Models and Spiritual Maps*, edited by Jensine Andresen and Robert Forman, 17–73. Bowling Green: Imprint Academic.

———, ed. 2001. *Religion in Mind: Cognitive Perspectives on Religious Belief, Ritual, and Experience.* Cambridge and New York: Cambridge University Press.

Andresen, Jensine, and Robert K. C. Forman, eds. 2000. *Cognitive Models and Spiritual Maps: Interdisciplinary Explorations of Religious Experience.* Bowling Green: Imprint Academic.

Astin, Alexander, Helen Astin, and Jennifer Lindholm. 2011. *Cultivating the Spirit: How College Can Enhance Students' Inner Lives.* San Francisco: Jossey-Bass.

Austin, James H. 1998. *Zen and the Brain.* Cambridge: MIT Press.

———. 2006. *Zen-Brain Reflections.* Cambridge: MIT Press.

———. 2009. *Selfless Insight.* Cambridge: MIT Press.

Bache, Christopher. 2008. *The Living Classroom: Teaching and Collective Consciousness.* Albany: State University of New York Press.

Baier, Karl. 2009. *Meditation und Moderne.* 2 vols. Würzburg, Germany: Königshausen and Neumann.

Barbezat, Daniel, and Mirabai Bush. 2014. *Contemplative Practices in Higher Education: Powerful Methods to Transform Teaching and Learning.* San Francisco: Jossey-Bass.

Barnhart, Bruno, and Joseph Wong, eds. 2001. *Purity of Heart and Contemplation: A Monastic Dialogue between Christian and Asian Traditions.* New York and London: Continuum.

Beauregard, Mario, and Vincent Paquette. 2006. "Neural Correlates of a Mystical Experience in Carmelite Nuns." *Neuroscience Letters* 405: 186–90.

Begley, Sharon. 2006. *Train Your Mind, Change Your Brain.* New York: Ballantine.

Bell, Catherine. 1997. *Ritual: Perspectives and Dimensions.* Oxford and New York: Oxford University Press.

Benson, Herbert. 1975. *The Relaxation Response.* New York: Morrow.

Berger, Peter L. 1990 (1967). *The Sacred Canopy: Elements of a Sociological Theory of Religion.* New York: Anchor Books.

Berger, Peter L., and Thomas Luckmann. 1966. *The Social Construction of Reality.* New York: Doubleday.

Bourdieu, Pierre. 1977. *Outline of a Theory of Practice.* Translated by Richard Nice. Cambridge and New York: Cambridge University Press.

Brookfield, Stephen. 1995. *Becoming a Critically Reflective Teacher.* New York: Jossey-Bass.

Brown, Daniel. 1977. "A Model for the Levels of Concentrative Meditation." *International Journal of Clinical and Experimental Hypnosis* 25.4: 236–73.

———. 1986. "The Stages of Meditation in Cross-Cultural Perspective." In *Transformations of Consciousness*, edited by Ken Wilber et al., 219–83. Boston: Shambhala.

Brown, Daniel, and Jack Engler. 1984. "A Rorschach Study of the Stages of Mindfulness Meditation." In *Meditation: Classic and Contemporary Perspectives*, edited by Deane Shapiro and Roger Walsh, 232–62. New York: Aldine.

Brown, Sid. 2008. *A Buddhist in the Classroom.* Albany: State University of New York Press.

Bush, Mirabai, ed. 2011. *Contemplation Nation: How Ancient Practices Are Changing the Way We Live.* Kalamazoo: Fetzer Institute.

Cabezón, José. 2006. "The Discipline and Its Other." *Journal of the American Academy of Religion* 74.1: 21–38.

Cabezón, José, and Sheila Davaney, eds. 2004. *Identity and the Politics of Scholarship in the Study of Religion.* London and New York: Routledge.

Calais-Germain, Blandine. 2007. *Anatomy of Movement.* Rev. ed. Seattle: Eastland Press.

Calhoun, Adele Ahlberg. 2005. *Spiritual Disciplines Handbook.* Downers Grove: InterVarsity Press.

Cardeña, Etzel, Steven Jay Lynn, and Stanley Krippner, eds. 2000. *Varieties of Anomalous Experience: Examining the Scientific Evidences*. Washington: American Psychological Association.

Chester, Michael, and Marie C. Norrisey. 1985. *Prayer and Temperament: Different Prayer Forms for Different Personality Types*. Rev. ed. Charlottesville: Open Door.

Coburn, Thomas, Fran Grace, Anne Klein, Louis Komjathy, Harold Roth, and Judith Simmer-Brown. 2011. "Contemplative Pedagogy: Frequently Asked Questions." *Teaching Theology and Religion* 14.2: 167–74.

Craig, Barbara. 2011. "Contemplative Practice in Higher Education: An Assessment of the Contemplative Practice Fellowship Program, 1997–2009." Northampton: Center for Contemplative Mind in Society.

Csikszentmihalyi, Mihaly. 1990. *Flow: The Psychology of Optimal Experience*. New York: Harper.

Csikszentmihalyi, Mihaly, and Isabella Selega Csikszentmihalyi, eds. 1988. *Optimal Experience: Psychological Studies of Flow in Consciousness*. Cambridge: Cambridge University Press.

D'Aquili, Eugene, and Andrew B. Newberg. 1999. *The Mystical Mind: Probing the Biology of Religious Experience*. Minneapolis: Fortress Press.

Davanger, Svend, Halvor Eifring, and Anne Grete Hersoug. 2008. *Fighting Stress: Reviews of Meditation Research*. Oslo, Norway: Acem Publishing.

David, Caroline Franks. 1989. *The Evidential Force of Religious Experience*. Oxford: Clarendon Press.

Davidson, Julian M. 1984. "The Physiology of Meditation and Mystical States of Consciousness." In *Meditation: Classic and Contemporary Perspectives*, edited by Deane N. Shapiro and Roger N. Walsh, 376–95. New York: Aldine.

Davidson, Richard, and Anne Harrington, eds. 2002. *Visions of Compassion: Western Scientists and Tibetan Buddhists Examine Human Nature*. Oxford and New York: Oxford University Press.

De Wit, Han. 1991. *Contemplative Psychology*. Translated by Marie Louise Baird. Pittsburgh: Duquesne University Press.

Deikman, Arthur J. 1982. *The Observing Self: Mysticism and Psychotherapy*. Boston: Beacon Press.

Dewey, John. 1997 (1938). *Experience and Education*. Reprint. New York: Free Press.

Dumoulin, Heinrich. 1990. *Zen Buddhism: A History*. Vol. 2: Japan. Translated by James Heisig and Paul Knitter. New York: Macmillan.

Dreyer, Elizabeth, and Mark Burrows, eds. 2005. *Minding the Spirit: The Study of Christian Spirituality*. Baltimore: Johns Hopkins University Press.

Engel. Klaus. 1997a. *Meditation: Volume 1 History and Present Time*. Berlin: Peter Lang.

———. 1997b. *Meditation: Volume 2 Empirical Research and Theory*. Berlin: Peter Lang.

Epstein, Mark. 1995. *Thoughts without a Thinker*. New York: Harper Collins.

Epstein, Mark, and Jonathan Lieff. 1986. "Psychiatric Complications of Meditation Practice." In *Transformations of Consciousness*, edited by Ken Wilber et al., 53–63. Boston: Shambhala.

Evans, Donald. 1989. "Can Philosophers Limit What Mystics Do?" *Religious Studies* 25.1: 53–60.

Ferrer, Jorge, and Jacob Sherman, eds. 2008. *The Participatory Turn: Spirituality, Mysticism, Religious Studies*. Albany: State University of New York Press.

Fischer, Roland. 1971. "A Cartography of the Ecstatic and Meditative States." *Science* 174.4012: 897–904.

———. 1980. "A Cartography of the Ecstatic and Meditative States." In *Understanding Mysticism*, edited by Richard Woods, 286–305. Garden City: Doubleday Image Books.

Fitzgerald, Timothy. 2000. "Experience." In *Guide to the Study of Religion*, edited by Willi Braun and Russell T. McCutcheon, 125–39. London and New York: Cassell.

Forman, Robert K. C., ed. 1990. *The Problem of Pure Consciousness*. Oxford and New York: Oxford University Press.

———, ed. 1998. *The Innate Capacity*. Oxford and New York: Oxford University Press.

———. 1999. *Mysticism, Mind, Consciousness*. Albany: State University of New York Press.

Fraleigh, Sondra Horton. 1996. *Dance and the Lived Body*. Pittsburgh: University of Pittsburgh Press.

Friedman, Harris, and Glenn Hartelius, eds. 2013. *The Blackwell Handbook of Transpersonal Psychology*. West Sussex, England, and Malden, MA: Wiley-Blackwell.
Frohlich, Mary. 2001. "Spiritual Discipline, Discipline of Spirituality: Revisiting Questions of Definition and Method." *Spiritus* 1.1: 65–78.
———. 2007. "Critical Interiority." *Spiritus* 7.1: 77–81.
Fromm, Erich. 2002 (1976). *To Have or to Be?* New York: Continuum.
Gallagher, Shaun, and Jonathan Shear, eds. 1999. *Models of the Self*. Bowling Green: Imprint Academic.
Gendlin, Eugene. 1997 (1962). *Experiencing and the Creation of Meaning: A Philosophical and Psychological Approach to the Subjective*. Evanston: Northwestern University Press.
Gill, Jerry. 1984. "Mysticism and Mediation." *Faith and Philosophy* 1: 111–21.
Gill, Sam. 2005 (1987). "Prayer." In *Encyclopedia of Religion*, edited by Lindsay Jones, 7367–72. 2nd ed. Detroit: Macmillan Reference.
Gimello, Robert. 1978. "Mysticism and Meditation." In *Mysticism and Philosophical Analysis*, edited by Steven T. Katz, 170–99. Oxford and New York: Oxford University Press.
———. 1983. "Mysticism in Its Contexts." In *Mysticism and Religious Traditions*, edited by Steven T. Katz, 61–88. Oxford and New York: Oxford University Press.
Glazer, Steven, ed. 1999. *The Heart of Learning: Spirituality in Education*. New York: Jeremy P. Tarcher.
Goleman, Daniel. 1977. *The Varieties of Meditative Experience*. New York: E. P. Dutton.
———. 1988. *The Meditative Mind*. Los Angeles: J. P. Tarcher.
Goleman, Daniel, and Robert Thurman, eds. 1991. *MindScience: An East-West Dialogue*. Boston: Wisdom.
Goodman, Felicitas. 1990. *Where the Spirits Ride the Wind: Trance Journeys and Other Ecstatic Experiences*. Bloomington: Indiana University Press.
Grimes, Ronald. 1995. *Beginnings in Ritual Studies*. Rev. ed. Columbia: University of South Carolina Press.
Grof, Stanislav, and Christina Grof, eds. 1989. *Spiritual Emergency: When Personal Transformation Becomes a Crisis*. New York: Tarcher/Putnam.
Grosz, Elizabeth. 1994. *Volatile Bodies: Toward a Corporeal Feminism*. Bloomington and Indianapolis: Indiana University Press.
Guyton, Arthur, and John Hall. 2006. *Textbook of Medical Physiology*. 11th ed. Philadelphia: Elsevier Saunders.
Hadot, Pierre. 1995. *Philosophy as a Way of Life: Spiritual Exercises from Socrates to Foucault*. Hoboken: Blackwell.
Harrington, Anne, and Arthur Zajonc, eds. 2006. *The Dalai Lama at MIT*. Cambridge: Harvard University Press.
Hart, Tobin. 2004. "Opening the Contemplative Mind in the Classroom." *Journal of Transformative Education* 2.1: 28–46.
Haruki, Y., Y. Ishii, and M. Suzuki, eds. *Comparative and Psychological Study on Meditation*. Delft, Netherlands: Eburon.
Heidegger, Martin. 1977. *The Question Concerning Technology, and Other Essays*. Translated by William Lovitt. San Francisco: Harper and Row.
Heiler, Friedrich. 1932. *Prayer: A Study in the History and Psychology of Religion*. Oxford: Oxford University Press.
Hewes, Gordon W. 1955. "World Distribution of Certain Postural Habits." *American Anthropologist* 57: 231–44.
———. 1957. "The Anthropology of Posture." *Scientific American* 196: 123–32.
Higher Education Research Institute (HERI). 2005. "The Spiritual Life of College Students: A National Study of College Students' Search for Meaning and Purpose." UCLA HERI Spirituality in Higher Education Research Report.
———. 2006. "Spirituality and the Professoriate: A National Study of Faculty Beliefs, Attitudes, and Behaviors." UCLA HERI Spirituality in Higher Education Research Report.

Hill, Clifford, ed. 2006. "Contemplative Practices and Education." Special Issue of *Teachers College Record* 108.9.

Hood, Ralph W., Jr., ed. 1995. *Handbook of Religious Experience*. Birmingham: Religious Education Press.

Houshmand, Zara, Anne Harrington, Clifford Saron, and Richard Davidson. 2002. "Training the Mind: First Steps in a Cross-Cultural Collaboration in Neuroscientific Research." In *Visions of Compassion*, edited by Richard Davidson and Anne Harrington, 3–17. Oxford and New York: Oxford University Press.

Ibish, Yusf, and Ileana Marculescu, eds. 1977. *Contemplation and Action in World Religions*. Houston: Rothko Chapel.

Iwamura, Jane. 2000. "The Oriental Monk in American Popular Culture." In *Religion and Popular Culture in America*, edited by Bruce David Forbes and Jeffrey H. Mahan, 25–43. Berkeley: University of California Press.

James, William. 1890. *The Principles of Psychology*. 2 vols. New York: Holt.

———. 1999 (1902). *The Varieties of Religious Experience*. New York: The Modern Library.

Johnson, Mark. 1987. *The Body in the Mind: The Bodily Basis of Meaning, Imagination, and Reason*. Chicago: University of Chicago Press.

Johnson, Don Hanlon. 1995. *Bone, Breath, and Gesture: Practices of Embodiment*. Berkeley: North Atlantic Books.

Kabat-Zinn, Jon. 1990. *Full Catastrophe Living*. New York: Delacorte Press.

———. 1995. *Wherever You Go, There You Are*. New York: Hyperion.

Katz, Steven T., ed. 1978a. *Mysticism and Philosophical Analysis*. Oxford and New York: Oxford University Press.

———. 1978b. "Language, Epistemology, and Mysticism." In *Mysticism and Philosophical Analysis*, edited by Steven T. Katz, 22–74. Oxford and New York: Oxford University Press.

———, ed. 1983a. *Mysticism and Religious Traditions*. Oxford and New York: Oxford University Press.

———. 1983b. "The 'Conservative' Character of Mysticism." In *Mysticism and Religious Traditions*, edited by Steven T. Katz, 3–60. Oxford and New York: Oxford University Press.

Komjathy, Louis. 2007. *Cultivating Perfection: Mysticism and Self-Transformation in Early Quanzhen Daoism*. Leiden: Brill.

———. 2011. "Field Notes from a Daoist Professor." In *Meditation and the Classroom: Contemplative Pedagogy in Religious Studies*, edited by Judith Simmer-Brown and Fran Grace, 95–103. Albany: State University of New York Press.

———. 2012. "Mysticism." In *Encyclopedia of Global Religion*, edited by Mark Juergensmeyer and Wade Clark Roof, 855–61. Thousand Oaks: Sage.

———. 2013. *The Daoist Tradition: An Introduction*. London and New York: Bloomsbury Academic.

———. 2014. "THRS 394: Contemplative Traditions Syllabus." http://home.sandiego.edu/~komjathy. Accessed on June 1, 2014.

Kripal, Jeffrey. 2001. *Roads of Excess, Palaces of Wisdom: Eroticism and Reflexivity in the Study of Mysticism*. Chicago: University of Chicago Press.

———. 2006. *The Serpent's Gift: Gnostic Reflections on the Study of Religion*. Chicago: University of Chicago Press.

Lakoff, George. 1987. *Women, Fire, and Dangerous Things: What Categories Reveal about the Mind*. Chicago: University of Chicago Press.

Lakoff, George, and Mark Johnson. 1980. *Metaphors We Live By*. Chicago: University of Chicago Press.

———. 1999. *Philosophy in the Flesh: The Embodied Mind and Its Challenge to Western Thought*. New York: Basic Books.

Lindholm, Jennifer, Melissa Millora, Leslie Schwartz, and Hanna Song Spinosa. 2011. *A Guidebook of Promising Practices: Facilitating College Students' Spiritual Development*. Berkeley: Regents of the University of California.

Lopez, Donald S., Jr. 1999. *Prisoners of Shangri-La: Tibetan Buddhism and the West.* Chicago: University of Chicago Press.

Luisi, Pier Luigi. 2009. *Mind and Life: Discussions with the Dalai Lama on the Nature of Reality.* New York: Columbia University Press.

Lutz, Antoine, and Evan Thompson. 2003. "Neurophenomenology: Integrating Subjective Experience and Brain Dynamics in the Neuroscience of Consciousness." *Journal of Consciousness Studies* 10: 31–52.

Lutz, Antoine, John Dunne, and Richard Davidson. 2007. "Meditation and the Neuroscience of Consciousness: An Introduction." In *The Cambridge Handbook of Consciousness*, edited by Philip Zelazo et al., 499–551. Cambridge and New York: Cambridge University Press.

Maitland, Jeffrey. 1995. *Spacious Body: Explorations in Somatic Ontology.* Berkeley: North Atlantic Books.

Martin, Craig, and Russell McCutcheon, eds. 2012. *Religious Experience: A Reader.* Sheffield, England: Equinox.

Maslow, Abraham H. 1964. *Religions, Values, and Peak Experiences.* New York: Viking.

———. 1999 (1968). *Toward a Psychology of Being.* New York: John Wiley and Sons.

Mauss, Marcel. 1935. "Les techniques du corps." *Journal de Psychologie Normale et Pathologique* 35: 271–93.

———. 1979. "Body Techniques." In *Sociology and Psychology*, translated by Ben Brewster, 95–123. London: Routledge and Kegan Paul.

McCown, Donald, Diane Reibel, and Marc Micozzi. 2010. *Teaching Mindfulness: A Practical Guide for Clinicians and Educators.* New York: Springer.

McCutcheon, Russell, ed. 1999. *The Insider/Outsider Problem in the Study of Religion.* London and New York: Cassell.

———. 2001. *Critics Not Caretakers: Redescribing the Public Study of Religion.* Albany: State University of New York Press.

McGinn, Bernard. 1991. *The Foundations of Mysticism.* New York: Crossroad.

Metzinger, Thomas, ed. 2000. *Neural Correlates of Consciousness: Empirical and Conceptual Questions.* Cambridge: MIT Press.

Mischell, Theodore, ed. 1977. *The Self: Psychological and Philosophical Issues.* Oxford: Basil Blackwell.

Mitchell, Donald, and James Wiseman, eds. 2003. *The Gethsemani Encounter: A Dialogue on the Spiritual Life by Buddhist and Christian Monastics.* New York and London: Continuum.

Murphy, Michael. 1992. *The Future of the Body: Explorations into the Further Evolution of Human Nature.* New York: Penguin Putnam.

Murphy, Michael, Steven Donovan, and Eugene Taylor. 1999. *The Physical and Psychological Effects of Meditation.* Sausalito: Institute of Noetic Sciences.

Nagatomo, Shigenori. 1992. *Attunement through the Body.* Albany: State University of New York Press.

Naranjo, Claudio, and Robert Ornstein. 1977. *On the Psychology of Meditation.* Baltimore: Penguin Books.

Newberg, Andrew, Michael Pourdehnad, Abass Alavi, and Eugene d'Aquili. 2003. "Cerebral Blood Flow during Meditative Prayer: Preliminary Findings and Methodological Issues." *Perceptual and Motor Skills* 97: 625–30.

Ornstein, Robert, ed. 1973. *The Nature of Human Consciousness.* San Francisco: W. H. Freeman.

———. 1996 (1972). *The Psychology of Consciousness.* New York: Penguin Books.

Orsi, Robert. 2002. *The Madonna of 115th Street: Faith and Community in Italian Harlem.* 2nd ed. New Haven: Yale University Press.

———. 2005. *Between Heaven and Earth: The Religious Worlds People Make and the Scholars Who Study Them.* Princeton: Princeton University Press.

Oscar-Berman, Marlene, and Ksenija Marinkovic. 2004. "Alcoholism and the Brain: An Overview." National Institute of Alcohol Abuse and Alcoholism. http://pubs.niaaa.nih.gov/publications/arh27-2/125-133.htm.

O'Sullivan, Edmund, Amish Morrell, and Mary Ann O'Conner. 2002. *Expanding the Boundaries of Transformative Learning.* New York: Palgrave.

Palmer, Parker. 2007 (1997). *The Courage to Teach: Exploring the Inner Landscape of a Teacher's Life.* San Francisco: Jossey-Bass.

Palmer, Parker, and Arthur Zajonc. 2010. *The Heart of Higher Education: A Call to Renewal.* San Francisco: Jossey-Bass.

Paper, Jordan. 2004. *The Mystic Experience: A Descriptive and Comparative Analysis.* Albany: State University of New York Press.

———. 2005. *The Deities Are Many: A Polytheistic Theology.* Albany: State University of New York Press.

Persinger, Michael. 1987. *Neuropsychological Basis of God Beliefs.* New York: Praeger.

Phillips, Dewi. 1965. *The Concept of Prayer.* London: Routledge and Kegan Paul.

Plante, Thomas, ed. 2010. *Contemplative Practices in Action: Spirituality, Meditation, and Health.* Santa Barbara: Praeger.

Proudfoot, Wayne. 1985. *Religious Experience.* Berkeley: University of California Press.

Rendon, Laura. 2009. *Sentipensante (Sensing/Thinking) Pedagogy: Education for Wholeness, Social Justice and Liberation.* Sterling: Stylus.

Rogers, Carl. 1961. *On Becoming a Person: A Therapist's View of Psychotherapy.* New York: Houghton Mifflin.

Roth, Harold D. 2006. "Contemplative Studies: Prospects for a New Field." *Teachers College Record* 108.9: 1787–1815.

———. 2008. "Against Cognitive Imperialism: A Call for a Non-Ethnocentric Approach to Cognitive Science and Religious Studies." *Religion East & West* 8: 1–26.

Russell, Robert John, Nancy Murphy, Theo C. Meyering, and Michael A. Arbib, eds. 1999. *Neuroscience and the Person: Scientific Perspectives on Divine Action.* Berkeley/Vatican City: Center for Theology and the Natural Sciences/Vatican Observatory.

Sacks, Oliver. 1992. *Migraine.* Rev. ed. New York: Vintage Books.

Said, Edward W. 1979. *Orientalism.* New York: Vintage Books.

Schilbrack, Kevin, ed. 2004. *Thinking through Rituals: Philosophical Perspectives.* London and New York: Routledge.

Scholem, Gershom. 1995 (1941). *Major Trends in Jewish Mysticism.* New York: Schocken Books.

Senge, Peter, Otto Sharma, Joseph Jaworski, and Betty Sue Flowers. 2004. *Presence: Exploring Professional Change in People, Organizations, and Society.* Cambridge: Society for Organizational Learning.

Shapiro, Deane H., and Roger N. Walsh, eds. 1984. *Meditation: Classic and Contemporary Perspectives.* New York: Aldine.

Shapiro, Shauna, Kirk Brown, and John Astin. 2011. "Toward the Integration of Meditation into Higher Education: A Review of Research Evidence." *Teachers College Record* 113.3 (March 2011): 493–528.

Sharf, Robert. 1995. "Buddhist Modernism and the Rhetoric of Meditative Experience." *Numen* 42.3: 228–83.

———. 1998. "Experience." In *Critical Terms for Religious Studies,* edited by Mark C. Taylor, 94–116. Chicago: University of Chicago Press.

Shear, Jonathan, ed. 2006. *The Experience of Meditation: Experts Introduce the Major Traditions.* St. Paul: Paragon House.

Simmer-Brown, Judith, and Fran Grace, eds. 2011. *Meditation and the Classroom: Contemplative Pedagogy for Religious Studies.* Albany: State University of New York Press.

Smart, Ninian. 1965. "Interpretation and Mystical Experience." *Religious Studies* 1.1: 75–87.

Smith, J. Z. 1982. *Imagining Religion: From Babylon to Jonestown.* Chicago: University of Chicago Press.

———. 2004. *Relating Religion: Essays in the Study of Religion.* Chicago: University of Chicago Press.

Solberg, Erik Ekker. 2004. *Psycho-Biological Effects of Meditation.* Oslo, Norway: Unipub AS.

Tanahashi, Kazuaki. 1985. *Moon in a Dewdrop: Writings of Zen Master Dōgen.* San Francisco: North Point Press.

Tart, Charles, ed. 1969. *Altered States of Consciousness.* New York: John Wiley and Sons.

Thompson, Evan, ed. 2001. *Between Ourselves: Second-Person Issues in the Study of Consciousness*. Bowling Green: Imprint Academic.
———. 2010. *Mind in Life: Biology, Phenomenology, and the Sciences of Mind*. Cambridge: Belknap Press.
Underwood, Frederic. 2005 (1987). "Meditation." In *Encyclopedia of Religion*, edited by Lindsay Jones, 5816–22. 2nd ed. Detroit: Macmillan Reference.
University of Alberta Evidence-Based Practice Center (UAEBPC). 2007. "Meditation Practices for Health: State of the Research." Agency for Healthcare Research and Quality, U.S. Department of Health and Human Services, *Evidence Report/Technology Assessment* 155.
Varela, Francisco. 1996. "Neurophenomenology: A Methodological Remedy to the Hard Problem." *Journal of Consciousness Studies* 3: 330–50.
Varela, Francisco, Evan Thompson, and Eleanor Rosch. 1993. *The Embodied Mind: Cognitive Science and Human Experience*. Cambridge: MIT Press.
Varela, Francisco, and Jonathan Shear, eds. 1999. *The View from Within: First-Person Approaches to the Study of Consciousness*. Bowling Green: Imprint Academic.
Wallace, B. Alan. 2000. *The Taboo of Subjectivity: Toward a New Science of Consciousness*. Oxford and New York: Oxford University Press.
———. 2007. *Contemplative Science: Where Buddhism and Neuroscience Converge*. New York: Columbia University Press.
Walsh, Roger. 1993. "Phenomenological Mapping and Comparisons of Shamanic, Buddhist, Yogic, and Schizophrenic Experiences." *Journal of the American Academy of Religion* 61.4: 739–69.
Walvoord, Barbara. 2007. *Teaching and Learning in College Introductory Religion Courses*. Malden: Blackwell.
Ward, Jamie. 2009. *The Student's Guide to Cognitive Neuroscience*. 2nd ed. New York: Psychology Press.
Wasserstrom, Steven. 1999. *Religion after Religion: Gershom Scholem, Mircea Eliade, and Henry Corbin at Eranos*. Princeton: Princeton University Press.
West, Michael. 1987. *The Psychology of Meditation*. Oxford: Clarendon.
Wilber, Ken. 1977. *The Spectrum of Consciousness*. Wheaton: Quest Book.
———. 2000. *Integral Psychology: Consciousness, Spirit, Psychology, Therapy*. Boston: Shambhala.
Wilber, Ken. 2006. "Foreword." In *The Experience of Meditation: Experts Introduce the Major Traditions*, edited by Jonathan Shear, ix–xii. St. Paul: Paragon House.
———, Jack Engler, and Daniel Brown, eds. 2006. *Transformations of Consciousness: Conventional and Contemplative Perspectives on Development*. Boston: Shambhala.
Wilber, Ken, Terry Patten, Adam Leonard, and Marco Morelli. 2008. *Integral Life Practice: A 21st-Century Blueprint for Physical Health, Emotional Balance, Mental Clarity, and Spiritual Awakening*. Boston: Integral Books.
Wulff, David M. 1997. *The Psychology of Religion: Classic and Contemporary*. 2nd ed. New York: Wiley.
Yandell, Keith E. 1994. *The Epistemology of Religious Experience*. Cambridge and New York: Cambridge University Press.
Yuasa Yasuo. 1987. *The Body: Toward an Eastern Mind-Body Theory*. Translated by Nagatomo Shigenori and T. P. Kasulis. Albany: State University of New York Press.
———. 1993. *The Body, Self-Cultivation, and Ki-Energy*. Translated by Nagatomo Shigenori and Monte S. Hull. Albany: State University of New York Press.
Zajonc, Arthur. 2009. *Meditation as Contemplative Inquiry: When Knowing Becomes Love*. Great Barrington: Lindisfarne Books.
Zelazo, Philip, Morris Moscovitch, and Evan Thompson, eds. 2007. *The Cambridge Handbook of Consciousness*. Cambridge and New York: Cambridge University Press.
Zinberg, Norman, ed. 1977. *Alternate States of Consciousness*. New York: The Free Press.

Chapter 2

Contemplative Traditions

Louis Komjathy

"Contemplative traditions" refers, first and foremost, to the contemplative strains or dimensions of religious traditions. Similar to the category of "mystical traditions," "contemplative traditions" draws our attention to a particular aspect of religious adherence and commitment. The term is thus not intended to function in a manner parallel to "wisdom traditions" or "spirituality" in various modern contexts, wherein intellectual colonialism, appropriation and domestication, as well as decontextualization and reconceptualization are often involved. Instead, the present volume attempts to demonstrate the ways in which contemplative practice is always rooted in a particular worldview, community, context, and tradition. It specifically endeavors to provide accurate and nuanced presentations of religiously-committed and tradition-based contemplative practice, including the complex dimensions of the informing religious and soteriological systems. In this way, and as herein employed, "contemplative practice" is a distinct category, but not one that is wholly separable from the larger parameters of religious adherence and soteriological practice. At the same time, the categories of contemplative practice and contemplative experience make space for investigation of various modern phenomena, including "nonsectarian practice," "unchurched spirituality," as well as secular and therapeutic meditation. In fact, this book includes chapters on the Relaxation Response as advocated by Herbert Benson (b. 1935) and techniqueless meditation as taught by J. Krishnamurti (1895–1986). Beyond the narrow confines of seated meditation, contemplative practice might also include various somatic disciplines, such as Alexander Technique, Applied Kinesiology, Authentic Movement, Autogenic Training, Feldenkrais Method, Pilates, Trager Approach, and so forth (see, e.g., Johnson 1995; Murphy 1992). In this respect, one might also study martial arts (see, e.g., Palmer 2002; Raposa 2003). In addition, as mentioned in the previous chapter with respect to contemplative studies, contemplative practice might include art, dance, music, photography, theater, and so forth, with the defining characteristics and specific qualities requiring inquiry and reflection.

Nonetheless, the present volume is informed by and located within the field of religious studies. Particular attention is given to religiously-committed and tradition-based contemplative practice, specifically through representative texts from various religious traditions. As discussed later, each contributor has utilized a standardized interpretive framework and approach in order to explore the contextual nuances of the associated practice, community, and tradition. Our "contemplative traditions" are thus the contemplative approaches within a larger religious and soteriological system, and this volume argues that this is true of any contemplative practice. Views, influences, and contexts are always informing, embedded within and expressed through particular practices and experiences.

In the present chapter, I discuss the meaning and defining characteristics of "contemplative traditions." In particular, I provide some information on the entire spectrum of tradition-based contemplative practice in order to locate the works selected in this volume. Next, attention is given to the dimensions of contemplative practice, specifically the ways in which contemplative practice is located in larger religious and soteriological systems. Here I emphasize the multidimensional nature of religious practice, with contemplative practice being only one element. This is followed by a brief discussion of "contemplative experience," or types of experiences that occur or that are deemed significant within the context of contemplative practice. I draw a distinction between contemplative experience, mystical experience, and religious experience. In addition, I discuss some of the types of experiences that are claimed to occur during committed and sustained practice. Next, I suggest that we may study contemplative practice through the lens of "psychologies of realization," that is, the types of psychologies utilized within contemplative traditions. In particular, I suggest that many contemplative traditions map human potential and more "advanced" ontological conditions. That is, committed and prolonged contemplative practice aims at and often results in distinctive transformative effects. I then discuss "contemplative literature" and the contents of the present volume. Finally, attention is given to future prospects. While the previous chapter was more abstract and theoretical, this chapter is more concrete. I focus on specific examples of contemplative practice and contemplative experience and on contemplative traditions. Throughout this presentation, I draw upon the micro-studies of contemplative literature that form the core of this volume.

Contemplative Traditions

In the present volume, "contemplative practice," which includes meditation, contemplative prayer, and other cognate disciplines (see ch. 1), encompasses and approximates a variety of tradition-specific technical terms. Like the historical use of "contemplation" and "meditation," this dimension of tradition-based religious practice deserves further study, especially with attention to the contextual meaning and practical nuances of the terms. Important technical terms used to designate contemplative practice as herein employed include *bhāvanā* (Pali: development), a Buddhist term for meditation or mental development; *contemplatio* (Lat.: to look at/to observe), a Christian term for maintaining silent awareness of God; *dazuo* (Chn.: seated meditation), a Chinese and Daoist term for "meditation" broadly understood and an umbrella category for various specific practices; *dhyāna* (Skt.: concentration), a Buddhist term for concentration or meditative states; *hesychia* (Grk.: stillness), a Christian term for stillness, seclusion, and inner prayer; *hitbodedut* (Heb.: mental seclusion), a Jewish term for secluded, inward prayer; *jhāna*, the Pali equivalent of *dhyāna*; *muraqaba* (Ar.: to watch over), an Islamic term for Sufi contemplation; *samādhi* (Skt.: absorption), a Hindu and Buddhist term for concentration, meditative absorption, and yogic stasis; *shouyi* (Chn.: guarding the One), a classical Daoist technical term for apophatic meditation that eventually became a general category for "meditation" broadly understood; *yoga* (Skt.: to yoke and, by extension, to unite), a principally Hindu term for spiritual discipline aimed at liberation; *zazen* (Jpn.: sitting *dhyāna*), a Buddhist term for Zen meditation; and so forth. Here we must consider the degree to which these are general categories like "contemplative practice" and "meditation" or designations for specific methods such as *vipassanā*. It is also important to reflect on the extent to which they refer to techniques and/or experiences. As discussed in the chapters of the present book, there are many tradition-specific terms related to various methods with diverse soteriological aims. For example, as utilized by Harold Roth and myself, "Daoist apophatic meditation" approximates a variety of classical Daoist terms, including *baoyi* (embracing the One), *shouyi* (guarding the One), *xinzhai* (fasting the heart-mind), and *zuowang* (sitting-in-forgetfulness), all of which refer to a stillness-/emptiness-based practice characterized by a contentless, nonconceptual, and nondualistic state and aimed at mystical union with the Dao. Tradition-based and religiously-committed practices are thus located in larger religious and soteriological systems, a central topic of this volume.

In terms of "meditation" strictly defined, in the modern West the term is most often conflated with Buddhist forms, and Buddhist meditation has received the most attention in the Western academy. Viewed from a more neutral perspective, it is clear that Buddhist practice has been privileged, perhaps in a manner paralleling an earlier Christian bias. The reasons for this are complex. Regardless, there can be no debate that the Buddhist tradition, broadly and inclusively conceived, includes some of the most developed and diverse forms of contemplative practice: from calming and mindfulness practices, through loving-kindness and reflection on death, to emptiness and visualization. If familiar with Buddhist meditation, readers of the present volume will most likely think of Vipassanā, especially as taught by lay Burmese Theravāda teachers; Zazen, especially as taught within modern Japanese Sōtō and Rinzai lineages; and perhaps Tibetan Buddhist methods, especially as taught by contemporary Tibetan teachers as well as academic and neuroscientific researchers. Originating in ancient Indian Buddhism and a central practice of Theravāda Buddhism in South and Southeast Asia, Vipassanā (insight meditation) involves investigation of the entirety of one's psychosomatic experience with particular attention on the Buddhist "three characteristics of existence," namely, suffering, impermanence, and no-self (see ch. 6 herein; Shaw 2006, 2009). That is, Vipassanā is informed by and apparently confirms the "truth" of foundational Buddhist doctrine.[1] Originating in Chinese Chan, a Chinese school of Mahāyāna (Greater Vehicle) Buddhism that was eventually transmitted to Korea (Son), Japan (Zen), and Vietnam (Thien), Zazen (Chn.: *zuochan*; seated [*dhyāna*] meditation) generally consists of two types, although counting breaths (1–10) is a common shared beginner's practice. Traditionally speaking, Zen meditation is practiced within a meditation hall (Jpn.: *zendō*) and monastic community.[2]

Zen meditation usually involves spiritual guidance, especially through formal interviews (Jpn.: *dokusan*), under a meditation master and intensive periods of meditation (Jpn.: *sesshin*). Generally speaking, in the Sōtō (Chn.: Caodong) lineage, one practices "silent illumination" (Chn.: *mozhao*), also referred to as "just sitting" (Jpn.: *shikan taza*) (see, e.g., Bielefeldt 1990; Leighton 2000; Tanahashi 1995, 2004).[3] This is stillness-/emptiness-based meditation, wherein practitioners seek to return to their original nature, often referred to as "Buddha-nature" (Skt.: *tathāgata-garbha*; Chn.: *foxing*). It is deeply indebted to classical Daoist apophatic meditation and classical Daoist

Figure 2.1. Interior of Korean Sŏn (Zen) Buddhist Meditation Hall[2]
Source: Jogye Order of Korean Buddhism.

views (see ch. 3 herein), especially as documented in the *Zhuangzi* (Book of Master Zhuang). In the Rinzai (Chn.: Linji) lineage, the central practice utilizes *kōan* (Chn.: *gong'an*), or enigmatic sayings aimed to shatter the discriminating mind and facilitate a psychospiritual breakthrough (see, e.g., Heine and Wright 2000).[4] A typical beginner's *kōan* is "Mu," Jōshū's (Chn.: Zhao Zhou's) answer to the question "Does a dog have Buddha-nature?" In Zen *kōan*-practice, one meditates on the given saying, question, or phrase.

Tibetan Buddhist meditation practice is complex and diverse. As a form of Vajrayāna (Diamond/Thunderbolt) or Tantric Buddhism, it may include emptiness-based practices, as in Dzogchen (Great Perfection), and/or complex visualization practices, as in various forms of "deity yoga" (see, e.g., Snellgrove 1959; Wayman and Tajima 1992; Hopkins 2009). The latter includes the "identification" of the practitioner with specific buddhas and bodhisattvas, wherein he or she comes to embody specific powers and qualities such as wisdom and compassion. While "Buddhist meditation" is most likely to be viewed through practices such as modern Burmese Vipassanā, modern Japanese and American Zen, and various forms of modern Tibetan Buddhist meditation, this volume demonstrates that there are other, less well-known Buddhist practices, such as Pure Land visualization (see ch. 9 herein). Buddhism also has some of the most sophisticated and systematic presentations of meditation and meditative experience. Some of these include the possibly first-century CE *Vimuttimagga* (Path of Freedom) by the Sri Lankan Theravāda monk

Upatissa (see Ehara et al. 1977), the fifth-century *Visuddhimagga* (Path to Purification) by the Indian Theravāda monk Buddhaghoṣa (see Nanamoli 1999), and the *Lam-rim chen-mo* (Great Treatise on the Stages of the Path to Enlightenment) by Tibetan Buddhist monk Tsong-kha-pa (1357–1419) (see Wayman 1997; LCTC 2000–2004).

Equally complex and diverse are Christian contemplative practices, although they are likely to be less familiar to academic researchers outside of Christian studies. Beyond certain Christian contexts, these methods are often unfamiliar to both Christians and "non-Christians" alike.[5] With respect to the former, this is because contemplative practice has frequently been the province of Catholic and Eastern Orthodox monastics. With respect to the latter, it is often the case because of an implicit or explicit bias, including the assumption that meditation is an "Eastern" or "Asian" discipline. There are complex issues related to Orientalism here. In any case, Christian contemplative practice, broadly and inclusively conceived, especially includes Eastern Orthodox and Roman Catholic forms of contemplative prayer. The former is usually associated with the Hesychast practice of the Jesus Prayer, which involves repeated recitation of "Lord Jesus Christ, Son of God, have mercy on me" (see ch. 8 herein). Catholic forms of contemplative prayer are most often associated with particular religious orders and their corresponding charism (associated spiritual quality and/or commitment). Some prominent and influential examples include Dominican prayer, Ignatian prayer, Teresian prayer, Thomistic prayer, and so forth. Most of these are not included in the present volume (see, e.g., Holder 2009; also Chester and Norrisey 1985). A major omission is Ignatian prayer, especially as expressed in the Examen, which is a simplified version of the *Exercitia spiritualia* (Spiritual Exercises; see Ganss 1991) especially popular in contemporary Catholicism. Composed by Ignacio de Loyola (St. Ignatius; 1491–1556), a Spanish Catholic priest and eventual founder of the Society of Jesus (Jesuits), the *Exercitia spiritualia* describes a set of Christian meditations, prayers, and mental exercises divided into four thematic weeks of variable length and designed to be carried out over a period of twenty-eight to thirty days. In the modern world, in addition to Ignatian retreats, Saint Ignatius's practice has become simplified into a daily practice called the Examen, or "examination of conscience" (see, e.g., Aschenbrenner 1972; Skehan 1991; Gallagher 2006). Rooted in "A Method for Making the General Examination of Conscience" in the First Week of the *Exercitia spiritualia* (see Ganss 1991, 134–35), it is a reflection exercise that usually consists of the following five steps:

1. Gratitude. I note the gifts that God's love has given me this day, and I give thanks to God for them.

2. Petition. I ask God for an insight and a strength that will make this examen a work of grace, fruitful beyond my human capacity alone.

3. Review. With my God, I review the day. I look for stirrings in my heart and the thoughts that God has given me this day. I look also for those that have not been of God. I review my choices in response to both, and throughout the day in general.

4. Forgiveness. I ask for the healing touch of the forgiving God who, with love and respect for me, removes my heart's burdens.

5. Renewal. I look to the following day and, with God, plan concretely how to live it in accord with God's loving desire for my life. (Gallagher 2006, 25)

In contrast, Dominican contemplative prayer as documented in the *Novem modi orandi sancti Dominici* (Nine Ways of Prayer of Saint Dominic) is largely lost in the modern world (see ch. 11 herein). The practice involves taking various postures in imitation of Jesus Christ and of Saint Dominic. Perhaps surprisingly, there are also examples of Protestant Christian contemplative practice, with Quaker contemplative prayer and silent worship being most prominent (see ch. 4 herein). Quaker silent worship is especially fascinating as it may be read as a form of communal mysticism (see, e.g., Gorman 1973; Birkel 2004). In the modern world, we also find examples of "ecumenical practices" such as Centering Prayer and Taizé Prayer. Developed by three Catholic Trappist monks, Thomas Keating (b. 1923), William Meninger (b. ca. 1925), and M. Basil Pennington (1931–2005), Centering Prayer most often involves repetition of a selected Christian word or phrase (*mantra*), such as "Jesus," "abba," and so forth. It draws its inspiration from a variety of sources, including the Desert Fathers and Mothers of early Christian monasticism, the Benedictine monastic practice of *lectio divina*, and spiritual classics such as the anonymous, fourteenth-century *The Cloud of Unknowing* and the writings of Teresa of Ávila (1515–1582) and Juan de la Cruz (John of the Cross; 1542–1591), both of whom were Spanish Catholic monastics associated with the Carmelite order (see Holder 2009). Taizé Prayer was developed by the Taizé Community, which is an ecumenical monastic order associated with Frère Roger (1915–2005) and based in Bourgogne, France. It primarily involves chanting and singing in a form somewhat similar to Gregorian chant.[6]

Daoism is another tradition with diverse and sophisticated contemplative practices. Although research is still in preliminary stages (see Kohn 1987, 1989; Robinet 1993; Roth 1999; Komjathy 2007, 2013a, 2013b), we may identify at least the following five major types: (1) apophatic or quietistic meditation, for which there are various technical terms such as "quiet sitting" (*jingzuo*), "fasting the heart-mind" (*xinzhai*), "sitting-in-forgetfulness" (*zuowang*), or "guarding the One" (*shouyi*); (2) visualization (*cunxiang*); (3) ingestion (*fuqi*); (4) inner observation (*neiguan*); and (5) internal alchemy (*neidan*), which also includes "female alchemy" (*nüdan*). Although each major type of Daoist meditation survives into the modern world, especially in more integrated training regimens, each has corresponding historical source-points as well as associated movements and seminal texts. Apophatic meditation was first practiced in the inner cultivation lineages of the classical period (4th–2nd c. BCE); visualization and ingestion became especially prominent in the Shangqing (Highest Clarity) movement during the early medieval period (3rd–6th c. CE); and inner observation and internal alchemy emerged inside a variety of movements during the late medieval period (7th–14th c.). The present volume includes a chapter on classical Daoist apophatic meditation (ch. 3) and on late imperial Daoist internal alchemy (ch. 12).

Less well-researched contemplative traditions associated with major "world religions" include those of Confucianism, Hinduism, Islam, Jainism, Judaism, Shinto, and Sikhism. This is not to mention contemplative practice in "indigenous traditions," including various Native American groups.

Although most often associated with humanism, morality, and perhaps ritual, Confucianism eventually developed distinctive contemplative practices such as "quiet sitting" (*jingzuo*) and a form of systematized ethical reflection. Emerging during the late medieval period of Chinese history, the former was influenced by Chan Buddhist and Daoist forms of meditation (see Taylor 1978, 1988). The history of the latter is somewhat obscure, but it resembles the Catholic Ignatian practice of the Examen in certain respects. Specifically, Confucian adherents utilized "ledgers of merit and demerit" (*gongguo ge*) in which they recorded their moral successes and failures daily in order to examine and rectify themselves. Initial research suggests that the practice was influenced by the Chinese Buddhist and Daoist practice of atonement (*chanhui*) and Daoist purification practices (*zhai*) in preparation for Daoist ritual, specifically by Daoist priests (see Brokaw 1991). However, a classical Confucian precedent may be found in various passages of the *Lunyu* (Analects), with the following perhaps being most noteworthy: "Each day I examine myself in three ways: In doing things for others, have I been disloyal? In interactions with friends, have I been untrustworthy? Have I failed to practice what has been transmitted?" (1.4).

Hindu meditation is most well known in the West through modern practices associated with the International Society for Krishna Consciousness (ISKCON; "Hare Krishnas"), Self-Realization Fellowship (SRF), Transcendental Meditation™ (TM™) movement, Vedanta Society, and *yoga* loosely defined. The present volume includes a chapter on Hindu classical Yoga as described in the *Yoga Sūtras* (Yoga Aphorisms), which demonstrates the ways in which traditional Indian yoga is a soteriological system aimed at liberation (*moksha*), or more technically "perfect solitude" and "complete detachment" (*kaivalya*). A clear omission is Hindu *bhakti* practices, such as those associated with Vaishnavite and Shaivite devotionalism, as well as Tantric and diverse Yogic practices, specifically Kundalinī Yoga (see, e.g., Brooks 1996; White 1998; Bryant 2007). While such a tradition-based approach is viable and important, on the level of types, there are parallels with Dominican Catholic prayer, Pure Land Buddhist visualization, and Daoist internal alchemy (see ch. 1 and further discussion here). This of course is not to deny the radically different soteriologies related to different objects of devotion.

Figure 2.2. *Sema* of the Mevlevi Sufi Lineage
Galata Mevlevihanesi (Mevlevi Lodge), Istanbul, Turkey
Source: International Mevlana Foundation.

Islam is rarely discussed as a "contemplative tradition," but there are clear examples of contemplative practice in Islam, especially in various Sufi lineages (orders) (see Schimmel 1975; also ch. 7 herein). Perhaps the most famous example not included in this book is *sema* (Ar.: *samāʿ*; lit., listening), or "whirling," as practiced in the Mevlevi lineage (Whirling Dervishes), which is associated with Jalāl ad-Dīn Rūmī (1207–1273) (see Chittick 1984).[7] Considered as an expression of *dhikr* (*zikr*; remembrance), this is a form of contemplative and mystical dance. Islamic contemplative practice also raises a number of interesting questions. We are inspired to consider the parameters of inclusion of the comparative category of "contemplative practice" or "meditation," including areas of overlap with "prayer," "ritual," "mysticism," and so forth. For example, Ibn al-ʿArabī (1165–1240) wrote a number of texts that could be read as "contemplative" (see Hirtenstein 2009; Twinch and Beneito 2008).[8] However, here one must again consider the accuracy of such categorization, including the degree to which the texts describe cosmological speculation and mystical experience, rather than practical details on contemplative practice.

Jewish contemplative practice is also a relatively understudied area of research (see Blumenthal 1978; Kaplen 1978, 1989). This may be because Jewish meditation is intricately tied to Jewish mysticism, the latter of which has received a vast amount of scholarly attention. However, little research has been done on the *actual techniques* utilized in Jewish contemplative and mystical circles. Jewish meditation is most often associated with Kabbalah, which is an esoteric practice traditionally of the Jewish spiritual elite. The present volume includes a chapter on Lurianic Kabbalistic meditation (see ch. 5). As evident in the late sixteenth-century *Shaarei Kedusha* (Gates of Holiness), Kabbalistic meditation most often involves magical reconfigurations of Hebrew letter combinations (alphabetic permutation), which is based on a specific theological understanding of the Hebrew language. Many of these types of practices have been lost outside of textual records and/or reconstructed in the modern world. In fact, the largest number of modern "Jewish contemplative practices" are not Jewish. A visible minority of Jews, at least ethnic Jews, practice Vipassanā and Zazen. As is the case with other religious traditions, especially Christianity, more research is required on this phenomenon, including the various reconceptualizations required to create soteriological and theological congruency with the religious tradition in question.

As far as my reading goes, there are few if any Western-language studies of Jain, Shinto, and Sikh contemplative practice.[9] The same is true with respect to "indigenous traditions" and new religious movements (see Williamson 2010). I hope that the present volume inspires and perhaps provides a model for furthering such research.

Dimensions of Contemplative Practice

There is a danger of isolating contemplative practices from the larger soteriological systems and religious traditions in which they are historically and culturally embedded. This includes the problematic tendency of reducing contemplative practice to technique and, especially in the modern West, to physiological effects. This tendency is especially apparent in contemporary neuroscientific accounts, which largely ignore important elements of contemplative practice such as community and place (see ch. 1). A more comprehensive, integrated, and sophisticated approach recognizes that contemplative practice does not occur outside of other religio-cultural parameters, including the specific contours of the individual and communal lives involved. It appears that "meditation"

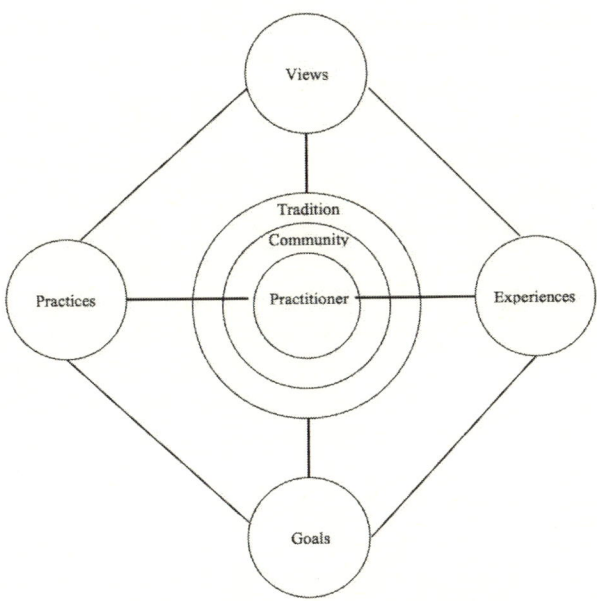

Figure 2.3. Dimensions of (Religious) Praxis

as an isolated practice and separate "tradition" is largely, if not wholly, a modern phenomenon. As the chapters in this book indicate, contemplative practice always occurs within particular contexts. This is equally true of modern secular, "nonsectarian," "spiritual" and therapeutic techniques (see chs. 13 and 14 herein). In the case of tradition-based and religiously-committed forms, contemplative practice always includes specific worldviews, soteriological systems, and religious traditions. Thus, from a religious studies perspective, we must be attentive to the larger training regimen and approach of a given practice.

As discussed briefly in chapter 1, a more sophisticated approach would recognize the complex dimensions of contemplative practice. We may consider the relative importance of community and tradition. We may also consider the informing views, associated practices and experiences, as well as guiding aspirations and projected goals. As discussed in more detail later, this would include being attentive to the potential benefits of different contemplative practices. As I have suggested elsewhere (Komjathy 2007; see also Moore 1978), there is a complex interplay and interrelationship among informing worldviews, specific practices, related experiences, and projected goals. We may think of these in terms of individual adherents and/or religious communities, and we may also consider the ways in which adherents are located within specific communities and traditions. When I say that the four primary dimensions of (religious) praxis are interrelated, I mean that each informs and expresses the other. Worldviews inform practices, experiences, and goals, but these are embodiments, literally and symbolically, of those worldviews. Arguably, though requiring further research, specific experiences only occur within the context of specific worldviews and practices. At the very least, specific practices and experiences only make sense within a larger framework of doctrine and imagined accomplishment and outcome. Moreover, it is probable that specific practices actually result in technique-specific experiences. There is thus a complex interrelationship among view, practice, and experience.[10] While these insights are more easily recognized by and applied to studying content-based practices, such as those informed by and expressing theistic views, they are equally relevant for studying apparently contentless methods. For example, although the conceptual framework of Herbert Benson's Relaxation Response may be so familiar as to seem like a self-evident given with scientific verification, it has a particular history, distinctive worldview, and unique set of goals (see ch. 13 herein). In particular, it is rooted in Mind-Body Medicine and therapeutic meditation, wherein disease is associated with "stress" and meditation is identified as a "relaxation technique" and form of "stress management."

It is thus important to recognize the multidimensional nature of contemplative practice. We should not reduce contemplative practice to method or technique. Instead, we should be attentive to at least the following dimensions:

1. Prerequisites
   a. Community
   b. Ethical foundations
   c. Instruction/training
   d. Initiation/ordination
   e. Lineage
   f. Place
   g. Resources
   h. Teachers
   i. Time

2. Posture[11]
   a. Lying down
   b. Moving/walking
   c. Sitting
   d. Standing

3. Breathing
   a. Regulated
   b. Unregulated

4. Technique

5. Style
   a. Individual
   b. Communal
   c. Lay
   d. Monastic
   e. Vocal
   f. Silent

6. Duration and format

7. Location[12]
    a. Cave
    b. Desert
    c. Home
    d. Community center
    e. Forest
    f. Monastery
    g. Mountain
    h. Temple

8. Aesthetics and material culture
    a. Architecture
    b. Art
    c. Clothing
    d. Paraphernalia

9. Religious system
    a. Cosmology
    b. Dietetics
    c. Ethics
    d. Ritual
    e. Scripture study
    f. Soteriology[13]
    g. Theology[14]

That is, tradition-based and religiously-committed forms of contemplative practice reveal that something "more" or "larger" is involved. This is so much the case that I would suggest that there is always a theological dimension, an ultimate concern and spiritual orientation. This includes existential and ontological dimensions of human existence, the potential of human beings to become fully so. Here one example will suffice. As documented in the *Novem modi orandi sancti Dominici* (Nine Ways of Prayer of Saint Dominic) (see ch. 11 herein), Dominican prayer takes place within the larger contours of Dominican monastic life and the Liturgy of Hours (Divine Office). The latter is the official set of prayers prescribed by the Catholic Church to be recited at the canonical hours by the clergy, religious orders, and laity. That is, Dominican prayer takes place within a larger ritual and liturgical structure. In addition, this type of Dominican prayer requires a Catholic altar with a crucifix, that is, a freestanding representation of Jesus Christ crucified on the cross. One prays using various postures in front of this altar and Christian symbol. Here we find a clear example of the aesthetic and material culture dimensions of contemplative practice. Moreover, each dimension expresses and is informed by a specific soteriology, in this case salvation through Jesus Christ and the Catholic Church.

Finally, we may recognize the ways in which contemplative practice is frequently only undertaken under the training and spiritual direction of a teacher and community. For example, in the nineteenth-century Eastern Orthodox *Rasskaz strannika* (Tale of a Pilgrim) (see ch. 8 herein), the anonymous Pilgrim searches for a spiritual father to direct his practice of the Jesus Prayer. Traditionally speaking, Hesychast prayer is a monastic practice only undertaken under the spiritual direction of an elder. The latter is supposed to have a high-level of attainment and a capacity to assist his students' spiritual progress. The same is true with respect to Daoist internal alchemy (see ch. 12 herein). In the preface to his *Huiming jing* (Scripture on Wisdom and Life-Destiny), Liu Huayang (1735–1799) emphasizes the importance of finding a master. It was only after he received instruction under the Daoist immortal Wu Shouyang and the Chan monk Huyun that Liu completed the alchemical process and attained enlightenment. In these and other contemplative traditions, training and spiritual direction under a teacher are essential. However, community relationships are always complex, and discipleship may result in various problems and dilemmas. A teacher may not have the commitment or capacity to assist a student. Students may also come to idolize or blindly follow a given teacher. Thus, J. Krishnamurti (1895–1986) advises one to abandon reliance on teachers and community and to renounce attachment to specific teachings and traditions (see ch. 14 herein). Krishnamurti warns about the potential of "spiritual teachers" to become sources of delusion and disorientation.[15] These varied perspectives direct us to consider the relative importance of teachers and community in specific training regimens and religious approaches. They also inspire one to consider the contributions and limitations of tradition-based and community-dependent forms of contemplative practice.

Contemplative Experience

The relevance and importance of "experience" in religious traditions and the meaning of the category are frequently debated topics in religious studies (see, e.g., James 1999 [1902]; Proudfoot 1985; Sharf 1998; Bagger 1999; Fitzgerald 2000; Komjathy 2007; Taves 2009; Martin and McCutcheon 2012). For present purposes, "experience" refers to the subjective and lived dimension of human existence. It relates to various dimensions of personhood, including corporeal, psychological, cognitive, spiritual, intersubjective, and cultural aspects. In terms of the present volume, specific types of experience are most relevant, especially religious, mystical, and contemplative experiences. "Religious experience" refers to experiences that occur within religious contexts and/or experiences that are deemed "religiously significant." Religious experience may refer to more "ordinary" or "mundane" experiences (e.g., a feeling of communal belonging) to more "extraordinary" or "anomalous" experiences (e.g., ecstasy or euphoria). There are some parallels with the category of "anomalous experience" (see, e.g., Cardeña et al. 2000). "Mystical experience" refers to experiences of that which a given individual or community identifies as sacred or ultimately real (Komjathy 2012). Mystical experiences are generally located within specific religious communities and traditions, and they would thus be a subcategory of religious experience. However, there are "nonreligious" or "trans-tradition" mystical experiences, such as disappearing into Nature. Finally, "contemplative experience" refers to experiences that occur within the context of contemplative practice, are associated with particular practices, and/or are deemed significant by contemplatives. Like religious experiences, contemplative experiences may be more or less "ordinary." Like mystical experiences, contemplative experience may, in certain contexts, be a subcategory of religious experience, but there are secular forms of contemplative experience. In addition, and as discussed later, while some conflate mystical experience with contemplative experience, or assume that contemplative practices are means to initiate mystical experiences, the relationships are extremely complex.

From my perspective, it is quite clear that contemplative practice involves specific types of experience, which we may label "contemplative experience."[16] This may include specific outcomes, such as capacities, skills, benefits, and so forth. As discussed later, contemplative practice may result in transformed existential and ontological conditions as well as new *ways of experiencing*. I label such outcomes of religious praxis as "ontologies" or "psychologies of realization." That is, there is a soteriological and theological dimension of most religiously-committed and tradition-based contemplative practice (see previous discussion). By not simply reducing contemplative practice to technique and physiological effects, we may focus on contemplative experience in a broad frame. Specifically, we may be attentive to the particular types of experience associated with specific practices, the relative importance of such experiences, and the potential benefits that result from contemplative practice. In the process, we may decouple "contemplative experience" from "mystical experience" and consider the relative importance of the latter in different training regimens (see also ch. 1 herein).

As Robert Gimello (1978) has emphasized, meditation and mysticism are frequently conflated. Gimello helpfully suggests that the two must be distinguished and that the relative importance of mystical experience in contemplative traditions should be carefully examined. Specifically, we should recognize that mystical experiences are often viewed as byproducts and even potential distractions in contemplative practice. We thus should not begin with the *assumption* that contemplative practices are methods for initiating mystical experiences. Rather, we should consider the types of experiences that occur within the parameters of contemplative practice, including their connection to soteriological and theological dimensions of the informing religious system. While it seems clear that practice and experience are connected, more research is required on the actual experiences associated with specific practices. Nonetheless, contemplative practice does result in identifiable benefits and experiences, broadly conceived.

In terms of contemplative experience, specific methods have recognizable and reproducible effects. In concert with access to experienced teachers and communities,[17] this may be one of the main arguments for tradition-based contemplative practice: Such techniques have been tested, confirmed, transmitted, and reconfirmed over a lengthy period of time. Their positive effects and potential challenges have been thoroughly explored. In any case, on the most basic level, there are discernable qualities for both particular methods and associated experiences. For example, devotional practices frequently result in a greater sense of reverence and communion. As in the case of Pure Land Buddhist visualization (see ch. 9 herein) and Dominican Catholic prayer (see ch. 11 herein), one develops a deeper sense of connection with Amitābha Buddha and Jesus Christ, respectively. Similarly, Hindu classical Yoga (see ch. 10 herein) and the Relaxation Response (see ch. 13 herein) aim to transform consciousness in particular ways. On some level, each of these practices is a form of trophotropic meditation that facilitates hyperquiescent/hypoaroused states, which are characterized by relatively low-levels of physiological activity (see chs. 1 and 13 herein). Practitioners enter deeper states of stillness, which the *Yoga Sūtras* describes as meditative absorption (*samādhi*) and Herbert Benson labels the Relaxation Response. Whether these are "higher-level" experiences is an open question, but it appears that consistent and prolonged practice of a given technique will eventually result in associated experiences and changed internal conditions.

On some level, we may consider "relaxation," "feelings of communion," and such as general qualities and common characteristics of various methods. This is not to suggest that these are universal; their ubiquity rather points toward "ordinary" or "common" experiences. At the same time, we must recognize that such experiences *may be defined* in unique ways in religious traditions and that categories such as "extraordinary" or "anomalous" may lead to mischaracterization. For example, although some religious traditions emphasize the possibility of abiding in contentless consciousness (Pure Consciousness Events [PCEs]; see Forman 1990, 1999), this type of subjectivity may only appear radically different from the perspective of the ordinary mind (see, e.g., Griffiths 1986).[18] As discussed in more detail further on, we thus need to be attentive to the psychological dimensions of contemplative practice and contemplative experience. This relates to consciousness studies broadly defined. In any case, it is clear that there are specific types of experiences associated with specific contemplative practices. For example, the *Yoga Sūtras* (Yoga Aphorisms; see ch. 10 herein) describes a process through which one purifies consciousness, eventually resulting in the separation of pure spirit (*purusha*), which is divine, from materiality (*prakrti*), which is samsaric and illusory in some sense. Such is liberation (*moksha*) according to Hindu classical Yoga. Similarly, and not coincidentally, Krishnamurti describes the attainment of "freedom from the known," a state in which one maintains choiceless awareness and apparently abides in pure being.

In terms of "mystical experience," some contemplative texts describe encounters with things deemed sacred or ultimate. In my way of thinking, this would be a specific type of contemplative experience. For example, Quaker contemplative prayer and silent worship involve abiding in silence, a receptive space (see ch. 4 herein). However, in contrast to other traditions such as classical Daoism and Sōtō Zen Buddhism, this silence is not the be-all and end-all of practice. Rather, it creates the space for the Presence of God to manifest. In terms of Quaker silent worship, during which Friends sit in silence together, the meeting is said to be "gathered" when there is a felt sense of sacred community and God's Presence. This practice might thus be thought of as both communal contemplative practice and communal mysticism. In terms of mystical experience, it would be primarily unitive. Along different lines, both the *Rasskaz strannika* (Tale of a Pilgrim; see ch. 8 herein) and the *Huiming jing* (Scripture on Wisdom and Life-Destiny; see ch. 12 herein) describe encounters with deceased masters and spiritual elders. The anonymous Pilgrim describes receiving "dream-teachings" from his deceased spiritual father, while Liu Huayang, in his preface, suggests that he learned Daoist *neidan* from a deceased monk and Daoist immortal named Wu Shouyang. Perhaps most radically, the *Guan wuliang shoufo jing* (Sutra on Visualizing the Buddha of Infinite Life; see ch. 9 herein) describes a sequential visualization practice, in the middle of which Amitābha, the Buddha of Infinite Life, supposedly appears to the practitioner. In addition, the text repeatedly emphasizes that various visions are associated with each visualization practice. One might read this as experiential confirmation of the efficacy of the practice and the theological reality of the Pure Land and Amitābha. Finally, the text explains that the vision of Amitābha Buddha is the same as the one that will occur upon the death of Pure Land Buddhists. In this way, one might read the text as preparation for dying and death. Here one also thinks of the "nine cemetery contemplations" found in the *Satipatthāna Sutta* (Discourse on the Foundations of Mindfulness; see Analayo 2004; Shaw 2006, 2009; also ch. 6 herein) as well as the practice of "sending out the yang-spirit" through the crown-point in Daoist internal alchemy (see ch. 12 herein). Although beyond the present volume, the connection between contemplative practice and dying, death, and afterlife is a fascinating topic. Like mystical experience, it brings up a whole set of interpretive questions, including the possibility that Pure Land visualization, like the famous *Bardo Thodol* (Liberation through Hearing during the Intermediate State; "Tibetan Book of the Dead"), describes near death experiences (NDEs). The latter is much debated in religious studies, specifically whether they are simply the physiological productions of a dying brain, a coping mechanism if you will, or experiences of something transcendent with soteriological and theological import (see, e.g., Bailey and Yates 1996). In any case, these examples are sufficient to reveal that the relationship between contemplative practice and mystical experience is complex. We find a spectrum of views in contemplative traditions: from elevation and advocacy through relative recognition to disregard and rejection. We should thus be attentive to the entire spectrum of contemplative practice and its potential overlap with mystical experience. This includes the relative importance as well as soteriological and theological import of such experience. Is it confirmation? Is it distraction? Could it be both simultaneously? The answers to such questions differ among discourse communities, both religious and academic. These considerations also point toward a clearer distinction between the categories of "contemplative experience" and "mystical experience": The former may include the latter, but contemplative experience is not synonymous with mystical experience. Contemplative experience encompasses any subjective occurrence deemed significant within the context of contemplative practice, which sometimes involves direct experience of that which is identified as sacred or ultimately real. Contemplatives and contemplative communities often understand such experiences as having epistemological, soteriological, and theological import. They may provide evidential support for the informing views and primary goals of contemplative practice.

Interestingly, most contemplative traditions claim that contemplative practice will result in specific benefits. For example, according to the texts of classical Daoism (see Roth 1999; ch. 3 herein), Daoist apophatic meditation and inner cultivation will result in the following: increased vitality, serenity, equanimity, clarity, numinosity, and so forth. Similarly, Daoist internal alchemy often results in cosmological integration, encounters with immortals, mystical participation, and numinous abilities. These are often referred to as "signs of successful training," "experiential confirmation," and "boons along the way" (see Komjathy 2007). Here one also thinks of the Six Perfections (*pāramitā*) mentioned in the *Guanjing* (see ch. 9 herein), which include generosity, morality, patience, effort, meditation, and wisdom. These are traditionally understood as six kinds of practice by which a bodhisattva attains Buddhahood. However, one might also understand them as qualities developed through Mahāyāna Buddhist practice. Even in a secular materialist and therapeutic form of meditation such as the Relaxation Response (see ch. 13 herein), one finds a similar trajectory of method-specific outcomes, which include relaxation, higher resiliency to stress, better health, increased self-control, and so forth. Although one may be tempted to read these as quantifiable "scientific evidence," it is noteworthy that contemplative traditions make similar claims about subjective experience. That is, one's fellow practitioners, community, and tradition confirm the efficacy of the contemplative practice.

However, are "contemplative experiences" and "benefits" the primary purpose of contemplative practice? Or is the relationship more complex? Interestingly, the *Yoga Sūtras* extensively describes specific *siddhi*, "accomplishments" or "attainments," as resulting from the practice of Hindu classical Yoga (see ch. 10 herein; also ch. 9). As a technical term, *siddhi* is often rendered as "paranormal abilities" or "supernatural powers,"[19] but these translations beg the question of "normalcy" and "naturalness" (see, e.g., Laing 1967). In standard Hindu conception, and also appearing in Buddhism, the *siddhi* include abilities such as the following: (1) the ability to go anywhere at will (teleportation and/or multilocality) and to transform oneself or objects at will, (2) the ability to see anything at any distance (clairvoyance), (3) the ability to hear anything at any distance (clairaudience), (4) the ability to know others' thoughts (telepathy), (5) the ability to know the former lives of oneself and others, and (6) the ability to destroy all negative passions. According to the text, these seem to be expected byproducts of the practice but ones that should not be actively pursued or obsessed over. In fact, there is a danger that they will lead to complacency or obstruction in spiritual progress. One finds a parallel concern in Daoist internal alchemy (see Komjathy 2007). Here again it is appropriate to consider Robert Gimello's points about tradition-specific views concerning the results of contemplative practice. A common theme throughout many contemplative traditions is the ever-present danger of chasing after "extraordinary experiences." Some contemplatives and contemplative communities also identify harmful, perhaps even demonic, influences. This has led to debate about the orthodoxy and sources of various experiences. Beyond fairly well-known examples from medieval Catholicism and charges of heresy, one particularly fascinating modern example is the official Vatican document titled *Normae S. Congregationis pro doctrina fidei de modo procedendi in diiudicandis praesumptis apparitionibus ac revelationibus* (Norms of the Sacred Congregation for the Doctrine of the Faith on the Manner of Proceeding in Judging Presumed Apparitions and Revelations), which was issued in 1978 and internally circulated to Catholic bishops. Some key requirements for "authentic apparitions and revelations" include both "positive" and "negative criteria." The former include moral certainty concerning the event and the particular circumstances in which it occurred, such as the personal qualities of the person involved, the theological orthodoxy of revelations, and subsequent positive effects (e.g., healthy devotion and enduring spiritual fruits). The negative criteria include factual inaccuracies, doctrinal errors, monetary motivations, immoral acts committed by the person and/or his or her associates, as well as psychic disorders or psychopathic tendencies. As the modern evaluation of these is located within the hierarchically ordered and ecclesiastical structure of the Catholic magisterium, there are, of course, complex issues of power and authority involved in the production, circulation, and application of such documents. In a more modern context, Chögyam Trungpa (1939–1987) warned his students about "spiritual materialism," or the tendency to turn spirituality into a form of mundane being and ego inflation. This connects to the ubiquitous Western tendency toward an acquisitive mode of being (see later discussion), which appears in various forms of "spiritual capitalism" and "spiritual colonialism" (Lau 2000; Carrette and King 2004; also the technical glossary herein).

Another helpful distinction in studying contemplative experience, especially the benefits and results of contemplative practice, centers on "states" (Ar.: *haal*; pl.: *ahwal*) and "stages" (Ar.: *maqaam*; pl.: *maqaamat*), with the latter also appearing as "conditions" and "stations," respectively. Here I borrow these terms from Islamic mysticism, often referred to as "Sufism" (see ch. 7 herein). Traditionally speaking, stages are moments on the contemplative or mystical path (*tariqa*), while states are conditions or experiences that may occur at various stages. Interestingly, Sufis generally hold that states are gifts from Allah; if they do occur, they are forms of grace and beyond the agency of the practitioner. A representative Sufi approach follows seven stages: (1) repentance, (2) abstention, (3) asceticism, (4) poverty, (5) patience, (6) confidence, and (7) contentment (see Schimmel 1975). Some common states in Sufi lineages include contraction, ecstasy, expansion, intimacy, intoxication, joy, loneliness, and so forth. Such claims are noteworthy in a number of respects. First, some of the states, such as loneliness or longing, might be considered "negative" outside of a Sufi context; however, along the Islamic mystical path, they are often identified as "positive," in the sense of being bestowed by Allah. Loneliness may be understood as a sign that one is oriented toward the sacred. Second, they draw our attention to the supposed sources of, or triggers for, experience (see Komjathy 2012). For present purposes, the state-stage distinction inspires one to consider the degree to which particular contemplative practices emphasize stages, or a sequence of spiritual progress, and states, or particular conditions, qualities, and experiences. One of the clearest examples of a stage-based practice in the present volume is Daoist internal alchemy (see ch. 12), which describes a sequence of techniques aimed at psychosomatic transformation. As discussed in the corresponding chapter, the late imperial Chinese text of the *Huiming jing* is a simplified version of earlier forms of *neidan* practice (see Komjathy 2013a). The emphasis on stages in some contemplative traditions suggests that there are different informing views, views often assumed in contemporary discussions of so-called "advanced meditation."

Here a few additional comments about stages may be helpful. While the comparative study of contemplative practice is only just beginning, some preliminary work has been done. As outlined by Brown (1986), based primarily on Tibetan Mahāmudrā, Hindu classical Yoga (see ch. 10 herein), and Theravāda Vipassanā (see ch. 6 herein), meditation has the following cross-cultural stages: (1) preliminary ethical practices, (2) preliminary body-mind training, (3) concentration with support, (4) concentration without support, (5) insight practice, and (6) advanced insight practice and enlightenment (see also Roth 1999, 135–36; Wilber 2000, 129–35). While we must exercise caution when applying such interpretive frameworks derived primarily from the study of Buddhist meditation, they are helpful for directing us to consider both the relevance of the concept of "stages" and the specific sequences of stage-based training. We may then consider the degree to which there is overlap between different systems. As discussed in more detail later, attentiveness to such claims may, in turn, take us into questions concerning human potential and the capacities or "levels of consciousness." This relates to claims about the possibility of spiritual development. Traditional Buddhist expressions and systematizations are found in the *summa* mentioned earlier. For example, the fifth-century *Visuddhimagga* (Path to Purification) outlines the "Seven Stages of Purification" (*satta-visuddhi*), namely, (1) Purification of Conduct (*sīla*), (2) Purification of Thought (*citta*), (3) Purification of View (*ditthi*), (4) Purification by Overcoming Doubt (*kankha-vitarana*), (5) Purification by Knowledge and Vision of What Is Path and Not Path (*maggamagga-nanadassana*), (6) Purification by Knowledge and Vision of the Course of Practice (*patipada-nanadassana*), and (7) Purification by Knowledge and Vision (*nanadassana*). Each purification is required for the attainment of the subsequent stage.

Psychologies of Realization

As mentioned, every form of contemplative practice is informed by and expresses a specific psychology. A more complete understanding of contemplative practice and contemplative experience would have to be multiperspectival and interdisciplinary (see ch. 1). In terms of the present topic, it would utilize the related disciplines of psychology and neuroscience, which are increasingly being placed inside of the emerging, interdisciplinary field of consciousness studies. In the present section, I focus on psychology and consciousness broadly conceived.

In *Orientalism and Religion*, Richard King makes a helpful distinction between "epistemologies of limitation" and "epistemologies of enlightenment." The former are epistemologies that restrict the potential of human beings to achieve some form of unmediated awareness. In contrast, epistemologies of enlightenment map a way out of cultural and linguistic conditioning through religious praxis and develop a nondual and unconstructed or unconditioned awareness (1999, 179). We find the former expressed in the whole spectrum of Western disciplines: from Neo-Kantian views of mind through conventional Freudian perspectives that pathologize the human condition. Developing King, I have suggested that we focus on "epistemologies of possibility," or more appropriately on "ontologies of realization" (Komjathy 2007, 63–97, 256–61). This modification emphasizes being over knowing and holds open the possibility that the latter may itself be a limitation. "Ontologies of realization" point toward claims concerning transformed modes of being, or ontological conditions often achieved through religious praxis in general and contemplative practice in particular. In the present context, I will emphasize "psychologies of realization" related to contemplative traditions, although I would not reduce the corresponding attainments to psychological ones.

In terms of humanistic and transpersonal psychology, with the former often referred to as the "third force" in psychology, emphasis has been placed on "human potential" and "actualization" (see ch. 1 herein). For present purposes, key theorists include Mihaly Csikszentmihalyi, Arthur Deikman, Erich Fromm, Stanislav Grof, Abraham Maslow, Carl Rogers, and Ken Wilber, among others. Although diverse, such psychological approaches place stronger emphasis on the existential dimensions and "spiritual" capacities of human beings; attention is given to meaning and purpose and the capacities of individuals to become fully human and alive. This includes the recognition and development of hidden and perhaps unknown capacities, "higher levels of consciousness" if you will. In particular, the most influential humanistic and transpersonal psychologists have emphasized different modes of being. These are existential states characterized by a greater sense of personal fulfillment and interpersonal wellness. Humanistic and transpersonal psychology thus places emphasis on "self-actualization" and "authenticity," with the latter category strongly influenced by French existentialism.

For example, Carl Rogers has discussed the process of "becoming fully human," in which one engages in a process of self-actualization. In the latter, one is less inclined to accept dissatisfying relationships and situations. One also expresses "unconditional positive regard" toward self and other (see Rogers 1961). In a parallel manner, a distinction has been made concerning actualized modes and deficient modes. Deikman distinguishes between a "receptive mode" and an "active mode";[20] Maslow between Being-cognition and deficiency-cognition; and Fromm between a "being-mode" and a "having-mode" (see ch. 1 herein). While possibly problematic in terms of the privileged qualities and characteristics, these insights may inspire us to consider claims about human potential and "higher levels" of being in different contemplative traditions. We may consider the various psychological capacities (see Wilber 1997, 2000) and somatic ones (see Murphy 1992). Thus, Robert Forman and his colleagues (1990) have discussed Pure Consciousness Events (PCEs), while Eugene d'Aquili (1940–1998) and his colleagues (1999) have proposed a higher level of consciousness attained through contemplative practice called Absolute Unitary Being (AUB). As I have mentioned throughout my introductory comments, attention must be given to the specific and diverse claims within different contemplative traditions. It appears that different traditions emphasize different spiritual abilities, qualities, and experiences. This type of inquiry is the work of comparative religious studies.

As mentioned in chapter 1, Han de Wit has proposed a new psychological approach, namely, "contemplative psychology" (1991). Contemplative psychology has certain parallels with tradition-based psychologies, but the latter are located *within* religious traditions and in the perspectives of adherents. Contemplative psychology, on the other hand, draws insights from religious traditions in an effort to create an integrated psychological system focusing on spiritual development (cf. Wilber 2000). In this way, contemplative psychology tends to be comparative, interreligious, and syncretistic. As stated by De Wit, "In using the term *contemplative psychology*, we are referring to the *psychological* insights, knowledge and methods that we find *within contemplative traditions themselves*" (1, italics in original). Moreover, "The term *contemplative psychology* refers rather to the psychological insights and beliefs that are often implicitly present in the vision of religions, and that become concretized in the authentic religious practices of individuals" (12, italics in original). Furthermore,

> This brings us to the main purpose of this introductory study in contemplative psychology: to make explicit and clarify the nature and position of the psychological *know-how* that contemplative traditions contain. . . . The clarification of the psychological aspects of contemplative traditions may also contribute to *a general understanding of the value of contemplative traditions and their psychological perspectives*, both from a practical and from a scientific psychological or methodological point of view. (14, italics in original)

For De Wit, contemplative practice utilizes and activates a special set of psychological states or conditions. It involves a specific type of knowing (contemplative epistemology), which includes first-person experience (31–32). However, this is not uncritical adherent discourse, that is, the discourse of apologetics and dogmatics; rather, it is a more systematic investigation of one's life through experiences within contemplative practice. The goal, ideally, is to become more conscious, integrated, and, from one perspective, realized. De Wit identifies this as a path to that which religious traditions identify as emancipation, enlightenment, fulfillment, liberation, salvation, and so forth (18). This recalls my earlier points about contemplative practice as located in soteriological systems. For De Wit, an existential and psychological shift occurs through contemplative practice. Such shifts are documented in the psychological views of religious traditions. Contemplative psychology in turn attempts to map the "higher" levels of human functioning.

Drawing inspiration from humanistic, transpersonal, and contemplative psychology, we may be attentive to the various psychologies associated with specific forms of contemplative practice and contemplative experience. Here I would add that a postcolonial approach would be cautious about domesticating religious traditions and about making normative or totalizing statements concerning psychology. There are complex contemplative *psychologies*. Like the associated soteriologies and theologies, these may be equally convincing, but mutually exclusive. In any case, the primary point here is the importance of investigating system-specific psychologies. Here two specific examples will suffice. According to the *Yoga Sūtras*, consciousness contains various "defilements," which are associated with the "five abstentions" or "moral restraints" (*yama*). The latter include nonviolence, truthfulness, abstention from stealing, celibacy, and abstention from craving (see ch. 10 herein). By extension, the opposite states obscure consciousness and bind one to suffering caused by desire. By practicing Hindu classical Yoga, one becomes free of samsaric consciousness. Along parallel lines, members of the inner cultivation lineages of classical Daoism identified the heart-mind as the emotional, intellectual, and spiritual center of human personhood (see ch. 3 herein). In its ordinary habituated and agitated condition, the heart-mind is characterized by hyper-emotionality, excessive intellectual rumination, and spiritual disorientation. The basic contemplative psychology of classical Daoism recognizes the potential disruptive influence of sensory engagement as well as emotional and intellectual reactivity. Moreover, attachment to one's own ideas and knowing, deeply connected to language and thought, leads to dissipation and spiritual disorientation. However, as the fourth-century BCE "Neiye" (Inward Training) chapter of the *Guanzi* (Book of Master Guan) informs us, "Within the heart-mind there is yet another heart-mind," which has "an awareness that precedes language" (ch. 14). This heart-mind is the "lodging place of the numinous" (ch. 13; also ch. 8). From a classical Daoist perspective, this is our "innate nature" (*xing*) and "inner power" (*de*), or the capacity to realize the Dao and the way in which the Dao manifests in individual beings. From this perspective, human beings have an innate connection with the sacred, and contemplative practice is a path of return to that reality. Various religious traditions, in turn, identify increased capacities, such as aliveness, compassion, discernment, energetic sensitivity, equanimity, pain tolerance, and so forth. In this respect, we should note that it appears that the emphasis on "compassion" as the *sine qua non* of contemplative practice is largely influenced by Christian, Tibetan Buddhist, and post-1960s American counterculture conceptions. We should investigate the particular conceptions and qualities of "compassion" in different traditions. It is also important to consider the ways in which particular practices lead to particular ontological conditions, with associated values, commitments, and qualities (see earlier discussion).

Contemplative Literature

Here "contemplative literature" is used as a more inclusive category of literature than the more conventional "meditation manual," "guide to prayer," and so forth. Contemplative literature primarily refers to textual sources that discuss contemplative practice. As with other categories of literature, the meaning of contemplative literature needs to be addressed. The present volume is particularly concerned with literature that provides instruction on specific methods and systems. However, in certain cases, such as the *Novem modi orandi sancti Dominici* (Nine Ways of Prayer of Saint Dominic), the categorization may obscure as much as reveal the text's purpose. It appears that this text was intended as much as a canonization testimonial as a guide to Dominican prayer (see ch. 11 herein). Similarly, there is a way to read the *Ānāpānasati Sutta* (Discourse on Mindfulness of Breathing) and the *Guan wuliang shoufo jing* (Sutra on Visualizing the Buddha of Infinite Life) (see chs. 6 and 9 herein) as manuals of Buddhist doctrinal enculturation. Such is the work of close reading and nuanced textual analysis. This volume thus provides resources for the careful study of contemplative practice. In addition, most of the texts are not only representative but also highly influential and/or thought-provoking. Thus, a secondary meaning of "contemplative literature" may be literature deserving contemplation, of careful reading and deep reflection.

As with other categories of literature, contemplative literature cannot but be encountered as text, and a whole host of issues emerges. Similar to the problematic study of mystical experience through "mystical literature" (see, e.g., Smart 1965), there are issues with studying contemplative practice and contemplative experience through contemplative literature. Specifically, the reader wonders to what degree the described method was actually practiced. The contributors to the present volume attempt to explicitly address this question. Along the same lines, one wonders to what degree the texts are descriptive or prescriptive. Such are perennial questions in the interdisciplinary field of religious studies.

On a more strictly literary level, one may be attentive to a wide variety of formalistic features, including audience, authorship, context, date, genre, imagery, language, provenance, setting, symbolism, themes, tone, viewpoint, and so forth. Especially noteworthy with respect to contemplative literature are authorship, provenance, and genre. Many of the works in the present volume are anonymous or pseudonymous. The informing motivations deserve careful reflection. In terms of provenance, the setting presented often differs from the actual context of composition. Perhaps most interesting, we have a diverse set of genres: from actual practice manuals to travelogues and public talks. One question that emerges in the study of contemplative literature is the connection between the advocated practice, associated ontological conditions, and literary genre. To what degree does the format of the text approximate the practice itself? For example, the *Yoga Sūtras* (Yoga Aphorisms; see ch. 10 herein) is a sparse, aphoristic text. It advocates a purification of consciousness that eventually results in pure awareness. The writing style and textual format approximate the practice and experience on some level. In this respect, one also wonders about a text like the *Rasskaz strannika* (Tale of a Pilgrim; see ch. 8 herein). The text presents itself as a travelogue, in which the unnamed Pilgrim wanders through Russia in search of a spiritual father. As the text advocates unceasing practice of the Jesus Prayer, it appears that the text again approximates the associated practice and experience. Recalling the aforementioned points about tradition-specific and contemplative psychologies, one may reflect on the connection between literary composition and consciousness. Do specific styles of writing reveal something profound about the mind behind the writing? Are there distinctive qualities expressed in contemplative literature? And are these expressions of a "contemplative mind," of a mind transformed through contemplative practice?

Turning to the present volume, this work is a comparative anthology on contemplative practice from a wide variety of traditions. The texts were initially selected by me in consultation with experts on the associated literature and traditions. Rather than explain the evolution and journey of the volume, suffice it to say that the design required extensive preliminary research, and the organization went through a number of incarnations. In the end, I was fortunate to secure the participation of experts on the texts and traditions. It is our belief that the chapters form a dynamic whole, which may also be read individually as authoritative studies on each work and/or collectively as comparative exercises in contemplative studies. The selected texts are ones that are particularly fascinating and thought-provoking, both in terms of the associated traditions and the comparative study of contemplative practice and contemplative experience. As advocated in chapter 1, my approach to contemplative studies, and thus the one primarily expressed in this volume, aims to be more inclusive and comprehensive. Rather than restrict the category of "contemplative practice" arbitrarily or prematurely (e.g., as essentially attentional and/or trophotropic), this volume examines a wide-ranging spectrum of meditation and contemplative prayer. This includes practices like "prayer" and visualization, which some theorists might exclude.

This edited volume utilizes a comparative religious studies approach; it is informed by the interdisciplinary field of religious studies. This approach to contemplative practice and contemplative experience has a number of unique features. As scholars of religion, the contributors have the requisite skills and knowledge base for the resultant scholarship. Here language proficiency, deep engagement with the associated tradition, and comprehensive knowledge of relevant secondary scholarship are essential. In addition, to varying degrees, the contributors are conversant with the field of religious studies as such; the scholarship is informed by and contributes to theoretical and methodological issues in the field. However, here the texts, practices, and associated traditions are primary. As the reader will note, some of the contributors are more clearly located in area studies than others. There are moments when the volume is weakly comparative, as when there is comparison of datasets; at other times, it is more strongly comparative, as when theoretical insights are applied to or derived from the specific text. This volume in turn represents a pioneering effort in the emerging interdisciplinary field of contemplative studies, specifically from a religious studies perspective. The contributors primarily utilize a textual and historical Contextualist approach (see ch. 1 herein). The contributors have, in turn, employed a standardized interpretive framework, a chapter template, which was created by me. Each chapter follows a parallel format comprised of an introduction followed by an annotated translation and/or selection. Each introduction consists of six sections: (1) biographical and historical background, (2) associated religious tradition and textual corpus, (3) religious and soteriological system,[21] (4) textual survey of primary text, (5) legacy and influence, and (6) interpretive issues related to the comparative study of contemplative practice and contemplative experience. The first section discusses authorship and the origin of the primary text; it includes relevant information related to context of composition. The second section provides information on the associated religious tradition and movement as well as on the overall textual corpus in which the primary text is located. The third section discusses the specific practice documented in the primary text. It also examines the larger religious and soteriological system in which the practice is undertaken and which the practice embodies. The fourth section provides an outline and analytical overview of the text's contents and organization. At times, there is overlap with the previous section. The fifth section discusses the lasting influence of the text. It also addresses the degree to which the corresponding method is still practiced, including the types of reconceptualizations that have occurred. The sixth and final section examines relevant interpretive issues, especially with respect to comparative religious studies.

As discussed in more detail later, the texts and practices are representative of the associated tradition. However, given a variety of historical developments and cultural influences, they may be radically unfamiliar to many readers, even adherents of the associated religious tradition. In addition to attentiveness to issues of representativeness, there are also various subtexts involved. Specifically, among less specialized studies, one notices a fairly consistent tendency to ignore or to equate diverse practices and to engage in manipulative, perhaps deceptive, selection practices. For example, popular and general audience publications consistently exclude theistic, devotional, and visualization materials. Along similar lines, they frequently evidence a lack of familiarity with the associated tradition and the way in which the selected practice is understood within such contexts. In addition, such presentations most often advocate Perennial Philosophy, including an assumed normative monistic theology (see ch. 1 herein). In contrast, the present volume contains a more inclusive and comprehensive presentation of contemplative practice. It thus subverts and undermines the nearly ubiquitous tendency to domesticate and colonialize tradition-based contemplative practice. It provides material that challenges totalizing readings of contemplative literature and contemplative traditions. Thus, the contributors not only provide access to representative works, but the selections also provide resources for a fuller appreciation of the diversity and nuanced dimensions of tradition-based and religiously-committed contemplative practices. The work of comparative inquiry involves the recognition of *both* similarity and difference. It accepts and respects otherness as otherness while simultaneously seeking to understand alternative perspectives and views. This "dialogic imagination," and perhaps lived practice in the form of participant-observation and interreligious dialogue, may reveal a shared humanity characterized by difference and diversity, a context wherein the other is free to be and flourish as other. We may, in turn, recognize the following subtexts of the present volume: contemplative studies, religious studies, popular American culture, and so forth.

The volume consists of twelve primary chapters, which form its core. In sequential order, the topics and authors are as follows: (1) classical Daoist apophatic meditation by Harold Roth, (2) Quaker Christian silent prayer by Michael Birkel, (3) Lurianic Jewish Kabbalah by Shaul Magid, (4) Southern Buddhist meditation by Sarah Shaw, (5) Naqshbandi-Mujaddidi Sufi contemplation by Arthur Buehler, (6) Eastern Orthodox Christian prayer by John McGuckin, (7) Pure Land Buddhist visualization by Kenneth Tanaka, (8) Hindu classical Yoga by Edwin Bryant, (9) Dominican Catholic prayer by Paul Philibert, (10) Wu-Liu Daoist internal alchemy by Louis Komjathy, (11) modern therapeutic meditation by Louis Komjathy, and (12) techniqueless meditation by Constance Jones. The observant reader will note a number of things from this list. First, the volume's scholarship is international in scope. Second, there is not equal coverage concerning each tradition: there are two chapters on Buddhism, three chapters on Christianity, two on Daoism, one on Hinduism, one on Islam, one on Judaism, and two on modern and only loosely affiliated practices. I discuss this "lack of balance," this apparent bias or idiosyncrasy, in more detail later. Finally, though perhaps less obvious, many of the contributors have direct personal experience with the practices and associated traditions, and some are even "scholar-practitioners." This was not a primary criterion for their invitation to contribute; in fact, it only became apparent later in the editorial process. In any case, it is a welcome element (see further discussion).

In keeping with the previous points about contemplative literature, we may further map the volume's contents in terms of text, author, date, original language, practice, tradition, and audience (see fig. 2.4). As a final point on contemplative literature in general and the selections herein in particular, we may reflect more deeply on what might be labeled "contemplative reading" (see Komjathy 2013a; also Stock 1998, 2001; Griffiths 1999). On some level, this term parallels the perhaps less palatable notions of "scripture study" and *lectio divina*. Contemplative reading is careful reading, reading that is considerate, reflective, and perhaps orientated toward something more. Contemplative reading contrasts with the modern trend toward "consumptive" and "voracious reading" and with the movement toward the "post-literacy" of "virtual reality" and fragmented "downloads of information." Whether the primary texts in the present volume are read as historical artifacts or guides to practice, they will take time to read. They will need be to be read and probably reread slowly, deliberatively, contemplatively. You will need some degree of interest, commitment, and concentration. As was the case with its forging in various places at different times, reading this book requires consistent and prolonged engagement. This is perhaps even more the case for those, whether "seekers" or not, who would read it for spiritual insights and guidance. If one engages these texts as religious expressions and biographical dispensations, rather than as simply material or historical artifacts, one finds a new, perhaps hidden, landscape. This involves taking seriously the approach to reading and scripture study advocated by members of the tradition. To read with attentiveness, discernment, and application is to become open to the potential transformative effect of the texts themselves. Such is contemplative reading, a way of approaching texts as more than texts. Rather, they are documentations of individual and communal lifeworlds, expressions of lived religiosity, as well as offerings and petitions to those who choose to engage in deep inquiry.

Text	Author	Date	Language	Practice	Tradition	Audience
Laozi (Book of Venerable Masters), *Zhuangzi* (Book of Master Zhuang), etc.	Elders of the inner cultivation lineages	4th-2nd c. BCE	Classical Chinese	Apophatic meditation	Inner cultivation lineages of classical Daoism	Miscellaneous
A Guide to True Peace	Anonymous (William Backhouse [1779-1844] & James Janson [1784-1821])	1813	English	Contemplative prayer	Religious Society of Friends (Quakers; Protestant Christianity)	Quakers
Shaarei Kedusha (Gates of Holiness)	Hayyim Vital (1543-1620)	Late 16th c.	Hebrew	Kabbalistic contemplation	Lurianic line/ Safed school of Jewish meditative and theosophical Kabbalah	Lurianic Kabbalists
Ānāpānasati Sutta (Discourse on Mindfulness of Breathing)	Discourse attributed to Śākyamuni Buddha (5th c. BCE)	5th c. BCE?	Pali	Samatha/ Vipassanā	Ancient/ Theravāda Buddhism	Theravāda monastics
Suluk-i Mujaddidiyya (Mujaddidi Wayfaring)	'Abdullah Shah (1872-1964)	Mid-20th century	Urdu	Sufi contemplation	Naqshbandi-Mujaddidi order of Islam	Naqshbandi-Mujaddidi Sufis
Otkrovennyi rasskaz strannika dukhovnomu svoemu ottsu (The Candid Tale of a Pilgrim to His Spiritual Father; abbr. *Rasskaz strannika*)	Mikhail Kozlov (1826-1884) and others	Late 19th century	Russian	Hesychast prayer	Eastern Orthodox Christianity	Russian Orthodox Christians
Guan wuliang shoufo jing (Sutra on Visualizing the Buddha of Infinite Life; abbr. *Guanjing*)	Kālayaśas (383-442) (Discourse attributed to Śākyamuni Buddha)	Early 5th c. CE (2nd c. BCE?)	Chinese (Sanskrit)	Pure Land visualization	Pure Land school of Mahāyāna Buddhism	Mahāyāna Buddhist monastics and laypeople
Yoga Sūtras (Yoga Aphorisms)	Attributed to Patañjali (2nd c. CE?)	3rd c. CE?	Sanskrit	Classical Yoga	Yoga School of Hinduism	Hindu renunciants
Novem modi orandi sancti Dominici (Nine Ways of Praying of Saint Dominic; abbr. *Novem modi orandi*)	Anonymous Dominican monastics	13th c.	Latin	Dominican prayer	Order of Preachers (Dominicans) of Roman Catholic Christianity	Dominican monastics and papal canonization committee
Huiming jing (Scripture on Wisdom and Life-destiny)	Liu Huayang (1735-1799)	1799	Classical Chinese	Internal alchemy	Wu-Liu sub-lineage of Quanzhen (Complete Perfection) Daoism	Chan Buddhist and Longmen (Dragon Gate) Daoist monastics
The Relaxation Response	Herbert Benson (b. 1935)	1975	English	Relaxation Response	Mind-body Medicine	General audience
This Light in Oneself	Talks given by Jiddu Krishnamurti (1895-1986)	1968-1983	English	Techniqueless meditation	Krishnamurti	General audience

Figure 2.4. Comparative Chart of Contents of *Contemplative Literature*

Future Prospects

As mentioned previously, the present volume includes representative and historically significant works from a variety of religious traditions, with particular attention to so-called "world religions." The volume includes two chapters on Buddhism, three chapters on Christianity, two on Daoism, one on Hinduism, one on Islam, one on Judaism, and two on modern and only loosely affiliated practices. Thus, it may appear "unbalanced" from certain perspectives; in fact, some of the contributors themselves expressed reservations about the lack of coverage. I have taken these concerns seriously, but the volume is primarily intended as an (advanced) introductory reader and comparative sourcebook on contemplative practice. It is not meant to be comprehensive or even "balanced," if one understands the latter solely in terms of traditions. In fact, such an approach would require multiple volumes, a much larger project timeframe, as well as a larger group of international scholars. Moreover, as the majority of research to date has focused on Buddhist meditation and Christian prayer, this apparent lack of balance perhaps accurately reflects the current state of research.

No single volume can provide complete, balanced, or equal coverage of such a complex topic as contemplative traditions. For example, readers of this volume may be surprised by the absence of Zen Buddhist meditation. My response is that this form of meditation has received a high degree of attention and is highly accessible, including primary sources translated into English (see previous discussion). In addition, the foundational Chan Buddhist meditation practice is deeply indebted to and influenced by classical Daoist apophatic meditation (see ch. 3 herein). The selection is indeed idiosyncratic: It was chosen by me, in the same way that I designed the interpretive framework. However, the contributors agreed with the selection (in certain cases they were given the option of selecting different texts) and with the interpretive framework. That is, in the end, the selection and our methodology were collaborative. In addition, my process of editing each chapter was informed by editing the other chapters; some issues or elements addressed in one chapter subsequently were included in others and even changed my way of thinking about contemplative practice. In this way, the editing and writing processes were also collaborative. At the same time, some of the contributors expressed concerns that certain practices would be elevated to the status of "normative." That is, rather than recognizing that classical Yoga or Lurianic Kabbalah were only one form of Hindu and Jewish contemplative practice, respectively, readers might have the false impression that these are *the* representative practices. There are a number of responses. For the moment, we may recognize that based on the criterion of tradition, isolated from others, this volume is no doubt deficient. Thus, I have provided a partial overview of the spectrum of tradition-based and religiously-committed contemplative practice in this chapter (see previous discussion). When practical and appropriate, I have also asked the contributors to do the same in their chapters, particularly through the works cited and further reading section.

While the volume is representative, it is not comprehensive. Other texts and traditions could have been included. As mentioned previously, for the present volume, I was particularly interested in relatively unfamiliar, underrepresented, and radically diverse forms of contemplative practice. Informed by a Contextualist and pluralistic perspective, this approach to selection provides access into a complex spectrum of contemplative practice. Thus, the criterion of "types" in concert with "traditions" has informed the volume. For example, Hindu Vaishnavite and Shaivite forms of devotionalism, uncovered here, are much closer to Dominican prayer (ch. 11 herein) and Pure

Land visualization (ch. 9 herein) than to Hindu classical Yoga (see ch. 10 herein). The former are theistic and devotional, while the latter is primarily enstatic and trophotropic, though it does have a theistic dimension as well. Such attentiveness to similarities and differences with respect to "types" is not to deny the radically different soteriologies related to different objects of devotion. Similarly, Chan/Zen Buddhist "just sitting," also uncovered here (see previous discussion), is more similar to classical Daoist apophatic meditation than to Theravāda Buddhist *samatha/vipassanā* (ch. 6 herein) and Pure Land visualization (ch. 9 herein). Thus, both tradition-centered and typological approaches have their contributions and limitations.

These comments reveal a variety of trajectories for future work in contemplative studies from a religious studies perspective. As with many projects, perceived deficiencies open up new vistas. First and foremost, I hope that the present volume will inspire more scholarship on contemplative practice and contemplative experience from a sophisticated and nuanced perspective. While we have some detailed and reliable work on specific texts on meditation and prayer, we have yet to see comprehensive studies of different "contemplative traditions." In addition to more research on particular practices and texts, we also need broader studies. In this respect, one can imagine parallel volumes to the present one on each major contemplative tradition. Thus, there could be a volume on Buddhist contemplative literature, Christian contemplative literature, Confucian contemplative literature, and so forth. This would follow the "tradition-centered approach" of the present volume, with particular attention to so-called "world religions." However, it would move from interreligious to intrareligious comparison. In the process, one would find that there is as much diversity *within* supposedly unified or distinct religions as between them.

Another question that emerges in the process of inquiry about contemplative practice and contemplative experience is the degree to which actual practice is required. Many of the primary texts in the present volume are no longer in circulation. If the associated methods are practiced, it is often in various reconceptualizations and reconstructions.[22] Thus, like religious adherence more generally, "practitioners" may have important contributions to make, but they may overlook important details. The relationship between scholarship on religion and actual religious adherence is a complex topic (see, e.g., McCutcheon 1999; Cabezón and Davaney 2004). My own position is that scholarship that engages the whole range of interpretation, from social scientific reductionism through sympathetic engagement to scholar-practitioner and critical adherent views, will lead to the most comprehensive understanding. Each approach has its contributions and limitations. A generous approach would thus include, but not privilege, the voice of adherents. In any case, one can imagine a parallel volume written by scholar-practitioners and/or critical adherents,[23] ideally teachers, of specific techniques. In this respect, it might be more successful to focus on modern practice rather than to get into the thorny issue of historical precedents. Much of what is presented as "ancient" in the modern world has a very recent pedigree. In addition to various forms of "spiritual colonialism" and "spiritual capitalism" (see Lau 2000; Carrette and King 2004; also the technical glossary herein), the context of modernity reveals various attempts at "traditionalization," or the process of constructing something new as ancient (see, e.g., Hobsbawm and Ranger 1992). Along these lines, a profitable study of modern teachers and methods would also be welcomed.

This volume also appears relatively conventional from certain perspectives. As mentioned, the "major" religious traditions form its center. However, a "trans-tradition" approach would open up many new possibilities. One could imagine a volume on contemplative practice in "indigenous traditions." This also could result in an independent volume on Native American contemplative practices. Researchers might also focus on "nonsectarian practice," "unchurched spirituality," as well as secular and therapeutic meditation. Beyond the narrow confines of seated meditation, another volume could address various somatic disciplines, such as Alexander Technique, Applied Kinesiology, Autogenic Training, Feldenkrais Method, Pilates, Trager Approach, and so forth (see, e.g., Johnson 1995; also Murphy 1992). In this respect, one might also study martial arts (see, e.g., Palmer 2002; Raposa 2003). In addition, as mentioned in the previous chapter, contemplative practice may include art, dance, music, photography, theater, writing, and so forth. A volume could address the ways in which these disciplines are approached from a "contemplative perspective."

Finally, the perceptive reader also will note a "gender bias" in this volume. While "women's voices" are included in the chapters by Sarah Shaw (ch. 6) and Constance Jones (ch. 14), none of the primary texts in the present volume were written by or specifically for women. Here some qualification may be made with respect to a hyper-feminist viewpoint, specifically one rooted in a presentist fallacy (i.e., taking the present as the evaluative criterion for the past). The degree of inclusivity or exclusivity, including with respect to women, is an important consideration. This is equally true with respect to the *rationalizations* and *motivations* behind exclusion. In certain cases, there is strong justification for spiritual elitism, or the exclusion of those without commitment, initiation, and so forth. However, the exclusion of women from many practice communities is often rooted in patriarchal biases and untenable, especially by modern standards. Here it is reasonable to investigate the informing worldviews to determine the conception of women and the "feminine." Most germane to the present volume, we find that women are often included, implicitly, in texts addressed to the laity. More interesting, women find a more elevated position in some of our texts. For example, in the inner cultivation lineages of classical Daoism (see ch. 3 herein), there is evidence of female Daoist elders. Along similar lines, the Quaker text titled *A Guide to True Peace* incorporates materials and draws inspiration from the French Catholic Quietist Jeanne Marie Guyon (1648–1717) (see ch. 4 herein). In this respect, it is also important to recognize that the Religious Society of Friends was an egalitarian Christian denomination from the beginning, including prominent female leaders such as Margaret Fell (1614–1702), Mary Fisher (ca. 1623–1698), and Elizabeth Hooton (1600–1672) among the so-called Valiant Sixty. In addition, the *Novem modi orandi sancti Dominici* (Nine Ways of Prayer of Saint Dominic) may have been partially composed based on the oral testimony of a Dominican Catholic nun named Sister Cecilia (d.u.) of the Monastery of Saint Agnes in Bologna (see ch. 11 herein). The *Guan wuliang shoufo jing* (Sutra on Visualizing the Buddha of Infinite Life) is addressed primarily to Queen Vaidehī and Mahāyāna Buddhist laywomen (see ch. 9 herein), and it may be that this type of Pure Land practice was specifically intended for women. Nonetheless, texts written specifically by and for women are a major omission, and one can imagine a volume that addresses this topic. Here one thinks of texts such as *El Castillo Interior* (The Interior Castle) and *Camino de Perfección* (The Way of Perfection) by the Spanish Carmelite nun Teresa of Ávila (1515–1582) (see, e.g., Frohlich 1993; Holder 2009) and various late imperial Chinese Daoist works on female alchemy (*nüdan*) (see Valussi 2002). One would also like to see historical studies of "female contemplative practice," as it appears that much of the relevant literature is relatively late.

What this volume does provide is a representative and diverse sample of significant, fascinating, and thought-provoking texts on contemplative practice from a variety of contemplative traditions. Here the engaged reader learns how to sit in silence with the classical Daoist inner cultivation lineages and nineteenth-century British Quakers, to practice Hebrew letter permutations with sixteenth-century Lurianic Kabbalists in Jerusalem, to engage in *samatha* (calming) and *vipassanā* (insight) with the early Indian Buddhist community, to practice Sufi contemplation and visualization with twentieth-century Naqshbandi-Mujaddidi Sufis, to recite the Jesus Prayer with nineteenth-century Russian Orthodox monastics and pilgrims, to visualize the Pure Land with sixth-century Chinese Pure Land Buddhists, to purify consciousness and free spirit from materiality through Hindu classical Yoga in third-century India, to follow the model of Jesus Christ and Saint Dominic among thirteenth-century Spanish Dominicans, to practice Daoist internal alchemy among Chan Buddhist and Daoist monastics in eighteenth-century China, to enter relaxation and decrease stress in twentieth- and twenty-first-century America, and to forget technique, tradition, and teachers while listening to J. Krishnamurti's public talks in the modern world. One finds the ways in which specific practices and experiences are rooted in and informed by specific contexts, traditions, and worldviews. One finds that contemplative practice includes diverse and complex methods, methods associated with various contemplative traditions and documented in contemplative literature.

Notes

The present chapter has benefited from the comments of Jorge Ferrer (California Institute of Integral Studies), Andrew Fort (Texas Christian University), Fran Grace (University of Redlands), Jeffrey Kripal (Rice University), Kevin Schilbrack (Appalachian State University), and the volume's contributors. I am also grateful for grant support from the Wabash Center and the University of San Diego. My gratitude notwithstanding, all views and interpretations are my own.

1. Vipassanā, at least in name, is a method with wide dissemination in the modern world. Prominent practitioners and teachers include Ba Khin (Burmese; 1899–1971), Mahasi Sayadaw (Burmese; 1904–1982), Achaan Chah (Thai; 1918–1992), S. N. Goenka (Burmese; 1924–2013), as well as their Euro-American associates, Joseph Goldstein, Jack Kornfield, Larry Rosenberg, Sharon Salzberg, and so forth. Observant readers will note the large number of Jews, at least individuals who are ethnically Jewish, who practice Vipassanā. Perhaps paralleling the Jesuit Catholic practice of Zazen, this phenomenon deserves further research. Cf. chapter 5 herein.

2. Interestingly, different forms of communal contemplative practice involve different postural and spatial arrangements. Rinzai monks tend to sit facing inward, toward each other, while Sōtō monks tend to sit facing outward, toward the wall.

3. One of the most concise and profound meditation manuals is the "Fukan zazen-gi" (Universally Recommended Instructions on Zazen), often referred to as "Rules for Zazen," by Eihei Dōgen (1200–1253).

4. Throughout this chapter, my references focus on historical and authoritative textual sources. However, in most cases, the majority of the contemplative practices discussed here have received attention among contemporary practitioners and teachers. On Zen meditation, see especially the works of Philip Kapleau, John Daido Loori, Kazuki Sekida, Sheng Yen, Omori Sogen, and Shunryu Suzuki.

5. There are various biblical precedents for "Christian meditation," including in the Gospels. Some important and influential passages include 1 Kings 18:42; Psalm 46:10; Matthew 6:5–6; Matthew 7:7–8; 1 Thessalonians 5:17. One of the most important resources for inquiry into Christian, and to a lesser extent Jewish and Islamic, contemplative practice is the Classics of Western Spirituality series through Paulist Press. See also chapters 4, 8, and 11 herein.

6. Here one also thinks of prominent and influential Catholic contemplatives such as John Main (1926–1982), O.S.B., Thomas Merton (1915–1968), O.C.S.O., Richard Rohr (b. 1943), O.F.M., and David Steindl-Rast (b. 1926), O.S.B. This list of course does not include the widespread phenomenon of Christians practicing "non-Christian" methods. Some prominent methods include Transcendental Meditation, Vipassanā, Zazen, and so forth. Interestingly, Centering Prayer and the "contemplative revival" in certain sectors of the lay Christian community partially emerged as a response to the increasing prominence of Asian traditions of meditation (see, e.g., Keating 1994, 11–21). There has, in turn, been a backlash among some

conservative Christians. Especially fascinating, at least from a religious studies perspective, are the official Vatican documents titled *Epistula ad totius Catholicae Ecclesiae Episcopos de quibusdam rationibus christianae meditationis* (Letter to the Bishops of the Catholic Church on Some Aspects of Christian Meditation; *Orationis Formas*), which was issued in 1989, and *Jesus Christ, the Bearer of the Water of Life: A Christian Reflection on the New Age*, which was issued in 2003. These types of documents are located in the conservative Catholic "counter-ecumenical" movement, including under the former Cardinal Joseph Ratzinger (Pope Benedict XVI; b. 1927; r. 2005–2013), then prefect of the Sacred Congregation for the Doctrine of the Faith (1981–2005), as a reversal of the Second Vatican Council (1962–1965). See http://www.vatican.va/roman_curia/congregations/cfaith/doc_doc_index.htm. There has also been a fundamentalist and evangelical Christian backlash to the emergence of a "Christian meditation" movement, especially with respect to "contemplative prayer" in general and "Centering Prayer" in particular.

7. The *sema* is a form of kinesthetic contemplative practice. Like other performative and movement-based practices, it is difficult to present in written publications. For a discussion of dance as contemplative practice, see Fraleigh 1996. One might also profitably consider the central importance of music in this and other forms of contemplative practice, including "contemplative music" itself.

8. The most detailed studies of Islamic contemplative practice, including its technical specifics, with which I am familiar have been written by Arthur Buehler. See chapter 7 herein. However, as these materials are quite late, one wonders about earlier Sufi expressions. See, for example, Sells 1995.

9. For some relevant information on Jain meditation, see Jaini 1979. On the Shinto practice of *misogi* (purification), see Yamamoto 1999.

10. This is not to deny the potentially inherent transformative effects, especially on a subjective level, of contemplative practice or the ways in which specific experiences, often outside of the parameters of tradition, inspire contemplative practice and a deeper sense of meaning and purpose.

11. As briefly touched upon in chapter 1 herein, there are many body-configurations, including hand gestures (Skt.: *mudrā*). See Komjathy 2007.

12. This dimension asks one to consider the relative importance of place and contemplative spaces.

13. As employed herein, "soteriology" is a comparative category that refers to discourse on or theories about actualization, liberation, perfection, realization, salvation, or however an individual or community identifies the ultimate purpose of human existence. Soteriology is most often rooted in a specific "theology."

14. As herein employed, "theology" is a comparative category that refers to discourse on or theories about the "sacred," with the latter being another comparative category for that which a given individual or community identifies as "ultimately real." In terms of religious studies, one must, in turn, identify the tradition-specific term and the associated defining characteristics.

15. In this respect, Krishnamurti might be profitably compared to other contemporaneous iconoclastic spiritual teachers, such as Rajneesh (Osho; 1931–1990) and Chögyam Trungpa (1939–1987), including both the ways in which they subvert their own claims to authority and the degree of discrepancy with their own teachings. See, for example, Rawlinson 1998; Forsthoefel and Humes 2005; Williamson 2010.

16. In this context, it is important to consider the degree to which practice is emphasized over experience, or vice versa.

17. Here we should again be attentive to the individual and communal dimensions of contemplative practice. As discussed in chapter 1, a more comprehensive and integrated approach to contemplative studies recognizes the importance of critical first-person (subjective), intersubjective (interpersonal), and third-person ("objective") approaches. That is, we should be careful not to reduce contemplative experience to personal experience. In terms of tradition-specific training, it is often dialogic.

18. Moreover, from a comparative perspective, other religious traditions would clearly find "content-less" states of consciousness meaningless. For example, someone like the Catholic mystic Hildegard of Bingen (1098–1179) and the Islamic mystic Rūmī (1207–1273) might see it as absence of God's presence, specifically as manifested in love and grace. There are thus two primary approaches to contemplative experience. First, study particular experiences in the context of specific religions and training regimens, which I would label

a "tradition-centered approach." Second, study the entire spectrum of contemplative experience from a comparative perspective without privileging any type of experience. In the latter "comparative approach," one must inhibit the tendency to privilege, whether implicitly or explicitly, tradition-specific claims or categorizations.

19. From a comparative and cross-cultural perspective, one also thinks of the place of the "spiritual senses" in Christianity. See, for example, Gavrilyuk and Coakley 2012.

20. Unlike the other dyads, Deikman's active and receptive modes may not be dichotomous and antithetical. One may live in a realized "bimodal consciousness," which has some rough equivalence to introvertive and extrovertive mystical experience (see Stace 1960). The former involves unitive and enstatic types of mystical experience, while the latter involves returning to individuated being and retaining, in the flow of daily life, a profound sense of unity. For an attempt to apply Deikman to classical Daoism, see Roth 1999, 2000. In discussing the process of Daoist apophatic meditation (see ch. 3 herein), Roth outlines the training as follows: (1) preamble, in which the practices that prepare for the later stages are discussed; (2) *sorties*-style arguments, in which the stages of meditation are presented in a consecutive fashion; and (3) *denouement*, which discusses the noetic and practical benefits of having attained the stages. The latter is especially interesting as it suggests that in the "active mode" one lives through and applies contemplative practice. It is "contemplation in action." Deikman also speaks of "deautomatization," or disengaging and inhibiting "automatic" reactions. This is a process of transcending conditioning and habituation.

21. In the present book, "soteriology" is a comparative category that refers to actualization, liberation, perfection, realization, salvation, or however the ultimate purpose or goal of human existence is defined. "Theology" is a comparative category that refers to the study of, discourse on, or theories about the sacred, with the sacred being another comparative category. See chapter 1 and the technical glossary.

22. "Reconstructed practice" refers to practices that were lost in earlier moments of history and then reconstituted at later moments. It also includes contemporary attempts to reconstruct lost practices (see, e.g., Goodman 1990; Gore 1995; Goodman and Nauwald 2003), an extremely complex exercise fraught with many perils. The latter include the possibility of radical misinterpretations and inaccuracies, the creation of historical fictions. In terms of "reconceptualization," it is of course important to consider the ways in which this process is always occurring. For example, the Relaxation Response is a reconceptualization of Transcendental Meditation (TM), which is a reconceptualization of Hindu *mantra* meditation. More research of this process and phenomenon is required.

23. "Critical adherents" once again indicates the importance of education, training, and reflection. Dogmatists, polemicists, and apologists would be interesting topics of study but less relevant for a sophisticated and nuanced understanding.

Works Cited and Further Reading

Adiswarananda, Swami. 2003. *Meditation and Its Practices: A Definitive Guide to Techniques and Traditions of Meditation in Yoga and Vedanta*. Woodstock: Skylight Paths.
Analayo. 2004. *Satipatthana: The Direct Path to Realization*. Cambridge: Windhorse.
Aschenbrenner, George. 1972. "Consciousness Examen." *Review for Religious* 31: 13–21.
Bagger, Matthew C. 1999. *Religious Experience, Justification, and History*. Cambridge and New York: Cambridge University Press.
Bailey, Lee, and Jenny Yates, eds. 1996. *The Near-Death Experience: A Reader*. London and New York: Routledge.
Bielefeldt, Carl. 1990. *Dōgen's Manuals of Zen Meditation*. Berkeley: University of California Press.
Birkel, Michael L. 2004. *Silence and Witness: The Quaker Tradition*. Maryknoll: Orbis Books.
Blumenthal, David R. 1978. *Understanding Jewish Mysticism*. New York: Ktav.
Brokaw, Cynthia. 1991. *The Ledgers of Merit and Demerit: Social Change and Moral Order in Late Imperial China*. Princeton: Princeton University Press.

Brooks, Douglas. 1996. *Auspicious Wisdom: The Texts and Traditions of Śrīvidyā Śākta Tantrism in South India*. New Delhi: Manohar Publishers.
Brown, Daniel. 1986. "The Stages of Meditation in Cross-Cultural Perspective." In *Transformations of Consciousness*, edited by Ken Wilber et al., 219–83. Boston: Shambhala.
Bryant, Edwin, ed. 2007. *Krishna: A Sourcebook*. Oxford and New York: Oxford University Press.
———. 2009. *The Yoga Sutras: A New Edition, Translation, and Commentary*. New York: North Point Press.
Buehler, Arthur F. 1998. *Sufi Heirs of the Prophet: The Indian Naqshbandiyya and the Rise of the Mediating Shaykh*. Columbia: University of South Carolina Press.
———. 2011. *Revealed Grace: The Juristic Sufism of Ahmad Sirhindi (1564–1624)*. Louisville: Fons Vitae.
Buhnemann, Gudrun. 2011. *Eighty-Four Asanas in Yoga: A Survey of Traditions*. New Delhi: D.K. Printworld.
Buswell, Robert. 1993. *The Zen Monastic Experience*. Princeton: Princeton University Press.
Cabezón, José, and Sheila Davaney, eds. 2004. *Identity and the Politics of Scholarship in the Study of Religion*. London and New York: Routledge.
Cardeña, Etzel, Steven Jay Lynn, and Stanley Krippner, eds. 2000. *Varieties of Anomalous Experience: Examining the Scientific Evidence*. Washington: American Psychological Association.
Carrette, Jeremy, and Richard King. 2004. *Selling Spirituality: The Silent Takeover of Religion*. London and New York: Routledge.
Chadwick, Owen, ed. 1958. *Western Esotericism*. Philadelphia: Westminster Press.
Chariton, Igumen. 1997. *The Art of Prayer: An Orthodox Anthology*. London: Faber and Faber.
Chester, Michael, and Marie Norrisey. 1985. *Prayer and Temperament: Different Prayer Forms for Different Personality Types*. Rev. ed. Charlottesville: Open Door.
Chittick, William. 1984. *The Sufi Path of Love: The Spiritual Teachings of Rumi*. Albany: State University of New York Press.
Conze, Edward. 1997 (1956). *Buddhist Meditation*. New Delhi: Munshiram Manoharlal.
D'Aquili, Eugene, and Andrew B. Newberg. 1999. *The Mystical Mind: Probing the Biology of Religious Experience*. Minneapolis: Fortress Press.
De Wit, Han. 1991. *Contemplative Psychology*. Translated by Marie Louise Baird. Pittsburgh: Duquesne University Press.
Deikman, Arthur J. 1982. *The Observing Self: Mysticism and Psychotherapy*. Boston: Beacon Press.
Donner, Neal, and Daniel Stevenson. 1993. *The Great Calming and Contemplation: A Study and Annotated Translation of the First Chapter of Chih-I's Mo-ho chih-kuan*. Honolulu: University of Hawaii Press.
Ehara, N. R. M., Soma Thera, and Kheminda Thera. 1977. *The Path of Freedom: Vimuttimagga*. Kandy: Buddhist Publication Society.
Fitzgerald, Timothy. 2000. "Experience." In *Guide to the Study of Religion*, edited by Willi Braun and Russell T. McCutcheon, 125–39. London and New York: Cassell.
Forman, Robert K. C., ed. 1990. *The Problem of Pure Consciousness*. Oxford and New York: Oxford University Press.
———, ed. 1998. *The Innate Capacity*. Oxford and New York: Oxford University Press.
———. 1999. *Mysticism, Mind, Consciousness*. Albany: State University of New York Press.
Forsthoefel, Thomas, and Cynthia Ann Humes, eds. 2005. *Gurus in America*. Albany: State University of New York Press.
Fraleigh, Sondra Horton. 1996. *Dance and the Lived Body*. Pittsburgh: University of Pittsburgh Press.
Frohlich, Mary. 1993. *The Intersubjectivity of the Mystic: A Study of Teresa of Avila's "Interior Castle."* Oxford and New York: American Academy of Religion/Oxford University Press.
Gallagher, Timothy. 2006. *The Examen Prayer: Ignatian Wisdom for Our Lives Today*. New York: Crossroad.
Ganss, George. 1991. *Ignatius of Loyola: Spiritual Exercises and Selected Works*. Mahwah: Paulist Press.
Gavrilyuk, Paul, and Sarah Coakley, eds. 2012. *The Spiritual Senses: Perceiving God in Western Christianity*. Cambridge and New York: Cambridge University Press.
Gethin, R. M. L. 2001 (1992). *The Buddhist Path to Awakening*. Oxford: Oneworld.

Gimello, Robert. 1978. "Mysticism and Meditation." In *Mysticism and Philosophical Analysis*, edited by Steven T. Katz, 170–99. Oxford and New York: Oxford University Press.

———. 1983. "Mysticism in Its Contexts." In *Mysticism and Religious Traditions*, edited by Steven T. Katz, 61–88. Oxford and New York: Oxford University Press.

Goodman, Felicitas. 1990. *Where the Spirits Ride the Wind: Trance Journeys and Other Ecstatic Experiences*. Bloomington: Indiana University Press.

Goodman, Felicitas, and Nana Nauwald. 2003. *Ecstatic Trance: New Ritual Body Postures*. Haarlem: Binkey Kok.

Gore, Belinda. 1995. *Ecstatic Body Postures: An Alternate Reality Workbook*. Rochester: Bear and Company.

Gorman, George. 1973. *The Amazing Fact of Quaker Worship*. London: Quaker Home Service.

Gregory, Peter, ed. 1987. *Traditions of Meditation in Chinese Buddhism*. Honolulu: University of Hawaii Press.

Griffiths, Paul. 1986. *On Being Mindless: Buddhist Meditation and the Mind-Body Problem*. LaSalle: Open Court.

———. 1999. *Religious Reading: The Place of Reading in the Practice of Religion*. Oxford and New York: Oxford University Press.

Habito, Ruben. 2006. *Healing Breath: Zen for Christians and Buddhists in a Wounded World*. Somerville: Wisdom.

———. 2013. *Zen and the Spiritual Exercises*. Maryknoll: Orbis Books.

Hadot, Pierre. 1995. *Philosophy as a Way of Life: Spiritual Exercises from Socrates to Foucault*. Hoboken: Blackwell.

Heine, Steven, and Dale Wright. 2000. *The Koan: Texts and Contexts in Zen Buddhism*. Oxford and New York: Oxford University Press.

Hirtenstein, Stephen. 2009. *The Four Pillars of Spiritual Insight*. Oxford: Anqa.

Hobsbawm, Eric, and Terence Ranger, eds. 1992. *The Invention of Tradition*. Cambridge: Cambridge University Press.

Holder, Arthur. 2009. *Christian Spirituality: The Classics*. London and New York: Routledge.

Hopkins, Jeffrey. 2009. *Tantric Techniques*. Ithaca: Snow Lion.

Jaini, Padmanabh. 1979. *The Jaina Path of Purification*. Berkeley: University of California Press.

James, William. 1999 (1902). *The Varieties of Religious Experience*. New York: The Modern Library.

Johnson, Don Hanlon. 1995. *Bone, Breath, and Gesture: Practices of Embodiment*. Berkeley: North Atlantic Books.

Kadloubovsky, E., and G. E. H. Palmer. 1992. *Writings from the Philokalia: On the Prayer of the Heart*. London: Faber and Faber.

Kaplen, Aryeh. 1978. *Meditation and the Bible*. Newburyport: Weiser.

———. 1985. *Jewish Meditation: A Practical Guide*. New York: Schocken Books.

———. 1989. *Meditation and Kabbalah*. Newburyport: Weiser.

Katz, Steven T., ed. 1978a. *Mysticism and Philosophical Analysis*. Oxford and New York: Oxford University Press.

———. 1978b. "Language, Epistemology, and Mysticism." In *Mysticism and Philosophical Analysis*, edited by Steven T. Katz, 22–74. Oxford and New York: Oxford University Press.

———, ed. 1983. *Mysticism and Religious Traditions*. Oxford and New York: Oxford University Press.

Keating, Thomas. 1994. *Intimacy with God: An Introduction to Centering Prayer*. New York: Crossroad.

King, Richard. 1999. *Orientalism and Religion: Postcolonial Theory, India and 'The Mystic East.'* London and New York: Routledge.

King, Winston. 1992. *Theravada Meditation: The Buddhist Transformation of Yoga*. Delhi: Motilal Banarsidass.

Kiyota, Minoru, ed. 1978. *Mahayana Buddhist Meditation: Theory and Practice*. Delhi: Motilal Banarsidass.

Kohn, Livia. 1987. *Seven Steps to the Tao: Sima Chengzhen's Zuowang lun*. Monumenta Serica Monograph 20. St. Augustin/Nettetal: Steyler Verlag.

———, ed. 1989. *Taoist Meditation and Longevity Techniques*. Ann Arbor: Center for Chinese Studies, University of Michigan.

Komjathy, Louis. 2007. *Cultivating Perfection: Mysticism and Self-Transformation in Early Quanzhen Daoism*. Leiden: Brill.

———. 2011. "The Daoist Mystical Body." In *Perceiving the Divine through the Human Body: Mystical Sensuality*, edited by Thomas Cottai and June McDaniel, 67–103. New York: Palgrave Macmillan.

———. 2012. "Mysticism." In *Encyclopedia of Global Religion*, edited by Mark Juergensmeyer and Wade Clark Roof, 855–61. Thousand Oaks: Sage.

———. 2013a. *The Way of Complete Perfection: A Quanzhen Daoist Anthology*. Albany: State University of New York Press.

———. 2013b. *The Daoist Tradition: An Introduction*. London and New York: State University of New York Press.

———. 2014. "THRS 394: Contemplative Traditions Syllabus." http://home.sandiego.edu/~komjathy. Accessed on June 1, 2014.

Laing, R. D. 1967. *The Politics of Experience*. New York: Pantheon Books.

Lamrim Chenmo Translation Committee (LCTC). 2000–2004. *The Great Treatise on the Stages of the Path to Enlightenment: Lam Rim Chen Mo*. 3 vols. Ithaca: Snow Lion.

Lau, Kimberly. 2000. *New Age Capitalism: Making Money East of Eden*. Philadelphia: University of Pennsylvania Press.

Leggett, Trevor. 1995. *Realization of the Supreme Self: The Bhagavad Gita Yogas*. London and New York: Kegan Paul.

Leighton, Taigen Dan. 2000. *Cultivating the Empty Field: The Silent Illumination of Zen Master Hongzhi*. Rev. ed. North Clarendon: Tuttle.

Martin, Craig, and Russell McCutcheon, eds. 2012. *Religious Experience: A Reader*. Sheffield: Equinox.

McCutcheon, Russell, ed. 1999. *The Insider/Outsider Problem in the Study of Religion*. London and New York: Cassell.

Moore, Peter. 1978. "Mystical Experience, Mystical Doctrine, Mystical Technique." In *Mysticism and Philosophical Analysis*, edited by Steven T. Katz, 101–31. Oxford: Oxford University Press.

Murphy, Michael. 1992. *The Future of the Body: Explorations into the Further Evolution of Human Nature*. New York: Penguin Putnam.

Nanamoli, Bhikku. 1999 (1975). *The Path of Purification: Visuddhimagga*. Seattle: BPS Pariyatti Editions.

Nyanaponika, Thera. 1973. *The Heart of Buddhist Meditation*. Newburyport: Weiser.

Palmer, Wendy. 2002. *The Practice of Freedom: Aikido Principles as a Spiritual Guide*. Berkeley: Rodmell Press.

Paravahera Vajiranana. 1962. *Buddhist Meditation in Theory and Practice*. Kuala Lumpur: Buddhist Missionary Society.

Proudfoot, Wayne. 1985. *Religious Experience*. Berkeley: University of California Press.

Raposa, Michael. 2003. *Meditation and the Martial Arts*. Charlottesville: University of Virginia Press.

Rawlinson, Andrew. 1998. *Book of Enlightened Masters: Western Teachers in Eastern Traditions*. LaSalle: Open Court.

Robinet, Isabelle. 1993. *Taoist Meditation: The Mao-shan Tradition of Great Clarity*. Translated by Julian Pas and Norman Girardot. Albany: State University of New York Press.

Rogers, Carl. 1961. *On Becoming a Person: A Therapist's View of Psychotherapy*. New York: Houghton Mifflin.

Rosenberg, Larry. 2004. *Breath by Breath: The Liberating Practice of Insight Meditation*. Boston: Shambhala.

Roth, Harold D. 1991. "Psychology and Self-Cultivation in Early Taoistic Thought." *Harvard Journal of Asiatic Studies* 51.2: 599–650.

———. 1997. "Evidence for Stages of Meditation in Early Taoism." *Bulletin of the School of Oriental and African Studies* 60.2: 295–314.

———. 1999. *Original Tao: Inward Training (Nei-yeh) and the Foundations of Taoist Mysticism*. New York: Columbia University Press.

———. 2000. "Bimodal Mystical Experience in the 'Qiwulun' Chapter of the *Zhuangzi*." *Journal of Chinese Religions* 28: 31–50.

Schimmel, Annemarie. 1975. *Mystical Dimensions of Islam*. Chapel Hill: University of North Carolina Press.

Sells, Michael. 1995. *Early Islamic Mysticism: Sufi, Qur'an, Mi'raj, Poetic and Theological Writings*. Mahwah: Paulist Press.

Sharf, Robert. 1995. "Buddhist Modernism and the Rhetoric of Meditative Experience." *Numen* 42.3: 228–83.

———. 1998. "Experience." In *Critical Terms for Religious Studies*, edited by Mark C. Taylor, 94–116. Chicago: University of Chicago Press.

Shaw, Sarah. 2006. *Buddhist Meditation: An Anthology of Texts*. London and New York: Routledge.

———. 2009. *An Introduction to Buddhist Meditation*. London and New York: Routledge.

Skehan, James. 1991. *Place Me with Your Son: Ignatian Spirituality in Everyday Life*. 3rd ed. Washington: Georgetown University Press.

Smart, Ninian. 1965. "Interpretation and Mystical Experience." *Religious Studies* 1.1: 75–87.

Snellgrove, David. 1959. *The Hevajra Tantra: A Critical Study*. Oxford: Oxford University Press.

Stace, Walter. 1960. *Mysticism and Philosophy*. London: Macmillan.

Stock, Brian. 1998. *Augustine the Reader: Meditation, Self-Knowledge, and the Ethics of Interpretation*. Cambridge: Harvard University Press.

———. 2001. *After Augustine: The Meditative Reader and the Text*. Oxford and New York: Oxford University Press.

Tanahashi, Kazuaki. 1995. *Moon in a Dewdrop: Writings of Zen Master Dōgen*. San Francisco: North Point Press.

———. 2004. *Beyond Thinking: A Guide to Zen Meditation*. Boston: Shambhala.

Taves, Ann. 2009. *Religious Experience Reconsidered: A Building-Block Approach to the Study of Religion and Other Special Things*. Princeton: Princeton University Press.

Taylor, Rodney. 1978. *The Cultivation of Selfhood as a Religious Goal in Neo-Confucianism*. Missoula: Scholars Press.

———. 1988. *The Confucian Way of Contemplation: Okada Takehiko and the Tradition of Quiet-Sitting*. Columbia: University of South Carolina Press.

Twinch, Cecilia, and Pablo Beneito. 2008. *Contemplation of the Holy Mysteries*. Oxford: Anqa.

Valussi, Elena. 2002. "Beheading the Red Dragon: A History of Female Inner Alchemy in China." PhD diss., University of London.

Wayman, Alex. 1997. *Calming the Mind and Discerning the Real: Buddhist Meditation and the Middle View*. Delhi: Motilal Banarsidass.

Wayman, Alex, and Ryujun Tajima. 1992. *The Enlightenment of Vairocana*. Rev. ed. Delhi: Motilal Banarsidass.

Wayne, Alexander. 2007. *The Origin of Buddhist Meditation*. London and New York: Routledge.

White, David. 1998. *The Alchemical Body: Siddha Traditions in Medieval India*. Chicago: University of Chicago Press.

Wilber, Ken. 1977. *The Spectrum of Consciousness*. Wheaton: Quest Books.

———. 2000. *Integral Psychology: Consciousness, Spirit, Psychology, Therapy*. Boston: Shambhala.

Wilber, Ken, Terry Patten, Adam Leonard, and Marco Morelli. 2008. *Integral Life Practice: A 21st-Century Blueprint for Physical Health, Emotional Balance, Mental Clarity, and Spiritual Awakening*. Boston: Integral Books.

Williamson, Lola. 2010. *Transcendent in America: Hindu-Inspired Meditation Movements as New Religion*. New York: New York University Press.

Yamamoto, Yukitaka. 1999. *Kami no Michi: The Way of the Kami*. Stockton: Tsubaki America.

Part II

Contemplative Traditions

Chapter 3

Daoist Apophatic Meditation

Selections from the Classical Daoist Textual Corpus

Harold D. Roth

The selections in the present chapter derive from a variety of texts associated with classical Daoism, that is, the earliest communities of the Daoist religious tradition dating between the fourth and second centuries BCE (see Komjathy 2013b). Specifically, this chapter contains selections on classical Daoist apophatic meditation derived from the *Neiye* (Inward Training) and *Xinshu shang* (Techniques of the Mind I) works contained in the *Guanzi* (Book of Master Guan), *Laozi* (Book of Venerable Masters), *Zhuangzi* (Book of Master Zhuang), and *Huainanzi* (Book of the Huainan Masters). Written in classical Chinese and deriving from the mostly anonymous teachings of various elders of the inner cultivation lineages (see Roth 1999a, 1999b), these works primarily describe an emptiness-based form of meditation that leads to transformative experiences that have a foundational dimension of being contentless, nonconceptual, and nondualistic. The texts advocate a form of "inward training" or "inner cultivation" in which practitioners enter a state of stillness, a state that some identify as one's innate nature, as the Dao manifesting in one's being. The texts are, in turn, addressed to a variety of audiences: from members of the classical Daoist inner cultivation lineages to contemporaneous political leaders and projected Daoist sage-kings. The *Laozi* and *Zhuangzi*, in turn, became foundational scriptures of the Daoist tradition, wherein they are recognized as the *Daode jing* (Scripture on the Way and Inner Power) and *Nanhua zhenjing* (Perfect Scripture of Master Nanhua), respectively. Some of the sayings and all of the practices from the *Neiye* were influential on later Daoist texts and movements. In certain cases, classical Daoist contemplative perspectives also influenced some of the Chinese Buddhist schools, especially that of Chan (Jpn.: Zen).

Elders of the Inner Cultivation Lineages of Classical Daoism

With the selections of this chapter, we present a number of important surviving contemplative texts from classical Daoism. These texts contain the outlines of a consistent contemplative practice that spanned several centuries. As far as we can tell, this tradition was a loosely organized group of semi-independent teacher-student lineages, all of which involved a common practice of "inner cultivation" (Roth 1999a). This practice centered on sitting still and concentrating on the circulation of the vital energy (*qi* [*ch'i*]). Practicing this assiduously and over considerable lengths of time produced a gradual emptying out of the usual contents of consciousness—thoughts, feelings, perceptions—until a state of complete emptiness was attained. For this reason, we adapt the Christian mystical term "apophatic" (approaching the Absolute through "negative" means) as an appropriate descriptive adjective for these practices of emptying the mind.

There are four works from which we draw our relevant passages. The *Guanzi* (*Kuan-tzu*; Book of Master Guan)[1] is a large collection of seventy-six texts largely devoted to political and economic thought that was compiled over roughly two centuries starting around 330 BCE (see Rickett 1985, 1998). Attributed to the seventh-century prime minister of the state of Qi, Guan Zhong (ca. 720–645 BCE), it is really a collection of the various writings produced by scholars at the "Jixia (Chi-hsia) Academy" in that state (see Meyer 2010–2011). These individuals were a group of thinkers on the government payroll who were asked simply to debate one another and to offer the best advice to the kings of Qi on how to govern most effectively. The center at which they worked, the "Jixia Academy," was the first of several significant local court intellectual centers. It continued, with only a short decade-long interruption, until the state fell to Qin in 221 BCE, thus unifying the Chinese empire. This collection, entitled *Guanzi*, was likely compiled over a period of almost two centuries, as thinkers who considered themselves the intellectual heirs of Qi philosophers continued to add writings until about 130 BCE (Rickett 1985). While most of the collection is devoted to works on political and economic thought, the *Neiye* is one of four short texts devoted to the exploration of breathing meditation and the insights it produces, the four so-called Xinshu (Techniques of the Mind) texts.

The two works that we select from this collection are the *Neiye* (*Nei-yeh*; Inward Training; abbr. NY) and *Xinshu shang* (*Hsin-shu shang*; Techniques of the Mind I; abbr. XSS), which appear as chapter 49 and chapter 36, respectively, of the received *Guanzi*. These works deal first and foremost with the practice of apophatic meditation and the informing worldview, specifically the view that the universe is infused with the creative and unifying power of the Dao. Secondarily they present recommendations on how to apply these insights to governing. We have no reliable information about who wrote these texts.

The significance of the *Neiye* in the history of the Daoist tradition has only recently been recovered, as scholars have completely reexamined its relationship to the *Laozi*, previously held to be the oldest text of the tradition (Baxter 1998). It is a text made of twenty-six distinct units of rhymed verse, whose rhymes and style indicate that it is in the same category as the *Laozi*, forming the two most complete examples of what I have previously referred to as "early Daoist wisdom poetry" (Roth 1999a). Because it shows much less evidence of being reworked from earlier material, the *Neiye* is likely older then the *Laozi* and dates to around 350 BCE. It is thus the earliest work on breath meditation in China and hence all of East Asia (Roth 1999a).

The *Xinshu shang* (Techniques of the Mind I) is probably a mid-third-century BCE work that is part of the tradition of the *Neiye* in that it shares the same cosmology and contemplative practices. Written in a different era with the goal of offering concrete advice on how to govern, it commends the techniques of "inner cultivation" to the ruler as the essential foundation of skillful government.

The *Laozi* (*Lao-tzu*; abbr. LZ), which is conventionally translated as the "Book of Master Lao" but is better understood as the "Book of Venerable Masters" (Komjathy 2008, 2013b), has traditionally been attributed to Laozi (Master Lao), whose name also means "old master" and/or "old child." However, we now know that Laozi is a pseudo-historical figure, a composite character derived from a variety of sources. There is no historical or textual justification for the veracity of "the legend of Lao Dan (Lao Tan)," and it was probably adapted from an earlier story by the group who produced the text from earlier, perhaps oral, collections of rhymed verse around 275 BCE (Graham 1990b). It is shortly after that when we first read about the existence of this text and its teaching in contemporaneous works like the *Han Feizi* (Book of Master Han Fei) and *Xunzi* (Book of Master Xun). Producing this text from earlier materials and attributing it to a teacher superior to that of their main rivals in the Qin court and other local courts in the middle of the third century BCE was a stroke of polemical genius that left an indelible mark on Chinese civilization. Nonetheless, we cannot say reliably who might have written this work, although it was almost certainly the result of the activities of a group of people (LaFargue 1992, 1994). We may now recognize the received *Laozi* as a multivocal anthology consisting of an original weaving together of a variety of earlier oral and written sources that likely derived from different elders of the classical Daoist inner cultivation lineages (Komjathy 2008, 2013b). No matter how they were derived, the teachings contained in the *Laozi* on contemplative practice and its results give important testimony to the breadth of practices in the earliest Daoist communities. Moreover, as discussed later, there can be no doubt that the *Laozi*, under its later, honorific title of the *Daode jing* (*Tao-te ching*; Scripture on the Way and Inner Power), became the most influential text from classical Daoism, both within and beyond the tradition.

The primary extant or "received" edition of this text derives from the recension of Wang Bi (Wang Pi; 226–249), a member of the Xuanxue (Hsüan-hsüeh; Profound Learning) movement, around 240 CE. However, two editions of an earlier complete recension were found in a tomb sealed in 168 BCE at Mawangdui, a village near Changsha in Hunan Province (Henricks 1989). While the work was traditionally attributed to a shadowy sixth-century BCE figure known as Lao Dan, who legend says taught Kongzi (Master Kong; "Confucius") how to do ritual, this likely results from a clever adaptation of this story by Daoists around 250 BCE to demonstrate the superiority of this figure, whom they claimed as their founder (Graham 1990b). So the text did not take its present form of eighty-one short verses until this point in time. These verses, often rather hyperbolically called "chapters," are themselves the product of internal compilation, each one constituted of two or more distinct text blocks taken from earlier oral materials, such as the textual parallels found at Guodian in a tomb sealed circa 310 BCE (LaFargue 1992, 1994; Allan and Williams 2000; Roth 2000a; Henricks 2005). The only evident internal division within the eighty-one chapters is that in the received tradition chapters 1 through 37 are known as the *daojing* (Classic of the Way), while chapters 38 through 81 are called the *dejing* (Classic of Inner Power). These two sections are reversed in both editions of the recension found at Mawangdui, but it is not clear what the significance of this is. These manuscripts also contain many textual variants with the received versions, but few substantially alter the meaning of the text. Most are additional grammatical particles that help parse the unpunctuated text into sentences.

While the *Guanzi* texts on contemplation and the *Laozi* are almost exclusively constituted of rhymed verse, the *Zhuangzi* (*Chuang-tzu*; Book of Master Zhuang; abbr. ZZ) contains a majority of didactic narratives, as well as some prose essays and poetic writings. Compiled over perhaps a century and a half following the death of the evidently charismatic founding teacher of this particular lineage in about 290 BCE, this work contains a number of major strata. These include the teachings of the historical founder, Zhuang Zhou (Chuang Chou), later called "Zhuangzi" (Master Zhuang) (chapters 1–7), and the writings of several generations of his spiritual descendants, totaling in all thirty-three chapters in the received editions (Graham 1990c). Redacted by Guo Xiang (Kuo Hsiang; d. 312 CE), another member of the Xuanxue movement, the received *Zhuangzi* is a work in thirty-three chapters (originally fifty-two in number) that are often traditionally divided into the following three sections: (1) Inner Chapters (1–7), which are generally acknowledged to contain the teachings of the historical figure Zhuang Zhou, the founder of this particular lineage of classical Daoism; (2) Outer Chapters (8–22), which contain the collected writings of direct lineal descendants of Zhuang Zhou spanning the period from his death around 290 BCE to the completion of the *Lüshi chunqiu* (Spring and Autumn Annals of Master Lü) around 235 BCE; and (3) Miscellaneous Chapters (23–33), which contain some materials from the earlier strata combined with writings of the Syncretist thinkers who transmitted the text from the Qin court to the Han state of Huainan and completed the text there around 135 BCE (Graham 1990c; Roth 1991a).

Like the *Laozi*, the received *Zhuangzi* is therefore best understood as a multivocal anthology consisting of a several textual layers, layers that derive from the followers of the historical Zhuang Zhou as they interpreted his teachings in light of others from different elders of the classical Daoist inner cultivation lineages (Roth 2003, 181–219). Our selections come from the first seven chapters, generally accepted to be the writings of the historical Zhuang Zhou, and from chapter 15, "Geyi" (Ingrained Opinions), from the Syncretist authors who likely compiled the book at Huainan. This chapter may be the final one completed and shares striking resemblances to some of the chapters of the *Huainanzi*, a Han dynasty compendium. The contemplative practices evidenced in these early chapters resonate throughout the work and may be regarded as the central organizing principle around which the entire work formed. This can be seen in comparing them to the ideas in the selections from chapter 15 that we include here.

The classical Daoist period ends with the presentation of the completed *Huainanzi* (*Huai-nan-tzu*; Book of the Huainan Masters; abbr. HNZ) by its sponsor, Liu An (ca. 179–122 BCE), the second king of the major Han dynasty state of Huainan, to his nephew, the young Emperor Wu (r. 141–87 BCE) in 139 BCE, and with the fall of his government in 122 BCE. The title of the text refers to a particular geographical area, namely, the area south of the Huai River, which is located between the two dominant Chinese rivers, the Yellow River and Changjiang (Yangzi) River. The inheritors of this variety of inner cultivation texts and contemplative practices, the authors of the *Huainanzi*, present a grand synthesis of the best ideas of all early intellectual and religious traditions within the contemplative framework of inner cultivation: a cosmology of the Dao and practices of apophatic meditation (Roth 1992). Intended as a compendium of everything that the enlightened ruler needs to know in order to nurture the people and foster the creative processes of the cosmos, its twenty-one chapters detail the significance and methods of the inner cultivation of the ruler and the cosmological foundations that he needs in order to reinforce the natural homologous relations of macrocosm and microcosm between Heaven, Earth, and human beings. Doing this ensures that the universe will function harmoniously and human beings will flourish. Each chapter is addressed to a specific topic: cosmology, astronomy and astrology, geography, energetic resonance (theories of the activities of *qi*), inner cultivation, history, principles of rulership, military theory, and so forth (see Major et al. 2010). Our selections are principally drawn from the most important "root chapters" of the work, which provide its cosmological foundation and detail its contemplative practices.

It may legitimately be asked, "What could tie together such a varied group of texts written over a timespan of two centuries?" Each of these texts exhibit a characteristic set of conceptual categories that prove their origins within a distinctive teaching tradition. These categories and the technical terms within them provide a kind of "intellectual fingerprint" that shows these works to be the closely related products of a number of early Daoist contemplative lineages of teachers and students.

The first category is that of cosmology. These texts share a common understanding of the Dao, or Way, as the foundational unifying power or force in the cosmos. It interfuses each phenomenon as the essential invisible thread that enables each to develop spontaneously along its distinctive path of growth and to respond to its environment. It also transcends all phenomena as their ultimate source. The immanence of the Way leads to the second distinctive category, that of inner cultivation. These texts all demonstrate a belief that the Way can be directly experienced—"merged with"—through a series of apophatic practices that involve concentrating the mind on the circulation of the vital energy (*qi*) (Roth 1991b). These practices lead the adept to gradually empty out the normal contents of her consciousness until she directly merges with the Way and becomes a "True Person" (*zhenren*), a "Realized Person" (*zhiren*), and—particularly when this high degree of cultivation is applied to government—a sage (*shengren*), a sage-king (*shengwang*), or a moral paragon (*junzi*) (Littlejohn 2009, 26–51).[2] The direct apprehension of the Way, however, while quite an attainment, is never enough: one must apply the transformed consciousness that this introvertive experience yields to life in the external world, attaining what the *Zhuangzi* calls "flowing cognition" (*yinshi*) (Roth 2010). The specific details of the classical Daoist religious and soteriological system, in the sense of attunement with the Way, are discussed later in this chapter.

Classical Daoism and the "Family of the Way" (*Daojia*)

Until relatively recently the works detailed earlier were not seen to be related to one another in a significant fashion. The *Laozi* and the first seven "Inner Chapters" of the *Zhuangzi* were believed to be the sole foundational works of the entire Daoist tradition. The later organized Daoist religion, which really begins in the closing decades of the second century CE and which holds a much greater variety of teachings, some of which seem to directly contradict these two works, almost inexplicably for many scholars, still continued to assert the *Laozi* and *Zhuangzi* as its origins. Generations of literati scholars made a hard-and-fast distinction between these imagined original "philosophical" texts and the largely superstitious peasant-based "religious" Daoism of the later formal institutions. However, as this chapter and the primary texts demonstrate, there can be little debate that classical Daoism was a "religious community" that advocated and employed a specific religious and soteriological approach to human existence. Lineages of master-disciples were also involved. Thus, one of the main distinctions between classical Daoism and early organized Daoism was the emergence of a higher degree of social organization and an enduring institution (see Komjathy 2013b). We may, in turn, recognize the "inner cultivation lineages" of classical Daoism as the beginning of the Daoist tradition as such, an indigenous Chinese religious tradition characterized by complexity and diversity.

Scholarship that began with the 1973 discovery of an alternate recension of the *Laozi* at Mawangdui has exploded the so-called "philosophical Daoism–religious Daoism" distinction as a literati myth that was likely established after the rise of the institutionalized Daoist religion had incorporated these two works as their foundations. In analyzing these works and trying to place them within a larger tradition, many questions were raised about the nature of this tradition and what constituted its distinctive characteristics and whether or not it even existed. In the end, scholars came to appreciate that there were many more texts that contained distinctively Daoist ideas than just the *Laozi* and *Zhuangzi* and in analyzing them came to appreciate just what these distinctive characteristics were. As we have seen in the previous section, these texts contain distinctive categories of ideas and practices under the general headings of "cosmology," "inner cultivation," and "political thought" (see also later discussion).

These common categories of ideas and practices attest to the existence of at least a minimal social organization of teachers and students who trained in these practices and shared the cosmological and psychological ideas that emerged from them. They certainly elaborated their ideas, as most individual practitioners within traditions innovate within their own sets of life experiences, and so there is not absolute consistency within these texts across the two centuries of their development. However, indeed, the authors of the later texts of this classical Daoist tradition—chapters 8 through 33 of the received *Zhuangzi* and the *Huainanzi*—show clear evidence of not only being cognizant of the ideas and practices in the earlier texts but also of having actual copies of the texts themselves. Some of them also may have been actual lineal descendants of earlier teachers, not just on the level of intellectual genealogies but also on the level of direct contemplative technical training within particular lineages. Given the relative scarcity of copies of texts and the challenges of actually making them (Tsien 1962; also Komjathy 2013b), the fact of their references to one another attests to the existence of a lineage-based social organization that transmitted them, despite the contentions of some recent historians that the entire notion of "Daoism" before the end of the second century CE is a retrospective classification without basis in fact (Queen 2001; Csikszentmihalyi and Nylan 2003). While it is true that in the second century BCE "Grand Historian" Sima Tan (ca. 165 BCE–110 BCE) coined the actual term *daojia* (lit., Family of the Way; rendered in English as Daoism), there is ample evidence that his clear identification of the characteristics of this tradition was based on his direct knowledge of this as a living tradition (Roth 1991b, 1999a).

These inner cultivation lineages of classical Daoism, in turn, shared a particular conception of the sacred, namely, the Dao (Tao; Way). From a classical and foundational Daoist perspective, the Dao has four primary defining characteristics as: (1) the Source of everything; (2) an unnamable mystery; (3) an all-pervading sacred presence (*qi*); and (4) the universe as transformative process (Nature) (Komjathy 2013b). That is, Daoists understand the cosmos, world, and self as differentiated expressions of the Way. According to our texts, there are various methods of inner cultivation, also referred to as "inward training" and "techniques of the mind," that enable one to attune oneself with the Way. This is also referred to as "returning to the Source" (*guigen*) and cognate terms. One specific practice, discussed in more detail later in this chapter, involves apophatic meditation. By entering a state of emptiness and stillness, one may rediscover one's innate connection to the Way. Here it is important to recognize that one's inner stillness is a manifestation of the Way *as* Stillness (see LaFargue 1992). For present purposes, it is also important to remember that, from my perspective, classical Daoism consisted of various "inner cultivation lineages," or master-disciple communities. Training and supervision under teachers and elders within a communal context would have been a defining characteristic. At the same time, it appears that the practice was primarily individualistic, as our texts advocate the central importance of self-cultivation and realization.

Ways to the Way: Classical Daoist Apophatic Meditation and Its Results

The foundational ideas of classical Daoist meditation begin and end with the concept of the Dao (Tao; Way) as the ultimate source of the cosmos; inner power (*de*) as its manifestation in terms of concrete phenomena and experience; the heart-mind (*xin*) as the psychosomatic (emotional, intellectual, and spiritual) center of human personhood; nonaction (*wuwei*) as its definitive movement; and formlessness (*wuxing*) as its characteristic mode. There is also a common self-cultivation vocabulary that includes stillness and silence (*jimo*), tranquility (*jing*), emptiness (*xu*), and a variety of apophatic, self-negating techniques and qualities of mind that lead to a direct apprehension of the Way.

In terms of personhood and informing psychology, and drawing upon the so-called Xinshu (Techniques of the Mind) chapters, we must recognize that classical Daoist inner cultivation and apophatic meditation centers on the "heart-mind" (*xin*), usually translated as "mind" herein. The ancient seal script version of the character is revealing, as it depicts the actual heart, which is also referred to as "the center" (*zhong*). From a classical and foundational Daoist perspective, *xin* is understood both as a physical location in the chest (the heart as "organ" [*zang*]) and as relating to thoughts (*nian*) and emotions (*qing*) (the heart as "consciousness" [*shi*]). As verse XIV of the *Neiye* informs us, "Within the heart-mind, there is yet another heart-mind. That inner heart-mind is an awareness that precedes language." This could be interpreted in various ways, including that the physical heart contains the mind and/or that the ordinary or conditioned mind contains the numinous or realized mind. In any case, the mind is the emotional and intellectual center of the human person. It is associated with consciousness and often identified as the storehouse of spirit (*shen*). In its original or realized condition, the mind has the ability to attain numinous pervasion; in its disoriented or habituated condition, especially in a state of hyper-emotionality or intellectualism, the mind has the ability to separate the adept from the Dao as Source. Often associated with "innate nature" (*xing*), the original condition of the mind is characterized by stillness, and this inner stillness is a manifestation of the Dao as Stillness (see LaFargue 1992).

Classical Daoist meditation featured practices that involved sitting still and gradually emptying out the usual contents of the mind until no specific thoughts, feelings, or perceptions remained. In the state of nondual consciousness attained through the apophatic emptying of the mind, the adept was completely open to the awareness of a solitary unifying force that was apprehended as the basis of this consciousness: this is what is famously identified as the Dao or Way. Because constant change is an inherent part of the Chinese universe for the Daoists as well as for other early cultural traditions, this direct nondual awareness of the Dao in the depths of sitting meditation was transient. When the adept emerged from this state and returned to the dualistic world, she was able to apprehend that world in a thoroughly transformed fashion. No longer attached to the limited perspective that derived exclusively from her own individual self, she maintains an awareness of this Dao as the very foundation of her consciousness and of the world

96 / Harold D. Roth

with which she interacted. As all things change and flow, so too does her awareness constantly flow; learning how to master these constantly changing situations while remaining grounded in an awareness of the Dao was the challenge and the goal of classical Daoist practice. "It is rather easy to stop walking," writes Daoist mystic Zhuangzi, commenting on the relative ease of calming the mind through breathing meditation, "but much more difficult to walk without touching the ground." He elsewhere refers to this as "free and easy wandering" (*xiaoyao you*). Thus the classical Daoist adept practiced apophatic meditation not only for its own sake but for the practical transformative benefits it brought to her in everyday life. These goals were self-reinforcing and directly experiential; they were not thought of as conducive to some future distant soteriological goal of liberation or of going to a better place after death.

In terms of classical Daoist "inner cultivation," simply put, the basic practice is to unify or focus attention on one thing, often the inhalation and exhalation of the breath for a sustained period of time. Through this, one comes to gradually empty out the thoughts, perceptions, and

Figure 3.1. Western Han (202 BCE–9 CE) Statue of *Se*-zither Player
Chu Tomb at Tuolanshan (dat. 2nd c. BCE; disc. 1989)
Xuzhou Museum, Jiangsu
Source: Fitzwilliam Museum (Cambridge, United Kingdom)

emotions that normally occupy the mind and to develop an awareness of the presence of the Way that resides at the ground of human consciousness. We can analyze these apophatic or "self-negating" practices into a number of basic categories.

To begin, inner cultivation involves proper posture: An aligned and stable sitting position for body and limbs is frequently recommended. Although the classical Daoist works are somewhat vague on the exact posture, roughly contemporaneous archaeological materials suggest that the posture involved sitting on one's heels in a manner paralleling the more familiar Japanese *seiza* position (see, e.g., Harper 1995). The hands probably rested on the lap. This posture fosters the gradual empting out of the various types of conscious data, thoughts, emotions, and perceptions that are primary concern of apophatic meditation. This is aptly symbolized by the phrase from the famous narrative in *Zhuangzi* about "sitting and forgetting" (*zuowang*).[3] Along these lines, the *Neiye*, the oldest extant source on these practices, recommends the following advice on posture:[4]

1. Align the physical form (*zhengxing*) (XI)

2. Align the four limbs (*zheng siti*) (VIII, XIV, XIX)

3. Keep the body calm and unmoving (*xing'an buyi*) (XXIV)

Once in this posture, cultivating the breath or vital energy (*qi*) is a foundational practice in all of the major sources of inner cultivation. It is often spoken of as concentrating or refining the *qi* (*zhuanqi*), as in the *locus classicus* from *Laozi* 10. Focusing on one's breathing is, in essence, a concentration of the attention. The *Neiye* gives a number of recommendations for this mode of concentration:

1. Breathe following inherent patterns (*qili*) (V)

2. Guide the breathing (*qidao*) (VIII)

3. Relax and expand breathing (*kaiqi er guang*) (XXIV)

4. Concentrated breathing (*zhuanqi*)[5] (XIX)

5. Coiling/contracting–uncoiling/expanding of the abdominal breathing muscles (XVII)

6. Revolving the breath (another form of 5) (XXIV)

In the *Neiye*, as in all classical Daoist texts, *qi* is both the actual breath that we inhale and exhale and also the actual quasi-material stuff out of which all things are constituted. Some prefer to translate it as "vital breath" or "vital energy." It is essential to all things, both living and inert; and it exists on a continuum of density from the compact and heavy to the ethereal and light. All aspects of the human psyche have a typical *qi* associated with them; it forms a kind of physiological substrate to all psychological states, a strikingly parallel concept to modern neuroscience. The most rarified states of contemplation—tranquility and emptiness—have the most quintessential *and* ethereal *qi*.

The *Neiye* also discusses further ways to refine one's attention to the breath:

1. Unify your awareness, concentrate your mind (*yiyi zhuanxin*) (XIX)

2. Be concentrated and unified (*neng zhuan hu, neng yi hu*) (XIX)

3. Focus on the One/one thing and discard the myriad disturbances (*shouyi er qi wanke*) (XXIV)

This phrase, *shouyi* (to focus on the One/one thing), in the *Neiye* is the oldest extant enunciation of a technique that was to prove important throughout the classical and later Daoist—and even Chan Buddhist—traditions.⁶ In the *Neiye* it refers to focusing the attention on one thing and not letting it be disturbed by various mental distractions. This one thing could be the Way, often referred to in classical Daoist literature by this epithet of "the One." These techniques of keeping the body still, focusing the attention on various aspects of the breathing, and gradually eliminating distractions caused by a variety of psychological events are known elsewhere in classical Daoist literature. In the *Laozi* we find the repeating trope: "VERB (hold fast to/embrace/guard): OBJECT (the One/the center/the central practice/the Way/the Mother)" as in chapters 5, 10, 14, 15, 22, 32, 37, and 52. The associated Chinese technical terms include *baoyi* (embracing the One), *shoudao* (guarding the Way), *shoumu* (guarding the Mother), *shouyi* (holding fast to the One), *shouzhong* (guarding the Center), *zhiyi* (grasping the One), and so forth. A good example is the following line from chapter 22: "Therefore sages embrace the One and are models for the empire."

In addition to proper posture and concentration of breath and attention, these inner cultivation texts also present a wide variety of techniques that have the effect of emptying out the normal contents of consciousness and hence approaching the Dao by apophatic means. Principal among these is the very frequent admonition in the *Neiye* to restrict or eliminate desires (*jingyu*; *jieyü*) (e.g., XXV, XXVI), which occurs in similar form in the *Laozi* as "to minimize or be without desires" (*guayu*; *wuyu*) (chs. 1, 19, 37, 57). The *Zhuangzi, Guanzi* (e.g., *Xinshu shang*), and *Lüshi chunqiu* also contain similar and identical phrases.⁷ Other related apophatic techniques include restricting or eliminating emotions, a staple of the *Neiye* (III, VII, XX, XXI). A representative example is verse XXV: "When you are anxious or sad, pleased or angry, the Way has no place to settle within you." Restricting or eliminating thought and knowledge is also commended in the inner cultivation texts; so too is restricting or in some cases completely eliminating sense perception.

Taken together these passages recommend an apophatic regimen that develops concentration by focusing on the breathing and stripping away the common cognitive activities of daily life, something that must, of practical necessity, be done when not engaged in these activities, hence while sitting unmoved in one position. There are a wide variety of metaphorical descriptions of these apophatic regimens. These include the idea that following the Way involves "daily relinquishing" (*risun*) in chapter 48 of the *Laozi*, "fasting of the mind" (*xinzhai*) in chapter 4 of the *Zhuangzi*, and "sitting and forgetting" (*zuowang*) in chapter 6 of the *Zhuangzi*. Both *Zhuangzi* 23 and *Lüshi chunqiu* 25.3 talk of "casting off the fetters of the mind" (*jie xin miu*). Another common phrase with a few close variations is "to discard/reject/relinquish wisdom/knowledge/cleverness and precedent/scheming" (*qu/qu/qi/shi zhi/zhi/qiao gu/gu/mou*).⁸ Finally, who can forget such beautifully evocative parallel metaphors for these apophatic mental processes as "diligently cleaning out the abode of the vital essence" (*jingqu jingshe*) and "sweeping clean the abode of the spirit" (*saoqu shenshe*) in *Xinshu shang* and "washing clean the profound mirror" (*diqu xuanjian*) from *Laozi* 10. The latter metaphor is echoed in *Zhuangzi* 5: "None of us finds our mirror in flowing water, we find it in still water. . . . If your mirror is clear, dust will not settle. If dust settles, then your mirror is not clear."[9]

In terms of resultant states, there are temporary experiences of a transformative nature. The direct results of engaging in these apophatic psychological practices are remarkably similar across many early texts of the inner cultivation tradition, thus indicating a consistency of actual methods and some sharing of ideas and texts. It is useful to borrow an important contrast from cognitive psychologists and talk about these results in terms of "states," which pertain to the inner experience of individual practitioners and tend to be transient, and of "traits," which pertain to more stable character qualities developed in interactions in the phenomenal world (see, e.g., Cahn and Polich 2006).

Probably the two most common resultant states of classical Daoist inner cultivation practices are "tranquility" (*jing*)—the mental and physical experience of complete calm and stillness—and "emptiness" (*xu*)—the mental condition of having no thoughts, feelings, and perceptions yet still being intensely aware. States of tranquility and emptiness are both closely associated with a direct experience of the Way, perhaps the penultimate result of apophatic inner cultivation practices. There are a number of striking metaphors for this experience of unification of individual consciousness with the Way; three use the concept of "merging" to express it. Chapter 56 of the *Laozi* contains advice on apophatic practice (e.g., "Block the openings and shut the doors [of the senses]") and identifies the ultimate result as "profound merging" (*xuantong*). *Zhuangzi* 6 parallels *Laozi* 56: therein Yanhui teaches Kongzi ("Confucius") about the apophatic practice of "sitting and forgetting," the penultimate result of which is "merging with Great Pervasion" (*tong yu datong*).[10] Chapter 2 of *Zhuangzi* also engages this metaphor for the Way, stating that the "Way pervades and unifies" (*Dao tong wei yi*) phenomena as different from one another as a stalk from a pillar, a leper from the beauty Xishi.[11] It also is important to note that these profound states of experience of the Way are quite often linked with preserving the spirit internally or becoming spirit-like (*shen/rushen*).[12] They are further associated with a highly refined and concentrated form of vital energy called the "vital essence" (*jing*) in verses V, VIII, and XIX of the *Neiye* and in various other classical Daoist sources (see Roth 1991b).[13] As *Neiye* VIII explains, "The vital essence: it is the essence of the vital energy."

Other resulting traits include ongoing cognitive alterations. As the direct result of the experience of these various dimensions of union with the Way—which, if we understand them correctly, are internal experiences attained in isolation from all interactions with the phenomenal world—adepts develop a series of what are best thought of as traits, more or less continuing alterations in one's cognitive and performative abilities that were highly prized by rulers and literati subjects alike for obvious reasons.

Perhaps the most famous of these is the idea that one can take no deliberate and willful action from the standpoint of one's separate and individual self, and yet nothing is left undone (*wuwei er wu buwei*). This works because adepts have so completely embodied the Way that their actions are perfectly harmonious expressions of the Way itself in any given situation. While this is one of the most famous phrases in the *Laozi*, it appears in other early sources of inner cultivation, including the Outer and Miscellaneous Chapters of the *Zhuangzi* and three inner cultivation essays in *Lüshi chunqiu*.[14]

These traits of immediate and uncontrived responsiveness describe well one of the ideas for which the *Laozi* is famous, namely, spontaneity (*ziran*), which has also been translated as "naturalness" and "suchness." A quality of the Way, the phenomenal world, and the cultivated sage in chapters 17, 23, 25, and 51, it refers to their natural, instantaneous, and nonreflective responses. In a fundamental fashion, this almost magical ability to spontaneously accomplish all without seeming to exert any deliberate action is frequently associated with a great deal of inner power (*de*), an idea often associated with charisma. Inner power, or potency, is a kind of aura of spontaneous efficacy that develops in a person and is visible for all to see through repeated experiences of tranquility, emptiness, and merging with the Way. We find it in all of the early sources of inner cultivation theory, often in conjunction with apophatic techniques.

Additional cognitive improvements are also found in classical Daoist inner cultivation sources. These include perceptual acuity and cognitive accuracy, mental stability, impartiality, and the ability to "roll with the punches" that is so valued in the *Zhuangzi*'s notion of *yinshi*. A. C. Graham translates this in a very literal fashion: "the that's it which goes by circumstance." The concept is really that of "flowing cognition," totally changing and transforming to the situation, and it is exemplified in many of the narratives of the *Zhuangzi*: the "free and easy wandering" of chapter 1, the monkey keeper handing out nuts in chapter 2, Cook Ding in chapter 3, Cripple Shu in chapter 4, Wang Tai in chapter 5, Master Lai in chapter 6, and Huzi (Gourd Master) in chapter 7, among others. All of them respond without egotism, without selfishness, without insisting on any one fixed point of view: that is how they survive and flourish. This kind of indifference to fortune or misfortune and creative spontaneous responsiveness to all situations is characteristic of people "in whom inner power is at its utmost."[15]

So the basic contours of inner cultivation are as follows: Apophatic practices of sitting still and concentrating on one's breathing lead to gradual reductions in desires, emotions, thoughts, and perceptions. States of experience result from these reductions that make one feel tranquil, calm, still, and serene. These are states in which one's consciousness is empty of its usual contents and in which one feels unified with the Way. These states lead to a series of beneficial cognitive changes and the development of new traits such as acute perception, accurate cognition, selflessness and impartiality, the ability to spontaneously be in harmony with one's surroundings no matter what the situation, and the ability to be flexible and adjust to whatever changes may come one's way. Figure 3.2 provides a summary of these practices and results.

Despite the lack of precise identities among the specific terms assembled and discussed here, there is a remarkable consistency in their basic interrelationships and relatively focused range of meanings.[16] This, I would argue, indicates the presence of a distinctive cultural tradition that transmitted both ideas *and* practices. However, it is a tradition that was dynamic in its ability to change as the historical circumstances demanded. Thus, several later inner cultivation works were composed that centered on the political application of these apophatic techniques.

One of the primary areas of change in the classical Daoist inner cultivation tradition is the application of its practices to the fundamental concern of the late Warring States Chinese thinkers, namely, rulership. The *Laozi* (e.g., chs. 37 and 46) begins to address how some of the traits derived from inner cultivation practices are beneficial for rulership. For one, they give sage-rulers a distinct lack of attachment to themselves and their own desires, which leads to making better decisions in governing (e.g., chs. 22 and 49). Later texts such as the *Xinshu xia* (Techniques of the Mind II) and chapters 13 and 33 of the *Zhuangzi* demonstrate thinking aimed at applying the techniques, states, and traits of inner cultivation to governing. They developed catchphrases for these applications. For example, the "Way of Tranquility and Adaptation" (*jingyin zhi dao*)

CULTIVATION PRACTICES	
Posture	**Apophatic Techniques**
Aligning the body 正形/正四體 Keeping the body still 形安而不移	Restricting desires 寡欲/節欲/無欲 Restricting thoughts 出聰明/屈知/棄知/去知
Breathing	**Apophatic Techniques**
Concentrate 專氣 Order 氣理 Guide 氣導	Restricting Perceptions 塞其兌閉其門/遺其耳目/墮支體離形/出聰明
Attention	**Apophatic Metaphors**
Focus on one 守一 Focus on center 守中	Mind fasting 心齋 Sitting and forgetting 坐忘 Casting off mental fetters 解心繆 Sweeping clean numinous lodge 掃除神舍 Cleaning off the profound mirror 滌去玄鑑 The Way of Tranquility and Adaptation 靜因之道
RESULTANT STATES	
Tranquility 靜 Emptiness 虛 Calmness 安 Equanimity 齊 Repose 寧 Stillness 寂 Silence 漠 Serenity 恬	Detachment 淡 Refined/concentrated 精 Spirit-like 神 Hold fast to the One 執一 Attain Empty Way 得虛道 Halting the Way 止道 Guarding/Returning to the Ancestor 守/反宗
RESULTANT TRAITS	
Nonaction 無為 All done 無不 potency 德 Resonance 感應 Spontaneity 自然 Perceptual acuity 鑑於大清 Instant and accurate knowledge 見知不惑	Suppleness 弱 Pliancy 柔 Psychological order 定心/治心 Selflessness 無私 Impartiality 公 Simplicity 素 Wholeness 樸 Psychological Skill 心術 Flowing cognition 因是

Figure 3.2. Summary of Inner Cultivation

appears in the former, while "tranquil and sagely, active and kingly" (*jing er sheng, dong er wang*) and "internally a sage, externally a king" (*neisheng waiwang*) appear in the latter.[17] This trend continued into the *Huainanzi*, which embellished this unlikely mix of apophatic inner cultivation practices and results and political thought into a sophisticated new synthesis.

Inner Cultivation according to the Textual Corpus of Classical Daoism

As mentioned, the selections in the present chapter derive from the *Neiye*, *Xinshu shang*, *Laozi*, *Zhuangzi*, and *Huainanzi*. In this section I summarize their distinctive ideas about contemplative practice and its results. The *Neiye* (Inward Training; abbr. NY) appears as chapter 49 of seventy-six texts in the received *Guanzi*, a massive collection of works devoted mostly to political and economic thought that were written in the intellectual center that was established in the state of Qi around the year 330 BCE. Estimates date the *Neiye* to the very oldest stratum of the *Guanzi* and so in the latter half of the fourth century BCE. The text is written in a distinctive literary style: four- or five-syllable (and character) rhymed verse, a style shared with about 70 percent of the received *Laozi*. However, unlike the *Laozi*, the verses of the *Neiye* do not show any evidence of editorial work or the building up of verses into new and distinct semantic units (LaFargue 1992; Baxter 1998). This has led some scholars to theorize that the *Laozi* represents a collection of orally transmitted verses that could have developed during the prior century or more, what I have previously referred to as "early Daoist wisdom poetry" (Roth 1999a). Likely prior to both the *Laozi* and the oldest stratum of *Zhuangzi*, the *Neiye* contains the oldest extant Chinese and hence East Asian discussion of breath meditation and the insights into the universe that it confers.

So what does the *Neiye* say about these subjects? The work commends a range of breath meditation practices, such as "circulating the vital energy (*qi*)" and "expanding and contracting, coiling and uncoiling," which I interpret to mean focusing the attention on the process of breathing as it is felt in the abdomen. The work also advocates "relaxing and expanding the mind" and "concentrating the breathing." From my perspective, these all refer to different methods to pay attention to one's breathing as a technique to be done while keeping the body in a stable

Neiye I, II, IV, VIII, XI, XIII, XV, XVI, XVII, XIX	*Laozi* 1, 10, 15, 16, 22, 25, 42, 48, 56
Xinshu shang I, III	*Zhuangzi* 2, 4, 3, 6
Huainanzi 1.1, 1.8, 1.9, 1.14, 2.13, 7.4, 7.7, 11.6, 14.22	

Figure 3.3. Selections from the Classical Daoist Textual Corpus

and aligned seated posture. Such practices invariably return a series of important results. First and foremost is the yielding of profound experiences of tranquility and concomitant mental stability (NY VIII). According to the authors of this text, with one's attention unwavering, perceptions acute, and body stable, one will create a "lodging place for the vital essence." Herein and elsewhere in this classical Daoist contemplative corpus, vital essence (*jing*) is defined as a highly refined form of vital energy or vital breath (*qi*). It would not be wrong to conceive of it as a kind of physiological substrate associated with profound states of stillness, emptiness, and tranquility within the system of what one classical Chinese medical scholar calls the "Phase Energetic" system (Porkert 1973). In this comprehensive system, later developed further in Chinese medical texts like the *Huangdi neijing suwen* (Yellow Emperor's Inner Classic: Basic Questions; see Unschuld and Tessenow 2011) and the philosophical compendium *Huainanzi*, all phenomena are constituted of five categories and two modes of *qi*. The five are Wood, Fire, Earth, Metal, and Water; the two are yin and yang. The Five Phases are types of *qi* and have distinctive characteristics: Fire *qi* is hot, rises, burns; Earth qi is solid, stable, firm; Water qi soaks, flows, softens; and so on. The yin modality is dark, obscure, feminine, and receptive; the yang modality is bright, clear, masculine, and assertive. The vital essence is highly refined *qi*, refined through the process of systematic breath cultivation, that is, paying attention to the breathing while sitting in a stable posture and not moving. According to verse VIII of the *Neiye*,

> You can thereby make a lodging place for the vital essence.
> The vital essence: it is the essence of the vital energy.
> When the vital energy is guided, the vital essence is generated . . .

Vital essence not only occurs in the tranquil consciousness of the adept; it is an important quality with the cosmos writ large (NY I and II). Another key linkage here is the association of vital essence with the development of inner power (*de*). In the classical Daoist corpus this is often paired with the Way as its concrete manifestation within phenomena. This manifestation of the Way within human beings is metaphorically spoken of as the "halting of the Way" that comes and goes from one's awareness. What we also find here is, unlike in the *Laozi* or *Zhuangzi*, the Way seems to have similar concrete characteristics to those of the vital essence as a cosmic force:

> The Way has no fixed position;
> It abides within the excellent mind.
> When the mind is tranquil and the vital energy is regular,
> The Way can thereby be halted.
> That Way is not distant from us;
> When people attain it they are sustained.
> That Way is not separated from us;
> When people accord with it, they are harmonious.
> Therefore: Concentrated! as if you could be roped together with it.
> Indiscernible! as if beyond all locations.
> The true state of that Way:
> How could it be conceived of and pronounced upon?

> Cultivate your mind, make your thoughts tranquil,
> And the Way can thereby be grasped.
> (NY V)

So while the Way cannot be conceived of through dualistic thought, its apparent movement into and out of the awareness of the adept can be "halted" through the techniques of breath cultivation and mental tranquility. Elsewhere in the *Neiye* this is referred to using another significant term, namely, "spirit" (*shen*) (NY XIII). Spirit in the *Neiye* refers to a foundational layer of the mind that is conscious of both the world of phenomena and the Way experienced within the adept. Like the Way, it comes and goes, is beyond conception, and is the source of psychic order. Beyond dualistic thought and conscious control, it is inherent and has a physiological substrate: vital essence. Later in the *Huainanzi*, these two terms become combined to help distinguish vital essence in general from the specific vital essence associated with spirit, the fount of awareness of the Way. This combined term is "quintessential spirit" (*jingshen*).

Our selections from the *Xinshu shang* (Techniques of the Mind I; abbr. XSS), which is chapter 36 of the received *Guanzi*, introduce a key concept in the classical Daoist world, that of *li*, the inherent underlying patterns of the cosmos. Originally derived from the naturally occurring fracture lines within an uncarved block of jade, *li* can be thought of as the natural guidelines according to which things develop, operate, and transform. For example, the sun has a pattern through which it moves in the sky and returns every day. The stars have patterns of movement around the North Star. The seasons revolve through a set pattern during the year. The important thing about patterns is that they are discoverable, reliable, and predictable. They contribute to the early Chinese concept of a universe of order, structure, and harmony (see Needham 1956; Schwartz 1985; Graham 1989) and play a role similar to that of natural laws in Western cosmology.

In the *Xinshu shang*, the various perceptual organs comply with their inherent patterns only when we empty the mind of lusts and desires that interfere with their activity. This allows them to function spontaneously and harmoniously. In verse I, we read the following:

> When the mind keeps to its Way,
> The nine apertures will comply with their inherent patterns.[18]
> When lusts and desires fill the mind to overflowing,
> The eyes do not see colors, the ears do not hear sounds.
> When the one above departs from the Way,
> The ones below will lose sight of their tasks.
> Therefore we say, "The Techniques of the Mind are to take no action and yet control
>   the apertures."

Like its older companion, the *Neiye*, this text speaks of the cultivation of spirit within through an apophatic practice of concentrating on the breathing, emptying the mind, and becoming tranquil (XSS III).

The *Laozi* (Book of Venerable Masters; abbr. LZ) contains eighty-one "chapters," which are, in reality, verses that seem to have been woven together by the compilers from earlier circulating collections of rhymed verse. Distinct sections were linked together by connective phrases like "thus" and "therefore it is said" to sometimes create new meanings (LaFargue 1992). Repeatedly describing a cosmos of harmony infused by the ineffable Way, in a parallel fashion to the authors of the *Neiye*, the *Laozi* advocates its own process of apophasis in various passages (LZ 48 and 56). In these passages, apophasis inevitably leads to a return to the world and living within it without action. That is, one acts from the Way and not from the standpoint of a fixed and limited sense of self and self-interest. This fits well with the balance between sitting in meditation and then returning to act in the world of things that we see throughout the text.

Another important contrast with the *Neiye* is that the Way as a concept acting in the world does not have any parallels in the Phase Energetic system, no concept of it being a substance similar to or manifested through vital essence or realized through spirit. These latter concepts prove to be key ideas in the contemplative practices that developed in the later institutionalized Daoist religion; their absence in the *Laozi* has contributed to the misapprehension of a great gap between its cosmology and inner cultivation practices and those of later Daoism.

The contemplative exemplars in the *Laozi* are more strongly emphasized than in the *Neiye*. A representative example, which discusses the qualities of those who have cultivated the Way, is the following:

> Of old those who manifested the Way
> Were minutely subtle and profoundly pervasive,
> They were too deep to be known.
> Because they could not be known,
> We can only give a makeshift description:
> Tentative, as if fording a river in winter,
> Cautious, as if in fear of neighbors;
> Solemn, like guests;
> Melting, like thawing ice;
> Undifferentiated, like the Uncarved Block;
> Vast, like a valley;
> Murky, like muddy water.
>
> When muddy water is made tranquil, it gradually becomes clear.
> When the calm is made active, it gradually springs to life.
> Those who embrace this Way
> Do not wish to become full.
> It is only because they do not wish to become full
> That they can wear out and yet be newly made.
> (LZ 15)

Finally, there are many contemplative metaphors in the text: the "Uncarved Block" (*pu*) refers to the pure undifferentiated potentiality of the One Way but also to the total innocence of the adept and the people in their natural state. The empty vessel refers to the empty consciousness of the adept. The "Mysterious Female" (*xuanpin*) refers to the receptive and yielding qualities of the Way and the sage who realizes it. The space between Heaven and Earth being like a bellows is a metaphor for paying constant attention to the bellows-like inhalation and exhalation of the breath cycle. The "Spirit of the Valley" (*gushen*) symbolizes the empty mind. "Profound merging" (*xuantong*) is a merging with the Way. "Washing clean your mysterious mirror" reminds us of the *Neiye*'s "cleaning out the lodging place of the spirit" and *Xinshu shang*'s "sweeping clean the dwelling of the honored spirit." Both are metaphors for apophatic practice.

One final item to note about the *Laozi* is that, unlike the *Neiye*, it provides advice to the ruler on how to govern effectively by practicing the apophatic techniques commended in the text.

As discussed in the first section in this chapter, the received text of the *Zhuangzi* (Book of Master Zhuang; abbr. ZZ) contains thirty-three chapters, the first seven of which are usually thought to contain the ideas of the charismatic founder of this particular lineage of classical Daoist teaching, the person named Zhuang Zhou (ca. 290 BCE). These Inner Chapters are written in a unique style with distinctive grammatical patterns and technical terms, but perhaps more importantly, with a signature sense of humor about the most profound contemplative experiences that human beings can have. This humor is sometimes ironic, such as in the famous passage advocating apophatic meditation in which the disciple Yan Hui actually becomes the teacher of Kongzi ("Confucius") (ZZ 6). So Zhuangzi is here advocating a sitting meditation practice that leads ultimately to a merging with the Way as the "Great Pervasion" (*datong*) that puts him squarely within the classical Daoist contemplative tradition. But he does so with a characteristic sense of humor that is found nowhere else in this literary corpus, including in later sections of the same work. This passage also exemplifies another important feature of this work when compared to our prior sources: the use of didactic narratives and dialogues. Of course classical Daoist "wisdom poetry" still finds its way into the *Zhuangzi*, but narratives and short prose sections predominate.

Like the *Laozi*, the *Zhuangzi* emphasizes that the Way is not something to be experienced exclusively through sitting meditation; it is also something that is to be experienced directly through acting in the world after one has "merged with the Great Pervasion" and has become completely freed from attachment to fixed and self-based ways of looking at things. This view appears again in chapter 2 of the *Zhuangzi*. Here Zhuangzi directly criticizes the fixed positions of rival philosophers from the socially oriented Confucian and the utilitarian Mohist traditions, who remain convinced that theirs is the only possible correct way of conceiving of the world. He advocates, instead, breaking through to a new mode of enlightened cognition that confers the ability to change and flow from situation to situation because, having experience the Way, one is freed from the limited perspective of any individual viewpoint. He conceives of this as being grounded in the Way at the center of a vast cosmic circle.

The *Zhuangzi* contains many narratives featuring perfected human beings who can best be described as "masters of flowing cognition." They are often physically deformed, tradesman or craftsmen who develop a great technical proficiency through the calmness and clarity of mind that accrues to their having directly experience the Way through apophatic practices. This is the common thread that ties the entire collection together and is best exemplified by a passage from chapter 15 titled "Geyi" (Ingrained Opinions), one of the last additions to this work that was added by disciples in this lineage for over a century and a half until it reached its final form circa 130 BCE in the court of Liu An, the second king of Huainan, who was the sponsor and likely editor of his eponymous work, the *Huainanzi*. In chapter 15 of the *Zhuangzi*, we read the following:

> Thus is it said "imperturbable calm, utter stillness, empty absence (of thoughts), having no activity: these are the neutral basis of Heaven and Earth, the very stuff of

the Way and inner power." Thus it is said, "The sages find rest therein; when resting they are completely relaxed; when completely relaxed, they are imperturbably calm." When completely relaxed and imperturbably calm, then anxieties and misfortunes cannot enter and aberrant *qi* cannot seep in.

Therefore their inner power stays whole and their spirits are unimpaired. Thus it is said that the sages

> "In their living accord with the course of Heaven,
> In their dying transform as do things.
> In tranquility they share the inner power of yin;
> In activity they surge together with yang.
>
> They will not initiate to gain advantage;
> They will not instigate to avoid difficulties.
> Only when stimulated do they respond (*ganying*);
> Only when pressed do they move.
> Only when it is unavoidable will they arise.
> They discard wisdom and precedent (*qu zhi yu gu*);
> They comply with the Patterns of Heaven (*tianli*). . . ."[19]

This passage shows the influence not only of the Inner Chapters of the *Zhuangzi* but also many of the concepts and techniques of the inner cultivation tradition as found in our earlier sources such as the *Neiye* and *Xinshu shang*.

Finally, as mentioned earlier, the *Huainanzi* (Book of the Huainan Masters; abbr. HNZ) is a Syncretic Daoist compendium of everything that the enlightened ruler needs to know in order to govern efficaciously and nurture his subjects. While taking the best ideas of all the earlier classical Daoist works and placing them within a comprehensive framework of Daoist cosmology and inner cultivation practice and results, there are several of its chapters in which Daoist ideas predominate. These include "Yuandao" (Originating in the Way; ch. 1), "Chuzhen" (Activating the Genuine; ch. 2), and "Jingshen" (Quintessential Spirit; ch. 7).

The *Huainanzi* authors greatly benefited from having access to all the earlier Daoist sources and actually being the compilers of one of them, namely, the *Zhuangzi* (Roth 1991a). So it is not surprising that they present an even more evocative depiction of how the Way acts in the world than any of their predecessors. The beginning of chapter 1 and section 6 of chapter 2 are key passages because they point to how the Way acts within the world through non-action and thereby assists all things in their spontaneous self-generation. This works because there is an inherent underlying set of natural guidelines or laws in the world. This is *li*, the patterns of the cosmos through which all things develop during the course of their lives and which guide the spontaneous interactions among phenomena to produce a harmonious world order. Sages, because of their apophatic meditation, are distinctly able to accord their spontaneous actions with the Way because they comply with inherent patterns. These inherent patterns, along with the distinctive natures of things, form a "normative natural order" that itself is sacred and worthy of worship, according to the *Huainanzi* authors (HNZ 1.17; see also Roth 2007, 2012–2013). Herein the

Huainanzi demonstrates its familiarity with the earlier apophatic inner cultivation practices from our classical Daoist sources. Such ideas permeate these chapters of the text (see, e.g., HNZ 1.9).

So the *Huainanzi* authors advocate that the state be governed by rulers who have cultivated themselves through Daoist apophatic techniques so that they can refrain from deliberately interfering with this normative natural order that functions quite well without such interference. In this manner they are practicing the principle of *wuwei*, effortless activity, and thus are acting "microcosmically" in a parallel manner to how the Way acts macrocosmically. This is an interesting working out of the emphases that we find in both the *Laozi* and *Zhuangzi* of manifesting the Way within the phenomenal world, in this instance applied to the challenges of governing. In this manner, the *Huainanzi* embraces the cosmology, the apophatic techniques, the beneficial results, and the spiritual exemplars of the earlier sources of classical Daoism. In some ways, it also fills them out and provides a much more developed theory of their application to rulership.

Further Inquiries on the Way

These four texts, the *Guanzi*, *Huainanzi*, *Laozi*, and *Zhuangzi*, had varying influences within the Daoist tradition. The *Laozi* and *Zhuangzi* became the two most famous works of its classical period, but famous at least as much for their literati interpretations as philosophies of the lifestyle of retiring from Chinese society and resisting its enormous pressures to conform as they were as representatives of Daoist contemplative practices (Graham 1990d, 10–12). Scores of commentaries on these texts as philosophies were written by literati of every dynasty and tradition and most have never been translated (see Robinet 1998, 1999). The *Laozi* commentary of Wang Bi (Wang Pi; 226–249 CE) is perhaps the most famous (Wagner 2003; Lynn 2004), and the *Zhuangzi* commentary of Guo Xiang (Kuo Hsiang; d. 312) (Fung 1964) remains the most renowned. Both are famous as much for being statements of their authors' own distinctive philosophical systems as for accurate interpretations of the texts. Both authors are regarded as key thinkers in the third-century CE intellectual movement known as Xuanxue (Profound Learning). Made up largely of Chinese literati members of powerful clans, some of whom were disaffected critics who eventually fell afoul of the authorities, and romantically calling themselves the "Seven Sages of the Bamboo Grove," many spent their days drinking, philosophizing, and writing poetry. If they had a *raison d'être* other than living in the moment, however, it is the one clearly laid out by Guo Xiang's teacher, Xiang Xiu (Hsiang Hsiu; fl. 3rd c. CE), who himself wrote a commentary on the *Zhuangzi* (later incorporated by Guo into his own). This involved the attempt "to recover" this work for the Chinese intelligentsia after it had been appropriated by the "superstitious" followers of the Daoist religion (Zürcher 1972).

Perhaps more relevant for understanding continuities within the Daoist tradition, the early Tianshi (Celestial Masters) movement, one of the most important communities in early organized Daoism, incorporated the *Laozi* in various ways. Members compiled, studied, and applied the so-called Nine Practices (*jiuxing*), which were nine key principles derived from the *Laozi* (see Bokenkamp 1997; Komjathy 2008, 2013b). Similarly, Zhang Lu (d. 215 CE), the third Celestial Master, may have composed a commentary on the text. This is the *Laozi xiang'er zhu* (Commentary Thinking through the *Laozi*; DH 56; S. 6825), which is only extant in a Dunhuang manuscript. The text has been studied and translated by Stephen Bokenkamp (1997). Many more examples could be given, but here we must be content with another important example. In the context of early Quanzhen (Complete Perfection) Daoism, the *Daode jing* became one of three primary scriptures, with the other two being the sixth-century *Yinfu jing* (Scripture on the Hidden Talisman; DZ 31) and eighth-century *Qingjing jing* (Scripture on Clarity and Stillness; DZ 620) (see Komjathy 2007, 2013a).

The texts collected in the *Guanzi* were not directly influential in either the literati tradition or in the later religious tradition, but they do contain the earliest statements of the contours of the contemplative breath cultivation that seems to have continued into the institutionalized Daoist religion. The ideas of vital essence (*jing*), vital energy (*qi*), and spirit (*shen*) that are the cornerstones of many later Daoist contemplative practices are laid out clearly, particularly in the *Neiye*. Furthermore, the *Xinshu shang* contains one of the earliest attempts to apply these apophatic inner cultivation techniques to governing.[20]

The *Huainanzi* was the last attempt by classical Daoists to convince the Chinese emperor that Daoist philosophy could serve as the ruling ideology of the state. It was presented by its sponsor, Liu An (ca. 179–122 BCE), to his nephew, the young Emperor Wu (r. 141–87 BCE), in 139 BCE in hopes that its very specific recommendations on how to rule harmoniously would be adapted. Within a half decade, however, Confucian teachings became the ruling ideology of the Chinese state, and the *Huainanzi* was set aside when Liu An was accused of sedition and put to death in 122 BCE, with his entire library confiscated into the imperial collection (Major et al. 2010, 2–13). Nonetheless, the text's ideas of a normative natural order pervaded by the unifying power of the Way and the importance of adjusting human activities to this order remained extremely influential as Daoism first went underground during the Han dynasty and later reemerged as two millenarian rebellions in the latter half of the second century CE (see Michaud 1958; Stein 1979; Bokenkamp 1997; Hendrischke 2007). The ideal of Great Peace (*taiping*) created on earth by a ruler who has cultivated the Daoist contemplative arts that so dominated the *Huainanzi* was a powerful motivating force in these rebellions. In addition, the strong emphasis that the *Huainanzi* authors placed on the concept of *li* as the underlying patterns and laws of the universe seems to have directly influenced the *Taiping jing* (Scripture on Great Peace), one of the oldest extant sources for the organized Daoist religion (Hendrischke 2006). Further, because the *Huainanzi* contained the most elaborate and beautiful passages on the nature and activities of the Way in all of classical Daoist literature, it continued to serve as an important source for the later Daoist tradition, even if it was treated by literati as a textual source for unique flora and fauna, both real and mythical (Roth 1992).

It is impossible within the limits of this chapter to fully enumerate all the myriad of ways in which views and practices from these classical Daoist works were influential throughout the later Chinese literati and Daoist religious movements, but we will attempt a general sketch. First and foremost, the cosmology of the ineffable Way as the source and continuing sustaining force of the cosmos and inner power as its manifestation within each phenomenon are a palpable presence throughout all the many forms and traditions that Daoism developed throughout the subsequent two millennia of its development (see Komjathy 2013b). Within the literati traditions, as the late A. C. Graham has so clearly enunciated, the *Laozi* and *Zhuangzi* with their profound cosmologies, emphases on Nature, and commendation of individual self-cultivation, came to give paradigmatic support of a life of personal reflection, retreat, and restoration in contradistinction to the extremely strong pressures for service to the state that the Confucian tradition places upon lettered Chinese (Graham 1990d, 10–12). Other particularly influential concepts that pertain throughout the tradition are effortless action (lit., non-action; *wuwei*) and spontaneity (*ziran*) important in the *Laozi*, *Zhuangzi*, and *Huainanzi*. One also finds emphasis on Nothingness or Nonbeing (*wu*), instead of on Something, and the importance of tranquility and emptiness attained through apophatic inner cultivation practice and as generalized philosophical qualities (see Komjathy 2008). Finally, the Phase Energetic cosmologies of yin and yang and the Five Phases of *qi* and the principle of resonance and mutual causation of things in the same phrase or category that is important in classical Daoism, especially in the *Huainanzi*, proved to be extremely influential throughout many later Daoist movements and lineages.

The images of human perfection found in the classical Daoist textual corpus, particularly in the verses of the *Laozi* and the narratives of *Zhuangzi* and *Huainanzi*, have had lasting influence throughout the Daoist tradition. While the details of each of them has varied to some extent, we can point to some general definitions:

1. The Genuine (*zhenren*) are adepts who have become one with the Way through practices of inner cultivation.

2. Numinous beings (*shenren*) are spirit-like humans with otherworldly qualities and abilities who escape human understanding.

3. The Perfected (*zhiren*) are humans who have attained the pinnacle of realization.

4. Sages (*shengren*) are wise adepts who apply their realization of the Way to everyday problems, particularly those of rulership. They are sometimes spoken of as "sage-kings" (*shengwang*), who have qualities of wisdom and cognition that derive from achievements in apophatic inner cultivation practices.

There are, in addition, several key phrases used to designate these practices that resonate throughout the tradition:

1. *Yangxing* (nourishing innate nature)

2. *Yangsheng* (nourishing life or vitality)

3. *Yangshen* (nourishing spirit)

4. *Yangxing* (nourishing the body)

5. *Yangshen* (nourishing the whole person)

6. *Daoshu* (techniques of the Way)

As we have seen, these apophatic practices, including attending to the breath, breath control or cultivation, nurturing the body through gymnastic techniques of circulating the *qi* (lit., guiding and pulling; *daoyin*), and dietary practices, were key dimensions of the classical inner cultivation lineages. In classical Daoism, all are recommended; the only exception involves nourishing the body, which is criticized as practiced by health freaks and mere longevity seekers who cultivate the body but ignore spirit (see ZZ 15 and HNZ 7).

Finally, there are some lasting images of deep cultivation, mysterious states of the cosmic origins, and human perfection found in classical Daoist texts that also resonate throughout the tradition. These include the following:

1. The "mysterious female" (*xuanpin*), which becomes a key concept in later Daoist internal alchemy (*neidan*), in which it is interpreted to be the foundational vital energy of the cosmos (*yuanqi*) and supreme Nonbeing (Pregadio 2008, 1138)

2. The "valley spirit" (*gushen*), the empty consciousness of Daoist adepts through which the Way flows

3. The "Uncarved Block" (*pu*), which symbolizes the pure undifferentiated potentiality and innocence of cunning found in the Way and in adepts who have realized it

4. The "empty vessel" (*qi*) or "wheel hub" (*gu*), which represents the cultivated mind of the sage devoid of normal contents and being a channel through which the Way is manifest

5. The "axis of the Way" (*daoshu*), which relates to the experience of adepts grounded in the Way as the axis at the center of all the limited viewpoints of the narrow-minded and attached

6. The Way as water, symbolizing its qualities of flowing, interpenetrating, and persistence

7. The mirror metaphor for clear and unbiased consciousness of the Perfected

8. Guarding the One (*shouyi*), the meditative practice of concentrating on one thing and/or on the Way itself

The basic principles of apophatic inner cultivation meditation continue from classical Daoism into organized Daoism. These persist in the ways in which this practice was conceived: in terms of refining vital energy through attentive control of in-breathing and out-breathing until rarefied states of tranquility associated with the ethereal vital essence are attained and spirit is stabilized or realized. Taking their cues from such classical models as "sitting and forgetting" (*zuowang*) and "the fasting of the mind" (*xinzhai*), later Daoist masters elaborated on these methods in works such as the *Xisheng jing* (Scripture of the Western Ascension; DZ 666; Kohn 1991b), attributed to the pseudo-historical figure Yin Xi (ca. 6th c. BCE), and the *Zuowang lun* (Discourse on Sitting-in-Forgetfulness; DZ 1036; Kohn 1987) by the twelfth Shangqing (Highest Clarity) Patriarch Sima Chengzhen (647–735), and later in the Song dynasty contemplative practices of the inner alchemy tradition (Pregadio 2008, 1114, 1309). These works added visualization techniques to the apophatic inner cultivation practices of classical Daoism (Pregadio 2008, 762; Komjathy 2013b).

The influence of classical Daoism upon the various schools of Chinese Buddhism, especially Chan, is complex and difficult to detail with precision. What can be said is that many Chan texts of the formative period in the Sui and early Tang dynasties and many of the collected sayings (*yulu*) of the later Tang and Song dynasty masters demonstrate an awareness of classical Daoist texts. These include the *Laozi* to a certain extent, and even more so the *Zhuangzi*.[21] It is certainly possible to demonstrate several more definite historical avenues through which

Daoist ideas seeped into Chinese Buddhism. In the early Buddho-Daoist period (2nd–5th c. CE), translators of Buddhist texts were in the habit of "matching concepts" (*geyi*) and used classical Daoist ideas to render the new Buddhist technical terms such as nirvana, emptiness (*śūnyatā*), intuitive wisdom (*prajñā*), meditative concentration (*samādhi*), and so forth (Zürcher 1972). Then there were the later, post-Kumārajīva (334–413) Buddho-Daoist philosophers such as Sengzhao (374–414), who embedded classical Daoist ideas throughout his treatises and his commentary on the famous Mahāyāna text, the *Vimalakīrti-nirdeśa sūtra* (Discourse of Vimalakīrti; Robinson 1967). In addition, Sengzhao was quite influential in early Chan Buddhism, and so it is possible that classical Daoist ideas entered the tradition via this route (Sharf 2002, 37–38). Sharf also details evidence of a substantial influence of the Tang dynasty Chongxuan (Twofold Mystery) Daoist exegetical movement on two of the most important early Chan schools, namely, the East Mountain school of the fourth and fifth patriarchs of Chan (Daoxin [580–652] and Hongren [601–74]) and on the founder of the Ox Head school (Niutou Farong [594–657]) (Sharf 2002, 39–43). These figures are quite influential on the *Tanjing* (Platform Sutra) attributed to the supposed sixth patriarch of Chan, Huineng (638–713), and hence on later Chan masters who all draw their line of descent directly from him (see Yampolsky 1967).

Contemplative Being-in-the-World

Scholars of the comparative study of mystical experience have disagreed about the nature of early Daoist mysticism. Yearley, concentrating on the *Zhuangzi*, argues that therein there is neither the Christian "mysticism of union," in which a union occurs between an "unchanging Real and the changing but still real particular individual;" nor the Indian (Hindu-Buddhist) "mysticism of unity," in which the mystic attains unity by uncovering an inherent identity with a monistic principle that is the sole reality of the universe (Yearley 1983, 130–31). Rather, the *Zhuangzi* espouses what Yearley calls an "intraworldly mysticism," in which "one neither obtains union with some higher being nor unification with the single reality. Rather, one goes through a discipline and has experiences that allow one to view the world in a new way" (131).

Responding to Yearley while adapting Stace's contrasting categories of "introvertive" and "extrovertive" (Stace 1987), I have previously critiqued Stace for overemphasizing the former at the expense of the latter (Roth 2010). Instead, I have argued for a "bimodal mystical experience" in the *Zhuangzi* and in all of classical Daoism, one that involves two complementary dimensions: introvertive and extrovertive. The former involves focusing the attention and emptying the mind of its usual contents until an ultimate state is reached of complete union with the Way. The latter is bringing the dispassionate clarity of mind that comes from this experience into a transformed reinhabitation of the phenomenal world in which one attains a constantly flowing cognition. Through this flowing cognition, one may respond spontaneously and harmoniously to all new situations, best exemplified by *Zhuangzi*'s monkey keeper and in the several important "skill" passages that appear in the text.

There exists considerable support for the "bimodal model" of mystical experience in the contemplative literature of the classical Daoist tradition. Stace's first category of "introvertive mystical experience" provides an excellent way to categorize the apophatic inner cultivation practices and results that so pervade this literature (see Stace 1987, 111, 131). As we have seen, classical Daoists follow practices well described as "introvertive": these involve sitting still in a stable position and concentrating on the breath as it cycles in and out or focusing the attention on a mental object, a thought or sacred word as in *mantra* meditation in India. As one does this, the normal contents of consciousness gradually empty out and one comes to experience a tranquility and mental emptiness that, as one's practice develops, becomes quite profound. Eventually one comes to fully empty out the contents of consciousness until a condition of unity is achieved. This condition is spoken of with a number of related phrases, such as "attaining the One," "attaining the empty Way," "profound merging," "merging with the Great Pervasion," and so on. This fits well Stace's category of "introvertive mystical experience."

After such unitive experiences, Daoist adepts return and live again in the dualistic world in a profoundly transformed fashion, often characterized by an unself-conscious ability to spontaneously respond to whatever situation one is facing. This new mode of being in the world is frequently characterized by the following famous phrase from *Laozi*: "doing nothing, yet leaving nothing undone" (*wuwei er wu buwei*). Moreover, as we have seen, this is associated with profound cognitive transformations such as clear perception, unbiased thinking and decision-making, mental focus, and lack of self-consciousness. The *Zhuangzi* places a strong emphasis on this transformed mode of living in the world, referring to it in many passages that emphasize the flowing cognition of the sage, one that attains the "axis of the Way" and the "point of rest on the Potter's Wheel of the Heavens." In such a condition, all the myriads of individual viewpoints are seen as relatively true to the standpoint of their observers, while simultaneously being of equivalent epistemic value to the Daoist adept. We also see similar emphases in the *Huainanzi*'s many descriptions of perfected Daoists who "sink and float, plunge and soar, through life along with the Way."

This latter mode of transformed cognition bears some resemblance to Stace's category of "extrovertive mystical experience," in which the mystic experiences "the unifying vision—all things are One" coupled with "the more concrete apprehension of the One as an inner subjectivity, or life, in all things." For him, this unity is directly perceived within the experience and will later be variously interpreted depending on the "cultural environment and the prior beliefs of the mystic" (Stace 1987, 66). This mode fits well with Yearley's "intraworldly mysticism."

While embracing Yearley's insights into what he calls "intraworldly mysticism," I see them as a corrective rather than a replacement for Stace's phenomenological model. That is, his "intraworldly mysticism" is not an entirely new mode of mystical experience but rather a uniquely classical Daoist form of Stace's extrovertive mode. As such, it is integrally related to the introvertive mode, although I would most certainly concur with Yearley that the unity attained fits into neither of his two categories of Indo-European mystical experience. For classical Daoists, the Stacian "objective referent" of this introvertive mystical experience—the Way—is not a static metaphysical absolute but rather a continuously moving unitive force that can be merged with when consciousness is completely emptied through inner cultivation practice. It can then serve as a constant guiding power throughout the many activities and circumstances of daily life. This classical Daoist mode of flowing cognition bears resemblance to the mode of "optimal experience" identified by the famous psychologist Mihaly Csikszentmihalyi as "flow" (Csikszentmihalyi 1988).

Recent neuroscientific research on contemplative practice has concluded that there are two fundamental aspects that seem to parallel the bimodal mystical experience of classical Daoism: concentrative and receptive (Austin 2011, 42–43). The former involves concentrating one's attention in a deliberate manner, developing one-pointed attention that is more self-referential in that it involves focused awareness of one's body and mind. This deliberate choice to pay attention often leads to deep inner absorptions. The latter is effortless, sustained, unfocused attention leading to a more open universal awareness. The former is a "top-down" meditation, while the latter is a "bottom-up" meditation. In addition, Austin outlines various successful modes of "mindfulness meditation" that entail the focusing of the attention and developing both perceptual and emotional stability over time. Based on neurological research using various brain-scanning devices, including functional magnetic resonance imagery (fMRI), magnetic encephalography (MEG), and positron emission tomography (PET), he further hypothesizes that there are two primary and complementary neural pathways in the brain. The first is the "egocentric pathway" that works with a ventral attentional system that focuses on awareness within the body and in the space immediately surrounding it. The second is the "allocentric pathway" that works as a dorsal attentional system that focuses on awareness of objects that are more distant. The former reinforces our self-centeredness, is voluntary in terms of using the will, and works primarily with language. The latter reinforces our other-centeredness, functions involuntarily, and does not rely on linguistic processing. Austin theorizes that in the process of meditational training the egocentric pathway gradually loses its dominance in information processing to the allocentric pathway (Austin 2011, 29–39).

These preliminary neuroscientific theories fit well with the dual modes of contemplative practice and experience we have found in classical Daoism, namely, the silent and still, apophatic, inner-focused emptying of consciousness and the flowing and active kataphatic return to the world of dualities leading to a spontaneous and harmonious cognition. For practices, the terms concentrative and receptive map well onto the apophatic and kataphatic practices of classical Daoism. Furthermore the decrease in the predominance of the self-centered egocentric pathways in the brain that Austin postulates as resulting from systematic meditation and the corresponding increase in the other-centered allocentric pathways map well onto the self-forgetting and mind-fasting of classical Daoist meditation and the selflessness and spontaneity of the flowing cognition we also find there. Small wonder that the positive life changes that accompany these contemplative experiences were appealing to the local rulers who supported Daoist teachers at the intellectual centers formed during the third and second centuries BCE in the states of Qi and Qin and eventually at the court of Liu An in Huainan.

Notes

1. The present chapter utilizes Pinyin romanization, the official romanization system of the People's Republic of China and now the international standard. I supply Wade-Giles correlates for some important and relatively familiar Chinese terms. The informed reader will note that the Pinyin-derived Dao, Daoism, Daoist more commonly appear as the Wade-Giles-derived Tao, Taoism, Taoist. The pronunciation is the same.

2. I use the third-person female pronoun (she) in order to be inclusive in terms of gender. Although some may see this as anachronistic in terms of ancient China, there is evidence of female Daoist masters in classical Daoism. For example, chapter 6 of the *Zhuangzi* contains instructions from Nüyu (Woman Yu), also translatable as "Crooked-Backed Woman" and "female recluse." In addition, there is nothing to suggest any inherently exclusivist elements of the practice, other than a commitment to the practice. Women have played major roles in the larger Daoist tradition, which is relatively inclusive in terms of gender equity. See Despeux and Kohn 2003; Komjathy 2013b.

3. *Zhuangzi* 6/19/20–1. All *Zhuangzi* references are to the *Zhuangzi zhuzi suoyin* (Lau 2000). In these Institute for Chinese Studies critical texts, emendations are given in the following format: (*a*) [*x*]: "character *a* is emended to character *x*." The translation is modified from Graham 1981, 92.

4. Verse numbers follow Roth 1999a.

5. The same phrase as *Laozi* 10.

6. This phrase is often translated as "guarding the One." In the later Daoist tradition, it becomes a technical term for meditation in general. See Kohn 1989; Komjathy 2013b.

7. See, for example, *Zhuangzi* 9/23/29, 12/29/16, 20/53/24–25, 23/65/6, 25/76/17.

8. Such phrases are widespread in early inner cultivation texts. See, for example, *Lüshi chunqiu* 3.4/15/1, 25.3/162/20–21; *Zhuangzi* 15/41/27; and my analysis in Roth 1997. *Lüshi chunqiu* references are to Lau 1994.

9. *Guanzi* 13.1/95/29; *Laozi* chapter 10; *Zhuangzi* 5/13/18, 27. *Guanzi* references are to Lau 2001.

10. *Zhuangzi* 6/19/21.

11. *Zhuangzi* 2/5/1.

12. See, for example, *Neiye* IX, XII, XIII; *Lüshi chunqiu* 3.4; and the "Jingfa" chapter (ch. 6) of the *Huang-Lao boshu*.

13. Perceptive readers will note that this classical Daoist conception of *jing* appears to diverge from uses in classical Chinese medicine and in the later Daoist tradition. For example, in Daoist internal alchemy (*neidan*), the term often appears as one of the internal Three Treasures (*sanbao*), namely, vital essence (*jing*), vital energy (*qi*), and spirit (*shen*). In this expression, each one is subtler than the former. In such contexts, vital essence is usually associated with one's foundational vitality and understood as finite in quantity. However, from at least a certain classical Daoist perspective, it appears that vital essence, as concentrated *qi*, may be increased and replenished through specific types of inner cultivation.

14. *Zhuangzi* 18/48/7, 22/60/14, 25/76/6; *Lüshi chunqiu* 25.3/162/23.

15. Paraphrased from *Zhuangzi* 9/23/27.

16. In an earlier work, I have presented evidence for a remarkable consistency across texts as early as the *Huang-Lao boshu* (ca. 300 BCE) and as late as the *Huainanzi* (139 BCE) in terms used for stages of meditation. See Roth 1997.

17. *Guanzi* 13.1/96/14; *Zhuangzi* 13/34/22, 33/98/1.

18. This means that the sense organs will function properly and spontaneously if they are not interfered with by the mind. This occurs because each has an inherent pattern of activity that derives from its individual characteristics and its relation to the whole body. In texts of this period, *li* is often translated as "patterns" or "inherent patterns." However, "patterns" in English has a stronger determinative force than *li* does. A pattern is a regular form or order (e.g., behavioral pattern) and suggests that things or activities must conform to it exactly with little room for individual variation. *Li* admit of freedom within structure; *li* guide the spontaneous responses that develop from the natures of things. It is important to remember this whenever "inherent patterns" appears.

19. Lau 2000, 15/41/24–7. See also Graham 1981, 265.

20. More work needs to be done on potential influence on the later tradition. For example, it is noteworthy that the phrase *shouyi* (guarding the One), which appears in NY 9, 19, and 24 as well as ZZ 11, becomes a general name for Daoist meditation in the later tradition (Kohn 1989). For some preliminary thoughts on connections between the *Neiye* and organized Daoism, see Kirkland 2004, 39–52, 67–73.

21. For instance, one finds frequent allusions to the "dropping away of body and mind," such as in the writings of Eihei Dōgen (1200–1253), the Japanese founder of the Sōtō lineage of Zen Buddhism. This phrase derives from the passage on "sitting and forgetting" in chapter 6 of the *Zhuangzi*. Interestingly, in his "Sansui-kyo" (Mountains and Waters Sutra), Dōgen also explicitly refers to chapter 11 of the *Zhuangzi*: "At the time the Yellow Emperor visited Mt. Kongdong [Kongtong] to pay homage to Guangcheng

[Expansive Completion], he walked on his knees, touched his forehead to the ground, and asked for instruction" (Tanahashi 1985, 106). Here Dōgen is emphasizing the primacy of mountains, and mountain contemplatives by extension, over social concerns and political power. At the same time, the passage from the *Zhuangzi* also explicitly discusses Daoist apophatic meditation and the importance of mountain seclusion and solitary practice. For some insights into Master Guangcheng, see Komjathy 2013b.

Works Cited and Further Reading

Allan, Sarah, and Crispin Williams, eds. 2000. *The Guodian Laozi: Proceedings of the International Conference, Dartmouth College, May, 1998*. Early China Special Monograph Series no. 5. Berkeley: Institute for East Asian Studies, University of California, Berkeley.

Austin, James. 2011. *Meditating Selflessly: Practical Neural Zen*. Cambridge: MIT Press.

Baxter, William H. 1998. "Situating the Language of the *Lao Tzu*: The Probable Date of the *Tao Te Ching*." In *Lao-Tzu and the Tao-Te-Ching*, edited by Livia Kohn and Michael LaFargue, 231–54. Albany: State University of New York Press.

Bokenkamp, Stephen. 1997. *Early Daoist Scriptures*. Berkeley: University of California Press.

Cahn, B. Rael, and John Polich. 2006. "Meditation States and Traits: EEG, ERP, and Neuroimaging Studies." *Psychological Bulletin* 132.2: 180–211.

Csikszentmihalyi, Mark, and Michael Nylan 2003. "Constructing Lineages and Inventing Traditions through Exemplary Figures in Early China." *T'oung Pao* 89: 59–99.

Csikszentmihalyi, Mihaly. 1991. *Flow: The Psychology of Optimal Experience*. New York: Harper.

Despeux, Catherine, and Livia Kohn. 2003. *Women in Daoism*. Cambridge: Three Pines Press.

Fung, Yu-lan. 1964. *Chuang Tzu: A New Selected Translation with an Exposition of the Philosophy of Kuo Hsiang*. Peking: The Commercial Press.

Graham, A. C. 1981. *Chuang Tzu: The Inner Chapters*. London: Allen and Unwin.

———. 1989. *Disputers of the Tao: Philosophical Argumentation in Ancient China*. La Salle: Open Court.

———. 1990a. *Studies in Chinese Philosophy and Philosophical Literature*. Albany: State University of New York Press.

———. 1990b. "The Origins of the Legend of Lao Tan." In *Studies in Chinese Philosophy and Philosophical Literature*, by A. C. Graham, 111–24. Albany: State University of New York Press.

———. 1990c. "How Much of *Chuang Tzu* Did Chuang Tzu Write?" In *Studies in Chinese Philosophy and Philosophical Literature*, by A. C. Graham, 283–321. Albany: State University of New York Press.

———. 1990d (1960). *The Book of Lieh Tzu*. New York: Columbia University Press.

Harper, Donald. 1995. "The Bellows Analogy in *Laozi* V and Warring States Macrobiotic Hygiene." *Early China* 20: 381–91.

———. 1998. *Early Chinese Medical Literature: The Mawangdui Medical Manuscripts*. London and New York: Kegan Paul International.

Hendrischke, Barbara. 2006. *The Scripture on Great Peace*. Berkeley: University of California Press.

Henricks, Robert. 1989. *Lao-Tzu: Te Tao Ching: A New Translation Based on the Recently Discovered Mawang-tui Texts*. New York: Ballantine.

———. 2005. *Lao Tzu's Tao Te Ching: A Translation of the Startling New Documents Found at Guodian*. New York: Columbia University Press.

Kirkland, Russell. 2002. "Self-Fulfillment through Selflessness: The Moral Teachings of the *Daode jing*." In *Varieties of Ethical Reflection: New Directions for Ethics in a Global Context*, edited by Michael Barnhardt, 21–48. New York: Lexington Books.

———. 2004. *Taoism: The Enduring Tradition*. London and New York: Routledge.

Kohn, Livia. 1987. *Seven Steps to the Tao: Sima Chengzhen's Zuowang lun*. St. Augustin: Steyler Verlag.

———. 1989. "Guarding the One: Concentrative Meditation in Taoism." In *Taoist Meditation and Longevity Techniques*, edited by Livia Kohn, 125–58. Ann Arbor: University of Michigan, Center for Chinese Studies.

———. 1991a. *Early Chinese Mysticism: Philosophy and Soteriology in the Taoist Tradition*. Princeton: Princeton University Press.

———. 1991b. *Taoist Mystical Philosophy: The Scripture of Western Ascension*. Albany: State University of New York Press.

Kohn, Livia, and Michael LaFargue, eds. 1998. *Lao-Tzu and the Tao-Te-Ching*. Albany: State University of New York Press.

Komjathy, Louis. 2007. *Cultivating Perfection: Mysticism and Self-Transformation in Early Quanzhen Daoism*. Leiden: Brill.

———. 2008 (2003). *Handbooks for Daoist Practice*. 10 vols. Hong Kong: Yuen Yuen Institute.

———. 2013a. *The Way of Complete Perfection: A Quanzhen Daoist Anthology*. Albany: State University of New York Press.

———. 2013b. *The Daoist Tradition: An Introduction*. London and New York: Bloomsbury Academic.

LaFargue, Michael. 1992. *The Tao of the Tao Te Ching*. Albany: State University of New York Press.

———. 1994. *Tao and Method: A Reasoned Approach to the Tao Te Ching*. Albany: State University of New York Press.

Lau, D. C. 1982. *Chinese Classics: Tao Te Ching*. New York: Penguin.

———, ed. 1992. *Huainanzi zhuzi suoyin*. The Institute for Chinese Studies Chinese Text Concordance Series. Hong Kong: Commercial Press.

———, ed. 1994. *Lüshi chunqiu zhuzi suoyin*. The Institute for Chinese Studies Chinese Text Concordance Series. Hong Kong: Commercial Press.

———, ed. 2000. *Zhuangzi zhuzi suoyin*. The Institute for Chinese Studies Chinese Text Concordance Series. Hong Kong: Commercial Press.

———, ed. 2001. *Guanzi zhuzi suoyin*. The Institute for Chinese Studies Chinese Text Concordance Series. Hong Kong: Commercial Press.

Lee, Jung H. 2007. "What Is It Like to Be a Butterfly? A Philosophical Interpretation of Zhuangzi's Butterfly Dream." *Asian Philosophy* 17.2: 185–202.

Littlejohn, Ronnie L. 2009. *Daoism: An Introduction*. London and New York: I. B. Tauris.

Liu, Xiaogan. 1994. *Classifying the Zhuangzi Chapters*. Translated by William Savage. Ann Arbor: Michigan Monographs in Chinese Studies.

Lynn, Richard John. 2004. *The Classic of the Way and Virtue: A New Translation of Laozi as Interpreted by Wang Bi*. New York: Columbia University Press.

Mair, Victor. 1983. *Experimental Essays on the Chuang Tzu*. Honolulu: University of Hawaii Press.

———. 1990. *Tao Te Ching: The Classic Book of Integrity and the Way*. New York: Bantam.

———. 1994. *Wandering on the Way: Early Taoist Tales and Parables from Chuang Tzu*. Honolulu: University of Hawaii Press.

———. 2010. *Experimental Essays on the Zhuangzi*. Dunedin: Three Pines Press.

Major, John S., Sarah Queen, Andrew S. Meyer, and Harold D. Roth. 2010. *The Huainanzi: A Guide to the Theory and Practice of Government in Early Han China, by Liu An, King of Huainan*. New York: Columbia University Press.

Meyer, Andrew. 2010–2011. "'The Altars of Soil and Grain Are Closer Than Kin': The Qi Model of Intellectual Participation and the Jixia Patronage Community." *Early China* 33–34: 37–99.

Michaud, Paul. 1958. "The Yellow Turbans." *Monumenta Serica* 17: 47–127.

Miller, James 2003. *Daoism: A Short Introduction*. Oxford: Oneworld.

Needham, Joseph, with Wang Ling. 1956. *Science and Civilisation in China*. Vol. 2: *History of Scientific Thought*. Cambridge: Cambridge University Press.

Porkert, Manfred. 1973. *The Theoretical Foundation of Chinese Medicine.* Cambridge: MIT Press.

Pregadio, Fabrizio, ed. 2008. *The Encyclopedia of Taoism.* 2 vols. London and New York: Routledge.

Queen, Sarah A. 2001. "Inventories of the Past: Re-Thinking the 'School' Affiliation of the *Huainanzi.*" *Asia Major,* Third Series, 14.1: 51–72.

Rickett, Allyn. 1985/1998. *Guanzi: Political, Economic, and Philosophical Essays from Early China.* 2 vols. Princeton: Princeton University Press.

Robinet, Isabelle. 1997. *Taoism: Growth of a Religion.* Berkeley: University of California Press.

———. 1998. "Later Commentaries: Textual Polysemy and Syncretistic Interpretations." In *Lao-tzu and the Tao-te-ching,* edited by Livia Kohn and Michael LaFargue, 119–42. Albany: State University of New York Press.

———. 1999. "The Diverse Interpretations of the *Laozi.*" In *Religious and Philosophical Aspects of the Laozi,* edited by Mark Csikszentmihalyi and Philip J. Ivanhoe, 127–59. Albany: State University of New York Press.

Robinson, Richard. 1967. *Early Madhyamika in India and China.* Madison: University of Wisconsin Press.

Rosemont, Henry, Jr., ed. 1991. *Chinese Texts and Philosophical Contexts: Essays Dedicated to Angus C. Graham.* LaSalle: Open Court.

Roth, Harold D. 1991a. "Who Compiled the *Chuang Tzu?*" In *Chinese Texts and Philosophical Contexts,* edited by Henry Rosemont Jr., 79–128. LaSalle: Open Court.

———. 1991b. "Psychology and Self-Cultivation in Early Taoistic Thought." *Harvard Journal of Asiatic Studies* 51.1: 599–650.

———. 1992. *The Textual History of the Huai-nan Tzu.* Ann Arbor: Association for Asian Studies Monograph #46.

———. 1996. "The Inner Cultivation Tradition of Early Taoism." In *Religions of China in Practice,* edited by Donald S. Lopez Jr., 123–48. Princeton: Princeton University Press.

———. 1997. "Evidence for Stages of Meditation in Early Taoism." *Bulletin of the School of Oriental and African Studies* 60.2: 295–314.

———. 1999a. *Original Tao: Inward Training and the Foundations of Taoist Mysticism.* New York: Columbia University Press.

———. 1999b. "*Laozi* in the Context of Early Daoist Mystical Praxis." In *Religious and Philosophical Aspects of the Laozi,* edited by Mark Csikszentmihalyi and Philip J. Ivanhoe, 59–96. Albany: State University of New York Press.

———. 2000a. "Some Methodological Issues in the Study of the Guodian *Laozi* Parallels." In *The Guodian Laozi,* edited by Sarah Allan and Crispin Williams, 71–88. Berkeley: Institute for East Asian Studies, University of California, Berkeley.

———. 2000b. "Bimodal Mystical Experience in the 'Qiwu lun' Chapter of the *Zhuangzi.*" *Journal of Chinese Religions* 28: 31–50.

———. 2003. *A Companion to Angus C. Graham's Chuang Tzu.* Honolulu: University of Hawaii Press.

———. 2007. "Nature and Self-Cultivation in *Huainanzi*'s 'Original Way.'" In *Polishing the Chinese Mirror: Essays in Honor of Henry Rosemont, Jr.,* edited by Marthe Chandler and Ronnie Littlejohn, 270–92. New York: Global Scholarly.

———. 2010 (2000). "Bimodal Mystical Experience in the 'Qiwulun' Chapter of *Zhuangzi.*" In *Experimental Essays on the Zhuangzi,* edited by Victor Mair, 199–214. Dunedin: Three Pines Press.

———. 2012–2013. "The Classical Daoist Concept of *Li* (Pattern) and Early Chinese Cosmology." *Early China* 35–36: 157–84.

Schwartz, Benjamin. 1985. *The World of Thought in Ancient China.* Cambridge: Harvard University Press.

Sharf, Robert. 2002. *Coming to Terms with Chinese Buddhism: A Reading of the Treasure Store Treatise.* Kuroda Institute in East Asian Buddhism 14. Honolulu: University of Hawaii Press.

Stace, Walter. 1987 (1960). *Mysticism and Philosophy.* Los Angeles: Jeremy P. Tarcher.

Stein, Rolf. 1979. "Religious Taoism and Popular Religion from the Second to the Seventh Century." In *Facets of Taoism*, edited by Holmes Welch and Anna Seidel, 53–81. New Haven: Yale University Press.

Tanahashi, Kazuaki, ed. 1985. *Moon in a Dewdrop: Writings of Zen Master Dōgen*. San Francisco: North Point Press.

Tsien, Tsuen-Hsuin. 1962. *Written on Bamboo and Silk: The Beginnings of Chinese Books and Inscriptions*. Chicago: University of Chicago Press.

Unschuld, Paul, and Hermann Tessenow. 2011. *Huang Di Nei Jing Su Wen: An Annotated Translation of Huang Di's Inner Classic—Basic Questions*. 2 vols. Berkeley: University of California Press.

Wagner, Rudolph 2003. *A Chinese Reading of the Tao Te Ching: Wang Pi's Commentary on the Lao Tzu with Critical Text and Translation*. Albany: State University of New York Press.

Yampolsky, Phillip. 1967. *The Platform Sutra of the Sixth Patriarch*. New York: Columbia University Press.

Yearley, Lee. 1983. "The Perfected Person in the Radical *Chuang-tzu*." In *Experimental Essays on the Chuang-tzu*, edited by Victor Mair, 125–48. Honolulu: University of Hawaii Press.

Zürcher, Erik. 1972. *The Buddhist Conquest of China: The Spread and Adaptation of Buddhism in Early Medieval China*. 2 vols. Leiden: E. J. Brill.

Selections from the Classical Daoist Textual Corpus*

Elders of the Inner Cultivation Lineages[1]

Selected, Translated, and Annotated by Harold D. Roth

Cosmology

Neiye (Inward Training)[2]

Verse I

The vital essence of all things:[3]
It is this that brings them to life.
It generates the five grains below
And becomes the constellated stars above.
When flowing amid the heavens and earth,[4]
We call it ghostly and numinous.
When stored within the chests of human beings,
We call them sages.
(*Sibu congkan* [SBCK] 16/1a5–6; Roth 1999a, 46)

---

*Paralleling the third section in my introduction, I organize these translations according to four categories: (1) Cosmology; (2) Inner Cultivation: Theory and Techniques; (3) Contemplative States: Transient and Transformative; and (4) Contemplative Traits: Long-Lasting Benefits. Relevant details on editions and translations appear in the annotation of the first appearance. Translations from the *Neiye* (Inward Training) and *Huainanzi* (Book of the Huainan Masters) derive from Roth 1999a and Major et al. 2010, respectively. They are used with permission from Columbia University Press, for which I wish to express my gratitude: *Original Tao*, by Harold D. Roth. Copyright 1999 Columbia University Press. Reprinted with permission of the publisher. *The Huainanzi*, by John S. Major, Sarah A. Queen, Andrew Seth Meyer, and Harold D. Roth. Copyright 2010 Columbia University Press. Reprinted with permission of the publisher.

1. Although associated with Guan Zhong (Guanzi [Master Guan]; ca. 720–645 BCE), the *Neiye* (Inward Training) and *Xinshu shang* (Techniques of the Heart-Mind I) are anonymous works. Although traditionally attributed to Laozi (Master Lao) and Zhuangzi (Master Zhuang), the *Laozi* (Book of Venerable Masters) and *Zhuangzi* (Book of Master Zhuang) are multi-vocal anthologies with a variety of historical and textual layers. The *Huainanzi* (Book of the Huainan Masters) is a compendium completed around 139 BCE under the patronage of Liu An (179?–122 BCE), the King of Huainan. The *Laozi* has been translated too many times to document, but some reliable translations include those of Addiss and Lombardo, Henricks, Komjathy, LaFargue, Lau, Mair, and so forth. Standard translations of the *Zhuangzi* include those of A. C. Graham, Victor Mair, and Burton Watson. For a complete translation of the *Guanzi*, see Rickett 1985 and 1998. A complete translation of the *Huainanzi* has been published by Major et al. 2010.

2. These translations from the *Neiye* (Inward Training) section of the *Guanzi* (Book of Master Guan) follow Roth 1999a, with slight modifications for consistency of translation. See also Komjathy 2008, Handbook 1, which is indebted to Roth 1999a. The original Chinese text is from the *Sibu congkan* (SBCK) edition published in 1920 by the Commercial Press in Shanghai. See also Lau 2001.

3. In the context of the *Neiye*, vital essence (*jing*) is a form of concentrated vital energy (*qi*). It may be understood as a kind of physiological substrate associated with profound states of stillness, emptiness, and tranquility.

4. *Tian*, here rendered as "the heavens" and later as "Heaven," refers, first and foremost to the sky and secondarily to the cosmos. From a classical and foundational Daoist perspective, the universe is an impersonal transformative process based on yin-yang interaction.

Verse II

Therefore this vital energy is:[5]
Bright!—as if ascending the heavens;
Dark!—as if entering an abyss;
Vast!—as if dwelling in an ocean;
Lofty!—as if dwelling on a mountain peak.

Therefore this vital energy
Cannot be halted by force,
Yet can be secured by inner power.[6]
Cannot be summoned by speech,
Yet can be welcomed by the awareness.
Reverently hold on to it and do not lose it:
This is called developing inner power.
When inner power develops and wisdom emerges,
The myriad things will, to the last one, be grasped.
(SBCK 16/1a6–10; Roth 1999a, 48)

Verse IV

Clear! as though right by your side.
Vague! as though you are not going to get it.
Indiscernible! as though beyond the limitless.
The test of this is not far off:
Daily we make use of its inner power.
The Way is what infuses the physical form,
Yet people are unable to fix it in place.
It goes forth but does not return,
It comes back but does not stay.
Silent! none can hear its sound.
Suddenly stopping! it abides within the mind.[7]

---

5. Also translated as "energy," "pneuma," and "subtle breath," vital energy (*qi*) is both the actual breath that we inhale and exhale and also the quasi-material stuff out of which all things are constituted. It is essential to all things, both living and inert; and it exists on a continuum of density from the compact and heavy to the ethereal and light. All aspects of the human psyche have a typical *qi* associated with them; it forms a kind of physiological substrate to all psychological states, a strikingly parallel concept to modern physics and neuroscience. The most rarified states of contemplation, tranquility and emptiness, have the most quintessential *and* ethereal *qi*.

6. Also translated as "integrity," "potency," "potentiality," and "virtue," inner power (*de*) is a kind of aura of spontaneous efficacy that develops in a person and is visible for all to see through repeated experiences of tranquility, emptiness, and merging with the Way. It is the Way manifesting through and expressed by advanced practitioners, especially sages (*shengren*). In certain respects, it is thus connected with vital essence (*jing*), vital energy (*qi*), and innate nature (*xing*).

7. Throughout the present selections, I translate *xin* as "mind," but it may also be understood as "heart-mind." From a classical and foundational Daoist perspective, *xin* is understood both as a physical location in the chest (the heart as "organ" [*zang*]) and as relating to thoughts (*nian*) and emotions (*qing*) (the heart as "consciousness" [*shi*]). The mind is the emotional and intellectual center of the human person. It is associated with consciousness

Obscure! you do not see its form.
Surging forth! it arises with me.
We do not see its form,
We do not hear its sound,
Yet we can perceive an order to its accomplishments.
We call it "the Way."
(SBCK 16/1b2–9; Roth 1999a, 52)

Laozi (Book of Venerable Masters)[8]

Chapter 1

A way that can be objectified
Is not an eternal Way;
A name that can be named
Is not an eternal name.

The nameless was the beginning of heaven and earth;
The named was the mother of the myriad creatures.

Hence always negate desires to contemplate its secrets;
But always affirm desires in order to observe its manifestations.

These two are actually identical
Yet are named differently as they come forth.
It is their identity that we call "profound."[9]
More profound than even this,
It is the gateway of the myriad subtleties.

Chapter 25

There is something formed in obscurity,
Born before heaven and earth.
Silent and void,
It stands alone and does not change,
Goes round and does not weary.

---

and often identified as the storehouse of spirit (*shen*). In its original or realized condition, the mind has the ability to attain numinous pervasion; in its disoriented or habituated condition, especially in a state of hyper-emotionality or intellectualism, the mind has the ability to separate the adept from the Way as Source. Often associated with "innate nature" (*xing*), the original condition of the mind is characterized by stillness, and this inner stillness is a manifestation of the Dao as Stillness (see LaFargue 1992).

8. My translations are indebted to Lau 1982, with modifications to bring out the contemplative aspects of the passages.

9. Here "profound" translates *xuan*, which may also be rendered as "dark" or "mysterious." It is a Daoist technical term used to refer to the Dao (Way). Thus, the latter lines could be understood as describing the Way as a "mystery within a mystery," as a twofold mystery.

It is capable of being the mother of the world.
I do not know its name
So I nickname it "the Way."

I give it the descriptive name of "the great."
Being great, it is further described as receding,
Receding, it is described as far away,
Being far away, it is described as turning back.

Hence the Way is great;
Heaven is great;
Earth is great;
The king is also great.
Within the realm there are four things that are great,
And the king counts as one.

Humans model themselves on earth,
Earth models itself on heaven,
Heaven models itself on the Way,
And the Way on that which is naturally so.[10]

Chapter 42

The Way generates one;
One generates two;
Two generates three;
Three generates the myriad creatures.[11]

The myriad creatures carry yin on their backs and embrace yang in their arms and are the blending of the vital energies of the two . . .[12]

Zhuangzi (Book of Master Zhuang)[13]

Chapter 2

"Without Other there is no Self; without Self, no choosing one thing rather than another." This is somewhere near it, but we do not know in whose service they are being employed. It seems

---

10. Here "naturally so" translates *ziran* (*tzu-jan*), which has also been rendered as "naturalness," "self-so," "spontaneity," "suchness," and so forth. A quality of the Way, the phenomenal world, and the cultivated sage, *ziran* refers to natural, instantaneous, and nonreflective responses. In a fundamental fashion, this almost magical ability to spontaneously accomplish all without seeming to exert any deliberate action is frequently associated with a great deal of inner power.

11. "Myriad creatures" (*wanwu*) is a classical Daoist term for everything in existence.

12. Yin and yang are the two fundamental Chinese cosmological principles and forces. They form patterns of interrelationship in the transformative process that is the universe. There are various associations. The yin modality is dark, obscure, feminine, and receptive; the yang modality is bright, clear, masculine, and assertive.

13. My translations are often indebted to those of Graham 1981 but diverge in the priority I give to understanding the contemplative experiences underlying the passages that I have selected. I have utilized the Chinese text contained in Lau 2000.

that there is something genuinely in command; the only trouble is we cannot find a sign of it. That as "Way" it can be walked is true enough; but we do not see its shape; it has identity but no shape. . . . If we seek without success to grasp what its identity might be, that neither adds to nor detracts from its genuineness. (Chinese text in Lau 2000, 2/4/1–4; see also Graham 1981, 51)

Huainanzi (Book of the Huainan Masters)[14]

1.1

As for the Way:
It covers Heaven and upholds Earth.
It extends the four directions
and divides the eight end points.
So high, it cannot be reached.
So deep, it cannot be fathomed.
It embraces and enfolds Heaven and Earth;
It endows and bestows the Formless.
Flowing along like a wellspring, bubbling up like a font,
it is empty but gradually becomes full.
Roiling and boiling,
it is murky but gradually becomes clear.
Therefore,
Pile it up vertically: it fills all within Heaven and Earth.
Stretch it out horizontally: it encompasses all within the Four Seas.
Unwind it limitlessly: it is without distinction between dawn and dusk.
Roll it out: it expands to the six coordinates.
Roll it up: it does not make a handful.
It is constrained but able to extend.
It is dark but able to brighten.
It is supple but able to strengthen.
It is pliant but able to become firm.
It stretches out the four binding cords and restrains yin and yang.
It suspends the cosmic rafters and displays the Three Luminaries.[15]
Intensely saturating and soaking,
Intensely subtle and minute.
Mountains are high because of it.
Abysses are deep because of it.

---

14. All translations from the *Huainanzi* are from Major et al. 2010, with slight modifications for consistency of translation. Specific passage translators are indicated in the parenthetical references and notes. References are given to the Chinese text in Lau 1992 in the form chapter/page/line. Three literary forms are indicated by indentation: block prose is flush left; parallel prose is indented; poetry is further indented.

15. The Three Luminaries (*sanming*) usually refer to the sun, moon, and stars.

Beasts can run because of it.
Birds can fly because of it.
The sun and moon are bright because of it.
The stars and timekeepers move because of it.
*Qilin*s wander freely because of it.[16]
Phoenixes soar because of it.
(Chinese text in Lau 1992, 1/1/3–8; Roth in Major et al. 2010, 48–49)

Inner Cultivation: Theory and Techniques

Neiye (Inward Training)

Verse VIII

If you can be aligned and tranquil,
Only then can you be stable.
With a stable mind at your core,
With the eyes and ears acute and clear,
And with the four limbs firm and fixed,
You can thereby make a lodging place for the vital essence.
The vital essence: it is the essence of the vital energy.
When the vital energy is guided, the vital essence is generated,
But when it is generated there is thought.
When there is thought, there is knowledge,
But when there is knowledge there is a cessation.
Whenever the forms of the mind are filled with knowledge,
You lose the ability to generate the vital essence.
(SBCK 16/2a9–2b1; Roth 1999a, 60)

Verse XI

When your body is not aligned,
Inner power will not come.
When you are not tranquil within
Your mind will not be in order.
Align your body, summon your inner power,
Then it will come cascading on its own.
(SBCK 16/2b6–8; Roth 1999a, 66)

---

16. Sometimes translated as "unicorn," the *Qilin* is a mythological Chinese creature.

Verse XIII

There is a spirit naturally residing within you;[17]
One moment it goes, the next it comes,
And no one is able to conceive of it.
If you lose it, you are inevitably disordered;
If you attain it, you are inevitably well-ordered.
Diligently clean out its lodging place
And its vital essence will naturally arrive.
Still your attempts to imagine and conceive of it.
Relax your efforts to reflect on and control it.
Be reverent and diligent
And its vital essence will naturally stabilize.
Grasp it and don't let go
Then the eyes and ears won't overflow
And the mind will have nothing else to seek for.
When a properly aligned mind resides in your center,
The myriad things will be seen in their proper perspective.
(SBCK 16/2b9–3a1; Roth 1999a, 70)

Verse XVII

For all [to practice] this Way
You must coil, you must contract,
You must uncoil, you must expand,[18]
You must be firm, you must be regular [in the practice].
Hold fast to this excellent [practice]; do not let go of it.
Chase away the excessive [perception]; abandon trivial [thoughts].
And when you reach its ultimate limit
You will return to the Way and its inner power.
(SBCK 16/3b6–8; Roth 1999a, 78)

Verse XIX

By concentrating your vital energy as if numinous,
The myriad things will all be contained within you.

---

17. Spirit (*shen*) has many potential meanings. In the context of the *Neiye*, it appears to be an animating force and/or a numinous presence. From a traditional Chinese perspective, it is the spiritual faculty associated with the physical heart and consciousness in a more abstract sense. For some of my reflections on translating technical terms in the *Neiye*, see Roth 1999a.

18. From my perspective, these lines refer to specific types of breath-regulation methods. Alternatively, they may refer to the practice of Daoyin (lit., "guiding and pulling"), that is, stretching and breath-work aimed at health, healing, and/or longevity. See, for example, Harper 1998.

Can you concentrate? Can you unite with them?
Can you not resort to divining by tortoise or milfoil[19]
Yet know bad and good fortune?
Can you stop? Can you cease?
Can you not seek it in others,
Yet attain it within yourself?
You think and think
And think further about this.
You think, yet still cannot penetrate it.
The ghostly and numinous will penetrate it.
It is not due to the power of the ghostly and numinous,
But to the utmost refinement of your essential vital energy.
When the four limbs are aligned[20]
And the blood and vital energy are tranquil,
Unify your awareness, concentrate your mind.
Then your eyes and ears will not be overstimulated.
And even the far-off will seem to be close at hand.
(SBCK 16/4a2–7; Roth 1999a, 82)

Laozi (Book of Venerable Masters)

Chapter 16

Attaining emptiness is the apogee [of our practice];
Holding fast to the center is its governing mode.[21]
The myriad things arise side by side
And residing here, I see them slowly return.
The forms of the heavens are great in number
But each returns to its root.
Returning to the root is called tranquility;
Tranquility is called returning to life-destiny.

---

19. As mentioned in my introduction herein, this posture probably involved sitting on the heels in a manner paralleling the more familiar Japanese *seiza* posture. One would presumably align the shoulders with the hips, and the hands probably rested on the lap. Such conjecture is based on contemporaneous archaeological materials. See, for example, Harper 1995. For my discussion of the "Fourfold Aligning" as a central dimension of inward training see Roth 1999a.

20. Ancient Chinese divination, especially associated with the Shang dynasty, involved the use of tortoise shells (plastromancy), ox scapula (scapulomancy), and milfoil (yarrow stalks). Sometimes the former are referred to as "pyromancy" (divination by fire) because both methods involved heating with fire until cracks formed. In the present context, Daoists seem to be suggesting that one does not need formal divination practices, as everything will become clear and/or accepted through inner cultivation.

21. "Holding fast to the Center" translates *shouzhong*, which is also rendered as "guarding the Center." Parallel technical names for Daoist apophatic meditation include "embracing the One" (*baoyi*; LZ 10, 22) and "guarding the One" (*shouyi*; NY 9, 19, 24 and ZZ 11). The latter term became a general name for Daoist meditation in the later tradition. See Kohn 1989; Komjathy 2013b.

Returning to life-destiny is called constancy;
Knowing constancy is called illumination.

Chapter 48

In the pursuit of learning we increase every day,
But in the pursuit of the Way we decrease every day.
We decrease and further decrease until we reach the point of non-action.[22]
Through non-action, nothing is left undone.

Chapter 56

Those who understand it[23] do not talk about it; those who talk about it do not understand it.
    Block the openings;
    Shut the doors;
    Blunt the sharpness;
    Untangle the knots;
    Soften the glare;
    Let your wheels move only along old ruts.[24]
    This is known as profound merging.[25]

Chapter 10

Amid the psychic turmoil [of daily living][26]
Can you embrace the One (*baoyi*) and not let go?
In concentrating your vital energy
Can you become as supple as a babe?
Can you wash clean your mysterious mirror
And leave no blemish?

---

22. Nonaction (*wuwei*) is a classical Daoist principle and practice. It may be understood as effortless activity, noninterventionism and noninterference, as well as doing nothing extra. From a classical and foundational perspective, the *practice* of *wuwei* leads to the *state* of *ziran*, or naturalness.

23. That is, "Those who understand the following saying . . ."

24. This line seems to suggest effortlessness. At the same time, one might read it as a directive to follow patterns established by one's elders, community, and tradition.

25. Also translated as "mysterious pervasion," "profound merging" (*xuantong*) refers, first and foremost, to a state of mystical union with the Dao. As I have suggested elsewhere (Roth 2000b and 2010), there is an introvertive dimension (meditative absorption) and an extrovertive dimension (embodied being-in-the-world). One expression of the latter is the transformative and beneficial influence of sages (*shengren*).

26. This line more literally reads, "In carrying the *ying* and *po* . . ." Various commentators interpret the line differently. One of the more influential readings comes from Heshang gong (Master Dwelling-by-the-River) who suggests that *ying* refers to *hun* ("ethereal soul"). This would mean that the line is referring to the ancient Chinese "two-soul model," namely, that of the ethereal soul or yang-ghost (*hun*), associated with the liver, dreaming, and postmortem ancestral identity, and the corporeal soul or yin-ghost (*po*), associated with the lungs, emotionality, and postmortem corporeal decay. In any case, the method seems to be advocating psychosomatic harmonization and integration.

Can you love the people and govern the state
Without resorting to action?
When the Gates of Heaven open and shut[27]
Are you capable of keeping to the role of the female?
As your discernment penetrates the four quarters
Are you capable of doing so without [dualistic] knowing?

It gives them life and rears them.
It gives them life yet claims no possession;
It benefits them yet exacts no gratitude;
It is the steward yet exercises no authority.
Such is called profound inner power.[28]

Zhuangzi (Book of Master Zhuang)

Chapter 2

Wherever we walk how can the Way be absent? Whatever the standpoint, how can a hypothesis be unallowable? The Way is hidden by formation of the lesser; saying is darkened by its foliage and flowers. And so we have the "That's it" and "That's not" of the Confucians and Mohists, by which what is *it* [true] for one of them for the other is not, and what is *not* [false] for one of them for the other is *it* [true]. If you wish to affirm what they deny and deny what they affirm, the best means is illumination (*ming*).

No thing is not Other; no thing is not It. If you treat yourself as Other,[29] they do not appear. . . . This is why sages[30] . . . open things to the lucid light of Heaven; theirs too is a flowing cognition.[31] (Chinese text in Lau 2000, 2/4/12–14; see also Graham 1981, 52)

---

27. There are various interpretations of the "Gates of Heaven" (*tianmen*). On the most basic level, as the head is associated with "heaven," it may refer to the nostrils (gate of breath) and/or to the senses (gate of perception). A more esoteric Daoist reading identifies the location as the crown-point (gate of celestial *qi*). In any case, the method emphasizes passivity and receptivity.

28. Profound inner power (*xuande*) is a specific quality and presence developed through Daoist inner cultivation. As *xuan* is associated with the Dao itself, it appears that this is a state wherein one has merged with the Dao and become infused with its numinous presence.

29. The author is recommending a profound form of detachment from one's ego in which the various thoughts and feelings that constitute it have no more emotional hold on a person than the thoughts and feelings of other people.

30. Sages (*shengren*) are the ideal of classical Daoism, the exemplar of inner cultivation. They are the highest-level practitioners who have become embodiments of the Dao in the world. The classical Daoist textual corpus contains various descriptions of their qualities.

31. As I have suggested elsewhere (Roth 2000b and 2010), flowing cognition (*yinshi*) involves spontaneously and effortlessly responding to any situation in an adaptive and beneficial way. This is the "extrovertive" or embodied expression of the "introvertive" or contemplative practice and experience.

Chapter 4

[Confucius[32] addressed Yan Hui, saying,]
"Unify your attention;
Rather than listening with your ears, listen with your mind;
Rather than listening with your mind, listen with your breathing (*qi*);
Listening stops at the ears; the mind stops at what it can objectify;
As for your breathing, it becomes empty and waits to respond to things.
The Way gathers in emptiness.
Emptiness is attained through the fasting of the mind (*xinzhai*)."[33]

[Yan Hui responded,] "When I have never yet been the agent of an action, suddenly an action emerges from me. After I have acted, there has never begun to be a 'Hui.'[34] Is this what you mean?"

[Confucius responded,] "Perfect! I shall tell you. . . . It is easy to stop walking, but much more difficult to walk without touching the ground.[35] What has humanity for an agent is easily falsified, what has Heaven for an agent is hard to falsify. You have heard of using wings to fly. You have not yet heard of flying by being wingless; you have heard of using the wits to know, you have not yet heard of using ignorance to know." (Chinese in Lau 2000, 4/9/25–10/9; see also Graham 1981, 68–69)

Chapter 6

[Yan Hui:] "I'm making progress."
[Confucius:] "In what way?"
[Yan Hui:] "I have forgotten about Ritual and Music."[36]
[Confucius:] "Ok: but you still have a long way to go."
On another day he saw Confucius again.
[Yan Hui:] "I'm making progress."
[Confucius:] "In what way?"

---

32. Kongzi (Master Kong; "Confucius"), the nominal founder of the social philosophy associated with him, "Confucianism," is frequently and ironically used as a subject of narratives in the *Zhuangzi*. Here he expresses the teaching of Zhuang Zhou. Yan Hui was one of Confucius's senior disciples, often identified as his favorite.

33. "Fasting of the mind" (*xinzhai*) is one of the classical Daoist technical terms for what I am referring to as "apophatic meditation," that is, a contemplative method that is primarily contentless, nonconceptual, and nondualistic. It involves emptying and stilling the heart-mind, the psychological center of human personhood, of emotional and intellectual activity.

34. Here Yan Hui perfectly expresses the Daoist ideal of spontaneous action in one moment and not objectifying that action in the next. This keeps one rooted in the present moment. He also enters into a transpersonal state, wherein he is freed from the limitations of separate identity.

35. That is, becoming empty is easy; flowing cognition is hard. The apophatic emptying of consciousness is easy; flowing cognition is hard.

36. Ritual and Music as well as the subsequent Benevolence and Rectitude are key Confucian values and concerns.

[Yan Hui:] "I have forgotten all about Benevolence and Rectitude."
[Confucius:] "Ok: but you still have a long way to go."
On another day he saw Confucius again.
[Yan Hui:] "I'm making progress."
[Confucius:] "In what way?"
[Yan Hui:] "I just sit and forget."[37]
[Confucius:] "What do you mean by 'sitting and forgetting'?"
[Yan Hui:] "I let organs and members drop away,[38] dismiss eyesight and hearing,[39] part from the body and expel knowledge,[40] and merge with the Great Pervader.[41] This is what I mean by 'sitting and forgetting.'" (Chinese text in Lau 2000, 6/19/17–21; see also Graham 1981, 92)

Xinshu shang (Techniques of the Mind I)[42]

I

[Basic Text]
The position of the mind in the body
[Is analogous to] the position of the ruler [in the state].
The functioning of the nine apertures
[Is analogous to] the responsibilities of the officials.
> When the mind keeps to its Way,
> The nine apertures will comply with their inherent patterns.[43]

---

37. "Sitting and forgetting" (*zuowang*), also translated as "sitting-in-forgetfulness," is one of the classical Daoist technical terms for what I am referring to as "apophatic meditation," that is, a contemplative method that is primarily contentless, nonconceptual, and nondualistic. One practices forgetting until even forgetting is forgotten. Interestingly, in the later Daoist tradition, Sima Chengzhen (647–735), the twelfth Shangqing (Highest Clarity) Patriarch, wrote a text partially inspired by this passage in the *Zhuangzi*. This is the famous and influential *Zuowang lun* (Discourse on Sitting-in-Forgetfulness; DZ 1036). See Kohn 1987.

38. To let "organs and members drop away" (*duo zhi ti*) means to lose visceral awareness of the emotions and desires, which, for the members of the early Daoist inner cultivation lineages, have "physiological" bases in the various organs.

39. To "dismiss eyesight and hearing" (*chu cong ming*) means to deliberately disengage sense perception.

40. To "part from the body and expel knowledge" (*lixing quzhi*) means to lose bodily awareness and remove all thoughts from consciousness.

41. To "merge with the Great Pervader" (*tong yu datong*), also translated as "great pervasion," seems to imply that, as a result of these practices, Yan Hui has become united with the Dao.

42. All *Guanzi* references are to the *Sibu congkan* edition (SBCK). See also Lau 2001. Translations are based on my unpublished manuscript. Emendations are taken from Hsü Wei-yü, Wen I-to, and Kuo Mo-jo's *Guanzi jijiao* (*Kuan-tzu chi-chiao*) (Peking: Chung-hua, 1955), 633–49.

43. This means that the sense organs will function properly and spontaneously if they are not interfered with by the mind. This occurs because each has an inherent pattern of activity that derives from its individual characteristics and its relation to the whole body. In texts of this period, *li* is often translated as "patterns" or "inherent patterns." However, "patterns" in English has a stronger determinative force than does *li*. A pattern is a regular form or order (e.g., behavioral pattern) and suggests that things or activities must conform to it exactly with little room for individual variation. *Li* admits of freedom within structure; the *li* guide the spontaneous responses that develop from the natures of things. It is important to remember this whenever "inherent patterns" appears.

> When lusts and desires fill the mind to overflowing,
> The eyes do not see colors, the ears do not hear sounds.
> When the one above departs from the Way,
> The ones below will lose sight of their tasks.

Therefore we say, "The Techniques of the Mind are to take no action and yet control the apertures." (SBCK 13/1a5–8)

[Commentary]
The position of the mind in the body
[Is analogous to] the position of the ruler [in the state].
The functioning of the nine apertures
[Is analogous to] the responsibilities of the officials.

The eyes and ears are the organs of seeing and hearing. When the mind does not interfere with the tasks of seeing and hearing, the organs will be able to keep to their duties.
When the mind has desires, things pass by and the eyes do not see them; sounds are there, but the ears do not hear them. Therefore [the statement] says:

> When the one above departs from the Way,
> The ones below will lose sight of their tasks.

Therefore [the statement] calls the mind "ruler."
(SBCK 13/2a7–2b1)

Huainanzi (Book of the Huainan Masters)

1.8

> Therefore,
> Those who penetrate the Way return to clarity and tranquility.[44]
> Those who look deeply into things end up not competing with them. If you use calmness to nourish your nature, and use quietude to stabilize your spirit, then you will enter the Heavenly Gateway.[45]
> What we call "Heavenly"
> > Is to be pure and untainted,
> > Unadorned and plain.

---

44. "Clarity and tranquility" (*qingjing*), also translated as "clarity and stillness," is a central characteristic of classical Daoist inner cultivation and a major connective strand throughout the Daoist tradition. For example, it appears as one of the Nine Practices in early Tianshi (Celestial Masters) Daoism and part of the title of the highly influential eighth-century *Qingjing jing* (Scripture on Clarity and Stillness; DZ 620), which was seminal in early Quanzhen (Complete Perfection) Daoism. See Komjathy 2007, 2008, and 2013b.

45. For the meaning of "Heavenly Gateway," also translated as "Gates of Heaven," see footnote 27. Here it is possible that the phrase refers to a deeper state of cosmological attunement, perhaps paralleling the Daoist concept of the "heavenly pivot" (*tianji*).

And to never begin to be tainted with impurities.
What we call "human"
>>Is to be biased because of wisdom and precedent.
>>Devious and deceptive,
It is what looks back to past ages and resorts to the vulgar. . . .
Thus sages
>>Do not allow the human to obscure the heavenly
>>And do not let desire confuse their genuine responses.
>>They hit the mark without scheming;
>>They are sincere without speaking;
>>They attain without planning;
>>They complete without striving.

Their vital essence circulates to the Numinous Storehouse,[46] and they become human along with that which fashions and transforms them. (Chinese text in Lau 1992, 1/4/8–10; Roth in Major et al. 2010, 57–58)

1.9

Therefore,
>>Sages internally cultivate the root [of the Way within them]
>>And do not externally adorn themselves with its branches.
>>They protect their quintessential spirit[47]
>>And dispense with wisdom and precedent.
>>In stillness they take no deliberate action, yet there is nothing left undone.
>>In tranquility they do not try to govern, but nothing is left ungoverned.
>>What we call "no deliberate action" is not to anticipate the activity of things.
>>What we call "nothing left undone" means to adapt to what things have [already] done.
>>What we call "not to govern" means not to change how things are naturally so.
>>What we call "nothing left ungoverned" means to adapt to how things are mutually so.
>>The myriad things all have a source from which they arise;
>>[The sages] alone understand how to guard this root.
>>The hundred endeavors all have a source from which they are produced;
>>[The sages] alone understand how to guard this gateway.
>>Thus exhausting the inexhaustible,
>>Reaching the limit of the infinite,
>>Illuminating things without bedazzling them,
>>And inexhaustibly responding to things like an echo [responds to sound]:

This is what we call "being released by Heaven." (Chinese text in Lau 1992, 1/4/18–26; Roth in Major et al. 2010, 59–60)

---

46. Numinous Storehouse (*lingfu*) often refers to the heart, which is associated with spirit (*shen*). However, as the *Huainanzi* emphasizes vital essence, here it most likely refers to the kidneys.

47. "Quintessential spirit" translates *jingshen*, which often appear separately as "vital essence" (*jing*) and "spirit" (*shen*). In the *Huainanzi*, *jingshen* refers to the specific vital essence associated with spirit, the fount of awareness of the Way.

2.13

>Tranquility and calmness are that by which innate nature is nourished.
>Harmony and vacuity are that by which inner power is nurtured.
>When what is external does not disturb what is internal, then our innate nature attains what is suitable to it.
>When the harmony of innate nature is not disturbed, then inner power will rest securely in its position.
>Nurturing life so as to order the age,
>Embracing so as to complete our years,

This may be called being able to embody the Way.
Those who are like this:

>Their blood and pulse have no sluggishness or stagnation;
>Their five orbs have no diseased vital energy;[48]
>Calamity and good fortune cannot perturb them;
>Blame and praise cannot settle on them like dust;

Thus can they reach the ultimate. [However,] if you do not have the age, how can you succeed? If you have the right character but do not meet your time, you will not even be able to safeguard your person. How much less so one who is without the Way! (Chinese text in Lau 1992, 2/17/8–11; Roth and Meyer in Major et al. 2010, 103–4)

7.4

>The apertures of perception [eyes and ears] are the portals of the quintessential spirit.
>The vital energy and attention are the emissaries and servants of the five orbs.
>When the eyes and ears are enticed by the joys of sound and color, then the five orbs oscillate and are not stable.
>When the five orbs oscillate and are not stable, then the blood and vital energy are agitated and not at rest.
>When the blood and vital energy are agitated and not at rest, then the quintessential spirit courses out [through the eyes and ears] and is not preserved.
>When the quintessential spirit courses out and is not preserved, then when either good fortune or misfortune arrives, although it be the size of hills and mountains, one has no way to recognize it.

But

>If you make your ears and eyes totally clear and profoundly penetrating and not enticed by external things;
>If your vital energy and attention are empty, tranquil, still, and serene and you eliminate lusts and desires;

---

48. The five orbs (*wuzang*), also translated as "five yin-organs," correspond to the five organs of the human physiology that were thought to be critical generative and coordinating junctures for the dynamic matrix of *qi* that composed the mind-body system: liver, heart, spleen, lungs, and kidneys. Sometimes the gallbladder replaces the heart, with the latter considered the "ruler." The five orbs refer to organic systems, not just to the physical viscera; hence we speak of the hepatic, pulmonary, splenic, choleric, and renal orbs.

> If the five orbs are stable, reposed, replete, and full and not leaking [the vital energies];
> If your quintessential spirit is preserved within your physical frame and does not flow out;
>
> Then even gazing back beyond bygone ages and looking further than things that are to come; even these things would not be worth doing, much less discriminating between bad and good fortune.
>
> Therefore it is said, "The farther you go, the less you know."[49] This says that the quintessential spirit cannot be allowed to be enticed by external things.... (Chinese text in Lau 1992, 7/55/27–7/56/8; Roth in Major et al. 2010, 244)

11.6

> For this reason, whenever one is about to take up an affair, one must first stabilize one's awareness and purify one's spirit.
>
> > When the spirit is pure and awareness is stable
> > Only then can things be aligned ...
> > One who is suffused with grief will cry upon hearing a song;
> > One suffused with joy will see someone weeping and laugh.
> > That grief can bring joy
> > And laughter can bring grief—
>
> Being suffused makes it so. For this reason, value emptiness.
> (Chinese text in Lau 1992, 11/96/6–9; Meyer in Major et al. 2010, 405)

14.22

> > The sage has no conscious deliberations;
> > He has no fixed ideas.
> > He neither welcomes what arrives
> > Nor sends off what departs.
> > Though others occupy positions north, south, east, and west,
> > he alone is established at the center. . . .
>
> Thus,
> > He does not encourage what he likes,
> > Nor does he avoid what he dislikes;
> > He simply follows Heaven's Way.[50]
> > He does not initiate,
> > Nor does he personally assume authority;
> > He simply complies with Heaven's Patterns.
> > (Chinese text in Lau 1992, 14/135/10–14; Queen in Major et al. 2010, 547)

---

49. This line is also found in chapter 47 of the *Laozi*.

50. "Heaven's Way" (*tiandao*), also translated as the "Way of Heaven," refers to the universe as transformative process, and cosmological attunement by extension. According to this cosmological model of Daoist cultivation, one aligns oneself with the larger patterns of yin-yang and the Five Phases, specifically the seasons. Interestingly, chapter 13 of the *Zhuangzi* is titled "The Way of Heaven." See also chapters 15 and 23. In the later Daoist tradition, a key discussion appears in the sixth-century *Yinfu jing* (Scripture on the Hidden Talisman; DZ 31). See Komjathy 2008, Handbook 7.

Contemplative States: Transient yet Transformative

Xinshu shang (Techiniques of the Mind I)

III. Verse and *Internal Commentary*

The Way is not distant yet it is difficult to reach its limit.
The Way is located within the Heavens and the Earth.
So vast, there is nothing outside it.
So minute, there is nothing inside it.
This means there is no gap between them.
It dwells together with human beings yet it is difficult to find.
Only the sage is able to find this empty Way.
If you empty out your desires,
The spirit will enter its lodging.
If you sweep out what is impure,
The spirit will stay in its dwelling.
> *What the sage controls is the concentration of his vital energy.*
> *When you get rid of desires, you become expansive.*
> *When you are expansive, you become tranquil.*
> *When you are tranquil, then your vital energy will be concentrated.*
> *When it is concentrated then it [your mind] will attain complete solitude.*
> *When it attains complete solitude, it will be illumined.*
> *When it is illumined, then it will be spirit-like.*
> *The spirit is the most honored one.*
> *Therefore, if the chamber is not cleaned out,*
> *Then the honored one will not lodge there.*[51]
> (SBCK 13/1a10–12, 2b5–10)

Zhuangzi (Book of Master Zhuang)

Chapter 6

[The Crooked-Backed Woman began describing her training of Buliang Yi:] "After I taught him for three days: he was able to put the world outside him; after seven days: he could put the things we live on outside him; after nine days: he could put life itself outside him. And then he could: 'break through to the Brightness of Dawn, could be without past and present, could enter the undying and the unliving.' That which kills off the living does not die; that which gives birth to the living has never been born. As for the sort of thing it is, it is there to escort whatever departs, is here to welcome whatever comes, it ruins everything and brings everything about. Its name is 'At home where it intrudes.' . . ." (Chinese text in Lau 2000, 6/17/11–20; see also Graham 1981, 87)

---

51. Here the "honored one" may refer to spirit, with the "lodging place" being the heart. Alternatively, it could refer to vital energy (navel region) or vital essence (kidneys).

Huainanzi (Book of the Huainan Masters)

1.14

> Joy and anger are aberrations from the Way;
> worry and grief are losses of inner power.
> Likes and dislikes are excesses of the mind;
> lusts and desires are hindrances to nature.
>> Violent anger ruins the yin;
>> extreme joy collapses the yang.
>> The suppression of vital energy brings on dumbness;
>> fear and terror bring on madness.
>> When you are worried, aggrieved, or enraged,
>> sickness will increasingly develop.
>> When likes and dislikes abundantly pile up,
>> misfortunes will successively follow.
>
> Thus,
>> when the mind is not worried or happy, it achieves the perfection of inner power.
>> When the mind is inalterably expansive, it achieves the perfection of tranquility.
>> When lusts and desires do not burden the mind, it achieves the perfection of emptiness.
>> When the mind is without likes and dislikes, it achieves the perfection of equanimity.
>> When the mind is not tangled up in things, it achieves the perfection of purity.
>
> If the mind is able to achieve these five qualities, then it will break through to spirit-like illumination.[52] To break through to spirit-like illumination is to realize what is intrinsic.
> Therefore,
>> if you use the internal to govern the external,
>> then your various endeavors will not fail.
>> If you are able to realize internally,
>> then the external can be attended to.
>> If you realize it internally,
>> then your five orbs will be in repose;
>> worries and anxieties will be at peace.
>> Your sinews will be powerful, and your muscles will be strong;
>> your ears and eyes will be acute and clear.

---

52. "Spirit-like illumination" (*shenming*), also translated as "spiritual illumination" and "divine radiance," refers to a state of consciousness wherein one is infused with the Dao. Associated with spirit (*shen*) and the mind (*xin*), it is transpersonal and characterized by clarity and stillness, perhaps even actual luminosity.

Though you are placid and calm, you do not waver.
Though you are hard and strong, you do not break.
There is nothing you overshoot
and nothing you fall short of.
When you dwell in the small, you will not be cramped;
when you dwell in the great, you will be unrestrained.
Your soul will not be agitated;
your spirit will not be troubled.
Clear and limpid, still and calm,
you will become a hero to the entire world.
(Chinese text in Lau 1992, 1/7/4–11; Roth in Major et al. 2010, 66–68)

Contemplative Traits: Long-Lasting Benefits

Neiye (Inward Training)

Verse XV

For those who preserve and naturally generate vital essence,
On the outside a calmness will flourish.
Stored within, we take it to be the wellspring.
Flood-like, it harmonizes and equalizes
And we take it to be the fount of the vital energy.
When the fount is not dried up,
The four limbs are firm.
When the wellspring is not drained,
Vital energy freely circulates through the nine apertures.
You can then exhaust the heavens and the earth
And spread over the four seas.
When you internally have no delusions,
Externally there will be no disasters.
Those who internally keep their minds unimpaired,
Externally keep their bodies unimpaired,
Who do not encounter heavenly disasters,
Nor meet with harm at the hands of others,
Call them sages.
(SBCK 16/3a8–b1; Roth 1999a, 74)

Verse XVI

If people can be aligned and tranquil,
Their skin will be ample and smooth,
Their ears and eyes will be acute and clear,
Their muscles will be supple and their bones will be strong.

They will then be able to hold up the Great Circle of the Heavens
And tread firmly over the Great Square of the Earth.
They will mirror things with great purity.
And will perceive things with great clarity.
Reverently be aware of the Way and do not waver,
And you will daily renew your inner power,
Thoroughly understand all under Heaven,
And exhaust everything within the Four Directions.
To reverently manifest the effulgence of the Way:
This is called "grasping it within."
If you do this but fail to return to it,
This will cause a wavering in your vitality.
(SBCK 16/3b1–5; Roth 1999a, 76)

Laozi (Book of Venerable Masters)

Chapter 22

Bowed down then preserved;
Bent then straight;
Hollow then full;
Worn then new;
A little then benefited;
A lot then perplexed.

Therefore sages embrace the One (*baoyi*) and are models for the empire.
They do not show themselves, and so are conspicuous;
They do not consider themselves right, and so are illustrious;
They do not brag, and so have merit;
They do not boast, and so endure.
It is because they do not contend that no one in the empire is in a position to contend with them.
The way the ancients had it, "Bowed down then preserved," is no empty saying.
Truly it enables one to be preserved to the end.

Chapter 15

Of old those who manifested the Way
Were minutely subtle and profoundly pervasive,
They were too deep to be known.
Because they could not be known,
We can only give a makeshift description:
Tentative, as if fording a river in winter;
Cautious, as if in fear of neighbors;
Solemn, like guests;
Melting, like thawing ice;

Undifferentiated, like the Uncarved Block (*pu*);[53]
Vast, like a valley;
Murky, like muddy water.

When muddy water is made tranquil, it gradually becomes clear.
When the calm is made active, it gradually springs to life.
Those who embrace this Way
Do not wish to become full.
It is only because they do not wish to become full
That they can wear out and yet be newly made.

Zhuangzi (Book of Master Zhuang)

Chapter 2

"What is It is also Other; what is Other is also It." Therefore someone says, "This is true, that's false" from one point of view; here we say "That's true, this is false," from another point of view. Are there really It and Other? Or really no It and Other? Where neither It nor Other finds its opposite is called the Axis of the Way. Once the axis is found at the center of the circle, there is no limit to responding with either, on the one hand no limit to what is It, and, on the other, no limit to what is not. Therefore I say: "The best means is illumination (*ming*)." (Chinese text in Lau 2000, 2/4/18–20; see also Graham 1981, 53)

Chapter 2

To wear out your wits fixating on one way of seeing things without realizing that it's really no different from any other, we call "three every morning." A monkey keeper handing out nuts said, "Three every morning and four every evening." The monkeys were all in a rage. "All right then," he said, "Four every morning and three every evening." The monkeys were all delighted. Without either the name or the reality [of the nuts] being at all diminished, the monkeys' pleasure and anger were utilized by the keeper: his cognition, indeed, was flowing cognition. Therefore, sages harmonize things with their flowing cognition and relax into the center of the Potter's Wheel of the Heavens.[54] This is what we call "activating both positions." (Chinese text in Lau 2000, 2/5/3–6; see also Graham 1981, 54)

Chapter 2

Last night Zhuang Zhou dreamed he was a butterfly, spirits soaring he was a butterfly, and he did not know about Zhou. When all of a sudden he awoke, he was Zhou with all his wits about

---

53. Or, "unadorned simplicity." The *locus classicus* of this technical term is *Laozi* 19 and 28, in which it signifies a condition of undifferentiated selflessness and desirelessness. Interestingly, the phrase "embracing simplicity" (*baopu*; LZ 19) became the Daoist name of Ge Hong (287–347), the early medieval Daoist external alchemist and systematizer of the Taiqing (Great Clarity) movement.

54. The "Potter's Wheel of the Heavens" (*tianjun*) refers to the universe as transformative process, with the corresponding power of formation.

him. Now he does not know whether he was Zhou who dreamt he was a butterfly or a butterfly who is dreaming he is Zhou. Between Zhou and the butterfly there must be some dividing: just this is what is meant by the transformation of things. (Chinese text in Lau 2000, 2/7/21–23; see also Graham 1981, 61)

Chapter 3

What your humble servant is fond of is the Way: I have distanced myself from all thoughts of "skill." When I first began to butcher oxen I saw nothing but oxen wherever I looked. After three years I stopped seeing the ox as a whole. These days your humble servant is guided by the intuitive spirit in me and I don't even [deliberately] use my eyes to see; my senses know where to stop and then loose the intuitive drive from within me. I rely completely on the Patterns of Heaven,[55] I cleave along the main seams, I am guided by the great cavities, I go along with what is inherently so. . . . That's why after nineteen years the edge of my cleaver is as fresh as though it were just sharpened on the grindstone. (Chinese text in Lau 2000, 3/8/4–7; see also Graham 1981, 63–64)

Huainanzi (Book of the Huainan Masters)

7.7

Those whom we call the Perfected are people whose inborn nature is merged with the Way.
Therefore,
> They possess it but appear to have nothing.
> They are full but appear to be empty.
> They are settled in this unity and do not know of any duality
> They cultivate what is inside and pay no attention to what is outside.
> They illuminate and clarify Grand Simplicity;
> Taking no action, they revert to the Unhewn.[56]

They embody the foundation and embrace the spirit in order to roam freely within the confines of Heaven and Earth.[57] Untrammeled, they ramble outside this dusty world and wander aimlessly in their taskless calling.[58] Unfettered and unhindered, they harbor no clever devices or cunning knowledge in their minds.

Thus death and life are great indeed, but they do not alter them. Although Heaven and Earth support and nourish, they are not protected by them. They discern the flawless and do not get mixed up with things. While seeing the chaos of affairs, they are able to preserve their origin.[59]

> Beings like these
> > negate obsession and fear

---

55. The "Patterns of Heaven" (*tianli*) refers to the cosmological cycles based on yin-yang and the Five Phases, especially as manifested in seasonal changes.
56. That is, the "Uncarved Block."
57. This line and the previous six are found almost verbatim in *Zhuangzi* 12/32/21–22.
58. This parallels *Zhuangzi* 6/18/21–22 and 19/52/20–21.
59. This parallels *Zhuangzi* 5/13/12–13.

and cast aside sensory perceptions.⁶⁰
Their mental activity is concentrated internally
and penetrates through to comport with the One.
> At rest, they have no objectives;
> in motion, they set no goals.
> Artlessly they go forth;
> peacefully they come back.
> Their bodies are like withered wood;
> their minds are like dead ashes.⁶¹
> They forget the five orbs;
> lose their physical frames;
> know without studying;
> see without looking;
> complete without acting;
> and differentiate without judging.

When stimulated, they respond;
when pressed, they move;
when it is unavoidable, they go forth,⁶²
like the brilliant glow of a flame,
like the mimicry of a shadow.

Taking the Way as their guiding thread, they are necessarily so. Embracing the foundation of Grand Purity, they contain nothing, and things cannot disturb them. Vast and empty, they are tranquil and without worry.

> Great marshes may catch fire, but it cannot burn them.
> Great rivers may freeze over, but it cannot chill them.
> Great thunder may shake the mountains, but it cannot startle them.⁶³
> Great storms may darken the sun, but it cannot harm them.

For this reason,
> they view precious pearls and jade as being the same as gravel.
> They view the supremely exalted and maximally favored [at court] as being the same as wandering guests [scholars].
> They view [the beauties] Mao Qiang and Xi Shi as being the same as funerary figurines.⁶⁴

---

60. For "obsession and fear," the Chinese text reads, literally, "liver and gall," but this actually refers to the negative mental states associated with the hepatic (liver) and choleric (gall bladder) orbs of *qi* within the human being. In the Chinese medical literature, these states are said to be "obsession" for the hepatic and "fear" for the choleric. See *Grand dictionnaire Ricci de la langue chinoise* (Paris: Institut Ricci, 2001), 6: 621. The corresponding phrase in the parallel line, "sensory perceptions," literally reads "ears and eyes."

61. The *locus classicus* for this vivid description of a profound state of tranquility attained through meditation is *Zhuangzi* 2/3/14.

62. These three lines parallel *Zhuangzi* 15/41/26–27.

63. These lines parallel *Zhuangzi* 2/6/17–18.

64. Mao Qiang and Xi Shi were famed beauties of Yue, credited with having helped to bring about the destruction of the state of Wu by distracting King Fuchai (r. 495–477 BCE) with their charms. Their names became emblematic of perfect feminine beauty.

> They take life and death to be a single transformation
> and the myriad things to be a single whole.
> They merge their vital essence with the Root of Great Purity
> and roam freely beyond the boundless.
> They have vital essence but do not [recklessly] expend it;
> and have spirit but do not [thoughtlessly] use it.
> They identify with the artlessness of the Great Unhewn
> and take their stand amid the supremely pure.

Thus,
> their sleep is dreamless;[65]
> their wisdom is traceless.
> Their corporeal soul does not sink;
> their ethereal soul does not soar.[66]

They repeatedly cycle from end to beginning, and we cannot know their starting and stopping points.
> They behold the dwelling place of Total Darkness
> and contemplate the lodging place of Total Brightness.
> They rest in the realms of the Unfettered
> and roam in the fields of the Nebulous.
> At rest, they have no appearance.
> In place, they have no location.
> In movement, they have no form.
> In stillness, they have no body.
> They are present yet seem to be absent.
> They are alive yet seem to be dead.
> They emerge from, and enter into, the Dimensionless[67]
> and employ ghostly spirits as their servants.

They plunge into the Fathomless
and enter the Nonexistent.
In order that their different forms evolve into one another,
> Ending and beginning like a circle,
> of which no one can trace an outline.

This is how their quintessential spirit is able to verge upon the Way; this is the roaming of the Perfected. (Chinese text in Lau 1992, 7/57/10–7/58/3; Roth in Major et al. 2010, 248–50)

---

65. The idea that the Perfected sleep without dreaming and wake without cares is found in *Zhuangzi* 6/16/2 and 15/41/29.

66. According to ancient beliefs, at death the *po* eventually sank into the ground, and the *hun* eventually rose into the sky. This text maintains that it is not the case for perfected human beings.

67. This alludes to *Laozi* 43: "The most flexible in the world can gallop through the most rigid: that which has no substance enters that which has no space."

Chapter 4

Quaker Silent Prayer

A Guide to True Peace

Michael Birkel

A Guide to True Peace is a brief Quaker text that promotes a contemplative form of silent prayer that is without conscious effort of thought or use of images. Written anonymously in English by two British Friends in 1813, this little book exerted a lasting influence on the Religious Society of Friends, or "Quakers" as they are better known.[1] Friends do not have monastic orders or ordained clergy with particular commitments to a specialized form of contemplative practice, so *A Guide to True Peace* was composed with the entire Quaker community in mind.

The *Guide* and Christian Quietism

Little historical record has been preserved of the two Friends who produced *A Guide to True Peace*. *A Guide to True Peace: Or, the Excellency of Inward and Spiritual Prayer* first appeared in 1813. Two British Quakers, William Backhouse (1779/1780–1844) and James Janson (1784–1821), edited the work. As the title page indicates, the work is "compiled chiefly from the writings of Fénelon, Archbishop of Cambray, Lady Guion [Guyon], and Michael de Molinos." Backhouse and Janson did their work anonymously; their names nowhere appear in the book. Anonymity was a frequent practice among Quakers, not so much as a way of avoiding public responsibility for one's work but rather as an expression of positively valuing collective identity and even a decentralized, nonhierarchical authority.

Backhouse and Janson were fairly successful in maintaining their anonymity, not only in producing this work but in larger life as well. Quakers at that time published an annual remembrance of Friends who died each year. In the *Annual Monitor for 1844, or Obituary of the Members of the Society of Friends in Great Britain and Ireland*, William Backhouse is described as follows:

> The character of this dear friend, can scarcely be more appropriately delineated, than in the language of our Holy Redeemer when he said concerning Nathaniel, "Behold an Israelite indeed in whom is no guile." Integrity and simplicity adorned his Christian walk; and in him the poor and afflicted found a faithful and sympathizing friend. . . . For many years he filled the station of Elder, but believing himself called upon to speak in the character of a Gospel Minister, he yielded to the impression, and was recorded as such, in the year 1842. (*Annual Monitor* 1844, 20–21)

It was the wider Quaker body that published the *Annual Monitor*. The more local body was known as the monthly meeting because it met monthly to conduct business related to church affairs. This smaller body recorded memorials, also called testimonies, of Friends who had died. The Testimony of the Darlington Monthly Meeting concerning William Backhouse notes that he compiled "in conjunction with his brother-in-law, James Janson, a small work entitled a 'Guide to True Peace,' extracted from the writings of Fenelon and other pious authors." These two small notices exhaust the known published materials concerning the editors of *A Guide to True Peace*.

More important than the particulars of the lives of these compilers is an understanding of the Quakerism of their time, whose spiritual ideals they represented, as evidenced particularly in the case of Backhouse since Friends publicly acknowledged him as an approved minister of the gospel.

Quakerism arose amid the great social, political, and religious experimentation of the era of the English Commonwealth, the Interregnum of the mid-seventeenth century.[2] This was a time of great social and religious freedom—some more conservative voices would say "anarchy"—and political revolution. England was undergoing a civil war as Puritan roundheads and the forces of the traditional gentry fought for control of the country. Religiously, there was great diversity. With regard to church structure, the extremes ranged from congregational autonomy to episcopal authority. Worship patterns varied from fully scripted liturgies to complete abandonment of familiar form. Theological variety was similarly wide-ranging. Amid all this excitement, the Religious Society of Friends (RSF), a form of Protestant Christianity,[3] had its birth.

Early Quakers are often classed among the religious radicals of Puritan England. They did away with hierarchy, clergy, formal ritual, and outward sacrament and instead focused on inward experience of the divine. Friends gathered for worship in silence, waiting and attending to one another in outward stillness until one or more discerned a leading to speak to the gathered worshipers. The content of such utterances was without plan or conscious preparation and was intended to minister to the spiritual condition of others who were present. Particularly upsetting to many of their contemporaries was the early Quaker conviction that women were as likely as men to serve in this way as ministers of the gospel. Quaker spirituality was characterized by its distinctive ethical ideals, which included a focus on human equality, on material simplicity and plainness, on honesty and integrity, and on nonviolence. The first generation of Quakers shared with other religious radicals the vision of remaking human society.

The earliest Friends got into trouble with local political and religious authorities for their views and practices, but this resistance hardened into state-sponsored persecution once the monarchy and the Church of England were reestablished in 1661. In the years that followed, most other radical groups vanished, but Quakers formed structures of community that enabled them to survive the transition from a popular but emerging movement to a recognizable institution. Friends also responded to persecution by maintaining their radical ethics yet also withdrawing from wider society. The early hopes for a restored society were exchanged for a quiet existence in some isolation from the larger world. Quakers were easily recognized by their "peculiarities" of dress and address. They wore plain, unadorned garments. Based on their belief in human equality, earliest Friends addressed all others, Quaker and other-than-Quaker, by the singular pronoun "thee" or "thou" rather than the plural "you" that was reserved for social superiors. By the early nineteenth century, "thee" and "thou" had mostly disappeared from English speech, though Quakers continued to use these forms, and this practice marked them as Quakers. Quakers were expected to marry only other Quakers. They established schools to educate their own children. As dissenters from the state church, they were barred from university training and particular professions. They tended to do business mostly with one another. Theirs was a separate existence in many ways, though in other dimensions of life Quakers were accepted and participative in wider affairs, such as in the exploration of the natural sciences. The English scientific association, the Royal Society, admitted Friends in numbers far larger than their percentage of the British population.

By the time of the publication of *A Guide to True Peace*, Quakers had lived in this relative religious isolation for over a century, but this situation was about to change. The tides of the wider religious world were about to sweep over Friends, including both liberal and evangelical modes of faith and practice. Quakers were soon to cooperate with others in philanthropic activity, as it was known in that day, such as in efforts to end slavery. In some ways, *A Guide to True Peace* reflects the older strains of eighteenth-century Quaker ideals, even as the book continued to exert a powerful influence throughout the nineteenth and twentieth centuries.[4]

Nineteenth-century Quakerism was in many ways a far cry from seventeenth-century Roman Catholicism. Although the practice of private, contemplative prayer could be very close, the political risks were quite different.

A Guide to True Peace is, in turn, indebted to Continental Quietism.[5] Quietism was a term imposed from the outside, the product of its opponents who based their understanding of it more on condemnations of positions attributed to this pious movement rather than on the texts composed by those within it. As with many so-called heresies, it was not an organized group of people, nor in fact was it a developed theology, and church authorities who accused others of Quietism often meant specific teachings that those called Quietists did not themselves hold.

The central idea of the Quietists was that a quiet, receptive frame of the soul was the highest form of spiritual practice. In order to attain this inward stillness, practitioners sought to let go of all conscious thought and activity. The intent was to renounce one's own will so that only the will of God remained. For some but not all, it seems, even the desire for salvation could be an obstacle to this perfect renunciation and indifference: one should be so yielded to God that one would be ready to be damned, if that were God's will. In this state of deep stillness, one could experience pure love and union with God.

Opponents saw these ideas as dangerous, especially for the spiritually "weak," who could be tempted to moral laxity or to pantheistic notions. Additionally, a spirituality that focused so much on interior states could feel threatening to institutional leaders because formal religious structures might appear expendable. Mystics in many traditions, as a result, have been viewed with suspicion by religious authorities.

As mentioned, *A Guide to True Peace* explicitly acknowledges the influence of and draws upon the earlier works of Molinos, Guyon, and Fénelon.[6] Miguel de Molinos (1628–1697) was born in a small village in Aragón in Spain. He eventually studied in Valencia, where he was first ordained as a Catholic priest and later earned a doctorate. He then moved to Rome, where he gained fame as a spiritual director and as the author of the *Guía espiritual* (Spiritual Guide), which was published in 1675. The Italian edition of the work, in accordance with prevailing custom, received the required ecclesiastical approval from members of the powerful religious orders: Jesuit, Franciscan, Capuchin, Carmelite, Dominican, and Trinitarian. Translations into Latin, French, German, Dutch, and English followed. Pope Innocent XI (Benedetto Odescalchi; 1611–1689; r. 1676–1689) numbered among his admirers, initially. It was a time of intense rivalry among practitioners of different forms of prayer, however, and Molinos's form of quiet, receptive prayer came under attack. Although Molinos grounded his work in earlier, approved mystics such as the German Johannes Tauler (ca. 1300–1361) and the Spaniard Juan de Yepes Alvarez (John of the Cross; 1542–1591), his writings were regarded as dangerously imprecise by some and fully heretical by others. In his trial, his accusers presented him with a lengthy list of propositions, ostensibly drawn from his teachings but not explicitly found in them. Molinos abjured these heretical statements and was pardoned, which saved him from execution, though the court still sentenced him to life imprisonment. Nine years later, in 1696, he died in a papal prison.

Teachers of contemplative modes of prayer fared no better in France at that time. Theological suspicion conspired with ecclesial and court intrigue against the French Quietists Jeanne Marie Bouvier de la Motte Guyon (1648–1717) and François de Salignac de la Mothe-Fénelon (1651–1715).[7] The two were close friends, and initially Guyon served as Fénelon's guide in the inward life.

Guyon was wed at age sixteen to a wealthy aristocrat of thirty-eight years. Twelve years of unhappiness followed, marked by misery and numerous deaths, finally including that of her husband. Widowed at twenty-eight, Guyon then remained a lay Catholic but devoted herself to the practice of contemplative prayer under the guidance of François La Combe (1640–1715), a priest of the Roman Catholic Barnabite order. Both Guyon and La Combe endured persecution as a result. By this time the French monarch, Louis XIV (1638–1715; r. 1643–1715), had declared his opposition to the Quietism of Molinos, and so both church and state joined forces to combat suspected heresies. Guyon had published *Moyen court et très facile pour l'oraison* (A Short and Very Easy Method of Prayer), which resulted in her arrest. She went on to write other important works and to further imprisonments, including one at the notorious fortress of Bastille. Her sufferings did not deter her commitment to the inward life. As Dianne Guenin-Lelle has astutely noted,

> Ironically it was her identity as a woman and as a layperson that allowed Guyon the freedom to perform a most subversive act that neither Molinos nor Fénelon as priests could undertake: She was able to cultivate followers, sometimes known as disciples, educating them in her spiritual path. This happened after her final release from prison, during the last years of her life. (2002, 27)

Fénelon came from an aristocratic family of modest means, studied for the Roman Catholic priesthood, was ordained in the Sulpician order, and served as tutor to the royal court, eventually rising to the office of Archbishop of Cambrai. His nemesis in the Gallic church was a fellow archbishop, Jacques-Bénigne Bossuet (1627–1704). In the late 1690s the two came into serious conflict, at first over the teachings of Guyon and then over Fénelon's defense of his friend in his work *Maximes des saints* (Maxims of the Saints), which was eventually condemned as heretical, resulting in Fénelon's permanent banishment from the royal French court.

The Religious Society of Friends and Quaker Quietism

It may seem odd to offer as an example of Quaker contemplative practice a text that is largely drawn from Roman Catholic authors—Molinos, Guyon, and Fénelon all continued to regard themselves as deeply and loyally Catholic, even though others considered them to be heretical. However, it is typical within Quakerism for writers to be hesitant to spell out religious methods too precisely. Quaker spirituality relies heavily on a sense of immediate spiritual inspiration, both in group worship and in private devotion. To offer too detailed a spiritual method would risk "quenching the Spirit," restricting the freedom of God to move worshipers to speak or act in unanticipated ways. Elsewhere, I have outlined what I consider to be a practice of meditative reading of scripture among historical Quakers. There again Quakers have traditionally preferred "to show rather than to tell." A method of meditative reading can be drawn out from how earlier Friends used the Bible in their works of spiritual nurture, but the method itself is never fully made explicit (Birkel 2005). Likewise with contemplative prayer, Friends William Backhouse and James Janson were satisfied to allow others to do most of the talking. Moreover, among Quakers it was common to read non-Quaker spiritual writers. In the era of Backhouse and Janson popular writers included the German mystics Johannes Tauler (ca. 1300–1361) and Jakob Böhme (1575–1624), the author (whose identity is disputed but traditionally believed to be Thomas à Kempis [ca. 1380–1471]) of *The Imitation of Christ*, the (also contested) author of the *Spiritual Homilies* attributed to Macarius of Egypt (ca. 300–391), and spiritual writers of the Puritan commonwealth such as John Everard (ca. 1584–1641), John Saltmarsh (d. 1647), and William Dell (ca. 1607–1669).[8] In light of that practice, it should be no surprise that Friends also read the Continental Quietists.

The historical relationships between Quakers and Continental Quietists are complex and interwoven. Clearly the writings of Guyon and Fénelon appealed to Friends. In 1772 Bristol Quaker schoolmaster James Gough translated Guyon's autobiography. As J. Rendel Harris notes, "The translation was issued anonymously but that it was the work of a Friend is sufficiently clear from the attempts which are made to cover Madame Guyon's teaching with the authority of Barclay's Apology" (Harris 1899, 318). Robert Barclay (1648–1690) was an early Friend whose *Apology* became the standard text on Quaker theology and doctrine.

Sarah Lynes Grubb (1773–1842), a contemporary of Backhouse and Janson, while traveling in the ministry wrote a letter to her husband in 1815 that she had been studying her "little French book" with the hope of "reading of Fenelon and Guion some day in their own tongue" (1863, 152). For a woman of limited education to attempt in her forties to acquire another language in order to read the French Quietists in the original indicates the measure of her appreciation for their spiritual teachings.

These facts are established. Earlier influences, confluences, and cross-fertilizations are less fully documented but suggestive. Dorothy Lloyd Gilbert and Russell Pope, writing in 1940, found traces of early Quaker Robert Barclay (1648–1690), often hailed or criticized as the first Quaker Quietist, in Jacques-Bénigne Bossuet's anti-Protestant tracts (Gilbert and Pope 1940, 95). Barclay's *Apology* became the canonical Quaker theological treatise soon after its publication and held that place of honor for some two hundred years. Bossuet, who refers to Quakers as the most well-known fanatics (*les fanatiques les plus avérés*), is the same cleric who attacked Fénelon. Gilbert and Pope note that, while there is no extant work by Bossuet that equates Quakers and Quietists, his English translators made the connection explicit when publishing one of his tracts in 1698 under the title *Quakerism à la Mode, or A History of Quietism, Particularly That of the Lord Bishop of Cambray and Madame Guyonne*. Gilbert and Pope also find echoes of Barclay in Fénelon's oeuvre (Gilbert and Pope 1940, 95). More recently, Elaine Pryce has cogently argued that Barclay's Quietism was representative of wider Quaker theology rather than a stark innovation (Pryce 2010b, 216). In short, the Quietist influence upon later Quakers, such as Backhouse and Janson, may simply have been returning the favor. But the exchange may be even more complex. As a young Scottish Protestant, before joining Friends, Barclay studied for some time at the school led by his namesake and uncle, Robert Barclay. The elder Barclay was rector at the Jesuit Scots College, which at that time was in exile in France. Scholars of mysticism find the roots of Quietism's contemplative practice in earlier Western Christian mystical writers from the early monastic writers such as John Cassian (ca. 360–435) to the quiet but orthodox Saint Francis de Sales (1567–1622), whose writings were much in vogue when the younger Robert Barclay was a student in France (Molinos 2010, 23, 28; Fénelon 2006, 14–15). Barclay's *Apology* refers to earlier mystics such as Johannes Tauler and contains unattributed traces of Cassian (Barclay 1831, 351; Birkel 2007, 47–51). It is therefore possible that Barclay's Quietist impulse that nourished Fénelon and Guyon may in turn have been fed by the mystical works that he read in France under the tutelage of his Catholic educators. *Peut-être*.

In terms of sources used in *A Guide to True Peace*, Backhouse and Janson did not translate the sources from the original French or Spanish but instead made use of existing translations, usually word-for-word when quoting Guyon and Molinos. The editors of *A Guide to True Peace* used an anonymous English translation of the *Spiritual Guide* of Molinos, which was published in London in 1688 and based on the 1685 Italian edition published in Venice. For Guyon, they drew on Thomas Digby Brooke's 1775 translation of *A Short and Easy Method of Prayer*. The source of the excerpts from Fénelon is difficult to determine exactly because the citations are often not verbatim. The most likely source seems to be the anonymously edited *Pious Thoughts Concerning the Knowledge and Love of God: And Other Holy Exercises: by the Late Archbishop of Cambray. Together with a Letter of Christian Instruction by a Lady. Done Out of French*, which was printed in London for W. and J. Innys in 1720.

Even though Fénelon's name comes first on the title page of *A Guide to True Peace* (maybe because his material is quoted first), the book draws much more from Guyon's *Short and Easy Method of Prayer*. Material that is specific to Catholic piety is understandably omitted, such as references to the sacrament of Confession. Most references to biblical books that are canonical for Catholics but apocryphal for Protestants are removed; at times another scriptural citation is substituted. (The earliest editions of *A Guide to True Peace* followed the scriptural citations in the Catholic sources. By the "first American edition" of 1816 the editors noted, "In the first edition of this work, some of the quotations from Scripture were from the Vulgate Version; none are now admitted but such as are taken from the authorized English Version." The Authorized Version is better known in the United States as the King James Version [dat. 1611], the standard English Protestant Bible until the mid-twentieth century.)

Based on the excerpts found in *A Guide to True Peace*, Molinos can come across as an inordinately harsh writer, but this does not adequately represent the fullness of his *Spiritual Guide*, which also contains lofty appeals to love and spiritual union (Molinos 2010, 164, 181–82). He warns against harsh corporeal penances (129–30). Yet Molinos does dwell at length on issues of inner purgation and spiritual aridity, more so than does Guyon in her *Short and Easy Method of Prayer*, and it is on these passages that Backhouse and Janson tend to draw.

This is in keeping with Quaker spiritual tradition of their day. Quakers were yet to emerge from their withdrawn, quasi-separatist existence, and in their countercultural and antiworldly stance it was common for them to speak of "bearing the cross." This attitude toward inward suffering extended not only to the social costs of observing the "peculiarities" of dress and address mentioned earlier; it also embraced the inward life. Earliest Friends had spoken of "the Lamb's War," borrowing the at-first-glance self-contradictory image from the book of Revelation to refer to the real, though not physically violent, conflict between good and evil that takes place within the human heart. These Friends spoke of this encounter with the Christ Within as the Inner Light. For them the experience of this Light was first one of terror, as Christ illumined for them their own capacity for evil that humans generally would prefer to pretend does not really exist. To encounter the Light of Christ was to battle this human propensity for self-deception. After a time of struggle, this conflict yielded to a victory of good over evil, to a state of inner peace and divine love, and to a profound sense of community with others who had endured that same experience of the Lamb's war and victory.

Among early Friends in the seventeenth century, this inner conflict could last months or even longer but eventually led to a clear sense of triumph that lent confidence to early Quaker belief that they could reform human society in conformity with their ethical ideals, or testimonies as they called them, of peace, equality, simplicity, and the like. The decades of persecution that followed the return of the English monarchy led Friends to withdraw from wider society and challenged this confidence, both inwardly and outwardly. Just as Quakers by the early eighteenth century tended to separate from a world that they were no longer persuaded they could remake in a godly fashion, likewise they inclined to see bearing the inward cross as a long, slow process of interior purification. Taming the wayward human will was now a lifelong task of vigilance and discipline. This development in Quaker spirituality may help to explain the attraction of the excerpts chosen from Molinos.

Although *A Guide to True Peace* has exerted a powerful influence in the history of Quaker spirituality, it cannot properly be said to occupy a place in the "Quaker canon" because there is no formal canon among Friends, apart from the Bible. Certain writings from earlier Quakers, such as the spiritual autobiography or *Journal* of George Fox (1624–1691) and Robert Barclay's exposition of doctrine known as his *Apology*, have been found on many a Quaker bookshelf for the last three centuries, but they do not constitute an official canon, and *A Guide to True Peace* never attained such status. Among contemporary Quakers, many would continue to regard the Bible as in some sense authoritative, but among the liberal branch of Friends this authority has waned immensely. On the whole, as a denomination Quakerism is rather decentralized.

Quaker Silent Prayer and Quietist Spirituality

The central themes in *A Guide to True Peace* center around a practice of prayer and a theological concept of human nature. The two are naturally connected, although imageless contemplative practices are found in many theological traditions.

A Guide to True Peace promotes a practice of apophatic prayer, that is, prayer that is without content as much as is humanly possible. The idea behind this form of prayer is that instead of experiencing God directly, human beings are prone to construct an image of God and then worship that image, which may bear little resemblance to what God really is and is at any rate certainly inadequate. Christian apophatic prayer practices hold that God, like Nature as understood by scientists in the seventeenth century, abhors a vacuum. When one empties the mind of all distracting thoughts and feelings, God will fill the vacuum with divine presence. A sermon attributed to Johannes Tauler can serve as an example of this doctrine:[9]

> For the going forth to occur—that is, an elevation outside and above ourselves—we must renounce our own will, desire, and activity, so that only an open mindfulness of God remains. . . . If someone prepares the ground, then beyond doubt God must come and fill it totally, or the heavens would burst and fill the emptiness. God would not leave anything empty. Such a thing would be against God's nature and justice. (Tauler 1910, 9–10; author's translation)

The guidelines for practicing this prayer are very simply stated. The purpose of *A Guide to True Peace* is to teach "a species of prayer which may be exercised at all times, which doth not obstruct outward employments, and which may be equally practiced by all ranks and conditions of people" (ch. 3). In order to be suitable to all sorts, it must be a form of prayer not "of the head, but of the heart" (ch. 3). It is a prayer "of inward silence, wherein the soul, abstracted from all outward things, in holy stillness, humble reverence, and lively faith, waits patiently to feel the Divine presence, and to receive the precious influence of the Holy Spirit" (ch. 5).

Although this form of prayer is applicable under all circumstances, it can also be practiced in specific times of "retirement." The method for the latter occasions is this: "Consider yourselves as being placed in the Divine presence," looking intently to God and resigned to receive whatever God may give (ch. 5). At the same time, "Fix your minds in peace and silence; quitting all your own reasons, and not willingly thinking on any thing," no matter how good it may seem (ch. 5). If distractions occur, simply turn gently from them and wait in patience to feel God's presence (ch. 5).

If "something of inward stillness, or a degree of the softening of the Divine Spirit, is mercifully granted," one should appreciate it and be attentive to it, but not fan one's own flames in an effort to heighten the experience. Extraordinary experiences and sweet consolations bring delight, but they are not the goal. Genuine prayer is the act itself, the attentive desire, the patient gaze toward God, not fleeting moments of pleasure:

> True prayer consists, not in enjoying the light, and having knowledge of spiritual things, but in enduring with patience, and persevering in faith and silence; believing that we are in the Lord's presence, turning to him in our hearts with tranquility and simplicity of mind. (ch. 6)

Seeking consolations through self-exertion leads to deception. Those who pray must learn to discern such fabricated "meltings of the affections from the operations which purely proceed from the Divine Spirit" (ch. 6).

A Guide to True Peace counsels its readers to pray in equanimity, "Not that ye may enjoy spiritual delights, but that ye may be full or empty, just as it pleaseth God" (ch. 5)—for "inquietude is the door by which the enemy gets into the soul, to rob it of its peace" (ch. 15). Disinterested love of God distinguishes true prayer.

This little manual of prayer speaks of union of the soul with God through resignation, surrender of one's will, submission to the cross, and annihilation. Yet the soul is not to make itself dead but rather to become as receptive as it can to God's work within it (ch. 14).

Contemporary works on prayer make a distinction between ceaseless prayer, which uses a *mantra* (sacred sound) amid all waking activities, and modes of interior prayer such as Centering Prayer. In the former, a phrase is repeated to bring one into mindfulness of God in all of life, reshaping all action into a conscious prayerfulness. The goal here is to remember the words of the prayer as much as possible, to maintain an awareness of divine presence. In the latter, a phrase or image is used in a focused way, in a time set aside for prayer alone. In this kind of interior prayer, the goal is ultimately to move beyond the words of the prayer into an apprehension of God's presence at a level that is deeper than the discursive power of the mind. Because of this distinction, some modern proponents of these methods of prayer suggest that the phrases chosen for each kind of prayer should be different so that one maintains an awareness of the different purposes of these two ways of praying. Thomas Keating (b.1923), one of the founders of the Centering Prayer movement, distinguishes between Centering Prayer, for which one should choose a word of one or two syllables, and active prayer, which should be five to nine syllables in length (Keating 1986, 124).

A Guide to True Peace combines these two modes of prayer, suggesting that this species of prayer can function both as a constant background in all occasions and as a concentrated, focused contemplative practice. *A Guide to True Peace* differs from modern methods, though, in that in either mode of prayer, the content is imageless and wordless. *A Guide to True Peace* advances background prayer to a more fully apophatic practice (Birkel 2004, 79).

In the Quietist tradition, among others, the understanding of humanity that lies behind this contemplative practice is one of suspicion about human nature. Human beings are sinful, distant from God, and their inclinations are untrustworthy. The chasm between humankind and God is immense. The only way to conform the human will to the divine will is to obliterate the former. This may sound pessimistic regarding human nature, but at the same time Quietists held that perfection and union with God were desirable, possible, and attainable through the contemplative practice of apophatic prayer.

In terms of differences, some terms common to Quaker and Catholic Quietists had a different resonance in each community, so that when Friends read Guyon, Fénelon, or Molinos, they understood some matters differently.

One difference of course is the familiarity with silence. Because Friends met in silence for congregational worship, the adoption of a practice of silent contemplation is not as distant from collective worship as it would be from the Catholic liturgical tradition. Another difference would be how spiritual nurture was undertaken. Quakers had the office of elder, someone recognized by the community as a person gifted in the spiritual guidance of others. Although elders collectively held power in Quaker structures, including the power to initiate discipline against an errant community member, their status was quite different from that of an ordained priest to whom one confessed one's private sins for the ministration of divine forgiveness and sacramentally mediated grace.

Quakers did not adhere to the doctrine of original sin—the traditional Western Christian notion of a sinful state that is the natural condition of humankind and an inheritance from the fallen condition of Adam and Eve after their primordial disobedience in the Garden of Eden when they ate the forbidden fruit. Quakers were fully persuaded of the human potential for sin, but they held that human beings were responsible before God only for the evils that they had personally committed. People were not born into a state of sin, according to Friends.

Each religious community has a different balance of freedom and restriction. Catholics, for example, were free to dance and to gamble within limits but faced a precisely defined set of theological boundaries. To proclaim too much or too little of a theological idea ran the risk of heresy and Inquisition. As mentioned earlier, it seems to have been Molinos's lack of precision rather than intentional heresy that raised suspicion at first. Quakers, on the other hand, refrained from dancing or wagering but enjoyed wider theological freedom. As a result, some of the subtleties of the Quietists' texts from which *A Guide to True Peace* is compiled would hardly have registered with Quaker readers. The defense, for example, that all people are called to silent contemplative prayer was a controversial concept within Catholicism, where other, less apophatic forms of prayer were considered safer for uneducated laity. For most Quakers, silent individual prayer could seem a natural companion to their form of meeting for worship. In fact, the mode of prayer advocated in *A Guide to True Peace* may have sounded much like the advice given by early Quaker leader George Fox in an often-quoted letter of spiritual counsel, written in 1658 to Elizabeth Claypole (1629–1658), the daughter of Oliver Cromwell (1599–1658) who led England during its brief intermission from monarchy. In this letter, Fox promotes an apophatic practice that aimed at releasing all modes of thinking. Claypole was experiencing spiritual trials and inner turmoil, and George Fox's letter was intended as a guide to true peace.

> Be still and cool in thy own mind and spirit from thy own thoughts, and then thou wilt feel the principle of God to turn thy mind to the Lord God, whereby thou wilt receive his strength and power from whence life comes, to allay all tempests, against blusterings and storms. . . . Therefore be still a while from they own thoughts, searching, seeking, desires and imaginations, and . . . stay thy mind upon God . . . do not look at the temptations, confusions, corruptions, but at the light which discovers them, that makes them manifest; and with the same light you may feel over them, to receive power to stand against them . . . looking at the light . . . will give victory and you will find grace and strength; there is the first step to peace. That will bring salvation. (Fox 1952, 346–48; see also Ambler 2002)

Meeting for communal silent worship is the practice most often associated with the Religious Society of Friends. Traditionally, this occurs in Quaker "meeting houses," which include a contemplative space, a simple, undecorated room in which benches or chairs are usually placed in an organization pattern (square or circle) facing an empty center. In this respect, it is important to recognize that individual contemplative prayer among Quakers is not the same as gathering for meeting for worship. In meeting for worship, the community gathers in silence and seeks to quiet the mind and heart.

However, in meeting for worship the focus is on the gathered community. Friends come together and individually "center down" or seek to quiet themselves and turn inward. They "mind

Figure 4.1. Quaker Meeting House of Brigflatts (Cumbria, England)[10]
Source: Brigflatts FMH

Figure 4.2. Interior of Brigflatts Meeting House
Source: Brigflatts FMH

the Light" or wait expectantly for divine guidance. If one of the worshipers discerns that she or he has been given a message to share with the community, words are uttered. Such words are considered as ministering to those gathered in worship.[11] In pure apophatic practice, any ideas that come to the mind are considered a distraction to be released. In the collective practice of meeting for worship, there is an expectation that some in the group will feel called to minister to the whole body of worshipers. It is therefore essential to engage in discernment: When an idea comes to the mind, is it a distraction, a revelation for oneself, or a message to be shared in what is known among Friends as "vocal ministry"? As mentioned earlier, Quakers prefer to show rather than tell, so as not to "quench the Spirit." Friends have been reluctant to codify a set of rules for discernment as, for example, is found in the Ignatian spiritual tradition. Friends would learn this first of all by participating in meeting for worship. With regard to written sources, journals of ministers at times described the inward experience of discerning whether or not to speak. Again, the preferred mode of imparting spiritual teaching was by illustration rather than by elaboration of a detailed method.

The experience of ministering to others, moreover, was not limited to words. As they worshiped together, some Friends would find that as they centered down into a place of stillness, they would come to experience the collective dimension of worship. In traditional Quaker language, they would come to "a feeling sense of the condition of others," whether of particular individuals in the meeting or of the community as a whole. In the silence these sensitive Friends would feel the joys, sorrows, conflicts, and triumphs of others. They would be present to them in prayer and in silent awareness. Friends who came to meeting with a particular burden that felt lighter after worship would know that others had silently borne their trials in the time of worship. Ministry in silence can be as powerful and transformative as spoken ministry. In moments of rare grace, the whole meeting may feel powerfully knit together. Friends call such an experience a "gathered" or "covered" meeting.

Robert Barclay described it this way:

> Each made it their work to retire inwardly to the measure of Grace in themselves. . . . They come thereby to enjoy and feel the arisings of this Life, which, as it prevails in each particular, becomes as a flood of refreshment and overspreads the whole meeting . . . and we enjoy and possess the holy fellowship and 'communion of the body and blood of Christ,' by which our inward man is nourished and fed. (Barclay 1831, 354)

Barclay's use of sacramental language is common for Quakers in describing meeting for worship. Similarly, Friends spoke of being baptized into a feeling state of those gathered. Quakers refrain from the practice of external sacramental rituals but believe that they experience the same reality of divine presence inwardly.

John Woolman (1720–1772) was an important Quaker leader in the subsequent century. His works were standard on Quaker bookshelves almost from the time of their first printing in 1774. One can reasonably assume that Backhouse and Janson, as pious Quakers of a slightly later generation, would have been familiar with the words of John Woolman.

Although there is no firm evidence that Woolman read Molinos, Guyon, or Fénelon, there is an element of his piety that suggests that he and other Quakers of his era would have found

Quietist writings to speak a familiar dialect. As will be seen when turning to the central ideas of *A Guide to True Peace*, the following passage from John Woolman shares many terms: silence, resignation, will, perfection, suffering, and purity.

> The sincere in heart who abide in true stillness . . . have a knowledge of Christ in the fellowship of his sufferings. . . . While aught remains in us different from a perfect resignation of our wills, it is like a seal to a book wherein is written that good and acceptable and perfect will of God concerning us, Rom. 12.2. But when our minds entirely yield to Christ, that silence is known which followeth the opening of the last of the seals, Rev. 8.1. In this silence we learn abiding in the divine will and there feel that we have no cause to promote but that only in which the Light of Life directs us in our proceedings. [We learn] that the only way to be useful in the church of Christ is to abide faithfully under the leadings of his Holy Spirit in all cases, and being preserved thereby in purity of heart and holiness of conversation, a testimony to the purity of his government may be held forth through us to others. (Woolman 1775, 78–79)[12]

John Woolman was a social reformer as well as a mystic, dedicated to ending the practice of enslavement, to fair treatment for the indigenous peoples of North America, and to justice for the poor. An important difference from Continental Quietist thought in the passage from John Woolman is its concern for ethical action directed by divine leadings. Woolman integrated the inward and outward lives, and so the natural product of silent prayer and submission to divine will is the governance of Christ in practical affairs that led to greater human justice. Guyon and Fénelon practiced good works, but their works on prayer did not make explicit how ethics derived from contemplative practice. While these Continental Quietists called for care for the poor and afflicted, they did not espouse a plan for ending poverty itself, as John Woolman did in his essay *A Plea for the Poor* (Birkel 2003, 11–16).

William Backhouse and James Janson stood on the threshold of a major change in Quaker history, the lowering of the "hedge" that separated Friends from wider society. In the nineteenth century and beyond, Quakers were to cooperate with other-than-Quakers in common concerns of social reform. Even as Quakers borrowed from Guyon, Fénelon, and Molinos, they remained faithful to their hopes for a social transformation.

A Guide to True Peace fits into the larger Quaker framework of soteriology in several ways. Quakers subscribed to a realized eschatology: salvation from sin, knowledge of God, and even perfection were possibilities in this life. These were not simply hopes postponed for an afterlife. Just as the experience of divine revelation, such as the biblical prophets and apostles experienced, was not simply a thing of the past but presently available through the guidance of the Inward Light, so too the realities that most other Christians anticipated for the end of time were present possibilities. This was on the one hand an extreme interiorization of the Christian message, though Quakers also hoped for and labored toward a more just human society. This focus on inward, present experience extended to Quaker understanding of the saving work of Jesus on the cross. Many other Christians focused on the historical crucifixion and death of Jesus as the locus of salvation. Early Quakers acknowledged that the historical event of the cross made redemption available, but salvation became a personal reality only as the cross was inwardly experienced through encountering the Inward Christ or the Light. The contemplative mode of inward prayer advocated by *A Guide to True Peace* prepared one for this experience. By setting aside all other thoughts and desires, this prayer served as a cross to one's own will. By opening the way to an experience of divine union and even perfection, this interior mode of prayer participated in the salvific process.

Instructions on Prayer from the *Guide*

The preface to *A Guide to True Peace* begins with a verse from the Gospel of John much loved and often quoted by Friends. The verse comes from the story of Jesus meeting the Samaritan women by a well. The two converse about proper worship: Samaritans worship on the mountain of Gerizim, while Jews worship at the Temple in Jerusalem. Jesus proclaims that true worship is in spirit and in truth. Quakers saw themselves as fulfilling this scriptural verse. Other Christian bodies disputed about the proper external form of worship, including the shape of liturgy, proper clerical vestments during services, the furnishings of a church building, and the meaning of the bread and cup in communion. Quaker worship, based on gathering in silent expectation of divine presence, required no consecrated building, no ordained priesthood, and no outward rituals. For them, these silent gatherings were worship in spirit and in truth. To begin *A Guide to True Peace* with these words was to put a Quaker stamp of approval on the book that was to follow, even though much of the text borrowed from non-Quaker sources.

The first words of chapter 1, even though they are taken from Fénelon, make reference to biblical sources that were precious to Friends, especially the phrase from the Gospel of John that speaks of the true Light that enlightens everyone coming into the world. This passage has a central place in Quaker theology, where it is used to confirm the Quaker teaching of the Inner Light of Christ that is available to every human being. This universal accessibility of God is not dependent on an outward ritual of baptism or even of hearing the gospel. It is possible to know the reality of divine presence and its guidance without first learning the particularities of the Christian message. As early Friends put it, one can know the mystery without the history. Again, to begin with this echo from the Gospel of John is to signal to (Quaker) readers that what is to follow conforms with the truth as Quakers understand it. The work begins with a gentle invitation to the practice of silence, to hear the Inward Teacher. God speaks to all, and the *Guide* warns its readers that those who are too full of themselves will not hear these divine admonitions.

Contrasting concepts of faith dominate the second chapter: faith as assent to the truth of another's testimony, and faith as trust. The latter is the more essential in the practice of inward prayer because there will be many times of dryness, when it seems that nothing is happening. A trusting faith enables the practitioner to persevere.

The third chapter speaks of the need for a form of prayer that can be practiced in all situations and by all sorts of people. It must therefore be an exercise of the heart rather than the head. In this way it will not be impeded by outward activities but can continue as a background to all activities. Here the *Guide* first notes the dual purpose of this kind of contemplative practice: it is to be an activity carried on throughout the day as well as in times of committed focus on the prayer.

Preface	9. On Self-denial
1. The Spirit of God Dwells in the Heart of Man	10. On Mortification
2. On Faith	11. On Resignation
3. On Prayer	12. On Virtue
4. All Are Capable of Attaining to Inward and Spiritual Prayer	13. On Conversion
5. On Attaining to True Prayer	14. On Self-annihilation
6. On Spiritual Dryness	15. Man Acts More Nobly under the Divine Influence, Than He Can Possibly Do by Following His Own Will
7. On Defects and Infirmities	16. On the Possession of Peace and Rest before God
8. On Temptations and Tribulations	17. On Perfection, or the Union of the Soul with God

Figure 4.3. Sections of *A Guide to True Peace*

The following chapter continues in the same vein, arguing for the importance of this kind of prayer and that all people are capable of practicing it. Again, the Quaker conviction that God is available to all and that all people can be called to minister would have resonated with this line of thought. This fourth chapter contains what might be considered the heart of the message of the *Guide*: seek God in the heart, focus on that presence, return to that focus when distracted, and do and suffer all for God.

If chapter 4 holds the heart of the message of this book, chapter 5 offers what might be considered the method for this prayer of inward silence: wait, imagine (consider) oneself in God's presence, maintain a focus on that presence, assent (resign) to whatever happens without specific expectation, do not intentionally think of anything, and when distracted return gently to that presence. If something wonderful happens, receive and value it, but neither be attached to it nor try to enhance that pleasant experience by personal efforts.

Because this kind of prayer seeks to empty the mind, it is the safest form of spiritual practice. Here the *Guide* seems to echo traditional Christian teaching about apophatic prayer. From at least the time of ancient Christian monasticism, the understanding of the soul held that evil comes to the mind from the outside, so temptation must seek an entrance into human consciousness. This occurs through the senses, through the human capacity for images and fantasies. To refrain from the intentional use of the imagination is to refuse entry to these temptations. To let go of all images is to be safe from illusions of grandeur, from distractions from sexual energy, and from indulgence in anger, pride, and other potential disturbers of the peace of the soul.

This chapter also warns the reader not to fight distractions but simply to release them. A vigorously combative response to distractions only enhances their power and increases vexation. Even in the midst of distractions, love is present. The spiritual life embraces more than merely the surface of consciousness. One does not cease to love, even when one has strayed from a focus on the loved one. Finally, one should go to prayer without expectation of spiritual delights. This will enable one better to endure the times of dryness when nothing seems to happen or God seems absent. In short, chapter 5 contains many of the finest gems of the *Guide*.

Chapter 6 deals with the challenges of spiritual dryness and assures the reader that God is at work within, even when that is not easily known. Quoting Molinos, *A Guide to True Peace* notes that it is better not to know precisely what is happening within. These words seem akin to the thoughts of Gerald May on the dark night of the soul for the sixteenth-century Spanish Carmelite mystics Teresa of Ávila and John of the Cross, whom Molinos read. May understood the hidden transformation that occurs within the obscurity of the dark night to be a good thing. An experienced psychiatrist as well as a spiritual director, May wrote that (like periods of dryness for the *Guide*) the process of the dark night must be obscure:

> Since the night involves relinquishing attachments, it takes us beneath our denial into territory we are in the habit of avoiding. We might feel willing to relinquish compulsions we acknowledge as destructive, but . . . what about the attachments we love? . . . If we are honest . . . we have to admit that we will likely try to sabotage any movement toward true freedom. If we really knew what we were called to relinquish on this journey, our defenses would never allow us to take the first step. Sometimes the only way we can enter the deeper dimension of the journey is by being unable to see where we are going. . . . in spiritual matters it is precisely when we *do* think we know where to go that we are most likely to stumble. (May 2005, 71–72).

The *Guide* encourages the reader to persevere in times of spiritual aridity, asserting that to go to prayer with the intention of praying, despite whatever distractions intervene, is in fact to pray in spirit and in truth, echoing the opening words of the *Guide*.

The seventh chapter warns the reader not to grow vexed when distractions are plentiful. Such vexation springs from pride—an idea reminiscent of an insight of Francis de Sales. In his *Introduction to the Devout Life*, Francis judiciously observed that harshness can be a disguise worn by pride, by inflated self-importance, by an arrogance that violates self, neighbor, and God.

> One of the excellent practices of gentleness which we could learn to do is never to be vexed at ourselves or against our imperfections. Its subject is we ourselves. Even though it is reasonable that we must be sorry and displeased when we commit some faults, yet we must refrain from a harsh, vexed, gloomy, and angry displeasure. Many make a great mistake in this regard. . . . These vexations, harshness, and anger which we have against ourselves tend to pride. They had no other origin than self-love which is disturbed and anxious at seeing ourselves imperfect. (De Sales 1995, bk. 3, ch. 9)

Chapter 8 concerns itself with trials, noting that the greatest temptation is to have no temptations because then one falls into a state of spiritual languor and half-heartedness. Again the *Guide* cautions against fighting with temptations and urges simply turning away and within. A perfectly purified and annihilated soul leaves nothing for a tempter to act upon.

Suffering and self-denial are the concerns of the ninth chapter. Here the *Guide* begins its consideration of the theme of resignation, that quality of yieldedness that has a long history in Christian spirituality. The concept suggests submission, relinquishing one's own will, serenity, and equanimity.

The fourteenth-century Dominican mystic Johannes Tauler, who was widely read among Quakers in the nineteenth century, describes resignation (German: *Gelassenheit*) in his Second Sermon on Pentecost. For Tauler, resignation entails leaving behind everything, even one's hope to enjoy the presence of God, in order to conform one's will to the will of God.

> A person is completely stripped of one's self in complete and genuine resignation to God. One sinks deeply into the ground of the divine will, to linger in this poverty and nakedness, not for a week or a month, but rather, if God wills, for a thousand years or a full eternity. Or if God were to wish to have one forever in hellfire, in eternal pain, so that one could thoroughly yield oneself therein, children, that would be true resignation . . . with this resignation one sets one's foot truly into eternal life, and after this pain one never again comes into another, neither into hell nor into any other suffering, and it is impossible that God would ever forsake this person. (Tauler 1910, 108; author's translation)

Jakob Böhme, whom Friends also read across the centuries, employed this mystical tradition of utter abandonment to the will of God and titled one of his final treatises *Von der wahren Gelassenheit* (On True Yieldedness). As Quakers who favored Böhme read *A Guide to True Peace*, they may have heard overtones of his teachings on resignation such as these:

> The will of the creature should, with all reason and desire, totally sink into itself . . . so that God might do with it how and what God wishes. . . . All that is in or on you must also depart from all self-knowing and willing. . . . Thus one's own desire presses into the nothing, that is, only into the doing and acting of God that God wishes in it; and the Spirit of God presses out through the desire of yielded humility. Thus the human self looks to the Spirit of God in the trembling and joy of humility. And so it may see everything that is in time and eternity. Everything is near to it. (Böhme 2010, 104–6)

Chapter 10 is on mortification, a term that held different connotations among the Quaker readership and a Catholic audience. Physical austerities were common practice among the latter. Even the gentle Francis de Sales recommended use of the lash, referred to by the euphemism "the discipline," in his letters of spiritual direction (De Sales 1988, 134–35). Such practices of self-flagellation were generally anathema to most Protestants, and they were not part of the Quaker spiritual tradition. When the *Guide* states a preference for only interior practices of mortification, the Quaker reader would have heard it in the context of, for example, the following words from early Friend Isaac Penington (1616–1679): "For it is not a notion of Christ without (with multitudes of practices of self-denial and mortification thereupon) which can save; but Christ heard knocking, and let into the heart" (Penington 1761, 1: 119–20).

The theme of resignation returns in chapter 11, here described as the key to the inner court, which is perfection. Submission to the divine is the guide to peace.

The very brief twelfth chapter devotes its mere hundred words to the theme of virtue, which grows from within, from resignation.

Chapter 13 turns to conversion and explains that it is a total change to an inward life. As elsewhere, the *Guide* insists that the soul's task is simply to cooperate with divine grace, not to exert its own powers violently. God, at the center within, gently attracts one inward, thus purifying the soul. All attention should therefore be directed to cultivating inward silence.

Annihilation, the means to union with God, is the theme of the fourteenth chapter. Since the time of the apostle Paul (see the sixth chapter of the Epistle to the Romans), Christian spirituality has spoken of the need for dying and rising with Christ. This total surrender is, echoing the opening words of the *Guide*, worship in spirit and in truth. Lest this sound severe, the text reminds the reader that this experience brings joy and is the fulfillment of all blessing.

The fifteenth chapter defends Quietism against charges that the soul is in effect deadened by silent contemplation. On the contrary, one is more alive than ever. A ship may seem clumsy in harbor but is buoyant and easily steered upon the open sea. Likewise the soul is at first resistant to spiritual change but sails without strain as the spiritual journey progresses. As one allows God to be the inner pilot, one's course grows smooth, peaceful, and joyful, even in the midst of external storms. The chapter concludes with an exhortation to submit to annihilation.

Chapter 16 relates how, as God gradually takes possession of one's whole being, a sense of divine presence and of serenity comes to characterize all daily tasks. Again the *Guide* cautions against aggressive exertion: the interior is not a fortress to be stormed but a realm of peace acquired only by love. Divine love clothes all, and one faces death with equanimity. The soul identifies with Paul's assertion, "I have been crucified with Christ. It is no longer I who live but Christ who lives in me" (Galatians 2:20).

Perfection is the focus of the seventeenth and final chapter. It is defined as union with God, resulting in a freedom of spirit—a phrase that echoes a distinctive theme in Salesian spirituality (De Sales 1988, 49–53). The path to this union does not lie in the active, imaginative forms of prayer called "meditation" in seventeenth-century Catholicism but only in apophatic contemplative practice that leads to purification and annihilation. This perfection seems to be an unshakeable state, which is a surprising claim in a document edited by Quakers who did not subscribe to the doctrine of, as the Calvinists of that time termed it, the perseverance of the saints. Quoting Molinos, the *Guide* waxes rhapsodic in its portrayal of this state of perfection, a condition distinguished by its joy, peace, freedom, purity, equanimity, simplicity, and ceaseless prayer. This is the biblical pearl of great price.

Reading the *Guide* in Later Quakerism

According to Howard Brinton, between 1813 and 1877 *A Guide to True Peace* underwent at least twelve editions and reprintings, which attests to its ongoing influence among Quakers (Fénelon et al. 1946, vii). In addition, Molinos, Guyon, and Fénelon continued to be mentioned in Quaker writings.

Samuel McPherson Janney (1801–1880) was a Virginia Quaker minister, educator, and reformer who established schools for African Americans and worked for the abolition of slavery. In his *Memoirs* he wrote these favorable words: "Fenelon and Lady Guion were contemporaries with George Fox and William Penn. They were eminent for their purity and self-denial; few have been more devoted than they were to the service of God" (Janney 1881, 238). Stephen Grellet (1773–1855), while traveling in the ministry to the city of Rome, refers to Molinos and the prison that held him (Grellet 1867, 2:71). John Greenleaf Whittier (1807–1892), Quaker poet and social reformer, wrote of "sainted Guion" (Whittier 1904, 214). Hannah Whittall Smith (1832–1911), an important voice in the Holiness movement among Evangelical Friends, referred to Fénelon and Guyon in her autobiography, *The Unselfishness of God and How I Discovered It*:

> I possessed a book which distinctly taught that God's children were not only commanded to bring forth the fruits of the Spirit, but also that they could do so; and which seemed to reveal the mystical pathway towards it. It was called "Spiritual Progress," and was a collection of extracts from the writings of Fenelon and Madame Guyon. This book was very dear to me, for it had been a gift from my adored father, and always lay on my desk beside my Bible. (Smith 1903, 231)

Caroline Stephen (1834–1909) was a significant voice in British Quakerism in the Victorian era. Her writings were among the first of modern Friends to consciously identify Quakers as part of the wider stream of Christian mysticism. Her influential work *Quaker Strongholds* refers to all three of the Continental Quietists in a description of the Quaker concept of the Inner Light.

> "The kingdom of heaven is within you." Personal religion is a real and a living thing only in proportion as it springs from this deep inward root. The root itself is common to all true believers. The consciousness of its "inwardness" is that which distinguishes the mystic. . . . If, however, a certain correspondence between the inward and outward does really exist . . . the faculty of discerning it must needs be a gift. I believe, indeed, that the power in this direction which distinguishes such mystics as, *e.g.*, Thomas a Kempis, Jacob Boehme, Tauler, Fenelon, Madame Guyon, George Fox, William Law, St. Theresa, Molinos, and others is essentially the same gift which in a different form, or in combination with a different temperament and gifts of another order, makes poets. It is the gift of seeing truth at first-hand, the faculty of receiving a direct revelation. (Stephen 1891, 37)

J. Rendel Harris (1852–1941) was a scholar of the New Testament and also the first director of studies at Woodbrooke in Birmingham, England, a center of renewal for British Friends. In an essay titled "The Mysticism of Madame Guyon," he described Guyon as "a mother in Israel" and "the teacher from whom I have received more help and guidance in the things of God than from any other person" (Harris 1899, 313). The same essay goes on to acknowledge that despite the attractiveness of many of her teachings to Protestants, Guyon remained a Catholic and subscribed to "superstitions" (in the eyes of Protestants) of that church, though he is reluctant to condemn her for that. In a poem reflecting on her time in prison to which she was sent, in Harris's words, "for the crime of loving God too much," she wrote that she was pleased to be there because that was God's will. Is it really possible, Harris asks, that such great resignation "can be the mark of decadence in religion?" (Harris 1899, 337).

Both Stephen and Harris stood at a turning point in Quaker history. The Religious Society of Friends had divided in the nineteenth century in North America but not in Britain. Among American Friends, the major bodies reflected either liberal or evangelical movements in the wider religious society. A third, considerably smaller branch of Quakerism, known as Conservative Friends, maintained the Quietist impulse that nourished William Backhouse and James Janson. In England, evangelical theology and piety had dominated British Quakerism through much of the nineteenth century, witnessed in the life and thought of such Quakers as Elizabeth Fry and Joseph John Gurney. As the twentieth century approached, British Friends were turning toward a liberal and mystical interpretation of their faith. A North American ally in this transition, and arguably the most immensely influential Quaker throughout the twentieth century, was Rufus Jones. Because Jones held such weight in Quaker circles, it is worth considering his thought in some detail.

Rufus Jones (1863–1948) was a scholar of mysticism, a professor of philosophy, a social reformer, a historian of Quakerism, a public lecturer who traveled widely among Quakers and others, and a prolific author of more than fifty books.[13] His attitude toward the Quietists was at best ambivalent and in the final analysis negative. On the one hand, he could appreciate Molinos as "a remarkable spiritual expert" (Jones 1921, 43) and praise the "extraordinary insight" of Fénelon and "the rare sanity of his spiritual counsel" (52). On the other, as a devotee of the American philosopher and psychologist William James (1842–1910), whose work in psychology Jones taught for many years, he did not hesitate to diagnose Quietists as pathological and mentally disordered (Jones 1917, 36). While psychologists in recent times have been more reticent to classify psychological conditions across centuries and cultural norms, it was a common practice in the early twentieth century. William James, for example, was appreciative of early Quaker George Fox but had no professional qualms to pronounce that "from the point of view of his nervous constitution, Fox was a psychopath or *détraqué* of the deepest dye" (James 1903, 7).

Jones judged Quietism as insufficient because to him it lacked moral vigor aimed at improving society:

> The deep and ineradicable difficulty with this entire formulation of the spiritual life is its inability to get out of the dark region of negation into the real world of concrete experience and moral action. . . . Quietism needed the warm and tender objective realities of the Gospel as filling for its abstract and empty fervor. It lacked some concrete way of turning its moments of fecundity into the permanent stuff of moral character and ethical endeavor. It was a noble mood, but it was too rare and abstract to be translated into real human life. (Jones 1917, 46, 51)

Jones's objections here show how as a theological liberal he placed a premium on moral reform. He reflected the wider concerns of his day and found the past wanting. Elaine Pryce has noted this and further points that Rufus Jones was in fact mistaken about Quietism's incompatibility with social action: Guyon established a hospital funded by her own resources, and Fénelon was an advocate of the poor and the socially vulnerable (Pryce 2010a, 529).

Jones's further misgivings about Quietism revolve around his understanding of personality, which for him was the center not only of humanity but also divinity: "Every analysis of personality discovers the fact that God and man are inherently bound up together. Personal consciousness looms up out of an infinite background. Probe deep enough into any self and you come upon God" (Jones 1923, 176). For Jones, there must be a "basis for a unifying personality which binds into one organic and *vital* whole the divine and the human, *making a new spiritual creation*" (Jones 1923, 175). He noted,

> To become spiritual is to become a divine-human person—to be a person in whom the human nature and the Divine Nature have become organic and vital. The truth which comes will then be no injected revelation, no foreign irruption, but the genuine fruit and output of a personal life which unites in itself the finite and the infinite in one ever-expanding personality. (Jones 1923, 176)

This is so important to Rufus Jones because personality is salvific. God is an "Infinite Person" (Jones 1906, 107). The redemptive quality of Christ is that he brought to light the "personal aspect" of God (Jones 1938, 101). For Jones, the mystical experience is one of what he perceived as increased vitality and enhanced personality. The Quietists' suspicion of human will, desire, and activity, as well as their goal of annihilation, struck Jones as destructive, psychologically unhealthy, and ultimately contradictory to his understanding of the redemptive work of Christ. In all this he reflected the thinking of his day, particularly the school of North American liberal theology known as "personalism," in which, as noted by religious historian Gary Dorrien, the real was the personal (Dorrien 2003, 286–355).

Jones offered the following assessment of the Continental Quietists:

> Nothing is more clear than that they succeeded in so far as they retained and ennobled their concrete personalities and their interesting individual characteristics, and that they failed in so far as they suppressed, and annihilated themselves and arrived at abstract love, non-desire, and no-willing. (Jones 1921, 54)

Despite the enormity of Rufus Jones's influence, there were other voices. His student Howard Brinton (1884–1973), a major Quaker voice in his own right, edited a reprinting of *A Guide to True Peace* in 1946. This edition remained in print for some sixty years. In other works, published after the death of Jones, Brinton described the period of Quietist influence on Friends as the era of cultural creativity and mystical inwardness among Quakers (Brinton 1952, 181).

In recent years, some scholars have thoughtfully challenged Jones's negative evaluation of Quietism, paving the way for a renewed appreciation of Quietist spirituality, especially as it shaped Quaker spiritual practice (Damiano 1989; Spencer 2007; Pryce 2010a).

With respect to contemporary Quakers, a Friend from the Conservative tradition, which has preserved the Quietist dimension of Quakerism, once told me how when she completed her high school years she was given a copy of *A Guide to True Peace*, almost as a kind of recognition of her coming into adulthood and therefore her readiness for contemplative practice.

Among liberal Quakers today, some still read *A Guide to True Peace* with benefit, but many find its concept of human nature too foreign. Liberal theology tends to focus on human potential rather than human sinfulness, and *A Guide to True Peace* strikes liberal readers as having too negative a view of the self. It has not yet found many sympathetic interpreters that might open for liberals the treasures of this little gem, but perhaps this present essay can be a step in that direction. Liberal Quakers often turn elsewhere for guidance on contemplative practice: some to the Centering Prayer movement, others to the works of Thomas Kelly (1893–1941) (Kelly and Steere 1941, 29–50), who wrote compellingly of simple prayer, and still others to wider traditions, such as Buddhist mindfulness meditation or Sufi contemplative practices.

Among evangelical Friends, recently there has been a revival of interest in Christian spirituality. The work of Carole Spencer is important to mention in this regard (Spencer 2007, 186, 269–70). As there has been a rise of interest in spiritual direction, in meditative practices of reading scripture (*lectio divina*), there has arisen an appreciation of contemplative prayer such as that found in *A Guide to True Peace*. Like some liberals, evangelicals have become more comfortable with the spiritual treasures of Roman Catholic origin.

In short, *A Guide to True Peace* no longer holds a central position in Quaker spiritual practice, but it remains available and often speaks to those who will take the time to become acquainted with its dialect of the inward life. Personal affinity and inquiry play a distinctive role in Quaker spirituality, particularly in its more liberal strands that value attending to one's inner guide.

Minding the Light in Contemplative Studies

Apophatic practices, even as they aspire to universal experiences beyond words, take place in specific communities with particular modes of language. *A Guide to True Peace*, even though it is drawn chiefly from Catholic sources, is distinctively Quaker both by omission and inclusion. The former includes omission of Catholic biblical texts regarded by Protestants (including Quakers) as noncanonical, of references to sacramental traditions, and of uniquely Catholic practices of piety. The latter includes the assumption that the universal nature of the Light means that even those who have never heard the biblical message are nonetheless capable of encountering and achieving acceptance with God, a conception of perfection more as a moment-by-moment openness to divine leading rather than a focus on absolute sinlessness, and an understanding of this contemplative form of prayer as an individual preparation for a collective spiritual practice centered in a gathered silence.

A Guide to True Peace continued to be read among the various branches of Friends after the schisms of the nineteenth century. It was reprinted throughout that century and found a home again in the twentieth. This text is currently alive on the internet, on websites hosted by non-Quakers, as any search engine will reveal. All this points to *A Guide to True Peace*'s enduring capacity to speak to many theological points of view, both within Quakerism and beyond its borders. The work's universal dimension appeals to readers who do not share its specific theological framework. The simplicity of its method of contemplative prayer transcends its historical context, just as the words of the seventeenth-century Catholic Quietists Jeanne Guyon, François Fénelon, and Miguel de Molinos transcended theirs and spoke to William Backhouse and James Janson, who gathered their words into *A Guide to True Peace*.

Even so, the theology of *A Guide to True Peace* merits consideration. The nature of the self, human limitation and failure, the possibility of restoration, and the concept of perfectibility, however understood, deserve thoughtful reflection. Such reflection allows people to get in touch with what they may feel to be questions that lie at the heart of the mystery of what it is to be human.

The larger volume of which this chapter is a part seeks to make a contribution to the comparative study of religion. *A Guide to True Peace* already is comparative: it brings together different religious traditions and shows how one community makes use of texts from another, with appreciation and respect, although certainly with some difference of interpretation. As such, by virtue of its own example of a text that transcends conventional boundaries, it invites others into the conversation of the proper exploration of religious practices from other traditions. *A Guide to True Peace* will surely not completely meet all contemporary criteria for how to do this appropriately, yet it can serve as a historical model, from two hundred years ago, of an exchange of contemplative practice between religious communities.

Notes

1. In this chapter, "Quakers" and "Friends" are used interchangeably, as they are among Quakers. The Religious Society of Friends draws its name from the Gospel of John in the Christian Bible, where Jesus calls his disciples his friends (John 15:15). The term "Quaker" was originally a term of derision, referring to the experience of some early Friends of physically shaking during the experience of communal worship.

2. For an introduction to the history of Quakers, see Barbour and Frost 1994; Dandelion 2007.

3. Among the Protestant denominations, Quakers are often classified among the Radical Reformation, as opposed to Protestant bodies that are state-sponsored churches. Additionally, because of their pacifist convictions, Quakers are also designated among the Historic Peace Churches, which include such groups as the Mennonites and the Church of the Brethren.

4. For more on developments in Quakerism during these centuries, as some embraced the evangelical movement and others adopted liberal Protestantism and an identity as part of the history of mysticism, while both groups reintegrated themselves into mainstream society, see Barbour and Frost 1994, 169–208; Dandelion 2007, 80–171.

5. Even-handed treatments of Quietism remain rare. For some recent discussions of the movement, see Louis Dupré's "Jansenism and Quietism" in Dupré et al. 1989 and Bernard McGinn's "Miguel de Molinos and the *Spiritual Guide*: A Theological Reappraisal" in Molinos 2010, 21–39. Dupré notes that Quietism drew upon the spirituality of the very orthodox Saint Francis de Sales (1567–1622).

6. Backhouse and Janson made use of existing English translations of Molinos's *Spiritual Guide*, Guyon's *A Short and Very Easy Method of Prayer*, and a compilation from Fénelon entitled *Pious Thoughts Concerning the Knowledge and Love of God: And Other Holy Exercises: by the Late Archbishop of Cambray*.

7. For a recent scholarly introduction to Guyon, see Patricia A. Ward's "Madame Guyon" in Lindberg 2005. See also Bruneau 1998. For some helpful information on Fénelon, see Fénelon 2006.

8. Interestingly, William Dell published *The Way of True Peace and Unity* (dat. 1649).

9. Some dispute Tauler's authorship and attribute this text to Meister Eckhart (ca. 1260–ca. 1327). See, for example, McGinn 2005, 586.

10. I am grateful to the warden and Quaker community of Brigflatts for permission to use these images. This Meeting House was first built in 1675, during the formative years of the Quaker community. As it is located in Cumbria, England, it is associated with the geographical and religio-cultural context in which William Backhouse and James Janson anonymously compiled *A Guide to True Prayer*.

11. For an introduction to Quaker communal worship based in gathered silence, see Taber 1992; Birkel 2004.

12. I have slightly modified the orthography of this paragraph for the ease of contemporary readers.
13. For a brief biography and an extensive bibliography, see Bernet 2009.

Works Cited and Further Reading

Ambler, Rex. 2002. *Light to Live By: An Exploration of Quaker Spirituality.* Philadelphia: Quaker Books.

Annual Monitor for 1844, or Obituary of the Members of the Society of Friends in Great Britain and Ireland. 1844. Edited by Sarah Backhouse and Samuel Tuke. York: W. Alexander.

Barbour, Hugh, and J. William Frost. 1994. *The Quakers.* Richmond: Friends United Press.

Barclay, Robert. 1831 (1678). *An Apology for the True Christian Divinity: As the Same Is Held Forth, and Preached by the People, Called, in Scorn, Quakers: Being a Full Explanation and Vindication of Their Principles and Doctrines, by Many Arguments, Deduced from Scripture and Right Reason, and the Testimony of Famous Authors, Both Ancient and Modern, with a Full Answer to the Strongest Objections Usually Made against Them, Presented to the King.* New York: Benjamin C. Stanton.

Bernet, Claus. 2009. *Rufus Jones (1863–1948): Life and Bibliography of an American Scholar, Writer, and Social Activist.* Frankfurt am Main: Peter Lang.

Birkel, Michael L. 2003. *A Near Sympathy: The Timeless Quaker Wisdom of John Woolman.* Richmond: Friends United Press.

———. 2004. *Silence and Witness: The Quaker Tradition.* Maryknoll: Orbis Books.

———. 2005. *Engaging Scripture: Reading the Bible with Early Friends.* Richmond: Friends United Press.

———. 2007. "Dean Freiday, Robert Barclay, and John Cassian." *Quaker Religious Thought* 110: 47–51.

Böhme, Jakob. 2010. *Genius of the Transcendent: Mystical Writings of Jakob Boehme.* Translated by Michael L. Birkel and Jeff Bach. Boston: Shambhala.

Brinton, Howard H. 1952. *Friends for 300 Years: The History and Beliefs of the Society of Friends Since George Fox Started the Quaker Movement.* New York: Harper.

———. 1972. *Quaker Journals; Varieties of Religious Experience among Friends.* Wallingford: Pendle Hill.

Bruneau, Marie-Florine. 1998. *Women Mystics Confront the Modern World: Marie De L'Incarnation (1599–1672) and Madame Guyon (1648–1717).* Albany: State University of New York Press.

Damiano, Kathryn A. 1989. *On Earth as It Is in Heaven: Eighteenth-Century Quakerism as Realized Eschatology.* PhD diss., Union of Experimenting Colleges and Universities.

Dandelion, Pink. 2007. *An Introduction to Quakerism.* Cambridge: Cambridge University Press.

———. 2010. "Guarded Domesticity and Engagement with 'The World': The Separate Spheres of Quaker Quietism." *Common Knowledge* 16.1:95–109.

De Sales, Francis. 1995. *Introduction to the Devout Life.* Translated and edited by Antony Mookenthottam, Antony Kolencherry, and Armind Nazareth. Bangalore: SFS.

De Sales, Francis, and Jeanne-François Chantal. 1988. *Francis de Sales, Jane de Chantal: Letters of Spiritual Direction.* Translated by Péronne Marie Thibert. Selected and introduced by Wendy M. Wright and Joseph F. Power. Mahwah: Paulist Press.

Dorrien, Gary J. 2003. *The Making of American Liberal Theology: Idealism, Realism, and Modernity, 1900–1950.* Louisville: Westminster John Knox Press.

Dupré, Louis K., Don E. Saliers, and John Meyendorff. 1989. *Christian Spirituality: Post-Reformation and Modern.* New York: Crossroad.

Fénelon, François S. L. M. 1720. *Pious Thoughts Concerning the Knowledge and Love of God: And Other Holy Exercises: by the Late Archbishop of Cambray. Together with a Letter of Christian Instruction by a Lady. Done Out of French.* London: W. and J. Innys.

Fénelon, François S. L. M. 2006. *Fénelon: Selected Writings.* Translated by Chad Helms. Mahwah: Paulist Press.

Fénelon, François S. L. M, Jeanne M. B. L. M. Guyon, Miguel Molinos, William Backhouse, and James Janson. 1946. *A Guide to True Peace: Or, the Excellency of Inward and Spiritual Prayer*. New York: Harper and Brothers/Pendle Hill.

Fénelon, François S. L. M., Jeanne M. B. L. M. Guyon, Miguel Molinos, William Backhouse, and James Janson. 1979. *A Guide to True Peace: Or, the Excellency of Inward and Spiritual Prayer*. Wallingford: Pendle Hill.

Fox, George. 1952. *The Journal of George Fox*. Edited by John Nickalls. Cambridge: Cambridge University Press.

Gilbert, Dorothy, and Russell Pope. 1940. "Quakerism and French Quietism." *Bulletin of Friends' Historical Association* 29.2: 93–96.

Grellet, Stephen. 1867. *Memoirs of the Life and Gospel Labours of Stephen Grellet*. Edited by Benjamin Seebohm. Philadelphia: H. Longstreth.

Grubb, Sarah. 1863. *A Brief Account of the Life and Religious Labors of Sarah Grubb, (formerly Sarah Lynes): A Minister of the Gospel in the Society of Friends*. Philadelphia: Friends' Book Store.

Guenin-Lelle, Dianne. 2002. "Friends' Theological Heritage: From Seventeenth-Century Quietists to *A Guide to True Peace*." *Quaker Theology* 6: 20–36.

———. 2003. "Jeanne Guyon's Influence on Quaker Practice: A Guiding Voice in Silence." In *La spiritualité, L'epistolaire, Le merveilleux au Grand Siècle: actes du 33e congrès annuel de la North American Society for Seventeenth Century French Literature, Tome III*, edited by David Wetsel et al., 39–49. Tübingen, Germany: Gunter Narr Verlag.

Guyon, Jeanne Marie Bouvier de La Motte (M. B. L. M.). 1800. *A Short and Easy Method of Prayer*. London: H. R. Allenson.

Guyon, Jeanne Marie Bouvier de La Motte. 1804. *The Exemplary Life of the Pious Lady Guion*. Translated by Thomas D. Brooke. Philadelphia: Joseph Crukshank.

Guyon, Jeanne Marie Bouvier de La Motte. 2012a. *The Prison Narratives of Jeanne Guyon*. Translated by Dianne Guenin-Lelle and Ronney Mourad. Oxford and New York: Oxford University Press.

Guyon, Jeanne Marie Bouvier de La Motte. 2012b. *Jeanne Guyon: Selected Writings*. Translated by Dianne Guenin-Lelle and Ronney Mourad. Mahwah: Paulist Press.

Harris, Rendel J. 1899. "The Mysticism of Madame Guyon." *The London Quarterly and Holborn Review* 92: 313–37.

James, William. 1903. *The Varieties of Religious Experience: A Study in Human Nature*. London: Longmans, Green.

Janney, Samuel M. 1881. *Memoirs of Samuel M. Janney: Late of Lincoln, Loudoun County, Va., a Minister in the Religious Society of Friends*. Philadelphia: Friends' Book Association.

Jones, Rufus M. 1906. *The Double Search: Studies in Atonement and Prayer*. Philadelphia: J. C. Winston.

———. 1917. "Quietism." *The Harvard Theological Review* 10.1:1–51.

———. 1921. *The Later Periods of Quakerism*. London: Macmillan.

———. 1923. *Social Law in the Spiritual World: Studies in Human and Divine Inter-Relationship*. London: Swarthmore Press.

———. 1938. *The Eternal Gospel*. New York: Macmillan.

Keating, Thomas. 1986. *Open Mind, Open Heart: The Contemplative Dimension of the Gospel*. New York: Amity House.

Kelly, Thomas R. 1941. *A Testament of Devotion*. Edited by Douglas V. Steere. New York: Harper and Brothers.

Lindberg, Carter, ed. 2005. *The Pietist Theologians: An Introduction to Theology in the Seventeenth and Eighteenth Centuries*. Malden: Blackwell.

London Yearly Meeting of the Religious Society of Friends (LYM). 1845. *Testimonies Concerning Deceased Ministers: Presented to the Yearly Meeting of Friends Held in London, 1845*. London: Edward Marsh.

May, Gerald G. 2005. *The Dark Night of the Soul: A Psychiatrist Explores the Connection between Darkness and Spiritual Growth.* San Francisco: HarperCollins.

McGinn, Bernard. 2005. *The Harvest of Mysticism in Medieval Germany (1300–1500).* New York: Crossroad.

Molinos, Miguel. 1699. *The Spiritual Guide: Which Dis-Intangles the Soul, and Brings It by the Inward Way, to the Getting of Perfect Contemplation and the Rich Treasure of Internal Peace.* London: n.p.

———. 1990 (1699). *The Spiritual Guide Which Disentangles the Soul.* Grand Rapids: Christian Classics Ethereal Library.

———. 2010. *The Spiritual Guide.* Translated by Robert P. Baird and Bernard McGinn. Mahwah: Paulist Press.

Penington, Isaac. 1761. *The Works of the Long-Mournful and Sorely-Distressed Isaac Penington: Whom the Lord in His Tender Mercy, at Length Visited and Relieved by the Ministry of That Despised People, Called Quakers; and in the Springings of That Light, Life and Holy Power in Him, Which They Had Truly and Faithfully Testified of, and Directed His Mind to, Were These Things Written, and Are Now Published as a Thankful Testimony of the Goodness of the Lord unto Him, and for the Benefit of Others.* London: Printed by B. Clark for J. and T. Kendall.

Pryce, Elaine. 2010a. "'Negative to a Marked Degree' or 'An Intense and Glowing Faith'? Rufus Jones and Quaker Quietism." *Common Knowledge* 16.3: 518–31.

———. 2010b. "'Upon the Quakers and the Quietists': Quietism, Power and Authority in Late Seventeenth-Century France, and Its Relation to Quaker History and Theology." *Quaker Studies* 14.2: 212–23.

Smith, Hannah W. 1903. *The Unselfishness of God and How I Discovered It: A Spiritual Autobiography.* New York: Fleming H. Revell.

Spencer, Carole D. 2007. *Holiness: The Soul of Quakerism: An Historical Analysis of the Theology of Holiness in the Quaker Tradition.* Eugene: Wipf and Stock.

Stephen, Caroline E. 1891. *Quaker Strongholds.* London: E. Hicks.

Taber, William P. 1992. *Four Doors to Meeting for Worship.* Wallingford: Pendle Hill.

Tauler, Johannes. 1910. *Die Predigten Taulers.* Edited by Ferdinand Vetter and Karl Schmidt. Berlin: Weidmann.

Ward, Patricia A. 1998. "Madame Guyon and Experiential Theology in America." *Church History* 67.3: 484–98.

Whittier, John G. 1904. *The Complete Poetical Works of John Greenleaf Whittier.* Boston: Houghton, Mifflin.

Woolman, John. 1775. "Epistle to The Quarterly and Monthly Meetings of Friends." In *The Works of John Woolman: In Two Parts.* London: Printed and sold by James Phillips.

A Guide to True Peace: Or, the Excellency of Inward and Spiritual Prayer[*]

Anonymous[1]

Annotated by Michael Birkel

Preface

It was said by our blessed Redeemer, that "They who worship the Father, must worship him in Spirit and in Truth" (John 4:24).[2] Now the object of this work is to explain, in a simple and familiar manner, how this only true worship can be acceptably performed, and inward, spiritual Prayer rightly attained. Few authors have written with greater clearness than those from whose works this little volume has been chiefly compiled; they, therefore, have been preferred: at the same time, it has been thought necessary to simplify, and render more intelligible, some of their terms, in order that they may be more generally understood.

Whilst some, into whose hands this little treatise may fall, may receive it as a messenger of glad tidings, there will, doubtless, be others, who may not feel disposed to place much dependence on the simple manner here pointed out, of drawing near to their Creator; let such, however, not judge according to the appearance; but, laying aside all reasoning thereon, in humility and simplicity make trial of it, and feel for themselves, whether what is herein stated will not prove to be something more than an empty dream of the imagination, or a cunningly devised fable.[3] And, if they do this in a sincerity of heart, they will soon have to acknowledge, to their great consolation, that these are indeed substantial, efficacious, and incontrovertible truths; and that this is the true way to become purified from our many defilements, to be instructed in heavenly mysteries,[4] to taste of the wine of the kingdom,[5] and to partake of that bread which nourishes up unto everlasting life.[6]

---

[*]The present text is the complete 1816 edition, the first American edition, published in New York, New York, by the Quaker printer Samuel Wood and Sons. The original British edition of 1813 was published in Stockton-on-Tees, England, by Christopher and Jennett, while the second, revised and enlarged, British edition (1815) was published in York, England, by W. Alexander. The American edition replaces citations of the "Vulgate Version" of the Christian Bible with the "English [Authorized] Version" (King James Bible; dat. 1611), with the latter being the standard English Protestant Bible until the mid-twentieth century. The text is now in the public domain. Unless otherwise indicated, I have supplied all of the annotations. I have also retained the received orthography, including the British spellings, of the original edition.

1. Originally published in English in 1813, the text was edited anonymously by the British Quakers William Backhouse (1779/1780–1844) and James Janson (1784–1821). It subsequently went through a variety of anonymous reprints.

2. In the first edition of this work, some of the quotations from Scripture were from the Vulgate Version; none are now admitted but such as are taken from the authorized English Version. Biblical references in the body of the text appear in the original edition. Biblical references supplied by myself appear in footnotes.

3. 2 Pet. 1:16.

4. Cf. Matt. 13:11.

5. Cf. Matt. 26:29.

6. Cf. John 6:27.

1: The Spirit of God Dwells in the Heart of Man[7]

It is certain from Scripture, that the Spirit of God dwells within us, that a "manifestation of this Spirit is given to us to profit withal," 1 Cor. 12:7, and that this is "the true Light, which lighteth every man that cometh into the world."[8] John 1:9. "This is the grace of God, which bringeth salvation, and which hath appeared unto all men; teaching us, that denying ungodliness and worldly lusts, we should live soberly, righteously, and godly, in this present world." Titus 2:12. But we make too little account of this internal Teacher,[9] which is the soul of our soul, and by which only we are able to form good thoughts and desires. God ceases not to reprove us for evil, and to influence us to that which is good; but the noise of the world without, and of our own passions within, deafen us, and hinder us from hearing him.

We must retire from all outward objects, and silence all the desires and wandering imaginations of the mind; that in this profound silence of the whole soul, we may hearken to the ineffable voice of the Divine Teacher. We must listen with an attentive ear; for it is a still, small voice.[10] It is not indeed a voice uttered in words as when a man speaks to his friend; but it is a perception infused by the secret operations and influences of the Divine Spirit, insinuating to us obedience, patience, meekness, humility, and all the other Christian virtues, in a language perfectly intelligible to the attentive soul. But how seldom is it that the soul keeps itself silent enough for God to speak! The murmurs of our vain desires, and our self-love, disturb all of the teachings of the Divine Spirit. Ought we then to be surprised, if so many persons, apparently devout, but too full of their own wisdom, and confidence in their own virtues, are not able to hear it; and that they look upon this internal Word[11] as the chimera of fanatics? Alas! what is it they aim at with their vain reasoning? The external word, even of the gospel, would be but an empty sound without this living and fruitful Word in the interior, to interpret and open it to the understanding.

Jesus Christ saith, "Behold, I stand at the door, and knock—if any man hear my voice, and open the door, I will come in unto him, and sup with him and he with me." Rev. 3:20. His knocks are the monitions of his Spirit; which touch us, and operate in us. And to attend to these monitions and follow them, is to open unto him.

He speaks in impenitent sinners; but these, engrossed in the eager pursuit of worldly pleasures, and the gratification of their evil passions, are not able to hear him. His word with them passes for a fable. But woe to those who receive their consolation in this life. The time will come when their vain joys shall be confounded.

---

7. Sources paraphrased in this chapter come from Fénelon 1720, 29–34.

8. This biblical text has been central to Quakers, who hold that God is accessible to each human being. Friends have used many names for this concept over their history, such as the Inner Light, Light Within, Inward Christ, "that of God in everyone." This belief is key to the silent form of Quaker communal worship, in which the community gathers in expectant waiting for the experience of divine presence and guidance.

9. The Inward Teacher is another Quaker term for the Inner Light.

10. 1 Kings 19:12.

11. In the beginning of the Gospel of John, Christ is identified as the Word ("Logos") that was with and was God. For Quakers therefore "internal Word" refers to the Inward Christ or Inner Light.

He speaks in sinners who are in the way of conversion: these feel the remorses of their conscience, and these remorses are the voice of the Spirit, which upbraids them inwardly with their vices. When they are truly touched, they have no difficulty to comprehend the secret voice, for it is this that so pierces them to the quick. It is that two-edged sword within them, of which Paul[12] speaks, which goes even to the dividing of soul from itself: "The word of God is quick and powerful, and sharper than any two-edged sword; piercing even to the dividing asunder of soul and spirit, and of the joints and marrow; and is a discerner of the thoughts and intents of the heart." Heb. 4:12.

He speaks in persons enlightened, learned, and whose life, outwardly regular, seems adorned with many virtues; but often these persons, full of themselves, and of their knowledge, give too much ear to themselves to listen to his teachings. God, who seeks only to communicate himself, finds no place (so to speak) where to introduce himself into these souls, that are so full of themselves, and so over-fed with their own wisdom and virtues. He hides his secrets from the wise and prudent, and reveals them to the low and simple: Jesus said, "I thank thee, O Father, Lord of heaven and earth! because thou hast hid these things from the wise and prudent, and hast revealed them unto babes." Matt. 11:25. It is with the humble and childlike that he delights to dwell, and to disclose to them his ineffable secrets. It is these who are more peculiarly qualified for receiving in a greater measure the gift of faith; for, being willing that the pride of Reason should be laid in the dust, they obstruct not the entrance of this gift of their vain arguments; but believe with simplicity and confidence.

2: On Faith

There are two sorts or degrees of faith:—the first is that by which the mind gives its assent to the truth of a thing on the testimony of another; the second is of a more exalted nature, being of Divine origin, and is a gift of the Holy Spirit.—By the first, we believe in the existence of God, and in the truths which he has revealed to us in the Holy Scriptures.[13] It is an essential principle in the beginning of the spiritual path; for "he that cometh to God, must believe that he is God, and that he is a rewarder of them that diligently seek him." Heb. 11:6. And if we put our whole trust in him, and endeavour in all things to obey him, we shall be in a state of preparation for the reception of that true and living faith which is "the gift of God." Eph. 2:8.

It is only by this faith that we shall be enabled to overcome all our spiritual enemies, and clearly to understand those mysteries which are incomprehensible to human reason; for reason, being born of man, is weak and uncertain and easily errs; but faith, being born of God, cannot err; reason, therefore, must follow and submit to faith, not go before and control it.

---

12. Paul is the ancient Christian missionary, to whom many of the Epistles in the New Testament are attributed.

13. "Holy Scriptures" refers to the Bible, the collection of sacred Christian texts. (Many but not all Quakers, however, throughout their history, have declined to refer to the Bible as holy because they have held that the Spirit of God who revealed the Scriptures is still available to lead those who will attend to this Inward Teacher. This practice was not meant to diminish the value Scriptures but rather to point to the possibility of ongoing revelation by the same Spirit.)

It is by faith that, "being justified, we have peace with God through our Lord Jesus Christ." Rom. 5:1. And when this precious gift has been granted to us, it produces in us hope, love, confidence, joy and holiness of heart.[14] We shall then be enabled to feel an entire dependence on the goodness, power, justice, and mercy of God, and a confidence in his promises; as well as more fully to experience and comprehend the operations of his spirit on the mind.

Faith is an essential requisite for the proper performance of all our duties to the Supreme Being; indeed, without it we cannot possibly please him, Heb.11:6, neither should we ever be induced to seek him, or believe in the influence of his holy Spirit upon our souls. It is by faith that we are supported in our path to peace, and are enabled to persevere through the difficulties and besetments, which we may have to encounter on our way: it is through this holy principle that we suffer the pains of dryness,[15] and want of consolation, without fainting; being thereby strengthened to "endure, as seeing him who is invisible." Heb. 11:27. And it is only by faith that we can attain to the practice of true, inward, and spiritual prayer.

3: On Prayer[16]

Prayer is an intercourse of the soul with God.[17] It is not a work of the head but of the heart; which ought always to continue. It is the medium through which life and food are conveyed to the soul, and the channel through which the gifts and graces of the Holy Spirit[18] flow and are communicated. Every secret aspiration of the soul to God is prayer: all therefore are capable of prayer, and are called thereto, as all are capable of, and are called to salvation.

Paul hath enjoined us to "pray without ceasing;" 1 Thes. 5:17; and Jesus saith, "I say unto all, watch and pray." Mark 13:33, 37, and 14:38. Come, then, all ye that are athirst, to these

---

14. See Rom. 5:2; 1 Pet. 1:8; Eph. 3:12; and Acts 15:9.

15. The term "dryness" refers to the experience of aridity in prayer, when spiritual practice brings no obvious results, no sense of pleasure or even of divine presence.

16. Sources quoted in this chapter come from Guyon 1800, chapter 1.

17. "God is a Spirit; so is the mind. Bodies can have intercourse; so can souls. When minds are in an assimilating state of purity, they have union with their Maker. This was the bliss of Paradise; sin interrupted, and holiness must restore it. To the soul thus distressed, the Creator communicates himself, in a manner which is as insensible to the natural eye, as the falling of dew; but not less refreshing in its secret powers than the dew is to vegetation.—*Anonymous Essay on Devotion.*" This note is in the original text. The sources cited are difficult to determine. The earliest reference that I have found is in *The Boston Weekly Magazine*, October 12, 1805, 3.51:1. It is also printed in Jesse Kersey, *A Treatise on Fundamental Doctrines of the Christian Religion: In Which Are Illustrated the Profession, Ministry, Worship, and Faith of the Society of Friends* (Philadelphia: Published by Emmor Kimber, no. 93, and Solomon W. Conrad, no. 87, Market-Street; Samuel Wood, 1815). The Philadelphia *Friends Intelligencer* 27.5:551 (Tenth Month 29, 1870) notes, "There is so much of truth and beauty in the following article from the *English Review* for December 1791, that it merits republication in this age."

18. In traditional Christian teaching, God is one in being but encountered as three experienceable realities, namely, Father, Son, and Holy Spirit. Doctrine on this threeness yet oneness of God emerged slowly over the early centuries of Christianity, and official teaching on the Holy Spirit is least developed of all. Among Quakers, there was a rejection of the term "Trinity" because it does not appear in the Bible and because the word historically generated endless theological disputation that Quakers did not always judge to be spiritually useful. Early Friends, however, continued to use the biblical terms of Father, Son, and Holy Spirit. More recently, many liberal Quakers have moved away from traditional teaching on the divinity of Christ as the Son of God. The ancient Christian church felt the continuing experience of the presence of the Holy Spirit to guide and sustain their community, and early Quakers, who saw themselves as primitive Christianity revived, renewed this emphasis on the Holy Spirit.

living waters, Rev. 22:17;[19] nor lose your precious moments in "hewing out cisterns that will hold no water." Jeremiah, 2:13. Come, ye famishing souls who find naught whereon to feed; come, and ye shall be fully satisfied. Come, ye poor afflicted ones, who groan beneath your load of wretchedness and pain, and ye shall find ease and comfort. Come, ye sick, to your Physician, and be not fearful of approaching him, because you are filled with diseases; expose them to his view, and they shall be healed.

Children draw near to your Father, and he will embrace you in the arms of love. Come, ye poor, stray, wandering sheep, return to your Shepherd. Come, ye who have been seeking happiness in worldly pleasures and pursuits, but have failed to find in them that satisfaction ye expected: come, and learn how to be truly happy here, and eternally happy hereafter.—Come, sinners, to your Saviour. Come, ye dull, ignorant, and illiterate; ye who think yourselves the most incapable of prayer: ye are more peculiarly called and adapted thereto. Let all, without exception, come; for Christ hath called all.

You must however learn a species of prayer which may be exercised at all times, which doth not obstruct outward employments, and which may be equally practised by all ranks and conditions of men; by the poor as well as the rich, by the illiterate as well as the learned. It cannot, therefore, be a prayer of the head, but of the heart. It is a species of prayer which nothing can interrupt but irregular and disorderly affections. And though you may think yourselves ever so dull, and incapable of sublime attainments, yet, by prayer the possession and enjoyment of God is easily obtained; for he is more desirous to give himself to us than we can be to receive him.

Prayer is the guide to perfection, and the sovereign good; it delivers us from every vice, and obtains for us every virtue: for the one great means to become perfect is to walk in the presence of Infinite Purity.[20] He himself has said, "Walk in my presence, and be thou perfect." Gen. 17:1. It is only by prayer that we are brought into, and maintained in his presence; and when once we have fully known him, and the sweetness of his love, we shall find it impossible to relish any thing so much as himself.

4: All Are Capable of Attaining to Inward and Spiritual Prayer[21]

If all were solicitous to pursue the spiritual path, shepherds, while they watched their flocks, might have the spirit of the primitive Christians, and the husbandman at the plough maintain a blessed intercourse with his Creator; the manufacturer, while he exhausted his outward man with labour, would be renewed in internal strength; every species of vice would shortly disappear, and all mankind become true followers of the good Shepherd.[22]

Oh, when once the heart is gained, how easily is all moral evil corrected! It is for this reason, that God, above all things, requires the heart. It is the conquest of the heart alone, that can extirpate those dreadful vices which are so predominant amongst men; such as drunkenness,

---

19. Cf. John 7:37, 4:10.

20. The expression "Infinite Purity" refers to God.

21. Sources quoted in this chapter come from Guyon 1800, chapters 23–25.

22. In the Gospel of John 10:1–18, Jesus is described as the good shepherd who knows his sheep (believers) and lays down his life for them.

blasphemy, lewdness, envy, and theft. Christ would become the universal and peaceful Sovereign, and the hearts of all mankind would be wholly renewed.

The decay of internal piety is unquestionably the source of the various errors that have risen in the world; all of which would speedily be sapped and overthrown, were inward religion to be established.—If, instead of engaging our wandering brethren in vain disputes, we could but teach them simply to believe, and diligently to pray, we should lead them sweetly unto God.

Oh, how inexpressibly great is the loss sustained by mankind, from the neglect of the interior!

Some excuse themselves by saying that this is a dangerous way; pleading the incapacity of simple persons to comprehend spiritual matters. But Isaiah[23] saith, "The wayfaring men, though fools, shall not err therein." Isa. 35:8. And where can be the danger of walking in the only true way, which is Christ? John 14:6. Of giving ourselves up to him, fixing our eye continually on him, placing all our confidence in his grace, and turning with all the strength of our souls to his pure love?

The simple, so far from being incapable of this perfection, are by their docility, innocency and humility, peculiarly adapted and qualified for its attainment; and as they are not accustomed to reasoning, they are less employed in speculations, less tenacious of their own opinions. Even from their want of learning, they submit more freely to the teachings of the Divine Spirit; whereas others, who are blinded by self-sufficiency, and enslaved by prejudice, give great resistance to the operations of Grace.[24]

We are told in Scripture that, "unto the simple, God giveth understanding;" Psalm 119:130; and we are also assured that he careth for them: "The Lord preserveth the simple." Psalm 116:6. Christ said, "Suffer little children to come unto me, for of such is the kingdom of heaven." Matt. 19:14.

The simple are incapable of reasoning; teach them, therefore, the prayer of the heart, not of the head; the prayer of the Spirit, not of man's invention.

Alas! by wanting them to pray in elaborate forms, and to be curiously critical therein, we create their chief obstacles.—The children have been led astray from the best of Fathers, by endeavouring to teach them too refined, too polished a language.

The simple and undisguised emotions of filial love are infinitely more expressive than the most studied language. The spirit of God needs none of our arrangements and methods: when it pleaseth him, he turns shepherds into prophets; and, so far from excluding any from the temple of prayer, he throws wide open the gates, that all may enter in; while "Wisdom crieth, Whoso is simple let him turn in hither; as for him that wanteth understanding, she saith to him, Come, eat of my bread, and drink of the wine which I have mingled." Prov. 9:3–5.

To teach man to seek God in his heart, to think of him, to return to him whenever he finds he has wandered from him, and to do and suffer all things with a single eye to please him, is the natural and ready process; it is leading the soul to the very source of Grace, wherein is to be found all that is necessary for sanctification.[25]

---

23. Isaiah was a prophet, or spokesperson of God, in ancient Israel. A book of the Bible bears his name.

24. In Christian theology, "grace" refers to the merciful generosity of God. In classical Protestant thought, it is grace, or God's initiatory goodwill, alone that saves humankind from sin.

25. The term "sanctification" means "to render holy." It was understood, though in different ways among Protestant theologians, to refer to the process of being redeemed from sin and made righteous before God.

O that all would at once put themselves into this way, that Christ's kingdom might be established in their hearts! For as it is the heart alone that can oppose his sovereignty, it is by the subjection of the heart that his sovereignty is most highly exalted. And since none can attain this blessed state, save those whom God himself leads and places therein, we do not pretend to introduce any into it, but only to point out the shortest and safest road that leads to it: beseeching you not to be retarded in your progress by any external exercises; not to rest in the shadow instead of the substance. If the water of eternal life is shown to some thirsty souls, how inexpressibly cruel would it be, confining them to a round of external forms, to prevent their approaching it: so that their longing shall never be satisfied, but they shall perish with thirst!

O ye blind and foolish men, who pride yourselves on science, wisdom, wit and power! How well do you verify what God hath said, that his secrets are hidden from the wise and prudent, and revealed unto *the little ones—the babes!* Matt. 11:25.

5: On Attaining to True Prayer[26]

The sort of prayer to which we have alluded is that of inward silence; wherein the soul, abstracted from all outward things, in holy stillness, humble reverence, and lively faith, waits patiently to feel the Divine presence, and to receive the precious influence of the Holy Spirit. And when you retire for this purpose, which should be your frequent practice, you should consider yourselves as being placed in the Divine presence, looking with a single eye to him, resigning yourselves entirely into his hands, to receive from him whatsoever he may be pleased to dispense to you; calmly endeavouring, at the same time, to fix your minds in peace and silence; quitting all your own reasonings, and not willingly thinking on any thing, how good and how profitable soever it may appear to be. And should any vain thoughts present themselves, you should gently turn from them; and thus faithfully and patiently wait to feel the Divine presence.

If, while you are thus engaged, something of inward stillness, or a degree of the softening influence of the Divine Spirit, is mercifully granted you, you should prize these manifestations of the presence of God in your souls; and be carefully and reverently attentive thereto; being cautious, however, not to endeavour to increase them by your activity; for, by so doing, you will draw the mind off from that state of holy stillness and humble watchfulness, which you should be solicitous as much as possible to maintain: by fanning the flame there is danger of extinguishing it, and thus depriving the soul of that nourishment which was intended for it.

A lively sense of this presence will extricate us speedily from numberless mental wanderings, remove us far from external objects, and bring us nigh unto that Almighty Power, which is to be found in our inmost centre; which is the temple wherein he dwelleth. 1 Cor. 3:16. And when we are thus fully turned inward, and warmly penetrated with a sense of his presence, we should in stillness and repose, with reverence, confidence, and love, suffer the blessed food of which we have tasted, to sink deep into the soul.

The prayer of inward silence is the easiest and most profitable path, because, with a simple view, or attention to God, the soul becomes like a humble supplicant before its Lord; or as a child that casts itself into the safe bosom of its mother. It is also the most secure, because it is

---

26. Sources quoted in this chapter come from Guyon 1800, chapters 4, 2, and 14.

abstracted from the operations of the imagination; which is often beguiled into extravagancies, and is easily bewildered and deceived; the soul being thereby deprived of its peace.

It will at first be difficult, from the habit the mind will have acquired of being always from home, roving hither and thither, and from subject to subject, to restrain it, and free it from those wanderings which are an impediment to prayer. Indeed those wanderings of the imagination, with which beginners are for some time tried, are permitted in order to prove their faith, exercise their patience, and to show them how little they can perform of themselves; as well as to teach them to depend upon an Almighty Power alone for strength to overcome all their difficulties; "for by" his own "strength shall no man prevail"; 1 Sam. 2:9, and if they place all their hope in him, and faithfully persevere, every obstacle will be gradually removed, and they will find that they will be enabled to approach him with facility, and that inward silence is not only attended with much less difficulty, but at times will be found to be easy, sweet, and delightful. They will know that this is the true way of finding God; and feel "his name to be as ointment poured forth." Cant. 1:3.

And although we should at all times be very watchful and diligent in recalling our wandering thoughts, restraining them, as much as may be, in due subjection; yet a direct contest with them only serves to augment and irritate them; whereas, by calling to mind that we are in the Divine presence, and endeavouring to sink down under a sense and perception thereof, simply turning inward, we wage insensibly a very advantageous, though indirect, war with them.

Those who have not learned to read are not, on that account, excluded from prayer; for the great Teacher who teacheth all things is Christ himself. John 14:26. They should learn this fundamental rule, that "the kingdom of God is within them;" Luke 17:21, and that there only it must be sought.

"The kingdom of God is within you," saith the blessed Jesus. Abandon, therefore, the cares and pleasures of this world, and turn to the Lord with the whole heart, and the soul shall find rest. Matt. 11:28–29. If we withdraw our attention from outward things, and keep it fixed on the internal Teacher, endeavouring to obey him in whatsoever he may require of us, we will soon perceive the coming of the kingdom of God: Matt. 6:10, for the kingdom of God is that "peace and joy in the Holy Ghost," Rom. 14:17, which cannot be received by sensual and worldly men.

It is for want of inward retirement, and prayer, that our lives are so imperfect, and that we are neither penetrated nor warmed with the divine light of truth, Christ the light. John 1:9. We should therefore be in the daily practise of it; and there are none so much occupied, as not to be able to find a few moments of inward retirement. The less we practise silent prayer, the less desire we have for it; for our minds being set upon outward things, we contract at last such habit, that it is very hard to turn them inward.

"The Lord is in his holy temple, let all the earth keep silence before him." Heb. 2:20. The silence of all our earthly thoughts and desires is absolutely indispensable, if we would hear the secret voice of the Divine Instructor. Hearing is a sense formed to receive sounds, and is rather passive than active, admitting, but not communicating, sensation; and if we would hear, we must lend the ear for that purpose: so, CHRIST THE ETERNAL WORD, Rev. 19:13, without whose divine inspeaking the soul is dead, dark, and barren, when he would speak within us, requires the most silent attention to his all-quickening and efficacious voice.

We should forget ourselves and all self-interest, and listen and be attentive to the inspeaking voice. Outward silence is very requisite for the cultivation and improvement of inward; and, indeed, it is impossible we should become internal, without the love and practice of outward silence and retirement. And unquestionably our being thus internally engaged is wholly incompatible with being busied, and employed in the numerous trifles that surround us.

When through inadvertency or unfaithfulness we become dissipated, or as it were uncentered, it is of immediate importance to turn again gently and peacefully inward; and thus we may learn to preserve the spirit and unction of prayer throughout the day: for if the prayer of inward silence were wholly confined to any appointed half-hour, or hour, we should reap but little fruit.

It is of greatest importance for the soul to go to prayer with confidence; and such a pure and disinterested love, as seeks nothing from the Father, but the ability to please him, and to do his will: for a child who only proportions his diligence to his hope of reward, renders himself unworthy of all reward. Go, then, to prayer, not that ye may enjoy spiritual delights, but that ye may be full or empty, just as it pleaseth God. This will preserve you in an evenness of spirit, either in desertion or in consolation, and will prevent your being surprised at dryness, or the apparent repulses of Him who is altogether love.

Constant prayer is to keep the heart always right towards God. Strive then not to suffer your minds to be too much entangled with outward things, endeavouring to be totally resigned to the Divine Will; that God may do with you and yours according to his heavenly pleasure, relying on him as on a kind and loving father; and though you be taken up with your outward affairs, and your minds thereby prevented from being actually fixed on him, even then you will always carry a fire about you that will never go out; but which, on the contrary, will nourish a secret prayer, that will be like a lamp continually lighted before the throne of God.[27]

A son who loves his father does not always think distinctly of him; many objects draw away his mind, but these never interrupt the filial love; whenever his father returns into his thoughts, he loves him, and he feels, in the very inmost of his heart, that he has never discontinued one moment to love him, though he has ceased to think of him. In this manner should we love our heavenly Father. It is by coming under the influence of the Divine Spirit that we are enabled to call God Father, and that we can indeed become his sons.

True religion is a heaven-born thing, it is an emanation of the truth and goodness of God upon the spirits of men, whereby they are formed into a similitude and likeness of himself, and become "partakers of the Divine nature." 2 Pet. 1:4. A true Christian is every way of a most noble extraction, of a heavenly and divine pedigree, being born, as John expresseth it,[28] "from above."[29] And in another place he saith, "Behold what manner of love the Father hath bestowed upon us, that we should be called the sons of God." 1 John 3:1.

If considerations such as these are not sufficient to convince us of the folly of our attachment to perishing things, and to stimulate us to press after those which obtain for us such great and glorious privileges, we must, indeed, be sunk into a state of deep and deplorable insensibility;

---

27. Cf. Rev. 4:5.

28. John was a disciple of Jesus. A gospel and three epistles in the Christian New Testament bear his name, although this is contested by most modern biblical scholarship.

29. John 3:3.

out of which, even "if one were to rise from the dead"[30] for that purpose, it would be impossible to arouse us.[31]

6: On Spiritual Dryness[32]

No sooner shall we have given ourselves up to serve the Lord in this inward way, than he will begin to purify us and try our faith, in order to draw us nearer to himself. And, for this purpose, he will lead us through the paths of dryness and desertion; so that, when we endeavour to fix our minds in silence, in order to feel after our God, we will not experience the comfort and refreshment we expected; but, on the contrary, will be more than usually beset with a multitude of troublesome and importunate imaginations; insomuch, that we shall begin to think that we labour to no purpose, and that the prayer of internal silence is an attainment to which we need not aspire, seeing that our imagination is so ungovernable, and our minds so void of good. But this state of dryness is very profitable, if it be suffered with patience.

The Lord makes use of the veil of dryness, to the end we may not know what he is working in us, and so we may be humble; because, if we felt, and knew, what he was working in our souls, satisfaction and presumption would get in; we should imagine we were doing some good thing; and this self-complacency would prevent our spiritual advancement.

And, though in the prayer of mental stillness, we may feel ourselves to be in a dry and comfortless state, not being able to get rid of our troublesome thoughts, nor experience any light, consolation, or spiritual feeling, yet let us not be afflicted, nor desist from our undertaking; but resign ourselves at that time with vigour, and patiently persevere as in his presence; for while we persevere in that manner, our souls will be internally improved.

We need not believe that when we come from prayer in the same manner as we began it, without feeling ourselves profited thereby, that we have been toiling in vain. True prayer consists, not in enjoying the light, and having knowledge of spiritual things, but in enduring with patience, and persevering in faith and silence; believing that we are in the Lord's presence, turning to him our hearts with tranquillity and simplicity of mind.

We must be aware that nature is always an enemy to the spirit; and that when she is deprived of sensible pleasures, she remains weak, melancholy, and full of irksomeness. Hence, from the uneasiness of thoughts, the lassitude of body, importunate sleep, and our inability to curb the senses, every one of which would follow its own pleasure, we will often feel impatient again to mingle in the concerns of time. Happy are we if we can persevere amidst this painful trial!

---

30. Luke 16:31.

31. "Note—If you wish to receive real profit from the holy Scriptures and other spiritual books, you must peruse them with deep attention, and introversion of mind, observing, whatever you have chosen, to read only a small part of it; endeavouring to taste and digest it, to extract the essence and substance thereof; and proceed no further, while any savour or relish remains in the passage: when this subsides, take up your book again, and proceed as before, seldom reading more than half a page at a time; for it is not the quantity that is read, but the manner of reading, that yields us profit. Those who read fast, reap no more advantage than a bee would do by only skimming over the surface of a flower, instead of waiting to penetrate into it, and extract its sweets. If this method were pursued, we should be more fully disposed for retirement and prayer. Guion." Note in original.

32. Sources quoted in this chapter include Molinos 1699, paragraphs 27, 71, and 66; Guyon 1800, chapters 5 and 21.

Remember, that "they who wait upon the Lord shall renew their strength; they shall mount up with wings as eagles; they shall run and not be weary, they shall walk and not faint." Isaiah 40:31.

The prayer of internal silence may be well typified by the wrestling, which the Scriptures say the patriarch Jacob had all night with God,[33] until the day broke and he blessed him.[34] Wherefore, the soul is to persevere, and wrestle with the difficulties that it will meet with in inward prayer without desisting, until the Sun of internal light begins to appear, and the Lord gives it his blessing.

If you go to prayer with the spirit and intention of praying, so long as you retract not that intention, although, through misery and frailty, your thoughts may wander, you will, nevertheless, pray in spirit and in truth. Almighty Power, in due time, will help you to overcome all your difficulties; and, when least you think, will give you holy purposes, and more effectual desires of serving him. Distrust not him, therefore, but only yourselves; and remember that, as the apostle saith, "He is the father of mercies, and God of all comforts." 2 Cor. 1:3. His comforts are sometimes withdrawn, but his mercy endureth forever. He hath deprived you of what was sweet and sensible in his grace, because you required to be humbled.

Be of good courage, then, and though it may seem to you that you toil without gaining much advantage, yet you must recollect we must plough and sow before we can reap; and if you persevere in faith and patience, you will reap an abundant reward for all your labours. Would you be so unreasonable as to expect to find without seeking; or for it to be opened to you, without your taking the pains to knock?[35] As well might the husbandman expect to see his fields waving with grain, without his having been at the trouble to put the seed into the ground.

It is no hard matter to adhere to God while you are in the enjoyment of his comforts and consolations; but if you would prove your fidelity to him, you must be willing to follow him through the paths of dryness and desertion. The truth of a friend is not known while he is receiving favours and benefits from us; but if he remain faithful to us when we treat him with coldness and neglect, it will be proof of the sincerity of his attachment.

Though Almighty Goodness hath no other desire than to impart himself to those that love and seek him, yet he frequently conceals himself from us, that we may be roused from sloth, and induced to seek him with fidelity and love. But, with what abundant goodness doth he recompense our faithfulness! and how sweetly are these apparent withdrawings of himself succeeded by the consolations of his love! David[36] saith, "I waited patiently for the Lord; and he inclined unto me, and heard my cry. He brought me up also out of a horrible pit, out of the miry clay, and set my feet upon a rock, and established my goings. And he hath put a new song in my mouth; even praise unto our God." Psalm 40:1–3.

In seasons of the withdrawings of his presence, we are apt to believe that it will be a proof of our fidelity, and evince the ardour of our love, to seek him by an exertion of our *own* strength

---

33. The story of Jacob ("Israel"), the grandson of Abraham with whom God made a covenant and the father of twelve sons who lent their names to the twelve tribes of ancient Israel, is told in the biblical book of Genesis.

34. Gen. 32:24.

35. Matt. 7:7.

36. David was a king of ancient Israel and is regarded by Christians as a forebear of Jesus. The biblical poems collected in the book of Psalms are traditionally attributed to David, although modern scholarship questions this.

and activity; and that this exertion will induce him the more speedily to return. But this is not the right procedure when we are in this state: with patient resignation, with self-abasement with the repeated breathings of an ardent but peaceful affection, and with reverential silence, we must wait the return of our beloved. Thus only we shall demonstrate that we seek nothing but himself, and his good pleasure; and not the selfish delights of our own sensations.

It is very common for us, when we feel the sweetness of the grace of God, to fancy that we love him; but it is only in the withdrawings of his presence that our love can be tried, and the measure of it known. It is at these seasons that we are convinced of the weakness and misery of our nature, and how incapable we are, of ourselves, to think or do any good. There are many who, when they experience meltings of heart, shedding of tears, and other sensible delights, imagine that they are the favourites of the Almighty, and that then they truly possess him; and so pass all their lives in seeking after those pleasurable sensations; but they should be cautious lest they deceive themselves, for these consolations, when they proceed from nature, and are occasioned by their own reflections, or self-admirings, hinder them from discerning the true light, or making one step towards perfection. You should therefore be attentive to distinguish those meltings of the affections from the operations which purely proceed from the Divine Spirit; leaving yourselves to be led forward by him, who will be your light in the midst of darkness and dryness.

It is of no small advantage, patiently to suffer the want of consolation, and the trouble and importunities of a wandering imagination: it is an offering up of one's self in a whole burnt offering and sacrifice. And as many times as you exercise yourselves, calmly to reject your vain thoughts, and peacefully to endure your dark and desolate state, so many crowns will the Lord set upon your heads.

It is of great importance that you endeavour, at all times, to keep your hearts in peace; that you may keep pure that temple of God. The way to keep it in peace is to enter into it by means of inward silence. When you see yourselves more sharply assaulted, retreat into that region of peace; and you will find a fortress that will enable you to triumph over all your enemies, visible and invisible, and over all their snares and temptations. Within your own soul resides divine aid, and sovereign succour. Retreat within it, and all will be quiet, secure, peaceable, and calm. Thus, by means of mental silence, which can only be attained by divine help, you may look for tranquillity in tumult; solitude in company; light in darkness; forgetfulness in pressures; vigour in despondency; courage in fear; resistance in temptation; peace in war; and quiet in tribulation.

7: On Defects and Infirmities[37]

Should we so far get off our guard, as again to wander among externals in search of happiness, or sink into dissipation, or commit a fault, we must instantly turn inward; for having departed thereby from our God, we should as soon as possible return unto him, and patiently suffer whatever sensations he is pleased to impress: for he has declared, "As many as I love, I rebuke and chasten." Rev. 3:19.

---

37. Sources quoted in this chapter derive from Guyon 1800, chapter 18.

On the commission of a fault, it is of great importance to guard against vexation and disquietude, which spring from a secret root of pride, and a love of our own excellence; we are hurt by feeling what we are; and if we discourage ourselves, or despond, we are the more enfeebled; and from our reflections on the fault, a chagrin arises, which is often worse than the fault itself.

The truly humble soul is not surprised at its defects or failings; and the more miserable and wretched it beholds itself, the more doth it abandon itself unto God, and press for a nearer and more intimate alliance with him, that it may avail itself of an eternal strength. We should the rather be induced to act thus, as he himself hath said: "I will instruct thee and teach thee in the way which thou shalt go: I will guide thee with mine eye." Psalm 32:8.

8: On Temptations and Tribulations[38]

We are at times so base, proud, and ambitious; and so full of our own appetites, our own judgment and opinions, that if temptations and tribulations were not permitted to try, humble, and purify us, we should never arrive at a state of acceptance.

The Lord, seeing our misery, and perverse inclinations, and being thereby moved to compassion, withdraws his strength from us, that we may feel our own weakness; suffering us to be assaulted by violent and painful suggestions of impatience and pride, and divers other temptations; and some, who have long been in the practise of sin, by gluttony, luxury, rage, swearing, despair, and a great many other besetments; in order that they may know themselves, and be humble. With these temptations, Infinite Goodness humbles our pride; giving us, in them, the most wholesome medicine.

"All our righteousnesses," as Isaiah saith, "are as filthy rags;" Isaiah 64:6, through the vanity, conceitedness, and self-love, with which they are defiled. It is, therefore, necessary that they should be purified with the fire of temptation and tribulation; that so they may be clean, pure, perfect, and acceptable in the sight of God.

The Lord polishes the soul which he draws to himself, with the rough file of temptation; freeing it thereby from the rust of many evil passions and propensities.—By means of temptation and tribulation he humbles, subjects, and exercises it; showing it its own weakness and misery. It is thus that he purifies and strips the heart, in order that all its operations may be pure, and of inestimable value. Oh, how happy would you be, if you could quietly believe that all the trials and temptations, wherewith you are assaulted, are permitted for your gain and spiritual profit!

But you will perhaps say, that when you are molested by others, or wronged and injured by your neighbor, that this cannot be for your spiritual advantage; seeing that it is the effect of their faults and malice. This is no other than a cunning and hidden device of the enemy; because, though God wills not the sin of another, yet he wills his own effects in you; and the trouble which accrues to you from another's fault should improve you by increasing your patience, and exercising your forbearance and charity.

Consider, how the Lord makes use of the faults of others for the good of your souls. Oh, the greatness of the divine wisdom! who can pry into the depth of the secret and extraordinary

---

38. Sources quoted in this chapter derive from Molinos 1699, paragraphs 51–53 and 63; Guyon 1800, chapter 19.

means, and the hidden ways, whereby he guides the soul which he desires to purge, transform, and dignify?

It is often the greatest temptation to be without temptation; because we are then most liable to fall into a state of lukewarmness; wherefore we ought not to repine when it assaults us; but with resignation, peace, and constancy, shut our hearts against it. If we would serve God, and arrive at the sublime region of internal peace, we must pass through this rugged path of temptation and tribulation; and therein become polished, purged, renewed, and purified.

A direct contest and struggle with temptations rather serves to augment them; and withdraws the soul from that adherence to God, which it should ever be its principal occupation to strive after and maintain.—The surest and safest method of conquest is simply to turn away from the evil, and draw yet nearer and closer to our Sure Refuge: a little child, on perceiving a monster, does not wait to fight with it, and will scarcely turn its eyes towards it; but quickly shrinks into the bosom of its mother, in total confidence of safety: so, likewise, should the soul turn from the dangers of temptation to its God. "God is in the midst of her," saith the psalmist, "she shall not be moved; God shall help her, and that right early." Psalm 46:5. "The name of the Lord is a strong tower, to which the righteous flee and are safe." Prov. 18:10.

If we do otherwise, and in our weakness attempt to attack our enemies, we shall frequently feel ourselves wounded, if not totally defeated: but, by casting ourselves into the presence of God, and relying solely on him, we shall find supplies of strength for our support. This was the succour sought for by David: "I have set," saith he, "the Lord always before me: because he is at my right hand, I shall not be moved. Therefore, my heart is glad, and my glory rejoiceth: my flesh, also, shall rest in hope." Psalm 16:8–9. And, it is said in Exodus 14:14, "The Lord shall fight for you, and ye shall hold your peace."

Although "God cannot be tempted with evil, neither tempteth he any man;" James 1:13, yet it is evident that temptations are permitted for our good, and, if rightly endured, tend to our refinement; "therefore, count it all joy, when ye fall into divers temptations; knowing this, that the trying of your faith worketh patience." James 1:2. And in all our besetments, however painful they may feel to us, or of whatever nature they may be, we should remember that it is said, "Blessed is the man that endureth temptation: for when he is tried, he shall receive the crown of life, which the Lord hath promised to them that love him." James 1:12.

You cannot be hurt by men or devils, if you keep always near to God; for, "who is he that will harm you, if ye be followers of that which is good." 1 Peter 3:13. But if you are hurt, it is your pride, your passions, and your many unsubdued evil propensities, that rise up and injure you; and as long as these remain, the enemy will make use of them, and seek to draw your minds away from adherence to an all-sufficient Preserver.

"Every man is tempted, when he is drawn away of his own lust, and enticed." James 1:14. Therefore, know your own state, and the need you have to be purified by means of temptation, and keep always on the watch, lest the unwearied enemy gain access to your souls by his insinuations and pleasing allurements, which he will suit to your present situation and condition: for, in your passage through life, there are many things which he will offer you as temptations; endeavouring to produce in you an inordinate inclination and desire for them; which if you give way to whilst you are in this manner tempted, great will be the danger of your being wholly overcome.

If the malignant enemy is not resisted in his first attack, he enters by gradual advances, and takes entire possession of the heart: and so long as opposition is deferred by habitual negligence, the power of opposing becomes every day less, and the strength of the adversary proportionably greater. Therefore, when you feel in yourselves a strong and eager desire after any thing whatsoever, and find your inclinations carry you too precipitately to do it, strive to moderate yourselves by retreating inward, and seeking after tranquillity of mind. To do all things well, we must do them as in the Divine presence, otherwise we shall soon get off our right center, and be in danger of being wholly overthrown.

Oh, blessed soul! if thou wouldst but be content and quiet in the fire of temptation and tribulation, and suffer thyself to be fully proved and tried, in patiently enduring the assaults of the enemy and the desertion of heavenly good, how soon wouldst thou find thyself rich in celestial pleasures! how soon would the divine bounty make a rich throne in thy soul, and a goodly habitation for thee to refresh and solace thyself in! Know, that although the Lord may for a season *visit*, yet taketh up his *abode* in none but peaceful souls; and those in whom the fire of temptation and tribulation hath consumed *all* their corrupt propensities; the Lord reposeth not himself any where, but where quietness reigns, and self-love is banished.

If, from chaos, his omnipotence has produced so many wonders in the creation of the world, what will he not do in thy soul, created after his own image and likeness, if thou keep constant, quiet, and resigned, with a true sense of thine own nothingness?

"Cast not, therefore, away thy confidence, which hath great recompence of reward," Heb. 10:35, but keep constant; O blessed soul! keep constant; for it will not be as thou imaginest: nor art thou at any time nearer to God, than in such times of desertion, and trial of thy faith; for, although the sun is hid in the clouds, yet it changes not its place, nor loses any part of its brightness. The Lord permits these painful temptations and desertions to purge and polish, to cleanse and disrobe of self; that thou mayst become by these trials entirely his, and give thyself up wholly to serve him.

Oh, how much is there to be purified in a soul that must arrive at the holy mountain of perfection, and of transformation with God! For, whilst any portion of evil, any thing of self, remains in us, we must be subject to temptation. When self is annihilated, there is then nothing left for the tempter to act upon. Oh, how resigned, naked, denied, annihilated, ought the soul to be, that would not hinder the entrance of the divine Lord, nor his continual communion with it!

9: On Self-Denial[39]

He who expects to arrive at perfection, or a union of the soul with God, by means of consolation and comfort, will find himself mistaken. For, having sinned, we must expect to suffer, and be in some measure purified, before we can be in any degree fitted for a union with God, or permitted to taste of the joy of his presence.

Be ye patient, therefore, under all the sufferings which your Father is pleased to send you. If your love to him be pure, you will not seek him less in suffering than in consolation. Be not like those, who give themselves to him at one season, and withdraw from him at another. They give themselves only to be caressed; and wrest themselves back again, when they come to be crucified; or at least turn to the world for consolation.

---

39. Sources quoted in this chapter derive from Guyon 1800, chapters 7 and 8.

No, ye will not find consolation in aught but a free and full surrender of your will to the Divine will. Who savoureth not the cross, savoureth not the things that be of God; Matt. 16:23, and a heart that savours the cross finds the bitterest things to be sweet; "to the hungry soul every bitter thing is sweet." Prov. 27:7. God giveth the cross, and the cross giveth us God.

We may be assured, that there is an internal advancement, where there is an advancement in the way of submission to the cross.

As soon as anything presents itself as a suffering, and you feel a repugnance against it, resign yourselves immediately unto God with respect to it, giving yourselves up to him in sacrifice; and you will find that, when the cross arrives, it will not be so very burdensome, because you had disposed yourselves to a willing reception of it. Jesus himself was willing to suffer its utmost rigours. We often bear the cross in weakness, at other times in strength: all should be equal to us in the will of God.

If any other way but bearing the cross, and dying to his own will, could have redeemed man from a fallen and corrupt state, Jesus would have taught it, and established it by his example. But of all that desire to follow him, he has required the bearing of the cross; and without exception has said to all, "If any man will come after me, let him deny himself, take up his cross, and follow me." Matt. 16:24. Why then do you fear to take up the cross, which will direct you to the path which leads to the kingdom of God?

From the cross are derived heavenly meekness, true fortitude, the joys of the spirit, the conquest of self, the perfection of holiness! There is no redemption, no hope of the continuation of the divine life in us, but by our taking up the cross to our carnal appetites and inclinations: for all consists in the death of self, and there is no means to obtain life and peace, but by thus dying to corruption.

Why do you seek any other path to glory, but that in which you are called to follow the "Captain of your Salvation?"[40] His life was a continual cross, and desirest thou a perpetuity of repose and joy? The more perfectly you die to yourselves, the more truly will you begin to live to God; if you would then enjoy true peace here, and obtain hereafter the unfading crown of glory, it is necessary that in every place, and in all events, you should bear the cross willingly. To suffer, therefore, is your portion; and to suffer patiently, and willingly, is the great testimony of your love and allegiance to your Lord.

Prepare then your spirit to suffer patiently the many inconveniences and troubles of this life; for these you will find, and can never avoid, though you run to the ends of the earth, or hide yourself in its deepest caverns; and it is patient suffering only that can either disarm their power, or heal the wounds they have made. But while every tribulation is painful and grievous, and it is your desire to avoid it, you cannot but be wretched; and what you labour to shun will follow you wherever you go.—The patient enduring of the cross, and the death of self upon it, are the indispensable duty of fallen man; and it is thus only he can be delivered from his darkness, corruption, and misery, and be restored to the possession of life, light, and peace.

Knowing then the excellencies of the Father's love, having no other desire but that of ardently reaching after him, of dwelling ever with him, and of sinking into nothingness before him, we should accept indiscriminately all his dispensations, whether obscurity or illumination, fruitfulness or barrenness, weakness or strength, sweetness or bitterness, temptations, wanderings, pain, weariness, or doubtings; and none of all these should retard our course.

---

40. Heb. 2:10.

10: On Mortification[41]

All endeavours merely to rectify the exterior impel the soul yet farther outward into that about which it is so warmly and zealously engaged; and thus its powers are diffused and scattered abroad; for its application being immediately directed to externals, it thus invigorates those very senses it is aiming to subdue.

This species of mortification[42] can never subdue the passions, or lessen their activity. The only method to effect this is inward silence; by which the soul is turned wholly and altogether inward, to possess a present God. If it direct all its vigour and energy towards this centre of its being, the simple act separates and withdraws it from the senses; the exercising of all its powers internally leaves the senses faint and impotent; and the nearer it draws to God, the farther is it separated from the senses, and the less are the passions influenced by them.

In mortification of the eye and ear, which continually supply the busy imagination with new subjects, there is little danger of falling into excess: we have only to follow where the divine Spirit guides.

The soul has double advantage by proceeding thus: for, in withdrawing from outward objects, it draws the nearer to God; and the nearer its approaches are made to him, besides the secret sustaining power and virtue it receives, it is farther removed from sin; so that, at length, to have the mind turned inward, becomes, as it were, habitual.

11: On Resignation[43]

We should give up our whole existence unto God, from the strong and positive conviction, that while we are faithfully endeavouring to follow him, the occurrence of every moment is agreeable to his immediate will and permission, and just such as our state requires. This conviction will make us resigned in all things; and accept of all that happens, not as from the creature, but as from himself.

But I entreat you, who sincerely wish to give up yourselves to God, that after you have made the donation, you will not snatch yourselves back again: remember, a gift, once presented, is no longer at the disposal of the donor. Resignation is a matter of the greatest importance in our progress; it is the key to the inner court; so that whosoever knows truly how to resign himself, soon becomes perfect: we must, therefore, continue steadfast and immovable therein; and not listen to the voice of natural reason. Great faith produces great resignation; we must confide in God, "hoping against hope." Rom. 4:18.

Resignation is casting off all selfish care, that we may be altogether at the Divine disposal. All Christians are exhorted to resignation; for it is said to all, Be not anxious for to-morrow; for your heavenly Father knoweth all that is necessary for you. Matt. 6:32–34. "In all thy ways

---

41. Sources quoted in this chapter derive from Guyon 1800, chapter 10.

42. The term "mortification" literally means "to make (oneself) dead." The word usually refers to practices of physical self-denial and asceticism, such as fasting, sexual abstinence, self-inflicted pain, and other self-imposed disciplines of hardship. Quakers for the most part have not engaged in physical mortification, and so the editors of *A Guide to True Peace* willingly include these words from Guyon.

43. Sources quoted in this chapter derive from Guyon 1800, chapters 6 and 17; Molinos 1699, paragraph 30.

acknowledge him, and he shall direct thy paths." Prov. 3:6. "Commit thy works unto the Lord, and thy thoughts shall be established." Prov. 16:3. "Commit thy way unto the Lord, trust also in him, and he shall bring forth thy righteousness as the light, and thy judgment as the noonday." Psalm 37:5–6.

This virtue is practised by continually losing our own will in the will of God; by being resigned in all things, leaving what is past, in oblivion, what is to come, after having faithfully done our part, to his direction, and devoting the present moment to him, by attributing nothing that befalls us to the creature, but regarding all things as in his ordering, and looking upon all, excepting only our sins, as infallibly proceeding from him. Surrender yourselves, then, to be led and disposed of, just as he pleaseth.

We must willingly cooperate with, and second, the designs of God, which tend to divest us of all our own operations, that in the place thereof his may be instituted. Let this, then, be done in you; and suffer not yourselves to be attached to any thing, however good it may appear; for it is no longer good, if it in any measure turns you aside from that which God willeth of you.

The Divine will is preferable to all things else. And it is our conformity to this yoke that introduces us into the regions of internal peace. Hence, we may know that the rebellion of our will is the chief occasion of all our disquiet, and that this is the cause why we suffer so many straits and perturbations. Oh! if we did but submit our wills to the Divine will, and to all its disposals, what tranquillity should we feel! what sweet peace! what inward serenity! what supreme felicity, and foretastes of blessedness! Let us shake off, then, all attachment to the interests of self, and live on faith and resignation alone.

12: On Virtue[44]

It is thus that we acquire virtue with facility and certainty; for as God is the fountain and principle of all virtue, in proportion as we approach to the possession of him, in like proportion do we rise into the most eminent virtues. Indeed, he that hath God, hath all things; and he that hath him not, hath nothing. All virtue is but as a mask, an outside appearance, mutable as our garments, if it does not spring up from this divine source; and then, indeed, it is genuine, essential, and permanent. "The King's daughter," saith David, "is all glorious within." Psalm 45:13.

13: On Conversion[45]

"Turn ye, turn ye from your evil ways for why will ye die, O house of Israel?" Ezek. 33:11. "Turn ye unto him from whom ye have revolted." Isa. 31:6. To be truly converted is to avert wholly from the creature, and turn wholly unto the Creator.

For the attainment of salvation, it is absolutely necessary that we should forsake outward sin, and turn unto righteousness: but this alone is not perfect conversion, which consists in a total change of the whole man, from an outward to an inward life.

---

44. Sources quoted in this chapter derive from Guyon 1800, chapter 9.

45. Sources quoted in this chapter derive from Guyon 1800, chapter 11.

When the soul is once turned to God, it finds a wonderful facility in continuing steadfast in its conversion; and the longer it remains thus converted, the nearer it approaches, and the more firmly it adheres to God; and the nearer it draws to him, of necessity, the farther it is removed from that spirit, which is contrary to him: thus the soul is so effectually established and rooted in its conversion, that a state of conversion becomes in some measure natural to it.

Now, we must not suppose that this is effected by a violent exertion of its own powers; for the soul is not capable of, nor should it attempt, any other co-operation with Divine grace, than that of endeavouring to withdraw itself from external objects, and to turn in inward: after which, it has nothing farther to do, than to continue steadfast in its adherence to God.

He has an attractive virtue, which draws the soul more and more powerfully to himself, the nearer it approaches towards him, and in attracting, he purifies and refines it; just as it is with a gross vapour exhaled by the sun, which, as it gradually ascends, is rarified and rendered pure: the vapour, indeed, contributes to its exhalation only by its passiveness; but the soul co-operates with the attraction of Purity, by a free and affectionate correspondence. This turning of the mind inward is both easy and efficacious, advancing the soul naturally, and without constraint, because God himself is the centre which attracts it.

All our care and attention should therefore be to acquire inward silence: nor let us be discouraged by the pains and difficulties we encounter in this exercise, which will soon be recompensed by such abundant supplies of Divine strength as will render the exercise perfectly easy, provided we are faithful in meekly withdrawing our hearts from outward objects and gratifications, and returning to our centre, with affections full of tenderness and serenity.—When at any time the passions are turbulent, a gentle retreat inward unto a present God easily deadens and pacifies them; and any other way of contending with them, rather irritates than appeases them. Divine Power, in time past, instantly calmed a boisterous and raging sea; and can we now doubt, if we sincerely apply to him in our distress, that he will still the tumults of the agitated soul?

14: On Self-Annihilation[46]

The soul becomes fitted for union with God, by giving up self to the destroying and annihilating power of divine love.—This, indeed, is a most essential and necessary sacrifice in the Christian religion, and that only by which we pay true homage to the sovereignty of God. By the subjection of self within us, we truly acknowledge the supreme existence of our God; for unless we cease to exist in self, the spirit of the Eternal Word cannot exist in us. Now it is by the giving up of our own life, that we give place for his coming; and, in dying to ourselves, he himself liveth and abideth in us. Gal. 2:20.

We should, indeed, surrender our whole being unto Christ; and cease to live any longer in ourselves, that he himself may become our life; "that being dead, our life may be hid with Christ in God." Col. 3:3. By leaving and forsaking ourselves, we are lost in him; and this can be effected only by the annihilation of self, which being the true prayer of adoration, renders unto "God, and unto the Lamb, blessing, and honour, and glory, and power, for ever and ever." Rev. 5:13.

---

46. Sources quoted in this chapter derive from Guyon 1800, chapter 20.

This is the prayer of truth: it is "worshipping God in spirit and in truth," John 4:23, because we here come to know the Spirit to help our infirmities, and make intercession for us; Rom. 8:26, and being thus influenced by the pure spirit of God, we are thereby drawn forth and freed from our own carnal and corrupt manner of praying. We can pay due honour to the Almighty only in our own annihilation; which is no sooner accomplished, than he, who never suffers a void in nature, instantly fills us with himself.

Did we but know the virtues and the blessings which the soul derives from this species of prayer, we should willingly be employed therein without ceasing. It is the pearl of great price; it is the hidden treasure; Matt. 13:44–46, which, whoever findeth, selleth freely all that he hath to purchase it: it is the "well of living water, which springeth up into everlasting life:" John 4:14, it is true adoration, and comprehends the full performance of the purest evangelical precepts.

Jesus assureth us that the "kingdom of God is within us;" Luke 17:21, and this is true in two senses: first, God becometh so fully the Master and Lord in us, that nothing resisteth his dominion: then is our interior his kingdom. And again, when we possess God, who is the supreme good, we possess his kingdom also, wherein there is fulness of joy, and where we attain the end of our creation. The end of our creation, indeed, is to enjoy our God, even in this life; but, alas! how few there are who ever come to know the pure joy which his presence gives.

15: Man Acts More Nobly under the Divine Influence, than He Can Possibly Do by Following His Own Will[47]

Some persons, when they hear of the prayer of silence, falsely imagine that the soul remains dead and inactive; but unquestionably it acteth therein more nobly and more extensively than it had ever done before; for God himself is its mover, and it now acteth by the agency of his spirit. When Paul speaks of our being led by the spirit of God, it is not meant that we should cease from action; but that we should act through the internal agency of his grace. This is finely represented by the prophet Ezekiel's vision of the wheels which had a living spirit;[48] and whithersoever the Spirit was to go, they went, they ascended and descended, as they were moved: for the spirit of life was in them, and they turned not when they went. Ezek. 1—Thus the soul should be equally subservient to the will of that vivifying spirit wherewith it is enlightened, and scrupulously faithful to follow only as that moves. Our activity should, therefore, consist in endeavouring to acquire and maintain such a state as may be most susceptible of divine impressions, most flexible to all the operations of the Eternal Word.

Whilst a tablet is unsteady, the painter is unable to delineate a true copy: so every act of our own selfish spirit is productive of false and erroneous lineaments; it interrupts the work, and defeats the design, of this adorable Painter: we must then remain in peace, and move only when he moves us. Jesus Christ hath the life in himself, John 5:26, and this is the life of every living soul.

As all action is estimable only in proportion to the dignity of the efficient principle, this action is incontestably more noble than any other. Actions produced by a divine principle are

---

47. Sources quoted in this chapter derive from Guyon 1800, chapters 21, 24, and 20; Molinos 1699, paragraph 133; Guyon 1800, chapter 22; Molinos 1699, paragraph 52; Guyon 1800, chapter 21.

48. Ezek. 1:8. Ezekiel was a prophet of ancient Israel. The biblical book bearing his name begins with an extraordinary vision of wheels within wheels.

divine; but creaturely actions, however good they may appear, are only human. Christ, the word, hath the life in himself: and being communicative of his nature, he desireth to communicate it to man. We should, therefore, make room for the influx of this life, which can only be done by ejection of the fallen nature, and the suppression of the activity of self. This is agreeable to the assertion of Paul: "If any man be in Christ, he is a new creature: old things are passed away; behold all things are become new!" 2 Cor. 5:17. But this state can be accomplished only by dying to ourselves, and to all our own activity, that an heavenly influence may be substituted in its stead.

Man may, indeed, open the window; but it is the Sun himself that must give the light. Jesus has exemplified this in the gospel: Martha did what was right, but because she did it in her own spirit, he rebuked her. The spirit of man is restless and turbulent; for which reason it does little, though it would appear to do much.—"Martha," said Jesus, "thou art careful, and troubled about many things; but one thing is needful; and Mary hath chosen that good part which shall not be taken from her." Luke 10:41–42.[49] And what was it that Mary had chosen? Repose, tranquillity, and peace. She apparently ceased to act, that the spirit of Christ might act in her; she ceased to live, that Christ might be her life.

Peter,[50] in the warmth of his affection, told Jesus that, for his sake, he was ready willingly to lay down his life; but, at the word of a young damsel, he denied him.

The many troubles in life come from the soul not abiding in its place, and not being content with the will of God, and what is afforded therein, from time to time. Many souls may be resigned as to the general will, and yet fail as to the present moment: being out of the will of God, they fall: they renew such falls as long as they continue out of the divine will; when they return into it, all will go on well. God loves what is done in his own order, and of his own will and time; and while you faithfully give yourselves up thereto, you will do all things right.

All men have more or less of ardent desires, except those who live in the divine will. Some of these desires may appear to be good; but unless they be according to the will of God, he who rests in the divine will, though he be exempt from all these desires, is infinitely more peaceful, and glorifies God more. This shows us how necessary it is to renounce ourselves, and all our own activity, to follow Christ; and we cannot follow him, without being animated with his Spirit. Now that his Spirit may gain admission in us, it is necessary that our own spirit should be first subdued: "He that is joined unto the Lord," saith Paul, "is one spirit." 1 Cor. 6:17.

All things should be done in their season: every state has its commencement, its progress, and its consummation; and it is an unhappy error to stop in the beginning. There is even no art but what has its process; and at first we must labour with diligence and toil, but at last we shall reap the harvest of our industry. When the vessel is in port, the mariners are obliged to exert all their strength that they may clear her thence, and put to sea; but at length they turn her with facility, as they please. In like manner, while the soul remains in sin and creaturely entanglements, very frequent and strenuous endeavours are requisite to effect its freedom; the cords which hold it must be loosed; and then, by strong and vigorous efforts, it pushes off gradually from its old port; and, in leaving that at a distance, it proceeds to the haven to which it wishes to steer.

---

49. In the story in Luke, Martha and Mary are two sisters whom Jesus visits. Martha busies herself with many tasks, but Mary sits at the feet of Jesus and listens to his teachings. Jesus praises Mary for choosing the better part "that will not be taken from her." In later Christian understanding of this story, Martha became a symbol of the active life and Mary the contemplative.

50. Peter was one of the disciples of Jesus and a major leader of the ancient Christian community.

When the vessel is thus put in motion, in proportion as she advances on the sea, she leaves the land behind; and the farther she departs from the old harbour, the less difficulty and labour is requisite in moving her forward: at length, she begins to get sweetly under sail: and now proceeds so swiftly in her course, that the oar, which is become useless, is laid aside. How is the pilot now employed? He is content with spreading the sails and holding the rudder. To spread the sails is to lay the mind open before God, that it may be acted upon by his Spirit; to hold the rudder is to restrain the heart from wandering from the true course, recalling it gently, and guiding it steadily to the dictates of the blessed spirit, which gradually gain possession and dominion of it; just as the wind by degrees fills the sails, and impels the vessel.

While the winds are fair, the mariners rest from their labours, and the vessel glides rapidly along without their toil, and when they thus repose, and leave the vessel to the wind, they make more way in one hour, than they had done in a length of time by all their former efforts: were they now even to attempt using the oar, they would not only fatigue themselves, but retard the vessel by their ill-timed labours.

This is the manner of acting we should pursue interiorly: it will, indeed, advance us in a very short time, by the divine influence, infinitely farther than a whole life spent in reiterated acts of self-exertion: and whosoever will take this path, will find it easier than any other.

If the wind be contrary, and blow a storm, instead of putting out to sea, we must cast anchor to hold the vessel. Our anchor is a firm confidence and hope in Divine Power,[51] waiting patiently the calming of the tempest, and the return of a more favourable gale, as David "waited patiently for the Lord, and he inclined unto him, and heard his cry." Psalm 40:1. We must, therefore, be resigned to his Spirit, giving up ourselves wholly to his divine guidance; never suffering ourselves to be disquieted by any accident: for inquietude is the door by which the enemy gets into the soul, to rob it of its peace: neither should we concern or busy ourselves with what others say and do, for this will be a great cause of disturbance to us.

Let us pacify all the motions of our heart, as soon as we see it in agitation.—Let us quiet all pleasure that comes not from a pure source. Let us do away all unprofitable thoughts and musings. Let us diligently seek God within us, and we shall infallibly find him, and with him, joy and peace; such joy and peace as will endure in the midst of suffering, and which, flowing from an inexhaustible source, becomes a perpetual fountain of delight.—"Peace I leave with you," said Christ, "my peace I give unto you: not as the world giveth, give I unto you." John 14:27.

Did we but know the blessedness of hearkening unto God, and how greatly the soul is strengthened and invigorated thereby, all flesh would surely be silent before him; Zech. 2:13, all would be still as soon as he appeareth. But to engage us further in a boundless resignation, he assures us, by the same prophet, that we should fear nothing in thus giving up ourselves to him, because he takes a care of us, surpassing the highest tenderness of which we can form an idea: "Can a woman," saith he, "forget her sucking child, that she should not have compassion on the son of her womb? Yea, she may forget; yet will I not forget thee." Isaiah 49:15. Oh! blessed assurance, full of consolation! Who, after this, shall be fearful of resigning themselves wholly to the dispensation and guidance of their God!

All men seek for peace, but they seek where it is not to be found. They seek it in the world, which is ever promising, but can never give us solid peace; for, wherever we go, we shall carry

---

51. Cf. Heb. 6:19.

this fruitful source of every perplexity, our own unsubdued and selfish will. The love of liberty is one of the most dangerous passions of the heart. If we follow this propensity, instead of true liberty, it reduces us to slavery. As our passions are the worst of tyrants, if we obey them partially, we must always be in a perpetual strife and contest within; and if we entirely give ourselves up to them, it is horrid to think to what extremities they will lead; they will torment the heart, and, like a torrent, sweep all before them, and yet never be satisfied. True liberty is to be found only in him, whose truth shall set us free, John 8:32, and who shall make us experience that to serve him is to reign.

That piety by which we are sanctified, and entirely devoted to God, consists in doing his will precisely in all circumstances of life. Take what steps you please, do what deeds you will, let them shine with lustre, yet you shall not be rewarded but for having done the will of your sovereign Master. Although your servant did wonders in your house, yet if he did not what you required, you would not value his service, and you might justly complain of him as a bad servant.

There is no good spirit but that of God: that spirit, which removes us from the true good, is but a spirit of illusion, however flattering it may appear. Who would be carried in a magnificent chariot on the road to an abyss! The way which leads to a precipice is frightful, although it should be covered with roses; but the way that leads to a crown is delightful, although it should be thick set with thorns. He has given his good spirit to instruct us; Neh. 9:20; therefore, let us no longer follow our own will, but his; so that not only our religious actions, but also all others, may be done with no other view but that of pleasing him: then will our whole conduct be sanctified; then will our deeds become a continual sacrifice; and incessant prayer, and uninterrupted love will occupy the heart: therefore, let us submit to the annihilation of our own will, that his will may reign in us! For it is his prerogative to command, and our duty to obey.

16: On the Possession of Peace and Rest before God[52]

The soul that is faithful in the exercise of that love and adherence to God already described is astonished to feel him gradually taking possession of its whole being; and now enjoys a continual sense of that presence which is become, as it were, natural to it. This presence diffuses an unusual serenity throughout all our faculties—it calms the mind, and gives sweet repose and quiet, even in the midst of our daily labours: but then we must be resigned to him without reserve.

We must, however, urge it as a matter of the highest importance, to cease from self-action and self-exertion, that divine Power may act alone: he saith by the mouth of his prophet David, "Be still, and know that I am God." Ps. 46:10. Yet those greatly err, who accuse this species of prayer of idleness, a charge that can only arise from inexperience. If they would but make some efforts towards the attainment of it, they would soon experience the contrary of what they suppose, and find their accusation groundless.

This appearance of inaction is, indeed, not the consequence of sterility and want, but of fruitfulness and abundance; this will be clearly perceived by the experienced soul, which will know and feel, that its silence is full and unctuous, and the result of causes totally the reverse of apathy and barrenness. The interior is not a stronghold, to be taken by storm and violence;

---

52. Sources quoted in this chapter derive from Guyon 1800, chapter 12.

but a kingdom of peace, which is to be gained only by love. Let us then give ourselves up to God without apprehension of danger. He will love us, and enable us to love him; and that love, increasing daily, will produce in us all other virtues. He alone can replenish our hearts which the world has agitated and intoxicated, but never could fill.

He will take nothing from us but what makes us unhappy. We shall only be made to alter a little in our actions, and correct the motive of them, by making all referable to him. Then the most ordinary and seemingly indifferent actions will become exercises of virtue, and sources of consolation. We shall behold in peace the approach of death, as the beginning of life immortal; and as Paul saith, "We shall not be unclothed; but clothed upon, and mortality shall be swallowed up of life." 2 Cor. 5:4.

Let us therefore no longer fear to commit ourselves wholly to him. What risk do we run, in depending solely on his goodness? Ah! he will not deceive us, unless by bestowing an abundance beyond our highest hopes: but those who expect all from themselves will inevitably be deceived, and must suffer this rebuke by the prophet Isaiah: "Behold all ye that kindle a fire, that compass yourselves about with sparks; walk in the light of your fire, and in the sparks that ye have kindled.—This shall ye have of mine hand: ye shall lie down in sorrow." Isa. 50:11.

The soul advanced thus far hath no need of any other preparative than its quietude: for now the Divine presence, which is the great effect, or rather continuation of prayer, begins to be powerfully felt, and the soul experiences what the apostle Paul saith, that "Eye hath not seen, nor ear heard, neither have entered into the heart of man, the things which God hath prepared for them that love him." 1 Cor. 2:9. The soul certainly enjoys transcendent blessedness, and feels that it is no longer she that lives, but Christ that liveth in her; Gal. 2:20, and that the only way to find him is to turn the mind inward. We no sooner do this, than we are filled with the consolations of his presence: we are amazed at so great a blessing, and enjoy an internal converse, which external matters cannot interrupt.

The same may be said of this species of prayer, that is said of wisdom: "All good things come together with her." Wisdom 7:11. For the virtues now flow from us into action with so much sweetness and facility, that they appear natural and spontaneous.

17: On Perfection, or the Union of the Soul with God[53]

The most profitable and desirable state in this life is that of Christian perfection, which consists in the union of the soul with Infinite Purity, a union that includes in it all spiritual good; producing in us a freedom of spirit, which raises us above all the events and changes of this life, and which frees us from the tyranny of human fear; it gives an extraordinary power for the well performing of all actions, and acquitting ourselves well in our employments; a prudence truly Christian in all our undertakings; a peace and perfect tranquillity in all conditions; and, in short, a continual victory over self-love and our passions.

It is impossible to attain Divine union solely by the activity of meditation,[54] or by the meltings of the affections, or even by the highest degree of luminous and elegantly composed

---

53. Sources quoted in this chapter derive from Guyon 1800, chapter 24; Molinos 1699, paragraphs 206, 120, 154, 210, 211, and 214; Guyon 1800, chapter 20.

54. In traditional terminology, "contemplation" refers to apophatic spiritual practices that aspire to empty the mind of thoughts and images, while "meditation" refers to practices that engage the capacity for imagination and reason.

prayer; for, according to Scripture, "no man shall see God and live." Exod. 33:20. Now all the exercises of discoursive prayer, and even of active contemplation, being performed in the *life* of our own will, we "cannot thereby see God;" for all that is of man's own power or exertion must first die, be it ever so noble, ever so exalted.

John relates, "that there was silence in heaven." Rev. 8:1. Now heaven represents the centre of the soul, wherein, ere the divine Majesty appears, all must be hushed to silence. All efforts, nay the very existence, of self-love must be destroyed; because it is the natural will that is opposed to God, and all the malignity of man proceeds from it, insomuch, that the purity of a soul increases, in proportion as the natural will becomes subjected to the Divine will.

Therefore, the soul can never arrive at Divine union but by the annihilation of its will; nor can it ever become one with the Father, but by being re-established in the purity of its first creation. God purifies the soul by his wisdom, as refiners do metals in the furnace. Gold cannot be purified but by fire, which gradually separates from it, and consumes, all that is earthy and heterogeneous: it must be melted and dissolved, and all impure mixtures taken away, by casting it again and again into the furnace: thus it is refined from all internal corruption, and even exalted to a state incapable of further purification. It now no longer contains any adulterate mixture; its purity is perfect, its simplicity complete: and it is fit for the most exquisite workmanship. Thus we may see that the divine Spirit, as an unremitting fire, must devour and destroy all that is earthly, sensual and carnal, and all self-activity, before the soul can be fitted for, and capable of, union with it.

"I will make a man more precious than fine gold." Isaiah 13:12. But when the Word which was in the beginning begins to burn, destroy, and purify, then the soul, not perceiving the salutary designs of these operations, shrinks from them; and as the gold seems rather to blacken than brighten when first put into the furnace, so the soul conceives that its purity is lost, and that its temptations are its sins.

But while we confess that the enjoyment of God is the end for which we were created; that "without holiness" none can attain it; Heb. 12:14; and, that to attain it we must necessarily pass through a severe and purifying process; how strange is it, that we should dread and avoid this process, as if that could be the cause of evil and imperfection in the present life, which is to be productive of glory and blessedness in the life to come!

Let all, then, press forward towards the mark,[55] suffering themselves to be guided and governed by the spirit of grace, which would infallibly conduct them to the end of their creation, the enjoyment of the blessed Presence.

It may perhaps be said that some may feign to have attained this blessed state; but, alas! none can any more feign this than the wretch, who is on the point of perishing with hunger, can for a length of time feign to be full and satisfied: some wish or word, some sigh or sign, will inevitably escape him, and betray his famished state.

"Be ye perfect, even as your Father which is in heaven is perfect." Matt. 5:48. The soul, remaining in its disorderly will, is imperfect; it becomes more perfect, in proportion as it approaches nearer to the Divine will. When a soul is advanced so far that it cannot in any thing depart therefrom, it then becomes wholly perfect, united with, and transformed into, the divine nature; and being thus purified and united to Infinite Purity, it finds a profound peace, and a sweet rest, which brings it to such a perfect union of love, that it is filled with joy. It conforms

---

55. Phil. 3:14.

itself to the will of its great Original in all emergencies, and rejoices in every thing to do the divine good pleasure.

The Lord draws near to such a soul, and communicates himself inwardly to it. He fills it with himself because it is empty, clothes it with his light and with his love, because it is naked; lifts it up, because it is low; and unites it with himself.

If you would enter into this heaven on earth, forget every care and every anxious thought, get out of yourself, that the love of God may live in your soul; so that you may be enabled to say with the apostle: "I live, yet not I, but Christ liveth in me." Gal. 2:20.—How happy should we be if we could thus leave all for him, seek him only, breathe after none but him; let him only have our sighs! O, that we could but go on without interruption towards the enjoyment of this blessed state! God calls us thereto. He invites us to enter into our inward centre, where he will renew and change us, and show us a new and heavenly kingdom, full of joy, peace, content, and serenity.

The spiritual, abstracted, and retired soul hath here its peace no more broken, though outwardly it may meet with combats, and may sometimes be naked, forsaken, fought against, and desolate, because, from the infinite distance, tempests never reach to that serenest heaven within where pure and perfect love resides. For, although the prince of darkness may indeed make violent assaults against it; yet it makes head against them, and stands like a strong pillar; no more happening to it than happens to a high mountain in a storm. The valley is darkened with thick clouds, fierce tempests of hail, and thunder; while the lofty mountain glitters by the bright beams of the sun, in quietness and serenity, continuing clear like heaven, immovable, and full of light: such a soul, indeed, is as "mount Zion,[56] which cannot be removed, but abideth forever." Psalm 125:1.

In this throne of quiet are manifest the perfections of spiritual beauty: here we shall enjoy the true light of the secret and divine mysteries of Christ, perfect humility, the amplest resignation, the meekness and innocency of the dove, liberty and purity of heart; here is witnessed joyful simplicity, heavenly indifferency, continual prayer, total nakedness, perfect disinterestedness, conversation of heaven. This is the rich hidden treasure; this is the pearl of great price.[57]

The End

---

56. Mount Zion is a hill in Jerusalem, the site of the Temple built by King Solomon in ancient Israel. Symbolically, it can refer to heaven in the afterlife or to the interior presence of God in this life.

57. Matt. 13:46.

Chapter 5

Jewish Kabbalah

Hayyim Vital's *Shaarei Kedusha*

Shaul Magid

> Reading in translation is like kissing through a veil.
> —Hayyim Nahman Bialik

> Translation is one of the greatest miracles . . . leading into the heart of the sacred order from which it springs . . ."
> —Gershom Scholem, letter to Franz Rosenzweig, March 7, 1921

The *Shaarei Kedusha* (Gates of Holiness) is a late sixteenth-century work of Jewish Kabbalah in four parts. Originally written in Hebrew, the text was composed by Hayyim ben Joseph Calabrezi Vital (1542–1620), a rabbi and mystic in the Galilean city of Safed, Palestine, and the foremost disciple of Isaac Luria (the Ari; 1534–1572). The text is thus associated with the Lurianic line of Jewish meditative and theosophical Kabbalah. This line is also referred to as the "Safed school." The *Shaarei Kedusha* is an esoteric text. The fourth part, which is the focus of the present chapter, is an extended essay on contemplative techniques and the devotional prerequisites for attaining prophecy. It was intentionally excised from the standard printings of *Shaarei Kedusha* and was circulated in manuscript in small Kabbalistic groups. It was published for the first time by the contemporary Jerusalem Kabbalist rabbi Yaakov Moshe Hillel in a collected work titled *Ketavim Hadashim shel R. Hayyim Vital* (New Writings from Rabbi Hayyim Vital) in 1988. The text describes a highly complex form of Jewish meditation, largely lost in the modern world, that includes magical reconfigurations of Hebrew letter combinations. Rooted in traditional rabbinic/mystical Judaism, the text was written for Vital's own community and for members of the line of Lurianic Kabbalah.

Sixteenth-Century Safed, Isaac Luria, and Hayyim Vital

In contemporary Israel, the city of Safed, nestled in the Galilean hills, is the center of the Jewish mysticism tourist industry. Considered a "development town" by the state, modern-day Safed is a place of many layers combining impoverished immigrants, a mosaic of countercultural artists and ultra-Orthodox Jews, and a dwindling Arab population. The tourist industry is centered on the artist colony and the old cemetery where some of the great luminaries of Safed's past are buried. The central figure remains the charismatic Kabbalist Isaac Luria, who spent less than eighteen months in Safed before succumbing to a plague in the summer of 1572. Perhaps somewhat ironically, Hayyim Vital, who was instrumental in making Luria the figure he is today, is not buried in Safed but in Damascus, Syria.

This history of Safed certainly lends itself to its present celebrity status but is also more multivalent (see David 1999; Fine 2003, 41–77). It was a center of enormous Kabbalistic and rabbinic activity in the middle decades of the sixteenth century as well as the home of some well-known Sufi masters (see Fenton 1994). It is considered one of the four "holy cities" of Erez Israel, with the others being Jerusalem, Tiberias, and Hebron. There is no mention of Safed in the Hebrew Bible and only scant mention in rabbinic literature.[1] In the Middle Ages, it is mentioned by various Jewish travelers on pilgrimage in the Holy Land. By the early 1500s Safed began to emerge as a central locale for many immigrants from Spain and Portugal and as arguably the most important city in Palestine during the early Ottoman period (see, e.g., David 1991, 1992). It became a textile and manufacturing center given its proximity to Damascus, which was the urban center of that part of the empire (see Avisur 1962; David 1988). Safed's Jewish population grew tremendously during that period. According to one account, between 1567 and 1568 there may have been as many as 1,800 Jewish families, which is quite large given the size of the city (see Fine 2003, 47). It became a central location of Jewish jurisprudence. Jacob Berab (ca. 1474–ca. 1541) and the more well-known Joseph Caro (1488–1575), who emigrated from Turkey, functioned as rabbinic authorities. Caro's *Shulhan Arukh* (Code of Jewish Law; lit., Set Table) was composed in Safed and became the standard code of Jewish law to this day. In the 1530s Kabbalists from the European continent began arriving in Safed (there was an old adage that the messiah will rise in Safed). One important figure was Shlomo Alkabetz (1505–1576) who emigrated from Salonika. Alkabetz is most well known as the author of the Sabbath-eve hymn "Lekha Dodi" (Go Out My Beloved), but he was also the transmitter of Kabbalah that he had learned in an important circle of Kabbalists in Salonika. He became the brother-in-law and teacher of Moshe Cordovero, who rose to become the most important Kabbalist in Safed until the arrival of Luria in 1570.

Moshe Cordovero (1522–1570) (known as RAMAK) was the leading Kabbalist in Safed in the sixteenth century, at least until Luria arrived less than a year before Codovero's death in 1570. Cordovero's magnum opus *Pardes Rimonim* (Pomegranate Orchard) was a compendium of medieval Kabbalistic doctrine filtered through his distinctive dialectical approach founded on the notion that for God to reveal Godself, God had to be concealed. His position was Neoplatonic in that he believed in an emanation of cosmic forces downward as opposed to Luria who proffered a theory of divine rupture that contained more gnostic elements. He may have been most popularly known as the author of a series of works on ethics founded on Kabbalistic principles.[2]

These mystical figures in Safed began attracting many young Kabbalists from the Jewish Diaspora, which resulted in one of the most vibrant Kabbalistic communities that the Jewish world has ever known. As a Safed native, the precocious Hayyim Vital took advantage of his surroundings, studying with these older luminaries and rising to become a young protégé in this community.³ In addition to the metaphysical work going on, these mystics, many of whom were in Erez Israel for the first time, initiated an ascetic lifestyle in preparation for what they believed was the beginning of the messianic age. One outgrowth of this was an attempt to reinstitute formal rabbinic ordination as a prerequisite for reconstituting the Sanhedrin that had been disbanded after the destruction of the Temple in 70 CE (see Katz 1986; Fine 2003, 51–53). After the demise of the Sanhedrin, or official legal court, during the times of the Jerusalem Temple in the first century of the Common Era, official rabbinical ordination that was required to be a member of the Sanhedrin ceased as it was no longer relevant. Reestablishing official ordination was viewed as a prelude to coming of the messiah and the final redemption. This is noteworthy because Vital was very much a part of this circle and was one of the few who eventually did receive formal ordination.

As we can see, Hayyim Vital was at the center of what was arguably one of the most vibrant decades of Jewish literature in post-rabbinic history, both exoteric and esoteric. In the course of about forty years, from the mid-1530s until the mid-1570s, the scholars in Safed literally revolutionized Jewish life. During this time, the Jewish legal tradition achieved a universally accepted code of law in the *Shulhan Arukh* (Code of Jewish Law), a Kabbalistic corpus that collected and summarized early Kabbalah in the works of Moshe Cordovero, and a revolutionary metaphysical system that became the foundation of subsequent Kabbalah and Hasidism in the works of Isaac Luria. In addition, during this time certain customs were initiated that became standard Jewish practice. This included the Kabbalat Shabbat service for Friday evening, the custom of staying awake through the night studying Torah on Shavuot (Pentecost), and the more esoteric custom of Tikkun Hazot, a nightly midnight vigil to mourn the destruction of the Temple. This nocturnal ritual was developed and practiced by mystics to lament the destruction of the Temple and hasten its rebuilding through liturgical dirges, lamentations, and meditations while sitting on the floor and placing ashes on one's head (Magid 1996a). While the latter did not gain universal appeal, it was common among pious circles in subsequent centuries.⁴ Hayyim Vital's *Shaarei Kedusha* (Gates of Holiness) should thus be seen as the product of an individual who absorbed both the earlier Kabbalistic tradition as well as its new articulation, an individual who stood inside a community intent on completing Jewish exile by means of ascetic piety in preparing for the reemergence of prophecy, at a time when members of his elite circle viewed their time as on the precipice of a seismic shift that required immediate and radical action. The Kabbalists in Safed were pious, even extremely so, but they were not a cautious group; they believed audacity was required to complete their task.

Descended from a family of Italian Jews from Calabria, Hayyim Vital (1542–1620) was likely born in Safed. His father was a well-known scribe. As a young man Vital studied with the popular preacher Moshe Alshekh (1508–1593) and later with the celebrated Kabbalist Moshe Cordovero.⁵ Vital always had esoteric interests and as a young man spent two years studying alchemy, probably in Damascus, an activity he later regretted (see, e.g., Boss 1994). His life changed in 1570 when an unknown and charismatic young Kabbalist named Isaac Luria Ashkenazi (the Ari; 1534–1572) immigrated to Safed from Egypt (Fine 2003, 19–40). Cordovero died in the summer of 1570, and in the spring of 1571 Vital joined a group gathering around the charismatic Luria. He had already studied Kabbalah with Cordovero and soon asserted himself as

Luria's closest disciple (Fine 2003, 333–50). The relationship between master and disciple appears to have been a complicated one. According to Vital's account, Luria held that he had messianic potential, and he claimed that Luria told him that he (Luria) came into this world only to teach Vital the true Kabbalah.[6]

Isaac Luria was born in Jerusalem. His father died when he was a child and his mother moved with him to Egypt to live with her wealthy brother Mordecai Frances. Luria was raised in Egypt and became a young prodigy of David ibn Zamra, one of the leading jurists at that time. As far as we know, he began studying Kabbalah at an early age. A common story has it that Luria spent almost ten years living on an island in the Nile Jazirat al-Rawda (the island was owned by his uncle), returning home only for Shabbat, where he studied esoteric wisdom. We have no record of his teacher in Kabbalah. He immigrated to Safed in 1570 to study with Moshe Cordovero. A few months after commencing with his study, differences between him and his teacher began to surface regarding interpretations of the *Zohar*, and very soon afterward Cordovero died. Luria quickly became a central figure in Safed, and many of Cordovero's students, Vital included, drifted over to Luria and became his main disciples.

Luria is best known for his innovative use of the doctrine of *zimzum*, an idea that God contracted Godself to create an empty space for creation. Once God emanates light into that space that is void of divinity, the light was too strong for the vessels to contain it and the vessels ruptured, sending sparks of divinity into the netherworld. Evil thus emerges from this broken world, and the Jew, through acts of piety (*mitzvoth*), redeems these trapped sparks from the grips of evil to redeem the world. His second innovation was to expand the cosmology of the ten *sephirot* (divine emanations) into cosmic constellations or faces (*parzufim*) that interact with one another throughout the day, shifting in order to allow divine light to flow through them and into the world. Vital became Luria's major interpreter after years of battling with other more seasoned disciples. He attained almost a clear advantage of Luria's other students when Vital's son, Samuel, began publishing Vital's rendition of the Lurianic system soon after Vital's death.[7]

Vital had a very high opinion of himself, which explains his obsession in arguing for hegemony over Luria's teachings. He makes this quite explicit in his diary published as *Sefer Hizyonot* (Book of Visions), which was likely written between 1609 and 1612.[8] After Luria's death in the summer of 1572, Vital resided in various locations, including Jerusalem, where he served as rabbi, and in Damascus, periodically returning to Safed. A series of plagues ravaged Safed, and its vibrant Jewish life dwindled in the later decades of the sixteenth century. Many of Luria's students scattered. Some traveled to Poland or Italy; others went to Jerusalem or Damascus, which was a vibrant commercial city at that time and in close proximity to the Land of Israel; and still others moved to various locations in the Ottoman Empire (1299–1922). Vital spent his years after Luria's death editing and revising his version of the Lurianic system as well as dedicating time to the rabbinate in Jerusalem and teaching and writing about both exoteric and esoteric matters. He was known to be a prickly individual, not easy to get along with, and very critical of anyone who challenged his messianic self-fashioning. His *Sefer Hizyonot* is replete with disparaging remarks about many of his colleagues in Safed and Damascus, accusing them of all kinds of debauchery and ignorance of the true Kabbalistic tradition. He even suggests that he failed to be revealed as the true messiah due to the sins of the Jews of Damascus.[9] After a series of very serious and extended illnesses, Vital died in Damascus in the spring of 1620 at the age of seventy-seven.[10]

His son Samuel and grandson Moshe became the inheritors and editors of Vital's literary estate and were responsible for the body of Vital's rendition of Luria's teaching that were later printed as the *Etz Hayyim* (Tree of Life) and *Shemoneh Shearim* (Eight Gates). With the publication of these works, Vital became the dominant lens through which to study Lurianic Kabbalah. Gershom Scholem claims that although Vital "possessed no truly creative powers, [he] was one of the most important influences on the development of later Kabbalah, attaining this position as the chief formulator of the Kabbalah of Luria" (Scholem 1974, 448). Scholem here is speaking only of his contribution to Kabbalistic metaphysics, but we can see his point even in reading the *Shaarei Kedusha*. There is little that is original in this work, albeit his juxtaposition of older sources and his interpretive explanations are often illuminating. The style is taken from pietistic works written by older contemporaries such as Elijah da Vidas (1518–1592) and his one-time teacher Moshe Cordovero. His meditative techniques are quite similar to Abraham Abulafia (1240–after 1291) (discussed later in this chapter), although, again, he offers some new interpretations. However, the *Shaarei Kedusha*, especially its unpublished fourth part, came to represent one of the most concise and illustrative examples of late Kabbalistic contemplative practice of this period with a focus on the renewal of prophecy that was later taken up by various Kabbalists and Hasidic masters.

It is curious that Gershom Scholem's biographical sketch of Vital only mentions the *Shaarei Kedusha* in passing and does not tell us when it was written. In addition, Scholem does not mention the enigmatic fourth part that was still in manuscript when he wrote his essay. Moreover, Joseph Avivi wrote two massive bibliographical studies on Lurianic Kabbalah, *Binyan Ariel* (Building of Ariel) and *Kabbalat Ha-Ari* (Kabbalah of the ARI, Isaac Luria), which treat Vital's work extensively but which all but ignore the *Shaarei Kedusha* (Avivi 1987, 2008). This is somewhat ironic in part because the *Shaarei Kedusha* became one of the most widely read works attributed to Vital. If we had more exact data on when it was written, whether he continued working on it after meeting Luria, and if it was edited by his son and grandson after his death, we would be able to ascertain its somewhat idiosyncratic nature. The fact that Vital knew Elijah da Vidas, the author of the popular pietistic work *Reshit Hokhma* (Beginning of Wisdom), the style of the first three parts of *Shaarei Kedusha* makes perfect sense. It was clearly written at a time when works of pious asceticism were common. Given that Vital studied with Cordovero, who seemed quite aware of the ecstatic Kabbalah of Abraham Abulafia, it makes sense when we read the fourth part in which Abulafia is prominent. We must remember that at this time Abulafia's works were all in manuscript form and his Kabbalistic system had suffered from severe criticism in the centuries after his death. By the sixteenth century, the theosophical Kabbalah of the *Zohar* (that appeared after Abulafia's death), a series of texts that develop a cosmology very different than Abulafia's "letter mysticism," had become the template of all subsequent Kabbalistic activity. Thus in including Abulafia's works Vital was acting in an audacious manner. There are those who posit that the fourth gate remained unpublished until very recently because of its overt use of Abulafian techniques. Scholem notes that Vital had a strong interest in early Kabbalah; he claims that a manuscript exists that was likely the product of his own hand discovered in 1930 (Scholem 1974, 448). If this is so, the anthological section of part 4 of the *Shaarei Kedusha*, which comprises it largest section, may be part of a project that Vital never brought to completion. Finally, whether or not we accept Gershom Scholem's thesis regarding the messianic underpinnings of Lurianic Kabbalah as a response to the Spanish expulsion in 1492, it seems clear that messianism was part of the religious culture in Safed at that time.[11] And Vital certainly viewed himself as a messianic figure and one fit to receive the revelation of the Holy Spirit and even prophecy.[12] In that light, Vital's focus on the renewal of prophecy that is part of the messianic process in classical Judaism, both in part 3 and part 4 of the *Shaarei Kedusha*, would fit neatly into Vital's project in the text.

Rabbinic Judaism and Lurianic Kabbalah

Rabbinic Judaism refers to the body of literature written and redacted by an elite group of Jews—often viewed as the spiritual inheritors of the Pharisees—from the second to the sixth centuries CE. The products of this literary enterprise are known as Talmud and Midrash. The Talmud refers to two separate but overlapping corpora known as the Babylonian and the Jerusalem Talmuds, the former being the dominant record of rabbinic teachings redacted in Babylonia (an area including Persia and parts of modern-day Iran and Iraq) from the fourth to sixth centuries. Midrash refers to a body of nonlegal, homiletic literature appearing in various forms during the same period also extending in some cases to the early Middle Ages. The most well-known Midrash is known as Midrash Raba (2nd–5th c.) and consists of a running commentary to the Pentateuch (Fraade 2007).

The focus of Rabbinic Judaism is the adjudication and practice of law as the central tenet of Jewish living. Nonlegal dimensions of Rabbinic Judaism include creative interpretations of biblical passages, stories of the rabbis, and a small amount of what can be called proto-mystical doctrine. By that I mean stories of miraculous events and feats performed by the rabbinic sages. Rabbinic Judaism has no systematic mystical system, and scholars are unsure whether such systems existed among Rabbinic Jews until the Middle Ages.

The mystics in Safed were solidly Rabbinic Jews in that they accepted the rabbinic corpus as authoritative and lived by its precepts (Scholem 1965, 5–31). Much of their mystical Judaism is built on interpretations of biblical and rabbinic texts. Jewish mystics of this period were strict adherents to rabbinic law and often offered supererogatory interpretations of normative practice (Hallamish 1988). As a result of their strict adherence to Rabbinic Judaism, many of their contemplative techniques are developed in conjunction with the performance of *mitzvot* (commandments) or ritual acts prescribed by the rabbinic sages (Hallamish 2000). Sometimes they are practiced as part of the act itself, for example, in the shaking of the *lulav* and *etrog* (palm branch and citron fruit) on Sukkot (Festival of Booths/Tabernacles) and sometimes as an accompaniment to the ritual act, for example, in traditional liturgy (Kallus 2002). There are also a few cases where new rituals are invented to accompany contemplative practice, for example, in the midnight prayer vigil Tikkun Hazot (Rectification at Midnight) or all-night study ritual of Shavuot and Hoshanah Raba, the final day of Sukkot (Scholem 1965, 118–57).

In many cases, mystics also served as legal authorities, as was the case with Cordovero, Vital, and to a lesser extent Luria (Hallamish 1992). Many served on rabbinic courts, rendered legal decisions, and conferred with their nonmystical legal colleagues on matters of law and custom (Katz 1989, 45–58). That being said, Jewish mystics, especially of this period, often studied in secluded circles (sometimes known as *kloyzim*), were very strict about who was included in these circles, and demanded a high level of secrecy in terms of their program of study. As a result, it is unclear how many citizens of Safed knew about this mystical revolution that was going on in their environs. Many of these groups were largely nocturnal, gathering when most of Safed's residents were asleep. The townspeople knew of the main figures such as Cordovero and Vital, especially because Cordovero was a leading rabbinic figure and Vital was a longtime resident of Safed, but as to the nature of their devotional practices and teaching, it is not clear how much of their mystical activities were known in their lifetime. This may be especially the case in Safed since the city at that time was an amalgam of many new immigrants from various parts of the Jewish world. Jews from Portugal, Egypt, Salonika, Italy, Poland, and other locales immigrated to Safed in the sixteenth century. Some came as a result of the demographic shift after the expulsions from Iberia; others came because of Sultan Bayazid II's (r. 1481–1512) tolerant attitude toward Jews; and still others because of the mystical tradition that the messiah will come from Safed. As a result, many probably did not even share a common language (Hebrew was not the *lingua franca* in Safed) (David 1988, 1991, 1992, 1999).

Lurianic Kabbalah was an innovative metaphysical system founded on the principles of *zimzum* (divine contraction) and *shvirat ha-kelim* (the rupture of the vessels). In brief, Luria posited that creation began with an act of divine contraction whereby God removed Godself to create a space void of God that would then be infused with a diluted light of divinity giving birth to the material world. In fact, this process seemed to fail. The void (not totally void of God but rather the place of a much-diminished divine light that served as vessels to hold the emanated light from beyond the empty space) could not hold the emanated light and the "vessels" shattered, sending shards deeper into the dark void, known as the *tehom* (depths), which became the place of the demonic (Fine 2003, 124–49). The demonic was fed by this divinity and gained strength as a result of this failed attempt at creation. Our world is thus already the place of an exiled God, or exiled divinity (Magid 2002, 172–75). The purpose of Torah and *mitzvot* is that through abiding by divine command Jews slowly redeem these lost sparks from their embedded place in the demonic and raise them up to their appropriate place in the Godhead (Jacobs 1989). Moreover, these acts realign the cosmos that is malfunctioning due to the fallen state of creation. Lurianic Kabbalah, more than most Kabbalistic systems before it, is devoted to *mitzvot* as the tools of the mystic to redeem the sparks and realign the cosmos in order for the creation to complete itself in the redemptive era. It is thus a highly ritualistic contemplative system, one that embeds meditative practice with bodily actions connected to the web of Jewish legal literature (*halakha*). It is thus not surprising that Joseph Karo (1488–1575), a significant resident of Safed in this period and also a mystic, composed the *Shulhan Arukh* (Code of Jewish Law) that became the standard legal guidebook of post-medieval Judaism (Werblowsky 1980).

The central texts of the Lurianic school are Vital's *Etz Hayyim* (Tree of Life) and *Shemoneh Shearim* (Eight Gates), edited by his son Samuel. Many other students of Luria wrote their own works that are studied today, but the Vitalean rendition of Luria's teachings have dominated modern Kabbalah (Meroz 1993). In many cases, these other Lurianic texts were interpreted through the lens of Vital's collections, thus diminishing the more multivalent nature of Luria's work in the decades after his death in 1572. Scholars like to draw these distinctions, especially regarding the works of Israel Sarug (d. 1610), whose relationship to Luria is matter of scholarly debate (Meroz 1992). Sarug's work made its way to Italy and became popularized by numerous Kabbalists, most notably Menahem Azariah da Fano (1548–1620), once a student of Cordovero, who was instrumental in disseminating Lurianic manuscripts in Europe. Sarug's system differed from Vital's in numerous ways that are not really relevant to our consideration of the *Shaarei Kedusha*.

As a result of the ritualistic nature of Lurianic Kabbalah, many compendia were composed refracting the Lurianic metaphysical myth through the lens of ritual and law. The *Shaarei Kedusha* was thus written in the midst of a highly ritualized and mystical environment. As distinguished from many of the other treatises written at this time, the *Shaarei Kedusha* does not focus on the practice of ritual per se but rather on preparations for a mystically ritualized life. Leaning heavily on the metaphysical literature that Vital and others wrote, the *Shaarei Kedusha* focuses on the personality and discipline necessary to enact these contemplative practices, on cultivating the contemplative personality. The *Shaarei Kedusha* thus constitutes a kind of early modern pietism based on a newly formed mystical doctrine embedded in an ascetic and highly charged form of normative Judaism.

The Journey to YHVH through Hebrew

The search for an experience of God in Judaism reaches back to the Hebrew Bible and the prophets. Moses's desire to "see God" (Exod. 33:18) and the prophets' attempt to experience the divine stand as a central motif of biblical religion. Even in the rabbinic tradition, which is more interested in creating normative practice than fostering religious or mystical experience, we have many instances where rabbinic sages utilize methods in order to break through the divide separating the corporeal realm and the supernal heavens (e.g., Babylonian Talmud Hagigah 14b). In this sense, Kabbalah as mystical doctrine is not a deviation from Ancient Israelite religion, although its focus on experience as the *sine qua non* of its religious worldview does depart from its rabbinic antecedents, if not in essence then surely in emphasis.

That being said, Kabbalists were by and large also legal scholars, and Kabbalistic doctrine is built on the foundation of the obligatory nature of religious praxis (known as *halakha* [Jewish law]) (see, e.g., Katz 1983, 3–60). The Kabbalists exhibit an interesting mix of radicalism and conservatism; at times their radicalism is embedded in a highly conservative devotion to law as the vehicle of mystical experience. There are some notable exceptions, such as Abraham Abulafia (discussed later in this chapter), but for the most part Kabbalists were defenders and strict keepers of the law.[13] However, as in the case with many mystical traditions, there is also a tension between the law and experience in Kabbalah, and this tension is palpable in many Kabbalistic texts.

Kabbalah began in earnest sometime in the twelfth century in Provence with a circle of mystics around an enigmatic figure known as Isaac the Blind (see Scholem 1962, 248–89; cf. Sendor 1994).[14] Around this time we also find perhaps the first Kabbalistic text known as *Sefer Ha-Bahir* (Book of Illumination) (Scholem 1962, 49–198). This text, framed as a rabbinic Midrash, begins to develop the doctrine of the ten *sephirot* (divine pronunciations/attributes/emanations), although in the *Bahir* these *sephirot* do not constitute fully developed distinct divine emanations as they do in the *Zohar* (Book of Radiance), which is the great text of Kabbalah that was the product of the late thirteenth century. While the *Bahir* makes mention of its characters having mystical experiences that then translated into esoteric teachings, one could not call it a contemplative text, and the techniques are too oblique to constitute any contemplative method.[15] Descriptions of mystics sitting with their heads between their knees and entering the supernal realm are likely taken from descriptions of prophecy that appear in the rabbinic corpus.

The *Zohar* revolutionized Kabbalah with its intricate doctrine of the ten *sephirot* and complex cosmology, cosmogony, and theodicy (Green 2004). While the *Zohar* speaks often about its characters having mystical experiences, and its theosophy certainly assumes as much, it does not devote much time to exploring contemplative techniques. Its interests are primarily theosophical, exploring the highways and byways of the cosmic universe that is situated between God (as *eyn sof*, the Infinite) and the corporeal realm.

Lurianic Kabbalah, of which Vital was a central expositor, extends Zoharic theosophy to new levels of complexity. In addition, and more relevant to our concerns here, it introduces certain contemplative techniques, described as *kavannot* (mystical intentions) that accompany the performance of *mitzvot* (see Matt 1986, 367–404). In this sense, Lurianic Kabbalah introduces a practical or perhaps applicatory dimension to the theosophical Kabbalah of the *Zohar*. Yet even here, most of the discussion centers on internal computation and the intricate tracing of cosmic movement rather than actual physical techniques for attaining the desired experience (Kallus 2002; Giller 2008).

One of the interesting dimensions of Vital's *Shaarei Kedusha* is that here he moves Lurianic theosophy much closer to the practical realm. In this text, which can be viewed as a kind of guidebook for mystical practice according to the Lurianic system, Vital simplifies the complex theosophy and focuses on applying it in a contemplative framework. Much of the first three parts discuss the prerequisites for attempting to attain a mystical experience. Here he leans heavily on the approach of two ethical texts by his former teacher Moshe Cordovero, namely, the *Tomer Devorah* (Palm Tree of Deborah) and *'Or Neerav* (Concealed Light). Vital, like his teacher, argues that the mystic must be punctilious in his performance of *mitzvot*, must be conversant in the large body of rabbinic and classical literature, and must exhibit a sincere passion for the mystical quest. Moreover, he must be careful in his dealings with others, even more so than the nonmystic. Ethical infractions, even if they are not legal transgressions, can disqualify one from the mystical life. He must also be an expert in mystical doctrine and must be assiduous in ascetic practices such as fasting, sleep deprivation, weeping, and minimizing sexual contact to prescribed times, that is, solely for the sake of procreation or pleasing his wife (*'onat isha*). Vital's ascetic worldview would be familiar to Christian monastic and Muslim Sufi mystics, viewing the body and its appetites in a negative light, trying to separate his spiritual self (soul) from his carnal self (body), and striving to nullify the self as much as possible in preparation for the nullification (*bittul*) that is endemic to the mystical experience.

While the *Shaarei Kedusha* is rooted in a combination of Cordoverean ethical discipline and Lurianic theosophy, neither Cordovero nor Luria go into great detail about the practical dimensions of contemplative practice. It is here where the *Shaarei Kedusha*, especially its fourth part, should be of interest to scholars of contemplative practice and mysticism. While Vital alludes to certain practical applications of contemplation in the third part of his text, focusing there on *devekut*, or communion with the divine, in the fourth part he is more explicit in terms of practical techniques. In order to better transition from theosophy to contemplation, Vital introduces certain techniques expounded by the iconoclastic medieval mystic Abraham Abulafia, utilizing them within the theosophical system of Cordovero and Luria.

Abulafia's work is explicit in offering details of breathing techniques, visualizations of letter permutations, and body movements to simulate Hebrew letters in motion, all as methods to facilitate the meditative and contemplative experience (see Idel 1988a, 13–54). Abulafia did not accept the theosophical Kabbalistic systems of his time uncritically (he worked before the *Zohar* took its final form but other theosophical systems were already extant in southern Europe) and developed a distinct kind of letter mysticism based on letter visualization combined with a neo-Aristotelian philosophical worldview.[16] He is, for example, much more sympathetic to Moses Maimonides's (1135–1204) philosophical *Moreh Nevukhim* (Guide for the Perplexed) than mystics influenced by the *Zohar*. His correlation between the intellect and the soul is more in line with Maimonides than many of the more Neoplatonic mystics.

In any event, Vital does not incorporate Abulafia's system as such but tries to merge it with the systems of his teachers, albeit he must draw from Abulafia's letter mysticism to make it all work. Abulafia suffered severe critique by major rabbinic figures during his lifetime, which also continued after his passing. As a result, none of his texts were printed until the nineteenth century when the German scholar Adolph Jellenik included some of them in his compendia of mystical literature. Thus Vital's use of Abulafia was viewed negatively by many of his readers, even as Vital's credentials remained intact. This is one reason given why the first publishers of the *Shaarei Kedusha* conspicuously left out the fourth part in their printing of the text. As mentioned earlier, the fourth part remained in manuscript until it was published in the 1980s by Yaakov Moshe Hillel of Jerusalem. Hillel's published version contains a justificatory introduction, which unfortunately could not be included in my translation due to space considerations (see later discussion herein). It is important to note, however, that the publisher felt the need to justify why it is now appropriate to publish this text when previous generations of scholars forbade it. One reason given is that much of the Abulafia corpus was being published elsewhere in Jerusalem at the same time, thus erasing the informal ban of Abulafia's works.[17]

One of the significant consequences of the appearance of Abulafia's works and of the full text of the *Shaarei Kedusha* is the accessibility it rendered to those interested in meditation from a Jewish perspective. From the late 1970s and early 1980s until today a plethora of books have been written on "Jewish meditation," many utilizing these texts now available for the first time. While many of the new books on Jewish meditation are not scholarly but popular works, the availability of works such as the fourth part of the *Shaarei Kedusha* and Abulafia's books makes a significant contribution to this enterprise.[18]

For Kabbalists in general, the Hebrew language is an essential part of their mystical system, whether we are talking about more theosophical Kabbalah (the *Zohar*) or the letter mysticism of Abulafia. The status of the Hebrew language as mystical/magical or normative was an issue in classical Rabbinic Judaism as well as the medieval Jewish philosophical tradition (see, e.g., Idel 1989, 1–28). There are numerous Midrashic statements that suggest that the Hebrew letters preceded creation; for example, "Just as the Torah was given in Hebrew (*lashon ha-kodesh*), so too the world was created with Hebrew (*lashon ha-kodesh*)" (Midrash Genesis Raba 31:8). The important pre-Kabbalistic mystical tract *Sefer Yezeriah* (Book of Creation) is a discussion about the mystical meanings of Hebrew letters, and this book was widely read and commented on throughout the history of Kabbalah. The commentary by the early Kabbalist Isaac the Blind was one of the most important early works of Kabbalah.

Even in the theosophical Kabbalah that emerged from the *Zohar* and later Lurianic Kabbalah that influenced Vital and the *Shaarei Kedusha*, the mystical dimensions of Hebrew remained central.

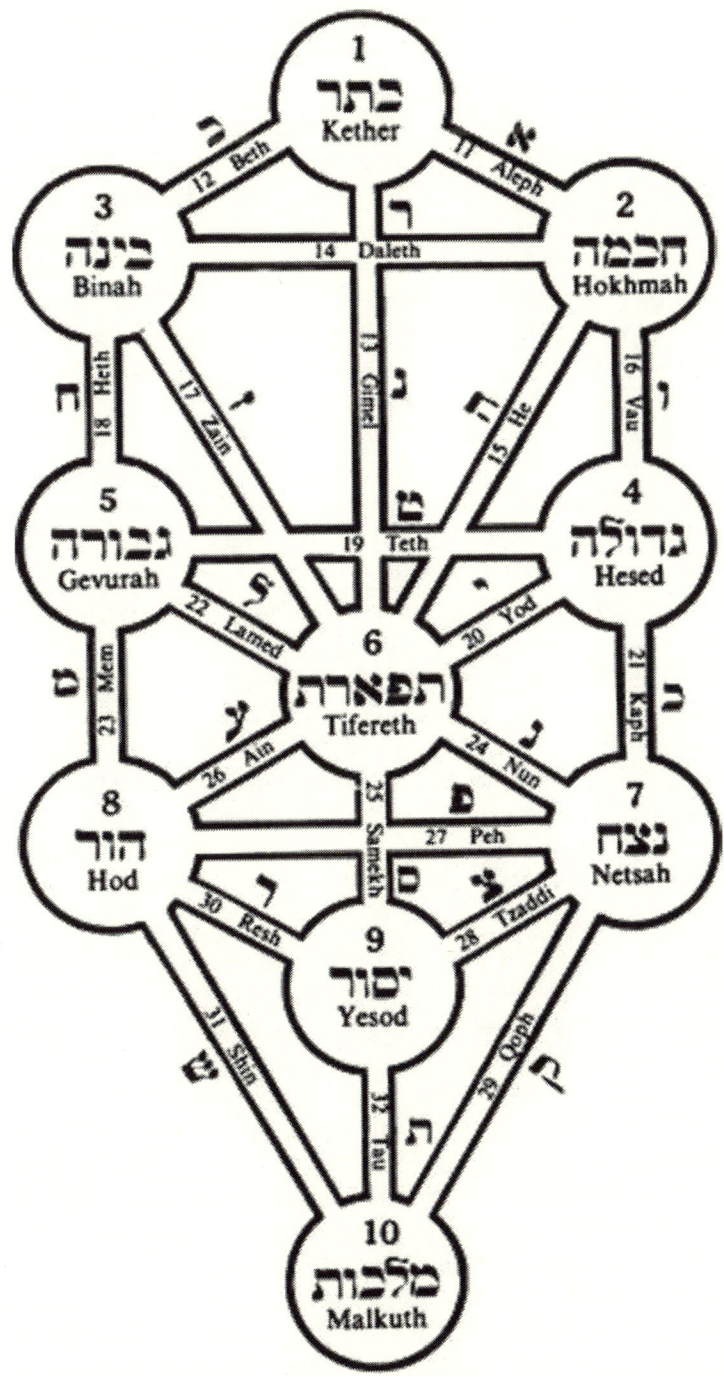

Figure 5.1. *Etz Hayyim* (Tree of Life)
The Ten *Sephirot*

While theosophical Kabbalah is more focused on the ten *sephirot*, the Hebrew letters and their various permutations and numerical value are central to the meditative techniques. Each Hebrew letter is given a numerical value producing a system of numerology linking ostensibly disparate worlds of expressions. Since in Hebrew all letters are consonants, vocalization variants enable Kabbalists to manipulate language to create new connections and cultivate meditative techniques through the manipulation of letters. The notion that God is embedded in the Torah (as the Hebrew language) suggests what some have called a "Logos Theology" of textual embodiment whereby God is accessed through the language of Torah (see, e.g., Boyarin 2004, 112–27; Wolfson 2005, 190–261). In this regard the *Shaarei Kedusha* is similar to other Kabbalistic works of its genre, except for the fact that it openly incorporates Abulafian letter techniques into its theosophical system of the *sephirot*, which, by the sixteenth century, had become the normative template of Kabbalah.

The text of the fourth part of *Shaarei Kedusha* does not introduce any new terminology. It garners terms used by earlier Kabbalists and presents them in a frame that enables Vital's contemplative program to take form. For our purposes the terms most relevant are *sephirot* (divine pronunciations/attributes/emanations), *hitbodedut* (contemplation), *devekut* (cleaving), *hishtavut* (equanimity), *ruah ha-kodesh* (holy spirit), and *nevuah* (prophecy). I will briefly discuss these terms and my choice to translate them as I did.

The regnant system of Kabbalah in the sixteenth century was based on the principle of the ten *sephirot*. Briefly, this is a cosmology that describes God as *eyn sof* (the Infinite; lit, without end) and spends little time on this unknowable dimension of divinity. Its focus is on the cosmos that it views as the mediation between the Infinite unknowable God and the universe/world. The ten *sephirot* are ten emanations, sometimes referred to in scholarship as "the godhead," that refract divine light as they descend into the corporeal world. This Kabbalah, sometimes known as theosophical Kabbalah, tracks divine light through these *sephirot* and uses ritual and contemplative techniques to move these *sephirot* in the proper positions to maximize the influx of divine light through them and into the world. This system is founded on the principle of theurgy, that is, that human action, in this case the performance of ritual commandments (*mitzvot*), has direct impact on the *sephirotic* world. Accompanying these acts are contemplative meditations, or *kavvanot*, that direct the divine flow as it filters downward through the *sephirotic* realm as a consequence of mandated ritual acts. These techniques also enable the Kabbalist to achieve an awareness of this divine flow as it filters through the cosmic realm.

Hitbodedut is perhaps the most complicated term and arguably the central term in Vital's text. Its etymology in Hebrew comes from BDD, "to be alone." The closest English equivalent might be "solitude." In medieval Kabbalah, especially in the works of Isaac of Acre (late 13th/early 14th c.) who had a strong influence on Vital, the term is used as a condition for contemplation (see Idel 1988, 128–31). With the term *hishtavut* (equanimity), also common in Isaac of Acre's writings, Vital employs two terms that Jewish mystics likely adopted from Sufism (see Fenton 1994, 1995).[19] The term *hitbodedut* has other meanings in the Jewish mystical tradition. For example, in Bratslav Hasidism (beginning in early 19th-c. Ukraine), the term *hitbodedut* means something quite different. Nahman of Bratslav (1772–1810) urged his followers to go out alone into the fields or forests and talk to God in the vernacular. This was not a particularly contemplative exercise and often resulted in gesticulating and the screaming cries of adepts as they emptied their insides through verbal catharsis. Habad Hasidism, a Hasidic group that

Category	Sephirot
Above-consciousness	1. Keter: Crown
Conscious Intellect	2. Hokhmah: Wisdom 3. Binah: Understanding (Da'at: Knowledge)
Conscious Emotions	Primary Emotions 4. Hesed: Kindness 5. Gevurah: Judgment 6. Tifereth: Beauty Secondary Emotions 7. Netsah: Eternity 8. Hod: Splendor 9. Yesod: Foundation 10. Malkhut: Kingship

Figure 5.2. Categories and Associations of the Ten *Sephirot*

emerged at about the same time, coined the term *hitbonenut* to imply a more contemplative state. This term comes from the root BNN, "to utilize the mind (*bina*) in contemplation," or, as some translate it, "meditation." Vital uses the term *hitbodedut* in its more medieval usage to imply both solitude as the condition and contemplation as the telos of the adept's process toward mystical experience. *Hitbodedut* as contemplation thus uses the condition (to be alone) to describe the act (to contemplate).

Devekut is a much more common term, and thus more multivalent, and has attracted more attention among scholars (see, e.g., Scholem 1949–1950; Pachter 1984; Carmilly-Weinberger 2008). The term took on specific resonance in Safed in the sixteenth century when Vital was active. There is much debate as to what this term actually implies. Moshe Idel (1995, 86–89) suggests that it comes quite close to the foreign term *unio mystica*, an experience of unity with the divine. Vital's use of the term in the *Shaarei Kedusha*, especially in the fourth part, seems closer to a notion of a symmetry whereby the adept aligns himself perfectly to receive the flow from above. It is a condition of receiving the Holy Spirit and thus the condition of prophecy.[20] He envisions this state not only as the apex of the religious quest but also as a positive biblical commandment, "And cleave to him" (Deut. 10:20). In part 3, Vital identifies *devekut* with prophecy quite explicitly. "The prophet cleaves (*mitdabek*) to the Holy Name through the drawing down of prophecy and divine effluence to the lower realm."[21] One of the things distinctive about Vital's fourth part is the merging of "letter combination" techniques and *devekut*, the experience of unity with the divine. This has precedent in Abraham Abulafia, but Vital's explicit use of the term *devekut* as a consequence of the techniques deployed became popular in subsequent Kabbalah and later in Hasidism (see Idel 1995, 61).

Hishtavut, or equanimity, is a common medieval trope of ascetic pietism and one that Vital likely gleaned from his reading of Isaac of Acre and through Elijah da Vidas's *Reshit Hokhma*.[22] The term applies to an ascetic exercise that erases any judgment between one thing and another. In the fourth part Vital cites a story in a quasi–Zen Buddhist dialogic exchange whereby a master questions an aspiring mystic as to what he thinks of the person who honors him and the person who denigrates him. The young man says, "I feel pleasure from the one who honors me and pain from the one who denigrates me. But I do not bear a grudge." The master sends him on his way saying, "As long as they are not equal in your eyes, until you feel no difference between being honored and being denigrated, you are not ready for your thoughts to be bound to the upper spheres when you enter contemplation." Equanimity is thus a state of selflessness where the mystic becomes a nonjudgmental vessel that receives everything equally. It is thus not an integral part of the mystical experience but an integral condition for its occurrence.

Ruah ha-kodesh (Holy Spirit) and *nevuah* (prophecy) are complicated terms in that they seem sometimes to be used interchangeably in the *Shaarei Kedusha*, but they do not mean the same thing, at least not in a formal sense. Simply stated, prophecy is a communication from God that enables one to step outside the linear time of history and thus know the future.[23] Prophetic proclamations have legal weight, and the rabbis even enable the prophets to temporarily annul a divine decree. Experiencing the Holy Spirit does not contain the same dispensation but also does not carry the same authoritative weight. The Holy Spirit does not become inaccessible after prophecy, and the rabbis and their spiritual progeny leave open the possibility of receiving the Holy Spirit even after the destruction of the Temple in 70 CE.[24] In the fourth part of the *Shaarei Kedusha*, Vital writes, "After a person achieves this state of cleaving, he will achieve equanimity (*hishtavut*).[25] If he achieves equanimity, he can achieve contemplation. After achieving contemplation, he can merit the Holy Spirit, and from there he can achieve prophecy, meaning that he can know the future." Here prophecy appears as the stage following the Holy Spirit. Yet we also read, "This is why prophecy and the Holy Spirit are called slumber (*tirdama*), dream (*halom*), or vision (*hazon*)," without an explicit distinction between them. In the third part of the *Shaarei Kedusha*, Vital remarks that prophecy and the Holy Spirit are both operational and necessary. "Prophecy and the Holy Spirit must be found in our world and easy to achieve. The difficulty is finding those who are fit for this."[26] Vital's explicit claim of proximity between the normative notion of receiving the Holy Spirit and the more precarious notion of the renewal of prophecy, all situated within technical methods of actualizing both, puts the *Shaarei Kedusha*, especially its fourth part, in a place between the theosophical Kabbalah from the *Zohar* to Luria and the ecstatic and prophetic Kabbalah of Abraham Abulafia. As mentioned earlier, while we cannot know for certain, perhaps it was the desire to keep these two approaches separate that contributed to the decision not to publish the fourth part of Hayyim Vital's treatise.

Entering the Gates of Holiness

The *Shaarei Kedusha* (Gates of Holiness) by Hayyim Vital (1542–1620) was originally written in four parts (*halakim*), with each part consisting of various "gates" (*shearim*). These four parts include twenty-five gates or sections in total. The division of Kabbalistic texts into separate parts is not uncommon, especially in the Lurianic school. In *Shaarei Kedusha* each gate, or *sha'ar*, serves to build the case toward Vital's understanding of applied Kabbalah. The historical grounding in the first three parts is necessary because Vital is well aware that his applied techniques in part 4 are not common and would likely be open to criticism. It should also be noted that these four parts may not have been written as they are printed but are, rather, at least in part the work of the editor of the manuscripts.

The first three parts of the *Shaarei Kedusha* cover ground common in other pietistic texts of the period. The first part discusses the nature of human sin and explains the different levels of righteousness that lead one to the status of the *zaddik* (righteous one) or *hasid* (pious one). The second part is devoted to the question of punishment for transgressions and the rewards of fulfilling the precepts of the Torah. The third part is concerned primarily with prophecy, the ways to achieve it, its various levels, and the experience of communion with God (*devekut*) and *ruah ha-kodesh* (the Holy Spirit).

The history of the unpublished fourth part of Hayyim Vital's *Shaarei Kedusha* is somewhat of an anomaly in the Jewish textual tradition. We have many cases where publishers chose not to print texts because their authors were deemed by some authorities as suspect, or, in other cases, where the texts were anonymous and thus the veracity and orthodoxy of the text could not be fully verified. In this case, we have a text that was accepted as written not only by a reputable Kabbalist but one of the most prolific and well-regarded Kabbalists in one of the most explosive periods of Kabbalistic creativity.[27] Moreover, this text did not stand alone but was the concluding part of a larger text, the *Shaarei Kedusha*, that has been reprinted many times since its initial printing in Constantinople in 1644. It remains a popular Kabbalistic text even for those not literate in the Kabbalistic tradition and has been mentioned approvingly by the greatest traditional and ultra-traditional minds in Jewish modernity.

All of this raises the following questions: Why *did* the printers of the *Shaarei Kedusha* choose not to print this fourth part, and why have subsequent printers until the 1980s continued to exclude this part from printings of the *Shaarei Kedusha*? Such questions did not go unanswered in various printers' introductions. Apparently, even before its first printing, Abraham ben-Asher, the copier of Vital's manuscript in Egypt, wanted to conceal this final part.[28] In the editor's introduction to the first edition we read, "This fourth part will not be transcribed nor printed because its contents exclusively contain divine names, divine letter permutations, and secrets that make it inappropriate to be published."[29] In addition, and this may be a more compelling reason not to publish this part, the editor mentions that this part relies on the "letter Kabbalah" (or, as Moshe Idel prefers, the "ecstatic Kabbalah") of Abraham Abulafia. By the sixteenth century Abulafia's Kabbalah had suffered such harsh criticism even in Kabbalistic circles that it was never published. Moshe Idel has shown, however, that even as Kabbalists such as Moshe Cordovero had ostensibly completely absorbed the theosophical Kabbalah based on the *Zohar*, elements of Abulafian Kabbalah were embedded in his work.[30] Thus we can see that Abulafia's work was being read in manuscript. Being a student of Cordovero, Vital was surely exposed to this material. What distinguishes the fourth part of the *Shaarei Kedusha*, however, is the explicit way in which Abulafian techniques are developed.

What any reader of the following translation will see is that this text as published is not exclusively divine names and letter permutations, and mention of Abulafia is quite minimal,

Part I	Part III
1. Explanation of the fault that was caused by transgression of the *mitzvoth* (1)	1. On the nature of the worlds, including a brief introduction for understanding the nature of prophecy (15)
2. Explanation of continuous fault due to improper conduct (2)	2. On the nature of humanity (16)
3. Explanation of the virtues of the righteous and of the pious. Teaches how to obtain them (3)	3. On the prophecy impeders (17)
4. Explanation of the details of the virtue of the righteous one (*tzadik*) (4)	4. On the prophecy stipulations (18)
5. Explanation of Hasidic virtue and how it will always be before your eyes (5)	5. On prophecy quality and concerns (19)
6. Summary of the previous gates and explanation how the Hasid should conduct his life in order to prevent his downfall (6)	6. On the prophecy levels (20)
Part II	7. A guide to the Holy Spirit in our times (21)
1. Reproofs (7)	8. Explanation concerning the sanctification in our time (22)
2. Reproofs of discipline of our sages of blessed memory (8)	**Part IV**
3. Untitled (9)	1. Necessary conditions for divine apprehension (23)
4. The punishment for bad character traits and the reward for good character traits (10)	2. Practical matters of divine apprehension (24)
5. The punishment for those who possess forbidden character traits (11)	3. Practical matters (contemplative techniques) (25)
6. The punishments for those who transgress the negative *mitzvot* (12)	
7. On the observance of the positive *mitzvot* and of good conduct (13)	
8. The gate of repentance, which is divided into three parts (14)	

Figure 5.3. Sections of the Received *Shaarei Kedusha*

although admittedly his influence may exist throughout. In fact, explicit Abulafian material only fills a small section of the text. I decided not to include this section (constituting about six printed pages) because its very nature makes it difficult if not impossible to convey in another language (see, e.g., Fine 1982).

What does flow more systemically in this text is the question of prophecy and the aspiration to attain prophecy through various contemplative techniques that include fasting, breathing, and the visualization of permutations of Hebrew letters. While prophecy as a formal category ended in Ancient Israel with the return of the exiles in fifth century BCE and the rabbinic tradition limits prophecy to the land of Israel (with the exception of Ezekiel who prophesied outside Erez Israel), Jewish mystics have continuously, and subtly, drawn a connection between mystical experience and prophecy (see, e.g., Fine 1982).[31] Vital is quite explicit in the third part of *Shaarei Kedusha* about the possibility for, and even necessity of, prophecy in his time, but it is only in the fourth part that he presents contemplative techniques of how to attain prophecy.[32] This suggests that the editors were less concerned with theoretical discussions regarding the renewal of prophecy, discussions that exist intermittently throughout Kabbalistic literature, especially after the Spanish expulsion in 1492, than with practical and technical discussions about how to achieve it. While we may never know for sure what Vital had in mind and what was in the minds of the printers who refused to print this fourth part (regardless of what they say), we can assume that it was read as somehow more problematic than similar discussions by Kabbalists from Isaac of Acre in the thirteenth century to Judah Albotini (1453–1519) in the fifteenth century and then Moses Cordovero in the sixteenth century.[33] In addition, Vital's reputation as a preeminent Kabbalist of this period was not tarnished by this text.

As printed, the fourth part of the *Shaarei Kedusha* is made up of three basic sections: (1) "necessary conditions for divine apprehension," (2) "practical matters of divine apprehension," and (3) "practical matters (contemplative techniques)." The translation that follows only includes parts 1 and 2. Part 1 consists of two printed pages; part 2 consists of eighteen printed pages; and part 3 consists of nine printed pages.[34] As Avishai Bar-Asher has shown, making assumptions about the text as a whole is problematic in that these three parts are likely three (or more) different "texts" that were written by Vital (some may have been changed by his son and grandson, both editors of his work). Bar-Asher divides the texts into two distinct textual layers: (1) preparations and practical techniques for achieving the Holy Spirit and (2) a collection of earlier Kabbalistic texts on human apprehension of the divine.[35] For example, the collection of earlier Kabbalistic material on acquiring the Holy Spirit and prophecy may have been written much earlier, consisting of material that Vital collected about contemplation as he was making his way through the Kabbalistic corpus (see Bar-Asher 2012). He may not have intended this to be a preface to his Abulafian techniques that may have been written much later. In and of itself, section 2 should not have been problematic for any Kabbalistic editor as it collects and collates a series of canonical Kabbalistic texts on the theme of apprehending the divine and attaining prophecy. Section 1 speaks of the necessary prerequisites of the contemplative life, in many cases restating what was stated in part 3 of the *Shaarei Kedusha* and any number of other canonical Kabbalistic texts. Hence, however the text was constructed, in whatever order, and in whatever time frame, it would appear that the choice not to print the fourth part was due to the inclusion of section 3 on techniques used by the contemplative to cultivate and foster prophecy. While other Kabbalists apart from Abulafia write about prophecy, they mostly do so in general and generic terms. This is true of Vital's teachers Moses Cordovero and Isaac Luria. It is worth noting that before meeting Luria, Vital had dabbled in alchemy and other exercises that came close to what is known as practical Kabbalah (*kabbalah ma'asit*) (see Boss 1994). He later turned against all practical Kabbalah, and in the *Shaarei Kedusha* and many other places he spoke vociferously against it.[36]

While we cannot know for sure, given Vital's predilection for experimentation and his messianic ambitions, it is indeed plausible that he collected a series of earlier texts on contemplation and the aspiration for prophecy to use for some practical contemplative purpose. Hence the manuscripts that place the collection of texts before the technical section make more sense than the manuscripts that place the technical section first. We also know from his diary that Vital considered himself to be a unique, even messianic, soul, and thus the reinstitution of prophecy would not be far from view.[37]

The practice of collating earlier sources was well known to Vital. Vital's family was from Italy, and he was intimately familiar with Italian Kabbalah. Moshe Idel describes what he calls "mosaic kabbalists—namely, those combining the ideas of several kabbalistic schools. . . . They are more concerned with absorbing, digesting, arranging, and re-arranging the pertinent sources in larger literary creations . . ." (Idel 2011a, 110). Section 2 appears to take this form, although, again, we cannot know Vital's intent in composing it. The fact that some of the texts that he collects speak approvingly of Abulafia (including his teacher Cordovero), and that he also cites Judah Hayyat's overt critique of Abulafia, suggests Abulafia is in his sights.[38] One of the striking things about the *Shaarei Kedusha* is how much Vital remained in some way a student of Moses Cordovero. Cordovero's mention and, more importantly here, his possible application of Abulafian techniques may be the shadow under which the *Shaarei Kedusha* was written (Idel 1988a, 138).[39]

Thus the text as we have it here, that is, classic preparatory conditions for contemplation to receive the Holy Spirit, earlier justifications of contemplation as a means to receive the Holy Spirit, and then practical meditative techniques to receive the Holy Spirit, makes perfect sense. Whether or not this was Vital's intent we do not know, but it seems to have been the intent of the transcriber of the manuscript that was used for the Ahavat Shalom edition.

The text as printed thus serves simultaneously as a justification for, and guide to, prophecy. Moshe Idel quite explicitly claims, "According to the author [Vital] the fourth and final stage of the process of purification, whose ultimate purpose is the attainment of prophecy, includes seclusion in a special house" (Idel 1988b, 135). Combining preparations for contemplation (which were considered normative by Kabbalists of his time),[40] justification for this exercise, and then techniques to achieve it, provides the reader with an abbreviated version of pious directives and support for the "orthodoxy" of such an endeavor and finally a technical guide for the aspiring contemplative. Again, we cannot determine if this was Vital's intent because the text as printed was not organized by him. However, it does appear that he was attempting (whether in this text specifically or more generally) to bring together the mystical piety he learned from his teachers, utilizing a mosaic method common in earlier Italian Kabbalah with an Abulafian approach toward achieving prophecy. He may have learned this from Cordovero. It is clear from what we know of Vital's youth that he was not exclusively interested in metaphysics or even theurgy. However, once he became a disciple of Isaac Luria around 1571, much of his work focused on the complex theurgic and cosmological system that Luria espoused.

The first section of part 4 of the *Shaarei Kedusha* is very short and introduces the reader to the ethical conditions necessary to achieve a mystical or prophetic experience through a series of citations from medieval mystics (e.g., Moshe Nahmanides, Isaac of Acre, *Sefer Hasidim* [Book of the Pious] by Rabbi Judah the Pious, and the anonymous *Brit Menuha* [Covenant of Composure]). Traits such as humility, equanimity, and the need to constantly direct one's thoughts to God are mentioned and briefly discussed.

The second section of part 4 is a more practical guide to contemplation. It examines in detail the postures and intention of prayer and the visualization of separating oneself from one's body. Much of it is devoted to exercises to control one's thoughts. This is also done through citation of earlier sources, but here Vital finds his voice and elaborates on these matters. However, unlike contemplative guides in other traditions, we still do not have a detailed practical guide of implementation. These matters are written about in general terms; only basic rubrics are discussed. Clearly, though, the ethical conditions for contemplation in section 1 now lead to more internal matters between the adept and his relationship to his own body and the spiritual ascent.

The third and final section of part 4 of the *Shaarei Kedusha* opens with a citation from Abulafia and is focused more on the techniques of letter mysticism including letter permutation meditation, the recitation of angelic names, and the use of numerology to link disparate words for the purposes of *yihud* or *zeruf oriot* (unifications of letters). This type of Kabbalah specifically involves combining the twenty-two letters (consonants) of the Hebrew alphabet (remember that vowels are not written) in various ways, especially, in the case of the *Shaarei Kedusha*, into the seventy-two names of God. The notion of manipulating letters, often by rearranging them in different combinations, either to spell out different words, puns, or angelic names, is a common practice in medieval Kabbalah that was used extensively by Abulafia. It also exists in the Lurianic school, especially in the later recensions of the Sharabi school in eighteenth-century Palestine.

One of the striking lacunae in the *Shaarei Kedusha* more generally and the fourth part in particular is that overt reference to Isaac Luria is almost entirely absent. After Luria's death in 1572, Vital came to be the most prolific and, according to him, the only legitimate representative of Luria's teachings.[41] It could be, as some claim, that some or even much of the *Shaarei Kedusha* was initially written before Vital met Luria around 1570. However, Vital lived for decades after

א (A)	ל (L)
בּ/ב (B/V)	מ (M)
ג (G)	נ (N)
ד (D)	ס (S)
ה (H)	ע (')
ו (V)	פּ/פ (P/F)
ז (Z)	צ (TZ)
ח (CH)	ק (Q)
ט (T)	ר (R)
י (Y)	ש (SH)
כּ/כ (K/KH)	ת (T)

Figure 5.4. Letters of the Hebrew Alphabet

Luria's death in 1572 and continued working on various projects.[42] Why, then, did he not integrate Luria's approach into what would become one of Vital's most widely read texts? We have very little information regarding Luria's exposure to or opinion of Abulafia. We must remember that Luria spent all but the last eighteen months of his adult life in Egypt. He briefly studied with Cordovero, who was quite old when Luria arrived in Safed, before going off on his own, and he did know David Ibn Zamra in Egypt, who mentioned Abulafia numerous times in his work.[43] Yet even if we accept the fact that Abulafia was indeed a part of the Kabbalistic world of Safed in the mid–sixteenth century, Luria's short stay there may suggest that he was not exposed to Abulafia in any significant way and, even if he was, his teachings as recorded by his many disciples show almost no influence of Abulafia whatsoever.[44]

Lurianic Contemplative Practice in Later Jewish Kabbalah

The combination of adaptations of Lurianic Kabbalah in Italy, among Sabbateans in southern and Eastern Europe, Lithuanian Jewish mystics in the circle of the Gaon of Vilna (Rabbi Elijah ben Shlomo Zalman; 1720–1797), and the rise of Hasidism resulted in Lurianic Kabbalah as the dominant, almost exclusive, school of Kabbalah in modernity. While medieval Kabbalists were still studied and scholars have shown the evidence of Abulafia's and Cordovero's systems in later Kabbalah, much of this was refracted through the Lurianic system. Even in the study of the *Zohar*, Lurianic commentaries on the *Zohar* dominated later readings of the text in traditional circles. Almost all contemporary academies of Kabbalah in Israel today are exclusively based on the Lurianic system with other works coming to compliment, not contest, Lurianic dominance (Garb 2012). In scholarly circles, of course, things are quite different, and, somewhat surprisingly, Lurianic Kabbalah has not been a central focus of study. While Gershom Scholem argued in his *Major Trends in Jewish Mysticism* that Lurianic Kabbalah was of central importance in terms of what he described was its metaphysical construct of history as divine rupture and repair, and while he acknowledged its dominance in traditional circles during his lifetime, he did not devote a major study to Lurianic Kabbalah.

In any case, the dominance of Lurianic Kabbalah coupled with its inordinate complexity made texts such as the *Shaarei Kedusha* extremely popular. This is because the *Shaarei Kedusha* presents the Lurianic system in broad strokes without delving into the details that one finds in Vital's other works, such as the *Etz Hayyim* (Tree of Life) and *Shemoneh Shearim* (Eight Gates). It was especially popular with Hasidim whose focus was by and large more devotional than scholastic.

The recently published fourth part of the *Shaarei Kedusha* begins with an extensive and substantive editor's introduction. This introduction by Netanel Safrin, a senior member and editor at Yaakov Moshe Hillel's Ahavat Shalom Yeshiva in Jerusalem, contains his justification for printing this text after it remained in manuscript for centuries and speaks to the larger question of Abulafia's influence in contemporary Kabbalah, both in traditional and nontraditional circles that may have inspired bringing this text to light.[45] The choice to print this fourth part and Safrin's justification is worth examining briefly. To begin, Yaakov Moshe Hillel, the yeshiva dean (*rosh yeshiva*) at Ahavat Shalom Yeshiva, has written openly against the publication of Abulafia's works (see Meir 2007, 241n522). However, elsewhere he offers a common justification for the publication of Kabbalah that we are living in the "footsteps of the Messiah" and the study of Kabbalah will provide the necessary *tikkun* (rectification) to move that process along.⁴⁶

The editor's introduction begins with a lengthy quotation from Moses Maimonides's (1134–1204) *Moreh Nevukhim* (Guide for the Perplexed). This makes sense for two reasons. First, because Maimonides is considered such a canonical figure, the placement of this problematic text in a Maimonidean frame immediately gives it credibility. Second, Abulafia was a close and devoted reader of Maimonides, even devoting numerous studies to interpret Maimonides in a Kabbalistic fashion (Luria almost ignores Maimonides).⁴⁷ The citation from Maimonides's *Guide for the Perplexed* III 52:53 is a classic text for Kabbalists since Maimonides speaks of contemplation on the divine name as a condition for being under the influence of divine providence. We read,

> If a person turns his mind and perceives the divine in its true ways, and is joyous in which he achieves, it is impossible for that person to succumb to the evils of the world, for he is with the Name and the Name is with him. But when his mind turns from the Name, he becomes separated from it, and the Name becomes separated from him. In that instant, all the evils of the world could potentially find him.

While it is unlikely that Maimonides meant what Kabbalists such as Abulafia interpreted him to mean, this introduces a quasi-Abulafian approach to the contemporary reader in a way that could be easily digested. It is somewhat ironic that Luria had little use for Maimonides, almost never citing him, and Vital was not a particular devotee of Maimonides either, specifically his philosophical treatise *Guide for the Perplexed*. Safrin then cleverly filters this approach through a principle of Moshe Isserles, the sixteenth-century Polish legalist, in his gloss to the canonical *Shulhan Arukh* (Code of Jewish Law) followed by a reference to Lurianic Kabbalah that is almost entirely missing from this treatise. Only then does he mention Vital's fourth part of the *Shaarei Kedusha*, thus setting it solidly within the ideational and legal framework of normative Judaism.

The most revealing part of this introduction, however, is the editor's justification for publishing this previously unpublished text now. Acknowledging that Abraham Ben-Asher, the transcriber of the *Shaarei Kedusha*, explicitly excluded this fourth part from his manuscript, Safrin remarks that this decision was made before the publication of the Lurianic corpus, much of which contains precisely the letter combinations (*zeruf otiot*) that Ben-Asher feared. Regarding mention of Abulafia, Safrin cites the well-known denigration of Abulafia and his writings, yet he also remarks on how some of these same individuals make reference to similar Kabbalistic ideas. The denigration of Kabbalah accompanied by the reference to Kabbalah is not uncommon. We see similar instances of this in the works of the Italian rabbis Elijah del Medigo (1458–1493) and Leon Modena (1571–1648), both of whom criticize Kabbalah while obviously being quite knowledgeable about its ideas and even use Kabbalah in various ways in their work.⁴⁸ By equivocating the critique of Abulafia and suggesting that in our time, that is, after the proliferation of the Lurianic corpus that is replete with the very dimensions of Kabbalah that Abraham ben-Asher cites as the reason not to transcribe the fourth part, Safrin accomplishes two distinct but related things. First, he contextualizes and thus diffuses the prohibition against publishing the text. Second, he views the text as part of the Lurianic lineage, which, as any reader can see, cannot be justified in the text itself. By linking Abulafia's "letter combination" with Lurianic contemplative techniques (*kavvanot*), the editor essentially situates this text as a legitimate companion to the contemporary study of Kabbalah.

The context of this publication, as well as the editor's justification to publish it, is important. What remains unanswered in Safrin's introduction is why while publishing the Lurianic corpus began slowly in the eighteenth century and really took off in the later decades of the nineteenth century, this fourth part remained unpublished until the 1980s! Here Zeev Gries's comment is significant:

> In those years [the 1970s until today] the socialistic, profane nature of the social and cultural life of the Jewish state was challenged by the rise of traditional sentiments of many young and adult Jews. . . . Since then, the ongoing process of secularization of Jewish life was and is coupled with a growing interest in traditional Jewish literature. (Gries 2008, 114)

The choice to publish this text now seems part of a larger shift in printing Kabbalistic literature in the later decades of the twentieth century, in large part due to the changing nature of ultra-Orthodox society influenced by, among other things, a renewed interest in the Jewish mystical tradition, both in Israel and the Diaspora; the increased influence of Mizrahi tradition where Kabbalah was almost always normative; as well as a more independent-minded readership no longer as tightly bound to older models of authority. Among other things, this new movement toward what I would call a kind of "anarchic traditionalism"[49] all but broke the spell of the decree against Abulafian Kabbalah, thus diffusing any remaining resistance to the printing of the fourth part of the *Shaarei Kedusha*.[50]

The interest in meditation that largely came to Israel from the American counterculture and young Israelis' interest in Asian religions as a result of post-army travel created prime conditions for the introduction of Abulafian Kabbalah in general and contemplative Kabbalah in particular. Of particular interest is the understudied influence of the American rabbi Aryeh Kaplan (1934–1983), whose books such as *Meditation and the Bible* (1978) and *Meditation and Kabbalah* (1982) freely use Abulafian techniques.[51] While Yaakov Moshe Hillel remained opposed to the publication of Abulafia's writings and was openly opposed to noninitiates studying Kabbalah more generally, he sanctioned the publication of the fourth part of the *Shaarei Kedusha*. Safrin's introduction addresses this apparent discrepancy by setting this part solidly within the normative Lurianic trajectory.

Translating the Untranslatable: A Note on Kabbalistic Translation

I briefly discussed the importance of Hebrew and language in Kabbalah earlier in this chapter. Hebrew lends itself to word play because all the letters in Hebrew are consonants enabling variant vocalizations to change a word's meaning or make two distinct words appear connected. Given that almost all Kabbalistic texts are written in Hebrew, even as the *lingua franca* of most of its authors was not, in many cases word play and linguistic allusions are built into the very fabric of the texts, even when the author is explaining a particular Kabbalistic idea. This poses serious challenges to the translator, who must somehow lift the language of the text from its embedded place in the ambiguity of Hebrew word play. Moreover, since many of the contemplative techniques involve the manipulation and visualization of Hebrew letters, translating these techniques can be difficult and, without knowledge of the language, comprehending much less performing these techniques is a challenge, if not an impossibility.

Yet given all these caveats, in some way the modern study of Kabbalah began with translation. In 1923 the young Gershom Scholem completed *Das Buch Bahir*, his doctoral dissertation from the University of Munich, which included an annotated German translation and commentary of the early Kabbalistic treatise *Sefer Bahir*.[52] Over the course of the twentieth century, many translations of Kabbalah followed. The beginning of the twenty-first century witnessed the first major critical translation of the *Zohar* when Daniel Matt published the first volume of the projected twelve-volume *The Pritzker Zohar* in 2004. I mention this only because there has been a robust debate among scholars of Kabbalah if this esoteric wisdom founded so deeply on language, specifically the Hebrew language, *can* be translated into another language without losing the blood (i.e., the language) that flows through its veins. Kabbalah is certainly not the only metaphysical and experiential wisdom that is tied deeply to the language in which it is expressed, but it surely is one of them.[53] And thus it is curious that the academic study of this ancient lore begins with . . . a *translation*. It is thus appropriate to discuss my translation of a sixteenth-century Kabbalistic text on contemplation by briefly reflecting on the question: What precisely does a translator do when he or she translates an esoteric text, a text whose very form of communication is to conceal precisely what it reveals? The sixteenth-century Kabbalist Isaac Luria put it succinctly when he defined his role as a teacher as "revealing one handbreadth and concealing a thousand."[54]

The two epigraphs that introduce this chapter gesture toward two approaches to the question of translation by the national Israeli poet Hayyim Nahman Bialik (1873–1934) and the scholar of Kabbalah Gershom Scholem (1897–1982), both of whom thought deeply about the Hebrew language and its relationship to the tradition that it articulates.[55] Both comments reflect Kabbalistic images of the erotic nature of language and the desire of one who utters it. And both were translators, in the formal and informal sense of the word.[56] Both lamented the secularization of the holy tongue yet recognized its inevitability. For Scholem, the secularization process *had* to fail. He writes,

> One believes that language has been secularized, that its apocalyptic thorn has been pulled out. But that is surely not true. The secularization of language is only a *façon de parler*, a ready-made phrase. It is impossible to empty out words filled to bursting, unless one does so at the expense of language itself.[57]

Bialik viewed language itself as a failure, not a failure to recognize the experience of divine unity but, quite the opposite, the failure to recognize the true reality of Chaos (Bialik uses the Hebrew term *blimah* that refers to nonsubstance, lit., without whatness). The secularization of language is a tragedy because it ties language so tightly to the everyday world that it hides that truth of humanity (see Bialik 2000, 89–94). Not unlike Nietzsche, Bialik suggests that we use language to escape the truth. As Azzan Yadin writes, "The ontological foundations of Bialik's critique of language have now been laid bare. Ultimate reality is Chaos, while the common language of generalization and abstractions enveloped man [sic] in a false sense of security and stability, distracting him from this difficult truth" (Yadin 2001, 195).

However, the epigraph from Bialik, echoing the Midrashic tradition that also informed the Kabbalists, suggests that language is a kiss, perhaps between the speaker and the one spoken to. Perhaps between the speaker and the language itself. Translation dampens the fire of erotic desire as a veil separates flesh from flesh, Word from flesh, leaving the lovers—the language and the speaker, the speaker and the listener—in a state of perennial unconsummation. Translation for Bialik is to be close, to almost touch, and yet never taste the flesh of the other, of the language. For Bialik, translation is a compromise of that which is already a compromise. Bialik's pessimism regarding language is countered by what he thinks brings language to life by destabilizing it: poetry. For "the masters of poetry . . . the profane becomes sacred, and the sacred profane" (2000, 89). For both Scholem and Bialik, in different ways, the best use of language is to free it from the rigidity of objects and generalization, to free language from simply describing the world. For Bialik, this is through poetry. For Scholem, this is exemplified in Kabbalah, the one use of language that gets at its very core: names. He cites approvingly the thirteenth-century rabbinic leader and Kabbalist Moses Nahmanides when he introduces his commentary to Genesis by claiming that the entire Torah—narrative, law, history—is simply one continuous recitation of "names of God." For Scholem, Kabbalah is the great resister of the secularization of language.[58]

Scholem's letter cited in the epigraph to this chapter was written to Franz Rosenzweig (1886–1929), who was in the midst of a massive translation project of the Hebrew Bible (into German) with Martin Buber (1878–1965), a project that sought to revolutionize not only the German but also the original Hebrew text.[59] Scholem's quotation suggests translation is an act of penetration, to enter the heart of another language, perhaps to dwell there, if only for a moment.[60] But all this comes at a price. In another letter to Rosenzweig from late 1926 Scholem writes about the danger of the modernization of Hebrew, itself a form of translation. He writes, "It is absolutely impossible to empty out words which filled to bursting, unless one does so at the expense of the language itself."[61] Nevertheless, somehow he also wrote that translation is a kind of miracle, which can "enter into the heart of the sacred order from which it springs." Perhaps for Scholem it is only because this "miracle" is possible that we do it at all. And even the "miracle" is not without a price. All miracles, perhaps, have a price. One of the grave dangers of language for Scholem, perhaps a product of its secularization, is when language becomes too familiar. The *Unheimlichkeit* (uncanniness) of language in some way protects its sacrality. It is not insignificant that even when Scholem mastered the New Hebrew of Palestine and then Israel he continued to write in other languages (German and English) throughout his life. Galili Shahar makes the following suggestion worth considering: "Scholem's 'real language,' one can argue, lies in the gap between the languages; the sources of his speech is the difference, the tension, the unfamiliarity of German and Hebrew" (2008, 307). In his lamentation about the secularization and popularization of the New Hebrew, Scholem writes, "Our children no longer have another language, and it is only too true to say that they, and they alone, will pay for the encounter which we have initiated without asking, without even asking ourselves." Monolingualism defuses the tension and, in doing so, undermines the *Unheimlichkeit* necessary for the sacred. Perhaps this "gap between the languages" is precisely where the translator resides.[62]

It would seem that of all texts to translate, mystical texts would be the most difficult because (1) they are often the most intimately tied to language; and (2) because mystics are engaged in saying the unsayable in their original language (see, e.g., Sells 1994). How much more so given the distance, or veil, created by translation? In his recent collection of translations of Kabbalistic poetry, Peter Cole suggests the following:

> Another way of putting this is that mysticism—*and, curiously, translation*—tries to say what it seems can't quite be said, what is hardest to say, or what some feel shouldn't be said. By surrounding the unsayable with techniques of speech or silence, the mystical work seeks to construct allegories of inwardness and understanding, to catch at least a reflection of that elusive essence of experience and so to tell us what it might mean to be more profoundly awake to our loves and all they ride on. (2012, xviii; italics added)

Cole suggests symmetry between mystical texts and translation worth considering. What would it mean to translate a text that acknowledges its failure to adequately express its own meaning, or, put otherwise, a text that acknowledges the unbridgeable distance between experience and expression? In this sense, the text *itself* is a translation, and thus a translation of it would not be blasphemous but only continuing what the text sets out to do. Perhaps for the Kabbalists, translation, given all its inadequacies, *is* tradition (the term Kabbalah literally means "to receive" or, more colloquially, "tradition").

In order to avoid being accused of reifying mystical texts, what Cole suggests here is arguably true of all texts. In contrast to Bialik's veil, I think translation has its own Eros; rather than demystifying the kiss, it adds another layer of flesh, or metaphor, onto the kiss. Here Martin Kavka's recent essay on translation says it well:

> We do not decide to translate. We find ourselves translating simply because we are living among varied and varying communities. We find ourselves translating in different ways at different times because the others among whom we live change. The aim of translation therefore cannot be some permanent mapping of concepts onto one another. The meaning of those concepts will change over time, so translation will never exhaust itself. (2012, 196)

The notion that translation is a matter of living in the world, many worlds, and not an act of our choosing, captures what I have done in the following translation. In the act of translation I find myself fluctuating between rendering and creating, choosing and reacting, agonizing and breathing. The former (rendering, choosing. agonizing) are acts of volition, the latter (creating, reacting, breathing) I do even against my will. I find myself in the "gap between the languages," making one familiar yet in the act of translating, recognizing (and experiencing) the *Unheimlichkeit* of both (to me, and to each other). The translator must ponder a word in the original and, in doing so, must consider what the word represents. This can, borrowing Scholem's volcanic metaphor, enable a word's multiple meanings to erupt to the surface.[63] The translator must make a choice, but that choice does not necessarily repress the eruption as much as give it foreign form, protecting its unfamiliarity, even as it may veil its multifarious nuances.

Those of us who translate in the formal sense know the difference between reading, even closely, and translating. The former can be a caress while the latter is, as Scholem intimated, an act of penetration, "leading into the heart of the sacred order from which it springs." But so as not to get overly heated about doing what we do not choose, Kavka tells us more.

> This account of translation allows us . . . both to affirm a boundary between cultures and at the same time acknowledge that the boundary is contingent. It allows for translation—cultures are neither incommensurable (making translation impossible) nor identical (making it unnecessary)—and at the same time it acknowledges that at various historical moments, the ways in which we want to translate might change. (2012, 204)

And so the wind in the sails of any rigid notion of the sacred is mitigated by the notion that the text and tradition itself are an exercise in translation. Following Bialik, one could argue that translation is compromise as language is compromise. Kavka argues translation is freedom.[64] It not only frees the translator; it liberates the text being translated from the confines of incommensurability. It enables a reader to miraculously penetrate the sacred order of the text, not necessarily to understand it on its own terms (even reading it in the original language will not do that) but to experience something of its fleshy core. In addition, translation takes a text across a border; it enables it to enter our habitus, a world that is changing. There is an Eros and intimacy in reading a text in the language in which it was written. But Eros and intimacy are not identical. Translation is an intimate, even penetrating, act. The translated text may lose that intimacy, but it does not necessarily lose an erotic quality; it becomes an Eros of unfamiliarity. Its very existence is, as Scholem states, miraculous, not in its reproducing the original (that would not be "miraculous"; it would be impossible or, even, undesirable) but in opening the text to change, change in the way that all texts change when they are read anew.

Is translation for Bialik and Scholem more like the secularized New Hebrew spoken in the *shuk* (marketplace) or the Hebrew of the poet or Kabbalist? It is likely something in-between, in the "gap of the languages" where familiarity (the secular) and the unfamiliar (the sacred) meet, and clash, and in their clashing coexists their intimate entwining.

As a final note, it is worth asking how much the publication of the fourth part of the *Shaarei Kedusha* has influenced contemporary forms of Jewish meditation. While this is a subject worth a separate study, my inclination is to suggest that it has not had much of an impact. The reasons lie perhaps in the ideational worldview of the text, a worldview that is wed to a Neoplatonic division of body and soul, ascetic practices and strict adherence to the law that does not conform to the New Age context of much of contemporary Jewish meditation (Garb 2012). Moreover, this work only appeared in a literal translation in 2006 even though it was referred to in earlier studies in Jewish meditation. The practice of Kabbalistic meditation today among those outside the small circles of adepts who may engage in such practices in secret is primarily an amalgam of Buddhist-influenced practices adopting Jewish models and motifs. Here some Abulafian techniques appear in truncated fashion to conform to body movement, visualization, and breathing techniques that practitioners glean from Buddhism and Hinduism as presented to a Western audience. This is not to say that Kabbalistic texts, the fourth part of the *Shaarei Kedusha* being an important exemplar, cannot provide a deeper and more nuanced variation on contemporary Jewish meditation. I think they can. In fact, it is my hope that, for those interested in this practice from both scholarly and applied perspectives, this introduction and annotated translation of the fourth part will provide a window into exploring the sources, context, and applied method of Vital in regard to the contemplative life.

Notes

1. See Jerusalem Talmud Rosh Ha-Shana 2:1, 58b.

2. For a short biographical sketch, see Scholem 1974, 401–4. For more extensive works on his Kabbalistic doctrines, see Ben-Shlomo 1965 and Sack 1995.

3. Vital's family was from Calabria, Italy. It is unclear if Vital was born in Italy and, if so, when he came to Safed as a young child.

4. On ritual innovation of Safadean Kabbalah, see Scholem 1965, 118–57.

5. For two helpful biographical sketches of Vital, see Scholem 1974, 443–48 and Faierstein 1999, 3–31.

6. There are numerous places where Vital elaborates on his relationship to Luria. For one extensive discussion, see Vital's *Sha'ar Ha-Gilgulim* (Gate of Reincarnation) (Jerusalem, 1988), 39.

7. On Luria, see Fine 2003; Magid 2008.

8. For an English translation of this text, see Faierstein 1999.

9. *Sefer Hizyonot*, 5.19; cf. Faierstein 1999, 9.

10. Damascus was the largest Jewish community and a large commercial center in closest proximity to Safed. Many Jews from Safed immigrated to Damascus after the demise of the Jewish community in Safed in the late sixteenth century resulting from various plagues that decimated the community there.

11. On Scholem's theory, see his *Major Trends in Jewish Mysticism* (1961), 244–86. On Moshe Idel's critique, see Idel 1993, 1998, 154–82.

12. See, for example, Vital's *Shaar Gilgulim* (1988), 134–36.

13. On Abulafia's *unio mystica* and law, see Moshe Idel's "Abraham Abulafia and *Unio Mystica*" in Idel 1988, 1–32.

14. Kabbalah literally means "to receive" and is sometimes used as a euphemism for "tradition." In the High Middle Ages, the term Kabbalah came to refer to a genre of literature encompassing Jewish mysticism. This literature explored metaphysical, pietistic, and ritual forms of Jewish mystical practice. Kabbalistic circles consisted of esoteric and often elitist communities that included specific lineages and schools expounding specific teachings and practices. In the Renaissance and early modernity, Kabbalah was also adopted by some Christian mystics to support Christian doctrines. Today Kabbalah continues to function in many Jewish communities, both traditional and progressive. On the history of Jewish Kabbalah, see Scholem 1961, 1962, 1974; Blumenthal 1982; Dan and Kiener 1986; Idel 1988b, 1990b; Hallamish 1999; Giller 2011.

15. On mystical techniques in early Kabbalah, see Idel 1990b, 74–111.

16. For a detailed analysis of the similarities and differences between Abulafia's letter mysticism and the mysticism of the *sephirot* in Zoharic Kabbalah, see Wolfson 2000a, 94–185.

17. Abulafia's corpus is being published in Jerusalem by Amnon Gross. To date more than twenty volumes have appeared.

18. On some contemporary discussion of Jewish meditation, see Kaplan 1982, 1995; Verman 1996; Giller 2011, 145–54.

19. On *hitbodedut* as a condition, see *Shaarei Kedusha Ha-Shalem*, 3:8, 127.

20. As stated by Moshe Carmilly-Weinberger, "Later it [*devekut*] became a very important tool in Hasidic circles. With the mutation and permutation of the Hebrew letters it became possible to create and

rebuild a connection to God, the 'unio mystica.' . . . They tried many ways. Did they succeed? One positive result is that *devekut* led to prophecy" (2008, 18).

21. Shaarei Kedusha Ha-Shalem, 3:2, 106.

22. On the term in Isaac of Acre, see Fishbane 2009, 253–59.

23. The term has a much more complex meaning in philosophical and mystical literature. See, e.g., Kreisel 2001; Idel 2009.

24. The concept of the Holy Spirit in Christianity is drawn from this classical Jewish notion. See Gunkel 1979. The connection between the Holy Spirit in Christianity and *ruah ha-kodesh* is made explicit in the Jewish convert to Christianity, Immanuel Frommann (d. 1735) in his commentary to Luke (written in Hebrew). See Wolfson 2011.

25. The notion of equanimity is a central tenet of Sufi mysticism that was an important part of Isaac of Acco's work. Moshe Idel notes that aside from other similarities between Abulafian Kabbalah and Sufi mystics, neither Abulafia nor the anonymous medieval Kabbalistic work written sometime at the end of the thirteenth century by one of the pupils, *Sha'arei Zedek* (Cracow, 1881, rpt. *Sha'arei Orah with Shaarei Zedek and Sefer Ha-Nikud*, Jerusalem 1994), ever mention equanimity (Idel 1988, 107). The term is mentioned in Eleazar Azikri's (1533–1600) *Sefer Haredim* where Azikri mentions Isaac of Acre as well as Isaac Luria. See Idel 1988, 132. Vital never mentions Luria in his discussion of equanimity in the *Shaarei Kedusha*. The Sufi influence on the circle of Kabbalists in sixteenth-century Safed is explored in Fenton 1994, 170–79; 2000. Equanimity as a state of mystical experience was also practiced by the Christian Hesychasts in Eastern Europe. The term *hesychia* means "calmness" and was a central devotional practice of these reclusive ascetics, whose movement began in the fourteenth century. This may also relate to Abulafia. See Wolfson 2012, 196n28. There is some speculation concerning whether or not these monks had any influence on early Hasidism. See Idel 2011b.

26. Shaarei Kedusha Ha-Shalem, 3:3, 108

27. Most scholars who work on Vital accept the *Shaarei Kedusha* as from his hand. See, for example, Ben-Menahem 1982. In a new essay on part 4, Avishai Bar-Asher (2012) questions the veracity of authorial attribution of at least the first three sections. However, Bar-Asher acknowledges that he has no evidence aside from manuscript inconsistencies to back up his theory. Hence, we will proceed as if *Shaarei Kedusha* is the product of Vital. There is one very literal and nonacademic translation of the fourth part of the *Shaarei Kedusha* that I consulted when rendering my translation. See Hadani and Getz 2006.

28. See *Shaarei Kedusha* (Constantinople, 1644), 1. Cf. Bar-Asher 2012. There are essentially four extant manuscripts: British Library Add 19788; British Library Or. 9167; Moscow, Ginzburg 691; and Bar Ilan University 1211.

29. *Shaarei Kedusha* (Constantinople, 1644), 35b. In the Moussaief ms. 22878 the transcriber notes at the conclusion of the third part, "The conclusion (i.e., the fourth part) was not printed *because of its holiness*." Cited in Bar-Asher 2012.

30. See, e.g., Idel 1985, 117–20; 1988, 126–40; 1990, 59–73.

31. This is not only true of mystics. See, e.g., Heschel 1996; Schweid 1999, esp. 9–20; Kreisel 2001, 1–26. There is also much written on prophecy in the thought of Abraham Isaac Kook (d. 1936). See Bin-Nun 2007. Prophecy also becomes a central motif in the twentieth-century Hasidic master Kalonymous Kalman Shapira of Piasczno, particularly in his *Mevo Shearim* (Jerusalem, 1962).

32. See, e.g., *Shaarei Kedusha Ha-Shalem* (Jerusalem, 2005), 3:3, 108–10. The connection between prophecy and the advent of the messianic era is also at play here as Vital (like Abulafia) had his own messianic aspiration. See, e.g., Idel 1998, 164–69.

33. Albotini's Kabbalistic work *Sulam ha-Aliyah* (Ladder of Ascent) was written sometime in the early sixteenth century and was not published in full until the twentieth century, although it was well known beforehand. Along with the anonymous *Sha'arei Zedek*, likely written by a student of Abulafia, the *Sulam*

ha-Aliya is one of the best-known Kabbalistic texts that openly utilizes meditative techniques drawn from Abulafia's writings. To the best of my knowledge, the most recent edition is *Sulam ha-Aliyah/Shaarei Zedek* (Jerusalem: Shaarei Ziv Institute, 1989).

34. This is according to the 1988 Ahavat Shalom edition. The Amnon Gross 2005 edition *Shaarei Kedusha Ha-Shalem* places section 3 before section 2. This seems somewhat odd given that section 2, which consists of long quotations of medieval Kabbalists affirming the legitimacy of prophecy and contemplation, would be better placed as a prerequisite for the actual contemplative techniques.

35. Bar-Asher (2012) notes that there are various other small sections in the printed text that may not be a part of either of these two groups. There are essentially three manuscripts that all printed editions utilize and these manuscripts differ quite extensively.

36. See, for example, *Shaarei Kedusha Ha-Shalem* (Jerusalem, 2005), 3:6, 123.

37. For an annotated English translation of Vital's diary published as *Sefer Hizyonot* (Book of Visions), see Faierstein 1999, 41–243.

38. It may be that Vital already was exposed to Abulafia through Cordovero at a young age. See Idel 1988b, 128–31.

39. Idel notes that the Italian Kabbalist Mordecai Dato's *Iggeret Ha-Levanon* mentions Cordovero's use of Abulafian techniques. "Know that the man, Moses Cordovero, took for himself the vocation of letter and vowel combination. He practiced it successfully and successfully trained others in this art." On Abulafia's influence on Cordovero, see Scholem 1961, 378n14; 1974, 181.

40. Vital studied with Elijah da Vidas, author of the pietist classic *Reshit Hokhma* (Beginning of Wisdom) first published in Venice in 1579. The text, a dense collection and analysis of rabbinic and Kabbalistic sources, was so popular that Jacob Poyetto published a condensed version, *Reshit Hokhma Ha-Qazar*, in Venice in 1600. For a partial translation of Poyetto's text, see Fine 1984, 92–156. Moses Cordovero's *Tomer Devorah* (Palm Tree of Deborah) and *Hanhagot* (Rules of Mystical Piety) are more basic approaches toward similar ends. We can assume that Vital was very aware of a body of literature that focused on contemplative behavior. Very little, however, delineated the technical aspect of the contemplative's prophetic aspirations.

41. See, for example, Vital's *Sefer Hizyonot* (Jerusalem, 1866). An abbreviated and corrupt version of this text appeared as *Shivhei Rabbi Hayyim Vital* (Ostrag, 1826). In English see Faierstein 1999, 3–30.

42. Gershom Scholem (1974, 447) notes, for example, that in Vital's commentary to the *Zohar* written before he met Luria, he added occasional remarks in a Lurianic vein after his association with him. However, his pre-Lurianic commentary to the Torah *Etz Ha-Daat Tov* (1864) remains void of Lurianic influence. See also Avivi 1981; Magid 2008, 75–110.

43. See David Ibn Zamra, *Teshuvot Radbaz*, volume 5, number 34. Abulafia is also mentioned numerous times in Ibn Zamra's *Magen David* (1710).

44. On Abulafia in Safed, see Idel 1988, 131–40. In his introduction to Abulafia's *Sefer Ha-Heshek*, Mattisyahu Safrin writes of numerous earlier Kabbalists who cite Abulafia as a justification for printing Abulafia's works. He also mentions Vital's own introduction to the *Shaarei Kedusha* (see *Shaarei Kedusha Ha-Shalem*, 3) where Vital writes of his receiving a tradition directly from Luria. Safrin implies that this refers to Abulafia, but in fact Vital is simply making a point about revealing and concealing secrets in his writings. Abulafia is absent from Luria's writings as far as we know.

45. For a general discussion, see Huss 2008. On the work of Ahavat Shalom publishing and its director Yaakov Moshe Hillel, see Meir 2001, 2007.

46. Hillel, "Introductory Remarks" to *Sefer Kisei Eliyahu*, 38, 39; cited in Meir 2007, 258n613.

47. See Abulafia's *Sitrei Torah* (Jerusalem, 2002) and Idel 1990a, esp. 54–76.

48. Del Medigo's criticism of Kabbalah can be found in his *Behinat Ha-Dat*, originally published in Basil in 1589. A critical edition was done by Jacob J. Ross. See *Behinat Ha-Dat of Elijah Del-Medigo* (Tel

Aviv: Chaim Rosenberg School of Jewish Studies, 1984). Cf. Bland 1992. Modena's attack on Kabbalah, *Ari Nohem*, is analyzed in Dweck 2011. One can also see this phenomenon later in the eighteenth century in Eastern Europe in the work of Ezekiel Landau of Prague. On this see Flatto 2010.

49. By "anarchic traditionalism" I mean the emergence of ultra-traditional communities that do not fit into existing hierarchical communal structures, be they Hasidic courts or existing mystical communities. They are often led by young charismatic figures who do not rise up through the normative ranks of authority and who draw from a plethora of mystical schools and traditions instead of being wed to one particular approach. The eclecticism of such communities makes them popular with more marginal individuals such as *baalei teshuva* (newly religious).

50. One can see this phenomenon in the rise of independent Kabbalists in Jerusalem who are not bound to any one tradition and engage in syncretistic Kabbalism. Two examples are the anonymous work *Yam Shel Hokhma* by Yizhak Meir Morgenstern and the anonymous collection *Bilvavi Mishkan Evaneh* by Itamar Schwartz. On Schwartz, see Wolfson 2011a. On this phenomenon more generally, see Garb 2011. Garb writes, ". . . the mystical-spiritual Haredi world, and specifically the Hasidic community, is undergoing a renaissance or revival, which includes return to early Hasidic forms of spirituality such as non-dynastic leadership. . . . hyper-nomian practices; cultivation of intense ecstatic states and extensive re-interpretation of classical texts" (125).

51. Kaplan's *Meditation and Kabbalah* (1982, 190–98) also includes a translation of the last two gates of part 3 of the *Shaarei Kedusha* (*Shaarey Kedushah*). For some biographical data and discussion on Kaplan, see the three-part posting "Aryeh Kaplan: A Lost Homily from his Iowa Pulpit and Outreach at SUNY-Albany," on Alan Brill's "The Book of Doctrines and Opinions: Notes on Jewish Theology and Spirituality," http://kavvanah.wordpress.com/2012/01/30/aryeh-kaplan-a-lost-homily-from-his-d-c-pulpit-and-outreach-at-suny-albany. Accessed on June 1, 2014. There is also the contemporary Jewish Renewal movement that utilizes certain Kabbalistic techniques wedded to Buddhist practices in order to foster contemplation. Renewal, however, is more committed to Hasidic techniques that are often much less technical. One does not find much Abulafian influence in contemporary Renewal spirituality, although the recent publications of the Abulafian corpus from manuscript may change this.

52. For some studies of Scholem, see Bloom 1975; Biale 1979; Wasserstrom 1999; Jacobson 2003.

53. The relationship between Kabbalah and language was a central issue in Gershom Scholem's early career. See, for example, Scholem 1982. Many others have included their voices in this important issue. See Bloom 1975; Idel 1992; Katz 1992; Abrams 2000; Wolfson 2005, 1–45.

54. See Hayyim Vital's "Introduction" to *Shaar Ha-Hakdamot* (printed as the Introduction to *Etz Hayyim*). *Etz Hayyim* (Jerusalem: Makor Hayyim, n.d.), 4c/d.

55. The Scholem epigraph is cited in Cole 2012, xiv.

56. For Bialik's seminal essay on language, see his "Gilluy vekhissuy balashon" in Bialik 1948, 191–93. In English see Bialik 1973, 2000, 11–26. Cf. Yadin 2001. On Scholem and language, see Cutter 1990; Shahar 2008.

57. See "Confession on the Subject of Our Language" in Derrida 2002, 226; cited in Shahar 2008, 301. More ominously, Shahar notes that for Scholem, "The Zionist attempt to transform Hebrew, the language that carries God's words, into a spoken and useful language, is an enterprise with horrific implications." Further, he notes that for Scholem, "secular language can be understood as equivalent to 'practical magic,' a vulgar misuse and a 'demonic' praxis of the sacred" (311). For another analysis of Scholem's letter, see Derrida 2002, 189–227. An English translation of Scholem's letter can be found on pages 226–27 in Derrida 2002 and Wiskind 1990. Another translation with the German original appears in Cutter 1990, 416–18; Moses 2009, 168–69.

58. In a 1974 essay titled "My Way to Kabbalah," Scholem notes that he initially intended to write a dissertation on the linguistic theory of Kabbalah but realized he was not adequately prepared. See Scholem 1997, 21.

59. David Biale notes the irony in the fact that Scholem wrote his letter on the essence of Hebrew in German. See Biale 1979, 205. See also the communication between Buber and Rosenzweig on translation collected in *Scripture and Translation* (1994).

60. I think the phallocentric allusion of translation as "penetration," while perhaps not conscious on Scholem's part, may speak to a particular inclination of the early scholars of Kabbalah. The feminine in Kabbalah remains a matter of scholarly debate, but early scholars, and perhaps Scholem in particular, very much aligned with the Kabbalists whom they were interpreting (who were exclusively men) and who used highly gendered language to describe the cosmos. For important studies on Kabbalah and gender, see Liebes, 1994, 67–119; Wolfson 1996; Idel 2005.

61. Letter, Gershom Scholem to Franz Rosenzweig, 1926. For a translation of this letter, see Cutter 1990, 417–18.

62. This comes close to Walter Benjamin's comment in "The Task of the Translator." See Benjamin 1968, 76–77.

63. Scholem's 1926 letter to Franz Rosenzweig begins, "This country is a volcano! It harbors the language!"

64. This is not to say that Kavka is disagreeing with Bialik. He is just looking at translation from a different perspective.

Works Cited and Further Reading

Abrams, Daniel. 2000. "Presenting and Representing Gershom Scholem: A Review Essay." *Modern Judaism* 20.1: 226–43.

Avisur, Shmuel. 1962. "Safed Center of the Manufacture of Woven Woolens in the Sixteenth Century" [Hebrew]. *Sefunot* 6: 41–69.

Avivi, Joseph. 1981. "The Lurianic Writings of Rabbi Hayyim Vital" [Hebrew]. *Moriah* 10.7–8: 77–91.

———. 1987. *Binyan Ariel*. Jerusalem: Center for the Study of Sephardic Judaism.

———. 2008. *Kabbalat Ha-Ari*. 3 vols. Jerusalem: Ben Zvi Institute.

Bar-Asher, Avishai. 2011. "Penance and Fasting in the Writings of Rabbi Moses de León and the Zoharic Polemic with Contemporary Christian Monasticism" [Hebrew]. *Kabbalah* 25: 293–319.

———. 2012. "'This Fourth Part Shall Not Be Transcribed or Printed': The Problem of Identifying the Final Part of *Shaarei Kedusha*" [Hebrew]. *Alei Sefer* 23: 37–49.

———. 2014. "Kabbalistic Interpretations of the Secret of the Garment in the Sixteenth Century" [Hebrew]. *Daat* 76: 191–213.

Ben-Menahem, N. 1982. "The Writings of R. Hayyim Vital: A Bibliographical Study" [Hebrew]. *Temirin* 2: 31–319.

Ben-Shlomo, Joseph. 1965. *The Mystical Theology of Moses Cordovero* [Hebrew]. Jerusalem: Bialik Institute.

Benjamin, Walter. 1968. *Illuminations: Essays and Reflections*. New York: Schocken.

Biale, David. 1979. *Gershom Scholem: Kabbalah and Counter History*. Cambridge: Harvard University Press.

Bialik, Hayyim Nahman. 1948. *Kol Kitvei H. N. Bialik*. Tel Aviv: Dvir.

———. 1973. "The Explicit and Allusive in Language." Translated by Avraham Holtz. *Literature East and West* 15.3: 498–508.

———. 2000. *Revealment and Concealment: Five Essays*. Jerusalem: Orbis.

Bin-Nun, Yoel. 2007. "God within the Soul: The Dwelling of the Holy Spirit According to Rabbi Abraham Isaac Kook" [Hebrew]. In *Darkei Shalom: Studies in Jewish Thought in Honor of Shalom Rosenberg*, edited by Benjamin Ish-Shalom, 353–76. Jerusalem: Beit Morasha.

Bland, Kalman. 1992. "Elijah del Medigo's Averroist Response to the Kabbbalas of Fifteenth-Century Jewry and Pico della Mirandola." *Journal of Jewish Thought and Philosophy* 1: 23–53.

Bloom, Harold. 1975. *Kabbalah and Criticism*. New York: Seabury Press.
Blumenthal, David R. 1978. *Understanding Jewish Mysticism: A Reader*. Vol. 1. Jersey City: Ktav.
———. 1982. *Understanding Jewish Mysticism: A Reader*. Vol. 2. Jersey City: Ktav.
Boss, Gerritt. 1994. "Hayyim Vital's 'Practical Kabbalah and Alchemy': A 17th-Century Book of Secrets." *Journal of Jewish Thought and Philosophy* 4: 54–112.
Boyarin, Daniel. 2004. *Border Lines: The Partition of Judeo-Christianity*. Philadelphia: University of Pennsylvania Press.
Brodt, Eliezer. n.d. "R. Chaim Vital and His Unknown Work *Sefer Ha-Pe'ulot*." http://seforim.blogspot.com/2010/07/r-chaim-vital-and-his-unknown-work.html. Accessed on June 1, 2014.
Buber, Martin, and Franz Rosenzweig. 1994. *Scripture and Translation*. Bloomington: Indiana University Press.
Carmilly-Weinberger, Moshe. 2008. "The Element of '*Devekut*' (*unio mystica*) and Prophecy in Philosophy and Kabbalah." *Studia Judaica* 16: 17–21.
Chavel, Charles, ed. 1964. *Kitvei Ramban*. Jerusalem: Mossad Ha-Rav Kook.
Cohen-Alloro, Dorit. 1987. *The Secret of Garment and the Image of the Angel in the Zohar* [Hebrew]. Jerusalem: Magnus Press.
Cole, Peter. 2012. *The Poetry of Kabbalah: Mystical Verse from the Jewish Tradition*. New Haven: Yale University Press.
Cutter, William. 1990. "Ghostly Hebrew, Ghastly Speech: Scholem to Rosenzweig, 1926." *Prooftexts* 10.3: 413–33.
Dan, Joseph, and Ronald Kiener. 1986. *The Early Kabbalah*. Mahwah: Paulist Press.
David, Abraham. 1988. "Demographic Changes in the Safed Jewish Community in the Sixteenth Century." In *Occident and Orient: A Tribute to the Memory of A. Schreiber*, edited by Robert Dan, 83–93. Leiden: Brill.
———. 1991. "Safed as the Center for the Re-Settlement of Anusim" [Hebrew]. *Proceedings for the Second International Conference for Research of the Sephardic and Oriental Heritage 1984*, edited by Haim Beinart, 183–204. Jerusalem: Misgav Yerushalayim.
———. 1992. "The Spanish Exiles in the Holy Land." In *The Sephardic Legacy*, vol. 2, edited by Haim Beinart, 77–108. Jerusalem: Magnus.
———. 1999. *To Come to the Land: Immigration and Settlement in 16th-Century Eretz Israel*. Translated by Dena Ordan. Tuscaloosa: University of Alabama Press.
Davis, Avram, ed. 1997. *Meditation from the Heart of Judaism: Today's Masters Teach about Their Practice, Discipline, and Faith*. Woodstock: Jewish Lights.
Derrida, Jacques. 2002. *Acts of Religion*. Edited by Gil Anidjar. London and New York: Routledge.
Diamond, Eliezer. 2004. *Holy Men and Hunger Artists: Fasting and Asceticism in Rabbinic Culture*. Oxford and New York: Oxford University Press.
Dweck, Yaakob. 2011. *The Scandal of Kabbalah: Leon Modena, Jewish Mysticism, Early Modern Venice*. Princeton: Princeton University Press.
Faierstein, Morris. 1999. *Jewish Mystical Autobiographies: Book of Visions and Book of Secrets*. Mahwah: Paulist Press.
Fenton, Paul. 1994. "The Influence of Sufism on Safed Kabbalah" [Hebrew]. *Mahanayim* 6: 170–79.
———. 1995. "Solitary Meditation in Jewish and Islamic Mysticism in the Light of a Recent Archeological Discovery." *Medieval Encounters* 1–2: 271–96.
———. 2000. "Influences Soufies sur le Development de la Qabbale a Safed: Le Cas de la Visitation des Tombes." In *Experience et Écriture Mystiques dans les Religions du Livre*, edited by Paul Fenton and Roland Goetschel, 163–90. Leiden: Brill.
Fine, Lawrence. 1975. "Techniques of Jewish Mystical Meditation for Achieving Prophecy and the Holy Spirit in the Teachings of Isaac Luria and Hayyim Vital." PhD diss., Brandeis University.

———. 1982. "Recitation of the Mishnah as a Vehicle for Mystical Inspiration: A Contemplative Technique Taught by Hayyim Vital." *Revue des études juives* 141: 188–92.

———. 1984. *Safed Spirituality: Rules of Mystical Piety, the Beginning of Wisdom*. Mahwah: Paulist Press.

———. 1992. "Purifying the Body in the Name of the Soul: The Problem of the Body in Sixteenth-Century Kabbalah." In *People of the Body: Jews and Judaism from an Embodied Perspective*, edited by Howard Elberg-Schwartz, 117–42. Albany: State University of New York Press.

———. 2003. *Physician of the Soul, Healer of the Cosmos: Isaac Luria and His Kabbalistic Fellowship*. Stanford: Stanford University Press.

Fishbane, Eitan. 1994. *The Kiss of God: Spiritual and Mystical Death in Judaism*. Seattle: University of Washington Press.

———. 1995. "The Imagination of Death in Jewish Spirituality." In *Death, Ecstasy and Other Worldly Journeys*, edited by John Collins and Michael Fishbane, 181–206. Albany: State University of New York Press.

———. 2009. *As Light before Dawn: The Inner World of a Medieval Kabbalist*. Stanford: Stanford University Press.

Flatto, Sharon. 2010. *The Kabbalistic Culture of Eighteenth-Century Prague: Ezekiel Landua (the "Noda Biyehuda") and His Contemporaries*. Oxford: The Littman Library of Jewish Civilization.

Fraade, Steven. 2007. "Rabbinic Midrash and Ancient *Jewish* Biblical Interpretation." In *The Cambridge Companion to Talmud and Rabbinic Literature*, edited by Charlotte Fonrobert and Martin Jaffee, 99–120. Cambridge: Cambridge University Press.

Garb, Jonathan. 2011. "Toward the Study of the Spiritual-Mystical Renaissance in the Contemporary Ashkenazi Haredi World in Israel." In *Kabbalah and Contemporary Spiritual Revival*, edited by Boaz Huss, 117–40. Beer Sheva: Ben Gurion University Press.

———. 2012. "Contemporary Kabbalah and Classical Kabbalah: Breaks and Continuities." In *After Spirituality: Studies in Mystical Tradition*, edited by Philip Wexler and Jonathan Garb, 19–46. New York: Peter Lang.

Giller, Pinhas. 2001. *Reading the Zohar*. Oxford and New York: Oxford University Press.

———. 2008. *Shalom Shar'abi and the Kabbalists of Beit El*. Oxford and New York: Oxford University Press.

———. 2011. *Kabbalah: A Guide for the Perplexed*. London and New York: Continuum.

Green, Arthur. 1997. *Keter*. Princeton: Princeton University Press.

———. 2004. *A Guide to the Zohar*. Stanford: Stanford University Press.

Gries, Zeev. 2008. "The Printing of Kabbalistic Literature in the Twentieth Century." *Kabbalah* 18: 113–32.

Gunkel, Hermann. 1979. *The Influence of the Holy Spirit: The Popular View of the Apostolic Age and the Teaching of the Apostle Paul*. Translated by R. A. Harrisville and P. A. Quanbeck II. Minneapolis: Fortress Press.

Hadani, Yaron Ever. 2006. *Shaarei Kedusha: Gates of Holiness*. Vancouver: Providence University.

Hadani, Yaron Ever, and Elyakim Getz. 2006. *Ktavim Chadashim: New Writings*. Vancouver: Providence University.

Hallamish, Moshe. 1988. "Kabbalah in the Legal Decisions of R. Joseph Karo" [Hebrew]. *Daat* 21: 88–102.

———. 1992. "Luria's Status as a Halakhic Authority" [Hebrew]. *Jerusalem Studies in Jewish Thought* 10: 259–85.

———. 1999. *An Introduction to Kabbalah*. Albany: State University of New York Press.

———. 2000. *Ha-Kabbalah be-Tifillah be-Halakha u-be-Minhag*. Ramat Gan: Bar Ilan University Press

Heinemann, Isaac. 1949. *Ta'amei Ha-Mitzvot*. 2 vols. Jerusalem: Horev.

Heschel, Abraham Joshua. 1996. *Maimonides and Other Medieval Authorities*. Edited by Morris Faierstein. Hoboken: Ktav.

Huss, Boaz. 2008. "The Formation of Jewish Mysticism and Its Impact on the Reception of Rabbi Abraham Abulafia in Contemporary Kabbalah." In *Religion and Its Others*, edited by Heicke Bock et al., 142–62. Frankfurt and New York: Campus Verlag.

Idel, Moshe. 1983. "'We Have No Kabbalistic Tradition on This.'" In *Rabbi Moses Nahmanides: Explorations in His Religious and Literary Virtuosity*, edited by Isadore Twersky, 51–74. Cambridge: Harvard University Press.

———. 1985. "Rabbi Moshe Cordovero and R. Abraham Abulafia." *Daat* 15: 117–20.

———. 1986. "The Land of Israel in Medieval Kabbalah." In *The Land of Israel: Jewish Perspectives*, edited by Lawrence Hoffman, 170–87. South Bend: University of Notre Dame Press.

———. 1988a. *The Mystical Experience in Abraham Abulafia*. Albany: State University of New York Press.

———. 1988b. *Studies in Ecstatic Kabbalah*. Albany: State University of New York Press.

———. 1989. *Language, Torah, and Hermeneutics in Abraham Abulafia*. Albany: State University of New York Press.

———. 1990a. "Maimonides and Kabbalah." In *Studies in Maimonides*, edited by Isadore Twersky, 31–82. Cambridge: Harvard University Press.

———. 1990b. *Kabbalah: New Perspectives*. New Haven: Yale University Press.

———. 1992. "Reification of Language in Jewish Mysticism." In *Mysticism and Language*, edited by Steven T. Katz, 42–79. Oxford and New York: Oxford University Press.

———. 1993. "One from a Town, Two from a Clan: The Diffusion of Lurianic Kabbalah and Sabbateanism." *Jewish History* 7.2: 79–104.

———. 1994. "Kavvanah and Colors: A Neglected Kabbalistic Responsum" [Hebrew]. In *Studies in Jewish Philosophy Presented to Sara O. Heller Wilensky*, edited by Moshe Idel et al., 1–14. Jerusalem: Magnus Press.

———. 1995. *Hasidism: Between Ecstasy and Magic*. Albany: State University of New York Press.

———. 1998. *Messianic Mystics*. New Haven: Yale University Press.

———. 2004. "*Nishmat Eloha*: The Divinity of the Soul in Nahmanides and His School" [Hebrew]. In *Midrash Ha-Hayyim* [Hebrew], edited by A. Arzi et al., 338–81. Tel Aviv: Yediot Ahronot.

———. 2005. *Kabbalah and Eros*. New Haven: Yale University Press.

———. 2007. *Ben: Sonship in Jewish Mysticism*. London and New York: Continuum.

———. 2009. "Definitions of Prophecy: Maimonides, Abulafia, and Beyond" [Hebrew]. In *Maimonides and Mysticism Presented to Moshe Hallamish*, edited by Avraham Elkayam and Dov Schwartz, 5–18. Ramat Gan: Bar Ilan University Press.

———. 2011a. *Kabbalah in Italy, 1220–1510*. New Haven: Yale University Press.

———. 2011b. "R. Israel Ba'al Shem Tov 'In the State of Walachia.'" In *Holy Dissent*, edited by Glenn Dynner, 79–87. Detroit: Wayne State University Press.

Jacobs, Louis. 1989. "The Uplifting of Sparks in Later Jewish Mysticism." In *Jewish Spirituality II*, edited by Arthur Green, 64–98. New York: Crossroads.

Jacobson, Eric. 2003. *Metaphysics of the Profane: The Political Theology of Walter Benjamin and Gershom Scholem*. New York: Columbia University Press.

Kallus, Menachem. 2002. "The Theurgy of Prayer in the Lurianic Kabbalah." PhD diss., Hebrew University of Jerusalem.

Kaplan, Aryeh. 1978. *Meditation and the Bible*. York Beach: Samuel Weiser.

———. 1982. *Meditation and Kabbalah*. York Beach: Samuel Weiser.

———. 1995. *Jewish Meditation: A Practical Guide*. New York: Schocken Books.

———. 1997. *Sefer Yezirah: The Book of Creation*. York Beach: Samuel Weiser.

Katz, Jacob. 1986. "The Controversy about Ordination between Rabbi Jacob Berab and Rabbi Levi ibn Habib" [Hebrew]. In *Halakha ve Kabbalah*, edited by Jacob Katz, 213–36. Jerusalem: Magnus Press.

———. 1989. "Halakha and Kabbalah as Competing Disciplines of Study." In *Jewish Spirituality II*, edited by Arthur Green, 34–63. New York: Crossroads.

Katz, Steven. 1983. "The 'Conservative' Character of Mystical Experience." In *Mysticism and Religious Traditions*, edited by Steven T. Katz, 3–60. Oxford and New York: Oxford University Press.

———. 1992. "Mystical Speech and Mystical Meaning." In *Mysticism and Language*, edited by Steven T. Katz, 3–41. Oxford and New York: Oxford University Press.

Kavka, Martin. 2012. "Translation." In *The Cambridge Companion to Religious Studies*, edited by Robert Orsi, 186–208. Cambridge and New York: Cambridge University Press.

Kreisel, Howard. 2001. *Prophecy: The History of an Idea in Medieval Jewish Philosophy*. Dordrecht: Kluwer Academic.

Liebes, Yehuda. 1994. "Zohar and Eros" [Hebrew]. *Alpayim* 9: 67–119.

Lorberbaum, Yair. 2004. *Image of God: Halakha and Aggada* [Hebrew]. Tel Aviv: Schocken Books.

Magid, Shaul. 1996a. "Conjugal Union, Mourning, and Talmud Torah in R. Isaac Luria's *Tikkun Hazot*." *Daat* 36: 52–72.

———. 1996b. "From Theosophy to Midrash: The Lurianic Reading of the Garden of Eden." *AJS Review* (Spring/Summer): 37–75.

———. 2002. "Origin and Overcoming the Beginning: *Zimzum* as a Trope of Reading in Post-Lurianic Kabbalah." In *Beginning/Again: Toward a Hermeneutic of Jewish Texts*, edited by Aryeh Cohen and Shaul Magid, 163–215. New York: Seven Bridges Press.

———. 2008. *From Metaphysics to Midrash: Myth, History, and the Interpretation of Scripture in Lurianic Kabbala*. Bloomington: Indiana University Press.

———. 2012. "Early Hasidism and the Metaphysics of *Malkhut*." In Yaakov (Lifhitz) Koppel's *Shaarei Gan Eden, Kabbalah* (Spring): 245–68.

Margolit, Mordecai, ed. 1993. *Leviticus Raba*. 2 vols. New York: Jewish Theological Seminary of America.

Matt, Daniel. 1986. "The Mystic and the *Mitzvot*." In *Jewish Spirituality I*, edited by Arthur Green, 367–404. New York: Crossroad.

Meir, Jonathan. 2007. "The Revealed and the Revealed within the Concealed: On the Opposition of the Followers of Rabbi Yehudah Ashlag and the Dissemination of Esoteric Literature" [Hebrew]. *Kabbalah* 16: 241–58.

———. 2011. "The Boundaries of Kabbalah: R. Yaakov Moshe Hillel and the Kabbalah of Jerusalem." In *Kabbalah and Contemporary Spiritual Revival*, edited by Boaz Huss, 163–80. Be'er Sheva: Ben Gurion University Press.

Menzi, Donald, and Zwe Padeh. 1999. *The Tree of Life—The Palace of Adam Kadmon: Chayyim Vital's Introduction to the Kabbalah of Isaac Luria*. Northvale and Jerusalem: Jason Aronson.

Meroz. 1992. "R. Israel Sarug, Student of the Ari: Reconsidered Anew" [Hebrew]. *Daat* 28: 41–56.

———. 1993. "Faithful Transmission verses Innovation: Luria and His Disciples." In *Gershom Scholem's "Major Trends in Jewish Mysticism" Fifty Years After*, edited by Peter Schafer and Joseph Dan, 257–76. Tubingen: Mohr.

Moses, Stephan. 2009. *The Angel of History: Rosenzweig, Benjamin, Scholem*. Stanford: Stanford University Press.

Nadav, Yael. 1959. "The Eschatology of R. Moshe de Leon in the Book *Mishkan Ha-Edut*" [Hebrew]. *Ozar Yehudi Sefarad* 2: 72–73.

Pachter, Mordecai. 1984. "The Concept of '*Devekut*' in the Homiletical Ethical Writings of 16th-Century Safed." *Studies in Medieval History and Literature* 2: 171–230.

Ross, Jacob J. 1984. *Behinat Ha-Dat of Elijah Del-Medigo*. Tel Aviv: Chaim Rosenberg School of Jewish Studies.

Sack, Bracha. 1995. *The Kabbalah of Rabbi Moshe Cordovero* [Hebrew]. Jerusalem: Bialik Institute.

Scholem, Gershom. 1949–1950. "*Devekut* or Communion with God." *Review of Religion* 14: 115–39.

———. 1961. *Major Trends in Jewish Mysticism*. New York: Schocken Books.

———. 1962. *The Origins of the Kabbalah*. Translated by Allan Arkush. Princeton: Princeton University Press.

———. 1965. *On the Kabbalah and Its Symbolism*. Translated by Ralph Manheim. New York: Schocken Books.

———. 1974. *Kabbalah*. New York: Dorset Press.
———. 1981. "The Concept of *Kavvanah* in Early Kabbalah." In *Studies in Jewish Thought: An Anthology of German Jewish Scholarship*, edited by A. Jospe, 165–80. Detroit: Wayne State University Press.
———. 1982. "The Name of God and Linguistic Theory of the Kabbalah." *Diogenes* 79: 59–80.
———. 1997. *On the Possibility of Jewish Mysticism in Our Time and Other Essays*. Edited by Avraham Shapiro. Philadelphia: Jewish Publication Society.
Schweid, Eliezer. 1999. *Prophets: For Their People and Humanity* [Hebrew]. Jerusalem: Magnus.
Sells, Michael. 1994. *Mystical Languages of Unsaying*. Chicago: University of Chicago Press.
Sendor, Meir. 1994. "The Emergence of Provencal Kabbalah: Rabbi Isaac the Blind's Commentary on *Sefer Yezeriah*." 2 vols. PhD diss., Harvard University.
Shahar, Galili. 2008. "The Sacred and the Unfamiliar: Gershom Scholem and the Anxieties of the New Hebrew." *The Germanic Review* 83.4: 299–320.
Soloveitchik, Haym. 2002. "Piety, Pietism, and German Pietism: *Sefer Hasidim* and the Influence of Hasidei Ashkenaz." *Jewish Quarterly Review* 92.3–4: 455–93.
Travis, Yakov. 2002. "Rabbi Ezra of Gerona: On the Kabbalistic Meaning of the Mitzvot." PhD diss., Brandeis University.
Twersky, Isadore. 1979. *Rabad of Posquieres: A Twelfth-Century Talmudist*. Philadelphia: Jewish Publication Society.
Verman, Mark. 1996. *The History and Varieties of Jewish Meditation*. Lanham: Jason Aronson.
Vital, Hayyim. n.d. *Etz Hayyim*. Jerusalem: Makor Hayyim.
———. 1988. *Shaar Gilgulim*. Jerusalem: Sidrat Kitvei Rabben ha-ARI z"l.
———. 2005. *Shaarei Kedusha Ha-Shalem*. Jerusalem: Amnon Gross.
Wasserstrom, Steven. 1999. *Religion after Religion: Gershom Scholem, Mircea Eliade, and Henry Corbin at Eranos*. Princeton: Princeton University Press.
Weinstein, Avi. 1995. *Gates of Light: Sha'are Orah*. Lanham: AltaMira.
Werblowsky, R. Z. 1980. *Joseph Karo: Lawyer and Mystic*. Philadelphia: Jewish Publication Society.
Wiskind, Ora. 1990. "Our Language: A Confession." *History and Memory* 2.2: 97–99.
Wolfson, Elliot. 1980. "The Secret of the Garment in Nahmanides." *Daat* 24: 25–49.
———. 1988. *The Book of the Pomegranate: Moses de Leon's Sefer Ha-Rimon*. Atlanta: Scholars Press.
———. 1989. "'By Way of Truth': Aspects of Nahmanides' Kabbalistic Hermeneutics." *AJS Review* 14: 103–78.
———. 1995. "Weeping, Death, and Spiritual Ascent in Sixteenth-Century Jewish Mysticism." In *Death, Ecstasy, and Other Worldly Journeys*, edited by John Collins and Michael Fishbane, 207–44. Albany: State University of New York Press.
———. 1996. *Through a Speculum That Shines*. Princeton: Princeton University Press.
———. 2000a. *Abraham Abulafia–Kabbalist and Prophet: Hermeneutics, Theosophy, and Theurgy*. Los Angeles: Cherub Press.
———. 2000b. "Judaism and Incarnation: The Imaginal Body of God." In *Christianity in Jewish Terms*, edited by Frymer-Kensky et al., 239–53. Boulder: Westview Press.
———. 2005 *Language, Eros, Being: Kabbalistic Hermeneutics and Poetic Imagination*. New York: Fordham University Press.
———. 2011a. "Building a Sanctuary of the Heart: The Kabbalistic-Pietistic Teachings of Itamar Schwartz." In *Kabbalah and Contemporary Spiritual Revival*, edited by Boaz Huss, 141–62. Be'er Sheva: Ben Gurion University Press.
———. 2011b. "Immanuel Frommann's Commentary to Luke." In *Holy Dissent*, edited by Glenn Dynner, 171–222. Detroit: Wayne State University Press.
———. 2011c. *A Dream Interpreted within a Dream*. New York: Zone Books.

———. 2012. "Textual Flesh, Incarnation, and the Imaginal Body: Abraham Abulafia's Polemic with Christianity." In *Studies in Medieval Jewish Intellectual and Social History*, edited by David Engel et al., 189–226. Leiden: Brill.

Yadin, Azzan. 2001. "A Web of Chaos: Bialik and Nietzsche on Language, Truth, and the Death of God." *Prooftexts* 21.2: 179–203.

Shaarei Kedusha (Gates of Holiness)*

Hayyim Vital (1542–1620)

Selected, Translated, and Annotated by Shaul Magid

The First Gate

(The necessary conditions required for an individual to be prepared to apprehend the divine)

א¹—Rabbi Pinhas ben Yair taught, "Enthusiasm leads to cleanliness, cleanliness leads to purity, purity leads to restraint, restraint leads to holiness, holiness leads to humility, humility leads to fear of sin, fear of sin leads to acquiring the Holy Spirit, the Holy Spirit leads to resurrection of the dead, resurrection comes through Elijah the Prophet." There are numerous versions of this teaching that I did not include (Mishna Sota 9:15).[2]

ב—We read in a letter by Rabbi Moses ben Nahman (Nahmanides)[3] that he sent his son from Acco to Barcelona, *Listen my son, to the teachings of your father and do not leave the Torah of your mother* (Proverbs 1:8), behave in a way that all your works are pleasant to everyone at all times. This is the way to avoid anger, which is a terrible trait that brings one to sin, as the sages teach that one who is angry is plagued by all manner of Gehenna, as it says, "All who get angry are plagued with all kinds of hell, as it further says, *Remove anger from your heart and let evil pass over your flesh* (Ecclesiastes 11:10)" (b.T. Nedarim 22a).[4] "There is no evil without Gehenna, as it says, *God made everything for a purpose, even the wicked for an evil day* (Proverbs 16:4)." Thus when one is liberated from anger, humility will enter the heart, which is the best of the best, as it says, *The foundation of humility is the fear of God* (Proverbs 22:4). And from humility one will come to fear of God so that the heart will always ask "from where did you come?" and "where are you headed?" And you will always live as if you are like a worm in your life, and even your death. And one will always know before whom he will give an accounting, before the King of

---

*The present translation is a partial rendering of part 4 of the *Shaarei Kedusha*. It does not include the final six pages of the text, which are devoted to letter diagrams and charts of letter combinations (*zeruf otiot*). Translating this material would be of little help. Instead, I have reproduced an example of the charts as they appear in the original text in order to give the reader a visual of the meditative template. I have utilized the Hebrew text contained in Vital 2005, with the source manuscript being unclear. Kaplan (1982, 190–98) translates the last two gates of part 3. A complete, but fairly literal and nonacademic translation with no annotations has been published by Hadani (2006), which consists of the first three parts, and by Handai and Getz (2006), which consists of the fourth part.

1. In classical Hebrew, like Greek, numbers are represented by letters. Like many other Kabbalistic texts, the *Shaarei Kedusha* divides its subsections using Hebrew letters as numbers. I have thus followed this in the translation.

2. See, for example, in b.T. Sota, 49b, Avodah Zara, 20b, Jerusalem Talmud, Shabbat, 1:3.

3. *Igrot Ha-Ramban 'im Perush Igrot Petuha* (Jerusalem, 2009) letter no. 5, 18–20.

4. Cf. b.T. Berakhot, "Anger is the root of all evil (*kelippot*)." Cf. b.T. Pesahim, 113b.

Glory,[5] as it says, *Even the heavens in their innermost reaches cannot contain You* (1 Kings 8:27).[6] Even in the heart of the individual, as it says, *For I fill both heaven and earth declares the Lord* (Jeremiah 23:24). When one thinks about all of this, one will have fear of the creator and distance oneself from sin. Embodying these traits will bring happiness. When one acts with humility, one will be embarrassed by and fearful of sin. At that time, the Holy Spirit and the shining of God's countenance will descend upon him, and this is the life of the World to Come.[7]

Now my child you should know and understand that arrogance destroys worlds because grandeur (*pe'er*) is the garment of the heavenly King, as it says, *The Lord is King who is robed in grandeur* (Psalm 93:1). How does a person become arrogant? If through wealth, *God is the one who makes one wealthy* (1 Samuel 2:7). If through honor, that too is God's as it says, *Wealth and honor are before You* (1 Chronicles 29:12). How does one give homage to the grandeur of God? If through wisdom, *He deprives trusted me of speech and takes reason away from the elders* (Job 12:20). We thus see that everything is equal before God. Through God's will the arrogant will fall and the downtrodden will be raised. Hence you should submit yourself to the Blessed One.

I will now explain to you the way to consistently act with humility: All your words should be pleasant, your head should be bowed, and your eyes gazing only downward. Your heart should be directed heavenward, and do not stare at a person when speaking to him. Every individual should be greater than you in your eyes; give honor to the rich and poor alike, if he should be poor and you rich, or if you are wiser, it should appear to you that you owe him and that he deserves more than you. For example, if he sins, it should be considered accidental. If you sin, it should be considered intentional.

One should concentrate all of one's actions, words, and thoughts at all times in one's heart as if one is standing before God (*hamakom*)[8] and God's *shekinah*[9] is upon him, because God's glory encompasses the world. One's words should be filled with awe and trepidation like a servant before his master. One should be humbled (lit., embarrassed; *mitbayesh*) in the presence of all people. If called, do not answer with a loud voice, rather answer pleasantly, as if he is standing before his master, the Holy Blessed One.

---

5. See Mishna Avot 2:14.

6. This is an adaptation of Mishna Avot 3:1, "Akaviah ben Mehalelel taught: Recalling three things will prevent you from sin; Know from where you came, know where you are going, and know before whom you stand in judgment. Where did you come from? From a putrid drop. Where are you going? To the worms. Before whom do you stand in judgment? Before the Holy One, Blessed be He."

7. See *Shaarei Kedusha* 3:2, 101 and 107; *Shaarei Kedusha* 3:3, 108–10. There Vital makes a case that the descent of the Holy Spirit or what he calls there "prophecy" is a natural and even inevitable outcome of acting in this matter. The reasons, he argues, is that the human/Adam is constructed of permutations of divine letters that are always seeking to return to their source in the Godhead. See *Shaarei Kedusha* 3:5, 117. But see *Shaarei Kedusha Ha-Shalem*, 2:2, 39, citing Midrash Eliyahu Raba where man, woman, gentile, slave, and maidservant are all included. I am grateful to Elliot Wolfson (New York University) for pointing this out. What prevents that (re)union of divinity and divinity within the human are the barriers erected through sin. When those are lifted, the (re)union happens naturally.

8. On "place" (*hamakom*) as a euphemism for God, see Genesis Raba 69:9 and the popularization of that in the Passover Haggadah, "Blessed be the Place, Blessed be He."

9. The *shekinah* is a term used to denote divine presence in the world. It is sometimes used to define the lowest realm of the sephirotic worlds, likened to the lowest *sephirah* of *malkhut* (kingship), and sometimes more generally as "divine presence."

Be strident to constantly be engaged in (lit., read) Torah, which will enable one to fulfill it. When one completes one's study, one should consider how what one has learned can be applied. One should be careful to scrutinize one's actions both morning and night. In that way all one's days will contain repentance.¹⁰ One should remove all thoughts from the heart during prayer and direct the heart solely to God. One should think about what one wants to say before saying it. If one does this consistently with everything in one's life, one will not sin. In that way, all one's behavior will be with integrity (*kol ma'asekha yesharim*), one's prayers will be granted and fulfilled, and they will be received before God, as it says, *You will direct your heart and you will incline your ear* (Psalm 10:17). Read this missive (*ha-igerret*) once a week, not less than that, in order to always go in God's way in order to succeed in everything you do and you will merit the World to Come, the realm of the righteous. The day that you read it you will be answered from heaven as your heart desire.¹¹

ג—Isaac of Acre (late 13th–14th c.) wrote according to Moshe, a student of Joseph Gikatilla (1248–1305), what he heard directly from Gikatilla.¹² One who is committed to changing one's ways, striving after humility in a sincere manner, one who is truly humble and one who hears criticism and does not respond, that person will immediately merit the *shekinah*. He will not have to learn from others because in that state the spirit of God will teach him.

ד—I found written in Tractate Kallah, "Said Abba Elijah, 'The Torah will only be abandoned by one who is not meticulous about his devotion (*kapdan*). I will also not reveal any Torah to someone who is not meticulous about his devotion. Happy is one who encounters such a person and has the opportunity to sit with them. He will surely merit the World to Come.'"¹³

ה—It is written in the book *Brit Menuha* (Covenant of Comfort) (second half of the fourteenth century) according to the first path:¹⁴ Wisdom appears in three places. The first is northward in the place of judgment where arrogance is subsumed and it stands trembling before God. This place is called the Place of Fear and also called burning (*tivarah*). It is the name אגלא (*agilah*) that is included in Torah (*torah*); it acts without the need of purification (*taharah*); it extends the thread of fear (*yirah*).¹⁵ The second place where wisdom shows its face is in humility. Its name is called serenity (*menuhah*). It is the name ליהדריא (*yehadriel*) of the God of Israel. The third place

---

10. See the exact locution in another Safadean Kabbalist of this period and older contemporary of Vital, Elijah da Vidas in his *Reshit Hokhma* (Jerusalem, 1972), "Gate of Humility," chapter 6, 235c.

11. This ends the citation from Nahmanides's letter to his son.

12. According to Abraham Azulai, he was also a student of Nahmanides. On Isaac of Acre, see Fishbane 2009. For an English translation of Gikatilla's famous work *Shaare 'Orah*, see Weinstein 1995. In Hebrew see *Shaare 'Orah*, two volumes, J. Ben-Shlomo ed. (Jerusalem: Bialik Institute, 1996).

13. Tractate Kallah cited here is actually Kallah Rabbati, one of the minor Talmudic tractates that can be found in standard editions of the Babylonian Talmud, volume 16 containing Tractate Avodah Zara. This citation can be found at the end of chapter 5, 53d in standard editions.

14. *Brit Menuha* is likely from Abraham Isaac of Granada attributed to Hamai Gaon. It was first published in 1648. *Brit Menuha* deals extensively with meditations according to letter combinations and the vocalizations (*nekudot*) of the Hebrew language. See, for example, Scholem 1974, 65, 105. The previous citation can be found in *Brit Menuha* (Jerusalem: Torat Ha-Nezah, 1979), 7b and top of 7c.

15. Note that all four words (*agilah, torah, taharah*, and *yirah*) rhyme.

where wisdom shows its face is in joy. Its divine name is מפרישמה (*mafrishma*). The three levels are thus fear, humility, and joy. Anyone who wants to learn wisdom must be connected to these levels. They should fear sin, be humble, and be satisfied with their lot.[16] When one completes these three stages, one will achieve [esoteric] wisdom.

ו—Says the contemplative (*hamitboded*): If one wants to be successful at contemplation in order to achieve well-being (*shalom*), one must fulfill these three things and distance oneself from their opposite. Only then will one achieve well-being. This is all the more so regarding reward after death. They are the following: be satisfied with one's portion, love solitary meditation, and avoid positions of authority and honor.[17]

ז—It is written in the *Sefer Hasidim* (Book of the Pious) (no. 363): Be careful to speak the complete truth at all times and your dreams will be fulfilled like prophecy.[18]

ח—There is the story of a person who fasted often, acted righteously, and supported orphans but sought after positions of authority. He came to a group of contemplatives who had achieved prophecy. He approached the leader of the group and asked, "Master, can you kindly explain to me why after all my righteous acts I have not merited prophecy to tell the future like yourself?" The contemplative replied, "Take a pouch of nuts and figs and tie it around your neck. Go out to the public square of a city in front of all the dignitaries, gather together a group of children, and ask them, 'Do you want me to give you nuts and figs? If so, come and strike me with your hand on my neck and then on my cheek.' Do this repeatedly and then return to me and I will guide you on the path of apprehending the truth." The inquirer replied, "Master, how can a person as important as me do such a thing?!" He replied, "You think that is such a big deal? That is a small thing compared to what you will have to do to see the light of truth." The inquirer rose and left in despair.

ט—Elijah da Vidas (1518–1592), the author of the *Reshit Hokhma* (Beginning of Wisdom) (1558), told me in the name of his teacher Moses Cordovero (1522–1570), author of the *Pardes Rimonim* (Orchard of Pomegranates) (1592):[19] One should distance oneself from all manner of sin that causes the light of the *shekinah* to depart from the soul of the sinner. If a person acts in an evil manner, his soul will be severed from the light of the *shekinah* and it will remain in darkness. If he is righteous, one will find that the light of the *shekinah* accompanies him.

---

16. See Mishna Avot 2:8 and 4:1.

17. See Mishna Avot 6:6.

18. The *Sefer Hasidism* was from the circle of Judah the Pious known as the Hasidei Ashkenaz in the German Rhineland (early thirteenth century). Two editions exist from two different manuscripts: *Sefer Hasidim*, edited by Reuven Margolit (Jerusalem: Mosad Ha-Rav Kook, 1957), and *Sefer Hasidism*, edited by Judah Ha-Kohen Wistinetsky from the Parma manuscript (Jerusalem: Vageshel, 1998). Neither of these editions contain Vital's citation in no. 363. On the *Sefer Hasidim*, see Soloveitchik 2002. For an analysis of the interpretation of dreams in the *Sefer Hasidism*, see Wolfson 2011c, 155–56.

19. Elijah da Vidas and Moses Cordovero were both active in Safed at the same time in the sixteenth century. Vital studied with Cordovero, the leading Kabbalist in Safed before the arrival of Isaac Luria in 1570. Da Vidas's *Reshit Hokhma*, one of the most popular pietist (*mussar*) texts to come from that period of Safed, was first published in Cracow in 1593. Cordovero's *Pardes Rimonim* was first published in 1592.

ר—Isaac of Acre wrote: One of the conditions of separation (*perishut*) and contemplation (*hitbodedut*)[20] is distancing oneself from all manner of fault, malice, or sin, all of which cause the light of the *shekinah* to depart from the soul of the sinner. If individuals act in an evil manner, a distance is created between their souls and the *shekinah*, and they will remain in darkness. If they act in a goodly manner, the light of the *shekinah* will be found in their midst.[21]

The Second Gate

(Explaining the process of apprehending God)

This is the second category in the three paths to achieve divine apprehension. I will not explain any specific action in terms of the recitation of divine names but only in regard to thought or prayer.

You already know that all manner of apprehending the divine requires solitude so that the mind will not be distracted. The individual must be alone with his thoughts until the last moment and peel away his body from his mind/soul until he no longer feels that he is a material being but a purely spiritual entity. The more one is able to do this, the stronger one's apprehension will become. If one is disturbed by a noise or a movement, one's thought process will cease. Or, if one has thoughts of material existence, one's thought process will be disrupted and one's communion with the upper spheres will be severed, at which point one will apprehend nothing. This is because the holy spheres above do not rest on one who is attached to physicality, even tangentially.[22] This is why prophecy and the Holy Spirit are called slumber (*tardama*), dream (*halom*), or vision (*hazon*). In the end even though a person may be fit to attain the Holy Spirit, if he does not accustom himself to sever his body from his soul, he will not achieve it. This is the secret as to why the disciples of the prophets used musical instruments (drums and fifes) (1 Samuel 10:5).[23] They were able to enter into a sustained state of contemplation and separation of body and soul by means of the sweetness of the music. At that moment, the musician ceased playing and the prophets continued in their state of communion and prophesied. This is the first condition.

The second condition is that one must dispose of anything that would cause an interruption in contemplation. The first condition only speaks about physical things or natural things that disrupt contemplation. Now we are speaking about spiritual things that disrupt contemplation. These include all manner of defiled things from the evil inclination (*yezer hara*) that attach themselves to a person and are strengthened through sinful acts.

---

20. *Hitbodedut*, or concentration, is a central tenet of Vital's treatise and a common trope for medieval Kabbalistic exercises of achieving the Holy Spirit and prophecy. See, for example, Idel's "*Hitbodedut* as Concentration in Ecstatic Kabbalah" in his *Studies in Ecstatic Kabbalah* (1988b), 103–69.

21. It is unclear if this reference is from Isaac's more popular *Me'irat Eynayim* or his *Ozar Hayyim*. In any case, the linkage of separation (*perishut*) and contemplation (*hitbodedut*) is a signature notion in Isaac's work. See, for example, Fishbane 2009, 248–82. Isaac's further connection of these two to prophecy had obvious influence on Vital in this treatise.

22. *Ke-khut ha-sa'arah*. Literally, by a thread.

23. Cf. 2 Kings 3:15

Therefore one who comes to contemplate God must first repent from all manner of sin and be scrupulous to avoid sin in the future.[24] Afterward one must accustom oneself to remove the evil character traits that are embedded in oneself, such as anger, depression, rigidity, frivolity, and the like. After one heals the sick soul from sin, one should remove the power of defilement from interrupting communion with the upper spheres. By these means one will accustom oneself to nullify physicality as we mentioned in the first condition, and after all this one will succeed in cultivating communion with the upper spheres, as I will explain according to what I have found in holy books and in the words of the contemplatives themselves. Regarding this second condition that is focused on removing the forces of defilement, this is accomplished through repentance and the removal of negative character traits.[25] We have already explained this in the first category according to what I have found in the holy books. Since I have already taught you these two conditions, I will mention certain behaviors that cultivate communion with the upper spheres that are applicable only after one has accomplished the first two conditions.

א—The contemplative should find solitude, wrap himself in a prayer shawl, and sit with his eyes closed.[26] He should separate himself from his material existence as if his soul has left his body and ascended to heaven. After achieving this separation he should recite any Mishna[27] he chooses, repeating it again and again as quickly as he can, as long as the recitation is clearly articulated and he does not skip any words.[28] During this recitation he should concentrate on binding himself with the rabbinic sage (Tanna) whose teaching is recorded in that Mishna. Through this exercise he should imagine (*titkhaven*) that his mouth is a vessel out of which the letters of that Mishna emerge. And [he should further imagine that] the sound that comes forth from that vessel, which is his mouth, are the sparks of his inner soul that pour forth and recite that Mishna.[29] This will make a chariot that will house the soul of the sage whose teaching is recorded in that Mishna. And his soul will envelop the soul of the one performing the recitation. If he is successful in his recitation of the language of the Mishna, and if he is adequately prepared, it is possible that his mouth will find a place in the soul of that [rabbinic] sage and will be enveloped there in his act of recitation. At that point, as he recites the Mishna, he [the rabbinic sage] will speak through his mouth and grant him peace. At that time, all of the thoughts and queries that he might have will be answered by that sage. He will speak through his mouth, and his ears will

---

24. See Fine 1992. Cf. *Shaarei Kedusha* 3:3, 110.

25. See, for example, in Elijah da Vidas, *Reshit Hokhma*, "Gate of Repentance," 100–27. Cf. Cordovero, *Tomer Devorah* (London, 2003). This new edition reprints the first Venice edition. Vital seemed to have modeled the *Shaarei Kedusha* after Cordovero's popular works, the *Tomer Devorah* and *'Or Ne'erav*, although he rarely cites them in his fourth part, relying on much earlier Kabbalistic literature. Much of parts 1, 2, and 3 of *Shaarei Kedusha* resemble both *Tomer Devorah* and *'Or Neerav* in tone, while the fourth part takes on a more practical contemplative tone.

26. This is a common technique in Kabbalah of which Vital was surely aware. See Moshe Idel's "*Hitbodedut* as Concentration in Ecstatic Kabbalah" in Idel 1988b, 134–36.

27. The Mishna is the earliest compilation of rabbinic texts, redacted in the second century in Palestine.

28. On recitation of the Mishna and mystical experience in Vital, see Fine 1982.

29. See *Shaarei Kedusha* 3:3, 115. There Vital speaks about an angel speaking through the contemplative as an example of prophecy using 2 Samuel 23:2, the same verse he uses here. In Abraham Ibn Hasdai's Hebrew translation of the Persian mystic Al Ghazali (1058–1111), there is mention of repetition of God's name allowing "one's tongue to move by itself." This notion of repetition, in Vital of any Mishna, is a product of Sufi influence, given that in the Kabbalistic imagination, Mishna (as Oral Torah or Torah of the Mouth) is of divine origin. See Idel 1988b, 106.

hear his words. He no longer will be speaking, but the sage will be speaking through him. This is the secret meaning of the verse, *The spirit of God has spoken through me; His message is on my tongue* (2 Samuel 23:2).[30]

If the contemplative is not yet fully prepared for this high level, his experience might be otherwise. In the quick repetition of his recitation his words will come forth without any intention and he will achieve a hypnotic state. In that state he will see a vision and his question will be answered, either in a hint or with clarity. This all depends on one's preparedness. If one does not achieve one of these two experiences, one should know that one is not yet ready for this. Or, perhaps, one did not adequately separate oneself from the material world.

ב—One must purify one's soul from all manner of spiritual defilement and cleanse oneself from all manner of theft, bribery, and the like, as it says, *Who may stand in God's holy place?* (Psalm 24:3). *He who has clean hands and a pure heart.* One should be cleansed through and through, as it says, *and a pure heart;* only then, *he will carry away a blessing from God,* this refers to prophecy (Psalm 24:3–4), as it is written, *And he took up his theme* (Numbers 23:7) and bound his spirit above. Afterward this will be brought down below. First, one should think about the reasons for the commandments in their exoteric meaning and only then in their esoteric meaning.[31] Study Torah, perform the *mitzvot*, and cease from idle chatter throughout the day. One should immerse in a ritual bath (*mikve*), dress in white garments in a clean place, and avoid all manner of defilement. One should avoid contact with a corpse and cemeteries, avoid all manner of anguish and depression, and wrap oneself in joy.[32] One should separate from material needs and allow one's thought to ascend the heavenly spheres until the seventh sphere called *aravot*.[33] Imagine that above the sphere of *aravot* there is another sphere of pure whiteness. There one should imagine this is the place of YHVH written in Assyrian script in very large letters.[34] Each letter is like a

---

30. This seems to be an example of soul impregnation (*ibbur*), which is a popular theme in Lurianic Kabbalah whereby a disembodied soul enters a person's body to perform some kind of function, either to rectify itself or to aid the individual. In this case, one calls down by repeating his teaching cited in the Mishna a departed sage who then speaks Torah through the mouth of the contemplative.

31. Reasons for the commandments, or *ta'amei ha-mitzvot,* occupy a central place in medieval Jewish philosophical and later Kabbalistic thinking. Moses Maimonides devotes close to one third of his magnum opus *Guide for the Perplexed* to this issue. See Heinemann 1949; Katz 1980; Matt 1986. Medieval Kabbalists such as Ezra of Gerona focused their attention on *ta'amei ha-mitzvot* that continued in the *Zohar* corpus. See Ezra of Gerona's "Commentary to Song of Songs" (erroneously attributed to Moses Nahmanides) in Chavel 1964, 2:485–517. Cf. Travis 2002. The latter dissertation includes a critical Hebrew edition and translation of Ezra's treatise on the *mitzvot*. Menahem Recanati's (fourteenth century) *Ta'amei Ha-Mitzvot* (Basel, 1581; reprint London: L. Honig and Sons, 1962) is a classical rendition of postmedieval Kabbalistic *ta'amei ha-mitzvot*. This exercise continues throughout the Lurianic corpus and into Hasidism.

32. Avoiding a cemetery has to do with contracting *tumat met,* or a state of spiritual defilement, by coming into contact with a corpse. Even though these laws no longer apply since the possibility of becoming pure requires a Temple ritual no longer possible (thus everyone is in this state of defilement), contemplatives and pietists still try to avoid contact with the dead unless they are required to do so by taking part in a burial ritual that is considered an obligatory *mitzvah*.

33. See b.T. Hagigah 12b and Zohar 2.56b.

34. Assyrian script, or *ketav ashurit,* is the script that is used to write Torah scrolls and all ritual objects, for example, *tefillin, mezuzot,* among others. See b.T. Shabbat 115b, Megillah 9a. Cf. Jerusalem Talmud Megillah 1:11, 71b, where Assyrian is considered the script best suited for writing.

mountain, white like snow.³⁵ One should then connect the letter Y [of YHVH] with the letter H, and H with Y, and V with the first H. And the first H with the V. And the V with the final H and the final H with the Y.

ג—The contemplative who sits in solitude with his eyes closed should preferably also don the prayer shawl (*talit*) and phylacteries (*tefillin*).³⁶ After emptying one's thoughts, one should think of one word, any word, in all its letter permutations. For example, if one chooses the word "land" (ארץ), imagine it in the following manner: ארץ, רצא, ראץ, צאר, צרא. One can do this with any word, as long as it is done following the linear manner of permutations. At that point one should separate oneself from the material world as if one's soul has left the body and has ascended and become enveloped in those letter permutations. One should continue to ascend from sphere to sphere until the seventh sphere, which is called *aravot*. Imagine there is a sphere above *aravot*, a sphere of pure white like snow and that the letter permutations imagined occupy that sphere, written in Assyrian script with white fire.³⁷ Each letter [should be imagined] as a mountain or a hill. Then one should imagine asking questions from those permutations that are written there. They will answer his question, or place their spirit in his mouth, or he will fall asleep and the answer will come in a dream or as we have mentioned in section 1.³⁸

ד—I have found something similar to what I wrote in section 1 that I will reproduce in an abbreviated fashion here: *For who would otherwise dare approach Me* (Jeremiah 30:21) . . . and when I was young . . . I saw the deficiency of those in my time in this lofty wisdom. People do not study it. I therefore *set my face like a flint* (Isaiah 50:7) and I engaged *the man dressed in linen* (Daniel 12:7) . . . I ran quickly toward my teacher and bowed my face to the ground. . . . in the way of veneration according to Kabbalah, as I received it directly, and I called out "Answer me my righteous God, amen."³⁹

The enlightened know that this [what is referred to in the previous paragraph] is the wisdom of Kabbalah that was utilized by many. I have seen many books regarding the secrets of Torah. However, the practice (*shimush*) that can be drawn from this is largely concealed except for individuals who received it directly from their teachers.⁴⁰ I greatly desired this and so I begged

---

35. Snow as a metaphor for purity is used in prophetic and liturgical literature. See, for example, Isaiah 1:18; *Mahzor for Yom Kippur*, "Morning Blessings," "whiten like snow the sins of your people"; *Mahzor for Yom Kippur*, "Repetition of the Amidah for Yom Kippur," "Whiten our sins like wool . . ."

36. This is a common practice in Jewish pietistic literature.

37. On "white fire," see Rabbi Moses Cordovero, *Pardes Rimonim*, vol. 2 (Jerusalem, 1962), 24:14, 52d, 51a and Cordovero, *Or Ne'erav* (Jerusalem, 1999), part 7, chapter 1, 59.

38. This contemplative exercise concentrating on letter permutations activates a downward flow of spirit that reveals the answer to the contemplative's question. This is a very Abulafian technique. However, see *Shaarei Kedusha*, 3:6, 123, where Vital speaks forcefully against practical Kabbalah by bringing examples of Solomon Molcho and Joseph della Rena, whom he claims were destroyed because of their use of practical Kabbalah.

39. The source of this account is unclear. Vital writes that he "found it in a book" but never reveals its source. This seems odd because throughout this treatise he is careful to mention his sources.

40. This appears to be the main purpose of this treatise. Vital wants to articulate the contemplative practicum of Kabbalistic theosophy that he has woven together from medieval sources refracted through his Lurianic lenses. There is an important distinction here between "practical Kabbalah," or *kabbalah ma'asit*, and what I would call "operative Kabbalah," or *kabbalah shimushit*. The former focuses on the use of amulets or prayers to change the course of human events. The latter is focused on the use of Kabbalistic principles to foster experience of divine worlds and thus gain access to knowledge not attainable through ordinary means.

my teacher [to reveal it to me]. I will give you some advice: Know, my brother, that when you enter into the operational dimension (*shimush*) of Kabbalah, do it in this fashion. Take the ten *sephirot* and all that is in them. For example, take the words that are specific to particular *sephirot* as explained in the books of Kabbalah. Take each word alone. Take the first word and rotate it and do the same to each word as it is written in the *Sefer Yezeriah* (Book of Creation) (4:12).[41] Every word has a three-letter root from which can be constructed six "houses" (*batim*). And these six houses can further produce twenty-four houses. For example, the first *sephirah* is called *ani* or "I" (אני). From this word one can make six permutations: א״ני, י״נא, נא״י, ני״א, אי״נ, אנ״י. You can do this with every word (using its three-letter root) until you complete this exercise with all ten *sephirot*. Regarding this letter rotation, you can write each one according to its level, which is called "the secret of levels."[42] Be careful not to err in these permutations because an error will cause much anguish. One must also master the secret of the vowels that bring the words to life (lit., into motion). The letters are likened to matter and the vowels are the form, as is explained in the way of vocalization. When one wants to place vowels onto the permutated letters, begin with the word itself and then the permutations. (Author's addition: I have forgotten to explain this well in this book. You should look for it elsewhere). If not for the great effort it would take, I would have written most of them according to the names and *sephirot*. If one finds other words, subject them to the permutations according to the examples that I have provided. Doing this to other words may not help but it will do no harm. When one completes all these rotations and permutations and wants to use them for some purpose, gaze above and below and be sure of the *sephirot* to which they relate.

At the beginning of any month, one should fast, immerse in a ritual bath, purify one's thoughts, and focus on one of the Psalms or the preliminary prayers in the liturgy. You will be answered from heaven. Recall all the words in their rotations and their vocalizations with their vowels from the upper ones to the lower ones.[43]

When one lays down to sleep, one should recite the prayer "May it be God's will . . . ," concentrating on one of the words in that prayer and on the *sephirah* from which it is drawn.[44] One should remember one's query to know a dream or the future or perhaps to understand other matters. Be careful not to eat any animal product the entire night if one eats after the completion of the fast (the fast is from sunrise to an hour after sunset).

I found this in close proximity to what I already mentioned: On the first of the month when the [new] moon begins to move toward its fullness, the higher forces are drawn down to the lower spheres. And you, my brother, read what I taught you three times and know that it

---

41. *Sefer Yezeriah*, standard edition (Brooklyn, NY, 1988), 54, 55. In English, see Kaplan 1997, 4:15–16 and 185–93.

42. "The secret of levels" seems to refer to the hierarchical structure of ascending and descending Kabbalistic theosophy, from below (or smallness) to above (or greatness). See, for example, in *Mevo le-Hokhmat ha-Kabbalah*, part 1, Fourth Gate, chapter 2.

43. The beginning of the month in the lunar calendar is considered to be a minor holiday in rabbinic tradition that includes special prayers of thanksgiving. Kabbalists have made much of this moment, symbolizing the birth of the new moon, with many fasting on the eve of the new month and celebrating on the first day of the new month with a festive meal and additional psalms.

44. This refers to the "Keriat Shma ʿal ha Mita," or bedtime Shema liturgy. Lurianic Kabbalists make much of this prayer and its theosophical implications. *Pri Etz Hayyim* devotes eleven long chapters to this liturgy. See, in Vital, *Pri Etz Hayyim* in *Kitvei Ha-Ari* (Jerusalem, 1986), 13:319–43.

contains deep secrets that those before you did not know. Then you will know the difference between the God of Abraham and the God of Nahor.[45] This does not come from us for we also only understood it after much effort. When one strives for this, one will know the names of the various levels, the ways of vocalization, and how they can be used. And I swear that this will be for you alone. This is all I found.

ה—In the *Sefer Meirat Eynaim* (Book of the Shining of the Eyes) it is written:[46] I, Isaac the young, son of Samuel from Acco say—In regard to either the elite or the masses, whomever wants to know the secret of tying his soul above and binding his thoughts to the supernal God in order to acquire uninterrupted thought and eternal life (*Olam Ha-Bah*; lit., the world that is coming), in order that God should be with him in this world and the next, he should do the following. He should place before his mind's eye the letters of the divine name as if they were written in a book in Assyrian letters. Each letter should be imagined as enormous, without limit. This is to say, when the letters of the divine name are placed before his mind's eye, he will see them but his thoughts will be in infinity (*eyn sof*).[47] His gaze and thoughts will be united. The is the secret of true cleaving (*ha-davuk*) as it is mentioned in the Torah: *And cleaving to him* (Deuteronomy 30:20), *And cleave to him* (Deuteronomy 10:20), *And you are cleaving* (Deuteronomy 4:4). As long as a person's soul cleaves to God in that manner, no evil will befall him nor will he err, not intellectually, not emotionally, and he will not be subject to accidents. When he is in that state [of *eyn sof*], he is above the physical world of accidents. In order to honor God be sure only to attempt this state of cleaving in a clean place, not in alleyways or other unclean places, not with unclean hands, and not in the presence of any idols, etc.

I once heard from a God-fearing wise man that witnessed the pious Rabbi Isaac, son of Rabbi Abraham ben David (Isaac the Blind), whom he served.[48] This man said of Rabbi Isaac, in all his days he never saw his own nakedness because he was blind. When he had to go somewhere he always asked a disciple to accompany him. When they would pass by a place of idolatry, he would quicken his pace. It appeared to me that he did this to honor God because his mind was in a constant state of cleaving, and due to the impurity of the idol he was forced to arrest this state of cleaving that is founded on purity. He thus hurried along in order to return to his previous state.

---

45. The distinction is first expressed in Genesis 31:53. Cf. *Zohar*, 1.165a and 213b. Nahor was the father of Terah, who was the father of Abraham. See Genesis 11:24. Nahor was also the brother of Abraham (Genesis 11:27), who was the father of Laban. Abraham's cousin Laban is viewed in Genesis as a worshiper of idols. Hence, "the god of Nahor" often refers in classical Judaism to idolatry. See Joshua 24:2.

46. The *Meirat Eynaim* is a Kabbalistic work by Isaac of Acre. The reference here can be found in the critical edition of *Meirat Eynaim* by Amos Goldreich, "*Sefer Meirat Eynayim* of R. Isaac of Acco," [Hebrew] (PhD diss., Hebrew University, 1981), 217–18. See Fishbane 2009, 253–59, where Fishbane addresses Sufi influence on Isaac's theory of contemplation. Cf. Fenton 1995.

47. *Eyn sof*, literally, "without limit," refers to that dimension of God that is unknowable and beyond all differentiation, the realm of the divine above the cosmos. This seems to imply that if his thoughts are in *eyn sof*, the letters that he imagines will appear as *eyn sof* (without limit) as well.

48. Rabbi Isaac ben Avraham (1160–1235), also known as Yizhak Sagi Nahor (Isaac the Blind), was a leader among Provencal Kabbalists in the twelfth century, the circle that produced the *Bahir* (Book of Illumination). The latter is arguably the first Kabbalistic work that served as the foundation of the Kabbalah of *sephirot*. See Scholem 1962, 248–89. Cf. Sendor 1994. On his father, Abraham ben David of Posquieres (Rabad), a famous Talmudist and mystic, see Scholem 1962, 205–27; Twersky 1979.

If you will ask: Why should we cleave our thought to this name (YHVH) more than all other divine names? It is because this name is the Cause of all Causes (*ilat ha-ilot*) and the source of all reason and includes everything in it, from *keter* (crown) until the *atarah* (*malkhut*, the diadem of *yesod*), from *eyn sof* to *eyn sof*.⁴⁹ This name (YHVH) is the source of all existence, from *keter* to the smallest mosquito, blessed be the name of God's kingdom for all eternity. Regarding this divine name, the psalmist sang: *I place this Name (YHVH) before me always, He is at my right hand; I shall not be moved* (Psalm 17:8). His eyes and his heart are constantly directed toward this name as if it was written before him. And when he says "my right hand" (*mi'yamini*) it is like *'ish yamini* (Esther 2:5), that is, one from the tribe of Benjamin (*Binyamin*), as if to say Binyamini. This also has the literal meaning of from the right side that is *gedulah* as is known.⁵⁰ The reception of that name is from the place of *gedulah*. We know generally that the name YHVH usually refers to *tiferet*, but it is mostly received from *gedulah*. Hence the verse, *I place this Name (YHVH) before me always* means that this emerges from the "right side" (*yamini, gedulah*). By means of putting the right side before me I will not err and be subject to accidents.⁵¹

From the works of Todros ha-Levi (ben Joseph Abulafia) (1255–1285) in his *Ozar ha-Kavod* (Storehouse of Glory) referring to a homiletic passage we read, "A person should always enter two doorways before praying" (b.T. Berakhot 8a).⁵² This means that he should enter through two doorways from the place where he is standing, that is, *gedulah* (greatness/kindness) and *gevurah* (judgment). And he should then enter *bina* (understanding) and should direct his prayers to her. And his thoughts should always be bound to *tiferet* because *tiferet* is what is alluded to in "from the place that he is standing" (b.T. Berakhot 8a). This is because the name YHVH is *tiferet*, which is the numerical value of "place" (*makom*; 186). This is referred to in the Passover Hagaddah in the words "Blessed be the Place, blessed be He."

After a person achieves this state of cleaving, he will achieve equanimity (*histavut*).⁵³ If one achieves equanimity, one can achieve contemplation. After achieving contemplation, one can

---

49. This is an odd phrase that I have not found anywhere else in Kabbalistic literature. I am not certain what Vital means here. *Keter* refers to that dimension where *eyn sof* and the cosmic world meet. In some Kabbalistic texts, *keter* implies *eyn sof*, and in other places it refers to the first place of divine differentiation, albeit one that cannot be discerned as in the lower *sephirot* such as *hokhma* (wisdom) or *bina* (understanding). Hence *keter* is that ambiguous place where infinity and divine finitude merge.

50. Often the right side is known as *hesed*, but it is also known as *gedulah*, as in *Sefer Yezirah* and the *Bahir*. See *Sefer Yezirah* 2:10.

51. In theosophical Kabbalah, from the *Zohar* to Cordovero and then to Luria, the downward flow from the highest spheres comes through *hesed/gedulah* to *tiferet*, which is the place of resolution of the right and then left side. YHVH is the name describing *tiferet*. Vital here suggests that the verse is connected to the right (right hand, in Psalms), meaning that YHVH in *tiferet* is rooted in the "right side," which is *gedulah*.

52. The *Ozar Ha-Kavod* was published in Warsaw in 1808. It is Todros Abulafia's Kabbalistic commentary on the homiletic (*aggadic*) portions of the Talmud.

53. The notion of equanimity is a central tenet of Sufi mysticism, which was an important part of Isaac of Acre's work. Moshe Idel notes that aside from other similarities between Abulafian Kabbalah and Sufi mystics, neither Abulafia nor the anonymous medieval Kabbalistic work written sometime at the end of the thirteenth century by one of the pupils, *Sha'arei Zedek* (Cracow, 1881; reprint, *Sha'arei Orah with Shaarei Zedek and Sefer Ha-Nikud*, Jerusalem, 1994), ever mention equanimity. See Idel 1988b, 107. The term is mentioned in Eleazar Azikri's (1533–1600) *Sefer Haredim*, where Azikri mentions Isaac of Acre as well as Isaac Luria. See Idel 1988b, 132. Vital never mentions Luria in his discussion of equanimity in the *Shaarei Kedusha*. The Sufi influence on the circle of Kabbalists in sixteenth-century Safed is explored in Fenton 1994 and 2000. Equanimity as a state of mystical experience was also practiced by the Christian Hesychasts in Eastern Europe. The term "Hesychia" means "stillness" and was a central devotional practice of these reclusive ascetics, whose movement began in the fourteenth century. This may also relate to Abulafia. See Wolfson 2012, 196n28. There is some speculation concerning whether these monks had any influence on early Hasidism. See Idel 2011a.

merit the Holy Spirit, and from there one can achieve prophecy, meaning that one can know the future.[54]

Regarding the secret of equanimity, I was told a story by Rabbi Avner wherein one of the (aspiring) contemplatives asked him to be accepted by him as a contemplative. He said to him, "You are blessed by God for your intentions are good. Tell me, have you reached a state of equanimity?" He responded, "Teacher, explain what you mean." He responded, "If there are two men, one who honors you and one who denigrates you, are they equal in your eyes?" He replied, "No, I feel pleasure from the one who honors me and pain from the one who denigrates me. But I do not bear a grudge." Avner responded, "My son, go in peace. As long as they are not equal in your eyes, until you feel no difference between being honored and being denigrated, you are not ready for your thoughts to be bound to the upper spheres when you enter contemplation. Therefore, go and train yourself in true humility until you reach a state of equanimity, and then you will be prepared for contemplation."

Equanimity is achieved by means of attaching one's thoughts to God, which is the secret of cleaving, as we explained. When one's thoughts cleave to God, one will not dwell on whether one is being praised or denigrated, and one will pay no need to soothsayers, magicians, or diviners.

Recall that when God was with [King] Saul, his thoughts were bound to God, *And Saul had forbidden [recourse] to ghosts and familiar spirits in the land* (1 Samuel 28:3). Similarly, he did not notice that the scoundrels denigrated him because he was ruling over Israel (1 Samuel 10:27). When God departed from him, he turned into another person and went to inquire about diviners (1 Samuel 28:7). And he also became enraged at the righteous priests who were not guilty of any sin and spilled their innocent blood (1 Samuel 22:17).

Balaam began as a magician.[55] When he came to bless Israel, the *shekinah* descended upon him and he was enveloped by the Holy Spirit, and at that moment his thought cleaved to God and he never sought out magicians again (Numbers 24:1).[56] From all of this we learn that a person must subjugate himself in order to merit this state of cleaving to God. This can be done by a devoted commitment to *mitzvot* combined with a strong effort to achieve humility: One's eyes should always gaze downward while one's heart reaches heavenward.

۱—The secret of cleaving with full concentration requires seeing oneself as a disembodied soul when one is praying or reciting psalms in order to draw down the Holy Spirit. For the enlightened one who comes to contemplation in order to accept upon himself the Holy Spirit, it is required that everything he apprehends and every bit of light that he sees from the beginning of his contemplative state will be considered as if it is only darkness from the side of defilement.[57] This is, in fact, true at the outset because his sins create a barrier except in the case where he is already

---

54. Linking the spiritual achievement of cleaving (*devekut*) to attaining the Holy Spirit and to prophecy, which is central in these texts, seems to be under the influence of Abraham Abulafia's prophetic Kabbalah.

55. See b.T. Sanhedrin 106a.

56. Balaam is a somewhat odd example for Isaac of Acre to use to illustrate acquiring the Holy Spirit. Throughout Jewish tradition, Balaam is viewed as a villain, based on the reference to him in Deuteronomy 23:5: *and because they hired Balaam son of Beor . . . to curse you.* In Lurianic Kabbalah, he is somewhat redeemed, albeit only through a process of soul transmigration. See Magid 2008, 143–95.

57. That is, he will refuse to recognize his exalted state. This appears to be part of the devotional practice of self-nullification, here meaning the nullification of one's mystical experience.

a *zaddik gamur* (completely righteous person).⁵⁸ If he is in the Diaspora (outside the Land of Israel), even if he is a *zaddik gamur* with no barriers, the defiled state of the Diaspora and dwelling among the nations will separate him from true apprehension of the divine.⁵⁹ Therefore, when one senses he has achieved a little, he should intensify his contemplative practice. And even in that intensification he should view that apprehension as rooted in defilement. He should continue in this way until he sees that the spirit from the place of holiness begins to speak through him, against his will, words of pure Torah. When he achieves this state, he should continue and force himself to draw down this Holy Spirit again and again until he collapses from exhaustion.

When he reaches that state of collapse, he should strengthen himself and recite the following with great force: "Master of the universe, your holy throne has been revealed to me. I have not done this for my honor but to honor your Name and to give honor to your unity so that I should know you in order to serve you; so that I should bless your name and your dominion like David your servant and faithful messiah and his son Solomon. *And you, Solomon, my son, know your father and serve him* (1 Chronicles 28:9). Make yourself present to me, seek me out, I am your faithful servant, strengthen me and enlighten my eyes lest I pass away. Hide your face from my sins, and may all my sins be blotted out. God created me with a pure heart and an upright spirit that should be renewed in me. Return to me the joy of your salvation and support me with a willing spirit." One should continue this way until he knows that the spirit is engraved in him and has become bound in a way that the covenant becomes inseparable. This is the secret of the verse, *And I will maintain my covenant with him in an everlasting covenant* (Genesis 17:19). This is the secret meaning regarding each time the covenant is mentioned with respect to the (biblical) patriarchs.

ז—In the book *Ma'arekhet Ha-Elohut* (Structure of Divinity)⁶⁰ it is written: Now that you know the structure of the human (*zurat ha-adam*), you are able to understand if you have received a true vision of prophecy that was revealed to the prophets. The Talmudic sages called this prophetic vision the full-bodied divine body (*shiur koma*; lit., the measure of height). This is the secret of one who knows the Creator (*Yozer Bereshit*). This is the meaning of the verse, *Let us make the human in our image and our likeness (kadmutenu)* (Genesis 1:26). On this vision it is said: . . . *And spoke parables through the prophets* (Hosea 12:11). Isaac gave this a sign, the word image (*temunah* = 501) is the same numerical value (*gematria*) as "the face of the human" (*parzuf adam* = 501).

---

58. The notion of the *zaddik gamur* is one who has permanently overcome his battle with his evil inclination. See *Zohar* 2.117b; Vital, *Sha'ar Ha-Gilgulim*, with Bnei Aaron (Jerusalem, 1990), "Introduction," 10, 85.

59. The relationship between Jewish devotion and the Land of Israel versus the Diaspora is based on the Talmudic dictum, "One who lives in Israel is like one who has a God and one who lives outside the land of Israel is as if he does not have a God," b.T. Ketubot 110b. Cf. b.T. Baba Batra 158b, "The air of the Land of Israel makes one wise." In Kabbalah more generally, see Idel 1986.

60. *Ma'arekhet Ha-Elohut* (1558, reprinted Jerusalem, Nezah Books, 1963), 143, 144. *Ma'arekhet Ha-Elohut* was written by an unknown author at the beginning of the fourteenth century. The commentary to this work by Yehudah Hayyat, *Minhat Yehuda*, is an important resource for the nexus of philosophy and Kabbalah in the Middle Ages. The editor of the printed edition notes that this citation is full of errors and that he copied it from the original text. I have translated this passage from the printed edition of Vital consulting the Jerusalem reprint of *Ma'arekhet Ha-Elohut*.

I found this in the writings of Rabbi Eleazar of Garmiza.[61] When it is written *temunah* (image) it means that all you saw was a voice (*kol*) (Deuteronomy 4:12). One who receives this vision should contemplate the notion of corporeality that is mentioned regarding God in the Torah and contemplate the notion of "passing" and "standing," as it is written, *And God passed by before him and stood with him there* (Exodus 34:5, 6) and all the other verbs describing divine movements. With what I described regarding the image of the human, a wise person can understand that a *zaddik gamur* is worthy to prophesy and will live forever for it is like a kind that finds its own kind (*min be-mino*) and is awakened . . .[62]

Rabbi Judah Hayyat discussed this in his commentary to the *Ma'arekhet Ha-Elohut* (Structure of Divinity).[63] This Kabbalah is founded on two principles. The first is that the form (*temunah*) of the divine name is called *atarah* (crown) because it is like a mirror (*aspaklaria*) that receives from all other mirrors that are set upon it.[64] There are seven chambers in this mirror, one chamber for each attribute (*middah*), and no human being has ever ascended beyond these seven. Each prophet occupies the chamber that is appropriate to his prophetic level. Moses ascended all of these levels.[65] Moses apprehended the chamber of [divine] will. On him it is written . . . *and he beholds the likeness* (*temunah*) *of God* (Numbers 12:8). Nothing from any of the seven chambers

---

61. It seems this reference is to Rabbi Eleazar ben Judah of Worms (1175–1238), *Sefer Rokeah* (Jerusalem, 1967), 22. See in Wolfson 1996, 222. Rabbi Eleazar was from the circle known as the German pietists. He was both a Talmudist and a Kabbalist. His most well-known works were the *Sefer Rokeah*, first published in Fano in 1505, and his commentary to the *Sefer Yezeriah*, first published in full in Przemysl in 1889. I am not sure which text this citation comes from in the *Ma'arekhet Ha-Elohut*. In his introduction to the first printing of Abulafia's *Sefer Ha-Heshek*, the editor Mattityahu Safrin notes that Abulafia's Kabbalah is based on the writings of Rabbi Eleazar of Worms. See *Sefer Ha-Heshek* (Jerusalem, 1999), 8.

62. The principle of *min be-mino* means various things in rabbinic literature. In discussions of dietary laws we read that two selfsame elements, one permitted and one forbidden (e.g., untithed wheat mixed with tithed wheat), make the mixture prohibited even in the smallest amount, whereas two different elements (e.g., untithed wheat mixed with tithed barley) is only prohibited if the untithed grain gives recognizable taste to the mixture. See, for example, Mishna Halah 3:10; Orlah 2:6; Birurim 3:10. The idea that two selfsame elements do not constitute an interruption can be found in b.T. Sukkah 37b and Zevahim 110a. Here it appears to mean that the *zaddik gamur* has found his source and is thus awakened to experience the source of his perfected state. The notion of him "living forever" is interesting here. Whether it is simply euphemistic or points to some notion of Jewish *theosis* is unclear. The question of *theosis*, here the divinization of the contemplative, is a complicated story of Kabbalism. The notion of a human being transformed into pure spirit has its roots in the inter-testamental literature such as the similitudes in the book of Enoch, 4 Ezra, and other sources. While these sources do not inform medieval Kabbalah in any direct way, we can find gestures toward these ideas in Abulafian Kabbalah. For differing views on this idea in Kabbalism, see Wolfson 2000b; Idel 2007.

63. Hayyat's commentary *Minhat Yehudah* appears in most editions of the *Ma'arekhet Ha-Elohut*. The *Minhat Yehuda* was in many ways a more important text than the *Ma'arekhet Ha-Elohut*. Hayyat's work was one of the most important works that transmitted Spanish Kabbalah to Italy. See, for example, Idel 2011a, 212–17. Vital's use of Hayyat here may also speak to the ways in which he wants to bring together the theosophical Kabbalah of Spain (which Hayyat represents) with the prophetic Kabbalah of Abulafia. Hayyat is openly critical of Abulafia at the conclusion of his introduction to the *Minhat Yehuda*, calling his work nonsense and warning his reader not to read his books. As has been argued, Abulafia seems to stand in the center of this fourth part of the *Shaarei Kedusha*. For Hayyat's remarks on Abulafia, see *Ma'arekhet Ha-Elohut 'im Perush Hayyat*, 3b.

64. On this mirror (*aspaklaria*) as a term describing prophecy, specifically the prophecy of Moses, see Yalkut Shimoni to Leviticus, 1:432, and Midrash Yalkut Shimoni to Hosea, 12: 538. In Kabbalah see *Zohar* 1:141a, 2. 23b, and 2,228a, among many other references. In Lurianic Kabbalah, see *Etz Hayyim* 6:5, 6, 8:5, 32:1, 35:2, 42:13, 47:6.

65. The notion of Moses's superior prophecy is based on Deuteronomy 34:10 and codified in Maimonides's "Laws on the Foundations of the Torah," *Mishneh Torah*, volume 1, chapter 7. See Kreisel 2001, 148–315.

was hidden from Moses. Just as in a conventional mirror one can see one's own form, so too in this supernal mirror (*aspaklaria*) that is called "the form of God" (*temunah*) each one gazes into it and understands his specific attribute in that chamber, all according to his level of perception. One person sees this through a barrier (*mehiza*), while another only sees it through two barriers, and another through three. In general, the number of barriers is determined by one's level of perception. One who is aided by his soul and whose inner senses are purified does not require more than a thin barrier of separation to gaze at the "shining mirror" (*aspaklaria ha-meira*) that resembles the burning sun. However, one who has the "eyes of a bat" requires many barriers to gaze upon this light because he cannot take in too much light at once, and he will become blind if he gazes at this great light without many barriers.[66] Moses, however, did not require any barrier, as it says, *He gazed upon the divine form* (Numbers 12:8).[67] It seems that these two kinds of prophecy (one through barriers and one without) is already hinted at in the prophet Hosea when he says, *When I spoke to (lit., on; 'al) the prophets; for I granted many visions* (Hosea 12:11). If we focus on the word *'al* (on) we can ask that the verse should have said, *When I spoke to ('im) the prophets*. The use of the word *'al* hints at the first type of prophecy that is superior to all others and is called a "mirror that shines" (*aspaklaria nehorah*). This is only found in Moses, the master of all prophets upon whom it is said, *And God spoke to Moses face to face* (Exodus 33:11) and, *With him I speak mouth to mouth, plainly and not in riddles, and he beholds the likeness of God* (Numbers 12:8).

The second type of prophecy is transmitted in parables, riddles, and images that the prophet imagines. If that prophet is weak in his capabilities, the parables and imaginings are intensified. This is because this prophet requires many barriers, as I explained. This is hinted at when the verse says, *I granted many visions* (Hosea 12:11). This refers to a mirror that does not shine (*aspaklaria sh-eyno meira*; i.e., a mirror that does not emanate its own light). The word in Hosea "vision" (*hazon*) teaches this; similar to the use of *hazon* in *A harsh vision (hazon) was announced to me* (Isaiah 21:2). This is also the case with Abraham before he circumcised himself. Of him it is said, *Sometime later the word of God came to Abraham in a vision* (Genesis 15:1). *And by means ('al yad) of the prophets I used imaginings* (Hosea 12:11). That is, by means of many or fewer barriers. The use of parables and riddles in the prophets correspond to the spiritual prowess of each prophet. The term *yad* [lit., hand, but also, by means of] is taken from the verse, *but if he does not have sufficient means ('im lo mazah yado)* (Leviticus 25:28).[68]

---

66. As a nocturnal creature, the bat was thought to have eyes very sensitive to light. Some even believed that bats were blind. In fact, bats are not blind and have highly developed vision, although they do not use their eyes but sound waves to navigate direction.

67. On this see b.T. Berakhot 7a.

68. Distinguishing between the prophecy of Moses and all other prophets is commonplace and rooted in Maimonides's discussion in the *Mishneh Torah* and more in depth in his *Guide for the Perplexed* 2:32–48. For additional sources in Maimonides writings, see Kreisel 2001, 157–209. What is distinctive here is the way that Vital uses the Maimonidean discussion to speak not about prophecy but about contemplative experience. Using the template of prophecy to speak about mystical experience is very much in line with Abraham Abulafia's teachings, which is why Abulafia's work is sometimes called "prophetic Kabbalah." See Idel 1988a, 73–178.

The second principle is the notion that the divine name, including its emanation, is the human.[69] The human is also the essential component of the divine chariot. And the corporeal human (*adam takhton*; humankind) is the seat of the supernal divine *anthropos* (*adam ha-elyon*). The physical limbs in the corporeal human point to (*romzim*; lit., hint) the spiritual limbs above that have divine power. It is not for naught that the Torah says, *Let us make man in our image* (Genesis 1:26).[70] After we determine that this "image" (*temunah*) in the verse is the image of the divine *anthropos* and that the prophet is the corporeal human who, during prophecy, is almost transformed into a spiritual being, his physical senses dissipate; when he sees the image of a human it is like he sees the image in a glass mirror. However, not every prophet sees the same thing; everyone sees according to his own spiritual organ from which the soul of the prophet was emanated. Moses apprehended all dimensions of that image, as it says, *And he gazed upon the image of God* (Numbers 12:8).

It is written [in Hayyat's commentary]: In Menahem Recanati's (1250–1310) *Recanati 'al Ha-Torah*[71] it is written: Contemplate this great secret I am about to reveal to you regarding the rabbinic teaching that the patriarchs died with a kiss (b.T. Baba Batra 17a). When the righteous enter into states of contemplation and engage in lofty secrets, they visualize (*medamim*; lit., imagine) with their imaginative faculties as if the things they imagine are engraved right before their eyes. When their souls become tied to the supernal soul, things increasingly become revealed on their own, like one who opens a faucet, resulting in water pouring in an uncontrolled manner. The connected thought is the source, the pool, and the running spring. This is why connecting one's thought to something evil is worse than the sin itself, as our sages teach, "The thought of sin is worse than sin" (b.T. Yoma 29a). The sages teach further that when Ben Azai was sitting and expounding on the Torah and a fire was swirling around his head, Rabbi Akiva approached him and said, "Ben Azai, what is going on (lit., why is this day different than all others)? I heard you sit and study and fire blazes around you. I thought in my room that perhaps the chariot has descended." Ben Azai replied, "We see that the Torah is likened to fire, as it says, *These are My words, like fire* (Jeremiah 23:29). I sit and study, and things descend and rejoice in my presence."[72] The reason is that when his [Ben Azai's] soul is bound to the supernal soul, lofty things are engraved in his heart and he imagines them as if someone is putting the words in his mouth. When one achieves a state where one's thought is bound in the world of emanation (the highest of the four worlds), the emanation from that lofty place descends upon one and things

---

69. This point in particular is developed in the third part of *Shaarei Kedusha*. Whether this only applies to the divine *anthropos* (Adam Kadmon [original man]) or also to the corporeal human is not specified here. However, the latter seems also to be the case, given that Vital is speaking here about the unitive process of contemplation where the elemental components (the names of God) of the human body return to their supernal source.

70. This literal rendering of Genesis 1:26 is a classic Kabbalistic move that severs it from the medieval philosophical tradition. For Maimonides metaphorical reading of Genesis, see his *Guide for the Perplexed* 1:1. On the history of *zelem elohim* (image of God), see Lorberbaum 2004.

71. *Sefer Recanati* (Jerusalem, 1961), 37d–38b. Recanati was one of the most important Italian Kabbalists in the fifteenth century. His Kabbalistic commentary on the Torah, finished in 1523, exemplified Kabbalah in that period in Italy. See Idel 2011a, 106–38.

72. See Midrash Leviticus Raba 16:4 and Song of Songs Raba 1:53.

begin to multiply, and through the joy that ensues things are revealed to one. This is what the sages mean when they say, "The *shekinah* does not dwell upon one who is depressed . . . but only in a place of joy" (b.T. Shabbat 30b). (Perhaps this joy overwhelmed him so much that he began to cry until his soul desired to leave his body. This is the notion of "death by a kiss" that teaches of the deep connection of the object of love. At that instant his soul becomes united with the *shekinah*. Thus we find in the *Zohar* at times when secrets are revealed that a sage will rise and begin to cry, sometimes so profusely that he faints [*aseifat nishmato*], as it says [regarding the biblical Jacob], *he drew [veya'asef] his feet into the bed* [Genesis 49:33]. If these secrets are placed on his heart, his spirit [*ruho*] and soul [*nishmato*] will be drawn up).[73]

Know that thought spreads forth and ascends [only] to the place of its origin. When it reaches its destination, it stops and cannot ascend further. This can be likened to a spring that rushes forth from a mountain. If one would make a dam to prevent the water from flowing, the water could only return to the place where it emerged and no further. Thus one who forces one's thought [to places it should not go] will be damaged in one of two ways: either one will become confused and destroy the body; or by attempting to force one's thought to bind itself to something it cannot apprehend, one's soul will separate itself from the body and return to its source [i.e., one will die]. This is what the sages mean when they say, "That which is beyond you, you should not seek out" (Hagigah 13a). Hence the early pietists (*hasidim rishonim*) only ascended to their place of origin, which resulted in prophecy whereby the prophet would contemplate and direct his heart to bind itself to its place of origin above. By this means the prophet was able to know the future. And this is the meaning of *You shall serve Him and cleave to Him* (Deuteronomy 10:19) and *cleave to him* (Deuteronomy 10:13).

ח—The philosophers say the following regarding prophecy: It is not unusual that an individual can see visions while he is awake like the visions of a dream. This is all possible through the nullification of feeling external stimuli in a wakened state by imaging the forms of the letters of the YHVH that stand before him. Sometimes he may hear a voice, wind, speech, thunder, and all manner of noise. He may also see many images, smell with his olfactory sense, taste with all his powers of taste, and touch with all his powers of touch. He also may float in the air. All this may happen as long as the letters remain before his eyes and he remains enveloped in their color. This is called the "deep slumber of prophecy" (*tirdamat ha-nevuah*). When the visions of God's glory depart from him, so will prophecy.

ט—Rabbi Moses Nahmanides writes in his *Sha'ar Ha-Gamul* (Gate of Reward): The sages teach that God will make a circle for the righteous in the Garden of Eden and God will sit among them (b.T. Ta'anit 31a).[74] This alludes to the pleasure and reward in the future during the

---

73. This bracketed section is added by the editor of Recanati's *Sefer Recanati*, 38b. The notion of "death by a kiss," which is how the Torah described Moses's death, is a central motif in Spanish and Italian Kabbalah. Moshe Idel claims that this notion of "death by a kiss" as describing "the cleaving of the individual soul to the supernal soul" was not known to Spanish Kabbalists before Recanati (Idel 2011a, 115). Both mystical death and the act of crying as fostering mystical experience are ideas common in classical Kabbalah. See, for example, Fishbane 1994 and 1995; Wolfson 1995.

74. Nahmanides's "*Sha'ar Ha-Gamul*" in "*Torat Ha-Adam*," *Kitvei Ramban*, C. Chavel ed. (Jerusalem: Mosad ha-Rav Kook, 1964), 2:299.

resurrection of the dead. The *shekinah* is seen as if it points a finger from this circle, which is an apprehension of the spiritual levels and the pleasure of solitude derived from physical pleasure. This is to say that these individuals will reach the spiritual level of Moses, our teacher, whose soul so dominated his body that his physical powers were nullified, whereby he was continually enveloped in the Holy Spirit such that his sight and hearing were purely from his soul and not the physical eye. This was the case with the other prophets only occasionally when their bodies became depleted and their souls transcended their bodily power when the Holy Spirit came upon them.[75] And the soul will see what [the angels] Michael and Gabriel saw. This is the true seeing and the true hearing. The heretical philosophers (lit., those who nullify our Torah) do not have convincing arguments to undermine our claims that Gabriel has real eyesight or hearing, which is called an apprehension that he receives from Michael. Our sages teach, "All the souls speak to one another" (b.T. Berakhot 18:b). This does not mean literal speech but rather the transmission of knowledge. (We have thus completed our task of explaining the secrets of prophecy and the visions of angels).

ל—Nahmanides writes in his *Commentary to the Torah*:[76] "Everything that is written regarding the vision or speech of an angel is all in a vision or dream because angels do not have physical senses. Thus experiencing an angel is not considered prophecy."[77] Rather, such a vision is called "a revelation of the eyes." But in places where angels are mentioned as humans, such as in *Behold Abraham saw three humans before him* (Genesis 18:2), that is not even a vision but rather the "honor [of God]" that was created as angels. This is called by those who know these matters "the garments of the angels."[78] This can be seen even by those whose senses are still rooted in their physical being if their souls are pure enough, such as the pious and the disciples of prophets.

In Nahmanides's *Commentary to the Torah* in the portion of Balak it is written:[79] The angels of God are called "separate intellects," they cannot be seen in a physical manner because they have no physical existence. When they were "seen" by prophets or those with the Holy Spirit such as Daniel, they were apprehended with a sight rooted in the soul/intellect [perhaps "the mind's eye"] when that individual had achieved a prophetic state or the lower state of the Holy Spirit.

In Nahmanides's *Commentary to the Torah* in the portion of Re'eh it is written:[80] *If a prophet arises among you* (Deuteronomy 13:2). It is likely that this verse refers to the following truth:[81] There are certain individuals who have prophetic potential to tell the future, but they do not

---

75. On the distinction between Moses and the other prophets in this regard, see Maimonides, "Laws on the Foundation of the Torah," *Mishneh Torah*, volume 1, chapters 6 and 7.

76. Nahmanides on Genesis 18:1 in *Ramban 'al Ha-Torah*, C. Chavel ed. (Jerusalem: Mosad ha-Rav Kook, 1959), 1:104.

77. This is contesting the position of Maimonides. See Maimonides's *Guide for the Perplexed* 2:41. Vital abbreviates Nahmanides's words here where Nahmanides explicitly criticizes Maimonides.

78. This term appears in a few other Kabbalistic works, for example, Rabbi Menahem Mendel of Skhlov (a disciple of the Vilna Gaon) in his *Raza De-Heimanuta* included in *Kitvei Ha Rav Menahem Mendel of Skhlov* (Jerusalem, 2001), 1:10a; and Rabbi Joseph Shlomo del Medigo in his *Mazref le-Hokhma* (Warsaw, 1890), 108.

79. Nahmanides on Numbers 22:23 in *Ramban 'al Ha-Torah*, 2:290.

80. Nahmanides on Deuteronomy 13:2 in *Ramban 'al Ha-Torah*, 2:404.

81. The use of the term "truth" in Nahmanides often alludes to a Kabbalistic understanding. See, for example, Idel 1983; Wolfson 1989.

know where these powers come from. They seclude themselves and the Holy Spirit comes upon them and tells them such and such will happen to this person in the future. The philosophers call this individual a Ka'hin (soothsayer). They have no idea how this happens but it does indeed happen. Perhaps the soul (*nefesh*) of the person attaches itself to one of these separate intellects. And this person is the one called a prophet (in the preceding verse).

יא—The Secret of Prophecy:[82] First the contemplative sees a vision and his power increases toward knowing its origin. His spirit is tied above and is then drawn downward. At first, he thinks of exoteric reasons and then slowly he thinks of the esoteric ones. This requires white glass in order that the material realm will not impede the prophetic apprehension.[83] The secret of the visionary (*hozeh*) is in the strengthening of the power of the north; the secret of the seer (*zofeh*) is in the strengthening the power of the south. This is all in accordance with the individual and the context (lit., time). The secret of the soothsayer (*ro'eh*) is in the strengthening of the in-between. All of the aforementioned are called prophets, for their prophecy is from their lips and they bring the future into the present from the spirit that rests upon them. The prophets contain two types of spirit, for a vessel is needed to pour into a vessel. This is how prophecy works. Sometimes when the soul is dreaming it sees dreams, sightings, and visions. And it hears voices and murmurings that are concealed in the soul. And fools are given this type of prophecy, which does not come from them but from the strength of the dreaming soul. Wise ones will seek to find the experience at its source but will sometimes be unsuccessful. Working in this manner a spirit from above will rest upon them in order to make known to them the truth of the matter. Those who do not know how to distinguish between the true and false way are subject to another spirit that will cause them to err. This is like the spirit of *navot* that is mentioned in the Book of Kings (1 Kings 22:23).[84] Sometimes there is true prophecy, but the prophet does not recognize it, such as Jonah's prophecy of Nineveh being destroyed (Jonah 3:4). The truly enlightened one must purify his body and separate from all manner of defilement, clean his hands, as it says, *with clean hands* (Psalm 24:4). He must refine his heart, as it says, *with a pure heart* (Psalm 24:4). Only then will he be able to carry prophecy which is a blessing in itself, as it says, *And portions were served to them before him, but Benjamin's portions was several* (Genesis 44:34). Jerusalem is called, *The burden of the Valley of Vision* (Isaiah 22:1); in it he (Benjamin) will have his portion. This is also similar to, *The burden of the word of God* (Malachi 1:1).

יב—In the *Sha'ar Ha-Kavvanot* (Gates of Intention) according to the early Kabbalists:[85] "Everyone who earns something on his own will retain what he has earned."[86] So too if you pray or intend to achieve something in a true manner, you should imagine yourself as a light that is surrounded

---

82. This is a section of Rabbi Joseph Angelet's "Twenty-Four Kabbalistic Secrets," extant only in manuscript. See the JTSA Mic. 1915. This passage is cited and discussed in Wolfson 1996, 276–77.

83. On "white glass" and prophecy, see Vital, *Sha'arei Kedusha*, 3:3 in *Shaarei Kedusha Ha-Shalem* (Jerusalem, 2005), 110; and Vital, *Shivhei R. Hayyim Vital* (Jerusalem, 1989), 14.

84. *So the Lord has out a lying spirit in the mouths of all these prophets of yours; for the Lord has decreed disaster upon you* (1 Kings 22:23).

85. On this early Kabbalistic text, see Scholem 1981. Scholem attributed this text to Rabbi Azreil of Gerona. Wolfson thinks it was written a bit later. See Scholem 1962, 416–19; Wolfson 1996, 301.

86. I have not been able to locate this citation.

by light from every corner. In the midst of that light is a throne of light and upon it is the light of *nogah* (splendor). Opposite it is a throne and upon it is a light called the "light of goodness."[87] When you stand between these two thrones, if you want to take revenge, turn to the light of *nogah*; if you want to be merciful, turn to the light of goodness.[88] Open your lips opposite the throne and then turn to the right and you will find *hod* (majesty), which is the light of *bahir* (illumination); on the left you will find the light of *hadar* (glory), which is the light of *mazhir* (shining). Between them and above them you will find the light of *kavod* (honor) and around them you will find the light of *hayyim* (life), and above that *keter* (crown). This is the light that crowns those who seek knowledge, sheds light on the imagination, and enlightens the vision out of the completeness of God's honor, will, and blessing. Peace and prosperity come to those who guard the path of God's unity. God hides Godself and reproves the recalcitrant to those who turn from the way of light. One who strives toward knowing the truth should cleave one's thoughts and will that are derived from the strength of his dream without measure. Through the power of drawing down the strength of his intention, one's willful knowledge, the imagined quality of his thoughts, and the force of his power of inquiry—when one is not disturbed—will also strengthen one's ability to draw from *eyn sof* and will result in success in all his spiritual endeavors. He will learn how to marginalize the limited nature of his will from its essence and his intention will overpower theirs. He will be able to think deeply in order to undermine the distorted path and renew the path of his proper will. He will be able to overpower those limited forces using the complete honor (*kavod*) that is drawn from the supernal light, a light that has no image, form, quality, measure, length, breadth, value, or finitude; a light that cannot be investigated, a light that has no number, no end, and no limit.

Thus when one rises from one level to the next according to the power of one's concentration with the intention of reaching *eyn sof*, one must [constantly] direct one's concentration toward this end such that the supernal will can envelop one's own will. It is not only that one's will should be enveloped in the divine will [but also the divine will should be enveloped in one's will]. Divine effluence does not descend into the human realm unless one is scrupulous in remaining proximate to the supernal will through the trait of equanimity in cleaving to divine unity. Only then will divine effluence descend to complete the contemplative's task. The perfection of one's will in its proximity to the supernal will is not only for its own sake. When the supernal will attaches itself to one's desire or will, by means of this equanimity it reveals that which was heretofore concealed. In this manner of proximate wills [divine and human], the supernal will adds strength to the object allowing it to complete any task. This is true even of the *nefesh*, the portion of the soul that is not part of the supernal will.[89] On this we read, *He who earnestly seeks*

---

87. The "light of goodness" (*'or ha-tov*) is the mature light (*gadlut*) of the *kelippat nogah*, or the light vulnerable to corruption, from the side of goodness. See Hayyim Della Rosa (d. 1786), *Torat Hakham* (Salonika, 1948), 89a. Della Rosa was one of the leading Kabbalists in the first generation of the Beit El school of Rabbi Shalom Sharabi, whose interpretation of the Lurianic system dominated the Sephardic world.

88. It is unclear what is intended here. According to Della Rosa, the "light of goodness" is also part of the light of *nogah*. Since the "light of goodness" is the upper sphere of *nogah*, perhaps he means that "taking revenge" refers to gazing at the lower sphere of *nogah*.

89. In Zoharic Kabbalah the soul is divided into three parts, *nefesh*, *ruah*, and *neshama*. Lurianic Kabbalah adds two more parts, *hayye* and *yehidah*. The *nefesh* is considered to be the lowest portion of the soul, the portion most closely aligned with corporality and the physical desires of the human. Its root lies in the Hebrew word "breath" (*neshima*). *Nefesh* is sometimes used to refer to one's self or one's personality.

what is good pursues what is pleasing (Proverbs 11:27).⁹⁰ That is, one's ability to achieve what one desires correlates to the cleaving of one's will to the supernal will. At that time, one's desire will be enveloped in the supernal will and one can draw this to anything one wants using the powers of concentration. This effluence is drawn from "the one who crowns," who holds the secret of desire and existence, from the spirit of *hokhma* (wisdom) and *bina* (understanding) and from the strength of *da'at* (knowledge). When one is enveloped in this spirit (*hokhma, bina,* and *da'at*), one's intentions (*kavanato*) will become clear and manifest in actions. The effluence will be drawn from power to power, and from reason to reason, until one accomplishes what one desires. This is how to understand why the sages of old would wait one hour before commencing to pray.⁹¹ They did so in order to dispel any foreign thoughts and to focus on the proper concentrations and behaviors. They would then pray for one hour in order to articulate those concentrations linguistically. And they would wait one hour after prayer to ponder how to properly translate those concentrations, now completed, to speech and action. In their status as righteous ones (*hasidim*) their *torah* is thus fulfilled [preserved] and their deeds are fulfilled [blessed]. This is one of the ways of prophecy: one must first accustom oneself to the rising levels of prophecy. This is accomplished through the completion of these concentrations. One must concentrate on establishing these things in a deep manner and fully articulate each word that leaves one's mouth, which includes the elements of fire, air, and water, as in voice (*kol*), spirit (*ruah*), and speech (*dibur*) in a perfect union in order to form each letter fully in one's mouth.⁹² Then he will be with the King and will achieve his essence.

What follows is the right way if one wants to accomplish anything: for prayer, blessing, or its opposite,⁹³ one must [first] imagine oneself as light. And surrounding this light is a throne of light. On that throne there are the ordered forms of light, as is known. One should concentrate one's thoughts from one attribute to another in ascending order, the order in which the light was emanated until *eyn sof*. One should focus one's concentration as if one and the roots of all things are unified in a single source. This is possible because the nature of all things is to return to its source.⁹⁴ By means of unifying and enveloping one's will in this thought, one will draw down with full force what is needed to accomplish one's intentions (*kavanato*), all according to the explanation of one's speech and the signs of one's behavior when there is no thought interference. This will begin the concatenation of effluence from attribute to attribute in the

---

90. The NJPS TANAKH's idiomatic translation of this verse does not capture Vital's nuance. The verse uses the term *razon* (will) in a way to illustrate Vital's point. A more Vitalian translation might be: "He who seeks what is good will desire the [supernal] will in all things."

91. See b.T. Berakhot 32b. Cf. Maimonides's *Mishneh Torah*, "Laws of Prayer and the Priestly Blessing," 4:16.

92. The formation of the letters in one's mouth is considered a crucial part of this verbal contemplative practice as the mouth serves as a portal for the transition from thought to language (speech), which activates divine power. The production of language is the materialization of divinity in this form of contemplative Kabbalah, and thus the process of forming letters in one's mouth is part of that process. The classical tradition divides the sounds that constitute the Hebrew letters as corresponding to the "five parts of the mouth."

93. This apparently refers to bringing about a curse.

94. This is a general metaphysical principle in theosophical Kabbalah drawn from Neoplatonic teaching. All emanations seek/desire/strive to return to the source of their emanation. This is the natural state of affairs. Sin impedes this process by either (1) creating barriers preventing returning light, or (2) by forcing the source of emanation to retreat to a place that is beyond reach. The notion of "returning light" (*'or hozer*) is a fundamental principle of Kabbalah at least from Moshe Cordovero to Luria and beyond. See, for example, in Cordovero, *Pardes Rimonim* (Jerusalem, 1972), Gate 20, chapter 10, 94d–95a; and in Lurianic Kabbalah, *Ozrot Hayyim* (Jerusalem: Makor Hayyim, n.d.) "Gate of Akudim," chapter 5, 4a/b.

order of emanation until *eyn sof*. This will establish a fitting place for what is necessary in the mercy of supplications, in all the remaining attributes from *eyn sof* to *eyn sof*.[95] At that time, one's thought will be accomplished *in actu*. When one begins to pray, whether in asking for mercy or in supplications, including all that we have mentioned, from *eyn sof* to *eyn sof*, one should concentrate on drawing down effluence from the place of the supernal fountain (lit., from the place of the fountain). Prayer (*tefila*) is the very language of drawing down. Prayer is the blessing that is sent as an emissary to the place of emanation (*azilut*). One should thus concentrate on the unity of the letters of divine name YHVH with the vocalizations that have been transmitted directly from generation to generation. First one should concentrate on the crown of the letter *yud* (י), which is a hint for the letters *zayin* (ז) and *ayin* (ע). The vocalized form includes all ten paths [of the *sephirot*]. Then one should concentrate on the remaining letters of YHVH, *vav* (ו) and *hey* (ה), which point to the light of wisdom (*hokhma*), which is the *telos* of cleaving to the nothingness of thought (*ayin ha-makhshava*) and the two *heys* of the YHVH since it draws by itself. This is the power of green (*yarok*) in the shape of a bucket (*dli*) that pulls (*doleh*) from the waters of creation without interruption.[96] This also includes the force of whiteness (*ha-luvan*) and the strength of red (*edom*).[97] Regarding the two *vavs*, these two hint at two arbitrators in the form of a pillar, including the six lights connected to the bucket that draws them. The final *hey* of YHVH draws from the supernal fountain like something that absorbs everything like the flowing *alef* (א). (This concludes the words of the early Kabbalists from *Sha'ar Ha-Kavannot*).

Hayyim [Vital] said:[98] According to my limited understanding regarding the lights discussed previously that are situated from below to above, the "throne of light" is the *sephirah* of *malkhut* itself and the light of *nogah* that is upon it is its soul (*neshama*). This is all one divine name (*havayah ehat*). The other throne is *yesod* and its soul is the "good light." From there upward it is not necessary to mention any throne but only the lights themselves that are souls and called *havayot*[99] because the thrones were already mentioned in the first two cases; these are the "light of illumination" (*bahir*), which is the *havayot* of *nezah*, and the "light that shines" (*mazhir*), which is the *havayot* of *hod*. The "light of honor" (*kavod*) is the *havayot* of *tiferet*. The "light of life" (*'or ha-hayyim*) is the *havayot* of *bina*. It is also possible that the [light] of life includes *hokhma* and *bina*. The "light that crowns" (*makhtir*) is the *havayot* of *keter*. We still need to know that all of these *havayot* have specific vocalizations, but I do not know them because the later Kabbalists have a different way of ordering the vocalizations of the ten *havayot* of the ten *sephirot* from what appears in the *Tikkune Zohar* (*tikun* 70).

---

95. This term "from *eyn sof* to *eyn sof*" appears numerous times in this text, cited earlier in the early *Sha'ar Ha-Kavanot* text. Its source is not known to me. One possibility is that *malkhut* is sometimes viewed as containing *eyn sof*. This is explicit, for example, in the eighteenth-century Kabbalist Rabbi Yaakov Koppel of Mezritch (Ukraine) in his *Sha'arei Gan Eden*. On this see Magid 2012.

96. On red and green light, see Vital, *Shivhei R. Hayyim Vital* (Jerusalem, 1989), 5.

97. On the role of colors in Kabbalistic contemplation and theurgy, see Hallamish 1999, 145–46; Idel 1994.

98. It seems that because this portion of the text is replete with quotations from earlier sources, Vital introduces this section with "Hayyim said" to indicate that what follows is his own voice.

99. It seems that Vital refers to souls here as manifestations of (divine) names, with *havaya* referring to the Tetragramaton or the name YHVH. In Lurianic Kabbalah all divine manifestations, be they *sephirot*, combinations of *sephirotic* clusters (*parzufim*), among others, are often referred to as *havayot*, manifestations of the divine name YHVH. See, for example, *Zohar* Hadash 87b: "The entire Torah is only names of God."

נ״ב—I found in Nahmanides's *Iggeret Ramban* something regarding the union of husband and wife:[100] Behold look at these concealed matters that appear in the Talmud. The rabbis taught, Ben Azai was sitting and studying surrounded by fire. Rabbi Eliezer was sitting and expounding (Torah) and horns of light shone from his head like the horns of light of Moses.[101] Know that all these things refer to the same thing. When the supernal spring is drawn down from its elevated place to a lower place, its water has the power to rise to another elevated place juxtaposed to the place of its origin. It is well known among the Kabbalists that human thought originates in the Soul Intellect (*nefesh sikhlit*) that is drawn from the higher spheres. This thought has the power to separate (from the individual) and return to its roots. It then cleaves to its place of origin in the Higher Light creating a unity between itself and its source. When this thought subsequently returns to its place below, it does so in the image of one line (*kav ehad*) and that supernal light is drawn down with it. The force of the thought that draws down the Higher Light also draws with it the *shekinah*. At that time the "light of illumination" (*'or ha-bahir*) is drawn down and covers the place where the thinker sits. This is how the ancient pious ones were able to achieve this state of cleaving and were subsequently blessed according to the power of their thought. This is the meaning of the verse, *The jar of flour did not give out* (1 Kings 17:16) *and a jar of water* (1 Kings 19:6) of Elijah. And I will pour *the oil* of Elisha (2 Kings 4:5–7).

After these things the sages were compelled to say the following: When a husband and wife engage in sexual union and the husband's thoughts cleave to the higher realm, that thought draws down the supernal lights that dwell in that drop of semen upon which the husband concentrates, like [Elisha's] jar of oil. Thus the drop of semen becomes connected to the light of illumination that is the secret meaning of the verse, *Before I created you in the womb I knew you* (Jeremiah 1:5). This is because the light of illumination was already connected to the semen of that righteous person at the time of union due to the contemplative nature of his thought that was attached to the supernal realm, which drew down the light of illumination [into the drop of semen that inseminated the woman]. Understand this well and you will understand the great secret regarding "the God of Abraham, the God of Isaac, and the God of Jacob."[102] This also applies when the righteous engage in eating, drinking, sexual intercourse, and other physical matters. The sages asked the question, "What will become of Torah?" (b.T. Kiddushin 66b). The answer lies in the fact that the patriarchs acted purely (*le-shem shamayim*) in all of their physical behavior. Their thoughts were not severed from the supernal light even for an instant. Hence Jacob merited twelve sons who were all righteous without blemish. They were all worthy of being vessels of God. This is because Jacob's thoughts were in a constant state of cleaving with the upper worlds, even during sexual union. Understand this well. On this King Solomon said in one of his most potent proverbs, *In all your ways* know *Him* (Proverbs 3:6). The sages say on, *In all your ways know Him*, even in the most mundane aspects of human behavior.[103] You already know that the term "know" refers

---

100. The reference is to chapter 5 of *Iggeret ha-Kodesh* (Holy Epistle) that is included in *Kitvei Ramban*, C. Chavel ed., 2:331–35. This epistle was attributed to Nahmanides (Ramban), but today scholarly opinion claims that it was not authored by Nahmanides but perhaps by one of his disciples.

101. *Pirkei de-Rebbe Eliezer with the commentary of R. David Luria* (Jerusalem, 1990), 2:4.

102. This is the doctrinal patriarchal proclamation that serves as the standard locution in traditional Jewish liturgy. It also serves as the classic expression of biblical monotheism, for example, in Blaise Pascal's *Pensées*.

103. See *Midrash Shokher Tov* to Psalm 119.

to the union of the Soul Intellect with the upper spheres and also to the union of husband and wife. You also know that we do not consider a person truly "knowing" something until there is a union between the subject and the object known.[104] Understand this well. Thus think deeply about the verse, *In all your ways know Him.* Depend on it and *He will make your paths straight* (Proverbs 3:6). If one lives in this way, the supernal light will always be bound to one's actions and one's priorities will always be in proper order. This is what the sages mean when they say, "And all of your actions should be for the sake of heaven" (Mishna Avot 2:2).

After you know all this, reflect on the rabbinic dictum "thoughts of sin are even more challenging than sin itself" (b.T. Yoma 29a).[105] When a person thinks about sinful things, his mind and soul become embedded in the dross of the supernal realm. Since his soul is by definition bound to heaven, the dross of heaven defiles it. However, if he actually commits the sin in this world in a thoughtless manner, the punishment is lighter than the thought of sin. On the latter, he becomes bound to the upper worlds and comes closer to heresy. Here you can better understand thoughts as sin during sexual intercourse. In such a case, that thought embeds itself in the semen and creates a foundation of evil that is called *zarim* (evil ones). On this we read, *The wicked (zaro) are defiant from birth* (Psalm 58:4). If you aspire toward righteousness, understand the implications described here. With this key you will also understand the story of the pious one who sat at the gates of the ritual bath (b.T. Baba Meziah 84b).[106]

Know that because the pious cleave their thoughts to the supernal reality, everything they think or contemplate comes to pass, whether good or bad. This is what the sages meant when they wrote, "He cast his eyes upon him and he became a pile of bones" (b.T. Berakhot 58a). And we also read, "And he told her, 'Return to dust'" (b.T. Ta'anit 24a). Further we read, "Everything that the sages turned their gaze upon, either death or poverty followed" (b.T. Moed Katan 17a). This also relates to prayer and animal sacrifices in the secret of cleaving to the supernal realm. This also relates to the episode of Balaam the villain (Numbers 22–24), upon whom it was said, *He whom you bless is blessed and he whom you curse is cursed.* (Numbers 22:6). Thus he wanted to consider Israel carefully in order to bind his thoughts to the supernal realms and drawn down evil tidings upon them. Hence it is written, *Balaam looked up and saw Israel encamped according to tribes* (Numbers 24:2). He needed to be scrupulous and thus we read [regarding Balak], *Come now, I will take you to another place* (Numbers 23:27). This is because a villain must carefully consider the one upon whom he intends to bestow a blessing or a curse. He binds his thoughts above with the intention of drawing down from the supernal fountain. This is the meaning of . . . *he who holds visions of the Almighty* (Numbers 24:4). The villain also needs actions. Thus Balaam asked for seven altars to be built and a bull and a ram to be sacrificed on each. This was all in order for him to summon energy and his thought in order to accomplish his evil intent. Hence

---

104. On this see Moshe Cordovero's *Or Ne'erav* (Jerusalem, 1999), part 6, 42–55.

105. Compare this to Jesus's teaching recorded in Matthew 5:27, *And you have heard the words of Exodus, "Do not commit adultery." Yet I say, if a man looks at a woman with lust, he has already slept with her in his heart.*

106. The Talmudic discussion reads as follows: Rabbi Yohanan used to sit by the gate of the bath, so that when the daughters of Israel would return from taking their ritual bath (after which they can have sex with their husbands), they should meet him, and bear children like to him in beauty and scholarship. And when the rabbis asked: Are you not afraid of an "evil eye"? He answered, I am a descendant of the children of Joseph, and no "evil eye" can do harm to them; as it is written "Joseph is a fruitful bough, a fruitful bough by the eye" (Genesis 49:22).

it says, *And he [Balak] took him [Balaam] to field of zofim* (from the word "to gaze") (Numbers 23:14) so that he [Balaam] could gaze upon them and drawn down his evil intent from above.[107]

I will now write a brief summary of what is written in Joseph Gikatilla's *Sha'arei Orah* (Gates of Light):[108] Know that even though we say that achieving a desired end requires contemplation of specific divine names related to that desire, we do not mean to say that one should only contemplate the name and nothing more. Rather, one should contemplate the name related to that thing and focus on drawing down its supernal source that is called "divine will" (*razon*). One's contemplative focus should move from one *sephirah* to another until it reaches *eyn sof*, which is the upper point of the letter *yud* (י) of the YHVH.[109] When one reaches there, one should make one's request from that place of divine will and then draw down that divine will into this world until it reaches its earthy domain, which is represented by the divine name *Adonai* (אדני).[110] In this manner all of the *sephirot* are blessed through one's contemplation, and one will subsequently be blessed by them. At the outset one should concentrate on elevating [one's desire] upward to enable the name *adonai* to penetrate the final "H" of YHVH. One should then continue upward until one reaches *eyn sof* [the upper point of the letter *yud*] and make one's request there, as we explained. From there one should descend to the name *Adonai*.

י"ד—Regarding the names *nezah*, *hod*, and *tiferet*, Gikatilla wrote: This is the secret of elevation of the *sephirot* and their unification until they reach the desired place. It is like one who wants to grasp on to and bind oneself to the supernal light. The natural inclination of that which is lower is to rise to that which is higher.[111]

Regarding the name *hokhma* he wrote: When *malkhut* rises up to *bina*, it attaches itself to *hokhma* that is also called "thought" (*makhshava*). This thought does not descend into the world but is perpetually bound to *keter* because both constitute the first letter of the YHVH, the *yud* and the upper point of the *yud*. This is the meaning of the rabbinic euphemism, "It arose in thought" (b.T. Menahot 29b). "Gazing at the throne," however, is a euphemism for descending. This is because at the outset it ascends to a high place where it receives divine effluence and then

---

107. This paragraph exhibits the extent to which Vital believes in the potential to summon divine power even for evil purposes as well as, and as easy as, for good purposes. Using Balaam as a proof of this phenomenon is quite suggestive of the tendency among many in that circle to support the notion that good and evil are drawn from similar places. God does not seem to intervene in this regard. This use of divine powers by Gentiles also emerges in healing practices. In Talmudic literature we have numerous instances of Jews seeking out "heretics" (*minim*) because of their healing skills. See, for example, b.T. Avodah Zara 27b and Jerusalem Talmud, Shabbat 14d.

108. Joseph Gikatilla (1248–ca. 1325) from Castile. He was one of the most influential Kabbalists of thirteenth century. He began as a student of Abraham Abulafia (hence his place in Vital's work here is very instructive), and his first major work *Ginat Egoz* (1615) displays a definite Abulafian influence. He then turned to theosophical Kabbalah, and his most famous work, the *Shaarei Orah*, written sometime after 1293 and first published in 1559, is an exhaustive explanation of the *sephirot*. For a concise biographical sketch, see Scholem 1974, 409–11. The *Shaarei Orah* was published in a new two-volume edition edited by Joseph ben Shlomo in Jerusalem in 1970. For an English translation, see Weinstein 1995.

109. Gikatilla was one of the most prominent advocates of identifying *eyn sof* with the highest *sephirah* of *keter*. *Keter* is often placed as the upper point of the Hebrew letter *yud*. On the Kabbalistic controversy of this identification, see Green 1997.

110. The divine name *Adonai* is considered the presence of God in the world, sometimes called *malkhut*, sometimes *shekinah*. This name is in closest proximity to the world and thus is the name that is pronounced as phonetically written to beseech divine favor.

111. *Shaarei Orah*, Ben Schlomo ed., 1:181.

with that same force generated by the ascension it descends and "gazes at the throne" (i.e., from a distance). Understand the depth of this process. The throne represents the seven lower *sephirot*.[112]

ט—Rabbi Moshe de León wrote in his *Mishkan Ha-Edut* (Tabernacle of Testimony):[113] When the prophet secludes himself with his prophetic wisdom to unify with the supernal forms, he ignores all matters of physicality and matters of this word. Only when he is able to achieve this level of severance from physicality does he become bound to the upper forms.

In the "Second Gate" of *Mishkan Ha-Edut* de León writes: The sustaining soul (*nefesh zomakhat*) sustains the body with the blood that circulates from it.[114] After death and the decomposition of the body, this dimension of the soul remains. The animal soul, the source of all base thoughts, is called the "seat of desire."[115] Upon it is it written, *The person who sins, he alone shall die* (Ezekiel 18:20).

In the "Third Gate" [of the *Mishkan Ha-Edut*] Rabbi Moshe de León writes something significant about the *nefesh*, *ruah*, and *neshama* [the three levels of the soul]: The lowest level called *nefesh* is the soul of the four elements [fire, air, water, wind] and includes the inorganic, vegetative, animate, and human dimensions. This is all rooted in the drop of the father's semen that includes the fundamentals of his body and soul. The two higher levels of *ruah* and *neshama* are not from the father but directly from God. *Ruah* comes from divinity that is given to humans either from "the world of action" (*asiah*) or from *malkhut*, which is also called the "feminine waters" (*mayim nukvin*). The *nefesh* comes from *tiferet* or from the side of the "masculine waters" (*mayin dekhurin*). This is the way it is explained in the section of the *Zohar* called "Saba de-Mishpatim."[116]

In the *Zohar* it is explained in a different manner. In the *Zohar*, the vital *nefesh* and *ruah* are both called *nefesh* because both are rooted in the "world of action" (*asiah*). The *neshama* is rooted in the "world of formation" (*'olam yezeriah*) and is called the "male *ruah*." The true *neshama* is from the "world of creation" (*'olam ha-beriah*). In fact, both of these approaches are true. In the "First Gate" [of the *Mishkan Ha-Edut*] it is explained precisely in this way: the *nefesh*, *ruah*, and *neshama* are from the lower worlds, the constellations (*galgalim*), and the world of angels. Note that all these worlds [of which we are now speaking] are contained in the "world of action" (*asiah*). Hence the *nefesh* and *ruah* mentioned earlier are called *nefesh*, and the *neshama* is called the *ruah* of [the world of formation] *yezeriah*, which is the realm of angels, and the *neshama* is from *beriah* (world of creation).[117] Understand that there is no discrepancy between the two

---

112. *Shaarei Orah*, Ben Schlomo ed., 2:94, 95.

113. Rabbi Moshe de León was born in Castile in 1240. He was most famous for claiming to have discovered the *Zohar*. It has later been determined by scholars that he was instrumental in writing the *Zohar*. Scholarly debate continues on the role de León played in the composition of the *Zohar*. His *Mishkan Ha-Edut* (1293) was a work largely devoted to the soul after death and also contains a commentary on the vision of Ezekiel. He was the author of many other original works on Kabbalah as well. See the short biography in Scholem 1974, 432–34. Cf. Wolfson 1988.

114. On this discussion in *Mishkan Ha-Edut*, see Nadav 1959, 72–73; Bar-Asher 2011. This "sustaining soul" is close to the notion of an organic soul, for example, that which sustains all organic life. Rabbi Menahem Mendel of Skhlov (eighteenth-century Lithuania) defines it as that which sustains the life of a tree. See his "Commentary to Mishmat Ha-sidim" in his *Kitvei R. Menahem Mendel of Skhlov* (Jerusalem, 2001), 1:165.

115. This is also called the *yezer ha-ra*, or the evil inclination.

116. See *Zohar* 2.94. On this section of the *Zohar*, see Giller 2001, 33–68.

117. This sentence is confusing because Vital, in line with Lurianic doctrine, views the categories of the soul (*nefesh, ruah, neshama*) as representing worlds (*asiah, beriah, yezeriah, and azilut*), as contained within them and also within each category (*nefesh* of *nefesh*, *ruah* of *nefesh*, etc.). So while generally, for example, we can call *nefesh* the world of *asiah*, the world of *asiah* also contains a *nefesh*, *ruah*, and *neshama* of its own. Moreover, each *nefesh* contains a *nefesh*, *ruah*, and *neshama* of its own. In that case, the *nefesh* of one world can be considered the *ruah* of another world.

positions. When a person dies, the vital soul and the blood are absorbed into the other organs. When the body decomposes, the vital soul remains in the decomposed matter. Upon this it is said, *And his souls still mourns* (Job 14:22). This is the "sustaining soul." The animal soul, however, departs from the body and hovers above the grave. The remaining dimensions of the "intellectual soul" (*neshama sikhlit*) rooted in the constellations of *asiah* (mentioned earlier) that are sometimes called *ruah* in relation to its foundations, dwell in the earthy (or lower) Garden of Eden. The *ruah* of *yezeriah* that is called *neshama* in relation to the "intellectual soul" dwells in the supernal (or upper) Garden of Eden.[118]

In "Part Four" of the *Mishkan Ha-Edut* it is written: We can learn from the enlightened and from the prophets that strive to understand spiritual matters how they constantly fast and weaken their bodies in all manner of ascetic behavior. It is only with the weakening of the body that the soul can be empowered.[119] The weakening of the body is proportionate to the strength of the soul, as it is written, *Have no fear Daniel, from the first day that you set your mind to get understanding, practicing abstinence before your God, your prayer was heard . . .* (Daniel 10:12). Similarly, we read in the teachings of the sages, "One rabbi fasted forty days so that he might meet with Rabbi Shimon bar Yohai."[120] It is also the case that living righteous ones (*zaddikim*) cannot see dead righteous ones except by means of fasting.[121] Evidence of this can be brought from a sick person whose animal soul is seriously weakened and can, in that state, achieve spiritual insight. In that weakened state his "intellectual soul" gains strength and can have visions of the supernal realms. This is also written in "Part Six."[122] There de León adds, When angels temporarily descend into this world, they take human form, drawing from the four elements. Even though they are corporeal, they are only revealed to the individuals to whom they were sent.

De León also wrote the following: It is only the *ruah* [dimension of the soul] that separates from the body at death. This *ruah* is called the "intellectual soul" (*neshama sikhlit*) as we explained. This is due to the destructive drop (*tipat herev*), the angel of death. The sustaining soul (*nefesh zomakhat*) and the animal soul remain in the body. Both die as a result of the drops of the angel of death.[123] However, they still retain a small portion of life that can be perceived in dreams. This is the meaning of "a dream is one sixtieth of prophecy" (b.T. Berakhot 57b).[124]

---

118. On the distinction between the upper and lower Garden of Eden, see Magid 1996b.

119. Asceticism is a formidable idea in classical Kabbalistic piety. See, for example, Elliot Wolfson's "Eunuchs Who Keep the Sabbath: Erotic Asceticism/Ascetic Eroticism" in his *Language, Eros, Being* (2005). On this passage in *Mishkan Ha-Edut*, see Bar-Asher 2011, 314. Asceticism is not foreign to the Talmudic sages either. See Diamond 2004.

120. *Zohar* 1.4. Forty days is considered a full cycle for mystical experience and also repentance. This is based on Moses being in heaven forty days before returning with the tablets. See, for example, b.T. Shabbat 89a; b.T. Ta'anit 28b.

121. On the role of fasting in rabbinic asceticism, see Eliezer Diamond 2004, 93–120.

122. This actually appears in "Part Four" of the *Mishkan Ha-Edut*. I want to thank Avishai Bar-Asher for clarifying the error.

123. This may refer to the seminal drop of demonic forces.

124. The whole notion of some life remaining in the body becomes, for the Kabbalists, the condition for resurrection. The body is thus never totally devoid of life, and this imperceptible life-force remains dormant until the time of resurrection.

טו—In the book *Sod Ha-Kedusha* (Secret of Holiness) I have found the following:[125] A person must sanctify his limbs and mark them with *mitzvot* in order to become a throne for the *shekinah*. Human limbs are like an ark in which the *shekinah* resides.[126] All positive commandments hold the secret of sanctity, and when a person does one *mitzvah* he sanctifies himself in that particular *mitzvah*. The more *mitzvot* one fulfills the more the sanctity increases. In this case, the limbs become like the Holy Tabernacle and its sacred vessels, as it is written about them, *And I will dwell in them* (Exodus 25:8). The *mitzvah* of Torah study (*talmud torah*) is the greatest of all and represents the tablets inside the ark, which represent both the written and oral Torah.[127] These are, respectively, *tiferet* and *malkhut*.[128] All of the limbs that are in the ten *sephirot* are included in them. By this means one literally binds oneself within a true state of cleaving (*devekut*) with the *shekinah*, as it is written, *And cleave to him* (Deuteronomy 11:22).[129]

יו—I found something regarding the essence of prophecy: Prophecy is the effluence that flows from God through the Active Intellect through the power of speech and afterward through the imagination that constructs parables and images. Moses's prophecy, however, was not facilitated by the imaginative faculty but directly from the Active Intellect to the highest level of the human intellect.[130] Hence Moses (Deuteronomy 9:9) and Elijah (1 Kings 19:8) fasted for forty days in accordance with the forty days required to form matter to weaken their physical state in order to receive complete prophecy. The intellect stands above the lower portion of the soul (*nefesh*), which is the life force generated from the heart. The sustaining soul is generated from the liver, and the soul that directs the power of speech is from the mind.

---

125. It is not clear to which text Vital is referring here. Elliot Wolfson initially suggested it might be the *Iggeret Ha-Kodesh* (Holy Epistle) that was attributed to Nahmanides and is included in the two-volume collection of his work edited by Charles Chavel. However, he noted to me in personal correspondence that Vital refers explicitly to the *Iggeret Ha-Kodesh* later in the text, which problematizes that theory. Many scholars today think that the *Iggeret Ha-Kodesh* was written by Gikatilla. While the exact passage cited here is not found in the printed edition of the *Iggeret Ha-Kodesh*, Vital could have been paraphrasing. One strike against this suggestion is that Vital does quote the *Iggeret Ha-Kodesh* by name earlier in this text. I want to thank Elliot Wolfson for his help with this textual conundrum.

126. This is likely based on Exodus 29:46, *I am the Lord your God who brought you out of the land of Egypt that I might abide (shekhanti) among you.*

127. See Mishna Peah 1:1. The contextual meaning of the *mishna* is that Torah study is one of those *mitzvoth* that has no boundary. However, in rabbinic literature and onward it is taken to mean that Torah study is equal to all the other *mitzvot* in the Torah. See b.T. Kiddushin 39b.

128. On the Tablets being *tiferet* and *malkhut*, see Moshe Cordovero, *Pardes Rimonim*, 2: "Gate 23," chapter 12, 23c.

129. There may be a subtle shift in the conventional notion of the passage in Exodus 29:46. Many understand that passage to mean that the *shekinah* dwells among the Israelites (*I will dwell among you*). Vital seems to be reversing the hierarchy. When one performs the *mitzvot*, the human body becomes bound to the *shekinah*. By juxtaposing Exodus 29:46 with Deuteronomy 11:22, Vital suggests, perhaps, that Exodus 29:46 refers to the mystical experience of a kind of apotheosis whereby the human body becomes "divinized" through its attachment to the *shekinah*.

130. The notion of Moses's prophecy as that which transcends the imaginative faculty is found in Maimonides's *Mishneh Torah*, "Laws on the Foundation of the Torah," chapters 6 and 7 and Maimonides's *Guide for the Perplexed* 2:32–48. Cf. Howard Kreisel 2001, 182–204, 210–56.

ח—I found a response from the book *Shaar Kevod Ha-Shem* (Gate of Divine Glory) by Ephraim ben Israel ben al-Nakawa: It is written in the works of the astronomers that there are individuals who can see spiritual forms in a wakened state, seeing them in bodily form. These forms speak to them and tell them the future. The reason for this is that these individuals receive divine effluence from above from the time of their birth. The text goes on to say: Those who see these forces in bodily form do not see them empirically. Rather, everything they see is inside of them like one who sees his form in a mirror or some clear surface. He is, in fact, seeing his own image. This is also the position held by Abraham Ibn Daud (1110–1180?) and Ravad (Avraham ben David of Posquieres; 1123–1198).

ט—In another work I found description of the *sephirotic* tree:[131] Now I will explain to you the secret of "enclothment" (*malbush*). First know that the human form is an image of God (*zelem*) and God created the human that way for God's glory, as it is written, *All who are linked to My name, whom I have created, formed and made for My glory* (Isaiah 43:7). God breathed breath (*neshama*) into the human's nostrils from above. That was stretched so that it could take the form of a human body. Hence the entire human body was filled with divine glory in order that it could draw down from the spirit and divine intellect, bind itself to them, and walk in the way of true wisdom. In order to illustrate that the human form is honorable, God commanded us to make the form of the cherubim in human form. And just like God breathed into our nostrils the breath from above (*neshama elyona*; lit., the supernal soul), so did God with the cherubim, *tiferet* and *atarah*. Upon the Torah it is written, *The Torah of God is perfect, restoring the soul (nefesh)* (Psalm 19:8). That is, it is restored to the place of its origin. In this way, God does a kindness to the righteous and prepares for them a spiritual garment (*malbush*) even loftier than those of the angels. They cannot decide for themselves nor can they pray for themselves and their offspring until God enclothes them in a second garment. This second garment has discernment, and thus they can pray for themselves and their offspring. On this it says, "They know their own pain but they do not know the pain of others."[132] If the soul merits this [second] garment it can pray for itself and its offspring. We find this in [b.T.] tractate Ketubot (103a) regarding Rabbenu ha-Kodesh [Rabbi Yehuda the Prince, the second-century sage known to be redactor of the Mishna] who, after his death, used to return to his home every Friday afternoon [before Shabbat]. We also read of Rabbi Ahai bar Josiah (b.T. Shabbat 152b). These righteous ones were given this garment that always hovers over their grave.

כ—Regarding the secret of enclothment (*sod ha-malbush*):[133] After the soul is enclothed in the body in this world, and after it separates postmortem, it returns and is enclothed in a precious

---

131. This section is derived from Shem Tov Ibn Gaon's *Keter Shem Tov*, which is reprinted in Judah Koriat's *Meor ve Shemesh* (Livorno, 1839). I want to thank Elliot Wolfson for this source. Cf. Idel 2004, 350.

132. See Zohar 1:225a/b. This seems to be a paraphrase of a Zoharic discussion. The citation as it appears in Vital's text does not appear in the *Zohar*.

133. The notion of the garment (*malbush*) is a complex and central idea in the *Zohar*. See, for example, Cohen-Alloro 1987. This section is derived from Joseph Angelet's *Twenty-Four Secrets*. See Bar-Asher 2014. The reproduction of the Angelet text in Vital is at the end of this essay. See also Wolfson 1980 and 1996, 276–77.

garment that appears as an image of an astral body (*guf aviri sapiri*—a sapphire-like ethereal body). There is one who wears the garment of Elijah, a spiritual garment that remains after it has been removed from his skin [i.e., after death]. This is apparent to the pure of heart. And there are some that only appear to the pure of spirit when the soul is strong, as it is hinted at in *I slept with my fathers* (Genesis 47:30) "in body and spirit."[134] The secret of this "body" is the foundation of the garment that is drawn from the supernal spirit. And this is what is meant by "And Jacob our father did not die" (b.T. Ta'anit 5b). This is because he was enclothed in a more perfect garment since "his bed was complete (*shelamah*)."[135] One can understand this regarding Joshua, who was described as wearing soiled clothing (Zechariah 3:4) because his children were not acting properly until, by separating from their gentile wives, his soiled clothes were removed. Jacob our father did not die because he had reached a state of perfection (*middat ha-emet*) and still stands to pray for the well-being of his children. Do not say he did so because his sons sold their brother Joseph, because Joseph had already forgiven them. Moreover, the brothers were already forgiven through their time in exile [in Egypt]. When the world needs mercy, all the patriarchs are enclothed and stand in prayer for the sake of their progeny, as is explained in a homiletic passage regarding Elijah, "Abraham was woken [from his eternal rest] and prayed" (b.T. Baba Meziah 85b). Rabbi Hiyya and his son's actions were similar (b.T. Baba Meziah 85b). Perhaps they too merited the very same spiritual garments. When a person's thoughts are bound above, he can see people that stand in these spiritual garments, according to their level of apprehension. We see this in sick people whose bodies are weakened and, as a result, their spiritual senses are heightened and they can see the image of a person in the form of an astral body, as in the passage, *Prepare a throne for Hezekiah* (b.T. Berakhot 28b), when he saw an image of what he [intellectually] apprehended. Similarly, "And they were born under one star" (b.T. Baba Batra 12b), that both were attached to the same place above. Regarding Rabbi Hiyya who said, "Do not bury me in a white shroud (lest I am not worthy and am like a bridegroom amid mourners) or a black shroud (lest I am worthy and am like a mourner amid bridegrooms), but bury me in court garments from overseas" (b.T. Shabbat 114a). This is because how one is buried will determine how one will serve God after death. Actions below have their impact on actions above. This also relates to being "buried on a mat of reeds" (b.T. Berakhot 18b). Even though one is clothed in one's good deeds, the body should be likened to the soul. The analogy between Hiyya and Abraham, Isaac, and Jacob requires further investigation. And why not bury him in a white shroud? Perhaps the court shroud is in-between (white and black) and he preferred the middle way to ascend because that was fitting for him? When he saw those who came to greet him [postmortem] and the ways in which they were dressed, Abraham being an example, he realized the principle, "The smaller follows the greater." We can also learn of

---

134. See *Zohar* 1:224. Vital slightly misquotes the passage here. In the *Zohar* it reads, "I slept with my fathers in the body of my *nafsha* (lower soul) and the spirit of my *neshama* (upper soul)." Here and in other places the likelihood is that Vital is quoting from memory and thus misquotes certain passages.

135. Here "his bed" refers to his sexual activity. See Midrash Leviticus Raba 36:5. "Abraham still had impurity (*pesolet*) as he produced Ishmael and Ketura. Isaac still had impurity (*pesolet*) as he produced Esau. Jacob's bed was complete as he produced only righteous sons." See Margolit 1993, 2:850.

the secret of the soul according to Rabbi Eliezer Ha-Gadol in his *Orkhot Hayyim* (Paths of Life)[136] where he says the soul is enclothed in spiritual ether and how, in his majestic garments, it ascends monthly and weekly.

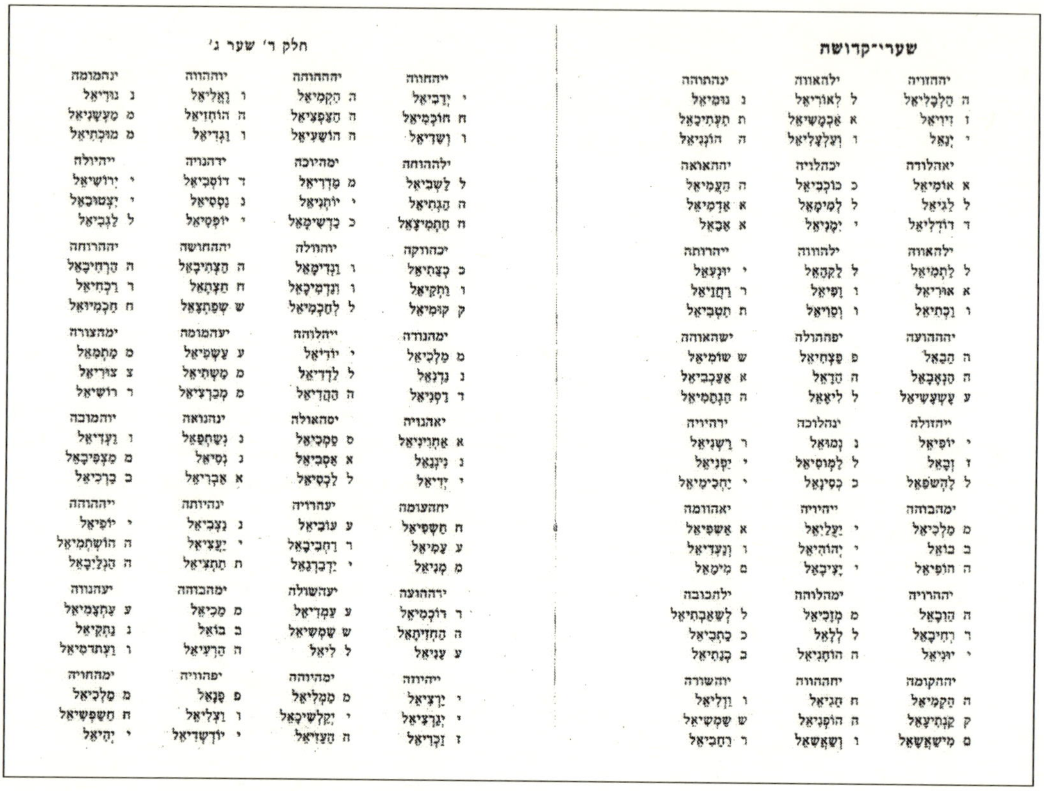

Figure 5.5. Chart of Kabbalah Letter Permutations

---

136. The *Orhot Hayyim* is also known as *The Testimony of R. Eliezer the Great*, which is attributed to Rabbi Eliezer ben Hurcanus, a second-century sage. The *Orhot Hayyim* includes midrashim and pious directives. It was first published in Salonika in 1521.

Chapter 6

Southern Buddhist Meditation
The *Ānāpānasati Sutta*

Sarah Shaw

The *Ānāpānasati Sutta* (Discourse on Mindfulness of Breathing) is an ancient Buddhist text on mindfulness of breathing, including meditative elements of *samatha* (calming) and *vipassanā* (insight). Originally composed in Pāli by his early followers, the text describes a discourse supposedly given by Siddhattha Gotama,[1] the historical Buddha (Awakened One). Like other *sutta*s (Skt.: *sūtra*), the text presents itself as context-specific teachings addressed to an assembly of monks, members of the early Buddhist religious community.

The Historical Buddha and the Early "Discourses"

The *Ānāpānasati Sutta* presents itself as a "discourse" (*sutta*) of the historical Buddha, the founder of Buddhism, which we may think of as the religious tradition emphasizing awakening (*budh*). Also known as the Buddha Gotama or Śākyamuni (Sage of the Śākya) Buddha, Siddhattha Gotama lived, taught, and practiced in Northern India in the fifth century BCE, dying around 404 BCE at the age of eighty-four. Born as the son of a local *rājā* (king), the baby was, according to legends, inspected by several seers at his birth. They predicted that he would be either a universal monarch—a great king who rules by justice, not force—or a Buddha, a completely awakened one, with the ability to lead and teach others the way to be free from suffering.[2] The last seer foresaw only one destiny, that of Buddhahood. On the basis of many past lives practicing the perfections of generosity, morality, meditation, wisdom, vigor, forbearance, truthfulness, resolve, loving-kindness, and equanimity, he was ready in his last life, the last seer foretold, to find *bodhi* (awakening) for himself and to teach a graduated path to others. Protected from seeing suffering, illness, old age, or death by a father anxious to preclude his renouncing kingship, Gotama then lived a life of sensory pleasures and abundance. He continued on such a worldly path until, on a ride out from the palace, he saw the "four messengers," also known as the "four great sights": an ill man, an old man, a dead man, and a wandering ascetic, indicating the possibility of a different, freer way of life. Inspired by these, Gotama renounced his palace and future role and spent six years as a renunciant trying to find wisdom and peace. At first he tried two meditations, later integrated into his own system, on no-thingness and on neither perception nor nonperception. These, he concluded, did not in the end "lead to peace" (see M I 164). After this, he tried major self-mortifications, fasting, as well as bizarre and punitive practices, which represented a type of practice that characterized a certain Indian asceticism of the time (see Bronkhorst 1993). These, he saw, lead to neither happiness nor peace and produce no wisdom.

Finally, he decided that it is fear of happiness that animates such endeavors. Remembering an incident as a child when he had spontaneously and happily found himself in meditation, entering what he called the first *jhāna* (meditation), accompanied by initial thought, discursive thought, joy, happiness, and one-pointedness, he wondered if this offered the way to freedom and enlightenment (*Mahāsaccaka Sutta*; M I 246–47). The first *jhāna* (see the glossary of Pāli terms at the end of this chapter) seemed to offer a different approach to the acquisition of wisdom.[3] The commentaries and the introduction to the *Jātaka*s (Birth Stories) say also that this state had been produced by a spontaneous practice of mindfulness of breathing, the subject of the *sutta* in this chapter. "Why am I frightened of the happiness that has nothing to do with sensual pleasures and unskillful states?" He asked himself, and decided to take some food and try a different path.

Figure 6.1. Statue of Seated Buddha
Gal Vihara, Polonnaruwa, Sri Lanka[4]
Source: Bernard Gagnon (Wikimedia Commons)

This he did, and with a body and mind now balanced, he attained enlightenment at the base of a banyan tree (later referred to as the "bodhi [enlightenment] tree") in what is now called Bodh Gaya (in present-day Bihar, India).[5] He successively practiced four *jhānas*—possibly discovered by him—before applying his mind to the liberating insight that freed him from all defilements of the mind, and further rebirth.

The bare story of his life itself poses an extensive critique of contemporary Indian meditative and ascetic systems and is taught to this day as an enactment of Buddhist principles. In a doctrine that Gotama articulated as the "middle way" (*majjhimā paṭipadā*), the practice of self-mortification was rejected, as involving the active denial of contentment and peacefulness, while the practice of sensory indulgence was also renounced, as involving the active engagement with samsaric existence. In the forty-five years after his enlightenment, or awakening, the principle of the middle way, an ongoing, dynamic balance between apparently opposing qualities, is suggested or explained through a number of axes in early texts: the middle way also provides a path between greed and hatred (M I 15); between eternalism, the view that the self is permanent, and annihilationism, the view that there is no continuity of experience from one life to another; and between the view that "all exists" (*sabbaṃ atthi*) and the view that "nothing exists" (*sabbaṃ natthi*; see for instance S II 17).[6] In one teaching, in which the term "middle way" is never used, its principle of creative equipoise is nonetheless aptly expressed. An overly zealous meditator, Soṇa, who cannot achieve results in meditation because he is exerting too much effort, is told to compare his mind and body to the strings of a lute, an instrument that the young man had been accustomed to play: too lax, and the note is off key; too tight, and the note is again harsh and wrong. When the strings are at the right tension, however, they produce a beautiful note, rightly tuned (A III 374).

As part of the teaching of the middle way, the Eightfold Path to liberation was formulated in what the tradition termed the first discourse ("Sermon at Deer Park") as a way of freeing the mind: it can be followed by anyone, and skillful states in accordance with the path can arise at any time, for anyone, as part of daily life or public and private practice (see Shaw 2006, 194–98). The Eightfold Path, in essence, comprises a series of interdependent areas or fields of operation: each relates to the others, but each also requires a different kind of effort and attention. Right view and right intention, for working on views and the alignment of the heart, are associated with the cultivation of wisdom (*paññā*). Right speech, right action, and right livelihood describe ethical behavior in the world (*sīla*). Right effort, right mindfulness, and right concentration support concentration (*samādhi*). This last includes what many moderns call "meditation." All of these factors come under the broad heading of "practice," or *bhāvanā*, things to be cultivated so that the practitioner can find awakening for him- or herself.[7] Broadly speaking, the practice of calm (*samatha*) is associated with the last three factors, and that of insight (*vipassanā*) with the first two, in that they involve the purification of views and intention. The cultivation of both calm and insight needs elements from all of these. The observation of generosity, kindliness in daily life, and *sīla* are advised for both. For monks, this involves keeping the monastic rules—the Vinaya—and for laypeople, the five foundational ethical precepts, namely, the avoidance of taking life, stealing, indulging in harmful sexual activity, lying, and intoxication

Over the next forty-five years, those who listened and learned from the Buddha comprised a varied group: in common with other teachers of the time, Siddhattha Gotama was an itinerant teacher, and, accompanied by some of his followers, taught, guided, and debated with highly diverse sets of individuals, either alone or in groups. These ranged across local *rājās*, Brahmins, warriors, farmers, servants, and women. His decision to teach all of these categories of people as equals—it is said to be a characteristic of all Buddhas that they address others as equal—was itself revolutionary at the time (see Gombrich 2009, 32–81). Indian society was codified by caste: only men of the Brahminical classes were permitted to learn, recite, and pass on the Sanskrit texts, which were considered, in their *śruti* (heard or revealed) classification, as unchanging emanations from the divine, accessible only to the few. Other people were considered in some way limited in their capacity to participate in salvific activity: lower castes had to accrue good *kamma* to ascend the hierarchical ladder for another lifetime; women were not thought capable of attaining enlightenment. Like Mahāvīra, the leader of the Jains, however, the Buddha thought that all castes, and both sexes, were capable of enlightenment. Moreover, admitting women into the monastic orders, he saw no inherent barrier to most humans' capacity to attain enlightenment. Such attainment was only influenced by willingness, disposition, and some traits or features of temperament, the result of kammic action in past lives, which might aid or hinder the path of any one individual in the attempt to find salvation for him- or herself. He also strongly rejected self-mortification and denial, reputedly associated with the Jains of the time.

The *Ānāpānasati Sutta*, our primary text, is contained in the Pāli Canon, which is the primary textual collection of ancient Buddhist writings and the canon of Southern Buddhism. Dating orally composed texts is difficult. Although there are different accounts of the transition to writing, they were probably not committed to written form until the beginning of the first millennium (Norman 1994, xxiii–xxix). The Buddhist tradition claims that this collection was compiled after the Buddha's death based on orally transmitted teachings, which had previously been preserved through recitation. Tradition tells us that the Pāli Canon was originally "compiled" (recited) during the First Buddhist Council, which was attended by those of his followers who had also attained enlightenment. The primary division of the Pāli Canon consists of the so-called Three Baskets (*Tipiṭaka*), or three types of teaching: the *Vinaya*, the code of conduct for monks and nuns; the *Sutta*s, the discourses in which the Buddha is described as talking with, responding to, and teaching others; and the *Abhidhamma*, the higher or philosophical teaching. It is the second, the *Sutta-piṭaka*, that principally provides an account of the various situations in which he taught, spoke, and interacted with disciples, lay and monastic, and houses the most commonly taught texts. The *Ānāpānasati Sutta* is from one of these *sutta* collections.

As discussed in more detail later in this chapter, these crafted and organized texts do not have an "author" in our modern sense. According to the tradition, they represent the recollections of Ānanda, the attendant and companion of the Buddha, whose capacious memory allowed him to recollect them at the First Council after the Buddha's death. This council, to which only those who were awakened were allowed to attend, was famously barred for Ānanda: he was known as one of the followers of the Buddha who had never attained enlightenment. Desperate to attend, he struggled hard at his meditation, but eventually had to concede defeat and gave up. Between standing up and lying down the night before the council as he went to bed, he finally attained his goal, and so he attended the meeting. There he was able to recollect all of the Buddha's discourses and recount them to the others. We cannot know whether or not this commentarial story (DA I 9ff.) is true, but it has been generally considered to give a living, personal touch to the practices and some sense of contact with the Buddha as teacher. The *sutta*s are one expression of a culture that has always valued "reminders" (*cetiya*), such as trees made from cuttings from the original enlightenment tree, as at Bodh Gaya (in present-day Bihar) and Anuradhapura (near present-day Colombo, Sri Lanka). Most *sutta*s start with "Thus have I heard" (*evaṃ me sutaṃ*). This is in itself a kind of reminder: the "I" is, in one sense, at any time, the person chanting it. This would have been the case from the time of the *saṅgha* (Buddhist community) who heard it from Ānanda at the First Council, where the Buddha's discourses were recounted, to the present. Indeed chanting and rehearsed recitation (*sajjhāya*) are the key to the texts' transmission and character: the *sutta*s were not committed to writing at least until the first century BCE, and perhaps later. Before this time and, indeed, in practice continuously after, it would have needed a first-person "I" to hear each text, not read it, from someone else. The original "I," who heard the text and made a continuous third-person narrative from the events recounted at the First Council, seems to be a generic term for the members of the *saṅgha* as well as Ānanda. Clearly a great deal of skill and artistry contributed to their composition: in practice they must have been carefully crafted and "authored," perhaps over a lengthy period of time, as they were chanted, and probably evolved, in the centuries after the Buddha's death (Cousins 1983; Gombrich 2009, 97–110; Skilling 2009). In this respect, we must recognize that the teachings and practices that the contemporary reader encounters as "texts" have a complex history. They present themselves as oral teachings of the historical Buddha that were later preserved and transmitted through recitation.

The Early Saṅgha and Southern Buddhism

On some level, one might read the *Ānāpānasati Sutta* as an independent work, as it presents itself as a context-specific teaching of Siddhattha Gotama. However, the text derives from the early Buddhist religious community and has been preserved in the Pāli Canon, which is in turn associated with Southern Buddhism, sometimes referred to as Theravāda (Teachings of the Elders). Scholars tend not to use the pejorative term Hīnayāna (Lesser Vehicle), on the grounds that it is a sectarian label. As Roebuck indicates in her succinct discussion of the early Buddhists, "The innovation of the Mahāyāna school was not, then, the teaching of the Bodhisatta path, but the fact that this was recommended as a goal for all meditators, not just a minority who felt a particular vocation for it" (2010, xxv). Modern scholars now tend to follow Skilling's avoidance of the use of anachronistic terms such as "Theravāda" too: the epithet was not in widespread use until the twentieth century and applies a misleading label to the diverse situation and schools of early Buddhist practice.[9]

The center of the early Buddhist community was Siddhattha Gotama himself, and within the discourses we encounter an experienced teacher debating, guiding, and giving meditational advice in various settings. Indeed, in the one included here, the historical Buddha appears as particularly adaptive, creative, and above all practical. He sets up an order of monks that ignores caste, establishes an order of women, and through redeploying the vocabulary of Brahmins and ascetics of the time moves outside the parameters of conventional philosophical discourse (see, e.g., Gombrich 2009, 180–92). From the outset of his career as a teacher, he frequently enjoins the practice of the "divine abidings" (*brahmavihāra*). In addition to loving-kindness and compassion, he also emphasizes and embodies the equally important qualities of sympathetic joy, the ability to delight in the happiness of others, and equanimity, a quality of feeling untainted by partiality. In

Figure 6.2. Wall Mural Depicting the "Sermon at Deer Park"
Dambulla Cave Temple, Sri Lanka[8]
Source: Bernard Gagnon (Wikimedia Commons)

the early texts, which form the corpus of what is now known as Southern or Theravāda Buddhism, the divine abidings are all enjoined, though there is repeated emphasis on the practice of loving-kindness to all beings and behaving with compassion and kindliness to others (Aronson 1980).[10] The abidings are taught as meditation practices, to be developed in seclusion, and as features of daily life and a basis for dealing with others.

It is in the accounts of his actual behavior and interactions with others, however, that we feel most strongly Siddhattha Gotama's capacity to act and think creatively in different situations, specifically as a teacher guiding an emerging religious community and attentive to the needs of specific students. This is especially evident in his responsiveness and aptness in teaching meditation according to needs presented to him. As an elucidator, he makes frequent recourse to simile and metaphor, drawing on vocabulary, interests, and themes that would be familiar to his pupils; level of attainment and capacity are also crucial, with some querents (seekers) being given one meditation or group of practices when they first see him, then, on subsequent occasions, different ones according to new developments, and quite different ones again when insight and preparedness are ripe.[11] A system of temperament and the practice of assigning meditation objects by the "good friend," a crucial element in Southern Buddhism, are seen from the earliest layers of the canon.[12]

What is historically distinctive about the Buddha's meditation system? Realistically we cannot know for certain. Certainly his approach, advocating the middle way, does seem to differentiate him from other thinkers of the time, as does his teaching meditation to all classes, including women, regarded as equals in their capacity to find awakening. The practice of the first *jhāna*—and one can perhaps infer the other three form of *jhāna*s too—is claimed in one autobiographical account to be linked to soteriological insight in a way that does not seem to have been done before. However, we do not have texts for many other traditions at the time. The Buddhist tradition holds that the wisdom, or insight, element is distinctive, and that certain meditations are peculiar to Buddhism. Meditation on dead bodies does seem to have been peculiar to the Buddhist tradition.[13] We do not have a great deal of evidence to ascertain actual practice, but many, as Wynne argues, also seem to be adaptations of and departures from earlier methods (see Wynne 2007). In two respects, however, the way that the Buddha teaches meditation appears clearly distinctive. The first is in the very diversity of techniques that are accommodated, reshuffled, and incorporated into his system. His famous advice to the struggling meditator Meghiya, which involves the Buddha giving a number of highly varied practices to suit different needs, offers a paradigm of this adaptive skill (Ud 34–37; Shaw 2006, 24–28). This sense of a creative synthesis of practices appears unusual and unique to early Buddhism. The second is in the careful assignation of subjects to temperament, as individuals are taught a graduated path in accordance with their needs and level of attainment at the time.[14]

Whatever the origins of his meditations, attentiveness to individual needs is the most notable, and apparently unparalleled, characteristic of the way that meditation is taught throughout the *Sutta-piṭaka* and the later commentarial stories. This is especially apparent when we consider the actual situations in which the Buddha is described teaching others. When he is teaching a group of monks, he instills a sense of urgency (*saṃvega*) and vigor. This is accomplished by emphasizing a meditation that death may come at any time, and an enumeration of the variety of ways that death may occur, both to oneself and to others (see A III 303–6). To a devout and conscientious layman, however, suffering from fear of death, the advice given seems intended to reassure: the man is reminded of earlier acts of generosity and kindness, themselves recollections that are included within Buddhist meditative instructions, and confirmation given that his future rebirth will be happy (see S V 370–1). To a housewife, the Buddha compares meditative practices suitable for daily life to various kinds of cleaning (see A I 206–11; Shaw 2006, 129ff.). To arrogant Brahmins, he works primarily on views, reformulating their own doctrines with satiric wordplay, in an attempt to realign their orientation away from the practice of ritual and sacrifice, to an internal consciousness of the importance of volition (*cetanā*) and its efficacy as a means of bringing about skillful action in word, thought, and deed (see Gombrich 2009, 180–92). In talking to and about kings, he carefully refrains from attack on their authority, insisting however on the superiority of the holy life. He does obliquely warn of the dangers of kingship. In this respect, he occasionally tells stories about his own past lives, where he had avoided kingship in order to avoid the terrible consequences of inflicting punishments on others (see *Mūgapakkha Jātaka*; J no. 537). He also discusses earlier idealized monarchies, when as a universal monarch, a destiny that some seers had said was a possibility for Siddhattha Gotama himself, he had ruled by "*dhamma* not force"; here he recalls maintaining the well-being of his subjects and ensuring that they had food, drink, and a workable system of justice (see *Mahāsudassana Sutta*, D II 169–99). Such models perhaps inspired the third-century BCE King Aśoka's attempts to reform his own behavior and to implement less punitive measures. This inspiration included enjoinders to respect those in other traditions who practiced justice themselves and apparently even resulted in the abolition of the death penalty (Gombrich 1988, 127–36). Some elements of the Buddha's teaching and meditative system appear new; some adapted from contemporary practices. One defining feature of the way that the Buddha teaches the path to liberation and meditation is, however, in careful applicability to individual needs.

The "authors" of the Pāli Canon are the unknown members of the community of monks and nuns who recorded the teachings, and gave them descriptive context and life, communicated within a richly far-ranging diversity of genres and types of text. In terms of authorship and the compilation of the Pāli Canon, we should remember that the reason why the Buddha is presented in so many kinds of situations, and in so many debates and dialogues—in one, a commentator observes that his face lights up in argument (see M I 250–1)—is that he is not in fact the author of the received ancient Buddhist texts but rather the principal voice. A parallel might be found in the use of Socrates as the principal speaker in a Platonic dialogue. All Buddhas, fully awakened ones, need not only a teaching but also a group of followers for the teaching to survive. The *saṅgha* must learn, preserve, and transmit the teachings. It must remember what the Buddha did and said. Although the *Sutta-piṭaka* was described from the earliest times as "the word of the Buddha" (*Buddhavacana*), its distinctive appeal is that it is not just his words: it is a descriptive, contextualized series of creatively imagined settings, with sometimes quite different atmospheric backgrounds and modes of text, for different purposes and teaching. Through each of what are called *sutta*s, the Buddha and sometimes his followers teach and interact with others. So one text, the *Mahāsudassana Sutta* (Discourse on the Universal Monarch; D II 169–99), provides an extended storytelling of one of Gotama's past lives, involving visualization of a palace and an ideal city for the listener to create in his or her mind. Some, like the *Satipaṭṭhāna Sutta* (Discourse on the Foundations of Mindfulness; M I 55–63), are spare, mostly instructive discourses with practical instructions for practitioners. Still others, like a little untitled text in which a demon attacks a chief monk (Ud 39–41), are comic stories of mildly bantering interchanges between his followers, which nonetheless reveal all kinds of detail about the nature of the enlightened beings, called *arhat/arahant* (worthy ones), that they describe.[15] The canon includes lyrical poems, dramatic debates, and lengthy philosophical analysis based on question and answer: all of these emphasize that the Buddha's teaching takes root and is enacted in specific, sometimes problematic situations. In this respect, highly varied genres are employed as the best way of highlighting points of discussion among different social groups and providing teachings for kinds of temperaments (*carita*) at various stages of attainment. Such diverse textual parallels provide a window into the historical and religious context of early Buddhism; they reveal a dynamic religious community led by an experienced teacher, considered an awakened being, attentive to the importance of training and to the needs of particular individuals.

Scriptural recitation has historically been the lifeblood of Southern Buddhist practice, and individual texts are chanted in specific ways that have also been developed over centuries. As mentioned earlier, what eventually became the textual collection known as the "Pāli Canon," or *Tipiṭaka*, began as a descriptive collection of discourses of the historical Buddha, which were then recited from memory during various assemblies and on important occasions. At any event, the continued prevalence of the chanted textual method up to the present in Southeast Asia, at all festive occasions and at all times, means that the "I"s who now hear the expression "Thus have I heard," and chant it, feel themselves actively participating in and continuing a lineage that dates back to the earliest beginnings of the Buddhist community. This might be understood as the textual equivalent of the way in which a cutting from the Bodhi tree perpetuates contact with the original tree of the enlightenment.[16] In part for this reason, the chanting of texts and the listening to them, both considered auspicious forms of *bhāvanā* (cultivation or spiritual development), is a reminder not just of the Buddha but of the Triple Gem of the Buddha, the *dhamma* (teaching), and the monastic members of the *saṅgha*, who composed, preserved, and chanted the texts.

Peter Skilling's recent observation about the early Buddhists is equally true for present-day Southern Buddhists:

> The fact that the narrative was produced by *saṃgītikāras* [chanters] did not diminish its authority. On the one hand, the narrative was the vessel for the precious *buddhavacana* [word of the Buddha]; on the other, the *saṃgītikāras* who participated in the earliest councils were believed to be all *arhat*s. That is, the product—the Buddha's words—was packaged by an elect elite (and further guaranteed by their *praṇidhijñāna* [personal knowledge based on resolve]). What could be more authoritative? The whole text, the *buddhavacana* in its narrative setting, was imbued with power and came to be recited to bring blessings, prosperity, and protection. (2010, 15; see also Skilling 2009)

It is worth bearing these features in mind when we consider that the meditation discussed in this chapter has primarily been taught through oral/aural methods, from one person to another. According to Southern Buddhism, awakening or enlightenment is usually found through hearing the teaching, at some point, from someone else: chanting or hearing these texts, regarded as so auspicious, is felt to be one expression of strong supporting conditions (*upanissaya*), conditions that help one to attain liberation and a new stage of meditation. One such condition is personal contact with a teacher or "good friend."

Thus, before considering the *sutta* and its associated practice, it is important to recognize that the very act of listening to any recited text is considered an auspicious form of *bhāvanā*. This was true in the early Buddhist community, and it remains true in contemporary Southeast Asia and Sri Lanka, with the audience and the chanters all participating in a collective exercise felt to be a central support and part of the meditative process. For modern Westerners, especially those unfamiliar with this Buddhist view and practice, it is important to understand the close relationship between what we call "meditation" and other activities felt necessary to support and balance it. The latter include *dhamma* discussion, listening to chanting, chanting itself, visiting temples, giving food to monks, and even having fun on a festival day. All of these are aspects of *bhāvanā*, and all are considered essential accompaniments to meditation itself. In this respect, we might also reflect on the degree to which such activities are themselves "contemplative practices" and thus, in the process, expand our conception of meditation. If one watches people at temples on a festival day (*uposatha*) as texts are being chanted, some will be listening attentively, some joining in, some meditating, some snoozing, and some keeping children entertained or looking out of a window. There is, of course, a place for solitary meditation, and retreats are held that emphasize this. However, someone may also practice meditation quietly while the festival is going on, and such people can be seen in any Southern Buddhist temple on a major occasion. Conversely, most meditation retreats involve daily visits to communal meditation halls to listen to talks, to chant and hear texts, as well as to participate in communal meals and meditation practice.[17] Even if, and perhaps sometimes because, everyone is silent, the presence of others doing the same thing creates a collective atmosphere that can be dipped in and out of for private practice. As we will see in the text considered here, this sense of a balance between the communal and the solitary, and of the need for supporting activities as well as private meditation, seem to have been present from the outset of the tradition.

Indeed in a nonliterate but not necessarily uneducated society, the effect of the "world" of a particular text would be particularly powerful and the *sutta* would be listened to with some attentiveness and familiarity. In this respect, some key words and phrases, found in many such texts and often with pericopes, or sections of text, would be repeated in the same way in different *suttas*.[18] So, the instructions for mindfulness of breathing given in the *Ānāpānasati Sutta* are found in the same way in various *suttas*. As Gethin has demonstrated, the chanted form of a text offers those listening to participate in the instructions given and to respond to words, such as *sati*, *samādhi*, *paññā*, which would key listeners in to the qualities named (Gethin 1992b). This would be particularly the case in the *sutta* under discussion here: mindfulness of breathing is one of the few practices with lengthy explanation of procedure given as the practice is described. Even if the texts are heard with only moderate attentiveness—at *Mahāpirit*s for instance,[19] when the chants go on all night—the effect of the words, the rhythms, and the repetitions seem to seep through to the unconscious mind: something about the chanting makes phrases, words, and little bits of teaching memorable and part of one's semi-conscious imaginative life. The nearest analogy seems to be with the status and role of biblical teaching and readings, admittedly vernacular, in the West. In my own lifetime, most schoolchildren learned large sections of the Bible, and most Christians, particularly in rural communities, would use the language of the King James Bible in daily expressions. It was just part of the way that perceptions about the world and social, interior, and public life are and were articulated. It is my impression that the same process occurs in Southeast Asia. Certainly the epithet "one who has heard much" (*bahussuta*) is constantly used as a term of praise for a practitioner by the Buddha (A II 6 and A III 113): just having heard texts on many occasions is of central importance for the path, as it keys the practitioner in to a particular meditation when he or she wishes to pursue it.[20]

So when the *sutta* on mindfulness of breathing is chanted, as it often it is, some laypeople will be participating, but perhaps only a few take it as the basis for practice. Some, however, will see it as a practice to follow, because they have done it before, are doing it at that time, or will do on a subsequent occasion. In Southeast Asia all men become monks for a short period, and many learn meditation then, even if they do not continue with it. Some take the ancient pattern of seeing meditation as especially beneficial for the old; groups of elderly women in Thailand, and some younger women as well, can often be seen visiting temples, chanting, and meditating together. Although the extent to which laypeople have historically practiced "meditation" in the modern Western sense of the term is still open, and realistically has probably varied, something of this pattern, of some joining in and others supporting the process in other ways, can be inferred from descriptions of lay practice at the time of the Buddha. One *sutta* describes hundreds of laypeople, both men and women, meditating "dressed in white, who enjoy the pleasures of the senses [a usual description of lay life] and yet carry out my instruction, listen to my advice, have gone beyond doubt, become free from uncertainty, have found complete confidence, and become independent of others in the dispensation of the teacher" (M I 491).

The *Ānāpānasati Sutta* is found in a collection known as the *Majjhimanikāya* (Middle Length Discourses), which is part of this *Sutta-piṭaka*. The former collection stands in contrast to the *Dīghanikāya* (Longer Length Discourses), *Saṃyuttanikāya* (Connected Discourses), and *Aṅguttaranikāya* (Graduated Discourses). Before the advent of writing, groups of monks charged with maintaining the chanted traditions, the *bhāṇakas*, would take responsibility for a single collection. Possibly influenced by these separate lineages, each collection acquires a certain overall identity and character, even though some texts are found in several collections. The literary distinctiveness of each can be seen in structure, ordering, content, and sometimes style. Among these, the *Majjhimanikāya* is perhaps the most accessible and popular of the four *nikāya*s (collections). It contains descriptions of situations, dialogues, and teachings for specific situations. It is divided into three sets of fifty, though the last contains fifty-two, and presents some of the most famous texts, such as the *Satipaṭṭhāna Sutta* (Discourse on the Foundations of Mindfulness; no. 10) and *Kāyagatāsati Sutta* (Discourse on Mindfulness of Body; no. 119), as well as the one discussed here, on breathing mindfulness (no. 120). Bhikkhus Ñāṇamoli and Bodhi write of this collection, which they refer to as MN, as follows:

> If the MN were to be characterized by a single phrase to distinguish it from the other books of the Pali canon, this might be done by describing it as the collection that combines the richest variety of contextual settings with the deepest and most comprehensive assortment of teachings. (2001, 20).

The collection also contains many texts in which disciples teach within the *sutta*s, with their words approved by the Buddha. Many types of individuals and situations are also addressed. The collection depicts what seems to be the public, interactive face of early Buddhism, demonstrating the health of the Buddhist monastic community as it goes about its round of teaching, discussion, alms rounds, and meditation in practice. The collection also contains many dialogues between the Buddha and people from all walks of lives, where he makes extensive use of apt simile and offers some of the more easily assimilable teachings. His followers also have a strong presence.[21]

A spirit of dialogue permeates all of the *sutta* collections and discourses given within them, even though the dialogue involved is sometimes rhetorical: many *sutta*s involve the Buddha posing a question and then answering it. Sometimes this is in the manner of a catechism (religious education); at other times it is addressed to and answered by a querent; perhaps most frequently it appears to be a literary device, possibly peculiar to an oral/aural tradition. In the *Ānāpānasati Sutta*, this can be seen by the posing of questions by the Buddha, who then answers them himself. Other oral features found throughout the canon are the extensive use of both redundancy and repetitive formulae. As discussed in more detail later in this chapter, the listening to chants is itself regarded as a meditative activity, and taking repetitions, with slight variations to a list according to different categories, are part of the whole process of chanting and listening.

As mentioned, the *Ānāpānasati Sutta* (Discourse on Mindfulness of Breathing) presents itself as a discourse of the historical Buddha on the practice of mindfulness of breathing. Addressed to an assembly of monks, it is contained in the *Sutta-piṭaka* section of the Pāli Canon. We may in turn

Three Characteristics of Existence (tilakkhaṇa)	Four Foundations of Mindfulness (satipaṭṭhāna)	Five Faculties (pañcindriyāni)	Seven Factors of Enlightenment (sattā bojjhaṅgā)
1. impermanence (anicca) 2. dis-ease (dukkha) 3. non-self (anattā)	1. body (kāya) 2. feeling (vedanā) 3. mind (citta) 4. phenomena (dhammā)	1. faith (saddhā) 2. vigor (viriya) 3. mindfulness (sati) 4. concentration (samādhi) 5. wisdom (paññā)	1. mindfulness (sati) 2. investigation (dhammavicaya) 3. effort (viriya) 4. joy (pīti) 5. tranquility (passadhi) 6. concentration (samādhi) 7. equanimity (upekkhā)

Figure 6.3. Some Key Dimensions of Southern Buddhist Meditation

locate it within a larger corpus of ancient Buddhist texts on meditation. The first four stages of the practice are described in the *Satipaṭṭhāna Sutta* (Discourse on the Foundations of Mindfulness; M III 55–63; see Shaw 2006, 76–85). The stages described in the text are also constantly used in other texts (see, e.g., the various texts included in the section on mindfulness of breathing in the *Saṃyuttanikāya*; S V 311–341, passim). Two great meditation manuals, Buddhaghosa's *Visuddhimagga* (Path of Purification) and Upatissa's *Vimuttimagga* (Path of Freedom) accord the subject extensive treatment (see Vism VIII 145 and PF 156–66).

Samatha, Vipassanā, and the Path to Liberation

The *Ānāpānasati Sutta* describes a foundational Buddhist contemplative practice referred to as "mindfulness of breathing" (*ānāpānasati*). The practice is taught in sixteen stages and involves paying attention to the breath as it moves in and out of the body, through a variety of different methods. The stages of the practice are regarded as comprehensive within the early Buddhist path, providing both calm and insight. Key to the practice is the cultivation of mindfulness, a factor in Buddhism notoriously difficult to translate (see Shaw 2006, 76ff.), but which is compared in one *sutta* to the gatekeeper of a city who "refuses entrance to those unknown but admits those he knows for the protection of those inside" (A IV 110). Mindfulness (*sati*) is certainly related to insight, and hence to *vipassanā* meditation. It is, however, also regarded as essential for the pursuit of *samatha* and *jhāna* (meditation). According to the *Abhidhamma*, mindfulness only occurs in moments of skillful consciousness and indeed may be perceived as a defining feature of that. It is not considered possible to attain any skillful state or meditation without the presence of mindfulness, which in *jhāna* becomes one of the five faculties of faith, vigor, mindfulness, concentration, and wisdom, all regarded as essential for the correct practice of meditation (DhS 12–16). This is worth bearing in mind when considering meditations for the pursuit of both calm and insight.

The goal of the Buddhist path is awakening (*bodhi*), the liberation of the mind through the eradication of the defilements and the latent tendencies of many lives that govern this and future rebirths. The historical Buddha taught that humans are trapped in *saṃsāra*, the apparently endless cycle of birth, death, and rebirth, which is determined by *kamma* (Skt.: *karma*), the universal law of moral cause and effect. The existential and soteriological response to this situation is the encouragement of the cultivation of steps that may in time lead to *nibbāna* (Skt.: *nirvāna*), or liberation from *saṃsāra*. *Nibbāna* is not regarded quite as a "destination" as in the sense of a train stop, or an annihilation of events: rather it is seen as the complete expression of felicities that may be found also on the path to awakening too, as well as in its attainment.[22] Its most commonly associated adjective is simply "happy" (see, e.g., J I 392). From an early Buddhist perspective, awakening is found through the union of calm, an emotional purification, and insight, the ability to see—without fear, hatred, or attachment—the three signs or characteristics of existence: impermanence (*anicca*), dis-ease (*dukkha*; also translated as suffering), and non-self (*anattā*). The mind searches for calm, contentment, or stillness (*samatha*), but it also needs to see "things as they are" (*yathābhūtaṃ*) through insight (*vipassanā*). In this way, one can become free from attachment to things as permanent, pleasant, or "mine." At some level both need and support the other: selflessness is a feature of the divine abidings and the state of *jhāna*, the meditation that the Buddha rediscovered before awakening. This is described at each of its stages as involving wisdom too, both as a power and a faculty (DhS 1ff.; see Cousins 1984). Moreover, perhaps as can be seen from the evidence of daily life, insight without a sense of stability and peace will not lead to awakening but to fear, panic, and imbalance of mind; insight requires the practitioner to already have a sense of contentment and unification, the fifth factor of *jhāna* (*ekaggatā*; see also Shaw 2006, 3–4).

The Buddha constantly taught both insight and calm. Specific instances within the texts usually involve calm preceding insight, but not always.[23] One early text describes four routes to awakening: the practice of calm before insight, the practice of insight before calm, the two "yoked" together, and an excitement with the *dhamma* that produces realization (A II 157). Those who work by developing calm have from early times been described as following the "wet" method; those who follow the insight path are described as using the "dry" method (see Cousins 1984). This can sometimes lead to misunderstanding between those who favor one and who find the other slightly strange. Generalizations are risky, but it could be said that insight practitioners primarily value a kind of clarity of perception (*saññā*), while calm practitioners tend to value the intuitive and precision of feeling (*vedanā*). Both approaches are validated within the canon; both strands are said to come together at the first and subsequent stages of enlightenment, when the mind enters the liberating *jhāna* of awakening.[24] According to the *Abhidhamma*, at this moment every single path factor comes into play (see DhS 277, 296). The vitality of the tension between *samatha* and *vipassanā* is ongoing, with some schools favoring one to be cultivated first, particularly with regard to the practice of mindfulness of breathing, which is the practice described in the *Ānāpānasati Sutta*. Mindfulness of breathing is unusual in that it can be taught with an emphasis on either or both elements at first. It is worth mentioning that all Buddhist meditation schools teach, in addition to the sitting practice itself, the need for good behavior, loving-kindness and compassion in the world, generosity, as well as listening to scriptural recitation and textual discussion. One text enjoins as follows: "Hearing *dhamma* at the right time, discussion of *dhamma* at the right time, calm (*samatha*) at the right time, insight (*vipassanā*) at the right time" (A II 141). From the point of view of the early texts, it should also be noted that practitioners of all kinds are described, including the "four assemblies": monks, nuns, laymen, and laywomen. The best conditions for meditation are those in which ordination has been taken. The monk or nun lives what is known as the higher or the "holy life," regarded as "free from dust" (S V 351). Clearly it was, at the time of the composition of the texts, usual for laypeople to practice too, often in groups, and their attainments and merits are also described.[25] Some preparation for meditation, such as following the five basic precepts and, under certain conditions for laypeople, eight or ten precepts, is also enjoined (see Shaw 2006, 12–15).

Returning to Buddhist meditation proper, and specifically considering the so-called forty objects of Buddhist meditation, we find that there is nothing that cannot be an object for meditation (*kammaṭṭhāna*) of some kind. From a Buddhist perspective, any event can inspire insight into the three signs of impermanence, dis-ease, and non-self, that is, the three marks of existence. So the commentarial *Dhammapada* (Verses of the Teaching) stories describe meditators reaching their final goal after practicing meditation and then being supported by various phenomena and experiences. For example, some see a candle flickering and its flame dying away, foam arising and falling across the surface of water, flowers in all stages of bud, growth, and decay. Others hear some words of teaching that happen to come to them at the right time, and with the right effect. At these moments the practitioners become enlightened. Indeed, the very same objects that produce soteriological insight are sometimes used to establish calm first. A representative example is the story of the goldsmith's son who develops calm meditation and proficiency in *jhāna* by reflecting on a beautiful golden flower. Then, following the Buddha's further guidance and encouragement, he moves on to insight by seeing the flower wither before him (see Roebuck 2010, 198). The Buddha often intercedes to help people over difficult patches and to encourage them to take the next step.[26]

From the outset of the tradition, a meditative system is established, however, involving objects particularly suitable to cultivate and to develop, with corresponding stages, the qualities to reach this stage of ripeness for awakening, described in the aforementioned stories. According to the fifth-century commentator Buddhaghosa, a Brahmin Buddhist monk who lived and worked in Sri Lanka, there are forty objects that are particularly efficacious for arousing calm. These include the following: (1) the ten *kasiṇa*s (visual objects), meditations on a mandala of earth, water, air, fire, blue, yellow, red, white, light, or limited space; (2) the ten impure (*asubha*) objects, on the stages of decomposition of a corpse; (3) the ten recollections, which comprise recollection of the Buddha, his teaching (*dhamma*), his community (*saṅgha*), restraint (*sīla*), generosity, gods (*devas*), death, body, breath, and peace; (4) the four divine abidings of loving-kindness, compassion, sympathetic joy, and equanimity; (5) the four formless spheres, of infinite space, of infinite consciousness, of no-thingness, and of neither perception nor nonperception; (6) the perception of the loathsomeness of food; and lastly (7) the defining of the four elements. These are assigned quite specifically to particular temperaments, often in conjunction with others that might balance their effect (see Vism III 74–133; Vajirañāṇa 1975, 98, 103ff.; Shaw 2006, 8ff.).

As Vajirañāṇa, a leading twentieth-century monk and scholar, notes, the practice of mindfulness of breathing, the twenty-ninth object selected by Buddhaghosa, is regarded from the outset of the tradition as the "root" (*mūla*) meditation object (1975, 227). As we have seen, it is associated with the final awakening of Buddha Gotama, the historical Buddha, and, it is said, with all Buddhas before him. The meditation associated with the text reproduced here was recommended by the Buddha as a complete method for attaining liberation, and he praises it as the noble abode (*ariyavihāra*), the divine abode (*brahmavihāra*), and the Buddha abode (*Tathāgata vihāra*; S V 326). Its immediacy and availability marks it out from the other objects: it is the only object of the forty that, according to Buddhaghosa, is apprehended in its early stages solely by touch, as the practitioner has to feel the breath as it enters his body, rather than by sight or hearing.[27]

It is from the point of view of the development of both calm and insight, however, that this practice is considered particularly important, for it arouses both, and hence describes elements with the potential to take the practitioner to enlightenment. Pursued in one way it can be developed for calm, as it becomes a basis for the practice of all four *jhāna* (*rūpa*) meditations. We have encountered the first meditation described in the Buddha's life story: it is accompanied by initial and discursive thought, joy, happiness, and one-pointedness. The first *jhāna* is compared in the texts to pieces of soap combined with water by a bath attendant so that they make a cohesive ball. The second meditation involves the dropping of the first two factors, of initial thought (*vitakka*) and discursive thought (*vicāra*). It is described as "inwardly calmed," because the factors associated with speech have been left behind; possessing unification (*ekodibhāva*), it is associated with tranquil confidence (*sampasādanam*). It is compared to a natural pool of clear water, where streams bubble in but which is inwardly contained. The third meditation abandons the factor of joy, and the mind becomes equable (*upekkhako*), with mindfulness and clear comprehension now strong. It is compared to brightly colored lotuses, growing and blossoming in clear water. The fourth meditation drops even happiness: the meditator relinquishes pleasure and pain and enters into a state of mindfulness and equanimity, undisturbed by discomfort or ease. He is compared to a man sitting covered in a pure white cloth, covered from head to foot (see D I 71–85). Adverting to the peaceful and joyful aspects of the breath is said to be capable of taking the meditator through all of these stages; this is accomplished through the development of the object (*nimitta*) that arises on the basis of the practice. The object of the breath, with its rise, fall, and impermanence, always contains some element of insight and the development of the faculties of mindfulness and wisdom. When these are brought into balance with confidence or faith (*saddhā*), vigor and concentration (*samādhi*), the practitioner can move through all four *jhāna*s. From then, if he or she so wishes, it is possible to cultivate enjoyment of the great powers of the mind (*abhiññā*), or the exercise of formless meditations (see, e.g., Cousins 1973, 1984; Gunaratana 1985). The meditator may also, however, move on to insight, or in some cases, develop this more at the outset. This is the gradual discernment of the three signs of impermanence, dis-ease, and non-self. The breath is also a natural object for this, as it is for the joyful alertness required for calm: it rises and falls; is not always even, smooth, or "satisfactory"; and is not owned. It cannot be held on to or grasped and never stays still or static. As far as we can tell, the historical Buddha valued the simply expressed and the vernacular, and this description tries to conform to the spirit of his formulation. Perhaps we could say, in modern terms, that the breath is an object that through the variety of its characteristics may be developed in such a way as to arouse both calm and insight.

Mindfulness of Breathing according to the *Ānāpānasati Sutta*

As has become clear, the *Ānāpānasati Sutta* is an early discourse of Siddhattha Gotama, the historical Buddha, wherein he discusses "awareness" or "attentiveness" (*sati*) of inhalation and exhalation (*ānāpāna*). The first notable feature of the *Ānāpānasati Sutta* is its evocation of community: the teaching is given to a large group of monastic practitioners, who are already well established in the Buddhist path. The discourse is given on the night of the full moon, an occasion still marked in Buddhist countries by visits to the temple. Two additional contexts are involved. First, the *sutta* opens with the community meeting on Pavāraṇā, the day that marks the end of the eleventh lunar month of Vassa and the annual Buddhist rain retreat. The assembled monks would thus have been on their annual rain retreat, a three-month period of intensive meditation during which there might be less contact with the laity. However, the actual teaching on mindfulness of breathing occurs during the festival of Komudī, the full moon day of the fourth lunar month of Kattika. This is the time when the white lotus is in full flower, which represents awakening or enlightenment in Buddhism. Komudī is the last full moon of the rains, when the monastic orders would have been getting ready to move back into their usual life and contacts, with daily interaction with the laity. Those who are listening to the discourse have been practicing, teaching, and learning from each other, preparing themselves for this evening; many have streamed in from round about, hearing that the Buddha is going to speak. There are those present at all stages on the path to enlightenment, and the Buddha delineates all of them. They include the enlightened, who have freed themselves from the "fetters" that bind to existence; the nonreturners, who have eradicated the five lower fetters and will not be reborn again; the once-returners, who have eradicated the three lower fetters and will obtain enlightenment within one lifetime; and the stream-enterers, those who will attain enlightenment within seven lifetimes.[28] Among these, and others, are many who have practiced at various levels the thirty-seven constituents of awakening: the four foundations of mindfulness, the four right efforts, the four bases of spiritual success, the five faculties, the five powers, the seven factors of awakening, and the noble Eightfold Path (see Gethin 1992a). The Buddha lists all of these, and the various meditations that are undertaken by those present. The latter include the divine abidings, the impure, the perception of impermanence, and mindfulness of breathing. It is as though the range of attainment, diversity of approach and difference in practice within the *saṅgha*, at the end of the period put aside for meditation, is being purposefully praised and validated, as is the continued teaching of newcomers and practitioners at every level being taught "the distinctive excellence" (*uḷara pubbenāpara visesa*) of each stage of a particular practice.

Having aroused great confidence in his audience, the Buddha speaks in praise of mindfulness of breathing, a practice that leads, he says, to all of the four foundations of mindfulness, and then to the seven factors of awakening (see later discussion herein). He asks the following rhetorical questions: What are the benefits of mindfulness of breathing? How is it to be cultivated and "made much of" (*bahulikata*), an expression sometimes translated as "practiced frequently"? How is it of great fruit and great reward?

The Buddha begins with specific instructions about what the meditator needs to do in order to undertake the practice; this is done in a series of instructions found in many places in the canon (see, e.g., D II 290; M I 59; S V 317). One must find an "empty space," perhaps at the roots of a tree or in a forest; sit cross-legged; make the body straight; and "set up mindfulness before [oneself]."[29] The practitioner following these instructions goes through sixteen stages—presumably the "distinctive excellences" of each stage of this practice (listed in the following tetrads). The description itself, through its rhythms, repeated words, and pace, seems to have been composed to support the meditational advice it enjoins. The list is associated with the four foundations of mindfulness (*satipaṭṭhāna*), aroused through practice on the breath. The sixteen stages of the practice are listed here in their tetrads, with some explanation and comment on supporting material for each stage.

First Tetrad: Mindfulness of Body

1. Mindfully he knows: I breathe in a long breath. Mindfully he knows: I breathe out a long breath.

2. Mindfully he knows: I breathe in a short breath. Mindfully he knows: I breathe out a short breath.

3. Then he trains for each successive stage of the practice: Experiencing the whole body I breathe in. Experiencing the whole body I breathe out.

4. Making tranquil the bodily formation I shall breathe in. Making tranquil the bodily formation I shall breathe out.

These first four stages are listed in the *Satipaṭṭhāna Sutta* (Discourse on the Foundations of Mindfulness) under mindfulness of body. In that text, though not here, the attention of the meditator is compared to a skilled wood-turner, who knows if he is turning a long turn or a short one (M I 56). There are a number of features, even of the first line of these instructions, which have been the subject of debate since the earliest times and which give some indication of the subtle practical implications involved in the exegesis of just a few lines of texts involving meditational advice. For instance, is *ānā* the in-breath or the out-breath, and *pāna* the out-breath or the in-breath? There was an ancient controversy on this issue, with the Vinaya (Monastic Rules) and Upatissa's *Vimuttimagga* (Path of Freedom), a commentary extant only in an early Chinese translation, placing the out-breath first (see PF 157, 160). Most sources, however, take the in-breath first, on the grounds that it is the first breath taken at human birth (see Vajirañāṇa 1975, 230–33). Indeed, the practice is usually translated and undertaken with the in-breath as the first breath. There is another feature that has historically had practical implications: there is no "middle"-length breath as one might expect, that of the usual daily breath, which suggests that the stages are carefully distinguished from the outset. Modern calm (*samatha*) schools and teachers often make a distinction between making "long" and the "short" breaths at the early stages of the practice, in order to allow more flexibility and confidence in the practitioner with regard to entering and leaving various meditations. In contrast, insight (*vipassanā*) schools and teachers, which do not take the practice to the cultivation of *jhāna*, tend to encourage the practitioner to let the breath do what it wants, the emphasis being rather on watching aspects of the rise and fall of the breath from the abdomen (cf. Nyanaponika Thera 1962, 109ff; Buddhadāsa 1997, 54–55). From the point of view of the literary immediacy of the text, it is noteworthy that the first two stages of the instruction are given in the present tense, and the meditator "knows" the length of breath, perhaps indicating that these stages are intended to anchor the practitioner in his or her present state. All of the other fourteen are in the future, prefaced by the words "he trains," suggesting a graduated movement on from these first two. This point is, oddly enough, not discussed in commentaries and critiques of the practice, so any comments here are conjectural. These stages are practiced in various ways, but the tetrad forms the basis of most modern meditative systems on the breath. As the renowned twentieth-century Thai Buddhist meditation teacher, Buddhadāsa (1906–1993), writes of them,

> knowing the long breath, knowing the short breath, knowing how the breath regulates the body, and contemplating the breath in order to calm the body. These four steps are not difficult if we sincerely observe and genuinely study in a scientific way. (Buddhadāsa 1997, 53)

Second Tetrad: Mindfulness of Feeling

1. Experiencing joy (*pīti*), I shall breathe in. Experiencing joy, I shall breathe out.
2. Experiencing happiness (*sukha*), I shall breathe in. Experiencing happiness, I shall breathe out.
3. Experiencing the mind formations, I shall breathe in. Experiencing the mind formations, I shall breathe out.
4. Making tranquil the mind formation, I shall breathe in. Making tranquil the mind formation, I shall breathe out.

While the first tetrad is associated with establishing mindfulness of the body and the breath itself, the second is associated with establishing mindfulness of feeling. It involves the active cultivation of the two *jhāna* factors of joy and happiness, suggesting that the meditator encourages them as a basis for becoming aware of the state and condition of the mind (*citta*). These are then made tranquil, just as the body had been made tranquil in the first tetrad. Joy is compared in one text to a thirsty man in a desert seeing a pool of water; happiness is the feeling that arises when he has drunk and washed in it. This sense of refreshment, culminating in feeling of tranquility in the mind, is felt to be a central part of practice on the breath.

Third Tetrad: Mindfulness of Mind

1. Experiencing the mind, I shall breathe in. Experiencing the mind, I shall breathe out.
2. Gladdening the mind, I shall breathe in. Gladdening the mind, I shall breathe out.
3. Concentrating the mind, I shall breathe in. Concentrating the mind, I shall breathe out.
4. Liberating the mind (*vimocayaṃ cittaṃ*), I shall breathe in. Liberating the mind, I shall breathe out.

The third stage is associated with establishing mindfulness of the mind (*citta*), which is successively experienced, gladdened, concentrated, and finally liberated. Buddhadāsa provides the following comment on this stage:

Liberating the mind means not letting the mind become attached to anything. We make the mind let go of anything it is grasping. Such a mind is spotlessly clean; it is free. Liberating the mind from all attachments has two aspects: the mind can let go of all these things, or we can take those things away from the mind. The results are the same. We take away all the things that the *citta* should not hold on to. Then we observe if there is anything to which the *citta* continues to cling. If so, we try to release those things from the mind. (1997, 86–87)

Fourth Tetrad: Mindfulness of Dhammas

1. Contemplating impermanence (*anicca*), I shall breathe in. Contemplating impermanence, I shall breathe out.

2. Contemplating dispassion (*virāga*), I shall breathe in. Contemplating dispassion, I shall breathe out.

3. Contemplating cessation (*nirodha*), I shall breathe in. Contemplating cessation, I shall breathe out.

4. Contemplating letting go (*vossaga*), I shall breathe in. Contemplating letting go, I shall breathe out.

In this last tetrad, all four components are prefaced by the same verb, *anupassati*, which means "to look on," "to contemplate," or "to observe." This tetrad is suggestive of the movement of the mind to the watching of the rise and fall of all events, free from partiality. Here *dhamma* refers to phenomena. After the body, feelings, and mind have all been established in mindfulness, this last tetrad is particularly associated with *vipassanā* (insight) meditation, just as the first three are associated with *samatha* (calm) meditation. Indeed just noting the succession of the stages is a good way of understanding the relationship between the two approaches to meditation: from the establishment of the practice and the tranquillization of the body in the first tetrad to the "letting go" of the last, where, like the breath, any attachments are relinquished. From the earliest moments of Buddhist history, the first twelve stages have been particularly associated with establishing calm in the mind, and the last four with insight (PF 163).

Once one has become established in the four foundations of mindfulness, one applies the seven factors of awakening to the practice of mindfulness of breathing. The seven factors of awakening are mindfulness, investigation, effort, joy, tranquility, concentration, and equanimity. As documented in the *Ānāpānasati Sutta* and other relevant Buddhist texts on meditation, they appear to have a special relationship with the practice of mindfulness of breathing. This is true even though they are often mentioned more generally as important to the path, characterizing its attainment, fruit, and development (see Gethin 1992a, 168ff.). In the *Ānāpānasati Sutta*, each factor is described as leading naturally to the next, and all seven factors are necessary for cultivation on the path. They seem to arise as products of mindfulness of breathing practice and also as ways of ensuring that the practice is cultivated in a healthy and natural way. The seven factors of awakening are famously associated with balance, and the bringing of good health to the mind and body: there are stories in the canon of *arhat*s being healed from illness after hearing them being chanted (S V 79–82); to this day in Southeast Asia a short chant based on them is recited over sickbeds. Elsewhere they are described as "clothes" that a king or a minister might wish to wear on a particular occasion: sometimes mindfulness is needed, sometimes investigation, and sometimes joy (see S V 70–72).

To a certain extent, through its interplay of calm and insight and the way that the seven factors are to be applied and interact with one another for each tetrad, the *Ānāpānasati Sutta* seems to have encouraged the diversity of practice and emphasis at each stage that is perhaps one of the most striking features of the modern practice of mindfulness of breathing as it is taught by various modern schools. Further developments within the practice are provided by an ancient commentarial division of the practice into stages of counting, following, touching, and settling (PF 159–60). Buddhaghosa adds another four that complete the practice for the practitioner, allowing him to set it down and to use any given meditation practice as a basis for insight and for a return to daily life: observing, turning away, purification, and looking back (Vism VIII 189). While different approaches encourage the breath to be viewed in various ways, the practice itself is felt to be a unified and self-sufficient means of obtaining liberation and insight:

> Practice is like a seed; it is the cause of merit. Fulfillment is like the flower or a fruit, because it proceeds from a similar thing. If mindfulness of respiration is practiced, the four foundations of mindfulness are fulfilled. If the four foundations of mindfulness are practiced, the seven enlightenment factors are fulfilled. If the seven enlightenment factors are practiced, freedom and wisdom are fulfilled. (PF 163–64; see also S V 329)

Breathing with the Buddhist Tradition

Mindfulness of breathing meditation has occupied a central position in the Buddhist tradition from the time of the earliest community to the present. From the earliest texts and accounts of the Buddha's own reliance on mindfulness of breathing, individual practitioners are described. The Buddha frequently recommends the practice to meditators. This commonly occurs in *suttas* that are addressed generally to "monks," a generic term for the entire monastic community on some occasions but also a reference to specific individuals. The monk Meghiya, who goes to meditate without seeking advice, finds himself beleaguered by distracting thoughts, desires, and annoyances. He is given a selection of practices by the Buddha, each designed to address imbalances in his mental state and temperament: the practice of loving-kindness to address ill will, the practice on the impure to address desire, mindfulness of breathing to address distracting thoughts (*vitakka*), and an insight practice on non-self to address the conceit "I am" (*asmimāna*). Indeed, one *sutta* describes a group of monks, who, in excessive enthusiasm for meditation on the impure, start to become deeply disturbed, so that the suicide rate rockets. Upon returning from a retreat, the Buddha finds those the remaining monks and immediately teaches them all mindfulness of breathing. This is clearly regarded as the antidote to imbalance: the monks are restored to equilibrium and well-being, with unhappiness and self-disgust dispelled by mindfulness of breathing, just "as a monsoon rain cloud dispels the heat" (S V 322). Another canonical text associates this practice, when used for *samatha*, with an unwavering mind and body, so that neither trembles (S V 316). The meditation is said to be particularly suitable for temperaments characterized by distracting thoughts (see, e.g., A I 449; PF 69). Oddly enough, the *Abhidhamma* does not mention the practice, apparently including it under the closely related practice on the air element.³⁰ The early Sri Lankan commentator on meditation, Upatissa, whose dates are unknown but who possibly composed his manual in the century before that of Buddhaghosa (see Ehara et al. 1977, xlii), writes the following with regard to mindfulness of breathing, specifically associating it with the element of air:

> Why is air contact pleasant? Because it calms the mind. It is comparable to the soothing of a heavenly musician's mind with sweet sounds. By this discursive thinking is suppressed. And again, it is like a person walking along the bank of a river. His mind is collected, is directed towards one object, and does not wander. Therefore in mindfulness of respiration, the suppression of discursive thought is taught. (PF 166)

Some meditations are considered especially suitable for the moment of death, helping the possibility of a fortunate future rebirth; these include recollection of the Buddha, the *dhamma* (teachings) and the community of monks, one's own generosity, and good deeds that have been performed in one's life. These are considered ways to bring confidence and composure to the practitioner at this time. Buddhist monks often visit those who are about to die and chant with and for them. Mindfulness of breathing is also singled out in the texts as helpful to practice at this time: "Rāhula, when mindfulness of breathing is developed in this way, those breathings that are final, are known when they cease; they do not cease unknown" (M I 425–26).

The *Ānāpānasati Sutta* is prominent in the schools of Southern Buddhism, but most traditions of Buddhism also practice some form of mindfulness of breathing. In some cases, the practice is based on this *sutta* or related Sanskrit versions (*Ānāpānasmṛti Sūtra*). In others, the practice follows adaptations of the associated exercises. Ascertaining the history and meditative influence of this particular *sutta/sūtra* would be a useful research exercise in itself: tracing its centrality in the tradition, as Glenn Wallis has suggested, would show how meditation, practice, text, and historical transmission have been linked in various Buddhist contexts.³¹ Indeed, one of the earliest extant Buddhist manuscripts (dat. 148–170 CE) of the *Ānāpānasati Sutta* is a longer Sanskrit version, which had been taken by An Shigao (d. 168 CE), the Parthian monk, to China. As the Chinese were already familiar with breathing exercises associated with Daoism, this text might have had an immediate and obvious appeal.

From the outset, there seem to have been early variations of the practice. Vasubandhu's *Abhidharma-kośabhāṣyam* (Compendium of Abhidharma), for instance, lists cultivation of the impure and mindfulness of breathing as preliminary practices. As in the Pāli Canon, mindfulness of breathing is recommended for those with distracting thoughts (*adhivitarka*). Adapting the methods described by the commentaries, it goes through the stages of counting, following, touching, and settling, along with observing (*upalakṣaṇā*), changing (*vivartanā*) to observation of the skillful roots and purification (*pariśuddhi*) (AKBh 341.6–8; Pradhan 1975).³² What has come to be known as the *Yogalehrbuch*, a fifth-century Sanskrit manuscript of unknown origin found in Kizil, delineates a variety of meditation objects, differing slightly from the Southern Buddhist forty but retaining many comparable elements, including the full sixteen stages of the breathing mindfulness practice. This text introduces a visual element linked to the instructions for mindfulness of breathing as they are given in the *Ānāpānasati Sutta* and elsewhere. The associated practice allows images that the practitioner develops in the mind's eye to arise and dissolve, presumably training flexibility in the use of handling visual phenomena in the mind, as well as linking them to the rise and fall of the breath.[33] Exercises associated with the breath also have been adapted in Chan (China), Son (Korea), and Zen (Japan) schools (Nan 1997, 80ff.). Tiantai Buddhism also uses the text for arousing calm and insight: its founder, Zhiyi (538–597), compiled various treatises on the practice, adapting the techniques and exploring the nature of various qualities and kinds of breath in meditation for calm and insight in the *Mohe zhiguan* (Great Calming and Contemplation; see Luk 1964, 110; Donner and Stevenson 1993). In Tibet, the practice of mindfulness of breathing forms the basis of Mahāmudrā (Great Seal) meditation (Zahler 2009, 80ff.). The practice and text appear to have been less influential in Tibet initially, though they do play a role in the Gelug, Kagyu, and Nyingma schools. Mindfulness of breathing is also part of contemporary Tibetan Buddhist meditation practice; it is primarily taught as a means of stilling the mind and establishing mindfulness at the outset of the schools' respective trainings.[34] The modern Western Gelug teacher B. Alan Wallace (Santa Barbara Institute for Consciousness Studies), for instance, teaches a variation of the method based on observation of the breath through the movement of the abdomen.[35]

Within the Mahāvihāra (Great Monastery) tradition of Southern Buddhism, the text has largely been pursued following the injunctions of Buddhaghosa in his *Visuddhimagga* (Path of Purification; see previous discussion). Upatissa's *Vimuttimagga* (Path of Freedom), which may be the product of the Abhayagiri monastery (Anurādhapura, Sri Lanka), a temple more obviously influenced by the newer Indian meditative systems, also accords a great preeminence to the text (see Ehara 1977, 35–44). In the modern period, the *Ānāpānasati Sutta*, our Pāli text, has been frequently translated and explained. A number of renowned twentieth-century works have dealt with the practice of mindfulness of breathing as it is presented in our primary source. For instance, in *The Heart of Buddhist Meditation* (1962), Nyanaponika Thera (Siegmund Feniger; 1901–1994), the German-born Sri Lanka–ordained Theravāda monk, takes a largely *vipassanā* approach to the practice. In *Breathing Mindfulness for Serious Beginners* (1997), Buddhadāsa (1906–1993), the famous Thai monastic meditation teacher and author, outlines the methods employed in his monastery and emphasizes a *samatha* approach to the practice, culminating in insight in the last tetrad.

Other schools and teachings within the Southern Buddhist traditions have emphasized the *sutta* and its techniques, including teachers such as Ajahn Mun (1870–1949), Ajahn Maha Boowa (1913–2011), Ajahn Chah (1919–1992) and his students Ajahn Sumedho and Ajahn Viradhamma. In these schools, the *Ānāpānasati Sutta* retains a central position in teaching Buddhist practice and principle, at every stage of the path. Maha Boowa, the great Forest teacher of Northeast Thailand, used the method to teach an emphasis on the arousing of wisdom as a means of obtaining concentration (*samādhi*). Buddhadāsa emphasized the *samatha* and *samādhi* elements of the practice, as did Ven. Saddhatissa (1914–1990), a Sri Lankan Theravāda monk, who said that many Westerners needed to establish calm first (Saddhatissa 1971, 81). The Burmese teachers U Ba Khin (1899–1971) and Mahasi Sayadaw (1904–1982) worked within a tradition emanating from Burma in the nineteenth century, which continued in the twenty-first century under the direction of S. N. Goenka (1924-2013). This popular school takes a strongly *vipassanā* approach to mindfulness of breathing. A lay *samatha* school in Britain and in the United States follows the teachings of Boonman Poonyathiro (b. 1932), who brought the *samatha* practice to the West in the early sixties, and who teaches the formless spheres and the further developments of *samatha* entirely through observation of the breath.[36]

There are many variations of the practice, both in those traditions and schools that conform closely to the instructions of the *sutta*, and in those where some adaptation, a feature of Buddhist meditation since the earliest times, is suggested. Some modern *samatha* practices, for instance, link the syllables Bu and Ddho to the in-breath and out-breath, respectively. They vary long and short in- and out-breaths within one cycle of breath, thus linking mindfulness of breathing techniques to the recollection of the Buddha. There are comparable variations throughout Southeast Asia: work on *yantra*s (meditational diagrams) also links the breath and the cultivation of the factors of *jhāna* to the Na Mo Bu Dha Ya chant (see Dennison 1996, 1997). In Southern Buddhism, the practice of mindfulness of breathing lies at the center of most modern schools. This occurs throughout the corresponding training, and it is sometimes linked to esoteric meditative practices and further developments of both calm and insight.

Variation in technique certainly indicates slight doctrinal difference, but it is more the product of a richly inventive and adaptive self-sufficiency of systems, methods that have been found to work well in particular temples and monasteries. The suggested methods adopted by a particular school are taught and recommended by them; teachers and other practitioners follow the same method and will recognize problems when they arise, thus knowing how to guide and direct the meditator through the different stages where necessary. Schools where there is an emphasis on calm, for instance, stress this in their teachings from the outset, suggesting the need for a joyful awareness and alertness throughout the various stages as the practice develops. Insight elements are an inevitable part of the practice leading to *jhāna*, however, as the faculty of wisdom is needed to support the others of faith, mindfulness, effort, and concentration. In practice, where calm is taught first, this tends to happen simply through some attention to the rise, fall, and impermanence of the breath. Thus a practitioner who has developed peace and contentment within *jhāna* then moves easily to insight. Those schools based more on insight methods may not follow this approach. Rather, they usually teach, say, loving-kindness practice, as in the Goenka schools, and the practice of recollection of the Triple Gem, to ensure that meditators develop their meditation in a balanced way. This diversity can be explained through the factors of enlightenment, so variously applied within the text itself. So, an insight-based method might place considerable emphasis on the first factors of mindfulness, investigation, and vigor, not encouraging at the outset the pursuit of the practice for the cultivation of joy, tranquility, and concentration (see S V 104; Vism IV 42ff.). These might be supplied by other supplementary practices given to the meditator—such as recollection of the Triple Gem—that encourage confidence and cheerfulness. Similarly, other devotional activities or even a receptiveness in the posture itself may help to develop such qualities. A *samatha* school, however, encourages the seven factors of awakening as a process, with particular emphasis on calm, joy, and tranquility. This does not mean that the other factors are rejected in either case.

In terms of modern interpretations, applications, and modifications, there are many published and indeed unpublished variations on a practice that has proven very popular, both in the corresponding source cultures and in new environments. The following passage, a good example of an approach to the practice that is published in a very accessible introduction to Buddhist doctrine, is indicative of the way that it has been integrated into the teaching of Buddhism for the general public and for those who study the subject academically. Walpola Rahula

(1907–1997), a Sri Lankan Theravāda monk and author of the highly influential *What the Buddha Taught* (1959), was a leading Buddhist scholar and practitioner of the twentieth century; the work in which this extract appears is regarded as a classic introduction to Buddhism.

> You breathe in and out all day and night, but you are never mindful of it, you never for a second concentrate your mind on it. Now you are going to do just this. Breathe in and out as usual, without any effort or strain. Now, bring your mind to concentrate on your breathing-in and breathing-out; let your mind watch and observe your breathing in and out; let your mind be aware of your breathing in and out. When you breathe, you sometimes take deep breaths, sometimes not. This does not matter at all. Breathe normally and naturally. The only thing is that when you take deep breaths you should be aware that they are deep breaths, and so on. In other words, your mind should be so fully concentrated on your breathing that you are aware of its movements and changes. Forget all other things, your surroundings, your environment; do not raise your eyes and look at anything. Try to do this for five or ten minutes. (Rahula 1967, 70)

This passage demonstrates the way in which the initial instruction is applied in a modern teaching.

It is not possible here to explore in detail the practical differences between the schools and various teachers. Most stress the importance of consultation with a teacher, or "good friend," for guidance on features such as the way of breathing, how to adjust lengths of breaths, and whether the posture that has been adopted is suitable. Some variations on the practice need a very stable posture, and it is considered a good idea to build up vigor over time to do the half-lotus posture to undertake them. Others allow more variations, but usually teachers can give advice on how to sit and how to prepare the legs for sitting. Other pieces of advice that may be needed include duration of practice. The recommended length of time may vary according to experience and sometimes between a *vipassanā* type of practice and a *samatha* one. For *samatha* practice, where it is important not to strain the mind, the practices may not be as long at first; *vipassanā*-based practices are often longer in the early stages. Yet more features to consider are good or suitable times of day to practice and whether, for instance, it works better with a separate space set aside or a shrine. The texts merely say "an empty space," and there would be some collective practice as well. This is clearly something where climactic, practical, and social expectations may differ. As the *sutta* indicates, there are "distinctive excellences" at each stage of graduated meditations, and the way a particular school approaches this may differ widely. A good meditation teacher will help the person through the stages they need and guide the direction that the practice needs to take for their temperament and disposition.

In terms of modern adaptations, Buddhist teachers tend to follow the model of the Buddha, who frequently made similes from features that were familiar to people's lives, and who drew upon people's experience to describe difficulties and problems with practicing meditation. Ven. Dhammasāmi, who teaches a *vipassanā* method, applies the foundations of mindfulness to work in an office environment (Dhammasāmi 1999). Boonman Poonyathiro, a Thai *samatha* mindfulness of breathing teacher, compares the hindrances and distractions that beset the meditator to "gangsters" trying to prevent the practitioner from traveling from one place to another; this image has a counterpart in the canonical comparison of the hindrances to thugs attacking a border town (A

IV 106ff.). This search for new imagery and modes of comparison tends to keep the tradition alive, as do reading texts on the subject, supplementary activities such as *dhamma* talks, group discussions, group practices, and chanting. The idea of the "good friend," central to the ancient understanding of how meditation should always be taught, tends to be a characteristic of groups that follow a mindfulness of breathing practice: a sense of community is still a great help. Indeed, these features are worth keeping in mind if a practitioner is looking for a teacher and school, as they have traditionally been regarded as symptomatic of the health and continued capacity of a school to take people through the sometimes tricky stages involved. Seeking help from those more experienced is constantly enjoined in early texts and in modern practice (see S V 78; A IV 30–32; A III 316).

Exercises observing the breath, which often have their roots in the traditions that have used this *sutta*, have also become integrated into modern psychotherapeutic practice.[37] Some argue that the Southern Buddhist tradition has historically and textually put a great deal of emphasis on the company and advice from the good friend for meditation teaching, and that such systems may not help "well" people in the long term. As Jenny Kwok, a practicing psychotherapist and Buddhist scholar, has noted, the factors of awakening, mindfulness, investigation, vigor, joy, tranquility, concentration, and equanimity, are central to Southern Buddhist practice but not necessarily encouraged by the psychotherapeutic traditions. The latter tend to place emphasis on diminishing unhappy symptoms rather than cultivating features of the mind fostered by a meditation that actively arouses calm and joy.[38] This may, however, represent a further stage of the Western familiarity with Buddhist principles: the success rates of such therapies, which use a few basic techniques, are remarkably high and are a credit to those who have adapted them, especially in the foundational Buddhist concern for the alleviation of suffering. Clearly more research in this area is needed.

Breathing Outside the Buddhist Tradition

So how can we conclude this discussion? Meditation on the breath is regarded in modern contexts as both communal and solitary, monastic and lay. In modern practice it is conducted as sitting practice, apart from daily activities, but awareness of the breath during the day is encouraged in many schools too, for both monastic and lay practitioners. The *Ānāpānasati Sutta* is delivered to a group of monks; the practice described in it is, however, found throughout the canon, and was presumably practiced at the time of the Buddha by those laymen and laywomen described as practicing the four foundations of mindfulness (M I 491). It is both an external object, in that the breath comes from outside, and an internal one, in that it is felt within the body. Clearly it is portable; it needs no device or phenomenon such as a dead body or a made-up disc (*kasiṇa*) as a starting point. It is, unusually for meditation objects, favored both as a means of calm and of insight. But observation of the breath is, of course, not peculiar to Buddhism. Other systems, in other traditions, involve repetitive elements and bringing back of the mind to a simple formula in association with the breath. Within Buddhist understanding, this process is described as the mind (*nāma*) finding in the breath a relationship with matter (*rūpa*) that allows the practitioner to discern the relationship between the two and derive the stages of meditation within that (see Vajirañāṇa 1977, 227ff.). The breath may then be used as an object to develop calm in all the *jhāna*s, or as means of insight, or both.

Close delineation of each stage of the practice and ways it is used to describe each level of the path do seem to be a hallmark of Buddhist practices associated with the breath. Indeed, perhaps the single most important observation to be drawn from studying these various approaches and types of practical exploration of the text is just that: there are a wide number of methods involved in the associated practice. Features of the practice, in modern schools, tend to be adjusted to needs. This might seem an unsatisfactory conclusion within the parameters laid down in a work of this kind, but flexibility and applicability to specific temperaments are noteworthy features in any contemplative system, suggesting not only a stated but also an enacted commitment to compassionate teaching. From the point of view of the Buddhist understanding of consciousness, all skillful states are accompanied by either loving-kindness, compassion, sympathetic joy, or equanimity (DhS 33). Meditation on the breath is considered a means of purifying the mind of hindrances that obstruct the full development of these qualities. In so doing it is regarded as particularly suited to the practitioner wishing to attain liberating wisdom (S V 326), with the last tetrad of the sixteen stages particularly associated with the culmination of this process. Many modern approaches seem to accord with the basic principles expounded in the text, and modern schools tend to be self-sufficient in the sense that they describe themselves as providing their own guidance, correctives, and encouragements at various stages of the path.

A practical analogy is perhaps most effective in summarizing what is really primarily understood as a method, as well as a means of liberation. As Peter Harvey comments,

> Learning meditation is a skill akin to learning to play a musical instrument: it is learning how to "tune" and "play" the mind, and regular, patient practice is needed to do this. Progress will not occur if one is lax, but it cannot be forced. For this reason, meditation practice is also like gardening: one cannot force plants to grow, but one can assiduously provide them with the right conditions, so that they develop naturally. For meditation, the "right conditions" are the appropriate application of mind and the specific technique being used. (1990, 244–45)

Abbreviations

A	*Aṅguttaranikāya*. Collection from the *Sutta-piṭaka* of teachings grouped by ones, twos, threes, fours, and so forth, and so termed "gradual" teachings.
D	*Dīghanikāya*. Collection from the *Sutta-piṭaka* of "long" teachings.
DA	*Dīghanikāya-aṭṭakatthā*. Commentary on D.
DhS	*Dhammasaṅgani*. The first book of the *Abhidhamma*, the third "basket" of the teaching.
DPPN	*Dictionary of Pāli Proper Names*. Dictionary compiled by G. P. Malalasekera.
J	*Jātaka*. The 547 stories of the Buddha's past lives as the Bodhisatta, the being "attached to awakening."
M	*Majjhimanikāya*. The *sutta*s of "middle length."
MA	Commentary on M.
Nidd	*Niddesa*. Late canonical text influenced by the *Abhidhamma*.
Patis	*Paṭisambhidāmagga*. Late canonical text influenced by the *Abhidhamma*.

PF	*Path to Freedom.* Translation of *Vimuttimagga* by Ehara and colleagues. An early commentary on meditation.
S	*Saṃyuttanikāya.* Collection from the *Sutta-piṭaka* of "connected" or "kindred" texts, so called because they are grouped together with close thematic links and verbal affinities.
Ud	*Udāna.* A small collection within the *Sutta-piṭaka*.
Vism	*Visuddhimagga.* Fifth-century meditation manual, sometimes known as *The Path to Purification.* Composed by Buddhaghosa, the most famous early commentator on Buddhist meditation and text. Cited according to the translation of Ñāṇamoli.

Notes

1. Following the primary language of early or Southern Buddhism, the present chapter uses Pāli, rather than Sanskrit, with the latter being the primary language of Northern Buddhism and some forms of Eastern Buddhism.

2. For accounts of the variations in the Buddha's early life story, see Strong 2001, 35–48, 156–59.

3. See the commentary to this *sutta* (MA 467) and the introduction to the *Jātakas* (Ja I 58): "The Bodhisatta, looking around here and there, and not seeing anyone, stirred with a sense of urgency, went into the cross-legged posture, took up the in-breath and the out-breath and attained the first *jhāna*."

4. Gal Vihara, also known as Gal Viharaya, is a rock temple of the Buddha situated in the ancient city of Polonnaruwa in north-central Sri Lanka. It was constructed in the twelfth century under the patronage of King Parākramabāhu I (1123–1186; r. 1153–1186). Polonnaruwa was designated as a UNESCO World Heritage Site in 1982. Sometimes referred to as the *samādhi* (concentration) posture, the body position of the statue includes the *jhāna muddā* (Skt.: *dhyāna mudrā*), or "concentration hand configuration," which is the standard one used in Southern Buddhist meditation. It sometimes involves touching the tips of the thumbs together.

5. Bodh Gaya, the place where the historical Buddha attained enlightenment, is one of four key sacred sites associated with ancient Indian Buddhism. The other three and their associations are as follows: Kushinagar (Uttar Pradesh, India), where the Buddha attained *parinibbana* after death; Lumbinī (Rupandehi, Nepal), where the Buddha was born; and Sarnath (Uttar Pradesh), where the Buddha gave his first sermon and the Buddhist community began.

6. Gethin (1992, 197–201) gives a close analysis of the occurrence of the term, its association with the Eightfold Path, and its varied use in the Pāli Canon.

7. See Gethin 1992a, 190–226; Harvey 1990, 6872; Saddhatissa 1971, 45–57; Shaw 2009, 1–17.

8. Situated in the central part of Sri Lanka, Dambulla was established as a Buddhist monastery in the third century BCE, and the caves were converted into a temple in the first century BCE. It was designated as a UNESCO World Heritage Site in 1991. The wall mural depicts the "Sermon at Deer Park," the first teaching of the historical Buddha, which occurred at Isipatana. The latter is now known as Sarnath, which is located about eight miles, or thirteen kilometers, northeast of Varanasi (Benares), in Uttar Pradesh, India.

9. See Peter Skilling's superb analysis of the problems of "labeling" early Buddhisms (2009). For the purposes of this chapter, the terms Northern, Southern, and Eastern have been applied to the various kinds of Buddhisms that have historically developed in different regions.

10. Aronson's study demonstrates the constant presence of vocabulary associated with compassion, kindness, and the divine abidings throughout early Buddhist discourse, specifically as relating to injunctions to meditation, behavior, and mental activity (Aronson 1980). See also Gombrich 2009, 75–91, in which the doctrinal centrality and soteriological importance of loving-kindness and compassion are stressed.

11. For some examples and comment, see Shaw 2006, 53–56 (Tissa), 189–93 (Rāhula), and 194–98.

12. See Ud 34–37; Nidd I 360.

13. See Vajirañāṇa 1975, 166–67; S V 320; and Vin III 68. This meditation and the careful limits on its practice are discussed in Shaw 2006, 101–8.

14. For diversity of meditation objects, see Vajirañāṇa 1975, 57–75; Shaw 2006: 92ff. For the assignment of objects to temperament (*carita*), see Vajirañāṇa 1975, 98; Shaw 2006, 8ff; Nidd I 360; PF 54–62; and Vism III 74–103.

15. For excerpts from these, see Shaw 2006, M I 55–63, 37–38; Shaw 2009, 54–55.

16. The chanting of the whole of the *Tipiṭaka* (Three Baskets), the Pāli Canon, has always been regarded as greatly meritorious. It takes about three months for a group of monks, taking one another's place, to chant it continuously, as sometimes happens for particularly auspicious occasions. In Burma, there are now ten monks fully trained in the memorization of all of the texts, a process that takes many years: they are tested every ten years on random samples. Author's ethnographic field observations on the basis of consultation with the Shan monk residents at the Oxford Buddhist Vihāra in 2010.

17. This statement is based on the author's visits to temples and meditation centers in Sri Lanka, Bangkok, and Sisaket (Northeast Thailand), and observation of practice on a number of Southern Buddhist retreats, in monastic and lay contexts, in Britain.

18. Richard Gombrich has noted that in Sri Lanka, for instance, the Buddhist tradition chanted texts, and complex narratives probably did offer a complete soteriological system that the area had not known previously (see Gombrich 1988, 137ff.). Indeed, learning, textual study, and the monastic orders have traditionally been inextricably linked in Southeast Asia and Sri Lanka. However, it should be remembered that, a society based on oral rather than written transmission of texts is not necessarily uneducated, unsophisticated, or incapable of abstract thought. This supposition is often found in Western analyses of the social function of literacy and writing.

19. A *Mahāpirit* is an extended chanting ceremony, felt to be particularly efficacious, that often takes a whole night. The monks involved sit within a canopy made for the event.

20. To gain a good sense of Southeast Asian ritual and practice, and the importance of chanting within that context, see Swearer 2010. At an anecdotal level, when accompanying a group of Westerners chanting a long *sutta* in 2008 (the *Samatha* group chanting the *Mahāsamaya Sutta* with Ajahn Maha Laow), I noticed groups of Thais flocked to participate in what was regarded as a salvific and meditative activity and often afterward congratulated the British chanters on the high quality of their Thai pronunciation. In fact, the words of the *sutta* were in Pāli, not Thai, and had they been translated into that language, they would have been quite different: the tonal and spelling variations in Thai do not really provide the same relationship between the original and the local vernacular that can be found even when Latin, say, moves to English. But for these Thais, so much hearing of the *dhamma* in Pāli has made them feel that Pāli *is* part of Thai in some sense, as the language of the temple, still used in some discourse among monks, rather as Latin is in some Roman Catholic contexts. Hearing chanting in the background is very much part of Southeast Asian life and has become a mild lay form of practice and cultivation (*bhāvanā*). In Sri Lanka in particular, it is impossible to go anywhere without hearing a radio with chanting going on in the background: women listen while doing the housework, shopkeepers waiting for customers, taxi drivers waiting for trade. Many lay Buddhists thus regard it as a useful background to their daily lives, helping them on their way to the ultimate goal of liberation.

21. Ānanda delivers seven teachings, Mahākaccana four, and Moggallāna two. There is also a dialogue between Sāriputta and Puṇṇa Mantāṇiputta, and another one wherein a nun delivers a discourse on meditation to the man who had been her husband in the lay life.

22. For more on this subject, see Collins 1998. Collins challenges the modern Western assumption that *nibbāna* represents a goal that is only accessible to a few, at a certain time, and suggests rather that the happiness of the goal may be present in many ways, in diverse forms, on its path too. See also Gethin 1992b; Shaw 2006, 194ff.

23. This is discussed in Cousins 1973, 1984; Shaw 2009, 116–23. For further discussion and the examples of Meghiya and Rāhula, see Shaw 2006, 18ff., 24–28, 189–93. See also Harvey 1990, 246–57.

24. For some very useful comments on this, see the important article by Soma Thera, PF 353–62, titled too modestly "Appendix: Contemplation in the *Dhamma*" (1959).

25. The extensive and rich subject of lay meditation at the time of the Buddha is outside the scope of this discussion. That it existed and that it produced fruits is clear from description of the practice and meditative attainments of those among the laity, men and women, described in the earliest strata of texts (M I 340, M I 491, A I 23–26; see Shaw 2006, 12–15).

26. See Valerie Roebuck's helpful summary of *Dhammapada* stories in Roebuck 2010, 113ff. The goldsmith's son was unable to find success in meditation at all, so the Buddha, seeing that he needed a beautiful object as he had spent so many lives as a goldsmith, conjures up a golden flower for him. His success through the stages of calm meditation is rapid, and only then does the Buddha make the flower decay. After that, attuned to his meditation object, the goldsmith's son sees a bank of flowers with some budding and others in decay: he gains further insight, and, encouraged by a magical visit from the Buddha, attains his final goal.

27. The subsequent development of the *nimitta* (mark or condition), the visual sign that works within this practice at a later stage when calm has been established, involves an internal "seeing" of what is in the mind's eye. Buddhaghosa differentiates this feature in one passage from other objects (Vism III 119).

28. These are the four stages of enlightenment or awakening. The "fetters" (*saṃyojana*) represent ten ways that the mind can exhibit attachment to various forms of self, views, and external forms. See PF 318 and Vajirañāṇa 1975, 418, for a full account of these.

29. This does not have to mean, as is commonly supposed, the full-lotus posture (*padmāsana*); the commentaries never state this. More usually a half-lotus is adopted, or, if the practitioner is unable to sustain this posture, a usual cross-legged posture. Modern-day practitioners sometimes sit in chairs for specific practices. This is largely dependent on the school in which one practices (see Shaw 2006, 15–18). Other postures are also employed in Thai temples, such as folding the legs to one side.

30. Vajirañāṇa discusses this issue and the occurrence of the corresponding meditation in the canon. See Vajirañāṇa 1975, 228.

31. Glenn Wallis has suggested this recently (pers. comm., 2008).

32. I am grateful to Florin Deleanu for his explanation of this method at his scholarly and lively course on Yogācāra meditation at the Oxford Centre for Buddhist Studies, Oxford University, in September 2010.

33. A Sanskrit transliteration of this fragment of text is given in Schlingloff 2006, 79ff.

34. I am grateful to Ulrike Roesler (Oxford University) for discussion about this.

35. See Spring 2011 audio teachings with B. Alan Wallace: http://podcasts.sbinstitute.com/spring2011/?p=106. Accessed on June 1, 2014.

36. The school is taught under the auspices of the Samatha Trust, United Kingdom, and the Samatha Foundation of North America.

37. Here one also thinks of the modern therapeutic meditation method of Mindfulness-Based Stress Reduction (MBSR). This is a modified form of modern *vipassanā* meditation developed by Jon Kabat-Zinn (b. 1944), the founding director of the Center for Mindfulness in Medicine, Health Care, and Society at the University of Massachusetts Medical School.

38. This point was made by Jenny Kwok in a lecture delivered at the Bangkok Conference for the Saṅgarāja's ninety-sixth birthday, Chulalongkorn University, October 3, 2009.

Works Cited and Further Reading

Anālayo. 2004. *Satipaṭṭhāna: The Direct Path to Realization*. Cambridge: Windhorse.
Aronson, Harvey. 1980. *Love and Sympathy in Theravāda Buddhism*. Delhi: Motilal Banarsidass.

Bodhi, Bhikkhu. 2000. *The Connected Discourses of the Buddha*. 2 vols. Oxford: Pali Text Society.
Bronkhorst, Johannes. 1993. *The Two Traditions of Meditation in Ancient India*. Delhi: Motilal Banarsidass.
Buddhadāsa, Bhikkhu, and Bhikkhu Santikāro. 1997. *Mindfulness with Breathing: A Manual for Serious Beginners*. Bangkok: Evolution/Liberation, and Boston: Wisdom.
Chah, Ajahn. 2006. *Talks on Meditation: A Collection of Talks on Cultivating the Mind*. Kandy: Buddhist Publication Society.
Coleman, James. 2002. *The New Buddhism: The Western Transformation of an Ancient Tradition*. Oxford and New York: Oxford University Press.
Collins, Steven. 1998. *Nirvana and Other Felicities: Utopias of the Pali Imaginaire*. Cambridge and New York: Cambridge University Press.
Conze, Edward. 1956. *Buddhist Meditation*. London: George Allen and Unwin.
Cousins, L. S. 1973. "Buddhist *Jhāna*: Its Nature and Attainment according to the Pāli Sources." *Religion* 3: 115–31.
———. 1983. "Pāli Oral Literature." In *Buddhist Studies, Ancient and Modern*, edited by Philip Denwood and Alexander Piatigorsky, 1–11. London: n.p.
———. 1984. "*Samatha-yāna* and *Vipassanā-yāna*." In *Buddhist Studies in Honour of Hammalava Saddhatissa*, edited by Gatare Dhammapala et al., 56–68. Nugegoda: Hammalava Saddhatissa Felicitation Volume Committee.
Dennison, Paul. 1996. "Na Yan: An Introduction." In *Samatha: Insight from a Meditation Tradition*, edited by J. Callow, vol. 2, 16–18. Llangunllo: Samatha Trust.
———. 1997. "Na Yan Continued." In *Samatha: Insight from a Meditation Tradition*, edited by in J. Callow, 3: 19–23. Llangunllo: Samatha Trust.
Dhammasāmi, Ven. 1999. *Mindfulness Meditation Made Easy*. Penang: Inward Path.
Donner, Neal, and Daniel Stevenson. 1993. *The Great Calming and Contemplation: A Study and Annotated Translation of the First Chapter of Chih-I's Mo-Ho Chih-Kuan*. Honolulu: University of Hawaii Press.
Ehara, N. R. M., Soma Thera, and Kheminda Thera. 1977. *The Path of Freedom (Vimuttimagga)*. Kandy: Buddhist Publication Society.
Gethin, R. M. L. 1992a. *The Buddhist Path to Awakening: A Study of the Bodhi-pakkhiyā Dhamma*. Leiden: Brill.
———. 1992b. "The Mātikas: Memorization, Mindfulness, and the List." In *In the Mirror of Memory: Reflections on Mindfulness and Remembrance in Indian and Tibetan Buddhism*, edited by Janet Gyatso, 149–72. Albany: State University of New York Press.
———. 1998. *The Foundations of Buddhism*. Oxford and New York: Oxford University Press.
Gombrich, Richard F. 1988. *Theravada Buddhism: A Social History from Ancient Benares to Modern Colombo*. London and New York: Routledge Kegan Paul.
———. 2009. *What the Buddha Thought*. London and Oakville: Equinox.
Gunaratana, Mahathera H. 1985. *The Path of Serenity and Insight: An Explanation of the Buddhist Jhānas*. Delhi: Motilal Banarsidass.
Harvey, Peter. 1990. *Introduction to Buddhism: Teachings, History, and Practices*. Cambridge and New York: Cambridge University Press.
Horner, I. B.1967. *Middle Length Sayings*. 3 vols. London: Luzacs.
Keown, Damien. 1996. *Buddhism: A Very Short Introduction*. Oxford and New York: Oxford University Press.
Khemā, Ayyā. 1988. *Within Our Own Hearts: Twelve Dhamma Talks on Meditation Practice*. Kandy: Buddhist Publication Society.
Luk, Charles. 1964. *The Secrets of Chinese Meditation*. London: Rider and Company.
Mahasi Sayadaw. 1990. *Satipaṭṭhāna Vipassanā: Insight through Mindfulness*. Kandy: Buddhist Publication Society.
Malalasekera, G. P. 1974. *Dictionary of Pāli Proper Names*. 2 vols. London: Pali Text Society.

Nan, Huai-Chin. 1997. *Basic Buddhism: Exploring Buddhism and Zen.* Newburyport: Red Wheel/Weiser.
Ñāṇamoli, Bhikkhu. 1991. *The Path of Purification: Visuddhimagga: The Classic Manual of Buddhist Doctrine and Meditation.* 5th ed. Kandy: Buddhist Publication Society.
Ñāṇamoli, Bhikkhu, and Bhikkhu Bodhi. 2001. *The Middle Length Discourses of the Buddha.* Boston: Wisdom.
Ñāṇarama, M. Mahāthera. 1997. *The Seven Contemplations of Insight: A Treatise on Insight Meditation.* Kandy: Buddhist Publication Society.
Norman, K. R. 1994. "What Is Pali?" In *A Pāli Grammar*, by Wilhelm Geiger, xxiii–xxix. Edited by K. R. Norman. Oxford: Pali Text Society.
Nyanaponika Thera. 1962. *The Heart of Buddhist Meditation: A Handbook of Mental Training Based on the Buddha's Way of Mindfulness.* London: Rider and Company.
Pradhan, Prahlad, ed. 1975. *Abhidharmakośabhasyam of Vasubandhu.* Patna: K. P. Jayaswal Research Institute.
Rahula, Walpola. 1967. *What the Buddha Taught.* 2nd ed. Bedford: Gordon Fraser.
Roebuck, Valerie. 2010. *The Dhammapada.* London: Penguin Classic Series.
Rosenberg, Larry. 2004. *Breath by Breath: The Liberating Practice of Insight Meditation.* Boston: Shambhala.
Saddhatissa, Ven. H. 1971. *The Buddha's Way.* London: George Allen and Unwin.
Shaw, Sarah. 2006. *Buddhist Meditation: An Anthology of Texts.* London and New York: Routledge.
——— . 2009. *An Introduction to Buddhist Meditation.* London and New York: Routledge.
Schlingloff, Dieter. 2006. *Ein Buddhistisches Yogalehrbuch Textband Akademie. Verlag Sanskrittexte aus den Turfanfunden.* Berlin: Ludwig auer Donauworth.
Skilling, Peter. 2009. "Redaction, Recitation, and Writing: Transmission of the Buddha's Teachings in India in the Early Period." In *Buddhist Manuscript Cultures: Knowledge, Ritual, and Art*, edited by Stephen C. Berkwitz et al., 53–75. London and New York: Routledge.
——— . 2010. "Scriptural Authenticity and the Śrāvaka Schools: An Essay towards an Indian Perspective." *The Eastern Buddhist* 41.2: 1–47.
Strong, John S. 2001. *The Buddha: A Short Biography.* Oxford: Oneworld.
Sumedho, Ven. 1985. *Mindfulness: The Path to the Deathless: The Meditation Teachings of Venerable Ajahn Sumedho.* Great Gaddesden: Amaravati.
Swearer, Donald. 2010. *The Buddhist World of Southeast Asia.* Rev. ed. Albany: State University of New York Press.
Tanabe, George T., Jr. 2004. "Chanting." In *Encyclopedia of Buddhism*, edited by Robert Buswell, Jr., 1.137–39. 2 vols. New York: Macmillan.
Vajirañāṇa, P. Mahāthera. 1975. *Buddhist Meditation in Theory and Practice.* 2nd ed. Kuala Lumpur: Buddhist Missionary Society.
Wynne, Alexander. 2007. *The Origins of Buddhist Meditation.* London and New York: Routledge.
Zahler, Leah. 2009. *Study and Practice of Meditation: Tibetan Interpretations of the Concentrations and Formless Absorptions.* Ithaca: Snow Lion.

Ānāpānasati Sutta (Discourse on Mindfulness of Breathing)*

Account of a Discourse Attributed to Gotama Buddha

Translated and Annotated by Sarah Shaw

Thus have I heard. At one time the Exalted One was living in Sāvatthī[1] in the Eastern Park, in the palace belonging to Migāra's mother,[2] along with many distinguished elder disciples: the Venerables Sāriputta, Moggallāna, Mahākassapa, Mahākaccāna, Mahākoṭṭhita, Mahākappina, Mahācunda, Anuruddha, Revata, Ānanda, and other distinguished elder disciples.[3]

Now on that occasion elder monks were teaching and giving instruction to younger monks. Some elder monks were teaching and training ten monks, some were teaching and training twenty monks, some were teaching and training thirty monks, some were teaching and training forty monks. And the new monks who had been taught and trained by the elder monks became aware of the distinctive excellence of each stage in its sequence.

At that time, the *uposatha* day of the fifteenth,[4] on the full-moon night of the Pavāraṇā festival,[5] the Exalted One was sitting in the open air, surrounded by the community of monks. Then, after surveying the silent community of monks, he addressed them in this way: "I am pleased with this progress, monks. My heart is pleased with this progress. So arouse even more energy to attain the unattained, to realize the unrealized. I shall wait here at Sāvatthī for the full moon at the time of the blossoming of the white lotus [Komudī] in the fourth month."[6]

The monks from the countryside heard the report that the Exalted One would wait there at Sāvatthī for the full moon of the white lotus, in the fourth month. And so they streamed

---

*The present translation is a complete rendering of the *Ānāpānasati Sutta* (no. 118, M III 78–78), a Pāli text of uncertain date but associated with the early Indian Buddhist community. Other translations include Horner 1967, 3:121–29; Ñāṇamoli and Bodhi 2001, 941–48; Rosenberg 2004. Commonly occurring technical terms may be found in the technical glossary at the end of my translation.

1. Sāvatthī is one of the six great cities mentioned in Pāli canonical texts in association with the Buddha and the most frequent location for *sutta*s. The commentaries say that he spent twenty-five of his forty rainy seasons there (DPPN II 1127).

2. Migāra's mother is the laywoman Visākhā, whose hospitality to monks was renowned; she was considered an ideal for other laywomen, being generous, supportive, youthful (despite living to a great age), and happy (A IV 348).

3. Among the distinguished elder disciples mentioned are the following: Sāriputta, the Buddha's foremost disciple, famed for insight (A I 23); Moggallāna, famous for psychic powers, who is the other chief disciple (A I 23), usually shown in art on the left of the Buddha, where Sāriputta is on the right; Mahākassapa, famous for his asceticism and observances of form (A I 23); Anuruddha, most highly skilled in the use of the psychic power of the divine eye (A I 23); and Ānanda, the Buddha's companion and attendant throughout his career, whose recollections formed the basis of the Pāli Canon. The point being made appears to be that those closest to the Buddha were present at the time.

4. The *uposatha* day corresponds to the seventh, fourteenth, twenty-first, and twenty-eighth days of the lunar cycle. It is a day of purification, on the days preceding the full moon, the new moon, and the quarter days in-between. The full-moon day in particular is commonly celebrated in Southern Buddhist countries with the laity wearing white, taking extra precepts, and spending the day at a temple chanting, meditating, and listening to talks.

5. Pavāraṇā is the ceremony that concludes the rainy season.

6. Komudī is the full-moon day of the month of Kattika, when white water lilies bloom.

into Sāvatthī to see the Exalted One. And those who were the elder monks taught and trained the new monks still more. Some elder monks taught and trained ten monks, some taught and trained twenty monks, some taught and trained thirty monks, and some taught and trained forty monks. And the new monks who had been taught and trained by the elder monks also became aware of the distinctive excellence of each stage in its sequence.

Now, at that time the Exalted One was sitting in the open air surrounded by the community of monks on the night of the full moon of the white lotus, the *uposatha* day of the fourth and final month of the rains. Then, after surveying the silent community of monks, he addressed them in this way:

"Monks, this assembly is not chaff. This assembly is free from any chatter. This assembly is settled, the most excellent heartwood. Such is this community of monks, monks, such is this assembly, an assembly that is worthy of gifts, worthy of hospitality, worthy of reverence, an incomparable field of merit for the world: such is this community of monks, monks, such is this assembly. It is such an assembly that even a small gift becomes great and a great gift greater: such is this community of monks, monks, such is this assembly. It is such an assembly that is difficult to see in this world: such is this community of monks, monks, such is this assembly. For just a glimpse of such an assembly, monks, it would be worth traveling many leagues with a bag of provisions on one's shoulder: such is this community of monks, such is this assembly.

"There are in this community of monks those who are arahants, with the corruptions destroyed, who have lived the holy life, who have done what has to be done, laid down the burden, attained their own goal, destroyed the fetters of existence, and who are freed by right knowledge: there are such monks in this community of monks.[7] There are in this community of monks those who, with the five fetters connected with this side of existence destroyed, will be born spontaneously in the Pure Abodes and from there attain *nibbāna*, without returning from that world;[8] those who have destroyed three fetters, who, with the reduction of greed, hatred, and delusion are once-returners, who will return once to this world to make an end of suffering;[9] those who have destroyed three fetters, stream-enterers, not bound for an unhappy rebirth and destined for awakening;[10] those who live dedicated to the cultivation of the four foundations of mindfulness, the four right efforts, the four bases of success, the five faculties, the five powers, the seven factors of awakening, the Noble Eightfold Path, loving-kindness, compassion, sympathetic

---

7. The arahants are those who have attained final awakening. They have destroyed all of the ten "fetters" (*samyojana*) of becoming: belief in self, doubt, attachment to precepts and vows, sensual desire, ill will, desire for existence in a form realm, desire for existence in a formless realm, conceit, restlessness, and ignorance (S V 61–63). At death they attain *nibbāna* (lit., putting out [of a flame]), the goal of the Buddhist path. It is a term frequently associated with happiness (*sukha*). For this and other stages of the path, see Ñāṇamoli and Bodhi 2001, 41–45.

8. This refers to those who have removed the first five "fetters." Such individuals are known as nonreturners and will take rebirth only once more, in the higher heaven known as the Pure Abodes, before attaining awakening.

9. This refers to the first category of those who have removed the first three of the aforementioned fetters, who will take rebirth only once more, in a heaven or a human realm, before attaining awakening. They will never again experience any unhappy or lower rebirths.

10. This refers to those who have "entered the stream." They too have eradicated belief in self, doubt, and attachment to precepts and vows and will experience awakening within seven lifetimes. They will never again experience any unhappy or lower rebirths.

joy, equanimity, meditation on impurity, the perception of impermanence: there are such monks in this community of monks.[11]

"There are, monks, in this community of monks, those who live dedicated to the cultivation of mindfulness of breathing. When mindfulness of breathing is cultivated and made much of, it is of great fruit and great reward. When mindfulness of breathing is cultivated and made much of, it fulfills the four foundations of mindfulness; when the four foundations of mindfulness are cultivated and made much of, they fulfill the seven factors of awakening.[12] When the seven factors of awakening are cultivated and made much of, they fulfill knowledge and liberation.

"And how, monks, is mindfulness of breathing cultivated? How is it made much of? How is it of great fruit and great reward? Here, monks, a monk goes to a forest, or the roots of a tree or an empty place, and sits, folding his legs in a cross-legged position, making his body straight and sets up mindfulness in front of him.[13]

"Mindful, he breathes in; mindful, he breathes out. As he breathes in a long breath, he knows, 'I am breathing in a long breath,' or, as he breathes out a long breath, he knows, 'I am breathing out a long breath.' As he breathes in a short breath, he knows, 'I am breathing in a short breath.' Or, as he breathes out a short breath, he knows, 'I am breathing out a short breath.' He trains thus: 'Experiencing the whole body, I shall breathe in'; he trains thus: 'Experiencing the whole body, I shall breathe out.' He trains thus: 'Making tranquil the bodily formation, I shall breathe in'; he trains thus: 'Making tranquil the bodily formation, I shall breathe out.'

"He trains thus: 'Experiencing joy, I shall breathe in'; he trains thus: 'Experiencing joy, I shall breathe out.' He trains thus: 'Experiencing happiness, I shall breathe in'; he trains thus: 'Experiencing happiness, I shall breathe out.' He trains thus: 'Experiencing the mind formation, I shall breathe in'; he trains thus: 'Experiencing the mind formation, I shall breathe out.' He trains thus: 'Making tranquil the mind formation, I shall breathe in'; he trains thus: 'Making tranquil the mind formation, I shall breathe out.'

---

11. There are a variety of technical terms here. The first thirty-seven, the four foundations of mindfulness (body, feeling, mind, and *dhammas* [phenomena]), the four right efforts, the five faculties, the five powers, the seven factors of awakening, and the noble Eightfold Path together refer to the thirty-seven factors contributing to awakening. For a full study of all of these, see Gethin 1992a. The four foundations of mindfulness are all fulfilled by the instructions in this *sutta*, as we have seen in my introduction, with one tetrad for body, feeling, mind, and *dhammas*, respectively. The next four factors described after the thirty-seven are loving-kindness, compassion, sympathetic joy, and equanimity, which are termed divine abidings (*brahmavihāras*). They can be pursued as meditations or as practices in daily life: one of these is present in all skillful consciousness; each one, developed as a meditation whereby the object of meditation becomes limitless, applied to all beings, can be taken as an object that leads to *jhāna* too. See DhS 253–62; Shaw 2006, 163–72. The meditation on the impure is a traditional practice on the dead body (see Shaw 2006, 101–8). The perception of impermanence (*anicca*) is an insight practice, in which the meditator perceives the first of three marks of existence: the twelfth stage of the practice under discussion in this text involves perceiving this mark with regard to the in-breath and the out-breath. The other two marks of dis-ease (*dukkha*) and non-self (*anattā*) are not specifically mentioned here, as indeed they are not in the instructions for breathing mindfulness either. Presumably, by mentioning all these different practices, a sense of the diversity of types of practitioners and their methods is intended to be communicated.

12. The seven factors of awakening are as follows: mindfulness, investigation, vigor, joy, concentration, tranquility, and equanimity. Their cultivation is considered essential to any path to the attainment of awakening. See Gethin 1992a, 146–89.

13. The text simply says "cross-legged" posture, and does not specify the full lotus. In modern practice, the half-lotus is usually adopted, though not by those who struggle with it. See Shaw 2006, 16.

"He trains thus: 'Experiencing the mind, I shall breathe in'; he trains thus: 'Experiencing the mind, I shall breathe out.' He trains thus: 'Gladdening the mind, I shall breathe in'; he trains thus: 'Gladdening the mind, I shall breathe out.' He trains thus: 'Concentrating the mind, I shall breathe in'; he trains thus: 'Concentrating the mind, I shall breathe out.' He trains thus: 'Liberating the mind, I shall breathe in'; he trains thus: 'Liberating the mind, I shall breathe out.'

"He trains thus: 'Contemplating impermanence, I shall breathe in'; he trains thus: 'Contemplating impermanence, I shall breathe out.' He trains thus: 'Contemplating dispassion, I shall breathe in'; he trains thus: 'Contemplating dispassion, I shall breathe out.' He trains thus: 'Contemplating cessation, I shall breathe in'; he trains thus: 'Contemplating cessation, I shall breathe out.' He trains thus: 'Contemplating letting go, I shall breathe in'; he trains thus: 'Contemplating letting go, I shall breathe out.' That is how, monks, mindfulness of breathing is cultivated and made much of, so that it is of great fruit and great reward.

"And how is mindfulness of breathing cultivated? How is it made much of, so that it fulfills the four foundations of mindfulness? At whatever time, monks, a monk breathes in a long breath and knows, 'I am breathing in a long breath,' or, as he breathes out a long breath, and knows, 'I am breathing out a long breath.' At whatever time a monk breathes in a short breath, and knows, 'I am breathing in a short breath.' Or, as he breathes out a short breath, and knows, 'I am breathing out a short breath.' At whatever time he trains thus: 'Experiencing the whole body, I shall breathe in'; he trains thus: 'Experiencing the whole body, I shall breathe out.' At whatever time he trains thus: 'Making tranquil the bodily formation, I shall breathe in'; he trains thus: 'Making tranquil the bodily formation, I shall breathe out.' At that time, monks, a monk practices contemplating the body in the body, ardent, clearly comprehending, and mindful, putting away longing and discontent in the world. I say that this is a particular body among bodies: that is, the in-breath and the out-breath.[14] Therefore, monks, at the time when a monk practices contemplating the body in the body, ardent, clearly comprehending, and mindful, he puts away longing and discontent in the world.

"At whatever time, monks, a monk trains thus: 'Experiencing joy, I shall breathe in'; and he trains thus: 'Experiencing joy, I shall breathe out.' At whatever time a monk trains thus: 'Experiencing happiness, I shall breathe in'; and he trains thus: 'Experiencing happiness, I shall breathe out.' At whatever time he trains thus: 'Experiencing the mind formation, I shall breathe in'; and he trains thus: 'Experiencing the mind formation, I shall breathe out.' At whatever time he trains thus: 'Making tranquil the mind formation, I shall breathe in'; and he trains thus: 'Making tranquil the mind formation, I shall breathe out.' At this time, monks, a monk practices contemplating feeling amid feelings, ardent, clearly comprehending, and mindful, putting away longing and discontent in the world. I say that this is a particular feeling among feelings: that is proper attention to the in-breath and the out-breath.[15] Therefore, monks, at the time when a

---

14. The "breath" is considered by the commentaries to be a body among others (MA IV 140), so that "the body in the body" is the body of the air element within the body as a whole. So, it is technically the body of the air element, among the "bodies" of earth, water, and fire. Or, it is one of the twenty-five classes of matter (*rūpa*) and thus provides the element of form within the practice that is perceived by the mind (*nāma*). See Horner 1967, 125n1.

15. The feeling that is pleasant that is associated with the in-breath and out-breath (MA IV 140).

monk practices contemplating feeling among feelings, ardent, clearly comprehending, and mindful, he puts away longing and discontent in the world.

"At whatever time, monks, a monk trains thus: 'Experiencing the mind, I shall breathe in'; and he trains thus: 'Experiencing the mind, I shall breathe out.'[16] At whatever time he trains thus: 'Gladdening the mind, I shall breathe in'; and he trains thus: 'Gladdening the mind, I shall breathe out.' At whatever time he trains thus: 'Concentrating the mind, I shall breathe in'; and he trains thus: 'Concentrating the mind, I shall breathe out.' At whatever time he trains thus: 'Liberating the mind, I shall breathe in'; and he trains thus: 'Liberating the mind, I shall breathe out.' At that time, monks, a monk practices contemplating the mind as the mind, ardent, clearly comprehending, and mindful, putting away longing and discontent in the world.[17] I do not say, monks, that the cultivation of mind that is mindfulness of the in-breath and out-breath is for one of confused mindfulness or the one who lacks clear comprehension. Therefore, monks, at the time when a monk practices contemplating the mind as the mind, ardent, clearly comprehending, and mindful, he puts away longing and discontent with regard to the world.

"At whatever time, monks, a monk trains thus: 'Contemplating impermanence, I shall breathe in'; and he trains thus: 'Contemplating impermanence, I shall breathe out.' At whatever time he trains thus: 'Contemplating dispassion, I shall breathe in'; and he trains thus: 'Contemplating dispassion, I shall breathe out.' At whatever time he trains thus: 'Contemplating cessation, I shall breathe in'; and he trains thus: 'Contemplating cessation, I shall breathe out.' At whatever time he trains thus: 'Contemplating letting go, I shall breathe in'; and he trains thus: 'Contemplating letting go, I shall breathe out.' At that time, monks, a monk practices contemplating *dhamma* among *dhamma*s, ardent, clearly comprehending, and mindful, putting away longing and discontent in the world.[18] He, having seen, with wisdom, the abandonment of longing and discontent, is one who looks on with perfect equanimity. Therefore, monks, at the time when a monk practices contemplating *dhamma* among *dhamma*s, ardent, clearly comprehending, and mindful, he puts away longing and discontent with regard to the world. Cultivated and made much of in this way, monks, mindfulness of breathing brings to fulfillment the four foundations of mindfulness.

"And how, monks, do the four foundations of mindfulness, which have been cultivated and made much of, bring to fulfillment the seven factors of awakening?

"At whatever time, monks, a monk practices contemplating the body in the body, ardent, clearly comprehending, and mindful, putting away longing and discontent in the world, then the mindfulness established in him at that time is not confused. At whatever time, monks, that the mindfulness established in a monk is not confused, at that time the awakening factor that is mindfulness is stirred in him, at that time he cultivates the awakening factor that is mindfulness, the awakening factor that is mindfulness comes to fulfillment.

---

16. See Ñāṇamoli and Bodhi 2001, 1330n1120.

17. Contemplation of the mind as the mind (*citte cittānupassī*), or as Buddhadāsa describes this, "contemplating or experiencing the mind in all its aspects" (1997, 79). For further comment, see Ñāṇamoli and Bodhi 2001, 1330n1124.

18. The word *dhamma* has a number of meanings in various contexts, meaning variously what is right, what is in accordance with law, the teaching of the Buddha, and sometimes simply "events" or phenomena. Here it has this latter meaning, that is, phenomena associated with the breath, within the context of other *dhamma*s, phenomena in general. See Ñāṇamoli and Bodhi 2001, 53ff. For the practitioner's viewpoint of this tetrad, see Buddhadāsa 1997, 91–98, 102–3.

"This monk, mindful in such a way, looks into, takes up, and comes to examine that state with wisdom. At whatever time, monks, a monk who is mindful in this way looks into, takes up, and comes to examine that state with wisdom, at that time the awakening factor that is investigation of *dhamma* is stirred in him, at that time he cultivates the awakening factor that is investigation of *dhamma*, the awakening factor that is investigation of *dhamma* comes to fulfillment.[19]

"When he looks into, takes up, and comes to examine that state with wisdom, at that time unflinching vigor is stirred in him. At whatever time, monks, unflinching vigor is stirred in a monk who looks into, takes up, and comes to examine that state with wisdom, at that time the awakening factor that is vigor is stirred in him, at that time he cultivates the awakening factor that is vigor, the awakening factor that is vigor comes to fulfillment.[20]

"When vigor is stirred, the joy that is free from sense-desire arises.[21] At whatever time, monks, the joy that is free from sense-desire is stirred in a monk who looks into, takes up, and comes to examine that state with wisdom, at that time the awakening factor that is joy is stirred in him, at that time he cultivates the awakening factor that is joy, the awakening factor that is joy comes to fulfillment.

"In the one who has a joyful mind, both the body becomes tranquil and the mind becomes tranquil.[22] At whatever time, monks, both the body and the mind become tranquil in the one who has a joyful mind, at that time the awakening factor that is tranquility is stirred in him, at that time he cultivates the awakening factor that is tranquility, the awakening factor that is tranquility comes to fulfillment.

"The mind of the one whose body is tranquil and happy comes to concentration.[23] At whatever time that the mind of one whose body is tranquil and happy comes to concentration,

---

19. Translating the term *dhammavicaya* poses challenges. It includes investigation of *dhamma*, states, events, the teaching, and "things as they are." For a full examination of this factor, see Gethin 1992a, 147–54.

20. Vigor or strength (*viriya*) is a crucial factor in a number of Buddhist lists. It is the second faculty in meditation, the second power, and, here, the third factor of awakening. It is also the fifth perfection to be developed by the Bodhisatta as he prepares for Buddhahood, represented in the *Mahājanaka Jātaka* (Jātaka 539; J VI 30–68). In this story, after being shipwrecked, the Bodhisatta swims valiantly on his own for seven days before being carried by a goddess to Mithilā, where he is the rightful king. As a mental factor (*cetasika*), it occurs in both skillful and unskillful consciousness but is itself neutral: when associated as it is with the sixth factor of the Eightfold Path, right effort (*sammāvāyāma*), it is linked to the removal of unskillful states, keeping them at bay, cultivating skillful states, and sustaining these when they arise. See Gethin 1992a, 72–73.

21. Joy (*pīti*) may arise within sense-sphere activities but also in meditation and in the states freed from the sense-sphere: in sense-sphere consciousness it may be skillful but, of course, is sometimes unskillful too when, say, joy in doing something wrong is present. The type that occurs in meditation is of five kinds, varying in intensity: momentary, minor, showering, uplifting, and pervading. Buddhaghosa tells a delightful anecdote of a woman not allowed to visit a shrine by her parents because she is pregnant. She is filled with so much joy, however, on seeing the butter lamps glitter in the darkness that she floats up in the air and lands right in front of them at the shrine. This is described as the fourth kind of joy (see Vism IV 97). The fifth kind does not seem to have this effect, as the body is pervaded like a bladder or a cave inundated with water. See also Gethin 1992a, 154–55.

22. Tranquility (*passadhi*) is closely associated with joy and regarded as its natural fulfillment or outlet. See Gethin 1992a, 155–56.

23. Concentration (*samādhi*) is another frequent term in Buddhist lists. It is the third faculty, the third power, and, rightly developed, becomes the last path factor, right concentration (*sammā-samādhi*). Connected to the word *sama*, meaning calm or even, it is the bringing together in unification of the mind on one object. Correctly cultivated, it leads to *jhāna* and to the full development of the mind's potential in meditation. See Shaw 2006, 59–75.

at that time the awakening factor that is concentration is stirred in him, at that time he cultivates the awakening factor that is concentration, at that time the awakening factor that is concentration comes to fulfillment.

"The one who has concentrated his mind in this way looks on that concentrated mind with equanimity.[24] At whatever time, monks, the one with concentrated mind looks upon that concentrated mind with equanimity, the awakening factor that is equanimity is stirred in him, at that time he cultivates the awakening factor that is equanimity, at that time the awakening factor that is equanimity in him comes to fulfillment.

"At whatever time that a monk practices contemplating feeling among feelings, ardent, clearly comprehending, and mindful, putting away longing and discontent in the world, then the mindfulness established in him at that time is not confused. At whatever time, monks, that the mindfulness established in a monk is not confused, at that time the awakening factor that is mindfulness is stirred in him, at that time he cultivates the awakening factor that is mindfulness, the awakening factor that is mindfulness comes to fulfillment.

"This monk, mindful in such a way, looks into, takes up, and comes to examine that state with wisdom. At whatever time, monks, that a monk who is mindful in this way looks into, takes up, and comes to examine that state with wisdom, at that time the awakening factor that is investigation of *dhamma* is stirred in him, at that time he cultivates the awakening factor that is investigation of *dhamma*, the awakening factor that is investigation of *dhamma* comes to fulfillment.

"When he looks into, takes up, and comes to examine that state with wisdom, at that time unflinching strength is stirred in him. At whatever time, monks, that unflinching strength is stirred in a monk who looks into, takes up, and comes to examine that state with wisdom, at that time the awakening factor that is strength is stirred in him, at that time he cultivates the awakening factor that is strength, the awakening factor that is strength comes to fulfillment.

"When strength is stirred, the joy that is free from sense-desire arises. At whatever time, monks, that the joy that is free from sense-desire is stirred in a monk who looks into, takes up, and comes to examine that state with wisdom, at that time the awakening factor that is joy is stirred in him, at that time he cultivates the awakening factor that is joy, the awakening factor that is joy comes to fulfillment.

"In the one who has a joyful mind, both the body becomes tranquil and the mind becomes tranquil. At whatever time, monks, that both the body and the mind become tranquil in the one who has a joyful mind, at that time the awakening factor that is tranquility is stirred in him, at that time he cultivates the awakening factor that is tranquility, the awakening factor that is tranquility comes to fulfillment.

"The mind of the one whose body is tranquil and happy comes to concentration. At whatever time that the mind of one whose body is tranquil and happy comes to concentration, at that time the awakening factor that is concentration is stirred in him, at that time he cultivates

---

24. The factor of equanimity is of profound importance in Buddhist meditative training, representing not the rejection of feeling but its purification and transcendence (Shaw 2006, 62–65). Equanimity is present in mild form in some unskillful and skillful consciousnesses, where it is simply neutral feeling. Developed, however, it is associated with the fourth *jhāna*. Here its quality is evoked by the image of the man covered from head to foot in a pure white clean cloth. It is also seen as the fourth divine abiding, after loving-kindness, compassion, and sympathetic joy, and the last of the ten perfections cultivated by the Bodhisatta on his path to Buddhahood.

the awakening factor that is concentration, at that time the awakening factor that is concentration comes to fulfillment.

"The one who has concentrated his mind in this way looks on that concentrated mind with equanimity. At whatever time, monks, the one with concentrated mind looks upon that concentrated mind with equanimity, the awakening factor that is equanimity is stirred in him, at that time he cultivates the awakening factor that is equanimity, at that time the awakening factor that is equanimity in him comes to fulfillment.

"At whatever time, monks, that a monk practices contemplating mind as mind, ardent, clearly comprehending, and mindful, putting away longing and discontent in the world, then the mindfulness established in him at that time is not confused. At whatever time, monks, that the mindfulness established in a monk is not confused, at that time the awakening factor that is mindfulness is stirred in him, at that time he cultivates the awakening factor that is mindfulness, the awakening factor that is mindfulness comes to fulfillment.

"This monk, mindful in such a way, looks into, takes up, and comes to examine that state with wisdom. At whatever time, monks, that a monk who is mindful in this way looks into, takes up, and comes to examine that state with wisdom, at that time the awakening factor that is investigation of *dhamma* is stirred in him, at that time he cultivates the awakening factor that is investigation of *dhamma*, the awakening factor that is investigation of *dhamma* comes to fulfillment.

"When he looks into, takes up, and comes to examine that state with wisdom, at that time unflinching strength is stirred in him. At whatever time, monks, that unflinching strength is stirred in a monk who looks into, takes up, and comes to examine that state with wisdom, at that time the awakening factor that is strength is stirred in him, at that time he cultivates the awakening factor that is strength, the awakening factor that is strength comes to fulfillment.

"When strength is stirred, the joy that is free from sense-desire arises. At whatever time, monks, that the joy that is free from sense-desire is stirred in a monk who looks into, takes up, and comes to examine that state with wisdom, at that time the awakening factor that is joy is stirred in him, at that time he cultivates the awakening factor that is joy, the awakening factor that is joy comes to fulfillment.

"In the one who has a joyful mind, both the body becomes tranquil and the mind becomes tranquil. At whatever time, monks, that both the body and the mind become tranquil in the one who has a joyful mind, at that time the awakening factor that is tranquility is stirred in him, at that time he cultivates the awakening factor that is tranquility, the awakening factor that is tranquility comes to fulfillment.

"The mind of the one whose body is tranquil and happy comes to concentration. At whatever time that the mind of one whose body is tranquil and happy comes to concentration, at that time the awakening factor that is concentration is stirred in him, at that time he cultivates the awakening factor that is concentration, at that time the awakening factor that is concentration comes to fulfillment.

"The one who has concentrated his mind in this way looks on that concentrated mind with equanimity. At whatever time, monks, the one with concentrated mind looks upon that concentrated mind with equanimity, the awakening factor that is equanimity is stirred in him, at that time he cultivates the awakening factor that is equanimity, at that time the awakening factor that is equanimity in him comes to fulfillment.

"At whatever time, monks, that a monk practices contemplating *dhamma* among *dhamma*s, ardent, clearly comprehending, and mindful, putting away longing and discontent in the world, then the mindfulness established in him at that time is not confused. At whatever time, monks, that the mindfulness established in a monk is not confused, at that time the awakening factor that is mindfulness is stirred in him, at that time he cultivates the awakening factor that is mindfulness, the awakening factor that is mindfulness comes to fulfillment.

"This monk, mindful in such a way, looks into, takes up, and comes to examine that state with wisdom. At whatever time, monks, a monk who is mindful in this way looks into, takes up, and comes to examine that state with wisdom, at that time the awakening factor that is investigation of *dhamma* is stirred in him, at that time he cultivates the awakening factor that is investigation of *dhamma*, the awakening factor that is investigation of *dhamma* comes to fulfillment.

"When he looks into, takes up, and comes to examine that state with wisdom, at that time unflinching strength is stirred in him. At whatever time, monks, that unflinching strength is stirred in a monk who looks into, takes up, and comes to examine that state with wisdom, at that time the awakening factor that is strength is stirred in him, at that time he cultivates the awakening factor that is strength, the awakening factor that is strength comes to fulfillment.

"When strength is stirred, the joy that is free from sense-desire arises. At whatever time, monks, that the joy that is free from sense-desire is stirred in a monk who looks into, takes up, and comes to examine that state with wisdom, at that time the awakening factor that is joy is stirred in him, at that time he cultivates the awakening factor that is joy, the awakening factor that is joy comes to fulfillment.

"In the one who has a joyful mind, both the body becomes tranquil and the mind becomes tranquil. At whatever time, monks, that both the body and the mind become tranquil in the one who has a joyful mind, at that time the awakening factor that is tranquility is stirred in him, at that time he cultivates the awakening factor that is tranquility, the awakening factor that is tranquility comes to fulfillment.

"The mind of the one whose body is tranquil and happy comes to concentration. At whatever time that the mind of one whose body is tranquil and happy comes to concentration, at that time the awakening factor that is concentration is stirred in him, at that time he cultivates the awakening factor that is concentration, at that time the awakening factor that is concentration comes to fulfillment.

"The one who has concentrated his mind in this way looks on that concentrated mind with equanimity. At whatever time, monks, the one with concentrated mind looks upon that concentrated mind with equanimity, the awakening factor that is equanimity is stirred in him, at that time he cultivates the awakening factor that is equanimity, at that time the awakening factor that is equanimity in him comes to fulfillment.

"Ardent, clearly comprehending, and mindful, putting away longing and discontent in the world, then the factor of mindfulness established in him at that time is not confused, at that time the awakening factor that is equanimity in him comes to fulfillment. When the four foundations of mindfulness are cultivated in this way and made much of, monks, in this way the seven factors of awakening are fulfilled.

"And how, monks, when the seven factors of awakening are cultivated and how, when they are made much of, do they fulfill knowledge and deliverance? Here, monks, a monk cultivates the awakening factor that is mindfulness dependent on seclusion, dependent on dispassion, dependent on cessation, that leads to letting go.²⁵ A monk cultivates the awakening factor that is investigation of *dhamma* dependent on seclusion, dependent on dispassion, dependent on cessation, that leads to letting go. A monk cultivates the awakening factor of strength dependent on seclusion, dependent on dispassion, dependent on cessation, that leads to letting go. A monk cultivates the awakening factor of joy dependent on seclusion, dependent on dispassion, dependent on cessation, that leads to letting go. A monk cultivates the awakening factor of tranquility dependent on seclusion, dependent on dispassion, dependent on cessation, that leads to letting go. A monk cultivates the awakening factor of concentration dependent on seclusion, dependent on dispassion, dependent on cessation, that leads to letting go. A monk cultivates the awakening factor of equanimity dependent on seclusion, dependent on dispassion, dependent on cessation, that leads to letting go. When the seven factors of awakening are cultivated in this way, monks, when they are made much of, they fulfill knowledge and liberation."

Thus spoke the Exalted One. Delighted, these monks rejoiced in what the Exalted One had said.

Glossary of Key Pāli Terms

ānāpāna: In-breath and out-breath.

arūpa: Formless. The states known as the sphere of infinite space, the sphere of infinite consciousness, the sphere of no-thingness, and the sphere of neither perception nor nonperception are the four formless attainments (*arūpasamāpatti*), available to the meditator who has attained the four formless (*arūpa*) attainments.

bhāvanā: Cultivation, practice, and meditation in particular. That the term describes meditation and other associated activities is suggested by its link with the verb.

bhāveti: To develop or cultivate. This verb is applied to the whole Eightfold Path, which is said to need "to be cultivated."

bojjhaṅga: Factor of awakening. There are seven of these, frequently associated with the practice of mindfulness of breathing.

dhamma: What is right, what is lawful, the teaching of the Buddha, or phenomena. "Things as they are."

ekaggatā: One-pointedness or unification. Known as the fifth factor of *jhāna*. It remains stable in the fourth *jhāna* when other factors have been dropped.

jhāna (Skt.: *dhyāna*): Meditative state of unification and peacefulness that forms the basis of the Buddha's meditative teaching. There are four *jhāna*s in the fourfold system and eight in the system that includes the formless attainments. The *Abhidhamma* takes a fivefold system, with *vitakka* dropped for the second and *vicāra* for the third.

kammaṭṭhāna: Literally, "place of work." An object of meditation. The ancient commentator Buddhaghosa lists forty of these, with the practice of mindfulness of breathing being the twenty-ninth.

---

25. *Viveka, virāga, nirodha,* and *vossagga*.

passadhi: Tranquility. The fifth of the seven factors of awakening.

pīti: Joy. The third of the five *jhāna* factors and the fourth of the seven factors of awakening. It is the only factor common to both lists.

rūpa: Form. Opposed to *nāma*, or mind. A descriptive term for the first four *jhānas*, *rūpa* denotes states where matter is present only in a subtle form. This "form" or subtle matter is then left behind for the formless attainments (Vism X).

samādhi: Concentration. The sixth of the seven factors of awakening.

samatha: Calm. From the same root as *samādhi*, meaning "calm" or "even." It refers in Pāli texts to the cultivation of *jhānas*, and is considered to complement the practice of insight (*vipassanā*).

sati: Awareness or attentiveness. Also translated as "mindfulness." Associated with the Sanskrit word for "memory" (*smṛti*), its meaning is more comprehensive than "mindfulness," being associated with awareness, attentiveness, and watchfulness. *Sati* is the first of the seven factors of awakening. In the early texts, there are said to be four "foundations of mindfulness" (*satipaṭṭhāna*). These are body (*kāya*), feeling (*vedanā*), mind (*citta*), and the teaching, or the teaching as it is manifest in the rise and fall of states (*dhamma*). The *Satipaṭṭhāna Sutta* (Discourse on the Foundations of Mindfulness), the famous teaching on the four foundations of mindfulness, includes the first tetrad of the stages of mindfulness of breathing under mindfulness of body. The *Ānāpānasati Sutta* develops this and associates each tetrad with one of the four foundations of mindfulness.

sukha: Happiness. The fourth of the five *jhāna* factors.

sutta: Discourse. Buddhist texts claimed to contain the teachings or discourses of the historical Buddha. The early transmitted teachings have traditionally been divided into three "baskets": the monastic code (*Vinaya-piṭaka*), texts given on specific occasions (*Sutta-piṭaka*), and the higher or philosophical teachings (*Abhidhamma-piṭaka*).

upekkhā: Equanimity. Associated with the fourth *jhāna* and the seventh of the seven factors of awakening.

vicāra: Exploration of the object; sustained thought. The second factor of *jhāna*, it sustains interest in the object of meditation. With the first factor, it is dropped in the second *jhāna* of the fourfold system.

vipassanā (Skt.: *vipaśyanā*): Insight. The term is an amalgam of the word for "seeing" and the prefix *vi*, which has connotations of separateness and multidirectionality. The term is used as well to communicate a sense of depth of seeing. Associated with mindfulness and wisdom, it denotes the strand of meditative practice that complements the cultivation of calm (*samatha*).

viriya: Vigor or strength. The third of the seven factors of awakening.

vitakka: Thinking of or initial thought. As the first factor of first *jhāna*, it is used in a positive sense as the applying of the mind to the object. In other contexts, the word is sometimes associated with distracting thoughts (see Ud 34–37).

Chapter 7

Sufi Contemplation
'Abdullah Shah's *Suluk-i Mujaddidiyya*

Arthur F. Buehler

The *Suluk-i Mujaddidiyya* (Mujaddidi Wayfaring) is a mid-twentieth century-text on sufi contemplation (*muraqabat*). Originally written in Urdu, the text was composed by 'Abdullah Shah (1872–1964), a prominent member of the Naqshbandi-Mujaddidi sufi lineage.[1] More popularly known as "the Muhaddith of the Deccan," 'Abdullah Shah lived, taught, and died in Hyderabad, which is located in Andhra Pradesh, India. The text describes a contemplative practice that includes guidance under a shaykh (Ar.: *shaykh*; fem.: *shaykha*; Per.: *pir*, all meaning elder) who functions as a spiritual guide and sufi master. It specifically describes a form of sufi contemplation that utilizes color visualization of the body's subtle centers and was primarily intended for use within the Naqshbandi-Mujaddidi sufi lineage.

'Abdullah Shah and Twentieth-Century Indian Sufism

Abu'l-Hasanat Sayyid 'Abdullah Shah Naqshbandi-Qadiri (1872–1964; Hyderabad, Deccan, India),[2] whose name will be shortened to 'Abdullah Shah, was a religious scholar specializing in hadith, the recorded sayings of the Prophet Muhammad (ca. 570–632). The honorific Abu'l-Hasanat (the father of meritorious acts) was given to him because of his famous hadith teacher Abu'l-Hasanat 'Abdulhayy (d. 1886) of Farangi Mahal in Lucknow (Uttar Pradesh, India) (Muhammad 'Abdussattar 1998, 57). Because of his five-volume compendium of hadith, titled *Zujajat al-masabih* (Lanterns' Glass) (see 'Abdullah Shah 1952), 'Abdullah Shah was better known in scholarly circles as "the Muhaddith of the Deccan," with Muhaddith being an honorific title for someone specializing in studying hadith. 'Abdullah Shah spent his life teaching at the 'Ali Aqa mosque in Hyderabad and wrote many books, including a detailed exposition on Naqshbandi-Mujaddidi contemplative practices, titled *Suluk-i Mujaddidiyya* (Mujaddidi Wayfaring) (see 'Abdullah Shah 1958), upon which the following translation is based. 'Abdullah Shah studied the religious sciences with his father, Mawlana Hafiz Sayyid Muzaffar Husayn, whose honorifics indicate that he was a religious scholar (*mawlana*) and had memorized the Qur'an (Muhammad 'Abdussattar 1998, 37). Some of his other teachers in Hyderabad were Shah Anwar Allah Faruqi, Mansur 'Ali Khan, 'Abdulrahman Saharanpuri, Habiburrahman Saharanpuri, and Shah Piran (d. 1950) (Muhammad 'Abdussattar 1998, 57).

'Abdullah Shah's first sufi shaykh was Miskin Shah (d. 1899; Hyderabad, Deccan), a well-known sufi of Hyderabad. Later, on the death of the latter, 'Abdullah Shah became a disciple of Muhammad Badshah Bukhari, a Naqshbandi-Qadiri shaykh and disciple of Shah Sa'dullah Husayni Naqshbandi-Qadiri, whose lineage goes back to Ghulam 'Ali Shah (1743–1824; Delhi) by way of Abu Sa'id (d. 1835; Delhi) (Muhammad 'Abdussattar 1998, 75, 643).[3]

Ghulam 'Ali Shah was the paramount Naqshbandi-Mujaddidi shaykh in India during the first quarter of the nineteenth century. His father, Shah 'Abdullatif, was a descendant of 'Ali b. Abi Talib (the Prophet's cousin and son-in-law) and a disciple of Shah Nasiruddin Qadiri Dihlwi who initiated him into the Qadiri, Chishti, and Shattari lineages. From the ages of eighteen to twenty-two he was involved in formal religious studies. Some of his teachers included the following: Diya'ullah and 'Abdul'adil, successors to the great-great-grandson of Muhammad Ma'sum (the chief successor to Ahmad Sirhindi), Muhammad Zubayr Sirhindi Mujaddidi (d. 1740; Sirhind, Punjab, India), Mir Dard (1721–1785), Fakhruddin Chishti (d. 1784), Shah Nanu Majdhub, and Ghulam Sadat Chishti ('Abdulghani Mujaddidi 1983, 571). Mirza Jan-i Janan (assassinated 1781) initiated Ghulam 'Ali Shah at the age of twenty-two. He continued studying hadith and Qur'an exegesis for the next sixteen years with his sufi guide (Ra'uf Ahmad Rafat 1914, 141). This was an atypical initiation in that Mirza Jan-i Janan initiated Ghulam 'Ali Shah into the Qadiriyya but gave his new disciple the exercises of the Naqshbandiyya-Mujaddidiyya ('Abdulghani Mujaddidi 1983, 572). Later, Ghulam 'Ali Shah explained that his shaykh had done this because most of Ghulam 'Ali Shah's ancestors were connected with the Qadiriyya and one can be initiated into any sufi lineage and still use Mujaddidi methods.[4] After fifteen years Ghulam 'Ali Shah received unconditional permission to teach (*ijazat-i mutlaq*). The next year his mentor died and Ghulam 'Ali Shah became his chief successor (*sajjada nishin*).

Ghulam 'Ali Shah built the sufi lodge at the site of his shaykh's tomb in the area of Delhi, which is still known as Chitli Qabr. The tomb of Mirza Jan-i Janan provided a basis for his authority, and Ghulam 'Ali Shah was quite aware of this situation.[5] There were about two hundred permanent residents in the sufi lodge and on Fridays and special occasions perhaps there would be twice this many.

'Abdullah Shah's lineage is directly linked to that of Ghulam 'Ali Shah, indicating the connections between Hyderabad and Delhi in the nineteenth century. 'Abdullah Shah's lineage and Naqshbandi teaching are continuing today under the leadership of Abu'l-Khayr Rahmatullah Shah. Without visiting the group there is no way to know if they are practicing the contemplative practices outlined in 'Abdullah Shah's *Suluk-i Mujaddidiyya*.[6]

Islam, Sufism, and the Naqshbandi Lineage

How is sufism central to the practice of Islam? The easiest way to answer this is to quote the famous hadith of the Prophet Muhammad known as Gabriel's hadith. It is so famous that it is the first account in some hadith collections. In shortened form it tells about a man with very white clothing and very black hair coming up to the Prophet and his companions. No mark of travel was visible on him, and no one recognized him. Sitting down before the Prophet he said, "Tell me Muhammad about submission to God (*islam*)." Muhammad replied, "Submission means that you should bear witness that there is no god but God and that Muhammad is God's messenger, that you should perform the ritual prayer, pay alms, fast during Ramadan, and make the pilgrimage to the House if you are able to go there." The man said, "You have spoken the truth." Then he said, "Now tell me about faith (*iman*)." Muhammad replied, "Faith means that you have faith in God, his angels, his books, his messengers, and the last day and that you have faith in the measuring out, both its good and its evil." Remarking that the Prophet had spoken the truth, he then said, "Now tell me about doing what is beautiful (*ihsan*)." Muhammad replied, "Doing what is beautiful means that you should worship God as if you see him, for even if you do not see him, he sees you." When the man left, Muhammad informed his astonished companions that the angel Gabriel had come to teach them about their religion.

Here is religion in a nutshell: it is what one does (*islam*), what one thinks (*iman*), and what one intends in one's heart (*ihsan*; also translated as "virtue"). The point here is that each of these three religious dimensions is interconnected with the other dimension, like a tree's roots, branches, and fruit. Being a perfected or complete human being involves an integration of these three dimensions. Sufism is that third dimension, the fruit of action and faith. Those who deny sufism (e.g., Wahhabi fundamentalists) do not recognize this integral "heart dimension" in Islam.[7] With multiple orthodoxies in the Islamic world, the Western Orientalist notion (taken up by the Wahhabis) that sufism is not an integral dimension of submission to God (*islam*) is itself a counter-orthodoxy, but one that comprises a small minority of Muslims (at most 15 percent).[8]

Such a three-dimensional conception of Islam assumes that different persons have varying potential and ability for spiritual accomplishment. The vast majority of Muslims seek salvation through their daily practices, informed by a faith commitment. Sufism, on the other hand, encompasses the activities working toward the field of consciousness and experience represented by acting in a beautiful manner. Such an enterprise assumes a firm foundation in faith and in the practice of submitting to God before achieving an extraordinary degree of proximity to God. Surely not all who call themselves sufis are able to achieve this advanced goal and not all of the few who reach this stage are necessarily sufis.

Gabriel's hadith should make clear that there is no conflict between "orthodoxy" and sufism. Sufis simply intensify and expand the notion of submitting to God by seeking to remember God more continuously (enter the second dimension of *iman*) and deeply (enter the third dimension of *ihsan*) in their lives than the Muslim masses who perform the five pillars of *islam*. Ritual prayer, fasting, giving alms, and going on the pilgrimage to Mecca are all ways of remembering that there is no god but God. Sufi practices of remembering God (*dhikr*) build on common Muslim practice, the most basic being a repetition of "Allah" or "*La illaha illa Allah*" (There is no god but God). These and other exercises prepare the aspirant to calm the discursive mind and develop subtle faculties, if not subtle bodies, to travel in other realms in contemplative witnessing (*mushahida*; *muraqaba*).[9]

Historically the word *sufi* was first used in an eighth-century Islamic context for ascetics wearing woolen cloaks—like their Christian counterparts—in the deserts of the Near East.[10] Eventually by the tenth century this activity developed into a branch of the Islamic religious sciences, into what has become known as "sufism" in the West. "The process of becoming a sufi" (*tasawwuf*) in the Sunni world (the mainstream Muslim community) and "philosophical mysticism" (*'irfan*) in the post-seventeenth-century Iranian Shi'i world (the major sect in Islam) are conflated by the English term "sufism." The activities of sufis are generally acknowledged by historians to be responsible for the spread of Islam in the Eastern Islamic world, including present-day Turkey, India, Indonesia, and Africa. Investigation into the historical processes of Islamization, still going on today, indicate that the sufi message is more expansive yet inclusive of the doctrinal, orthopraxic religion known as Islam. That is, although sufism historically has been practiced almost exclusively by Muslims, it has also gone beyond the human-created boundaries of the religion of Islam to include anyone who seeks to submit to God, the technical meaning of the word *muslim* in Arabic.[11]

The practice of sufism involves the inner aspect of *islam* (the submission to God/ultimate reality), including transformation of the human spirit and ethics/character development. To the extent that sufis desire closeness or intimacy with God, sufism can be vaguely translated as Islamic mysticism. Insofar as these interior experiences and transformations are not apparent to others (in contrast to woolen clothing), sufism can be said to be the esoteric aspect of Islam. From a transrational perspective, sufism is the study and cultivation of one's actual experience with God. In a more poetic fashion, one could say that sufism is the intentional act of plunging into a wave from the Infinite Ocean and being drawn back with it toward the Eternal Source.

In sufi contemplative practice, like other contemplative practices and experimental endeavors, there is usually a development from lesser to greater sophistication. What this means is that there are very general discussions of contemplative experiences in the early sufi literature of the tenth to twelfth centuries, which become quite detailed in seventeenth- to nineteenth-century Naqshbandi sources. The reader can appreciate the *scientific* nature of the sufi path here. The aspirant is first given tasks to perform in the "laboratory" of subjective experience. The "laboratory results" are checked with his mentor, who then verifies whether the aspirant's experiences do or do not coincide with the consensus of those "verifiers" who have used the same Naqshbandi methods. This is how serious contemplative practices operate. Every so often someone like Ahmad Sirhindi comes along and renews the entire contemplative methodology with more developed techniques (see Buehler 1998, 98–130).

In the early sufi literature there are entire books on stations (sing. *maqam*; pl. *maqamat*) along the sufi path and altered states of consciousness (sing. *hal*; pl. *ahwal*) that imply some kind of systematic treatment of the subject.[12] They outline ten stations that (in order) include the following: repentance, trusting in God, poverty, patience, gratitude, fear, hope, love, inner knowledge, and satisfaction. These are some very general markers on the sufi path for the average sufi wayfarer. More detailed treatments of sufi contemplative experience are outlined by Naqshbandis in their contemplative exercises (*muraqabat*). Often they pass through the *reflections* of the stations of the prophets and visit various spirits of prior sufis and notables of the Islamic tradition (see Buehler 2011).

Sufis clarify their experiences by comparing them with other types of sufi experience. The compendium of Ibn al-'Arabi's (1165–1240; Damascus, Syria) works (particularly his *Meccan Revelations*) outlining his visionary experiences was often consulted by advanced sufis seeking to verify their experiences after their mentors had passed away. Books written by experienced sufis have functioned to describe what has happened to them as they traverse the stations. There are probably innumerable stations—the ten "standard" stations discussed previously are very basic markers. The maps of the realms in which sufis travel are very approximate, even in the most detailed expositions of the Naqshbandis.[13]

The goal for the sufi is to become a complete/perfected human being. To be whole or complete means to realize the fullness of our own nature, physically, emotionally, mentally, psychically, and spiritually. Sufism is about cultivating unconditional love and becoming truly human. From a sufi perspective this comes about by realizing who one is ultimately, which is the total reflection and image of God's names and attributes. Sufis assert that this wholeness is a human being's natural state and that an experience of fragmented selves is an indication of separateness from God. To embark upon the path of sufism one usually finds a teacher or shaykh, formally makes a commitment through an initiation ritual, and then proceeds to incorporate a contemplative discipline into one's life as a practicing Muslim.

Initiation (*bay'a*) with a sufi shaykh with a two-handed handclasp follows the Prophetic precedent of the Companions making a pact with Muhammad at Hudaybiya in 628. By clasping the shaykh's hand one is symbolically shaking the hand of all the previous shaykhs and therefore ultimately clasping Muhammad's hand. Historically there are three types of initiation in the Naqshbandiyya. The *first* is repenting from sins and swearing on the Prophet and the rest of the Naqshbandi lineage that one will perform the ritual duties expected of an adult Muslim and avoid major sins. The *second* kind is an affiliation of blessedness (*tabarruk*) with the intention of receiving the blessings transmitted through the Naqshbandi (or another) lineage from Muhammad. In the past the shaykh often gave a sufi robe to the initiate on this occasion. Sometimes this type of affiliation is one in which the shaykh becomes an intermediary between the believer and God. Multiple sufi affiliations (after finishing the exercises of the primary lineage) often are of this type. This is why our author, 'Abdullah Shah, is called a Naqshbandi-Qadiri. Naqshbandi is his primary lineage and the set of practices that he teaches, while Qadiri is his secondary lineage and practice. What is usually understood to be initiation is the *third* type where the contemplative practice is added to the prerequisites of the first two. This involves a much more committed seeker who necessarily needs to obey the shaykh as the seeker develops both an inner and outer connection to the Prophet. Such is the beginning of a very close spiritual companionship.

Another oft-mentioned triad associated with explicating sufism is Islamic law (Ar.: *shari'a*; Per.: *shari'at*), the sufi path (*tariqa*), and the real reality (*haqiqa*) (see Schimmel 1975). For Muslims, Islamic law represents the wide path outlining (what are perceived to be) the timeless God-given rules that govern everyday life for all humans. It is the path leading to salvation. The sufi path is a narrower path leading to the real reality, the experience of the Ultimate. These three interrelated aspects of Islam have been depicted as the one circle of Islamic law with a multiplicity of radii or sufi paths leading to the reality at the center. In transformative terms, Islamic law is medical science: the sufi path is preventing disease and taking medicine, and experiencing reality is eternally perfect health.[14] The latter metaphor implies a necessary doctor or guide who has eternally perfect health. These triads clearly show the role of Islamic ritual practices in sufism (i.e., the five pillars of Islam outlined in Gabriel's hadith).

Jurists, whose knowledge is based upon book learning, often have contested sufis' experience-based religiosity (though one can be both a sufi and a jurist). Jurists are interested in the external symbols and outward behavior that are associated with maintaining and outwardly legitimizing Islamic social structures through a system of law, schools, and mosques. For this reason their activities and interests overlap considerably with that of the rulers who have the power to enforce such concerns and who need such legitimacy to keep their power. It is the jurists (often called *ulama*) who justify war in the name of *jihad* and who provide the basis of salvation to give meaning to such endeavors (martyrs go immediately to heaven).[15] This outer level supplies soteriological formulae, important psychologically, to enforce the dictates of society (if you do these things, you go to heaven; otherwise you go to hell). This approach utilizes fear to motivate people, which contrasts with the sufi approach of love. The jurist's expression of religion integrates and stabilizes society. *Shariat* (commonly translated as Islamic law) is the "kernel" that protects, legitimizes, and tempers the precious "seed" of spiritual practice. This is the conventional dualistic sufi explanation. The Naqshbandi-Mujaddidi conception of *shariat*, outlined in the following discussion, goes beyond this formulation.

Spiritual practice is required for the integration and stabilization of the outer social structure and presumes movement, change, and transformation within the individual. Instead of *jihad* as war, sufis stress the "inner struggling (*jihad*) in the path of God," controlling the desires and ignorance of one's lower carnal nature (*nafs*). Although ignored by those utilizing religion for their own sociopolitical ends, there is a well-known hadith that Muhammad related after the Muslims gained a military victory against a much larger force at the Battle of Badr (624 CE). He mentioned to the returning warriors that now they were returning from the "lesser *jihad*" of fighting others to the "greater *jihad*" of fighting their ego-selves. The transformation process of taming one's ego-self is a major goal of sufism, implying an unfolding, a transcending of prior states and perceptions. Often this transformation in the sufi environment is associated with the spiritual experiences associated with performance of sufi contemplative practices (see Buehler 2011).

Lineage (Ar.: *silsila*; lit., chain; *tariqa*; lit., method or path) is important to understand the construction of sufism since the tenth century. Creating spiritual lineages, continuous chains of pious sufis leading back to the Prophet, sufis met juristic challenges to their authority. Thus, by the eleventh century a number of international pan-Islamic sufi lineages named after their founder-figures came into existence, including the Qadiriyya lineage from 'Abdulqadir al-Jilani (1077–1166; Baghdad, Iraq), which is the most widespread lineage in the Islamic world. Other major lineages include the Suhrawardi lineage from Abu Hafs al-Suhrawardi (1144–1234; Baghdad), the Chishti lineage in India from Mu'inuddin Chishti (1141–1236; Ajmer, Rajasthan, India) famous for its qawwali songs, the Naqshbandi lineage from Baha'uddin Naqshband (1318–1389; Bukhara, Uzbekistan) famous for its pioneering contemplative practices and political involvement, and the Mevlevi lineage from Jalaluddin Rumi (1207–1273; Konya, Turkey), so named because Mevlana (our master) is the honorific given to Rumi in Turkish. It is famous for its so-called "whirling dervish" ritual, better described as "coming face to face with God" (*mukabeleh*).

'Abdullah Shah, the author of the *Suluk-i Mujaddidiyya*, outlines a Naqshbandi-Mujaddidi contemplative practice. Originally a Central Asian sufi lineage, the Naqshbandi lineage was named after its eponymous founder-figure, Baha'uddin Naqshband (1318–1389; Bukhara, Uzbekistan), continuing "the way of the Masters" that had begun with 'Abdulkhaliq Ghujduwani (d. 1179). In Central Asia the Naqshbandis were closely allied with the sedentary middle and lower classes and linked many different groups, for example, artisan guilds in towns and village peasants. Naqshbandi shaykhs were to be respected and their assistance had soteriological implications. Timur Tamerlane (1336–1405; r. 1370–1405), the founding member of the Timurids, chose to be buried next to Baha'uddin's sufi guide, Amir Kulal (d. 1370). 'Ubaydullah Ahrar (1404–1490) became the most significant Naqshbandi in Central Asia, as he became one of the largest landowners and *de facto* ruler of most of the eastern Timurid kingdom. His lineal and spiritual descendants dominated the Indian Naqshbandiyya, as they became allied with the first Indian Mughal ruler, Babur (1483–1530; r. 1526–1530). By the time of Akbar's rule (r. 1556–1605) in India, Naqshbandis had intermarried with many of the leading Mughal families.

The Naqshbandiyya subsequently became transformed by Ahmad Sirhindi (1564–1624; Sirhind, Punjab, India), the founder-figure of the Naqshbandiyya-Mujaddidiyya (henceforth Mujaddidi/Mujaddidiyya) lineage.[16] Sirhindi, initiated into the Qadiri lineage by his father Abdulahad, met his paramount Naqshbandi shaykh Khwaja Baqibillah (1563–1603) in Delhi. After a short period of three months, Baqibillah gave him permission to teach. This became the beginning of Sirhindi's mission to revitalize Islam by seeking to implement the universal symbols of Islam, having the Mughals implement Islamic law, and admonishing them to behave according to the Prophetic model. This ran counter to Akbar's pragmatic policies of opening up Mughal leadership to all influential members of Indian society regardless of religious identity or ethnicity. Although Akbar ignored Sirhindi, many members of Akbar's court were Sirhindi's students. Akbar's successor, Jahangir (r. 1605–1627), imprisoned Sirhindi for a year, apparently because of the latter's claim to have reached a station higher than the first caliph, Abu Bakr (d. 634). In the context of contemplative practice, Sirhindi vastly expanded the contemplative repertoire of the Naqshbandiyya. Apparently it was the top sufi contemplative technology of the day. Kalimullah Jahanabadi (1650–1729), a prominent Chishti shaykh of Delhi, says,

> The Naqshbandi path is very widespread. Since all paths are found in you, why should you remain a stranger to the way of meditation? Train people in this way also, for by God! It is the shortest of paths. There is no doubt concerning the greatness of this order. (Ernst and Lawrence 2002, 28)

A disciple of Ghulam 'Ali Shah in Delhi, Khalid al-Kurdi/al-Baghdadi (1779–1827; Damascus, Syria), became the founder-figure of the Naqshbandiyya-Khalidiyya lineage, which altered Mujaddidi contemplative practices and spread throughout the Ottoman lands. The Mujaddidi lineage is still active in the eastern Islamic world and is now found in most parts of the world, having globalized like other sufi lineages. Mujaddidi contemplative practices are remarkably diverse, even in Mujaddidi lineages of the same city. Istanbul, for example, has the Iskandarpaşas, the Süleymancis, and separate practices led by Shaykh Mahmud Ustaosmanoğlu and Osman Nuri Topbaş.

Shaykh Ahmad Sirhindi is the pioneer for the contemplative practices discussed here. His best-known writings are his *Maktubat* (Collected Letters), which comprise 536 letters in three volumes. The vast majority of these letters discuss contemplative practice and related sufi concerns.[17] As Mujaddidi shaykhs traveled throughout the eastern Islamic world with copies of these letters, Mujaddidi practices made their mark in sufi communities. When an envoy from Kokand (near Tashkent, present-day Uzbekistan) arrived in 1833 at the palace of Sultan Mahmut II (r. 1808–1839) in Istanbul, Turkey, he presented three books to the Sultan: a Qur'an, Ahmad Sirhindi's *Collected Letters*, and the *Collected Letters* of Sirhindi's son and formal successor, Khwaja Muhammad Ma'sum (d. 1668; Sirhind, India), along with other presents of clothes and shawls from Central Asia (Ahmet Lütfi 1873–1912, 4:77).[18]

Turkish Mujaddidis accord Sirhindi's *Collected Letters* a status alongside the Qur'an and Jalaluddin Rumi's *Mathnawi-yi ma'nawi* (Couplets of Reality). The contemplative methods that Ahmad Sirhindi pioneered supplanted almost all prior Naqshbandi practices worldwide within two generations. The lineage that he founded, the Naqshbandiyya-Mujaddidiyya, is still vibrantly active today globally and all through the eastern Islamic world, as evidenced by, for example, the recent translation of Sirhindi's *Collected Letters* into Chinese.[19]

Sirhindi had a unique view of the three dimensions of Islam. For him there was only one domain, the *shariat*. In my recent translation (Buehler 2011) this is the only word that has not been translated (although technically it has become an English word, sharia/*shariat* in this essay, *shariat*) because in most contexts it is translated conventionally as simply Islamic law. In ultimate terms, Sirhindi defines *shariat* as being equal to the sum of submission to God (*islam*), faith (*iman*), and virtue (*ihsan*)—analogous to one's way of life (*din*; usually translated as "religion") in Gabriel's hadith.[20] The *shariat* is the locus or organizing principle for all of Islamic life. Nothing is actually outside of the *shariat* (Sirhindi 1972, 1.40:104).[21] "Until these three dimensions of the *shariat* are experienced then one cannot say that the *shariat* is confirmed. When it is, one reaches satisfaction of God. Perfection of the *shariat* is virtue. Sufis who only have visions and traverse the stages and end in the station of satisfaction are shut off from the perspective of the *shariat*" (Sirhindi 1972, 1.36:98). For Sirhindi, *shariat* is not the wide path leading to the narrow sufi path to Reality. "Reality (*haqiqat*) and the sufi path (*tariqat*) are the path and reality of *shariat*; *shariat* is not distinct from Reality and the sufi path or vice versa (Sirhindi 1972, 1.57:30).[22]

Generally speaking, there are very few sufi texts that deal with specific contemplative practices in any detail whatsoever. Usually practices are mentioned in passing.[23] It appears that information on contemplative practice was not disseminated in written form but rather passed from master to disciple orally as part of the initiatory tradition. This surely is the case with the Naqshbandiyya up to Ahmad Sirhindi's time. Following Sirhindi's example, Mujaddidi shaykhs wrote letters concerning the details of Mujaddidi cosmology and spiritual practice answering their disciples' questions. Mir Nu'man, one of Sirhindi's disciples, wrote the first Mujaddidi "manual" of spiritual practice (see Mir Nu'man 1965). In this short thirty-two-page treatise, he describes the positions of the subtle centers and the colors associated with each one, the origins of each subtle center, and the stages of contemplation. There are no details of how to go about remembrance of God, the practice of negation and affirmation, nor any other detailed instructions for the disciple.

In the nineteenth century, particularly among Ghulam 'Ali Shah's lineage, an entirely new genre of sufi literature emerged. 'Abdullah Shah's *Suluk-i Mujaddidiyya*, our primary text, is one of the most modern works of this genre. 'Abdullah Shah's great-grandfather shaykh, Abu Sa'id, wrote the *Hidayat al-talibin* (Aspirants' Guidance), which was said to be used (twenty years ago) at Khundian Sharif in the Punjab of Pakistan. Muhammad 'Inayatullah, whose grandfather shaykh was Ghulam 'Ali Shah, named his book on Mujaddidi practice after his shaykh, Muhammad Irshad Husayn (see Muhammad 'Inayatullah 1959). Unlike any of its predecessors,[24] it begins by emphasizing the superiority of the Mujaddidiyya and the necessity of a shaykh. The first half is devoted to a description of the Mujaddidi cosmology and stages along the Mujaddidi path; the second explains many sufi technical terms used by Mujaddidi shaykhs. A short hagiography of Irshad Husayn completes the eighty-one-page Persian treatise.

Eight generations from Ghulam 'Ali Shah, Zawwar Husayn (d. 1980) developed the genre to its fullest. Written for a general audience, the first part of the *'Umdat al-suluk* (Pillar of Wayfaring) explains each aspect of Mujaddidi sufism with copious Qur'anic and hadith references (see Zawwar Husayn 1984). There are fifty-two Qur'anic proofs and forty-one hadith citations to support the common practice of remembrance of God (*dhikr*) alone. This is followed by the responsibilities of a shaykh and conditions for being a good disciple. The second section of the book, which is intended for a more specialized audience of sufi practitioners, discusses the Mujaddidi path and technical terminology. One of the most modern productions of this genre is the *Manahij al-sayr* (Methodologies of Wayfaring) by the late Abu'l-Hasan Zayd Faruqi (d. 1993; Delhi). It discusses sufi terminology and the specifics of the Mujaddidi path in an academic fashion, a synthesis of preceding, mostly out-of-print books. Abu'l-Hasan, who graduated from Cairo's Al-Azhar University in 1935, was a prolific author in Urdu, Persian, and Arabic. Living in the Chitli Qabr compound founded by Ghulam 'Ali Shah, Abu'l-Hasan was authorized to teach the Mujaddidi path at the age of fifteen by his father Abu'l-Khayr 'Abdullah.

Dimensions of the Mujaddidi Universe

One important perspective of the Mujaddidi universe is the map of the macrocosm. A sufi aspirant is not a religio-cultural blank slate as she proceeds wayfaring on the sufi path. Indeed, the Mujaddidi path is defined by the requisite articles of creedal faith and Islamic ritual practices in addition to the Mujaddidi cosmological conceptual map, pioneered by Ibn al-'Arabi (1165–1240; Damascus, Syria) (see Chittick 1982). Part of Mujaddidi wayfaring is having access to one's spiritual ancestors' wisdom and assistance, so there is good reason to stay connected to and not veer too far from the well-trodden path of the Prophet Muhammad. Contemplative witnessing is the method by which one transcends time and returns to the experiential roots of the Islamic tradition. It is a wide path in that it is open to all who agree with the assumptions and do the practices. At the same time, it is a narrow path like a railroad track. Guided Mujaddidi contemplative witnessing takes one to the metahistorical Prophetic source, Muhammad. Other paths go to other places.

The Mujaddidi cosmological universe opens out from the Absolute undifferentiated Essence as the first entification (*ta'ayyun-i awwal*) emerges.[25] It is also known as "the exalted pen," "the Muhammadan reality," and "the first Intellect." Also called the relative essence, it functions as the source of divine energy for the spirit, mystery, arcanum, and superarcanum subtle centers.[26] When Sirhindi talks about Essence (*dhat*), he means this first entification, the Muhammadan reality, which is sometimes called the "divine world" (*'alam-i lahut*).[27] It includes the interface (*barzakh*) between creation and undifferentiated Essence, the quality of comprehensive synthesis (*sha'n-i jami'*), which is collectively all the attributes, qualities, and aspects. The second entification, sometimes called the "world of omnipotence" (*'alam-i jabarut*), contains God's names and attributes in addition to the active attributes that direct divine energy to the heart subtle center. Traveling in the names and attributes occurs in this entification. The third entification, usually called the "world of divine command" (*'alam-i amr*), is also called the "world of angels" or the "world of sovereignty" (*'alam-i malakut*). This is where five subtle centers are located. It is the domain of the shadows of the names and attributes.

The lower limit of this entification is the world of image-exemplars, the fourth entification and transitional intermediary zone between the world of command and the fifth entification, the

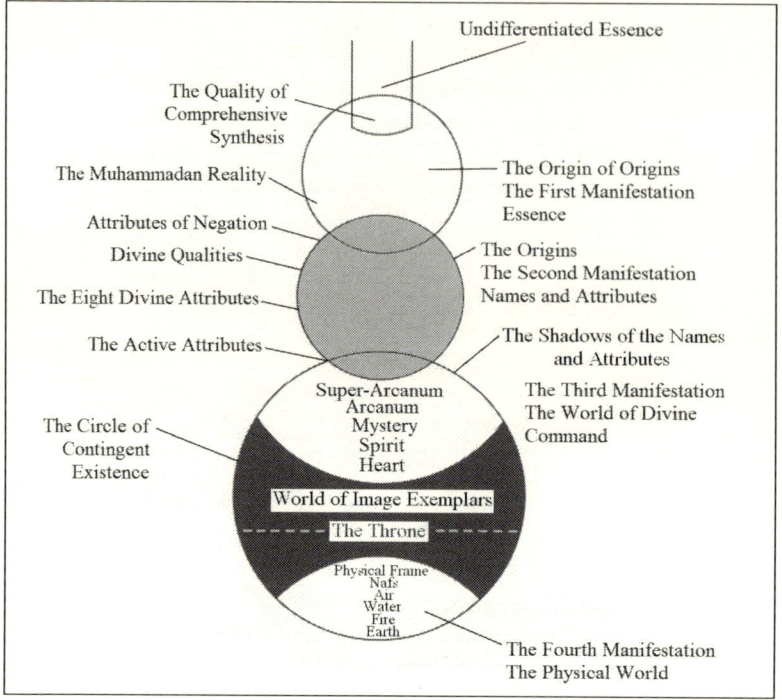

Figure 7.1. Mujaddidi Cosmology

world of corporeal bodies. The upper limit of the corporeal world is the Throne, below which are the two subtle centers of the physical frame and soul/ego-self, the elements, humans, animals, plants, and minerals. The bottom circle is the circle of contingent existence, which is the human realm, the confluence of the lower three entifications.

The Mujaddidi universe also emphasizes the body as microcosm.[28] The subtle realm associated with the human body, or what could be called subtle bodies, are expressed as *latifa*s, literally, "subtleties." Two of them are located in the world of creation (the physical frame and the ego-self), and the other five are located in the world of command (heart, spirit, mystery, arcanum, and superarcanum). In a training environment, where aspirants need specifics, these subtle bodies are given locations on the body and are called "subtle centers" with colors associated with them. Apparently, the locations and colors of these subtle centers varies widely from shaykh to shaykh. Faqirullah Shikarpuri (d. 1781) explains that the five subtle centers of the world of command interpenetrate the physical body and are perceived according to the capacity of each individual wayfarer (Shikarpuri 1978, 565).

Since Ahmad Sirhindi grew up in a Hindu majority region and because the word *chakra* is better known in the West than *latifa*, nonspecialists tend to jump to conclusions about so-called Indian influences on the Mujaddidi microcosm. The conceptualization of a subtle center comes from Junayd (830–910; Baghdad) and his contemporaries. These subtle centers were further developed by Najmuddin Kubra (1445–1221); his student Najmuddin Razi (d. 1256); and a

Subtle Center	Color
Heart	Yellow
Spirit	Red
Mystery	White
Arcanum	Black
Superarcanum	Green

Figure 7.2. Subtle Centers and Associated Colors Utilized in Mujaddidi Visualization

transmitter of the Central Asian Kubrawi tradition, 'Ala'uddin Simnani (1261–1336). By this point there was a sevenfold correspondence between subtle centers, colors, prophets, and levels of the cosmos, which was also articulated by Muhammad Parsa (d. 1420), a successor of Baha'uddin Naqshband.[29]

These subtle centers become activated sequentially from the heart to the physical frame through an intentional flow of spiritual/divine energy (*fayd*) directed from the shaykh to the student. Each of these subtle centers needs to be reciting "Allah" before the seeker proceeds to "the recollection of negation and affirmation." The negation is "There is no god" and the affirmation is "but God." Naqshbandis say that this three-part exercise was taught to 'Abdulkhaliq Ghujduwani by Khidr, an immortal who crosses paths with prophets and sufis in the Islamic tradition. Holding the breath below the navel, the seeker brings up the word *la* from below the navel to the middle of the forehead. Then the word *ilah* is mentally conveyed to the middle of the forehead, then to the right shoulder, ending with the final forceful mental motion that "hits" the heart from the right shoulder with *illa Allah*. When the seeker is proficient in this exercise, she is ready to travel toward God in the contemplations (*muraqabat*). The cross-legged body posture with the hands facing down on the knees is the same for all these exercises.

The context of these exercises and transmission is spiritual companionship (*suhbat*), with the actual flow of energy often described as spiritual attention (*tawajjuh*; *himmat*; *tasarruf*). For this process to work properly there needs to be an attunement between the shaykh and student. It is this concept of divinely emanating power that is used to explain how sufi shaykhs positively influence people's behavior or cure others of undesirable conditions and illnesses. Sometimes this energy (often perceived as divine grace) can be transmitted through the breath, like blowing in a glass of water, a handshake, or touching the head or places on the chest. But when "hearts are near" this process can occur with no physical contact whatsoever (see Buehler 1998, 131–38).

There is a critical difference between the Mujaddidi path that begins with subtle centers in the world of command and many other sufi methods. First, visions are considered to be for beginners only and, because there is both truth and falsehood in these visions, a shaykh's discriminatory ability is crucial. Second, physical and mental austerities are not perceived to diminish the power of the ego-self (*nafs*) because their effects only manifest in the outer realm.[30] Effective transformational practice involves knowing the relationship between the spirit subtle center (*ruh*) and the ego-self. Unless work is done in the world of command first, the journey back to God will take longer than a person's physical lifespan. Initially the spirit subtle center is lost in the ego-self, and one has to do contemplative practices in the world of command in such a way that one can reach the station of difference (*maqam-i farq*) where the spirit ascends and the ego-self descends.[31]

Once this occurs it is possible to work on the ego-self, which is where most other sufi lineages begin. That is not to say that work on the ego-self is postponed until the spirit subtle center and ego-center are separated. Spiritual companionship has many dimensions, and one of the most important is ego accountability. Some object to the necessity of a spiritual mentor and say that they can rely on their "inner teacher." There is such a thing as an inner teacher, but only spiritual Einsteins are able to access this guidance and dispense with a live shaykh. The vast majority have the ego pretending to be an inner teacher and need an *external* teacher to provide feedback in ways that are sometimes uncomfortably sudden wake-up calls. We are reminded of Satan, who, believing himself to be superior to a being of clay, refused to bow down to Adam (Q. 38:71–85). This is equivalent to accepting the first half of the Muslim profession of faith, "There is no god but God," but not accepting the second half, "and Muhammad is God's Messenger." Only accepting the transcendental aspect of this profession is easy for the ego. Anyone can love an invisible, distant God; it is entirely a different matter to love a living human being. As soon as an actual prophet comes and calls one to task, the ego balks.

The sufi shaykh, as an heir of the Prophet, fulfills a similar function by calling people to God and confronting seekers' egos with actual life trials if need be. It is easy to be complacent and proud while worshiping a transcendent God or venerating the Prophet. On the other hand, a live sufi shaykh will not allow the seeker to hide. Unfortunately, religious scholars and jurists who believe they are submitting to God on the basis of memorizing the Qur'an, hadith, and other book knowledge and who reject any need for *personal* guidance are using intellectual knowledge to avoid the confrontation of their egos. There is no substitute for spiritual companionship (*suhbat*). Contemplative practice without this aspect is just a technique. Again, the ego contrives innumerable ego defenses. If seekers trace the resistance against the authority of a spiritual teacher (not including those who have unresolved issues with their father/mother), they usually discover that it is the ego at the root of the situation. Rejecting an authentic shaykh is the natural course of action for the ego. The *last thing* that the ego wants is to be dethroned from its hegemonic position. This also may explain why so many seekers over the centuries have ended up with charlatans as shaykhs. There is a world of difference between superficial but seductive charisma and the subtle manifestation of transformative divine energy, a difference not only unnoticed by many sufi aspirants but also by most scholars who have used the vague, unnuanced term "charisma" when writing about sufism.[32]

In terms of the Mujaddidi path, Sirhindi has said that other sufis begin their wayfaring in the created world and end in the world of command, experiencing only lesser intimacy with God (*walayat-i sughra*). In contrast, Naqshbandis begin in the world of command and end in the created world, hence their adage, "The end is included in the beginning." This is the prophetic path because the domain of the prophets is to invite others to God in the created world. The *shariat* is linked to the created world and is brought to humans by prophets. The apparent "lowness" of the created world with respect to all of the other, subtler realms is only apparent. A person who returns from an ascent to the first entification is only outwardly in the world. Inwardly he or she is with God. This return to the world as the end of the path was already pioneered in the sufi world (a millennium after the bodhisattva ideal of Mahāyāna Buddhism) by Ibn al-'Arabi (1160–1240; Damascus) and 'Ala'uddin Simnani (1261–1336) (see Landolt 1996, 251–64). The following description of the path is approximate because there are no discrete lines and points of arrival. If one looks at figure 7.2, there are large overlaps between the entifications. These are examples of interfaces (sing. *barzakh*) that Sirhindi discusses in his letters. This means that there are many unclear boundaries, for example, between wayfaring to God and wayfaring in God as well as between inner and outer wayfaring. The terms used and the figures in the book are only maps. The map is not the experiential territory.

Before beginning spiritual wayfaring, a common person living in consensus reality is in a state of abiding (*baqa'*) in ignorance. The world preoccupies him or her both on the inside and outside. This is called the "first abiding." The Mujaddidi cyclical fourfold path begins by wayfaring to God (*sayr ila Allah*) in the world of command, the shadows of God's names and attributes. The first mode of wayfaring occurs in the outer world (*sayr-i afaqi*), going farther and farther, followed by inner wayfaring (*sayr-i anfusi*), going closer and closer. Finishing the latter mode roughly coincides with the completion wayfaring to God (*sayr ila Allah*). Sirhindi associates much of this wayfaring to God with the wayfarer's experience of "unity of being" (*wahdat-i wujud*), which is where the majority of sufis get stuck. This is a place of ecstasy, and, as was the case with Ahmad Sirhindi, one often is given conditional permission to teach at this point. Here the aspirant experiences God on the outside and the world on the inside.

Then one begins to proceed in the stage called "lesser intimacy with God" (*walayat-i sughra*), the closeness to God almighty attained by God's protégés along the path of "wayfaring in God" (*sayr fi'llah*), finally arriving at the end of the circle of shadows of the necessary names and leaving the circle of contingent existence. Continuing, one arrives at the level of God's necessary names and attributes. This is the end of ascent in the "lesser intimacy of God" and is associated with what Sirhindi called "the unity of contemplative witnessing" (*wahdat-i shuhud*). The processes of annihilation and abiding in God (*fana'* and *baqa*) are associated with this ascent (Sirhindi 1986, 63). Although there are stations and states that come up on the path (see previous discussion), these are not used as markers on the Mujaddidi path. At the summit of ascent, one is with God both on the inside and outside. Sirhindi defines this as the end of the path of lesser intimacy with God (*walayat-i sughra*). If one continues, then there is only descent and the prophetic path begins. Both inner and outer wayfaring are in the domain of lesser intimacy with God.

The third part of the journey involves a descent "returning to the world of creation for God and by means of God" (*sayr 'an Allah billah*); this is the beginning of greater intimacy with God (*walayat-i kubra*). This is where one begins to purify the spirit from the ego-self (*nafs*), associated with the station of separation after synthesis (*maqam al-farq ba'd al-jami'*).[33] This is when a person is once again able to recognize multiplicity (*farq*, or separation of conventional objects) in conventional reality after having the perception that "all is God" (*jam'*; *jam'-i jam'*). The journey culminates in the fourth and last cycle to live as an extraordinarily ordinary person in the created world (*sayr fi'l-ashya*). Although one experiences the multiplicity of the world, it is experienced as a mirror of the One. Here unity is experienced in the multiplicity, and multiplicity is experienced as a unity. This is the place where one is with God on the inside and with the world on the outside. It is the "best of both worlds" where one can see with two eyes, the right eye of unity and the left eye of multiplicity (Izutsu 1994, 19). It is following the prophetic path of inviting others to God.

320 / Arthur F. Buehler

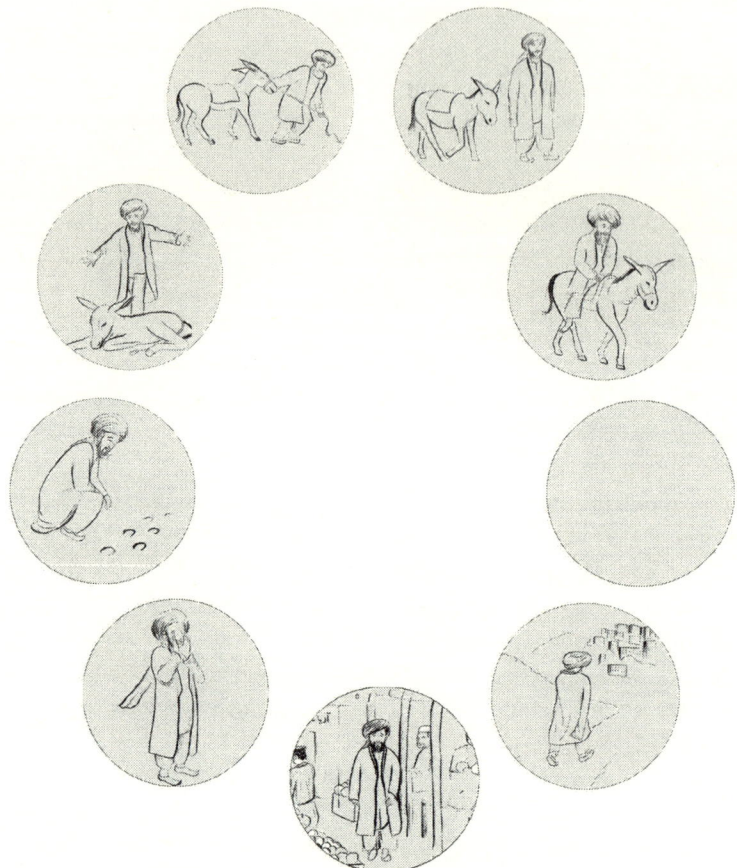

Figure 7.3. The Mujaddidi Path
Source: Shamim Homayun

1. Nasruddin[34] in the market (the first abiding) (center bottom)
2. Nasruddin looking for his donkey (starting to deal with the ego-self) (moving counterclockwise)
3. Nasruddin finding footprints of the donkey (starting to work on the subtle centers)
4. Nasruddin finds the donkey (there is more awareness of the ego-self—the beginning of wayfaring to God)
5. Nasruddin catches his donkey though the donkey is recalcitrant (grappling full-on with the ego-self)
6. The donkey is calm following Nasruddin (the beginning of a tranquil ego-self)
7. Nasruddin is riding the donkey (a tranquil ego-self—the beginning of wayfaring in God)
8. This picture is just a white empty circle (beginning of separation of the spirit and ego-self from the heart—complete ascent)
9. Nasruddin walking back to town without the donkey (returning to the world of creation for God and by means of God)
10. The same picture as number 1 in the bazaar (the second abiding—extraordinarily ordinary)[35]

'Abdullah Shah's *Suluk-i Mujaddidiyya*

'Abdullah Shah's *Suluk-i Mujaddidiyya* (Mujaddidi Wayfaring) was first published in Urdu in 1958. The first edition was published in Hyderabad, Deccan, India by Da'irat Machine Press. The treatise was written in Urdu because the British deposed the previous *lingua franca* of the Mughal Empire, Indo-Persian, from its linguistic pedestal in 1857. Urdu, which is written in the Arabo-Persian script, became the *lingua franca* of Indo-Pakistani Muslims, as Hindi, written in Devanagari script, has become the *lingua franca* of Hindus. Usually books of this genre are produced for local practicing Mujaddidis, and I was fortunate that a copy arrived to the Iqbal Academy in Lahore from Hyderabad nine years after it was published.

Of the published Mujaddidi texts on contemplative practice, the *Suluk-i Mujaddidiyya* is one of the most coherent and organized. The book is broken up into seventy-one sections which I will summarize in order. The text translated in this chapter is taken from the beginning of the book, which discusses the basic practices of remembrance of God, bonding with the shaykh, and visualizing the shaykh. In the subsequent section, which is not translated here, the author explains the divine energy (*tawajjuh*) transmitted between the shaykh and disciple, ecstatic attraction to God, and recognizing a perfected spiritual master (*shaykh*). This discussion is followed by outlining the necessity of initiation and two kinds of wayfarers, those desired by God and those desiring God, and how to cultivate beautiful behavior when in the presence of the shaykh. The next sections detail sufi terminology such as expansion (*bast*) and contraction (*qabd*) as altered states of consciousness. The treatise then outlines the well-known eight principles formulated by 'Abdulkhaliq Ghudjduvani (d. 1179): (1) awareness of breath, (2) being conscious of following in the footsteps of the Prophet, (3) traveling on the inward spiritual path, (4) solitude in society, (5) constant repetition of God's name, (6) returning to the world after performing remembrance of God, (7) guarding one's spiritual progress, and (8) concentration on God. These are followed

Introduction	The Spirit Subtle Center
The First Exercise: Remembrance of God	The Mystery Subtle Center
The Second Exercise: Contemplation	The Arcanum Subtle Center
The Third Exercise: Bonding with the Shaykh	The Superarcanum Subtle Center
Visualizing the Shaykh	The Ego/Self Subtle Center
The Method of Focusing Spiritual Energy	The Physical Frame Subtle Center
Ecstatic Attraction to God	The Practice of Negation and Affirmation
Subtle Centers	The Contemplation of Being Together with God
The Heart Subtle Center	The Circle of Contingent Existence

Figure 7.4. Sections of the *Suluk-i Mujaddidiyya* Translated in the Present Chapter

by the three additional principles that Baha'uddin Naqshband added, namely, awareness of time, counting of *dhikr* repetitions, and a heart constantly attentive to God. Then there is a discussion of how one becomes initiated. Although it seems out of order, the next section discusses the contemplation of exclusive unity.[36]

Following this section, the second part of the translation begins with a discussion of the subtle centers, negation and affirmation, and the contemplations of lesser intimacy with God and those of being together with God. The last part of the second translated section, logically out of order because it has nothing to do with the contemplations per se, is a cosmological digression on the circle of contingent existence. This is the first half of the book. The second half details the remaining twenty-three advanced contemplations.[37] The first six contemplations go to the origins of each of the subtle centers followed by various contemplations on love and various perfections (e.g., prophethood, messengership), cosmologically advancing through various realities (e.g., the Qur'an, ritual prayer, and the prophets Abraham, Moses, and Muhammad) before contemplating the Undifferentiated. After completing his discussion of contemplative practices, 'Abdullah Shah provides a thirteen-page section with spiritual guidance from notable sufi shaykhs along with a Mujaddidi litany often recited as a group before sunset prayer. This is "The Seal of the Naqshbandi-Mujaddidi Masters."[38] It involves an eighteen-step recitation of various Qur'anic *sura*s (chapters) and names of God punctuated by blessing the Prophet Muhammad. The book ends in typical fashion with the initiatic lineage of 'Abdullah Shah's Qadiri and Naqshbandi lineages ('Abdullah Shah 1958, 120–24).

Contemporary Mujaddidi Practice

As mentioned earlier, without doing field research there is no way to know if these contemplative exercises are still being practiced by 'Abdullah Shah's successors. Scholars who spend extended time with practicing sufis, few as they are, generally agree that changes in the modern world affect sufi practice in ways paralleling other aspects of life in the twenty-first century. These changes have yet to be documented. The changes occurring in Mujaddidi contemplative practice between the nineteenth and twentieth centuries in the Punjab are indicated by "the rise of the mediating shaykh," the subtitle of my *Sufi Heirs* (1998). What this means is that qualified directing shaykhs had been replaced very often with hereditary shaykhs. Given the uncompromising nature of Mujaddidi contemplative practice, it was not possible to fake the transmission of spiritual energy. So instead of being directing shaykhs, who literally trained seekers to progress along the path and *ordered* them to do things that would tame their egos, almost all sufi succession became hereditary. This meant that there was a new generation of hereditary shaykhs who became mediating shaykhs soon after the turn of the century. These mediating shaykhs had no choice but to abandon the contemplative practices outlined in this chapter, along with the accompanying divine/spiritual energy. Instead, seekers were required to harmonize their hearts to the shaykh, who then mediated between them and God (hence mediating shaykh). Instead of years of disciplined contemplative practice and effort dealing with one's ego-self, all one had to do was recite litanies of the Mujaddidi lineage going back to Muhammad (Buehler 1998, 202). With a mediating shaykh, seekers cultivated a love of the shaykh who then interceded with God on their behalf.

I found out about this firsthand. My principal mentor in Lahore during my research in Pakistan (1990–1992), the late Hakim Muhammad Musa Amritsari (d. 1999), sent me out to various places in Lahore every week for a year to learn about Indo-Muslim culture. Then he sent me out to sufi lodges in the Punjab and the Northwest Frontier Province (now called Khyber Pakhtunkhwa). This latter task was Hakim Sahib's way of introducing me to a common ongoing phenomenon (occurring globally, as I later discovered from my colleagues) of so-called "sufi activity." Having visited a couple dozen Mujaddidi sufi lodges in those provinces, I was very surprised to observe that they had apparently dispensed with transformative contemplative practices and formal ethical guidance. I returned very depressed and disillusioned to Lahore after six months and was hoping that I had missed something. Instead, Hakim Sahib, with a laugh, said that they were just going through the motions, and it had been this way for a couple of generations at least. Because the study of contemplative practice and human transformation is in its infancy, there is no way of verifying Hakim Sahib's evaluation of these changes.

The institutional expression of the directing shaykh was predicated on a particular worldview and specific political system. British colonial rule supported a modern scientific worldview, a worldview that was propagated through English-medium schools to train cadres of Indian bureaucrats. Almost all traditional religious schools and sufi lodges had closed by the turn of the century with the disappearance of Mughal patronage in 1858. Many sufi shaykhs utilized the new print media and the British train network to become trans-Indian shaykhs. Changes in the sociopolitical realm affected contemplative practice directly. Not only were there fewer sufi lodges but fewer people had the time to spend many hours a day doing contemplative practices pioneered three centuries earlier. In uncertain, changing times it was better that one's son was in charge of the sufi lodge and adjacent buildings than the most spiritually qualified aspirant.

My colleagues have confirmed that Mujaddidi practices are still being done in Uzbekistan, Bengal, and Xinjiang. Both in Turkey and Afghanistan there are many practicing Mujaddidi groups, as there are in Indo-Pakistan. This activity is mirrored in the continued dissemination and the translation of Sirhindi's intricate manual of contemplative practice, *Maktubat* (Collected Letters). Some Mujaddidis are known publically, such as Shaykh Mahmud Effendi in Istanbul or Shaykh Azad Rasool in Delhi, but Mujaddidis in many countries prefer to remain anonymous due to government pressure. Although the internet will provide hundreds, if not thousands, of Mujaddidi websites to those who are so inclined, typically Mujaddidis have preferred in their silent recollection of God to keep a low profile.

With the proselytization of the Ibn Arabi Society and the exemplary work of Michel Chodkiewicz and William Chittick, Ibn al-'Arabi (1165–1240) is relatively well known in the West. For all practical purposes, no one has heard of Ahmad Sirhindi. Ibn al-'Arabi is a towering figure in the history of sufism, arguably *the* towering literary figure along with Jalaluddin Rumi.[39] What the aficionados of Ibn al-'Arabi do not emphasize is that his work, particularly Ibn al-'Arabi's *magnum opus* (out of hundreds of books), the *Meccan Revelations*, is for very advanced practitioners. Indeed, the level of this text is so advanced that I seriously wonder about the value of translations that we have of Ibn 'Arabi into English or Persian.[40] The level of awareness of one who translates the experiences of an Ibn al-'Arabi or an Ahmad Sirhindi needs to correlate with the awareness of the author to a great extent.

On the practical day-to-day level, Sirhindi's main work, unlike that of Ibn al-'Arabi, was teaching and supervising the teaching of a large number of disciples. Sirhindi pioneered a set of contemplative practices that have been transmitted to us in the twenty-first century. His complete *Collected Letters* has been translated into at least five languages. Ibn al-'Arabi's *Meccan Revelations*, on the other hand, has provided a map of sufi experience and technical vocabulary used by subsequent sufis (including Sirhindi), in addition to being a visionary compendium of human experience. It is unparalleled in sufi literature. However, for almost eight hundred years it has not been translated. Only recently has it been quasi-translated into Persian (because much of the vocabulary is kept in the original Arabic without Persian explanation). It is not a manual for contemplative practice nor was it meant to be. As Sadruddin Qunawi (1207–1274), Ibn al-'Arabi's foremost disciple and interpreter, said in his last testament, "Ibn al-'Arabi's path ends with me." *Collected Letters* is often a dialogue with Sirhindi seeking to provide wayfaring advice to specific individuals on the path. Sirhindi metaphorically seeks to help wayfarers get on the airplane and fly. *Meccan Revelations* is a glorious atlas of the visionary world of sufism useful to very experienced wayfarers who have already been traveling on the airplane for a while (frequent flyers) and who seek to confirm their visions when they cannot ask their shaykh.

Bringing Awareness to Contemplative Studies

With respect to placing Mujaddidi practice in a larger comparative framework, this is a fascinating topic that unfortunately requires considerably more data than is available at the present time. To get this data and to provide frameworks to compare this data will require researchers to actually cultivate the different kinds of consciousness states outlined in the texts. Any meaningful type of comparison at this point is mere armchair scholarship, akin to philosophers, who have never left their narrow rational-cognitive worlds, making questionable judgments of post-rational (transrational) experience on the basis of (usually poorly translated) texts (see Buehler 2013). Points of comparison could start with the physiology of subtle bodies and energy states. It is possible that *prāṇa* and *qi* have much in common in their close relationship with the physical body just as *shaktipat* (*śaktipāta*) and *tawajjuh* (both defined as transmission of spiritual energy) may have similar frequencies in subtler human bodies. *Shaktipat* in the Siddha Yoga lineage (see Muller-Ortega 1997) apparently is the phenomenological equivalent to the Mujaddidi spiritual energy transmission outlined earlier in this chapter. Up until now no scholar has differentiated these two sets of energy phenomena. Indeed, these and many other phenomena are basically ignored in the academic study of religion. According to some advanced martial artists, transmitting *qi* involves physical contact, while I can attest that *shaktipat* and *tawajjuh* operate without physical contact. All of these phenomena are energies, but apparently the latter pair are of a "higher frequency" because they do not need physical contact. The point here is that scholars not only are clueless about these phenomena, but, even more regrettably, they apparently are blind to such phenomena.

It is shocking for me to witness the narrow context in which religious studies still operates in the twenty-first century. Since the 1980s, it was expected that anthropologists read the texts of those whom they study, but somehow this principle was not applied in a corresponding manner to those working with texts. The nineteenth-century sufis whom I studied in *Sufi Heirs* could not be visited in 1990, but equivalent consciousness events, transmitted via the Mujaddidi lineage, could be witnessed. That is how I began my inquiry. Those who are not intimately acquainted with Indo-Muslim culture or Mujaddidi sufi practices mostly assume that my *Sufi Heirs* is a textual study simply because that is the cover story. The book utilizes almost a hundred sources previously unknown to Western scholarship. However, for those readers who *know*, interspersed in the text are allusions to very arcanum points of Islamic or cultural practice. These points did not come from any book; they came from three years' immersion in Indo-Pakistani Muslim culture (thanks to the guidance of Hakim Sahib). The chapter devoted to Mujaddidi contemplative practice, repeatedly cited in this chapter, is generally ignored by my scholarly colleagues in their fourteen reviews of *Sufi Heirs*. It simply did not register. However, when I talk to Mujaddidi sufi shaykhs, some of whom ask their students to read that chapter on contemplative practice, they say that *Sufi Heirs* is the only work in English that they consider to accurately represent the Mujaddidiyya. This is because apparently I had accurately translated and contextualized the texts, not because of any special experiential knowledge. That translation and contextualization, however, was the result of closely working with practicing sufis. My point is that those who work with contemplative texts need an expanded context of inquiry beyond books.

We know next to nothing of the phenomenology and realms discussed in the following translation: Do wayfarers visit other realms that "objectively" exist, or are they simply creating subtle "films" that reflect religio-cultural constructs? Are subtle centers heuristic devices for cultivating subtle bodies, or are they actual energy centers that are latent in all human bodies? If these issues are ever going to be seriously researched, then we scholars need to get out of our textual armchairs and personally interact with contemplatives, ideally exploring other realms of consciousness with them. This bleak situation of scholarly ignorance is not a coincidence. In the postmodern academy we are aware of ethnocentrism, the narrowness of cultural experience, but we are hardly aware of our pervasive *cognocentrism*, the narrowness of conscious experience. Like color-blind people, those who have never experienced the nonordinary conscious realities of sufis do not realize how these psychospiritual realities can color the context of many sufi texts and open entirely new areas of inquiry.

Here we may "go beyond the armchair." Exploring other modes of human consciousness is not a function of material resources or elaborate infrastructure. It is simply a matter of deciding to "look through the telescope of altered states," which allows one to experience a vast inner universe analogous to how a telescope allows one to see the outer universe more clearly. By making subjective experience a taboo in academic inquiry (see Wallace 2000), scholars are similar to their Italian counterparts who refused to access the appropriate tools of their time. Galileo, writing to Johannes Kepler in 1610, observes, "My dear Kepler, what would you say of the learned here, who, replete with the pertinacity of the asp, have steadfastly refused to cast a glance through the telescope? What shall we make of this? Shall we laugh, or shall we cry?" (De Santillana 1978, 9). The learned whom he was discussing were not the Jesuits, whom Galileo knew to be "friends of science and discovery," but the professors at the university. They were the ones he feared (De Santillana 1978, 8).

In retrospect, modern scholars can explain Galileo's standoff situation in terms of paradigm shifts and the resistance of those of one paradigm to shift to another one. Thanks to the work of Thomas Kuhn and others (Kuhn 1996; Popper 2002), we have noticed a pattern over the last four hundred years. In short, the evidence and explanatory power of the new paradigm eventually reach a tipping point such that everyone except the most stubborn utilize the new paradigm's methodology and insights. Some have called the shift to an expanded paradigm in contemplative practice and consciousness studies "the consciousness revolution," or what William James referred to as "radical empiricism" (see Laszlo et al. 2003).

Being averse to investigating experience outside of the narrow confines of the rational-discursive mind, which I call "armchair consciousness," is not academic in origin. It is deeply embedded in the underlying paradigm of scientific materialism, one tenet of which is the "single-state fallacy."[41] Thomas B. Roberts, the person who coined the term "single-state fallacy," introduces it with a dialogue, which I am going to paraphrase (Roberts 2006, 104–5). You have a friend who just bought a new Apple computer after using a Windows-only computer, and you ask him why he bought it. He tells you that he is going to play chess with it, and you say, "Cool, why not try out the game, The Journey to the World Divine? It works better on a Mac." He repeats that he is going to play chess with it. You ask him for his email address to send him the details, and he says again that he is going to play chess with his new computer. However, you do not get it, and you start to recommend all kinds of even more amazing software. He angrily shouts, "No! No! I am going to play chess with my new computer."

Most people who use computers understand that a modern computer has an ever-expanding variety of uses, and to use a computer for one application is to limit oneself considerably. In a similar fashion, the single-state fallacy is assuming that all worthwhile abilities reside within our normal waking consciousness. Over the last thirty years, the data has been accumulating from a variety of disciplines to demonstrate the fallacy of a single-state consciousness, given almost limitless possibilities in the rainbow of human-consciousness. This data has been streaming in from multiple methodologies that include the study of altered states pioneered by Charles Tart, transpersonal psychology pioneered by Ken Wilber, mind-body medicine/psychiatry pioneered by Stanislav Grof, anthropology of consciousness pioneered by Edith Turner, and the philosophy of consciousness pioneered by Robert K. C. Forman.[42]

All of these researchers study various consciousness states that overlap with what is very loosely labeled "religious experience."[43] These are the states of consciousness that shamans, Vedic rishis, prophets, "saints," sages, sufis, and "mystics" have experienced and reported over many millennia. Without these states of consciousness, beyond the single-state, there would have been no religions. It is precisely these post-rational (transrational) experiences, often written into what become scriptures, that are the foundations of just about all religions on the planet. Logically, one would think that academics in the discipline of religious studies would be at the cutting edge of the academic study of altered states and human consciousness.

However, life does not operate according to logic, especially when one is conditioned—or hyperconditioned in the case of academics—in an outdated cognocentric flatland paradigm. Just about all of us were trained to approach our subjects from a postmodern set of presuppositions. None of these presuppositions allows for a differentiation between the rational and the pre-rational nor the rational and the post-rational. It is chocolate or vanilla, the two-dimensional realm of the rational or irrational? The study of contemplative practice cannot avoid (I hope) the post-rational realms of human experience. However, the conundrum is that the discipline of religious studies, encompassing literally all humanities and social science methodologies, generally does not acknowledge the post-rational.

It is time to move on to further embarrassments. This is the (other) huge elephant in the room that no one sees.[44] This elephant has a name: Ken Wilber. Huston Smith has described Ken Wilber (in book blurbs) as "the most seminal transpersonal psychologist to date," and "No one—not even Jung—has done as much as Wilber to open up Western psychology to the durable insights of the world's wisdom traditions" (Wilber 1996, back cover). In 2003, I checked the citation index from 1979, when Wilber published his first book at the age of thirty, to 2003 in order to see how many of my colleagues in religious studies had cited one of Wilber's twenty-two books. There were less than a dozen who had cited Wilber in twenty-four years. It seems that hardly any of my colleagues who teach psychology of religion or "mysticism" have ever heard of him. Either that or they are intentionally and systematically ignoring or excluding his perspectives. The only other people to mention Wilber in this very thick book on contemplative practice are the editor and one of the other contributors.

For scholars of contemplative studies, Wilber has provided an incomparable array of conceptual tools to investigate the development of human consciousness. This includes a quadrant system of epistemology, each with its line(s) of development, applications of values development (Spiral Dynamics) with a documented cross-cultural validity and practicality (it was used to dismantle apartheid in South Africa), and tentative maps of post-rational realms that seek to provide universal maps instead of the tradition-specific maps we now have (like figure 7.1). In terms of sheer pioneering trailblazing, no one in the last twenty years has come remotely close to contributing as much to building an infrastructure for the study of contemplative experience.

This does not mean Wilber and his contributions do not have their problems. Until 2002 I admired Wilber's ability to acknowledge his mistakes and improve his frameworks and perspectives. This process has apparently come to a halt. Even though Wilber provides a set of refreshing vistas and tools of inquiry, these fall far short of his grandiose claims of being "integral." Among other things, this so-called "integral vision" is severely compromised by his willful disregard of sufism and the Islamic tradition in general, much less any serious critiques of his ideas.

Jorge Ferrer (Ferrer and Tarnas 2001) has some critiques of Wilber's work even though he speaks more from the armchair of philosophical speculation than Wilber, whose work displays his extended contact with contemplatives.[45] Much to his credit, Ferrer has put his participatory approach into action by collaborating and engaging with other academics. Ironically, Ferrer also ignores the sufi tradition when arguably it is one of the best examples of a participatory approach focusing on intersubjective practice and development. It is, perhaps, no coincidence that the long-awaited debut of the Contemplative Studies Group of the American Academy of Religion in 2011 had a panel discussing Ferrer's contributions and completely ignored Wilber.

New vistas require methodologies that go beyond egoic armchair consciousness. It is easy to see how Orientalists of one kind or another over the last centuries have distorted what they saw, but it is not so easy to see how many of us in contemplative studies are simply distorting our subject in a more sophisticated fashion than our predecessors. Increased awareness usually does not occur until one transforms one's perspective with a more expansive context. That shift will require a scholar who can steer clear of intellectual certainty, absolute relativism, and religious belief to engage in a self-aware process of investigating consciousness while nuancing the historical and sociocultural dynamics of the specific context.[46] Formulating "methodologies of the subjective," critical to any involved study of contemplative practice and experience, will enable us to reassess the human and greater-than-human worlds that are open to all. Those of us who study the ordinary and extraordinary beings engaged in contemplative practice, and the texts that they have shared, are ideally positioned to expand the ontological matrix, thereby enchanting the largely disenchanted world of postmodern humanities in the academy.

Notes

1. Lowercase for sufi is intentional. As for "sufi orders" we have a case of an Orientalist holdover. At some point, most Western scholars finally stopped calling sufi lodges "monasteries" (a recent book has even called them convents!), but they have kept the usage of "sufi orders." There are orders of monks and nuns in Christianity and Buddhism with very clear and often common rules and contemplative practices. In sufi practice, celibacy is rare and there is very little "order" in sufi practices. Multiple Naqshbandi-Mujaddidi groups stemming from the same sublineages exist in one city, like Istanbul or Delhi, with minimal overlap (read dis-order) in contemplative practices. Sufi lineage is a more precise term and includes the shaykh and those initiated by him. "Sufi" is not capitalized for the same reason that mystic and jurist are not capitalized. "Sufism," already a reification in English, is not capitalized either because the Arabic word that it is translated from (*tasawwuf*) is more a verb meaning "the process of becoming a sufi" than a noun.

2. Sayyids are the lineal descendants of the Prophet and respected by both Sunnis and Shi'is across the Islamic world. The Naqshbandi sufi lineage is named after Baha'uddin Naqshband (1318–1389; Bukhara, Uzbekistan); the Naqshbandi-Mujaddidi sufi lineage is named after Ahmad Sirhindi (1564–1624; Sirhind, India) who was called the renewer (*mujaddid*) of the second Islamic millennium. The Qadiri sufi lineage is named after 'Abdulqadir al-Jilani (1077–1166; Baghdad, Iraq). Multiple lineages are common and the contemplative practices of the first lineage generally predominate (in 'Abdullah Shah's case Naqshbandi) over the second, in this case Qadiri.

3. The (apparently) sole "biographical source" of 645 pages dedicated to 'Abdullah Shah has about 6 pages of biographical information. There are no studies on Islam and sufism in the nineteenth- and twentieth-century Deccan except for a preliminary study focusing on Aurangabad (560 km from Hyderabad), which entirely neglects contemplative practice (as does almost all scholarship on sufism). See Green 2006, 10–11.

4. See Dihlawi 1997, 126. In Ghulam 'Ali's words, "Four rivers flow in the Naqshbandiyya-Mujaddidiyya. Two flow from the Naqshbandiyya, one from Qadiriyya, and one half each from the Chishtiyya and Suhrawardiyya" (Dihlawi 1997, 126). Cf. Dihlawi 1997, 236.

5. Note Dihlawi 1997, 91, where Ghulam 'Ali Shah reminds travelers visiting Chitli Qabr from Samarqand (Temirtau, Kazakhstan) that he is not worthy of such attention and that they really are coming to experience the presence of Mirza Jan-i Janan.

6. Indeed, entire chapters of books are written on Naqshbandi contemplative practices that the sufi author himself neither practices nor teaches. See Buehler 1998, 240.

7. The Wahhabi movement is named after Muhammad ibn 'Abdulwahhab (1703–1792). It is financed and centered in Saudi Arabia with an agenda to theologically remold the practice of Islam by declaring every development after the ninth century to be outside the fold of Islam, whether legal, literary, philosophical, artistic, or spiritual. In short, its members seek to erase a millennium of multicultural Islamicate heritage like they have already done in Mecca. It is extremely well financed with a worldwide agenda (e.g., the Taliban in Afghanistan) and has now evolved into various groups who often call themselves Salafis. See Abou el-Fadl 2005.

8. Carl Ernst has convincingly shown these connections in his *Shambhala Guide to Sufism* (1997). As a further note, there is a range of *practices* associated with sufism that are contested by Muslims who would not identify themselves as being Salafis or Wahhabis. The Wahhabis thought nothing of killing hundreds of thousands of suspected sufis and religious scholars and their students leading up to their takeover of Saudi Arabia in 1928.

9. The word "meditation" is purposely not used here, not only because it does not convey the Arabic root meaning of intense focused viewing, but because it has been used so uncritically in the scholarly literature to make it a meaningless term. The different levels of Mujaddidi contemplative witnessing are outlined in Buehler 1998, 249–253.

10. In addition to Ernst's *Shambhala Guide* mentioned earlier, two recommended introductions to sufism are Schimmel 1975 for a sensitive historical overview and Sells 1995 for selected translations from early sufi texts.

11. A recent example is Irena Tweedie's Mujaddidi guide. A Hindu, she did not even know that he was a sufi, much less a Mujaddidi sufi (from Mirza Jan-i Janan's lineage), until late in her training. See Tweedie 1995.

12. There is a splendid translation of 'Abdullah Ansari Hirati's *Sad Maydan* by Nahid Angha (2011). This book is the first Persian book to discuss stations and altered states.

13. In a translation of only 13 percent of Sirhindi's *Collected Letters* there is mention of over twenty stations above and beyond the ten "standard" stations. See Buehler 2011.

14. For an entire treatise on this approach to sufism see *Physicians of the Heart* (Meyer et al. 2011).

15. This is often how Q. 9:111 is interpreted, in addition to other Qur'anic verses and hadith.

16. Mujaddidi comes from Sirhindi's followers proclaiming him *mujaddid-i alf-i thani*, that is, the "renewer of the second Islamic millennium."

17. See letters 1.260 and 1.287 in Buehler 2011.

18. I am indebted to Professor Abu-Manneh of the University of Haifa for this reference.

19. See Ma 2005. For the story of this remarkable translating effort see the forthcoming book by Eloisa Concetti and Thierry Zarcone: *Sufism in Xinjiang and Inner Asia in 19th–20th Century: Ahmad Sirhindi's Maktubat and the Naqshbandiyya*.

20. Note Ansari's (1986, 71) discussion and translation of another letter in this regard.

21. From here forward the abbreviated notation will be Sirhindi, volume number, letter number, page number. For example, Sirhindi 1972, 1.40:104.

22. Here is the tension between the intoxication of annihilation in God, privileging an ascent beyond consensus reality (*fana' fi'llah*), and the sobriety of remaining in God (*baqa' bi'llah*), a descent from the intoxicated heights, firmly rooted in everyday life.

23. After my *Sufi Heirs* (1998), English-language studies dealing with sufi lineages, for example, Ernst and Lawrence 2002 and Huda 2002, began to consider contemplative practices in their monographs. It is hard to get a sense of the actual practices because of the relative lack of detailed primary sources in these two lineages compared to the Mujaddidiyya. Compare the generalities of the Chishti manual *The Alms Bowl* translated by Scott Kugle in his *Sufi Meditation and Contemplation: Timeless Wisdom from Mughal India*, with the precise details of 'Abdullah Shah's translation or with the relevant chapter in my *Sufi Heirs*. Weismann's otherwise acceptable work on the Naqshbandi lineage (Weismann 2007) is marred by its total disregard for any discussion of contemplative practice. To the best of my knowledge Sirhindi's *Collected Letters* is the most detailed manual of actual contemplative experience *and* contemplative methodology in the sufi tradition. If the reader does a keyword search and finds the misleading *Contemplative Disciplines in Sufism*, realize that it is poorly plagiarized from Shah Wali'ullah's books by Mir Valiuddin, a former professor of philosophy at Osmania University.

24. For a more exhaustive treatment of the subject see Buehler 1998, 234–40.

25. Entification is the process of undifferentiated Essence becoming an entity of some sort.

26. This is not obvious from figure 7.1, which is slightly misleading because about 40 percent of the first entification overlaps with the second entification.

27. There is no fixed cosmological system. For example, Faqirullah Shikarpuri, whose modified diagram appears here as figure 7.1, equates nondifferentiated Essence with the world of divinity. See Shikarpuri n.d., 30.

28. Here I provide a brief overview in order to contextualize the section on Mujaddidi contemplative practice. For a comprehensive treatment of the subject see Buehler 1998, 98–130. For information on some of the different locations of subtle centers see Tosun 2005, 155.

29. At least one of these Central Asian sufis, Simnani, had contacts with Buddhists. One would not expect sufis to be acknowledging their sources if they were to come from another religion. Contemplative

technology, like technology in other areas, spreads and is transformed. The difficulty is finding the historical sources that document these specific interchanges. Without this documentation, it is reasonable to consider independent formulations of the human microcosm. This subject is further articulated in Buehler 1998, 105–11.

30. Sirhindi also notes the non-effectiveness of non-Naqshbandi sufi practices that do not involve the world of command, the realm of purifying the heart. See letter 1.260 in Buehler 2011.

31. An aspect of this principle is discussed in the context of sufi lineages in letter 1.260 in Buehler 2011, where Sirhindi says, "Those of other sufi lineages purify their ego-self and perform strenuous exercises, traversing the beginnings of the appearance of the material world, saying that this is the beginning of the world of command."

32. A noteworthy exception (and there may be others) is Tony Stewart's use of "spiritual charisma." See Stewart 2010.

33. There is a discussion of this station in Sirhindi 1972, 1.285.45–46, explaining how the attributes and qualities are in the world of command and how the spirit (*ruh*) is an interface between two aspects, form (*chun*) and formlessness (*be-chun*).

34. Nasruddin was a Seljug satirical sufi who most likely lived during the thirteenth century in Akşehir, present-day Turkey. He is a famous sage-fool figure known throughout the Middle East and Central Asia.

35. These illustrations might be profitably compared to the Ten Oxherding pictures in Chan/Zen Buddhism.

36. It is out of order because one activates the subtle centers and perfects the affirmation and negation practice before going on to any of the contemplations.

37. All of the contemplations are detailed in Buehler 1998, 241–48, while the intentions of these contemplations are outlined in Buehler 1998, 249–53.

38. Fritz Meier discusses this litany in the second part of his *Zwei Abhandlungen über die Naqšbandiyya* (1994).

39. Arguably in terms of textual usage, the historically widespread use of Sirhindi's *Collected Letters* in the eastern Sunni Islamic world is comparable to Rumi's *Mathnawi*.

40. If one reads "Translator's Preface: Disclaimers and Confessions" (Buehler 2011), there is an extended discussion of how I also wonder about my translations of Sirhindi's *Collected Letters*.

41. Mark Blainey calls this "monophasic consciousness" in contrast to "polyphasic consciousness." See Blainey 2010.

42. Most of these authors have written many useful books. For those unacquainted with their works, consult the list of works cited and further reading for suggested starting points.

43. Charles Tart also studied psi phenomena, which are another distinct set of phenomena.

44. The first is the vast spectrum of uninvestigated human transrational consciousness events chronicled in (probably) millions of manuscripts over millennia that are being ignored by scholars.

45. There is a qualitative difference between working with contemplatives and actually being an accomplished contemplative. Wilber and his followers often allude to Wilber's own vast personal contemplative experience, but experienced sufis gauge contemplative experience by actual transformations manifested in open-hearted behavior rather than by the number of years sitting on the meditation cushion or allegedly stopping one's brainwaves.

46. Here I am paraphrasing Jeffery Kripal (Rice University) from his stellar *Authors of the Impossible* (2010, 26).

Works Cited and Further Reading

'Abdulghani Mujaddidi. 1983. "Halat-i Hadrat Shah Ghulam 'Ali Dihlawi." Urdu translation by Muhammad Iqbal Mujaddidi. Appendix One in Ghulam 'Ali Dihlawi. *Maqamat-i Mazhari*. Urdu translation by Muhammad Iqbal Mujaddidi. Lahore: Urdu Science Board.

'Abdullah Shah. 1952. *Zujajat al-masabih.* 5 vols. Hyderabad: Taj Press.
———. 1958. *Suluk-i Mujaddidiyya.* Hyderabad: Da'irat Machine Press.
Abou el-Fadl, Khalid. 2005. *The Great Theft: Wrestling Islam from the Extremists.* San Francisco: Harper.
Ahmet Lütfi. 1873–1912. *Tarih-i devlet-i 'aliye-i osmaniye.* 8 vols. Istanbul: Dar al-Taba'a al-Amire.
Angha, Nahid. 2011. *Stations of the Sufi Path: The "One Hundred Fields" (Sad Maydan) of Abdullah Ansari of Heart.* London: Archtype.
Ansari, Abdul Haq. 1986. *Sufism and Shari'ah: A Study of Shaykh Ahmad Sirhindi's Effort to Reform Sufism.* Leicester: The Islamic Foundation.
Blainey, Mark. 2010. "The Future of a Discipline: Considering the Ontological/Methodological Future of the Anthropology of Consciousness, Part II: Towards an Ethnometaphysics of Consciousness: Suggested Adjustments in SAC's Quest to Reroute the Main(Stream)." *Anthropology of Consciousness* 21/2: 113–138.
Buehler, Arthur F. 1998. *Sufi Heirs of the Prophet: The Indian Naqshbandiyya and the Rise of the Mediating Shaykh.* Columbia: University of South Carolina Press.
———. 2011. *Revealed Grace: The Juristic Sufism of Ahmad Sirhindi (1564–1624).* Louisville: Fons Vitae.
———. 2013. "Researching Sufism in the Twenty-First Century: Expanding the Context of Inquiry." In *The Bloomsbury Companion to Islamic Studies,* edited by Clinton Bennett, 93–118. London and New York: Bloomsbury Academic.
Chittick, William C. 1982. "The Five Divine Presences: From al-Qunawi to al-Qaysari." *Muslim World* 72.2 (April): 107–28.
De Santillana, Giorgio. 1978. *The Crime of Galileo.* Chicago: University of Chicago Press.
Dihlawi, Ghulam 'Ali. 1997. *Sharh-i durr al-ma'arif: minhaj al-raghibayn illa makubat imam al-muttaqin Imam Rabbani mujaddid-i alf-i thani.* Edited by Ayyub Ganji. Sanandaj: Intisharat-i Kurdistan.
Ernst, Carl. 1997. *The Shambhala Guide to Sufism.* Boston: Shambhala.
Ernst, Carl, and Bruce B. Lawrence. 2002. *Sufi Martyrs of Love.* New York: Palgrave Macmillan.
Faruqi, Abu'l-Hasan Zayd. 1983. *Manahij al-sayr.* Urdu translation by Muhammad Na'imullah Khiyali. *Madarij al-khayr.* Delhi: Shah Abu'l-Khayr Academy.
Ferrer, Jorge, and Jacob Sherman, eds. 2008. *The Participatory Turn: Spirituality, Mysticism, Religious Studies.* Albany: State University of New York Press.
Ferrer, Jorge, and Robert Tarnas. 2001. *Revisioning Transpersonal Theory: A Participatory Vision of Human Spirituality.* Albany: State University of New York Press.
Forman, Robert K. C., ed. 1997. *The Problem of Pure Consciousness: Mysticism and Philosophy.* Oxford and New York: Oxford University Press.
Frager, Robert. 1999. *Heart, Self and Soul: The Sufi Psychology of Growth, Balance, and Harmony.* Wheaton: Quest Books.
Graham, William A. 1977. *Divine Word and Prophetic Word in Early Islam: A Reconsideration of the Sources, with Special Reference to the Divine Saying or Hadith Qudsi.* New York: Walter de Gruyter.
Green, Niles. 2006. *Indian Sufism since the Seventeenth Century: Saints, Books, and Empires in the Muslim Deccan.* London and New York: Routledge.
Grof, Stanislav. 2000. *Psychology of the Future: Lessons from Modern Consciousness Research.* Albany: State University of New York Press.
Huda, Qamar. 2002. *Striving for Divine Union: Spiritual Exercises for Suhrawardi Sufis.* London and New York: Routledge.
Izutsu, Toshihiko. 1994. *Creation and the Timeless Order of Things: Essays in Islamic Mystical Philosophy.* Ashland: White Cloud Press.
Kripal, Jeffery. 2010. *Authors of the Impossible: The Paranormal and the Sacred.* Chicago: University of Chicago Press.
Kuhn, Thomas. 1996. *The Structure of Scientific Revolutions.* Chicago: University of Chicago Press.

Landolt, Hermann. 1996. "Le 'Double Èchelle' d'Ibn 'Arabi chez Simnani." In *Le Voyage Initiatique en Terre d'Islam: Ascensions cèleste et itineraries spirituals*, edited by Mohammad Ali Amir Moezzi, 251–64. Louvain-Paris: Peeters.

Laszlo, Ervin, Stanislav Grof, and Peter Russell. 2003. *The Consciousness Revolution*. Las Vegas: Elf Rock.

Ma Tingyi. 2005. *Yindu Yimamu Ranbani zhu*. 3 vols. Hong Kong: Tianma.

Meier, Fritz. 1994. *Zwei Abhandlungen über die Naqšbandiyya*. Istanbul: Franz Steiner.

Meyer, Wali Ali, Bilal Hyde, Faisal Muqaddam, and Shabda Muqaddam. *Physicians of the Heart: A Sufi View of the 99 Names of Allah*. San Rafael: Sufi Ruhaniat International.

Mir Nuʿman. 1965. *Risala-yi suluk*. Karachi, Pakistan: Barqi Press.

Muhammad ʿAbdusattar. 1998. *Tadhkirah-i Hadrat Muhaddith-i Dakkan*. Hyderabad: Minar Book Depot.

Muhammad Dhawqi. 1985. *Sirr-i dilbaran*. 4th ed. Karachi: Mashhur Offset Press.

Muhammad ʿInayatullah. 1959. *Maqamat-i irshadiyya* [1911]. Urdu translation by Muhammad Allah Khan. *Maʿarif-i ʿinayatiyya*. Lahore: Urdu Art Printers.

Muller-Ortega, Paul. 1997. "Shaktipat: The Initiatory Descent of Power." In *Meditation Revolution: A History and Theology of the Siddha Yoga Lineage*, by Douglas Brooks et al., 407–44. South Fallsburg: Agama Press.

Popper, Karl. 2002. *The Logic of Scientific Discovery*. 2nd ed. London and New York: Routledge.

Raʾuf Ahmad Rafat Mujaddidi. 1914. *Jawahir-i ʿAlawiyya* (Urdu trans.). Lahore: Nawal Kashur Kin Printing Works.

Roberts, Thomas B. 2006. *Psychedelic Horizons*. Charlottesville: Imprint Academic Philosophy Documentation Center.

Schimmel, Annemarie. 1975. *The Mystical Dimensions of Islam*. Chapel Hill: University of North Carolina Press.

Sells, Michael. 1995. *Early Islamic Mysticism: Sufi, Qurʾan, Miʾraj, Poetic and Theological Writings*. Mahwah: Paulist Press.

Shikarpuri, Faqirullah. 1978. *Qutb al-irshad*. Quetta, Pakistan: Maktaba-yi Islamiyya.

———. n.d. *Maktubat-i Faqirullah*. Edited by Mawlwi Karam Bakhsh. Lahore: Islamiyya Steam Press.

Sirhindi, Ahmad. 1972. *Maktubat-i Imam-i Rabbani*. Edited by Nur Ahmad. 3 vols. Karachi: Educational Press.

———. *Maʿarif-i laduniya*. 1986. Edited with Urdu translation by Zawwar Husayn Shah. Karachi: Idara-yi Mujaddidiyya.

Stewart, Tony. 2010. "The Subject and the Ostensible Subject: Mapping the Genre of Hagiography among South Asian Chishtis." In *Rethinking Islamic Studies: From Orientalism to Cosmopolitanism*, edited by Carl Ernst and Richard Martin, 227–44. Columbia: University of South Carolina Press.

Tart, Charles. 2009. *The End of Materialism: How Evidence of the Paranormal Is Bringing Science and Spirit Together*. Oakland: New Harbinger Publications.

Tosun, Necdet. 2005. *Imâm-i Rabbânî Ahmed Sirhindî: Hayatı, Eserleri, Tasavvufî Görüşleri*. Istanbul: Insan Yayınları.

Turner, Edith. 2006. "Advances in the Study of Spirit Experience: Drawing Together Many Threads." *Anthropology of Consciousness* 17.2: 33–61.

Tweedie, Irena. 1995. *Daughter of Fire: A Diary of a Spiritual Training with a Sufi Master*. Inverness: The Golden Sufi Center.

Wallace, B. Alan. 2000. *The Taboo of Subjectivity: Toward a New Science of Consciousness*. Oxford and New York: Oxford University Press.

Weismann, Itzchak. 2007. *The Naqshbandiyya: Orthodoxy and Activism in a Worldwide Sufi Tradition*. London and New York: Routledge.

Wilber, Ken. 2001 *Sex, Ecology, Spirituality: The Spirit of Evolution*. Boston: Shambhala.

Zawwar Husayn. 1984. *ʿUmdat al-suluk*. 5th ed. Karachi: Ahmad Brothers Printers.

Suluk-i Mujaddidiyya (Mujaddidi Wayfaring)*

'Abdullah Shah (1872–1964)

Selected, Translated, and Annotated by Arthur F. Buehler

Naqshbandi-Mujaddidi wayfaring (*suluk*) includes seven subtle centers (*lata'if*) and thirty-six contemplations (*muraqabat*).[1] In other words, it comprises seven subtle centers, three modes of intimacy with God (*walayat*), three types of perfections (*kamalat*), and seven realities (*haqa'iq*).[2] According to the refuge of those who arrive at the goal, the axis of those who have direct knowledge of Reality, the eternal beloved, the divine leader, the renewer of the second [Islamic] millennium, the leader of the Mujaddidi path (*tariqa*), the holy presence of Shaykh Ahmad Sirhindi Faruqi Naqshbandi Sirhindi,[3] the human being is composed of ten components. These are the four elements and the speaking ego (*nafs-i natiqa*),[4] heart, spirit, mystery, arcanum, and superarcanum, all of which are called the ten subtle centers. The four elements and the ego-self are in the world of creation, and the five subtle centers are connected to the world of command ('*alam-i amr*).[5]

God (Ar.: *Allah*) almighty created some creatures as mortal, material beings. All of the subtle bodies are connected to the lower material ones.[6] Some creatures were not created with mortal corporeal bodies. They are called incorporeal beings (*mujarridat*). The human spirit subtle center and the other subtle centers of the heart, mystery, arcanum, and superarcanum are incorporeal. The eminent sufis' meaning of the subtle centers being in the world of command is that they are above the Throne. It is said that the anything having a corporeal body belongs to the created world and the incorporeal belongs to the world of command. It is also understood that what is found in the world of command was created solely by means of the word "Be!" (*kun*).[7] That which was created by material means comprises the material world. The Qur'anic verse "God is creator and command" refers to both of these aspects.[8] According to those who have inner

---

*The present translation is a partial rendering of the Urdu original, *Suluk-i Mujaddidiyya* (Hyderabad, Deccan: Da'irat Machine Press, 1958), 2–23.

1. Wayfaring is traveling on the sufi path; the subtle centers are the heart, spirit, mystery, arcanum, superarcanum, ego-self, and physical frame. See my introduction for sources on twenty-three of the contemplations.

2. These three modes of intimacy with God and the three perfections are graded lesser, greater, and greatest. The seven realities are detailed later, where eight are listed.

3. Ahmad Sirhindi (1564–1624; Sirhind, Punjab, India) was the founder-figure of the Naqshbandiyya-Mujaddidiyya lineage. For details, see my introduction.

4. Air, water, fire, and earth. The *nafs-i natiqa*, literally, the "speaking-rational ego," is the human aspect of ego identity, I-ness, separating a person from what is conceived to be outside the ego-created I-ness. The spirit subtle center is its inner aspect, while the human's "animal self" is the outer aspect of the speaking-rational ego. See Muhammad Dhawqi 1985, 183, 280. Sufis have developed a sophisticated analysis of the *nafs*. See Frager 1999.

5. The world of command is one of the seven realities, the first realm beyond the physical world.

6. Literally, "higher bodies."

7. Qur'an 2:117.

8. Qur'an 7:54.

knowledge (*ahl-i 'irfan*), all beings are either in the material world or the world of command, the macrocosm. Human existence is the microcosm in such a way that the origins (*usul*) of the subtle centers of the material world are in the macrocosm below the Throne. In this manner the subtle centers of the world of command are in the macrocosm above the Throne. The subtle centers of the world of command correspond to those in the world of creation in the following manner: the heart and the ego (*nafs*) subtle center, the spirit and the element air, the mystery and the element of water, the arcanum and the element of fire, and the superarcanum and the element of earth. Another way of saying this is that the subtle centers of the world of creation are the shadows of the subtle centers of the world of command. For example, the ego subtle center is the shadow of the heart subtle center, the element air is the shadow of the spirit, and so on.

All human power comes from the configuration of these subtle centers and elements such that each one of the subtle centers has the quality of contrasting with aspects of the world of creation. The speaking-rational ego takes on [the quality of] I-ness. One should not keep on following wherever [the ego] leads, but one should make sure that all elements and subtle centers are obedient. God almighty, in God's complete power and governance with mature wisdom, gives one a special disposition and a consolidation of all the subtle centers (*hayat-i wahdani*) after putting these opposites aside. This gives one a special form protecting the various opposing parts. This integration [of parts] has the name of "Adam."[9] Considering the assemblage of opposites and consolidating all the subtle centers, [Adam] was bestowed the honor of being God's vice-regent, a great blessing not given to anyone else but him.

The origins of the seven subtle centers are in the macrocosm. The five subtle centers of the world of command, heart, spirit, mystery, arcanum, and superarcanum, are above the Throne beyond space-time (*la makani*) in the shadows of the self-disclosures of God (*tajalliyat*). Likewise,

1. The origin of the heart subtle center is the divine active manifestations. Its action is divine recollection.

2. The origin of the spirit subtle center is the divine immutable attributes. Its action is presence (*huduri*).

3. The origin of the mystery subtle center is the divine qualities (*shu'yunat*). Its action is the unveiling of sovereignty (*mukashafa-yi malakut*).

4. The origin of the arcanum subtle center is the divine negative attributes. Its action is the contemplative witnessing of the annihilation of annihilation (*mushahada-yi fana'-i fana'*).

5. The origin of the superarcanum subtle center is the divine quality of the totality of the perfect attributes. Its action is contemplation (*mu'ayana*).

All of the subtle centers in the world of command are inside the circle of possibility.

God almighty, after arranging the human form, positioned the five subtle centers of the world of command in the bodily frame so that the human would be a confluence of the material

---

9. Adam is the first human being and the first prophet in Islam.

world and the world of command. The human being becomes worthy of the name "microcosm" because the heart beats inside. It looks like a muscle in the human body that goes back and forth and looks like a pinecone-shaped lump of flesh located on the left side of the chest. The spirit subtle center is more subtle than the heart subtle center because it has more of a correspondence with the right [side]. For this reason it is located on the right side of the chest. The remaining subtle centers, the mystery, arcanum, and superarcanum are progressively more subtle and honored by being in the middle. The superarcanum is in the middle of the other four, the mystery is above the heart subtle center, and the arcanum is above the spirit subtle center. The Naqshbandi-Mujaddidi shaykhs (Ar.: elder) say that the ego subtle center corresponds to the physical senses and is located in the middle of the forehead between the eyes. This arrangement has the benefit of allowing the effects of remembrance of God and the divine/spiritual energy (*fayd*) of remembrance to reach all the subtle centers.[10]

The remembrance of God (*dhikr*) associated with the human frame occurs when all the four elements are purified. This is called the sultan of remembrance (*sultan-i adhkar*). Fire relieves the dominance of materiality and in earth one cannot help but have base materiality. On account of the unbalanced attributes of fire and earth, [these attributes] harmonize in a display of submission upon ascent. The other elements ascend and manifest the blessed attributes of God. Having become illumined, they establish the station of servanthood. Because of the ego's connections, one forgets the origins of the subtle centers. By means of much recollection of God and the spiritual energy (*tawajjuh*) of a perfect guide (*pir-i kamil*), one can become aware of the origins of the subtle centers and fly [toward them]. Having gone inside [oneself], one can start to destroy [egoic tendencies]. Eminent sufis are known for their unveiling [of divine mysteries] that the utilization of some subtle centers enables them to do. Compared to [the capabilities of] these subtle centers, an angel is weak. The ego subtle center is the weakest, and it is not that strong because it cannot do anything against animals or jinns.[11] People do not know this and have not cultivated the power of their own subtle centers. They think that the body is irrelevant, while inside of them the largest world has become hidden. From this situation people cannot know their own reality.

The human subtle center of the spirit has been created in the world of command. By the Creator's decree, it is connected to our shadow body (*jism-i zulmati*).[12] The spirit subtle center and the human body became joined in a special way to form the ego. For the wayfarer, the ego is such that it is arriving at the way station of the Buraq,[13] enabling him to finish [the stage of] wayfaring to God. He then advances to the way stations of wayfaring in God, the end of which is the death of the ego. Therefore human development is extensive. Angels do not have an ego and that is why their development is limited. Humans, by their fortune of having egos, can proceed like the highest angels (*mala' al-a'ala*). Sometimes [the ego] causes one to fall to the lowest of the low. The ego is a lightning-fast mount. It is the rider's job to keep the mount under control and on the path to the desired way station.

---

10. This divine/spiritual energy comes from the origins of the subtle centers and can be transmitted from the shaykh to the disciple in a process called *tawajjuh*.

11. Mentioned in the Qur'an, jinns are disembodied spirits that can possess people. The English word "genie" is derived from the Arabic *jinn*.

12. The physical realm is seen as the shadow of reality, so the physical human body is the shadow body.

13. The vehicle that some claim took Muhammad on his heavenly ascent.

The leader of the exalted Naqshbandi path is the holy presence of Baha'uddin Naqshband.[14] God almighty be pleased with him. His principles include following the Prophetic example (*sunnat*), determined action, avoiding innovations, and easy ways out [of fully completing the duties of a good Muslim]. There are three practices. The first is recollection of God; the second is the contemplations; and the third is bonding between the shaykh and the disciple (*rabita-yi shaykh*). The outcomes of this method are continual presence with God, awareness of the divine Essence, and correct principles of faith in harmony with the rightly guided community (*ahl-i sunnat wa-jamaat*). The technical word for this among the companions of the Prophet is virtue (*ihsan*). In sufism [it is called] contemplative witnessing (*mushahada*), concentrating on God (*yad dasht*), and the eye of certainty.

The Mujaddidi path is built on the principles pioneered by the holy presence of the leader Shaykh Ahmad Faruqi Sirhindi Mujaddidi, the renewer of the second Islamic millennium. May God almighty be pleased with him. Before him Naqshbandi wayfaring in the contemplations and learning only went as far as the subtle center of the ego. Afterward God almighty, with kindness and mercy, revealed the divine contemplations and realities to him. There are no limits on God almighty's perfections, nor is God's divine energy ever cut off. According to the Arabic dictum "Everything comes in its own time," it was time for [these divine contemplations and realities] to appear and for those close to [Sirhindi] to partake of divine energy. The discovery of reality [pioneered by Sirhindi] does not mean that the Naqshbandi notables before Shaykh Ahmad Sirhindi were deficient. Before Sirhindi all the Naqshbandi notables arrived to God. The difference is that his predecessors arrived at the Absolute Essence (*dhat-i mutlaq*) after wayfaring in a comprehensive way (*sayr-i ijmali*), while Ahmad Sirhindi was distinguished by wayfaring in the stations,[15] knowledge, and realities in a detailed manner (*tafsili*). Arriving at the holy threshold, he reached the goal.

After cleaning the subtle centers, the wayfarer has the good fortune to arrive at God. In order to clean the subtle centers, it is necessary in the Naqshbandiyya-Mujaddidiyya to do a lot of recollection of God and contemplative practice and imbibe a lot of divine/spiritual energy from the shaykh. Without this the wayfarer will not be able to successfully reach the goal.

Enacting the *shariat* is of two kinds, a strict interpretation of what are obligatory (*'azimat*) aspects and a permissive interpretation (*rukhsat*).[16] Being strict [with the *shariat*] is a basic tenet (*hukm*) and makes it difficult for the ego-self, while permissively performing [the duty] makes the legal tenet easy. For example, after the evening prayer it is permissible to sleep, but the strict interpretation of what is obligatory means that in the first part of the evening one should pray the late evening *sunnat* prayers (*tahajjud*).[17] In the same way it is permissible to fill one's stomach

---

14. Baha'uddin Naqshband (1318–1389; Bukhara, Uzbekistan) was the founder-figure of the Naqshbandi sufi lineage. For details, see my introduction.

15. The ten stations (in order) include: repentance, trusting in God, poverty, patience, gratitude, fear, hope, love, inner knowledge, and satisfaction. These are some very general markers on the sufi path for the average sufi wayfarer. In actuality, Naqshbandi wayfaring stations can occur apparently anywhere.

16. In this context *shariat* means the ritual injunctions for a Muslim's daily life.

17. Ritual prayer is divided into three categories: obligatory, praiseworthy or *sunnat*, and voluntary. *Tahajjud* prayers are the praiseworthy prayers done between the last obligatory prayer in the evening and before the first obligatory prayer in the morning.

when eating, but it is difficult to eat a little so that one still feels hungry.[18] When there is some hunger [in the late evening] it is difficult to get up. When one is traveling, it is permissible not to fast during [the fasting month of] Ramadan, but endeavoring to fast while traveling is difficult.

In the exalted Naqshbandi-Mujaddidi method, doing the contemplative practices and working against the ego enable one to avoid difficulty, allowing the seeker to choose a harmony between worship and other aspects of life. The shaykhs of the path take their students to the goal only by using exaltedly potent spiritual power. This effective spiritual power manifests in such a manner that one session of spiritual power with the shaykh is more beneficial than enduring dozens of forty-day retreats. One is commanded to follow the sacred *sunnat* and avoid innovations that are displeasing to God while not allowing permissive performance of religious duties as much as possible. Instead, one should act according to a strict interpretation of what is obligatory, which is beneficial and efficacious.

After the level of perfections of the great prophets (*ulu' al-'azm*), Mujaddidi wayfaring proceeds first toward the divine realities and then toward the prophetic realities.[19] God bless them and give them peace. In our sublineage,[20] the wayfarer does the contemplations of the divine realities before those of the prophetic realities. Other eminent Mujaddidi shaykhs do the contemplations of the prophetic realities before those of the divine realities. This difference in order is due to these realities being like two arcs facing each other with neither being higher or lower than the other.[21] Thus either sequence is correct.

In the exalted Naqshbandiyya-Mujaddidiyya, the wayfarer should strive to achieve four things: (1) being free of thoughts, (2) having continuous presence with God, (3) having an ecstatic attraction to God (*jadhba*), and (4) having significant inner experiences (*waridat*).

The First Exercise: Remembrance of God

Remembrance of God (*dhikr*) has been mandated in the noble Qur'an and blessed hadith since the preference, reliability, usefulness, and trust [of these sources] has been established. The evidence for remembrance of God is conclusive since its opposite is forgetfulness. Therefore, in truth, remembrance of God is that method (*tariqa*) where people remember God almighty's essence, attributes, and perfections. Remembrance of God is when one occupies one's tongue or thoughts and heart with God almighty. Among the modes of remembrance of God, Qur'an recitation gives one effective blessings, which are included in the recitation of litanies (*awrad*) or exercises taken from the Qur'an. Even the *shariat* injunctions are included [in this blessing]. Paying attention to encouraging good and discouraging evil is also included in the definition of remembrance of God. In the blessed Qur'an, God almighty's guidance "You remember me and I remember you"[22] happens when one remembers God.

---

18. The strict interpretation is to only fill the stomach one-third full.
19. The divine realities are as follows: the reality of the Ka'ba, the reality of the Qur'an, the reality of ritual prayer, and the reality of pure worshipedness (*ma'budiyyat-i sirfa*). The prophetic realities include the reality of Abraham, the reality of Moses, the Muhammadan reality, and the Ahmadi reality.
20. Literally, "family."
21. Literally, "bows."
22. Qur'an 2:152.

In the technical vocabulary of sufism, remembrance of God refers to imagining God's name in a part of the body or the entire body.[23] There are two ways of doing this: vocal and silent remembrance of God. From the perspective of the blessed hadith, silent remembrance is sixty degrees more preferred than vocal remembrance. Remembrance of God using the tongue sometimes has an effect on the heart, while in the beginning of silent remembrance there is an effect on the heart. That is why the exalted Naqshbandi method uses silent remembrance of God and why Naqshbandi shaykhs place great importance on it. God bless them. In the holy presence of Khwaja Baqibillah Naqshbandi's blessed assembly,[24] one time a disciple started saying "Allah, Allah" out loud. Baqibillah counseled the other disciples to tell him that he should think about behaving beautifully (*adab*) while remembering God and to do silent remembrance.

Doing silent remembrance and contemplation fosters the growth of the wayfarer. People think that during contemplation one does wayfaring in the world of sovereignty. In this there is a possibility of hypocrisy. Therefore the wayfarer should consider exercising caution.

> Remaining in the inner world, be a stranger to the outer world.
> In the world there are few who proceed so exquisitely.
> In the heart it is a complete secret—why is it all locked up?
> The heart waxes eloquent as the lips remain silent.

The exalted Naqshbandi-Mujaddidi lineage has two types of remembrance of God, repeating "Allah, Allah," negation and affirmation (*nafy wa-ithbat*), which is repeating *la illaha ila Allah* (There is no god but God); and contemplation of the exclusive unity (*ahadiyat*), the first of the contemplations.[25] One only repeats "Allah" for the subtle centers of the heart, spirit, mystery, arcanum, superarcanum, ego, and physical frame. When these subtle centers are activated, one then begins the practice of negation and affirmation. The contemplation of being together with God (*ma'iyat*) also involves the practice of negation and affirmation.[26] After this, one contemplates the five subtle centers of the world of command repeating "Allah." Up to this point one utilizes silent remembrance of God. Afterward until the end of wayfaring, one's remembrance of God can be silent or vocal. The goal of vocal repetition of negation and affirmation is to engage both the imagination and the tongue. The process is vocal to the extent that only the person reciting it can hear it. This is just like one does in [Sunni] ritual prayer or in repeating phrases when using the rosary.

There are two ways one can repeat "Allah." One is [repeating] "Allah" continuously, whether standing, sitting, or lying down, with or without ritual purity. This repetition is focused on the heart subtle center, which is the most important of the subtle centers because it is the foundation and inner bastion of the other subtle centers. This is evident after one purifies the heart subtle center. According to one of the noble sayings of the Prophet, "The human body has a lump of

---

23. The practice of repeating God's name occurs in places in the physical body corresponding to the locations of subtle centers, for example, the heart. When all of the subtle centers are activated, each hair on the body utters "Allah."

24. Khwaja Baqibillah (1563–1603; Delhi, India) was Ahmad Sirhindi's Naqshbandi shaykh.

25. The two types mentioned here are silent and vocal, not the three stages of practice.

26. For more details on *ma'iyyat*, see Buehler 1998, 244.

flesh [the heart] and when it is sound, the entire body is sound, and when it is corrupt, the entire body is corrupt."

The second, when one has some time to be alone in silence, is to visualize the shaykh's face as if he were right in front of you while imagining the tongue repeating "Allah" many times until one senses the effect of divine/spiritual energy. The modality of remembrance is one of observing carefully. One can do this remembrance any time, but the most effective time is the evening when it is quiet. Because of this, one progresses one hundred times as fast. In the beginning there will be [experiences] of blessed disembodied spirits and spirits of eminent deceased shaykhs along with [outbursts of] repentance and asking for forgiveness. Along with humility, these experiences are beneficial and have good effects. This is why the tranquility of the heart is such good fortune. When an aspirant does a lot of repeating of "Allah," his subtle centers and body become purified of [the ego's] coarse rebellion and the seeker ascends to the appropriate level [of development]. Now the aspirant can contemplatively witness his own origin (*asl*), which up to this point had been a theoretical possibility.

In this regard, the holy presence of the renewer of the second Islamic millennium [Ahmad Sirhindi], in his *Maktubat* (Collected Letters), God be pleased with him, guided people to first repeat "Allah" in the following manner.[27] First, eliminate all thoughts and inner talk. Then with firm resolve focusing on the heart, repeat softly "Allah, Allah." Imagine the tongue saying it such that you visualize the form of the heart. Instead of holding the breath, one follows the awareness of the heart (*wuquf-i qalbi*). It is necessary to say this because remembrance of God without careful observation of the heart's thoughts is ineffective. Instead there is [nothing but] inner talk. The holy presence of Khwaja Baha'uddin Naqshband did not find it necessary that one be aware of how many times one repeated "Allah" but instead made awareness of the heart one of the conditions of remembrance of God.

Sirhindi, in another letter, said that in the beginning one should focus on the pinecone-shaped heart because that lump of flesh is like a chamber for the true heart. When the repetition of "Allah, Allah" passes through the true heart, one should not voluntarily move a muscle. The entire body should be focusing on the true heart as one sits still. The goal of focusing on the true heart is to view the meaning of "Allah, Allah" in its incomparable formlessness, not in some corporeal form. The exaltedness of the almighty Essence is beyond attributes. One must not go from unity (*wahdat*) to looking at multiplicity. In other words, one should not go from transcendence to immanence. That which appears in the mirror of form is not the formless. That which shows [itself] in multiplicity is not the real One. True formlessness is outside the circle of form, and one needs to look outside the walls of multiplicity to find the real One.

Every so often during remembrance of God one can say, "[To arrive near] God is my purpose and my desire is His pleasure. Give me knowledge and love of Him." In one twenty-four-hour period one should repeat "Allah" twenty-four thousand times or as many times as one can as long as it is not less than six thousand. The minimum number for effective remembrance of God is twenty-four thousand because a person takes this many breaths in a twenty-four-hour period. One should be so aware in the process of remembrance that one should keep track of exactly how many times one inhales. The holy presence of 'Azizan 'Ali Ramitani Naqshbandi said that on

---

27. Ahmad Sirhindi's *Maktubat* is his main literary legacy and includes some of the most detailed instructions on sufi contemplative practice. See Buehler 2011.

the Day of Judgment each person would be asked about each breath he had taken.[28] That is why one should not be heedless of even one breath. For breaths that pass by unawares, the wayfarer, having repented, should try to follow each unaware breath so that he does not forget God in any subsequent breath. In this way one's practice progresses. Remembrance of God is performed by daily establishing the number of times to repeat [Allah], which is equally distributed between the subtle center of the heart and the next subtle center or contemplation [one will focus on].

Remembrance of God should include [acting in accordance] with the splendor of the outer *shariat* and with the inner fire of love (*muhabbat*). After achieving continuous presence with God (*hudur*), the wayfarer arrives at the reality of remembrance of God. Previously [the wayfarer] was only performing the appearance of remembrance of God. Continuous presence of God is one of the benefits that one receives from continuous remembrance of God. There are five degrees of continuous presence of God: (1) One becomes aware of the presence of God almighty from the effects of focusing on the heart subtle center as awareness of the world decreases; (2) One has less awareness of the world from the effects of focusing on the spirit subtle center, (3) One's awareness of the presence of God almighty predominates over the awareness of the world from the effects of the mystery subtle center; (4) One is aware of the presence of God almighty without any awareness of the world from the effects of the arcanum subtle center; and (5) One is aware of the presence of God almighty without any awareness of oneself or of the world from the effects of the superarcanum subtle center.

One should adhere to the practice of remembrance of God because remembrance is the magnet [enabling one to] arrive near God. The person who is an intimate of God almighty is one who arrives near to God almighty. An eminent person once advised that when one repeats "Allah, Allah" in remembrance, then one remembers this greatest name of God without realizing its reality and greatness because one is pronouncing the words according to one's own capacity. One is not pronouncing the blessed name according to its power and rank. The method of saying the worthy rank of Allah's name in its belovedness and greatness was something that the Prophet knew how to do. God bless him and give him peace. To the extent that one can learn from eminent shaykhs, at the time one is recollecting God the person realizes that God is hearing the remembrance. In what fashion can I remember God? Do I experience God by longing for God or do so without longing and yearning from the heart? What about that aforementioned thought that keeps coming—that God also keeps remembering me in the same way that I remember God. If I remember God sincerely, then God will remember me lovingly. Saying "Allah, Allah" has the thought of God being retained in the mind because one is repeating the name of the most exalted king and beloved. Period. Having the king and beloved's name in the forefront [of one's awareness] [enables one] to receive God's greatness, majesty, and love. One should conduct the practice of remembrance of God such that God's greatness, majesty, and love are cultivated in the heart. After some days, remembering God in this way facilitates a state to manifest that cannot be expressed in words.

The holy presence of Moses said, "Oh my God you are close like something that is too close to be seen, and so far away that it is difficult to grasp." God replied, "I am with the person who

---

28. 'Azizan 'Ali Ramitani (d. 1321) was the grandfather shaykh of Baha'uddin Naqshband.

remembers me, and I am as close to [that person] as his jugular vein,[29] when the nourishment of his spirit (*ruh*) is remembrance of God, when his soul's thirst is quenched by praising God almighty, and when his spirit is clothed with God's life-giving being."

Remembrance of God is a fortress into which Satan cannot enter.[30] As long as the wayfarer is engaged in remembrance of God, the wayfarer is protected from Satan. From remembrance of God the heart becomes delicate and soft while increasing one's inclination (*dhawq*) to worship and obey God. One realizes God almighty's favor. One's sins are erased. As the rust is removed from the heart, the [polished] mirror of the heart [reflects] nothing but the love of God. The person remembering God is always content and cheerful with a heart continually full of the inner knowledge of God (*ma'rifat*).

The Second Exercise: Contemplation

The word "contemplation" (*muraqaba*) comes from waiting attentively (*raqabat, raqubat*), linguistically meaning "guarding" and "waiting." From the perspective of *shariat*, [this means] that after having brought together all the external and internal senses, one pays attention to the limbs and organs of one's body. From the perspective of the path (*tariqat*), contemplation means waiting attentively for God's divine effulgences (sing.: *fayd*) and not being distracted by thoughts of other than God. Contemplation is the passageway where one keeps imagining divine effulgence to arrive. It is said that divine effulgence arrives at a subtle center when one feels the divine effulgence from God almighty in one of the subtle centers. Contemplation can be done with or without remembrance of God. The wayfarer closes her eyes and then, keeping all thoughts out of the heart, keeps focusing on the arrival of divine effulgence, attentively waiting for the divine effulgence of God's essence, attributes, or deeds by means of one's shaykh. The goal that is kept in mind overrides everything else such that there remains no feeling of one's own being. In the technical vocabulary of sufism, contemplation is deeply considering an attribute of God almighty. Contemplation without remembrance of God is especially effective for ascent. In our opinion, combining remembrance of God with contemplation is effective because one can perfect two practices at one time as one is able to realize the aforementioned divine effulgences and blessings (*barakat*). If one has enough time in one's daily life and enough determination, one can complete these two practices by doing them separately.

The holy presence of Ahmad Sirhindi said that in the same way that one cannot realize the essence of God almighty, one cannot realize the attributes of God almighty in contemplation. Those attributes that can be realized in contemplation are the shadows of the attributes. God be satisfied with him. Understand what is given. Through that understanding it will come in some manner. The holy presence of Junayd said that he learned contemplation from a cat.[31] One

---

29. Cf. Qur'an 50:16.

30. Satan has the same role of tempting people as in the Christian tradition. In the Islamic tradition he became Satan after refusing to bow down to Adam. See Qur'an 38:71–85.

31. Junayd (830–910; Baghdad, Iraq) was a major sufi of so-called classical sufism, who is considered to be the leader of the "sober" school of sufi practice.

day he noticed a cat sitting and waiting to pounce on a mouse. It was totally consumed in this activity to the point that not even a hair moved on the cat. Junayd said that he was surprised on seeing this and suddenly he heard a voice inside that said, "Your determination and goal are totally more exalted, so your total immersion [in contemplation] should be correspondingly more intense (*balatar*) than that of this cat." Junayd said that after this experience he used this method when contemplating and experienced a lot of divine effulgence.

After one experiences the power of light or manifestations of brightness, one realizes the results of contemplation in such a way that after not experiencing power and brightness, the splendor of the goal is unveiled with lights in a state of desert silence.

The Third Exercise: Bonding with the Shaykh

Both roots of the word *rabita* mean a connection or relationship.[32] The noble sufis call the word "bonding" when one holds the appearance of the shaykh's face in the heart like a cupbearer holds a cup. Our great shaykhs decided that the fastest method to arrive near God was bonding with the shaykh. The goal of bonding with the shaykh is perfect love and obedience along with a beautiful way of behaving (*adab*) in the shaykh's presence.[33] In the shaykh's absence one should visualize the shaykh and fix that in the mind. It is by means of the shaykh that the divine effulgences come to a person, which is one way of creating an inner and outer togetherness with God. To the extent that one develops an affinity with the shaykh, one's togetherness with God increases. The extent of one's servanthood is the strongest factor in receiving divine effulgences. Complete servanthood is bonding with the shaykh, which is called annihilating oneself in the shaykh. This is the first degree of perfection on the path.

Khwaja Muhammad Ma'sum Naqshbandi-Mujaddidi said that in the Mujaddidi method arriving completely is connected to bonding with the shaykh.[34] God bless him. A sincere seeker receives divine effulgences and blessings from the shaykh's inner being by lovingly following this method of focusing on the shaykh. Through an essential affinity one realizes the same being [of the shaykh].[35] According to the saying of the notables of the path, annihilation in the shaykh is the beginning of real annihilation. Whatever manner of recollecting God and however one gets to a place [in one's practice] are both dependent upon the bonding of love and annihilating oneself in the shaykh. One can effectively practice without the method of remembrance of God if one bonds with the shaykh guided by correct behavior in spiritual companionship (*suhbat*) and focusing on the shaykh.[36]

The holy presence of Ahmad Sirhindi said that if an aspirant were to bond with the shaykh without difficulty, then a spiritual relationship would be formed between them. God be pleased

---

32. Here the context is bonding with the shaykh (*rabita-yi shaykh*).

33. This context is explicitly when the seeker is in the physical presence sitting in front of the shaykh. However, *rabita* is not restricted by time or space or corporeality. Almost all sufi shaykhs I have known have continual contact with their deceased shaykhs.

34. Khwaja Muhammad Ma'sum Naqshbandi-Mujaddidi (d. 1668; Sirhind, India) was Ahmad Sirhindi's chief successor.

35. Literally, "color."

36. Spiritual companionship is a companionship in which divine/spiritual energy is being shared between the individuals involved, in this case the shaykh and the aspirant.

with him. This benefits the seeker and enables the seeker to derive benefit. There is no better method than bonding with the shaykh to arrive at God. In terms of effectiveness, bonding with the shaykh is better than remembrance of God because in the beginning it is difficult to receive divine energy completely without bonding with the shaykh. In another place Shaykh Ahmad Sirhindi advised that it is not strange for a seeker to become convinced of his shaykh's utmost perfection and excellence. This conviction is a result of love and inner affinity with the shaykh—the reason why the seeker benefits and is able to receive benefit from the shaykh. One must keep in mind that one should not prefer one's shaykh over all else such that it goes beyond the limits of the *shariat*. Whatever is against the *shariat* guidelines, for example, making it obligatory to have excess love [for one's shaykh], is frowned upon in reality. It is permissible to prefer others in addition one's shaykh, but on the sufi path it is incumbent on the qualified seeker to voluntarily develop a love in his heart. If this process comes about with difficulty or through one's own choice, then it is not permissible. Whatever results and type of benefits occur or do not occur, the domain of the seeker's success is being certain that the seeker's shaykh knows the way to arrive at God almighty quite well and that the shaykh can get the seeker there. Whoever does not depend on one's shaykh keeps experiencing a blocked path.

Contemplation should be done without remembrance of God so that one has complete focus (*tawajjuh*) on God. It is difficult to do contemplation without a lot of remembrance of God and spiritual companionship with those of the sufi group. This method depends on centering the work around love and bonding with the shaykh. Without bonding with the shaykh, remembrance of God, and meditation (*fikr*), one would not get anywhere. Love and bonding with the shaykh without remembrance of God is still effective. One should continue thinking of what pleases the shaykh while behaving to one's utmost best while in the presence of the shaykh. In the shaykh's absence one must visualize the shaykh, which is called bonding with the shaykh. This is one of the prerequisites of wayfaring. One is purified to the extent that one is able to follow the external *sunnat* and keep anything other than God away in one's inner experience. From spiritual companionship, one's inner being is cleansed by the constant focus on God. Shaykhs' spiritual energy (*tawajjuh*) [facilitates] one's heart to turn toward God almighty. Divine lights begin to appear in one's heart after witnessing the attraction of the shaykh's love.

Visualizing the Shaykh

The seeker is dependent upon finding a spiritual guide (*murshid*) first before being able to visualize him. Having created a green path [enabled] by the intermediary function (*barzakh*) of the shaykh, the seeker traverses the way stations and arrives at the real goal. From visualizing the shaykh, the sincere seeker contemplatively witnesses divine secrets.

> All the time I keep visualizing your blessed face.
> How could I explain what I see if someone were to ask?

A seed hidden under the ground later becomes manifest as a date palm, which is in truth the seed's original form. In the same manner, the form of visualizing the spiritual guide [like the seed] being planted in the field of the heart, will make all of the original form apparent.

> The thought that appears from the inside
> Is like a tree that grows from the ground.
> Each thought in the heart and body is wondering where it will end up.
> On the Day of Judgment one form will appear.

Therefore it is better that wayfarers do not think about conceptualizing what perfect guidance [on the path] is. The appearance of what is in this world becomes imprinted in the heart, and one dies with this visualized appearance. It is through this intended form [imprinted on one's heart] that one will have [to be evaluated] on the Day of Judgment.

While in remembrance of God, corrupt thoughts will come rushing in. To end these, one should totally focus on God almighty by means of remembrance of God so one can be free of these thoughts involving the ego. However, a beginner is not accustomed to focusing on God almighty, so thoughts will keep rushing in. It is human nature that one cannot pay attention to two things at the same time. One should set out in such a way that one is not able to concentrate on those [corrupt] thoughts. The shaykh has a humanness (*shakhsiyat*) that one can feel and one quickly feels love for him. Thoughts of the shaykh arise in this way such that they automatically ward off thoughts going in the direction of ego involvement, thereby necessarily inculcating a corresponding habit. From repeatedly visualizing the shaykh's face (*surat*) and perfections, love (*muhabbat*) for the shaykh is engendered and a strong connection (*nisbat*) develops [between the shaykh and the seeker]. For whatever reason, the seeker begins to be affected by the character and deeds of the shaykh because states result from actions. So [the seeker] begins to experience states. Visualization of the shaykh depends on these abridged secrets. But this is an incredibly difficult path. From visualizing the shaykh a lot, a likeness of the shaykh's body sometimes appears in front of a seeker. Sometimes this form resembles [the shaykh]. What is imagined is imagined. Sometimes some unseen subtlety (*latifa*) resembles the form [of the shaykh]. When a seeker is [physically] in front of the shaykh, he begins to learn how to be fully present and observant [in service to the shaykh] (*hadir wa nazar*). This is a relaxed form of association with God, though usually the seeker does not notice what happens when he is sitting in front of the shaykh.

Some ignorant seekers conceive of the shaykh as being the form of God almighty. This is also an association with God, but one that creates [Satanic] suspicions leading to thoughts that cause one to be led completely astray. It is very difficult for the seeker to follow the straight path [to God]. In short, it is this kind of error that one encounters on the way when doing the exercises. It [explains why] the elite proceed very carefully when visualizing the shaykh and [why] they experience so much love in the shaykh's presence and when they are engaged with remembrance of God. Common people are incapable of being fully present in the presence of the shaykh.

Visualizing the shaykh is the elegance of becoming annihilated in the shaykh.[37] This visualization comes by imagining and is not continuous. It is only after the visualization becomes continuous that one is able to realize one's level of annihilation in the shaykh. Continual

---

37. Annihilation (*fana*) is considered the annihilation of the ego-self. It is juxtaposed with abiding in God (*baqa*), which is the experience that one has when the ego-self becomes temporarily annihilated. On the sufi path there are many such experiences of annihilation/abiding until one is able to be in the world of duality with a unitary awareness. See the illustration of the Mujaddidi path in my introduction (fig. 7.3).

visualization and annihilation in the shaykh must involve the heart. The beginner visualizes mentally, while the intermediate wayfarer involves the heart in visualization. In order to involve the heart in this manner, it is necessary to purify the heart, which is achieved by having done a lot of remembrance of God. When the heart is not sound, it will not become illumined by the lights of remembrance of God.[38] The wayfarer will not be able to use the heart [in the practices] nor receive divine/spiritual energy from the shaykh. Afterward [that is, with a sound heart] continual visualization [occurs] as the shaykh is reflected and engraved in the wayfarer's heart by means of the shaykh's heart. It is believed that notable sufis can bring light to the hearts of wayfarers with a mere glance, who then reach the goal.[39] Common people do not have such sensitive hearts like those of wayfarers. In today's unsettled conditions and [an Islamic environment] not considering what is permitted and prohibited, these kinds of events do not happen anymore.

Concerning this situation, it is worthwhile to mention [the story of] the Byzantine (*rum*) and Chinese artisans.[40] Once upon a time there was a king and two artisans, one Byzantine and the other Chinese, who came to him praising their work. The king realized their worthiness and presented them with a hall in a palace where they could completely exhibit [their talents]. The hall was divided in half with a curtain in the middle, such that each artisan could not see the work of the other. So they began their work. When it was finished, the king came with his ministers to inspect what had been done. The curtain was raised and everyone was astonished at what they saw because each side of the hall was painted exactly the same down to the last detail. What had happened was that one wall was painted and the other wall was polished like a mirror, reflecting the other wall. One can get an idea about purifying the heart and the benefit of receiving divine effulgence from this example.

This is the situation of the wayfarer on the path. When one purifies the heart from impurities by repeated remembrance of God and spiritual energy of the shaykh, the heart becomes illumined by the lights of remembrance of God. The heart becomes like a mirror, pure and brightly polished, while reflecting the heart of the shaykh and the writing of the preserved tablet (*luh-i mahfuz*).[41] Then the wayfarer becomes aware of the how the universe is arranged. When this purification process is finished and one reaches perfection, one not only considers the created universe but the Creator of the universe whose manifestations and splendor pour into the wayfarer's heart.

> Visualizing the Friend in the mirror of the heart,[42]
> One sees brightness when the ego is diminished in strength.

In the shaykh's absence, the wayfarer should visualize him as if he were in his actual presence. If this quality is cultivated, then one can receive spiritual energy from the shaykh at a distance.

---

38. Literally, "afflicted with heart diseases."
39. Reading *mu'taqad* for *mutaqqad*.
40. From Rumi's *Mathnawi*, Book 1, verses 3480–3500.
41. The preserved tablet is said to be the heavenly prototype of the Qur'an.
42. Here "Friend" can mean God or one's male or female lover. Persian poetry is delightfully ambiguous.

The Method of Focusing Spiritual Energy

In the technical vocabulary of sufism, focusing spiritual energy (*tawajjuh*) means [transmitting] an inner power that affects someone else. The shaykh focuses this energy by putting his heart in front of the seeker's heart. Focusing on God and the intermediaries of the noble holy presences of the [Naqshbandi] shaykhs, he says, "Oh God may I experience God's lights of remembrance from the great shaykhs and may my heart have already been illumined by them. May You present this seeker's heart to the shaykhs so that the seeker's heart will become illumined by them." Then the shaykh strongly focuses spiritual energy toward the seeker's heart. While focusing spiritual energy, the shaykh notices the other subtle centers and contemplations and knows which station's divine energy to focus upon. First the shaykh feels the quality of a station's divine energy; then he transmits this to the seeker's inner being, knowing exactly where to direct it.

The seeker should first should purify her heart by thinking of nothing but God. After this, as one's inner self harmonizes with the shaykh's inner self, one mentally thinks, "God almighty's divine energy is coming to the shaykh. That divine energy is coming to me through the shaykh." Keeping this thought in mind, one experiences divine energy. One can also visualize the shaykh saying, "Having harmonized my heart with the shaykh's pure heart, divine energy comes from the shaykh's blessed heart to mine." It is just like water running in a canal. The visualization keeps on occurring in the heart as long as one does not block the flow.

Ecstatic Attraction to God

When a feeling of pulling starts to happen in the subtle centers, it is called "attraction" (*jadhb*). Hidden divine energy (*fayd-i ghaybi*) and having the intention of God (*ghayat-i haqq*) are called "attraction" or "arriving at God" in the context of having realized an inner connection. It is clear that attraction is an involuntary affair.

When the wayfarer experiences a connection of wholeness (*jami'at*) and presence of the heart (*hudur-i qalb*), the shaykh focuses divine energy [on the seeker] as a way to facilitate attraction to God. As the seeker's heart begins to experience an attraction upward, lights begin to appear. This is a sign that the heart is turning toward its own origin. Attraction in all of the subtle centers is experienced because the perfect shaykh is focusing blessed divine/spiritual energy. Each of the subtle centers are attracted to their origins.

It is known that the wayfarer's progress on the path depends on assiduous practice and receipt of a lot of spiritual energy from a perfect shaykh. When these two aspects become perfected, the wayfarer proceeds very rapidly, and to the extent that these aspects are lacking, progress slows down. The readiness of wayfarers is also a major factor such that a person with a high degree of readiness can progress rapidly even with occasional practice and little spiritual energy from the shaykh. Likewise, a person of diminished readiness will limp toward the goal even though he practices a lot and receives much spiritual energy. In this method the spiritual companionship and spiritual energy of the perfect shaykh is a great factor [in realizing the goal]. How can exertion and practice be effective without these two elements of [spiritual companionship and spiritual energy]?

In this notable method, attraction to God comes at the beginning of wayfaring. Therefore, progress in wayfaring is easy because of attraction to God. As long as there is no spiritual energy from a perfect shaykh, attraction to God will not be evident. The perfect shaykh, through his connection with the seeker, keeps pulling the seeker, way station by way station, to the goal. In a short time the seeker experiences exalted wayfaring. Even if traversing the path takes thousands of years, it is worthwhile. However, when there is attraction from God almighty, there is no conceivable limit to how fast one can traverse the path. One could travel on the path for thousands of years and not travel as far as one who is attracted to God travels in a moment.

Attraction to God is necessary for wayfaring in the sense that if there is to be ease in wayfaring, then there has to be an attraction to God. Conversely, for attraction to God, wayfaring has to be perfect. If the goal in wayfaring has to do with *shariat* affairs like repentance and asceticism, then one will not experience attraction to God. The attraction will remain incomplete. In this exalted method the seeker realizes the connection of both attraction to God and wayfaring. In the beginning stages the seeker realizes the connection of attraction to God, and then the seeker experiences traversing the path with ease.

Subtle Centers[43]

Using the light of this blessed saying of the Prophet (hadith), we will explain the subtle centers of the macrocosm. "In the human body of the sons of Adam there is a piece of flesh; and in this piece of flesh is the heart (*qalb*); and in the heart is the inner heart (*fu'ad*); and in the inner heart is the mystery (*sirr*); and in the mystery is the arcanum (*khafi*); and in the arcanum is the superarcanum (*akhfa*)."[44]

The Heart Subtle Center

The method of activating the heart is to close the eyes with the tip of the tongue on the upper palate while directing one's heart to God almighty and visualizing the face of one's shaykh. This is done with the tongue of the heart repeating "Allah, Allah." The heart is an interface between the world of creation and the world of command. When the wayfarer remembers Allah in the subtle center of the heart in this way, the heart becomes purified and the quality of the heart transforms by going from the world of humans to the world of sovereignty (*'alam-i malakut*).[45] [This is like the] saying "That which is between the body and spirit is a subtle thing." It is a hidden reality within the human being that is also called the world of sovereignty. By means of this saying the wayfarer can proceed gradually through the stages of ascent, realizing the fruits of remembrance of God. In this station one's heart can receive divine effulgence (*fayd*) from the holy level of the divine Essence by means of the spiritual guide. One can receive this divine effulgence by visualizing the heart in one's mind (*khiyal*), while focusing the heart subtle center on God almighty.

The origins of the five subtle centers of the macrocosm are above the Throne. The heart subtle center is attracted to ascend to its origin.[46] In this exercise one usually repeats "Allah" and

---

43. The translation from here to the end is from 'Abdullah Shah's *Suluk-i Mujaddidiyya*, 45–62.
44. The author, a noted hadith scholar, does not give a hadith citation for this.
45. Another word for the world of command.
46. Literally, "inclined."

visualizes the shaykh. The light from the heart subtle center is yellow. First and foremost the seeker must be truthful and sincere in order to minimize heedlessness and become more aware.

The Spirit Subtle Center

When palpable sensations begin in the heart, one can begin remembrance in the spirit subtle center. The spirit subtle center is located two finger widths under the right nipple. When the wayfarer becomes aware of the quality of the heart subtle center, he realizes that the spirit subtle center is also situated in the world of command. From here he goes from the world of image exemplars (*alam-i mithal*) to the world of spirits,[47] becoming knowledgeable in the names and attributes of God.[48]

The meaning of "spirit subtle center" is reality (*haqiqat*) and involves the transformation of a person's image exemplar.[49] The divine effulgences [associated with this subtle center] are the Muhammadan spirit's light associated with the world of dominion (*'alam-i jabarut*). The wayfarer can suddenly sometimes have a very subtle experience of not having a physical or imaginal body. When the wayfarer becomes overwhelmed in this way, she contemplatively experiences states associated with the station of dominion. This is the work of the human spirit with which friends of God have had the good fortune to be blessed. It is said that outwardly the friends of God are with us [in the physical world], but the quality of their [simultaneously] being in the world of spirits continues to be hidden [to others]. Even though the spirit subtle center is connected with the formless world (*'alam-i be-chun*), in reality it is facing the true formless One, which intersects the circle of form. Exalt God's affair. In other words, between the formless and form there is an interface (*barzakh*) that mixes the two. Therefore [in this interface] both aspects are valid. The color of the spirit subtle center is red.

The Mystery Subtle Center

When the spirit subtle center starts to become transformed, then one can begin remembrance in the mystery subtle center. It is located between the left nipple and the sternum.[50] The mystery subtle center means "secret" or "mystery."[51] It is the origin of the human spirit, which is also called the world of the divine Essence revealing itself (*'alam-i lahut*). The world of the divine Essence revealing itself means Muhammadan spirit but with a more subtle quality, whereby the wayfarer unintentionally experiences states beyond those of the previous subtle centers. What the wayfarer can understand after these states pass is that by reason of his ardent love of God he has come to have experiential knowledge of the divine (*ma'rifat*). The light of this subtle center is white.

---

47. The world of image exemplars is often located between the world of command and the physical world. The world of spirits is another name for the world of command.

48. According to Ahmad Sirhindi and the illustration of Mujaddidi cosmology in my introduction, these are the *shadows* of God's names and attributes.

49. A person's image exemplar is most likely the subtle body that is used to navigate in the world of command.

50. It is usually located two or three finger widths above the left nipple. For a discussion of how to reconcile the differences in subtle centers' locations as reported by different shaykhs, see Buehler 1998, 110–13.

51. Since *sirr* is used for other sufi terms and often translated as "secret," I have chosen to use "mystery" as a technical term for subtle centers.

The Arcanum Subtle Center

After the mystery subtle center, one begins remembrance of God in the arcanum subtle center. It is located between the right nipple and the sternum.[52] The arcanum subtle center involves the Muhammadan light associated with the world of undifferentiated Essence (*'alam-i hahut*). When the quality of this subtle center manifests, the wayfarer realizes God. The color of this subtle center is black.

The Superarcanum Subtle Center

After the arcanum subtle center, one begins remembrance of God in the superarcanum subtle center located at the sternum in the middle of the chest. These are the five subtle centers belonging to the world of command, which was created with the word "Be!"[53] [The superarcanum] is in the station above the Throne, the shadow of which is the human body, which in turn becomes purified through much remembrance of God. How the superarcanum returns to its origin is explained in detail by Ahmad Sirhindi in his *Maktubat*. God bless him.

The superarcanum subtle center corresponds to the undifferentiated Essence at the level of undifferentiated Essence. This Essence is described as "Glorious and Holy" or "Eternal."[54] It is beyond the beyond and then even beyond this. This Essence is free of attributes, qualities, and absolute limitations. This is the holy Essence whose only connection is guided by itself. God encompasses everything.[55] This subtle center has a green light.

The Ego-Self Subtle Center

After the superarcanum subtle center, one begins remembrance of God in the ego-self subtle center, which is located between the eyes in the middle of the forehead. The ego keeps the human being inclined toward self-centeredness (*ananiyat*) and hypocrisy, which the Qur'an calls the "commanding to evil."[56] One tries in this station to distance oneself from the commanding nature of the ego so that one can change one's [base] qualities. This is called cleansing the ego. After this, one becomes adorned with laudable character traits and attributes. The light of this subtle center after cleansing the ego is without quality. Note that the colors and lights of the subtle centers are only a part of the sufi path, and this is nothing more than a way to differentiate [the subtle centers].

The Physical Frame Subtle Center

After the ego-self subtle center, one begins remembrance of God in the physical frame subtle center (*qalab*), which is located all over the body. This is also called the "supreme way of remembrance of God."[57] The ego-self and physical frame subtle centers are in the created world, which was cre-

---

52. It is usually located two or three finger widths above the right nipple.
53. A Qur'anic reference: "Be and it is" (Q. 3:47).
54. These are divine names of God, some of which are mentioned in the Qur'an: *al-subbuh*, *al-quddus* (Q. 59:23 and 62:1), and *al-samad* (Q: 112:2).
55. Qur'an 4:126.
56. Qur'an 12:53.
57. Literally, "Sultan."

ated in degrees over six days. When the interior of the wayfarer is enlightened, then [the interior] qualities [mentioned earlier] become manifest [in the created world]. In this subtle center one cleanses the four elements of air, water, fire, and earth. In this station all the veins and nerves of the body and even the tips of each hair on the body all recollect God. There are three signs of a wayfarer's purifying the subtle centers: (1) The wayfarer does not feel lazy in obeying God's ordinances and in worship. There is no inclination for sinful behavior. The urge to become close to and experience God grows in the wayfarer's heart. (2) Without any intention on the part of the wayfarer, his subtle centers become activated (*dhakir*) and the wayfarer contemplatively witnesses the lights of God in them. The wayfarer experiences an incomparable joy when obeying God's ordinances and worshiping. And (3) the wayfarer begins to hear the sound of her subtle centers remembering God and begins to feel a complete pulsating in the heart. Unencumbered by stray and suspicious thoughts, the wayfarer has the good fortune of a pure heart. One becomes overpowered by the love of God and by following obediently the example of God's Messenger. God bless him and give him peace. These are the signs of a wayfarer's subtle centers being purified. When these seven subtle centers become activated, then there is never any heedlessness. There is no way for one to become lazy or forgetful in any way because one's desire to obey God's ordinances and to worship God has grown so much.

The Practice of Negation and Affirmation

After activating the seven subtle centers, one can begin the practice of negation and affirmation.[58] The method is to hold the breath in the navel area, directing the word *la* upward to the ego subtle center (between the eyes) and aiming *ilaha* toward the right shoulder, "striking powerfully" into the heart subtle center with the words *illa Allah* via the spirit, arcanum, superarcanum, and mystery subtle centers to the point of feeling the effect. In this last movement one keeps in mind that the one goal is the Pure Essence of God almighty. One does this three, five, seven, or more times (as long as it is an odd number) holding the breath. After releasing the breath, one says, "Muhammad is the Messenger of God." Then one visualizes divine effulgence on the physical frame, and a bit later one says humbly, "God is my purpose. Please give me your pleasure, love of you, and knowledge of you." If one is not able to hold the breath, then one can do the exercise without holding the breath. Ideally one should do this recollection exercise one thousand times each day. One can do it fewer times if necessary but not less than three hundred times a day. One repeats "Allah" from 9 p.m. to 9 a.m. and negation and affirmation from 9 a.m. to 9 p.m. Repeating "Allah" is beneficial for cultivating ecstatic attraction to God and love of God, while negation and affirmation is very effective for keeping away stray thoughts and inner purification.

In the Naqshbandi-Mujaddidi lineage, ecstatic attraction to God happens first in wayfaring and can be overpowering. For this reason, Naqshbandi-Mujaddidi shaykhs teach beginning wayfarers the repetition of "Allah." After they receive divine effulgence [from this practice], they are taught the procedures of negation and affirmation. For this reason the repetition of "Allah"

---

58. This is the first part of the attestation of faith for Muslims, "There is no god but God." A different method is outlined in Buehler 1998, 129–30.

is more effective when there is attraction to God—it creates warmth in the heart and desire for God. Doing negation and affirmation is more effective for wayfaring.

From the wayfarer's desire to cleanse the elements along with holding the breath at the navel is the usual practice of negation and affirmation. This is because the station of the elements is located below the navel. When one does much negation and affirmation practice, she feels a circle of light go from the navel to the forehead and from the forehead to the right shoulder, and from there to the area of the five subtle centers of the world of command. This is the quality as one begins [the practice]. As one advances, one negates all beings when saying *la* and affirms God almighty when saying *ila Allah* to the point that the remembrance of God and the person remembering are subsumed in God.[59]

The limbs of the body do not move when saying *la* as one negates all of creation. One imagines the pure Essence when affirming *illa Allah*. It is also necessary that when this *illa Allah* strikes the subtle center it also affects one's entire body. If it is painful to hold the breath, one can also do the negation and affirmation without holding the breath. When holding the breath, one does the negation and affirmation an odd number of times, for example, three, five, seven, nine, and so forth. After releasing the breath, one says mentally, "Muhammad is the Messenger of God. God bless him and give him peace." For a very short time thereafter one says mentally, "God is my purpose. Please give me your pleasure, love of you, and knowledge of you." If one is not holding one's breath, then the same thing is said an odd number of times.

Holding one's breath and counting an odd number of times is not necessary for the practice of negation and affirmation. It is necessary, however, to go through the movements.[60] The goal is to do negation and affirmation twenty-one times in one breath, which enables the wayfarer to arrive quickly. Holding the breath has an exalted quality of facilitating the warming of the heart, longing for God, unveiling, and expanding the heart (*inshirah-i sadr*) while keeping away stray thoughts. This is the way to experience tranquility of the heart and spiritual joy. An extremely effective method of realizing God almighty is through the method of negating all existence when saying *la* and affirming God when saying *illa Allah*. If this method of remembrance of God is not working, one should realize that one is deficient in beautiful behavior (*adab*) and in fulfilling the requirements of the practice. One should begin anew, assiduously adhering to all the required behavior and principles of practice. If God almighty wills it, the practitioner will be able to adhere to all the necessary details [of practice]. Some wayfarers are able to do the negation and affirmation more than twenty-one times in one breath. The first practice for divine knowledge (*'ilm-i laduni*) is counting an odd number of negation and affirmations. Divine knowledge means realizing a certain quality and manifesting God's secrets. Discovering this divine knowledge is associated with doing negation and affirmation in this manner. While doing this practice, one must think that one's only goal is God almighty's Essence. The linguistic meaning of this holy phrase is that one only worships God almighty. Negating worshipedness (*ma'budiyat*) is more complete and profound than negating having a goal (*maqsudiyat*). This is because each thing worshiped is a goal but not every goal is worshiped. When having a goal is negated, negating worshipedness is included because general negation includes negation of the particulars.

---

59. Here the practice is repeated word for word as described in the first five lines of this section.
60. Navel to forehead to shoulder to heart.

Khidr,[61] God give him peace, taught this practice of negation and affirmation along with holding the breath and counting odd numbers of repetitions to Khwaja 'Abdulkhaliq Ghujduwani (d. 1179),[62] God bless him. There is a branch of this practice whereby one repeats *la ilaha ila Allah* in a low voice while also thinking the words according to the requisite behavior and requirements of negation and affirmation.[63]

In Naqshbandi-Mujaddidi practices, it is permissible to do vocal repetition of negation and affirmation as a way of contemplating the ego-self. If the wayfarer wants to repeat *la ilaha ila Allah* in the mind, there is nothing that is disapproved. However, with mental repetition the wayfarer's tongue is shut off from the divine effulgence of remembrance of God. That is why a bit of vocal repetition is necessary. Also, vocal repetition promotes states of ecstasy. The wayfarer can experience divine lights through his senses and awareness. In the future stages on the path involving ecstasy, the wayfarer will be able to create a capacity to stabilize his awareness and senses through vocal repetition of *la ilaha ila Allah*.[64]

There are six conditions of practicing negation and affirmation: (1) One should keep in mind the meaning of the expression, "Except for the pure Essence there is no other goal." When one thinks of "no" [as in "There is *no* god but God"], one negates all of existence. When thinking "but God," one visualizes the Essence of God almighty. (2) One needs to focus on the heart and the heart needs to focus on God almighty. Without this, being present with God is not possible. (3) Observing one's awareness (*nigahdasht*) is a sufi technical term meaning to purify the heart from stray thoughts and what underlies them in the ego structure. Observing one's awareness is a method whereby one can achieve a synthesis (*jami'at*) and the connection of God's continual presence. Do not be heedless of the King for an instant. It is possible he looks [at you] and you are unaware. (4) One should keep track of how many times one says "There is no god but God" in one breath, and make sure that it is an odd number. (5) One should visualize the shaykh. And (6) one should turn to God every so often in the practice of remembrance of God (after the exhalation of each breath), stopping to say humbly, "God is my purpose. Please give me your pleasure, love of you, and knowledge of you." Then one continues in remembrance of God. The Naqshbandis call this returning to the world while performing remembrance of God (*baz gasht*).

Humility is the most important means [to achieving the goals] on the wayfaring path. This is because God almighty needs nothing but takes pleasure in his exalted palace in people's supplications. One sees one's efforts as completely nothing and without any reality, putting one's trust completely in the grace and generosity of God almighty.

> This kingdom is not built on strength.
> This conquest is only attainable through defeat.

---

61. Khidr is an immortal who crosses paths with prophets and sufis in the Islamic tradition. He is often identified with the companion of Moses in Qur'anic sura 18. In addition he has been identified as a prophet, one of the heavenly pillars (*awtad*), and the seventh substitute (of seven *abdal*).

62. 'Abdulkhaliq Ghujduwani (d. 1179) was the founder-figure of the sufi lineage called the "Masters" (*khwajagan*).

63. *La ilaha ila Allah* means "There is no god but God."

64. Typically in the texts, Naqshbandi identity is one of *silent* remembrance of God, whether "Allah" or *la ilaha ila Allah*. In practice, however, there is considerable flexibility in vocal and silent practice.

In short, heedlessness will not go away without trying and perseverance. In this manner the wayfarer will become drowned in a quality of exclusive unity (*ahadiyat*). This is when no sense of self remains and he realizes a total annihilation of self. This means that the wayfarer is at the level of still thinking about creation but not her own self. No kind of sensation of self remains. That is, one leaves behind one's own essence and attributes. In this meditation (*muraqaba*) the wayfarer affirms God almighty by intensive negation and affirmation involving the negation of oneself and all other than God.

Ahmad Sirhindi, the renewer of the second Islamic millennium, said that if there were no expression "There is no god but God," then who would explain the road to God. Who would lift the veil from the face of asserting the oneness of God (*tawhid*), and who would open the door to heaven? God be satisfied with him. The hoe of "no" [in "There is *no* god but God"] can dig out the mountain of human attributes. By this good fortune one negates the connection to the world and all the worthless things that are worshiped. In this manner the affirmation of God is an affirmation of worshiping something real. The wayfarer is helped by *la ilaha ila Allah* to traverse gradually the realm of no place. By means of this blessing, the wayfarer soars to this greatness. *La ilaha ila Allah* causes [the wayfarer] to go from the self-disclosures of God (sing.: *tajalli*) of the shadows to the self-disclosures of the names and attributes until he reaches the holy Essence. This great *la ilaha ila Allah* is like the uncreated shore of an ocean. Compared to this the world is but a drop. *La ilaha ila Allah* is the synthesis of the perfections of intimacy with God (*walayat*) and prophethood (*nubuwwat*).

In a holy saying of the Prophet it says, "Whomever says *la ilaha ila Allah* will enter heaven." People are astonished that just by saying this once a human being can enter heaven. This poor one [the author] knows well that it is a wondrous thing if the person saying this once were to go to heaven. But simply by saying *la ilaha ila Allah* once, all the Muslims were given this [grace], so there is the capacity [for this to happen]. From the blessings of *la ilaha ila Allah* that have been distributed to the entire world, the whole world keeps on blossoming and flourishing. It is also said that the blessings and greatness of *la ilaha ila Allah* manifest according to the level of the person saying *la ilaha ila Allah*. Your friend may look very good if your friendship is on the basis of sincerity. In another place the Prophet said that all the joys and delights of the world are nothing compared to the joy and sweetness of *la ilaha ila Allah*.

The Messenger of God, God give him blessings and peace, said in a blessed hadith that Moses, God give him peace, supplicated to God that God would teach him some words so that he could summon and remember God. God instructed him to say *la ilaha ila Allah*, whereupon Moses replied that all of God's servants say that and that he wanted some special words. Then God said that if all the seven heavens and earth including all of creation were placed on one pan of a balance scale and *la ilaha ila Allah* on the other, the latter would tip the scale. From this it is apparent that the practice of negation and affirmation is a powerful method to realize God. How important this practice is for the wayfarer!

One should know that at the time of saying "no" (*la*) [one thinks] of nothing but God, banishing stray thoughts and poor character traits one at a time. For example, in order to get rid of envy, one thinks that she no longer has any envy at the time of saying "no." At the time of saying *ila Allah* (but God), one thinks that God almighty's love permeates me. By continual practicing negation and affirmation in this manner and being humble toward God, blameworthy character traits will be removed over time if God wills. One's inner self will be cleansed and purified of reprehensible character traits and tendencies to act against God's rules for living in an upright manner (*shariat*).

The Contemplation of Being Together with God

When the aspirant experiences the effect of the practices of remembrance of God, that is, he experiences the sweetness of the practice without very many distracting thoughts along with an aversion to the world, it is appropriate to supplement the practice of negation and affirmation with the contemplation of being together with God (*muraqaba-yi ma'iyat*).[65] This latter practice is contemplating the meaning of the following Qur'anic verse in one's heart: "God is with you wherever you are."[66] One becomes worthy in this way of receiving the divine effulgence of the Essence. This effulgence comes via the shaykh's physical frame subtle center to the aspirant's physical frame subtle center.

> The transmission is incomparable beyond qualities.
> There is a longing for the soul to be with the Sustainer of people.

One becomes so engulfed in this contemplation that no other thought remains. Whether one is walking, standing, or sitting, this contemplation is kept in the mind so that one eats, listens, and talks less. When the wayfarer continually contemplates in this way for a few days, the love for God increases and the love for the world decreases so that the wayfarer can realize the supreme purpose.

As an interim note, the two contemplations of exclusive unity and togetherness are in the realm of lesser intimacy (*walayat-i sughra*), which is also called the intimacy of the friends of God (*awliya*). The wayfaring at this level is in the shadows of God's names and attributes. This is the station where the wayfarer is blessed with annihilation [of the ego] and abiding [in God], forgetting everything but God while realizing the intimacy of the friends of God. A friend of God is a person who has eliminated [temptations of] the ego-self, Satan, and the world, including her own desires, directing her heart and being to God almighty. There is no desire for anything in this world or the next world except God almighty.

In this station, one contemplates according to the meaning of "God is with you wherever you are,"[67] which is that this Essence that is with me is with all the atoms of creation and divine energy comes [to me] by means of the presence of the shaykh. This is the source of the divine energy of the subtle center of the physical frame and the practice of negation and affirmation.

God has such a communication with God's servants that it is beyond understanding. In this contemplation, being together with God is in lesser intimacy of God, which is where the assertion of unity of God and the secrets of togetherness with God are realized. In this lesser intimacy

---

65. In the "standard" version (standard being the system outlined in nineteenth- and twentieth-century books on the subject), the contemplation of being together with God is the seventh contemplation of twenty-six. See Buehler 1998, 249–53.
66. Qur'an 57:4.
67. Qur'an 57:4.

the wayfarer is facilitated in inner wayfaring (*sayr-i anfusi*).[68] An allusion is in the Qur'anic verse "[I am] inside you; can't you see?"[69]

The being together with God and creation is unambiguously proved in the Qur'an. This following example will make it easy to understand. In a ball made of clay one sees the earth, but in reality it is composed of atoms, which are hidden from view because of their subtlety. All we see is the clay. In the same manner the spirit, which is together with all aspects of the body, keeps the body going. The spirit, however, because of its subtlety, is hidden while the body outwardly manifests.

> The soul (*jan*) is not hidden from the body nor is the body hidden from the soul.
> A person, however, cannot see the soul.

Air and the spirit are with clay and the body, respectively, but they are not seen because of their subtlety. Thus God almighty is together [with us] in an ineffable and incommensurate (*bichun wa-bichigun*) manner, [which we do not comprehend because of] our limited understanding. Yet without a doubt God almighty is with us and with each atom of creation, undergirding all of it. This is because God is the absolute everlasting, the support of creation connected to permanency (*qayyumiyat*).

Up until this point the wayfarer's attention has been directed upward in a state of unveiling and ecstasy. Now it is directed inwardly toward the subtle centers while feeling divine energy comes from each side.[70] The wayfarer ineffably realizes the ineffable togetherness with God almighty along with visualizing how [this togetherness] encompasses all of creation. This is the sign that one has realized the level of lesser intimacy with God. The specifics of this station include the secrets of the unity of being (*tawhid-i wujudi*), [often paraphrased as] "All is God." [One experiences] longing, "ahh" exclamations, lament, ego-self loss, forgetting everything except God, along with an ineffable continual presence and togetherness with God almighty. If the wayfarer's eye of insight opens, then so do the secrets of *shariat* and divine comprehension. From an ecstatic state one can realize God almighty's togetherness.

In short, without effort, perseverance, and striving, one will not get rid of heedlessness.[71] In this fashion the wayfarer becomes subsumed in exclusive unity because there is no longer a sense of ego-self. The secrets of the unity of being are revealed to the wayfarer in this state. These secrets have a spiritual quality and are not associated with the physical body.

A blessed [divine] hadith from the Messenger of God,[72] God bless him and give him peace, heard from God says, "When my servant performs supererogatory works (sing.: *nafl*) to get closer to me, I draw many degrees closer to him until he starts to become dear such that his

---

68. The author says that in this inner wayfaring one is able to see all the lights of the subtle centers. For a more detailed exposition of inner and outer wayfaring, see Buehler 2011, Letter 2.42.

69. Qur'an 51:21. This translation is that of the author, who is using it to make a point. The Qur'anic context points to a meaning more akin to "Can't you see the truth [of these statements] inside you?"

70. For the subtle centers it more literally reads "six sides."

71. The negative particle *na* is missing in the text.

72. Divine sayings are considered as God's words but not a part of the Qur'an. See Graham 1977.

sight, hearing, hand, and foot become my sight, hearing, hand, and foot. Things come and go. If someone asks me for refuge, I give it to him; and if someone asks something of me, I give it to him. The person who says something against my friend should be ready to wage war on me."[73]

The Circle of Contingent Existence

After traversing the end of the subtle center of the physical frame, one begins wayfaring in the lesser intimacy, the circle of contingent existence.[74] Naqshbandi-Mujaddidis conceive of wayfaring in the world of command and the world of creation. The Essence is beyond and then beyond this. There are five subtle centers in the world of command and two in the world of creation. The world of command is above the majestic Throne and came into existence by the word "Be!" The created world is under the Throne, gradually created over six days. These two worlds are collectively called the circle of contingent existence. The majestic Throne is the dividing line between these two worlds.[75]

There is an innate imperative for a human being to return to God almighty. One's heart is inclined upward and one's eyes look toward the sky. God's grace and generosity along with God's wrath and rage are understood to come from above. In doing this there is a concealed secret that God almighty turns the creature's determination and will toward the sky and the Throne. Each person's mind when returning to God almighty has a tendency to be inclined toward the heart and the Throne. Rationally and according to the dictates of the *shariat*, God almighty is beyond space-time. God is beyond the beyond, and then beyond the beyond. In reality the great Throne is not the place of God almighty nor the place where God resides. The majestic Throne is the station from which God's dictates (*ahkam*) and divine self-disclosures proceed.

The great Naqshbandi shaykhs have explained the circle of contingent existence in the following manner: From remembrance of God all the subtle centers light up. This light becomes all collected together in the shape of a circle, which in sufi terminology is called the circle of contingent existence. One first feels a push upward in the circle of contingent existence and then has experiences in the heart that the wayfarer often describes as an annihilation of ego-self. This is a transformative experience, and that has also happened to others and is facilitated by intercession [of the chain of Naqshbandi shaykhs going back to Muhammad]. These experiences are called "the existence of nonexistence" (*wujud-i 'adm*) and are interpreted to be annihilation and ecstatic attraction to God (*jadhba*). It is at this time that various kinds of lights appear in the subtle centers. One does not experience absolute annihilation, although a realization of incomparable closeness to God manifests. Ahmad Sirhindi, the renewer of the second Islamic millennium, God be satisfied with him, interpreted [these experiences] in various circles.[76] The word "circle" is commonly used so that one knows that there are no corners or directions. Being close to God is similar in that there are no dividing lines or directions. Thus circles are suitable [as an analogy

---

73. This is a conflation of many hadiths, which is unexpected from a hadith scholar.
74. See the illustration of Mujaddidi cosmology (fig. 7.1) in my introduction.
75. This is not indicated well in the illustration of Mujaddidi cosmology (fig. 7.1).
76. See the illustration of Mujaddidi cosmology in my introduction (fig. 7.1).

to describe] closeness to God. The first circle is the circle of contingent existence. If the wayfarer has contemplative unveilings (sing.: *kashf*), then some of the world of image exemplars comes into view. Being able to experience [the world of image exemplars] necessarily depends on the capacity to have contemplative unveilings. The majestic Throne is also revealed in the same manner. The upper half of the circle of contingent existence contains the five subtle centers of the world of command, and the lower half is where the subtle centers of the created world can be seen.

Outer wayfaring (*sayr-i afaqi*) occurs in this circle of contingent existence. It is called "outer" because from inside oneself it is possible to observe outer lights and self-disclosures of God. These innumerable beautiful colors appear in all kinds of delightful forms. It is imperative that the wayfarer not be inclined to this [display] and ignore it. Something of many colors is the origin of multiplicity, and being without color is the origin of oneness (*wahdat*).[77]

When there is presence of heart and realization of wholeness (*jami'at*) and no thoughts in a four-hour period of time, then that is the sign that wayfaring in the circle of contingent existence is completed. Some notable sufis have decided that the wayfaring is ended in this circle when there are self-disclosures of God and lights. The consensus of the Naqshbandi-Mujaddidi shaykhs, God bless them, is that presence of heart, the realization of wholeness, being ecstatically attracted to God, and special experiences in the heart (*waridat*) are what is important, not self-disclosures of God, visionary experiences (*zuhur-i ashkal*), and lights.

Notable sufis have also added that the bottom half of the circle of contingent existence is where one does outer wayfaring, while the upper half is where one does inner wayfaring. Whatever is revealed from the surface of the earth to the majestic Throne is outer wayfaring. The sign of finishing in the lower half is contemplatively witnessing inner lights on the outside.[78] Inner wayfaring is unveiling of lights and secrets. The sign of finishing the upper half is complete realization of wholeness, frequent significant experiences in the heart, attraction to God, and the ascent of the subtle centers toward their respective origins. Wayfarers who experience unveiling (*sahib-i kashf*) are able to understand these altered states. In this era, because *halal* food is not easy to obtain, a wayfarer experiencing unveiling does not have clear vision. Most of those experiencing unveiling manifest it by ecstatic attraction. From being an unveiling-experiencing wayfarer with clear vision, one can progress to the next station [on the path]. In addition to being able to transform one's states, one can have a clear visionary experience. The unveiling-experiencing wayfarer who is ecstatically attracted, even though he cannot see clearly, is able to realize transformations and perceive changes in his states. This process is not visualized but is necessarily felt. If these aforementioned matters are not dealt with, then one will not be able to realize a connection with these stations [on the path].

---

77. Literally, "chameleon-like," for something of many colors.
78. The author glosses this as the unveiling the world of spirits, image exemplars, and the levels of the sky and earth.

Chapter 8

Eastern Orthodox Prayer

The *Rasskaz strannika*

John Anthony McGuckin

More commonly appearing in English as *The Way of a Pilgrim*, the *Otkrovennyi rasskaz strannika dukhovnomu svoemu ottsu* (Candid Tale of a Pilgrim to His Spiritual Father; abbr. *Rasskaz strannika*) is a late nineteenth-century travelogue that includes information on Eastern Orthodox Hesychast prayer, specifically the Jesus Prayer. Originally written in Russian, the text has a complex authorial and compositional history. Recent scholarship identifies the primary textual layer as composed by Archimandrite Mikhail Kozlov (1826–1884), a Russian Orthodox monk. The text is thus associated with the Hesychast strain of Eastern Orthodox Christianity and specifically with nineteenth-century Russian Orthodox monasticism. The received text consists of "four meetings" during which the unnamed Pilgrim seeks instruction on the admonition to "pray without ceasing." He eventually finds guidance from an unnamed *starets*, or spiritual Elder, who describes the practice of the Jesus Prayer, which is also known as the "Prayer of the Heart." The text appears to be a monastic composition intended for laypeople, especially the steady number of pilgrims staying in monastic guesthouses.

In Search of the Pilgrim

The well-known text concerning a poor pilgrim who makes his way through nineteenth-century Russia with only a knapsack filled with crusts of bread, a Bible, and (later) a copy of a book of spiritual writings from the early Greek Fathers known as the *Philokalia*[1] was received very enthusiastically throughout the twentieth century, both in Russia and in the English-speaking world. This was partly because it was believed that it was a record, almost mystically produced,[2] of an unlearned peasant, whose innocent devotion to interior prayer had refined his intellect and polished his communicatory capacity to such a pitch that he could be Everyman and speak directly to the heart of all his readers. In addition, the book seemed to stand as a plaintive testimony to so much that had been lost after the Russian Revolution of 1917, when the Bolsheviks so heavily damaged the Orthodox Church in both its fabric and its clerical personnel, especially venting their fury on the extensive monasteries that spread over all the land. The book seemed to be a perfectly captured sepia photogravure of Holy Mother Russia, or *Slavia Orthodoxa*;[3] this is Russia as the heartland of an Eastern Orthodox spirituality so tied to the earth that it rose out of the very stones. Was the Pilgrim not a pure representative of this? Was he not the quintessence of what Nikolai Gogol (1809–1852) tried to evoke literarily, was he not a fuller and more spiritually acute version of the Holy Fool Grisha, who appears to such effect in Lev Tolstoy's (1828–1910) reminiscences of *Childhood*,[4] or even the image of the wise Elder who occupies such a significant place in Fyodor Dostoevsky's (1821–1881) *Crime and Punishment* (a figure of his own monastic *starets* from the Optino Hermitage)? For such reasons, ordinary questions of literary criticism seemed to have been left aside throughout the twentieth-century reading of the collection of tales that make up the story of the Pilgrim. Interpretation was felt to be sacrilegiously intrusive, as it were, not a fitting response to the pure religious fervor that the Pilgrim both represented and attempted to spread. The book was about a devotion of the heart, not of the head, and so it seemed that many of its readers avoided exegetical questions. However, although the Pilgrim is indeed a quintessential character, still, a character he is. He is not a real authorial figure (except as a pseudepigraphical symbol). The tales are not his simple journal of real events. The stories are not even a written-down version of his (supposedly illiterate) recounting of his journeys and adventures to some learned cleric who transcribed them to edify others. The work is a fiction, a pastiche. Nevertheless, it is, for all that, as genuine as gold. The experiences that it recounts and the characters and attitudes that it represents are as real as we could wish: they ring with the actuality of a real spirituality as practiced for many generations and coming to a fruition in that long autumn of nineteenth-century Russia before its baptism in blood under the Bolsheviks (see McGuckin 2008, 47–52; also Wallace 1984). The book, even when understood as a fictionalized account of very real monastic notes, certainly does represent *Slava Orthodoxia* in shining clarity.

The book is a complicated product of learned monks; it is a tale of handwritten manuscripts in monastery libraries, copied by hand well into the nineteenth century, circulated in ways that another copyist would add to them as well as reproduce them, before they became more "fixed" by the printed editions that started to become more common at the very end of the nineteenth century. Several monastic figures, living in different Russian monastic centers, were involved, though Irkutsk, Kazan, the Optino Hermitage (near Moscow), the Vyshenskaia Hermitage (Tambov Province), and the Saint Panteleimon (Russian) Monastery on Mount Athos in Greece all form the center of the nexus that produced the final texts. All of the compilers and editors belonged to the same "school" of monastic spirituality, the Hesychast tradition that went back to early medieval Byzantium (coming to Russia in the ninth century). This was true of the two individuals who most stand out as manuscript "authors" in the modern sense of that term: Archimandrite[5] Mikhail Kozlov (1826–1884) and Hieromonk[6] Arsenii Troepol'skii (1804–1870). It is equally true of the most important editors of the final printed texts: Hegumen[7] Paisii Fedorov (fl. 1880s), Saint Theophan (Govorov) the Recluse (1815–1894), and Bishop Nikon Rozhdestvenskii (1851–1918) of Irkutsk.[8]

As discussed in detail later, a life in Hesychastic prayer and informed by Eastern Orthodox spirituality is "presumed" by all of the Russian monastics involved with the final preparation of the text that has been preserved and transmitted as the *Rasskaz strannika*. All of these individuals were Hesychasts, all of them steeped in the Bible and the traditions of the Jesus Prayer, and all of them eager to propagate it in terms accessible to the large "lay" readership of eighteenth- and nineteenth-century Russia. This laid two main avenues of audience open to them. The first was the large ring of houses of the minor nobility, or landed gentry, that existed in Russia at this time (see Wallace 1984). We notice how often this class of people appear in the book. This literature would have been read on Sundays, and the wider circle of listeners would have been the household servants (the very class to which the Pilgrim who is the main character belongs). It is a tale meant to bring together into a commonality of Christian feeling the landowner and the *muzhak* (peasant). The other audience envisaged by the monastic compilers was the hordes of actual Russian pilgrims who, before the catastrophic events of 1917, thronged the many monasteries across Russia that acted as way-stations for medical and social help as well as centers of prayer and pilgrimage in their own right.

At the core and center of the nexus of eighteenth- and nineteenth-century Russian monasteries that produced the *Rasskaz strannika*, there was (paradoxically) the monastery of Saint Panteleimon on Mount Athos in Greece. Athos was the recognized center and focus of Orthodox monastic life, the heart of the Hesychastic movement and the Jesus Prayer, and in the nineteenth century a monastery devoted exclusively to Russian pilgrims and monks. In the pilgrimage to Jerusalem that so many hundreds of thousands of Russians made annually, before the Revolution, there were two other essential stopping points: Constantinople (Istanbul, Turkey) and the Panteleimon Monastery. On Athos, and throughout most of the Russian and Romanian monasteries, the memory of an eighteenth-century leading Hesychast, Saint Paisy Velichovsky (1722–1794), was still vivid.

Saint Paisy had been the original translator into Slavonic of the Greek *Philokalia* (see further discussion), a compendium of Hesychastic theology from the medieval writers (it is the book that the Pilgrim treasures above all after his Bible).[10] He was a Ukrainian monk who worked out of the Moldavian (Romanian) Monastery of Neamt to disseminate three critical traditions of the Hesychasts: the incessant use of the Jesus Prayer as the soul of monastic observance, the need for obedience to the directions of a wise spiritual Elder, and the use of the *Philokalia* as the fundamental library on prayer that every monastic ought to know by heart. These three motives are at the very core of all that the text of the *Rasskaz strannika* sets out to advocate. It is this above all that locates the text, and the monastics who shaped it, in the Paisian tradition of Russian Hesychasm (see McGuckin 2009). In the late nineteenth century this tradition was especially strong in the Optino Hermitage near Moscow (a noted center from which several famous spiritual Elders wrote), the Panteleimon Monastery on Athos, and the Vyshenskaia Hermitage that was the base for Theophan the Recluse (one of the most prolific spiritual writers of nineteenth-century Russia). All three centers of Hesychast spirituality "had a hand" in the final shaping and popular dissemination of the *Rasskaz strannika*. In the course of the last few decades, the fascinating history of the various redactions of the text has been laid bare by the careful detective work of Aleksei Pentkovsky.[11]

The final version of the tales came to be put together in this way. The first basic text, no longer traceable in its manuscript form,[12] was a work written by Archimandrite Mikhail Kozlov (1826–1884) and titled *Iskatelia neprestannoi molitivy* (A Seeker of Unceasing Prayer). Father Kozlov was a convert to Orthodoxy from the Old Believers' (Old Ritualists) sect, which is discussed later in this chapter. The (now misplaced) manuscript was described by Archbishop

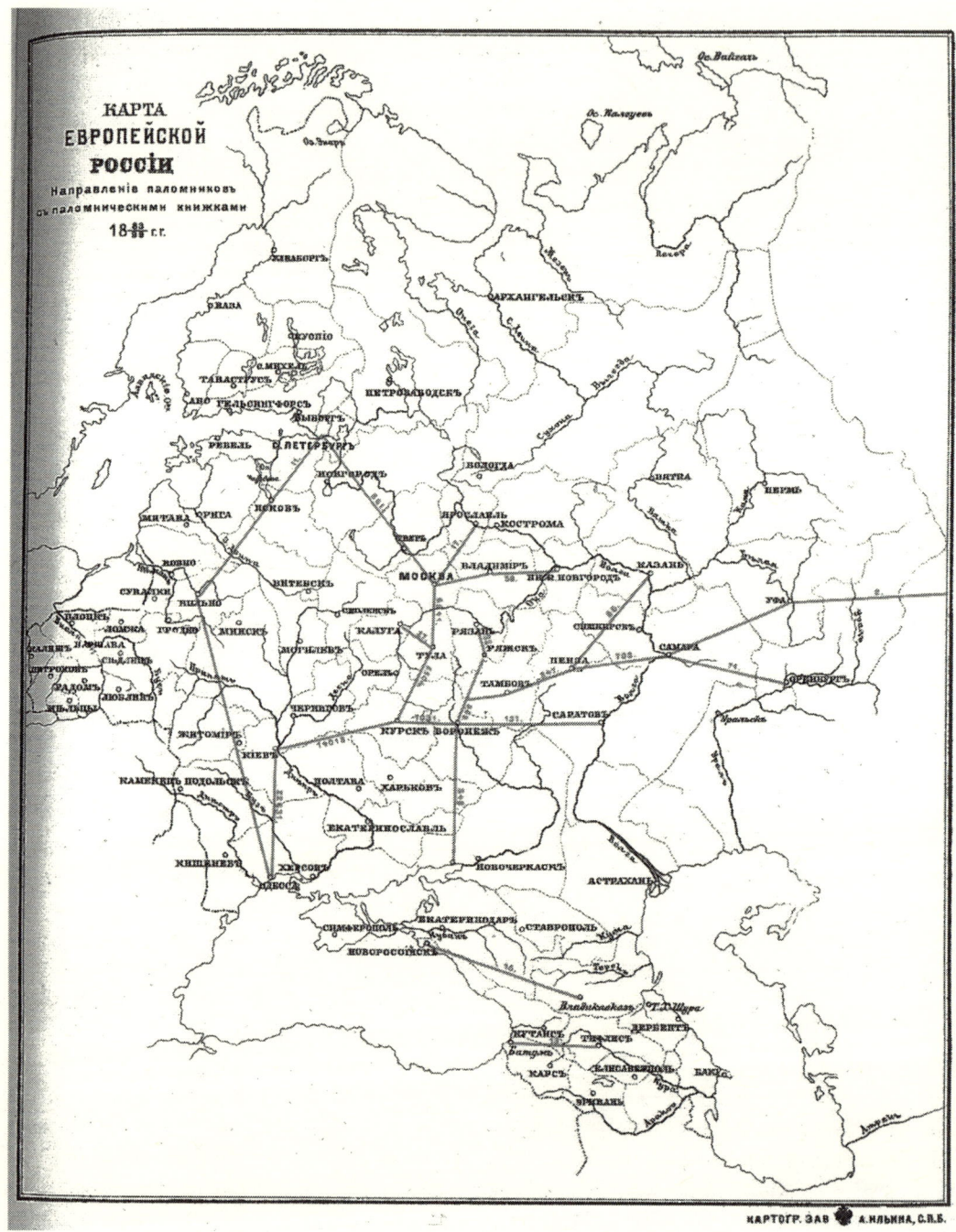

Figure 8.1. Nineteenth-Century Map of Russian Cities
Where Pilgrims Purchased "Pilgrims' Booklets"[9]
Source: Slavonic Library, University of Helsinki

AUTHORS AND TEXTS
Mikhail Kozlov (1826–1884) Panteleimon Monastery (Mount Athos, Greece) and Holy Trinity Monastery (Selenginsk, Russia) *Iskatelia neprestannoi molitivy* (A Seeker of Unceasing Prayer) (Ur-text)
Arsenii Troepol'skii (1804–1870) Saint Simon Monastery (Moscow, Russia), Pafnutii Borovski Monastery (near Moscow), among others *Pamiat'o molitvennoi* (Recollection of a Life of Prayer) and *Otkrovennoe poslanie* (*Otkrovennyi ilisa*; Candid Missive)
KEY EDITORS
Paisii Fedorov (fl. 1880s) Saint Michael the Archangel Monastery (Kazan, Russia)
Saint Theophan the Recluse (1815–1894) Vysha Monastery (near Tambov, Russia), among others
Nikon Rozhdestvenskii (1851–1918) Trinity Lavra of Saint Sergius (Sergiyev Posad, Russia)
KEY ARCHIVISTS
Amvrosii Grenkov (1812–1892) Optino Hermitage (Kozelsk, Russia)

Figure 8.2. Redaction Chart of the Received *Rasskaz strannika*

Veniamin Blagonravov (1825–1892) of Irkutsk, who knew the author. His few remarks tell us that this work contained a strong advocacy of the Jesus Prayer and set in the form of a poor pilgrim who starts off making many prostrations and saying the prayer vocally hundreds of times before he meets up with a wise Elder who shows him how to bring prayer down into his heart and so make it "unceasing." The story makes reference to several sermons on prayer that have no great impact on the seeker. The archbishop records that the story of prayer is portrayed in the book "through characters, in simple and lively conversations."[13] Seeing this note in the published letters of Archbishop Veniamin, at a later date, when he himself possessed the 1881 published book form of the *Rasskaz strannika*, Father Pavel Florensky (1882–1937) made his own note that the author of the *Rasskaz strannika* was none other than Mikhail Kozlov, which is a simplification of the true sequence of events that has been taken up by several later scholars.

Now this work, the *Iskatelia neprestannoi molitvy*, is unquestionably the core of the First Tale of the greater text, the *Rasskaz strannika*, and thus Kozlov is the original author of the primary layer of the text; he is its originating mind, as it were. There is no doubt that the Pilgrim's First Tale is the heart and soul of the whole book, even though Kozlov's work is no longer wholly synonymous with it. For later monastic advisors, Kozlov left out several things that needed to be and were "corrected" and amplified by additions; this process, in turn, gave rise to the finished (anonymous) book that we now have. Kozlov's Ur-text, as it were, is also found in parts of the remaining Tales Two through Five.[14]

The larger text of the *Rasskaz strannika*, however, is made up of four such tales. There is also an appendix, published at a later time, consisting of Tales Five, Six, and Seven. Tale Five in this appendix seems to belong to the same editorial hand that assembled the first four tales. But Tales Six and Seven are clearly from a different creative hand, being more dry and controversialist in character; the Pilgrim's character also fades away here, and they have never generally been loved as much as the core of the first four tales, even though the similarities of Tale Five permitted them to be regarded (at first) as collectively a simple continuation of the *Rasskaz strannika*. One of the earlier English versions of the two redactions tried to smooth over the evident differences by giving the first series of four its own invented title of *The Way of a Pilgrim* and the three appendix texts the title of *The Pilgrim Continues His Way* (see French 1991 [1931]). Both of these titles, which have no basis at all in the Russian text, have become widely known in the English-speaking world and tended to propagate the view of the first translators that this was an actual account of a peasant pilgrim, one that needed no exegesis to make it clear. In other words, they fell for the narrative devices in a rather unscholarly way and used a rather defective Russian text as the basis of their translations.

Returning to the author of the primary textual layer of the *Rasskaz strannika*, Father Mikhail became a monastic postulant in 1854 and transferred to the Panteleimon Monastery on Mount Athos in 1857, becoming tonsured as a monk there in 1858. He spent some time after that traveling through Russia collecting funds for his Athonite monastery. (We see the figure of just such a monk who teaches the Pilgrim about the *Philokalia* in Tale Five.)[15] In 1864 he returned to Mount Athos and entered a higher grade of monastic life there (the Mikro-Schema).[16] In 1868 he met up on Athos with Paisii Fedorov,[17] who would bring out the first printed text of *Rasskaz strannika* in 1881. In 1874 Kozlov returned once more to Russia and was ordained as a priest at the monastery of the Theotokos in the town of Sviiazhsk. From there he traveled throughout his local Kazan region, making a special focus of his work to try to bring about the return of the Old Ritualists to the communion of the Orthodox. At this time he possibly met again with Hegumen Paisii Fedorov, who was also working as a missionary in the Kazan province. In 1879 Father Mikhail was promoted to the highest monastic rank of Archimandrite and given charge of the Holy Trinity Monastery in Selenginsk. He died on January 30, 1884.

From his own life experience, therefore, Mikhail Kozlov was well rooted in the notions of the traveling pilgrims that moved through the Russian villages, begging for food and alms, and he used his experiences on the road to advocate for his readership (for he authored several other treatises and would have known well the problem of securing good material for the refectory readings in his monastery)[18] an easy form of lay spirituality of the Jesus Prayer. He seems to have placed particular stress on the way that the ordinary sermons in the churches rarely gave spiritual direction and often issued ideas on prayer that were completely wrong.[19] He advocated the vocal recitation of the Jesus Prayer along with many prostrations, so as to form a rhythm, a habit, of regularity in daily prayer in the secular life.

This is, no doubt, the tradition of the Jesus Prayer, and as such stands in the tradition of monastic Hesychasm. However, it caused raised eyebrows in other sections of monastic life, especially among the more serious Hesychastic monks of the tradition of Paisy Velichovsky. Such were the monks attached to the Optino Lavra near Moscow, who received an early copy of the work in manuscript form in 1879. Starets Amvrosii Grenkov (1812–1892) of Optino, a center dedicated to the memory and tradition of Paisy Velichovsky, was asked by one of his spiritual disciples, the nun Leonida of Moscow, to comment on a "tale of a pilgrim" who wanders the land and freely practices the Jesus Prayer. He reported back to her, in words that almost damn with faint praise, "There is nothing offensive in it."[20] He nonetheless made a copy of the manuscript for the Optino library, which eventually ended up having two manuscript copies, as well as knowledge of the 1881 first printed edition of the *Rasskaz strannika* issued by Paisii Fedorov.

What strict Hesychasts, such as Amvrosii, would have found "wanting" in this first draft of the advocacy of the vocalized Jesus Prayer were the other (shall we say six) quintessential hallmarks of the Velichovskian Hesychast tradition of the Prayer of the Heart (see McGuckin 2009): (1) the manner in which the Jesus Prayer must move from the lips (vocalization) to the interior heart (an internal rhythm of the heartbeat); (2) the ways in which the prayer can cause sensation (warmth, light, joy); (3) the dangers of other sensations that it might be evoked in an inexperienced practitioner (flashes of lights, pains, phantasmal and delusional visions, and feelings of superiority and pride); (4) the overarching need for anyone practicing this way of prayer to have an older experienced guide, an Elder who has lived through the life of prayer and speaks from direct experience; (5) the mystical way this Elder can and will serve as a spiritual Father or Mother (*starets*) to the younger disciple; and, finally, (6) the way in which the collection of texts known as the *Philokalia* can serve as a stand-in for a real spiritual Elder if one is not readily available (a real issue for those who did not live in or near monastic communities).

It was this sense of "something lacking" in Father Mikhail's first draft manuscript that led to the production of the amplified text that has now come down to us (in some varied formats and different redactions that need not delay us here)[21] as the *Rasskaz strannika*. The published text of this, even from its first appearance in print in 1881, supplied all the omissions of the larger Hesychast themes noted earlier in this chapter. In the published form, the Pilgrim now stands looking back on his earlier naïveté in making the Jesus Prayer a constantly vocalized devotion and sees his main enlightenment (through the prayers and teachings of a spiritual Elder who mystically helps him, even after death) as being the way that the prayer has to descend into the heart. The Pilgrim also becomes obsessed with his copy of the *Philokalia*, which serves him as a guide after the death of his Elder, and there are many references to the type of good sensation effects of the prayer and warnings against the bad sensations. The *Rasskaz strannika*, in short, now has it all; and what is more, it speaks of the interior life, the intimate sensations of the heart and the spiritual consciousness of one at prayer, in just as much graphic immediacy and authority as the Pilgrim was able to use to summon up the immediacy and authenticity of the "life on the road." Where did this all come from?

The answer to this question is our second major "source" in the making of the *Rasskaz strannika*. This was a monk who, like Father Mikhail, was a prolific and lively author, one who heavily used his own and others' spiritual writings to make up a series of new texts on the theme of prayer. If today we now blanch at this cavalier way of cutting and pasting the work of (even living) authors to make up new "anonymous" books, we need to remember that Orthodox monastic authors were often glad to preserve their anonymity and usually regarded themselves as mere conveyers of the "school of wisdom" (Hesychasm) to which they had been initiated; they did not see themselves as originative composers in a modern sense. This free-handedness in the approach to textuality and reusing texts was a typical, enduring medievalism of late eighteenth- and nineteenth-century Russian monastic circles. The author in question was Hieromonk Arsenii (Valentin) Troepol'skii (1804–1870).

Arsenii Troepol'skii was born into a family of minor Russian nobility in 1804 and studied in the philological faculty of Moscow University. In 1826 he entered the monastery of Saint Simon in Moscow as a monk and was ordained deacon in 1831 and priest in 1832. Throughout his life he moved extensively to different posts in many provinces: the Kozelsk Optino Hermitage in 1833, the Kiev Caves Lavra in 1835, the Saint Petersburg Trinity-Sergiev Lavra in 1837,[22] the Zaikonospasskii Monastery in Moscow later that same year, back to the Saint Simon Monastery in Moscow in 1842 to be the assistant superior, to Saint Sava Monastery in Novgorod in 1847, to Saint George Monastery in Balaklava in the Crimea in 1852, to Saint Nicholas Monastery in Kaluga province in 1854, and in 1857 to the Pafnutii Borovski Monastery in Naro-Fominsk village near Moscow. Father Arsenii died there on July 7, 1870. He was a highly learned[23] and practical man, occupying several positions of authority in the church administration. Moreover, in spite of all his travels across Russia, he also managed a productive literary life, issuing numerous works, mostly concerned with the advocacy of the life of interior prayer, the importance of the spiritual Elder (he makes detailed records of how important his own spiritual guides were), the nature of mystical experiences in prayer, and the significance of the *Philokalia* as a source of spiritual teaching. Here in a nutshell were all the very elements that some felt were missing from Father Mikhail Kozlov's *Iskatelia neprestannoi molitivy*.

One of the most significant works of Father Arsenii, which found its way into the mix that was to become the *Rasskaz strannika*, was his treatise titled *Pamiat'o molitvennoi zhizni startsa Vasiliska, monakha i pustynnika Sibirskikh lesov* (Recollection of a Life of Prayer of Elder Vasilisk, a Monk and Hermit in the Siberian Forests; abbr. *Pamiat'o molitvennoi*). This text, issued sometime in the later 1850s, propagated the teaching of the Siberian Hesychast hermit Vasilisk and lifted up for notice the numerous visions that the Elder recounted, laying great stress on the phenomenal sensory aspects associated with continuous use of the Jesus Prayer. These included the warming of the heart, feelings of great sweetness and peacefulness, as well as remarkable and self-evident manifestations of spiritual power arising quickly with the very use of the holy name of Jesus. When this work gathered attention, Starets Makarii of Optino wrote a small treatise titled *Predosterezhenie chitaiuschim dukohnye otecheskie knigi i zhelaiushchim prokhodit'umnuiu Iisusovu molitvu* (Warning to the Readers of Spiritual Books of the Fathers and Those Wishing to Study the Mental Jesus Prayer; abbr. *Predosterezhenie Iisusovu molitvu*). Makarii was alarmed by the stress on the sensations associated with the prayer and wanted his readers to be careful not to mistake physical for spiritual signs. He wanted anyone, particularly laity, thinking of embarking on a serious life of performance of the Jesus Prayer to be strictly under the guidance of a living, experienced Elder. Ignatius Brianchaninov's book on the Jesus Prayer makes exactly the same point, which is a possible reason why Father Arsenii departed so quickly from the monastery that they were both inhabiting in 1837.

Another important text of Father Arsenii was a short manuscript on the Jesus Prayer; this was the *Otkrovennoe poslanie pustinnogo otshelnika k svoemu startsu i nastavniku vo vnutrennei molitve* (Candid Missive of an Eremitic Anchorite to His Elder and Mentor in Interior Prayer; abbr. *Otkrovennoe poslanie*), which was his last work (dat. 1870) and which again stresses the profundity of the relationship between disciple and spiritual Elder. Here we also discern the seed that would grow on the back of Mikhail Kozlov's *Iskatelia neprestannoi molitivy* to expand into the more diverse and rounded narrative of the *Rasskaz strannika*. Also appearing as *Otkrovennyi ilisa*, the *Otkrovennoe poslanie* gives many details of Father Arsenii's life, especially reflecting on the time that he spent in the Optino Hermitage, and digests teachings on prayer from four other treatises on prayer that he tells the reader he has composed. It also adds generous quotations from the writings of the Philokalic Fathers on prayer; this is something we notice in the text of the *Rasskaz strannika*, but which was not in the work of Kozlov, according to its description by Archbishop Veniamin.

Pentkovsky (1999, 23) shows that there is also a precise and direct link between the two figures, Kozlov and Troepol'skii, in that the latter was aware of the manuscript *Iskatelia neprestannoi molitvy* and borrowed material from it in his *Otkrovennoe poslanie*. It was clearly Troepol'skii's way always to leave his name off his works, regularly to recycle writings using materials from previous redactions of his own, and of others, and to be possessed of a lively and expert narrative style. All of this may point toward him being the hand that was the shaper of the almost finished form of the *Rasskaz strannika* sometime in the 1860s.[24] The collection of Father Arsenii's complete writings existed in the Optino Hermitage library, in the form of a collation of his *Letters* on the Jesus Prayer, the *Otkrovennoe poslanie*, the *Pamiat'o molitvennoi*, and several other treatises on prayer that he composed, all bundled together under the title of *An Ascetic Miscellany* (see Pentkovsky 1999, 18). This would have allowed later redactors to access all his works with facility in one source, but the first editor and collator, the combiner and organizer of the materials for the *Rasskaz strannika*, was Father Arsenii himself. It is to his hand that the liveliness belongs and the details of the interior powers of the Jesus Prayer. It is thus ironic that in this pseudepigraphical way he circumvented the heavily dampening disapprobation of Starets Amvrosii (in his lifetime recognized as one of the leading spiritual Elders in Russia) and himself became, albeit under the cloak of anonymity, one of the most renowned (and beloved) of all modern Russian religious teachers of the Jesus Prayer.

Eastern Orthodox Christianity, Hesychasm, and the Philokalic Tradition of the *Rasskaz strannika*

The Eastern Orthodox Church always saw itself as the ancient and enduring form of Christianity that was indigenous to the Eastern (i.e., Greek-speaking) provinces of the Roman Empire. It was really a complex network of churches, sharing common doctrinal and liturgical traditions from the earliest days of Christianity. The Greek language was its solid cultural basis, so strong a foundation, in fact, that the very name and words of Jesus himself were transmitted not in Aramaic, Jesus's native tongue, but almost entirely in Greek. From the second century onward, when the ink of the Greek Gospels hardly had time to dry, the foundational creedal texts and liturgical prayers of the Christian faith were also fashioned and transmitted in Greek. The Eastern,

Greek-speaking churches held fiercely to their sense of ancient traditions. Eventually, by the fifth and sixth centuries of the Christian era, this sense of a federation of local churches, using the same language and rooted in evangelical and patristic precedent,[25] caused increasing friction between the Eastern and Western provinces of the Christian world, most notably between the Latin and Greek churches, and the various parts of Christendom started off down that long path that would finally lead to the full-scale separation of the Orthodox and the Catholics in the High Middle Ages, a separation that has lasted until the present day. In its glory days, before the expanse of Islam had eroded many of its ancient territories, Eastern Orthodoxy was centered in Byzantium, the capital of the later Roman Empire as based in Constantinople (present-day Istanbul, Turkey). In the ninth century a major evangelization movement was initiated by the empire that brought the Slavic world into communion (both religious and economic) with Byzantium; and it is from that date that Russia entered the Orthodox family of churches, soon to become one of the largest and most vital of all the world families of Orthodoxy. Russia took to monasticism most fervently, adopting the strict practices of Byzantine solitude (hermitism, or eremitism) with a considerable stress on the need for private and reclusive contemplation in the life of the serious spiritual seeker.

The Russian Orthodox Church began with its center in Kiev (Old Rus') but eventually moved to the capital of the leading princes at Moscow. Church institutions grew in stature and importance with the ascent of the Russian state itself, especially after the defeat of the Tatars, Mongol tribes who had for many centuries kept Russian Christians divided and in a permanent state of war. In the conjoined ascent of the Russian state and church, monasticism played a great part; there were many important monasteries all over the country, even into the early decades of the twentieth century. In the seventeenth century, reforming patriarchs, such as Nikon, tried to change the long-established patterns of prayer and ritual that the Byzantine missionaries had first brought to Russia, in favor of correcting their church books from current Greek practices. In the generations between the first evangelization of the Rus' and the seventeenth century, many small divergences had crept in between Greek and Russian Orthodox practices in liturgy and prayers. Many of the Russian churches accepted the reforms willingly,[26] but in numerous other parts of Russia a severe and violent resistance set in that regarded the "reform" as corruption of the faith; and the aftermath, after a church council in 1666, was a long-lasting division of Russian Christianity. The sect of the Old Believers, also known as the Old Ritualists, was born. They had much support among the poorer peasantry. State and church initiated persecutions against them by 1682, and one part of the movement turned more radical, rejecting the concepts of priesthood and sacraments;[27] another increasingly found sympathetic bishops and priests elsewhere, eventually becoming reorganized in 1847 by a dissident Greek archbishop, Amvrosy of Sarajevo, who provided them with two consecrated bishops and thus restored their clerical and sacramental infrastructure. In the time of the publication of our main text, the *Rasskaz strannika*, therefore, the Old Believers were undergoing a notable renovation, and part of the subtext of the book (part of its "theological mission," as it were) was surely to reach out from the heart of mainstream monastic-based Russian Orthodoxy to the *popovtsy* (clergy-based) Old Believers, who were felt to be potentially reconcilable.[28] Instead of the face of the state-church as a persecuting bureaucracy, the *Rasskaz strannika* offers an icon of mainstream Russian Christianity as having preserved the "pearl of great price" (Matt. 13:46), a living spirituality and an internal knowledge of the Spirit of God, which could serve as the true basis for a spiritual reunion among the separated communities of faith, and one that was rooted in the "authentic" past of the Russian men and women of the soil.

The tradition of Russian monasticism and spirituality that was common to both mainstream and Old Believers was known as Hesychasm. It was a long-established Byzantine spiritual school that had been brought to Russia in its Christian foundations. The word means "quietness," and it was a spiritual teaching that stressed the need to acquire peace of heart before the presence of the Holy Spirit within the soul could be sensed and understood. Hesychastic teaching was taken to great heights by the later Byzantine writers. Its chief notions were that the soul (*psyche*) was divided into various levels. The lower soul related closely to the body and was influenced strongly by bodily states; it dealt with matters that today we would describe as empathy, or feelings. The middle soul was concerned with rational ideas and understanding; it had an elevated spiritual function but was also much beset by the problem of the multitude of thoughts (*logismoi*) that clamored for attention in a human being, which could often suppress spiritual sensibility in the name of rationalism. The highest level of the soul (*nous*), which could be best translated as the "spiritual intellect," was a capacity given only to human beings and angels; it was an instinct for the divine presence and a capacity for knowledge of God. This knowledge was not simply another form of "reason" (*logos*) in a human person's cognitive capacity. It was precisely a divinely gifted *proprium* of divine awareness; and as such it was intrinsically and fundamentally related to the prayer life of the individual. In short, for the Byzantine Hesychasts, the doctrine of prayer was an unavoidable part of the definition of the very purpose of cognition. One began with awareness of the self in the world and progressed to the awareness of the self before God, in a triplex ascent that marked the emergence of the individual from animal consciousness to the awareness of being a divine icon enfleshed. Hesychasm also laid stress on the practical methods of quieting down the teeming thoughts of the second level of awareness (the rational thoughts or *logismoi*) so that the senses of the graced *nous* could emerge more completely. This is fundamentally the goal of the Prayer of the Heart, of which the Jesus Prayer is the most commonly known example. Hesychasm also strongly advocated the need for an experienced guide, as one walked this subtle and difficult road.

The teachings on prayer of Hesychastic saints, such as Symeon the New Theologian (949–1022), Gregory Palamas (ca. 1296–1359), Gregory of Sinai (ca. 1260–1346), and others, accumulated into a vast depository of advanced teachings on detailed practices of the inner life. They were read avidly by monastics. In the late eighteenth and early nineteenth centuries these collections passed out from handwritten manuscript form for the first time into print, in *Florilegium* of spiritual writings known as the *Philokalia* or *Dobrotolyubié*. From that time onward we see the teachings of Hesychasm having a wider expanse among the laity and rousing great interest. Hesychasm is a constant backdrop and presupposition of the *Rasskaz strannika*.

In its final versions, the *Rasskaz strannika* thus became a book linking three key ideas together: the seeking of the Prayer of the Heart through the Jesus Prayer, the reliance on a spiritual Elder (*starets*), and immersion in the *Philokalia*. We may, in turn, consider the *Rasskaz strannika* as a later Russian expression of the earlier Hesychast tradition documented in the *Philokalia*. This latter collection of books was put together by Athonite monks in order to meet the problems of having access to spiritual Elders who were truly experienced in the higher reaches of prayer. The idea was begun on Mount Athos at the end of the eighteenth century and reaches right through to the Russia of the time of the Pilgrim (and to today in the English edition of the volumes that have had a wide readership in modern times),[29] for one of the editors of the 1883 edition of the *Rasskaz strannika* (Theophan the Recluse) was actually himself a translator of a Slavonic version of the *Philokalia*.[30]

From the fourth century onward, the monastic movement grew in popularity in Christianity. Key centers of monastic life and organization were Egypt, Gaza, Palestine, Syria, and Asia Minor. By the end of the first millennium, the great Christian monastic centers had shifted to Constantinople (present-day Istanbul, Turkey) and to certain monastic colonies, such as Olympus and Athos. It was Athos that was destined to have the longest continuous survival, and as a result its libraries represented centuries of monastic writings on the nature of prayer. Monasticism was, above all else, about a life given over wholeheartedly to the service and worship of God (see later discussion herein). Prayer was the *raison d'être* of this celibate and ascetic lifestyle, and there was a deep and lively interest in the forms and methods of prayer. On Athos, a monk, certainly during a notable feast of the Christian calendar, might spend up to fourteen hours a day in the church. The level of prayer that we are speaking about here is far more intense than the occasional ten minutes spent randomly "saying prayers."

Not to be able to find a truly advanced spiritual teacher nearby would be a problem of significant proportions. It might be compared to an advanced musician who needed lessons to develop technique but who could find no one at all in that particular town who even played the same instrument. So it was that the monks developed from early centuries the regular custom of *lectio divina* (sacred reading), the close study of those who were acknowledged as past masters on the life of prayer. However, to have access to all of these works was also a problem: one needed a library of some considerable size. So it was that in the eighteenth century two monastic figures came up with a proposal to gather together all the best of the practical writings on interior prayer from the Greek Fathers and gather them into a smaller collection, a compendium, which could be bought by almost every monastery that wanted it. Bishop Makarios (Notaras) of Corinth (1731–1835) had the idea, and he commissioned a very energetic writer and editor, Hieromonk Nikodemos (1749–1809), who lived on Mount Athos, to gather the best texts and edit them. The final collection, entitled the *Philokalia* (Lover of Beauty), was published at Venice in 1782.

The book very quickly came to the attention of the renowned Ukrainian Starets Paisy Velichovsky (1722–1794), who a few years earlier had moved from Athos to gather disciples around him in Moldavia. He had noted in his journals that when he was struggling on Athos to develop the inner life of prayer, he had been able to find no experienced guides at all on the mountain; and so he had himself come up with the idea of transcribing every manuscript of the Fathers about prayer that he could lay his hands on. He had already started to translate the Greek texts into Slavonic for the benefit of his own Moldavian and Russian disciples, but when he heard of the Greek *Philokalia*, he redoubled his efforts and, using parts of it, brought out in 1793 a slightly smaller collection (twenty-four authors instead of the Greek thirty-six) translating the Greek title as *Dobrotolyubié*. Makarios and Nikodemos, like him, were Hesychast monks who laid immense stress on the inner spiritual life. However, it is Paisy, more than they, who actually made a life's mission out of spreading the Jesus Prayer as the chief means to achieve this inner and unceasing Prayer of the Heart, and it was his mission that had long-lasting results in the Slavonic lands.[31] By the nineteenth century, the Russian Saint Panteleimon Monastery on Athos became the new center of Hesychastic spirituality. It is no surprise that the earliest manuscript of the *Rasskaz strannika* is lodged there, or that the first printed edition came out under its auspices in the care of the Kazan dependency of Saint Panteleimon (Saint Michael's) led by Hegumen Paisii Fedorov.

Hesychastic Prayer and Eastern Orthodox Spirituality

The tradition of spiritual life expressed in the *Rasskaz strannika* gives high precedence to the Jesus Prayer, or the Prayer of the Heart, a form of interior prayer of the divine presence focused on the repetition of the Name of Jesus, along with a prayer for the Lord to have mercy. The phrase "Lord Jesus Christ, Son of God, have mercy on me"[32] is repeated many times in a quest for the rhythm of the prayer to move from the lips to the inner heart (a biblical cipher for spiritual consciousness) and then to be absorbed into our human awareness almost in the rhythm of the in-breathing (attached symbolically to the first half of the phrase invoking the holy name) and the out-breathing (attached to the petition for mercy) (see Ware 1992, 161–63). When the prayer has "entered the heart," it is seen as the achievement of the apostolic command to "pray unceasingly" (1 Thess. 5:17). More than a concept of prayerful petition, this stage of the prayer is seen as a unification with the presence of God, truly present in the created world in terms of his divine energies (*pneuma*); and so this "entering into God" is conceived in Orthodox spirituality as salvation and deification by grace. The latter term, a striking one based upon the New Testament text of 2 Peter 1:4, is developed extensively in the early Greek Fathers of the Church. It is a distinctive Orthodox approach to salvation, a soteriology that places its emphasis not so much on the redemptive suffering and cleansing blood of Christ on the Cross (a much-favored Western Christian theme, developing the sacrificial theology found in St. Paul) but rather on the idea (prevalent in the Gospel of John) that the Divine Word of God, Second Person of the Trinity, descended to earth to become incarnate as a Man, so that all Humanity might be lifted up once more to the presence of God from which they had fallen when they lost the innocence of Adam. As in the First Adam, all Humanity sinned and fell,[33] so in the Second Adam (Christ) Humanity would be given back its union with God, and in that gift of union (called deification by grace) would follow all the benefits of heavenly life. This Orthodox theme of deification[34] is similar, with several uniquely different aspects, to the Western Church's notion of sanctifying grace. Jaroslav Pelikan notes its underlying presence in the Pilgrim's story in this way:

> To a degree that many western Christians, both Roman Catholic and Protestant, may find surprising, prayer which "constitutes universally the essence or soul of every religion"[35] performs a function here that is so comprehensive as to include not only the sacrificial and fervent communication of human petition, praise, and thanksgiving to God, but a divine and indeed sacramental communication of grace to the human condition. (Qtd. in Pentkovsky and Smith 1999, xi)[36]

Running completely throughout this series of tales, therefore, is the common understanding that the Prayer of the Heart[37] is not simply a pious exercise peripheral to religious belief but rather the core of the Christian experience of salvation: the descending presence of God within the heart by the gift of the Holy Spirit. It is the presence of Christ in the soul that purifies and unites the individual human consciousness with God and brings the heavenly condition to earth, thus making the sinner into the redeemed creature wholly by the divine grace. The "effects of the prayer" are thus commonly listed in terms of light and warmth and joy. The light is the radiant glory of the divine Transfiguration.[38] The joy and warmth are understood as the signs of the indwelling presence of the Holy Spirit.[39]

The *Rasskaz strannika* assumes participation in the religious life of the Russian Orthodox Church. Practitioners of the Jesus Prayer are expected to be regularly confessing to their spiritual counselor, who will normally be a priest, and to regularly receive the sacrament of the Eucharist at the divine liturgy. Serious dedication to the life of prayer is understood to be rooted in an ascetically serious attempt to live out the ethics of the Gospel. The Pilgrim in the *Rasskaz strannika* is consistently offered as an ideal model of "churchgoer" as well as mystic.

In terms of its theory of prayer, the *Philokalia* is a deeply scriptural assembly of the broad stream of the Greek Fathers of the Church, and one that turns all the time around the idea that the very purpose of Christianity is to enter into the deepest relationship with the Word of God, the Second Person of the Trinity (Christ as Son), who, through the movements of the Holy Spirit in the core of the person, brings this reunion with God as the salvation that he offers to humanity. As we have already noted, this overarching idea of salvation through union with God (*henosis*) is one that is called by the Fathers "deification by grace" (*theosis kata charin*). One of the writers represented in the *Philokalia* is Saint Symeon the New Theologian (949–1022), and in his treatise *Kephalaia Praktika Kai Theologika* (153 Practical and Theological Texts) he expresses the idea as follows:

> What is the purpose of the Incarnation of the Divine Logos which is proclaimed throughout the Scriptures, which we read about but often without comprehending? Surely, it is that He has shared in what is ours so as to make us participants of what is His. For the Son of God became the Son of Man in order to make us human beings into Sons of God, lifting us up by grace to what He is by nature; giving us a new birth in the Holy Spirit and leading us directly into the kingdom of heaven. To put this another way: He gives us the grace to possess the Kingdom within ourselves (Luke 17:21), so that we do not simply hope to enter it, but rather, now fully possessing it, we can make the statement: "Our life is hidden with Christ in God" (Col. 3:3). (Palmer et al. 1979–1995, 4:48)

This is the core religious philosophy of prayer that the *Rasskaz strannika* also represents. It is the deifying presence of the Word of God in the soul of a human being, which is the reality of salvation. The Jesus Prayer is simply the call to the God of mercy to fulfill his offer of salvation in us, asking God to do something in us that he is more eager to accomplish than we are to receive (Luke 11:12–13). Moreover, the words of the prayer are significant too, in several ways, according to the teaching of the Fathers. The first thing that is noted is that the very words are an "epitome" or synopsis of the entire Gospel: they sum up humanity's entire cry for salvation in Jesus. The Hesychasts also note that this redeeming presence of God within a human being is what scripture means by the Kingdom of God[40] being "within." We can see this juxtaposition in the aforementioned citation from Saint Symeon. Moreover, throughout the scriptures there is a profound sense that the Name of God carries its own creative energy.

In the Old Testament the four unpronounceable letters of the divine Name (the *Tetragrammaton*, IHWH)[41] were seen as carrying the awesome "charge" of the divine person's power.⁴² "Calling on the Name" was the Old Testament phrase for prayer.⁴³ God will not give his Name, except enigmatically, to humans.⁴⁴ The Name is a cipher for God himself.⁴⁵ The Name carries in it protective power⁴⁶ and bears the "glory" (Heb.: *kabod*) of the divine presence (Heb.: *shekinah*) itself.⁴⁷ It is above all else in the Psalms, that fundamental prayer book of the Christian monks, that the concept of praying "In the Name" first emerges and takes shape.⁴⁸ It is summed up in the Psalms' approach to prayer as the "blessedness of entering into the Name" of God (Ps. 118:26). This is the heart of what the Orthodox Hesychasts envisaged as prayer conceived of as the mystical entering into the Uncreated Energy (*energeia*) of the Divine Presence. It does not contradict the common conception of prayer as a petition to God for assistance, or even a set of prayers offering praise or sentiments of repentance; rather, and above all else, the Hesychasts understood "true" or pure prayer to be the ascent to the glorification of God experienced as mystical⁴⁹ union with him, given in the Name, and that is recognized as the indwelling presence of the Divine Logos, or the Word of God incarnated. It is Jesus Christ risen from the dead and made gloriously immediate in the world through the energy and action of the Holy Spirit.

For the Greek Fathers, then, all prayer was made to the Father, through Christ as the High Priest of the Race, in the action and energy of the Holy Spirit. It is for this reason that we so often find the evocation of the Holy Trinity throughout the *Rasskaz strannika*. For Orthodox Christians, this was far more than a desiccated dogma; it was rather an understanding of the whole inner dynamic of how prayer worked toward the mystically indwelling presence of God. It was a permanent modality of the power of salvation that reconciled, in union, God and Humanity: to the Father, through the Son, in the Holy Spirit.

The Jesus Prayer, with its twin phrases of "Lord Jesus Christ, Son of God" and "Have mercy on me (a sinner)," was also seen to be a precise epitome of two of the key teachings of Jesus on prayer. It may be understood as a conflation of the parable of the Tax Collector and the Pharisee,⁵⁰ where the sinner becomes a model of true prayer because his prayer is a cry for mercy made out of humility (the second phrase of the Jesus Prayer), and the story of the Blind Man at Jericho,⁵¹ who is a symbol of the true disciple who becomes such (when the chosen Apostles themselves are faltering) by his courage and persistence in calling out the name of Jesus as Lord (the first phrase of the prayer).

In both evangelical accounts of the Blind Man, we note that the beggar begins by calling out "Jesus" and ends with naming him as Lord and Master. As the Apostle Paul put it succinctly, this exclamation of the Name of Jesus, as Lord, is itself the sign of the activity of the Holy Spirit of God: "For no one can say 'Jesus is Lord' except by the Holy Spirit" (1 Cor. 12:3). And in his Epistle to the Romans, Saint Paul also depicted how the energy of the Holy Spirit itself is at work in the inmost center of the believer, making prayer ascend in the sanctuary of the heart in a secret manner, which is beyond the capacity of words to describe:

> Likewise the Spirit helps us in our weakness; for we do not know how to pray as we ought, but the Spirit himself intercedes for us with sighs too deep for words. And he who searches the hearts of men knows what is the mind of the Spirit, because the Spirit intercedes for the saints according to the will of God. (Rom. 8:26–27)

The Jesus Prayer was advocated throughout the Hesychastic literature, therefore, as being a concise way to sum up the Christian sense of salvation through the presence of Jesus. Calling on the Name of Jesus, for an Orthodox Christian, was the same as calling on the Name of the Living

God, for the Word and the Father were substantially one (*homoousion*) in the mystery of the Holy Trinity. The Jesus Prayer was thus the fulfillment of Jesus Christ's own teaching about what life in the fullness of the Spirit would be like:[52] to be able to pray "In the Name" and "In the Spirit," and to have the power of God himself manifested in that prayer.

One last element that is of great concern to the teaching of the *Rasskaz strannika*, and which is a strong element of Hesychastic theology, ought to be mentioned here. This is the notion of how the Jesus Prayer progresses to become the true Prayer of the Heart. Throughout the Bible the term "heart" (Grk.: *kardia*) is the preferred word for the interior consciousness of a human being, especially as that arena (it is often called the altar of the heart, or the interior temple) is the secret domain where the remembrance of God arises, and where the indwelling presence of God is felt within the human worshiper (see McGuckin 1999). In later times, the idea of "soul"[53] predominated (to connote similar things), but the Hesychastic Fathers, especially the Syriac writers among them, always preferred to keep this default reference to "the heart" to convey the sense of the depths of a human being face to face with God. As Jesus himself taught, it was the heart (certainly not the eyes) that was the only organ that could "see" God (Matt. 5:8).

This is why the *Rasskaz strannika* spends much time trying to explain the way that progress in prayer means the "descent of the mind into the heart." It is a difficult idea to convey in words. Even as lively a text as the *Rasskaz strannika* has some difficulty getting round the notion, but it comes head-on at it in the episode of the discussion with the blind man on the road to Tobolsk (see Smith 1999, 126–27). It returns to it many times in different fashions and often calls up the support of the *Philokalia* itself, by introducing quotations from that source. One of the main texts in the *Philokalia* describing the method of the "descent" is the *Treis Odai Proseuches* (Three Methods of Prayer) attributed to Saint Symeon the New Theologian (see Palmer et al. 1979–1995, 4:64), and the *Rasskaz strannika* explicitly makes use of this. The descent basically refers to a recognized spiritual movement that occurs when the prayer ceases to be experienced as something done mechanically, or "remotely" by the lips or by the mind of the person who prays, and instead seems to enter the very fabric of the person's being in such a way that it becomes like the breathing, or the heartbeat, something innate, permanent, fused with the person's consciousness in a very deep way. At this stage or level, it even becomes a symbol of the sense that the individual and the Divine Lord present in the heart (like the Godhead in the Temple) have become one: all duality moves aside because of the divine condescension of grace. This is the goal of union toward which all the mystics aspired: not a state that could be achieved by any technique, however holy in itself, but only a gift of grace from God's part alone. In Eastern Orthodox Christian theology, human beings cannot "rise to God," but God can condescend to be directly present to them.

The *Treis Odai Proseuches* recommends certain physical techniques in the praying of the Jesus Prayer, and when it comes to the issue of the descent of the mind into the heart, it teaches that at the beginning of the prayer, which ought to be continued fervently many times,[54] and without allowing images[55] to arise in the mind, the one who prays ought to feel in his or her senses the place where the heart is beating and draw a focus of attention there. When the heartbeat thus becomes paramount, the person is told to try to draw down the mind (the mental faculties of conscious and imaginative thought) into the heart itself, as if it were a chamber or chapel, and to imprison it there. This involves keeping the mind still and silent, while the other senses of the soul are thus allowed to become operative.

The Greek Fathers of the *Philokalia* taught that there were actually three distinct forms of human consciousness operative: the first was the physical awareness of the body; the second was comprised of the mental faculties of thought and imagination (more refined than the body's senses but closely related to them); and the third was the spiritual consciousness or the instincts of the higher soul (*nous*). Each of the three stages of human awareness stepped up in refinement and quality from the level beneath it. Mental awareness was more acute than physical awareness (understanding something as distinct from simply touching it, for example), but so too was spiritual awareness much more acute than mental awareness. In modern English we do not really have words to distinguish between mental and spiritual awareness, but the Greeks had entirely different terms: *logos* and *nous*, which give rise to two different types of consciousness, namely, logical and noetic. What the Hesychast theologians are trying to say (and why it is so difficult for moderns who do not even have the semantic of the language surviving) is that one has to use the Jesus Prayer to move up and across three levels of awareness in the course of pure prayer.

One begins prayer with fervent exclamations on the lips, calling out the words of the Gospel, "Lord Jesus Christ, Son of God, have mercy on me!" This is a high prayer in and of itself. But it is only a beginning. It puts the human awareness into first gear as it were. As soon as the physical attention is engaged (one is standing attentively in prayer[56] and reciting the simple words with the lips), the person ought to move on to stage two. This is the capturing of the hundreds of imaginations (*logoi*) that arise in the mind (distractions or reminiscences or even any idea at all), on the grounds that any of our ideas about God are not God. The important thing about stage two (mental) awareness is to quiet it down, to silence the endless chatter of the imagination. The Jesus Prayer attempts to accomplish this by the technique of making the imagination feel itself enclosed in the heartbeat and the in-and-out flow of the breath while the vocal prayer is articulated. The mind is thus lulled to quietness like a baby fascinated by a rattle. Of course the mind will not want to stay "captive" this way for long and will often reassert itself. One might emerge from a time of prayer suddenly realizing that while the mouth has been reciting the prayer, the mind has been reeling off a to-do list. But when this happens, the process "of descent" is begun over again.

What the Hesychasts think is really important is arriving at the third stage of awareness: *noetic* sensibility. The *nous* is the very heart and soul of the human being, as originally made in God's image and likeness. The human being is a living sacrament of God. It is "natural" (in other words this is why humanity was made) for a human to stand in the presence of God in the *nous*. But the Fall from grace has habituated human beings to want to live anywhere else in their complex synthesis of being, other than in the *nous*, for the awareness of God is like that which drove Adam and Eve in fear away from the divine presence. The divine mercy of Christ, however, is now experienced, because of his sacrificial love, as no longer the terrifying presence of God but as the wonderful source of love and mercy. The redeemed *nous* is thus able to enter boldly into the presence of the Divine Christ and be made radiant in his deifying grace. Even so, the senses of the *nous* are so undeveloped in us that it takes much effort to still down the very loud voices of the body and the mind, so that we can learn the new language of the spiritual consciousness of our deepest selves. This is what the Jesus Prayer tries to facilitate: to offer the body and mind a simple form of prayer that quiets down their engagement and allows the *nous* to wake up and descend into the inner heart, as if into a holy shrine, and there encounter the God who has been waiting patiently all along. What transpires then, in the secret of the heart, at the level of noetic engagement with the Divine Word, is truly beyond words, and is often called, in the ancient Christian writings, the "Bridal Chamber of the Word," which suggests a level of intimacy and mystical secrecy that ought not even be attempted to be described. The genius of the *Rasskaz strannika* is that it manages to get this across in the most simple and charming of narrative devices: an entertaining travelogue. It accomplishes this without making the associated instructions and insights sound like a theology class or a lesson in Byzantine metaphysics.

Pilgrimage to the Interior and to God

Now arriving at our primary text, the *Rasskaz strannika*, or the *Candid Tale of a Pilgrim*, is so readable that it needs little exegesis, at least in terms of its structure. It is based around the recurring motif and symbol of pilgrimage. The main character journeys throughout Russia, stopping constantly at holy places and looking out for guides who may help him in his ascent to spiritual wisdom. The motif of the pilgrimage is a symbol of the larger metaphysical "calling" of each human soul to return to the heavenly homeland, since it is in exile upon this earth (see Heb. 13:14). There are four tales, or "meetings," that make up the core of the text. Three extra tales were later published (from a manuscript on Mount Athos that contained them) as an appendix. In the first English translations, the first core of the book was labeled *The Way of the Pilgrim*, while the appendix received the designation of *The Pilgrim Continues His Way*. Neither title derives from the Russian manuscripts or the printed Russian publications. Tale Five in the appendix is closely akin to the first four tales and is from the same hand. The Sixth and Seventh Tales are more scholastic, and more apologetic in style, and the character of the Pilgrim dwindles away as merely a single member of a scholarly discussion group. As discussed earlier, the *Rasskaz strannika* has been preserved and transmitted as an anonymous work, and it is best understood as a collaborative composition involving numerous Russian Orthodox monks and resulting in various redactions. It is a creation of nineteenth-century Russian monasticism aimed at the laity, especially the countless numbers of pilgrims staying in monastic guesthouses.

The book fits with an old genre,[57] but it is also unusual and possibly was designed for a very specific end. Each evening, both at Panteleimon and any other Russian monastic house, in the pilgrims' refectory where they ate, a junior monk would read spiritual works throughout the course of the meal, and no one was allowed to talk. During the monks' own meals, a similar practice was followed, and then the writings of the Fathers and theologians were read. One imagines that by the nineteenth century, the heavier works of the theologians had been replaced in the refectories, where there was a preponderance of lay visitors, with works of a simpler and more plot-centered type. It is to this world that the *Rasskaz strannika* belongs. It is a repackaging of the basics of Hesychast teaching but now set in a novelette "adventure" form by monastics all singing from the same hymn sheet, as it were. This is why several hands could be at work in the production of what emerges as the final printed format of the tales, while more or less a generic harmony of style and intent could be preserved.

The First Tale (eighteen pages in English translation), which is subtitled "How He Acquired the Gift of Interior Unceasing Prayer of the Heart," introduces us to the Pilgrim, his wandering lifestyle, and his extremely meagre possessions (a satchel containing bread crusts and a Bible). We learn how a phrase from scripture, "pray unceasingly,"[58] strikes him with great force; however, he is unable to find anyone, from the church reader to the local bishop, who can explain it satisfactorily to him. All of the teachings on prayer that he hears in the local parishes seem to him to be wrongheaded when he checks them against his Bible. He finds a nobleman who practices interior prayer but who does not think it suitable to reveal its secrets to someone as lowly as him. A kindly monk shows him some things from a book by Saint Dimitry of Rostov (1651–1709).[59] Finally, the Pilgrim stumbles on an experienced old monk, a *starets*, on the road to whom he opens his heart and from whom he learns the basic distinctions and forms of prayer. The Elder shows him how the Jesus Prayer fulfills the command to "pray unceasingly" and reveals to him the riches of the *Philokalia*. The Pilgrim starts off well and then loses heart. His Elder recommends that he says the prayer three thousand times a day, which rises to six thousand times a day, and eventually culminates in twelve thousand times a day. The Pilgrim follows the spiritual direction and accomplishes the prescribed practice in seclusion in his watchman's hut, where he has taken a summer job. The Elder then dies, and the Pilgrim determines to use his summer wages to buy the *Philokalia* for himself. Setting off on the road once more, and feeling the great sweetness and warmth from the Jesus Prayer, he is elated that he has the Bible and the *Philokalia*, and he trusts in the continuing spiritual help from his late Elder.

The Second Tale (thirty-three pages in English translation) is slightly longer and introduces us to a larger range of characters and adventures that the Pilgrim encounters on his way through Russia. He is beaten by robbers[60] and loses his satchel and books, which he finds again as soon as he reconciles himself to God's will. We hear various stories of conversion, but then he runs into hardships and his food stores diminish. He turns off the road and meets a forester who invites him to use a deserted hut in the woods for the winter. They share stories and the Pilgrim helps him with tales from the *Philokalia*. However, our Pilgrim wants to understand more about how the mind can descend into the heart but cannot make sense of his texts. His deceased Elder appears to him in a dream and instructs him about this essential, and advanced, aspect of the Jesus Prayer.[61] He wakes and describes the new sensations that this form of prayer evokes. More adventures are recounted. He tries to explain to people the benefits of the prayer and the *Philokalia*. He stays for a while as sacristan, a church watchman, but then he moves on. Meanwhile, a girl flees from the village to avoid an unwelcome marriage, seeking his protection, and the outraged family accuses him of impropriety. They bring him before the magistrate, who beats him. There is a regular subtheme in the book of the necessity for a disciple to retrace the suffering path of the master: patiently accepted suffering is presented as having redemptive value as a purification of soul. His Elder once more appears and consoles him with passages from the *Philokalia*, which he marks for him. The Pilgrim pays for the cure of his hurt legs by teaching a young boy to read and is able to offer healing to the local steward's wife by advice he receives from another visitation by his Elder. Becoming notorious after this, he sets off on the road once more, and the book ends with him in Irkutsk, Siberia, receiving the offer of a passage to Jerusalem via Odessa.

The Third Tale (four pages in English translation) is the shortest of all. It serves to give some biographical data about the Pilgrim, how he came to be disabled and eventually lost his farm, and his wife, and then took to the road as a pilgrim. It is ostensibly a dialogue with a monastic guide who asks for more information about him. The Pilgrim tells the interlocutor that he is off to Jerusalem, God willing, and we learn that he is thirty-three years of age. The tale ends with the following note: "Well dear brother you have attained the measure of the stature of Christ."[62]

The Fourth and last Tale of the core redaction is considerably longer (thirty-four pages in English translation), being about the size of the Second Tale. The Pilgrim starts to make his way towards Tobolsk, Siberia, accompanying a blind man and considering travel on to Jerusalem. They are given hospitality by a charitable noble family. He and the husband talk about the Philokalic texts. He is told about a former nobleman who had passed through earlier as a wandering penitent pilgrim. The blind man tells the Pilgrim that he too is a practitioner of the Jesus Prayer, and the Pilgrim starts to read the *Philokalia* to him on the road. The blind man learns the descent of the heart very quickly and even becomes clairvoyant, "seeing into" the hearts of others. The Pilgrim also enjoys many spiritual sensations from the prayer. He almost has an amorous adventure at a Post-house but escapes by a providential accident that converts the woman. He then meets a kindly priest and an old woman who tells him how the Jesus Prayer saved her from harm. A nobleman in a carriage in Kazan province tells him how the Jesus Prayer worked wonders in his family, and the Pilgrim informs him that the *Philokalia* has the fuller version of texts on prayer that he already knows. The book ends with the Pilgrim bidding farewell to the monk whom we met in the Third Tale, saying that he has already chatted too long and now has to find his fellow travelers to Jerusalem. A final few lines give a thumbnail portrait of his appearance: "This pilgrim was of medium build, with a body made lean by self-control and austere life. He had a handsome face, expressive eyes, and a broad and thick beard. He showed abundant love toward all and was affable with humility" (Smith 1999, 140).

The Pilgrim Continues His Journey

From its Russian publication and public dissemination in late nineteenth-century Russia to its first English-language translation (1931) by Reginald Michael (R. M.) French (1884–1984), the *Rasskaz strannika* has been highly popular and influential. There is no question that the work has an immense charm in its literary construct. The Pilgrim is so obviously presented as a model of "perfect piety" that he might have struck the modern reader as very stuffy if the whole book was not suffused with liveliness and an underlying wit and elegance. Part of the charm undoubtedly lies in the way that it catches the spirit of a lost world of Russia under the nobility. There are instances enough, however, to remind the reader (nineteenth century or contemporary) that all is not well on the social scene: the old and sick seem always to hover uncertainly on the brink of destitution and death. Life fortunes can change catastrophically in the blink of an eye. The roads are full of thieves, drunkards, and random violence. This book is as much Gorky as it is Tolstoy. One feels how fragile a life it is to be dependent on the thin charity of the villagers, or on the random kindnesses of the rich. The Pilgrim is not a simplistic escapist in all this: he is deliberately delineated in this way to show us an image (an icon) of what "dispossession" means, and the *Rasskaz strannika* is consistently trying to underline the deeper truth throughout that a human being, whether rich or destitute, is dependent on God for all things. Society will shape all men and women, whatever their circumstances or rank, but only the grace of the Gospel can redeem them and free them. The Pilgrim learns that conformity with God's Providence is the surest way to live in harmony: riches will not protect one in life. Prayer is the way to be conformed to God's will and to learn to live trustingly in his presence.

This, of course at the heart of monastic philosophy, is presented to us as being more than that; indeed, it is presented as being the sure guide to a peaceful and sanctified life. In this work a subtle Hesychast doctrine is painted in a charmingly approachable way. Above all, the plot does not distract; the characters are vivid but not extensively developed; the numerous citations of textual authorities and specific instructions are all introduced as if incidentally, never to the extent of becoming tedious. All is subordinated to the overarching suggestion: Why not get hold of the Philokalic texts yourself and use them to navigate toward a life marked by saying the Jesus Prayer?

It was this message that Franny, in J. D. Salinger's (1919–2010) novel *Franny and Zoey* (1961), clung to in her great existential distress. The book, and its teaching, were a comfort to her as she faced the mental turmoil of coming to terms with her brother's suicide. It is this message that still serves to make the book a luminous read for moderns and allows it to retain a freshness most surprising for a nineteenth-century text: so many of its peers are so dusty that they could hardly be picked up today. This, I suppose, is a sign of its perennial charism as a "spiritual classic." It is a work that offers a rare vision of Christianity from the inside, showing it from real and vivid experience as a religion of mystical prayer. It is a Christianity where miracles still occur daily, at least to those who have the eyes to see and the heart to hear. The book contains a promise, passed on by wise monks through the mouth of the Pilgrim but ultimately from Christ himself to the one who reads the book: Call on the name of Jesus, and the Spirit of God will straightway take up residence in your innermost soul. And nothing will ever be the same again.

Further Meetings with the Pilgrim

The *Rasskaz strannika* is certainly a fascinating document, and since its first (relatively recent) issuing in English translation it has had a steady stream of readers who have found it both heart-warming and useful in terms of the spiritual life, that is, advancing a personal life of prayer beyond the level of incessant "petitions" to God or the use of formulaic prayers. In the modern renewal of church life in Russia and the former Eastern Bloc countries after the fall of Soviet communism, the book has also had a strong new following. This indicates that the text is actually useful: it has things of proven worth to communicate about the lived state of the spiritual life. Now much of its context is quite clearly dead and gone. It may be charming to read about peasants and aristocrats in a long-vanished Tsarist Russia (just as soap operas about lords and ladies and servants still have entertainment value in our time and age), but no one would really like to see this world returned. What is perhaps actually attractive here in the *Rasskaz strannika* is the sense that a simple person, of no great intelligence but of great heart and spirit and endurance, wished to dedicate himself to the serious following of what was good and true and holy. That, perhaps, is the nub of the affair. And, surely, that still motivates countless people today who wish to press further in following high ideals and are genuinely curious about, and interested in, the pathways of a coherent and consistently sought-after spiritual life. Indeed, like that older seeker, many people of goodwill today, who set off along this pilgrim's path to learn about prayer, find a profound silence when they ask: "Can anyone help me here?" Even to raise an interest publicly in deepening a prayer life can raise the eyebrows of one's listeners. Too much seriousness in religion, one is often chided, can lead to weird zealotry. Many will warn off an inquirer: few can ever be found who not only understand the questions but also can provide solid encouragement and guidance. This is exactly what the Pilgrim found in his journeying and (almost giving up one suspects) decided to put the book in his knapsack as his paper *starets* instead. Things may not have changed much. Churches are full each week: One does not have to go too far to find one, but even then if one asks for special guidance in the forms of private prayer or meditation, even clergy may look askance. There are many churches that have an abundance of "parish talks" on the roster of activities, but rarely on any theme related to meditation or prayer. So the little book of the Pilgrim will perhaps continue its journeying through our generation too, lighting up the way (for a time) for more Frannys and Zoes, as Salinger described them, as new generations of seekers ask of the Christian tradition what deeper currents of spiritual wisdom it possesses.

The tradition of the Pilgrim is rooted, of course, in the Eastern Orthodox Church. That pathway of the Jesus Prayer is rooted in the larger scheme of what is known as the Hesychast movement. This extends back to classical Christian antiquity, but came to a refined restatement from the thirteenth century onward and began a new wave of monastic revivals. In the instance of the Pilgrim, this Hesychastic school was breaking out of the monastery and trying to make its way into ordinary, "secular" life. Hesychasm derives from the Greek word for "quietness" (*hesychia*). It sketches out a state of spiritual awareness where the body is first stilled by simple repetitive stances or actions (standing still, moving a prayer rope, and such), and the mind is given simple tasks of repetitive short phrases or words (Lord Jesus Christ, Son of God, have mercy—in the case of the Jesus Prayer) in order that the heart (by which the Hesychast school means the spiritual soul-awareness of a person [*aisthesis noetikos*], one's sense of God's presence to one and the world) may stand before God in a continuous awareness "beyond the range of words." This *stasis* (the Greek word means a drawn-out condition, a stable state) is barely possible given the fragmented nature of human psychical awareness. In prayer that is silent, imageless, and wordless, it takes only a matter of seconds before the normal freewheeling nature of the human imagination "fills the gaps" with psychic junk: daydreams, distractions, thoughts of a hundred different things. The Jesus Prayer that the Pilgrim uses, therefore, was meant as a mountaineer's rope—a way of ascending a difficult peak, a tool to rise out of normal states of ragged and dissipated consciousness into a sustained concentration on the awareness of God's immanent presence. The physical posture of the prayer, the mental fixation on a few simple words, and the ultimate release of the heart's deeper awareness to be focused on God: this is all the fabric of the structure of a system of prayer that is meant to be an aid to radical concentration, but concentration that is free, relaxed, nonideational. And that is the point: so that prayer might rise from being a matter of what we have to say to God into being enabled to hear what God might actually be saying to us.

In the Pilgrim's case, he was situated in "Holy Mother Russia" of the nineteenth century: *Slavia Orthodoxa*. He might not have found many sympathetic clerics, or even fewer perhaps who could help him along his mystical road, though he did find some. But week by week he passed on his journeys from church to church where the liturgy was being celebrated in lively congregations, where he could receive the sacraments of his church and in which community context his spiritual aspirations were perfectly well understood and honored. Today that substructure of a lively religious tradition has disappeared for many people. They cannot learn their religious traditions from an early age: they often do not have a native syntax of faith or customary spiritual practices on which they can draw. This is why spiritual practices are perhaps more difficult to access—precisely because of this lack of common context, or semantic accessibility.

Perhaps in this day and age it is the very simplicity of the Pilgrim's story and method of prayer that can help and inspire the new seeker. This is perhaps comparable to the great force that the Taizé community's spirituality had for the youth of postwar Europe, with its liturgical assemblies stripped down to simplest basics and its resonant chants of very short themes (meant originally so that youth groups of numerous different language zones could join in together).

That liturgical ethos opened up to lots of young people the sense that the words or chants of such simple themes were not ends in themselves but things that, being repeated for a significant amount of time, suddenly became "doors of consciousness," opening up the spiritual awareness to different levels of prayer that were not possible for those engaged in the use of many words or complex rituals. New movements also began elsewhere in the Roman Catholic Church in recent decades, often designated as "Centering Prayer," which were concerned with the same overall goal: simplification, peaceful concentration, attention to the Presence, use of increasingly wordless and imageless prayer. This kind of "mysticism" was democratized, taken down from the esoteric heights such a word seemed to command in former ages and given back to the ordinary people as a way of spiritual prayer and praxis that was far from esoteric and rather a most "normal" and homely, most intimate, way of self-discovery and spiritual expansion. The Pilgrim is a very down-to-earth mystic. Maybe that was his attractiveness to so many in the past. Perhaps that is to be his continuing role as a teacher for the future.

His great sorrow, as he states many times in his story, is the difficulty he has in finding a real "spiritual father" to guide him on his way. This tradition of spiritual eldership is something that is still inculcated in the Eastern Orthodox Church, though today it is largely rooted in the monastic clergy who become soul-guides for serious spiritual travelers. In countries such as Romania, Russia, Serbia, and Greece, I myself have witnessed many instances of such guides, who have large followings of lay disciples. In the West, monastic life has, for centuries, been in abeyance. It is hard to find an Orthodox monastic community (though they do exist); and if one does, the tradition of spiritual eldership is a secret thing chiefly reserved for the Orthodox faithful themselves and set within a sacramental basis. In Eastern Orthodox practice, spiritual "fathers" (*startsi*) are meant to guide men; spiritual "mothers" (*ammas, starissas*) to guide women; for the relationship is so intimate that the church always advised prudence so that romantic attachments should not get in the way, and there ought to be a significant age gap between the advisee and the advisor. The Elder's main qualification is meant to be experience. He or she has traveled the path beforehand, been tested, and learned.

So, the Pilgrim's problem remains a lively one: Where to go to find guidance on this difficult, often lonely, and largely "untrodden" path? The Pilgrim speaks of having his (now dead) spiritual father come to visit him in dreams and guide him. The bonds of love in God are often like this: untrammeled by "little things" like death or distance. However, for a beginner it remains, it is, very important to have some form of more experienced guide in the ways of prayer and spirituality, especially as one sets off in the early stages. It stands to reason. Who would ever set up as a carpenter and open a shop to show off homemade tables and chairs for sale if they had never taken a single class in woodworking? If they claimed to be wholly self-taught carpenters, we can imagine what kind of furniture they might be producing. They might indeed be very proud of it—but a trained eye might cast a much more jaundiced eye over the results that the enthusiastic devotee was not even able to see! Early mistakes in a new field quickly become habits that take years to remedy. This is said time after time by music teachers, for example, who pick up a "self-taught" musician and spend a long time trying to remedy basic beginners' errors that actually limit the possibility of development. Self-taught pianists or string players have often developed habits of finger positioning that physically limit their abilities; and to make real progress in playing a skilled teacher has to make them "unlearn" basics before teaching them the techniques that they needed from the outset. It is very much like this in the spiritual life. The

Russians have a word for the ideas that beset a beginner who is often filled with heartfelt zeal and fire, and determination in the spiritual life, and with all of this entertains a "deep inner sense of being right." They call it *prelest*, or self-delusion.

Religious zeal often breeds *prelest*. It can also alienate people from the usual (not to say "normal") surroundings of friends, family, and mundane jobs. It can dislocate, even damage a person. This is the primary role of the spiritual guide, the *starets* or *starissa*: they keep the eager seeker grounded. They offer wise advice as from someone who has "been there already" and save them from unbalanced mistakes. So, if the pilgrimage trail beckons, remember part of the message of the Pilgrim himself, and do not neglect the serious search for a wise guide as you go. They are not ten a penny, but perhaps God will make sure that they are not wholly absent either. Do not neglect the clergy of your own area, for here is a fund of serious spiritual seekers (or at least they were at one stage!). It does not take long to recognize those who remain spiritually serious and those who are wise and kind and helpful. If they are not these things, then nothing is lost. They were not the right guides for you anyway.

Like the Pilgrim, perhaps an archetype or model for all serious pilgrims, in the fascinating tale that we have been reviewing, there will always be those who want more from the spiritual life and are willing to "make the journey" to go looking for it. Christ in the Gospels promised that those who went out on such a pilgrimage would not waste their time. He said, "Ask, and it will be given you; seek, and you will find; knock, and it will be opened to you. For everyone who asks receives, and whoever seeks finds, and to the one who knocks it will be opened" (Matt. 7:7–8). This is an extraordinarily encouraging prospect and as good an invitation for a serious journey as perhaps has ever been issued.

Notes

1. The title of the *Philokalia* may be translated as "Lover of Beauty" or "Love of the Beautiful," and it more or less connotes a *Florilegium*, or portable library of the "best texts" of a certain type. We shall come back to the history and background of the *Philokalia* shortly. For more information, see McGuckin 2012.

2. There is an old Christian theme that the Lord himself will teach wisdom to the innocent beyond their natural capacity. See Mark 6:2–3; Luke 12:11–12; John 14:26.

3. The quintessence of "Slavic Orthodoxy"—a vision of how Christian Orthodoxy (from tenth-century Byzantium) gave birth to the Russian nation and endures as its soul and heart. It was an idea that filled the Russian Middle Ages, was renewed by the Slavophile movement of the nineteenth and twentieth centuries (the likes of Solovyev, Dostoevsky, Frank, and Berdyaev), and was at the heart of a monastic understanding of Russian history, from its first chroniclers (monastics) to the last great revival in eighteenth- to nineteenth-century Hesychast monasteries of the Philokalic tradition (the very centers that sponsored our primary text).

4. See chapters 5 and 12; Tolstoy n.d., 28–32, 50–52.

5. A title of honor for a senior, and spiritually advanced, monastic priest. Originally a designation of the senior monk of a whole province, it became an honorific title of a senior monk, though usually also of one who leads a monastic house.

6. A monk who is also a priest.

7. An abbot or superior of a monastery.

8. Nikon Rozhdestvenskii was especially instrumental in collecting the appendix tales (5–7).

9. Beginning in 1883, these "Pilgrims' Booklets" were sold by agents of the Imperatorskoe

Pravoslavnoe Palestinskoe Obshchestvo (Imperial Orthodox Palestine Society; IPPO; founded in 1882) for their travels to the Holy Land. These were coupon booklets that certified that the pilgrims had paid for third-class railroad and steamship tickets at a reduced price. Not all pilgrims to the Holy Land, however, purchased such booklets. The map, which covers the years 1883–1899, was first published as part of an article by V. N. Khitrovo, "Kakimi putiami idut russkie palomniki v Sv. Zemliu (Opyt statisticheskogo issledovaniia)" (Routes That Russian Pilgrims Are Taking to the Holy Land [An Attempt at a Statistical Study]), in the Soobshcheniia IPPO (St. Petersburg, 1900), volume 11, part 2. It is reproduced in *Tysiacha let russkogo palomnichestva* (One Thousand Years of Russian Pilgrimage; Moscow, 2009, 21). The latter is a catalogue of an exhibit on Russian pilgrimages held at the State Historical Museum in Moscow in 2009–2010. We are grateful to Irina Lukka and the Slavonic Library of the University of Helsinki for the image and to Christine D. Worobec, Distinguished Research Professor Emerita of Northern Illinois University, for her assistance in identifying the map.

10. See McGuckin 2009. Paisy's volume, called the *Dobrotolyubié*, reproduced twenty-four of the original thirty-six ancient authors that comprised the Greek *Philokalia* assembled on Athos by Saints Makarios and Nikodemos (see Palmer et al. 1979–1995). It is the *Dobrotolyubié* that our Pilgrim treasures.

11. For an English synopsis on his earlier research in Russian, see Pentkovsky 1999.

12. For a list and discussion of extant manuscripts, see Pentkovsky 1999, 4–7, *passim*.

13. See Pentkovsky 1999, 12, 38n38, 40n48.

14. The interest in the conversion of the Old Ritualists was a marked aspect of Father Mikhail's priestly mission and appears in Tale Five. See Smith 1999, 160.

15. Smith 1999, 161. I suspect that this is a later inclusion (Hegumen Paisii or Hieromonk Arsenii's choice?) of the authorial figure of Father Mikhail by allusion; it may be a painterly way of putting in an anonymous reference by a thumbnail portrait. It comes in a section focused on the importance of the *Philokalia* as a *vade mecum*, which is a theme found in the later tales, but not stressed in the first, and which seems not to have been a predominant concern of Father Mikhail's original text of the *Iskatelia neprestannoi molitvy*.

16. The Mikro-Schema is a monk of higher grade than postulant but lower than the highest (most ascetical grade) of monastics, the Great-Schema. The Mikro-Schema is usually a mark of a monk of some maturity and experience, who is still under the guidance of an older spiritual master.

17. His involvement in the story of the text's dissemination is briefly depicted by Pentkovsky in his introduction to *The Pilgrim's Tale* (1999). The monastery of Saint Michael, of which Father Paisii was head, was a dependency of Panteleimon.

18. All meals in the monasteries would be conducted in silence while a monk designated for the task would read from a spiritual work of popular and accessible format.

19. From Kozlov's perspective, "wrongheadedness" meant especially the view that one should try to live a good life first and then start improving a life of prayer. In contrast, for Kozlov, all repentance and all holiness lay in the life of prayer that God inspired as the first of all good actions. See Smith 1999, 49–55. Father Mikhail's willingness to admit (especially relevant since he was head of the mission to the Old Ritualists who criticized the Orthodox parish churches for just this very thing) that life in the local churches was deficient in many respects was something that eventually became "softened" in the final version of the *Rasskaz strannika*.

20. Cited in Pentkovsky 1999, 8, 39–40nn34–35. The reasons for his lack of enthusiasm relate to his earlier (1860) issuing of a "Warning" against the kind of spiritual experiences as found in the writings of the Siberian Elder Vasilisk, published by his disciple Zosima in 1859 and recommended by Hieromonk Arsenii Troepol'skii, whose *Otkrovennoe poslanie* (Candid Missive) represented in the *Rasskaz strannika* was the very text that Amvrosii was attacking (without naming it) in 1860. See Pentkovsky 1999, 16–17.

21. They are set out in a detailed, if somewhat circuitous, way in Pentkovsky 1999.

22. His superior there was Saint Ignatius Brianchaninov (1807–1867), who wrote a significant book on the tradition of the Jesus Prayer. See Brianchaninov 2006.

23. Several of his writings on prayer show a strong interest in Western thought, especially in the Ignatian method deriving from Ignacio de Loyola (St. Ignatius; 1491–1556), founder of the Society of Jesus (Jesuits) and author of the highly influential *Exercitia Spiritualia* (Spiritual Exercises).

24. Unless we are to presume, as Pentkovsky (1999, 27–28) tentatively suggests, that Hegumen Paisii Fedorov made the conflation of Kozlov and Troepol'skii before printing the text of the *Rasskaz strannika* in 1881.

25. "Patristic" is a term fundamental to Orthodox theology and self-identity, which means holding as "authoritative" and "seminal" the writings of the earliest bishop theologians and saints of the first centuries of church life. The word literally means "writings of the fathers."

26. Which ironically were often less Greek, being less Byzantine, than the eighteenth-century Greek practices that were being appealed to as "authentic" liturgical standards.

27. The so-called *bespopovtsy* or "priestless" sect.

28. The reconciliation did not really occur until the twenty-first century. It only started to mature after the fall of communism, but it is currently in process in Russia.

29. The text has been translated into English in four volumes. See Palmer et al. 1979–1995. The Greek text now exists in a five-volume edition (Athens: Astir-Papadimitriou, 1957–1963). For some selections of important writings on inward prayer from the *Philokalia*, see Kadloubovsky and Palmer 1992; Chariton 1997.

30. Theophan made a seven-volume version of the *Philokalia*, amplifying the Greek collation of thirty-six Fathers made by Nikodemos and Makarios and notably expanding on the previous Slavonic version made by Saint Paisy Velichovsky.

31. His early disciples developed the monastery of Neamt after his death as a major publishing house of Hesychastic literature. Several of them also returned to Russia to become founding Elders of the Optino Hermitage, a major force in the Hesychastic revival among the Russians of the eighteenth and nineteenth centuries.

32. Grk.: *Kyrie Iesou Christe, Yie tou Theou, eleison me.* Rus.: *Gospodi Isusi Christe, sine Bozhe, pomilui me.* The primary biblical precedent for the prayer is Luke 18:13. See also Ps. 9:13.

33. See 1 Cor. 5:14–16; 1 Cor. 15:22; 1 Cor. 15:45–50.

34. Developed by Saint Irenaeus (2nd c. CE) in his *Adversus Haereses* 5, preface; in Saint Athanasius's (4th c.) *De Incarnatione* 54.3; *Contra Arianos* 1.39; *De Decretis* 14; and in Saint Gregory of Nyssa's (late 4th c.) *Catechetical Oration* 25.

35. Pelikan is here quoting the *Rasskaz strannika*.

36. In the present chapter, all references to the original text are taken from T. Allan Smith's translation in the Paulist edition. It is unfortunate in some respects that the Paulist edition, which is the best English edition produced to date, has chosen to give *yet another translation of the title* (the existing English translations seem to make up a new one each time) in order, perhaps, to resonate with John Bunyan's (1628–1688) famous *Pilgrim's Progress* or to challenge the anti-monastic *The Pilgrim's Tale*, an anonymous sixteenth-century English poem. I will refer to the book in the abbreviated form of its first printed Russian title (1881), namely, *Rasskaz strannika*. It would be more accurate to refer to the text in English as *The Candid Tale of a Pilgrim*.

37. Of which there are several variants mentioned in the book (such as reciting a single phrase of scripture many times, or reciting simply the Holy Name of Jesus, or the petition "Lord have mercy"), but the Jesus Prayer ("Lord Jesus Christ, Son of God, have mercy on me") is seen as the highest and most perfect medium of the Prayer of the Heart.

38. See Mark 9:1ff., which was taken by the medieval Hesychast theologians as a symbol of the spiritual illumination that Jesus offered to the disciples who understood his offer of grace and were thus "enlightened" by him. Thus, not only was Jesus seen to be transfigured in light (the incarnation of the divine in the human), but this radiance was also seen as a gift communicated to the whole human nature that the Divine Word had assumed (deification by grace). The Incarnation was thus seen by the Hesychasts as the doctrine of salvation encapsulated. Saint Athanasius of Alexandria put it in an apophthegmatic form

in his Book *On the Incarnation* 54: "He [the Divine Word] became Man, so that Man might become god." Always it is presumed that this "becoming god" is in terms of the divine grace of restored union offered gratuitously by God to humankind. In the original Greek the wordplay on the transference between God and Man evokes both the universal (divine status, human nature) and the particular (the Divine Word being Jesus; the "Man" being Adam, of whom Jesus is the recapitulation and atonement).

39. John 15:11; John 16:22–24; John 17:13; Acts 24:32.

40. The New Testament notion of the Kingdom (*Basileia tou theou*) is not a static abstract noun, as the English translation would have it, but the active present sense of God's energized dominion in a person's life.

41. Observant Jews were forbidden to pronounce the Name of God. Only the High Priest could speak it, and only behind the veil of the Holy of Holies in the Temple, on the Day of Atonement.

42. Psalm 111:9; Jeremiah 10:6.

43. Genesis 21:33; Genesis 26:25; Psalm 116:4.

44. Genesis 32:29; Exodus 3:13–14.

45. 2 Samuel 7:13; Ezra 6:12.

46. Psalms 20:1, 54:1, 91:14, 118:10, 124:8; Zephaniah 3:13; Sirach 51:3.

47. Psalms 29:2, 79:9, 96:8; Micah 5:4.

48. Cf. Psalms 7:17, 8:1, 9:2, 18:49, 30:34, 44:8, 45:17, 52:9, 54:6, 61:8, 63:4, 86:9 and 12.

49. The Greek Fathers use the word "mystical" (*mustikos*) to describe the movings of the Spirit in the secret interiority of a person. The word itself means "private" or "silent." In later medieval Western Christian literature, it began to have a new set of meanings, namely, a separate metaphysical state of awareness contrasted with "natural" states as an entirely "supernatural" thing. However, this contrast is not found in the Greek Fathers. The presence of God in the deepest soul of a person is seen by them as the true natural condition of a human being as child of God. Returning to such an ontological condition is a return to the divine glory of grace and union that was lost in the Fall, a Fall whereby Adam was alienated not only from God but even from himself.

50. Luke 18:10–14: "The tax collector, standing far off, would not even lift up his eyes to heaven, but beat his breast, saying, God, be merciful to me a sinner! I tell you, it was this man who went down to his house justified rather than the other."

51. Mark 10:46–52; Luke 18:35–43.

52. See John 1:12, 14:13–14, 14:26, 15:16, 16:23–26, 17:6, 11–12, and 26.

53. Grk.: *Pneuma* or *nous* when it referred to the higher mystical senses of the soul.

54. Here we may note that the Pilgrim is advised to say the prayer many thousands of times, ending up reciting the prayer twelve thousand times per day, an extraordinary amount that demands a radical detachment from the ordinary tasks of earning a living (not a major concern to a hermit monk or impoverished pilgrim walker).

55. This stands in contrast to the Catholic Ignatian method of mental prayer, for example, which begins with the "imagining" of a scene (e.g., from the life of Christ).

56. Eastern Orthodox customarily stand for prayers. However, the Jesus Prayer is also often said crouched down in a half-kneeling posture and/or using a small wooden stool. On the latter, see "On Stillness" by Saint Gregory of Sinai and "Directions to Hesychasts" by Kallistos and Ignatios. A woolen rosary (prayer beads) is also used to count off the exclamations, with a whole prayer rope often being made up of one hundred knots.

57. One of the most famous monastic tales from medieval Rus' was the twelfth-century *Journey to the Holy Land* by Hegumen Daniil (d.u.), which is the first Russian text to characterize the monk as a pilgrim in the world. This idea of the wanderer, however, is an ancient monastic theme. See McGuckin 2000. Only a few decades before the making of the *Rasskaz strannika* in Kiev in 1853, the monk Alimpii copied down and published the mystical visions that were told to him by the Siberian peasant pilgrim Iakov Lanshakov. See Pentkovsky 1999, 33, 39n19, 45n111. Similarly, the monk Parfenii published an account of

his own wanderings as a pilgrim around Russia, Moldavia, and the Holy Land; the work is titled *Skazanie o stranstvii po Rossii, Moldavii, Turtsii I Sviatoi Zemle* (Moscow; 1855). The *Rasskaz strannika* dates its own travels to only a few years of this date (1859+), although the text was actually issued, in all likelihood, more than a decade later.

58. 1 Thess. 5:17. The device echoes the beginning of the famous narrative by Saint Athanasius of the conversion of Saint Antony, the first monk, who hears in church the text "Sell all that you have" (Matt. 19.21) and, taking it literally, begins his life of wandering in search of God.

59. The corresponding text is *The Spiritual Training of the Inner Person*.

60. Recalling a similar episode in the life of Saint Seraphim of Sarov (1759–1833), one of the great Hesychastic saints of Russia.

61. He is given the special "order" in which to read the *Philokalia*: (a) Nikiphoros the Monk; (b) Second Book of Gregory of Sinai, minus the short chapters; (c) *Three Modes of Prayer* and *Discourse on Faith* by Saint Symeon; and then (d) the works of Saints Kallistos and Ignatios. A summary of it all is available, he is told, in the *Abbreviated Description of the Mode of Prayer* by Saint Kallistos. See my annotations to the following translation. The didactic dream, peaceful and reverent in character, while unusual, is a recurrent motif in Orthodox spiritual discernment and found in many spiritual texts from the New Testament onward.

62. Eph. 4:13. Thirty-three is traditionally regarded by the Orthodox as the age at which Christ died.

Works Cited and Further Reading

Adnès, Pierre. 1974. "Prière à Jésus." In *Dictionnaire de Spiritualité*, edited by Marcel Viller et al., vol. 8, cols. 1126–50. Paris: G. Beauchesne et ses fils.

Alfeyev, Hilarion. 2000. *The Spiritual World of Isaac the Syrian*. Kalamazoo: Cistercian.

Bacovcin, Helen. 1978. *The Way of a Pilgrim and The Pilgrim Continues His Way*. Garden City: Image Doubleday.

Behr-Sigel, Elisabeth. 2012 (1992). *The Place of the Heart: An Introduction to Orthodox Spirituality*. Translated by Stephen Bingham. Yonkers: St. Vladimir's Seminary Press.

Bingaman, Brock, and Bradley Nassif, eds. 2012. *The Philokalia: A Classic Text of Orthodox Spirituality*. Oxford and New York: Oxford University Press.

Brianchaninov, Ignatius. 2006. *On the Prayer of Jesus*. Translated by Archimandrite Lazarus Moore. Boston: New Seeds Books.

Brock, Sebastian. 1987. *The Syriac Fathers on Prayer and the Spiritual Life*. Kalamazoo: Cistercian.

Chariton, Igumen. 1997. *The Art of Prayer: An Orthodox Anthology*. London and New York: Faber and Faber.

De Catanzaro, C. J. 1980. *Symeon, the New Theologian: The Discourses*. Mahwah: Paulist Press.

Fedorov, Hegumen Paisii, ed. 1881. *Otkrovennyi rasskaz strannika dukhovnomu svoemu ottsu*. Kazan: St. Michael's Monastery.

French, Reginald M. 1991 (1931). *The Way of a Pilgrim and The Pilgrim Continues His Way*. New York: Harper.

Gillet, Lev. 1987. *The Jesus Prayer*. Crestwood: St. Vladimir's Seminary Press.

Grayston, Donald. 2003. "Anti-Semitism in a Russian Spiritual Classic: The Pilgrim's Tale." *Spiritus* 3.1: 110–26.

Holy Transfiguration Monastery (HTM). 2011. *The Ascetical Homilies of Saint Isaac the Syrian*. 2nd rev. ed. Brookline: Holy Transfiguration Monastery.

Kadloubovsky, E., and G. E. H. Palmer. 1992. *Writings from the Philokalia: On Prayer of the Heart*. London and New York: Faber and Faber.

McGuckin, John Anthony. 1999. "The Prayer of the Heart in Patristic and Early Byzantine Tradition." In *Prayer and Spirituality in the Early Church*, edited by Pauline Allen et al., vol. 2, 69–108. 5 vols. to date. Queensland: Centre for Early Christian Studies, Australian Catholic University.

---. 2000. "Aliens and Citizens of Elsewhere: Xeniteia in East Christian Monastic Literature." In *Strangers to Themselves: The Byzantine Outsider*, edited by Dion Smythe, 23–38. London: Ashgate-Variorum Press.

---. 2008. *The Orthodox Church. An Introduction to Its History, Doctrine, and Spiritual Culture*. Oxford and New York: Wiley Blackwell.

---. 2009. "The Life and Mission of Saint Paisius Velichovsky (1722–1794): An Early Modern Master of the Orthodox Spiritual Life." *Spiritus* 9.2: 157–73.

---. 2012. "The Making of the *Philokalia*: A Tale of Monks and Manuscripts." In *The Philokalia: A Classic Text of Orthodox Spirituality*, edited by Brock Bingaman and Bradley Nassif, 36–49. Oxford and New York: Oxford University Press.

Monks of Saint Panteleimon. 1882. *Zamechatel'nyi rasskaz o blagodatnykh deistviiakh molitvy Iisusovu*. Moscow: Monastery of Saint Panteleimon.

Palmer, G. E. H., Philip Sherrard, and Kallistos Ware. 1979–1995. *The Philokalia: The Complete Text*. 4 vols. London and New York: Faber and Faber.

Pennington, M. Basil. 1978. *O Holy Mountain! Journal of a Retreat on Mount Athos*. Garden City: Doubleday.

---. 2003. *The Monks of Mount Athos: A Western Monk's Extraordinary Spiritual Journey on Eastern Holy Ground*. 25th anniversary ed. Woodstock: Skylight Paths.

Pentkovsky, Aleksei. 1992. "*Rasskaz strannika, iskatelia molitvy (podgotovka teksta i publikatsiia A Pentkovskogo)*." *Simvol* 27: 7–74.

---. 1999. "Introduction: From 'A Seeker of Unceasing Prayer' to 'The Candid Tales of a Pilgrim.'" In *The Pilgrim's Tale*, edited by Aleksei Pentkovsky and translated by T. Allan Smith, 1–46. Mahwah: Paulist Press.

Pentkovsky, Aleksei, and T. Allan Smith. 1999. *The Pilgrim's Tale*. Classics of Western Spirituality. Mahwah: Paulist Press.

Savin, Olga. 1991. *The Way of a Pilgrim and A Pilgrim Continues His Way*. Boston: Shambhala.

Smith, T. Allan. 1999. "The Tale of a Pilgrim, a Seeker of Prayer." In *The Pilgrim's Tale*, edited by Aleksei Pentkovsky and translated by T. Allan Smith, 49–227. Mahwah: Paulist Press.

Spidlík, Tomas. 1986. *The Spirituality of the Christian East*. Kalamazoo: Cistercian.

Tolstoy, Lev (Leo). n.d. *Childhood*. Moscow: Foreign Languages Publishing House.

Valachos, Hierotheos. 2003. *A Night in the Desert of the Holy Mountain: Discussion with a Hermit on the Jesus Prayer*. Translated by Effie Mavromichali. 2nd ed. Levadia: Birth of the Theotokos Monastery.

Wallace, Donald MacKenzie. 1984. *Russia on the Eve of War and Revolution*. Princeton: Princeton University Press.

Ware, Kallistos. 1992. "The Power of the Name: The Jesus Prayer in Orthodox Spirituality." In *The Place of the Heart*, edited by Elisabeth Behr-Sigel, 133–73. Torrance: Oakwood.

---. 1995. *The Orthodox Way*. Rev. ed. Yonkers: St. Vladimir's Seminary Press.

Ware, Timothy (Kallistos). 1993. *The Orthodox Church: New Edition*. New York: Penguin.

---. 1995. *The Orthodox Way*. Rev. ed. Crestwood: St. Vladimir's Seminary Press.

Otkrovennyi rasskaz strannika dukhovnomu svoemu ottsu (Candid Tale of a Pilgrim to His Spiritual Father)

Anonymous[1]

Translated by Sergey Trostyanskiy

Annotated by John Anthony McGuckin and Sergey Trostyanskiy

The First Tale

By God's mercy I am a Christian man, by my deeds a great sinner, and by occupation a homeless pilgrim of the lowest social rank. I wander from place to place. My possessions are the following: a sack of dry bread over my shoulders and the Holy Bible in my inside coat pocket. That is all.

On the twenty-fourth week after the Trinity Sunday[2] I entered the church at the midday service in order to pray. The Apostle was being read from the Epistle to Thessalonians in which it says: "Pray without ceasing."[3] This saying in particular gripped my imagination, and I started thinking: "How can it be possible to pray unceasingly, when it is necessary for each human being to exercise so many other activities in order to sustain life?" I consulted the Bible and saw with

---

*Abbreviated as *Rasskaz strannika*, which is most commonly (and problematically) translated into English as *The Way of a Pilgrim* but more accurately rendered as *A Candid Tale*. The present translation is a completely new and fresh rendition into English based on the Slavonic manuscript of Saint Panteleimon's Monastery on Mount Athos: Old Catalogue No: 317/1883 or Ms. афонской пантелеимоновской рукописи № 50/4/395. This was discovered in 1951 and soon thereafter recognized to be the original manuscript of the work. In the 1980s Monk Vasili compared this systematically with the first published edition of the *Rasskaz strannika* (Kazan, 1881) and with the third (Lavra) edition. The most recent Russian translation of the work has followed the Kazan edition (in preference to the changes introduced in the Lavriotic version). Scholars have since criticized the Kazan edition for several infelicities. However, few English translations, so far, have based themselves on this Panteleimon script, tending to put its version in the footnotes in the cause of "cleaning up the style." One of the reasons for this is that the language in many places was crude and colloquial. For a more detailed discussion of extant manuscripts, see the chapter introduction. The present selection of passages was chosen by John Anthony McGuckin in consultation with Louis Komjathy. The most commonly available, complete and reliable English translation is that of T. Allan Smith, which was published as *The Pilgrim's Tale* in Paulist Press's Classics of Western Spirituality series (1999). For some alternative translations, see French 1991 (1931); Bacovcin 1978; Savin 1991.

1. The text has been transmitted as an anonymous work. However, recent scholarship has suggested that an early version, possibly the earliest version, was written by Archimandrite (superior abbot) Mikhail Kozlov (1826–1884), a Russian Orthodox monk. However, as discussed in the introduction, the text is best considered as a collaborative composition involving numerous Russian Orthodox monks and resulting in various redactions.

2. In the Russian Orthodox Church, Pentecost (lit., fiftieth [day]) is referred to as Trinity Sunday or the Day of the Holy Trinity. It is the Greek name for the Feast of Weeks (Heb.: *shavuot*), a Jewish holiday that celebrates the bestowal of the Torah (Law) to Moses on Mount Sinai. In terms of the Christian liturgical year, Pentecost commemorates the descent of the Holy Spirit on the Apostles and other followers of Jesus Christ, as recounted in the Acts of the Apostles 2:1–31. In the Eastern Orthodox Church, Pentecost may refer to the entire fifty days from Easter, which commemorates the resurrection of Jesus Christ, to Pentecost.

3. 1 Thessalonians 5:17.

my own eyes the text I had heard: precisely that it is necessary to pray without ceasing, to pray always in the Spirit,[4] to lift up praying hands in each place.

I thought and thought, but I did not know how to solve this puzzle. So I went to the local priest's house.

"How can I pray without ceasing?" I asked the deacon. "What does it mean to pray without ceasing? How can such a thing be possible?"

He replied, "Just pray like it tells you in the Bible."

But I asked him again: "But how can I pray unceasingly?"

"Well now! Why are you bothering me with your questions?" the deacon said, and promptly left.

So I asked the priest. He told me: "Go to church more often, offer prayer services there, light the candles, and perform more prostrations."

I asked him: "But where does it talk about this in the Bible?"

He said: "How can a fool like you read the Bible! For the likes of you it is forbidden to read. It is only permissible for us priests to read this book." Having said this, he threw me out.

"What am I supposed to do now?" I thought. "Where can I find someone who can explain this for me? I'll go to the churches that have a reputation for good preachers, and maybe there I will hear good instruction."

In order to make sure that all I had heard was the right thing, I opened the Bible and there I read the following advice in Isaiah chapter 55: "Seek the Lord while he can be found, call upon him while he is near. Let the wicked man forsake his evil way and the unrighteous abandon his thoughts, and let him revert to the Lord, and he will be forgiven as He will overlook his sins."[5] Now here I saw quite the opposite sequence of things. First, it is necessary to seek God and call upon him in prayer. Then, when He approaches by this means, one must attempt to leave behind the works of sin with the Lord's help and turn back to Him, that is, toward the fulfillment of his commandments.

So, after having heard all these admonitions, and not having clarified the meaning of how to "pray unceasingly," I did not listen to any more public sermons but decided with God's help to search for an experienced and knowledgeable person, who could explain to me about incessant prayer, since I could not stop longing for this knowledge.

I wandered for a long time in different places. I kept reading the Bible, and I kept on asking myself whether I could find somewhere a spiritual instructor or a godly and experienced guide. One time I was told that in a certain village there lived a landlord who was striving to save his soul, who had a chapel in his house, and who stayed in the place, always praying to God and constantly reading soul-saving books. Upon hearing this news, I did not walk but rather ran to that village, and reaching it, I came to the landowner.

---

4. Ephesians 6:18; 1 Timothy 2:8

5. Isaiah 55:6–7.

"What do you want of me?" he asked.

"I have heard that you are a learned and godly man. And that is why I want to ask you, for God's sake, to explain to me what it means, in the Apostle, to 'pray unceasingly,' and how can it be possible to pray without cease? I would like to know this but I cannot understand it at all."

The landlord was silent for some time. Then he stared at me and said:

"Ceaseless interior prayer is an uninterrupted aspiration of the human spirit to flow into the heart of the divine. In order to explore this sweet activity, you need to bend the power of the will to it and ask the Lord more and more often to teach you to pray without ceasing."

"I do not understand your words," I said. "Please will you explain this to me more clearly?"

"This is too subtle for you," the landlord replied. "You will not understand. So just pray as you know how, and the prayer, of itself, will reveal to you how it can become ceaseless. To do this it needs its own proper time."

Having said this, he ordered his servants to feed me, gave me some funds for my travels, and let me go. But he did not explain to me the meaning of ceaseless prayer. So once more I went on my way. I thought and thought, kept on reading and musing over what the landlord had told me, but I could not understand it. I wanted so much to comprehend that I could not sleep at night.

The Elder[6] crossed himself and started to talk:[7]

"Give thanks to God, my beloved brother, for the way he has unveiled in you this deep longing to know the meaning of unceasing prayer. Recognize in this the will of God, and calm down; and know this, that you have indeed been given a trial to see if your will conformed to the voice of God. It has thus been given to you to understand that the heavenly light of inner prayer cannot be gained either by the wisdom of this world or by the grasp of speculation. On the contrary, it can only be attained by poverty of spirit and firsthand experience in all simplicity of heart. And so, it is no surprise that you could not hear anywhere about the essential work of prayer, or come to the knowledge of how to arrive successfully at its unceasing practice. And, to tell the truth, though many have preached much on prayer, and there are many writers discoursing about it, since all their arguments have largely been built on speculation or on deductions from natural reasoning, instead of on actual experience, they have really taught more about the peripheries of prayer rather than of its essence, and they have not understood its inner consistency of spirit. One speaks eloquently about the necessity of prayer; another about its efficacy and benefits; someone

---

6. *Starets*. Traditionally speaking, in the Eastern Orthodox practice of the Jesus Prayer, one has a spiritual director, often referred to as a "spiritual father." This is usually a senior monastic who is experienced with contemplative prayer, including potential problems and pitfalls, and who provides guidance concerning contemplative life.

7. In the preceding part of the text, the Pilgrim has encountered a variety of individuals in his search for the meaning of "pray unceasingly," which resulted in little success. In the present section, he finally meets "an old man, who from appearances looked like a cleric." The old man identifies himself as "a monk of the great habit," which technically indicates a higher degree of monastic commitment and perfection (see Pentkovsky 1999, n. 88), from a hermitage about six miles away. The monk invites the Pilgrim to accompany him and lodge at the monastic guesthouse. As they walk together, the Pilgrim recounts his previous experiences and his search for understanding, after which the monk begins more formal instruction.

else about the appropriate means of conducting prayer. But the means of prayer are more difficult to understand than all their aforementioned arguments, and they require a mysterious direct experience, not a mere scholastic facility. Moreover, which is even more pitiful, that vain restless wisdom tries to measure the things of God in terms of human criteria.

"So, many talk about the work of prayer in a completely perverted way, thinking that their preparations and merits make prayer, instead of the fact that prayer itself gives birth to merits and virtues. You have heard this in the sermons, and accordingly you were told not to touch prayer but instructed that you should first prepare yourself for true prayer by accumulating meritorious virtues and conquering the passions.

"But just so, they have wrongly identified the fruits and consequences of prayer with its means and ways, and in this way they have destroyed the power of prayer. For this totally contradicts the Holy Scripture since the Apostle Paul gives instructions on prayer in the following words: 'First of all I pray that prayer be made.'[8] Here the first exhortation in the Apostle's teaching on prayer is that the work of prayer itself is allocated the primary place. He says: 'I pray that prayer be made before all else.' There are many good deeds, which are required of a Christian, but the work of prayer must be performed before anything else, because without prayer no other good deed can be accomplished. Without persevering in frequent prayer it is impossible to find the way to God, to apprehend the truth, to crucify the flesh so full of passions and lusts, to be illumined in the heart by the light of Christ, or to attain salvific union with Him. Here I say 'frequent' prayer since the perfection and purity of prayer is beyond our capacity, as the holy Apostle Paul says: 'We do not know how, or what to pray for, since we do not know how to pray as we should.'[9] And so I am speaking here only about frequency. Perpetual prayer remains part of our capacity, as a means of attaining true purity of prayer, which is the mother of all spiritual good. For as Saint Isaac the Syrian says:[10] 'Own the mother and she will make you children.'[11] But learn how to acquire prayer first and then you will find it easy to attain all the virtues. Many people who are only slightly familiar with spiritual practices and the mystical teachings of the Holy Fathers have unclear conceptions and talk superficially about these matters."

While we were so engaged in conversation, we had almost come up to the hermitage, and we had not noticed it. So as not to lose this wise Elder, since I wanted an urgent answer to my question, I made haste to tell him:

"Most honest Father, I beg you to explain to me what unceasing inner prayer means and how to become proficient in it. I can see that you have a thorough expertise in this matter."

The Elder listened to my request lovingly and beckoned me into his cell. "Come into my room, and I will show you a book of the Holy Fathers, from which you can understand and learn prayer clearly and thoroughly, by God's help."

So, we entered his cell, and the Elder began by saying this:

---

8. 1 Timothy 2:1.

9. Romans 8:26.

10. Isaac the Syrian, also known as Isaac of Nineveh, was a seventh-century Assyrian bishop and theologian, particularly known for his ascetical writings. Regarded as a saint in the Eastern Orthodox Church, his writings survive in a number of collections. See, for example, Brock 1987; Alfeyev 2000; HTM 2011.

11. The reference is taken from the "Ascetical Discourses," a text of Saint Isaac's that is included in the Russian version (*Dobrotolyubié*) of the *Philokalia*.

"Unceasing inner prayer is a continuous and uninterrupted invocation of the divine name of Jesus by the lips, the mind, and the heart, all the while imagining His constant presence, and asking for His mercy, and doing so in all our works, in all places, in all times, even while we sleep. It is expressed in these following words: 'Lord, Jesus Christ, have mercy on me!'[12] If a person becomes habituated in this invocation, he will feel a deep comfort and desire only to make prayer in this way, as if he could not exist without this prayer; and then this prayer will itself overflow within him. Now is it clear to you what unceasing inner prayer is?"

With what joy I cried out: "My dear Father now it is very clear! But, for God's sake, teach me how to achieve this."

"We will read how to learn prayer from this book," he replied. "It is called the *Philokalia*.[13] It contains in itself a complete and detailed body of knowledge about unceasing interior prayer, as has been expounded by twenty-five Holy Fathers,[14] and it is so subtle and useful that it is venerated as the chief and highest instructor in the contemplative spiritual life. As the venerable Nicephorus said: 'It is the book that brings one into salvation, effortlessly and sweetly.' "[15]

"Is it really higher than the Bible then?" I asked him.

"No," he answered. "It is neither above nor holier than the Bible, but it contains in itself luminous explanations of things that are mystically contained in the Bible but are not fully adjusted to our limited minds because of their subtlety. I can offer you a good example of this. The sun is the greatest, most brilliant, and excellent source of light, but you cannot contemplate and examine it with the naked and unprotected eye. It is necessary to have a specific artificial lens, a million times smaller and dimmer than the sun, through which you can examine this magnificent king of the celestial bodies, admiring and tolerating its fiery rays. In the same way the Holy Scripture is the brilliant sun, but the *Philokalia* is that necessary lens.

"Now listen," he said. "I will read to you the instructions on how to master unceasing interior prayer."

---

12. Grk.: *Kyrie Iesou Christe, Yie tou Theou, eleison me*. Rus.: *Gospodi Isusi Christe, sine Bozhe, pomilui me*. The primary biblical precedent for the prayer is Luke 18:13. See also Psalm 9:13.

13. The title of the *Philokalia* may be translated as "Lover of Beauty" or "Love of the Beautiful." It more or less connotes a *Florilegium*, or portable library of the "best texts" of a certain type. It is a collection of texts from the fourth to fifteenth century by masters of the Hesychast tradition. Originally intended to provide guidance on the contemplative life to Orthodox monastics, the original Greek edition was compiled on Mount Athos (Greece) in the eighteenth century by Saint Nikodemos of the Holy Mountain (1749–1809) and Saint Makarios of Corinth (1731–1805). The received Greek text begins with "On Guarding the Intellect" (ca. 370?) by Isaiah the Solitary (d. 489/91) and ends with excerpts from the life of Maximos Kausokalybites (d. 1365–1380). The standard English translation is Palmer et al. 1979–1995, which includes four of a projected five-volume edition. For a critical discussion, see Bingaman and Nassif 2012. For selections on the Jesus Prayer, also known as the Prayer of the Heart, see Chariton 1997; Kadloubovsky and Palmer 1992.

14. The Slavonic version of the *Philokalia* consists of the texts of only twenty-four instead of the thirty-six authors of the original Greek edition (Venice, 1782). The Slavonic translation was published in 1793 in Moscow and republished in 1822 and 1833. Smith 1999, 220n33. This translation, titled *Dobrotolyubié*, was created by Saint Paisy Velichovsky (1722–1794), a Ukrainian monk and leading eighteenth-century Hesychast. It is Saint Paisy's Slavonic translation that the Pilgrim treasures. See the introduction to the present chapter.

15. Also appearing as Saint Nikiphoros, Nicephorus the Monk, who was born in Italy, was a thirteenth-century monastic who converted from Roman Catholicism and who lived for a time on Mount Athos. He described a method of breathing while praying to concentrate the mind within the heart in order to practice watchfulness, which has some parallels to Symeon the New Theologian's "Three Methods of Prayer." Nicephorus's writing "On Watchfulness and the Guarding of the Heart," which the Pilgrim cites here, is contained in the *Philokalia*. See Palmer et al. 1979–1995, 4:194–206.

The Elder opened the *Philokalia*, found an exhortation of Saint Symeon the New Theologian[16] and began to read: "'Sit in silence and solitude, bow down your head, and close your eyes; breathe more calmly; in your imagination look inside your heart and move the mind, that is the thoughts, from the head down into the heart. While breathing say quietly, or only in your mind: "Lord, Jesus Christ, have mercy on me." Try to banish thoughts, be patient and calm. Repeat this exercise often.'"[17]

After this the Elder explained all these things to me and showed examples of them, and we read more from the *Philokalia*, of Saint Gregory of Sinai,[18] and also from the venerable Callistus and Ignatius.[19] For all that we read in the *Philokalia* the Elder pointed to me the different places of the Bible, for the sake of verification, and said: "Look here and see where all these things have been taken from." I listened attentively and admiringly to all these things, memorizing them, and trying to fix in my memory all the details. In this way we sat through the entire night and, without having slept at all, we went on to Orthros.[20]

The Elder then dismissed me with a blessing and told me that while I was engaged in the study of prayer, I should visit him to make an open-hearted confession and manifestation of the self,[21] because it was never safe or profitable to engage oneself in this inner labor without having the guidance of a mentor. While I was standing in the church, I felt within myself a burning zeal to learn as seriously as I could about this unceasing interior prayer. So I kept on asking God to help me.

---

16. Born in Paphlagonia, Anatolia (present-day Turkey) and raised in Constantinople (present-day Istanbul, Turkey), Symeon the New Theologian (949–1022) was a Byzantine Christian monk who began his monastic study under Symeon the Studite (ca. 918–986) at the Monastery of Saint John the Forerunner at Stoudios (Stoudios Monastery; Constantinople). He later joined the community of the Monastery of Saint Mamas in Constantinople, eventually becoming abbot. His writings "On Faith," "153 Practical and Theological Texts," and "Three Methods of Prayer" are contained the *Philokalia*. See Palmer et al. 1979–1995, 4:16–75. See also De Catanzaro 1980.

17. A passage paralleling the present one appears in Symeon the New Theologian's "Three Methods of Prayer." See Palmer et al. 1979–1995, 4:72–73. See also the reference to Symeon in Gregory of Sinai's "On Stillness." Palmer et al. 1979–1995, 4:265. The Elder's advice is melded here with that of the saints in the *Philokalia*, symbolizing the oneness of the source of inspiration, which is a theme much to the fore in the *Rasskaz strannika*.

18. Originally born in Smyrna, Anatolia (present-day Turkey), Gregory of Sinai (1260s–1346) became a monk at Saint Catherine's Monastery (Sinai Peninsula; present-day Egypt). He eventually relocated to Mount Athos in 1310 and lived there until 1335. His writings "On Commandments and Doctrines, Warnings and Promises; on Thoughts, Passions and Virtues, and also on Stillness and Prayer: 137 Texts," "Further Texts," "On the Signs of Grace and Delusion, Written for the Confessor Longinos: Ten Texts," "On Stillness: Fifteen Texts," and "On Prayer: Seven Texts" are contained the *Philokalia*. See Palmer et al. 1979–1995, 4:212–86.

19. Callistus II Xanthopoulos (fl. fourteenth c.), also appearing as Callistus Xanthopulus or just Kallistos, was a Byzantine Hesychast monk who reigned as Ecumenical Patriarch of Constantinople in 1397. He was a disciple of Gregory of Sinai (1260s–1346) and lived for some time on Mount Athos. With his close monastic friend Ignatius of Xanthopoulos, he wrote a tract on the ascetical practices of the Hesychast monks. Their cowritten "Directions to Hesychasts, in a Hundred Chapters" and Callistus's own "Texts on Prayer" are contained in the *Philokalia*. See Kadloubovsky and Palmer 1992, 164–273.

20. Paralleling in certain respects Matins in the Western Christian liturgy, Orthros (Grk.: daybreak) is the last of the four night offices in Eastern Orthodox Christianity, with the other three being Vespers, Compline, and the Midnight Office. Traditionally, it is celebrated daily so as to end at sunrise. It primarily consists of psalms and litanies.

21. The "manifestation of the self" was part of the ascetical ritual of confession. As well as confessing one's faults and sins to the spiritual father, the ascetic was encouraged to open the whole range of the heart's inclinations and the manner of all the "thoughts." This opening up to the *starets* was quite a radical affair. It placed the confessor in the different relationship of "spiritual father" to the one who committed to such openness and trust.

I thought to myself: "How can I visit the Elder for guidance and spiritual confession since they will not let me stay at the monastery guesthouse for more than three days, and there are no dwelling places near the hermitage?" But eventually I learned that there was a village about four miles from the hermitage. So I went there to find a place for myself. God blessed me by showing me a place to stay. I was employed for the whole summer by a peasant, as a guard over his allotment, and I could live in a tent at the side of this garden. Glory to God! I had found a quiet place. And so I began to live and learn interior prayer, according to the method shown to me by the Elder, and I was able to go and see him.

For about a week in solitude I carefully studied unceasing prayer in this garden, exactly as the Elder had explained it to me. At first the work seemed to make progress. Then I began to feel heavily burdened. I felt lazy and bored. I was overcome with sleepiness, and different thoughts started hanging over me like a cloud. Sadly, I went back to the Elder and told him about my situation. He welcomed me back and chatted with me, saying this:

"Beloved brother, all this is the war of the dark world against you. For nothing in our lives is so threatening to it as the Prayer of the Heart; and this is why the dark world makes every effort to hinder you and turn you away from the study of prayer. But even so, the Enemy can act against us only in accordance with what God allows, and as God has thought necessary for us. It seems, then, that you still need a testing of your humility. So it is still too early for you to enter in so zealously to the highest gateways of the heart, in case you fall into spiritual greed.[22] Let me read to you an exhortation from the *Philokalia* about just such a case."

The Elder then found the teachings of the venerable monk Nicephorus and started reading: "If having worked a little, you cannot enter into the country of the heart in the way that has been explained to you, then do what I shall tell you now, and with God's help you will find what you are searching for. You know that the capacity of speech is situated in each person's larynx. Allow this capacity to chase away all thoughts (you are able to do this if you desire it) and grant it to say without ceasing: 'Lord, Jesus Christ, have mercy on me!' Try to say this phrase without stopping. If you carry on like this for some time, then without doubt the doorway of the heart will open itself because of this. This is proven from experience."[23]

The Elder then said: "Listen how the Holy Fathers instruct us in such a case. So now you have to obey their instruction. Say the Jesus Prayer orally as often as you can. Here is a rosary for you;[24] use it to begin with at least three thousand Jesus Prayers every day. Whether standing, sitting, walking, or lying down, say incessantly: 'Lord, Jesus Christ, have mercy on me.' Do not do it loudly, nor too quickly, but make sure you accomplish three thousand a day. Do not arbitrarily add to, or take away from, this number. God will help you by this means to attain to the unceasing work of the heart."

How joyfully I accepted this instruction and returned to my abode. I began to act in this way faithfully and exactly as the Elder had taught me. The first two days were very hard for me,

---

22. The text warns here about the spirit of acquisitiveness, or covetousness, that can attach itself even to spiritual matters. In the times when God gives consolations to the soul, it is easy to end up desiring these more than is appropriate for necessary progress. The old adage applies: "Seek the God of consolations, not the consolations of God."

23. From Nicephorus the Monk's "On Watchfulness and the Guarding of the Heart." See Palmer et al. 1979–1995, 4:206.

24. A woolen rosary (prayer beads) is often used to count, with a whole prayer rope frequently consisting of one hundred knots.

but then it felt so simple and desirable that when I stopped saying the Jesus Prayer I felt as it were some compulsion to continue with it; and it put itself into words so easily and simply, not as before when I felt as if I was under compulsion. I told this to the Elder, and he ordered me now to make six thousand prayers every day. He said: "Be calm, but try and perform this stated number of prayers as precisely as possible. And God will have mercy on you."

So the entire week, when I was secluded in my tent, I went through six thousand Jesus Prayers each day. I gave no mind to anything else and paid no attention to my thoughts, even though they tried to wage war against me. I only tried to put into effect the commandment of the Elder. And what was the result? I became so habituated to this prayer that as soon as I stopped reciting it, I felt something was lacking, as if I had lost something. So I started the prayer again, and at the same moment I would become calm and filled with gladness. When I met up with people, I no longer wanted to talk but preferred to be in solitude, so that I could recite the prayer. This was how used to it I had become, even in a week.

Since he had not seen me for ten days, the Elder came to visit me. I explained my condition to him. Having listened to me he said:

"Now you have become used to the prayer, make sure that you maintain and intensify this habit. Do not waste your time in idleness, but with God's help set yourself to make twelve thousand Jesus Prayers a day without falling off. Keep to your solitude, get up earlier, and go to bed later. But come to me every two weeks for advice."

And so I started to act as the Elder had commanded me. On the first day I could barely finish my twelve thousand rule, even late into the night. But on the next day I completed it easily and pleasurably. At first I felt tired during the unceasing recitation of the prayer and felt as if my tongue had become like wood, and my jaws felt as if they were frozen but not in an unpleasant way; and there was a slight soreness in my throat and a little pain in my left thumb that kept moving the rosary and also an inflammation through the whole wrist and all the way up to my elbow, though this too created a rather pleasant sensation. All of this simply urged me on to make the prayer even more intensely; so by this means over the course of five days I made exactly twelve thousand daily Jesus Prayers and so acquired the habit most pleasantly and zealously.

One day, early in the morning, it was as if the prayer itself woke me up. Once awake, I felt that my lips were moving of themselves and my tongue came to life of its own accord. I wanted to restrain it, but I could not. For a moment I began to recite the Morning Prayers,[25] but my tongue countermanded them, and all my desire was to turn to the recitation of the Jesus Prayer. As soon as I started to recite it, I felt such lightness and, given this encouragement, my tongue and lips freely took over the recitation by themselves, so to say! I spent that entire day in such joy. It was as if I were detached from everything else. It was as if I were on a different planet. By early evening I had completed twelve thousand prayers quite easily. I so much wanted to add more, but I did not dare to do more than the Elder had instructed. So it was that in the days that followed I continued to invoke the name of Jesus with such ease and longing.

---

25. These were the "set" prayers appointed for the hour of waking up. They always began with the Trisagion prayers, including the "Holy God, Holy Mighty, Holy Immortal" and the "Our Father," as well as a short set of verses comparing the soul's "awakening" to the nearness of the end of time with the body's waking up in the morning. The theme of the prayers is to give thanks to God for a new day and ask guidance to live the time evangelically. The text can be viewed online at www.goarch.org/chapel/liturgical_texts/daily_prayers.

Then I went to the Elder for confession and told him all these details. Having listened to me, he began by saying:

"Thank God that such eagerness and facility for prayer has opened up in you. This is a natural thing and arises from frequent exercise and practice. Imagine it like a cart. You subject the main wheel to a powerful jolt, and after that it runs on of its own accord. But in order to extend its movement, it is necessary to keep oiling and jogging it. Now you see what superb abilities our merciful God has provided for the experiential nature of man, and what kind of sensations can appear even besides grace, and in a soul that is still sinful and unpurified, as you have already experienced yourself. How excellent, adorable, and delightful it is when God blesses a person and opens up for them the gift of this self-activating spiritual prayer and cleanses the soul from passions. This condition is indescribable, and the revelation of this mystery of prayer is the foretaste of heavenly bliss on earth. This is given in the simplicity of a loving heart to those who seek after God! As of now, I permit you to offer as much prayer as you want, as much as is possible for you. All the time you are awake, try to dedicate yourself to prayer. So now, without bothering to count, invoke the name of Jesus Christ, and abandon yourself to God's will and wait for His help, for I believe that He will not leave you alone but will direct your way."

I adopted his instruction and thereafter spent all summer long in this unceasing verbal prayer, and I was very calm. I often had visions in my dreams that I was continuing in prayer. During the daytime, if I happened to meet anyone, then they all, without exception, seemed so kind to me, as if they were family, though I did not occupy myself with them greatly. My thoughts totally subsided of their own accord, and I ended up not thinking of anything else apart from prayer. My mind began to incline to all news concerning this, and my heart at times of its own accord began to experience warmth and delight. When I happened to come to church, then the long and empty service seemed so quick to me and was no longer tiring to my inner powers as used to be the case before. My solitary tent seemed to me now a magnificent palace. I did not know how to thank God for sending me, wretched sinner though I was, such a salutary Elder and mentor.

However, I did not enjoy the teachings of my lovable and divinely inspired Elder for long. He passed away at the end of that summer. I said my goodbyes to him in tears, and I thanked him for the fatherly teachings that he had given me in my wretched state. I begged for the rosary that he had always used in his prayers as a blessing. So it was that I was left alone once more. At last the summer had ended. Once again I had nowhere to live. The garden was broken up. The peasant paid me my wages, two rubles, and poured out a bag of hard biscuits for me to eat on my travels. And so I went out wandering in different places. But now my wanderings were not like the old days, made out of the need to beg, for now the invocation of the name of Jesus Christ comforted me on the move, and all the people seemed kinder to me, as if they had all started to love me.

One day I began to think about how to spend the money that I had received for looking after the garden and for what purpose I had been given it. And then it came to me: Wait! The Elder is no longer here, now there is no one to teach me! I will buy the *Philokalia*, and I will learn all about interior prayer from it. I made the sign of the cross over myself and kept on walking and praying. So it was that I reached a provincial town and started asking at the shopkeepers' tables about the *Philokalia*. I found it in one place, but they were asking three rubles, while I only had two. I bargained as best I could, but the merchant would not reduce the price. Finally he said: "Go to that church over there, and ask for the presbyter of the church.[26] He owns some kind of an old book. Perhaps he will relinquish it to you for only two rubles."

I went and there I actually bought the *Philokalia* for two rubles. It was all battered and dilapidated, but even so I was so happy. I fixed it up as best I could, covering it with a piece of cloth, and put it in my bag along with the Bible.

So now I walk on this way and incessantly say the Jesus Prayer, which is to me the sweetest, most precious thing on this earth. Sometimes I walk seventy miles a day or more, but I do not feel that I am walking; I feel only that I am making prayer. When a bitter chill penetrates my bones, I intensify my recitation of the prayer, and soon all gets warm again. If I am overcome by hunger, I start invoking the name of Jesus more often and soon forget that I needed to eat. When I become sick, and the rheumatism in my spine and legs starts up, I focus on listening to the prayer instead of the voice of pain. When people insult me, I turn my mind to how delightful the Jesus Prayer is, and at once the pain of the insult and the anger go away so that I just forget everything associated with it. I have become something of a half-wit. I do not care for anything anymore. Nothing preoccupies me. I no longer want to look on things of vanity but prefer to remain secluded and alone. It is now my habit to long for one thing only, that I can make unceasing prayer. When I am occupied in prayer, I feel so full of joy. God knows what is happening to me. Indeed, all these things are related to the human sensibility in us or, as my deceased Elder used to say, are natural and artificial effects related to our skill. But up to this moment I have not dared to approach or adopt the real study of prayer in the very interior of my heart because of my unworthiness and stupidity. I am waiting still for the hour of God's will. I am relying on the efficacy of the prayers of my departed Elder.

So, even though I have not yet attained to unceasing, self-energizing spiritual prayer in my heart, I nevertheless give glory to God, for now I clearly understand what the saying means that I first heard from the Apostle: "Pray unceasingly."

The Second Tale

So, in order to give some help to this brother and build up his faith,[27] I got out of the bag the *Philokalia*, opened up chapter 109 of the venerable Hesychius,[28] read it out loud, and started

---

26. Russian meaning "pope," the presbyter is a local priest attached to a church. While the quality of the local clergy in nineteenth-century Russia was variable, they were among the few people who could be expected to be literate in any village, thus among the few candidates likely to possess a book of any kind. The implicit criticism of the priest here is his apparent readiness (contrasted to the Pilgrim) to let the *Philokalia* go out of his possession.

27. Here the Pilgrim is in conversation with a peasant who is serving as the warden of the local forest. He invites the Pilgrim into his earthen hut for a meal. During the preliminary conversation, we learn that the warden is worried about the fate of his soul but begins to despair and doubt the existence of God.

28. Also appearing as Saint Hesychios, Hesychius the Priest, or Hesychius of Sinai (fl. eighth c.?) is an obscure Hesychast monk who served for a time as the abbot of Saint Catherine's Monastery (Sinai Peninsula; present-day Egypt). His writing "On Watchfulness and Holiness" is contained in the *Philokalia*. See Palmer et al. 1979–1995, 1:162–98. Chapter 109 appears on page 181.

explaining to him that abstaining from sins for the sake of the fear of torment is an unsuccessful and barren thing, and that it is impossible for the soul to free itself from mental sins by anything other than preserving purity of mind and heart.

"All of these things are acquired by interior prayer," I added, "not only on account of one's fear of the torments of hell but even because of our desire for the kingdom of heaven. For if anyone is focused on accumulating salvific actions, then even the Holy Fathers call this a mercenary affair. They say that the fear of torment is the path of the slave, while the desire for reward in the kingdom of heaven is the path of the mercenary. But God wants us to approach Him by the path of a Son; that is, we would obey Him honestly for the sake of his love and for our desire for Him, and thus find a salvific union with Him in our heart and soul. No matter how much you exhaust yourself, what kind of corporeal works and merits you undertake, if you do not always keep God in mind, and the unceasing Jesus Prayer in your heart, you will never calm down your thoughts but will always incline to sin for the slightest of reasons. So, brother, start to make the Jesus Prayer unceasingly; insofar as is possible and practical to you in this solitude, and you will soon see its benefits. Godless thoughts will stop bothering you, and faith and love for Jesus Christ will open up for you. You will learn how the dead will arise and the Dread Judgment will appear before you in the way that it will truly take place. In your heart there will be such lightness and joy from prayer that you will no longer be surprised; you will no longer be bored and will no more hesitate about the life of salvation."

Moreover, as far as I was able, I explained to him how to start and continue incessantly with the Jesus Prayer, what the Word of God commands about it, and how the Holy Fathers preach concerning it. It seemed as if he was in agreement with all this and calmed down a little. After that I took my leave of him and once more shut myself up in my shabby hut.

Oh my God! What joy, tranquility, and delight I felt, as soon as had I stepped over the threshold of "my cave," or rather this grave. It seemed to me like a vast and royal palace filled with every consolation and joy. With tears of joy I thanked God and thought to myself: "Now finally, with such peace and silence, I can carefully occupy myself with my proper work and beseech the Lord for enlightenment." So it was that with great attention I began by reading the *Philokalia*, all in the proper order, from beginning to end. In a short time I had read through everything and saw what kind of wisdom, holiness, and depth was contained in this book. But since its contents had been written about many different subjects, with various exhortations from the Holy Fathers, I was not able to understand all of it, or especially to combine in one place all the things I wanted to know about the nature of interior prayer, so as to understand from this the way of understanding that unceasing and self-energizing prayer in my heart. And I wanted this so very much, in accordance with the commandment of God given through the Apostle that says: "But covet earnestly the best of gifts"[29] and "Do not quench the spirit."[30]

I thought and thought about what I should do. My mind and my power of apprehension are not big enough, and there is no one here to explain this to me. Let me start bothering the Lord with prayer, and maybe the Lord will somehow fill me with thoughts. After this I did not do anything for the whole day except for concentrating on unceasing prayer. I never stopped even for

---

29. 1 Cor. 12:31.
30. 1 Thess. 5:19.

a short time. My thoughts calmed down and I fell asleep; and then I saw in a dream that I was standing in the cell of my deceased Elder. He was interpreting the *Philokalia*, and he said to me:

"This holy book is full of great wisdom. It is a mysterious treasure of comprehension of the secret destinies of God. It is not available for all men or in every place, but it contains, according to the capacity of each seeker, deep instructions for the wise and clear ones for the simple. And this is why for the likes of you who are unsophisticated, you should not read it in linear succession, as the treatises of the Holy Fathers are situated in it, for here, this order is theological. But for an uneducated man, who wants to be taught unceasing prayer out of the *Philokalia*, it is necessary to read it in the following way. First, read the book of Nicephorus the Monk (the second part).[31] Then read the whole book of Saint Gregory of Sinai, apart from the short chapters.[32] Then read Saint Symeon the New Theologian about three types of prayer and the word on faith.[33] After that read the book of Callistus and Ignatius.[34] In these Fathers is contained a complete exhortation and teaching on the interior Prayer of the Heart, one that is understandable for everyone. And if you want to find another very clear instruction on prayer, then look in part 4 for a brief exposition given by the most holy Patriarch Callistus of Constantinople."[35]

So now, as if I were holding the *Philokalia* in my hands, as it were, I started searching through these exhortations he referred to but somehow could not immediately find the passages. The Elder himself, having turned a few pages, said, "Here it is! I will mark it for you." And having picked up a piece of charcoal from the ground, he marked the surface of the book, in the margin where he had found the chapter.

I listened and tried to memorize all these details that the Elder had told me, as much as I could. Then I woke up, and since it was still before dawn, I lay down and went over in my memory all that I had seen in my dream, and all that the Elder had told me. Eventually I started to think: "God knows whether the soul of the deceased Elder really appeared to me, or whether my own thoughts were just marshaling themselves, since I have been thinking so much about the *Philokalia* and the Elder." Perplexed by this thought, I got out of bed. It was beginning to become light. And then what? I saw on the stone, which I had set up as a table in my hut, the open copy of the *Philokalia*. The very place that the Elder had pointed out to me was underlined by charcoal, just as I had seen it in my dream. Even the piece of charcoal was lying alongside the book. This astounded me because I could clearly remember that there was no book there last

---

31. On Nicephorus the Monk, see note 15 in this translation. As his writing "On Watchfulness and the Guarding of the Heart" is not clearly divided into parts, it is difficult to determine the exact passages. The Elder may mean the section written by Nicephorus himself. See Palmer et al. 1979–1995, 4:194–206, especially 204–6.

32. On Gregory of Sinai, see note 18 in this translation. Based on the present description, one presumably studies his writings "On Commandments and Doctrines, Warnings and Promises; on Thoughts, Passions and Virtues, and also on Stillness and Prayer: 137 Texts," "On the Signs of Grace and Delusion, Written for the Confessor Longinos: Ten Texts," "On Stillness: Fifteen Texts," and "On Prayer: Seven Texts" but not "Further Texts." See Palmer et al. 1979–1995, 4:212–86.

33. On Symeon the New Theologian, see note 16 in this translation. Here one is instructed to study his writings "Three Methods of Prayer" (Palmer et al. 1979–1995, 4: 67–75) and "On Faith" (Palmer et al. 1979–1995, 4:16–24) but not "153 Practical and Theological Texts."

34. On Callistus and Ignatius, see note 19 in this translation. Their text "Directions to Hesychasts, in a Hundred Chapters" appears in Kadloubovsky and Palmer 1992, 164–270.

35. The fourth part of Callistus's "Texts on Prayer" appears in Kadloubovsky and Palmer 1992, 271–73.

evening. It had been laid down near my pillow. And I also know this to be true: That there was no mark against that place indicated. All this made me believe in the truth of my dream and in the godliness of the blessed memory of my Elder. So I then began to read the *Philokalia*, following the same order that the Elder had indicated to me. I read it through once, then once more, and my reading kept fanning the flame of zeal and diligence in my soul, so that I could put into practice what I was reading about. It made clear to me what interior prayer was, what were the means toward it and what was its end, how pleasing it was to both heart and soul, and how one could recognize whether the sweetness came from God, from out of nature, or as a temptation.

So, first of all, I started to find the place where my heart was in accordance with the instruction of Saint Symeon the New Theologian. Having closed the eyes, I looked in my mind for the heart,[36] trying to depict it for myself, how it was on the left side of the chest, and so I listened attentively to its beating. In the beginning I exercised like this several times a day. At first I could notice nothing at all, only darkness; but soon after the heart started appearing to me, revealing itself by its inner motion. Then I started inhaling and exhaling the Jesus Prayer, to the heart by my breath, according to the instructions of Saint Gregory of Sinai and Callistus and Ignatius. That is, I began imagining and mindfully looking into the place of the heart and then breathing in saying, "Lord Jesus Christ," and then exhaling the air on the phrase "Have mercy on me." At first, I busied myself like this for an hour, and then for two hours, and after that I started the exercise more and more often until finally I used to spend almost the whole day in this pursuit. Whenever I felt attacked by oppressions or laziness, or was assailed by doubt, I immediately began to read those parts of the *Philokalia* that gave teachings about zealous action, and then the desire and zeal for prayer reasserted itself once more. After three weeks I started to feel some pain in my heart, and then some sort of most pleasant warmness in it, a sense of joy and tranquility. This was exciting and urged me on to exercise prayer with ever increasing diligence, so that all my thoughts were occupied by this and I experienced a great joy. Since that time I have begun to feel, from time to time, varied sensations in my heart and mind. At times a pleasant sensation, like simmering over, used to happen in my heart. It had such calmness, freedom, and comfort about it that I used to become entirely transformed and felt I had been turned into joy itself. Sometimes I felt a burning love for Christ and for all God's creation. Sometimes sweet tears of thankfulness to God, for having mercy on me a wretched sinner, sprung up in me of their own accord. At times I found my earlier foolish notions were so clarified in me that I could easily understand and meditate on things that I could not earlier even think about. Sometimes the heart's sweet warmth would flood over my entire being, and I felt the presence of God so tenderly all around me. At times I used to sense within myself the greatest joy from invoking the name of Jesus Christ, and then I learned what Christ had meant when he said, "The kingdom of God is within you."[37]

---

36. The Hesychast movement in the Eastern Orthodox Church made a distinction of the spiritual faculties in a human being. It distinguished the mental faculties (Grk.: *logismoi*; thoughts and imaginations) from the spiritual discernment of the ways of God (Grk.: *nous*). The *nous* is a higher faculty of perception dedicated to the seeking of the presence of God. Hesychast writers (using Syriac originals) locate the perceptions of the *nous* in the heart, with "heart" taken as the biblical symbol of faithfulness to God. What the text means here by "looking in the mind" for the place of the heart is quite literally to imagine the place in the body where the heart is located (like a chamber) and lead one's imaginative faculties down there so as to keep them hemmed in while prayer is taking place. Thus prayer is liberated from all manner of thoughts, imaginations, and phantasms.

37. Luke 17:21.

While experiencing these and similar pleasant consolations, I noticed that the effects of the Prayer of the Heart were unfolding themselves in three forms: in the spirit, in the feelings, and in revelations. In spirit, for instance, they were the sweetness of God's love, inner peace, delight of mind, purity of thought, a sweet remembrance of God. In the feelings, they were a pleasant warming of the heart, an overwhelming with sweetness throughout the body, a joyful sense of simmering in the heart, lightness and cheerfulness, a feeling of delight in life, a lack of sensibility to disease or afflictions. In terms of revelations, they were the enlightenment of the mind, an apprehension of Holy Scripture, an understanding of the language of creation, a renunciation of vanities, a knowledge of the delights of the interior life, as well as an assurance of the closeness of God to us and His love for us.

Having spent five months over this prayerful work in solitude, and having all the joyful sensations that I have just mentioned, I became so used to the Prayer of the Heart that I practiced it unceasingly, and, finally, I felt that the prayer itself, of its own accord, without any prompting by me, was working and expressing itself in my mind and heart, not only when I was awake but even in my dreams it was acting exactly in the same way. Nothing could interrupt it. It did not cease for a moment, no matter what I did. My soul gave thanks to God and my heart melted in unceasing joy.

The Fourth Tale

In the evening the lord himself came to call all of us together for dinner.[38] After dinner I told him that I was going on a journey with the blind man and that we would not need the carts because I would be able to read the *Philokalia* more comfortably. The master said, "I too love the *Philokalia*. I wrote a letter and prepared some money so that when I go to court tomorrow I can send them to Saint Petersburg in order to have a copy of the *Philokalia* sent to me in the first mail."

So, the following morning we went on the road, giving many thanks to these lords for the exemplary love and mercy they had shown. Both of them followed us for a mile out from their residence. Then we parted. The blind man and I went on, walking slowly and gradually, over ten to fifteen miles a day. The rest of the time we sat in secluded places and read the *Philokalia*. I read everything to him about the Prayer of the Heart according to the order that my deceased Elder had shown me. I started with the book of Nicephorus the Monk, then Gregory of Sinai, and so on. How eagerly and attentively he listened to all this, and how much he liked and enjoyed it! Then he started asking me such questions about prayer that my mind fell short in resolving them. Having read all the necessary things from the *Philokalia*, he started asking me earnestly to show him the way that the mind can find the pace of the heart, and how it can set up there the divine name of Jesus Christ, and how one can pray internally in the heart with sweetness. So I started to explain it to him:

---

38. In this section of the text, the Pilgrim is having a communal meal with an aristocratic lord and lady, a priest, servants, and beggars. Following a decision to travel to Tobolsk (Tyumen Oblast) with a blind man, with the intention of reading the *Philokalia* and discussing interior prayer, the Pilgrim begins to have a conversation with the lord.

"If you are not able to see anything, you have to imagine things mentally. Represent to yourself something you have seen before, such as a man, or part of yourself, such as an arm or a leg, that you can imagine as vividly as you would as if you had looked at it. Can you focus on this, and direct your blind eyes in this way?"

"I can," replied the blind man.

"Well, in the same way you should imagine your heart, bringing your eyes to it as if you were looking at it through the wall of your chest. Imagine it as vividly as possible, and listen carefully to the rhythm with your ears, how it beats time after time. The Holy Fathers call this 'the bringing of the mind captive into the heart.' When you have become accustomed to all this, then while you are gazing on the heart, start attaching the words of the Jesus Prayer to each heartbeat. In other words, with the first beat say, or think, 'Lord'; with the second one, 'Jesus'; with the third, 'Christ'; with the fourth, 'Have mercy'; and with the fifth, 'On me.' Repeat this many times over. This will be easy enough for you since you have already mastered the basics and the preliminary training. Finally, when you have become really familiar with all of this, start inhaling and exhaling the entire Jesus Prayer into the heart along with your breath, as the Fathers have taught us. In other words, while inhaling the air to your lungs, say vocally or mentally 'Lord Jesus Christ,' and while exhaling say 'Have mercy on me!' Do this more and more often and you will soon feel a fine and pleasant pain in the heart. Then there will appear within the heart a sensation of warmth and melting. In this way, with God's help, you will arrive at the state where the delightful interior Prayer of the Heart starts to work of its own accord. However, along with all this, be very careful about all manner of mental imaginations as well as certain phantasms and mental forms that may appear. Do not accept any of these imaginings in any way during interior prayer, as the Holy Fathers have insistently instructed us, but keep to a formless state of mind so that we may not fall into delusions."

The blind man listened to all these words with close attention and diligently started to put into effect the method I had indicated. At night, when we made stops at various shelters, he concentrated on this work for a long time. About five days later he started to feel a deep warmth and indescribable pleasure in his heart and along with it a great zeal to continue with this prayer unceasingly, for it was opening up within him the love of Jesus Christ. At times, he started seeing light, though without discerning any objects or things in it. Sometimes it appeared to him when he was in the act of entering the heart, and it was as if a vigorous flame of a burning candle was sweetly flashing inside his heart and even casting itself through his throat to the outside to give him light. By this flame he could see even some distant things, as once he used to be able to.

We were walking in the forest. The blind man was silent and entirely concentrated on prayer. Suddenly he said to me:

"What a fire there is in the town! Look at it! What a pity! The church has already caught fire, and the bell tower has collapsed."

I told him: "Now, stop imagining such vanities. This is a temptation for you. It is necessary to reject all imaginations. How is it possible to see what is taking place in the town? We are still twelve miles from it."

He was obedient and went on praying quietly. Toward evening we reached the town, and there I really did see several burned houses and the ruined bell tower that had been set up on wooden stilts. People were milling round, wondering how the fallen tower had not crushed anyone. It is my belief that this calamity had happened at exactly the same time when the blind man had told me about it. And then he started talking to me:

"You told me that this vision of mine was vanity, but it is true. Should we not thank and love the Lord Jesus Christ who reveals his grace to sinners, to the blind and foolish? And I thank you also, that you taught me this work of the heart."

I said to him: "Yes, love Jesus Christ, and thank him, for His grace is everywhere, in pure as well as in sinful hearts. No one can say the name 'Jesus is Lord' except in the Holy Spirit.[39] The Word of God is uttered by the Holy Spirit alone and that is why whoever says the name of God, and however he says it, the grace of the Holy Spirit is in it entirely. But even so, you must not accept phenomenal visions as direct revelations of grace, because these things can often happen in the natural order of things. The human soul is comparatively boundless, and so it can see in the darkness, as well as things far distant and close at hand. We should not lend our strength and effort to this psychic ability. Neither should we try to suppress it in the fetters of our weak bodies, nor by the entanglements of our speculations and scattered imaginings. But when we concentrate on ourselves, abstracting from all peripheral things so as to refine our mind, then the soul can finally act out its part in the highest degree. So this is really a natural capacity.

"I heard my deceased Elder say that even people who do not pray, either because they have some capacity or at times when they are sick, can see light even in the darkest room and how it emanates from all things. They are able to distinguish various objects in the dark, and even sense their own spirit's presence, and penetrate the thoughts of another person. But that which occurs during the Prayer of the Heart comes straight from the grace of God, and thus it is so delightful that no tongue can speak of it. It cannot be compared to anything in this material world. Everything to do with this sensible nature is so paltry in the face of the delightful feelings of grace in the heart."

My blind friend listened so carefully to me and became even more humble. The Prayer of the Heart developed so much for him and proved an ineffable delight for him. I was filled with such joy in my soul to see this and thanked God fervently for allowing me to see such a blessed servant of his.

We finally arrived at Tobolsk. I took him to the almshouse there. We said our warm goodbyes, and then I continued on my journey. I walked on slowly for about a month and had a deep feeling about how edifying and rewarding are living examples of the good. I read the *Philokalia* often, and kept checking over all that I said to the blind man about prayer. His example was so instructive to me that it kindled my desire to emulate him, in appreciation and love for the Lord. The Prayer of the Heart delighted me so much that I could not believe that there was anyone on earth happier than I was. I was puzzled as to what kind of pleasure there might be that is greater and deeper in the kingdom of heaven. I did not only feel all this in my soul, for even the exterior world began to appear to me in a charming manner. All things started to draw me into love and gratitude to God: people, trees, plants, animals, everything became dear to me. I kept on discovering in all things an icon of the name of Jesus Christ. Sometimes I felt as weightless as if I did not have a body, as though I was no longer walking but pleasurably floating in the air. At times it was as if I was entering inside myself and seeing all my insides, marveling at the wise composition of the human body. At times I felt joy as if I had been made the Tsar, and on having such consolations I wanted God to let me die sooner, so that I could pour myself out in thanksgiving at the foot of his throne in the world of spirits.

---

39. 1 Corinthians 12:3.

Perhaps I did not enjoy these feelings with sufficient modesty, so to say, or in accordance with God's will, because after a time I started to feel in my heart a kind of trembling and fearfulness. Might not some sort of trouble occur again, I thought, or some misfortune, such as when I taught the Jesus Prayer to that girl in the chapel? Thoughts like this fell down on me like a cloud, and then I recalled the words of the venerable John of Karpathos,[40] who taught that a wise man accepts disgrace and suffers adversities and trials for the sake of those who need his spiritual help. This was how I fought these thoughts, and I deepened my prayer, which dispelled them completely. With my confidence returning, I said to myself: "God's will be done! I am ready to suffer all things that Jesus may send to me because of my sins and my prideful temper. For those to whom I recently revealed the mystery of the heart's entrance into interior prayer were surely already prepared for it, even before I met up with them, by God's secret revelation of the mystery." The idea reassured me, and I was able to set off again in prayerful consolation and I had greater joy than ever.

For two days it rained, and the road turned into mud so deep one could hardly lift a foot from it. I was by then walking through the Steppe and in fifteen miles had not seen a single settlement. Finally as evening fell, I saw by the roadside a yard and was glad and thought to myself: "I'll ask here if I can take a rest and spend the night. Tomorrow morning we'll see what God wills. Maybe the weather will improve." So I went up and saw a drunken old man wearing a soldier's greatcoat sitting inside the yard on a bank. I bowed before him and said:

"May I ask anyone here if I may stay overnight?"

The old man shouted back: "Who can allow you if not me! I am in charge here! This is a postal station, and I am the caretaker."

So I said: "Then let me spend a night in your place, Father."

"Do you have a passport?" he said. "Show me your passport!"

I gave him my passport, and he held it in his hands and then asked me once more: "Where is the passport?"

"In your hands," I answered.

"Well then, let's go up to the house." There the caretaker put on his glasses and read the passport. And he said: "You can stay overnight. I am a good man. See, I will bring you a glass of wine."

I told him: "I have never taken a drink."

And he said: "Well, no matter. But at least stay with us for some dinner."

They sat down to table, he and the cook, a young woman who was also quite drunk, and they made me sit down with them. All through the dinner they were quarrelling and abusing each other, and in the end it turned into a real fight. The caretaker went to the inner porch to sleep in a closet there, and the cook started cleaning up, washing the cups and spoons, all the while cursing the old man.

---

40. John of Karpathos (ca. seventh c.) is an obscure Hesychast. He presumably came from the island of Karpathos, situated between Crete and Rhodes in the archipelago of the Sporades. It is believed that he lived there as a cenobitic monk and then became bishop of the island. He may be identical with the bishop John of the island "Karparthion" who signed the acts of the sixth Ecumenical Council (680–681), but this remains to be determined. The "monks in India" whom he addresses may have been living in Ethiopia. Palmer et al. 1979–1995, 1:297. His writings "For the Encouragement of the Monks in India Who Had Written to Him: 100 Texts" and "Ascetic Discourse Sent at the Request of the Same Monks in India" are contained in the *Philokalia*. See Palmer et al. 1979–1995, 1:298–326.

I sat there for quite some time, and then I thought to myself: "There is no sign that she is going to calm down any time soon." So I said to her: "Little Mother, where can I go to sleep? I am very tired form the journey."

"Here Father," she said. "I will prepare a place for you."

Having placed a chair next to the bench by the front window, she put felt down over it and laid out a pillow. I laid down, closed my eyes, and drifted away. The cook went on making noise for a long time still. Finally, when she had cleaned up, she put out the fire. Now what was going on? She lay down with me and started to caress me! I suddenly felt such desire that I did not know what to do! So I thought I had better start to pray, but the prayer wilted and would not come alive. There might have been a fatal fall occurring at that moment, when all of a sudden the whole window frame just above us, the frame, the glass, and plaster, flew apart and showered down on us with a terrible thunder and cracking. From behind the window there arose the loudest moaning and roaring. It scared me to death, and I shoved the woman off me with such force that she landed in the middle of the floor, and the whole house was shaking. I jumped up and fell straight on my knees and cried out to God. I thought that the earth was going to open up beneath me so as to swallow the wicked. At that moment I saw two coachmen bringing a man all covered with blood into the house. His face could hardly be made out. That terrified me even more. It turned out that he was a courier who had been galloping to change his horses here. His coachman had not properly opened the gates, and so he had clipped the window by the drawbar and overturned his carriage in the ditch that lay in front of our house. As the courier fell down into it, he cut his head on the sharpened stakes that pinned in the bank. The courier shouted out for us to bring him water and wine, so he could wash his wound. He soaked the cut in wine and then drank a glass for himself. And then he shouted, "Horses!" I stood beside him and said, "Father, how can you possibly drive on in such pain?" "A courier has no time to be sick," he answered. And off he galloped.

The woman was still unconscious. The caretaker dragged her over to the stove in the corner and covered her up with a mat. "She's had a skinful [of wine]," he said. "She'll come round tomorrow." And then the caretaker sobered himself up by downing another shot of vodka and went back to bed to continue his sleep.

I was left alone then. Oh my God! I was in such a state! Despondency and grief tormented me. I was full of pity, in case the woman passed away in such a bad state, for there was little sign of life noticeable in her, apart from heavy breathing. I started to pray and ask for the Lord's mercy. I put the Elder's rosary on the sick woman's head and started invoking the name of Jesus Christ. Soon the woman got up and began to pace from corner to corner, like a mad thing. Finally, she left the house. After praying I felt so weak and fell asleep just as dawn broke. And then I heard a voice, as if it was speaking to me from inside: "Timid man! Learn to grasp the ways of God's providence in human affairs! How many wonders there are! Can you not see how many lessons there are for you in all that has happened here? Be strong, and have faith in the omnipresent divine love of Jesus Christ! Read more carefully the seventh and twelfth chapters of Saint Gregory of Sinai and you will find consolation there."

Chapter 9

Mahāyāna Buddhist Visualization
The *Guan wuliang shoufo jing*

Kenneth K. Tanaka

More commonly appearing in English as the *Visualization Sutra* or *Contemplation Sutra*, the *Guan wuliang shoufo jing* (Sutra on Visualizing the Buddha of Infinite Life; abbr. *Guanjing*) is a Mahāyāna (Greater Vehicle) Buddhist scripture on visualization, specifically, visualization of the Buddha Amitāyus (Infinite Life) or Amitābha (Infinite Light)[1] and his Pure Land called "Sukhāvatī" (Ultimate Bliss). While presented as a record of oral teachings given by the historical Buddha, like other Mahāyāna *sūtra*s, the composer of the text is actually anonymous. It was possibly composed in Central Asia around the fourth century CE. The received text is a Chinese translation by the Central Asian missionary-monk and translator Kālayaśas (ca. 383–442), who composed it sometime between 424 and 442. The *Guanjing* in turn became an important text in the Jingtu (Jpn.: Jōdo; Pure Land) movement, a Chinese school of Mahāyāna Buddhism. It was later canonized as one of the so-called Three Pure Land Sutras. The text is intended for any Mahāyāna Buddhist, whether monastic or lay.

Listening to the Buddha in Fifth-Century China

The *Guan wuliang shoufo jing* (Sutra on Visualizing the Buddha of Infinite Life; abbr. *Guanjing*)[2] is written in classical Chinese, possibly from an earlier Sanskrit version, and has been considered by Mahāyāna Buddhists to be a transcription of oral teachings delivered by Śākyamuni Buddha (ca. 540–480 BCE), the historical Buddha. Also known as Siddhārtha Gautama, Śākyamuni Buddha is the founder of Buddhism. He lived in the northeastern part of the Indian subcontinent approximately five hundred years before the Common Era.

There are two categories of scriptures that are believed to contain the words of the historical Buddha: *sūtra* and *vinaya*. *Sūtra* is etymologically related to the English word "suture" and may be taken to mean a "string of words" of his sermons on the teachings based on his enlightenment experience. The *vinaya* (code of conduct) focuses on the Buddha's instructions on conduct and organization for his disciples, mostly of the community of monks and nuns. It specifically contains precepts and rules associated with foundational Buddhist commitments and monastic life.

Unlike the Bible and the Qur'an, these *sūtra*s are too numerous to be contained in one book, because they number in the hundreds. Most of the important *sūtra*s and *vinaya*s are contained in the various Buddhist canons that have been handed down through the centuries by different schools and traditions, with the main ones being those in Pāli, Chinese, and Tibetan languages. The Pāli canon, or *Tipiṭaka* (Three Baskets), belongs to the Theravāda (Teachings of the Elders) school, which is found primarily in Sri Lanka and Southeast Asia. The Tibetan canon was transmitted by various Tibetan schools in Tibet and the surrounding areas, often referred to as the "Tibetan cultural sphere." The Chinese canon was handed down by numerous schools in China and transmitted from there to Korea, Japan, and Vietnam. It is the Chinese canon that includes our primary text.

The *Guanjing*, like most of the *sūtra*s in the Chinese canon, belongs to the Mahāyāna branch of Buddhism, a new movement that took place around the beginning of the Common Era, or approximately 450 years after the death of the historical Buddha. The proponents referred to their movement as Mahāyāna (Greater Vehicle) in contrast to the earlier forms that they pejoratively called Hīnayāna (Lesser Vehicle). Today, it is no longer customary to use the latter term in referring to any "non-Mahāyāna" Buddhist groups or schools, most notably the Theravāda school that, as mentioned previously, is dominant in Sri Lanka and Southeast Asia.

Consequently, Mahāyāna *sūtra*s could not be the direct recording of the words of the Buddha but are the product of anonymous composers, most probably monks, who expressed their religious insights by attributing them as the words of the Buddha. In defense of the Mahāyānists, while these *sūtra*s are historically of later composition, the teachings at their core could very well be those of the Buddha that were transmitted orally through the centuries. It needs to be pointed out that core teachings of even the Pāli canon of the Theravādins—of Sri Lanka and Southeast Asia and the only surviving "non-Mahāyāna" school with claims of direct transmission back to the Buddha—were transmitted orally for roughly four centuries and were only put into writing around the same time as the emergence of Mahāyāna Buddhism.

Among the Mahāyāna *sūtra*s, the *Guanjing* requires added clarification with regard to its origin. Many Mahāyāna *sūtra*s are available in Sanskrit texts or in Tibetan translation of the Sanskrit original, thereby attesting to their Indian origin. However, no such Sanskrit text or Tibetan translation has been found for the *Guanjing* (Tanaka 1990, 38).[3] Hence, a long debate has ensued among specialists concerning the location of its composition.

The present Chinese text is presented as a translation by Kālayaśas (ca. 383–442) sometime between 424 and 442. Kālayaśas was an obscure Central Asian missionary-monk and translator, primarily remembered as the translator of the *Guanjing*. As mentioned, a Sanskrit version of this *sūtra* has not been found, nor is the *sūtra* cited by other Sanskrit texts. In addition, the absence of a Tibetan translation from Sanskrit further casts doubt on the view that there was a Sanskrit original of our text. Thus, most scholars today are in agreement that this *sūtra* was not composed in India. However, their views divide into two camps concerning its actual place of composition, one favoring Central Asia and the other China (Fujita 1976, 121–22).[4]

Those advocating Central Asian composition argue on the basis of the origin of the translator and the iconographic descriptions found in the *Guanjing*. Kālayaśas, the translator, was from Central Asia, as were the translators of other *sūtras* that belong to the same genre of "visualization *sūtras*" that bear the term "visualization" (*guan*) in their titles and have it as their main subject of discussion. Furthermore, the descriptions of the Buddhas and bodhisattvas in the *sūtra* reveal characteristics suggestive of actual images existing in Central Asia. For example, it has been proposed that the Śākyamuni Buddha of the tenth visualization actually depicts the thirty-five meter (approx. 120 foot) Buddha image located in the eastern part of Bāmiyan, like the sixth-century ones that the Taliban destroyed in March 2001 on the grounds that they were an affront to Islam. Representatives of this interpretation argue that these huge descriptions in the *sūtra* would be highly unlikely to have been based on Buddha images in China, since prior to the fifth century the images in China were virtually all very small, measuring only thirty to forty centimeters (approx. sixteen inches) in height.[5]

In contrast, arguments in support of the Chinese composition theory come primarily from textual evidence. For example, some of the passages in the *Guanjing* are very similar to those found in the earlier Chinese translations of other *sūtras*. This suggests that the Chinese composers of the text adopted these passages during its composition. For example, the passage that reads "the forty-eight vows of Bhikshu Dharmākara" may have been taken from another Pure Land text, the *Wuliang shoufo jing* (Sutra of the Buddha of Infinite Life).[6] In addition, a passage in the *Guanjing*, "We praise the names and the *opening titles* of the twelve divisions of the Mahāyāna sutras" (emphasis added), suggests that it was based on Chinese text, as *sutra* titles of Sanskrit texts do not generally appear at the beginning in a manner paralleling the Chinese texts (Fujita 1976, 126–31).

Other evidence to strengthen the Chinese composition theory is based on a proposal that the *Guanjing* is the result of amalgamation of four previously unrelated parts. On the basis of detailed textual analysis, Yamada Meiji sees the four parts as follows: (1) the preface based on the Ajātaśatru story, (2) the first thirteen visualizations, (3) the last three visualizations on the nine grades of rebirth, and (4) the conclusion. Yamada argues that each of the parts shows a clear preference for one or the other of the Chinese expressions for the Amitābha/Amitāyus Buddha, with one being "Amituofo" (a transliteration of the sound of the Sanskrit word "Amita Buddha") and the other being "Wuliang shoufo" (a Chinese translation of the meaning of Amita Buddha, the Buddha of Infinite Life). Part 1 employs almost exclusively the term "Amituofo," the second "Wuliang shoufo," the third "Amituofo," and fourth "Wuliang shoufo" (Yamada 1976).

While both composition theories have substantial merit, neither side has decisive evidence in its favor. It appears safe to assume that the *Guanjing* transmitted some core ideas, including the Queen Vaidehī narrative that was widely known among Buddhists in India and beyond as well as a form of visualization that was at that time actively practiced in Central Asia. One possible area is Turfan, which is located in the northeast section of the present-day Uyghur Autonomous Region of Xinjiang, China, and which historically has been an important trade center located on the northern branch of the Silk Route. As alluded to earlier, the *Guanjing* probably was not intact as a single entity but was amalgamated into the present form in a cultural milieu outside of India. Moreover, in the process of translation into Chinese, concepts and expressions assumed a Chinese coloring from the numerous Chinese scriptural translations that were consulted, including the other Pure Land texts and visualization *sūtras* discussed later in this chapter.

Mahāyāna Buddhism and the Early Pure Land Schools

The basic teachings of Pure Land Buddhism have their origins in the Indian subcontinent, but it was in China that the tradition emerged as a "school" to become one of the dominant streams in East Asia (Chn.: Jingtu; Jpn.: Jōdo; Kor.: Jeongto; Viet.: Tịnh Độ). Pure Land teachings have also been represented in some significant ways in Tibetan and Nepalese Buddhism.[7] Pure Land Buddhism focuses on a "transcendent" Buddha called Amitāyus (Infinite Life), also known as Amitābha (Infinite Light), and a "transcendent" realm called "Sukhāvatī" (Ultimate Bliss) Pure Land.[8] There are said to be innumerable pure lands, and Sukhāvatī is the specific pure land of Amitāyus.

Pure Land Buddhism belongs to Mahāyāna (Greater Vehicle), which is one of the two major divisions of Buddhism, the other being Theravāda (Teachings of the Elders). Buddhism was introduced into China in the first and second centuries CE via Central Asia (see Wright 1959; Ch'en 1964). This led to the adaptation of Buddhism to indigenous Chinese cultural values and the formation of new schools such as Pure Land and Chan (Jpn.: Zen). These movements were rooted in Mahāyāna Buddhism, which became the dominant forms of Buddhism throughout East Asia, specifically in China, Korea, and Japan, as well as in Vietnam. This is equally true of all the various Chinese schools, with Pure Land and Chan being the most prominent and influential throughout the centuries, especially since the ninth century.

For present purposes, a number of dimensions of Mahāyāna Buddhism are most relevant. Mahāyāna recognizes various transcendent Buddhas and bodhisattvas and associated Buddha-realms. That is, Mahāyāna Buddhism has a stronger devotional dimension with quasi-divine beings who function as salvific figures in the universe, who work selflessly for the alleviation of suffering and the liberation of all beings. Mahāyāna Buddhism also is characterized by a greater degree of inclusivity, specifically with respect to lay participation. From this Buddhist perspective, one does not need to become a renunciant or monastic; rather, householders not only have the capacity for enlightenment, but they also may attain enlightenment while living "ordinary" Buddhist lives. Thus, laypeople have higher status and greater recognition in Mahāyāna than in Theravāda Buddhism.

In addition, Mahāyāna Buddhism emphasizes the bodhisattva ideal. As beings of infinite wisdom and compassion, bodhisattvas postpone their own complete enlightenment (Buddhahood) in order to work selflessly for the liberation of all beings. This commitment is expressed in the famous bodhisattva vow: "No matter how limitless sentient beings are in number, I vow to save them all." Along these lines, one also finds a strong concern for "merit," basically positive karma accrued through virtuous activities, including the possibility of "merit transfer." Higher-level spiritual beings may use their "own" positive karma in order to assist others through merit transference. As discussed later in this chapter, one expression of this spiritual power is Bodhisattva Dharmākara's creation of the Sukhāvatī Pure Land and his ascendance as Buddha Amitāyus. Moreover, those who are reborn in the Pure Land do not stay there to enjoy eternal blissful existence but return as liberated bodhisattvas to other realms, including this earthly realm, to assist in the liberation of other sentient beings

These various dimensions of Mahāyāna Buddhism are connected to the teachings of "emptiness" (Skt.: *śūnyatā*; Chn.: *kong*) and interdependence, which are related to the Buddhist notions of "no-self" (Skt.: *anātman*) and "co-dependent origination" (Skt.: *pratītyasamutpāda*). As one is ultimately empty of "own-being" and, thus, is an integral part of an interconnected whole, one realizes that suffering, karma, enlightenment, and so forth are also not merely one's own. The suffering of other beings becomes one's own suffering, and one's enlightenment must lead to the enlightenment of all beings. This is expressed most clearly in the Mahāyāna Buddhist concern for universal liberation, and Sukhāvatī in the Pure Land tradition represents a realm where one can more easily make progress on the path to enlightenment. It becomes exponentially easier to pursue enlightenment in the Pure Land since beings residing there are freed from the restrictions of earthly life in an environment much more conducive to practice guided by Buddha Amitāyus and bodhisattvas.

In terms of historical development, there is no founder of the Pure Land school in China. However, we may identify a number of key figures. One of the earliest was Lushan Huiyuan (334–416), not to be confused with Jingying Huiyuan (523–592), the author of the earliest extant commentary on the *Guanjing* (see later discussion herein). Lushan Huiyuan was a Chinese Buddhist monk who resided in Donglin si (Temple of the Eastern Forest) on Lushan (Mount Lu; near Jiujiang, Jiangxi). Huiyuan is perhaps best known in Chinese history as the author of the *Shamen bujing wangzhe lun* (On Why Monks Do Not Bow before Kings; dat. 404). Huiyuan and his disciples were among the earliest known Chinese Buddhists to advocate the practice of contemplating Buddha Amitāyus in order to attain birth in the Western Pure Land of Sukhāvatī. Huiyuan's disciples included Huiguan, Sengji, and Fa'an, and he was identified retrospectively as the first Patriarch of Pure Land Buddhism.

As discussed briefly later, other key early figures in the development of Pure Land Buddhism in China included the Chinese monks Tanluan (476–542), Daochuo (562–645), and Shandao (613–681), among others. Tanluan wrote a commentary on the *Larger Sukhāvatī-vyūha Sūtra*. He taught that all beings could be born in the Pure Land of Amitāyus Buddha through sincere contemplation of the Buddha's name (Chn.: *nianfo*; Jpn.: *nembutsu*). He was followed by Daochuo, who advocated that in the Period of the Last Dharma (Chn.: *mofa*; Jpn.: *mappō*) people must rely on the "easy path" to enlightenment by placing complete trust in Amitābha; his view was based on the growing view that people no longer possessed the capacity to follow the more difficult path of personally accomplishing all the requirements for enlightenment by relying only on one's effort. Finally, Shandao, a disciple of Daochuo, primarily lived in Xiangji si (Xiangji Temple; near Xi'an, Shaanxi). He was one of the first individuals to advocate that salvation could be achieved simply by reciting the name of Amitābha Buddha as distinct from contemplation or visualization. He also wrote one of the most influential commentaries on the *Guanjing*. In certain lineage constructions, Tanluan is identified as the third Patriarch, Daochuo as the fourth Patriarch, and Shandao as the fifth Patriarch of Pure Land Buddhism.

As discussed in more detail later, Pure Land Buddhism also became transmitted to and developed in Japan by the famous Japanese Buddhist monks Hōnen (1133–1212), the founder of the Jōdo (Pure Land) school, and Shinran (1173–1263), the founder of Jōdo Shinshū (True Pure Land School).

Pure Land Buddhism eventually became systemized around a family of texts, although it is important to recognize that there were many other contemporaneous Pure Land texts and associated Chinese translations.[9] The systematized Pure Land "canon" includes the so-called Three

Pure Land Sutras, namely, the *Larger Sukhāvatī-vyūha Sūtra*, *Smaller Sukhāvatī-vyūha Sūtra*, and the *Guanjing* (Visualization Sutra), with the latter being our primary text. There are extant Sanskrit versions of the *Larger* and *Smaller Sukhāvatī-vyūha Sūtra*, but not of the *Guanjing*. Both of the Sanskrit texts are titled *Sukhāvatī-vyūha Sūtra*; however, given the length variations, they are conventionally referred to as the *Larger* and *Smaller Sukhāvatī-vyūha Sūtra*, or the *Larger* and *Smaller Pure Land Sūtra*. These two texts primarily describe the formation of the Pure Land, the practices required of the seekers for birth in it, and its exquisite qualities. The *Larger Sukhāvatī-vyūha Sūtra* also describes in a narrative story the transformation of Bodhisattva Dharmākara into Buddha Amitāyus, including the former's forty-eight vows to benefit all sentient beings (see Inagaki 1995, 32–39; also later discussion herein).[10] As the *Guanjing* is our primary text, I provide specific details later.

Along with the *Larger Sukhāvatī-vyūha Sūtra* (Chn.: *Wuliangshou jing*)[11] and the *Smaller Sukhāvatī-vyūha Sūtra* (Chn.: *Amituo jing*),[12] the *Guanjing* has long been considered one of the sacred scriptures of Pure Land Buddhism in East Asia. It requires mentioning that while no Pure Land school as a distinct tradition or doctrinal lineage appears to have developed in India, the Pure Land teachings existed in India, since the aforementioned two *sūtras*, the *Larger* and the *Smaller Sukhāvatī-vyūha*, are extant in Sanskrit. In fact, the idea of the existence of "transcendent" realms (Buddha-realms) far beyond the Sahā realm (this earthly realm) presided by "transcendent" Buddhas can be traced back as early as the second century BCE, having been advocated by pre-Mahāyāna schools such as the Mahāsaṃghikas and the Lokottaravādins.[13] However, it was not until the sixth century in China when we see the emergence of Pure Land Buddhism as a distinct tradition, as one among the various new Chinese schools of Mahāyāna Buddhism. These schools became the dominant traditions of Buddhism throughout East Asia and in the modern world.

Pure Land Buddhism can be defined as beliefs and practices that espouse for its aspirants the realization of the stage of non-retrogression (*avaivartika*) after death in a Pure Land called Sukhāvatī (Realm of Joy) or in the present life, as in the case of later Japanese Pure Land proponents such as Shinran (1173–1263).[14] When an aspirant attains this stage of non-retrogression, he or she does not fall backward to lower levels of spiritual development and becomes guaranteed of eventual realization of full enlightenment, the ultimate goal of Pure Land Buddhists in keeping with the goal common to all Buddhists.

The Pure Land *sūtras* describe the Sukhāvatī Pure Land as being located billions of Buddha-realms away in the western direction from this realm called "Sahā." Amitāyus (Infinite Light) Buddha or Amitābha (Infinite Life) Buddha (henceforth, Amitāyus, except when Amitābha is more appropriate) is the "transcendent" Buddha who presides over this Sukhāvatī Pure Land.

It needs to be qualified here that Amitābha and Sukhāvatī are among innumerable transcendent Buddhas and pure lands in Buddhist cosmology, including Akṣobhya Buddha and the Abhirati Pure Land located in the eastern direction (see Nattier 2000). However, on account of its unparalleled popularity in East Asia, "Pure Land Buddhism" normally refers to a tradition centered on a *specific* Buddha (Amitāyus) and a *specific* pure land (Sukhāvatī).

According to the central mythic narrative told in the *Larger Sukhāvatī-vyūha Sūtra*, Amitābha established the Sukhāvatī Pure Land as a result of fulfilling his forty-eight vows (*praṇidhāna*) to lead all sentient beings to realize perfect enlightenment in the Pure Land (see Inagaki 1995, 12–18). He made the vows when he was still a human being and bodhisattva named Dharmākara

(Storehouse of Dharma); his vows were followed by innumerable eons of disciplined cultivation until all aims of his vows were consummated. Having fulfilled his vows, he became Amitāyus Buddha and has dwelt in Sukhāvatī for the past ten eons to preach the Dharma (teachings) and to guide aspirants to reach full enlightenment.

Those born in the Sukhāvatī Pure Land do not enjoy lives of luxury and bliss, but they acquire an ideal environment for consummating their Buddhist practices that they could not fulfill in their earthly life. In this sense, Sukhāvatī is not a "paradise" but more of an ideal "training center" for realizing enlightenment under the tutelage of a Buddha and bodhisattvas in an environment freed from the trials and tribulations of earthly life. Birth in the Pure Land guarantees the attainment of the stage of non-retrogression and the eventual realization of the Mahāyāna goal of perfect enlightenment.

Upon attaining enlightenment, many go forward as bodhisattvas to other realms, including back to this earthly Sahā realm, to carry out the bodhisattva task of leading others to birth in Sukhāvatī and ultimately to enlightenment. This is explained in Dharmākara's twenty-second vow:

> For they will wear the armor of great vows, accumulate merits, deliver all beings from birth-and-death, visit Buddha-lands to perform bodhisattva practices, make offerings to Buddhas, Tathāgatas, throughout the ten directions, enlighten unaccountable sentient beings as numerous as the sands of the River Ganges, and establish them in the highest, perfect Enlightenment. (*Larger Sukhāvatī-vyūha Sūtra*; Inagaki 1995, 35)

This description, based on the mythic narrative, refers primarily to how the Pure Land was created and what happens to the aspirants *after* they are born in the Pure Land. However, the Pure Land *sūtra*s also discuss at length the practices needed while in this Sahā realm *before* one gains birth in the Pure Land. These include a wide range of practices: from visualization through observation of precepts to virtuous acts and oral recitation. The *Guanjing* in particular focuses on this point, for it exhorts aspirants to engage in a number of practices, most notably visualization.

Here it is important to note that the *Guanjing* dates to a historical moment before the emergence in China of the Pure Land movement itself. We may thus recognize two contexts in which to locate our primary text. As mentioned, the first is fifth-century China in which Central Asian missionary-monks like Kālayaśas translated, composed, and transmitted visualization texts such as the *Guanjing*. In terms of visualization and translation projects, this sociohistorical moment included a larger family of texts focusing on Amitāyus and Sukhāvatī.

The second context centers on the emergence and development of the Pure Land movement in China. Beginning around the same time as Kālayaśas's translation of the *Guanjing*, but becoming more established in the sixth and seventh centuries, the Pure Land movement involved Chinese monastics and laypeople increasingly committed to devotion to Amitāyus. In the earliest stages, this included both visualization and recitation practices. In this context, the *Guanjing* became the key Pure Land visualization manual, while the *Larger Sukhāvatī-vyūha Sūtra* and *Smaller Sukhāvatī-vyūha Sūtra* became key works describing the Pure Land. That is, the *Guanjing* increasingly became part of a standardized "Pure Land Buddhist canon." These were the textual sources that formed the foundation of the movement, at least on an elite monastic level. We may thus recognize the first context, the translation of the *Guanjing* by Kālayaśas, as laying one of the foundations for the second context, the emergence and development of the Pure Land as a distinct movement.

Seeking the Pure Land in Medieval China

The *Guanjing* advocates two categories of practice, which I classify as "ethical" and "spiritual" in nature. Ethical practice, termed the "three pure acts" or "three acts of merit," is discussed in the prologue section of this *sūtra* (see later discussion herein). In response to Queen Vaidehī's plight and her plea to be born in a better place, the Buddha[15] prescribes to Queen Vaidehī the three acts as a means of being born in the Pure Land.

The three pure acts include the following:

1. Caring for one's parents, attending to one's teachers and elders, compassionately refraining from killing, and carrying out the Ten Good Deeds

2. Taking refuge in the Three Treasures of the Buddha (the enlightened person), the Dharma (teachings taught by the Buddha), and the Sangha (the community of monks and nuns); keeping the various precepts; and refraining from breaking the rules of conduct

3. Raising the aspiration for enlightenment, believing in the law of causality, reciting the Mahāyāna *sūtra*s, and encouraging those who practice the teachings

The Ten Good Deeds alluded to here involve refraining from the following: (1) killing, (2) stealing, (3) committing sexual misconduct, (4) telling lies, (5) being duplicitous, (6) slandering, (7) equivocating, (8) being covetous, (9) being hateful, and (10) holding wrong views.

The Buddha then proceeds to prescribe the second category of practices, which I am calling "spiritual." There are in fact two forms within this practice, namely, visualization (*guan*; Jpn.: *kan*) and oral recitation (*nianfo*; Jpn.: *nembutsu*), which literally means "recollecting or remembering the Buddha." The primary concern of the *Guanjing* is, of course, visualization, and it devotes the bulk of its space to it. Oral recitation is referred to briefly, but its significance lies in the fact that the text is the earliest known Pure Land *sūtra* to mention this form of practice, which became the more dominant and pervasive form of practice within Pure Land Buddhism in the subsequent centuries and even to this day.

Let us first examine the practice of visualization. The sixteen visualizations discussed in the *Guanjing* are essentially distinguished on the basis of the various objects being visualized. The first visualization on the setting sun differs from all others since its object is the only one located in this Sahā world, while the objects of the remaining fifteen visualizations are of the Sukhāvatī Pure Land. The sixteen visualizations are as follows: (1) the setting sun, (2) water, (3) ground, (4) trees, (5) pond, (6) towers, and so on, (7) lotus throne, (8) images of Amitāyus and two bodhisattvas, (9) actual Amitāyus (the Buddha of Infinite Light), (10) Avalokiteśvara (the Bodhisattva of Compassion), (11) Mahāsthāmaprāpta (the Bodhisattva of Wisdom), (12) aspirants being reborn in the Pure land, (13) images of Amitāyus and two bodhisattvas in a comprehensive manner, (14) aspirants of the highest grade, (15) aspirants of the middle grade, and (16) aspirants of the lowest grade.[16]

In performing visualization, a practitioner can be seen to generally undergo four stages in its deepening process. While not all the visualizations in this *sūtra* are described as undergoing the exact same process, the four stages include imagining or forming of image (*xiang*), inspection (*guan*), vision (*jian*), and *samādhi* (*sanmei*) (Pas 1995, 174–78). First, one takes any one of the sixteen objects and forms its image in one's mind. Second, once the image is clearly formed, one carefully and meticulously inspects the detailed features of the formed image. Third, when this inspection is properly carried out, the vision of the object appears clearly before the practitioner, whether the eyes are open or shut.

As the vision is fully consummated, it leads to *samādhi* (meditative concentration), whereby the practitioner experiences psychological and spiritual tranquility and the sense of being embraced in great compassion, which is none other than the Buddha's mind. The following passage from the ninth visualization of the *Guanjing* describes this *samādhi* experience:

> Those who have envisioned them see all the Buddhas of the ten directions. Because they see the Buddhas, this is called the Buddha-Recollection Samādhi. By perceiving these, one also realizes the Buddha's mind. The Buddha's mind is great compassion. It embraces sentient beings with unconditional benevolence.

The Pure Land soteriological scheme generally conceived such *samādhi* states realized through visualization as assurances to practitioners that they were, indeed, guaranteed birth in the Pure Land at the end of their present lives and their ultimate perfect enlightenment.[17]

In my view, practitioners who attain this level of enlightenment have realized a certain insight that adequately fulfills their soteriological needs. That is to say, they have already realized their primary spiritual goal and, thus, the issue of birth in the Pure Land becomes a secondary concern. They would, of course, not refuse to go on to the Pure Land because they would be guaranteed not to retrogress to lower spiritual levels and be able to realize full enlightenment in an ideal setting. Nevertheless, the question of whether or not they are born in the Pure Land has become for them neither urgent nor a primary concern in the present life. As the two *Guanjing* passages cited at the end of this introduction suggest, through visualization a practitioner arrives at a state in which he awakens to the fact that "Amitāyus is not far away" but right here and that "his mind is itself the Buddha." These are indications, in my view, of some level of awakening experience.

Located in the context of early Mahāyāna Buddhist history, the Pure Land visualization documented in the *Guanjing* is one among the meditational techniques that sought *samādhi* states. These include, for example, the *śūramgama-samādhi* (concentration of the heroic Buddha in which defilements are destroyed) and the *pratyutpanna-samādhi* (concentration in which the Buddhas stand before one).[18] The textual background and content of the *Guanjing* suggest that it belongs to a group of so-called visualization *sūtra*s devoted to bodhisattvas and Buddhas. These visualization techniques gained popularity in India and, more notably, in Central Asia, particularly from about the fourth century CE forward. The Central Asian popularity of visualization may be partially seen in the inordinately large number of Central Asians involved in translating "visualization sutras" into Chinese in the early fifth century.[19]

We shall now look at the other spiritual practice, that is, oral recitation. Compared to the more difficult visualization, oral recitation is more accessible to aspirants because it can be carried out by virtually anyone without any discipline, even by those who are "spiritually inferior." In fact, the *Guanjing* suggests exactly that. Those on the lowest level of the nine grades of birth, who have committed the Five Grave Offenses (killing an arhat [worthy one; saint], killing one's father, killing one's mother, injuring a Buddha, or bringing discord to the Buddhist monastic community) and who cannot carry out the Ten Good Deeds, are instructed to concentrate their thought on the Buddha, but they are unable to carry out even this more basic practice. Thus, they are instructed one-on-one by their virtuous teachers to simply recite with sincere mind the name of Amitāyus, *namo Amituofo* (I take refuge in Buddha Amitāyus). In so doing, they are said to eradicate their karmic retribution of eight billion eons and are assured of birth in the Pure Land. Recitation, thus, brought with it the eradication of karmic retribution.

Examples of the prototype of recitation are also found in earlier pre-Mahāyāna Buddhist scriptures, but in most cases they involved elements of a magical nature that warded off imminent dangers. In one of the major early texts, the *Mahāvastu* (Great Story), for example, five hundred merchants in a boat were devoured by a giant fish but were saved when collectively they recited aloud: "We take refuge in the Buddha" (Komaru 1985, 430).[20]

In contrast, the type of recitation found in the *Guanjing* differs in its nature and application from the earlier worldly, self-serving forms. Rather, it is related to a genre of *sūtras* that dealt primarily with contemplation (Skt.: *anusmṛti*; Chn.: *nian*) and with Buddha names (*Buddhanāma*), which also advocated the type of recitation found in our primary text. Almost invariably these *sūtras* closely associated recitation with the practice of repentance (Chn.: *chanhui*). Recitation and repentance together led to the elimination of karmic retribution. In some instances, these practices also led to the realization of some levels of *samādhi*.

However, in the case of the *Guanjing*, recitation led not to *samādhi* but to confirmation of aspirants' belief in birth in the Sukhāvatī Pure Land. In either case, recitation had the capacity to lead aspirants to some form of elevated state of mind or spiritual experience that was understood as having eradicated karmic retribution and assuring birth in the Pure Land. Thus, this extremely accessible form of practice helped to encourage and perhaps to enable a much broader range of aspirants to realize birth in the Pure Land where they attained the ultimate goal of all Mahāyāna Buddhists: the attainment of Buddhahood and complete enlightenment.

Pure Land Visualization according to the *Guanjing*

The *Guanjing* begins with a prologue of the story of King Ajātaśatru and his parents, former King Bimbisāra and Lady Vaidehī. Upon learning from Devadatta about his father's failed attempt to kill him at birth, Ajātaśatru is enraged and, in effect, carries out a *coup d'état*. He then imprisons his father with the intent of starving him to death. His mother, Lady Vaidehī, however, succeeds in keeping Bimbisāra alive by secretly feeding him during her visits.

When Ajātaśatru discovers his mother's clandestine activity, he imprisons her as well out of extreme anger. Deeply distressed by her predicament, in which she and her husband are imprisoned by their own son, Vaidehī turns to Śākyamuni Buddha for counsel. The Buddha miraculously appears in her prison cell with two of his main disciples, Mahāmaudgalyāyana and Ānanda, as

Mahāyāna Buddhist Visualization / 417

Figure 9.1. Taima (Tall Hemp) Mandala[21]
Source: Metropolitan Museum of Art (New York, NY)

well as with other guardian gods. Then, prostrating and weeping bitterly before the Buddha, Vaidehī says to the Buddha, "O World-Honored One, what bad karma did I commit in former lives that I have given birth to such an evil son?" She then expresses her desire to take leave of this world and to be born in a realm with no suffering.

Then the Buddha, through his transcendental powers, illuminates the countless realms in the ten quarters of the universe. Vaidehī selects Amitāyus's Sukhāvati Pure Land as the realm of her choice.

The Buddha then proceeds to expound the required practices for aspirants' rebirth. As previously discussed, they include the "three pure acts" that are ethical in nature, for example, the caring for one's parents and teachers, the adherence to precepts, and the reciting of Mahāyāna *sūtra*s. The Buddha then leads Vaidehī and others to see Amitābha's realm and, in that process, to attain a level of awakening called the "Insight of Non-Arising of *Dharma*s," in which one realizes the insubstantiality or emptiness (Skt.: *śūnyatā*; Chn.: *kong*) of all phenomena.

Concerned for the salvation of future beings, who will not have the benefit of the Buddha's direct instructions, Vaidehī inquires about the method for their rebirth. In response, the Buddha proceeds to instruct her in the sixteen kinds of visualization. As previously mentioned, the first thirteen begin with the visualization of the setting sun in this earthly Sahā realm; then move to the physical features in the Pure Land such as the ground, trees, and lakes; and conclude with the features of Buddha Amitāyus and his attendants, Bodhisattva Avalokiteśvara and Mahāsthāmaprāpta.

The last three visualizations have as their object the people of the nine grades of rebirths, the level of their spiritual attainment, the quality of their death-bed welcome, and the length of time spent in Sukhāvatī before hearing the Dharma and attaining complete enlightenment. This section on the sixteen visualizations, which is four times longer than the prologue section, comprises the main body and the primary aim of this *sūtra*.

(1) Setting sun (in this world)	(9) Actual Amitāyus, the Buddha of Infinite Light
(2) Water (in the Pure Land; the same holds true for visualizations 3–12)	(10) Avalokiteśvara, the Bodhisattva of Compassion
(3) Ground	(11) Mahāsthāmaprāpta, the Bodhisattva of Wisdom
(4) Trees	(12) Aspirants being reborn in the Pure land
(5) Pond	(13) Images of Amitāyus and two bodhisattvas in a comprehensive manner
(6) Towers, etc.	(14) Aspirants of the highest grade (for being born in the Pure Land; the same holds true for visualizations 15 and 16)
(7) Lotus throne	(15) Aspirants of the middle grade
(8) Images of Amitāyus and two bodhisattvas	(16) Aspirants of the lowest grade

Figure 9.2. Sixteen Visualizations according to the *Guanjing*

In the epilogue, which is one-third the length of the prologue, Vaidehī attains the Insight of Non-Arising of *Dharma*s, while her five-hundred female attendants are prophesized by the Buddha that their birth in the Pure Land is imminent and guaranteed.

Visualizing Amitāyus Buddha in Later Pure Land Buddhism

The legacy of the *Guanjing* lies in two ways, though the two are not unrelated. The first way has to do with the scholastic tradition, in which numerous commentaries were written on this *sūtra* in East Asia, particularly in China. The second way lies in the area of living practice, as for centuries up to the present-day Pure Land followers, laymen and laywomen as well as some monks and nuns, have engaged in the oral recitation of the name of Amitāyus. Let us first take up the scholastic tradition.

In China, from the sixth to the thirteenth century, at least forty commentaries on the *Guanjing* are known to have been written. Most of them were compiled prior to the year 800 CE. They include commentaries by such eminent figures as Jingying Huiyuan (523–592), Tiantai Zhiyi (538–597), Jizang (549–623), and Shandao (613–681). Briefly, Huiyuan, Zhiyi, and Jizang were towering Buddhist figures of the sixth century with numerous writings to their credit. Huiyuan is said to have been affiliated with the advocates of the Yogācāra or Consciousness-Only schools, specifically Dilun and Shelun. As discussed later, his commentaries include the earliest extant one of the *Guanjing* (see Tanaka 1990). Zhiyi and Jizang are the founders of Tiantai (Celestial Terrace) and Sanlun (Three Treatise; Madhyamaka) schools, respectively, and they also have commentaries on the *Guanjing* attributed to them. Shandao, who came a hundred years later, is regarded as one of the most prominent Pure Land proponents in East Asia (see Pas 1995), and his influence is felt even today in China and, particularly, in Japan. More commentaries were also composed in Korea and Japan.

Among the Chinese texts, Huiyuan's commentary played a pivotal role in helping to bring attention to the *Guanjing*, which, by all accounts, was not very well known within the Buddhist community in sixth-century China. It was a "minor" text compared to the likes of *Nirvana Sūtra* and the *Lotus Sūtra*. Huiyuan thus helped to bring the text out from the corner closer to center stage. Huiyuan accomplished this by constructing an acceptable doctrinal framework that placed the teachings of this *sūtra* within a wider Buddhist context. This work then went on to serve as a basic referent for subsequent commentaries, so that, for example, the commentary by Shandao approximately one hundred years later did not have to explain or justify its categories and issues, because they had already gained legitimacy with the commentarial tradition that Huiyuan had established (Tanaka 1990, 108–12).

For example, Huiyuan employed the category of the "five essentials" (*wuyao*) to assess the *Guanjing* along with other major *sūtra*s of his time. The five essentials included the following: (1) whether the teachings are Mahāyāna or Hīnayāna; (2) whether the teaching is limited, gradual, or sudden; (3) the main import of the *sūtra*; (4) the categories on which the title of the *sūtra* is based; and (5) whether the teaching comes from the Buddha, his sagely disciples, holy recluses, celestial spirits, or apparitional beings. Huiyuan assessed the five essentials of the *Guanjing*, which are that it is (1) Mahāyāna teaching, (2) sudden teaching, (3) Buddha-Visualization Samādhi (*guanfo sanmei*), (4) person (Buddha) and doctrine (Discourse on the Visualization of the Buddha of Immeasurable Life), and (5) taught by the Buddha (Tanaka 1990, 117).

Another major category that drew the attention of the commentators was that of the "nine grades of birth in the Pure Land." In the *Guanjing*, the nine grades of birth are distinguished based on the quality of practice and the level of attainment. The highest is the "highest level of the highest grade of birth," and the lowest is the "lowest level of the lowest grade." Huiyuan proceeded to rank these nine grades within the broader, well-known Buddhist doctrinal framework, rendering the highest level of the highest grade as being equal to the Fourth Bhūmi Stage. On the other hand, the middle level of the middle grade was seen to be equal to the Outer Pṛthagjanas (*fanfu*; ordinary beings), while the lowest level of the lowest grade was deemed to be "those who have begun to train in the Mahāyāna path" (Tanaka 1990, 81–92).

This ranking of the nine grades of birth captured the imagination and the interest of virtually all subsequent commentators through the centuries, all of whom vied to put forth their own version of the ranking. Among them, the commentary by Shandao played a vital role for not only the Chinese Pure Land tradition but also for the Japanese Pure Land tradition. In essence, Shandao infused a stronger element of the workings of the "other-power" dimensions of Amitāyus, for he saw the Pure Land teachings to be for those ordinary beings of diminished capabilities (compared to monks and nuns). Consequently, he ranked the nine grades of birth much lower than Huiyuan. For example, the highest level of the highest grade was not of the Fourth Bhūmi Stage but a mere Mahāyāna Pṛthagjanas. As for the lowest level of the lowest grade, rather than Huiyuan's "those who have begun to train in the Mahāyāna path," Shandao saw them as being ordinary beings who commit such evil acts as the Five Grave Offenses and the Ten Evils (the failure to carry out the Ten Good Deeds discussed earlier) (see Tanaka 1990, 83–86; Pas 1995, 215–23).

Shandao thus enlarged the audience of those who could benefit from the Pure Land teachings, including those who commit the Five Grave Offenses, which included the killing of one's parents and injuring of the Buddha. To make this "soteriological egalitarianism" possible, Shandao simplified the practice for the aspirants by allowing for oral recitation of the name of Amitāyus and not requiring the conducting of Buddha visualization to which the *Guanjing* was devoted. Having so said, oral recitation was similarly found in the *Guanjing* as seen in the passage regarding the lowest of the lowest grade. A good teacher tells a person in this group that if he cannot concentrate on the Buddha, he can recite with sincerity and numerous times the Buddha's name:

> The good teacher then advises him, "If you cannot concentrate on the Buddha then you should say instead, 'Homage to Amitāyus Buddha.' In this way, he sincerely and continuously says, 'Homage to Amitāyus Buddha' (*namo Amituofo*) ten times. Because he calls the Buddha's Name, with each repetition the evil karma that would bind him to birth and death for eighty *koṭi*s of *kalpa*s is extinguished. When he comes to die, he sees before him a golden lotus flower like the disk of the sun, and in an instant he is born within a lotus bud in the Land of Utmost Bliss."[22] (sec. 30)

Shandao strove to make this simpler form of practice possible in his other writings and succeeded in spreading this teaching in and around Chang'an, then the capital of the Tang dynasty (618–907).

It must, however, be noted that Shandao's preference for the simpler oral recitation was made possible by his doctrinal shift in emphasizing the workings of Amitāyus's Vow Power to save all beings who meet the various conditions as taught in the other Pure Land text, the *Larger Sukhāvatī-vyūha Sūtra*. While the *sūtra* passage just quoted appears to argue that oral recitation by itself was sufficient for birth in the Pure Land, Shandao drew on the authority of the *Larger Sukhāvatī-vyūha Sūtra* along with the *Smaller Sukhāvatī-vyūha Sūtra* to buttress his advocacy of oral recitation (Pas 1995).

Thus, it is important to keep in mind that this simpler form of practice became widely accepted because, in part, Shandao was able to tie it to the workings of the other-power of Amitāyus Buddha. A case in point is seen in Shandao's reading of the eighteenth of the forty-eight vows made by Amitāyus when he was a bodhisattva named Dharmākara. He pledged,

> If, when I attain Buddhahood, sentient beings in the lands of the ten directions who sincerely and joyfully entrust themselves to me, desire to be born in my land, and call[23] my Name even ten times should not be born there, may I not attain perfect Enlightenment. Excluded, however, are those who commit the five grave offenses[24] and abuse the right Dharma. (*Larger Sukhāvatī-vyūha Sūtra*; see Inagaki 1995, 34)

With regard to this emphasis on the other-power dimension, some modern interpreters in the West see an influence of Nestorian Christianity,[25] which had made its way to this part of the world by the seventh century. However, there has been no convincing evidence to support this view. Most specialists see this development as a natural outcome of the Mahāyāna Buddhist teachings of ultimate reality expressed, for example, as *dharmakāya* (Dharma-body), which contains a function that automatically reaches out to sentient beings as expression of its great compassion.

Shandao's legacy remained significant in the subsequent centuries of Chinese Buddhism leading up to the present. From the tenth century onward, Buddhist practice came to be limited to Chan or Pure Land regardless of the various teachings that Buddhists primarily followed. Most monks and nuns carried out Chan practices, consisting mostly of sitting meditation, but they at times also engaged in the Pure Land practices of visualization and oral recitation.

On the other hand, many laypeople engaged in Pure Land devotional practices consisting primarily of oral recitation of the name of Amitāyus, *namo Amituofo*. This tradition can be seen today in Taiwanese Buddhism where many lay visitors to the temples are heard orally reciting this sacred phrase. In fact, the popularity of this phrase has become one of the main forms of greeting each other in an ordinary daily context as people put their palms together to utter "(namo) Amituofo." This is carried on outside any religious setting in the same way that speakers of English greet each other by saying, "Hello. How are you?"

Now, let us turn briefly to Korea. In Korea, the Pure Land practice of oral recitation has had a long history within its Buddhist development. As a case in point, Wonhyo (617–686), who continues to be revered today as a preeminent Buddhist figure in Korean Buddhist history, made enormous contributions to the propagation of Pure Land practice of oral recitation. As the well-known story of his life shows, Wonhyo left the monastic life on account of having broken the monastic precepts when he fathered a son. He then traveled among the people living in the thousands of hamlets of the Korean countryside, teaching them to recite orally the name of Amitāyus for gaining birth in the Pure Land. His proslytizing effort appears to have been enormously successful; modern historian Lee Ki-baek has gone so far as to postulate that eight or nine of every ten Koreans were converted to Buddhism as a result of Wonhyo's effort (Lee 1984, 83). Thus, Pure Land practice would end up becoming extremely popular in Korea, not only as a pervasive mode of practice for the common people but also as vital elements in the practices of many of the monastics, similar to the pattern that we saw in China. The sounds of oral recitation of the name "Amit'a bul" (Amitāyus Buddha) can be heard today in many of the temples in Korea (Tanaka 2005, 59–60).

A similar situation is evident in Vietnam. Oral recitation is a practice also found in contemporary Vietnamese Buddhism, for Pure Land teachings have enjoyed broad support through the centuries. This has led Cuong Tu Nguyen, a contemporary scholar, to make the observation, "Pure Land is probably the most common form of practice in Vietnamese Buddhism" (1997, 359). It is, therefore, not surprising to hear today a resounding melodic reciting of "A-di-da Phat" (Amitāyus Buddha) by the devotees at a Buddhist service at the Duc Vien Temple in San Jose, California. That the recent immigrants exhibit the oral recitation of the name of Amitāyus is a testimony to the ongoing popularity of this form of Pure Land practice in Vietnam that harkens back to the *Guanjing* (Tanaka 2005, 72–74).

In the case of Japan, Pure Land Buddhism, or Jōdo, developed into the most dominant form of Buddhism. Unlike in China, Vietnam, and Korea, Pure Land became a distinct school with large independent institutions.[26] The Kamakura period (1185–1333) is commonly regarded as the period when Pure Land Buddhism reached its maturity as an independent school by limiting its practice to that of oral recitation (*nembutsu*). This focus on one practice was motivated by the supposed arrival in 1052 of the Period of the Last Dharma (*mappō*), also referred to as the "end of the Dharma," during which it was believed that no other efficacious practice existed besides oral recitation. The prominent figures at the forefront of this movement were Hōnen (1133–1212) and Shinran (1173–1263).

Hōnen was a prominent monk of the Tendai (Chn.: Tiantai) school, which was the dominant school at the time. Despite his enormous effort, he failed to find spiritual resolution, but within his intense spiritual struggle, he came upon a passage from Shandao's commentary to the *Guanjing*, which read as follows:

> Only repeat the name of Amitābha with all your heart. Whether walking or standing, sitting or lying down, never cease the practice of it even for a moment. This is the very work that unfailingly issues in salvation, for it is in accordance with the Original Vow of that Buddha. (Taishō Canon 37.1753: 272)

This was the very answer for which he was searching, which soon prompted him to leave the Tendai teachings in order to focus on Pure Land teachings. And in 1175, Hōnen and his followers proclaimed themselves as a distinct school of Buddhism.

Hōnen struck a responsive chord, especially among the masses who had been relatively ignored by the older schools, whose biggest supporters were the imperial court, aristocrats, and the privileged classes. Hōnen's success in gaining new followers made the older Buddhist schools, including Tendai, nervous as they petitioned the civil authorities to restrict the new movement (SETP 1998, 6).

Despite the attempt to block Hōnen's following, the old schools were not able to stem the tide of the new movement. The new simple and caring message was a welcome break from the old elitist teachings. The followers simply had to recite the name of Amitāyus with faith in the Buddha's compassionate vow. The Pure Land teachings were now open to all people regardless of social class, education, wealth, and spiritual abilities. Hōnen's teachings even embraced those whose work made them violate the precepts, such as fishermen and the emerging Samurai (military) class, who had to routinely break the precept of not killing. After Hōnen's death in 1212, his disciples spread the teachings throughout the Japanese islands, forming an institution that survives today as the Jōdo (Chn.: Jingtu) school, the Japanese Pure Land tradition (see SETP 1998; Blum 2002).

One of these disciples was Shinran, who is the founder of Jōdo Shinshū (True Pure Land School), also referred to as Shin Buddhism, which is today the largest Buddhist school in Japan. Shinran continued the legacy of oral recitative *nembutsu* but placed greater emphasis than his teacher on the transformative experience in this life called *shinjin* (faith-mind), which assured one of birth in the Pure Land immediately upon death. This *shinjin*, he claimed, was the result of the workings of Amitāyus and not due to the self-effort of the aspirant, for he believed that humans were incapable of saving themselves, particularly in the Period of the Last Dharma. Thus, we see here an example of Shinran's radical other-power understanding that traces back to Shandao's teaching and to the Pure Land *sūtras*, including the *Guanjing*. Furthermore, Shinran's reliance on other-power is reminiscent of the emphasis on faith and antinomianism put forth a couple of centuries after Shinran by the Protestant reformer Martin Luther (1483–1546). There is an emphasis on faith and grace in Shinran's vision.

There are two further qualities about Shinran that are significant in the history of Pure Land Buddhism. One has to do with his deep awareness of the imperfections (reminiscent of "sin" in Christianity) of human nature. In an admission about himself, he wrote the following: "I know how grievous it is that I, Gutoku (stubble-haired ignorant one) Shinran, am sinking in an immense ocean of desires and attachments and am lost in vast mountains of fame and advantage" (Hirota 1997, 125). This realization about himself was a product of intense self-cultivation during the twenty years of his early life as a monk. Despite his greatest efforts, there was no satisfying result. Shinran found that his greed, hatred, and ignorance were deep-seated, without any hope of eradication through his own effort. This realization, however, was accompanied by the salvific compassion of Amitāyus, who accepted Shinran unconditionally precisely on account of his imperfect and foolish qualities.

The second feature of Shinran pertains to his leaving the celibate life to marry and to have a family, reminiscent of Wonhyo in Korea six hundred years earlier. Shinran was encouraged by Hōnen, who placed the greatest importance on finding a way of life that would allow one to recite the *nembutsu* and regarded the issue of celibacy and marriage a secondary concern; if one could not practice *nembutsu* as a celibate, one was encouraged to do so by getting married, and if unable to do so by being married, one was exhorted to recite it as a celibate.

As a result, the Jōdo Shinshū school has maintained the only tradition of married priests from its inception, while all other schools in Japan came to recognize married priests only since the Meiji period (1868–1912). It should, however, be noted that even though Shinran married and had children, he did not regard himself simply as a layman either, for he invested his self-identity in the phrase "neither monk nor lay" (*hisō-hizoku*) by which he often referred to himself.

Today, Jōdo Shinshū together with Hōnen's Jōdo school and other smaller Pure Land schools comprise the largest branch of Japanese Buddhism, claiming close to 40 percent of all Buddhists.

And what they have in common is their teaching and practice rooted in the *Guanjing*, particularly the practice of orally reciting the name of Buddha Amitāyus.

While oral recitation continues to be practiced widely in Japan as well as in China, Korea, and Vietnam, visualization appears to have ceased to be practiced in the Pure Land traditions. This is certainly true in the Jōdo and Jōdo Shinshū schools in Japan, whose teachings rest on the fundamental idea that recitation is appropriate but visualization is beyond the capabilities of ordinary beings fraught with imperfections.

The same can be said for contemporary Pure Land practices in other countries, where lay devotees to the temples are seen reciting the name of Buddha Amitāyus as an important element in their devotional activities. Monks and nuns also carry out oral recitation during their devotional worship, but when conducting their meditative practices, they normally carry out traditional Chan (Zen) style meditation, not Pure Land visualization. This is understandable because the contemporary monks and nuns in China, Korea, and Vietnam are generally ordained in the Chan lineages. It thus appears that visualization practices have ceased to be practiced within the Pure Land schools in contemporary East Asia; it is clearly the case in Japan.[27]

Today, the largest institution to represent the Jōdo Shinshū tradition outside Japan is the Buddhist Churches of America (BCA) with its headquarters in San Francisco, overseeing approximately one hundred temples and branches.[28] It also sponsors a seminary and graduate school, the Institute of Buddhist Studies (IBS), located in Berkeley, California. With its beginnings in 1899, the BCA temples made English their official language in 1944 and now see a growing number of priests and members who are not of Japanese ethnicity. The process of "Americanization" can be seen in BCA's active role in the Boy Scouts of America programs and the Institute of Buddhist Studies being certified to train Buddhist chaplains for the US armed forces.

With regard to its teachings and practices, there have been moves in recent years to adopt "meditation" in religious services as well as in spiritual practice sessions. This has alarmed the headquarters in Kyoto, for it is seen as "self-power" or Zen practice, thus deviating from the central doctrine of "other-power." Nevertheless, advocates in the BCA continue to promote meditation as "skillful means" in response to the overwhelming interest in meditation by those interested in Buddhism, with the ultimate aim of leading them to the Jōdo Shinshū teachings and insight.

Within this movement, there has not been any adoption of the traditional Pure Land visualization as seen in the *Guanjing*. Certainly, some have called for adopting Pure Land visualization rather than going "outside" the tradition to imitate Zen and Theravāda types of meditation.[29] They point to the presence of visualizations in the *Guanjing*, which after all is one of their canonical texts. However, here again, the Jōdo Shinshū tradition from its very inception had adopted oral recitation but not visualization, thus leaving BCA advocates of meditation without a doctrinal basis or the actual know-how for "resuscitating" the visualization practice. A possibility does remain in reaching out to the Tendai practice in Japan, which continues to preserve a form of Pure Land meditative practice.[30]

In assessing the status of *Guanjing* in the contemporary world, we cannot ignore its continuing vital role as a canonical *sūtra* of Pure Land Buddhism in East Asia and, as such, as particularly esteemed in the Jōdo and Jōdo Shinshū schools. Partly for that reason, it was first translated into English as early as 1894 by Takakusu Junjirō for the Sacred Books of the East series published by Oxford University Press (see Takakusu 1965). The *Guanjing* was included among the 139 texts from the Taishō Canon to be translated into English for the Tripitaka Translation

Series project sponsored by Bukkyo Dendo Kyokai (BDK) and the Numata Center for Buddhist Translation and Research (Berkeley, CA). It was translated by Inagaki Hisao and has appeared in *The Three Pure Land Sutras* (1995). The inclusion of this *sūtra* in two of the most prominent translation series reflects its importance among the Buddhist texts. To reinforce this view, there have been other English translations in recent years (see RUTC 1984; Gomez 1996).

The *Guanjing* has had an impact in the realm of art as seen earlier in the Taima Mandala. Similar mural representations of the Pure Land and the sixteen visualizations have been found on the walls of the Dunhuang caves (Gansu, China). In modern times, this *sūtra* has continued to inspire works of art in the creation of these murals among modern artists, particularly in Japan. Furthermore, though not in the realm of art, the story of King Ajātaśatru that appears in the opening section of the *Guanjing* inspired Kosawa Heisaku (1897–1968), a Japanese psychoanalyst and a direct disciple of Sigmund Freud (1856–1939), to expound a theory called the "Ajase (Ajātaśatru) complex." In contrast to the emphasis on the father-child relationship in the Oedipus complex, Kosawa's Ajase complex focused on the mother-child relationship, which he deemed was more relevant for Japanese culture. It has exerted a substantial influence on some segments of the psychotherapeutic community in Japan and has even attracted academic interest overseas (see Okonogi and Kitayama 2001).[31]

Between Consciousness and Reality

In the long history of Pure Land Buddhist development, scholar-monks discussed and debated on the question of the "whereabouts of the Pure Land." The debate primarily centered on two conflicting interpretations, which I shall refer to as "objective" and "subjective." There are other related sets of terms that characterize this relationship, including form and formless, mythological and demythological, celestial and psychological, futuristic and present, transcendent and immanent, phenomenal and noumenal, and hypostatized and nonhypostatized. Each of these carries varying shades of meaning, and each perspective expresses a dimension of the relationship between the two interpretations of Pure Land. I have, however, for this discussion chosen "objective" and "subjective" on account of their most comprehensive meaning.

The objective position, based on a literal reading of the Pure Land *sūtras*, including the *Guanjing*, sees Sukhāvatī as an independent realm outside the mind, epitomized by the stock phrase, "There exists a realm called Sukhāvatī billions of Buddha lands to the west." It denotes a specific location in the universe where practitioners actually go to be born upon death. Sukhāvatī is one among the numerous realms that fill the universe in the ten directions. In contrast, the subjective interpretation regards the Pure Land as an analogical expression of the purified or enlightened mind of the bodhisattvas and rejects its independent existence outside the mind. The scriptural authority most often cited in support of this view is the *Vimālakīrti-nirdeśa sūtra* (Discourse of Vimālakīrti), a major Mahāyāna scripture, which states, "If a Bodhisattva (a seeker of enlightenment) desires to obtain the Pure Land, he must purify his mind. In accordance with the purity of the mind, the Buddha Land is pure" (Taishō Canon 14.475: 538c5). This *sūtra* thus regards the Pure Land as none other than the expression of the enlightened state and does not take the position that the Pure Land has an ontic existence in a distant corner of the universe.

It was the Chan (Zen) tradition that took this view. Master Huineng (638–713), the Sixth Patriarch, in the *Platform Sūtra* elaborates on that passage from the *Vimalakīrti-nirdeśa sūtra*: "There is no doubt that the Western [Pure] Land can be seen here in China." And the great twentieth-century promulgator of Zen Buddhism in the West, D. T. Suzuki (1870–1966), echoed the same vision while speaking at the Buddhist Academy in New York in the spring of 1958:

> The Pure Land is not many millions and millions of miles away to the west. According to my explanation, the Pure Land is right here, even in this very hall. Amida is not presiding over a Pure Land beyond our reach. His Pure Land is this dirty earth itself. (Suzuki 1985, 2)

Moreover, for the Chan master, the objective Pure Land that existed "far to the west" was a teaching with concrete images meant to convert people of "inferior capacity." The Pure Land proponents did not object to this. Concreteness, they would assert, was the very hallmark of the Pure Land teaching. The anonymous Pure Land Buddhist author of the *Jingtu shiyi lun* (Ten Doubts Concerning the Pure Land), compiled in the late eighth century, expresses this in the metaphor of constructing a house, a favorite among Pure Land advocates. The metaphor extols the effectiveness of a tangible example that rests firmly on the ground but not in thin air.

> The *Vimalakīrti-nirdeśa sūtra* states, "Even though the Buddha knows that the Buddha Land and sentient beings are empty, he perpetually establishes the Pure Land in order to convert the multitude." In addition, the *Dazhidu lun* (Great Treatise on Wisdom Liberation) says, "A man who in constructing a mansion is successful when he builds it on a vacant ground but fails when he tries to build it in space."
>
> In the same way, the [Buddhas] always rely on the two truths to explain ultimate reality without destroying the provisional name. (Taishō Canon 47.1961: 78a)

Other Pure Land Buddhist proponents also challenged the subjective Chan interpretation of the Pure Land. One such person was Huiri or Cimin (d. 748), a prominent Pure Land Buddhist figure of the mid-Tang period. In his only surviving work, the *Lüezhu jinglun nianfo famen wangsheng jingtu ji* (Collection of Scriptural Passages on the Teachings of Buddha-Recollection for Rebirth in the Pure Land), Huiri responds to a host of Chan criticisms by citing an array of *sūtra*s and commentaries in support of the Pure Land position. In it, he first quotes the view of a Chan antagonist:

> There is a group of monks, nuns, laymen and laywomen who truly believe that the Pure Land really exists. The Pure Land is none other than the time when the mind is pure. Where does the Western Pure Land exist separate [from the mind]? (Taishō Canon 85.2826: 1236)

Huiri refutes the criticism by reminding the antagonist of the traditional Buddhist acceptance of eighty-four thousand equally legitimate paths for attaining the Buddhist goal. The Pure Land path is not only one of them but also a superb and important one at that. Huiri continues the argument primarily on the basis of the swiftness of Pure Land teaching in leading all beings to enlightenment, thereby enlisting a common Pure Land theme of universal salvation and speedy attainment frequently cited by the Pure Land proponents.

A more convincing rebuttal than that of Huiri is found in the second of the ten doubts, cast presumably by a Chan adherent, in the *Jingtu shiyi lun*:

> Since *dharma*s [fundamental psycho-philosophical elements that constitute human experience] are by nature empty and essentially do not arise, they are equanimous and tranquil. But now you have abandoned this and seek rebirth in the Western Pure Land of Amitāyus; how could it not go against the truth? Moreover, the [*Vimalakīrtinirdeśa*] *sūtra* says, "If one seeks the Pure Land, first purify the mind because when the mind is pure the Buddha Land is pure." How do you reconcile this? (Taishō Canon 47.1961: 78a)

To this, the Pure Land author responds:

> You claim we are not in accord with the truth when we seek the Western Land of Amitāyus's Pure Land since we seek one [position] while abandoning another. But you also are at fault for not being in keeping with the truth, for in adhering to your position of not seeking the Western Land, you have abandoned one position while becoming attached to another position. (Taishō Canon 47.1961: 78a)

In the classic Madhyamaka (Middle Way) school[32] mode of reasoning that rejects any and all positions (*dṛṣṭi*) as ultimately unreal, he attempts to disqualify the Chan argument by rendering it simply another self-serving, limited position that lacks the authority and justification for nullifying the Pure Land position. Then he proceeds to say, in so many words, that his Pure Land position transcends all position in the same manner as expounded in the *Diamond Sūtra*. Huiri argues that when one aspires to be reborn in the Pure Land, one comes to understand that the essence of rebirth is "nonbirth." This constitutes another way to express the extraordinary nature of rebirth in the Pure Land. His argument, however, does not appear to me to be convincing, for he elevates his position to a level that only those with wisdom are capable of comprehending, when the majority of Pure Land seekers are ordinary unenlightened beings, the very audience of Pure Land teaching.

It is clear that Pure Land Buddhist apologists did not subscribe to the *subjective* interpretation of the Chan proponents. However, this did not then automatically imply that the Pure Land advocates subscribed to the opposite view of an objective Pure Land. This becomes more evident when we look at their controversy with the followers of Maitreya Buddha, specifically with respect to Amitābha's Sukhāvatī Pure Land versus Maitreya's Tuṣita heaven.

Until around the year 700, Maitreya worship, at least in northern China, had competed with and even exceeded Amitāyus worship in popularity. This observation rests primarily on the tabulations of dated Buddha images found in the caves of northern China, such as the Longmen grottoes (Luoyang, Henan). They reveal that images of Maitreya far exceeded those of Amitāyus during the Six Dynasties and Sui periods (ca. 386–618). Not until well into the Tang period (ca. 700) did the number of Amitāyus images come to surpass those of Maitreya (Tsukamoto 1942, 564–95).

The competition was fueled partly by the tendency during this period, despite the distinct historical and doctrinal background of the two traditions, to regard both Maitreya and Amitābha worship as one and the same practice. The syncretic tendency is supported by numerous inscriptions on stone images that express concurrently salutations to Maitreya and the desire to be reborn in Amitāyus's Pure Land. The rivalry was intensified due in part to the elevation, by some, of Maitreya's Tuṣita Heaven to the status of a Pure Land, though this deviated from the Indian understanding. According to the early Indian Buddhist cosmology, Tuṣita is one of the heavens of the Desire realm within the Sahā realm, the "galaxy" in which we dwell. However, the Sukhāvatī Pure Land exists far beyond the Sahā realm.

During the seventh century, Pure Land advocates such as Daochuo (562–645), Jiazai (ca. 620–680), and Huaigan (d. 701)[33] asserted the superiority of Sukhāvatī over Maitreya's Tuṣita heaven. Their arguments relative to the present discussion can be summarized as follows:

1. Whereas Sukhāvatī transcends the Sahā realm, Tuṣita (one of the heavens in the Desire realm) still lies within the Sahā realm.

2. Whereas the lifespan in the Sukhāvatī is limitless like that of the Buddhas and transcends the cycle of *saṃsāra* (realm of births and deaths), a lifespan in Tuṣita lasts four thousand heaven years, and at the end of that time, one is forced back into the cycle of *saṃsāra*.

3. Whereas Sukhāvatī is a realm of non-retrogression (not backsliding to lower spiritual states), Tuṣita is not. Rebirth in Sukhāvatī assures not only attainment of Buddhahood but also non-retrogression to lower levels on the Buddhist cultivational, spiritual path.[34]

The argument for the superiority of Sukhāvatī rested primarily on the Sukhāvatī's transcendence of the Sahā realm in contrast to the Tuṣita heaven, which occupied a specific locus within the Sahā realm. The Pure Land proponents stressed Tuṣita's proximity and affinity to the human realm in order to point out Tuṣita's ties to *saṃsāra*. For example, in an interesting analogy, Jiazai claims that boys are reborn in Tuṣita on the laps of their fathers and girls on the laps of their mothers, while in the Sukhāvatī one is reborn among the lotus flowers (Taishō Canon 47.1960: 100b). The symbolism of mother and father was intended to strengthen the fact that life in Tuṣita did not differ qualitatively from the human realm, thus from *saṃsāra*.

In terms of reconciling the positions, we have seen the Pure Land proponents reject what they perceive to be two extreme views of Pure Land: the subjective and the objective. If the Pure Land is neither, how was it understood? One of the principal heuristic methods was to employ a major Mahāyāna concept of the twofold truths: ultimate truth (*paramārtha-satya*) and conventional truth (*saṃvṛti-satya*). In this scheme, the Pure Land possessed both an ultimate as well as a conventional dimension. The ultimate dimension was none other than the ultimate (*tathatā*; *dharmatā*), which was absent in Maitreya's Tuṣita heaven as we examined earlier. On the other hand, the conventional dimension proved to be the objective Pure Land, the very interpretation that the Chan Buddhists criticized.

The Pure Land commentators expended much energy in trying to reconcile these two dimensions. Tanluan (476–542),[35] for example, expressed this mode of existence as "subtle" (*wei*) and explained, "Though it is extra-phenomenal, it exists" (Taishō Canon 40.1819: 830a). The question that now demands asking concerns the manner in which the Pure Land exists extra-phenomenally. Shandao expressed this relationship in the concept of "giving direction and establishing form" (*shifang lixiang*) (Taishō Canon 37.1753: 267b).

Tanluan called it the "interpenetration of the expanded and the essential" (*guanglue xiangru*) (Taishō Canon 40.1819: 841b). The expanded refers to the seventeen decorated forms of the Pure Land, Amitāyus, and the two bodhisattvas described in the *Jingtu lun* (Treatise on the Pure Land) attributed to Vasubandhu (fl. 4th c.). These are forms that are in accord with the emotional and intellectual comprehensive ability of the unenlightened. The essential refers to "one dharma phrase" (*yifa ju*), which constitutes another term for ultimate truth. The two are mutually dependent. The decorated forms of Pure Land (expanded) and ultimate truth (essential) are mutually dependent. The former emerges based on the latter, while the latter is expressed through the former.

From the ultimate standpoint, the Pure Land is not to be taken as an existent place, in the way ordinary beings are predisposed to understanding it. The admonition against such a view of the Pure Land is found in the following passage from the *Jingtu shiyi lun*:

> A foolish person in hearing "birth" [in the Pure Land] understands it as "birth" and in hearing "nonbirth" understands it as "nonbirth." He, thus, fails to realize the identity of "birth" and "nonbirth" and of "nonbirth" and "birth." (Taishō Canon 47.1961: 78a)

Tanluan, almost two centuries earlier, similarly described, "That [Pure] Land is the Realm of Nonbirth" (Taishō Canon 40.1819: 839b).

Nevertheless, the Pure Land proponents acknowledged that the capacity of ordinary, unenlightened people left them no choice but to regard the Pure Land as ontically existent. In other words, ordinary beings adopted a literal reading of the *Larger* and *Smaller Sukhāvatī-vyūha Sūtras*. One such Pure Land proponent, Daochuo, for example, asked rhetorically, "If those of the lowest grade attain rebirth through reciting [the name of Amitāyus] ten times, how can they possibly not grasp it as real birth?" (Taishō Canon 47.1958: 11c).

The objective portrayal of the Pure Land accords with the emotional and intellectual makeup of ordinary beings whose capacity affords only a literal understanding of the *sūtra* description. What is often ignored is that for these seekers, initially at least, the objective Pure Land as described in the *sūtra*s was taken at face value as an absolute. For them there is no ultimate reality to be found "lurking behind" the Pure Land of cool breezes and bejeweled palaces. Direct insight into ultimate truth for them is beyond their ability, and only through their relationship with the Pure Land of form can ultimate reality be realized. However, the question remains as to how beings are able to realize enlightenment through "grasping at forms" of the Pure Land, which strikes as being antithetical to the fundamental Buddhist practice. Daochuo again argues,

> Therefore, although this is grasping on to form, such grasping does not constitute binding attachment. In addition, the form of the Pure Land being discussed here is identical to form without defilements, for that is true form. (Taishō Canon 47.1958: 18c)

Tanluan had earlier explained that, based on the theory of the "arising of *dharmatā*" as taught in the *Avataṃsaka Sūtra* (Flower Garland Sutra), the Pure Land is a manifestation commensurate with ultimate reality, the *dharmatā* (Taishō Canon 40.1819: 828c). The Pure Land emerges based on ultimate reality, while the latter is expressed through the former. Hence, the "grasping at form" is permitted on the strength of the form being "form that is true form."

The mechanism of this soteriological process is explained by Daochuo in an ingenious metaphor of "fire and ice."

> It is like lighting fire on top of ice. As the fire intensifies, the ice melts. When the ice melts, then the fire goes out. Those of the lowest grade of rebirth who are intent on attaining rebirth based solely on the power of reciting the Buddha's name with the resolve to be reborn in his land even though they do not understand the birthlessness of the dharma-nature, will attain the realm of birthlessness and will see the fire of rebirth spontaneously disappear at that time. (Taishō Canon 47.1958: 11c)

The fire and ice refer to the ignorant, passion-ridden people who aspire to be reborn in an existent, objective Pure Land. The melting of the ice refers to the soteriological process of their single-minded resolve to be reborn in Sukhāvatī, which eventually leads aspirants to the attainment of some level of wisdom. This attainment automatically extinguishes the fire based on the provisional notion that the aspirant actually is reborn in an objective Pure Land.

According to this explanation, an ordinary being is able to engage the ultimate realm without that person fully understanding the ultimate nature. This process skillfully utilizes the form (rooted in truth) to transcend form in order to enter the formless. When the formless is attained, the previous attachment to form disappears. The form is skillfully realized so that beings of low ability are "catapulted" to attain the realm of the ultimate even though they themselves do not possess the wisdom for directly apprehending the nature of reality.

The eminent Buddhist scholar Edward Conze (1904–1979) aptly described this process in terms of faith and wisdom:

> As soon as we judge it by the standard of self-extinction, the "Buddhism of Faith" is in the direct line of Buddhist orthodoxy. Surrender in faith involves a high degree of extinction of separate selfhood, partly because one does not rely on oneself, or one's own power, partly because one sees the futility of all consciousness and personal efforts and allows one to be "carried" to salvation, and partly due to superior merit or wisdom. . . . For it must never be forgotten that which is represented to the relatively ignorant in the form of a personal savior and of a paradise is exactly the same thing as that which is taught to the relatively learned as the Absolute itself. . . . A sincere heart and belief, unaware of the merit of its sincerity, is all that is needed. The Buddha's demand that, in order to be saved, one should learn to do nothing in particular, is fulfilled in this way as perfectly as in any other. (Conze 1975, 159–60)

In a sense, the Pure Land proponents steered a middle path to advocate that the Sukhāvatī Pure Land was not simply subjective (Chan or Zen position) or simply objective (Tuṣita heaven). It could not simply be subjective because the Pure Land teaching was directed to those incapable of realizing full enlightenment in the present life. Their aim in the Pure Land was the attainment of Buddhahood and was not an escape to an eternal paradise to enjoy the extension of pleasures in this life. In this respect, Pure Land Buddhists made no false claims of enlightenment in the present life and thus remained faithful to the Mahāyāna Buddhist goal. However, at the same time, the Pure Land was more than just another celestial body because it was rooted and enveloped in ultimate reality. Thus, it was a non-samsaric quality not found in Maitreya's Tuṣita that allowed those reborn to transcend the cycle of births and deaths and to be guaranteed Buddhahood.

In closing and in terms of the present volume, in the preceding debates on the nature of Pure Land and of Amitāyus, we cannot lose sight of the fact of the importance of one's practice. Whether through simple faith in tandem with oral recitation or through visualization, one nurtures and purifies the mind toward the ultimate Buddhist goal of enlightenment. Visualization in the *Guanjing* as a meditative technique utilizes form by creating in the mind the concrete features or images of the Pure Land. After creating or forming the image in one's mind, the aspirant observes and inspects them, sees them clearly, and attains the Buddha-Recollection Samādhi, which is none other than a purification of consciousness. Some may see elements of "theism" in the anthropomorphic Amitāyus and bodhisattvas in celestial realms, but as the objects of visualization, these theistic forms are provisional in nature; the ultimate aim is to achieve the purified or awakened mind. This point is nowhere better expressed than in the following well-known lines in the *Guanjing*:

Then the World-honored One said to Vaidehī, "Do you know that Amitāyus is not far away?" (sec. 7)

"Your mind produces the Buddha's image and is itself the Buddha. The ocean of perfectly and universally enlightened Buddhas thus arises in the meditating mind." (sec. 16)

Notes

1. This Buddha is referred to as either Amitāyus or Amitābha, though the former is more prominent in the *Guanjing*. Amitāyus and Amitābha are the aspects of the timeless life and of the universal life of Śākyamuni Buddha, respectively. They symbolize the transcendental dimensions of the historical Buddha in temporal and spatial terms (Fujita 1996, 14). This celestial Buddha is referred to as Amituo in Chinese, Amida in Japanese, and Amit'a in Korean.

2. The Chinese title of the text uses *guan*, which conventionally means "to observe." In a more technical Chinese Buddhist sense, it constitutes a translation for *vipassanā* (Skt.: *vipaśyanā*) (see, e.g., Gregory 1987; Donner and Stevenson 1993). In terms of Pure Land texts, *guan* normally means "observation," "contemplation," or "visualization." An edited text of the *Guanjing* appears as number 365 in volume 12 of the Taishō Canon (abbr. T.), a one hundred–volume collection of Buddhist literature mostly in classical Chinese and edited by Japanese scholars headed by the Japanese scholars Takakusu Junjirō (1866–1945) and Watanabe Kaigyoku (1872–1933) from 1924 to 1932.

3. A Uyghur fragment has been found but appears to be a translation from the Chinese. If there were a Sanskrit original, its reconstructed title might have been something akin to *Amitāyur-dhyāna-sūtra* (Sūtra of the Meditation of Amitāyus), the title of the first English translation of *Guanjing* by Takakusu Junjirō. See Takakusu 1965 (1894).

4. For a summary in English, see Tanaka 1990, 38–40.

5. For a representative and influential perspective, see Ono 1927, 33–34; 1937, 98–99. Nakamura Hajime also took a similar position. See, for example, Nakamura 1964, 2: 206. These views are summarized in Fujita 1976, 124–25.

6. Taishō Canon 12.360.

7. For Tibet, see Halkias 2013. See also Kapstein's contribution in Payne and Tanaka 2003, 20. For Nepal, see Lewis' contribution in Payne and Tanaka 2003, 254.

8. For some English language discussions of the origins and development of Pure Land Buddhism, see Tanaka 1990, 2005; Pas 1995; Foard et al. 1996; Gomez 1996; Blum 2002; Payne and Tanaka 2003.

9. In Japan, Hōnen is known as the person who treated the Three Pure Land Sūtras as a set.

10. For English summaries of these key Pure Land *sūtra*s, see Inagaki 1995, 4–17; Gomez 1996, 4–13, 23–59.

11. There are numerous Sanskrit manuscripts and modern editions, which are discussed in Fujita 2011, i–xxxvi. The first modern edition was published by Max Müller and Bunyū Nanjō (1883). There are five extant Chinese translations of this work, which appear as texts 360, 361, 362, 363, and 365 in the Taishō Canon. Among these, 360 has been adopted as the canonical text by East Asian Pure Land schools, especially in Japan. For English translations, see Inagaki 1995; Gomez 1996.

12. There are numerous Sanskrit manuscripts, one of which was transmitted to Japan as early as the ninth century. This text and manuscripts found more recently in Nepal were consulted to produce an edited text, which is also found in Fujita 2011. There are two extant Chinese translations of this work, which appear as texts 366 and 367 in the Taishō Canon; the former one, translated by the famous Kuchean Buddhist monk-translator Kumārajīva (334–413), is considered canonical by many Pure Land schools. For English translations, see Inagaki 1995; Gomez 1996.

13. These were two of the eighteen or twenty schools into which the Buddhist followers were divided approximately one hundred years after the death of the historical Buddha. Their doctrine developed a more liberal and expanded view of the Buddhist cosmology.

14. Shinran is the founder of Jōdo Shinshū (True Pure Land School) or Shin Buddhism, the largest of Japanese Pure Land schools. Much is available in English as can be seen in the references for this chapter. On Shinran's life see, for example, Bloom 1991; Dobbins 2002; on his writings, see Hirota et al. 1997; Bloom 2007; on his thought, see Ueda and Hirota 1989; from a comparative perspective, see Keel 1995; Hirota 2000.

15. Here we must remember that the text is presented as oral teachings of the historical Buddha, but that the text was composed at a later date and in a different context (see previous discussion in this chapter).

16. Those writers affiliated with Japanese Pure Land schools generally do not view visualizations 14, 15, and 16 as actual visualizations but as descriptions of the nine grades of people born in the Pure Land. While this reflects the interpretation of Shandao (613–681), one of the most prominent Chinese Pure Land masters, other Chinese commentators such as Jingying Huiyuan (523–592) do not agree with Shandao's interpretation, for they regard all sixteen as visualizations. From my perspective, the *Guanjing* supports the latter view. See Tanaka 1990, 84–85.

17. In the prologue of the *Guanjing*, Queen Vaidehī requests the Buddha to provide instruction on the way for future beings to be reborn in the Pure Land. The Buddha then teaches the visualization practices precisely because practitioners would be guaranteed rebirth in the Pure Land by accomplishing the *samādhi* states.

18. In fact, the vision of Amitābha Buddha is mentioned as one of the accomplishments in association with the *pratyutpanna-samādhi*. See Taishō Canon 13.417.

19. Five of these visualization *sūtra*s, including the *Guanjing*, contain the character *guan* (visualization) in their titles. The other four consist of Taishō Canon 277, 409, 452, and 642.

20. Komaru notes that the *Mahāvastu* passage is found in Senart 1882–1897, 245.

21. This version of the Taima Mandala is used with permission of ARTstor. The Japanese original is housed at the Metropolitan Museum of Art (Gallery 224). Dating to the late Kamakura period (1185–1333), it is a hanging scroll consisting of ink, color, and gold on silk. It was obtained by the Met in 1957 through the Rogers Fund. The original Taima Mandala, based on the *Guanjing* and possibly intended as a visualiza-

tion aid in Pure Land monastic halls, was completed around 763 in Japan. Housed at Taimadera Temple in Nara prefecture, the original is a woven tapestry that measures about thirteen feet or four meters square. In the later Pure Land tradition, these types of religious art were understood as representations of the Pure Land, with adherents having the goal of being born there. For a study of the Taima Mandala and related Japanese Buddhist material culture, see ten Grotenhuis 1999.

22. The Land of Utmost Bliss is the English rendering of Jileguo (or *Sukhāvatī*), the Pure Land of Amitāyus.

23. "Call" is synonymous with "recite." In either case, this English translation reflects what the translator Inagaki regards as Shandao's interpretation of the original *nian*, of which the broad meaning can include visualization, contemplation, and recitation. Given Shandao's overall understanding, this rendering (to call or recite) is correct.

24. They are patricide, matricide, killing an arhat, injuring a Buddha, and causing division in monastic order.

25. See Pas 1995, 315–18. Pas cites numerous scholars from the early twentieth century, such as K. Reichelt, S. Y. Saeki, and H. de Lubac.

26. Pure Land lineages, indicating a transmission line of teachings, existed in these countries. However, these lineages were not, as in Japan, large institutions comprised of a "mother" temple and thousands and even tens of thousands of "member" temples connected by allegiance to a common founder and shared teachings. In the case of China, the temples have tended to be more "independent," with their school or lineage affiliation being determined mostly on the basis of the personal commitment of the head monk of the temple.

27. It could be possible that there are "pockets" of temples continuing the practice unnoticed by scholars, but I have not heard of such reporting. However, if we go outside the Pure Land schools, visualization is actively practiced in most of the Tibetan Buddhist traditions. I know of nonmonastic, lay American Buddhists who engage in visualization on a routine basis as part of their spiritual practice. In addition, within the Japanese Tendai school, one of the main practices for the priests is the Continuously Moving Samādhi (*jōgyō zanmai*). It calls for the practitioner to circumambulate around an image of Amitāyus for a period of ninety days for the purpose of attaining the Buddha-Recollection Samādhi (*nembutsu zanmai*) previously discussed.

28. Other Jōdo Shinshū traditions include the Hompa Hongwanji of Hawaii, Higashi Honganji Mission of Hawaii, and Higashi Honganji Buddhist Temple. The Jōdo tradition is represented by Jodo Mission of Hawaii and Jodo-shu North America Buddhist Mission.

29. In reality, these "meditations" being adopted mostly consist of stilling the mind by quiet sitting for a short period of time, a far cry from the officially recognized Zen or Theravāda practices. This is due, in part, to the fact that BCA priests are not officially trained in these meditative practices, and they make no pretense of having been so trained.

30. As discussed earlier, this possibility exists because of historical and institutional affinity, specifically given the fact that Hōnen and Shinran were initially Tendai monks.

31. Although the story of King Ajātaśatru is found widely in other Buddhist texts, Kosawa probably learned of the story through *Guanjing*, as his mother was a devoted follower of Jōdo Shinshū teaching.

32. An Indian Mahāyāna school based initially on the thought of Nāgārjuna (2nd c. CE), who promoted teachings that rejected the extremes of annihilationist and eternalist positions. Its doctrine further advocated that all phenomena are empty of intrinsic existence (*svabhāva*), thus, regarding all positions (*dṛṣṭi*) to be ultimately unreal and at best relative or provisional.

33. As the author of a Pure Land treatise, the *Anle ji* (Collection of Passages concerning Birth in the Land of Peace and Bliss), Daochuo is known to have promoted the teaching of the arrival of the Period of the Last Dharma (*mofa*) and strongly advocated the practice of oral recitation, even prior to Shandao, as the practice appropriate for the period. As author of the influential treatise *Jingtu lun* (Pure Land Treatise), Jiazai

explained Pure Land teachings in the context of Mahāyāna doctrine such as the Three-Body theory. He also featured prominent Pure Land monastics and lay followers, including Tanluan and Daochuo, with stories of their extraordinary religious lives. After being affiliated with the Consciousness-Only school, Huaigan converted to Pure Land to study with Shandao and practiced Buddha-Recollection Samādhi. He authored the *Shi jingtu qunyi lun* (Discourse Clearing Numerous Doubts about the Pure Land Teachings) to discuss the status of Amitāyus, the Pure Land, and the cause of birth.

34. The summary is based upon the views of the aforementioned three figures, respectively. They can be found in Taishō Canon 47.1958: 78a, 1960: 53b, 1963: 100a.

35. Tanluan is said have abandoned his Daoist allegiance upon being given a Pure Land text called *Guanjing* by Bodhiruci, an Indian monk-scholar of high repute. His commentary to the *Wuliangshou jing youpotishe yuansheng*, attributed to Vasubandhu, reconciled Pure Land teachings with Mahāyāna doctrine and served as an inspiration for subsequent Pure Land proponents such Daochuo and Shandao.

Works Cited and Further Reading

Ama, Michihiro. 2011. *Immigrants to the Pure Land: The Modernization, Acculturation, and Globalization of Shin Buddhism, 1898–1941*. Pure Land Buddhist Studies. Honolulu: University of Hawaii Press.

Amstutz, Galen. 1997. *Interpreting Amida: History and Orientalism in the Study of Pure Land Buddhism*. Albany: State University of New York Press.

Atone, Joji. 2011. *The Promise of Amida Buddha: Honen's Path to Bliss*. Boston: Wisdom.

Bloom, Alfred. 1991 (1966). *Shinran's Gospel of Grace*. Ann Arbor: Association for Asian Studies.

———. 1981. *Tannisho: Resource for Modern Living*. Honolulu: The Buddhist Studies Center.

———, ed. 2004. *Living in Amida's Universal Vow: Essays in Shin Buddhism*. Bloomington: World Wisdom.

———, ed. 2007. *The Essential Shinran: A Buddhist Path of True Entrusting*. Bloomington: World Wisdom.

———, ed. 2013. *The Shin Buddhist Classical Tradition: A Reader in Pure Land Teaching, Volume 1*. Bloomington: World Wisdom.

———, ed. 2014. *The Shin Buddhist Classical Tradition: A Reader in Pure Land Teaching, Volume 2*. Bloomington: World Wisdom.

Blum, Mark L. 2002. *The Origins and Development of Pure Land Buddhism: A Study and Translation of Gyōnen's "Jōdo Hōmon Genrushō."* Oxford and New York: Oxford University Press.

Blum, Mark L., and Robert F. Rhodes, eds. 2011. *A Modern Shin Buddhist Anthology: Cultivating Spirituality*. Albany: State University of New York Press.

Blum, Mark L., and Shin'ya Yasutomi, eds. 2006. *Rennyo and the Roots of Modern Japanese Buddhism*. Oxford and New York: Oxford University Press.

Chappell, David. 1996. "The Formation of the Pure Land Movement in China: Tao-ch'o and Shan-tao." In *The Pure Land Tradition*, edited by James Foard et al., 139–71. Berkeley: Regents of the University of California.

Ch'en, Kenneth. 1964. *Buddhism in China: A Historical Survey*. Princeton: Princeton University Press.

Conze, Edward. 1975. *Buddhism: Its Essence and Development*. New York: Harper and Row.

Demiéville, Paul, Hubert Durt, and Anna Seidel, eds. 1978. *Répertoire du canon bouddhique Sino-Japonais: Edition de Taishō*. Paris: L'Académie des inscriptions et belles-lettres, Institut de France.

Dobbins, James C. 2002 (1989). *Jōdo Shinshū: Shin Buddhism in Medieval Japan*. Honolulu: University of Hawaii Press.

Donner, Neal, and Daniel Stevenson. 1993. *The Great Calming and Contemplation: A Study and Annotated Translation of the First Chapter of Chih-i's "Mo-ho chih-kuan."* Honolulu: University of Hawaii Press.

Foard, James, Michael Solomon, and Richard Payne, eds. 1996. *The Pure Land Tradition: History and Development*. Berkeley: Regents of the University of California.

Fujita, Kōtatsu, 1976. *Genshijōdo shisō no kenkyū*. Tokyo: Sankibō busshorin.

———. 1996. "Pure Land Buddhism in India." In *The Pure Land Tradition*, edited by James Foard et al., 1–42. Translated by Taitetsu Unno. Berkeley: Regents of the University of California.

———, ed. 2011. *The Larger and Smaller Sukhāvatīvyūha Sutras*. Kyoto: Hozokan.

Gomez, Luis. 1996. *The Land of Bliss: The Paradise of the Buddha of Measureless Light*. Honolulu: University of Hawaii Press.

Gregory, Peter, ed. 1987. *Traditions of Meditation in Chinese Buddhism*. Honolulu: University of Hawaii Press.

Halkias, Georgios. 2013. *Luminous Bliss: A Religious History of Pure Land Literature in Tibet*. Honolulu: University of Hawaii Press.

Hirota, Dennis. 1997. *No Abode: The Record of Ippen*. Honolulu: University of Hawaii Press.

———, ed. 2000. *Toward a Contemporary Understanding of Pure Land Buddhism: Creating a Shin Buddhist Theology in a Religiously Plural World*. Albany: State University of New York Press.

———. 2006. *Asura's Harp: Engagement with Language as Buddhist Path*. Heidelberg: Universitätsverlag Winter.

Hirota, Dennis, Hisao Inagaki, Michio Tokunaga, and Ryushin Uryuzu. 1997. *The Collected Works of Shinran*. Kyoto: Jōdo Shinshū Hongwanji-ha.

Inagaki, Hisao. 1994. *The Three Pure Land Sutras: A Study and Translation*. Kyoto: Nagata Bunshodo.

———. 1995. *The Three Pure Land Sutras*. Berkeley: Numata Center for Buddhist Translation and Research.

Keel, Hee-Sung. 1995. *Understanding Shinran: A Dialogical Approach*. Fremont: Asian Humanities Press.

Komaru Shinji. 1985. "Kanmuryōjukyō to shōmyōshisō." In *Bukkyō shisō no shomondai*. Tokyo: Shunjūsha.

Lee, Ki-baek, 1984. *A New History of Korea*. Translated by Edward G. Wagner. Cambridge: Harvard University Press.

Machida, Soho. 1999. *Renegade Monk: Hōnen and Japanese Pure Land Buddhism*. Translated and edited by Ioannis Mentzas. Berkeley: University of California Press.

Müller, Max, ed. 1879–1910. *Sacred Books of the East*. 50 vols. Oxford: Oxford University Press.

Müller, Max, and Bunyū Nanjō. 1883. *Sukhāvatī Vyūha, Description of Sukhāvatī, the Land of Bliss*. Anecdota Oxonieensia, Aryan Series, Volume 1, Part 2. Oxford: Oxford University Press.

Nakamura Hajime. 1964. *Jōdo sambukyō*. 2 vols. Tokyo: Iwanami shoten.

Nattier, Jan, 2000. "The Realm of Akṣobhya: A Missing Piece in the History of Pure Land Buddhism." *Journal of the International Association of Buddhist Studies* 23.1: 71–102.

Nguyen, Cuong Tu. 1997. *Zen in Medieval Vietnam*. Honolulu: University of Hawaii Press.

Okonogi Keigo, and Kitayama Osamu, eds. 2001. *Ajase Konpurekkusu* (Ajase Complex). Osaka: Sōgensha.

Ono Genmyō. 1927. *Daijō bukkyō geijutsu-shi no kenkyū*. Tokyo: Kano-bun'endō.

———. 1937. *Bukkyō no bijutsu to rekishi*. Tokyo: Kano-bun'endō.

Pas, Julian. 1995. *Visions of Sukhāvatī: Shan-tao's Commentary on the Kuan wu-liang-shou-fo ching*. Albany: State University of New York Press.

Payne, Richard, ed. 2009. *Path of No Path: Contemporary Studies in Pure Land Buddhism Honoring Roger Corless*. Berkeley: Institute of Buddhist Studies and Numata Center for Translation and Research.

Payne, Richard, and Kenneth Tanaka, eds. 2003. *Approaching the Land of Bliss: Religious Praxis in the Cult of Amitābha*. Honolulu: University of Hawaii Press.

Pye, Michael, ed. 2012. *Listening to Shin Buddhism: Starting Points of Modern Dialogue*. Sheffield and Bristol: Equinox.

———, ed. 2013. *Interactions with Japanese Buddhism: Explorations and Viewpoints in Twentieth-Century Kyōto*. Sheffield and Bristol: Equinox.

Rogers, Minor L., and Ann T. Rogers. 1991. *Rennyo: The Second Founder of Shin Buddhism*. Berkeley: Asian Humanities Press.

Ryukoku University Translation Center (RUTC). 1984. *The Sūtra of Contemplation on the Buddha of Immeasurable Life as Expounded by Śākyamuni Buddha*. Kyoto: Ryukoku University.

Senart, Émile. 1882–1897. *Le Mahāvastu: Texte Sanscrit.* Paris: Imprimerie Nationale.

Senchakushū English Translation Project (SETP). 1998. *Hōnen's Senchakushū: Passages on the Selection of the Nembutsu in the Original Vow.* Honolulu: University of Hawaii Press and Taishō University.

Shigaraki, Takamoro. 2013. *Heart of the Shin Buddhist Path: A Life of Awakening.* Translated by David Matsumoto. Boston: Wisdom.

Sugao, Kentaro, dir. 2013. *Streams of Light: Shin Buddhism of America* (DVD). Ebisu Films.

Suzuki, D. T. 1985. "Shin Buddhism: Part 1." *The Eastern Buddhist* 17.1 (Spring): 1–7.

———. 1997. *Buddha of Infinite Light.* Boston: Shambhala. (Reprint of *Shin Buddhism* [New York: Harper & Row, 1970]).

———. 2013. *Shinran's Kyōgyōshinshō: The Collection of Passages Expounding the True Teaching, Living, Faith, and Realizing of the Pure Land.* Oxford and New York: Oxford University Press.

Takakusu, Junjirō. 1965 (1894). "Amitāyur-dhyāna-sūtra: The Sūtra of the Meditation of Amitāyus." In *Sacred Books of the East, Volume 49: Buddhist Mahāyāna Texts,* edited by Max Müller, 159–201. Delhi: Motilal Banarsidass.

Takakusu, Junjirō, and Watanabe Kaigyoku, eds. 1929–1937. *Taishō shinshū daizōkyō* (Taishō Canon). Tokyo: Taishō issaikyō kankōkai.

Tanaka, Kenneth, 1990. *The Dawn of Chinese Pure Land Buddhist Doctrine: Ching-ying Hui-yüan's Commentary on the Visualization Sutra.* Albany: State University of New York Press.

———. 1997. *Ocean: An Introduction to Jodo-Shinshu Buddhism in America.* Berkeley: WisdomOcean.

———. 2005. *Pure Land Buddhism: Historical Development and Contemporary Manifestation.* Bangalore: Dharmaram.

Tanaka, Kenneth, and Eisho Nasu, eds. 1988. *Engaged Pure Land Buddhism: Essays in Honor of Professor Alfred Bloom.* Berkeley: WisdomOcean.

ten Grotenhuis, Elizabeth. 1999. *Japanese Mandalas: Representations of Sacred Geography.* Honolulu: University of Hawaii Press.

Tsukamoto, Zenryu. 1942. *Shina-bukkyo-shi kenkyu: Hokugi-hen* (Study on the History of Chinese Buddhism: Northern Wei Period). Tokyo: Kobundo.

Ueda, Yoshifumi, and Dennis Hirota. 1989. *Shinran: An Introduction to His Thought.* Kyoto: Hongwanji International Center.

Unno, Taitetsu. 1998. *River of Fire, River of Water: An Introduction to the Pure Land Tradition of Shin Buddhism.* New York: Doubleday.

———. 2002. *Shin Buddhism: Bits of Rubble Turn into Gold.* New York: Doubleday.

Watts, Jonathan, and Yoshiharu Tomatsu, eds. 2005. *Traversing the Pure Land Way: A Lifetime of Encounters with Honen Shonin.* Tokyo: Jodo-shu Press.

Wright, Arthur. 1959. *Buddhism in Chinese History.* Stanford: Stanford University Press.

Yamada Meiji. 1976. "Kangyō kō: Muryōju-butsu to Amida-butsu." *Ryūkoku daigaku ronshū* 48: 76–95.

Guan wuliang shoufo jing (Sutra on Visualizing the Buddha of Infinite Life)*

Account of a Discourse Attributed to Śākyamuni Buddha[1]

Translated from Sanskrit into Chinese by Kālayaśas[2]

Translated by Inagaki Hisao in Collaboration with Harold Stewart

1 Thus have I heard. At one time the Buddha was staying on Vulture Peak[3] in Rājagṛha with a great assembly of twelve hundred and fifty monks. He was also accompanied by thirty-two thousand bodhisattvas led by Mañjuśrī,[4] the Dharma Prince.

2 At that time, in the great city of Rājagṛha, there was a prince named Ajātaśatru. Instigated by his wicked friend Devadatta[5] he seized his father, King Bimbisāra,[6] confined him in a room with walls seven deep, and forbade all the court officials to visit the king.

---

*Abbreviated *Guanjing* (Visualization Sutra or Contemplation Sutra). No Sanskrit original has been found, but if we were to reconstruct its title, one possibility would be *Amitāyur-dhyāna-sūtra*. This text became one of the central texts of the Jingtu (Jpn.: Jōdo; Pure Land) movement. It is commonly included in the canon of the Pure Land schools of East Asia known as the "Three Pure Land Sutras" (see Inagaki 1995). The present English translation is a complete rendering based on Kālayaśas's Chinese translation of the text (Taishō Canon 12.36), which is the only extant version of this *sūtra*. This translation appeared in Inagaki 1995 and is used with the permission of the Bukkyō Dendō Kyōkai (Society for the Promotion of Buddhism; BDK) and the Numata Center for Buddhist Translation and Research. It follows the slightly revised translation (2003) available online through BDK, which is part of the BDK English Tripitaka Series. Inagaki translates the title in two different ways *Sutra on the Contemplation of Amitāyus* and *Sutra on the Visualization of the Buddha of Infinite Life*. As these renderings indicate, the Chinese character *guan* conventionally means "to observe," but here it has a more technical meaning of "to visualize." These may have significant interpretive and practical consequences. The text focuses on Amitāyus (Chn.: Amituo or Wuliang shoufo; Jpn.: Amida; Infinite Life) Buddha, also known as Amitābha (Infinite Light) Buddha. Originally the Buddhist monk Dharmākara (Storehouse of the Dharma) who created the "Sukhāvatī" (Ultimate Bliss) Pure Land from his accumulated merit, Amitābha Buddha oversees Sukhāvatī, a transcendent Buddha-realm. Unless otherwise indicated, all annotations are based on Inagaki Hisao's technical glossary and were supplied by Louis Komjathy with contributions from Kenneth K. Tanaka. Numbers in brackets indicate page numbers in Inagaki's original publication (1995, 93–118), with the first appearance corresponding to the beginning of a new page. For alternative translations, see Takakusu 1965 (1894); RUTC 1984.

1. Śākyamuni (sage of the Śākya [clan]) is the honorific name of Siddhārtha Gautama (ca. 563–ca. 483 BCE), the founder of Buddhism. As with other Buddhist *sūtras* (Pali: *suttas*), the text presents itself as a written record compiled by members of the early Indian Buddhist community based on oral teachings of the historical Buddha.

2. Inagaki's original publication has the following: "Translated into Chinese during the Liu-Sung Dynasty by Tripitaka Master Kālayaśas of Central Asia." Kālayaśas (ca. 383–442) was a Central Asian missionary-monk and translator. Tradition claims that he worked in Jianye (present-day Nanjing), Jiangsu (China), during the Yuanjia era (424–453) of the Liu-Song dynasty (420–479).

3. Vulture Peak is a mountain near Rājagṛha, the capital of the ancient Indian kingdom of Māgadha in the time of the historical Buddha, on which he often preached.

4. The bodhisattva who represents the wisdom and realization of all Buddhas. Contrasted with the bodhisattva Samantabhadra, who represents the meditation and practice of all Buddhas.

5. A cousin of the historical Buddha who became one of his disciples but who later tried to murder him and usurp the leadership of the Sangha.

6. Bimbisāra (558–491 BCE; r. 543–491) was the fifth king of the Śaiśnāga (Haryanka) dynasty in Māgadha and a follower of the Buddha.

Vaidehī, the king's consort, was devoted to him. After having bathed and cleansed herself, she spread over her body ghee and honey mixed to a paste with wheat flour, filled her ornaments with grape juice, and secretly offered this food and drink to the king. He ate the flour paste, drank the juice, and then asked for water. Having rinsed his mouth, he joined his palms in reverence and, facing Vulture Peak, worshiped the World-Honored One[7] from afar, and said, "Mahāmaudgalyāyana[8] is my close friend. I beseech you to have pity on me and send him here to give me the eight precepts."[9]

Then Mahāmaudgalyāyana flew as swiftly as a hawk to the king. Day after day he came like this to give the king the eight precepts. The World-Honored One also sent the Venerable Pūrna[10] to the palace to expound the Dharma to the king. Three weeks passed in this way. Because he had eaten the flour paste and heard the Dharma, he appeared peaceful and contented. [94]

3 Then Ajātaśatru asked the guard, "Is my father still alive?"

The guard replied, "Great King, his consort spreads flour paste over her body, fills her ornaments with grape juice, and offers these to the king. The monks Mahāmaudgalyāyana and Pūrna come here through the air to expound the Dharma to him. It is impossible to stop them."

Hearing this, Ajātaśatru became furious with his mother and said, "Because you are an accomplice of that enemy, Mother, you too are an enemy. Those monks are evil, for with their delusive magic they have kept this wicked king alive for many days." So saying, he drew his sharp sword, intending to kill her.

At that time the king had a minister named Candraprabha who was intelligent and wise. Together with Jīvaka[11] he made obeisances to the king and said, "Great King, according to a certain Vedic scripture,[12] since the beginning of this cosmic period there have been eighteen thousand wicked kings who have killed their fathers out of their desire to usurp the throne, but we have never heard of anyone who has committed the outrage of killing his mother. Your Majesty, if you commit such an outrage, you will bring disgrace upon the *kṣatriya* class.[13] As your ministers, we cannot bear to hear what people will say. As this would be the act of an outcaste, we could no longer remain here."

Having spoken these words, the two ministers grasped their swords and stepped back. Agitated and frightened, Ajātaśatru said to Jīvaka, "Are you not on my side?"

Jīvaka replied, "Your Majesty, please restrain yourself and do not kill your mother."

---

7. "World-Honored One" translates Bhagavān, which is one of the ten epithets of a Buddha.

8. One of the historical Buddha's foremost disciples, renowned for his supernatural powers.

9. Eight precepts of abstinence, which dictate that on certain days of the month lay Buddhists should abstain from killing; stealing; sexual acts; lying; drinking intoxicants; such idle pleasures as using perfumes, singing and dancing, wearing bodily decoration, and going to see dances or plays; sleeping on a raised bed; and eating after noon.

10. One of the ten great disciples of the Buddha, renowned for his skill in teaching the Dharma.

11. A nephew of King Bimbisāra who served as a royal minister. He was also a famous physician who once cured the Buddha of a serious illness.

12. An unidentified text in the four Vedas, which are the oldest scriptures of Hinduism.

13. The warrior caste. The second of the four primary castes, namely, Brahmin (priest), warrior, merchant, and servant.

Hearing this, the king repented and begged their forgiveness. Having thrown away his sword, he stopped short of killing his mother and instead ordered the court officials to lock her up in an inner chamber and not allow her to leave.

4 Vaidehī, thus confined, grew emaciated with grief and despair. Facing Vulture Peak, she worshiped the Buddha from afar and said, "O Tathāgata,[14] World-Honored One, you used to send Ānanda to comfort me. Now I am in deep sorrow and distress. Since there [95] is no way of my coming to look upon your august countenance, World-Honored One, I pray you send Venerable Mahāmaudgalyāyana and Venerable Ānanda[15] here to see me."

When she had said these words, tears of sorrow streamed down her cheeks like rain. Then she bowed toward the Buddha in the distance. Even before she raised her head, the World-Honored One, who was then staying on Vulture Peak, knew Vaidehī's thoughts and immediately ordered Mahāmaudgalyāyana and Ānanda to go to her through the air; he himself disappeared from the mountain and reappeared in the inner chamber of the royal palace.

After worshiping him, Vaidehī raised her head and saw Śākyamuni Buddha, the World-Honored One. He was the color of purple gold and was seated upon a lotus flower of a hundred jewels. He was attended by Mahāmaudgalyāyana on his left and Ānanda on his right. Śakra,[16] Brahmā,[17] the guardian gods of the world, and other *deva*s[18] were in the air about him. Scattering heavenly blossoms like rain, they paid homage to the Buddha.

When she saw the World-Honored One, Vaidehī tore off her ornaments and prostrated herself on the ground. Weeping bitterly, she said to the Buddha, "O World-Honored One, what bad karma did I commit in former lives that I have given birth to such an evil son? I wonder, World-Honored One, what karmic relations could have made you a relative of Devadatta?

5 "I beseech you, World-Honored One, to reveal to me a land of no sorrow and no affliction where I can be reborn. I do not wish to live in this defiled and evil world of Jambudvīpa[19] where there are hells, realms of hungry ghosts, animals, and many vile beings. I wish that in the future I shall not hear evil words or see wicked people. World-Honored One, I now kneel down to repent and beg you to take pity on me. I entreat you, O sunlike Buddha, to teach me how to visualize a land of pure karmic perfection."

Then the World-Honored One sent forth from between his eyebrows a flood of light that was the color of gold and illuminated the innumerable worlds in the ten directions. Returning

---

14. Tathāgata (Thus Come or Thus Gone) is one of the ten epithets of a Buddha. It is conventionally understood as the one who has come from suchness or gone to suchness, but it may also simply mean the one who was here.

15. The historical Buddha's cousin, close disciple, and personal attendant who was renowned for his ability to recite all of the Buddha's sermons from memory.

16. Indra, the lord of the Heaven of the Thirty-Three Gods. Originally a Hindu god but later considered a protector of Buddhism.

17. Originally the creator god in Hinduism. He was incorporated into Buddhism as a tutelary (guardian) god.

18. Gods or divine beings.

19. In ancient Indian cosmology, the triangular island continent south of Mount Sumeru that is inhabited by human beings.

to the Buddha, the light settled on his head and transformed [96] itself into a golden platform resembling Mount Sumeru.[20] On the platform appeared the pure and resplendent lands of all the Buddhas in the ten directions. Some of these lands were made of the seven kinds of jewels, some solely of lotus flowers; some resembled the palace in the Heaven of Free Enjoyment of Manifestations by Others,[21] while some were like a crystal mirror in which all the lands in the ten directions were reflected. Innumerable Buddha lands like these, glorious and beautiful, were displayed to her.

Vaidehī then said to the Buddha, "O World-Honored One, these Buddha lands are pure and free of defilement, and all of them are resplendent. But I wish to be born in the Western Land of Utmost Bliss of Amitāyus.[22] I beseech you, World-Honored One, to teach me how to contemplate that land and attain *samādhi*."[23]

6 The World-Honored One smiled, and from his mouth came five-colored rays of light, each shining on King Bimbisāra's head. Although the old king was confined, with his unhindered mind's eye he saw the World-Honored One in the distance. He knelt down in homage to the Buddha and effortlessly made spiritual progress until he reached the stage of non-returner.[24]

7 Then the World-Honored One said to Vaidehī, "Do you know that Amitāyus is not far away? Fix your thoughts upon and contemplate that Buddha land. Then you will accomplish the pure acts. I shall describe it to you in detail with various illustrations, so that all ordinary people in the future who wish to practice pure karma may also be born in that Western Land of Utmost Bliss. Whoever wishes to be born there should practice the three acts: first, caring for one's parents, attending to one's teachers and elders, compassionately refraining from killing, and doing the ten good deeds; second, taking the Three Refuges,[25] keeping the various precepts, and refraining from breaking the rules of conduct; and third, awakening aspiration for enlightenment,[26] believing deeply in the law of causality, chanting the Mahāyāna sutras, and encouraging people to follow their teachings. These three are called pure karma." [97]

The Buddha further said to Vaidehī, "Do you know that these three acts are the pure karma practiced by all the Buddhas of the past, present, and future as the right cause of enlightenment?"

8 The Buddha said to Ānanda and Vaidehī, "Listen carefully, listen carefully and ponder deeply. I, the Tathāgata, shall discourse on pure karma for the sake of all sentient beings of the future who

---

20. In traditional Buddhist cosmology, the great mountain in the center of the world. Often referred to as the axis mundi.

21. *Paranirmita-vaśa-vartin*. The sixth and highest heaven in the realm of desire, where demons are said to dwell. According to Buddhism there are three realms, namely, desire, form, and formlessness.

22. Sukhāvatī. It is the Pure Land of Amitāyus. There came to be innumerable Pure Lands in the Mahāyāna cosmology, but since the Pure Land of Amitāyus (Sukhāvatī) became the most dominant, it came to be referred to as "the Pure Land." Those who are reborn there find themselves in an ideal environment (presence of a Buddha and bodhisattvas to assist and freed from the restrictions of earthly life) to pursue practice for enlightenment.

23. Meditative absorption or mental concentration.

24. *Anāgāmin*. In the teachings of early Buddhism and particularly of Southern or Theravāda Buddhism, it is the third stage in the four stages of spiritual attainment, in which the seeker will never again be reborn in this world.

25. Taking refuge in the Buddha, the Dharma (Teachings), and Sangha (Community).

26. *Bodhicitta*. The aspiration for enlightenment. The intention to achieve Buddhahood.

are afflicted by the enemy, evil passions. It is very good, Vaidehī, that you have willingly asked me about this. Ānanda, you must receive and keep the Buddha's words and widely proclaim them to the multitude of beings. I, the Tathāgata, shall now teach you, Vaidehī, and all sentient beings of the future how to visualize the Western Land of Utmost Bliss. By the power of the Buddha all will be able to see the Pure Land as clearly as if one were looking at one's own reflection in a bright mirror. Seeing the utmost beauty and bliss of that land, they will rejoice and immediately attain insight into the non-arising of all *dharmas*."[27]

The Buddha said to Vaidehī, "You are unenlightened and so your spiritual powers are weak and obscured. Since you have not yet attained the divine eye,[28] you cannot see that which is distant. But the Buddha Tathāgatas have special ways to enable you to see afar."

Vaidehī said to the Buddha, "World-Honored One, through the Buddha's power, even I have now been able to see that land. But after the Buddha's passing sentient beings will become defiled and evil and be oppressed by the five kinds of suffering.[29] How then will those beings be able to see the Western Land of Utmost Bliss of Amitāyus?"

9 The Buddha said to Vaidehī, "You and other sentient beings should concentrate and, with one-pointed attention, turn your thoughts westward. How do you contemplate? All sentient beings except those born blind—that is, all those with the faculty of sight—should look at the setting sun. Sit in the proper posture,[30] facing west. Clearly gaze at the sun, with mind firmly fixed on it; concentrate your sight and do not let it wander from the setting sun, which is like a drum suspended above the horizon. Having done so, you should then be able to visualize it clearly, whether [98] your eyes are open or closed. This is the visualization of the sun and is known as the first contemplation. To practice in this way is called the correct contemplation, and to practice otherwise is incorrect."

10 The Buddha said to Ānanda and Vaidehī, "After you have accomplished the first contemplation, next practice the visualization of water. Envision the western direction as entirely flooded by water. Then picture the water as clear and pure, and let this vision be distinctly perceived. Keep your thoughts from being distracted. After you have visualized the water, envision it becoming frozen. After you have visualized the ice as transparent to its depth, see it turning into beryl. When you have attained this vision, next imagine that the beryl ground shines brilliantly, inside and out, and that this ground is supported from below by columns that are made of diamond and the seven kinds of jewels and hung with golden banners. These columns have eight sides

---

27. Depending on context, *dharma* may mean duty, teachings, truth, or phenomena. In the present context, it is the latter. "Non-arising of all *dharmas*" describes the ultimate nature of things from a Mahāyāna Buddhist perspective. Emphasizing the emptiness (*śūyatā*) of *dharmas*, the phrase suggests that although phenomena appear to arise and perish, when they are seen from the viewpoint of "ultimate reality," they do not. That is, nothing has a truly independent, self-sufficient existence.

28. One of the six "paranormal abilities," "supernatural powers," or forms of "extrasensory perception" (*siddhi*). These are six transcendent faculties of a Buddha, bodhisattva, or arhat: (1) the ability to go anywhere at will (teleportation and/or multilocality) and to transform oneself or objects at will; (2) the ability to see anything at any distance (clairvoyance); (3) the ability to hear anything at any distance (clairaudience); (4) the ability to know others' thoughts (telepathy); (5) the ability to know the former lives of oneself and others; and (6) the ability to destroy all negative passions.

29. Birth, sickness, old age, death, and separation from that which one loves.

30. Most likely the full-lotus posture (*padmāsana*).

and eight corners, each side being adorned with a hundred kinds of jewels. Each jewel emits a thousand rays of light, each ray in turn having eighty-four thousand colors. As they are reflected on the beryl ground, they look like a thousand *koṭis*[31] of suns, so dazzling that it is impossible to see them in detail.

"On this beryl ground, golden paths intercross like a net of cords. The land is divided into areas made of one or the other of the seven jewels, so the partitions are quite distinct. Each jewel emits a flood of light in five hundred colors. The light appears in the shape of a flower or a star or the moon; suspended in the sky, it turns into a platform of light on which there are ten million pavilions made of a hundred kinds of jewels. Both sides of this platform are adorned with a hundred *koṭis* of flowered banners and innumerable musical instruments. As eight pure breezes arise from the light and play the musical instruments, they proclaim the truths of suffering, emptiness, impermanence, and no-self.[32] This is the visualization of the water and is known as the second contemplation.

11 "When you have attained this contemplation, visualize each object quite clearly without losing the image, whether your eyes are closed or open. Except when sleeping, always keep it in [99] mind. To practice in this way is called the correct contemplation, and to practice otherwise is incorrect."

The Buddha said to Ānanda and Vaidehī, "When the visualization of the water has been accomplished, it is called the general perception of the ground of the Western Land of Utmost Bliss. If you attain a state of *samādhi*, you will see this ground so clearly and distinctly that it will be impossible to describe it in detail. This is the visualization of the ground and is known as the third contemplation."

The Buddha said to Ānanda, "Keep these words of the Buddha in mind, and expound this method of visualizing the ground for the benefit of the multitude of future beings who will seek liberation from suffering. If one has attained a vision of the ground of that land, the evil karma that would bind one to birth and death for eighty *koṭis* of *kalpas*[33] will be extinguished, and so one will certainly be born in the Pure Land in the next life. Do not doubt this. To practice in this way is called the correct contemplation, and to practice otherwise is incorrect."

12 The Buddha said to Ānanda and Vaidehī, "When you have accomplished visualization of the ground, next contemplate the jeweled trees. This is how to do so. Visualize each one and then form an image of seven rows of trees, each being eight thousand *yojanas*[34] high and adorned with seven-jeweled blossoms and leaves. Each blossom and leaf has the colors of various jewels. From the beryl-colored blossoms and leaves issues forth a golden light. From the crystal-colored issues forth a crimson light. From the agate-colored issues forth a sapphire light. From the sapphire-

---

31. A numerical unit sometimes defined as ten million.

32. Suffering (*duḥkha*), impermanence (*anitya*), and no-self (*anātman*) are the three characteristics of existence. *Duḥkha*, "suffering" or "unsatisfactoriness," is also the first of the Four Noble Truths.

33. An eon or an immeasurably long period of time.

34. A unit of distance in India, said to be equal to seven or nine miles (eleven or fourteen kilometers). Also the distance that the royal army could march in a day.

colored issues forth a green pearl light. Coral, amber, and all the other jewels serve as illuminating ornaments. Splendid nets of pearls cover the trees. Between these seven rows of nets covering each tree there are five hundred *koṭi*s of palaces adorned with exquisite flowers, like the palace of the Brahmā-king, where celestial children naturally dwell. Each of these children wears ornaments made of five hundred *koṭi*s of Śakra's pendant *maṇi*-gems,[35] which light up a hundred *yojana*s in all directions, like a hundred *koṭi*s of suns and moons shining together, and so it is impossible to [100] describe them in detail. Manifold jewels intermingle, producing the most beautiful colors.

"Rows of these jeweled trees are evenly arranged and their leaves are equally spaced. From among the leaves appear wonderful blossoms which spontaneously bear fruits of the seven kinds of jewels. Each leaf is twenty-five *yojana*s in both length and breadth. Like the celestial ornaments, the leaves are of a thousand colors and a hundred patterns. These trees have marvelous blossoms which are the color of gold from the Jambu River[36] and spin like firewheels among the leaves. From these blossoms appear various fruits, as from Śakra's vase,[37] and from the fruits issue forth great floods of light which transform themselves into banners and innumerable jeweled canopies. Inside the jeweled canopies can be seen reflections of all the activities of the Buddha throughout the universe of a thousand million worlds. The Buddha lands in the ten directions are also reflected in them.

"After you have seen these trees, visualize each detail in order: the trunks, branches, leaves, blossoms, and fruits, and let your vision of all of them be clear and distinct. This is the visualization of the trees and is known as the fourth contemplation. To practice in this way is called the correct contemplation, and to practice otherwise is incorrect."

13 The Buddha said to Ānanda and Vaidehī, "When you have accomplished visualization of the trees, next contemplate the ponds. This is how to do so. In the Western Land of Utmost Bliss, there are ponds of water possessing the eight excellent qualities, each made of the seven kinds of jewels which are soft and pliable. The water, springing from a wish-fulfilling king *maṇi*-gem,[38] forms fourteen streams. Each stream is the color of the seven kinds of jewels. Its banks are made of gold and its bed is strewn with diamond sand of many colors. In each stream there are sixty *koṭi*s of lotus flowers of the seven kinds of jewels, which are round and symmetrical, measuring twelve *yojana*s in diameter. The water from the *maṇi*-gem flows among the flowers and meanders between the trees. As it ripples it produces exquisite sounds, which proclaim the truths of suffering, emptiness, impermanence, and no-self, and of the *pāramitā*s.[39] Its sound also [101] praises the physical characteristics and marks of the Buddhas.[40] The wish-fulfilling king *maṇi*-gem emits a

---

35. A precious gem of globular shape with a short pointed top. According to Buddhist cosmology, Śakra is the ruler of the Trāyastriṃśa Heaven.
36. A mythological river that runs through the mango forest in the northern part of Jambudvīpa and that is famous for producing purple gold.
37. A divine vase that produces anything that its owner desires.
38. A legendary precious stone supposedly able to produce treasures at the owner's wish.
39. "Perfections." Usually appearing as the six perfections, which are the six kinds of practice by which a bodhisattva attains Buddhahood: (1) giving (*dāna*); (2) keeping precepts or morality (*śīla*); (3) patience (*kṣānti*); (4) effort (*vīrya*); (5) meditation (*samādhi*); and (6) wisdom (*prajñā*).
40. The thirty-two physical characteristics and eighty secondary distinguishing marks of a Buddha or bodhisattva. They include such things as golden skin, blue eyes, and a broad tongue. Buddhist texts also mention eighteen special qualities.

splendid golden light, which transforms itself into birds with the colors of a hundred jewels. Their songs are melodious and elegant, constantly praising the virtue of mindfulness of Buddha, Dharma, and Sangha. This is the visualization of the water possessing the eight excellent qualities and is known as the fifth contemplation. To practice in this way is called the correct contemplation, and to practice otherwise is incorrect."

14 The Buddha said to Ānanda and Vaidehī, "In each region of this jeweled land there are five hundred *koṭi*s of jeweled pavilions in which innumerable *deva*s play heavenly music. There are also musical instruments suspended in the sky, which, like those on the heavenly jeweled banners, spontaneously produce tones even without a player. Each tone proclaims the virtue of mindfulness of Buddha, Dharma, and Sangha. When this contemplation has been accomplished, it is known as the general perception of the jeweled trees, jeweled ground, and jeweled ponds of the Western Land of Utmost Bliss. This is a composite visualization and is called the sixth contemplation.

"Those who have perceived these objects will be rid of extremely heavy evil karma which they have committed during innumerable *kalpa*s and will certainly, after death, be born in that land. To practice in this way is called the correct contemplation, and to practice otherwise is incorrect."

15 The Buddha said to Ānanda and Vaidehī, "Listen carefully, listen carefully and ponder deeply. I will expound for you the method of removing suffering. Bear my words in mind and explain them to the multitude of beings."

When these words were spoken, Amitāyus appeared in the air above, attended on his left and right by the two *mahāsattva*s Avalokiteśvara[41] and Mahāsthāmaprāpta.[42] So brilliant was their radiance that it was impossible to see them in detail. They could not be compared even with a hundred thousand nuggets of gold from the Jambu River. [102]

After she had this vision of Amitāyus, Vaidehī knelt down in worship at Śākyamuni's feet and said to him, "World-Honored One, through your power I have been able to see Amitāyus and the two bodhisattvas, but how can sentient beings of the future see them?"

The Buddha said to Vaidehī, "Those who wish to see that Buddha should form an image of a lotus flower on the seven-jeweled ground. They visualize each petal of this flower as having the colors of a hundred kinds of jewels and eighty-four thousand veins like a celestial painting, with eighty-four thousand rays of light issuing forth from each vein. They should visualize all of these clearly and distinctly. Its smaller petals are two hundred and fifty *yojana*s in both length and breadth. This lotus flower has eighty-four thousand large petals. Between the petals there are a hundred *koṭi*s of king *mani*-gems as illuminating adornments. Each *mani*-gem emits a thousand rays of light which, like canopies made of the seven kinds of jewels, cover the entire earth.

"The dais is made of Śakra's pendant *mani*-gems and is decorated with eighty thousand diamonds, *kiṃśuka*[43]-gems, *brahma mani*-gems, and also with exquisite pearl nets. On the dais four columns with jeweled banners spontaneously arise, each appearing to be as large as a thousand

---

41. "Lord of Beholding." The name of a great bodhisattva who represents Amitāyus's great compassion and stands at his left side.

42. "Possessed of Great Power." The name of a great bodhisattva who represents Amitāyus's great wisdom and stands at his right side.

43. A kind of tree that bears beautiful red blossoms.

million *koṭi*s of Mount Sumerus. On the columns rest a jeweled canopy similar to that in the palace of the Yāma Heaven.[44] It is also adorned with five hundred *koṭi*s of excellent gems, each emitting eighty-four thousand rays shining in eighty-four thousand different tints of golden color. Each golden light suffuses this jeweled land and transforms itself everywhere into various forms, such as diamond platforms, nets of pearls, and nebulous clusters of flowers. In all the ten directions it transforms itself into anything according to one's wishes and performs the activities of the Buddha. This is the visualization of the lotus throne and is known as the seventh contemplation."

The Buddha further said to Ānanda, "This majestic lotus flower was originally produced by the power of the *bhikṣu*[45] Dharmākara's Vow.[46] Those who wish to see the Buddha Amitāyus should first practice this contemplation of the flower throne. In doing so, do not contemplate in a disorderly way. Visualize the objects one by [103] one—each petal, each gem, each ray of light, each dais, and each column. See all of these as clearly and distinctly as if you were looking at your own image in a mirror. When this contemplation is accomplished, the evil karma that would bind you to birth and death for five hundred *koṭi*s of *kalpa*s will be extinguished, and you will certainly be born in the Western Land of Utmost Bliss. To practice in this way is called the correct contemplation, and to practice otherwise is incorrect."

16 The Buddha said to Ānanda and Vaidehī, "After you have seen this, next visualize the Buddha. Why the Buddha? Because Buddhas, Tathāgatas, have cosmic bodies,[47] and so enter into the meditating mind of each sentient being. For this reason, when you contemplate a Buddha, your mind itself takes the form of his thirty-two physical characteristics and eighty secondary marks. Your mind produces the Buddha's image and is itself the Buddha. The ocean of perfectly and universally enlightened Buddhas thus arises in the meditating mind. For this reason, you should single-mindedly concentrate and deeply contemplate the Buddha, Tathāgata, Arhat, and Perfectly Enlightened One.

"When you visualize the Buddha, you should first form his image. Whether your eyes are open or closed, perceive a jeweled image of him, who is the color of gold from the Jambu River, sitting on that flower throne. When you have thus perceived a seated image of the Buddha, your mind's eye will open and you will clearly and distinctly see the seven-jeweled glorious objects of the Western Land of Utmost Bliss, including the seven-jeweled ground, the jeweled ponds, the rows of jeweled trees covered with heavenly jeweled curtains, and jeweled nets spreading over the sky. Perceive these as clearly and distinctly as if you were seeing an object in the palm of your hand.

"After you have seen this image, visualize on the Buddha's left a large lotus flower which is exactly the same as the one described above, and then another large one on his right. Visualize

---

44. The third of the six heavens in the realm of desire.

45. A fully ordained monk.

46. The Forty-Eight Vows taken by Dharmākara prior to becoming Amitāyus and creating the Pure Land. They appear in the *Larger Sukhāvatī-vyūha Sūtra* (see Inagaki 1995, 32–39). According to the Pure Land movement, the eighteenth is considered especially significant, as it guarantees rebirth in the Pure Land for those with sincerity and devotion: "If when I [Dharmākara] attain Buddhahood, sentient beings in the lands of the ten directions who sincerely and joyfully entrust themselves to me, desire to be born in my land, and call my Name even ten times should not be born there, may I not attain perfect enlightenment. Excluded, however, are those who commit the five gravest offences and abuse the right Dharma" (Inagaki 1995, 34).

47. The body of a transcendent Buddha that is manifested in response to the meditating mind of a sentient being.

an image of the Bodhisattva Avalokiteśvara sitting on the flower seat on his left, sending forth a golden light just like the Buddha image [104] described above, and then an image of the Bodhisattva Mahāsthāmaprāpta sitting on the flower seat on his right.

"When you have attained this vision, you will see these images of the Buddha and bodhisattvas sending forth golden rays, which illuminate the jeweled trees. Under each tree there are also three lotus flowers with images of a Buddha and two bodhisattvas sitting on them, so that the land is completely filled with such images.

"When you have attained this vision, you will perceive the streams, rays of light, jeweled trees, ducks, geese, male and female mandarin ducks, and so forth, all expounding the wonderful Dharma. Whether in meditation or not, you will always hear the wonderful Dharma. When you rise from meditation, you should remember what you have heard, not forget it, and confirm it with the sutras. If it does not agree with the sutras, it should be called an illusion, but if it does agree, it is called the attainment of the general perception of the Western Land of Utmost Bliss. This is the visualization of the Buddha image, and is known as the eighth contemplation. If you have attained this, the evil karma that would bind you to birth and death for innumerable *koṭi*s of *kalpa*s will be extinguished and, while in this life, you will attain the Buddha-Recollection Samādhi.[48] To practice in this way is called the correct contemplation, and to practice otherwise is incorrect."

17 The Buddha said to Ānanda and Vaidehī, "After you have succeeded in seeing these images, next envision the physical characteristics and the light of Amitāyus. Ānanda, you should realize that his body is as glorious as a thousand million *koṭi*s of nuggets of gold from the Jambu River of the Yāma Heaven and that his height is six hundred thousand *koṭi*s of *nayuta*s[49] of *yojana*s multiplied by the number of the sands of the Ganges River. The white tuft of hair curling to the right between his eyebrows is five times as big as Mount Sumeru. His eyes are clear and as broad as the four great oceans; their blue irises and whites are distinct. From all the pores of his body issues forth a flood of light as magnificent as Mount Sumeru. His aureole is as broad as a hundred *koṭi*s of universes, [105] each containing a thousand million worlds. In this aureole reside transformed Buddhas numbering as many as a million *koṭi*s of *nayuta*s multiplied by the number of the sands of the Ganges River. Each Buddha is attended by innumerable and countless transformed bodhisattvas.

"The Buddha Amitāyus possesses eighty-four thousand physical characteristics, each having eighty-four thousand secondary marks of excellence. Each secondary mark emits eighty-four thousand rays of light; each ray of light shines universally upon the lands of the ten directions, embracing and not forsaking those who are mindful of the Buddha. It is impossible to describe in detail these rays of light, physical characteristics, and marks, transformed Buddhas, and so forth. But you can see them clearly with your mind's eye through contemplation.

"Those who have envisioned them see all the Buddhas of the ten directions. Because they see the Buddhas, this is called the Buddha-Recollection Samādhi. To attain this contemplation

---

48. A state of concentration in which one visualizes Amitābha. Also an intense practice in which one recites the Name of Amitābha and thereby attains union with him.

49. A high number generally defined as either ten million or a hundred billion.

is to perceive the bodies of all the Buddhas. By perceiving these, one also realizes the Buddha's mind. The Buddha's mind is great compassion. It embraces sentient beings with unconditional benevolence. Those who have practiced this contemplation will, after death, be born in the presence of the Buddhas and realize insight into the non-arising of all *dharma*s. For this reason, the wise should concentrate their thoughts and visualize Amitāyus.

"In contemplating him, begin with one of his physical characteristics. Visualize first the white tuft of hair between his eyebrows until you see it quite clearly and distinctly. When you visualize it, all the eighty-four thousand physical characteristics will spontaneously become manifest. When you see Amitāyus you will also see innumerable Buddhas of the ten directions. Having visualized these innumerable Buddhas you will receive from each the prediction of your future Buddhahood. This is the general perception of all the physical characteristics of the Buddha and is known as the ninth contemplation. To practice in this way is called the correct contemplation, and to practice otherwise is incorrect." [106]

18 The Buddha said to Ānanda and Vaidehī, "After you have seen Amitāyus clearly and distinctly, next visualize Bodhisattva Avalokiteśvara. His height is eighty *koṭi*s of *nayuta*s of *yojana*s multiplied by the number of the sands of the Ganges River. His body is the color of purple-gold, and on the top of his head is a mound surrounded by an aureole with a radius of a hundred thousand *yojana*s, in which there are five hundred transformed Buddhas. Each transformed Buddha resembles Śākyamuni and is attended by five hundred transformed bodhisattvas and innumerable *deva*s. In the light emanating from his entire body are seen the sentient beings of the five realms of samsara in all their distinct physical forms. On his head he wears a heavenly crown made of Śakra's pendant *maṇi*-gems, on which stands a transformed Buddha (Amitāyus) measuring twenty-five *yojana*s in height.

"The face of Bodhisattva Avalokiteśvara is the color of gold from the Jambu River, while the tuft of hair between his eyebrows has the colors of the seven kinds of jewels, and from it issue forth eighty-four thousand different rays of light. In each of these rays dwell innumerable and countless hundreds of thousands of transformed Buddhas, each attended by countless transformed bodhisattvas, all of whom manifest in various forms at will, filling completely the worlds of the ten directions. Avalokiteśvara's arms are the color of red lotus flowers. They emit eighty *koṭi*s of exquisite rays of light in the shape of ornaments, in which are reflected all the glorious objects of that land. The palms of his hands are the color of five hundred *koṭi*s of various lotus flowers. Each of his ten fingertips bears eighty-four thousand signs like impressed patterns, each with eighty-four thousand colors. Each color in turn emits eighty-four thousand delicate rays of light, illuminating all beings. With his jeweled hands he welcomes and guides sentient beings.

"When he lifts one of his feet, the mark of a thousand-spoked wheel on its sole spontaneously changes into a pedestal, which emits five hundred *koṭi*s of light rays. When he puts his foot down, flowers made of diamond and *maṇi*-gems scatter, covering everywhere. All the other physical characteristics and marks that he [107] fully possesses are the same as the Buddha's, except for the mound on his head and the uppermost, invisible part, which are not equal to those of the World-Honored One. This is the visualization of the true physical features of the Bodhisattva Avalokiteśvara and is known as the tenth contemplation."

Then the Buddha said to Ānanda, "Those who wish to see the Bodhisattva Avalokiteśvara should follow the method of contemplation just mentioned. Those who practice this contemplation will not encounter any misfortune but will be freed from karmic hindrances and rid of the evil karma which they have committed during innumerable *kalpa*s of samsara. If you only hear the name of this bodhisattva, you will obtain immeasurable merit. And so, how much more merit will you acquire if you clearly visualize him! Those who wish to see the bodhisattva Avalokiteśvara should first envision the mound on his head and next his heavenly crown. Then they should visualize the other physical characteristics in order, as clearly as if they were looking at something in the palm of their hand. To practice in this way is called the correct contemplation, and to practice otherwise is incorrect."

19 The Buddha said to Ānanda and Vaidehī, "Next visualize the Bodhisattva Mahāsthāmaprāpta. The dimensions of this bodhisattva are the same as those of Avalokiteśvara. His aureole, two hundred and twenty-five *yojana*s in diameter, shines to a distance of two hundred and fifty *yojana*s. The light emanating from his entire body illuminates the worlds of the ten directions, making them shine like purple gold. This light can be seen by anyone who has a close karmic relationship with him. Even if one sees the light emanating from only one pore of his skin, one can perceive the pure and glorious lights of the innumerable Buddhas of the ten directions. That is why this bodhisattva is called Boundless Light. Furthermore, he has great power to illumine all beings with the light of wisdom in order to deliver them from the three evil realms. It is for this reason that he is also called Possessed of Great Power.

"The heavenly crown of this bodhisattva is adorned with five hundred jeweled lotus flowers, each having five hundred jeweled [108] pedestals. On each pedestal appear the pure and resplendent lands of the Buddhas in the ten directions with all their boundless and glorious features.

"The mound on his head, shaped like a lotus bud, has a jeweled vase in front. This is suffused with various lights which reveal all the activities of the Buddha. The rest of the characteristics of his body are exactly the same as Avalokiteśvara's. When this bodhisattva walks, all the worlds in the ten directions quake. Wherever the earth trembles, five hundred *koṭi*s of jeweled flowers appear, each as beautiful and brilliant as a flower in the Western Land of Utmost Bliss. When this bodhisattva sits down, all the seven-jeweled lands, from the land of the Buddha Golden Light in the nadir to that of the Buddha King of Light in the zenith, tremble simultaneously. From between these, manifested bodies of Amitāyus, Avalokiteśvara, and Mahāsthāmaprāpta, as innumerable as particles of dust, all assemble like clouds in the Western Land of Utmost Bliss, filling the entire sky. Sitting on lotus seats, they expound the wonderful Dharma to save suffering beings. To visualize thus is known as the contemplation of Bodhisattva Mahāsthāmaprāpta and is also called the contemplation of Mahāsthāmaprāpta's physical characteristics. To visualize that bodhisattva in this way is known as the eleventh contemplation. It extinguishes the evil karma that would bind one to birth and death for immeasurable and countless *kalpa*s. Those who practice this contemplation will no longer be subject to birth from the womb. They can journey to the pure and exquisite lands of the Buddhas. These contemplations are known as the complete contemplations of Avalokiteśvara and Mahāsthāmaprāpta. To practice in this way is called the correct contemplation, and to practice otherwise is incorrect."

20 The Buddha said to Ānanda and Vaidehī, "After you have contemplated thus, next visualize yourself as born in the Western Land of Utmost Bliss sitting cross-legged upon a lotus flower. Visualize this lotus flower as closed; as it opens, five hundred rays of colored light illuminate your body; then your eyes open and you see Buddhas and bodhisattvas filling the sky and hear the [109] sounds of the water, birds, and trees, and the voices of the Buddhas all expounding the wonderful Dharma in accord with the twelve divisions of the scriptures. When you rise from meditation, keep those things in mind and do not forget them. Seeing them thus is known as the visualization of the Western Land of Utmost Bliss of the Buddha Amitāyus. This is the comprehensive visualization and is known as the twelfth contemplation.

"Innumerable transformed bodies of Amitāyus, together with those of Avalokiteśvara and Mahāsthāmaprāpta, will always accompany those who contemplate thus. To practice in this way is called the correct contemplation, and to practice otherwise is incorrect."

21 The Buddha said to Ānanda and Vaidehī, "If you sincerely desire to be born in the Western Land, you should first picture a figure, sixteen feet tall, on the surface of a pond. The dimensions of Amitāyus as previously described are boundless and beyond the mental scope of ordinary beings. But by the power of the Original Vows of that Tathāgata, those who contemplate him will certainly succeed. You can acquire immeasurable merit simply by visualizing an image of that Buddha. And so, how much more merit will you acquire by visualizing his complete physical characteristics!

"Amitāyus, exercising supernatural powers at will, can freely manifest his various forms in the lands of the ten directions. At times he may appear as a large figure, filling the whole sky; at other times as a smaller figure, only sixteen or eight feet high. The figures that he manifests are all of the color of pure gold. The transformed Buddhas and jeweled lotus flowers in the aureole of each manifested form are like those described above.

"The bodhisattvas Avalokiteśvara and Mahāsthāmaprāpta have a similar appearance, wherever they are. Sentient beings can only tell one from the other by looking at the emblems on their heads. These two bodhisattvas assist Amitāyus in saving all beings everywhere. This is the miscellaneous visualization and is known as the thirteenth contemplation. To practice in this way is called the correct contemplation, and to practice otherwise is incorrect." [110]

22 The Buddha said to Ānanda and Vaidehī, "Those born in the Western Land are of nine grades. Those who attain birth on the highest level of the highest grade are sentient beings who resolve to be born in that land, awaken the three kinds of faith, and so are born there. What are the three? They are, first, sincere faith; second, deep faith; and third, the faith that seeks birth there by transferring one's merit. Those who have these three kinds of faith will certainly be born there.

"There are three other kinds of sentient beings who also attain birth. Who are the three? They are, first, those who have a compassionate heart, abstain from killing, and observe the precepts; second, those who chant the Mahāyāna sutras of greater scope; and third, those who practice the six forms of mindfulness.[50] They aspire to be born in that Buddha land by transferring there the merit of practice. With the merit acquired from doing these acts for one to seven days, they attain birth.

"When an aspirant is about to be born in that land through dedicated and undaunted practices, the Tathāgata Amitāyus arrives together with Avalokiteśvara, Mahāsthāmaprāpta, innumerable transformed Buddhas, a great assembly of a hundred thousand monks and *śrāvakas*,[51]

---

50. Six objects of concentration, namely, the Buddha, the Dharma, the Sangha, precepts, giving, and heaven with a desire to be born there.
51. "Hearers." Originally, a disciple of the historical Buddha who heard his teachings.

and innumerable *deva*s in seven-jeweled palaces. The Bodhisattva Avalokiteśvara, carrying a *vajra*-seat,[52] together with the Bodhisattva Mahāsthāmaprāpta, approaches the aspirant. Amitāyus releases a great flood of light that illuminates the aspirant's body and, along with the bodhisattvas, extends his hands in welcome. Avalokiteśvara and Mahāsthāmaprāpta, together with innumerable bodhisattvas, praise and encourage the aspirant. Seeing this, the aspirant rejoices so greatly as to dance. Then he sees himself sitting on the *vajra*-seat, and, following the Buddha, is born into that land in the time it takes to snap one's fingers.

"After being born in that land, he sees the Buddha's body complete with all its physical characteristics and also the bodies of the bodhisattvas equally complete with all their physical characteristics. Hearing the discourse on the wonderful Dharma sent forth by the light and the jeweled trees, he then reaches the [111] insight into the non-arising of all *dharma*s. In a single moment, he visits and worships all the Buddhas of the ten directions and receives from each of them the prediction of his future Buddhahood. Returning to the Pure Land, he is endowed with innumerable hundreds of thousands of *dhāraṇī*s.[53] Such a person is called one who attains birth on the highest level of the highest grade.

23 "Those who attain birth on the middle level of the highest grade do not necessarily uphold and chant the sutras of greater scope, but they comprehend the teachings of the Buddha so well that when they hear the supreme truths they are not dismayed. They have deep faith in the law of karmic cause and effect and do not slight the Mahāyāna. They transfer the merit acquired to the Western Land of Utmost Bliss, aspiring to be born there.

"When such an aspirant is about to die, Amitāyus appears before him, surrounded by Avalokiteśvara, Mahāsthāmaprāpta, and innumerable sages and attendants, carrying a purple-gold lotus seat. The Buddha praises him, saying, 'Son of the Dharma, because you have practiced the Mahāyāna and appreciate the supreme truths, I have come to welcome you.' So saying, he and a thousand transformed Buddhas extend their hands all at once toward the aspirant, who, seeing himself sitting on the purple-gold seat, joins his palms and praises the Buddhas. In an instant, he is born in a seven-jeweled pond of that land.

"The purple-gold seat has become like a great jeweled flower, which opens after one night. The body of the aspirant has become the color of purple gold and beneath his feet are seven-jeweled lotus flowers. The Buddha and bodhisattvas together release a flood of light that illuminates the aspirant's body. His eyes open, and because of the store of merit from his previous life, he hears voices everywhere expounding only the most profound and supreme truths. Descending from his golden seat, he bows with joined palms and praises the Buddha, the World-Honored One. After seven days, he immediately reaches the stage of non-retrogression[54] for realizing highest, perfect enlightenment. He is also able to fly in the ten directions, as he wishes, and to revere all the Buddhas and [112] learn various *samādhi*s from them. After the lapse of a smaller *kalpa*,

---

52. A seat made of adamant.

53. A magical phrase, spell, or incantation.

54. *Avinivartanīya*. The stage in which a practitioner no longer backslides to a lower stage and is thus able to proceed to enlightenment with greater confidence.

he attains the insight into the non-arising of all *dharma*s and receives from each Buddha the prediction of his future Buddhahood. Such a person is called one who attains birth on the middle level of the highest grade.

24 "Those who attain birth on the lowest level of the highest grade likewise accept the law of karmic cause and effect, do not speak slightingly of the Mahāyāna, and awaken aspiration for highest enlightenment. They transfer the merit acquired to the Western Land of Utmost Bliss, aspiring to be born there.

"When such an aspirant is about to die, Amitāyus, together with Avalokiteśvara, Mahāsthāmaprāpta, and a host of attendants, come to welcome him, bringing a golden lotus flower and manifesting five hundred transformed Buddhas. Those transformed Buddhas extend their hands all at once and praise the aspirant, saying, 'Son of the Dharma, since you have awakened pure aspiration for highest enlightenment, we have come to welcome you.'

"When he has viewed all this, the aspirant finds himself seated upon a golden lotus flower, which then closes. Following the World-Honored One, he immediately attains birth on a seven-jeweled pond. After a day and night, the lotus flower opens and, within seven days, the aspirant beholds the Buddha. Although he sees the Buddha's body, he is still unable to discern his physical characteristics and marks clearly. But after three weeks he sees them distinctly, and also hears all the sounds and voices proclaiming the wonderful Dharma. Then he can travel in all the ten directions to make offerings to the Buddhas and hear their profound teachings. After three smaller *kalpa*s, he acquires clear understanding of the one hundred *dharma*s and dwells in the stage of joy. Such a person is called one who attains birth on the lowest level of the highest grade. These three together are known as the contemplation of the highest grade of aspirants, and the fourteenth contemplation. To practice in this way is called the correct contemplation, and to practice otherwise is incorrect." [113]

25 The Buddha said to Ānanda and Vaidehī, "Those who attain birth on the highest level of the middle grade are the sentient beings who keep the five precepts,[55] observe the eight abstinences, practice in compliance with various precepts, and abstain from committing the five grave offenses[56] and other transgressions. They transfer the merit acquired to the Western Land of Utmost Bliss, aspiring to be born there.

"When such a person is about to die, Amitāyus appears before him, surrounded by a host of monks and radiating a golden light. He then expounds the truth of suffering, emptiness, impermanence, and no-self, and praises renunciation of the world as the way to escape from suffering.

"Seeing this, the aspirant greatly rejoices and finds himself seated upon a lotus flower. He kneels down, joins his palms, and worships the Buddha. Before he raises his head he attains birth in the Western Land of Utmost Bliss, where his lotus bud soon opens. When the flower opens,

---

55. Not to kill, steal, commit sexual misconduct, lie, or take intoxicants.

56. Patricide, matricide, killing an arhat, maliciously causing a Buddha's body to bleed, and causing disharmony in the Sangha.

he hears various sounds and voices extolling the Four Noble Truths. He immediately attains arhatship,[57] acquires the three kinds of transcendent knowledge[58] and the six supernatural powers, and realizes the eight *samādhi*s of liberation.[59] Such a person is called one who attains birth on the highest level of the middle grade.

26 "Those who attain birth on the middle level of the middle grade are the sentient beings who observe for at least a day and a night the eight abstinences, the precepts for a novice,[60] or the complete precepts of a monk or a nun, and do not violate any of the rules of conduct. They transfer the merit acquired to the Western Land of Utmost Bliss, aspiring to be born there.

"When such an aspirant, perfumed by the virtue of observing the precepts, is about to die, he sees Amitāyus coming toward him with his attendants, radiating a golden light and carrying a seven-jeweled lotus flower. He hears a voice in the sky above praising him, saying, 'Man of good deeds, since you are virtuous and have followed the teachings of the Buddhas of the three periods, I have come to welcome you.' The aspirant finds himself seated upon the [114] lotus flower. The flower having closed, the aspirant is born on a jeweled pond of the Western Land of Utmost Bliss. After seven days the lotus bud unfolds, and he then opens his eyes. With joined palms he pays homage to the World-Honored One, rejoices at hearing the Dharma, and reaches the stage of stream-winner. After half a *kalpa*, he becomes an arhat. Such a person is called one who attains birth on the middle level of the middle grade.

27 "Those who attain birth on the lowest level of the middle grade are good men and women who are dutiful to and care for their parents and do benevolent deeds for others. When such a person is about to die, he may meet a good teacher, who fully explains to him the bliss of the land of Amitāyus and the Forty-Eight Great Vows of the *bhikṣu* Dharmākara. Having heard this, he dies; and in as short a time as it takes a strong man to bend and straighten his arm he attains birth in the Western Land of Utmost Bliss. Seven days after his birth there, he meets Avalokiteśvara and Mahāsthāmaprāpta, rejoices at hearing the Dharma from them, and so reaches the stage of stream-winner. After one smaller *kalpa*, he becomes an arhat. Such a person is called one who attains birth on the lowest level of the middle grade. These three together are known as the contemplation of the middle grade of aspirants and the fifteenth contemplation. To practice in this way is called the correct contemplation, and to practice otherwise is incorrect."

---

57. "Worthy" or "noble one." A saint who has completely eradicated harmful passions and attained emancipation from the cycle of birth, death, and rebirth. The highest of the four stages of spiritual attainment. Also one of the ten epithets of a Buddha.

58. Three kinds of knowledge attained by a Buddha, bodhisattva, or arhat: (1) knowledge of the former lives of oneself and others, (2) the ability to know the future destiny of oneself and others, and (3) the ability to know all about the miseries of the present life and to remove their root cause, namely, harmful passions.

59. Meditation on the following: (1) the impurity of the body, to extinguish physical passions; (2) the impurity of external objects, to extinguish desire; (3) pure aspects of external objects, to extinguish passions; (4) boundless consciousness, to remove attachment to material objects; (5) boundless consciousness, to remove attachment to the void; (6) nonexistence, to remove attachment to consciousness; (7) the stage of neither thought nor nonthought, to extinguish attachment to nonexistence; and (8) the final *samādhi*, which extinguishes all thoughts and perceptions and enables the meditator to dwell in the stage of total extinction.

60. There are 5 precepts for laypeople, 10 precepts for novices, and 250 for fully ordained monks.

28 The Buddha said to Ānanda and Vaidehī, "Those who attain birth on the highest level of the lowest grade are the sentient beings who commit various evil acts but do not slander the Mahāyāna sutras of greater scope. When a foolish person such as this, who has committed much evil but feels no remorse, is about to die, he may meet a good teacher, who praises the titles of the twelve divisions of the Mahāyāna scriptures. By hearing these sutra titles, he is released from the burden of evil karma that would bind him to birth and death for a thousand *kalpa*s. Furthermore, this wise teacher advises him to join his palms and call, 'Homage to Amitāyus Buddha [*Na-mo-o-mi-t'o-fo*].'[61] Calling the Name of the [115] Buddha extinguishes the evil karma that would bind the dying person to birth and death for fifty *koṭi*s of *kalpa*s.

"The Buddha then sends his transformed body and those of Avalokiteśvara and Mahāsthāmaprāpta to the aspirant; they praise him, saying, 'Well done, man of good deeds! By calling the Name of the Buddha your evil karma has been extinguished, and so we have come to welcome you.' When these words are uttered, the aspirant sees a flood of light from that transformed Buddha fill his room. Having seen this, he rejoices and dies. Seated on a jeweled lotus flower, he follows the transformed Buddha and is born on a jeweled pond. In seven weeks the lotus bud opens and Avalokiteśvara, the bodhisattva of great compassion, and Mahāsthāmaprāpta Bodhisattva appear before him, releasing great floods of light, and explain to him the extremely profound teachings of the twelve divisions of the scriptures. Having heard these, the aspirant accepts them in faith and awakens aspiration for highest enlightenment. After ten smaller *kalpa*s, he acquires clear understanding of the one hundred *dharma*s and enters the first stage of a bodhisattva. Such a person is called one who attains birth on the highest level of the lowest grade. Thus he is born by hearing the Name of Buddha, Dharma, and Sangha—that is, the Three Treasures."

29 The Buddha said to Ānanda and Vaidehī, "Those who attain birth on the middle level of the lowest grade are the sentient beings who violate the five precepts, the eight precepts, or the complete precepts of a monk or a nun. A foolish person such as this steals from the Sangha, or takes the personal belongings of monks, or preaches the Dharma with impure motives, but feels no remorse. Thus he defiles himself by evil karma and because of this he is liable to fall into hell.

"When he is about to die and the flames of hell suddenly close in on him, he may meet a good teacher, who compassionately explains to him the ten supernatural powers of Amitāyus,[62] fully describing the majestic power of the light of that Buddha and his virtues in the observance of the precepts, meditation, wisdom, liberation, [116] and knowledge of liberation. When he has heard this, the evil karma that would bind him to birth and death for eighty *koṭi*s of *kalpa*s are

---

61. "Recitation of the Name." Literally, "recollecting" or "thinking about the Buddha" (Chn.: *nianfo*; Jpn.: *nembutsu*). An important Pure Land Buddhist practice. In Pinyin romanization, it is *namo Amituofo* ("I take refuge in the Buddha of Infinite Life"). In Japanese, it is pronounced *namu Amida Butsu*.

62. Perfect knowledge of the following: (1) distinguishing right and wrong; (2) knowing the karma of all sentient beings of the past, present, and future, and its outcome; (3) knowing all forms of meditation; (4) knowing the superior and inferior capacities of sentient beings; (5) knowing what they desire and think; (6) knowing their different levels of existence; (7) knowing the results of various methods of practice; (8) knowing the transmigratory states of all sentient beings and the courses of karma they follow; (9) knowing the past lives of all sentient beings and the nirvanic state of nondefilement; and (10) knowing how to destroy all harmful passions.

extinguished; thus, the fierce flames of hell turn into cool and refreshing breezes, wafting heavenly flowers. On each flower is a transformed Buddha accompanied by bodhisattvas welcoming him.

"In an instant, he attains birth within a lotus bud on a seven-jeweled pond. After six *kalpa*s the lotus bud opens, and then Avalokiteśvara and Mahāsthāmaprāpta comfort him with their noble voices and teach him profound Mahāyāna sutras. Upon hearing these, he immediately awakens aspiration for highest enlightenment. Such a person is called one who attains birth on the middle level of the lowest grade."

30 The Buddha said to Ānanda and Vaidehī, "Those who attain birth on the lowest level of the lowest grade are the sentient beings who commit such evils as the five grave offenses, the ten evil acts,[63] and all kinds of immorality. Owing to such evil karma, a fool like this will fall into evil realms and suffer endless agony for many *kalpa*s. When he is about to die, he may meet a good teacher, who consoles him in various ways, teaching him the wonderful Dharma and urging him to be mindful of the Buddha; but he is too tormented by pain to do so. The good teacher then advises him, 'If you cannot concentrate on the Buddha then you should say instead, "Homage to Amitāyus Buddha.'" In this way, he sincerely and continuously says, 'Homage to Amitāyus Buddha' [*Na-mo-o-mi-t'o-fo*] ten times. Because he calls the Buddha's Name, with each repetition the evil karma that would bind him to birth and death for eighty *koṭi*s of *kalpa*s is extinguished. When he comes to die, he sees before him a golden lotus flower like the disk of the sun, and in an instant he is born within a lotus bud in the Western Land of Utmost Bliss. After twelve great *kalpa*s, the lotus bud opens. When the flower opens, Avalokiteśvara and Mahāsthāmaprāpta teach him with voices of great compassion the method of extinguishing evil karma through the realization of the suchness of all *dharma*s. Hearing this, he rejoices and immediately awakens aspiration for [117] enlightenment. Such a person is called one who attains birth on the lowest level of the lowest grade. These three together are known as the contemplation of the lowest grade of aspirants and the sixteenth contemplation."

31 As the Buddha delivered these words, Vaidehī and her five hundred female attendants listened to his teaching. Having envisioned the boundless features of the Western Land of Utmost Bliss, of the Buddha [Amitāyus], and of the two bodhisattvas, Vaidehī rejoiced in her heart. Wonder-struck at this revelation, she attained great awakening with clarity of mind and insight into the non-arising of all *dharma*s. Her five hundred female attendants awakened aspiration for highest, perfect enlightenment and desired to be born in that land. The World-Honored One gave them all assurances that they would be born there and that they would then gain the *samādhi* of being in the presence of all the Buddhas. Innumerable *deva*s also awakened aspiration for highest enlightenment.

32 Then Ānanda rose from his seat, stepped forward, and said to the Buddha, "World-Honored One, what should we call this sutra and how should we receive and retain the essentials of its teaching?"

---

63. Killing, stealing, committing sexual misconduct, lying, uttering harsh words, uttering words that cause hatred and distrust among people, engaging in idle talk, envy, malice, and having wrong views.

The Buddha answered, "Ānanda, this sutra is called the Visualization of the Western Land of Utmost Bliss of the Buddha Amitāyus and of the Bodhisattvas Avalokiteśvara and Mahāsthāmaprāpta. It is also called the Purification and Elimination of Karmic Hindrances for Attaining Birth in the Presence of All the Buddhas. Hold fast to this sutra and do not forget it. Those who practice this *samādhi* will be able to see, during their lifetime, the Buddha Amitāyus and the two *mahāsattva*s. If good men or women simply hear the Name of this Buddha or the names of those two bodhisattvas, the evil karma that would bind them to birth and death for innumerable *kalpa*s will be extinguished. And so, how much more merit will they acquire if they concentrate on them! You should know that all who are mindful of that Buddha are like white lotus flowers among humankind; the bodhisattvas Avalokiteśvara and Mahāsthāmaprāpta [118] become their good friends. They will sit in the seat of enlightenment and be born into the family of the Buddhas."

The Buddha further said to Ānanda, "Bear these words well in mind. To bear these words in mind means to hold fast to the Name of Buddha Amitāyus."

When the Buddha had spoken thus, Venerable Mahāmaudgalyāyana, Venerable Ānanda, Vaidehī, and all the others greatly rejoiced to hear the Buddha's discourse.

33 Then the World-Honored One returned to Vulture Peak through the air. There Ānanda fully explained to the assembly what had happened. Innumerable humans, *deva*s, *nāga*s,[64] *yakṣa*s,[65] and all other beings greatly rejoiced to hear the Buddha's teaching. Having worshiped the World-Honored One, they departed.

---

64. A dragon. One of the eight kinds of superhuman beings that protect Buddhism.
65. A goblin. One of the eight kinds of superhuman beings that protect Buddhism.

Chapter 10

Hindu Classical Yoga

Patañjali's *Yoga Sūtras*

Edwin F. Bryant

A text of unclear provenance, the *Yoga Sūtras* (Yoga Aphorisms; abbr. YS) is a Sanskrit text on classical Yoga. Originally written in Sanskrit, the text was composed by Patañjali, an obscure figure who probably lived during the first or second century CE and who became identified in later times as the founder of the "Yoga school." In the *Yoga Sūtras*, Patañjali describes a fairly systematic process of meditative discipline aimed at liberation (*mokṣa*) through the purification of consciousness, perhaps most famously expressed as the "eight limbs" (*aṣṭāṅga*). Based on the various preconditions and religious commitments for the practice, the text appears to be addressed to Hindu ascetics and renunciants.

Patañjali and Second-Century-CE Hinduism

Patañjali (ca. 1st–2nd c. CE) was the compiler of the *Yoga Sūtras*, one of the ancient treatises on Indic thought that eventually came to be regarded as the basis of the "Yoga school," one of the "six classical schools of Indian 'philosophy.'"[1] Patañjali presents a teaching that focuses on realization of *puruṣa*—the term favored by the Yoga school[2] to refer to the innermost conscious self, loosely equivalent to the soul in Western Greco-Abrahamic traditions. This school emerged from the sixth century BCE as perhaps the most important development in post-Vedic India and has exerted immense influence over the philosophical directions and religious practices of what has come to be known as mainstream "Hinduism,"[3] both in its dominant forms in India and in its most common exported and repackaged forms visible in the West. Accordingly, Patañjali's *Yoga Sūtras* is one of the most important classical texts in Hinduism and thus a "classic" of so-called "Eastern," and therefore world, thought.

As with the reputed founders of the other schools of thought, very little is known about Patañjali himself. Tradition, first evidenced in the commentary of Bhoja Rāja in the eleventh century CE, considers him to be the same Patañjali who wrote the primary commentary on the famous grammar by Pāṇini and also ascribes to him authorship of a treatise on medicine. There is an ongoing discussion among scholars as to whether this was likely or not.[4] My own view is that there is not much to be gained by challenging the evidence of traditional accounts in the absence of alternative evidence to the contrary, especially evidence that is uncontroversial or at least adequately compelling. Other than this, a verse surfacing in the eleventh-century commentary of king Bhoja identifies Patañjali as an incarnation of *śeṣa*, a manifestation of the Supreme God Viṣṇu in the form of a cosmic serpent. In sum, we lack information on both the historical Patañjali and the provenance of the *Yoga Sūtras* attributed to him.

Patañjali's date can only be inferred from the content and context of the text itself. Unfortunately, as with most classical Sanskrit texts from the ancient period, early Sanskrit texts tend to be impossible to date with accuracy, and there are always dissenters against whatever dates become standard in academic circles. Most scholars seems to date the text shortly after the turn of the Common Era, around the first to second centuries CE, but it has also been placed as early as several centuries before the Common Era (see Larson and Bhattacharya 2008). Other than the fact that the text does not postdate the fifth century CE, the date of the *Yoga Sūtras* cannot be determined with exactitude. By the ninth century CE at the latest,[5] Yoga, as a tradition stemming from Patañjali's *Yoga Sūtras*, is situated as one of the "six schools of philosophy" and retained that status thereafter.

Yoga and the "Yoga School"

In terms of *yoga*'s origins, the Vedic period (1500–1200 BCE) is the earliest era in South Asia for which we have written records, and it provides the matrix from which later religious, philosophical, and spiritual expressions such as the "Yoga school" evolved in India, at least in the northern part of the subcontinent. *Yoga* evolved on the periphery of Vedic religiosity and beyond the parameters of mainstream Vedic orthopraxy. It is clearly in tension with Vedic (Brāhmaṇical) ritualism,[6] and its goals are in stark and explicit opposition to it (e.g., YS I.15–16).

Like other old world cultures, the dominant religious expression in the early Vedic period within which Yoga emerged was that of the sacrificial cult wherein animals and other items were offered to various gods through the medium of fire. One of the purposes of these rituals involved obtaining worldly boons such as offspring, cattle, victory over enemies, and so forth. While the intricacies of the Vedic sacrificial rite may seem alien to modern worldviews and practices, the mentality that supported it, what one may call materialistic religiosity—attempting to cajole or solicit higher powers for the purpose of receiving boons ultimately aimed at enjoying the pleasures of the material world through the medium of the sensual body—has remained constant throughout human history. It is for this reason that the post-Vedic reactions to this type of mentality, in the form of developments such as the various systems of *yoga*, remain perennially relevant to the human condition.

There is evidence as early as the oldest Vedic text, the *Ṛg Veda*, of a long-haired ascetic (X.136), indicating that there were *yogī*-like ascetics on the margins of the Vedic landscape. However, it is

Figure 10.1. Harappan Seal
Mohenjo-daro (Sindh, Pakistan)⁷
Source: J. M. Kenoyer/Harappa.com and Department of Archaeology and Museums, Government of Pakistan

in the late Vedic age, marked by the fertile speculations expressed in a genre of texts called the *Upaniṣads*, that practices that can be clearly related to classical Yoga are first explicitly expressed in literary sources (Bryant 2009, xixff.). The *Upaniṣads* reveal a clear shift in focus away from the sacrificial rite, which is relegated to an inferior type of religiosity, replacing it with an interest in philosophical and mystical discourse, particularly the quest for the ultimate, underlying reality, Brahman, underpinning the external world, which is localized in living beings as *ātman*.⁸ While the *Upaniṣads* are especially concerned with *jñāna*, or understanding Brahman, the Ultimate Reality, through the cultivation of knowledge, there are also several unmistakable references, especially in the *Katha Upaniṣad* and *Śvetāśvatara Upaniṣad*, to a technique for realizing Brahman (in its localized aspect of *ātman*) called *yoga*. These are clearly drawn from the same general body of related practices as those articulated by Patañjali.⁹ By the later (but pre-Patañjala) *Maitrī Upaniṣad*, we have a much more extensive discussion of *yoga*, including more specific references of the six *aṅga*s or "limbs" of *yoga*: Five of these "limbs" correspond precisely to the last five limbs of Patañjali's system (see YS II).¹⁰

The *Mahābhārata* (Tale of the Great Bhārata Dynasty), which culminates in one hundred thousand verses,[11] is the largest literary epic in the world, and, like the *Maitrī Upaniṣad*, preserves significant material representing the evolution of *yoga*. Usually dated somewhere between the ninth and fourth centuries BCE, this epic exemplifies the transition between the origins of *yoga* in the Upaniṣadic period (ca. 8th–4th c. BCE) and its expression in the systematized tradition of Yoga as represented by Patañjali.[12] Nestled in the middle of the epic, the well-known *Bhagavad Gītā* (Song of the Lord; ca. 4th c. BCE), devotes a good portion of its bulk to the practices of *yoga*, which it considers to be "ancient" (IV.3); indeed, Kṛṣṇa presents himself as reestablishing teachings that had existed since primordial times. While the *Gītā* tends to use the term *yoga* as synonymous with *karma yoga*, the discipline of action, the techniques of Patañjalian-type *yoga* are outlined throughout the entire sixth chapter, albeit subsumed under devotion to Kṛṣṇa. The *Gītā* refers to this type of practice as *dhyāna yoga*, the discipline of meditation,[13] as did most early Indic texts.

While a comprehensive discussion of the references to *yoga* in the larger *Mahābhārata* is beyond the scope of this chapter, there are a number of references to practices that are clearly relatable to the system of Yoga as taught by Patañjali. Most of these appear in the *mokṣadharma* section of book 12. The terms *yoga* and *yogī* occur about nine hundred times throughout the epic, expressed, as noted previously, in terms midway between the unformulated expressions of the *Upaniṣads* and the systematized practice as outlined by Patañjali. This, of course, indicates that practices associated with *yoga* had gained wide currency in the centuries prior to the Common Era, with a clearly identifiable set of basic techniques and generic practices, and it is from these that Patañjali drew for his systemization. For example, scholars have long pointed out a commonality of vocabulary and concepts between the *Yoga Sūtras* and Buddhist texts (see Larson and Bhattacharya 2008, 37ff.). All this underscores the basic point that there was a cluster of numerous, interconnected, and cross-fertilizing variants of meditational *yoga*, Buddhist and Jain as well as Hindu, prior to Patañjali. All of these drew from a common but variegated pool of terminologies, practices, and concepts (and indeed, many strains continue to the present day). One might envision a plethora of centers of learning and practice, spearheaded by charismatic renunciants, where parallel and overlapping philosophical doctrines and meditative practices, many going by the name of *yoga*, were evolving out of a common Upaniṣadic-flavored core.

The history of Yoga is inextricable from that of the Sāṁkhya tradition, one of the so-called "six schools" (see Bryant 2009, xxvff.). As discussed in more detail later, Sāṁkhya provides the metaphysical infrastructure for Yoga and thus is indispensable for understanding of Yoga. Usually translated as "enumeration" or "counting" due to its focus on the evolution and constituents of the twenty-four ingredients of *prakṛti*, material reality, Sāṁkhya might best be taken as the path striving to understand the ultimate truths of reality through knowledge, typically known as *jñāna yoga*, while Yoga focused on practice. Sāṁkhya seems to have been perhaps the earliest philosophical system to have taken shape in the late Vedic period, and, indeed, it has permeated almost all subsequent Hindu traditions: Vedānta, Purāṇa, Vaiṣṇava, Śaiva, Śakta, and even the medicinal traditions such as Āyurveda. Indeed some scholars see the classical Yoga of Patañjali as a type of neo-Sāṁkhya, updating the old Sāṁkhya tradition to bring it into conversation with the more technical philosophical traditions that emerged by the third to fifth centuries CE, most particularly Buddhist thought (see Larson and Bhattacharya 2008, 43ff.). Sāṁkhya and Yoga should not be considered different "schools" until very much later. In fact, the first reference to

Yoga itself as a distinct school seems to be the writings of Śaṅkara[14] in the ninth century CE. Their difference is not in metaphysics, ethics, or soteriology but in method: the terms *yoga* and *sāṁkhya* in the *Upaniṣads* and *Mahābhārata* simply refer to the two distinct paths of liberation through meditation and liberation through knowledge, respectively, rather than to distinct schools. The chief difference in the trajectory that Yoga took was its exclusive focus on the psychological mechanisms and techniques involved in *puruṣa*'s liberation (*mokṣa*), or more technically "perfect solitude" and "complete detachment" (*kaivalya*). Similarly Sāṁkhya concerned itself with the specificities of *prakṛti*'s ingredients, from which *puruṣa* was to be extricated.

We might note that *yoga* has been popularly translated as "union with the divine" and may refer to a number of different spiritual systems. The well-known *Bhagavad Gītā*, for example, discusses a number of practices that have been termed *yoga* in popular literature: *karma yoga* (*buddhi yoga*), the path of action; *jñāna yoga* (Sāṁkhya), the path of knowledge; *bhakti yoga*, the path of devotion; and *dhyāna yoga*, the path of silent meditation, the latter of which is the subject of Patañjali's text.[15] Moreover, terms such as *tantric yoga*, *siddhi yoga*, *nāḍa yoga*, and so forth, are now common in alternative spiritualities in the West. Typically, however, when the word is used by itself without any qualification, *yoga* refers to the path of meditation aimed at liberation, particularly as exemplified in the *Yoga Sūtras*, while the term *yogī* refers to a practitioner of this type of meditational *yoga*.

In addition to various "heterodox schools" such as Jainism and Buddhism, what came to be identified (in much later times) as six schools of orthodox thought[16] also eventually evolved out of the Upaniṣadic period.[17] (Of course, there were various other streams of thought, which did not gain this status but have nonetheless emerged as significant presences on the religious landscape of Hinduism.) They shared much of their overall worldview but dedicated themselves to different areas of human knowledge and praxis. While differing considerably on metaphysical and epistemological issues, they nonetheless did not necessarily reject the authority of the other traditions in other specific areas, especially where these did not conflict with their own positions. For example, the Nyāya (Logician) school accepts Yoga as the method to be used to realize the *ātman* as understood within that tradition (*Nyāya Sūtras* IV.2.42), and Vedānta primarily only objects to it to the extent that it does not accept Brahman as the ultimate source of *puruṣa* and *prakṛti*, not to its authenticity in meditative technique and practice (*Vedānta Sūtras* II.1.3 and commentaries). Thus, rather than a distinct school, prior to the second millennium, *yoga* referred, first and foremost, to a form of rigorous discipline and concentration for attaining liberation that was appropriated and tailored by different traditions according to their metaphysical understanding of the Self.

In any event, eventually an "orthodox school" of Yoga came to be identified with Patañjali, the compiler of these *Yoga Sūtras*. It took its place alongside other traditions that also had distinct *sūtra* traditions and became one of the "six schools of Indian philosophy" (see Nicholson 2011). These are Sāṁkhya, Yoga, Nyāya, Vaiśeṣika, Mīmāṁsā, and Vedānta.[18] These schools were deemed "orthodox" because they retained at least a nominal allegiance to the sacred Vedic texts; this stands in contrast to the "heterodox schools" such as Buddhism and Jainism that rejected them.

Indic schools, both "orthodox" and "heterodox," interacted intellectually and sometimes polemically, both debating and mutually enriching each other, and their emergence pushed the old Vedic cult further into the background. From this rich and fertile post-Vedic context, then, emerged an individual called Patañjali whose systematization of the heterogeneous practices of *yoga* came to become the standard canon for all subsequent practitioners; this system eventually became reified into one of the six schools of classical Indian philosophy. Here it is important to stress again that Patañjali is not the founder, or inventor, of *yoga*, the origins of which had long preceded him in primordial and mythic times. Patañjali systematized and authored what came to be the seminal text for *yoga* discipline from preexisting traditions. There was never one uniform school or Ur-Yoga (or of any Indic school of thought for that matter): there were a plurality of variants and certainly different conceptualizations of meditative practices that were termed *yoga*. For example, while Patañjali organized his system into eight limbs, the *Mahābhārata* also speaks of *yoga* as having eight "qualities" (*aṣṭaguṇita*; XII.304.7). Similarly, as early as in the *Maitrī Upaniṣad* of the second century BCE, there is reference to a six-limbed *yoga* (VI.18), as there is in the *Viṣṇu Purāṇa* (VI.7.91). *Yoga* is thus best understood as a cluster of techniques, some more and some less systematized, that pervaded the landscape of ancient India. These overlapped and were incorporated into the various traditions of the day, providing these systems with a practical method and technique for attaining an experience-based transformation of consciousness. However, in short, because he produced the first systematized treatise on the subject, Patañjali was to become the prime or seminal figure for the Yoga tradition after his times and accepted as such by other schools. For all intents and purposes, his *Yoga Sūtras* were to become the canon for the mechanics of generic *yoga*, so to speak, that other systems often adopted and then tinkered with and flavored with their own theological trappings. As discussed in more detail later, the fundamental characteristic of this practice involved meditative discipline aimed at liberation.

The *sūtra* writing style of the *Yoga Sūtras* is that used by the philosophical schools of ancient India, as evidenced in the *Vedānta Sūtras*, *Nyāya Sūtras*, and so forth. The term *sūtra*, from the Sanskrit root *sū*, and cognate with "sew," literally means a thread. It essentially refers to a terse and pithy philosophical statement in which the maximum amount of information is packed into the minimum amount of words. Knowledge systems were handed down orally in ancient India, and thus source material was kept minimalistic partly with a view to facilitating memorization. Being composed for oral transmission and memorization, the *Yoga Sūtras*, and *sūtra* traditions in general, allowed the student to "thread together" in memory the key ingredients of the more extensive body of material with which the student would eventually become thoroughly acquainted. Each *sūtra* served as a mnemonic device to structure the teachings and facilitate memorization, almost like a bullet point that would then be elaborated upon.

This very succinctness—the *Yoga Sūtras* contain about 1,200 words in 195 *sūtras*—indicates that the text was composed as a manual requiring unpacking. That the *sūtras*, or aphorisms, are in places cryptic, esoteric, and incomprehensible in their own terms points to the fact that they served as a manual to be used in conjunction with a teacher. Thus, while some of the *sūtras* are somewhat straightforward, the fact is that we cannot construe meaning for many *sūtras* from Patañjali's primary text. *Sūtras* such as I.17 are so obtuse that they are undecipherable in their own terms, and thus the text of the *Yoga Sūtras* requires commentaries, which are discussed later in this chapter. Thus, when we speak of the "Yoga school" we refer to Patañjali's *Yoga Sūtras* and the earliest commentary of Vyāsa, which always accompanies any study of the *sūtras*, along with other primary commentaries of the premodern era.

Classical Yoga as Hindu Soteriological System

Although situated as a work of the "Yoga school," one of (what later came to be known as) the six schools of classical Hindu philosophy, Patañjali's *Yoga Sūtras* is not so much a philosophical treatise as instructions on a psychosomatic technique of meditative practice. As a dualistic system that presupposes an ultimate and absolute distinction between matter and consciousness, it is concerned with presenting a psychology of mind and an understanding of human consciousness, along with a method of experiencing consciousness in its pure, unadulterated, and non-intentional potential, rather than with a metaphysics of manifest reality. In actuality, Patañjali's text reads more like a manual for the practitioner interested in plumbing the depths of human consciousness than a philosophical exposition on metaphysics.

To realize pure unchanging awareness as an entity distinct and autonomous from the mind (and, of course, body), thought must be stilled and consciousness extracted from its embroilment with the mind and its incessant thinking nature. The process to accomplish this is classical Yoga. More specifically, *yoga* entails concentrating the mind on one object without deviation, and it is this stilling of the mind that is classical Yoga.

So why might individuals take up the practice of this type of meditation? When not in its pure state, the soul (*ātman*), the actual source of consciousness or being, is mistaken to be the mind and body, which is animated by its presence (YS II.5). Consciousness is therefore identified with the experiences of the body and mind—birth, death, rebirth, disease, old age, distress, anxiety, and so on—even though these are merely transformations occurring in the inanimate and external body and mind encompassing it and therefore unconnected with consciousness. They are nothing other than the permutations of gross and subtle matter external to and enveloping the soul that are pervaded by the soul's awareness. Misidentifying with these permutations, the self (that is, the mind animated by consciousness) is thereby afflicted by suffering as a result of considering itself to be subject to birth and death, insecurity and stress, and so forth, and it is this misidentification, or ignorance, that is the root of bondage to the world and its consequent suffering (YS II.5–15). Yoga is therefore ultimately geared toward freeing consciousness from suffering (YS II.16), which is inherent in embodied life (perpetuated by incessant rebirth)[19] and is even defined as such in some ancient texts (e.g., *Vaiśeṣikha Sūtras* V.2.16). The Vedānta tradition goes a step further and states that bliss is inherent in the soul (*Vedānta Sūtras* I.1.12), and therefore, since the soul is eternal, once awareness resituates itself in its own nature, it attains a state of eternal beatific bliss. The latter far surpasses any temporary pleasures that might be attained through the material body and mind.

While the notion of a distinction between the material body and a conscious soul has a well-known history in Western Greco-Hellenistic and Abrahamic religion and thought, Yoga, as with other strains of Indic thought, differs from most comparable Western schools of dualism by regarding not just the physical body but the mind, ego, and all cognitive functions as also belonging to the realm of inert matter. It is imperative to absorb this essential and prerequisite metaphysical presupposition of Yogic (and, for that matter, much, but not all Indic) thought in order to understand the basics of Yoga. The dualism fundamental to Platonic or Aristotelian thought, or to Paul of Tarsus (ca. 5–ca. 67) or Augustine of Hippo (354–430), is not at all the dualism of Yoga. Perhaps René Descartes (1596–1650) most famously represents the generic

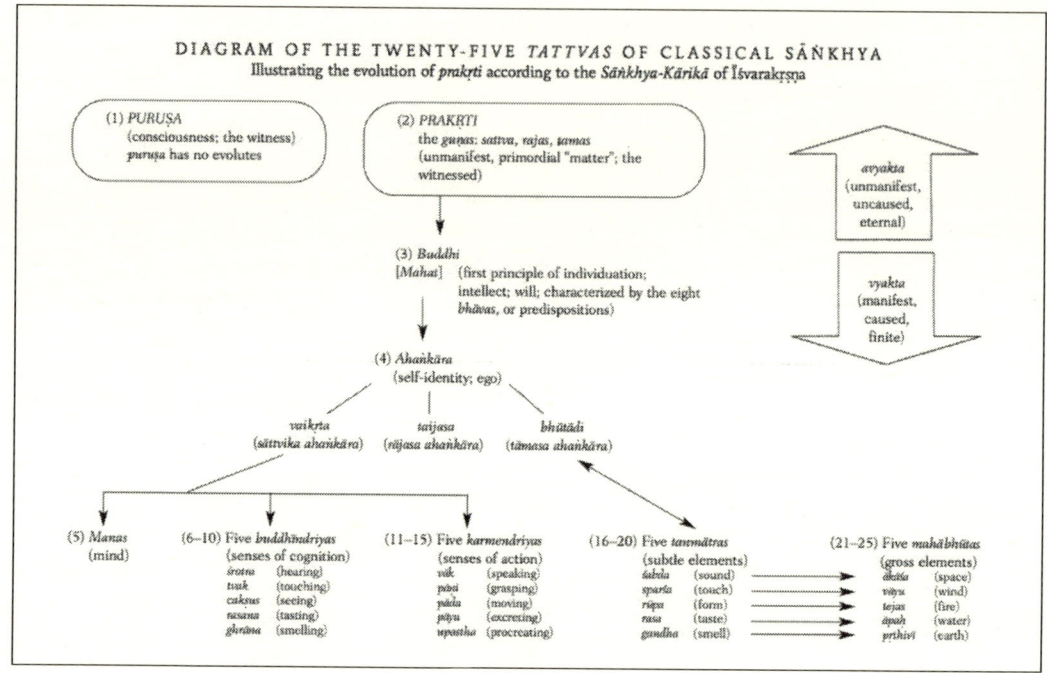

Figure 10.2. Classical Sāṁkhya and Yoga Psychology
Source: Larson 1979

Western notions of the dualism between self and body in his *Meditationes de prima philosophia* (Meditations on First Philosophy; dat. 1641): the self thinks and lacks extension, while the body is unthinking and extended. In other words, there are two types of realities in classical Western dualism: physical reality, which is extended in space and empirically perceivable, and mental reality, which does not have spatial extension and is not empirically perceivable but private.

In the Yoga tradition, the dualism is not between the material body and physical reality on one hand, and mental reality characterized by thought on the other. Rather, the dualism of Yoga is between pure awareness, on one hand, and all objects of awareness, on the other—regardless of whether these objects are physical and extended or internal and non-extended. In other words, in Sāṁkhya and Yoga, thought, feeling, emotion, memory, and so forth, are as material or physical as the visible ingredients of the empirical world. Pure consciousness, called *puruṣa* in this system, animates and pervades the incessant fluctuations of thought—the inner turmoil of fears, emotions, cravings—but the two are completely distinct entities.

There is thus a radical distinction between the mind, which is considered to be very subtle but nonetheless inanimate matter, and pure consciousness, which is the actual conscious animate life force. Animated by consciousness, it is the mind that imagines itself to be the real self rather than a material entity external to consciousness. The mind is therefore the seat of ignorance and bondage; *puruṣa*, in contrast, is "witness, free, indifferent, a spectator and inactive" (*Sāmkhya Kārikā* XIX). Therefore, while the goal of the entire classical Yoga system, and of Hindu and Jain soteriological (liberation-seeking) thought in general, is to extricate pure consciousness from its embroilment with both the internal workings of the mind as well as the external senses of the body, in fact, "No one is actually either bound or liberated, nor does anyone transmigrate; it is only *prakṛti* in its various manifestations who is bound, transmigrates, and is released" (*Sāmkhya Kārikā* LXII). *Puruṣa* is eternal and therefore not subject to changes such as bondage and liberation;[20] in the Yoga tradition, the quest for liberation, in other words human agency, is a function of the prakṛtic mind, called *citta* in the *Yoga Sūtras*, not of *puruṣa*. Yoga claims to provide a system by which the practitioner can directly realize his or her *puruṣa*, the soul, or innermost conscious self, through mental practices. Put differently, the enlightened *citta* realizes that the source of its own animation is not inherent within or stemming from itself but radiating from a conscious entity more subtle than and beyond itself. Just as "ignorance" (*avidyā*) is the mind considering itself to be the ultimate entity, and this causes saṃsāric bondage, so "enlightenment" is the same mind realizing that consciousness is a metaphysically distinct entity beyond itself with which it is confusing itself. The mind thus determines that if it is to transcend its suffering, it has to remove itself, so to speak, from distracting consciousness. It does so by stilling all its activities through concentrating on one object without deviation.

The *citta* can profitably be compared to the software, and the body to the hardware. Neither is "conscious" but rather forms of matter, even though the former can do very intelligent activities. Both software and hardware are useless without the presence of a conscious observer. Only *puruṣa* is truly "alive," that is, aware or conscious. When uncoupled from the mind, the soul, *puruṣa*, in its "pure state," that is, in its own constitutional autonomous condition untainted by being misidentified with the physical coverings of the body and mind, is free of content and changeless; it does not constantly ramble and flit from one thing to another in the way the mind does. To realize pure awareness as an entity distinct and autonomous from the mind (and, of course, body), thought must be stilled and consciousness extracted from its embroilment with the mind and its incessant thinking nature. Only then can the soul be realized as an entity completely distinct from the mind. The process to accomplish this is classical Yoga.

In conventional existence, *puruṣa*'s awareness of objects is mediated by means of *buddhi*, the intellect. As the discriminatory aspect of the *citta*-mind, the intelligence is the first interface between the soul and the external world. More specifically, the soul becomes aware of the outside world when images of sense objects are channeled through the senses, sorted by the *manas*, the thinking, feeling, and organizing aspect of *citta*; appropriated by the *ahaṁkāra*, the ego aspect of the *citta* that appropriates cognitions under the notions of "I" and "mine"; and presented to the intellect, the function of judgment and discrimination. Although inanimate, the intellect, in addition to its function of discrimination, "molds" itself into the form and shape of these objects of experience, thoughts, and ideas, and, due to the reflection of the consciousness of *puruṣa*, appears animated. Since the soul is "adjacent"[21] to the intellect (and the *citta* in general), the intellect is the immediate "covering" of *puruṣa*, hence, it is through the intellect that *puruṣa* becomes aware of these forms and therefore of the objects of the world. The pure consciousness of the soul pervades the *citta*, animating it with consciousness like a lightbulb—although distinct in its own right—pervades a nonluminous light-shade surrounding it with light, and makes it appear luminous.

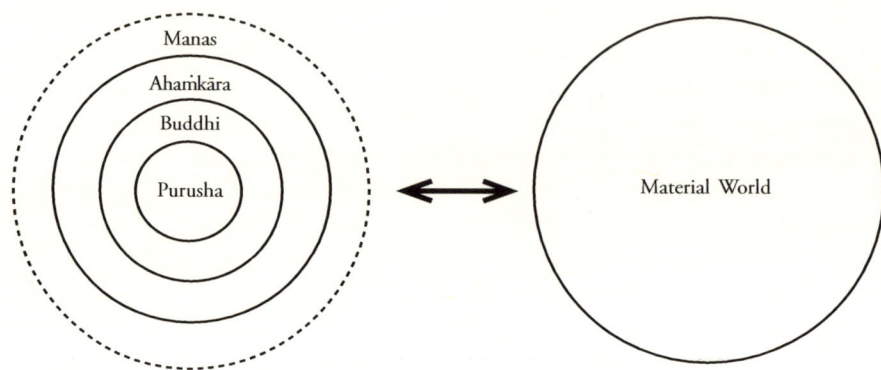

Figure 10.3. Yogic Consciousness

Pervaded by this consciousness, the *citta*-mind appears "as if" it itself was conscious in the same way that a metal ball placed into intense fire becomes molten and appears "as if" it were fire. However, the mind animated by consciousness is in reality unconscious, just as an object appears illuminated in its own right, but it is in actuality dependent on an outside light source for its illumination and visibility. Most importantly, the soul, the pure and eternal power of consciousness, never changes; as a "spectator" or "witness," it does not itself transform when in contact with the ever-changing states of mind. It simply becomes aware of them. Just as light passively reveals gross and subtle objects in a dark room and yet is not itself affected or changed by them, consciousness passively reveals objects, whether in the form of gross external physical objects or subtle internal thoughts (*vṛtti*), including the higher states of discrimination, but is not itself actually affected or "touched" by them. However, the awareness of the pure soul does permeate or shine on the *citta*, like a projector light permeating inanimate pictorial forms of a movie reel, thereby animating these pictures as if they had a life of their own. In so doing, the "animated" mind misidentifies consciousness with itself, identifying consciousness with the churnings of thought, as if consciousness were inherent within itself rather than the effulgence of an entity outside and separate from itself. This misidentification is ignorance and the cause of bondage in *saṃsāra*. It is the mysterious glue that binds the self to the world of matter in all Indic soteriological traditions.

According to some commentators, such as the fifteenth-century exegete Vijñānabhikṣu, the intellect functions like a mirror; just as light bounces off an illuminated reflective object back to its source, the consciousness of the soul bounces off this animated intellect, which presents a reflection to the soul. Because *sattva*, discussed later, is predominant in the intellect, it is highly translucent and thus able to reflect pure consciousness back to itself. Just as one becomes conscious of one's appearance in a mirror due to the mirror's translucency, the soul becomes conscious of its reflection in the animated intellect. However, since the intellect is constantly being molded into the images presented to it by the mind and senses, this reflection presented back to *puruṣa* is distorted or transformed by constantly changing forms (*vṛtti*), just as one's reflection in a mirror is distorted if the mirror is warped. The soul, that is, the actual source of consciousness, is misidentified with this distorted reflection by the mind, which considers awareness to be inherent within itself rather than a feature of *puruṣa*, an entity completely outside of and separate from itself. The soul is thus misidentified with the world of change through these changing states of mind (*vṛtti*), just as one may look at one's reflection in a dirty mirror and mistakenly think that it is oneself who is dirty.

The soul thus becomes misidentified with the experiences of the body and mind—birth, death, disease, old age, happiness, distress, peacefulness, and anxiety—even though these are merely transformations occurring in the inanimate and external body and mind, and therefore unconnected with *puruṣa*. They are nothing other than the permutations of gross and subtle matter external to the soul that are pervaded by the soul's awareness. However, awareness is misidentified with these permutations as a result of which the self (that is, the mind animated by consciousness) considers itself to be subject to birth and death, happiness and distress, and it is this misidentification, or ignorance, that is the root of bondage to the world. Classical Yoga involves inhibiting the mind's tendency of being molded into these permutations, the *vṛtti*, the impressions and thoughts of the objects of the world. This stilling of the mind is the practice of meditation outlined in the *Yoga Sūtras*.

A discussion of the metaphysics of this process requires an understanding of the infrastructure of Sāṃkhya metaphysics that underpins both the essential constituents of Yoga psychology and practice, as well as the supplementary aspects of the system such as the *siddhi*, or mystic powers, of chapter 3. As with the cluster of Yoga traditions, there were numerous variants of Sāṃkhya, but in generic Sāṃkhya, the universe of animate and inanimate entities is perceived as ultimately the product of two ontologically distinct categories; hence, this system is quintessentially *dvaita*, or dualistic in presupposition. These two categories are *prakṛti*, or the primordial material matrix of the physical universe, and *puruṣa*, the innumerable conscious souls or selves embedded within it. As a result of the interaction between these two entities, the material universe evolves in a series of stages. The actual catalysts in this evolutionary process are the three *guṇas*, literally, "strands" or "qualities," which are inherent in *prakṛti*. These are *sattva* (lucidity), *rajas* (action), and *tamas* (inertia). These *guṇas* are sometimes compared to the threads that underpin the existence of a rope; just as a rope is actually a combination of threads, so all manifest reality actually consists of a combination of the *guṇas*. These *guṇas* are mentioned incessantly throughout the commentaries on the text, as are the various evolutes from *prakṛti*, and thus require some attention.

Given the meditative focus of the text, the *guṇas* are especially significant to classical Yoga in terms of their psychological manifestation; the mind, and therefore all psychological dispositions, are *prakṛti*, and therefore also comprised of the *guṇas*—the only difference between mind and matter is that the former has a larger preponderance of *sattva* and the latter of *tamas*. Therefore, according to the specific intermixture and proportionality of the *guṇas*, living beings exhibit different types of mindsets and psychological dispositions. Thus, when *sattva* (from the root *as*, meaning to be)[22] is predominant in an individual, the qualities of lucidity, tranquility, wisdom, discrimination, detachment, happiness, and peacefulness manifest; when *rajas* (from the root *rañj*, meaning to color or to redden) is predominant, hankering, attachment, energetic endeavor, passion, power, restlessness, and creative activity manifest; and when *tamas* (from the root *tam*, meaning to stifle), the *guṇa* least favorable for classical Yoga, is predominant, ignorance, delusion, disinterest, lethargy, sleep, and disinclination toward constructive activity manifest.[23]

The *guṇas* are continually interacting and competing with each other, one *guṇa* becoming prominent for a while and overpowering the others, only to be eventually dominated in turn by the increase of one of the others (*Bhagavad Gītā* XIV.10). The *Yuktidīpikā*, a seventh-century Sāṃkhyan text, compares them to the wick, fire, and oil of the lamp, which, while opposed to each other in their nature, come together to produce light (13). Just as there is an unlimited variety of colors stemming from the intermixture of the three primary colors, different hues being simply expressions of the specific proportionality of red, yellow, and blue, so the unlimited psychological dispositions of living creatures (and of physical forms) stem from the intermixture of the *guṇa*s, specific states of mind being the reflections of the particular proportionality of the intermixture of the three *guṇa*s.

The *guṇa*s not only underpin the philosophy of mind in classical Yoga, but the activation and interaction of these *guṇa* qualities result in the production of the entirety of physical forms that also evolve from the primordial material matrix, *prakṛti*, under the same principle.[24] Thus the physical composition of objects like air, water, stone, fire, and so forth, differs because of the constitutional makeup of specific *guṇa*s: air contains more of the buoyancy of *sattva*, stones more of the sluggishness of *tamas*, and fire more of the energy of *rajas* (although its buoyancy betrays its partial nature of *sattva* as well). The *guṇa*s allow for the infinite plasticity of *prakṛti* and the objects of the world.

Returning to classical Yoga, one of its primary goals, discussed repeatedly by the commentators, is to maximize the proportion of the *guṇa* of *sattva* in the mind and correspondingly decrease that of *rajas* and *tamas*. When all trace of *tamas* and *rajas* is eliminated, the mind attains the highest potential of its prakṛtic nature—illumination, peacefulness, discernment, and inclination toward meditation and contemplation, all qualities inherent in *sattva*. When the *citta*-mind has cultivated a state of almost pure *sattva*,[25] the discriminative aspect of *buddhi*, intelligence, can reveal the distinction between the ultimate conscious principle, *puruṣa*, and even the purest and most subtle (but nonetheless unconscious) states of *prakṛti*. When manifesting its highest potential of *sattva* and suppressing its inherent potential of *rajas* and *tamas*, which divert consciousness away from its source, *puruṣa*, and into the external world of objects and internal world of thought, the pure *sattva* nature of the mind can recognize the distinction between *puruṣa* and *prakṛti* and redirect consciousness back inward toward this inner self (one of the penultimate goals of classical Yoga), just as a dusty mirror can reflect things clearly when cleansed from the coverings of dirt. In short, classical Yoga can also be viewed as the process of stilling the potential of *rajas* and *tamas*, and allowing the maximum potential *sattva* nature of the mind to manifest, and the commentators often promote it in this way. The specific means of doing this involves fixing the mind on an object of concentration without deviation. These are some of the foundations of the soteriological system of classical Yoga. This system aims at complete liberation, which is defined as the extraction of pure consciousness (*puruṣa*) from materiality (*prakṛti*).

Aphorisms on Discipline and Liberation

As mentioned, the *Yoga Sūtras* (Yoga Aphorisms) is attributed to Patañjali, an obscure figure who later became identified as the founder of the "Yoga school." The text describes a sequential meditative practice aimed at purification of consciousness, or, in keeping with the text itself, at the realization of *puruṣa* as pure consciousness beyond materiality. The received text consists of 195 aphorisms, cryptic and esoteric guidelines or maxims on meditative discipline. The text is divided into four sections (*pada*), with the following titles and corresponding number of aphorisms:

1. *Samādhi Pāda* (Meditative Absorption (51)	3. *Vibhūti Pāda* (Mystic Powers) (55)
2. *Sādhana Pāda* (Practice) (55)	4. *Kaivalya Pāda* (Absolute Liberation) (34)

Figure 10.4. Sections of the *Yoga Sūtras*

Chapter 1 occupies itself with a discussion of *yoga*, the various meditative states that accrue from its practice, and the various objects upon which the mind can concentrate. From a structural point of view, while situating the goal in chapter 1 before the practice to attain it in chapter 2 may challenge modern notions of narrative or pedagogical sequence, there is a logic to Patañjali's choice of informing his readership about the goal of the yogic journey before proceeding further with details of the journey itself and its accompanying mental landscape. In any event, according to Patañjali's definition in the second aphorism, *yoga* is the cessation (*nirodha*) of the activities or permutations (*vṛtti*) of *citta*-thought. The *vṛtti*s refer to any sequence of thought, ideas, mental imaging, or cognitive acts performed by either the mind, intellect, or ego as defined previously—in short, any state of mind whatsoever (I.I–5ff.). As has been stressed, the essential point for understanding classical Yoga is that all forms or activities of the mind are products of *prakṛti*, matter, and completely distinct from *puruṣa*, the soul or true self, which is pure awareness or consciousness (I.2–4; II.20).

The means prescribed by Patañjali to still the *vṛtti* states of mind or fluctuations of thought is meditation, defined as keeping the mind fixed on any particular object of choice without distraction (I.23–39). Īśvara, often referred to as the "Lord of Yoga," is a transcendent omniscient Being who comes highly recommended in this regard; Yoga is clearly, but non-dogmatically, a theistic system (I.23–29).[26] By concentration and meditation (or, by the power of Īśvara's grace), the distracting influences of *rajas* and *tamas* can be curtailed, and the *sattva* constitution of the mind can exhibit its full potential. In this state, the mind can concentrate without being distracted. Several verses in section 1 point to intense levels of concentration that begin by penetrating the subtler substructure of the object of meditation, proceed to penetrate past the very organ of cognition, the mind, as the *yogī*'s awareness approaches its ultimate source and final goal, *puruṣa*, or pure consciousness itself (I.17, 42–51). When the mind is focused on an object, whether on the object's gross manifestation or subtle substructure, or even on the mind itself as an organ of cognition, its corresponding states are known as stages of *samprajñāta samādhi*, also known as *sabīja samādhi* (absorption with seed).[27] When consciousness is completely uncoupled from the mind and from any meditative objects upon which it might concentrate, that is, when consciousness abides in its own pure, unintentional nature, the ensuing state is *asamprajñāta samādhi*, also known as *nirbīja samādhi* (absorption without seed; I.18, 51).

Ultimately, through the grace of Īśvara (II.45) or the sheer power of concentration, the mind can attain an inactive state where all thoughts remain only in potential but not active form. In other words, through meditation one can cultivate an inactive state of mind where one is not cognizant of anything. Consequently, once there are no more thoughts or objects on its horizons or sphere of awareness, consciousness has no other alternative but to become conscious of itself. In other words, consciousness can either be "object" aware or "subject" aware (loosely speaking).[28]

The point is that it has no option in terms of being aware on some level, since awareness is eternal and inextinguishable. By stilling all thought, meditative concentration removes all objects of awareness; awareness can therefore now only be aware of itself. It can now bypass or transcend all objects of thought, disassociate from even the pure sāttvic *citta*, and become aware of its own source, the actual soul itself, *puruṣa*. This is "self-realization" (to use a neo-Vedāntic term), the ultimate state of awareness, the state of consciousness in which nothing can be discerned except the pure self, objectless consciousness itself, *nirbīja/asamprajñāta samādhi*. This is the final goal of classical Yoga and thus of human existence.

In terms of specifics, chapter 1 begins by introducing the subject of the work and providing a definition of *yoga*, namely, the cessation of all *citta vṛtti*, the fluctuating states of the mind (1–2). This is followed by a discussion of the two possible functions of awareness—exclusive awareness of awareness itself or awareness of the *vṛtti*s (3–4)—a description of the *vṛtti*s (5–11), and how to control them by practice (13–14) and dispassion (15–16). Then comes the division of *samādhi* (the term that refers to the state of the mind when thought has, indeed, been stilled) into the important divisions of *samprajñāta samādhi* (17) and *asamprajñāta samādhi* (18) and how to attain it (20–22), after pointing to other states that might resemble it (19). Īśvara is then introduced as the easy method of attaining *samādhi* if one fixes the mind on Him by means of chanting the sacred syllable *om*[29] that represents him (23), along with his nature (24–26), name and its recitation (27–28), and the fruits accruing therefrom (29). The chapter describes the distractions of the mind (30) and their accompanying effects such as grief, and so on (31); outlines the means to combat these by dwelling on one truth (32), practicing benevolence, and so on (33), breath control (34), and other such means (35–39) that are conducive to *samādhi*. Additionally, the chapter explains the variety of *samāpatti* meditative states (a type of *samādhi* state) (41) with definitions (42–44) and their fruits (46–48) and object (49). The chapter concludes with a discussion of *samprajñāta samādhi*, the states when awareness is still being channeled through the mind and onto the objects of concentration, preceding the final stage of *asamprajñāta*. *Asamprajñāta samādhi* is the highest stage of the eighth and final limb of yoga presented by Patañjali to attain this lofty goal: when consciousness "abides in its own pure nature" (I.34).

The second chapter is called *kriyā yoga*, "the discipline of action,"[30] and deals with the lifestyle and practices that are prerequisites for the higher meditational states outlined in chapter 1. The chapter begins with a very succinct but precise outline of the mechanisms underpinning karma, human action and its consequent effects (namely, rebirths), the nature of human suffering, ignorance, and the means to dissolve all of this through discrimination. The chapter is best known for its discussion of the "eight limbs of Yoga" (*aṣṭāṅga yoga*), which are the practical means to develop discrimination. These include the following:

1. Abstentions/Moral restraints (*yama*)

2. Ethical observances (*niyama*)

3. Posture (*āsana*)

4. Breath control (*prāṇāyāma*)

5. Sensory withdrawal (*pratyāhāra*)

6. Concentration (*dhāraṇā*)

7. Meditation (*dhyāna*)

8. Meditative absorption (*samādhi*)

The first limb, *yama* or "restraints," consists of nonviolence, truthfulness, refrainment from stealing, celibacy, and refrainment from coveting. *Yama* are universal (II.31), were standard in the ascetic culture of ancient India, and are in fact identical with the five Jain vows and with four of the five Buddhist ones. They deal with how the aspiring *yogī* relates to others. Obviously, if one's goals are to remove consciousness from identification with the body and the mind, one must curb activities that pamper to the grosser urges of the body—violence, stealing, deceit, sexual exploitation, and coveting are acts that are generally performed with a view to improving one's bodily or material situation and with a disregard for the well-being of others. They must be resisted by one striving for transcendent goals. They form the core of Yogic ethics. But they are not just ethical or social. They also carry an essential metaphysical dimension: for the mind to be able to settle and concentrate, its *sattva* potential must be at a maximum. Since the mind can be considered as nothing other than a "reservoir" of *saṃskāra*s (*karmāśaya*), which are nothing other than impressions streaming in from the senses, classical Yoga requires the practitioner to direct attention to only submitting the mind to sāttvic sounds, tastes, sights, and so forth. Yoga is thus a culture and a lifestyle. Thus, for example, vegetarianism is not only an ethical issue relevant to the natural compassion of a *yogī* toward other helpless embodied beings, but food imbibed also translates into saṃskāric imprints. (Most vegetarian food contributes to the *sattva* potential of the mind, while meat creates *tamas*.)

Niyama or "observances" includes cleanliness, contentment, austerity, study [of scripture], and devotion to Īśvara. These deal with how the *yogī* cultivates his or her own lifestyle. Once the cruder and more destructive potentials of the body are curtailed by following the abstentions of the previous limb, consciousness can be turned more inward toward personal refinement. Each limb furthers and deepens this internal progression. The third limb, *āsana* or "postures," focuses on stretches and postures with a view to preparing the *yogī*'s body to sit for prolonged periods in meditation. In this respect, the classical *padmāsana*, or "full-lotus," posture is prioritized by the tradition (commentaries to II.46). It is this aspect of classical Yoga that has been most visibly exported to the West but all-too-often stripped from its context as one ingredient in a far more ambitious and far-reaching soteriological project.

While successful performance of the third limb begins the focusing of attention and stilling of the mind, the fourth limb furthers this process through fixing the mind on breath control (*prāṇāyāma*). By regulating and slowing the movement of the breath, the mind, too, becomes regulated and quiescent. The fifth limb, *pratyāhāra* or sensory withdrawal, deepens the process by removing consciousness from all engagement with sense objects (sight, sound, taste, smell, touch). The last three limbs are considered internal as opposed to the previous five "external" limbs (III.7); they include concentration (*dhāraṇā*), meditation (*dhyāna*), and complete meditative absorption (*samādhi*). These limbs, which Patañjali subdivides into seven rather esoteric stages (I.17, 42–51), are laid out at the beginning of chapter 3. The last three limbs are essentially increasingly focused degrees of concentrative intensity and culminate in the realization by awareness of its own nature, *asaṃprajñāta samādhi*, as outlined earlier. *Dhāraṇā* is compared to the dripping tap (that is, the mind is still distracted from its object of meditation); this stands in contrast to *dhyāna*, which is compared to the unbroken flow of thick unctuous oil.[31] In *samādhi*, at least as touched upon in this section of the text, the "object alone shines forth and the mind is devoid of its own reflective nature" (III.3).[32] As this chapter makes clear, the *Yoga Sūtras*, in fact, are primarily a manual for the practitioner, rather than an exposition of Yoga philosophy.

In terms of specifics, the second chapter begins with an introduction of *kriyā yoga* as consisting of austerity, study, and devotion to Īśvara (1), its effects (2), and a discussion of the *kleśa*s, the deep-rooted mental obstacles to Yoga, such as ignorance, ego, and desire, which it removes (3–11). Karma and its consequences are outlined, that is, the law of action and reaction (12–14), and the principle of suffering established (15–16). This is followed by the characteristics of the seer and the seen, *puruṣa* and *prakṛti* (17–22), the conjunction between them (23–24), and the definition of liberation (25–27). Next, the eight limbs of Yoga are introduced as the means to attain liberation (28–29), and the remainder of the chapter is dedicated to the first five of these: the restraints and their universality (30–31), observances (32), the means to counter tendencies contrary to the observances (33–34) and the side benefits accrued from observing them (35–45), postures (46–48), breath control (49–53), and withdrawal of consciousness from sense objects (54–55).

The third chapter focuses on the potential development of mystic powers (*siddhi*) that might accrue when the mind is in intense meditative states. Patañjali is not promoting such powers but warning yogic aspirants not to be distracted by them should they occur. One might note that the epic and folk literature of Hinduism (and even modern hagiographical literature of *yogī*s)[33] is replete with narratives of individuals who perform austere practices of mind control, with the motive of attaining mundane but supernormal power. This stands in contrast to the real goal of classical Yoga: experiencing one's highest and ultimate self. It is because such erroneously motivated practices were so widespread that one might infer that Patañjali felt moved to dedicate an entire chapter to this topic. He does so with some intellectual rigor, however, initiating the chapter with a rational explanation of how *siddhi*s can be understood metaphysically in terms of the substructural cause and effect principles of Sāṃkhya.[34]

The chapter begins by concluding the definitions of the last three limbs of classical Yoga (1–3), which are distinguished from the others by constituting *saṃyama*, another term for intense absorption in the object of meditation (4–6) and by being internal limbs (7–8). A discussion of the state of *nirodha*, the state of the stilled mind, ensues (9–12), followed by the metaphysics of the relationship between the substratum of matter and its characteristics (13–15). The remainder of the chapter is then dedicated to an extensive discussion of various mystic powers accrued from the performance of *saṃyama* on a variety of things (16–48), culminating in omniscience, followed by ultimate *kaivalya* liberation, the complete autonomy of consciousness (49–55).

The fourth chapter is the shortest, and among other things, features the Yoga tradition's response to Vijñāna Buddhism,[35] which must have been quite prevalent at the time to merit Patañjali's engagement with it, in an otherwise very curt and nonpolemical treatise. The chapter begins by listing other means of attaining *siddhi*s (1). This is followed by some comments on *prakṛti*'s relationship with its effects (2–3) and by the phenomenon of the creation of multiple minds by the *yogī* (4–5). A more advanced discussion of karma (6–7), *saṃskāra*s (8–11), as well as Time and the *guṇa*s (12–14) then ensues. The next section critiques Buddhist idealist notions of the mind (15–21), followed by a discussion of the classical Yoga view of the relationship between mind and consciousness (22–26) and of distractions to meditation (27–28). The chapter and thus the text ends with a type of *samādhi* called *dharma-megha* and its effects (29–33), and then ultimate liberation (34).

Reading the *Yoga Sūtras* in Later Hinduism and the Modern West

Knowledge systems in ancient India were transmitted orally, from master to disciple, with an enormous emphasis on fidelity toward the original set of *sūtra*s upon which the system was founded. The master unpacked the dense and truncated aphorisms to the students, and this system continues in traditional contexts today. Periodically, teachers of particular prominence wrote commentaries on the primary texts of many of these knowledge systems. Some of these gained wide currency to the point that the primary text was always studied in conjunction with a commentary, particularly since, as noted earlier, texts such as the *Yoga Sūtras* (and, even more so, the *Vedānta Sūtras*) contain numerous *sūtra*s that are incomprehensible without further elaboration, and hence were designed to be "unpacked." One must stress, therefore, that our understanding of Patañjali's text is completely dependent on the interpretations of later commentators: it is incomprehensible, in places, in its own terms.

In any event, in terms of the overall accuracy of the commentaries, there is an *a priori* likelihood that the interpretations of the *Yoga Sūtras* were faithfully preserved and transmitted orally through the few generations from Patañjali until the first commentary by the sage Vyāsa[36] in the fifth century CE. Indeed, some commentators, both traditional and modern, even hold Vyāsa's commentary to be that of Patañjali himself. In other words, unless compelling arguments are presented to the contrary, one must be cautious about questioning the overall accuracy of this transmission. Certainly, the commentators from Vyāsa onward are remarkably consistent in their interpretations of the essential metaphysics of the system for over fifteen hundred years, which is in marked contrast with the radical differences in essential metaphysical understanding that distinguishes commentators of the Vedānta school. While the fifteenth-century commentator Vijñānabhikṣu, for example, may not infrequently quibble with the ninth-century commentator Vācaspati Miśra, the differences generally are in detail, not essential metaphysical elements. And while Vijñānabhikṣu may inject a good deal of Vedāntic concepts into the basic dualism of the Yoga system, this is generally an addition (conspicuous and identifiable) to the system rather than a reinterpretation of it. There is thus a remarkably consistent body of knowledge associated with the Yoga school for the best part of a millennium and a half, and consequently one can speak of the "traditional understanding" of the *Yoga Sūtras* in the premodern period without overly generalizing or essentializing.

The first extant commentary (*bhāṣya*) by Vyāsa, typically dated to around the fourth to fifth century CE, was to attain a status that caused it to become almost as canonical as the primary text written by Patañjali himself. Consequently, the *Yoga Sūtras* has always been studied embedded in the commentary that tradition assigns to this greatest of literary figures. Practically speaking, when we speak of the philosophy of Patañjali, what we really mean (or should mean) is the understanding of Patañjali according to Vyāsa: it is Vyāsa who determined what Patañjali's abstruse *sūtra*s meant, and all subsequent commentators elaborated on Vyāsa. From one aphorism of a few words, Vyāsa might write several lines of comment, without which the *sūtra* remains incomprehensible. It cannot be overstated that Yoga philosophy is Patañjali's philosophy as understood and articulated by Vyāsa. Subsequent commentators base their commentaries on unpacking Vyāsa's *bhāṣya*—almost never critiquing the latter but rather expanding or elaborating upon it. This point of reference results in a marked uniformity to the interpretation of the *Yoga Sūtras* in the premodern period as noted earlier.[37]

There have been numerous commentaries in the premodern period from which we can mention the half-dozen or so that have made a significant contribution.[38] The next best-known commentator after Vyāsa was Vācaspati Miśra, a brahmin from the Bihar region of India, whose commentary, the *Tattvavaiśāradī* (Insight into Truth), can be dated with more security to the ninth century CE. Also important, although its authorship is debated, is the commentary called the *Vivaraṇa* (Exposition), attributed to the great Vedāntin Śaṅkara in the eighth to ninth century CE. A fascinating Arabic translation of Patañjali's *Yoga Sūtras* was undertaken by the famous Arab traveler and historian Al-Bīrūnī (973–1050), the manuscript of which was discovered in Istanbul in 1922.[39] Roughly contemporaneous with Al-Bīrūnī is the eleventh-century king Bhoja Rāja, poet, scholar, and patron of the arts, sciences, and esoteric traditions. Then, in the fifteenth century, another prolific scholar, Vijñānabhikṣu, wrote to my mind the most insightful and useful commentary after that of Vyāsa; this is the *Yogavārttika* (Explanation of Yoga). In the sixteenth century, another Vedāntin,[40] Rāmānanda Sarasvatī, wrote his commentary, called *Yogamaṇiprabhā* (Light of the Jewel of Yoga), which adds little to the previous commentaries, but there are valuable insights contained in the *Bhāsvatī* (Dawning Sun) by Harihārananda Āraṇya, written in Bengali in the nineteenth century. Although a traditional Sāṃkhya master, Harihārananda was exposed to Western thought and thus situated in a context nearer to our own.

In terms of classical Yoga and the contemporary cultural landscape of the West, almost everyone, by now, has heard of *yoga*. Indeed, with millions of people in some form or fashion practicing *āsana*, the physical aspect of *yoga* in the United States,[41] the teaching and practice of *yoga*, at least in its aspect of techniques of body poses and stretches, are now thoroughly mainstream activities on the Western cultural landscape. *Yoga* in its exported manifestations has tended to focus on the physical aspect of the system of classical Yoga, the *āsana*s or stretching poses and postures, which most Western adepts of *yoga* practice in order to stay trim, supple, and healthy. Patañjali himself, we must note, pays much less attention to the *āsana*s, which are the third stage of the eight stages or "limbs" of yoga; discussion of posture only comprises 10 words from 1,200, or less than 1 percent of the content of the text. Instead, Patañjali focuses primarily on meditation, the various stages of concentration of the mind, as a path to liberation. As we have seen, this involves the extraction of pure consciousness (*puruṣa*) from materiality (*prakṛti*). The body, sensuality, physical beauty, and so forth, of course are associated with *prakṛti*. "Yoga" practiced for health, fitness, and beauty is antithetical to the informing views and soteriological system of classical Yoga.

After its initial introduction to the West by Vivekānanda (1863–1902), a key figure in the establishment of the Vedanta Society, at the end of the nineteenth century (see De Michelis 2004),[42] *yoga*, particularly as stretching and breathwork but also as a meditative technique leading to enlightenment (*samādhi*), was popularized in the West by a number of influential Hindu teachers of *yoga* in the 1960s. Most of these individuals came from two lineages: those of Sivananda (1887–1963), and those of Krishnamāchārya (1888–1989). Sivananda was a renunciant, and his ashram tradition was transplanted by his disciples, especially Vishnu-devananda (1927–1993) and Satchidananda (1914–2002), each of whom founded their own independent missions in the West. These are the Sivananda Yoga Vedanta Centres and the Integral Yoga Institute, respectively (see Strauss 2005). Krishnamāchārya's three principal disciples each took his emphasis on the practice of *āsana* in their own direction. K. Pattabhi Jois (1915–2009) continued to promote his version of Ashtanga Vinyasa Yoga; Krishnamāchārya's son, T. K. V. Desikachar (b. 1938), developed Viniyoga; and, perhaps most influential of all, Krishnamāchārya's brother-in-law, B. K. S. Iyengar (b. 1918), established Iyengar Yoga.

While B. K. S. Iyengar and Satchidananda both wrote commentaries on the *Yoga Sūtras*, the others all referred frequently in their writings to the text as a source of authority. However, the *yoga* taught by (especially) the disciples of Krishnamāchārya, which prioritizes *āsana*s so prominently, has departed considerably in emphasis from classical Yoga, where only 3 of the 195 aphorisms focus on postures. As a consequence, *yoga* in the Western cultural landscape is almost exclusively associated with *āsana* and might be better referred to as "modern postural yoga" (De Michelis 2004). Indeed, recent research has shown that the phenomenon of modern postural yoga has much more to do with European gymnastics and Hindu nationalism in twentieth-century India than any imagined ancient Vedic Yoga (see Sjoman 1996; Alter 2004; Singleton 2010). Seeking an indigenous form of physical fitness that could hold its own against the introduction of British gymnastics and body-building techniques into the subcontinent, Hindus alighted on the *āsana*s of classical Yoga as a supposed indigenous alternative. In so doing, of course, they massively emphasized and inflated the third of the eight limbs and equally conspicuously minimized much of the rest of the actual system.[43] The more mainstream and acculturated forms of modern *yoga* have thus come to be associated with modern attitudes and modalities associated with psychophysical well-being rather than the radical enterprise outlined in the *Yoga Sūtras*, which is aimed at the absolute uncoupling of a transcendent consciousness from all forms of psychophysical embeddedness.

While we have focused here on the *Yoga Sūtras*, since, once fossilized as one of the six *darśana*s (views), it became referenced in orthodox Hindu scholastic circles as the authoritative manual of a systematized and generic rendition of concentrative practice, there were other forms of *yoga* in ancient India as touched upon earlier. All, however, subscribed to the *ātman/karma/ saṃsāra/mokṣa* paradigm of Hindu soteriology. Prominent forms of these are the *yoga*s of *bhakti* (devotion), *jñāna* (knowledge), and *karma* (selfless action), as exemplified in the *Bhagavad Gītā* (Song of the Lord). Moreover, albeit marginalized and excluded from traditional doxographical schemas (the *darśana*s were construed variously at different historical periods by Hindu, Buddhist, and Jain scholastics; see Nicholson 2011), there are also the *yoga*s of *tantra* or *siddha* as exemplified in the *Haṭha-yoga-pradīpikā* (Light on Hatha Yoga). While a discussion of these is beyond the scope of the present chapter, in terms of *yoga* on the Western landscape, one can mention in this regard Bhaktivedanta Swami (1896–1977), founder of ISKCON (International Society for Krishna Consciousness; Hare Krishna Movement), who, in the 1960s, traveled to the West and transplanted a form of monotheistic devotional *yoga* focusing on worship of Krishna (Kṛṣṇa) as supreme Godhead and featuring *mantra* recitation (*jāpa*) and chanting (*kīrtan*) as personal and congregational praxis, respectively (see, e.g., Bryant 2004). Similarly, Swami Muktananda (1908–1982), founder of SYDA (Siddha Yoga Dham Associates) Yoga, which is a monistic form of devotional *siddha yoga* focused on the divinity Śiva, also emphasized *mantra* recitation and other devotional activities (see Brooks et al. 1997).[44] Gurus such as these, who (most significantly in the case of Bhaktivedanta Swami) demonstrated less accommodation to modernity and its discourses, and far greater commitments to preserving and promoting a traditional and orthodox reading of the practices, theologies, and ideologies of their respective Hindu sectarian lineages, made little or no use of the *Yoga Sūtras* in their canons. They also had little interest in *āsana*-centered praxis (Syman 2010).

Nowadays, of course, *yoga* is completely mainstream in Western society and taught in every neighborhood and on every college campus, often completely stripped of its traditional worldview, soteriological system, and Indian trappings. However, a large percentage of *yoga* teachers trace their lineage to tradition-based teachers, and the more serious among such teachers or practitioners of postural yoga will have a valued copy of the *Yoga Sūtras*. Our primary text and the *Bhagavad Gītā* are the two books that most popularly represent transplanted "Hinduism." Here I might add that Patañjali's *Yoga Sūtras*, while likely written for ascetics, is not an overtly sectarian text in the sense of prioritizing a specific deity or promoting a particular type of worship, as is the case with many Hindu scriptures such as the *Bhagavad Gītā*. Therefore, as a template, its schematic essentials can be and have been appropriated and reconfigured by followers of different schools and traditions throughout Indian religious history. The text continues to lend itself to such appropriations, most recently in secular contexts of the West. In short, among those more serious about engaging the practice of Hindu classical Yoga on its own terms, Patañjali's *Yoga Sūtras* is a classical Hindu text that has received the most attention and interest outside of India. This is specifically the case among individuals interested in meditation and contemplative practice. It is one of the most important classical texts in Hinduism and thus a "classic" of Indian, and therefore world, thought.

Yoga as Yoga

As a concluding reflection then, while, from the perspective of its adherents, mainstream (and increasingly consumerized) forms of postural *yoga* have contributed enormously to the psychophysical well-being of those who practice them, the meditative (i.e., more primary) focus and concern of the Hindu classical Yoga and other tradition-based forms of *yoga* offer another prospective contribution to modernity. *Yoga* emerged from the margins of a highly consumption-focused ancient culture: Vedic ritualism was highly materialistic (i.e., primarily concerned with the pursuit and attainment of fulfillment and happiness through the gratification of the sensual body and mind). Vedic religion was essentially a technology of highly ritualized sacrificial acts accompanied by meticulously precise and formalized *mantra* recitation, the basic goal of which was to manipulate the physical environment through the forces that controlled it. It was a method through which boons associated with the "good life"—cows (the currency of the time), offspring, victory over enemies, and so on—could be attained. In short, the goal of early Vedic ritual, reflective of the perennial goal of human endeavor, was the fulfillment of desire. Put differently (and provocatively), one might argue that the only difference between many of the Vedic goals of life and our modern consumer-centered ones is in the methods employed in the attaining of the good life: the ancients adopted sonic- and ritual-centered technologies, and we machine engineered industrial ones. Constructed, glamorized, and manipulated by the media and other institutions of mass propagation, modern attitudes to what constitutes the basic goal of life may not be that different from some of the essential core presuppositions underlying the Vedic ones.

A radical critique of this attitude to life and meaning emerged on the margins of the mainstream culture in the form of the earliest teachings promoting *yoga*. These texts, such as the *Upaniṣads*, the *Bhagavad Gītā*, and the *Yoga Sūtras*, proposed an alternative paradigm of human existence and possibility. As the *Gītā* notes, desire is insatiable, burns like fire, and is our eternal enemy (III.39). It is the cause of suffering and malaise (YS II.15). From the perspective of these *ātman*-based traditions, one can never find fulfillment through the physical body and mind because these do not form the real basis or source of the "self"; rather, they are simply inanimate coverings. Ultimate and enduring happiness, meaning, and fulfillment come when the mind realizes the *ātman* as distinct from the body-mind mechanism and reconfigures and redirects its notion of self away from identification with these layerings and onto the *ātman* as the ultimate source of consciousness and awareness. It is out of ignorance of this ultimate *ātman* that embodied beings seek fulfillment through the gratification of the coverings that are misidentified as the self and potentially become victims of greed, excessive consumption, and extravagant accumulation as ultimate goals (*Gītā* XVI).

Taken to excess and with little sociopolitical restraints, these endeavors can easily translate into enormous damage being inflicted on the individual, social, political, cultural, economic, and environmental worlds that human and nonhuman beings inhabit. Indeed, from the perspective of the Indic soteriological systems, it is this ignorance of the self and the consequent proliferation of endless desires that perpetuates suffering and *saṃsāra* (YS II.3–15). And it is as a deconstructive critique of this perennial mindset that the Indic soteriological systems such as *yoga* emerged on the margins of the consumer cultures of their day and offer an alternative mode of being that remains perennially relevant to the human condition.

With respect to insights and challenges related to contemplative studies and religious studies, the *Yoga Sūtras* thus brings our attention to the radical alterity of tradition-based Indic contemplative practice, especially as rooted in specific religious and soteriological systems. Patañjali's system of *yoga*, a discipline aimed at the purification of consciousness and ultimately liberation, emphasizes a radical "mind-body" (*puruṣa-prakṛti*) dualism and utilizes a distinctive psychology. The latter includes a sophisticated map of human consciousness, which consists of both gross and subtle, material and immaterial dimensions. According to Hindu classical Yoga, through dedicated practice of meditation, the consciousness of a practitioner may enter the deep interior recesses of its own ultimate nature, *puruṣa*, the transcendent aspect of personhood that is immortal, eternal, untainted, autonomous, and free. This soteriological system contrasts sharply with various decontextualized and reconceptualized forms of modern "yoga." Hindu classical Yoga emphasizes that aspiring *yogīs*, individuals seeking the ultimate goal of liberation (*mokṣa*) from *saṃsāra*, must remove themselves from the phenomenal world, physical embodiment, sensory engagement, materialistic life goals, as well as various emotional and mental attachments and misconceptions. Viewed from a larger perspective, Hindu classical Yoga might thus inspire one to reflect on the extent to which concern for beauty, health, materialism, and so forth, is incompatible with contemplative practice. Perhaps the *Yoga Sūtras* encourages us to consider *yoga* as it was understood in the premodern period: a profound and sophisticated system of liberation rooted in committed and prolonged meditative praxis. This includes, ironically, liberation from the very things with which *yoga* has come to be associated, namely, the goals of a body-centered, consumer-based lifestyle.

Notes

This chapter incorporates some material from my book *The Yoga Sutras* (Bryant 2009).

1. The Sanskrit term *darśana*, which is typically translated as "philosophy," more accurately indicates a point of view. In actual fact, the *Yoga Sūtras* are more of an instruction manual for practitioners than a philosophical tradition. For historical analyses and overviews of the so-called six schools, see Hiriyanna 1995; King 1999a.

2. Throughout the present chapter, "Yoga" refers to the philosophical school, or the Yoga tradition, while *yoga* is used to indicate various practices or systems of *yoga*.

3. The term "Hindu" was introduced by invaders from the West to refer to people living on the other side of the Sindhu (Indus) River. It surfaces for the first time in Indic sources in the sixteenth-century Bengali text *Caitanya Caritāmṛta* to refer to communities engaged in Vedic-derived practices deemed distinct from those of the Muslims, the dominant power in Bengal. It is now used as a term of convenience to refer to an enormously variegated cluster of interrelated, but distinct practices that lay claim to some connection to the old Vedic texts discussed later in this chapter.

4. For a discussion of the problem of the "three Patañjalis," see Larson and Bhattacharya 2008, 54ff.

5. The first reference to Yoga as a school separate from Sāṃkhya is in the writings of the ninth-century Vedāntin Śaṅkara.

6. Here Vedic is used to refer to the oldest corpus of Sanskrit texts, namely, the four Vedas (hymns), *Brāhmaṇas* (ritual expositions), *Āraṇyakas* (forest books), and *Upaniṣads* (philosophical treatises). Much of what comes to be placed under the rubric of "Hinduism," especially the "traditional Indian worldview and soteriology," has its roots in the last of the four strata, the *Upaniṣads*, rather than the earlier ritualistic corpus. For an easily available flavor of the Vedic worldview, see Doniger O'Flaherty 1981.

7. First discovered in 1922 with further excavations in the 1930s and 1940s, Mohenjo-daro is now a UNESCO World Heritage Site (est. 1980). This seal is associated with Harappa culture, also known as the Indus Valley Civilization. It dates to around 2,600 BCE and thus relates to prehistoric Indus culture. As the Harappan (Indus) script remains undeciphered, there is debate concerning the actual meaning and symbolism of the various archaeological discoveries. Under one reading of the present figure, it is one of the earliest depictions of a *yogī* in full-lotus posture, although this is disputed. See, for example, Srinivasan 1975–1976; McEvilley 1981.

8. While the term "Brahman" is used primarily for the Absolute Truth in its all-encompassing aspect, and *ātman* for the more localized aspect of that same truth in the individual, the two terms are interchangeable in the *Upaniṣads*.

9. The earliest reference to *yoga* actually appears in the *Taittirīya Upaniṣad* (II.5.4), after a discussion of the five *kośas* or "layers" that make up an individual. However, it is unclear if this refers to a meditative technique.

10. This *Maitrī Upaniṣad* adds *tarka*, or "inquiry," to the last five limbs later found in Patañjali's *Yoga Sūtras* and reverses the order of *dhāraṇā* and *dhyāna* from that found in Patañjali's system.

11. While both traditional narrative and critical scholarship consider this epic to have developed over centuries, it reached its present size of one hundred thousand verses prior to the fifth century CE. This is confirmed by a land grant that mentions this number of verses.

12. For *yoga* in the *Mahābhārata*, see Brockington 2003 and 2005.

13. For example, XIII.25 and XVIII.52.

14. Śaṅkara is the earliest commentator on the *Vedānta Sūtras* who has left extensive writings.

15. The identification of these "four *yoga* systems" in the *Bhagavad Gītā* was first popularized in *Rāja Yoga* by Vivekānanda (1863–1902), who became popular in the West after his address to the Chicago World's Parliament of Religions in 1893. For a genealogy of neo-Vedānta, see De Michelis 2004.

16. Of course, there were various other streams of thought that did not gain this status but have nonetheless emerged as significant presences in the religious landscape of Hinduism. For a discussion of

the history of Sanskrit doxographies culminating in the formation of the "six schools" as presently known, see Nicholson 2011.

17. "Orthodox" here refers to the "Vedic schools" that claim at least nominal allegiance to the Vedic corpus. "Heterodox" refers to those that have no such association but, in the case of Jainism and Buddhism, develop their own canons.

18. Sāṁkhya and Vaiśeṣika are metaphysical schools; Nyāya is primarily associated with Hindu logic; and Mīmāṁsā and Vedānta are exegetical schools, with the former concerning itself with the earlier ritualistic corpus and the latter with the *Upaniṣads*.

19. Any action performed in the unenlightened state, that is, in a state of ignorance (defined in YS II.5 as identifying oneself with the body and mind covering, as opposed to pure consciousness), plants a seed of corresponding reaction, which requires subsequent births to come to fruition. However, when these fruits manifest in due course, they trigger a further response, causing fresh seeds of karma, in an ever-spiraling vicious cycle of action, reaction, re-reaction, and so forth. This cycle is known as *saṁsāra*, which is often translated as "reincarnation" or "transmigration."

20. It is an axiom in Indic thought that anything eternal cannot be subject to change. If the soul is eternal, it therefore cannot undergo changes for Sāṁkhya.

21. Since *puruṣa* is omnipresent, its "adjacency" with *buddhi* is not spatial; conceptualizing their relationship is one of the main philosophical problems of Hindu thought.

22. *Sat-tva* literally means "being-ness."

23. For a selection of characteristics associated with the *guṇa*s, see chapters 14, 16, and 18 of the *Bhagavad Gītā*.

24. When the *guṇa*s maintain what we might call an "equi-tension," *prakṛti* remains in a pre-creative state of dynamic potential called *avyakta*. Once the equilibrium is disrupted, however, creation takes place.

25. *Rajas* and *tamas* can never be completely eliminated due to the inherent constitution of *prakṛti*.

26. Īśvara in philosophical discourse refers to a supreme creator god. While creation is not a topic relevant to the focus of the *Yoga Sūtras*, I have argued elsewhere that we must assume that Patañjali is using the term in its long-established conventional meaning (see Bryant 2009, 88ff.). This stands in contrast to Eliade's (1969) notion of Īśvara as the "archetypal *yogī*."

27. The "seed" referred to here is the imprint left on the mind by the object of meditation. The mind is stilled by fixing itself upon an object of meditation. This object, like any object perceived by the mind in normal cognitive activities, leaves a seed or saṁskāric imprint. Once consciousness is uncoupled from the mind, the mind remains in a state of complete vacuity and, hence, retains no "seeds" (*nirbīja*).

28. I use the notion of the soul as pure "subjectivity," or the soul as "subject-aware," loosely throughout this commentary. The notion of "subject" is only meaningful in contrast to some interaction with an object. In ultimate *asaṁprajñāta samādhi*, by definition, there are no interactions with objects, so the notion of subjectivity becomes inapplicable. However, I find it useful to retain the usage with this caveat so as to underscore the transference in the focus of awareness in *yoga*, from "other" to pure "self."

29. *Om* has been correlated with the sonic manifestation of Brahman, the ultimate Truth of the *Upaniṣads*, since the time of these texts (ca. 8th–4th c. BCE). See, for example, *Taittirīya Upaniṣad* I.8.1.

30. The term *kriyā yoga* is rarely found in the early texts. *Kriyā* usually refers to ritual action.

31. Hariharānanda commentary (III.2).

32. The idea here is that the meditator is so focused on the object that he or she is not even aware of what the object is (which requires the activation of memory), nor of the fact that he or she is meditating. This is the second of the seven *samādhi*s.

33. See, for example, Paramahansa Yogānanda's (1893–1952) *Autobiography of a Yogi* (1st ed., dat. 1946).

34. Gross matter, in Sāṁkhya, is a "densification" of subtler matter, and this, in turn, of mind stuff, which underpins all manifest reality. In intense concentrative states, the *yogī* can merge his or her mind with this "cosmic" mental substrate and then rearrange the grosser effects emanating from it.

35. See Larson and Bhattacharya (2008, 37ff.) for a perspective arguing that the *Yoga Sūtras* was perhaps written to bring the old Sāṁkhya traditions in line with later philosophical developments, including a response to Vijñānavāda Buddhism, with the latter also known as Yogācāra or the "Consciousness-Only" school.

36. Vyāsa is the legendary sage who is reputed to have divided the one Veda into four, written the 100,000-verse *Mahābhārata* epic, and compiled the eighteen *Purāṇas*.

37. For a translation of Vyāsa along with a more recent commentary, see Āraṇya 1984.

38. For select translations of commentaries, see Larson and Bhattacharya 2008; Bryant 2009.

39. It had, however, been known since the publication of Al-Bīrūnī's more famous work, published in 1887, that he had translated the *Yoga Sūtras*. The latter is quoted copiously in the former work.

40. Rāmānanda Sarasvatī also wrote a commentary, called *Ratnaprabhā* (Light on the Gem), on Śaṅkara's commentary on the *Vedānta Sūtra*, the *Brahmasūtrabhāṣya* (Commentary on the Aphorisms of Vedānta).

41. *Business Magazine*, September 2002 issue, gives the number as 18 million. *Yoga Journal* in 2003 174 (May–June) estimated that 25.5 million people were "very interested," 35.5 percent of the population intended to try *yoga* in the coming year, and 109.7 million had a "casual interest."

42. Vivekānanda's well-known book, *Raja Yoga* (1st ed., dat. 1896), drew from Patañjali but was heavily influenced by both Western rationalism and esotericism, as well as neo-Hindu nationalism (De Michelis 2004). While Vivekānanda was the first to introduce *yoga* to the West in a relatively mainstream context, there are references to awareness of *yogī*s on the Western landscape as early as Greek classical sources; Alexander (356–323 BCE; r. 336–323 BCE) was perhaps the most notorious early Westerner to be fascinated with Indian ascetics. See Halbfass 1981.

43. Along with Western esotericism and scientific discourse, elements of British gymnastics were nonetheless still absorbed in this process (see De Michelis 2001; Singleton 2010). Mention should also be made of the fifteenth- to sixteenth-century *Haṭha-yoga-pradīpikā* (Light on Haṭha Yoga), which dedicates one of its four chapters to *āsana*s. Although this was a very marginal and barely known text in mainstream Hindu circles, it was one of the few premodern Sanskrit sources that could be produced to attempt to authenticate this sudden emphasis on postural *yoga*. It has thus gained a far greater readership in the modern period (and mostly in the West, at that) than would ever have been the case previously.

44. Also very influential in the 1960s and 1970s and still promoted internationally is Maharishi Mahesh's (1917–2008) Transcendental Meditation (TM) movement, an extremely simplified form of meditational practice.

Works Cited and Further Reading

Alter, Joseph. 2004. *Yoga in Modern India: The Body between Science and Philosophy*. Princeton: Princeton University Press.
Āraṇya, Swāmi Harihārananda. 1984. *Yoga Philosophy of Patañjali*. Albany: State University of New York Press.
Bhattacharya, Ram Shankar. 1985. *An Introduction to the Yoga Sūtra*. Delhi: Bharatiya Vidya Prakasansa.
Brockington, John. 2003. "Yoga in the Mahābhārata." In *Yoga: The Indian Tradition*, edited by David Carpenter and Ian Whicher, 13–24. London and New York: Routledge.
———. 2005. "Epic Yoga." *Journal of Vaishnava Studies* 14.1 (Fall 2005): 123–38.
Bronkhurst, Johannes. 1993. *The Two Traditions of Meditation in Ancient India*. Delhi: Motilal Banarsidass.
Brooks, Douglas et al. 1997. *Meditation Revolution: A History and Theology of the Siddha Yoga Lineage*. South Fallsburg: Agama.
Bryant, Edwin F. 2004. *The Hare Krishna Movement*. New York: Columbia University Press.

———. 2009. *The Yoga Sūtras of Patañjali: A New Edition, Translation and Commentary*. New York: North Point Press.
Carrette, Jeremy, and Richard King. 2004. *Selling Spirituality: The Silent Takeover of Religion*. London and New York: Routledge.
Chapple, Christopher. 2003. *Reconciling Yogas: Haribhadra's Collection of Views on Yoga*. Albany: State University of New York Press.
Dasgupta, Surendranath. 1922. *A History of Indian Philosophy*. Delhi: Motilal Banarsidass.
———. 1927. *Hindu Mysticism*. Delhi: Motilal Banarsidass.
De Michelis, Elizabeth. 2004. *History of Modern Yoga: Patañjali and Western Esotericism*. New York and London: Continuum.
Diamond, Debra. 2013. *Yoga: The Art of Transformation*. Washington: Smithsonian Institution.
Doniger O'Flaherty, Wendy. 1981. *The Rig Veda*. New York: Penguin.
Eliade, Mircea. 1936. *Yoga: Essai sur l'origine de la mystique Indienne*. Paris: Geuthner.
———. 1958. *Yoga: Immortality and Freedom*. Translated by Willard R. Trask. London: Kegan Paul.
———. 2009 (1969). *Yoga: Immortality and Freedom*. Translated by Willard R. Trask. Princeton: Princeton University Press.
Feuerstein, Georg. 1989. *The Yoga-Sutra of Patañjali: A New Translation and Commentary*. Rochester: Inner Traditions.
———. 1996. *The Philosophy of Classical Yoga*. Rochester: Inner Traditions.
———. 2001. *The Yoga Tradition: Its History, Literature, Philosophy, and Practice*. Prescott: Hohm Press.
———. 2003. *The Deeper Dimension of Yoga: Theory and Practice*. Boston: Shambhala.
Forman, Robert K. C., ed. 1990. *The Problem of Pure Consciousness: Mysticism and Philosophy*. Oxford and New York: Oxford University Press.
———, ed. 1998. *The Innate Capacity: Mysticism, Psychology, and Philosophy*. Oxford and New York: Oxford University Press.
Halbfass, Wilhelm. 1981. *India and Europe: An Essay in Understanding*. Basel: Schwabe and Co.
Hiriyanna, Mysore. 1995. *The Essentials of Indian Philosophy*. Delhi: Motilal Banarsidass.
Hopkins, E. W. 1901. "Yoga Technique in the Great Epic." *Journal of the American Oriental Society* 22: 333–79.
Jacobsen, Knut, ed. 2005. *Theory and Practice of Yoga: Essays in Honour of Gerald James Larson*. Leiden: Brill.
Jacobi, Hermann. 1911. "The Dates of the Philosophical Sūtras of the Brahmans." *Journal of the American Oriental Society* 31:1–29.
King, Richard. 1999a. *Indian Philosophy*. Washington: Georgetown University Press.
———. 1999b. *Orientalism and Religion: Postcolonial Theory, India and 'The Mystic East.'* London and New York: Routledge.
Larson, Gerald James. 1979. *Classical Sāṃkhya*. Delhi: Motilal Banarsidass.
———. 1999. "Classical Yoga as Neo-Sāṃkhya: A Chapter in the History of Indian Philosophy." *Asiatische Studien Études Asiatiques* 52.3: 723–32.
Larson, Gerald James, and Ram Shankar Bhattacharya. 2008. *Yoga: India's Philosophy of Meditation*. Encyclopedia of Indian Philosophies, Volume 12. Delhi: Motilal Banarsidass.
McEvilley, Thomas. 1981. "An Archaeology of Yoga." *RES: Anthropology and Aesthetics* 1: 44–77.
Nicholson, Andrew. 2011. *Unifying Hinduism: Philosophy and Identity in Indian Intellectual History*. New Delhi: Permanent Black.
Prasad, Jwala. 1930. "The Date of the *Yoga-sūtras*." *Journal of the Royal Asiatic Society* 84: 365–75.
Singleton, Mark. 2010. *Yoga Body: The Origins of Modern Posture Practice*. Oxford and New York: Oxford University Press.
Sjoman, N. E. 1996. *The Yoga Tradition of the Mysore Palace*. New Delhi: Abhinav Publications.

Srinivasan, Doris. 1975/76. "The So-Called Proto-Śiva Seal from Mohenjo-Daro: An Iconological Assessment." *Archives of Asian Art* 29: 47–58.
Strauss, Sarah. 2005. *Positioning Yoga*. Oxford: Berg.
Syman, Stefania. 2010. *The Subtle Body: The Story of Yoga in America*. New York: Farrar, Straus and Giroux.
Whicher, Ian. 1998. *The Integrity of the Yoga Darśana*. Albany: State University of New York Press.
Yamashita, Koichi. 1994. *Patañjala Yoga Philosophy: With Reference to Buddhism*. Calcutta: Firma KLM.

Yoga Sūtras (Yoga Aphorisms)*

Patañjali (ca. 1st–2nd c. CE)

Translated and Annotated by Edwin F. Bryant

Chapter One: Samādhi Pāda (Meditative Absorption)[1]

I.1
Now, the teachings of *yoga*[2] [are presented].

I.2
Yoga is the stilling of the changing states of the mind.

I.3
When that is accomplished, the seer abides in its own true nature.

I.4
Otherwise, at other times, [the seer] is absorbed in the changing states [of the mind].

I.5
There are five kinds of changing states of the mind, and they are either detrimental or non-detrimental [to the practice of *yoga*].

I.6
[These five states are] right knowledge, error, imagination, sleep, and memory.[3]

I.7
Right knowledge consists of sense perception, logic, and verbal testimony.

I.8
Error is false knowledge stemming from the incorrect apprehension [of something].

---

*The present translation is a complete rendering of the standard Sanskrit text. The translation with translations of various traditional commentaries first appeared in Bryant 2009. It is used with permission from North Point Press/Farrar, Straus and Giroux (FSG), and I am grateful for the opportunity to reprint it here. I wish to especially thank Victoria Fox and Jeff Seroy for their assistance. For some reliable alternative translations, see Āranya 1984; Feuerstein 1989; Larson and Bhattacharya 2008. "Translation of Sutras" from *The Yoga Sūtras of Patañjali: A New Edition, Translation and Commentary*, by Edwin F. Bryant.

1. When the mind is fixed on an object of concentration with undeviating absorption, various stages of *samādhi*, supernormal mental states, manifest sequentially, as the intensity of the focus deepens. There are six consecutive states grouped as *samprajñāta samādhi*, and a final state once the mind has been bypassed and consciousness abides in its own nature unmediated by the external mind. The latter is called *asamprajñāta samādhi*.

2. In Sanskrit texts, *yoga*, cognate with English "to yoke," generally refers to meditative techniques through which the mind can still itself such that one's innermost nature as pure consciousness (*puruṣa*) can be attained. This is defined in verses I.2–4.

3. As discussed in my introduction, in classical Yoga memory is the ability to recollect *samskāra*s.

I.9
Imagination consists of the usage of words that are devoid of an actual object.

I.10
Deep sleep is that state of mind which is based on an absence [of any content].

I.11
Memory is the retention of [images of] sense objects that have been experienced.

I.12
[These states of mind] are stilled by practice and dispassion.

I.13
From these, practice is the effort to be fixed in concentrating the mind.

I.14
Practice becomes firmly established when it has been cultivated uninterruptedly and with devotion over a prolonged period of time.

I.15
Dispassion is the controlled consciousness of one who is without craving for sense objects, whether these are actually perceived or described [in scripture].

I.16
Higher than renunciation is indifference to the *guṇa*s [themselves].[4] This stems from perception of the *puruṣa*, the soul.

I.17
Samprajñāta [*samādhi*] consists of [the consecutive] mental stages of absorption with physical awareness, absorption with subtle awareness, absorption with bliss, and absorption with the sense of I-ness.[5]

I.18
The other *samādhi* [*asamprajñāta-samādhi*] is preceded by cultivating the determination to terminate [all thoughts]. [In this state] only latent impressions remain.[6]

---

4. Since everything is made of the *guṇa*s (lit., strands or qualities), indifference to them indicates complete disinterest in any prakṛtic pleasures of the world. This can only occur when the mind has attained higher spiritual stages.

5. In these rarefied esoteric states of meditation, the mind is able to penetrate and perceive increasingly subtler metaphysical substructures of the object of meditation, then the instruments of perception themselves, and finally is able to "reflect" consciousness back to itself. However, all of these states are mediated by the mind and hence are not ultimate: the final goal is for consciousness to perceive its own nature directly and without mediation. The interpretation of these views is aided by traditional commentaries. See Bryant 2009.

6. This is a reference to the final goal of Hindu classical Yoga, where consciousness now abides in its own nature (I.3). The mind has now been bypassed, and all its *saṁskāra*s remain inactive.

I.19
For [some], those who are unembodied and those who are merged in matter, [the state of] *samprajñāta* is characterized] by absorption in [subtle] states of *prakṛti*.⁷

I.20
[But] for others, [the state where only subconscious impressions remain] is preceded by faith, vigor, memory, *samādhi*-absorption, and discernment.

I.21
[This state of *samprajñāta*] is near for those who apply themselves intensely.

I.22
Even among these, there is further differentiation [of this intensity into degrees of] mild, mediocre, and ardent.

I.23
Or, [this previously mentioned state is attainable] from devotion to Īśvara.⁸

I.24
Īśvara is a special soul. He is untouched by the obstacles [to the practice of *yoga*], karma, the fructification [of karma], and subconscious predispositions.⁹

I.25
In him, the seed of omniscience is unsurpassed.

I.26
Īśvara was also the teacher of the ancients, because he is not limited by Time.

I.27
The name designating him is the mystical syllable *om*.¹⁰

I.28
Its repetition and the contemplation of its meaning [should be performed].

---

7. This is taken to be a reference to *yogī*s who fail to attain the final goal of *yoga*, but who remain stranded in some high state of meditation, considering this to be ultimate.

8. Īśvara is the term for the supreme creator in most Hindu philosophical texts and the object of the *bhakti* devotional traditions, where he is the awarder of liberation, which is his role here. Patañjali does not dwell extensively on Īśvara in the present aphorisms, which are extremely brief and narrowly focused on meditative practices. However, he is clearly assuming awareness of *bhakti* practices here, and hence classical Yoga is considered a theistic practice. The *Bhagavad Gītā* provides a far more robust set of teachings associated with the wider role of Īśvara as well as of the path of devotion.

9. These are the *saṃskāra*s (imprints or impressions), which are discussed in my introduction.

10. In the *Upaniṣads*, *om* is correlated with Brahman as well as with Īśvara. See also *Bhagavad Gītā* VII.8, IX.17, X.25.

I.29
From this comes the realization of the inner consciousness and freedom from all disturbances.

I.30
These disturbances are disease, idleness, doubt, carelessness, sloth, lack of detachment, misapprehension, failure to attain a base for concentration, and instability [in practice]. They are distractions for the mind.

I.31
Suffering, dejection, trembling, inhalation, and exhalation accompany the disturbances.

I.32
Practice [of fixing the mind] on one object [should be performed] in order to eliminate these disturbances.[11]

I.33
By cultivating an attitude of friendship toward those who are happy, compassion toward those in distress, joy toward those who are virtuous, and equanimity toward those who are non-virtuous, lucidity arises in the mind.

I.34
Or [stability of mind is gained] by exhaling and retaining the breath.

I.35
Or else, focus on a sense object manifests, and this causes steadiness of the mind.

I.36
Or [steadiness of mind is gained when] the mind is free of pain and luminous.

I.37
Or [the mind becomes steady when it has] one who is free from desire as its object.

I.38
Or [the mind can become steady when it has] the knowledge attained from sleep and dreams as its support.[12]

I.39
Or [steadiness of the mind is attained] from meditation upon anything of one's inclination.

I.40
The *yogī*'s mastery extends from the smallest particle of matter to the totality of matter.

---

11. While Patañjali prioritizes the chanting of *om*, any object can be used for meditation. See I.39 and previous verses.
12. This peculiar *sūtra* is interpreted variously by different commentators. See Bryant 2009.

I.41
Samāpatti, complete absorption of the mind when it is free from its changing states, occurs when the mind becomes just like a transparent jewel, taking the form of whatever object is placed before it, whether the object be the knower, the instrument of knowledge, or the object of knowledge.[13]

I.42
In this stage, *savitarka-samāpatti*, absorption with physical awareness, is intermixed with the notions of word, meaning, and idea.[14]

I.43
Nirvitarka [*samāpatti*], absorption without conceptualization, occurs when memory has been purged and the mind is empty, as it were, of its own [reflective] nature. Now only the object [of meditation] shines forth [in its own right].[15]

I.44
The states of *samādhi* with "subtle awareness" and without "subtle awareness," whose objects of focus are the subtle nature [of things], are explained in the same manner.[16]

I.45
The subtle nature of things extends all the way up to *prakṛti*.

I.46
These aforementioned *samāpatti* states are [known as] *samādhi* "with seed."[17]

I.47
Upon attaining the clarity of *nirvicāra-samādhi*, there is lucidity of the inner self.[18]

I.48
In that state, there is truth-bearing wisdom.

---

13. *Samāpatti* is more-or-less synonymous with *saṁprajñāta-samādhi*, referring to the complete absorption of the mind with the object of meditation. It thus refers to a particular type of *samādhi* or meditative state.

14. In this state, the mind still retains some awareness of what the object of meditation is—its name and function in the grand scheme of things. In other words, memory is still active.

15. In this state, even memory is inactive, and, in its quest for absolute stillness, the mind is focused on its object of meditation without activating recognition and thus without awareness of what this object is.

16. This verse refers to two further states, where the mind's intensity penetrates the object of meditation to its deeper metaphysical nature of subtle matter. In *savicara*, there is still an awareness of space and time (the here and now); in *nirvicāra*, even these concepts are transcended, and the *yogī* becomes aware only of all-pervading eternal subtle matter.

17. Any object upon which the mind is focused, in any state of *saṁprajñāta-samādhi*, leaves an imprint (*saṁskāra*), hence, the "seed" referred to here. The first six stages of *samādhi* noted previously are thus "with seed," while the final is "without seed."

18. See annotation to I.44 (fn. 16).

I.49
It [*samādhi*] has a different focus from that of inference and sacred scripture, because it has the particularity of things as its object.[19]

I.50
The *saṁskāra*s born out of that [truth-bearing wisdom] obstruct other *saṁskāra*s [from emerging].[20]

I.51
Upon the cessation of even those [truth-bearing *saṁskāra*s], *nirbīja-samādhi*, seedless meditative absorption, ensues.[21]

Chapter Two: Sādhana Pāda (Practice)[22]

II.1
Kriyā-yoga, the path of action, consists of self-discipline, study, and dedication to Īśvara.[23]

II.2
[The *yoga* of action] is for bringing about *samādhi* and for weakening the impediments [to *yoga*].

II.3
The impediments [to *samādhi*] are nescience, ego, desire, aversion, and clinging to life.

II.4
Ignorance is the breeding ground of the other impediments, whether they are in a dormant, weak, intermittent, or fully activated state.

II.5
Ignorance is the notion that takes the self, which is joyful, pure, and eternal, to be the non-self [the body and mind], which is painful, unclean, and temporary.[24]

---

19. The three ways of "knowing" in I.7 are limited because sense perception, inference, and words only refer to generalities (knowing an object such as a "pot," for example, only allows us to know the pot as a member of a genus or species but give us very little about any particular pot as distinct from any other). In the more esoteric states of *samādhi*, one's awareness of the pot can penetrate its essence far more deeply, even to its subtle substructure as indicated earlier.

20. When the mind is cultivating absolute stillness, the *saṁskāra* that monitors the inner mental landscape to ensure no distracting thoughts arise.

21. When even the *saṁskāra* referred to in the previous verse is still, the mind has attained absolute stillness. There is now nothing external to consciousness to distract it, and thus consciousness can finally abide in its own nature, which is the goal of Hindu classical Yoga.

22. This chapter deals with the more preliminary preparatory practices that eventually lead to the esoteric states outlined in the first chapter.

23. *Kriyā* means action.

24. The "non-self" refers to the body and mind coverings of pure autonomous consciousness.

II.6
Ego is [to consider] the nature of the seer and the nature of the instrumental power of seeing to be the same thing.

II.7
Attachment stems from [experiences] of happiness.

II.8
Aversion stems from [experiences] of pain.

II.9
[The tendency of] clinging to life affects even the wise; it is an inherent tendency.

II.10
These impediments are subtle; they are destroyed when [the mind] dissolves back into its original matrix.

II.11
The states of mind produced by these impediments are eliminated by meditation.[25]

II.12
The stock of karma has the impediments as its root. It is experienced in present or future lives.

II.13
As long as the root [of impediments] exists, it fructifies as type of birth, span of life, and life experience [of an individual].

II.14
These [the type of birth, span of life, and life experience] bear the fruits of pleasure and pain, as a result of [the performance of] virtue and vice.

II.15
For one who has discrimination, everything is suffering on account of the suffering produced by the consequences [of action], by pain [itself], and by the *saṁskāra* memory imprints, as well as on account of the suffering ensuing from the turmoil of the states of the mind due to the *guṇa*s.

II.16
Suffering that has yet to manifest is to be avoided.

---

25. The term here is *dhyāna* (meditation), the seventh limb of classical Yoga discussed in this chapter, wherein the mind is approaching the more intense states of *samādhi* (meditative absorption).

II.17
The conjunction between the seer and that which is seen is the cause [of suffering] to be avoided.

II.18
That which is knowable has the nature of illumination, activity, and inertia.[26] It consists of the senses and the elements and exists for the purpose of [providing] either liberation or experience [to the soul, *puruṣa*].

II.19
The different stages of the *guṇa* qualities consist of the particularized, the unparticularized, the distinctive, and the indistinctive.[27]

II.20
The seer is merely the power of seeing; [however,] although pure, it witnesses the images of mind.

II.21
The essential nature of that which is seen is exclusively for the sake of the seer.

II.22
Although the seen ceases to exist for one whose purpose is accomplished [the liberated *puruṣa*], it has not ceased to exist altogether, since it is common to other [not-liberated] *puruṣa*s.

II.23
[The notion of] conjunction is the means of understanding the real nature of the powers of the possessed and of the possessor.

II.24
The cause of conjunction is ignorance.[28]

II.25
By the removal of ignorance, conjunction is removed. This is the absolute freedom of the seer.

II.26
The means to liberation is uninterrupted discriminative discernment.

II.27
The *yogī*'s true insight has seven ultimate stages.[29]

---

26. This is a reference to *sattva* (lucidity), *rajas* (action), and *tamas* (inertia), which are discussed in my introduction.

27. This is a technical way of schematizing the evolutes of *prakṛti*.

28. See II.5 for the definition of ignorance and II.17 for conjunction.

29. These seven stages are not central to this chapter. The interested reader may consult the traditional commentaries. See Bryant 2009.

II.28
Upon the destruction of impurities as a result of the practice of *yoga*, the lamp of knowledge arises. This culminates in discriminative discernment.

II.29
The eight limbs are abstentions (*yama*), observances (*niyama*), posture (*āsana*), breath control (*prāṇāyāma*), sensory withdrawal (*pratyāhāra*), concentration (*dhāraṇā*), meditation (*dhyāna*), and absorption (*samādhi*).

II.30
The abstentions are nonviolence, truthfulness, abstention from stealing, celibacy, and renunciation of [unnecessary] possessions.[30]

II.31
[These abstentions] are considered the great vow. They are not exempted by one's class, place, time, or circumstance. They are universal.

II.32
The observances are cleanliness, contentment, austerity, study [of scripture], and devotion to Īśvara.

II.33
Upon being harassed by negative thoughts, one should cultivate counteracting thoughts.

II.34
Negative thoughts are violence, etc.[31] They may be [personally] performed, performed on one's behalf by another, or authorized by oneself; they may be triggered by greed, anger, or delusion; and they may be slight, moderate, or extreme in intensity. One should cultivate counteracting thoughts, namely, that the end results [of negative thoughts] are ongoing suffering and ignorance.

II.35
In the presence of one who is established in nonviolence, enmity is abandoned.

II.36
When one is established in truthfulness, one ensures the fruition of actions.

II.37
When one is established in abstention from stealing, all jewels manifest.

---

30. These five *yama*s are identical to the five great vows of the Jains and overlap with four of the five Buddhist vows. They were more or less generic for aspiring ascetics and *yogī*s in ancient India.

31. The "etc." here refers to acts contrary to the five *yama*s. When "etc." appears in my translation, it follows the Sanskrit original; it does not indicate an abridgement.

II.38
Upon the establishment of celibacy, power is attained.

II.39
When renunciation of [unnecessary possessions] becomes firmly established, knowledge of the whys and wherefores of births manifests.

II.40
By cleanliness, one [develops] distaste for one's body and the cessation of contact with others.

II.41
Upon the purification of the mind, [one attains] cheerfulness, one-pointedness, sense control, and fitness to perceive the self.

II.42
From contentment, the highest happiness is attained.

II.43
From austerity, on account of the removal of impurities, the perfection of the senses and body manifests.

II.44
From study [of scripture], a connection with one's deity of choice is established.

II.45
From submission to Īśvara comes the perfection of *samādhi*.

II.46
Posture should be steady and comfortable.[32]

II.47
[Such posture should be attained] by the relaxation of effort and by absorption in the infinite.

II.48
From this, one is not afflicted by the dualities of the opposites.

II.49
When that [posture] is accomplished, breath control [follows]. This consists of the regulation of the incoming and outgoing breaths.[33]

II.50
[Breath control] manifests as external, internal, and restrained movements [of breath]. These are drawn out and subtle in accordance to place, time, and number.

---

32. The traditional commentaries advocate the *padmāsana*, or "full-lotus," posture. See Bryant 2009.

33. This is a reference to *prāṇāyāma*, wherein respiration is slowed in accordance with the next verse.

II.51
The fourth [type of breath control] surpasses the limits of the external and the internal.

II.52
Then, the covering of the illumination [of knowledge] is weakened.

II.53
Additionally, the mind becomes fit for concentration.

II.54
Sensory withdrawal occurs when the senses do not come into contact with their respective sense objects. It corresponds, as it were, to the nature of the mind [when it is withdrawn from the sense objects].

II.55
From this comes the highest control of the senses.

Chapter Three: Vibhūti Pāda (Mystic Powers)[34]

III.1
Concentration is the fixing of the mind in one place.[35]

III.2
Meditation is the one-pointedness of the mind on one image.[36]

III.3
Samādhi is when that same meditation shines forth as the object alone and [the mind] is devoid of its own [reflective] nature.

III.4
When these three are performed together, it is called *saṁyama*.[37]

III.5
From *saṁyama* comes insight.

---

34. *Vibhūtis*, also known as *siddhis*, are the supernormal powers that may accrue spontaneously in the higher states of meditation. Since there are many references to pseudo-*yogīs* engaging in *yoga*-type practices but with the goal of attaining power, rather than with the true goal of *yoga* in mind (liberation), Patañjali discusses them here with a view to dissuading sincere *yogīs* from being distracted by them.

35. In this sixth stage of *dhāraṇā* (concentration) the mind remains not yet fully stilled. The commentator Vyāsa compares it to a dripping tap: as gaps intersect the otherwise identical drops of water, so the mind focused on the object is still subject to distraction.

36. In the seventh stage, *dhyāna* (meditation), the mind, in contrast with the previous limb, is compared to the flow of oil: thick, unctuous, and unbroken.

37. This term refers to when the mind is sequentially applied through the last three limbs of *yoga*.

III.6
Saṁyama is applied on the [different] stages [of *samādhi*].

III.7
These three [concentration, meditation, and *samādhi*] are internal limbs compared to the previous limbs [of *yoga*].

III.8
Yet even these are external limbs in relation to "seedless" *samādhi*.

III.9
The state of restraint, *nirodha*, is when there is disappearance of outgoing [worldly] *saṁskāra*s, mental imprints, and the appearance of restraining *saṁskāra*s. These emerge in the mind at the moment of restraint.[38]

III.10
The mind's undisturbed flow occurs due to *saṁskāra*s.

III.11
The attainment of the *samādhi* state involves the elimination of all-pointedness [wandering] of the mind and the rise of one-pointedness [concentration].

III.12
In that regard, the attainment of one-pointedness occurs when the image in the mind that has just passed is the same as the image in the mind that is present.

III.13
In this way, the change in the characteristics, state, and condition of objects and of the senses is explained.

III.14
The substratum is that which underpins past, present, and future.

III.15
The change in the sequence [of characteristics] is the cause of the change in transformations [of objects].

---

38. The mind is normally drawn to thoughts connected with the outside world. This verse refers to the tension between those *saṁskāra*s seeking to restrain the mind and those seeking to think in normal ways. Through practice, the former are strengthened, until one can sit in meditation without the mind being distracted by the arising of thoughts.

III.16
When *saṁyama* is performed on the three transformations [of characteristics, state, and condition], knowledge of the past and the future ensues.[39]

III.17
Due to the correlation among word, meaning, and idea, confusion ensues. By performing *saṁyama* on them separately, knowledge of the speech of all creatures arises.[40]

III.18
By bringing [previous] *saṁskāra*s into direct perception comes the knowledge of previous births.

III.19
From [their] ideas, one can attain knowledge of others' minds.

III.20
That knowledge is not accompanied by its object, since this object is not the object [of the *yogī*'s mind].

III.21
By performing *saṁyama* on the outer form of the body, invisibility [is attained]. This occurs when perceptibility is obstructed by blocking contact between light and the eyes.[41]

III.22
Karma is either quick to fructify or slow. By *saṁyama* on karma, or on portents, knowledge of [one's] death arises.

III.23
By [*saṁyama*] on friendliness and such things, strengths are acquired.

III.24
[By practicing *saṁyama*] on strengths, [the *yogī*] attains the strength of an elephant, etc.

III.25
By directing the light of cognition, one obtains knowledge of subtle, concealed, and remote things.

---

39. This is a reference to the *yogī*'s ability to know past and future, by dint of perfect awareness of the present (i.e., of cause and effect, since the present is the product of the past and the cause of the future).

40. The ability to understand the speech of all creatures is a traditional supernormal power.

41. Since mind "stuff" is highly sāttvic and the source of derivative grosser manifestations of matter, it underpins its evolutes and can, according to this verse, in intense states of meditation, transform the nature of a body to a less tamasic and more sāttvic element such as air, such that light does not bounce back from it, rendering the body invisible.

III.26
By performing *saṁyama* on the sun, knowledge of the different realms in the universe arises.

III.27
[By *saṁyama*] on the moon, knowledge of the solar systems arises.

III.28
[By *saṁyama*] on the polestar, knowledge of the movement of the stars arises.

III.29
[By *saṁyama*] on the navel plexus of the body, knowledge of the arrangement of the body arises.

III.30
[By *saṁyama*] on the pit of the throat, the cessation of hunger and thirst arises.

III.31
[By *saṁyama*] on the subtle tortoise channel,[42] steadiness is attained.

III.32
[By *saṁyama*] on the light in the skull,[43] a vision of the *siddha*s,[44] perfected beings, is attained.

III.33
Or, by intuition, comes [knowledge of] everything.

III.34
[By *saṁyama*] on the heart, knowledge of the mind ensues.

III.35
Worldly experience consists of the notion that there is no distinction between *puruṣa* and pure intelligence, although these two are completely distinct. Worldly experience exists for another [*puruṣa*]. [By *saṁyama*] on that which exists for itself [*puruṣa*], knowledge of *puruṣa* arises.

III.36
From this, intuition as well as higher hearing, touch, vision, taste, and smell are born.

III.37
These powers are accomplishments for the mind that is outgoing but obstacles to *samādhi*.

---

42. This is a reference to the *nāḍis* (subtle channels), which play a prominent role in the *siddha/tantra/śakta* cluster of traditions but almost none in the classical Yoga tradition.
43. According to the commentator Vyāsa, this refers to an opening in the skull containing radiant light.
44. The *siddha*s are elevated beings who exist on subtle planes of reality and are generally invisible to normal gross vision.

III.38
By loosening the cause of bondage, and by knowledge of the passageways of the mind, the mind can enter into the bodies of others.

III.39
By mastery over the *udāna* vital air,[45] one attains [the power of] levitation and does not come into contact with water, mud, and thorns, etc.

III.40
By mastery over the *samāna* vital air,[46] radiance is attained.

III.41
By *saṁyama* on the relationship between the organ of hearing and the ether,[47] divine hearing is attained.

III.42
By performing *saṁyama* on the relationship between the body and ether, and by performing *samāpatti* on the lightness of cotton, one acquires the ability to travel through the sky.

III.43
The state of mind [projected] outside [of the body], which is not an imagined state, is called the great out-of-body [experience]. By this, the covering of the light [of the pure intelligence] is destroyed.

III.44
By *saṁyama* on the gross nature, essential nature, subtle nature, constitution, and purpose [of objects, one attains] mastery over the elements.

III.45
As a result of this, there are no limitations on account of the body's natural abilities; mystic powers such as the ability to become minute in size, etc., manifest; and the body attains perfection.

III.46
The perfection of the body consists of [possessing] beauty, charm, strength, and the power of a thunderbolt.

III.47
By the performance of *saṁyama* on the process of knowing, on the essence [of the sense organs], on ego, on inherence [of the *guṇa*s], and on the purpose [of the *guṇa*s] comes control over the senses.

---

45. There are five *prāṇa*s (life airs or vital breaths) in Hindu subtle physiology. The *udāna prāṇa* is upward flowing, manifesting up to the head, and so is instrumental to levitation.

46. The *samāna prāṇa* nourishes all parts of the body and is considered instrumental in generating a bodily aura.

47. Ether is one of the five gross elements, along with air, fire, water, and earth.

III.48

As a result of this comes speed like the speed of mind, activity independent of the bodily senses, and mastery over primordial matter.[48]

III.49

Only for one who discerns the difference between the *puruṣa* and the intellect do omniscience and omnipotence accrue.

III.50

By detachment even from this attainment [i.e., omniscience and omnipotence], and upon the destruction of the seeds of all faults, *kaivalya*, the supreme liberation, ensues.[49]

III.51

If solicited by celestial beings, [the *yogī*] should not become smug, because the tendency toward undesirable consequences can once again manifest.

III.52

By performing *saṁyama* on the moment, and its sequence, one attains knowledge born of discrimination.

III.53

As a result of this, there is discernment of two comparable things that are not distinguishable by species, characteristics, or location.

III.54

Knowledge born of discrimination is a liberator; it has everything as its object at all times simultaneously.

III.55

When the purity of the intellect is equal to that of the *puruṣa*, absolute liberation (*kaivalya*) ensues, the complete freedom of *puruṣa*.

Chapter Four: Kaivalya Pāda (Absolute Liberation)[50]

IV.1

The mystic powers arise due to birth, herbs,[51] mantras, the performance of austerity, and *samādhi*.

---

48. In this and similar verses, the classical Yoga tradition claims that accomplished *yogīs* essentially become omniscient and omnipotent.

49. *Kaivalya*, literally, "aloneness" or "autonomy," is the ultimate goal of classical Yoga. In this state, consciousness is finally withdrawn from all external objects and abides in its own nature. See I.3.

50. As mentioned earlier, *Kaivalya* refers to the ultimate liberated state when consciousness is uncoupled from the mind. See also I.3 and III.50.

51. The traditional commentators give the ancient *soma* herb as an example here, since the Vedic texts describe it as bestowing supernormal powers on those who imbibe it. Its exact referent and characteristics are a matter of controversy among scholars in the field.

IV.2
The changes [in bodily forms that take place] in other births are due to the filling in by *prakṛti*.

IV.3
The instrumental cause of creation is not its creative cause, but it pierces the covering from creation like a farmer [pierces the barriers between his fields].

IV.4
Created minds are made from ego only.

IV.5
There is one mind, among the many [created by the *yogī*], which is the director in the different activities [of the different bodies].

IV.6
From these [five types of minds that possess *siddhi*s], the one born of meditation is without the storehouse of karma.

IV.7
The karma of a *yogī* is neither white nor black; of everyone else, it is of three types.[52]

IV.8
From [these three types of karma] the activation of only those subliminal impressions that are ready for fruition [in the next life] occurs.

IV.9
Because they are identical, there is an uninterrupted connection between memory and *saṃskāra*, even though they might be separated by birth, time, and place.

IV.10
The *saṃskāra*s are eternal, because the desire [for life] is eternal.

IV.11
Since [*saṃskāra*s] are held together by immediate cause, motive, the mind, and the object of awareness, the *saṃskāra*s cease when the latter cease.

IV.12
The past and the future exist in reality, since they differ [from the present only] in terms of the time of [manifestation] of their characteristics.

---

52. The commentator Vyāsa notes that there are four types of *karma*: black comprises evil deeds; black and white, the norm, refers to the actions of most people, which are sometimes good and sometimes not; white consists of internal activities like meditation, study, and austerity. Finally, the accomplished *yogī* performs neither black nor white nor mixed *karma*: when all ignorance has been destroyed, there are no karmic reactions that accrue, even to the performer of actions. This principle of action based on knowledge of the true self is articulated most clearly in the *karma yoga* teachings of the second and third chapters of the *Bhagavad Gītā*.

IV.13

The past, present, and future have the *guṇa*s as their essence and are either manifest or latent.

IV.14

The things [of the world] are objectively real, due to the uniformity [of the *guṇa*s that underpin] all change.

IV.15

Because there is a multiplicity of minds [perceiving an object] but yet the object remains consistent, there is a difference in nature between the object and the mind [of the observer].[53]

IV.16

An object is not dependent on a single mind [for its existence]; if it were, then what happens to it when it is not perceived [by that particular mind]?

IV.17

A thing is either known or not known by the mind depending on whether it is noticed by the mind.

IV.18

The permutations of the mind are always known to its *puruṣa*, because of the soul's unchanging nature.

IV.19

Nor is the mind self-illuminating, because of its nature as the object of perception.

IV.20

There cannot be discernment of both [the mind and the object that it perceives] at the same time.

IV.21

If [the mind] were cognized by another mind, then there would be an infinite regress of one intelligence [being known] by another intelligence. Moreover, there would also be confusion of memory.

IV.22

Although it is unchanging, consciousness becomes aware of its own intelligence by means of pervading the forms assumed by the intelligence.

IV.23

The mind, colored by the seer as well as by that which is seen, knows all objects.

---

53. Verses IV.15–21 undertake a response to Vijñāna Buddhism, also known as Yogācāra or the "Consciousness-Only" school, which held an idealist metaphysics.

IV.24
That mind, with its countless variegated subliminal impressions, exists for another entity [other than itself], because it operates in conjunction [with other instruments].

IV.25
For one who sees the distinction [between the mind and the soul], reflection on the nature of the self ceases.

IV.26
At that point, the mind, inclined toward discrimination, gravitates toward ultimate liberation.

IV.27
During the intervals [in this state of discriminate awareness] other ideas [arise] because of previous *saṁskāra*s.

IV.28
The removal [of these previous *saṁskāra*s] is said to be like [the removal] of the impediments.

IV.29
For one who has no interest even in [the fruits] of meditative wisdom on account of the highest degree of discriminative insight, the *samādhi* called *dharma-megha*, cloud of virtue, ensues.[54]

IV.30
From this comes the cessation of the impediments to *yoga* and of karma.

IV.31
At this point, because of the unlimited nature of knowledge when all impurities have been removed from it, that which remains to be known is little.

IV.32
As a result, there is a cessation of the ongoing permutations of the *guṇa*s, as their purpose is now fulfilled.

IV.33
The progression [of any object through Time] corresponds to a [series of] moments. It is perceivable at the final [moment] of change.

IV.34
Ultimate liberation is when the *guṇa*s, devoid of any purpose for *puruṣa*, return to their original [latent] state; in other words, when the power of consciousness is situated in its own essential nature.

---

54. There are almost as many interpretations of the meaning of this metaphor as there are commentators. See Bryant 2009.

Chapter 11

Roman Catholic Prayer
The *Novem modi orandi sancti Dominici*

Paul Philibert

The *Novem modi orandi sancti Dominici* (Nine Ways of Praying of Saint Dominic; abbr. *Novem modi orandi*) is a mid- to late thirteenth-century work on Roman Catholic prayer, specifically as practiced by Saint Dominic and in the early Order of Preachers (Dominicans). Originally composed in Latin by an unidentified Dominican and associated with the Spanish Catholic Domingo Félix de Guzmán (St. Dominic; 1170–1221), the text presents itself as a testimonial by Saint Dominic's associates concerning his nine ways of praying, specifically as observed by these individuals on various occasions. The text is, in turn, associated with the religious order of Roman Catholicism founded by Saint Dominic known as the Order of Preachers. Written by a friar, the text drew from the canonization process of Dominic, which concluded in 1234, and provided guidance on prayer for Dominican friars and nuns. From the seventeenth to the mid-twentieth century, the work was largely neglected in the few libraries in which it still existed in manuscript form.

Saint Dominic and the Formation of the Order of Preachers

The *Novem modi orandi*, or "Nine Ways of Praying," was composed by some unidentified Dominican between 1234 and 1280, after the death of Saint Dominic. It derives from what might be labeled the "formative" or "early" period of the Order of Preachers. Dominic died in 1221. In 1260, Humbert of Romans (ca. 1200–1277), Master General of the Order, appealed for stories about the early friars. It seems likely that the author of the *Novem modi orandi* would have collected his material in Bologna after that date. The sixth way of praying mentions the witness of Sister Cecilia at San Sisto in Rome during the lifetime of Dominic, but the *Novem modi orandi* clearly draws from other witnesses as well, and likewise from many locales. This suggests that the manuscript as a whole was composed by someone within the Province of Lombardy who had access to all the collected stories being gathered in Bologna as a result of Humbert's appeal (Tugwell 1985, 70–74). As it is a detailed description of Saint Dominic's personal ways of praying, we should familiarize ourselves with his life.

Saint Dominic, a Spaniard, is most well known as the founder of the Order of Preachers, which was, along with the Order of Friars Minor (Franciscans), the first fundamentally apostolic religious order in the Roman Catholic Church.[1] The order came into being in response to the new challenges and pastoral needs of a growingly urban, cosmopolitan, and communitarian European church. A generation after Dominic's death, the order came to be known popularly as the Dominicans, although during his lifetime, Dominic made it perfectly clear that he did not consider it *his* order at all but rather an inspired initiative completely at the service of the church. Furthermore, the first generation of Dominicans were so consumed with the urgency of

Figure 11.1. Side Panel Depicting Saint Dominic
Pala di Perugia (Perugia Altarpiece; dat. 1437) by Fra Angelico (1395–1455), O.P.[2]
Source: Galleria Nazionale dell'Umbria (Perugia, Italy)

their preaching mission that they quite frankly neglected to promote or cultivate their founder's reputation for sanctity beyond the boundaries of their own communities. Among themselves, however, Dominic was loved and esteemed as both a model of sanctity and a beloved father (Vicaire 2004, 380ff.) The remarkable text considered here, the *Novem modi orandi*, is an excellent indication of what Dominic meant to the order that he founded. It is also particularly useful for contemporary readers because it offers so many clues to the life, piety, and ministry of the first generation of Friars Preachers.

Composed in the decades following Dominic's death and based upon testimony given by the witnesses at his process for canonization, the *Novem modi orandi* draws upon the customs and liturgical practices of the first friars and upon the stories that they circulated about their founder. It provides an extraordinary portrait of Saint Dominic that offers both instruction and motivation for coming generations of preachers. As I will remark later, this document is a coherent ensemble of texts and images that need to be read together, and as such it is unique for its time. It was created not as a program of spiritual exercises but rather as a kind of spiritual anthropology to explain the meaning of prayer. It is immediately evident that prayer for Dominic is not localized in words, thoughts, feelings, or repeated physical exercises, but it is rather the integration and orientation of the whole person toward identification with Christ as the head of his mystical body (the church). Even though the *Novem modi orandi* is not a program as such, it does have important things to teach about prayer and the contemplative way, including directives that are quite practical, as I will show. However, first it is important to situate Dominic and his life in a historical context, if readers are to understand both the genre of the text and the spirituality that it conveys.

Domingo Félix de Guzmán (St. Dominic; 1170–1221) was born in Caleruega, halfway between Osma and Aranda in Old Castile, in an area of Spain recently won back from the Moors. As a youth, he was trained as a cleric studying under a priest uncle in his neighborhood. As a student at Palencia, he drew attention to himself because of his generosity to the poor and his concern for others. As a priest, he joined the canons of the cathedral church at Osma and became subprior as still a young man. Diego, a friend, became bishop of Osma in 1201 and took Dominic with him on a long journey to the northern marches (today's Denmark) at the behest of the pope. They journeyed twice on a route that took them through southern France, where Diego and Dominic became acquainted with the Albigensian heresy (of which more will be said in time). The founding of an order for preaching was the outgrowth of Diego's and Dominic's response to the pastoral needs of those in the Albigensian territories of southern France.[3]

Today the best-known Dominicans of the medieval period are Albertus Magnus (Albert the Great; ca. 1200–1280), Thomas Aquinas (1225–1274), and Meister Eckhart (ca. 1260–1328), all of whom were principally academics, along with Catherine of Siena (1347–1380), a mystical writer with great influence on church affairs. However, their eminence in the universities was rooted directly in the earliest tradition of the order. If preachers are to preach what is true, first they must study and learn. That is why the Order of Preachers immediately took its place in theological study and teaching. Dominic himself insisted that his friars should study and have a study director in each priory. That is also why its great masters of theology, however distinguished, always maintained a practical pastoral orientation in their work. They saw themselves as essentially members of an order whose fundamental mission is the evangelization of a changing world (Tugwell 1979; Walgrave 1968, 285ff.).

What were the issues that the order's foundation addressed? There were several, including the evolution of an international church, the cultural transformation of Europe, and the spiritual ferment among the laity that led to problems of heresy. An understanding of these questions is essential for grasping the context of Dominic's life and the daring innovation at that time of a religious order devoted to preaching. The church, both in its international administration in Rome as well as in its pastoral life scattered throughout all the regions of Europe, was in flux and seeking a way to enter productively what many understood to be the beginning of a new age. Dominic and the mendicants became important agents for bringing about needed changes in the life of the church.

In order to understand this process, we must first understand the background to this period of change. In the middle of the eleventh century, a dramatic shift had taken place in the church in Europe. Earlier, in 800, Charlemagne (ca. 742–814; r. 768–814), the first emperor of what was to be called the "Holy Roman Empire," had been crowned by the pope as leader of the whole of the Western world. Due to his extraordinary military and administrative achievements, Charlemagne brought about political and religious unity across Europe, virtually serving as the head of the church in his domain and controlling all episcopal appointments, liturgical reforms, and disciplinary norms for monks and clerics. His legendary authority sustained this fragile unity for over a century (Brown 1996, 276–298; Barbero 2004).

With the collapse of the Carolingian Empire (800–888) with the Treaty of Verdun in 843, however, scores of small kingdoms and principalities eventually managed to reduce the episcopacy and church administration to tools of local feudal lords. Two vexing problems during this period of decline were simony, the buying and selling of church offices, and clerical marriage, leading to the troublesome inheritance of church properties by the offspring of clerics. The reform and renewal of monasteries, especially under the leadership of Cluny in Burgundy, a monastery in central France that became the center of an international federation of reformed monasteries that reached across Western Europe, introduced a spirit of religious observance that renewed monastic scholarship as well as Christian piety. However, the most neuralgic issue and the key concern for the papacy remained; that was lay investiture, the designation or appointment of bishops and abbots by secular lords. In response, Pope Gregory VII (ca. 1020–1085; r. 1073–1085) insisted that all religious offices fell under the direct control of the papacy. In 1075 he proclaimed that the pope held supreme power over all Christians and that he was the supreme judge, under God alone, of all kings and earthly rulers as well as of all prelates (bishops and abbots) (Kelly 1988, 154–56).

This expansion of leadership seized by the pope and the Roman curia, the pope's ecclesiastical bureaucracy, also led to a new style of general councils of the church. One of Gregory's successors, Innocent III (ca. 1160–1216; r. 1198–1216), is considered the strongest exponent of ecclesiastical power in the Middle Ages. He convoked the greatest reform council of the Middle Ages, Lateran IV (1215), and also encouraged both Francis and Dominic to form a new type of religious order. Still, during Innocent's time, the lower clergy were for the most part poorly educated and inadequately supervised. Therefore the question of what we would today call evangelization or catechesis (adult education in the faith) was a major preoccupation for the pope. The lay faithful's lack of a basic formation in the meaning of their Christian faith and of the Christian life was a devastating weakness in the church. This helps to explain the pope's personal interest in Dominic's project of a canonically approved order dedicated to preaching and evangelization (Kelly 1988, 186–88; Mandonnet 1945, 5ff.).

In the twelfth century, Western Europe was still sufficiently "Roman" that the language for the schools, for official communications, and for formal decrees and correspondence was everywhere Latin. One reason for this was that the texts used for education, especially the Bible, the laws or canons, and ancient classical and patristic texts, were in Latin—copied by scribes in monastic scriptoria or cathedral schools. Most people, even the nobility, were still illiterate.

However, the twelfth century was also the era of the Crusades, and the Crusaders returning to the West brought back with them, among other things, legends, stories, and songs that began to be recorded in the dialects of the returning heroes. Gradually, Latin yielded to emerging independent vernaculars. The Near East and the Islamic world also inspired art and architecture as the Crusaders brought back new ideas influencing the development of the Romanesque style and its expression not only in church buildings but also in sculpture and illuminated manuscripts (Stalley 1999).

More to the point for our interests here, the opening up of borders by the Crusades stimulated international commerce and urban growth. Commercial activity and its consequent wealth favored the competitive building of great cathedrals throughout Europe, requiring artisans endowed with a variety of skills. Their formation of guilds to protect themselves, to train apprentices, and to negotiate contracts was one of the key elements in the formation of communes, that is, urban centers where the working people themselves had a voice in determining their social life. All these factors played a part in transforming the lower level of European society from serfs into burghers, from agricultural laborers dependent upon their feudal lords to an urban populace with avenues to advancement through the crafts, military service, or trade (Chenu 2002).

This is the context into which Dominic sent his preachers. It was complicated by the fact that the Gregorian reform of the eleventh century had promoted high expectations among the laity for a clergy who would be holy, devoted, and pastorally effective. However, most of the clergy failed to live up to this expectation. At the same time, the laity poorly understood Christian teaching, so that people were more easily influenced by dramatic or novel approaches than by the familiar Catholic ministry that seldom or never attempted to explain the principles of the faith systematically.

This situation opened the door to a stream of heretical teachers who, by their piety and austerity, attracted laity looking for a more serious Christian life. The critically important heretical group here held a dualistic Manichaean doctrine positing a good God, who created the angels and human souls, and an evil God (Satan), who created the physical world. Called Albigensians (see Mandonnet 1945, chs. 5–6), they understood salvation as a process of becoming aligned with the good God by liberating the soul from the contamination of the flesh. This doctrine required an extreme asceticism in their leaders, which, to the eyes of the untutored laity, appeared more attractive than the laxity of the majority of Catholic clergy. Moreover, these Albigensian heretics were zealous preachers, and their influence flourished in the south of France during the middle of the twelfth century. They were known by the people as the *bons hommes* (good people), and they were remarkably successful as an alternative church with its own hierarchy rooted especially in the territory around Toulouse, Carcassonne, and Albi, their center (Tugwell 1995, 8–9).

Throughout the first decade of the thirteenth century, Dominic found himself engaged in preaching against the Albigensians under the auspices of Pope Innocent III. When Dominic and his bishop Diego d'Azevedo (d. 1207) had passed through the area while on a royal embassy for the King of Spain, they discovered Cistercian monks at work preaching against the heretics at the request of the pope.[4] Diego and Dominic gradually succeeded in persuading the Catholic preachers that they would have no chance of success in converting the people of the region unless they themselves undertook to live a life of austerity and simplicity and to travel poor, barefoot, and mendicant (begging their bread day by day) as the Albigensian preachers did. The full story of the Albigensians, also known as the Cathars (Pure), is too complicated to sketch here. They were dualists, believing in two transcendent principles of creation and life, a good spiritual Creator and an evil Material Principle. For them salvation meant becoming harmonized with the good God by liberating the soul from fleshly contamination through fasts and ascetical practices. As itinerant preachers, the Albigensians gained adherents among the poor, who were impressed with their renunciation of wealth and the denunciation of the powerful (Ladurie 1979). Suffice it to say that in time Dominic was charged by Rome to head up the preaching crusade among the Cathars and, with the encouragement of the Bishop of Toulouse (a former troubadour named Fulk), obtained papal authorization to found an order of preachers.

It is important to observe that Dominic sympathized with the people's ideal of an evangelizing clergy who lived in simplicity and holiness. He too thought that this had a proper place in the Catholic Church. As one author puts it, Dominic was "religiously on their wavelength" (Tugwell 1995, 18), meaning in sympathy with their desire for an exemplary and spiritually enriching Christian life. So fully did Dominic accept this point of view, that when he eventually founded his order, he based it upon a strict appreciation of what he and Diego knew as the *vita apostolica* (apostolic life). For Dominic, this meant living like the twelve apostles or seventy-two disciples (Luke 10:1) of Jesus of Nazareth, sent out without purse or baggage to preach the gospel far and wide, living austerely and piously. There was thus a necessary link between radical voluntary poverty and evangelical preaching. This idea runs through the *Novem modi orandi*, and it helps to explain what might otherwise seem to be extremism or exoticism.

Roman Catholicism, the Order of Preachers, and Early Dominican Writings

As mentioned, the Order of Preachers founded by Saint Dominic is a Roman Catholic religious order. In the first millennium, the Christian Church was a single universal communion of believers in Christ. There were diverse practices in liturgy and church administration in the Greek East and the Latin West as well as a more Platonic tendency in theology in the East. Both the Eastern and the Western Churches had monks and monasteries from the fourth century on. The bishop of Rome (pope) was recognized as having a primacy among his peers because his See (bishopric) was founded by Saint Peter, who was the leader of the Apostles. However, after 1054, because of doctrinal disputes between East and West concerning formulas for praying to God as the Blessed Trinity, the bishops of the Greek East refused to acknowledge the Roman pope's primacy. Some centuries later, after Luther's Reformation (1517), religious orders disappeared from the Protestant world, and the rich and complex ritual of Catholic sacraments was curtailed by Protestant Christians. Catholics, drawing from the theology of the first six centuries of Christian theologians, emphasize the sacramental principle of employing material signs in worship (bread and wine, oil, water, candles, etc.). Further, in addition to the celebration of seven sacraments in the church, Catholic religious have many ritual practices that they incorporate into their community prayers. We will note later in this chapter how a number of the practices of Dominic in the *Novem modi orandi* borrow from or extend such ritual practices used in community prayers.

The Roman Catholic Church has a wide variety of religious orders, ranging from contemplative monks and nuns to apostolic groups of priests, brothers, and sisters dedicated to teaching, healing, and service to the poor. In the thirteenth century, other mendicant groups sprang up, following the Franciscans and the Dominicans, whose mission was generally evangelization and revival preaching. At the time of the Reformation, the beginning of which is conventionally dated to 1517, the Society of Jesus (Jesuits) was founded by Ignacio de Loyola (St. Ignatius; 1491–1556), and its members soon began expressing their characteristic emphasis on education and theological and scientific research. In the sixteenth century, a wave of missionary expansion began in the church, leading to the commitment of many religious to foreign missions (like the well-known missions of the Franciscans in Mexico and California). Most of the religious orders of the eighteenth and nineteenth centuries had as their focus either the church's missionary expansion following the colonizing of India and Africa or the rebuilding of the church in post-revolutionary France and Western Europe following the French Revolution (1789–1799). The spirituality of these later groups is largely devotional and practical, whereas the older monastic and mendicant traditions maintain their contemplative roots and understand their ministry as a response of Christian charity arising from the compassion they learn in contemplation. That perspective helps us to understand the spirituality of Dominic and the Dominicans (Rapley 2011).

In terms of the founding of the Order of Preachers, by 1216, Dominic finally had a first community of sixteen preachers settled in the city of Toulouse, France, under the sponsorship of Bishop Fulk (d. 1231). Visiting Rome with Fulk, Dominic soon convinced Pope Innocent III to allow him to found a new order of preachers, but the pope charged Dominic to choose an existing rule for the order. Consequently, Dominic and the preachers in Toulouse adopted the Rule of Saint Augustine and, as their first constitutions, they adapted the customs and liturgical practices of the Premonstratensian Canons (priests attached to a cathedral following the customs of the monastery of Prémontré in northern France). Dominic had lived as a cathedral canon under the Rule of Saint Augustine in Spain for some years, and it was natural for him to embrace these practices and then situate them within the new way of life of an itinerant preacher. Fundamentally, this meant that the friars would commit themselves to the monastic office (regular periods of chanted prayer throughout the day), to a common life in a priory (a house of friars—or brothers—that had a prior rather than an abbot as its superior), and to a life of study in preparation for their preaching mission (Vicaire 2004, 164ff.).

Dominic was walking a fine line between innovation and orthodoxy. Just as in his early days as a preacher among the Cathars he had to win the confidence of the people by adopting a lifestyle that would appeal to heretics, so now, establishing a corps of evangelizing preachers who would be itinerant and freewheeling, he had to make sure that he would not upset the generality of Catholics. So Dominic wanted his new order to *look* like a religious order, and that included being good canons. Reassured by this successful institutionalization of the preachers, Pope Innocent's successor, Pope Honorius III (1148–1227; r. 1216–1227), granted Dominic papal bulls establishing the order and commending it to the bishops of Europe. Dominic finally received what he wanted most of all, the title "Order of Preachers" (abbr.: O.P.), which remains the official title of the Dominicans to this day.

In the spring of 1217, Dominic surprised everyone by dispersing the Toulouse community; he sent some of the friars to Spain and Italy and others to Paris, which left only a small community behind in Toulouse. Paris was to become the ideal place to recruit bright young scholars from all over Europe, and the Dominicans in Paris would soon become renowned for the teaching of Albertus Magnus, Thomas Aquinas, and other Dominican masters of theology at Europe's greatest university. It was there that Aquinas introduced Aristotelian philosophy into his theological method and where a great number of his immense corpus of writings was composed. His extremely influential theology first took root in Paris.

Within a few more years, the order expanded outside France, Spain, and Italy and spread to England, Hungary, Poland, and Scandinavia. The friars carried with them the Rule of Saint Augustine and the liturgical practices that became known as the Dominican rite, that is, the particular Dominican way of singing the psalms and the Mass as well as the rites and gestures that they used in celebrating the sacraments. These included detailed rubrics linking movement, posture, processions, and prostrations to the chanting of the Divine Office and the celebration of the Eucharist. These prescribed, for instance, genuflection on two knees at the *et incarnatus est* (and he became man) of the Credo; and in the Gloria, an inclination of the head when the Lord is thanked for his divine glory: *Gratias agimus propter magnum gloriam tuam* (We give you thanks for your great glory). Other examples were the rubrics to go barefooted in the procession to adore the cross on Good Friday and the daily practice of bowing profoundly while chanting *Gloria Patri et Filio et Spiritui Sancto* (Glory be to the Father and to the Son and to the Holy Spirit) at the end of each psalm in the office. More examples will be mentioned as they are alluded to in the text of the *Novem modi orandi*. It is clear that ritual movement and gestures of devotion were incorporated into the customary practice of Dominican community prayer from the beginning (Mandonnet 1945, 111–15). Humbert of Romans, the fifth Master General of the Order (1254–1263), consolidated the internal organization of the friars' life by standardizing their liturgical texts, commenting on the constitutions, and writing a huge work bearing the title *De eruditione praedicatorum* (On the Formation of Preachers) (Tugwell 1982, 181–370). From this time on, the Dominicans had a liturgy and a set of rules for community life recognized everywhere throughout the order.

The Order of Preachers eventually became divided into the friars (mendicant preachers), the nuns (cloistered contemplatives), the sisters (female religious), and lay members of the order (formerly known as tertiaries). This fourfold structure has been maintained in the order to the present day, although only the friars are strictly speaking under the jurisdiction of the male religious superiors. The nuns were the first of these groups to come into existence, assuming that one considers the gathering of female converts from the Albigensians at Prouille in 1206 as a convent of Dominican women. Dominic thought of the convent (later monastery) at Prouille both as a refuge for young women who were being driven by poverty into the hands of the heretics and also as a domestic base for preaching. In 2006, the Dominican nuns of the order celebrated their eight hundredth anniversary of foundation; they are now spread throughout the whole church wherever the order is present.

Dominic himself, however, left his followers neither a rule of his own devising nor a body of writings to guide them. During his last years, Dominic traveled tirelessly from priory to priory to help and encourage the early communities, so his legacy was personal and *viva voce*, that is, by word of mouth. There are, nonetheless, several brief early hagiographical writings as well as the testimony of nine Dominicans who knew Dominic personally and who testified in the process of canonization opened by Pope Gregory IX. Tugwell has collected these and commented upon them in his *Early Dominicans* (Tugwell 1982, 51–93). In 1954, Vicaire published a series of early documents, including those mentioned by Tugwell, that describe Dominic's life and work.

In addition to the works by Mandonnet, Tugwell, and Vicaire included in the works cited, there are other lives of Dominic written through the centuries, some of the most noteworthy being those by Lacordaire, Bede Jarrett, and Guy Bedouelle.

Dominican Contemplative Practice and the Religious Spirit of the Preachers

According to the *Novem modi orandi*, Dominican contemplative practice involves expanding the movement of spiritual love aroused in study and common prayer into a protracted period of silence, self-surrender or self-offering to God, and enjoyment of intimacy with God. Such prayer is a sort of overflow of affection and spiritual desire that can be expressed in simple attention, in internalized reflection, as well as in extraverted gestures like genuflections, prostrations, or imitation of Christ's extended arms on the Cross. The two things to notice here are, first, that this form of contemplation flows directly out of study and community prayer, and, second, that it engages the body in the "work" of contemplation, that is to say, the gesture is as expressive as the thought. The constitutions of the order call for daily private, mental prayer; in this sense, the *Novem modi orandi* is a way of describing how Dominic himself realized this dimension of the life.

Considering Dominican spirituality and charism, the Dominican constitutions clearly outline the fundamental orientation and spirit of the order. They begin by explaining, "The Order of Friars Preachers, founded by Saint Dominic, is known to have been established, from the beginning, specifically for preaching and the salvation of souls." They go on to say the following:

> Sharing the Apostles' mission, we also follow their way of life, in the form devised by St. Dominic. . . . Because of the Order's mission, personal talents and a sense of responsibility are especially esteemed and cultivated by the brothers. After the completion of his formation, each brother is treated as an adult, competent to teach others and to take on various responsibilities. . . . For this reason, the Order has decided that its rules do not bind under pain of sin, so that the brothers may accept them with mature understanding. . . . Consequently our government is communitarian in a manner peculiar to itself, for superiors ordinarily take office after election by the brothers and confirmation by a higher superior. Furthermore, when matters of greater moment are being determined, communities share in several ways in the exercise of self-government. (BCO 2001, 25–26)

This position of the order relative to the observance of the rules means that the prudent judgment of the individual brothers to attend to study rather than participate in a particular religious exercise in community overrides the question of obedience. A friar should obey the rule, but a given exception, judged by himself to be sensible in the light of his commitments to preaching or teaching, is not an act of disobedience or a sin. As to their purpose in life, the friars are committed "to the proclamation of the word of God, preaching everywhere in the name of our Lord Jesus Christ" (BCO 2001, 25).

At the heart of Dominican life is the primacy of the word of God, understood to be an *embodied* word, not only in the sense that Christ is understood as "the word made flesh" but in the further sense that God's word becomes a saving reality when it is welcomed into the heart and becomes the source of one's identity. An important twentieth-century Belgian Dominican, Edward Schillebeeckx (1914–2009), expressed the idea in this way: God's word has a "prophetic expandability" that can never be exhausted. No reading, preaching, or teaching will ever be adequate to unpack the fullness of what the revealed word contains. Those who live by the word of God (who live *in* the word) are constantly being shaped by the word to become a sacramental link to the God who speaks to us in Christ (Schillebeeckx 1962, 91ff.). Dominicans are expected, in this sense, to become in their own way sacramental embodiments of the word that they study and pray; and the constitutions pass on this phrase that had been used frequently of Dominic: the friars too should "speak to God or of God, among themselves or with their neighbors" (BCO 2001, 25, sec. 2). A passage of Thomas Aquinas from the *Summa Theologiae* (his "introduction" to theology), parallel to this consideration, has become a fundamental motto for the order: *contemplata aliis tradere* (give to others the fruit of your contemplation) (2a2ae, 188, 6, c; Aquinas 1973, 204).

This discussion illustrates the idea of contemplation in the Dominican tradition. For the friars, contemplation is not something extraordinary but integral to the successful internalization of the mission and practices of a friar preacher. First, its finality is not personal spiritual delight or moral growth but rather the deepening of a relationship with a living word destined to be preached for the salvation of others. Second, contemplative practice is not the exercise of exotic or esoteric activities meant to extract a person's mind from the world of human interactions but rather a *vita contemplativa* (contemplative life), a way of living that is integrated with reading, silence, and listening to and pondering the divine word. Third, Dominican contemplation is not about intellectual activity of a sort that is disengaged from social experience. It is, rather, what I refer to as "incarnate mindfulness," by which I mean embodying a person's presence to the dynamic power of the living word that is proclaimed, celebrated, pondered, and preached. From my perspective, this is the core message of Saint Dominic's "nine ways of praying."

The thrust here is practical and pastoral rather than theoretical. Most writing about contemplation among the Fathers of the Church and the early medieval monastic masters took a Platonic point of departure, aiming to cast off the material world as inferior or even corrupt and seeking to enter an ideal world untouched by the taint of materiality (see Shannon 1993). That such an otherworldly concept of contemplation is foreign to the Dominican approach can be seen in Thomas Aquinas's treatment of the question: a mixed life of contemplation and action "proceeds from the fullness of contemplation, such as preaching and teaching. . . . And this [mixed life] is preferred to simple contemplation, for just as it is better to illumine than merely to shine, so it is better to give to others the things contemplated than simply to contemplate" (2a2ae, 188, 6, c; Aquinas 1973, 205).

Whether measuring progress in contemplation by kataphatic or apophatic categories, the finality of Dominican contemplation always embraces the proposal and exposition of the divine word. As we will soon understand, this in no way implies superficiality but instead a stance that is, as in the *Novem modi orandi*, utterly Christological. Saint Dominic becomes thoroughly "lost" in the word and in his contemplation of Christ. But his contemplation also entails a deeper grounding in the real world rather than a release into a supposed world of disincarnate grace.

This principle is fundamental, if we are to understand what is going on in this characteristically Dominican account of prayer. As opposed to imagining the physical body as a burden and a source of impurity, this manuscript demonstrates how Dominic employed the body as an instrument of grace and a sacrament of faith. Nothing could be more anti-Manichaean. Christ's human body is, as Dominican Catherine of Siena (1347–1380) a century later would so often call it, our "bridge" between heaven and earth and the pathway through which all grace comes to us (Catherine of Siena 1980). In these terms, Dominic's ways of praying were meant to prepare his own body to share in Christ's bridge-building ministry.

The implication of this Christological stance is that ultimately the prayer of every Christian is "in Christ" in the sense of 2 Corinthians 5:17: "So if anyone is in Christ, there is a new creation." The Christian's prayer becomes joined to or melded with Christ's prayer and likewise often reduced to Christ's simple utterance, "Abba, Father" (see Rom. 8:15). The goal of such prayer is to trust intimately in the grace of being made a new being through Baptism, grafted onto Christ, and so also an instrument of Christ's presence and action in the world. Our very bodies and quotidian activities become the stuff of this enfolding into Christ. So all Dominicans, like Dominic himself, both *come* and *go*—come into these moments of deep awareness of Christ's presence, and then go to live ordinary lives as preachers, teachers, or sacramental ministers.

The Nine Ways of Praying of Saint Dominic

In order to accommodate a growing population of friars, building renovations were undertaken in the 1230s at the Dominican priory in Bologna, Italy, where Dominic had been buried in 1221. Motivated in part by these architectural modifications, the friars decided to relocate the body of the saint from its simple grave to a noble shrine inside the new church building.[5] By then, they were conscious that they had neglected the *cultus* of their founder, especially by comparison with the Franciscans. Francis of Assisi (1182–1226) had been canonized less than two years after his death (1228), and Antony of Padua (1195–1231), a prominent Franciscan, only a year following his death (1232). The reigning pope, Gregory IX (ca. 1150–1241; r. 1227–1241), had been a friend of Dominic and was well aware of the founder's holiness. Gregory gave approval to a formal process of inquiry in view of Dominic's canonization, a process that commenced in 1233 and concluded in 1234.[6] Many of the early friars who lived with Dominic came forward and bore witness during the process (Vicaire 1955, 2004, 376–95).

Their testimony, as far as it is relevant to the *Novem modi orandi*, bore witness that Dominic prayed constantly, that he prayed out loud and frequently wept, and that he prayed with bodily gestures. Most of the time, he spent much of the night in prayer, letting out groans, sighs, and cries that could be overheard by the friars. Many heard him pray: "Lord have mercy on your people—what is to become of sinners?" Gerard de Frachet (1205–1271), the author of the *Vitae Fratrum* (Lives of the Brethren) (1260–1262), consecrates a brief chapter to Dominic's private prayer. There he wrote the following description: "One of the friars, a man both discreet and virtuous, said that he observed Dominic seven times throughout the night in order to find out how the blessed father acted in his nightly vigil. He saw him praying sometimes standing, sometimes kneeling, sometimes prostrated, until finally he was overcome by sleep" (Aubin 2005, 13). What is common to all of the testimonies in the process of canonization is that Dominic wove his prayers together into a seamless whole that integrated his public prayer and his private prayer throughout the day and night. Gerard coined the lovely phrase that Dominic devoted his nights to God and his days to his friends (Koudelka 1972, 62–63).

After the death of Dominic in 1221, some of the friars gathered their remembrances of the ways in which Dominic prayed and illustrated them, giving them a unique literary form that included descriptive iconography. This is how the *Novem modi orandi* came into being. It is likely that the original document was widely copied and shared. In any case, there are four manuscripts that we know about containing illustrations showing Dominic's way of praying. The first is the Codex Carcassonensis written in Latin that was in the library of the Dominican priory of Carcassonne from the end of the thirteenth through the fourteenth century; it was still being mentioned in the seventeenth century, although today it has been lost. Second, there is the Codex Matritensis that belongs to the monastery of Dominican nuns of the Royal Monastery at Madrid. It comes from the same period, but it is difficult to get access to it, and it is also written in Castilian. Its illustrations were published, however, in *La Ciencia Tomista* in 1921 and are very sketchy ink drawings with slight polychrome ornamentation. The third is the Codex Rossianus 3 written in Latin, which can be found in the Vatican Library in Rome; it dates from the beginning of the fourteenth century. Tugwell claims that it belonged to the Carthusians of Porta Coeli in Valencia and was probably produced in the south of France at the beginning of the fourteenth century (Tugwell 1985).

Today the Codex Rossianus 3 is the best-known and most widely diffused edition, thanks to the initiative of Leonard Boyle, O.P., who was prefect of the Vatican Library in the 1990s and permitted a facsimile edition of the manuscript to be published. My translation follows the Codex Rossianus 3 as it is presented in the edition given in Simon Tugwell's monograph in *Mediaeval Studies*. These illustrations (used here) are minor masterpieces that include clues of great subtlety in their pictorial field. Here we should note that the original manuscript includes color illustrations, reproduced in black and white in this chapter. The reader may thus fail to experience their full aesthetic power, including the dramatic depiction of Christ's blood painted in red throughout the illustrations.

Finally, there is the Codex Bononiensis, dating from the fifteenth century, written in the Italian language of that period sometime before 1470, and including fourteen ways of praying. Its illustrations were published by Collomb and Balme in 1901 (Tugwell 1985; Aubin 2005, 14).

Simon Tugwell thinks that the original manuscript was composed sometime around the year 1280. Leonard Boyle estimates that it was written between 1234 (when the process of canonization was completed) and 1280 (the death of Albertus Magnus). In any case, the authorship is unquestionably Dominican. Jean-Claude Schmitt, the noted French medievalist, observes that the *Novem modi orandi* seems to be the first time that the prayer and practices of a saint were graphically illustrated in a manuscript, especially important for one so closely linked to those who knew Dominic and his community. This makes of this manuscript a document effectively without parallel in medieval religious literature. Black-and-white images of the Madrid and Bologna manuscripts can be found in Schmitt's critical essay, along with the Codex Rossianus 3 (Schmitt 1985, 215–20). The text has, in turn, been translated into English a number of times.[7]

An excellent and helpful commentary in French was published in 2005 by Catherine Aubin, a French Dominican sister and doctor of theology, who does a remarkable reading of the anthropological dimensions of the text. I am deeply indebted to her book, *Prier avec son corps*, for alerting me to the profound link between the nine modes of praying given in the text and the biblical sources that clearly inspired Dominic and the author(s) of the manuscript. She cites, among many others, this text that powerfully evokes the inspiration that moved Dominic in his prayer: "I give you thanks, O Lord, with my whole heart; you have heard the words of my mouth. I sing your praise in the presence of the angels, I bow down toward your holy temple and give thanks to your name for your steadfast love" (Ps. 138:1–2). Aubin also pays close attention to the significance of the members of the body in prayer and to the parallels between Dominic's prayer and the biblical texts (especially the Psalms) that he prayed constantly. For Dominic, then, the integration of the implicit gestures mentioned in the texts of the Psalms and of other biblical passages was as integral an act of fidelity to prayer as his singing, speaking, or meditating the words themselves. Further, we should remember that in the thirteenth century, people characteristically read out loud or at least moved their lips when they entered into a text. As Aubin notes, the use of the voice helps to deepen one's attention to the text and to that degree opens one's heart to the divine voice that speaks within it. Because of this integral link between text and gesture, as well as because of the need to decode the gestures illustrated in the manuscript, I provide explanatory commentary on each of the nine ways of praying according to the text.

The "ways" seven and nine include stories about Dominic extraneous to the precise description of his manner of praying, but they invoke instances in which Dominic went from prayer to wonder-working. Tugwell considers these to be a corruption of the original text, while Boyle seems to see them as characteristic of the period and the genre. In any case, I have included the stories, but placed them in brackets to indicate that they are, indeed, extraneous to the description of Dominic's prayer as such. In citing the Bible, I use the New Revised Standard Version, even though this translation differs slightly at times from the Vulgate used in the Codex Roassianus 3. I follow Aubin's identification of the biblical texts in the manuscript and usually borrow from her biblical notations in my explanations.

Moving into the *Novem modi orandi sancti Dominici* (Nine Ways of Praying of Saint Dominic; abbr. *Novem modi orandi*), the text consists of a brief preface followed by nine sections with the nine distinct modes of prayer. According to Tugwell, the manuscript of the Codex Roassianus 3 was intended to be presented with text and the corresponding illustration on two facing pages, which required the omission of two exemplary stories that were part of the original manuscript

(1) Bowing	(6) Standing with outstretched arms
(2) Full-body prostration	(7) Standing with upraised body and hands
(3) Self-flagellation	(8) Sitting and reading
(4) Repeated kneeling	(9) On a journey[8]
(5) Standing with gestures of the hands	

Figure 11.2. Nine Ways of Praying according to the *Novem modi orandi sancti Dominici*

(Tugwell 1996, 3–4). The present translation deviates from that format and includes the stories. As described in our text, the "Nine Ways of Praying of Saint Dominic" are as illustrated in figure 11.2. With the exception of the ninth, all of these are performed before an altar with a crucifix. Consequently there is a strong material dimension to the practices, including Catholic religious objects and architecture. Interestingly, some of the illustrations indicate that the corresponding crucifix (depiction of the crucified Jesus) is life-size. Thus, when Dominic or other Dominicans take the cruciform position, they stand facing a mirror image of Jesus Christ. Here we notice an expression of the Christological nature of this praxis, a devotionalism that involves a physical, emotional, intellectual, and spiritual identification with Christ. Also noteworthy is the fact that, strictly speaking, only flagellation and the bows made within the Divine Office were prescribed practices for the friars. Saint Dominic did not necessarily encourage or discourage the other practices (see, e.g., the sixth way).

Entering more deeply into the text, the first way involves bowing before the altar of a church or chapel. Traditional Christian theology understands the altar to be the principal symbol of Christ within the church—the bridge between heaven and earth (lifted above the ground, on which offerings are made to heaven). The Dominican rite for the Divine Office prescribed that at each recitation of the "Glory be to the Father," the friars should bow profoundly as a sign of reverence and adoration of the Holy Trinity (Father, Son, and Holy Spirit), whom they address in this prayer. So Dominic's gesture of prayer is an act of edification meant to incite imitation and understanding among his brothers. However, as mentioned before, all these gestures of prayer are also deeply Christological, and in them Dominic saw himself imitating Christ. In this instance, Dominic personifies Christ's great humility that was evident in his incarnation, humbling himself by abandoning his status as Son of God so as to become like us in our human flesh. Christ's humility was also manifest in his baptism, when the sinless one presented himself for a baptism of repentance and, in so doing, sanctified the rite of Baptism to make it a theandric event—an action of God in flesh. Finally, Christ's humility culminated on the Cross, where he was crucified as a criminal. Dominic accordingly turns his physical gesture into a nonverbal counterpart of this essential Christian theology, making of his gesture of humility a sacrament of Christ's sanctifying self-offering to his divine Father. Like seven other of the nine ways, this way is shown taking place in front of an altar on which a crucifix has been placed. In the picture, we see a jet of blood shooting out from the side of Christ, as if Christ is responding to Dominic with his own silent gesture of recognition. Further, the blood flowing from Christ's side, as seen in John 19:34, is a symbol of the Eucharist; and this prayer of Dominic, even though not taking place within a ritual context, can be interpreted as a prolongation of the Eucharist. Dominic's successor, Humbert of Romans (ca. 1200–1277), O.P., who was Master of the Order from 1254 to 1263, understood Dominic's gestures of humility in this sense: "[S]o that Christ, who humbled himself for our sake even unto death, may see us bowing humbly before his divine majesty" (Aubin 2005, 33; Humbert of Romans 1889). Here Dominic's body expresses his prayer, or conversely, his prayer conveys its meaning in the members of his body. Likewise, Dominic prays this verse of Sirach: "Humble me, Lord, to the utmost." Humility becomes the key that opens the door to a dialogue with God, because God needs for us to recognize that we are creatures taking our proper place before our Creator. This establishes a relation of receptivity and openness to grace. Once this door of humility has been opened, it is possible to enter into a dialogue with Christ, who meets us on this same path in the humiliation of his incarnation. Dominic, in this way, desires to make of his inclinations a visible sign of his intention to become and to be "another Christ," a human sacrament of the humiliated Christ who in his incarnation brings us all the graces of salvation and sanctification. This is, in turn, one of the "ways" that Dominic and the early friars clearly wanted the brothers of the order to understand and to imitate. While performing routine rituals, it is easy enough to go through the motions day after day. However, Dominic wanted the friars to feel in their bodies the urge to humble themselves by bending low and to feel what it means to make this motion of self-abasement an essential element of their prayer. He also wanted them to discover what only experience can make clear, that what the body says in performing this profound act of reverence cannot be said in words, but only in a gesture that comes from the heart and that revives the heart. This is the first step in harmonizing the body with the developing mindfulness that is awakened in prayer.

The second way involves full-body prostration before the altar and the Cross. This gesture externalizes the experiences of shame and heartbreak that sinners feel who are led to compunction, as the biblical citations make clear ("Have pity on me, for I am a sinner; what is evil in your sight I have done"). Here again, this aspect of Dominic's prayer represents his solidarity with sinners, rooted in his awareness of Christ's universal relation to all humankind and of Christ's desire to plead for their salvation. The manuscript says, "Jesus, seeing them, wept bitterly." Here Dominic enters into that Christological mystery of identifying with Christ who grieves for those who have not yet understood that he has come to embrace them in the saving mystery of his mystical body. The text says, "Blessed Dominic often prayed by throwing himself down on the ground with his face to the floor," a gesture that became a customary expression of humility within the Order of Preachers. Known as the *venia*, a Latin word signifying an indulgence or pardon for faults committed, the friars were expected to perform this gesture of self-abasement in front of the community when they committed faults or mistakes in the exercise of the liturgy, when they were corrected in chapter, and also when they received a new assignment or a commission to preach. (This practice of the *venia* still exists in many provinces of the order to this day.) It is, above all, a sign of readiness to take up the work of Providence and of vulnerability to the grace of obedience. Jordan of Saxony (ca. 1170–1237), O.P., Dominic's first biographer, stressed Dominic's desire to give to his friars a deep sense of compassion for sinners, asking them to pray for their salvation. Jordan says,

> For Dominic thought that he himself would not fully be a member of the body of Christ until the day that he could give himself completely, with all his energies, to the task of winning souls, just as the Lord Jesus—Savior of all people—consecrated himself completely to our salvation. (Aubin 2005, 60)

The manuscript tells us that Dominic wept and groaned mightily, as almost all the witnesses in the process of canonization testified. Dominic's tears, his body stretched on the ground, and his lamentations were the external expression of what drove him within, namely, a total self-involvement in this prayer. Humbert of Romans, once again, explained the meaning of Dominic's prostrations as a way of praying in the following way. A prostration is a cry for mercy, as in the words of Moses in Deuteronomy 9:25, "Throughout the forty days and forty nights that I lay prostrate before the Lord when the Lord intended to destroy you, I prayed to the Lord and said, 'Lord, do not destroy the people who are your very own.'" A prostration is also the expression of an attitude of humility, like the humility of Peter who fell down before Jesus, after the miraculous catch of fish, saying, "Go away from me, Lord, for I am a sinful man!" (Luke 5:8). Prostrations likewise express a penitential spirit; so the friars were taught to prostrate themselves when reciting the penitential psalms according to the text of Psalm 95:6, "Let us worship and bow down, let us kneel before the Lord, our maker!" The brothers learned to prostrate themselves also as a sign of adoration, just as the Magi did in the text cited in this manuscript. Friars today can still be found prostrate before the Cross or the tabernacle containing the reserved Eucharist, allowing their posture to be the core of their prayer. This gesture of prostration is also retained in the Dominican rite of profession, where the brothers who offer themselves to the order in a vow of obedience throw themselves to the ground with their arms extended and respond to the question of their prior, "What do you seek?" with the words "God's mercy and yours" (*Rituale Professionis Ritus* 1999, 53). A prostration of a similar kind is included in the rite of ordination for deacons, priests, and bishops. In all these instances, the candidates remain prostrated while the Litany of the Saints is sung over them by the assembly. To understand what this prayer really means, we have to stretch ourselves out on the ground in church or in our room and let our bodies speak to us. This is a gesture that involves our whole body and our whole being, and we can feel the ground with our belly, our arms, our legs, and the whole weight of our person. Once again, composing ourselves in this gesture allows our person to express something that can never fully be put into words. Like Dominic, though, someone praying in this position will probably wish to formulate some verbal prayer, such as "Lord Jesus Christ, son of the living God, have mercy on me, a sinner." And, finally, this gesture teaches something important: it is the whole person who prays—bones and muscles as well as thoughts and feelings.

The third way involves self-flagellation before the altar and the Cross. By contrast with the first two practices, this way of praying is prescribed for a particular liturgical context, namely, an act of devotion following Compline (the night prayer of the community). This practice is prescribed for ferial days, that is, for days on which no special feast is celebrated. Dominic uses a small whip known as a "discipline" to scourge himself. His is made of iron chains, whereas the friars are told to discipline themselves with wooden sticks or branches (probably to insist on the practice without making it so severe, particularly with concern for the weak, the elderly, or the infirm). If this practice appears masochistic to modern eyes, it nonetheless has deep-seated biblical roots. The Fathers of the Church referred frequently to the pedagogy of faith through which God led the people of Israel to an ever-deeper understanding of their election by being chastised for their sins of idolatry and unfaithfulness. Slavery, exile, and humiliation were not willed for God's people as such but were permitted so as to allow them to come to their senses in order to realize their irreplaceable role as witnesses to God's ways by standing before the nations as God's people. Even today in Judaism, the feast of Tabernacles celebrates the closeness that the Hebrew people on their exodus experienced with God as they were led toward the Promised Land. The trial of the exodus was recast as the blessing of the chosen people's new consciousness of their incomparable relation to the Lord. Similarly, in the New Testament, a text from the Letter to the Hebrews summarizes the parallel Christian intuition of the meaning of chastisement: "Endure trials for the sake of discipline. God is treating you as children; for what child is there whom a parent does not discipline? . . . Should we not be even more willing to be subject to the Father of spirits and live?" (Heb. 12:7, 9). In the medieval period, flagellation was understood as a way of imitating Christ's scourging at the pillar during his passion (Mark 15:15; John 19:1).

Pious medieval Christians sought to emulate Christ's irrepressible desire to save souls by uniting themselves to the experience of his passion. The word "discipline" was also used to describe other practices, like fasting and abstaining from meat during the season of Lent, the period of forty days of penance observed each year preceding the church's celebration of Easter. Someone who learned from "discipline" was in a special way a "disciple." In medieval Latin wordplay, the discipline as an instrument of penance became a form of education and correction. Once again, we are led to perceive how for the High Middle Ages the body had a role to play in prayer that went far beyond words and ideas. The shoulders and the back become instruments of prayer here, integral to our understanding of what Christ suffered for us and to identifying with him in his redemptive passion. For people today, this way of praying can have a particularly apt significance by making them conscious of their solidarity with those forced into captivity in prison camps, penitentiaries, and refugee camps. Moreover, without literally returning to the use of a whip or a discipline, it is possible to become conscious how much of the tension of our life of work and the stresses of our many anxieties come to reside in our neck, our shoulders, and our upper back. To change these real wounds or pains into a willing sacrifice of solidarity with Christ for the sake of those who suffer the wounds of war or the pain of illness, of bed-ridden captivity, or of chemotherapy, for example, is to enter into the spirit of this way of praying as Dominic understood it. What is essential here is to link our own corporal sufferings with the sufferings of Christ who came in our flesh to share and sanctify our human misery. The "discipline" or flagellation described here is no longer prescribed by the order's current constitutions, but voluntary penances are encouraged (and this may, of course, include some form of physical "discipline").

The fourth way involves repeated kneeling before the altar or Cross in a church or chapel. This mode describes Dominic "with his eyes fixed, [giving] the Crucifix his entire attention." In Latin, the phrase is *summo intuitu* (with the deepest concentration). Dominic's contemplation of the Cross overflows into his work of adoration, which involves yet again his imitation of Christ's actions. Luke's gospel describes the moment when Jesus in the Garden of Gethsemane withdrew from the disciples about a stone's throw, and then "he knelt down and prayed" (Luke 22:41). Matthew for his part describes Jesus returning to the disciples in the garden and, finding them asleep, chiding them, "So, could you not stay awake with me one hour?" (Mt. 26:40). Jesus uses his bodily members to worship his Father and in so doing offers an example that his disciples should follow. Dominic, for his part, becomes one with Christ in this physical act of adoration. The manuscript says that Dominic is also imitating the apostle James, making reference to a passage in Eusebius that repeats an old tale from Hegesippus reporting that James genuflected and prayed on his knees so much that his knee-pads became like those of a camel (Aubin 2005, 90). In early monasticism too, there was a custom of performing rituals of repeated genuflections, kneeling down completely and then rising up straight over and over. In the fifth century, Saint Patrick, for example, was reported to have genuflected hundreds of times a day; and to this day there is the custom of climbing Croagh Patrick, a mountain close to the town of Westport, that is the most popular pilgrimage for Irish Catholics. There are almost no trees on this mountain where Patrick prayed in retreat, and the paths uphill are full of heavy stones, so that the only way to get there is by hiking for several hours on that exhausting path. Every year on the last Sunday of July thousands of pilgrims hike uphill, some of them on their knees or without shoes. Such penances are understood locally as part of the tradition of Irish Catholicism. Closer to the spirit of the manuscript, however, are the multiple biblical resonances it evokes, such as that of the leper who "came to [Jesus] and kneeling said, 'If you choose, you can make me clean'" (Mark 2:40); or of the man who came to Jesus, "knelt before him, and said, 'Lord, have mercy on my son . . .'" (Mt. 17:14); or, in a different context, the hymn of Philippians 2:10: "At the name of Jesus every knee should bend, in heaven and on earth and under the earth." To give weight to his prayer, Dominic fell on his knees again and again to express his submission to the power of Christ, his dependence upon the grace of Christ, and his fealty to his Lord whom he serves. This last note, of course, mirrors the feudal customs of Dominic's times, when knights and vassals knelt before their lords to swear loyalty and accept assignments for duty. It was a sign both of respect and of affection. Saint Thomas Aquinas, O.P., in his treatment of prayer in the *Summa Theologiae*, explains that the desire for eternal life for another can become so intense that a real communion of love comes to be established between them. In this way, divine love so fills the heart of those who pray for others that they set their hearts on seeing the same hope that they have for themselves extended to the object of their intercession. This is reminiscent of the Buddhist figure of the bodhisattva who fixes his or her heart on gaining the Buddha-nature for all sentient beings and does not rest until that goal is achieved. Perhaps we can understand Dominic's insistent prayer here somehow in analogy to that tradition. But even deeper than that for Catholics, there is the evident concreteness of Dominic's prayer in this fourth way. He loves Christ as he loves a person present to him, and his action of prayer deepens his feeling of that presence and deepens his experience of love. In Catholic liturgy there are a number of strong times when repeated genuflections are prescribed and have a powerful impact on the faithful. On Good Friday, for example, in the Great Prayer of Intercession in which the church prays at length (ten times) for the needs of all the different segments and ranks of humanity, the faithful are repeatedly called to kneel (*Flectamus genua*—let us bend our knees) and then to stand (*Levate*—stand up) as a sign of their radical investment in this solemn prayer that is linked to the celebration of Christ's crucifixion. Likewise, on that same day, in coming to venerate the Cross, the faithful (with the friars barefoot) approach the Cross, first kneeling and then rising three times as a sign of adoration and of penance for their sins. In our day, such gestures are rare indeed; but Dominic's prayer makes us realize that we are missing something precious by entering so rarely into this corporal mode of worship. There is clearly a kind of spiritual athleticism in Dominic's way of going about it. But remember, of course, that this "way" may well have reference to the competitive exertions of the Cathar *perfecti* (leaders). Dominic outdoes even them in zeal. Above all, it is a form of edification for the friars, as well as a progressive internalization for Dominic himself of his utter devotion to his Lord. In all these cases, what is required more than anything else is the inner spirit of prayer and humility that lies at the heart of the gestures.

The fifth way involves standing before the altar and expressing his prayer with the gestures of his hands. This way of praying corresponds with Dominic's endeavor to enter into dialogue with God. Further, it represents the transition from the preparatory activities of the first four ways into a new posture of conversation with God. Think of this text in Daniel: "As he was speaking to me, I fell into a trance, face to the ground; then he touched me and set me on my feet. He said, 'Listen, and I will tell you what will take place'" (Dan. 9:18–19). This prayer of Dominic "upright and firmly supported by his feet" presupposes a relation of intimacy and confidence in God adapted to sustain a conversation. The manuscript describes Dominic as engrossed in this dialogue: "[Y]ou would have thought that it was a prophet in conversation with an angel or with God, sometimes talking, sometimes listening." He is seeing what the Lord God has to show him and then sorting through all its implications. For God's part, we can remember his command to Ezekiel: "'Mortal, stand up on your feet, and I will speak to you.' And when he spoke to me, a spirit entered into me and set me on my feet; and I heard him speaking to me" (Ez. 2:1–2). The previous four ways were closely focused upon Christ's passion and suffering, but here the symbolism is of resurrection. The verb for "stand" in Latin is *surgere*, with the symbolism being that of rising up from the defeat of suffering and death. Dominic is lifted up to see, to learn, and to prepare himself to preach. His arms and hands are mentioned several times: opened before him like the leaves of a book, joined together under his eyes, and finally lifted up near his ears as though to focus his hearing on something being said to him. These are images of concentration and attentiveness, as the citation of Psalm 132 mentions: "as the eyes of servants look to the hands of their masters." In each case, Dominic's hands are instruments to help him listen more deeply to the word of God. They are the physical extension of his attentiveness and his recollection. This way of praying expresses Dominic's practice of meditating that involves a murmuring of the words that he has received from God's revelation. As Psalm 37 says, "The mouths of the righteous utter wisdom, and their tongues speak justice: the law of their God is in their hearts" (Ps. 37:30–31). The languages of the ancients understood *meditation* (Lat.: *meditatio*) to mean learning and internalizing a message: "take care over" (Grk.: *melete*) and "become familiar with" (Lat.) (Aubin 2005, 125). Medieval monastic teachings considered meditation to be the recall and repetition of God's word and entering into a *rumination* (a metaphor taken from what cattle do in chewing over what they have ingested). It is worth noting that Dominican friars were expected to memorize the 150 psalms and the Pauline Letters during their novitiate. This interiorization of the word through memorization was a first step in internalizing its meaning. The three different positions of Dominic's hands in this fifth way express in a visual way the dynamic transformation taking place through this prayer. They signify the investment of Dominic's whole person—voice, eyes, glance, posture, and hand movements—in his gestures of attention and dialogue. Standing straight before the Cross and fixing his gaze on it signifies above all a powerful openness and vulnerability to the slightest movement of grace. Dominic awaits God's initiative. Just as Christ has risen from the dead, so Dominic also is lifted up from his prayers of compunction and compassion to partake of Christ's resurrection life. In grasping the meaning of this fifth way, the principal element is the symbolism of Dominic's absorbing and internalizing the word of God. He learns the word like a prophet learns a message to deliver to those to whom he is sent. He stands perfectly erect, firmly planted like an oak tree reaching out its branches to heaven. He ruminates and repeats to himself the message he understands, shaping it into a life-giving word for the people. What does that feel like? Stand up straight, breathe deeply from your diaphragm, lift your head high, open your hands before you. This is how you become an instrument of good news—a herald of the divine word. It allows the Spirit of God who brings mere printed words to life in faith to "work away" in the depths of our hearts; it allows the Spirit "to intercede with sighs too deep for words" and speak to our hearts the mind of God (Rom. 8:26–27).

The sixth way involves standing with outstretched arms before an altar supporting a crucifix; here the body takes on a cruciform posture. Early Christian iconography shows us many examples of the faithful praying in what we call the *orantes* (lit., those who are praying) position, with arms stretched out and lifted. For those who observe such a posture, it possesses a dramatic quality that calls attention to the intensity and reverence of the prayer. For those performing the act, it is a gesture of heightened awareness and unguarded self-giving. In the preface of the Mass, this familiar dialogue takes place: "Lift up your hearts," and "We lift them up to the Lord." This is what the gesture of arms extended and lifted symbolizes: the core of one's being elevated in prayer. This sixth way of praying also reminds us of the dramatic story of Moses, presiding over the battle with Amalek: "Whenever Moses held up his hand, Israel prevailed; and whenever he lowered his hand, Amalek prevailed" (Ex. 17:11). So powerful was this gestural prayer of Moses that when he became tired, Aaron and Hur held up his hands so that they remained steady. God worked his victory through the prayer of intercession of Moses and his extended arms. Early Christian writers saw this prayer of Moses as a foreshadowing of the cross of Christ. The efficacy of Moses's prayer depended upon the gesture of his extended arms, a gesture that takes on Christological significance. Christ is presented as the perfect *orans*—the perfect example of a person at prayer. Christ obtained a victory greater than that of Moses, the victory over death and over sin. Christ's arms and hands, stretched out to embrace the universe, became a powerful instrument communicating the enormity of divine mercy. Dominic, entering into Christ's prayer on the cross, conforms his gesture to that of the crucified, making his bodily posture itself an instrument of grace. The manuscript tells us that Dominic prayed this way particularly when he was aware that God was proposing to work some marvel through his intercession. The two miracles referred to in the text are incidents repeated in the early stories of Dominic in a variety of manuscripts (see Tugwell 1982, 118–19, 173–78). The first has to do with his either healing or raising from the dead a boy named Napoleon, the nephew of a Roman cardinal who fell off his horse and was brought to Dominic inanimate and unconscious. Dominic had the boy carried to a room where he could pray secretly over him and soon gave him back to his family safe and sound. The second story is about English pilgrims who were shipwrecked while crossing the Garonne River near Toulouse. Called to the site, Dominic extended his arms in the form of a cross and prayed, and they came forth from the river saved. The manuscript also refers to the story of Elijah restoring to life the son of the widow of Zarephath by stretching himself upon the dead child three times as he cried out to the Lord, "O Lord my God, let this child's life come into him again" (1 Kings 17:21). Here again the message is that God used the presence and physical members of the body of the prophet as an instrument for divine healing. This is to help us to understand the power of the gesture that Dominic assumes as he stretches out his limbs to allow God's power to enter and take possession of him. His gesture and his prayer are the same thing. To really understand the meaning of this sixth way of praying, we need to follow Dominic's example. In some quiet place before a crucifix, extend your arms in the form of a cross, reaching out with your hands into the space that lies beyond them. Try to understand that the posture itself is the prayer. Stay in that position for several minutes, and you will experience both the weight of your body and the psychic energy that rushes in to fill the extended space that you create. The manuscript puts edifying words from the Psalms on the lips of Dominic here again, but it is important to understand that for him (and for us) the prayer is essentially the gesture—which says more than what any words can say.

The seventh way involves standing with upraised body and hands before the altar and the Cross. This way of praying may be described as reaching out for heaven. The body, the arms, and the hands are lifted on high with such intensity that the saint's body is described as looking like an arrow shot from a bow. As a form of spiritual choreography, this gesture evokes the sort of self-offering described by Psalm 141: "Let my prayer be counted as incense before you, the lifting up of my hands as an evening sacrifice" (141:2). In imitation of Christ's self-offering on the cross, Dominic offers himself in union with Christ, his head. Christ as high priest is the definitive intercessor-mediator, who obtains for those grafted into him by Baptism not only God's mercy but also the grace of adoption as children of God. Following Christ, sacrifice no longer consists in offering gifts or bloody sacrifices but rather in offering our very selves in solidarity with him. So Dominic offers his freedom, whole and entire, placed at the disposition of God's Providence. Saint Dominic's gesture signifies this handing over of his life to the Father after the pattern of Christ. The manuscript describes Dominic being carried into rapture and obtaining in that state the gifts of the Holy Spirit for the members of his order. The point of the rapture is not so much to claim an extraordinary characteristic for Dominic but rather to underline the extraordinary strength of divine power here. Dominic is lifted up by the Spirit toward supernatural realities that can only be experienced through abstraction from sense experience. And the gift he receives is not for himself but for his friars, not for his own spiritual delight but to express his charismatic generativity. The attitude of this posture where the body vibrates like an arrow ready to fly off into space expresses the intensity of Dominic's prayer. Once again, the trunk of his body, his arms, his hands, and his head express the depth of his affection and the intensity of his desire. This seventh way pays particular attention to Dominic's hands. He is reaching out as though waiting to be grasped by hands from above. However, he also reminds us of the parting words of Jesus, "Father, into your hands I commend my spirit" (Luke 23:46). Dominic's hands are stretched out toward the merciful hands of God. Dominic, who so often appealed to Divine Providence for extraordinary help—in sending out the friars two by two, in counting on God's mercy to feed his brothers, in insisting on mendicant poverty—lived in the constant awareness that there was nothing in his life that he had not received gratuitously. In understanding this way of prayer, perhaps it is most important for us to grasp Dominic's robust appreciation of Providence. He dares to reach out for the most precious spiritual gifts while offering his entire life in a simple but intense gesture of total and absolute self-offering.

The eighth way involves sitting and reading in a quiet place. So much of Dominican life is linked to reading, studying, and preparing to preach that this eighth way of praying, although extraordinary in Dominic's rendition of it, represents a great slice of the life of a friar preacher. When mendicant friars distinguished themselves from monks and canons, *lectio divina* (reading divine texts), a meditative reading of the Scriptures or of sacred authors with the goal of being drawn into prayer, developed for Dominicans into the practice of study. A prayer written by Thomas Aquinas to be prayed before study is a good illustration of the sacred character of study in the Dominican tradition. Thomas composed these lines:

> Ineffable Creator, who are the true source of light and wisdom, cast upon my dark intellect a ray of your own brightness and dispel the twofold darkness of sin and ignorance in which I was born. You who can make the tongues of children eloquent, instruct my tongue and bless my lips. Give me keenness of understanding, a capacity to retain, method and ease in learning, accuracy in interpreting, and eloquence in speech. Instruct my beginning, direct my progress, and perfect the finished task. (DPB 330)

For Thomas, study was not some sort of verbal calculus but a dialogue with the one who revealed the mysteries of faith. This is perfectly consistent with Dominic's eighth way. The eighth way tells us that Dominic would periodically bow down with reverence and respect to the book that he was reading and even kiss it, especially if it were the book of the Gospels. The grace of this way of praying allowed him to leap beyond the limitations of human words and a written text and to hear and respond from his heart to a saving revelation that gave him joy. He dialogued with the sacred authors and with himself, expressing his emotions, his sadness, and his hopes in both tears and laughing. There is even the remarkable detail of his hiding his face in his capuce (his hooded head covering), reminiscent of Moses hiding his face at the burning bush "for he was afraid to look at God" (Ex. 3:6). Dominic's gestures are his response to the living word that he has taken from the book before him and his astonished awareness that he has been given the gift of coming to know "the mystery that has been hidden throughout the ages and generations" (Col. 1:26). It is important to note then that reading and study, which require attention, meditation, and contemplation, are included here among the ways of praying. If the reader is seeking to find God in what he reads, then all of his activity will be finalized or transformed by that intention. This eighth manner of praying describes a new kind of bodily posture for Dominic. He places himself before Christ in the words of the gospel with his whole being—body, soul, and spirit—because the Scriptures are the open book of the living word. The freedom with which he spontaneously responds with interest, joy, sadness, or excitement prompts gestures and emotions that help him to internalize what he reads and what he hears. The liturgy of the Mass includes the gesture of signing the Cross over the initial lines of the gospel and then kissing that place as a sign of reverence. Dominic obviously did something similar when he read the Scriptures. In his day, there were not many books around, and so a hand-lettered manuscript was a rare and precious thing. For us, inundated with texts, it is hard to reconstruct the sense of reverence that someone in Dominic's time must have felt in contact with a sacred book. However, as we try to internalize the meaning of this eighth way, it is perhaps helpful to remember Thomas Aquinas's instinct to pray for enlightenment before study and Dominic's practice of listening for the living voice of the Holy Spirit at work in that form of prayer that is *sacred* study. We should remember that what the heart learns in study is the key to understanding.

The ninth way involves preaching and travel to the place of preaching, the quintessential Dominican activity. The Christological dimension here is Dominic's imitation of Christ's repeated journeys along the roads of Galilee and Judea, with his disciples trailing behind him or going on ahead. When Jesus was on the road, he was on the way to announce the kingdom of God. Jesus "went on through cities and villages, proclaiming and bringing the good news of the kingdom of God. The twelve were with him" (Luke 8:1). He taught in their synagogues, healed all sorts of illnesses, and gave hope to those who heard him. A particularly powerful example of Jesus's itinerancy is his encounter with the two disciples on the road to Emmaus: he went along the road with them, but their eyes were only opened at the breaking of the bread (Luke 24:16ff.). Dominic's journeys show his extraordinary freedom of spirit; not only did he have no permanent priory of residence, he had no cell that was his own. Even though Dominic loved to stay with and pray with the friars as he passed through the cities where they were establishing themselves, in a habitual way, the highways were Dominic's cloister. As the text suggests, during his peripatetic contemplation, he penetrated to the depths of the mysteries he meditated and prepared his heart to explain God's revelation with power when he preached. The primitive constitutions of the order prescribed that when the brothers went out to preach, each should be given a companion (*socius*) to go with him. After receiving the prior's blessing, they left and went on their way, conscious that their goal was the evangelical mission of saving souls through the preaching of the gospel. The friars were supposed to carry no money nor to receive gifts but only to take what they needed to eat along the way and whatever clothing and books were necessary for their work. The witnesses at his process of canonization described Dominic as walking vigorously along the roads, loving to sing hymns and psalms, and stopping in whatever churches they passed along the way to pray on bended knee in secret. The text also describes Dominic's strange gesture of moving his hand in front of his face as if shooing away flies or brushing away hot ashes. This gesture seems to be a kind of physical externalization of a busy mind trying to concentrate and push away distractions or unwelcome thoughts. It suggests that Dominic existed at such times in a sort of noetic parenthesis in which he became largely oblivious of his surroundings and during which his gestures, even while walking, mirrored the intense psychic life he was living in his prayer. We should keep in mind that we are dealing here with a man of robust constitution and boundless energy. Even though he did completely wear himself out at the end, he had nonetheless walked across Europe on foot several times, often taking months to travel between points. The imagery of the illustration for the ninth way is unique in showing us three postures that are not explicitly described in the text. In the first posture, Dominic is conversing with his *socius* on the way, speaking of God or explaining his thoughts. In the second, Dominic is trailing somewhat behind his companion, caught up in his meditation and prayer. In the third posture, Dominic stands to the right of the frame of the image, the position usually taken by Christ in the previous illustrations. Catherine Aubin suggests that Dominic here blesses the friar who holds out to him a leather-covered bundle that is probably the manuscript of the gospels, commending his brother to read and understand and preach God's word. This is an imaginative reconstruction of the meaning of the image but not necessarily a deficient one. Certainly Dominic appears in a new role that in a sense completes and terminates all that has gone before. He is a living icon of the Christ whom he followed with all the resources of his person. In our frenetic world today, strolling along a country road or through a forest might offer us some sense of what Dominic experienced in his itinerant contemplation. The movement of the body while walking can be deeply relaxing, the exposure to the elements can be bracing or uplifting, and the commitment to devote significant time to reflection can create a break from the pressures of life. Our goal, as with Dominic, is to arrive at an ability to grasp and explain the hidden mysteries of God revealed by the Spirit in the quiet of our hearts. Mindful strolling is still one way to do this.

Saint Dominic's Ways in the Later Dominican Tradition and Beyond

For centuries, this manuscript was essentially forgotten by the friars of the Order of Preachers, whose minds were preoccupied with theological controversies at best and ephemeral cultural distractions at worst. When a distinguished Irish Dominican medievalist, Leonard Boyle, became prefect of the Vatican Library in the 1990s, however, he promoted interest in this text by making a facsimile edition (complete with illustrations) available. In previous decades, the Dominican historians M. H. Vicaire, O.P., and Simon Tugwell, O.P., had written important articles or chapters about the *Novem modi orandi*. So, at the end of the twentieth century, this document once again became a source of fascination and edification not only for Dominicans but also for others interested in the spiritual life.

This has been an important corrective, because in the 1970s in many provinces the friars of the Dominican Order had abandoned the very gestures mentioned in this manuscript: the inclination at the *Gloria Patri*, the various prostrations in the Dominican liturgy, and the *venia* (described earlier). Their doing so was a reaction against the dry formalism of nineteenth-century and early twentieth-century Dominican rituals (Walgrave 1968). However, today a younger generation of friars wants to experience the full power of the Dominican ritual, and so they are reintroducing many of these elements to Dominican community life. From that point of view, the *Novem modi orandi* is a valuable and instructive text for them.

Vicaire, who researched Saint Dominic's life through repeated visits to Fanjeaux, Prouille, Toulouse, and its surrounding area in the south of France, where Dominic lived for ten years before formally founding the Order of Preachers, published a French translation of the *Novem modi orandi* in 1954. His motive at the time appears to have been the dissemination of a then little-known source that revealed much about the spiritual life of Dominic. Since then, many others have mentioned this manuscript in passing. Catherine Aubin's book, *Prier avec son corps*, is a significant contribution, giving attention not only to the historical development of the text but also and above all to its theological meaning and its spiritual significance for contemporary believers. A French Dominican Sister and doctor in theology, who is a professor of spirituality at the Pontifical University of Saint Thomas (Angelicum) in Rome, Aubin provides important insights into our primary text and the associated contemplative way of life that it inspires.

At present, there is no requirement for the *Novem modi orandi* to be studied by young Dominicans in preparation for ministry. Each province of the order develops its own curriculum for initiating new members. However, it is fair to say that this rich and remarkable monument to the life and spirit of Saint Dominic will become better known as years go by, and it should prove to be instructive and edifying in circles reaching well beyond the members of the Dominican order.

Praying with Saint Dominic

In concluding, I would like to make three points. First I will speak about the fundamental message of the *Novem modi orandi*, then point out that the manuscript contains an implicit message about religious or spiritual development, and finally observe that its perspective on bodily prayer might be a welcome contribution in the Roman Catholic community (at least in the English-speaking world) as a new Roman Missal has been recently introduced (in Advent of 2011).

First, the phrase "incarnate mindfulness" (of my own coining, as far as I know) sums up for me the whole spectrum of these gestural prayers of Dominic. In the introduction to the manuscript, the medieval author explains how sometimes "the soul makes use of the members of the human body in prayer so that it might be drawn more devoutly toward God, and then the soul by causing the body to respond is also affected." There is no question that the underlying preoccupation of this document is to demonstrate that the bodily person as a whole is called into prayer. What we see in Dominic's gestures is precisely his soul making use of the members of his body to help him internalize the meaning of what he is doing. He also uses the momentum of his physical actions to penetrate more and more deeply the mystery that he contemplates. The word "mindfulness" seems appropriate to me, since it is a question here above all of being rendered vividly conscious of what one is about and performing it with reverence and attention.[9] We noted previously that in this Dominican tradition contemplation has reference less to acts of the mind than to a complete self-investment in a way of living that is circumscribed by the word of God and by preaching.

As a somewhat banal observation, it seems that one of the great problems today for intellectuals or even for spiritual seekers is that we are immersed in a world that is too busy and too impatient. One of the most remarkable observations about Dominic in his process of canonization was how much time he put into visibly praying. Indeed, the manuscript itself and its commentators remark upon how the *Novem modi orandi* described Dominic's unique way of *praying always*. The example of these gestures of Dominic, therefore, holds out the possibility of learning how to slow down, how to pay attention, how to let the body carry the burden of the praying, and how to create patterns or routines that integrate physical gestures in such a way as to extend the depth of our heart's desires and the intensity of our investment in the act of prayer. All of these are essentially ways of encoding mindfulness onto the members of our body.

Second, there is an implicit theory of spiritual transformation lying beneath the development of the *Novem modi orandi*. Catherine Aubin develops this persuasively by saying that the first four ways, bowing, prostrating, the discipline, and kneeling, represent a first stage. Here humility, compunction, discipline, and trust are developed along the line of an imitative self-abasement modeled upon the self-emptying of Christ (see Phil. 2:6–7). In each of these cases, the body is in contact with the ground and Dominic recognizes his groundedness in humility. The function of this first stage is to orient the person to his or her role as creature, by celebrating his or her dependence on and trust of the divine creator. Aubin says that this stage represents filial piety, leading to docility and to the confidence of a child toward his or her parent. The second stage consists of ways five, six, and seven, in which Dominic is in each case standing erect, entering into dialogue with Christ on the cross. The relation is more fraternal than filial, and this is seen in the emphasis upon dialogue and acts of thanksgiving. Aubin describes this as the relation of friendship grounded in mutual love. The third stage includes the eighth and ninth ways, in which Dominic moves from preparatory steps into the execution of his life of study and preaching. In the eighth way, Dominic is portrayed as externalizing with eccentric excess his love of Christ, breaking out into laughter and tears as well as secret conversation and exclamations. In the ninth way, he walks along the highways to get himself to the place where he will be able to give to others what he has contemplated (*contemplata aliis tradere*). He becomes the *father* to his *brothers* and to others to whom he is sent. Aubin describes this stage as *spousal* love, where Dominic embraces the church as the spouse of Christ (Aubin 2005, 228–30). Whether or not we follow Aubin's interpretation completely, it does seem clear that there are three distinct stages or groups within the *Novem modi orandi* and that they move from humility to dialogue and then to generativity. This is a helpful way of understanding what the manuscript as a whole is able to teach.

Finally, I would like to remark briefly that this kind of appreciation of the integral role of bodily gestures in Christian prayer could be an important help to Catholics who are obliged to appropriate the new Roman Missal that is introducing new ritual texts of greater complexity than the 1973 English Sacramentary (Mass book) and that will restore some traditional ritual gestures (for example, striking one's breast in the *Confiteor*). The individual Catholic believer, for example, will have a more ample understanding of genuflecting in the midst of the whole congregation if he or she has practiced the discipline of genuflection in the style of Dominic in private prayer. There are vast treasures here to be explored. My hope is that the riches of the spiritual source here opened will be harvested and refined to become spiritual treasures for yet another generation of faith.

In terms of the present volume, this treatise illustrates how corporal asceticism in medieval Catholic religious practices was as much sacramental as it was penitential. In other words, the prayer gestures, taxing as they were, were meant to conform the one practicing them to Christ and make him or her into a sort of sacrament or icon of Christ living in his mystical body, the Church. They were also penitential, of course, but their thrust was to link the penitent's prayer of atonement (or reparation) for the offense of sin to Christ's own prayer of atonement, believing that Christ's atoning work was the true value of such prayer. This illustrates the deeply corporate understanding of medieval spirituality—something very different from the more individual understanding of spirituality in the present day. Finally, for people in today's culture in which so many live almost completely sedentary lives, the *Novem modi orandi* portrays an integration of body, action, and mental prayer that might stimulate a healthy revival of corporal expression in both private and community prayer and contemplation. In the last analysis, this treatise opens a window upon a medieval experience of contemplation that is exotic and strange in its details but nonetheless surprisingly realistic about the need for the body to support the mind in prayer and for the mind to call the body into the exercise of prayer. In general, most monks and other religious in the thirteenth century would have utilized many of these same gestures—bowing at the doxologies (phrases praising God) in the Divine Office, genuflecting within the Catholic liturgies, making prostrations on solemn occasions and reverences to the Cross in personal, private expressions of piety. What the *Novem modi orandi* gives us, then, is a rare reading in depth of the theological and contemplative meanings of these rather common gestures of medieval religious life as well as a spiritual portrait of the founder of one of the most influential medieval religious orders, the Friars Preachers.

Notes

1. Throughout the present chapter, when "church" appears without qualification it refers to the Roman Catholic Church, within which the bishop of Rome (pope) and his curia (or bureaucracy) hold a universal jurisdiction for questions of doctrine and church policy (see further discussion later in this introduction).

2. The painting was originally executed for the Saint Nicholas Chapel in the Basilica of San Domenico (Perugia, Italy). Fra Angelica was an early Italian Renaissance painter and a Dominican friar. Interestingly, the Friary of San Marco, a Dominican monastery in Florence, Italy, where Fra Angelico lived from 1436 to 1445, contains various works painted there by Angelico. See, for example, Hood 1993. For present purposes, it is especially noteworthy that devotional frescoes portraying aspects of the life of Jesus Christ adorn the walls of each cell. Some of these depict Saint Dominic praying in a manner paralleling our primary text. Unfortunately, today San Marco is primarily a museum, rather than an active Dominican monastery, with the cells unoccupied.

3. For a basic account of the gradual founding of the order, see Tugwell 1982, 11–16. The Order of Preachers follows the Rule of Saint Augustine. Composed by Augustine of Hippo (St. Augustine; 354–430) for a community of priests around 400 CE, this rule antedated the Rule of Benedict, which was intended for monks without an explicit pastoral mission. Augustine's rule, similar in many practices to Benedict's, was envisaged for those who would do pastoral work in the church. The Rule of Saint Augustine covers the following points: love of God and neighbor as its aim, the way to pray, fasting and asceticism according to the abilities of each individual, modest clothing and deportment, common life and mutual care, mutual love and forgiveness, love as the spirit of governance, and spiritual freedom.

4. The Cistercians were an eleventh-century reform of the Benedictine Order founded at Citeaux (Lat.: *Cistercium*) in Burgundy. The monks who preached with Diego and Dominic were from the nearby Abbey of Fontfroide in the Midi.

5. Saint Dominic's body is still housed in a sculptural masterpiece, the *Arca di San Domenico* (Ark of Saint Dominic), designed by the Italian sculptor Nicola Pisano (ca. 1220–ca. 1284) in 1264; the priory in Bologna has set aside the room used by Saint Dominic as a shrine for veneration by the friars and by visitors.

6. Saint Dominic is the patron saint of astronomers and astronomy, with his feast day celebrated on August 8th.

7. The most readily available English version is contained in Tugwell's *Early Dominicans* and *The Nine Ways of Prayer of St. Dominic* (1982 and 1996), but the text is also available in Vicaire 1954 and in a full-sized facsimile edition published in Ireland by Dominican Publications in 2003.

8. Kolzow (1964) lists them as follows: (1) Inclinations, (2) Prostrations, (3) Penance, (4) Genuflections, (5) Contemplation, (6) Earnest intercession, (7) Supplication, (8) Thoughtful reading, and (9) Praying on a journey.

9. A recent comparative study of the Vietnamese Buddhist monk Thich Nhat Hanh and the German Dominican theologian and mystic Meister Eckhart points out how appropriate the word "mindfulness" is to both contemporary Buddhism's understanding of meditation and medieval Christian ideas of awakening through conversion. See Pierce 2005, chapter 2, "Mindfulness and the Eternal Now."

Works Cited and Further Reading

Aquinas, Thomas. 1973. *Summa Theologiae 2a2ae, 183–9*. Translated by Jordan Aumann. New York: McGraw-Hill.
Aubin, Catherine. 2005. *Prier avec son corps à la manière de saint Dominique*. Paris: Editions du Cerf.
Barbero, Alessandro. 2004. *Charlemagne: Father of a Continent*. Translated by Allan Cameron. Berkeley: University of California Press.
Bedouelle, Guy. 1987. *Saint Dominic: The Grace of the Word*. San Francisco: Ignatius Press.
Book of Constitutions and Ordinations of the Brothers of the Order of Preachers (BCO). 2001. Dublin: Dominican Publications.
Borgmann, Erik. 2001. *Dominican Spirituality: An Exploration*. Translated by John Bowden. London and New York: Continuum.
Boyle, Leonard. 1994. "Saint Dominic's Nine Ways of Prayer." *Archivum Fratrum Praedicatorum* 64: 5–17.
Brown, Peter. 1996. *The Rise of Western Christendom: Triumph and Diversity AD 200–1000*. Oxford: Blackwell.
Catherine of Siena. 1980. *The Dialogue*. Translated by Suzanne Noffke. Mahwah: Paulist Press.
Chenu, Marie-Dominique. 2002. *Aquinas and His Role in Theology*. Translated by Paul Philibert. Collegeville: Liturgical Press.
Colledge, Edmund, and Bernard McGinn. 1981. *Meister Eckhart: The Essential Sermons, Commentaries, Treatises, and Defense*. Mahwah: Paulist Press.
Dominican Prayer Book (DPB). 1962. 4th and rev. ed. Rome: Curia Generalizia O.P.
Hinnebusch, William. 1983. *Dominican Spirituality: Principles and Practice*. Dublin: Dominican Publications.
Hood, William. 1993. *Fra Angelico at San Marco*. New Haven: Yale University Press.
Humbert of Romans. 1888–1889. "Expositio Magistri Humberti Super Constitutiones fratrum Praedicatorum." In *Humberti de Romanis Opera de Vita Regulari*, edited by J. J. Berthier, 2:160–71. Rome: Monumenta Ordinis Praedicatorum Historica.
Jarrett, Bede. 1995. *Life of Saint Dominic*. New York: Doubleday.
Kelly, J. N. D. 1988. *The Oxford Dictionary of Popes*. Oxford and New York: Oxford University Press.
Kolzow, Andrew. 1964. "The Nine Ways of Prayer of St. Dominic." In *Saint Dominic: Biographical Documents*, edited by Francis Lehner, 147–59. Washington: Thomist Press.
Koudelka, V. J. 1972. "Les dépositions des témoins du procès de canonization de Saint Dominique." *Archivum Fratrum Praedicatorum* 42: 62–64.

Lacordaire, Henri-Dominique. 1880. *Life of Saint Dominic.* Translated by an English Dominican. London: Burns and Oates.

Ladurie, Emmanuel LeRoy. 1979. *Montaillou: The Promised Land of Error.* Translated by Barbara Bray. New York: Vintage Books.

Mandonnet, Pierre. 1945. *St. Dominic and His Work.* Translated by Sister Mary Benedicta Larkin. St. Louis: B. Herder.

McBrien, Richard P. 1994. *Catholicism.* San Francisco: HarperSanFrancisco.

McGinn, Bernard, with Frank Tobin and Elvira Borgstadt. 1986. *Meister Eckhart: Teacher and Preacher.* Mahwah: Paulist Press.

Murray, Paul. 2006. *The New Wine of Dominican Spirituality: A Drink Called Happiness.* London: Burns and Oates.

Pierce, Brian J. 2005. *We Walk the Path Together: Learning from Thich Nhat Hanh and Meister Eckhart.* Maryknoll: Orbis Books.

Rapley, Elizabeth. 2011. *The Lord Is Their Portion: The Story of Religious Orders and How They Shaped Our World.* Grand Rapids: Eerdmans.

Rituale Professionis Ritus. 1999. http://www.op.org.au/texts/prof_frat_03.pdf. Accessed on June 1, 2014.

Schillebeeckx, Edward. 1962. "Exegese dogmatik und dogmenentwicklung." In *Exegese und Dogmatik*, edited by Herbert Vorgrimler, 91–114. Mainz: Herder.

Schmitt, Jean-Claude. 1985. "Entre le texte et l'image: les gestes de la prière de Saint Dominique." In *Persons in Groups: Social Behavior as Identity Formation in Medieval and Renaissance Europe*, edited Richard C. Trexler, 194–220. Binghamton: Medieval and Renaissance Texts and Studies (vol. 36).

———. 1990. *La Raison des gestes dans l'Occident medieval.* Paris: Gallimard.

Shannon, William H. 1993. "Contemplation, Contemplative Prayer." In *The New Dictionary of Catholic Spirituality*, edited by Michael Downey, 209–14. Collegeville: Liturgical Press.

Stalley, Roger. 1999. *Early Medieval Architecture.* Oxford History of Art. Oxford and New York: Oxford University Press.

Taurisano, Innocenzo. 1922. "Quomodo Sanctus Patriarcha Dominicus Orabat." *Analecta Ordinis Praedicatorum* 15: 93–106.

Tugwell, Simon. 1979. *The Way of the Preacher.* Springfield: Templegate.

———. 1982. *Early Dominicans: Selected Writings.* Classics of Western Spirituality. Mahwah: Paulist Press.

———. 1985. "The Nine Ways of Prayer of St. Dominic: A Textual Study and Critical Edition." *Mediaeval Studies* 42: 1–124.

———. 1988. *Albert and Thomas: Selected Writings.* Classics of Western Spirituality. Mahwah: Paulist Press.

———. 1995. *Saint Dominic.* Strasbourg: Editions du Signe.

———. 1996. *The Nines Ways of Prayer of St. Dominic.* Rome: Ufficio Libri Liturgici.

Vicaire, Marie-Humbert. 1955. *Saint Dominique de Caleruega d'après les documents du XIIIe siècle.* Paris: Editions du Cerf.

———. 1964. *Saint Dominic: Biographical Documents.* Translated by Francis Lehner. Washington: Thomist Press.

———. 2004. *Saint Dominic and His Times.* Translated by Kathleen Pond. Green Bay: Alt.

Walgrave, Valentine. 1968. *Dominican Self-Appraisal in the Light of the Council.* Translated Sister Jean David. Chicago: Priory Press.

Zagano, Phyllis, and Thomas McGonigle. 2006. *The Dominican Tradition: Spirituality in History.* Collegeville: Liturgical Press.

Novem modi orandi sancti Dominici (Nine Ways of Praying of Saint Dominic)*

Anonymous[1]

Translated and Annotated by Paul Philibert

The holy doctors Augustine, Leo, Ambrose, Gregory, Hilary, Isidore, John Chrysostom, John Damascene, Bernard,[2] and other devout teachers, both Greek and Latin, wrote a great deal about prayer. They wrote in order to encourage praying and also to describe the need for it and its usefulness, as well as ways of praying and of preparing for prayer, and especially describing obstacles to prayer. Further, our brother Thomas Aquinas, the venerable doctor, and his master Albert, along with William [Peraldus],[3] have written about prayer in a way that is both noble and penetrating in the tract on the virtues and in their other books.

Sometimes the soul makes use of the members of the human body in prayer so that it might be drawn more devoutly toward God, and then the soul by causing the body to respond is also affected by the body and at times falls into ecstasy like Paul,[4] or experiences suffering like our Savior, or is transported beyond consciousness like David.[5] Blessed Dominic very often prayed in these ways, as we have been told.

The saints of the Old and the New Testaments also prayed in this way at times. This kind of prayer stimulates devotion, with the soul spurring on the body, and then the body the soul. This sort of prayer moved Saint Dominic to vehement weeping and so inflamed the fervor of his will that his mind was unable to restrain his body from showing signs of his devotion. As a result, incited by his mind at prayer, he threw himself into petitions and pleas and acts of thanksgiving.

Dominic devoutly practiced the customary ways of praying in common by celebrating Mass and singing the psalms, which he did whether in choir or while on the road.[6] In these prayers, he was often swept up beyond himself to speak with God and with the angels. In addition to these ways of praying, however, he also used to pray in the following ways.

---

*Abbreviated *Novem modi orandi* (Nine Ways of Praying). The present translation is a complete rendering of the Latin manuscript Codex Rossianus 3 (dat. early 14th c.), as presented in Simon Tugwell's monograph in *Mediaeval Studies* (1985). In the original manuscript, which is preserved in the Vatican Apostolic Library, the illustrations are in color, which produces a more powerful aesthetic effect. The text has been translated into English a number of times, including by Simon Tugwell (1982, 94–103, also 1996). See the introduction to this chapter. I am grateful to the Biblioteca Apostolica Vaticana/Vatican Apostolic Library for permission to use the illustrations.

1. Probably a friar of the Order of Preachers (Dominicans) founded by Domingo Félix de Guzmán (St. Dominic; 1170–1221). Said friar may have been an associate of Saint Dominic who personally observed his "ways of praying."

2. The first eight figures mentioned here are Church Fathers, that is, those early Christian writers whose teachings are considered the foundation of orthodox Christian doctrine. Saint Bernard of Clairvaux (1090–1153) was a French Cistercian abbot and spiritual writer.

3. On the famous German Dominican Albertus Magnus (Albert the Great; ca. 1200–1280) and Italian Dominican Thomas Aquinas (1225–1274), see the introduction to this chapter. William Perault (Latinized Peraldus or Peraltus; ca. 1190–1271) was a French Dominican who wrote the *Summa de vitiis et virtutibus* (General Treatise on Vices and Virtues), which was very influential in the thirteenth century.

4. 2 Corinthians 12:2–4.

5. 2 Samuel 6:12–16. David's dancing before the Ark is interpreted as a transport of joy and spiritual intensity.

6. From the beginning, Dominican friars celebrated Mass (the sacrament of the Eucharist) and the Divine Office (composed mostly of psalms) every day, singing the texts of these prayers with chant melodies. Dominic prayed in this way even when traveling.

The First Way of Praying

Figure 11.3. First Way of Praying: Bowing

First of all, Dominic humbled himself in front of the altar as if Christ, symbolized by the altar, were really and personally present there, and not only by way of a sign. "The prayer of the humble pierces the clouds."[7] Dominic also used to remind the brothers of this phrase of Judith: "You are the God of the lowly . . . upholder of the weak."[8] By humility the Canaanite woman got what she wanted,[9] as did the prodigal son. As for me, "I am not worthy to have you come under my roof."[10] "Humble me, Lord, to the utmost,"[11] for before you "I am severely afflicted."[12] In this way, standing up straight, our holy father bowed his head and the trunk of his body humbly toward Christ, who is his head. Remembering that he was but a servant and Christ his excellent master, he gave himself over completely to venerating Christ.

He taught the brothers to do this themselves when they passed in front of the humiliation of the crucified one, so that Christ, who was humiliated to the extreme for our sake, would find us humbled before his majesty. Likewise he instructed them to humble themselves before the whole divine Trinity when they solemnly chanted, "Glory be to the Father, and to the Son, and to the Holy Spirit." This way of praying, as seen in the image here, was the point of departure for his devotion—bowing profoundly.

---

7. Sirach 35:21.

8. Judith 9:11.

9. Matthew 15:22–28.

10. Matthew 8:8.

11. Sirach 7:17.

12. Psalm 119:107.

The Second Way of Praying

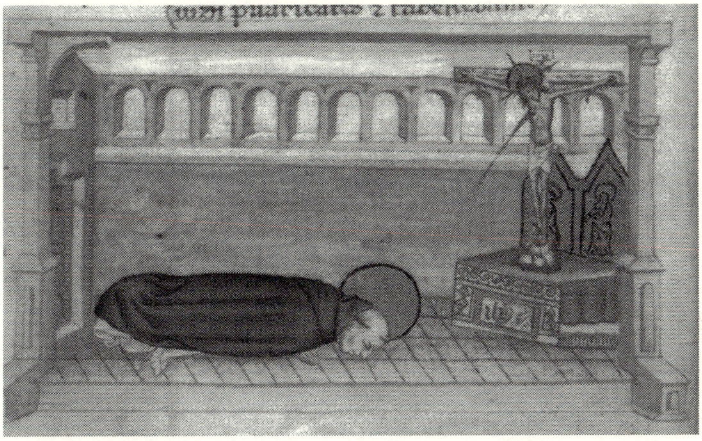

Figure 11.4. Second Way of Praying: Full-Body Prostration

In addition, Blessed Dominic often prayed by throwing himself down on the ground with his face to the floor; and he would be moved by compunction and would blush, saying these words from the gospel, sometimes loud enough for others to hear: "God, be merciful to me, a sinner."[13] And with deep piety and reverence he would also utter these words of David: "I have sinned greatly in what I have done."[14] He wept and groaned mightily. Then he would say: "I am unworthy to gaze on the heights of heaven because of the great number of my sins, because I have stirred up your anger and done what is evil in your sight." And then he would emphatically and devoutly recite this psalm: "We sink down to the dust; our bodies cling to the ground."[15] And also: "My soul clings to the dust; revive me according to your word."[16]

At times, desiring to teach the brothers how to pray reverently, he told them that the Magi, those pious kings, "on entering the house, saw the child with Mary his mother."[17] Now it is certain, he said, that we too have found the God-man with Mary his handmaid; so "Come, let us bow down, let us kneel before the Lord, our Maker."[18]

He exhorted the young by telling them, "If you can't weep for your own sins because you have none, there are still many sinners to be presented to God's mercy and love, for whom both prophets and apostles grieved; and for whom Jesus, seeing them, wept bitterly, and holy David also wept, saying, 'I look at the faithless with disgust because they do not keep your commands.' "[19]

---

13. Luke 18:13.
14. 2 Samuel 24:10.
15. Psalm 44:25.
16. Psalm 119:25.
17. Matthew 2:11.
18. Psalm 95:6.
19. Psalm 119:158.

The Third Way of Praying

Figure 11.5. Third Way of Praying: Self-Flagellation

For this reason, after getting up off the ground, he would take the discipline with an iron chain[20] and say: "Your discipline has set me straight on toward my goal." This is why the whole order prescribed that all the brothers, honoring the example of Saint Dominic, should take the discipline on their bare backs with wooden sticks[21] after Compline[22] on ferial days[23] while saying either "Have mercy on me, O God"[24] or "Out of the depths I cry to you, O Lord,"[25] either for their own sins or for the sins of those whose alms supported them. So no one, no matter how innocent, should be exempt from this holy example. The image shows this practice.

---

20. The instrument for whipping oneself was called "the discipline," and it could be made of chain or rope or the branches of a tree or a bush, as long as it allowed the brother to strike himself on the back in imitation of Christ's painful flogging at Pilate's direction (see John 19:1). Dominic's use of a chain entails the most painful option among these possibilities.
21. "Sticks" most likely refer to branches of a tree or bush.
22. Compline is the last liturgical service of the friars at the end of the day before setting off for bed.
23. "Ferial days" refers to weekdays without a special feast and so most ordinary days.
24. Psalm 51.
25. Psalm 130. See my commentary on the third way in the introduction.

The Fourth Way of Praying

Figure 11.6. Fourth Way of Praying: Repeated Kneeling

Next, Saint Dominic either before the altar or in the chapter room,[26] with his eyes fixed, would give the crucifix his entire attention, genuflecting again and again as much as a hundred times.[27] Sometimes between Compline and midnight he would rise and genuflect over and over[28] like the apostle James[29] and also like the leper in the gospel who said on bended knee, "Lord, if you choose, you can make me clean";[30] and like Stephen,[31] who knelt down and cried out in a loud voice, "Lord, do not hold this sin against them."[32] Then our holy father Saint Dominic would feel great trust in the mercy of God both for himself and for all sinners, and also for the protection of the novices whom he was sending out to preach to souls. At times he was not able to hold back his voice but was overheard by the brothers saying, "To you, O Lord, I call; do not refuse to hear me, for if you are silent to me, I shall be like those who go down to the Pit,"[33] as well as similar phrases from sacred Scripture.

At other times, he spoke within his heart, however, and his voice could hardly be heard at all; and he would remain on bended knees, caught up in awe sometimes for a long time. It also seemed because of the way he looked that at times his mind even penetrated into heaven, and suddenly he became filled with joy and wiped away tears that flowed freely. He became

---

26. The chapter room is where the friars gathered for community meetings or chapters (Lat.: *capitulum*), a term used for formal monastic assemblies, often on a daily basis. During the day, the chapter room was a quiet place where someone could find silence and seclusion.

27. That is, kneeling down completely and then rising up straight over and over.

28. Cf. Luke 22:45.

29. Dominic is described as imitating the apostle James who, according to the *Historia Ecclesiastica* (Ecclesiastical History) of Eusebius (ca. 265–340), genuflected and prayed on his knees so much that his knee-pads became "like those of a camel" (bk. 2, ch. 23: Loeb Library ed., 1.171).

30. Mark 1:40.

31. Acts 8:60 describes the deacon Stephen falling to his knees while being stoned to death and crying out to the Lord for the forgiveness of those who were murdering him.

32. Acts 7:59.

33. Psalm 28:1.

overcome with desire, like someone driven by thirst toward a spring of water, or like a traveler at last approaching home. Then he would become animated and vigorous and his movements would become controlled and agile as he stood and knelt once again.

He was so used to genuflecting that when he was on a journey, both when staying in an inn after the fatigue of traveling and even while on the road, while others were sleeping and resting, he went back to his genuflections as if to an art that was all his own and his own special ministry. He taught the brothers this way of praying more by his example of performing it than by explicitly teaching them.

The Fifth Way of Praying

Figure 11.7. Fifth Way of Praying: Standing with Gestures of the Hands

Sometimes our holy father Dominic, when he was in one of the priories,[34] would stand before the altar, not leaning on or being supported by anything, but with his body upright firmly supported by his feet. At times, he would open his hands before his chest as though he were looking at an open book, and then he acted as though he was in the presence of God reading with deep reverence and devotion. He seemed to meditate in his mouth the words of God and repeat them to himself with delight. He made his own the Lord's practice that we read about in Luke, where it says that Jesus "went to the synagogue on the Sabbath day, as was his custom, and stood up to read."[35] Also Psalm 106 says: "Phineas stood up and interceded and the plague was stopped."[36]

Sometimes he also clasped his hands together, holding them tightly joined before his eyes and bent himself forward. At other times he held his hands at the level of his shoulders, like the priest celebrating Mass, as if he wanted to focus his hearing to catch carefully what someone was saying to him. If you had seen his devotion while he was standing attentively and praying, you would have thought that it was a prophet in conversation with an angel or with God, sometimes talking, sometimes listening, sometimes reflecting quietly about what had been revealed to him.

While he was traveling, he would suddenly steal time for prayer in secret and would stand with his whole mind fixed on heaven. You would have heard him speaking sweetly and delicately some beautiful text drawn from the marrow and the richness of Holy Scripture that he seemed to have drawn out from the well of the Savior's wisdom. The brothers were deeply moved by his example, when they saw their father and master praying like this, and the more devout among them were taught in this way how best to pray reverently and continuously "as the eyes of servants look to the hand of their master, [and] as the eyes of the maid to the hand of her mistress,"[37] as the illustration shows.

---

34. The friars technically refer to their houses as *conventus* (sing.)/*conventi* (pl.), literally meaning "coming together" or an assembly by extension. Because Dominic renounced the term "abbot" (father) for the head of the Dominican community and choose instead the term "prior" (first among equals), Dominican houses came to be called "priories."

35. Luke 4:16.

36. Psalm 106:30.

37. Psalm 123:2.

The Sixth Way of Praying

Figure 11.8. Sixth Way of Praying: Standing with Outstretched Arms

Saint Dominic was also seen praying with his hands and arms extended in the form of a cross as far as he could make them go and as erect as possible, according to a witness who saw this and told me himself. This was how he prayed when God restored the boy Napoleon to life in response to his prayer in the sacristy of the convent of San Sisto in Rome;[38] likewise in church, during the celebration of Mass, he levitated,[39] as the devout and holy sister Cecilia[40] told us, who herself was present and saw this along with a crowd of others. Here Dominic was like Elijah[41] when he raised the widow's son, stretching himself over the body of the child. He prayed in the same way when he delivered the English pilgrims near Toulouse[42] when they nearly drowned in the river, as is written elsewhere. This is also how the Lord prayed while hanging on the cross, namely, with hands and arms stretched out, when "with loud cries and tears . . . he was heard because of his reverent submission."[43] The holy man of God, Dominic, did not use this way of praying very frequently. He did so only when he was aware by God's inspiration that some great wonder was going to come about by virtue of his prayer. Also he neither forbade the brothers to pray this way, nor did he encourage them to do so.

When he raised the boy from the dead,[44] praying and standing with his arms and hands stretched out in the form of a cross, we have no idea what he said at that time. Perhaps he spoke

---

38. A church in Rome founded in the fourth century and dedicated to Pope Saint Sixtus II (r. 257–258); Dominic brought different communities of nuns together there and formed them in the monastic life as Dominican nuns.

39. Levitation refers to the extraordinary phenomenon of someone being lifted up off the ground in a prayer of ecstasy. This uncommon form of ecstatic experience was a symbol of extraordinary docility to the word of God.

40. Sister Cecilia (1200–1290) was a member of the monastery of San Sisto and a special friend of Dominic; she left an account of the miracles of Dominic. See Tugwell 1982, 391–93.

41. In 1 Kings 17, Elijah restores life to the son of a poor widow by stretching himself out upon his body. See further discussion.

42. Dominic was standing at the edge of the Garonne River in Toulouse when a ship of English pilgrims foundered. As Dominic prayed with arms extended, the pilgrims were saved from drowning.

43. Hebrews 5:7.

44. On these various miracles and their relationship to Dominic's canonization process, see my introduction.

Elijah's words, "O Lord my God, let this child's life come into him again,"[45] just as he followed Elijah's manner of praying. But the brothers and sisters and cardinals, and the others present, were paying attention to Dominic's way of praying, which was unusual and remarkable for them, and they did not remember the words that he said, nor did they feel free to ask the holy and extraordinary Dominic about them later, because on this occasion he was a source of amazement and an object of reverence for them all.

Sometimes Dominic carefully, deliberately, devoutly, and with great attention recited the words of the psalter that mention this way of praying, namely, "Lord, God of my salvation, I cry out to you in the night . . . I call to you, Lord, all the day long: I stretch out my hands to you,"[46] and also, "Hear my prayer, O Lord; give ear to my supplication in your faithfulness; answer me in your righteousness," all the way down to, "I stretch out my hands to you; my soul thirsts for you like a parched land. Answer me quickly, O Lord."[47]

This makes clear for those devoted to prayer what our father taught by this way of praying, when he desired to give himself over to God by the force of his prayer in the most profound way, or rather when he became aware by secret inspiration that he would be powerfully moved by God with a particular grace for his own benefit or that of another. Here they can find themselves instructed by the teaching of David, the example of Elijah, the charity of Christ and the devotion of Dominic, as shown in this illustration.

---

45. 1 Kings 17:21.
46. Psalm 88:1, 9.
47. Psalm 143:1, 6.

The Seventh Way of Praying

Figure 11.9. Seventh Way of Praying: Standing with Upraised Body and Hands

Frequently at prayer Dominic was found reaching out for heaven, with his hands lifted high above his head like an arrow shot directly upward from a bow. His hands were either joined together or perhaps slightly opened as if to accept something being offered from above.

It is believed that he grew in grace at such times and was caught up in rapture,[48] so that his prayer obtained from God the gifts of the Holy Spirit for the order that he had founded and for himself and his brothers, along with the delight of putting the Beatitudes[49] into practice. As a result, in the deepest poverty, in moments of bitterness, in violent persecution, moved by hunger and thirst for justice, and in the anxiety of striving for mercy, the friars would all consider it a blessing to observe the commandments and to carry out the evangelical counsels. At such times the holy father seemed to be carried off into the holy of holies[50] and into the third heaven.[51] Following this kind of praying, whether correcting or dispensing or preaching, he acted like a prophet, as was noted in the *Miracles*.[52]

---

48. Here "rapture" translates the Latin *raptus*, meaning "seized," which implies passivity and docility to the powerful action of the Holy Spirit.

49. Matthew 5:1–12, which contains Jesus's Sermon on the Mount, refers to those who enact the values of the kingdom of heaven as "Blessed" (Lat.: *beati*), with the associated values listed as eight attitudes and behaviors (Beatitudes). Under one expression they include the following states and associated blessings: (1) The poor in spirit (kingdom of heaven), (2) Those who mourn (comfort), (3) The meek (inheritance of the earth), (4) Those who hunger and thirst for righteousness (fulfillment), (5) The merciful (mercy), (6) The pure in heart (vision of God), (7) The peacemakers (children of God), and (8) Those persecuted for righteousness (kingdom of God).

50. Referring metaphorically to the inmost sanctuary of the Temple in Jerusalem, but in Christian terms, to the court of heaven (as in Heb. 9:24).

51. A reference to Saint Paul's experience in 2 Corinthians 12:2 (see fn. 48). Being lifted up to heaven signifies that Dominic experienced communion with God. Paul used the phrase "third heaven" (verse 2) and then indicated in verse 4 that this is where Paradise is located.

52. This refers to the *Miracula beati Dominici* (Miracles of the Blessed Dominic), an account of Dominic's miracles witnessed by Sister Cecilia, a contemporary and beloved friend of the saint. See Tugwell 1985, 10, 13.

[Here is a brief story to give you an example. Once after praying in this way at Bologna,[53] the holy master Dominic sought the advice of the senior brothers about things that needed to be discussed, as was his custom; because, he said, good things may be revealed to one that are not revealed to another, as happened with the prophets. But then the sacristan[54] came and called one of the brothers taking part in this meeting to go to the chapel for women to hear a confession, and he foolishly added in a voice not loud enough to be heard by holy master Dominic, "A beautiful woman is asking for you; come quickly." Inspired by the Holy Spirit, Dominic then became troubled and the councilors regarded him with anxiety. Then he ordered the sacristan to return to him and he said, "What did you just say?" He replied, "I asked a priest to come to the church." And the father said, "Shame on you! Confess what you really said. God, who made all things, made me aware of your thoughts and the words that you imagined you spoke in secret." And he disciplined him right there forcefully and for a long time, so that those present were moved to compassion because of his bruises. Then he said, "Go on your way, my son; you have learned from this how to look at a woman so that you will not judge her by her appearance. Pray that God will give you chastity in your eyes." So clearly he knew what was hidden, and he corrected the folly of this brother and taught him through correction, as he had foreseen it all in prayer. The brethren were amazed that he said that this must be done; but the holy master replied, "Our righteousness, compared to that of God, is like a filthy rag."[55]][56]

So the holy father did not remain in this kind of praying for a long time but returned to himself as if he were coming from far away, and he seemed like a stranger to the world because of his appearance and his behavior. However, while he prayed, the brothers sometimes clearly heard him speaking, saying like the prophet: "Hear the voice of my supplication, as I cry to you for help, as I lift up my hands toward your most holy sanctuary."[57] The holy master taught his friars to pray like this by both word and example, citing this verse of the psalm, "Come, bless the Lord, all you servants of the Lord, who stand by night in the house of the Lord: lift up your hands to the holy place, and bless the Lord,"[58] and also, "I call upon you, O Lord; come quickly to me; give ear to my voice when I call to you. Let my prayer be counted as incense before you, and the lifting up of my hands as an evening sacrifice."[59] The image here will teach you to understand all this better.

---

53. The Dominican priory in Bologna, Italy, was an important center for the order; the first two General Chapters of the Dominicans were held there. Bologna was also an important medieval university town. Dominic died there in August 1221. Today the Basilica of San Domenico is located there, which houses the relics of Saint Dominic in the *Arca di San Domenico* (Ark of Saint Dominic) designed by the Italian sculptor Nicola Pisano (ca. 1220–ca. 1284) in 1264. The priory in Bologna has set aside the room used by Saint Dominic as a shrine for veneration by the friars and by visitors.

54. The sacristan is the friar in charge of tending to the care of the sacristy—the room where all the equipment and appurtenances for liturgies in the church are stored and prepared for use. The sacristan usually assures the availability of friars for leading services or serving the faithful in the sacraments.

55. See Isaiah 64:6.

56. The brackets indicate that this story and the one in the "ninth way" are extraneous to the precise description of Dominic's manner of praying and may be later additions.

57. Psalm 28:2.

58. Psalm 134:1–2.

59. Psalm 141:1–2.

The Eighth Way of Praying

Figure 11.10. Eighth Way of Praying: Sitting and Reading

Holy father Dominic had yet another way of praying that was beautiful, devout, and full of grace. After the canonical hours[60] and following the thanksgiving said in common after the meal, our father would go off quickly to some solitary place, a cell or elsewhere, to read or pray, alert and anointed with the spirit of devotion that had been aroused by the divine words that had been chanted in choir or read during the meal. There he would sit down to read or pray, recollecting himself and placing himself in the presence of God. He sat peacefully and opened some book before him, fortified with the sign of the cross. As he read, his mind would be moved by a kind of sweetness as if he were hearing the Lord speaking to him, as it says in the psalm, "Let me hear what God the Lord will speak, for he will speak peace to his people, to his faithful, to those who turn to him in their hearts."[61] As if he were debating with a friend and nodding his head, at one moment he appeared to be impatient and then at another quiet and listening, then again he would seem to be disputing and arguing, then laughing and weeping at the same time, fixing his gaze, then lowering it and quietly speaking and striking his breast. To some curious person who wanted to watch him from hiding, our father Saint Dominic appeared to be like Moses[62] when he had gone into the depths of the desert and saw the burning bush and the Lord speaking and calling out to him to humble himself. This man of God had the prophet's habit of moving quickly from his reading into prayer and from meditation into contemplation.[63]

---

60. "Canonical hours" is another expression for the Divine Office, which is also known as the Liturgy of Hours and the Breviary. These are the seven prayer sessions, composed mostly of psalms, which the friars prayed at intervals in community each day.

61. Psalm 85:8.

62. See Exodus 3:2ff. Moses was captivated by a bush in flames that was not consumed by the fire and there met God, who sent him on his mission to set the Hebrews free.

63. There is no strict technical definition of these two terms. In the context, however, it seems clear that *meditation* (Lat.: *meditatio*) refers to reflection where the mind is active and seeking to know the holy, while *contemplation* (Lat.: *contemplatio*) refers to an experience where the fruit of study or prayer is a spiritual gift beyond words.

When he was reading like this all by himself, he would venerate the book and bow toward it and sometimes kiss it, above all if it were the book of the gospels or if he had read words that Christ had spoken with his own mouth. Sometimes also he would hide his face and turn it aside, or put his face in his hands and cover it a bit with his capuce.[64] He could become very anxious and full of yearning, and even rise and bow slightly with respect as if he were thanking some very important person for the favors he had received. Then, refreshed and at peace again, he would go back to reading his book.

---

64. The capuce is the hood on the uppermost garment in the Dominican habit. It was (is) often worn by the friars during prayer and study, especially in drafty European priories where central heating is not dependable.

The Ninth Way of Praying

Figure 11.11. Ninth Way of Praying: On a Journey

Dominic observed this last way of praying when he was going from one country to another, especially when he was in a solitary place. He delighted himself with his meditations during his contemplation, and sometimes he remarked to his companions on the road, "It is written in the prophet Hosea, 'I will now allure her, and bring her into the wilderness and speak tenderly to her.' "[65] Also sometimes he went aside from his companions or went on ahead or more often fell back behind them; and following at a distance, he prayed and walked while a fire began to burn within his meditation. And then something unusual would happen when he prayed like this: it was as if he were brushing away hot cinders or chasing away flies from before his face; and because of this he often strengthened himself with the sign of the cross. The brothers thought that in this kind of praying the saint became attuned to the full meaning of sacred Scripture and to the very marrow of the meaning of God's words, arriving at a bold power to preach fervently about the intimate mysteries of the Holy Spirit hidden in the world.

[To mention but one of many stories, it once happened that the devil came to the church of the Friars Preachers in Bologna in the form of a vain and lustful young man and asked for a confessor.[66] Five priests were brought to him one after the other. This was because the devil so disturbed and badly excited the first confessor by what he said that the priest got up from hearing the confession and refused to listen to such dreadful things to the end. The second confessor did the same, and so did the third, the fourth, and the fifth. They went away quietly and did not ever want to reveal what happened in this confession, since from their point of view they thought it was a sacramental confession, although it was really the devil. Then, the sacristan

---

65. Hosea 2:14.

66. This refers to a priest able to hear his confession in the sacrament of Penance.

approached Saint Dominic who was present in the priory and complained to him that all five of these priests were unable to hear one sinner's confession. "This is a scandal," he added, "that the friars preach about penance and yet are unwilling to give the sacrament of penance to sinners." Then holy father Dominic got up from his reading, prayer, and contemplation, not unaware of what was going on, I think, and came to hear the devil's confession. When he entered the church, the devil approached him and immediately our holy father recognized who it was and said to him, "You evil spirit, why do you tempt God's servants under this pretense of piety?" And he reproached him severely. The devil disappeared at once, but he left a terrible stench of sulphur[67] behind in the church. The sacristan then quieted down and got over his anger with the priests.]

---

67. The stench of sulphur seems to be intended to evoke the stink of hell, as described in Revelation 14:10, where the damned are described as tortured in burning sulphur. In both cases (this manuscript and the book of Revelation), readers are well advised to remember that this is edifying religious literature, not journalism.

Chapter 12

Daoist Internal Alchemy

Liu Huayang's *Huiming jing*

Louis Komjathy

The *Huiming jing* (Scripture on Wisdom and Life-Destiny; ZW 131)[1] is a late eighteenth-century work on Daoist internal alchemy (*neidan*). Originally written in Chinese, the text was composed by Liu Huayang (1735–1799), a Chan Buddhist monk. In the *Huiming jing*, Liu describes an eight-stage practice aimed at complete psychosomatic transformation, often referred to as "immortality" or "transcendence" in Daoism. The *Huiming jing* might thus be read as a Daoist *neidan* text and/or as a Chan Buddhist text. It appears to be addressed to Liu Huayang's disciples and Chan Buddhist monks, but it later became "canonized" in the Wu-Liu lineage of Daoist internal alchemy. The latter is technically a sublineage of the Longmen (Dragon Gate) lineage of the Quanzhen (Complete Perfection) monastic order. The text eventually became highly influential in both Daoist circles and the modern Qigong (Ch'i-kung) movement.

Liu Huayang and Eighteenth-Century Chinese Religiosity

The *Huiming jing* was written by Liu Huayang (Chuanlu [Transmission Vessel]; 1735–1799), a Chan Buddhist monk. The text's and its author's location in the landscape of Chinese religious history is complex. On the one hand, the *Huiming jing* presents itself as a text on Daoist internal alchemy. On the other hand, it was written by a Chan Buddhist monk and represents a Chan Buddhist reconceptualization of Daoist techniques. Thus, the reader is faced with the question of religious affiliation. Does the text describe a "Buddhist practice influenced by Daoism" or "Daoist technique practiced by Buddhists"? Or, should we discard such rigid categories altogether? The matter becomes even more complex in terms of the text's subsequent history: it was incorporated into the Wu-Liu lineage, technically a sublineage of the Longmen (Dragon Gate) lineage of Quanzhen (Complete Perfection) Daoism. One must thus be attentive to Liu's personal history as well as his various cultural influences. In the present section, I discuss the relevant biographical and historical background, while the subsequent section focuses more on Liu's location at the intersection between Buddhism and Daoism, especially as expressed in his writings.

As Liu Huayang traces one element of his own lineage to Wu Shouyang (Chongxu [Infused Emptiness]; 1574–1644),[2] and as Liu eventually became associated with the Wu-Liu lineage, we should familiarize ourselves with these individuals. The name of the lineage refers to Wu Shouyang and Liu Huayang, that is, it is a lineage associated with these two teachers.

Liu Huayang, whose Buddhist religious and ordination name was Chuanlu (Transmission Vessel), was a native of Hongdu (present-day Nanchang), Jiangxi (southeast China).[3] He lived during the Qing dynasty (1644–1911), a Chinese historical period that, together with the Ming dynasty (1368–1644), is often referred to as the "late imperial period" of Chinese dynastic history. While the Ming dynasty was ruled by Chinese emperors, the Qing was a non-Chinese dynasty ruled by the Manchus, a "non-Han" ethnic group from the northeast who descended from the earlier Jurchens. As discussed in more detail later, in terms of the three primary Chinese religions (Confucianism, Daoism, and Chinese Buddhism), the late imperial period was characterized by popularization, simplification, and syncretism. Within this historical context, Liu first pursued a Confucian literati career, but he eventually became a Chan Buddhist monk at Shuanglian si (Temple of the Double Lotus; near Anqing, Anhui). Having failed to attain enlightenment, Liu left the temple in search of a master. According to his own apparently straightforward account in the preface to the *Huiming jing*,

> I set my determination [to meditate] every night during the second drum-sounding [9–11p.m.]. I prostrated myself on the ground, swearing an oath and praying with deep reverence. I beseeched the powers above to help me find what I was seeking. After half a year, I was fortunate to encounter Master Wu Chongxu, who transmitted secret instructions to me. Suddenly, I became totally awakened and understood the Way of Wisdom and Life-Destiny (*huiming zhi dao*). It is the numinous substance that is our original being and endowment. (ZW 131, 5.876)

This event occurred in 1780, when Liu received a spiritual transmission from Wu Shouyang, a Longmen Daoist who had died 136 years earlier! The account in turn allows for a number of unconfirmable conjectures regarding the "secret transmission." The most straightforward would be that this is a fabrication, a lineage construction, and "invented tradition" (see Hobsbawm and Ranger 1983). However, this viewpoint requires one to address the motivation behind the selection of Wu Shouyang and Liu's apparently strange decision to undertake Daoist internal alchemy practice under the guidance of a deceased Daoist master. As discussed later, Wu Shouyang was also a native of Nanchang, Jiangxi, so the local connection may be one major influence. Another possibility is that Liu Huayang had gained access to texts written by Wu. Under this reading, the secret transmission derived from Liu's own reading and study, from his practice of the methods contained in Wu's writings. On a more esoteric level, the secret transmission may have involved a mystical experience, meditative vision, dream, and/or spirit mediumship. With respect to the former, encounters with immortals (*xianren*), whether embodied or disembodied, are a common experience in Daoist internal alchemy practice (see Komjathy 2007). This is also true of meditative visions and of dream teachings and transmissions. In terms of mediumship, we know that there was a great amount of mediumistic and spirit-writing activity at this time and in this region. In fact, it resulted in a variety of textual productions such as the influential *Taiyi jinhua zongzhi* (Secret of the Golden Flower of Great Unity; abbr. *Jinhua zongzhi*) (see Esposito 2000) and possibly Wu's own *Jindan yaojue* (see later discussion in this introduction). Interestingly, the *Jinhua zongzhi* was eventually published together with the *Huiming jing*, our primary text (Baldrian-Hussein 2008a). So, it may be that Liu encountered Wu through some anomalous experience or religious activity. Interestingly, if the aforementioned account is read literally, it appears that the "encounter" was directly connected to Liu's consistent and prolonged practice of prostration and meditation. In any case, after practicing the transmitted methods for some time, Liu met the obscure Buddhist monk Huyun (Gourd Cloud; d.u.) in Kuanglu, Jiangxi. Huyun then provided instructions on the final stages of his training. Regardless of the historical accuracy of these details, they tell us something fundamentally important: Liu's own religious practice involved Daoist internal alchemy in combination with Chan Buddhist meditation. Liu died at Renshou si (Temple of Humane Longevity) in Beijing in 1799.

As mentioned, Liu Huayang claimed that he received a secret transmission from Wu Shouyang, and he practiced Daoist internal alchemy in a manner that was influenced by Wu's writings. Thus, although the first known reference to the "Wu-Liu lineage" appears much later, Liu's own account seems to add some justification for the association. Wu Shouyang (1574–1644)[4] lived roughly 150 years earlier than Liu, during the Ming dynasty. Wu, who had the Daoist names of Chongxu (Infused Emptiness) and Duanyang (Upright Yang), was born in Nanchang, Jiangxi (southeast China), the same place as Liu Huayang.[5] Wu's father, Wu Xide (d.u.), was a high-ranking local official in Nanchang. He attained the highest rank in the imperial civil service examination of 1562 and was subsequently appointed to various high posts in the imperial bureaucracy. He eventually received the position of prefect in Weimo, Yunnan, in 1578 but died there the following year. Wu Shouyang was only four years old. Wu's mother was born in 1552 and died in 1640, when Wu was sixty-four and only four years before his own death. The hagiographies differ on when Wu began his own Daoist training. Some, in typical Confucian fashion and emphasizing filial piety, claim that he waited until after the death of his mother; others, following a Daoist praxis-oriented and more monastic viewpoint, suggest that he began formal training while his mother was still alive. The dates of his various writings (discussed later) add support for the latter. In any case, it is significant that, in a traditional Chinese society wherein Confucian values were preeminent, Wu grew up without a father; as possibly the eldest son, Wu was responsible for caring for his mother.

As one might expect given his father's position and his location in Chinese society, Wu received a traditional Confucian education. He began studying the Confucian classics around the age of ten, and his uncle, Wu Lizhai (d.u.), who was interested in attaining immortality, supplied the young Wu Shouyang with Daoist books. By the age of twenty, it appears that Wu had developed a root in Buddhist contemplative practice centering on *samādhi* (meditative adsorption) and was familiar with the classics of Chinese culture, including Confucian literature. Having been repeatedly recommended for official court positions, Wu fled to Lushan (Mount Lu; Jiujiang, Jiangxi). There he met, trained with, and was ordained by Cao Changhua (Huanyang [Reverted Yang]; 1562–1622). This occurred in 1612,[6] when Wu was thirty-eight. Cao Changhua was a self-identified Longmen monk and a disciple of Li Zhenyuan (Xu'an [Empty Hut]; 1525–1579), with the latter having received training and ordination under Zhang Jingxu (Hupi [Tiger Skin]; fl. 1563–1582).[7] Cao emphasized the complementary nature of Buddhist and Daoist practice.[8] The

Zhang-Li-Cao line would make Wu Shouyang an eighth-generation Longmen monk. It appears that during this time Wu also studied with an obscure Daoist teacher named Li Niwan (d.u.), who trained him in thunder magic (*leifa*) in the Jin'gai mountains (near Huzhou, Zhejiang). From 1613 to 1618, Wu served as the tutor of Prince Ji, possibly Zhu Youjian (1611–1644), who eventually became the Chongzhen Emperor (r. 1627–1644), the last Ming emperor. During this time, Wu received the title of "national teacher." Perhaps influenced by the political turmoil of the time and anticipating the fall of the Ming, Wu then went into seclusion in the Tiantai mountains (Zhejiang). There a fellow eighth-generation Longmen Daoist named Zhao Zhensong (Fuyang [Returning Yang]; d. 1628) convinced him to seek instruction from Wang Changyue (Kunyang [Paradisiacal Yang]; ca. 1594–1680), the eventual founder of the official or "orthodox" Longmen lineage. This supposedly took place at the Daoist grotto-heaven (*dongtian*) of Qingxu located on Wangwu shan (Mount Wangwu; near Longgang, Shanxi). Wu reportedly attained immortality at this northern retreat after practicing techniques of the "reverted elixir" (*huandan*) (Boltz 1987, 200).[9] Wu later returned to Jiangxi and devoted himself to teaching and writing; the prefaces to his works date from between 1622 and 1640. In the latter year, Wu interrupted his religious activities in order to tend to his mother, who was in the final stages of life. After her death in 1640, Wu went into complete seclusion. Wu Shouyang died in 1644 at an unidentified location. His teachings were, in turn, preserved and transmitted by his senior disciples, Gu Yutao, Li Xiren, Wu Shouxu, Wu Taiyi, Zhao Zhixin, and Zhu Changchun.

In terms of Wu's teachings and writings, which later exerted some influence on Liu Huayang and members of the Wu-Liu lineage, Farzeen Baldrian-Hussein (2008c) provides the following summary:

> Wu Shouyang describes his Taoist [Daoist] practice as a long, painstaking, and expensive process, and criticizes adepts who soon get discouraged. Wu himself selflessly served Cao Changhua, sometimes going without food to bring meals to his master. He also raised funds for Cao by selling some of his own ancestral land. The theme of financial support appears frequently in Wu's writings and is included among the requirements for the final stages of the practice in order to overcome the four difficulties (*sinan*): time, financial resources, right companions, and choice of an auspicious site. (1047)

Anticipating Liu's own approach, Wu also emphasizes that the pursuit of immortality is basically analogous to the attainment of Buddhahood. In addition, he draws on a wide variety of texts, including the earlier Quanzhen and so-called Nanzong (Southern School) traditions of internal alchemy. Perhaps most relevant for the present discussion, Wu cites the *Huayan jing (Avataṃsaka Sūtra)*, which is discussed later. Finally, Wu emphasizes that the "way of the immortality" (*xiandao*) involves both *qi* and spirit; cultivation of the former leads to longevity, while cultivation of the latter leads to immortality (see later discussion).

Two additional elements related to Liu's life and sociohistorical context are important for understanding the production of the *Huiming jing*, namely, eighteenth-century Chinese Buddhism and Longmen Daoism. With respect to the former, especially in terms of Liu Huayang's form of Chan Buddhism, the situation is currently understudied. On the one hand, we may locate Liu Huayang in the "revitalization" and "reinvention" of Chan Buddhism occurring during the Qing dynasty (see Wu 2008). On the other hand, it is unclear the degree to which Liu Huayang was anomalous or representative of eighteenth-century Chan Buddhism. That is, the following question remains unanswered: To what degree were Chan Buddhist monks practicing Daoist internal alchemy? The same is true with respect to emphasis on the *Huayan jing*, a text more often associated with the Tiantai (Celestial Terrace) and Huayan (Flower Garland) schools of Chinese Buddhism. In any case, late imperial Chan Buddhism was primarily a monastic tradition, in which celibate monks and nuns lived in monasteries. The latter formed a vast network throughout China. In terms of Liu's own life, this is obvious from his ordination at Shuanglian si in Anqing, Anhui; his eventual training under Huyun in Kuanglu, Jiangxi; and his residence in Beijing during the final years of his life. Just as we may view Liu Huayang through the lens of late imperial Chan Buddhism, we may view the latter through the former. From this perspective, some Chan Buddhists were reading the *Huayan jing* and *Lengyan jing* (*Śūraṅgama Sūtra*) as the clearest expressions of enlightenment. These same Chan Buddhist monks were practicing Daoist internal alchemy in combination with Chan meditation. Interestingly, the associated *neidan* practice was reconceptualized according to a Chan Buddhist worldview. It would be a mistake, however, to see this as a "corruption" or "distortion" of Daoist internal alchemy practice. Late imperial expressions of the latter not only were characterized by extensive use of Chan Buddhist terms and views, but Liu's writings also eventually became incorporated into the Wu-Liu "Daoist" lineage and became highly influential in Daoist circles.

In terms of late imperial Daoism, and especially Daoism during the Qing dynasty, the Chinese religious landscape consisted of the two dominant institutional divisions of Daoism, namely, Quanzhen (Complete Perfection) and Zhengyi (Orthodox Unity), with the latter being an alternate name of Tianshi (Celestial Masters). The former is a monastic tradition consisting of celibate monks and nuns, while the latter is a householder tradition consisting of married priests and a larger lay community. Daoism during the Qing dynasty was dominated by the Quanzhen monastic order, especially its Longmen (Dragon Gate) lineage (see Esposito 2000, 2001, 2004; Goossaert 2007). Although conventionally associated with Qiu Chuji (Changchun [Perpetual Spring]; 1148–1227), one of the senior members of the early Quanzhen community, the official, "orthodox" Longmen lineage was actually established by Wang Changyue (Kunyang [Paradisiacal Yang]; ca. 1594–1680). As we saw earlier, some accounts of Wu Shouyang claim that he trained under the latter. In any case, Wang Changyue was abbot of Baiyun guan (White Cloud Monastery; Beijing) during the mid-seventeenth century. He established the official Longmen lineage as based on three ordination ranks associated with three corresponding monastic manuals and precept texts: (1) Wondrous Practice/Initial Perfection and the *Chuzhen jie* (Precepts of Initial Perfection; JY 292; ZW 404); (2) Wondrous Virtue/Medium Ultimate and the *Zhongji jie* (Precepts of Medium Ultimate; JY 293; ZW 405); and (3) Wondrous Dao/Celestial Immortality and *Tianxian jie* (Precepts of Celestial Immortality; JY 291; ZW 403) (see Kohn 2004; Komjathy 2013a). An expression of Quanzhen monasticism, within which the core religious commitments and monastic vows are celibacy, sobriety, and vegetarianism, the mainland Chinese Longmen lineage is characterized by precept study and application and by the practice of lineage-based internal alchemy. For present purposes, these details are significant because Wu Shouyang, Liu's divine teacher, and the Wu-Liu lineage are associated with Longmen. As mentioned, the Wu-Liu lineage is technically a sublineage of Longmen. From this perspective, Liu Huayang's lineage of internal alchemy was Longmen. Longmen flowed into Liu's system and into Chan Buddhism, which, in turn, flowed back into Longmen.

Buddho-Daoist Syncretism and the Wu-Liu Lineage

As has now become clear, or perhaps obscure, Liu Huayang, a Chan Buddhist monk practicing and teaching Daoist internal alchemy in concert with Chan meditation, is not easily categorized. He falls between the neat and tidy categories of "Buddhist" and "Daoist." He embodies and expresses one way in which Buddhists and Daoists interacted, namely, collaboration and mutual influence. While much has been written on historical patterns of interaction characterized by "conquest," competition, and debate, there can be little doubt that Chinese Buddhists and Daoists have peacefully inhabited the same sacred sites and positively influenced each other. The latter tendency is often referred to as "syncretism," or the combining of elements associated with a supposedly distinct religious tradition with those of another. Although overly simplistic, this phenomenon is characteristic of traditional Chinese religiosity and becomes especially prominent in the late imperial period. Syncretism is so strong in Chinese religiosity that some scholars prefer to discuss "Chinese religion" rather than Confucianism, Daoism, and Chinese Buddhism. However, this is largely a popular view of Chinese religion. There have been and remain ordained Daoists and Buddhists associated with their respective traditions. In the present case, Liu Huayang was a Chan Buddhist monk, while Wu Shouyang was a Quanzhen monk. Liu Huayang is, in turn, perhaps best characterized as a Chinese Buddhist adherent and a Daoist sympathizer. He clearly speaks primarily as the former. His form of religious practice might be best characterized as "Buddho-Daoist syncretism."

A close reading of the *Huiming jing* reveals specific elements of Liu Huayang's Buddho-Daoist syncretism. Liu Huayang was a Chan Buddhist monk, and Chan Buddhism is his primary worldview and interpretive framework. Even though Liu Huayang was practicing Daoist internal alchemy, he presents it from a Chan Buddhist perspective.

Chan Buddhism is a Chinese school of Mahāyāna (Greater Vehicle) Buddhism. The latter began as the second major "vehicle" of Indian Buddhism, was transmitted to and transformed in China, and became the dominant form of Buddhism throughout East Asia. It is the second piece of this story that is most relevant here, namely, the Sinification (making Chinese) of Mahāyāna Buddhism. Chan Buddhism follows Mahāyāna Buddhism in emphasizing foundational Buddhist views in combination with a stronger emphasis on "emptiness" (Chn.: *kong*; Skt.: *śūnyatā*) and interdependence as well as an increased recognition of the laity. As will be discussed in more detail later, Chan Buddhists identify all beings as capable of attaining enlightenment (perhaps as already enlightened), as having the potential to become buddhas (awakened beings). Chan Buddhism, better known in its later Japanese expression of Zen Buddhism, is one of the major Chinese schools of Buddhism, with the others being Huayan (Jpn.: Kegon; Flower Garland), Jingtu (Jpn.: Jōdō; Pure Land), and Tiantai (Jpn.: Tendai; Celestial Terrace) (see Wright 1959; Ch'en 1964). The name *chan* is a Chinese transliteration of the Sanskrit *dhyāna* (Pali: *jhāna*), which has a variety of contextualized meanings. In terms of Chan, it refers to meditation broadly conceived and to particular types of meditation, often referred to under the general name *zuochan* (Jpn.: *zazen*; lit., seated *dhyāna*). Although Chan Buddhism claims that its original transmission occurred between Śākyamuni Buddha, the historical Buddha, and his disciple Kāśyapa, the tradition was actually first established in China. It is traditionally associated with the obscure Central Asian missionary-monk Bodhidharma (ca. 6th c. CE), the imaged twenty-eighth Indian Patriarch and first Chinese Patriarch of Chan. While this account, like the construction of the tradition in terms of the so-called Gradual (Northern) and Sudden (Southern) Schools, has been disputed in modern scholarship (see, e.g., McRae 1987), it has been the primary emic (insider) view. In addition, Chan Buddhists have tended to claim that Chan is "a special transmission outside the sutras, not dependent on language and texts, pointing directly to mind." Emphasizing intensive meditation practice and experience, including enlightenment as an innate capacity, one's "original nature" or "face before birth," Chan Buddhists have tended to emphasize "mind-to-mind transmission." The latter points toward the central importance of teachers, training, transmission, and direct experience in the tradition. Finally, Chan Buddhism is primarily a monastic tradition, though, following texts such as the Mahāyāna *Vimalakīrti Sūtra* (Discourse of Vimalakīrti), it has recognized the possibility of attaining enlightenment as a lay practitioner.

Here we should be familiar with a number of other historical dimensions of Chan Buddhism. Chan Buddhism emerged through diverse influences. In addition to its connection with foundational Buddhism, Mahāyāna Buddhism, and Sinified Buddhism, Chan drew upon the Mahāyāna *Prajñā-pāramitā* (Perfection of Wisdom) literature and *Tathāgata-garbha* (Buddha-embryo) literature (see Dumoulin 1988). The former emphasizes the importance of *prajñā*, or "wisdom," especially in terms of recognizing the emptiness of separate existence and individuated personhood. The latter emphasizes the inherent capacity for enlightenment or Buddhahood in all beings, referred as the "Buddha-embryo" or "womb of Buddhahood." In Chan Buddhism, the intersection of these two doctrines is clearly expressed in the phrase, "If you see the Buddha on the road, kill him." One must "kill" the discriminating mind, based on subject/object dichotomies, and recognize that *one is the Buddha*. It is the ordinary or habituated mind that prevents one from realizing that one is already enlightened. At the same time, Chan Buddhism is a Chinese school of Mahāyāna Buddhism. In addition to the influence of earlier Indian Buddhism and Mahāyāna, Chan only emerged in a Chinese social context and under Chinese cultural influences. One key influence was classical Daoism, especially the *Zhuangzi* (*Chuang-tzu*; Book of Master Zhuang). Although yet to receive adequate scholarly attention, one could make a strong argument that Chan Buddhism is a form of Daoicized Buddhism. Through the influence of the *Zhuangzi*, one finds a strong Chan Buddhist emphasis on the Dao (Way); teacher-disciple transmissions, especially as expressed in "discourse records" (*yulu*); as well as a form of contentless, nonconceptual, and nondualistic meditation indebted to Daoist discussions of the "fasting of the heart-mind" (*xinzhai*) and "sitting-in-forgetfulness" (*zuowang*). In fact, one finds allusions to the *Zhuangzi* throughout Chan literature. For example, when speaking about Chan meditation, Chan Buddhists often speak about a "body of withered wood and mind of dead-ashes" as well as "casting off body and mind," phrases derived from chapters 2 and 6 of the *Zhuangzi*, respectively. In some sense, basic Chan meditation is a modified form of classical Daoist apophatic meditation.

In terms of his own expression of Chan Buddhism, Liu Huayang follows the aforementioned outline by emphasizing the importance and possibility of attaining enlightenment. As will be explored in more detail in the subsequent section, Liu understands all beings as containing the capacity for awakening. This viewpoint combines the Buddhist notion of *tathāgata-garbha* with the Daoist notion of the "immortal embryo" (*xiantai*), that is, the transcendent spirit created through Daoist internal alchemy practice. As Liu Huayang envisions and expresses it, Buddhist enlightenment is most clearly expressed in the *Huayan jing* and *Lengyan jing*, Chinese names for two earlier Indian Mahāyāna Buddhist *sūtra*s originally written in Sanskrit and eventually translated into Chinese. The former is the Chinese version of the *Avataṃsaka Sūtra* (Flower Garland Sutra;

see Cleary 1993), while the latter is the Chinese version of the *Śūraṅgama Sūtra* (Discourse on Indestructible [*Samādhi*]; see Luk 1966; BTTS 2009). The *Avataṃsaka Sūtra* occupied a central position in Huayan, named after the text, and Tiantai Buddhism. In these Chinese Mahāyāna schools, the text is believed to contain the most complete and highest expression of Śākyamuni Buddha's enlightenment. The *Śūraṅgama Sūtra* was highly influential in the Chan Buddhist circles. It emphasizes the attainment of higher levels of consciousness through the purification of defilements and delusion, and the importance of *samādhi* (meditative absorption or concentration) in the attainment of Buddhahood. In the *Huiming jing*, these texts are apparently cited as support for Liu's account of enlightenment, which is accomplished through the practice of Daoist internal alchemy.

Daoist internal alchemy (*neidan*) is a later form of Daoist meditation, which first became systematized during the later Tang (618–907) and early Song dynasties (960–1279). Before discussing Daoist internal alchemy, some basic information on Daoism, or the tradition of the Dao, is necessary. Daoism is an indigenous Chinese religion in which the Dao (Tao), translatable as "the Way" and "a way," is considered to be sacred or ultimately real. As a Daoist cosmological and theological category, the Dao has four primary characteristics, namely, it is the Source of everything, unnamable mystery, all-pervading sacred presence (*qi*), and universe as transformative process (Nature). In terms of historical development, scholars are divided about how best to discuss the tradition, but here we may make a simple four-part division: (1) classical Daoism, (2) early organized Daoism, (3) later organized Daoism, and (4) modern Daoism (see Komjathy 2013b). This replaces the inaccurate and outdated interpretive framework of so-called "philosophical Daoism" and so-called "religious Daoism." Classical Daoism refers to Daoism from the Warring States to the Early Han dynasty (4th–1st c. BCE), early organized Daoism to Daoism from the Later Han dynasty to the Period of Disunion (2nd–6th c. CE), later organized Daoism to Daoism from the Tang dynasty to the Qing dynasty (7th–early 20th c.), and modern Daoism to Daoism from 1912 to the present. As one would expect, there were many different Daoist communities and movements within these historical periods (see Komjathy 2013b, 2014).

Daoist internal alchemy first became systematized during the late Tang and early Song dynasties, or the late medieval period of Chinese dynastic history. The three earliest "schools" of Daoist internal alchemy are conventionally identified as Zhong-Lü, Quanzhen (Complete Perfection; a.k.a. Beizong [Northern School]), and Nanzong (Southern School) (see Needham et al. 1983; Boltz 1987; Pregadio and Skar 2000; Komjathy 2007, 2013a). The name Zhong-Lü refers to two teachers and immortals, namely, Zhongli Quan (Zhengyang [Aligned Yang]; ca. 2nd c. CE) and Lü Dongbin (Chunyang [Pure Yang]; b. ca. 798); Quanzhen refers to a state of complete psychosomatic transformation attained through successful *neidan* training; and Nanzong is a geographical designation related to a group of loosely related teachers. As mentioned earlier, Wu Shouyang was especially influenced by writings associated with the second two traditions. It is also noteworthy that the Wu-Liu lineage follows the Zhong-Lü tradition in identifying two teachers as its source and inspiration. What is important to recognize here is that late medieval *neidan* is radically different from late imperial *neidan*, the type of internal alchemy practiced by Wu Shouyang and Liu Huayang. The former is extremely complex, while the latter is a highly simplified version. Traditionally speaking, internal alchemy involves stage-based practices aimed at complete psychosomatic transformation, or "alchemical refinement." The early version of *neidan* assumes a composite view of self, wherein the postmortem fate of ordinary human beings is to dissipate into the cosmos. In order to attain postmortem existence, one must complete the process of alchemical training and transformation. One must *create* a transcendent spirit. The latter is referred to as the "embryo of immortality" (*xiantai*), "body-beyond-the-body" (*shenwai shen*), and "yang-spirit" (*yangshen*). As will become clear later, in Liu Huayang's late imperial and simplified form of "Daoist" *neidan* practice, a completely different view of self is involved. Following Buddhism more generally, Liu assumes reincarnation as an ontological given; this is a quasi-docetic view of self, wherein some aspect of consciousness continues to reincarnate. Following Chan Buddhism in particular, "self" is an illusion, and one ultimately disappears in emptiness; this is a composite or impermanence view of self, emphasizing enlightenment over afterlife.

Interestingly, Wu Shouyang's *neidan* system is associated with the Longmen lineage of Quanzhen Daoism. This became the inspiration for and influence on Liu Huayang's version. Eventually, these two teachers became associated with a new lineage of internal alchemy referred to as the Wu-Liu lineage, which is technically a sublineage of Longmen. As a combined name for a particular lineage of internal alchemy associated with Wu Shouyang and Liu Huayang, "Wu-Liu" first appeared in 1897, that is, about one hundred years after the death of Liu. In that year, a certain Deng Huiji (fl. 1890s) published the *Wu-Liu xianzong* (Immortal Tradition of Wu and Liu), alternatively translated as the "Lineage of the Immortals Wu and Liu" or "Wu-Liu Lineage of Immortality." As discussed later, the *Wu-Liu xianzong* collects two texts by Wu Shouyang and two by Liu Huayang. This lineage subsequently became identified as a subdivision of Longmen. While the designation of "Wu-Liu" appears relatively late, we have noted the ways in which Liu thought of himself as a disciple of Wu Shouyang.

Considering the associated textual corpus, there are two extant texts by Liu Huayang. First, there is the *Jinxian zhenglun* (Discourse on Confirmation of Golden Immortality; ZW 132), which was completed and printed in Anhui around 1790 and edited again in 1799 by Liu Huayang at Renshou si (Temple of Humane Longevity; Beijing). In addition to Liu's own preface, the received *Jinxian zhenglun* also includes prefaces by Gao Shuangjing (dat. 1790) of Nanchang, Jiangxi, and by the Buddhist monk Miaowu (dat. 1791). In terms of its title and contents, the *Jinxian zhenglun* sounds like a Daoist text, with *zhengyan* (experiential confirmation or verification) being a Daoist technical term for signs of successful training (see Eskildsen 2001, 2004; Komjathy 2007, 2013a). Divided into eighteen sections, the *Jinxian zhenglun* discusses the *neidan* practice of the Microcosmic Orbit and the refinement of vital essence and *qi*. Liu also discusses doubts and dangers associated with alchemical training. Second, there is the *Huiming jing* (Scripture on Wisdom and Life-Destiny; ZW 131), which is the primary text of the present chapter. Discussed in more detail later, the *Huiming jing* was completed in 1794 at Zhongjie an (Hermitage of Zhongjie [Devoted Purity]) in Wancheng (present-day Anqing), Anhui, and edited again in 1799 by Liu Huayang at Renshou si. In addition to Liu's own preface, which is one of the primary sources on his life, the received *Huiming jing* includes a preface by Sun Tingbi (dat. 1794) (Esposito 2000, 636; Baldrian-Hussein 2008a, 2008b). While the contents of the text are discussed here later, the title points in a syncretic direction. First, *jing* may refer to both a Buddhist *sūtra*, technically a discourse given by the historical Buddha, and a Daoist scripture, with Daoist *jing* usually considered to be revealed and/or inspired. With respect to the *Huiming jing*, it appears to be the latter, possibly through the influence of Wu Shouyang. The *huiming* of the title is syncretic: "wisdom" (*hui*) relates to (Buddhist) consciousness,[10] while "life-destiny" (*ming*) relates to (Daoist) longevity. As a composite term, *huiming* points toward the dual cultivation of innate nature and life-destiny as well as a state of complete psychosomatic integration. Here we should also note that Liu Huayang was still working on both texts during the final year of his life, a fact that is especially relevant with respect to the *Huiming jing*.

If we expanded the textual corpus to include the Wu-Liu lineage, especially as expressed in the *Wu-Liu xianzong*, we would include the four texts contained therein.[11] In sequential order, these are the *Tianxian zhengli*, *Xianfo hezong yulu*, *Huiming jing*, and *Jinxian zhenglun*. The first two are by Wu Shouyang, while the last two are the previously discussed texts written by Liu Huayang. Also known as the *Tianxian zhengli zhilun zengzhu*, the *Tianxian zhengli* (Correct Principles of Celestial Immortality; JY 242; ZW 127) was written in 1622, with commentaries by Wu Shouyang and his younger brother Wu Shouxu added in 1639. This text gathers and develops teachings on Daoist *neidan* transmitted to Wu from Cao Changhua. The *Xianfo hezong yulu* (Discourse Records from the Shared Lineage of Immortals and Buddhas; JY 240; ZW 126) was collected by Wu's disciples and again includes a commentary by his brother. This text also contains the "Wu zhenren xiuxian ge" (Song of Cultivating Immortality by Perfected Wu), an important poem for biographical information on Wu. The main theme of the text is that the pursuit of immortality is analogous to the attainment of Buddhahood.

Expanding the corpus still further, there are two other extant texts attributed to Wu Shouyang, namely, the *Jindan yaojue* (Essential Instructions on the Golden Elixir; JY 243; JHL 76; ZW 129) and the *Dandao jiupian* (Nine Essays on the Way of the Elixir; JY 244; JHL 78; ZW 130). An undated text, the *Jindan yaojue* is a series of essays on *neidan* principles with associated commentary, possibly by Wu's disciple Zhao Zhixin. This text may have been composed through spirit-writing (*fuji*). The *Dandao jiupian* contains a preface by Wu Shouyang dated to 1640. It presents itself as instructions given by Wu to Prince Ji.

In the present chapter, I focus on Liu Huayang's writings, especially the *Huiming jing*.

Seeking Enlightenment through Alchemy

Liu Huayang's Buddho-Daoist syncretism, especially as documented in the *Huiming jing*, involves the practice of Daoist internal alchemy in combination with Chan meditation. Liu in turn presents meditative praxis from a Chan Buddhist perspective, one in which Daoist views are reconceptualized along Chan Buddhist lines. Concisely stated, one is instructed on how to attain enlightenment through internal alchemy.

As discussed in more detail later, internal alchemy is the main form of meditation documented in the *Huiming jing*. It became one of the primary forms of Daoist meditation from the Song dynasty to the present. The indigenous term *neidan*, here translated as "internal alchemy," literally means "inner pill" or "inner cinnabar," with cinnabar (*dan*; *dansha*) being the chemical compound and substance mercuric sulfide (HgS). English equivalents borrowed from European alchemy are conventionally utilized to translate Chinese Daoist technical terms because Daoist *neidan* involves refinement and transmutation. *Neidan* emerged out of an earlier Daoist tradition called *waidan* (lit., outer pill), often translated as "external," "laboratory," or "operational alchemy." Becoming prominent during the Later Han dynasty (25–220) and Period of Disunion (220–589), *waidan* involved complex chemical compounding methods, processes, and apparatuses (see Needham et al. 1976), which aimed at creating "elixirs of immortality," or substances that would confer immortality. A highly specialized terminology was also utilized. In the case of *neidan*, the "elixir of immortality" was seen as residing *within* the body; it did not require the ingestion of external substances, as in *waidan*. Daoist *neidan* in turn utilizes complex and esoteric terminology to describe the body as well as the corresponding practices and associated experiences. Some of this terminology derives from earlier *waidan*, with the terms now referring to the body rather than external elements. Generally speaking, the goal of Daoist internal alchemy is complete psychosomatic transformation, or the creation of the "embryo of immortality" (*xiantai*). The latter is also referred to as the "body-beyond-the-body" (*shenwai shen*; i.e., the subtle or rarified body) and as the "yang-spirit" (*yangshen*; i.e., the transcendent spirit *created* through *neidan*).

As expressed in the *Huiming jing*, "Daoist" internal alchemy involves an eight-stage process,[12] although there is overlap in the first three stages. The practitioner begins by "sealing the body." One attempts to abide in a state of "nondissipation" (*wulou*; Skt.: *anāsrava*) or "cessation of outflow" (*loujin*; Skt.: *āsrava-ksaya*). Here Liu follows ascetic or monastic views emphasizing celibacy, with a Daoist layer involving the conservation of vital essence (*jing*), associated with semen in men.[13] The "outflows" (*lou*; Skt.: *āsrava*) are samsaric entanglements and forms of dissipation. As Liu explains in the tenth section of the received *Huiming jing*,

> When life-destiny becomes active, it flows out of the body. After it becomes totally dissipated, we die. . . . The root of life-destiny [vital essence and/or original *qi*] is in the kidneys. When active, it becomes water. The root of original nature [spirit and/or true awareness] is in the heart. When active, it becomes fire. If fire is immersed in water, wisdom and life-destiny do not depart. (ZW 131, 5.901)

In a Daoist context, "nondissipation" often refers to alchemical transformation, with various ordinary corporeal substances (e.g., mucus and sweat) transformed into more subtle substances (see Komjathy 2007, 2013a). From a Buddhist perspective, and perhaps most pertinent here, the state of cessation from outflow involves sensory disengagement and the elimination of desires. It is also often associated with the purification of "defilements" or "vexations" (*fannao*; Skt.: *kleśa*), such as covetousness, anger, ignorance, arrogance, doubt, and false views. That is, the apparently simple practice of "purification of consciousness" is actually quite complex. Enlightenment is characterized, at least to a certain extent, by the absence of outflow and defilements. According to the *Huiming jing*, the attainment of the state of nondissipation is preliminary, provisional, and foundational for engaging in more advanced *neidan* training.

The primary practice of the *Huiming jing* is the Microcosmic Orbit (*xiao zhoutian*), which is also translated as "Lesser Celestial Cycle." The practice is also referred to as the Waterwheel (*heche*) and Dharma Wheel (*falun*). This practice involves circulating *qi* through two corporeal meridians, or the subtle channels through which *qi* circulates. There are twelve organ meridians and eight so-called "extraordinary" meridians. The Microcosmic Orbit practice involves two of the latter. Specifically, one circulates *qi* up the Governing Vessel (*dumai*) and down the Conception Vessel (*renmai*). The former basically begins at the perineum, moves up the back centerline of the body to the crown-point, and ends in the cleft of the upper lip. The latter basically begins at the perineum, moves up the front centerline of the body, and ends in the cleft of the lower lip. In the Microcosmic Orbit, one circulates *qi* up the Governing Vessel and down the Conception Vessel in a continuous cycle. These meridians are connected by touching the tongue, often referred to as the Descending Bridge or Crimson Dragon, to the upper palate. After the completion of the practice, *qi* is stored in the lower abdomen or navel region, conventionally referred to as the lower "elixir field" (*dantian*). The practice is said to result in complete energetic integration, with the "embryo of immortality" (energetic presence) forming in the lower elixir field. As this subtle presence becomes stronger, the yang-spirit forms. The practice concludes with "wall-gazing" (*biguan*) and disappearance into the Void. The former is a name for Chan Buddhist meditation, more conventionally appearing as *zuochan*. Associated with Bodhidharma, who supposedly practiced wall-gazing for nine years, the practice involves stilling and emptying the mind (see Broughton 1999). It is a nonconceptual and contentless form of meditation. Although conventionally associated with the Caodong Chan (Jpn.: Sōtō Zen) practice of "silent illumination" (*mozhao*) and Dōgen's (1200–1253) practice of "just sitting" (*shikan-taza*) (see, e.g., Dumoulin 1990), the practice actually finds its earliest Chinese historical precedent in classical Daoist apophatic meditation. That is, there is way of reading Liu Huayang's Chan practice as a twofold reconceptualization of Daoist practice. In any case, it is common in Daoist *neidan* practice to complete the process of alchemical transformation by sitting in stillness and disappearing into unity.

In Liu Huayang's system, the Microcosmic Orbit is the primary *neidan* practice. This is a radical simplification of *neidan* training, with Liu also including illustrations in his manual. It parallels contemporaneous tendencies in late imperial *neidan* systems. However, in earlier Daoist internal alchemy, specifically in its early expressions in the late medieval period, the process of complete psychosomatic transformation is an extremely complex undertaking, with no guarantee of success. It included a complex mapping of human personhood, in which one's body consists of various vital substances, spiritual faculties, as well as hidden and subtle dimensions (see Komjathy 2007, 2013a). In terms of vital substances, the three primary ones are vital essence (*jing*), *qi* (both physical respiration and subtle breath), and spirit. Associated with health, corporeality, and the kidneys, vital essence is one's foundational or core vitality; on the most basic level, it relates to semen in men and menstrual blood in women. *Qi* is a subtle, cosmic vapor or "energy" that flows through the universe and self. Associated with consciousness and the heart, spirit relates to "divine" capacities; it is often understood as a more refined or conscious form of *qi*. Daoist internal alchemy also emphasizes the conservation and refinement of body fluids as well as other spiritual capacities such as the ethereal soul (*hun*) and corporeal soul (*po*). These substances are contained in a body defined largely in terms of the so-called organ-meridian system, in which *qi* circulates. There are also various subtle, mystical locations, with the following three being most important: (1) Ocean of *Qi*/lower elixir field (navel region), (2) Vermilion Palace/middle elixir field (heart region), and (3) Ancestral Cavity/upper elixir field (center of head). The "embryo of immortality" is incubated in the lower elixir field. After it becomes fully formed, it is directed to exit through the crown-point.

As one might expect from this complex view of self, Daoist internal alchemy involves a variety of methods aimed at "refining," "smelting," and "fusing" the elements together. Traditionally speaking, this is the goal of Daoist internal alchemy: the fusion of disparate elements of self into a unified spirit (not an ontological given), which is capable of transcending physical death. It is beyond the present chapter, and largely unnecessary for understanding the *Huiming jing*, to discuss the associated techniques. However, some include establishing a link between the heart and kidneys, refining the *qi* of the five yin-organs and uniting them into a single energetic presence, opening the eight extraordinary vessels, activating the Nine Palaces in the head, and so forth.

In Liu Huayang's presentation, Daoist internal alchemy practice is reconceptualized and viewed through a Chan Buddhist lens. As mentioned, Liu begins by emphasizing the importance of nondissipation, which occupies an important place in both traditions, and of the practice of the Microcosmic Orbit, an important *neidan* method. Interestingly, Liu refers to the latter as the "Dharma Wheel." "Turning the Dharma Wheel" is usually a Buddhist phrase for transmitting Buddhist teachings. In our text, it primarily refers to circulating *qi* through the Microcosmic Orbit. However, there are additional conceptual layers here. On the one hand, the *dharma* becomes associated with energetic presences in the body; the practitioner is literally circulating the *dharma* (Buddhist teachings/truth) in his or her own body. On the other hand, anyone who practices the Microcosmic Orbit is turning the Dharma Wheel; by practicing the method, one is converting to Buddhism on some level. As explored in more detail later, the next two sections of the *Huiming jing* discuss the formation of the embryo of immortality and of sending out the transcendent spirit. These are also elements of traditional Daoist *neidan* practice. However, in Liu Huayang's presentation, the former becomes associated with the aforementioned *tathāgata-garbha*, while the latter becomes associated with the appearance of enlightened consciousness. This is followed by the activation of the Transformation Body. The latter refers to one of the so-called Three Bodies, the threefold body or nature of a buddha: the Dharmakāya, Sambhogakāya, and Nirmānakāya, that is, the dharma-body, bliss-body, and transformation-body. These correspond to (1) the body of a buddha in its essential nature (cosmic), (2) the body of a buddha received for his own use and enjoyment (divine), and (3) the body of a buddha by which he can appear in any form (physical). In the depiction in the corresponding diagram, one can manifest in many different forms, which appear to be both physical (perhaps different incarnations) and spiritual (multilocation). The text finally discusses the Chan Buddhist meditation method of wall-gazing, which has some parallels to other *neidan* systems that end with contentless, nonconceptual meditation. Finally, one disappears into the Void. Thus the text literally begins with reference to the Dao, moves on to reference the Mahāyāna Buddhist *Huayan jing* and *Lengyan jing* as well as to describe Daoist *neidan* practice, and then concludes with Chan Buddhist wall-gazing. The latter eventually leads to disappearance into the Void. This reconnects the practice to both Buddhism and Daoism, while at the same time transcending any doctrinal distinctions or soteriological divisions. One thus begins as Daoist, participates in both traditions simultaneously, eventually relocates oneself in Chan Buddhism through the model of Bodhidharma, and then forgets personal and religious identity altogether. Through the practice, one has apparently transcended sectarian confines. Following Wu-Liu syncretism, one has realized the state wherein one is simultaneously immortal and buddha.

In terms of the larger religious and soteriological system within which the text is located and which it expresses, the *Huiming jing* was written by a Chan Buddhist monk under the influence of a deceased Daoist monk. While the text does not present itself as monastic, its context of composition and intended audience appear to be Buddhist monasticism. Liu's Buddho-Daoist syncretic practice thus assumes certain foundational religious commitments. These include foundational Buddhist ethics as expressed in the five precepts of no killing, no stealing, no sexual misconduct, no lying, and no intoxicants. In the case of monastics, the commitment to sexual propriety technically involves physical and cognitive celibacy. In a Chinese Buddhist and Daoist monastic context, one would also adhere to voluntary poverty and to vegetarianism, at least ideally speaking. At the same time, following Mahāyāna and Chan Buddhist views, Liu makes space for lay participation. As importantly, he is quite clear on the importance of correct instruction and internal cultivation, access to reliable teachings, and practice of efficacious methods. Commenting on the line "This is why realized individuals observe the cycles of movement and stillness and engage in cultivation," Liu explains,

> Ordinary people believe that one can engage in cultivation and refinement by leaving the family in order to live in the deep mountains and long valleys or in a remote hermitage or large monastery. They think that by sitting in stillness they can cultivate the Dao. This is absurd. They do not know that without authentic transmission, they will not understand the meaning and function of movement. As a result, their stillness resembles living death. They are like cats guarding an empty hole. (*Huiming jing*, ZW 131, 5.901)

Here Liu seems to suggest that quietistic meditation, like Confucian and Daoist quiet sitting (*jingzuo*) and Chan silent illumination (*mozhao*), are deficient without an alchemical dimension. Specifically, "movement" seems to refer to the activation of the body's subtle energetic networks and the circulation of original *qi* through them.

Placed in the larger context of the Wu-Liu system, Farzeen Baldrian-Hussein summarizes it as follows:

> The school arranges *neidan* practice into three stages (called *sancheng* or Three Accomplishments). In the first stage, mental concentration activates precosmic pneuma [pre-natal *qi*] (*xiantian qi*) within the lower Cinnabar Field (*dantian*), providing the basis for all alchemical action. The adept then continues on to "lay the foundations" (*zhuji*) using physiological methods to strengthen vital force [*qi*] and prevent its dissipation. This entails opening the inner channels and circulating the *qi* by the method known as the Lesser Celestial Cycle (*xiao zhoutian*).
>
> The second stage, the union of spirit and breath [*qi*] engenders the seed of the inner elixir, which is fixed and nourished in the middle Cinnabar Field. When the immortal embryo is complete, it is moved to the upper Cinnabar Field, crossing the Three Passes (*sanguan*) of the spinal column.
>
> The third and last stage includes the method of the Greater Celestial Cycle (*da zhoutian*) or intense concentration (*dading*), the egress of the spirit (*chushen*), and the suckling (*rubu*) of the infant. This leads one to the rank of "divine immortal" (*shenxian*). Three more transformations are needed to attain the rank of "celestial immortal" (*tianxian*). The final process of transfiguration is described as "facing the wall for nine years" (*jiunian mianbi*) or "refining spirit and reverting to emptiness" (*lianshen huanxu*). (Baldrian-Hussein 2008d, 1050)

The Macrocosmic Orbit, referred to as the Greater Celestial Cycle here, usually involves circulating *qi* through all of the eight extraordinary vessels. Whereas the Microcosmic Orbit emphasizes the body as torso, the Macrocosmic Orbit includes the limbs as well. The complete Wu-Liu system awaits a future study.

As a final set of points related to Liu's soteriological system, we may understand the associated benefits and experiences that result from alchemical training. One dimension of *neidan* practice involves "signs of successful training" and "boons along the way" (see Eskildsen 2001, 2004; Komjathy 2007, 2013a). These are one indication that one is making progress. As mentioned earlier, the title of Liu Huayang's *Jinxian zhenglun* alludes to "experiential verification" or "confirmation" (*zhengyan*), which is sometimes translated as "signs of proof." In terms of earlier *neidan* systems, the final section of the tenth-century *Chuandao ji* (Record of Transmitting the Dao; DZ 263, j. 14–16) is titled "Lun zhengyan" (On Experiential Confirmation; 16.27a–30b; Wong 2000, 143–48). It informs the Daoist adept that specific training regimens may result in specific types of experiences. After one conserves vital essence, opens the body's meridians, and generates saliva, one begins a process of self-rarefication and self-divinization. At the most advanced stages of alchemical transformation, one becomes free of karmic obstructions and entanglements and one's name becomes registered in the records of the Three Purities. The embryo of immortality matures, which includes the ability to manifest as the body-beyond-the-body and to have greater communion with celestial realms. After the adept's bones begin to disappear and become infused with golden light, he or she may receive visitations from divine beings. This process of experiential confirmation is said to culminate as follows:

> In a solemn and grand ceremony, you will be given the purple writ of the celestial books and immortal regalia. Immortals will appear on your left and right, and you will be escorted to Penglai. You will have audience with the Perfect Lord of Great Tenuity in the Purple Palace. Here your name and place of birth will be entered into the registers. According to your level of accomplishment, you will be given a dwelling-place on the Three Islands. Then you may be called a Perfected (*zhenren*) or immortal (*xianzi*). (16.30a; see also *Dadan zhizhi*, DZ 244, 1.17b–18a; *Neidan jiyao*, DZ 1258, 2.9a–13a, 3.10b–14a)

In Liu Huayang's system, some important signs of successful training include the activation of the body's meridians (subtle energetic networks), the presence and circulation of original *qi* (*yuanqi*) in the body, the formation of the embryo of immortality (energetic presence) in the lower elixir field (navel region), and the appearance of the yang-spirit. In addition, one gains the ability to manifest in multiple forms in multiple places at multiple times (multilocation). The latter relates to "numinous abilities" and "supernatural powers" (*shentong*; Skt.: *siddhi*) (see Komjathy 2007). However, rather than being the goal of *neidan* practice, such signs are generally regarded as by-products, and one is advised not to become attached to or actively seek extraordinary experiences. As Liu Huayang explains about the later stages of alchemical transformation, "*Chan* is stillness; thusness is innate nature. . . . Knowledge of past and present, fortune and misfortune, should not affect your practice. . . . In deep silence, there is constant illumination" (*Huiming jing*, ZW 131, 5.901). The ultimate goal of Daoist internal alchemy is the formation of transcendent spirit, which Liu Huayang's discusses in terms of *tathāgata-garbha*. In Liu's system, this refers to one's "original face" (*benlai mianmu*) or "original nature" (*benxing*), that is, one's innate capacity for (or innate state of) enlightenment. "After the fetus matures and *qi* is sufficient, with flowers fluttering down, the Child of the Buddha emerges in meditative absorption to rise beyond the Three Realms (*sanjie*). This is the emergence of the Tathāgata" (ZW 131, 5.905). One attains *samādhi* (meditative absorption), awakening, and *nirvāṇa*. One abides in a state/nonstate beyond the realms of desire, form, and formless. Although supposedly indescribable and incomprehensible, and open to a variety of interpretations, Liu refers to this "state" as complete dissolution and disappearance into the Dao.

Neidan Training according to the *Huiming jing*

The *Huiming jing* (Scripture on Wisdom and Life-Destiny; ZW 131), also known as the *Zuishang yisheng huiming jing* (Scripture on Wisdom and Life-Destiny of the Supreme Unified Vehicle), was written by Liu Huayang (1735–1799), a Chan Buddhist monk and Daoist sympathizer. Liu completed the text in 1794 at Zhongjie an (Hermitage of Zhongjie [Devoted Purity]) in Wancheng (present-day Anqing), Anhui. Liu edited it again in 1799 at Renshou si (Temple of Humane Longevity; Beijing). As discussed previously, in 1897, about one hundred years after Liu's death, Deng Huiji (fl. 1890s) included the *Huiming jing* in his edited anthology titled *Wu-Liu xianzong* (Immortal Tradition of Wu and Liu; abbr. WLXZ). The text in turn became a central work in the Wu-Liu lineage, a sublineage of the Longmen lineage of Quanzhen Daoism. It describes "Daoist" internal alchemy in combination Chan Buddhist meditation. Liu largely does this from a Chan Buddhist, or at least Buddho-Daoist syncretic perspective. In Liu Huayang's own words,

> Because I had a silent agreement transmitted from my teacher [Huyun], I compiled this book, titled the *Huiming jing*. The illustrations and diagrams establish signs that open up the secrets of the ancient buddhas, revealing the original pivot (*yuanji*) of the teacher-patriarchs. They are a raft that will guide later generations of students. (ZW 131, 5.876).

As found in the *Wu-Liu xianzong* and in late twentieth-century *Zangwai daoshu* (Daoist Texts outside the Canon; abbr. ZW), an "extra-canonical" Daoist textual collection (see Komjathy 2002), the *Huiming jing* is much more complex than it appears in the present chapter. The received text consists of two prefaces, which are followed by the text proper. The first preface was written by Sun Tingbi (fl. 1794), a Qing dynasty military and political leader in Zhejiang and Anhui, while the second is by Liu Huayang himself. Both date to 1794. The text proper may be divided in a number of ways. As appearing in the ZW edition, the *Huiming jing* consists of twenty sections, with asterisks (*) indicating material included in the present chapter (see fig. 12.1).

Sections 1 through 8 make up the primary textual layer of the *Huiming jing*; in fact, I would suggest that this is the actual text of the *Huiming jing*; the other sections could be considered "supplements" or "additions." Thus, the *Huiming jing* is a text in eight sections, and this is the text translated in the present chapter. In that form, the text also circulated independently in esoteric circles and was published in various collections. The next section, "Collected Explanations of the *Huiming jing*," is a clarification of the previous text (see Nicholson 2000). Although lengthy, complex, and more difficult than the *Huiming jing* proper, the text provides greater details and insights related to *neidan* training. The remainder of the received text appears to be a collection of various independent, perhaps loosely related works. Sections 10 through 14 were written by Liu Huayang himself. This fact is confirmed by the 1794 preface by Sun Tingbi, who explicitly

1. Diagram of the Cessation of Outflow*	11. Direct Discussion of the Correct Path of the Work
2. Diagram of the Six Phases of the Dharma Wheel*	12. Direct Discussion of the Correct Path of Stillness and Movement
3. Diagram of the Governing and Conception Vessels*	13. Miscellaneous Comments
4. Diagram of the Embryo of the Dao*	14. Resolving Doubts
5. Diagram of Sending Out the Fetus*	15. Zhang Ziyang's Scripture on the Eight Vessels
6. Diagram of the Transformation Body*	16. Elder Qianyang's Discussion of Breath Regulation
7. Diagram of Facing the Wall*	17. Further Discussion of Breath Regulation
8. Diagram of Disappearance into the Void*	18. Zhang Sanfeng's Discussion of Breath Regulation
9. Collected Explanations of the *Huiming jing*	19. Nine Stages of Refining the Heart-mind
10. Direct Discussion of the Correct Path of Cultivation	20. Li Hanxu's Sequential Transmissions on Later Heaven[14]

Figure 12.1. Sections of the Received *Huiming jing*

states that the text consists of fourteen sections in the same sequence as shown in figure 12.1. Most of these works have a primary layer that begins with "Liu Huayang said," followed by commentary that was most likely written by Liu. The last six sections (secs. 15–20) were not penned by Liu Huayang; they may have been added by Deng Huiji. Although the "Nine Stages of Refining the Heart-Mind" has been associated with Liu (see Wong 1998), it is attributed to Li Hanxu, an obscure Daoist who possibly lived from 1806 to 1856 and who was associated with the Xipai (Western Lineage).

As mentioned previously, Liu was working on the *Huiming jing* and *Jinxian zhenglun* during the final year of his life (1799). As translated in the present chapter, the *Huiming jing* consists of eight sections. The primary layer is eight illustrations with mnemonic poems. The secondary layer of the text is a commentary or explanation, which was also written by Liu Huayang. From my perspective, the text is incomplete. A simple perusal reveals that the lengthiest prose sections are at the beginning. Sections 6 through 8 lack prose altogether. It thus seems that Liu Huayang died before completing his explanations.

On the most basic level, the *Huiming jing* presents *neidan* training in terms of an eight-stage process. One could also divide the practice into a more standard three-stage process of elixir formation, which consists of gestation, childhood, and adulthood. The process of becoming

1. Sealing the Body (Non-dissipation)	5. Sending Out the Transcendent Spirit
2. Activating the Dharma Wheel	6. Manifesting the Transformation Body
3. Connecting the Governing and Conception Vessels	7. Entering Silence
4. Coalescing the Immortal Embryo	8. Disappearing into Emptiness

Figure 12.2. Eight Stages of Alchemical Transformation according to the *Huiming jing*

immortal is thus analogous to pregnancy, incubation, maturation, and independence. Following similar *neidan* accounts, this involves the formation of the "embryo" of immortality, which eventually grows into a "fetus." The former is a potentiality, which eventually becomes fully actualized. Both "embryo" and "fetus" translate the Chinese term *tai*, with the meaning depending on context. At the beginning of *neidan* training, it resembles an embryo (that which grows); toward the completion of the practice, it resembles a fetus (coming into being). The latter eventually becomes the "Child of the Buddha." According to the *Huiming jing* and as discussed earlier, the process begins with the cessation of outflow (sec. 1). One then practices the Microcosmic Orbit (secs. 2, 3). Following these stages, the elixir of immortality forms (sec. 4). After it reaches maturity, one can send out the yang-spirit through the crown-point (sec. 5) and manifest as the body-beyond-the-body (sec. 6). In the seventh and penultimate stage, one practices Chan Buddhist meditation (sec. 7), referred to as "wall-gazing" in the text. Finally, one disappears into the Void and merges with the Dao (sec. 8). Thus, the *Huiming jing* describes a variety of methods under the general category of *neidan* as well as corresponding experiences and attainments.

Before discussing the later influence of the *Huiming jing*, a few additional comments on the illustrations, recommended posture, practice space, and audience may be helpful. First, with respect to posture, Liu Huayang does not provide explicit instructions in our text. However, illustrations 4 through 7 depict the full-lotus posture (*jiafu zuo*; Skt.: *padmāsana* [lotus throne]), which was the standard and preferred posture in Buddhism and also became increasingly prominent in Daoist meditation from the Tang dynasty (618–907) onward. In addition, in section 11 of the received *Huiming jing*, Liu explicitly refers to this posture (see, e.g., ZW 131, 5.903). The full-lotus posture, often referred to as "sitting cross-legged," involves placing one foot on top of the opposite thigh with the sole facing upward and the heel close to the abdomen. The other foot is then placed on the opposite thigh in a symmetrical way. Various hand positions (*shouyin*; Skt.: *mudrā*) are used. In the case of Buddhist meditation, the standard *mudrā* and the one depicted in Liu's diagrams is the *dhyāna* mudra, which is also known as the *samādhi* or yogic *mudrā*. In this hand position, the right hand is placed on top of the left with the palms facing upward and the tips of the thumbs touching. The hands then rest on the lap, usually at the level of the navel. Interestingly, in diagrams 5 through 7 of the *Huiming jing*, the hands are located at the level of the heart, an iconographic feature that may be significant in terms of focusing on the heart and spirit.

The diagrams are also noteworthy in terms of the prescribed methods, views of self, and religious affiliation. In the first three diagrams, the human body appears as a torso (see also Komjathy 2008b, 2009). It is primarily the body as energetic circuit composed of the Governing and Conception Vessels. In diagram 4, the body includes the limbs. The diagram also has distinctively Buddhist characteristics. In particular, one notices the so-called head protuberance (*usnīsa*). This is one of the thirty-two "marks" or physical attributes (*laksana*) of a great spirit or realized being (*mahāparusa*). In this and the subsequent diagrams, the body now includes limbs rather than simply being a torso or energetic network. Moreover, like diagrams 5 through 7, it depicts the meditator in full-lotus posture. On initial examination, diagrams 5 through 7 seem to depict a Buddhist monk (shaven head) rather than a Daoist one (uncut hair and beard). However, the fact that the image lacks clothing (and also genitalia) might rather point in a different direction. They seem to follow Daoist notions of a return to "childhood" and cosmic integration, a return to the "primordial womb." In this respect, it is interesting that section 5 includes a reference to becoming a "child of the Buddha."

In terms of place, our primary text lacks specific guidance or recommendations. However, in section 11 of the received *Huiming jing*, Liu Huayang emphasizes the importance of a quiet location.

> When you set to work, locate yourself in a quiet room (*jingshi*).[15] Your body should be like withered wood. Your heart-mind should resemble cold ashes.[16] Make use of the numinous light. House innate nature and life-destiny together in the same palace. (ZW 131, 5.903)

Commenting on these lines, Liu further explains,

> Your meditation room should be located in a place where you will not be disturbed. When you meditate, forget form. After entering stillness, forget the heart-mind. Return the radiance and revert illumination.[17] Let original nature enter the Palace of Life-Destiny.[18] In this way original nature and life-destiny will be cultivated simultaneously. (ZW 131, 5.903)

Drawing upon his earlier suggestion that mountain seclusion or monastic residence is unnecessary, a perspective reiterated in his own preface to the *Huiming jing*, Liu seems to indicate that one can engage in meditative practice anywhere. Some primary supporting conditions include commitment, consistency, and a quiet place. The latter may be found or established in urban, rural, or wild environs.

Finally, with respect to community and audience, in his preface to the text Liu Huayang comments that he wrote the *Huiming jing* for "those who have karmic affinities" (ZW 131, 5.876). Based on the fact that Liu Huayang was a Chan Buddhist monk teaching his disciples, who were primarily other Chan Buddhist monks, one might assume that "those with karmic affinities" only refers to those following an ascetic and monastic path. However, as discussed previously, this contradicts certain foundational Mahāyāna and Chan commitments and viewpoints. It appears that Liu's intended audience is much broader.

> As I observe contemporary seekers of the Dao, I notice that there are discourse records from many schools. In these records there is true and false instruction. Beginning students do not know the Way of Wisdom and Life-Destiny (*huiming zhi dao*) of the Tathāgata. They thus mistakenly become ensnared in slogans and superficial oral Chan. They end up as base fools, repeatedly reaping harm from such discourse records. . . . Now, by means of simple, straightforward language, I am transmitting the Treasure of the Buddha, offering it as if on a tray to enable disciples in the world [to practice]. As you examine the *Huiming jing*, it is indeed the same as if I were telling it to you with my own mouth. It is only necessary to rouse your aspirations and dedicate all your energy—you do not need go to some other mountain to seek further help—and you will be able to establish and manifest the Buddha fruit. This was my original vow to suffer bitterly to find a teacher and awaken to the Dao. (ZW 131, 5.876)

The *Huiming jing* in turn seems to be intended for wider dissemination and circulation. It is among a unique handful of works that not only explicitly discuss internal alchemy but also contain illustrations of the related practices. The latter becomes increasingly the case during the late imperial period. In the *Huiming jing*, Liu explicitly and straightforwardly explains his form of *neidan* training and the process of alchemical transformation. In the process, he departs from earlier *neidan* esotericism and secrecy. Such esoteric terminology and symbolism prevented misuse and most often required training under a master with corresponding oral instruction (*koujue*). That is, traditionally speaking, there were oral commentaries and secret instructions that accompanied actual *neidan* texts. These were required for successful *neidan* practice. Although this viewpoint continues into the present day, Liu's *Huiming jing* makes the practice more accessible and public. In this respect, it is probably significant that Liu Huayang was working on the text in the final years of his life. He probably recognized that there was little time left for transmission and perhaps feared that his understanding and experience would be lost with his own death. There thus appears to be a greater willingness to "disclose the secrets." The wider context of reception and larger intended audience, including lay practitioners, are confirmed in the preface of Sun Tingbi, who funded the wood-block printing.

Reading the *Huiming jing* in Modern Chinese Society and in the Modern West

It seems that both Liu Huayang and Sun Tingbi were correct in their vision and estimation, as our primary text exerted a profound influence on the later Daoist tradition and on Chinese culture more generally. Here we may recall Liu's claim that the instructions of the *Huiming jing* "are a raft that will guide later generations of students." The selection of the text for the present chapter confirms this claim, though the extent to which readers will become enlightened through alchemy remains to be seen.

At the present time, the contemporaneous impact of *Huiming jing* is unclear. As discussed earlier, Liu did contribute to the lives and practice of his Chan Buddhist disciples, some Daoist spiritual companions, as well as to the local laity. For example, in his preface to the *Huiming jing*, Liu comments, "I secretly journeyed to Jiangzuo [Jiangsu]. Together with some Daoist companions we burned incense and cultivated ourselves. We studied in detail, and as a result Bichan, Liaoran, Qiongyu, and Zhenyuan attained perfection" (adapted from Nicholson 2000, 17; see also Nicholson 2000, 65–75). However, the immediate, subsequent influence of Liu's writings remains unclear. This issue partially relates to the history of various manuscripts, editions, and publications. At present, we do not know the extent to which the *Huiming jing* and *Jinxian zhenglun* circulated in early nineteenth-century Buddhist and Daoist circles. The former topic is especially interesting, though wholly understudied, namely, the extent to which Chan Buddhist monks were practicing Daoist internal alchemy.

About one hundred years after Liu's death, Deng Huiji, whose identity requires further research, included the *Huiming jing* in his edited anthology titled *Wu-Liu xianzong* (dat. 1897). As discussed previously, this text includes two texts by Wu Shouyang and two by Liu Huayang, and it appears to be the first time that the combined term "Wu-Liu" was used to refer to a sublineage of the Longmen lineage of Quanzhen Daoism. At present, it is difficult to know if the *Wu-Liu xianzong* was a formative influence on the establishment of the Wu-Liu lineage, or if it rather documented this phenomenon in late nineteenth-century China. In 1921, Zhanran Huizhenzi published another edition of the *Huiming jing* with the *Jinhua zongzhi* (Secret of the Golden Flower) (Baldrian-Hussein 2008a). This partially helps to explain the appearance of the two texts in Richard Wilhelm's German and then English *The Secret of the Golden Flower* (1962; see later discussion).

In terms of the Wu-Liu lineage, the *Huiming jing* became one of four "canonical" texts of that lineage. The Wu-Liu system of *neidan* and its history, especially with respect to Quanzhen in general and Longmen in particular, deserves a future study. The text seems to have received fairly wide circulation and exerted major influence from at least the early twentieth century to the present. Members of the Wu-Liu lineage read and applied the *Huiming jing* in their own *neidan* training.

However, like other popular works such as the anonymous *Xingming guizhi* (Precious Decrees on Innate Nature and Life-Destiny), Zhao Bichen's (1860–1942) *Xingming fajue mingzhi* (Illuminated Pointers to the Methods and Instructions of Innate Nature and Life-Destiny), and Liu Yiming's (1734–1821) *Daoshu shier zhong* (Twelve Daoist Works), the *Huiming jing* was not simply circulated in Daoist circles. It has occupied and continues to occupy a central place not only in Daoism but also in the larger Chinese culture and society. The text is influential in modern Qigong (*Qi* Exercise) circles. Although commonly misidentified as a "Daoist" movement (see Komjathy 2006), Qigong as such actually began in the middle of the twentieth century and reached its indigenous Chinese pinnacle with the "Qigong boom" occurring in the 1980s and 1990s (see Palmer 2007). There are various types of Qigong (see Komjathy 2006), including Daoist forms. Some Qigong sets also have relatively early provenances, with a root in earlier Chinese and Daoist Yangsheng (Nourishing Life) and Daoyin (Guided Stretching) methods (see Komjathy 2013b). In China, the Qigong movement has recently been in decline due to the criminalization of Falun gong (Dharma Wheel Exercises), a Buddhist-inspired form of Qigong, from 1999 to the present. This has led to Qigong in general being viewed with suspicion; it became politicized and potentially subversive to practice Qigong in the People's Republic of China. However, in the late twentieth century, Qigong became disseminated globally. In this global health and fitness movement, the *Huiming jing* is one text that describes *neidan*-inspired Qigong practice.

The text also receives fairly wide circulation in contemporary Daoist circles. For example, at various moments during my ethnographic fieldwork and participant-observation of contemporary Quanzhen monasticism (1998–present), Chinese Quanzhen monastics have referred to and recommended the *Huiming jing*. Most of these monastics were associated with the Longmen lineage, though they did not self-identify as members of the Wu-Liu lineage. From this contemporary, mainland Chinese Daoist perspective, the *Huiming jing* provides helpful guidance on foundational *neidan* training. At the same time, in ways that parallel contemporary Daoist views on other late imperial materials, Liu Huayang's Chan Buddhist identity and the syncretic religiosity expressed in the *Huiming jing* are sources of discomfort for many Daoists.[19]

Outside of China and the Chinese cultural sphere, the *Huiming jing* has also exerted influence in Europe and North America. The text first entered the popular Western imagination with Richard Wilhelm's *Das Geheimnis der Goldenen Blüte: Ein chinesisches Lebensbuch* (1929). Paralleling the British Sinologist and Christian missionary James Legge (1815–1897) in terms of Western engagement with (construction of) "Daoism," Richard Wilhelm (1873–1930) was a German Sinologist as well as Christian theologian and missionary. He spent time as a missionary in Qingdao, Shandong, beginning in 1899. After returning to Germany at the end of World War I (1914–1918), Wilhelm established the China Institute in Frankfurt am Main (see Wippermann et al. 2007; Walravens 2008).[20] Wilhelm is best known for his German translation of the *Yijing* (*I-ching*; Book of Changes; dat. 1923), which was subsequently translated into English by Cary Baynes in 1950 (see Wilhelm 1967). Most relevant for present purposes, Wilhelm published a German translation of the *Jinhua zongzhi* and the *Huiming jing* in 1929 (see Komjathy 2003). This German translation of the Chinese text was subsequently translated into English as *The Secret of the Golden Flower* by Cary Baynes in 1931 (see Wilhelm 1962). Although the Wilhelm-Baynes translation remains in print through Mariner Books (Houghton Mifflin Harcourt), it is most interesting in terms of Western intellectual history and as an intellectual artifact of earlier Western engagement with China and Daoism. Richard Wilhelm's translation also prepared the way for the general-audience English translation of Thomas Cleary (b. 1949), which was published by Shambhala.

Particularly interesting is the fact that Richard Wilhelm was a close friend of Carl Jung (1875–1961), the famous analytical psychologist. This influence partially led to Wilhelm at times reading the *Huiming jing* as proto-Jungian psychology. Carl Jung, in turn, contributed a foreword to Wilhelm's *The I Ching* and a commentary to *The Secret of the Golden Flower*. According to Jung,

> I first met Richard Wilhelm at Count [Hermann Alexander Graf] Keyserling's [1880–1946] during a meeting of the "School of Wisdom" in Darmstadt [Germany]. That was in the early twenties. In 1923 we invited him to Zurich and he spoke on the *I Ching* at the Psychology Club. (Jung 1989, 373)

Here we see Jung's interest in Western esotericism (see, e.g., Noll 1997; Shamdasani 1998, 2003), including later symbolic interpretations and applications of "alchemy" (see Jung 1980, 1983). The "School of Wisdom" began as an early intellectual circle of spiritualists who envisioned a "planetary culture" beyond nationalism and ethnocentrism as well as a "new world consciousness" (see www.schoolofwisdom.com). The Psychology Club was established by Jung himself in 1916 in Zürich, Switzerland; here Jung engaged in research, writing, and conversations related to his emerging analytical psychology (see www.psychologyclub.ch). Jung's commentary on the *Jinhua zongzhi* and *Huiming jing* is, in turn, quite extensive and beyond the scope of the present chapter. The commentary, significantly, appeared *before* the actual translation in the original German edition, but the order of the English edition was reversed at the request of Jung (Wilhelm 1962, ix). As Jung summarizes,

> The purpose of my commentary is to attempt to build a bridge of psychological understanding between East and West. The basis of every real understanding is man [humanity], and therefore I had to speak of human beings. . . . Therefore it seemed to me important above all to emphasize the agreement between the psychic states and symbolisms of East and West. . . . [At the same time,] Western consciousness is by no means consciousness in general; it is a historically conditioned and geographically limited factor, representative of only one part of mankind [humanity]. The widening of our consciousness ought not to proceed at the expense of other kinds of consciousness, but ought to take place through the development of those elements of our psyche which are analogous to the alien [Chinese] psyche, just as the East cannot do without our technology, science, and industry. (Wilhelm 1962, 136–37)

Jung primarily interprets Daoist alchemical symbolism as a window into the "collective unconscious." As he notes in the foreword to the second German edition,

> At that time [the publication of the first edition] it seemed unimportant to me that *The Secret of the Golden Flower* is not only a Taoist text of Chinese yoga [*sic*] but also an alchemical tract. However, a subsequent, deeper study of Latin [alchemical] tracts has corrected my outlook and shown me that the alchemical nature of the text is of prime significance.[21] (Wilhelm 1962, xiv)

As this chapter demonstrates, this is, of course, even more the case than Jung recognized; historical and cultural dimensions of the text are pivotal, especially in terms of Jung's concern for "psychology and consciousness." The subsequent influence of Wilhelm's and Jung's engagement with Daoist *neidan* literature deserves its own study.[22]

Wilhelm's translation of the *Huiming jing* also prepared the way for two additional translations, translations that provide a window into contemporary "American Daoism."[23] That is, there is an (non-Daoist) intellectual genealogy that begins with Richard Wilhelm and moves into contemporary America; this intellectual genealogy is rooted in Western colonialist, Christian missionary, and Orientalist legacies. The second English translation of the *Huiming jing* was published by Eva Wong (b. 1951) with Shambhala (Boston; dat. 1998).[24] Intended for hybrid spiritualists, health and fitness adherents, and Western Daoist sympathizers, the book is titled *Cultivating the Energy of Life: A Translation of the Hui-ming ching and Its Commentaries*. Like many of Shambhala's publications on Daoism, the translation and Wong's historical comments are deficient on academic grounds, though Wong does give readers access to an actual Daoist *neidan* text. For Wong,

> Once the perspective of the authors is understood, we need to free the text from its historical and philosophical context and listen to it as if it were a trusted teacher. When the text develops a personal meaning for us, it will begin to speak as a spiritual advisor. (1998, 6–7)

There also can be no doubt that Wong's popular translations, like those of Thomas Cleary, have exerted a major influence on the Western understanding of Daoism. Much more interesting here is the fact that Eva Wong is a Hong Kong emigrant and self-identified Daoist. Early on, she was a senior disciple of Moy Lin-shin (1931–1998), the founder of the Toronto-based Taoist Tai Chi Society (TTCS) and Fung Loy Kok (FLK). In fact, under the direction of Moy Lin-shin, Eva Wong helped to establish the Denver branch of TTCS/FLK. Eva Wong eventually split with Moy and his organization, becoming an independent Daoist practitioner in the early 1990s (see Komjathy 2004). With each subsequent Shambhala publication, there is a newly imagined Daoist identity and lineage. On the *Huiming jing*, Wong is described as "a practitioner of the Taoist arts and a translator of texts from the Chinese," and there is no mention of her connection to Moy and TTCS/FLK.

However, TTCS/FLK is acknowledged in James Michael Nicholson's master's thesis (2000), which is an academically reliable study and annotated translation of the received *Huiming jing* text.[25] A TTCS/FLK adherent, Nicholson earned his master's degree under Daniel Overmyer at the University of British Columbia (UBC). Although currently unclear, it seems that there was some connection between Overmyer and the UBC Department of Asian Studies and TTCS/FLK. Two other TTCS/FLK adherents, Paulino Belamide and Paul Crowe, earned advanced degrees there. Nicholson is explicit about his TTCS/FLK connection. The dedication of the thesis reads, "In memory of Master Moy Lin-shin, teacher of the Tao." Moreover, in the acknowledgments, Nicholson comments, "I would like to acknowledge the kind encouragement I received from my many friends in the Taoist Tai Chi Society." In addition to commenting on the deficiencies of the Wilhelm-Baynes translation (7–8), Nicholson also takes aim at Eva Wong (8–9), someone who broke with Moy, the "teacher of the Tao," and replaced him with texts as "trusted teachers" and "spiritual advisors." In summary, Nicholson comments, "As a result of all these problems, Wong's translation cannot be considered adequate treatment of the *Huiming Jing*, especially for those with an academic interest in precision" (9). While Nicholson's critique is valid on academic grounds, there is also a TTCS/FLK subtext. Many academics would have simply ignored or omitted Wong's work from serious consideration. Many specialists refuse to consider and especially to cite popular translations such as those of Wong and Thomas Cleary. Just being published by Shambhala would indicate unreliability with respect to Daoism. One might thus read Nicholson's comments along sectarian lines. It is not simply that Wong is "not an academic"; she is also a TTCS/FLK defector and apostate. That is, Nicholson's thesis aims not only to provide a more academically reliable translation of the *Huiming jing* but also, perhaps, to undermine and replace the work of a former member of TTCS/FLK. At the same time, like the present chapter, it is indebted to Wilhelm and Wong for elevating the *Huiming jing* to a status deserving study and translation. Here we see the complex contexts and subtexts of modern Western Daoist studies.

Transmuting Contemplative Studies through Internal Alchemy

Daoist internal alchemy is a radically different kind of practice; it contrasts sharply with more familiar modern forms of contemplative practice, especially those that emphasize "relaxation" as central. While one can find parallels with certain Indian expressions of Tantra and Yoga, placed in comparative perspective there are few methods and systems that resemble Daoist internal alchemy. In this way, the inclusion of Daoist *neidan* in the comparative study of contemplative practice inspires one to reflect on the meaning and application of "meditation" and perhaps to modify the term in ways that subvert the tendency, recognized or not, to privilege apophatic and trophotropic types of meditation. In combination with other methods, Daoist *neidan* thus has the potential to transmute the meaning of "contemplative practice" and the emerging, interdisciplinary field of contemplative studies by extension. Under a more conventional reading, Daoist internal alchemy is generally practiced using seated postures and involves increasing awareness, attentiveness, interiority, and psychosomatic aliveness. It is "meditation" conventionally understood. At the same time, during certain moments of *neidan* training, one apparently enters more hyper-aroused and ecstatic states, and one experiences the body as a subtle energetic network. According to traditional *neidan* accounts, one may even encounter gods and immortals and/or one's spirit may leave the body to explore the subtle realms of the cosmos. Here we see potential overlap with comparative categories such as mysticism and shamanism. It may be that this kind of training is ultimately training for death and afterlife as envisioned by Daoists. In this way, Daoist *neidan* is not as easily appropriated, domesticated, and reconceptualized as other forms of contemplative practice. As discussed momentarily, it apparently requires detailed understanding of the theory behind the practice as well as specific views of personhood, death, and afterlife. Given its complexity, it is unlikely that people will practice it without the guidance of a Daoist teacher and perhaps without a Daoist orientation, although there are a number of New Age Qigong teachers of *neidan* practice (see Komjathy 2004, 2006).

Daoist internal alchemy also brings the complex interplay among views of self, practice, and experience into high relief (see Komjathy 2007). Specifically, it reveals the socio-historical and cultural layers of "the body" as inscribed by religious traditions. The body of Daoist *neidan* practitioners is arguably a different body than the one utilized in other forms of contemplative practice. While it (at least provisionally) has a parallel structure and basic constituents (e.g., organs), the Daoist alchemical or subtle body has other layers and dimensions as well. Emphasis is placed on the importance of the internal Three Treasures (*nei sanbao*) of vital essence, *qi*, and spirit. In addition, fluids and the so-called organ-meridian system are central. The latter includes an integrated and interconnected system of energy channels running through the body. There are also hidden and secret regions of the body, which apparently are only accessed or activated through *neidan*-like practices (see previous discussion and Komjathy 2007, 2008b, 2009). Such an anthropology (theory of the human), like views of personhood more generally, informs the practice, and the practice embodies such views. As mentioned, from a traditional Daoist perspective, the postmortem fate of ordinary human beings is to dissipate into the cosmos; immortality or transcendence is *not* an ontological given. As the self is composite, it is only through alchemy, complete psychosomatic transformation, that one can fuse all of the disparate elements of self into a unified entity that is capable of transcending death. This is the transcendent spirit *created* through *neidan* practice. Interestingly, as we have partially glimpsed in Liu Huayang's *Huiming jing*, *neidan* training became reconceptualized through Buddhist influences. Specifically, inspired by a Mahāyāna Buddhist quasi-docetic viewpoint (consciousness as reincarnating), Daoists began to understand *neidan* training as necessary not for postmortem continuation but rather for more auspicious incarnations. Generally speaking, in Daoist contexts, the latter are understood as existences wherein one has greater access to Daoist teachers and teachings and greater opportunities for Daoist training and practice. From this perspective, the psychosomatic transformation facilitated by *neidan* practice leads to a more spiritually beneficial ontological condition. These dimensions of Daoist internal alchemy may inspire us to give more attention to conceptions of the body and the way in which they inform and are expressed in specific forms of religious practice. Contemplative practice may, in turn, be considered as a "somatic discipline."

Liu Huayang's *Huiming jing* also brings the issue of "influences" and "syncretism" to our attention. As mentioned, syncretism, which is a problematic category on a number of levels, generally refers the process of combining elements from supposedly distinct traditions or systems into a new expression or hybridization. In this respect, the *Huiming jing* is fascinating in a variety of ways. First, foundational Chan Buddhist meditation was influenced by classical Daoist apophatic meditation. Second, certain forms of Daoist *neidan* incorporated Buddhist views of self, especially with respect to reincarnation. Finally, Liu Huayang was a Chan Buddhist practicing "Daoist" internal alchemy methods in combination with Chan Buddhist meditation. In the *Huiming jing*, Liu primarily locates *neidan* practice in a Chan Buddhist worldview, while simultaneously utilizing Daoist maps of the subtle body. We thus find that categorizing the *Huiming jing* is a complex exercise. Is the text really about "Daoist" practice? There can be no debate that the methods and some of the views are Daoist. However, Liu is a Chan Buddhist primarily utilizing a Chan Buddhist, or at least Buddho-Daoist syncretic, soteriology. Perhaps "cross-pollination," rather than "syncretism," is a better characterization. In terms of the comparative study of contemplative practice, Liu Huayang's *Huiming jing* inspires us to be attentive to the various cultural, historical, and religious influences on particular practices. It may be that the meaning, purpose, and practice of specific methods changes depending on sociohistorical context and changing cultural influences. This depends on the degree of fluidity within and between traditions.

Finally, Daoist internal alchemy reveals an important distinction in contemplative practice, a distinction that may be helpful for contemplative studies. This is the distinction between basic and advanced practice. Here it is important to recognize that not all contemplative traditions utilize such a framework, and, normatively speaking, it may condition one to approach contemplative practice in terms of spiritual athleticism and spiritual exhibitionism (see technical glossary). Again, there are complex existential, ontological, and soteriological views here. Nonetheless, from a Daoist perspective, *neidan* is an advanced practice, which can be dangerous if not practiced correctly. Tradition-based Daoist *neidan* training is generally stage-based, utilizing a variety of complex practices in sequence and aimed at complete psychosomatic transformation. This type of contemplative practice generally utilizes Daoist stillness-based practices as foundational and preliminary for more advanced training. The adept begins and ends with sitting in silence and emptiness. This foundation is necessary so that one actually has the purity of intention as well as the degree of awareness and concentration necessary for *neidan* practice proper. As we have seen in the Wu-Liu lineage, *neidan* systems also tend to include other foundational elements such as virtue, sobriety, and celibacy, or at least temporary abstinence. In addition, Daoist *neidan* training is traditionally only undertaken under the guidance of a teacher and/or community, which provide spiritual direction and perhaps secret instruction. The latter is often lineage-based and requires ordination. Here we might make a distinction between basic or foundational practices as those that are relatively simple, easy, and safe. If a system contains so-called advanced practices, they would be relatively complex, difficult, and even dangerous. The latter is rarely discussed in the comparative study of contemplative practice, but the challenges, pitfalls, and perils of contemplative practice are frequent themes in contemplative traditions and contemplative literature. They may include more innocuous moments or events such as despair, discouragement, distraction, doubt, lethargy, loneliness, psychological releases, and so forth. However, some commonly identified major dangers include demonic possession, illness, insanity, psychological breakdown, spiritual disorientation, as well as premature death. Somewhere between these two, contemplatives may experience unfamiliar energetic transformations and tradition-specific spiritual events, the full significance of which only emerges through spiritual direction. We might thus consider the full spectrum of contemplative practice, both within and between religious traditions, as well as the benefits and detriments of such practice and the ways in which these are understood and addressed within the larger community and tradition. Such an approach would also consider the relative importance of teachers, community, and tradition for successful training.

Notes

1. Numbering systems for Daoist textual collections follow Komjathy 2002, with "JY" referring to the *Daozang jiyao* (Collected Essentials of the Daoist Canon; dat. 1906) and "ZW" referring to the *Zangwai daoshu* (Daoist Texts outside the Canon; dat. 1992/1995).

2. Daoists traditionally have a number of names. When known, at their first appearance I include religious and ordination names (*daohao*; *faming*) in parentheses with English translation and dates.

3. The primary biographical source on Liu Huayang is his own preface to the *Huiming jing*. Nicholson (2000) includes translations of the prefaces of both Liu and Sun Tingbi. The present account synthesizes information from Boltz 1987, 201–2; Esposito 2000, 633, 635–37; Baldrian-Hussein 2008b.

4. Other dates for Wu include 1552–1641, 1563–1632, and 1565–1644. On this issue, see Boltz 1987, n. 550; Baldrian-Hussein 2008c.

5. Some important biographical information on Wu Shouyang appears in his own prefaces and his autobiographical poem titled "Wu zhenren xiuxian ge" (Song of Cultivating Immortality by Perfected Wu), which appears in his *Xianfo hezong yulu*. Other information appears in a commentary to the latter text by his younger brother, Wu Shouxu (Zhenyang [Perfect Yang]; d.u.). There is also a biographical entry on him in the *Jin'gai xindeng* (Transmission of the Heart-Lamp from Mount Jin'gai; ZW 950) by Min Yide (1758–1836) (see Esposito 2000). I am grateful to Stephen Eskildsen (University of Tennessee, Chattanooga) for these references. The fact that Min Yide, a prominent eleventh-generation Longmen monk, dedicated attention to Wu substantiates his importance in the late imperial lineage and especially in Min's more local Jin'gai Longmen community. The present account synthesizes information from Liu 1984; Boltz 1987, 199–202; Qing 1996, 4.37–59; De Bruyn 2000, 613; Esposito 2000, 632–33, 635–37; Baldrian-Hussein 2008c.

6. Or in 1593 in other accounts.

7. At present, the identities of these self-identified Longmen Daoists are somewhat obscure. Brief biographical notes appear in Wu Shouxu's commentary on the *Xianfo hezong yulu*. See Liu 1984, 186; Esposito 2000, 632.

8. Wu records some of Cao Changhua's teachings in his *Tianxian zhengli*.

9. We must note that this account represents a simplification or standardization of Wu's biography. For example, Monica Esposito suggests that these may be competing biographies that reflect the internal polemics of contemporaneous Longmen: "All of this suggests that Wu Shouyang's original affiliation to a local Longmen branch was obscured by the official, standardized Longmen claim that linked him with Wang Changyue" (2000, 632).

10. In Daoist contexts, it is more common to find "innate nature" (*xing*), a technical term that also appears in Liu's writings.

11. For more details on this corpus, see Boltz 1987, 199–202; Esposito 2000, 636–37; Baldrian-Hussein 2008c. My discussion is indebted to these sources.

12. A future comparison between Liu Huayang's writings and those of Wu Shouyang might clarify the degree to which there is convergence or divergence. I use "Daoist" in quotation marks to highlight the question of affiliation.

13. There was also a roughly contemporaneous practice system known as *nüdan* (female alchemy), a particular form of *neidan* training for women that gave particular attention to the lived experience of female embodiment. Specifically, more emphasis was placed on the heart, breasts, uterus, and blood. As mentioned, Wu Shouyang was a Quanzhen Daoist monk, while Liu Huayang was Chan Buddhist monk. The *Huiming jing* was either intended for men or for anyone regardless of gender. As in earlier *neidan* works, there are few if any specific guidelines for women.

14. In the table of contents to the text, sections 19 and 20 appear in reverse order. An annotated translation of the entire text, including the prefaces and excluding the commentaries, appears in Nicholson 2000. Sections 10, 11, 12, and 19 have been translated in Wong 1998, 57–70, 71–89, 91–102, and 103–13, respectively. The phrase *zhengdao*, here rendered as "correct path," could also be translated as "aligning with the Dao."

15. This is an early Daoist technical term for a meditation and purification chamber. It is more conventionally translated as "pure chamber" or "chamber of quiescence."

16. As discussed earlier, these phrases derive from chapter 2 of the *Zhuangzi* (Book of Master Zhuang).

17. In Daoist meditation practice, "reverting the radiance" (*fanzhao*) usually refers to turning the gaze inward to illuminate the inner landscape of the body. In that context, the left eye is associated with the sun and the right eye with the moon.

18. Here the Palace of Life-Destiny (*minggong*), which recalls the Gate of Life (*mingmen*), seems to refer to the lower elixir field (navel region), the storehouse of *qi*. In other contexts, the Gate of Life refers to the point between the kidneys, the storehouse of vital essence.

19. The same is true with respect to late imperial connections between the imperial court, eunuch culture, and the Longmen lineage. See Komjathy 2008b, 2009.

20. Richard Wilhelm was also father of the famous Sinologist Helmut Wilhelm (1905–1990), who, like his father, was involved in Western esotericism and Jungian psychology. For example, Helmut Wilhelm participated in the Eranos Society (est. 1933; Ascona, Switzerland) (see www.eranossociety.org). Some major participants in this annual discussion included Carl Jung (1875–1961), Joseph Campbell (1904–1987), and Mircea Eliade (1907–1986). See Haki 2013; also Hanegraaff 2012. Interesting in terms of the present volume, the theme of the first Eranos meeting was "Yoga and Meditation East and West."

21. The use of *yoga* to describe Daoist practices is a misnomer and should be avoided. The term, which is an indigenous Indian Sanskrit one rooted in a radically different soteriology, was early on utilized by individuals like the famous British historian of science Joseph Needham (1900–1995) and the lay Chinese Buddhist scholar-practitioner Charles Luk (Lu K'uan Yü; 1898–1978) to discuss Daoist internal alchemy. See, for example, Luk 1973. So-called "Taoist Yoga," sometimes referred to under the names of "Flow Yoga" or "Yin Yoga," has now become systematized and marketed as part of contemporary American hybrid spirituality. For a critical and informed perspective, see Komjathy 2013b and 2014. See also the entry on "Taoist Yoga" and "Common Misconceptions concerning Daoism" on the Center for Daoist Studies website.

22. For an initial, albeit problematic, attempt to consider Jung's engagement with "Daoism," see Clarke 1994. Unfortunately, that study lacks the necessary religious literacy with respect to Daoism (see Komjathy 2013b, 2014). It is, nonetheless, helpful for considering Jung's constructions of "Daoism," even if Clarke does not adequately recognize them as such. Such, perhaps, is one of the pitfalls of an intellectual history approach. See also Kripal 2008.

23. According to Eva Wong,

Unfortunately, Wilhelm's translation (and the English version of Cary F. Baynes) was based on an incomplete text of the *Hui-ming ching*: the commentaries and the most important sections—the illustrations—were missing. Moreover, the Wilhelm-Baynes translation is severely biased by Jungian psychology and does not present the book from the Taoist spiritual perspective. Not only are the historical and philosophical connections with its major influences—the Complete Reality [Quanzhen] school of Taoism, Ch'an (Zen), and Hua-yen Buddhism—ignored, but the teachings of the Wu-liu sect, which form the spiritual foundation of the *Hui-ming ching*, are not acknowledged. (1998, 5–6)

24. As mentioned, Wong translated sections 1–8, 10–12, and 19 of the received *Huiming jing*.
25. Nicholson's study includes an annotated translation of the entire text, including the prefaces but excluding the commentaries.

Works Cited and Further Reading

Baldrian-Hussein, Farzeen. 2008a. "*Huiming jing*." In *The Encyclopedia of Taoism*, edited by Fabrizio Pregadio, 520–21. London and New York: Routledge.

———. 2008b. "Liu Huayang." In *The Encyclopedia of Taoism*, edited by Fabrizio Pregadio, 688–89. London and New York: Routledge.

———. 2008c. "Wu Shouyang." In *The Encyclopedia of Taoism*, edited by Fabrizio Pregadio, 1046–47. London and New York: Routledge.

———. 2008d. "Wu-Liu pai." In *The Encyclopedia of Taoism*, edited by Fabrizio Pregadio, 1049–50. London and New York: Routledge.

Boltz, Judith. 1987. *A Survey of Taoist Literature, Tenth to Seventh Centuries*. Berkeley: Institute of East Asian Studies.

Broughton, Jeffrey. 1999. *The Bodhidharma Anthology: The Earliest Records of Zen*. Berkeley: University of California Press.

Buddhist Text Translation Society (BTTS). 2009. *The Śūraṅgama Sūtra: A New Translation with Excerpts from the Commentary by the Venerable Master Hsuan Hua*. Ukiah: Dharma Realm Buddhist Association.

Chang, Garma. 1971. *The Buddhist Teaching of Totality: The Philosophy of Hwa Yen Buddhism*. University Park: Pennsylvania State University Press.

Ch'en, Kenneth. 1964. *Buddhism in China: A Historical Survey*. Princeton: Princeton University Press.

Clarke, J. J. 1994. *Jung and Eastern Thought: A Dialogue with the Orient*. London and New York: Routledge.

———. 1997. *Oriental Enlightenment: The Encounter between Asian and Western Thought*. London and New York: Routledge.

———. 2000. *The Tao of the West: Western Transformations of Taoist Thought*. London and New York: Routledge.

Cleary, Thomas. 1993. *The Flower Ornament Scripture: A Translation of the Avatamsaka Sutra*. Boston: Shambhala.

Cook, Francis. 1973. *Hua-Yen Buddhism: The Jewel Net of Indra*. University Park: Pennsylvania State University Press.

De Bruyn, Pierre-Henry. 2000. "Daoism in the Ming (1368–1644)." In *Daoism Handbook*, edited by Livia Kohn, 594–622. Leiden: Brill.

Deng Huiji, ed. 1987 (1897). *Wu-Liu xianzong*. Henan: Henan renmin chubanshe.

Dumoulin, Heinrich. 1988. *Zen Buddhism: A History*. Translated by James Heisig and Paul Knitter. Vol. 1: India and China. New York: Macmillan.

———. 1990. *Zen Buddhism: A History*. Translated by James Heisig and Paul Knitter. Vol. 2: Japan. New York: Macmillan.
Eskildsen, Stephen. 2001. "Seeking Signs of Proof: Visions and Other Trance Phenomena in Early Quanzhen Taoism." *Journal of Chinese Religions* 29: 139–60.
———. 2004. *The Teachings and Practices of the Early Quanzhen Taoist Masters*. Albany: State University of New York Press.
Esposito, Monica. 2000. "Daoism in the Qing (1644–1911)." In *Daoism Handbook*, edited by Livia Kohn, 623–58. Leiden: Brill.
———. 2001. "Longmen Taoism in Qing China: Doctrinal Ideal and Local Reality." *Journal of Chinese Religions* 29: 191–231.
———. 2004. "The Longmen School and Its Controversial History during the Qing Dynasty." In *Religion and Chinese Society*, edited by John Lagerwey, vol. 2, 621–98. 2 vols. Hong Kong: Chinese University of Hong Kong.
Goossaert, Vincent. 2007. *The Taoists of Peking, 1800–1949: A Social History of Urban Clerics*. Cambridge: Harvard University Press.
Hakl, Thomas. 2013. *Eranos: An Alternative Intellectual History of the Twentieth Century*. Translated by Christopher McIntosh. London and New York: Routledge.
Hanegraaff, Wouter. 2012. *Esotericism and the Academy: Rejected Knowledge in Western Culture*. Cambridge and New York: Cambridge University Press.
Hobsbawm, Eric, and Terence Ranger, eds. 1983. *The Invention of Tradition*. Cambridge and New York: Cambridge University Press.
Jung, Carl. 1980. *Psychology and Alchemy*. Translated by Gerhard Adler and R. F. C. Hull. Princeton: Princeton University Press.
———. 1983. *Alchemical Studies*. Translated by Gerhard Adler and R. F. C. Hull. Princeton: Princeton University Press.
———. 1989. *Memories, Dreams, Reflections*. Edited by Aniela Jaffé. Translated by Richard and Clara Winston. Rev. ed. New York: Vintage Books.
Kohn, Livia, ed. 1989. *Taoist Meditation and Longevity Techniques*. Ann Arbor: Center for Chinese Studies, University of Michigan.
———. 2004. *Cosmos and Community: The Ethical Dimension of Daoism*. Cambridge: Three Pines Press.
Komjathy, Louis. 2002. *Title Index to Daoist Collections*. Cambridge: Three Pines Press.
———. 2003. "Daoist Texts in Translation." Center for Daoist Studies website (www.daoistcenter.org/advanced.html). Accessed on June 1, 2014.
———. 2004. "Tracing the Contours of Daoism in North America." *Nova Religio* 8.2 (November 2004): 5–27.
———. 2006. "Qigong in America." In *Daoist Body Cultivation*, edited by Livia Kohn, 203–35. Cambridge: Three Pines Press.
———. 2007. *Cultivating Perfection: Mysticism and Self-Transformation in Early Quanzhen Daoism*. Leiden: Brill.
———. 2008a. *Handbooks for Daoist Practice*. 10 vols. Hong Kong: Yuen Yuen Institute.
———. 2008b. "Mapping the Daoist Body: Part I: The *Neijing tu* in History." *Journal of Daoist Studies* 1: 67–92.
———. 2009. "Mapping the Daoist Body: Part II: The Text of the *Neijing tu*." *Journal of Daoist Studies* 2: 64–108.
———. 2013a. *The Way of Complete Perfection: A Quanzhen Daoist Anthology*. Albany: State University of New York Press.
———. 2013b. *The Daoist Tradition: An Introduction*. London and New York: Bloomsbury Academic.
———. 2014. *Daoism: A Guide for the Perplexed*. London and New York: Bloomsbury Academic.

Kripal, Jeffrey. 2008. *Esalen: America and the Religion of No Religion.* Chicago: University of Chicago Press.
Liu Ts'un-yan. 1984. *New Excursions from the Hall of Harmonious Wind.* Leiden: Brill.
Luk, Charles (Lu K'uan Yü). 1966. *The Śūraṅgama Sūtra.* London: Rider and Company.
———. 1973. *Taoist Yoga: Alchemy and Immortality.* York Beach: Samuel Weiser.
McRae, John. 1987. *The Northern School and the Formation of Early Chan Buddhism.* Honolulu: University of Hawaii Press.
Needham, Joseph et al. 1976. *Science and Civilisation in China, Vol. 5: Chemistry and Chemical Technology, Part 3: Spagyrical Discovery and Invention: Historical Survey, from Cinnabar Elixirs to Synthetic Insulin.* Cambridge: Cambridge University Press.
———. 1983. *Science and Civilisation in China, Vol. 5: Chemistry and Chemical Technology, Part 5: Spagyrical Discovery and Invention: Physiological Alchemy.* Cambridge: Cambridge University Press.
Nicholson, James Michael. 2000. "The *Huiming jing*: A Translation and Discussion." Master's thesis, University of British Columbia.
Noll, Richard. 1997. *The Jung Cult: Origins of a Charismatic Movement.* New York: Free Press Paperbacks.
Palmer, David. 2007. *Qigong Fever: Body, Science, and Utopia in China.* New York: Columbia University Press.
Pregadio, Fabrizio, and Lowell Skar. 2000. "Inner Alchemy (*Neidan*)." In *Daoism Handbook*, edited by Livia Kohn, 464–97. Leiden: Brill.
Pulleyblank, Edwin. 1991. *Lexicon of Reconstructed Pronunciation in Early Middle Chinese, Late Middle Chinese, and Early Mandarin.* Vancouver: University of British Columbia Press.
Qing Xitai, ed. 1996 (1988–1995). *Zhongguo daojiao shi.* 4 vols. Chengdu: Sichuan renmin chubanshe.
Shamdasani, Sonu. 1998. *Cult Fictions: C. G. Jung and the Founding of Analytical Psychology.* London and New York: Routledge.
———. 2003. *Jung and the Making of Modern Psychology: The Dream of a Science.* Cambridge and New York: Cambridge University Press.
Walravens, Hartmut, ed. 2008. *Richard Wilhelm (1873–1930): Missionar in China und Vermittler chinesischen Geistesguts.* Nettetal: Steyler.
Wilhelm, Richard. 1923. *I Ging: Das Buch der Wandlungen.* Jena: Eugen Diederichs.
———. 1929. *Das Geheimnis der Goldenen Blüte: Ein chinesisches Lebensbuch.* Zürich and Stuttgart: Rascher Verlag.
———. 1962 (1931). *The Secret of the Golden Flower: A Chinese Book of Life.* Translated by Cary F. Baynes. Rev. ed. New York: Mariner Books.
———. 1967 (1950). *The I Ching, or Book of Changes.* Translated by Cary F. Baynes. 3rd, rev. ed. Princeton: Princeton University Press.
Wippermann, Dorothea, Klaus Hirsh, and Georg Ebertshäuser. 2007. *Interkulturalität im frühen 20. Jahrhundert: Richard Wilhelm—Theologe, Missionar und Sinologe.* Berlin: IKO-Verlag.
Wong, Eva. 1998. *Cultivating the Energy of Life: A Translation of the Hui-ming ching and Its Commentaries.* Boston: Shambhala.
———. 2000. *The Tao of Health, Longevity, and Immortality: The Teachings of the Immortals Chung and Lü.* Boston: Shambhala.
Wright, Arthur. 1959. *Buddhism in Chinese History.* Stanford: Stanford University Press.
Wu, Jiang. 2008. *Enlightenment in Dispute: The Reinvention of Chan Buddhism in Seventeenth-Century China.* Oxford and New York: Oxford University Press.

Huiming jing (Scripture on Wisdom and Life-Destiny)*

Liu Huayang (1735–1799)[1]

Translated and Annotated by Louis Komjathy

1. Diagram of the Cessation of Outflow[2]

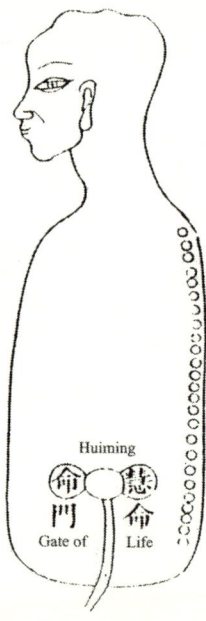

Figure 12.3. Stage 1 of Alchemical Transformation: Cessation of Outflow

---

*The present translation is based on the Chinese edition contained in ZW 131 (dat. 1794/1799), with "ZW" referring to the modern collection of Daoist texts known as the *Zangwai daoshu* (Daoist Books outside the Canon; dat. 1992/1995; see Komjathy 2002). The present text, the first section of the received *Huiming jing*, appears in 5:878–83. I have also consulted the independently circulated *Wu-Liu xianzong* (Deng 1987 [1897]). A popular audience translation of the *Huiming jing* appears in Richard Wilhelm's *The Secret of the Golden Flower* (Harcourt Brace, 1962) and Eva Wong's *Cultivating the Energy of Life* (Shambhala, 1998). In the case of the former, readers are reading an English translation of a German translation of the original Chinese text. For an annotated translation of the entire text, including the prefaces but excluding the commentaries, see Nicholson 2000.

1. Liu Huayang (Chuanlu [Transmission Vessel]; 1735–1799) was a Chan Buddhist monk and Daoist sympathizer eventually identified as the cofounder of the Wu-Liu lineage of internal alchemy (*neidan*). Associated with Wu Shouyang (Chongxu [Infused Emptiness]; 1574–1644) and Liu, the Wu-Liu lineage is technically a sublineage of the Longmen (Dragon Gate) lineage of Quanzhen (Complete Perfection) Daoism.

2. Or, "free from outflow," which also appears as "nondissipation" (*wulou*). The diagram identifies the Gate of Life (*mingmen*), located between the kidneys, as associated with wisdom and life-destiny (*huiming*). It shows the "path of dissipation" as descending from that location to outside the body. Here *loujin* is used in a Buddhist technical sense of "without outflow" (Skt.: *āsrava-kṣaya*), but "nondissipation" (*wulou*; Skt.: *anāsrava*) usually appears in an internal alchemy

If you want to complete the diamond-body beyond dissipation (*loujin*),
You must practice diligently to decoct the root of wisdom and life-destiny.[3]
In meditative absorption,[4] illumine and never depart from the ground of joyfulness;
In time, the perfected self will secretly reside in this location.[5]

Considering the essential subtleties of the Dao, nothing compares to innate nature and life-destiny.[6] In cultivating and refining these aspects, nothing compares to returning to oneness.[7] When providing guidance on uniting innate nature and life-destiny, the ancient sages and exalted worthies instructed using symbols. They did not dare to disseminate the teachings with direct explanations. Thus there is no one in the present time who engages in such dual cultivation.

In compiling and publishing these diagrams, I have not engaged in reckless dissemination. Rather, I combined notes from the *Lengyan jing*[8] on nondissipation with secret instructions from the Flower Garland[9] and various teachings from other scriptures in order to create accurate illustrations.

---

context. In any case, the perineum area, usually referred to as Huiyin (Meeting of Yin) or Dihu (Earth Door), is often associated with the lower elixir field and vital essence (*jing*), with the latter related to semen in men and menstrual blood in women. Vital essence, the basis of one's core vitality, in turn becomes dissipated through seminal emission in men and menstruation in women. As in the next two diagrams, the body, especially the Daoist subtle or alchemical body, in this stage of the practice is depicted as a torso.

3. I have translated the phrase *huiming* as "wisdom and life-destiny," but it is possible that the characters form a composite category related to vitality. There also appears to be an interesting view of "wisdom" as associated with the kidneys. As a form of Buddho-Daoist syncretism, it appears that the stabilization of vital essence, also associated with emotionality, is required for the emergence of spiritual insight, or wisdom.

4. "Meditative absorption" (*ding*), also translated as "concentration," renders *samādhi*. The latter is a Sanskrit technical term, here derived from Buddhism, for a deeper state of meditation.

5. Although initially difficult to determine, the paired couplets of these poems may be resolved by analyzing the tonal patterns of the lines based on their Early Middle Chinese pronunciation (see Pulleyblank 1991; Nicholson 2000, 128–32).

6. Associated with original spirit (*yuanshen*) and the heart, "innate nature" (*xing*) relates to one's consciousness and divine capacities. Associated with vital essence (*jing*), original qi (*yuanqi*), and the kidneys, life-destiny relates to one's foundational vitality and physicality, or corporeality more generally. The reference to the combined terms indicates complete psychosomatic transformation.

7. "Returning to oneness" (*guiyi*) is a Daoist technical term that may refer to either Daoist meditation or mystical union with the Dao. *Yi*, translatable as "the One," "oneness," and "unity," refers to the Dao. In terms of Daoist meditation, "embracing the One" (*baoyi*) and "guarding the One" (*shouyi*) are classical Daoist terms for Daoist apophatic meditation. In the later Daoist tradition, *shouyi* may be a generic name for "meditation" and/or may refer to a wide variety of specific methods (see Kohn 1989; Komjathy 2013b).

8. The Chinese version of the *Śūraṅgama Sūtra* (Discourse on Indestructible [Samādhi]), which was originally written in Sanskrit. This text is a Mahāyāna (Greater Vehicle) Buddhist sutra that was highly influential in the Chan (Jpn.: Zen; Meditation) school of Chinese Buddhism. The text emphasizes the attainment of higher levels of consciousness through the purification of defilements and delusion, and the importance of *samādhi* (meditative absorption or concentration) in the attainment of Buddhahood. See Luk 1966; BTTS 2009. Note that Wong (1998) fails to identify this sutra, both here and in diagrams 4 and 5.

9. Huayan (Flower Garland) refers to both a Chinese school of Mahāyāna Buddhism and the Buddhist text from which the name derives. The *Huayan jing* is the Chinese name for the *Avataṃsaka Sūtra* (Discourse on the Flower Garland). In both the Huayan (Jpn.: Kegon) and Tiantai (Jpn.: Tendai; Celestial Terrace) schools, this sutra is believed to be the perfect expression of enlightened consciousness. The text depicts the Buddha describing the universe as consisting of a hidden, complex structure and infinite realms that become revealed through meditative practice. The text also contains the famous "Indra's Jeweled Net" that expresses the Mahāyāna Buddhist emphasis on interpenetration and interconnection. See Cleary 1993; also Chang 1971; Cook 1973.

Through them one may understand that wisdom and life-destiny[10] are not outside the [mysterious] cavity. These diagrams are intended to assist adepts with similar aspirations to understand the celestial workings of dual cultivation. In this way, one will not be misled by side gates (*pangmen*).[11] The diagrams illustrate how to nourish and tend to the perfect seed, how to end patterns of dissipation, how to complete the precious relic (*sheli*),[12] and how to refine the great Dao.

This cavity is the cavern of empty Nonbeing. It has neither form nor shape. When the numinous *qi*[13] manifests, the cavity is complete. When its movement ceases, it becomes vague and indistinct.[14] It is the place where perfection is stored, the altar for cultivating wisdom and life-destiny. There are many names for it, including the Dragon Palace at the Ocean Floor, the Land of the Snowy Mountain, the Western Realm,[15] Original Pass, Country of Utmost Joy, and Village of Nondifferentiation. Even though there are many different names, they all refer to this single cavity. If adepts engaging in cultivation do not understand this single cavity,[16] they will wander through a thousand lifetimes and ten thousand eons (*kalpa*) without knowing how to find wisdom and life-destiny.

This cavity is great and amazing. Before we were born from our parents, we existed in embryonic form. Before birth, innate nature and life-destiny were a single substance in this cavity. Everything was joined in the center. These two aspects were fused and united. The smelting and refining was like fire in a furnace. It was the type of oneness that joins Great Harmony with celestial principle.[17]

Thus it is said that Prior Heaven (*xiantian*)[18] contains limitless cycles of respiration. Thus it is said that prior to birth, *qi* is abundant and the embryo is complete. Then the form stirs and the covering splits open. Like an elevated mountain crashing down, the fetus comes out. With

---

10. In Liu's system, it appears that "wisdom" (*hui*) is used interchangeably with "innate nature" (*xing*), though it is possible to read *huiming* as a compound related to vitality. The latter reading is supported by the fact that another Chinese character for wisdom (*zhi*) is associated with the kidneys in Chinese correlative cosmology based on the Five Phases (*wuxing*).

11. Erroneous views, mistaken approaches, deviant teachings, and deficient practices.

12. Skt.: *śarīra*. A Buddhist technical term referring to "relics," or miraculous objects that appear in the cremation remains of advanced Buddhist practitioners and enlightened beings. Here the term seems to refer to a capacity for spiritual realization and as evidence of alchemical transformation. It thus may be read as an alternative name for the "body-beyond-the-body" (*shenwai shen*), "embryo of immortality" (*xiantai*), and the "yang-spirit" (*yangshen*).

13. Liu Huayang uses the Daoist character for *qi* (*ch'i*), which may be translated as "vital" or "subtle breath," and more problematically as "energy" or "pneuma." Qi is the subtle vapor circulating through the universe and body. The standard character 氣 depicts "steam" (*qi* 气) over "rice" (*mi* 米). The Daoist character 炁 depicts "emptiness" (*wu* 无) over "fire" (*huo* 火/灬), suggesting subtle heat in the body.

14. Subtle. In a Daoist context, "vague and indistinct" (*miaomang*) also refers to the Dao.

15. The Western Realm may refer to Mount Kunlun (the Western Daoist paradise) and/or the Pure Land of Amitābha Buddha, the Buddha of Infinite Life. According to the text, these sacred realms are *inside* the practitioner's own body rather than located in some external site. They are different names for the Ocean of Qi (*qihai*), also referred to as the "lower elixir field" (*dantian*). This is the navel and lower abdomen region.

16. *Yiqiao*, here translated as "single cavity," might also be translated as "cavity of unity," with "one" (*yi*) referring to psychosomatic unity, mystical union, and the Dao as oneself.

17. The universe as primordial unity and cosmological process, wherein the structure and principles are harmonized. From a Daoist perspective, one may return to this original condition in one's own being.

18. Also translated as "Anterior Heaven," *xiantian* refers to a prenatal condition, that is, one before birth. In terms of Daoist practice, it relates to primordial or original *qi*, to complete cosmological integration and unity. It stands in contrast to Later Heaven, specifically the condition after birth wherein physical respiration and food are the primary sources of nourishment for ordinary people.

its first cry, innate nature and life-destiny separate and become two aspects. From this point on, innate nature cannot recognize life-destiny, and life-destiny cannot recognize innate nature. So, one moves from infancy to youth, from youth to old age, and from old age to death.

Therefore, the Tathāgata,[19] through his great compassion, disseminated a method of cultivation and refinement in order to teach people to return to the womb. By diligently preparing innate nature and life-destiny, our *qi* and spirit will enter the cavity. There they become harmonized and unified, complete as a perfect seed that resembles the vital essence of father and mother. When *qi* enters this cavity, it becomes harmonized and unified, so that the embryo is complete and embodies oneness.

The sovereign fire (*junhuo*) is inside the cavity; the ministerial fire (*xianghuo*) guards the gates; and the subject fire (*minhuo*) encircles the body.[20] When the sovereign fire issues forth, the ministerial fire supports it. When the ministerial fire manifests, the subject fire follows it. When the three fires go forward and outward, one completes human being. When they move in reverse and inward, one completes the Dao.

Thus the cavity of nondissipation is also the place that gives rise to sacredness.[21] If you do not cultivate this way (*dao*), you will be divided. If you cultivate dividedness and commit to that, there will be no benefit. Therefore, even if you have access to a thousand gates and ten thousand doors,[22] failure to understand that this cavity contains wisdom and life-destiny will lead to a vain search for external governance and control. You will waste time and effort. In the end, you will exhaust yourself and accomplish nothing.

---

19. The Tathāgata (Thus Come) refers to Siddhartha Gautama, the historical Buddha. In terms of the Chan tradition, it also appears as the *tathāgata-garbha*, the "Buddha-embryo" or "womb of Buddhahood." This is one's original nature, or capacity for enlightenment.

20. The "three fires" (*sanhuo*), also translated as the "ruling," "subordinate," and "common fire," respectively. The meaning of "fire" in Daoist internal alchemy is complex. On the most basic level, it refers to the Fire phase in correlative cosmology, which is associated with the heart and spirit. In Daoist *neidan* practice, it also refers to "firing times" (*huohou*), or the degree to which one exerts effort and uses intentionality in practice. In terms of the three fires, they are commonly identified as the "true fires of *samādhi*" (*sanmei zhenhuo*): (1) sovereign fire associated with the heart and spirit, (2) ministerial fire associated with the Ocean of *Qi* (navel region) and *qi*, and (3) subject fire associated with the kidneys and vital essence. Utilizing the Chinese bureaucratic idiom, the first is dominant, while the latter two, in sequence, are subordinate. One also encounters the sovereign fire and ministerial fire in Chinese medicine, though the subject fire appears to be uncommon. Within that context, the sovereign fire often refers to the heart, while the ministerial fire refers to the pericardium. Alternatively, the former designates kidney-yang, while the latter designates the Mingmen (Gate of Life), the area roughly between the kidneys. See Komjathy 2007, 2013a. Based on context, it appears that here the sovereign fire refers to the kidney-yang or original *qi* (*yuanqi*) in the lower elixir field (navel region); the ministerial fire refers to fire associated with Mingmen, which is a gate that also spreads to the liver, gall bladder, Triple Warmer (*sanjiao*), and pericardium; and the subject fire is the movement of *qi* throughout the entire organ-meridian system, which might also relate to the Triple Warmer's distribution of original *qi* (source-*qi*) through the body, including "source-points" (*yuanxue*). I am grateful to Kate Townsend of the Daoist Foundation for her insights here.

21. Or, "sagehood" (*sheng*).

22. Other approaches, lineages, and schools.

2. Diagram of the Six Phases of the Dharma Wheel[23]

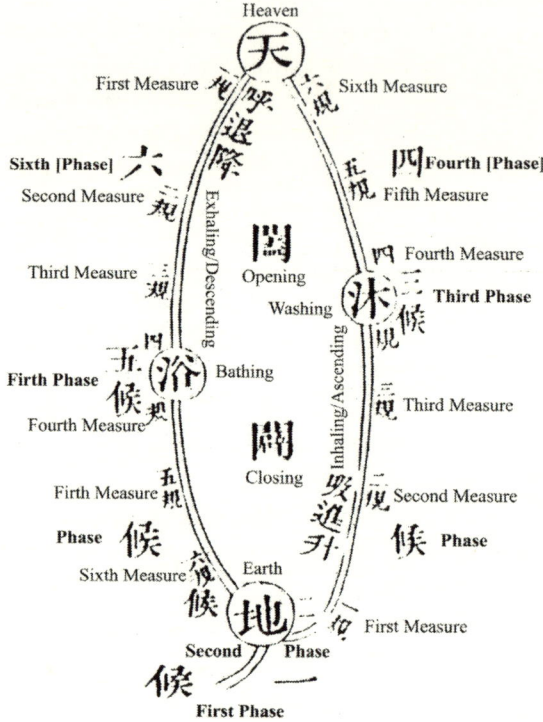

Figure 12.4. Stage 2 of Alchemical Transformation: Six Phases of the Dharma Wheel

Open up the road to the source [as revealed by] buddhas and patriarchs;
Work to manifest the City of Utmost Joy in the Western Realm.
By turning the Dharma Wheel during inhalation, you pay court to the heavens;[24]
When breathing through exhalation, you return to the earth.[25]

---

23. Recalling the previous diagram and transitioning to the next one, this illustration depicts the human torso viewed from the left side. It identifies the crown-point as "heaven" and the perineum region as "earth." The spine (Governing Vessel) and front center-line (Conception Vessel) are divided into "six measures" (*gui*), amounting to twelve in total. Moving from the base of the spine to the crown of the head, the former involves inhalation and ascent; moving from the crown of the head to the base of the spine, the latter involves exhalation and descent. The former is identified as "washing" (*mu*), while the latter is identified as "bathing" (*yu*). Also somewhat confusingly, the diagram uses the "six phases" (*hou*) mentioned in the poem to refer to specific corporeal locations: (1) urethra, (2) perineum, (3) mid-spine, (4) upper spine, (5) heart level, and (6) upper chest. In any case, this diagram directs the reader's attention to the central importance of the Governing Vessel and Conception Vessel, and to the practice of the Microcosmic Orbit (*xiao zhoutian*). The latter is also referred to as the Waterwheel (*heche*) and the Dharma Wheel (*falun*). For additional guidance on the practice from Liu Huayang, see ZW 131, 5.903; Wong 1998, 74.

24. Here "heaven" (*tian*), literally, "sky," refers to the head.

25. Here "earth" (*di*) refers to the perineum.

Timing is divided into six phases (*hou*);
In a single instance (*ke*), connect beginning and end.
The great Dao emerges from the Center;
Do not seek the original pivot on the outside.

For the wondrous application of the Dao, nothing is better than the Dharma Wheel; it circulates without ceasing. Nothing is better than following its path;[26] do not become obstructed or delayed. Nothing is better than the phases for keeping track; do not make mistakes. Nothing is better than the segmented wheel, which this diagram illustrates. When this method of great preparation is completed, the true face[27] will emerge from the west.[28] This is the key to everything; there is nothing beyond this.

To find the original wondrousness in the Center, nothing is better than practicing inhalation and exhalation. Considering such breathing patterns, it is essential to observe the openings and closings. In inhibiting the tendency to stray from the path, nothing is better than true intent and perfect awareness. In terms of starting and stopping, nothing is better than demarcating the territory. This involves abandoning self and according with others.

Even though this diagram completely divulges the secrets of the heavens, if ordinary and ignorant people attain it, they certainly will be unable to attain completion. This is because the heavens will not reveal the Dao to those who lack virtue and adhere to ignorance. Why is this? Because the relation between virtue and the Dao is like feathers to birds. One cannot function without the other. You must embody the four cardinal virtues of loyalty, filial piety, humaneness, and righteousness. You must also follow the five precepts.[29] After you are completely pure, you will attain the anticipated result. The *Huiming jing* contains everything essential, subtle, obscure and wondrous.[30] Study it carefully and you will assuredly attain perfection.

---

26. *Daolu* is open to interpretation. On the most basic level, it refers to a "road" or "path," but *dao* might also refer to the Dao itself. Thus, the phrase might be rendered as "path of the Dao."

27. A Chan Buddhist technical term for one's original nature (*benxing*).

28. Wilhelm (1962, 72) has, "This presentation contains the whole of the law, and the true features of the Buddha from the West are contained in it."

29. The five foundational Buddhist ethical commitments: no killing, no stealing, no lying, no sexual misconduct, and no intoxicants.

30. These terms most often refer to the Dao.

3. Diagram of the Governing and Conception Vessels[31]

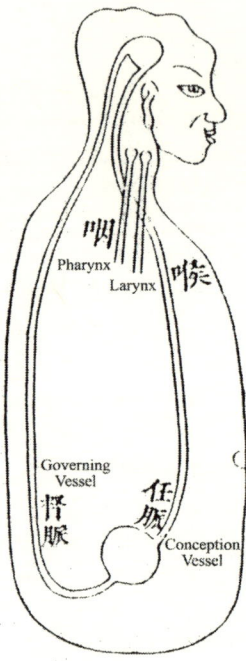

Figure 12.5. Stage 3 of Alchemical Transformation: Governing and Conception Vessels

Work to manifest the path of respiration of the Original Pass;[32]
Do not forget to initiate the circulation of the Dharma Wheel through the hundred meridians.[33]
Constantly direct the fire to nourish the cavity of perpetual life;
Remain attentive to the bright pearl[34] in the pass of deathlessness.

---

31. This diagram depicts the Governing Vessel (*dumai*) and Conception Vessel (*renmai*). In the Daoist Microcosmic Orbit practice described in the text, one circulates *qi* up the Governing Vessel, which basically moves from the perineum around the crown-point to the upper lip, and down the Conception Vessel, which basically moves from the lower lip to the perineum. Here the lower elixir field (*dantian*), or the navel region, is especially important, as it is the primary corporeal location where *qi* is stored. This diagram with additional comments also appears in section 17 of the *Jinxian zhenglu* (ZW 132, 5.955).

32. The Original Pass (*yuanguan*) usually refers to the lower elixir field.

33. "Meridians" refers to the channels or pathways through which *qi* circulates in the body. There are twelve organ meridians and eight "extraordinary" ones. The latter are especially important in Daoist internal alchemy.

34. "Bright pearl" refers to spiritual illumination and the elixir of immortality. In terms of Buddhism, it relates to enlightenment and liberation. In terms of Daoism, it relates to the creation of a transcendent spirit capable of surviving physical death.

This diagram and the previous one are actually the same. Why is such repetition necessary? Because I fear that those who are cultivating the Dao do not know their own bodies. The body contains a pathway known as the Dharma Wheel. Accordingly, I created this illustration to assist those with similar aspirations.

If people can connect these two channels, then the hundred meridians will also be connected. Similarly, a sleeping deer touches its nose to its anus to connect the Governing Vessel, and the crane and tortoise connect the Conception Vessel naturally. If these animals can live for a thousand years, then there is no reason why humans cannot. If adepts cultivating the Dao[35] turn the Dharma Wheel,[36] they will be able to circulate wisdom and life-destiny, attain longevity, and complete the Dao.

---

35. *Xiudao zhi shi*. Interestingly, this phrase recalls the standard Daoist name for Daoist priests and monastics (*daoshi*). The latter technical term literally means "adept of the Way," and Liu suggests "cultivating the Dao" is primary.

36. One might read this line as a brilliant Buddhist polemical and evangelical move. By referring to the Microcosmic Orbit practice as the Dharma Wheel, and as "turning the Dharma Wheel" also refers to providing Buddhist teachings, Daoist adepts become Buddhist converts, at least on some level, through this practice. Alternatively, under a Chan Buddhist reading, one does not need the "teachings" of the Buddha (sutras), as the body contains an inherent capacity for enlightenment, here also associated with the activation of the subtle body. However, one should also keep in mind that in the late medieval period Daoist internal alchemists utilized "Dharma Wheel" to refer to the Microcosmic Orbit (see Komjathy 2007, 2013a). Thus, from a Daoist *neidan* perspective, the Buddhist "dharma" becomes replaced by the subtle body, which circulates the numinous presence of the Dao. Ultimately, here we again see a complex Buddho-Daoist cross-pollination, in which Daoist reconceptualizations have become Buddhist reconceptualizations.

4. Diagram of the Embryo of the Dao[37]

Figure 12.6. Stage 4 of Alchemical Transformation: Embryo of the Dao

Apply the method without effort and diligently allow the illumination to penetrate;
Forget form and attend to the inside so that the perfect numen will grow.
Incubate the embryo of the Dao with fire for ten months;
Bathe and cleanse it in warmth for one year.

This illustration is based on the *Lengyan jing* (*Śūraṅgama Sūtra*),[38] which originally was a secret teaching. Ordinary Buddhist monks do not know about the embryo of the Dao because previously it was not described with illustrations. For the benefit of fellow practitioners, I will now explain the embryo of the Dao as embodied by the Tathāgata. Its substance and authenticity reside in inner work.

---

37. There is no additional information in the Chinese version of the diagram, and its content is straightforward. However, the attentive reader will notice that this diagram has Buddhist characteristics. In particular, one notices the so-called head protuberance (*uṣṇīṣa*). This is one of the thirty-two "marks" or physical attributes (*lakṣaṇa*) of a great spirit or realized being (*mahāparuṣa*). In this and the subsequent diagrams, the body now includes limbs rather than simply a torso or energetic network. Moreover, like the diagrams 5 through 7, it depicts the meditator in full-lotus posture, which was the standard and preferred posture in Buddhism and also became increasingly prominent in Daoist meditation from the Tang dynasty (618–907) onward.

38. See fn. 8.

This embryo has neither form nor shape. It is created from two substances: spirit and *qi* contained within oneself. First, spirit enters *qi*, and then *qi* envelops spirit. When spirit and *qi* coalesce together, and thinking becomes silent and unagitated, this is called the "embryo." After *qi* congeals, spirit becomes numinous. Thus the scripture says, "Personally maintain awakened responsiveness";[39] the two vapors become nourished. It also says, "Through daily commitment and constant nourishment," *qi* becomes sufficient and the embryo complete. Eventually, it emerges from the crown-point. We refer to this as "form becoming complete to emerge as a fetus." Our tradition considers it to be the child of the Buddha.

---

39. Quotations unidentified. Presumably the *Lengyan jing*.

5. Diagram of Sending Out the Fetus[40]

Figure 12.7. Stage 5 of Alchemical Transformation: Sending Out the Fetus

Beyond the body, there is another body called the Buddha form;
The numinous power of consciousness is beyond thinking, which is *bodhi*.[41]
A thousand-petaled lotus flower[42] emerges as an emanation of *qi*;
A hundred-rayed luminous presence appears as a coalescence of spirit.

---

40. Like the previous diagram and the subsequent ones, this diagram does not contain any additional information, and its content is self-explanatory. However, we might once again note that the illustration seems to depict a Buddhist monk (shaven head) rather than a Daoist one (uncut hair and beard). However, the fact that the image lacks clothing (and also genitalia) might rather point in a different direction. These images seem to follow Daoist notions of a return to "childhood" and cosmic integration, a return to the "primordial womb." In this respect, it is interesting that the paragraph ends with a reference to becoming a "child of the Buddha."

41. *Bodhi* refers to "awakening" or "enlightenment."

42. In the Buddhist tradition, the lotus flower represents enlightenment and pure consciousness. Here one may recall the famous "flower sermon" of Śākyamuni Buddha as told within the Chan tradition, which is actually a Chinese school. According to this legendary account, one day Śākyamuni Buddha gave a silent discourse during which he held up a lotus flower. While the entire monastic community sat dumbfounded, Kāśyapa, one of his senior disciples, smiled. So began the "secret mind-to-mind transmission" of Chan Buddhism. See, for example, Dumoulin 1988.

The *Lengyan zhou* (*Śūraṅgama* Incantation)[43] says, "At that time, a hundred precious rays of radiance issued from the World-Honored One's head; a thousand-petaled precious lotus flower issued from the radiance. The transformation Tathāgata sat on the precious flower. A hundred precious rays of light issued from his head, illuminating the ten directions and manifesting through the totality of sentient beings. Everyone welcomed the radiance-releasing Tathāgata, who was speaking divine incantations." This is the emergence of the yang-spirit. It is called the child of the Buddha.

However, if you do not attain the Way of Wisdom and Life-Destiny, but only helplessly recite the Chan teachings, you may gain personal reputation and worldly recognition, but this is a lesser path. In revealing the secrets of the *Lengyan jing*, I have preserved its teachings for later generations. Those who attain this way will immediately pass into the sacred realms. They will become liberated from the mundane world of dust.

---

43. *Zhou* is the Chinese translation of the Sanskrit *dhāraṇī*, which are magical incantations or invocations used especially in esoteric or Tantric Buddhism. The term is sometimes translated as "spell."

590 / Louis Komjathy

6. Diagram of the Transformation Body[44]

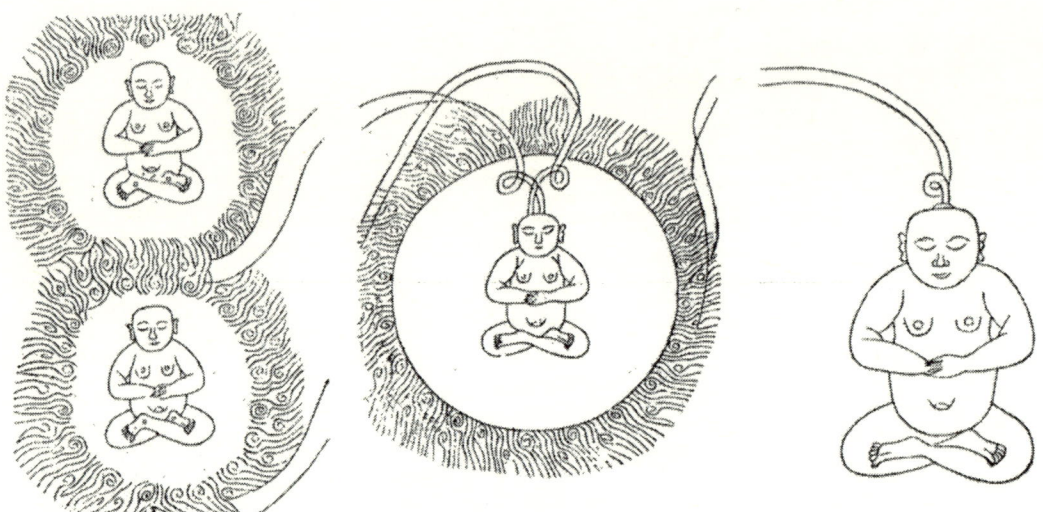

Figure 12.8. Stage 6 of Alchemical Transformation: Transformation Body

Interrupting thought and completing form, watch for the visible appearance;
Merged with the numinous and manifest traces, it becomes the empty Void.
Manifesting in Being and disappearing into Nonbeing,[45] one realizes the wondrous Dao;
Divided in form and appearing in bodies,[46] you merge with the perfect Source.

---

44. This diagram depicts the "transformation body," which is one of the so-called Three Bodies (*trikāya*). A Buddhist technical term, the Three Bodies refers to the threefold body or nature of a buddha: the Dharmakāya, Sambhogakāya, and Nirmāṇakāya, that is, the dharma-body, bliss-body, and transformation-body. These correspond to (1) the body of a buddha in its essential nature (cosmic), (2) the body of a buddha received for his own use and enjoyment (divine), and (3) the body of a buddha by which he can appear in any form (physical). In the depiction in the present diagram, one can manifest in many different forms, which appear to be both physical (perhaps different incarnations) and spiritual (multilocality).

45. This line recalls chapter 1 of the *Daode jing* (Scripture on the Dao and Inner Power): "Nameless (*wuming*): the beginning of the heavens and earth. Named (*youming*): the mother of the ten thousand beings." In more cosmological and metaphysical translations, these lines are rendered as follows: "Nonbeing (*wu*) names the beginning of the heavens and earth. Being (*you*) names the mother of the ten thousand things."

46. The meaning here seems to be that realized beings may manifest as multiple individual things and become merged with the totality simultaneously.

7. Diagram of Facing the Wall[47]

Figure 12.9. Stage 7 of Alchemical Transformation: Facing the Wall

The fire of spirit transforms its shape to become an appearance of emptiness *and* form;
The radiance of innate nature reverts its illumination to return to original Perfection.
The mind-seal hangs in the Void like the moon's shadowy purity;[48]
The raft reaches the other shore[49] like the sun's shining radiance.[50]

---

47. "Facing the wall" (*mianbi*) refers to emptiness-based meditation, during which one returns to nonconceptual and contentless awareness. The phrase alludes to the famous Chan story about Bodhidharma's (ca. 6th c. CE) legendary nine years of "wall-gazing," or meditation facing the wall in his hermitage. See Dumoulin 1988. In this diagram, the practitioner still exists as a separate being, as a self-body with form in meditation.

48. The moon represents enlightenment.

49. A famous Buddhist phrase for the attainment of *nirvāṇa*, or liberation from samsaric existence. "Raft" conventionally refers to the Buddhist teachings, while the traversed river represents *saṃsāra*.

50. The sun represents spiritual illumination and insight as well as numinous presence.

8. Diagram of Disappearance into the Void[51]

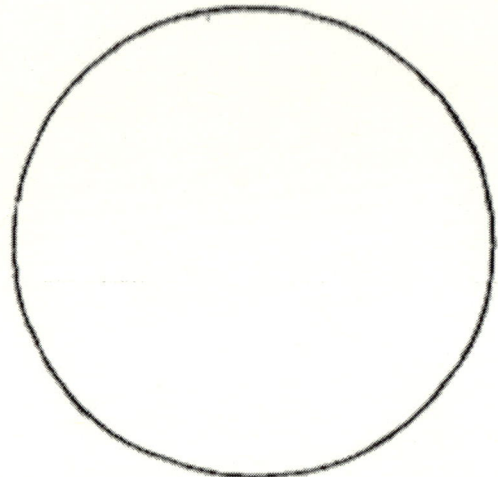

Figure 12.10. Stage 8 of Alchemical Transformation: Disappearance into the Void

One bright ray of light encircles the phenomenal world;
When both are forgotten, silence and stillness become numinous and empty.
In the great expanse of the empty Void, the celestial heart-mind shines;
In the pure clarity of the ocean's waters, the full moon glistens.

There is neither birth nor death;
There is neither past nor future.

Clouds scatter in the blue sky,[52] as the mountainscapes become clear;
Wisdom returns in meditative absorption, as the full moon shines alone.

---

51. The empty circle is a traditional Chan symbol for enlightenment and the end of separate selfhood. It represents emptiness or nothingness. One of the most famous examples appears in the Ten Oxherding Pictures. In the Daoist tradition, the empty circle represents the Dao and mystical union. In this respect, it is interesting that some Daoists interpret the character *yi* 一 (one) as a circle on its side. That is, it represents both individual beings (one) and the Dao as all-encompassing reality (One).

52. Cloudless sky represents meditative emptiness and pure consciousness.

Chapter 13

Therapeutic Meditation

Herbert Benson's *The Relaxation Response*

Louis Komjathy

The Relaxation Response method is a form of modern therapeutic meditation developed by the American cardiologist and Mind-Body pioneer Herbert Benson (b. 1935).[1] This meditation method first entered mainstream American society through Benson's publication of *The Relaxation Response* in 1975. Originally written in English and now a "classic" of Mind-Body Medicine and therapeutic meditation, *The Relaxation Response* describes a step-by-step relaxation technique and stress-management therapy as well as the corresponding trophotropic physiological state identified as the "Relaxation Response." The title of the book thus refers to both a general physiological condition as well as a specific method that elicits the former. The text was, in turn, written for a general audience and aims to have popular and perhaps universal appeal.

Herbert Benson and the Discovery of the "Relaxation Response"

Herbert Benson (b. 1935), MD, is an American cardiologist, Professor of Medicine at Harvard Medical School, and the founder of the Mind/Body Medical Institute, now the Benson-Henry Institute for Mind Body Medicine at Massachusetts General Hospital (Boston, Massachusetts).[2] As discussed throughout the present chapter, Benson is also author of the seminal and highly influential *New York Times* bestseller *The Relaxation Response*, which was first published by William Morrow in 1975.

Herbert Benson was born in Yonkers, New York, to Hannah Benson (maiden name Schiller; ca. 1900–1995) and Charles Benson (1902–1956). His parents were both Jewish immigrants to the United States. Hannah Benson emigrated from western Poland and was a stay-at-home mother. Charles Benson emigrated from Argentina, although he was born in Trieste, Italy. With little formal education and a background in horse training, Charles Benson came to the United States in the 1920s and initially continued to work breaking horses. Herbert Benson's parents met in New York City while attending night school. After marrying, they moved to Yonkers in the 1930s. Charles Benson made his living selling produce at his own fruit and vegetable stand. He eventually established a chain of about nine stores. After being forced out of retail, he began a wholesale produce business. These ventures ensured a relatively comfortable, upper-middle-class life for the family.

The Bensons had three children, including Herbert who was the youngest child. The young Herbert had a stable and relatively comfortable childhood and adolescence. The family originally was part of an Orthodox Jewish congregation, but they moved to Conservative Judaism (see Streett 2010, 29). This change partially occurred on account of Herbert Benson, who was diagnosed with a medical condition that only bacon could supposedly cure. The family in turn broke from the *kashrut* (kosher) dietary requirements and became Conservative Jews. When asked about any significant events from his childhood, Benson responded that there was a security and stability within the family and that his parents were very supportive. They gave the young Herbert freedom to explore his own interests. At the same time, his father inspired and nurtured a strong work ethic, which Herbert Benson describes as "notable" (see also Benson 1996, 15–16). Specifically, his father worried that the family's relative wealth might negatively influence the Benson children. Herbert Benson was, in turn, required to work in the family business. One day when he refused to perform menial labor (emptying trash) because of the extreme summer heat, his father took away his shovel and made him perform the task with his hands. On another occasion, a young boy was stealing fruit. The elder Benson caught him, at which point the boy said that his father was starving. After visiting the impoverished family, he sent a weekly basket of fruit and vegetables. For Herbert Benson, "[M]y father embodied a work ethic and humanity that was fundamental to my whole upbringing." Herbert Benson's father died at the age of fifty-four of rheumatic heart disease, partially as a result of his earlier contraction of rheumatic fever in South America. As discussed later, this event occurred when Herbert Benson was twenty-one years old, and it was one major influence on his decision to pursue medical studies and, specifically, to become a cardiologist.

Herbert Benson attended Wesleyan University, a private liberal arts college in Middletown, Connecticut. He chose Wesleyan because he felt that it was the finest school. He majored in biology/chemistry and for all intents and purposes was a premedical student. For as long has he could remember, Benson wanted to be a doctor. Reflecting on his undergraduate experience, he recalls that during his junior year he began to contemplate the existence of God. He took a course in religious studies, within which he wrote a paper on the topic. Not unexpectedly, he was making little progress on the paper but happened upon the work of William James (1842–1910), the American psychologist, philosopher, and author of the highly influential *The Varieties of Religious Experience* (1902). Benson identifies James's work as a "tremendous influence," both in his earlier life and into the present (see Benson 1996, 55, 147; Benson and Proctor 2010a, 48–52; Streett 2010, 29). Specifically, under Benson's reading, James's work suggests that people either have a universal pathology or that God exists. James's work, in turn, provided one of the primary inspirations for Benson's eventual identification of the "Relaxation Response." According to Benson, James's psychological investigations and philosophical reflections indicated that there were physiological dimensions of human experience that did not require "transcendental sources." It was also during his undergraduate years at Wesleyan that Benson had a mystical experience. On one warm spring day, he experienced "an overwhelming sense of unity." This inspired deeper existential reflections. Following a sense of calling to enter medical school and to become a doctor, Benson received his BA in biology in 1957.

Herbert Benson entered Harvard Medical School (HMS) that same year. As mentioned, his decision to pursue a career in cardiology was partially inspired by the death of his father from heart disease. Reflecting on his medical school experience, Herbert Benson characterizes it as "ordinary" and "uneventful," except obviously for the fact that he earned an MD. However, he was elected as president of his second-year class. "It was primarily a conventional education in which I received technical medical training. It also involved indoctrination into the dominant reductionist worldview of Western biomedicine" (Komjathy 2011b). Benson earned his medical degree in 1961 and began his practice as a cardiologist that year.

While treating cardiology patients as a medical resident, Benson noticed that their heart rates and blood pressures were significantly higher inside his office. This triggered a question concerning the source of and influences on the patients' condition. He wondered if the instruments and the environment were exerting harmful influences.[3] He also noticed the tendency of physicians to overmedicate patients. After two years of residency, Benson went back to Harvard Medical School to the Department of Physiology in order to determine whether or not he could identify specific triggers for negative physiological responses. With his colleagues, he attempted to develop an experiment to identify the sources and effects of stress. Using squirrel monkeys in a controlled experiment (see Benson et al. 1970), in combination with the paradigms of the American behaviorist and social philosopher B. F. Skinner (1904–1990), Benson found that the patterns of high blood pressure could be reinforced through external influences. Benson and his colleagues trained the monkeys either to raise or lower blood pressure using operant conditioning technology. They found that the monkeys who were "rewarded" for higher blood pressure went on to develop hypertension, basically due to their own behaviors. These experiments were conducted in the late 1960s.

Around the same time, practitioners of Transcendental Meditation™ (TM™) approached Herbert Benson about studying the positive effects of TM. The practitioners claimed that through TM practice they could modify their own physiology, with resulting beneficial effects and conditions. This contrasted with the contemporaneous medical context, wherein pharmaceutical drugs and/or surgery were the dominant therapeutic modalities. After much coaxing from young TM practitioners, Benson agreed to conduct research on TM, though some of his colleagues objected and warned him that he was "committing professional suicide." With the permission of his supervisor A. Clifford Barger (1917–1996), then Professor of Physiology at Harvard Medical School, Benson began his research. He instrumented the TM practitioners through various means in order to measure heart rate, metabolism, respiration, brain activity, and so forth. After conducting a three-part experiment, Benson and his colleagues determined that there were "dramatic changes" that occurred during TM meditation.[4] As Benson summarizes, "There was a decrease, and this is fundamental to this day, in the overall metabolism of the body. There was a decrease in heart rate and respiratory rate. And there were distinctive brain waves that were different from sleep." Also noteworthy is that the HMS room in which Benson was conducting his early experiments was the very same room where Walter B. Cannon (1871–1945), the American physiologist and discoverer of the "fight-or-flight response," had conducted his experiments. It was this identification that contributed to research on and understanding of stress.

Benson's early experiments with Transcendental Meditation in turn led to additional reflections. Specifically, Benson questioned the claim that TM was the only means to invoke positive physiological changes. He spent two more years studying religious and secular works related to meditation (see Benson 2000, 80–110). He wanted to know if the basic steps of TM had been described previously. According to Benson, he found that there are two fundamental and universal steps: (1) repetition, whether a word, a sound, a prayer, or an activity; and (2) passivity, specifically disengagement from distractions by returning to the selected repetitive sound or activity. These two steps effectively interrupted the train of everyday thinking. According to Benson, every culture and religious tradition throughout human history has utilized such practices. Seeking to create a satisfactory description of this common practice, Benson coined the phrase "Relaxation Response." As discussed in more detail later, this refers to both a specific physiological condition and specific method developed by Benson. Benson then developed a sequential method to invoke the Relaxation Response and reproduced the earlier experiment, this time with Harvard medical

Figure 13.1. Herbert Benson, circa 1996
Source: Margaret Kois Photography

students repeating the word "one."[5] This word originally was not chosen for any metaphysical meaning; rather, it was a simplification of a Zen Buddhist breath-control method that involved counting inhalations and exhalations. It was literally the number one. Utilizing the same forms of scientific measurement, Benson found the exact same physiological changes. Benson explains, "This was now science, and this is very important. Here was something that was measurable, predictable, and reproducible. This was science." Over the next forty or so years, Benson and his colleagues then studied the various conditions that were caused or exacerbated by stress.[6] The early inquiry in meditation, physiology, and stress in turn determined the trajectory of Benson's entire career, specifically his commitment to self-care and Mind-Body Medicine through stress management.

In the early years of Benson's work, there was strong resistance and even opposition to his research on Mind-Body Medicine and the Relaxation Response. He effectively had two careers: the first was his medical practice as a cardiologist;[7] the second was his work as a researcher in mind-body studies. It was not until 1988 that Benson thought that Mind-Body Medicine was adequately established and relatively stable. That year he established the Mind/Body Medical Institute at the Beth Israel Deaconess Hospital, which is one of the primary hospitals associated with Harvard Medical School. In 2006, the institute became part of the Massachusetts General Hospital (MGH), another major HMS-affiliated hospital (see Bull and Bull 2011), and was renamed the Benson-Henry Institute for Mind Body Medicine (BHI; see www.massgeneral.org/bhi; www.bensonhenryinstitute.org; also Bull and Bull 2011, 180–81). The Benson-Henry Institute is named after Herbert Benson and John William Henry II (b. 1949), founder of John W. Henry and Company and principal owner of the Boston Red Sox. Henry is a strong supporter of Mind-Body Medicine and a major financial contributor to the institute. The institute is associated with the entire MGH, not a single department, and is under the supervision of representatives of the hospital's various departments. For Benson, this is fundamentally important as early proposals wanted to place the institute only under the Department of Psychiatry. According to Benson, this was unacceptable because Mind-Body Medicine relates to medicine as a whole.

> The hospitals are characteristically divided into departments, such as gynecology, oncology, surgery, and so forth. Initially, MGH argued that we should be under psychiatry. We maintained that we should represent the entire hospital. So a thematic center of Mind-Body Medicine was established where we are responsible for the entire medical community and where we are overseen by a board comprised of representatives from the various departments. We are answerable to the entire hospital, not just one department. This is because mind interacts with body on all levels. (Komjathy 2011a)

The Benson-Henry Institute is a nonprofit scientific and educational organization dedicated to research, teaching, and clinical application of Mind-Body Medicine and its integration into all areas of health. According to the BHI website, it accomplishes these objectives through the following activities:

- Documenting and furthering the understanding of mind-body medicine through research
- Providing treatment for patients each year with stress-related illnesses through the institute

- Teaching medical students and training post-doctoral fellows and health care professionals to integrate mind-body interactions into their work through the Center for Training in Mind/Body Medicine

- Fostering the establishment of clinical and research programs in health care institutions through the BHI Affiliate Program

- Teaching students and educators life management skills through the Education Initiative

- Improving the health and productivity of the American workforce through the Center for Corporate Health (www.massgeneral.org/bhi)

The institute in turn offers various types of education and training, including the Relaxation Response Resiliency Program (RRRP), which is an outpatient comprehensive lifestyle program based on the principles and practices of Mind-Body Medicine. BHI is currently under the direction of Gregory L. Fricchione, MD, and consists of some nineteen staff members, including researchers and clinicians.

With the establishment of the Benson-Henry Institute in 2006, Herbert Benson became Director Emeritus, which is his current position. Although the institute is now owned by MGH, Benson retains his affiliation with that institute and remains Professor of Medicine at Harvard Medical School.[8] When asked about his role, he responded, "It's hard to say. I work full-time. I interface with various individuals and institutions under the supervision of the current director, Dr. Gregory L. Fricchione." He further added, "I just turned seventy-six, and it would be foolish for me to try to sustain leadership. It should be passed on so that the work continues among younger people." Benson remains involved on the level of research, teaching, and seeing patients. It remains a full-time job and collaboration.

Herbert Benson has two children and four grandchildren. He lives with his wife, Marilyn Wilcher, in Brookline, Massachusetts.

In terms of the larger cultural and historical context of Benson's work, and specifically *The Relaxation Response*, the location of his earlier research in 1960s and 1970s America is noteworthy. Like the mainstream American population more generally, the American medical establishment at the time was extremely conservative, especially concerning the superiority of allopathic (Western) medicine and the view that the "doctor knows best." There was a climate of conservatism, which included respect for authority and unquestioned faith in dominant social values and the political system. This changed with the 1960s counterculture movements and their subsequent cultural influences. These movements included various antiauthoritarian and alternative viewpoints and social experiments. They included an emphasis on civil rights, community, egalitarianism, peace, personal fulfillment, women's rights, and experimentation. The 1960s also saw the emergence of drug experimentation and alternative spirituality, specifically a great interest in "Eastern religion." Benson's early Harvard experiments on the physiology of meditation were located at the historical and cultural crossroads of pre- and post-1960s American culture. On the one hand, they were largely dismissed or opposed by the conservative American medical establishment. On the other hand, they were well positioned for the emerging interest in alternative health and spirituality. As will be discussed later, Mind-Body Medicine might be seen as embodying both pre-1960s conservatism and post-1960s radicalism. It remains rooted in a Western scientific paradigm while simultaneously advancing a more holistic view of self and healing.

Two additional elements of the sociohistorical and cultural context within which the Relaxation Response was identified and disseminated are significant. The first was and remains the ascendance of science as one of the primary modern worldviews. Science was in the process of becoming the new universal "religion." Within the conventional scientific paradigm, neutrality and objectivity are central values. This includes the primary importance of technology and quantification (measurability). Here "personal experience," perhaps indefinable and unmeasurable, is largely unreliable and perhaps even dangerous. Thus one finds an early interest in the "physiology of meditation," specifically the attempt to prove (or disprove) its effectiveness beyond subjectivity. However, effectiveness is a specific construct, and the scientific study of meditation has its own informing worldview and soteriological system.

The 1960s also saw increasing interest in "Eastern religion" and the gradual emergence of "alternative spirituality," that is, designer, hybrid spirituality. Within this context, various Asian teachers and Asian religions began to establish themselves. Although the American engagement with Asian religions has a complex history, including early interest among the American Transcendentalists, most scholars identify 1893 and the 1960s as pivotal dates. The former refers to the World's Parliament of Religions held at Chicago's World Fair, during which various Asian teachers introduced their traditions to a larger Euro-American public. The latter date refers not only to the 1960s counterculture but also to changes in American immigration laws that occurred in 1965 (see Tweed and Prothero 1998). In this year, the United States government eliminated severe restrictions on "Asian immigration," and a new wave of Asian immigrant religious teachers appeared. In this context, Maharishi Mahesh (1914–2008) and his Transcendental Meditation movement were major players (see Humes 2005; Williamson 2010). Simply stated, TM is a meditation method that utilizes the repetition of secret *mantra*s (sacred sounds) in order to purify consciousness and attain higher levels of consciousness. It is a modified form of Hindu *mantra* practice created by Maharishi Mahesh, the founder of the TM movement. For present purposes, TM is noteworthy for its self-characterization as "Vedic science" (not religion) and for its financial support of scientific research on meditation, specifically early problematic research aimed to demonstrate the effectiveness and superiority of TM. In this way, TM along with early scientific research on Vipassanā (Buddhist "mindfulness" meditation) helped to inspire such research, research that continues to this day with Zen Buddhist and Tibetan Buddhist meditation being the new "belle of the ball" of meditation researchers. In terms of the Relaxation Response, Benson conducted early experiments on the physiology of TM. Although he was not personally involved in the movement and never practiced TM himself, TM influenced Benson's own Relaxation Response method. Benson has consistently acknowledged his debt to TM (see Benson 2000, xv–xvi, 61–64, 112–15; Benson 1996, 100, 195, 233; Benson and Proctor 2010a, 57, 62), but he has also been quite clear that TM is not unique (see Benson 2000, 72, 128, *passim*). The subsequent development and dissemination of the Relaxation Response approach was assisted by the social climate of experimentation, spiritual seeking, and search for personal healing and wellness. That is, it was historically well positioned to contribute to the emerging alternative medicine and health and fitness movements, although Benson emphasizes his location in a Western scientific paradigm and allopathic medical approach (Benson 2000, xxxiii–vi). His envisioned "paradigm shift" involves recognition of mind-body connections (Benson 2000, xlvi–l) and an allopathic approach utilizing a "three-legged stool" of pharmaceutical drugs, surgery and other medical procedures, and self-care (Benson 2000, xii). This is primarily done under the supervision of an allopathic physician.

Mind-Body Medicine and Therapeutic Meditation

Herbert Benson's Relaxation Response method and related stress-management therapy are located, first and foremost, in the field of Mind-Body Medicine (MBM). As mentioned, Benson understands Mind-Body Medicine as a more comprehensive and holistic expression of allopathic medicine, that is, mainstream Western biomedicine. While other, later representatives and advocates of Mind-Body Medicine are associated with "alternative" or "complementary medicine," Benson himself prefers the allopathic affiliation and conception (Komjathy 2011a; see also Benson 2000, xxxiii–xxxvi). One might, in turn, focus on Mind-Body Medicine in terms the history of science (see, e.g., Kuhn 1962; Gould 1981; Popper 1992) and medical anthropology (see, e.g., Kleinman 1981, 1988). As a "religious tradition," Mind-Body Medicine includes elements from scientism (science as religion and dogmatic adherence) and allopathic medicine, including a strong emphasis on secular materialism and on personhood and experience defined largely in terms of physiology and technological quantification.

A comprehensive history of Mind-Body Medicine has yet to be written. However, Anne Harrington has published an initial account (Harrington 2008; cf. Benson and Proctor 2010a, 31–88). Here we must be attentive to both the history of Mind-Body Medicine as such and the specific location of Herbert Benson and *The Relaxation Response* within that history. According to Harrington, we may understand the history of Mind-Body Medicine in terms of chronological sequence and distinctive narratives, with particular attention to the cultural history of self-body and illness/wellness as well as to the relationship among personal beliefs, cultural values, and bodily experience. The dominant narratives include the power of suggestion (skeptical/debunking), the body that speaks (detective), the power of positive thinking (secular miracle), broken by modern life (lament), healing ties (redemption and nostalgia), and eastward journeys (exoticism). For Harrington, Herbert Benson primarily participates in the last narrative. In terms of a more straightforward history, and considered as a whole, Mind-Body Medicine is composed of an eclectic set of events and elements: from Mesmerism (animal magnetism), named after Franz Anton Mesmer (1734–1815), hypnosis and "suggestion"; through psychoanalytic practice, psychosomatic medicine, and physiology; French medical efforts to explain "miracles" and popular American faith-healing; the discovery of "stress" and practice of Biofeedback; increased concern for "social support" and "caring communities"; and finally to engagement with "Asian spiritual technologies" and the medicalization or secularization of meditation. This is not to say that every expression of Mind-Body Medicine contains these diverse influences; it is rather to highlight the complex history that led to the emergence of Mind-Body Medicine as such and to its broad popular appeal.

For our purposes, three dimensions of this broader cultural history are most relevant: the stress concept and experience defined physiologically; the increasing presence and influence of Asian religions (or at least Asian-inspired hybrid spirituality) in the West; and the history of the scientific study of meditation, including the emergence of "therapeutic meditation." In the case of the United States, there is an intersection point wherein scientific validation is considered relevant, perhaps even necessary, and wherein there is a concern for experience defined principally in physiological terms, with corresponding technological measuring instruments. These topics are thus related to the history of modern physiology and medical technology.

As discussed later, "stress" is a central element of the soteriology of Benson's version of Mind-Body Medicine. "Stress," at least as a concept and framework for understanding the human condition, did not exist before 1936, when the Austrian-Canadian endocrinologist Hans Selye (1907–1982)[9] published his initial research on rats (see Selye 1936, 1952, 1956, 1993; also Viner 1999; Harrington 2008, 148–52). Selye eventually conceptualized stress as a "General Adaptation Syndrome," that is, a nonspecific response of the body to any demand. According to Selye, stress in turn has three stages:

> (1) Alarm, wherein an animal perceives itself as under threat and prepares for action, either fight or flight (or freeze); in this stage, endocrine glands release hormones responsible for accelerating heartbeat and respiration, elevating blood sugar, increasing perspiration, dilating the pupils, and slowing digestion.
>
> (2) Resistance, wherein the body repairs any damage caused by the alarm reaction and all of the physiological changes associated with the first reaction are reversed.
>
> (3) Exhaustion, wherein a stressor persists beyond the body's ability to respond effectively and the mechanisms enabling adaptation begin to show signs of exhaustion, planting seeds for the emergence of stress-linked diseases. (Harrington 2008, 150–51)

Selye published a variety of popular works, and his influence has been so strong that "stress" and "stress-related disease" may seem like self-evident givens to readers of the present chapter. What we must keep in mind is that the stress concept has a history, and "stress" is a category superimposed onto particular physiological patterns and subjective experiences.

Selye's work was partially indebted to Walter B. Cannon (1871–1945), who discovered the "fight-or-flight response" around 1915 (see Cannon 1915, 1932; also Harrington 2008, 144–48).[10] Cannon was a professor of physiology in Harvard Medical School. Based on experiments on cats and dogs, Cannon found that cats agitated by the presence of dogs, the cats' "natural enemy," secreted a hormone called "adrenin," today usually referred to as the neurotransmitter "adrenaline" or "epinephrine." In Cannon's Darwinian perspective, the corresponding physiological changes increased an animal's capacity for survival:

> The increase of blood sugar, the secretion of adrenin, and the altered circulation in pain and emotional excitement have been interrupted in the foregoing discussion as biological adaptations to conditions in wild life which are likely to involve pain and emotional excitement, i.e., the necessities of fighting or flight. (Cannon 1915, 211)

In the "conditions of wild life," the animal, having mobilized its resources, either successfully masters the threat or fails to do so. If it succeeds, its physiology settles back to a pre-emergency state, a process of dynamic self-regulation that Cannon called "homeostasis." Eventually, Cannon also demonstrated ways in which specialized parts of the nervous system (now known as the sympathetic and parasympathetic systems) were centrally involved (see Benson 2000, 52–53). Perhaps more significant for understanding the "religious tradition" of Benson's Mind-Body Medicine, Cannon suggested that in modern industrialized and technological societies, many human beings were in a constant "emergency state," the fight-or-flight mode. With such emergency responses chronically stimulated, there are few opportunities for homeostatic mechanisms to restore our physiologies to a resting state. Over time, modern human beings are thus prone to falling ill in uniquely modern ways (Harrington 2008, 146–47). Here stress becomes identified as a source of disease, while relaxation, by extension, counteracts stress and therefore disease. Within Selye's and Cannon's research, one finds elements that would become signatures of scientific research on meditation, specifically a concern for "hormones," emphasis on the "nervous system," physiological correlates to experience, and competing conceptions of optimal human being (i.e., health and wellness). Both Selye's stress concept and Cannon's fight-or-flight response are, in turn, central to Benson's own system of Mind-Body Medicine (see Benson 2000, 1–54; BHI "Stress").[11] Benson defines the physiological state of the Relaxation Response (trophotropic) as the exact opposite of the fight-or-flight response (ergotropic), and the Relaxation Response method as a "stress-reduction" or "stress-management strategy."[12] One might thus read *The Relaxation Response* as *a response to* Cannon's fight-or-flight response.

The increasing presence and influence of Asian religions in America is another key development for understanding Benson's therapeutic meditation. As mentioned, Benson began early collaborative research with practitioners of Transcendental Meditation in the late 1960s. It was during this pivotal time in American history that Asian religions and related practices were becoming increasingly popular and accepted, as well as appropriated, commodified, and reconceptualized. Some major players in the early Western reception of Asian religions include A. C. Bhaktivedanta (Swami Prabhupada; Hinduism; 1896–1977), Thich Nhat Hanh (Vietnamese Buddhism; b. 1926), Jiddu Krishnamurti (Hinduism; 1895–1986), Maharishi Mahesh (Hinduism; 1914–2008), D. T. Suzuki (Japanese Zen Buddhism; 1870–1966), Shunryu Suzuki (Japanese Zen Buddhism; 1904–1971), Chögyam Trungpa (Tibetan Buddhism; 1939–1987), Vivekananda (Hinduism; 1863–1902), Paramahansa Yogananda (Hinduism; 1893–1952), as well as the Western popularizer Alan Watts (1915–1973) and the Beats (see, e.g., Tweed and Prothero 1998). Many of these individuals were instrumental in introducing "meditation" to America. As we know, Benson's early conception of the Relaxation Response method was a modified version of Maharishi Mahesh's Transcendental Meditation, which was itself a modified form of Hindu *mantra*-practice conceptualized as "Vedic science." Although Benson eventually distanced himself from TM claims of specialness, he continues to acknowledge his debt to his early TM research subjects and the TM method. So, while the Relaxation Response is neither Hindu nor TM, its emergence is intimately tied to the history of Asian religions in America, including American appropriative agendas.

Along the same lines, Maharishi Mahesh and the Transcendental Meditation movement played a major role in the scientific study of meditation and indirectly in the eventual emergence of therapeutic meditation. The history of scientific research on meditation, especially one attentive to cultural influences, informing concerns, and guiding motivations, has yet to be written (see Engel 1997a, 1997b; Murphy and Donovan 1999; Andresen 2000; also Harrington 2008, 205–55; Baier 2009). However, a simple perusal of early publications reveals Transcendental Meditation and South Asian Buddhist Vipassanā meditation as the primary methods studied. Part of this derived from Maharishi Mahesh's interest in proving that Transcendental Meditation was "scientific," that is, scientifically verifiable through laboratory experimentation and technological measurement. In fact, the Transcendental Meditation movement funded many of the early studies of "meditation" (TM) (see Engel 1997b; Murphy and Donovan 1999; Andresen 2000). Although this research has since been challenged on grounds of neutrality and objectivity, and as methodologically deficient in distinguishing *specific meditative techniques*, the early research established identifiable patterns. These include the actual validity of scientific study of meditation, experimentation, experience defined physiologically and eventually neuroscientifically, technological measurement, and so forth. That is, for meditation to be valid, it must be scientifically verifiable. Scientists, rather than advanced practitioners, are apparently the primary interpretive authorities. Here one may recall Benson's emphasis on measurability, predictability, and reproducibility as essential features of therapeutic meditation, of meditation as scientific.

In recent years, Tibetan Buddhist meditation techniques and Zen meditation to a lesser extent have become the preferred objects for the neuroscientific study of meditation. Although this research is far more sophisticated than the earlier research on TM, it follows a similar pattern: it is often supported by adherents of the source-tradition; frequently involves Western sympathizers or converts who assume elements of the informing worldview as self-evidently important (e.g., compassion); seeks scientific validation; and, in typical Orientalist fashion (see also Harrington 2008, 205–42, especially 207–8), excludes Western forms of contemplative practice. There are thus cultural and political subtexts to such research, including the Fourteenth Dalai Lama's (Tenzin Gyatso; b. 1935) own involvement. There can be little debate that Tibetan Buddhist meditation is the "new TM," and that the Dalai Lama is the "new Maharishi" (see also Lopez 1995, 1999; Iwamura 2000; Paine 2004). In this respect it is noteworthy that Herbert Benson was one of the early "East-West" conversation partners (see also Benson 1984, 29–82); Benson and the Dalai Lama met during the latter's three-day visit to Harvard University in 1979, the first semi-official (religious, not political) visit of the Dalai Lama to the United States. In some sense, this was the beginning of the dialogue between science and Tibetan Buddhism (see also Harrington 2008, 231–34). Later, in 1991, Benson participated in a conversation with the Dalai Lama at a Harvard Medical School symposium held at the Massachusetts Institute of Technology (MIT). The event was cosponsored by the Mind/Body Medical Institute and the Tibet House (see Dalai Lama et al. 1991). This type of East (meditation/spirituality)-West (science) dialogue has given rise to neuroscientific research on (Tibetan Buddhist) meditation by individuals like Francisco Varela (1949–2001; Mind and Life Institute), Richard Davidson (University of Wisconsin, Madison), and B. Alan Wallace (Santa Barbara Institute for Consciousness Studies; Shamatha Project), and to organizations like the Mind and Life Institute,[13] an organization established in 1987 in order to promote dialogue between Buddhism and science, or in their own conception "scientific understanding of the mind to reduce suffering and promote well-being" (see www.mindandlife.org; also Harrington and Zajonc 2006; Luisi 2010).[14]

As mentioned, such research is intricately tied to advances in medical technologies. While early scientific research on meditation utilized devices like EEGs (electroencephalography), more recent research prefers new neuroimaging technology like fMRI (functional magnetic resonance imaging) and CT (computed tomography), also known as CAT (computed axial tomography) (see Andresen 2000; Lutz et al. 2007). From this perspective, the actual brain regions and corresponding neural faculties (i.e., "consciousness") activated or deactivated during meditation may be mapped. That is, it may be possible to identify distinctive brain maps associated with specific meditation techniques.

The Relaxation Response method is a form of therapeutic meditation, that is, meditation as medicalized and secularized.[15] It is meditation extracted from its traditional contexts, communities, and traditions, and apparently reconceptualized as "nonreligious" and along instrumentalist lines. As documented in the inside endorsements of the twenty-fifth anniversary edition of *The Relaxation Response* (2000), "I am delighted that someone has finally taken the nonsense out of meditation. . . . This is a book that any rational person—whether a product of Eastern or Western culture—can wholeheartedly accept" (William Nolen, MD).[16] Again, the history of therapeutic meditation has yet to be written, but Herbert Benson's medicalized version of TM (Relaxation Response) represents one important source-point, if not the actual beginning (see also Harrington 2008, 214–22, 230–42; Baier 2009).[17] Therapeutic meditation may be restorative, remedial, and/or health-promoting. To benefit from the Relaxation Response method and other forms of therapeutic meditation, no belief is required. Religion is apparently unnecessary or irrelevant for efficacy. According to advocates, meditation is *a technique* (or series of techniques) with particular instructions, characteristics, and outcomes (e.g., relaxation). If practiced correctly, the corresponding physiological changes and health benefits will follow. Here we may recall that Benson sees every form of meditation as a method for eliciting the Relaxation Response as a physiological state. According to Benson, stress-management therapy focusing on the Relaxation Response is nonsectarian, even to the point that "there is no Benson method" (Komjathy 2011a). For Benson, although one may choose to use the "Benson-Henry Protocol," almost any practice may be used as a stress-management therapy as long as it has the two key elements of repetition and passivity.

Although during the 1970s the Relaxation Response method was the primary form of therapeutic meditation, by the 1980s other kinds of secularized and medicalized meditation appeared. Perhaps the most popular alternative to the Relaxation Response method is Jon Kabat-Zinn's (b. 1944) Mindfulness-Based Stress Reduction (MBSR), a medicalized version of South Asian Buddhist Vipassanā meditation. Paralleling Benson in certain ways, Kabat-Zinn is Professor of Medicine Emeritus and founding director of the Stress Reduction Clinic and the Center for Mindfulness in Medicine, Health Care, and Society at the University of Massachusetts Medical School. In Kabat-Zinn's vision, MBSR can be used both as a stress-reduction method and as palliative care, as a method to treat pain. Interestingly, the former application of MBSR was featured on Bill Moyers's five-part series *Healing and the Mind* (1993; see Harrington 2008, 222, 244–45), which was partially funded by the Fetzer Institute, an organization established in 1954 whose current mission is "to foster awareness of the power of love and forgiveness in the emerging global community" (see www.fetzer.org). The palliative dimension of therapeutic meditation later appeared in Moyer's four-part series *On Our Own Terms: Moyers on Dying* (2000). Although distinguishable, the Relaxation Response and MBSR agree that meditation is principally therapeutic, and one in turn finds ever-increasing numbers of publications with related titles such as *Meditation as Medicine*. Moreover, as Harrington comments,

> The original medicalization of meditation in the late 1960s and 1970s by people like Benson and Kabat-Zinn was a self-consciously secular effort aimed to distance the

practice from all its exotic Eastern associations. By the 1990s, however, there began to be signs of change afoot on this front [public interest in the health benefits of seated meditation], of a turn back to the East. The face of the East to which people turned this time was not India, not China; it was Tibet, perhaps the most exotic of the three. (2008, 230)

Another key point here is that in this context "meditation" became both *a technique* (or variety of techniques) and *a tradition* distinct and apparently extractable from a larger religious and soteriological system. That is, "meditation" became a new form of adherence;[18] one could apparently "practice meditation" without beliefs or conceptual commitments and even without recognition of different types of contemplative practice with different orientations and projected outcomes. Relaxation and stress reduction became the *sine qua non* of contemplative practice.

As we have seen, Herbert Benson's Relaxation Response method may be contextualized in terms of the history of Mind-Body Medicine, Asian religions in America, the scientific study of meditation (physiology and biochemistry), and therapeutic meditation. Interestingly, Herbert Benson has recently begun to identify the "lineage" of his form of Mind-Body Medicine, specifically as a development within allopathic medicine. According to Benson, there is a "tradition of mind-body studies at Harvard University" (Komjathy 2011a). This Harvard Medical School subculture begins with Harvard professor of physiology Oliver Wendell Holmes, Sr. (1809–1894); moves through the American psychologist and philosopher William James (1842–1910); Harvard professor of physiology Walter B. Cannon (1871–1945); Harvard professor of physiology A. Clifford Barger (1917–1996); and eventually arrives at Herbert Benson himself (see Taylor 2000; Benson and Proctor 2010a, 48–53). In one version of this account, Holmes embodies compassion, James mind and method, and Cannon science. Also noteworthy is the fact that Herbert Benson frequently emphasizes that he discovered the physiological state of the Relaxation Response in the very same Harvard laboratory where Walter B. Cannon discovered the fight-or-flight response (Taylor 2000; Taylor 2003, 45; Benson and Proctor 2010a, 52; Komjathy 2011a). This account in turn relates to the history of Harvard University, Harvard Medical School, and Harvard-affiliated hospitals (see, e.g., Bull and Bull 2011). From a comparative religious studies perspective, we may note the ways in which Mind-Body Medicine comes to resemble other religious movements through the use of the language of lineage and the construction of tradition. Similarly, one might also recognize the way in which Jon Kabat-Zinn began with a stance against Vipassanā as "existential" or "religious"[19] but has gradually come to resemble a guru, including the associated phenomenon of individuals self-identifying as "disciples of Kabat-Zinn" (author's field observations). That is, just as most therapeutic and secularized forms of meditation derive from earlier religiously-committed methods,[20] so too many advocates of therapeutic meditation come to resemble religious leaders with relatively insular quasi-religious communities. In this respect, one might understand "Mindfulness" as a new religious movement (NRM). One finds a similar pattern among scholars who "go native" and become spiritual teachers, and in the process replace nonacademically trained religious leaders and associated religious communities.

On this issue we should be clear. Herbert Benson emphasizes the Relaxation Response method as secular and therapeutic, as "nonreligious," although the so-called faith factor may play a role. Strictly defined, "religion" does not play a role in Relaxation Response practice. While

Benson self-identifies as a Reform Jew and attends synagogue on the high holy days, the "religious tradition" within which the Relaxation Response is located is not Judaism. Herbert Benson's Jewish affiliation is largely irrelevant, and anyone, religious or not, may supposedly benefit from the practice. Similarly, although the Relaxation Response method derives from Transcendental Meditation, it is not associated with either Hinduism or the TM movement and Maharishi Mahesh's "Vedic science," which might be categorized as a new religious movement. However, as I have attempted to demonstrate and as will become clearer in the next section, Mind-Body Medicine and therapeutic meditation, or even "meditation" as a distinct tradition, may be read from a comparative religious studies perspective. It has an informing worldview, distinctive set of practices, interpretive authorities (experts/professionals), identifiable form of community, soteriological system, ultimate concern, and so forth.

Finally, we should recognize that *The Relaxation Response* was first published in 1975 and represents Herbert Benson's first book-length publication, written with the assistance of Miriam Z. Klipper. Although there can be little debate that this book is a "classic" of Mind-Body Medicine and therapeutic meditation, Benson has expanded and modified his views and approaches over the course of his career. *The Relaxation Response* is the first and primary publication, but it is located in a larger textual corpus. In addition to a wide variety of scientific and popular articles (see Benson 2011), Benson has published the following important general-audience books in chronological order:

(1) *Beyond the Relaxation Response* (with William Proctor; 1984). Here Benson introduces the idea of the "faith factor," or faith and religious belief as a "placebo" that may positively influence stress-reduction practice and healing.

(2) *Timeless Healing: The Power and Biology of Belief* (with Marg Stark; 1996). Here Benson emphasizes the importance of "remembered wellness" (an alternative conception of the "placebo effect") and the possibility that belief may alter biology. Benson begins to move in the direction of claiming that we are "wired for God."

(3) *Relaxation Revolution* (with William Proctor; 2010). Here Benson suggests that reprogramming practices like the Relaxation Response method may actually change one's genetics. Benson also modifies the early Relaxation Response method, now referred to as the "Benson-Henry Protocol."

This is not to mention *The Mind/Body Effect* (1979), *Your Maximum Mind* (1987), *The Wellness Book* (1992), and *The Breakout Principle* (2003). On Benson's curriculum vitae (CV) these works are categorized as "education materials for patients and the lay community," which stand in contrast to "scholarship" or professional, medical research publications (see Benson 2011).[21] In writing popular publications, Benson has followed the precedent set by earlier scientific researchers such as Hans Selye and Walter B. Cannon. Although beyond the scope of the present chapter, we should also recognize that Benson's research publications are substantial. If one were going to expand the "canon" beyond Benson's own publications and include other "classics" of Mind-Body Medicine, Jon Kabat-Zinn's *Full Catastrophe Living* (1990; fifteenth anniversary edition 2005) would probably be among the first titles added. One would probably also need to include other practitioners of therapeutic meditation, such as Eugene Gendlin (Focusing) and Richard Miller (iRest [Integrative Restoration]).

Relaxation, Self-Care, and Stress Management

The Relaxation Response method is a simple therapeutic meditation technique and stress-management therapy aimed a relaxation. As mentioned, the original method is a secularized and medicalized version of Transcendental Meditation, that is, it is a mantric meditation practice. Like TM, the Relaxation Response method involves the continual repetition of a chosen phrase or sound, this time chosen by oneself. Although Benson emphasizes that there are various methods that can elicit the corresponding physiological response (xix, 73–79, 80–110; also below) and that there is "no Benson method" (Komjathy 2011a), *The Relaxation Response* provides specific instructions on a particular method (xviii–xxii, 11–12, 85–86, 126–30; see also Benson "Steps"; BHI "Eliciting"). In its original formulation, there are four basic or essential components: (1) a quiet environment, (2) a mental device, (3) a passive attitude, and (4) a comfortable position. There is a corresponding six-step (Benson 1975), eight-step (Benson 1984), or nine-step (Benson 1996, 2000) "generic method." One must repeat a self-chosen word, sound, phrase, prayer, or muscular activity. Additionally, one must passively disregard everyday thoughts and remain concentrated on repetition (xx–xxi; also Benson 1996, 134–37). "*A passive mental attitude appears to be the most essential factor in eliciting the Relaxation Response*" (86, italics in original). Although the sound or phrase for repetition is self-chosen, Benson early on utilized "one" (129; also xix–xx, 88, 135–36). As mentioned earlier, the choice of this word was a simplification of a Zen Buddhist respiratory technique that involved counting inhalations and exhalations, traditionally ten in number. The corresponding practice instructions appear in the selected passages after this introduction.

As time has gone on, and beyond *The Relaxation Response*, Benson has made a number of modifications. In its most recent formulation and refinement, only steps 2 and 3 (repetition and passivity) are identified as essential (Benson 1996, 134; Komjathy 2011a). Benson has also come to believe that the "faith factor" and "remembered wellness" play an important role in beneficial outcomes. These phrases refer to the power of belief to influence health and healing, including the results of therapeutic meditation. In his most enthusiastic moments, Benson emphasizes that belief changes biology and perhaps even genetics (Benson 1996; Benson and Proctor 2010a). In terms of Relaxation Response practice, and one's self-chosen word or phrase in particular, religious convictions may exert important influences. That is, individuals with religious commitments may combine personal beliefs with Relaxation Response training, specifically by choosing tradition-specific "*mantras*" (Benson 1984, 3–8, 103–17; Benson 1996, 134–37). In this regard, Benson emphasizes the importance of "expectation-belief," or one's anticipated results of meditation (see, e.g., Benson and Proctor 2010b, 6–7). Expectation-belief is a factor in both religious and secular therapeutic meditation.[22]

Returning to the actual Relaxation Response method, Benson eventually standardized it as follows:

Step 1. Pick a focus word or short phrase that's firmly rooted in your belief system.

Step 2. Sit quietly in a comfortable position.

Step 3. Close your eyes.

Step 4. Relax your muscles.

Step 5. Breathe slowly and naturally, and as you do, repeat your focus word, phrase, or prayer silently to yourself as you exhale.

Step 6. Assume a passive attitude. Don't worry about how well you're doing. When other thoughts come to mind, simply say to yourself, "Oh, well," and gently return to the repetition.

Step 7. Continue for ten to twenty minutes.

Step 8. Do not stand immediately. Continue sitting quietly for a minute or so, allowing other thoughts to return. Then open your eyes and sit for another minute before rising.

Step 9. Practice this technique once or twice daily. (Benson 1996, 136; see also Benson 2000, xxi–xxii)

Interestingly, he has recently proposed a new version called the "Benson-Henry Protocol" (BHP), which is practiced as follows:

Phase One: Relaxation Response Trigger

Step 1. Pick a focus word, phrase, image, or short prayer. Or focus only on your breathing during the exercise.

Step 2. Find a quiet place and sit calmly in a comfortable position.

Step 3. Close your eyes.

Step 4. Progressively relax all your muscles.

Step 5. Breathe slowly and naturally. As you exhale, repeat or picture silently your focus word or phrase, or simply focus on your breathing rhythm.

Step 6. Assume a passive attitude. When your thoughts intrude, simply think, "Oh, well," and return to your focus.

Step 7. Continue with this exercise for an average of 12 to 15 minutes.

Step 8. Practice this technique at least once daily.

Phase Two: Visualization

Use mental imagery, such as picturing a peaceful scene in which you are free of your mental condition, to engage in healing expectation, belief, and memory. This second phase will usually require an average of 8 to 10 minutes.

Total time for Phase One and Two will be 20 to 25 minutes per session.
(Benson and Proctor 2010a, 9–10, 91–108)

In this new version, there are now eight steps to the Relaxation Response method, with the previous step 8, emphasizing a slow return to ordinary consciousness, deleted. In addition, one may now simply observe the breath rather than use a *mantra*-based practice. In terms of the timeframe, "ten to twenty minutes" has now become "12 to 15 minutes" with an additional eight to ten minutes dedicated to visualization. This results in a twenty- to twenty-five-minute practice, rather than a ten- to twenty-minute one. In BHP, Benson also adds an "optional relaxation response exercise" in which one incorporates "three essential components," namely, a mental focusing device, a passive "oh, well" attitude, and sufficient time (12–15 minutes) (Benson and Proctor 2010a, 10, 95–98). In both versions, one sits in a comfortable position. In Benson-Henry Institute training, this usually involves a chair, but Benson recognizes other postures such as keeling, standing, and full-lotus (Benson 1996, 136). However, except in cases involving the treatment of insomnia, he advises against using a supine posture, as this often results in sleep (Benson 2000, 86, 128; Benson and Proctor 2010a, 137). Interestingly, what began as largely a mantric, attentional, and at times apophatic practice has become more concentrative, kataphatic, respiratory, and even devotional, with an additional visualization component. Here we may recall the aforementioned dimensions of the history of Mind-Body Medicine such as the power of suggestion and positive thinking as well as psychosomatic views of personhood.

The Relaxation Response method is a form of therapeutic meditation because it primarily emphasizes health, healing, and medical intervention. As described by Herbert Benson, it is a dimension of self-care, stress management, and Mind-Body Medicine. It has both a personal and a clinical application. In terms of self-care, the Relaxation Response can be self-administered and appears to be autodidactic (self-taught), at least through consultation of Benson's publications and other resources.[23] According to Benson, almost any activity can elicit the Relaxation Response; one may choose one's own method based on affinity and comfort; and one may use any word or phrase. The latter includes a religiously significant one that invokes the additional healing power of the faith factor (2000, xix–xx, xxix–xxxi; see also Benson 1984, 1996). In addition to the method described in *The Relaxation Response*, Benson suggests that the following activities can elicit the Relaxation Response, assuming that the two basic elements of repetition and passivity are included: Autogenic Training, Biofeedback and behavior modification, cycling, dance, diaphragmatic breathing, hypnosis with suggested deep relaxation, jogging, knitting, meditation (TM, Vipassanā, Zazen), progressive relaxation, Qigong, rowing, sentic cycles, swimming, Taiji quan (T'ai-chi ch'üan), walking, Yoga, and so forth (2000, xix, xxii, 56–64, 73–79; Komjathy 2011a). It can be evoked in almost any posture and vocally or silently. As we saw earlier, Benson eventually changed his views on the "essential features" for eliciting the Relaxation Response (2000, xix). Specifically, one supposedly does not need a quiet environment or a comfortable posture (2000, xix). That is, although the Relaxation Response method was inspired by Transcendental Meditation and is a form of therapeutic meditation, it now includes other types of activities, including movement awareness. One may use such practices to decrease stress and to increase well-being.

In terms of Mind-Body Medicine as a more comprehensive and holistic form of allopathic medicine, Benson envisions self-care methods as one part of a "three-legged stool" approach, which also includes pharmaceutical drugs as well as surgery and other medical procedures. As 60 to 90 percent of visits to physicians are for stress-related conditions, "medicine would call upon self-care for 60 to 90 percent of the everyday problems that patients experience. We [physicians and health care professionals] would draw appropriately upon the medicines and surgeries when necessary. All three legs are mandatory" (xii; see also Benson 1996, 23). All are essential for "health and well-being." Here we see the physician-centered approach characteristic of allopathic medicine, with potential practitioners of the Relaxation Response method identified as "patients." In this respect, Relaxation Response therapy may be prescribed by physicians for stress management; it is a form of medical treatment. According to Benson,

> Every illness has a mind/body component and some potential for benefit if you employ self-care techniques. But how do you determine the appropriate use of the advice in this book for your particular medical problem? Always start by discussing your medical complaint with your personal physician. (xliii)

Moreover, although one can use self-care techniques to manage stress,

> *no matter how encouraging the initial results, no person should treat himself for high blood pressure [or other stress-related medical conditions] by regularly eliciting the Relaxation Response. You should always do so under the care of your physician, who will routinely monitor your blood pressure to make sure it is adequately controlled.* (116–17, italics in original)

Thus, physicians committed to Mind-Body Medicine should ideally prescribe self-care techniques, including behavior modification, exercise, nutrition, relaxation methods, and social support (BHI "Mind Body Treatments"; Benson and Stuart 2010). For this, training is required, and there is a clinical application. Specifically, the Benson-Henry Institute offers various forms of education and training, including workshops on the Relaxation Response for patients and physicians.

The Relaxation Response may thus be used to treat a variety of medical conditions such as anger, anxiety, depression, hypertension, irregular heartbeat, pain, premenstrual syndrome, infertility, insomnia, irritable bowel syndrome, and so forth (xli–xlii; see also Jacobs 2001; Benson and Stuart 2010; Benson and Proctor 2010a). In Benson's system, these are often caused by stress, and stress is identified as a primary source of illness. There are, in turn, many sources of stress, including familial, financial, work, and psychological issues and conditions. In fact, *The Relaxation Response* contains a chart of stress related to adjusting to change, including specific events and their corresponding scale of impact (39–40; also Harrington 2008, 156). The regular elicitation of the Relaxation Response, in turn, leads to identifiable benefits. As mentioned, these include relatively lower heart rate, respiratory rate, and blood pressure. While there may be side effects of excessive meditation, such as hallucination and other psychological disturbances, "*We have not noted any of the above side effects in people who bring forth the Relaxation Response once or twice daily for ten to twenty minutes a day*" (137, italics in original). That is, the correct practice of the Relaxation Response method is a safe and effective form of stress management. It relieves stress and assists in restoring and/or maintaining health. At the same time, Benson believes that stress can only be reduced and managed. Due to the complexity of modern, industrialized and technological societies as well as individuals' lives, stress cannot be eliminated completely (BHI "Stress"; Komjathy 2011a). It is apparently an existential given.

As a final set of points, I would like to draw attention to the ways in which Benson's system of Mind-Body Medicine resembles a religious movement. Many elements could, of course, be highlighted: the professional clergy and interpretive authorities (physicians and scientists), in contrast to the laity (patients and/or "nonphysicians"); ordination and professionalization (credentialing and teacher certification); the larger discourse community (allopathic medicine and Mind-Body Medicine); more-encompassing training regimen (diet [nutrition], ethics, exercise, sleep); set of rituals (physician-patient interaction, drug-taking, surgery); quasi-sacred sites (hospitals and medical laboratories); system-specific terminology; and so forth.[24] We have already seen the ways in which the Relaxation Response method has a specific history and a distinctive set of cultural influences. That is, I have contextualized the practice. It is also interesting that this form of therapeutic meditation, like all forms of contemplative practice, has an informing worldview and identifiable soteriological system. The Relaxation Response system identifies a problem in human existence and society: like competing religious categories such "sin," "karma," "suffering," and so forth, "stress" appears as an existential and ontological given. As Benson describes in the opening pages of *The Relaxation Response*, "We are in the midst of an epidemic, one that is all too prevalent in the United States and other industrialized nations. The name of this epidemic is hypertension, the medical term for high blood pressure" (2000, 4). Within this worldview, stress has distinguishing characteristics, which may lead to dissatisfaction and disease. However, like any sophisticated soteriological system, there is an alternative: one may rather choose to embrace the goal, the projected outcome, of "relaxation," "health," and "well-being." For this, the Relaxation Response method and other stress-management therapies will enable one to elicit the Relaxation Response as physiological condition. As we now know, this state is the opposite of the fight-or-flight response (a stressful, "emergency" state). It is characterized by stable blood flow; increases in slow "brain waves"; and decreases in metabolism, blood pressure, heart rate, respiration rate, and muscle tension (Benson 2000, 74–75; also Benson 1996, 131). In this framework, one encounters an additional allopathic and scientific perspective, rooted in secular materialism: human health and well-being are the ultimate concern.[25] We may simply consider that *Timeless Healing* is dedicated "To life!" Of course, like any religious tradition, it is "life" defined in very particular ways. Within the Relaxation Response system, stress is the problem, relaxation the goal, and optimal well-being the ultimate concern.

Equally interesting, there are signs of successful training; Relaxation Response practice results in specific types of experience and benefits. In *Relaxation Revolution*, Benson outlines them as follows:

- If you feel more relaxed after you finish a Phase One session, the technique is working.

- If the [medical] symptoms you experience diminish or disappear, even momentarily, during or immediately after a session, the technique is working.

- If the symptoms you experience diminish within a week or two, the technique is working.

- If you feel that the stressors in your life bother you less now than they did when you started this mind body treatment process, the technique is working.

- If you feel that you are more in control of your life now than when you started, the technique is working.

- If you are observing the basic guidelines for eliciting the relaxation response, you can rest assured, in light of extensive scientific studies, that the technique is working—no matter how you may feel on a day-to-day basis. (Benson and Proctor 2010a, 99)

Key concepts in this map of successful practice include control, relaxation, scientific support, symptomatology, and stressors. In the most recent expression of Benson's Mind-Body system, the Relaxation Response method is just the first phase in an effective mind-body treatment strategy. So-called Phase Two will provide enhanced potential for healing:

> Experiencing Phase One on a regular basis—that is, simply evoking the relaxation response daily—will often lead to significant healing without any further action. But you will increase your chances for maximum healing by adding Phase Two—the visualization phase—to your mind body medicine kit. (Benson and Proctor 2010a, 99)

As a restorative method, therapeutic meditation may, in turn, be used to prevent or treat a whole range of medical conditions (see Benson 1984, 119–33; Benson 1996, 146–48; Benson 2000, front matter, xli–xliii; Benson and Proctor 2010a, 56–70).

In ways paralleling other American appropriations and reconceptualizations of religiously-committed forms of contemplative practice, Benson's system of therapeutic meditation also emphasizes simplicity and efficacy, especially with respect to health and healing. Similar to other simplified and popularized forms of meditation, the Relaxation Response method is presented as simple, easy, and effective. As the description on the back cover of *The Relaxation Response* (2000) promotes, "Requiring only minutes to learn, and just ten to twenty minutes of practice twice a day, *the relaxation response* has proven to be one of the most effective ways to relieve the tensions of modern-day living for a richer, healthier, more productive life." This in turn may be applied to any activity, including increasing the efficacy and productivity of American workers and supporting the American economy! The latter commitment is expressed in a subdivision of the Benson-Henry Institute named the Center for Corporate Health.[26]

Finally, closely connected with the aforementioned physiology of stress and relaxation as well as the corresponding benefits of therapeutic meditation, we may recognize the relationship among views of self, practice, and experience in Benson's stress-management system (cf. Komjathy 2007). We are already familiar with the Relaxation Response method, and we have also seen how modern physiology and allopathic medicine are constitutive elements of its informing worldview. Herbert Benson emphasizes that the Relaxation Response method is part of Mind-Body Medicine, but what is the "mind-body" in this system? First, it is mind as controlling power. Mind has power over body; by training the mind through stress-reduction practices, one may change one's body, here defined primarily in terms of physiology, biology, and genetics. That is, the "body" present in Benson's therapeutic meditation is largely that of modern science and allopathic medicine. It is comprised of physiological responses, hormones, neurotransmitters, and so forth. This view of self is moderately psychosomatic, with primacy given to mind or consciousness (uniquely defined). It also has materialist dimensions. Such a view of self in turn informs the practice, and the practice embodies this view of self. Closely connected with such views of self and practice, therapeutic meditation leads to particular types of experience, which are conditioned by and confirm those views. Here "experience" is largely defined in terms of the stress-relaxation or illness-health dyads, with the associated physiological correlates being scientifically identifiable and verifiable. There is an inherent tension, if not an actual contradiction in claims regarding experience: personal experience is simultaneously reliable and unreliable. On the one hand, practitioners of the Relaxation Response gain personal experience with the corresponding Relaxation Response condition. On the other, one needs conditioning, technological measurement devices, and scientific verification in order to understand the benefits. This is not to mention the presence of physicians as interpretive authorities. Moreover, experience is largely defined through modern physiology. One cannot help but wonder about the degree to which "nonadherents" of Mind-Body Medicine and therapeutic meditation find such views of self, practice, and experience convincing.

The Relaxation Response

Although Herbert Benson has published a great deal of material since the initial appearance of *The Relaxation Response* (1975) and its twenty-fifth anniversary edition (2000), *The Relaxation Response* remains Herbert Benson's most influential work. It was the *New York Times* number 1 nonfiction bestseller (December 21, 1975), remains in print in its sixty-fourth printing, has sold five million copies, and has been translated into fourteen languages, including French, Italian, Korean, and Japanese (Harrington 2008, 219; Benson 2011). In addition, most of Benson's seminal ideas, core views, and principal approaches are documented in the pages of *The Relaxation Response*.

The original edition of *The Relaxation Response* was published in 1975 by William Morrow. It was first published in English in the United States. It almost immediately became a national bestseller. It was reprinted in 2000 by Avon Books (now HarperCollins) in an updated and expanded twenty-fifth anniversary edition. We may thus consider the current edition as a work of both the 1970s and the 2000s.[27] The popularity and influence of *The Relaxation Response* are testified by the sheer volume of sales, by the fact that it has been continuously in print for almost forty years, and by its location as a "classic" of Mind-Body Medicine and therapeutic meditation. If one were going to identify a "canon" related to these topics, *The Relaxation Response* would be one of the first texts included.

The current edition of *The Relaxation Response* consists of the foreword to the twenty-fifth anniversary edition, eight untitled chapters, a calendar for scheduling personal practice, and a bibliography. The current text consists of the sections and illustrations shown in figure 13.2, with asterisks (*) indicating at least partial selections in the present chapter. With respect to the foreword, the careful reader will note that it must be recontextualized, as it dates from some twenty-five years after the original publication. The foreword covers Benson's vision for medicine (i.e., the three-legged stool); the historical development of the Relaxation Response; its connections to stress management and beneficial physiological changes associated with meditation; the essential components of the Relaxation Response method and steps for its elicitation; information on the social reception of the book; Benson's response to claims that the Relaxation Response is simply an example of the placebo effect; the eventual addition of the faith factor into the practice; Benson's vision for the next fifteen years; his thoughts on alternative medicine, advanced meditation, and the latest findings; the importance and application of self-care; the "paradigm shift" currently underway; and the Mind/Body Medical Institute. In short, the most recent foreword is an overview of the book, including its central concerns and findings, and a clarification of Benson's vision, amendments, and current work. Chapter 1 discusses the physiology and negative influence of stress and the way in which the Relaxation Response contrasts with the fight-or-flight response. Chapter

Foreword	Chapter 5
The Three-Legged Stool, From the Beginning, Mind Divorced from Body, Transcendental Meditation, Connections to the Fight-or-Flight Response, Essential Components, How to Elicit the Relaxation Response, A Best-Seller, Bridging the Divide, The Public's Enthusiasm, Only the Placebo Effect, The Faith Factor, The Next Fifteen Years, Alternative Medicine, A Fine Line, Advanced Meditation, The Latest Findings, How to Use Self-Care, Fear and Guilt, The Paradigm Shift Underway, The Mind/Body Medical Institute, Words of Thanks	Age-Old Wisdom*, Meditation: The Four Basic Elements*
Chapter 1	**Chapter 6**
Victims of Stress, The Hidden Epidemic*, The Fight-or-Flight Response*	Decreasing Blood Pressure*, Decreasing Drug Use
Chapter 2	**Chapter 7**
Vital Functions, A Disease with No Symptoms*	How to Bring Forth the Relaxation Response*, Personal Experiences with the Relaxation Response*
Chapter 3	**Chapter 8**
Who Develops Hypertension?, Internal Signs of Stress*	N/A
Chapter 4	**Illustrations and Tables**
Mental Control, Sleep v. Meditation, Dr. Hess's Crucial Experiments	Unblocked and Partially Blocked Artery, Single Cell Surrounded by Sea, Circulation, Cell Surrounded by Other Cells, Blood Pressure Measurement Method, Enlarged Heart Due to High Blood Pressure, Stress of Adjusting to Change (table), Physiology of Fight-or-Flight Response, Hypothalamic Area of Brain, Physiology of Relaxation Response, Oxygen-Consumption Changes of the Relaxation Response, Comparative Chart of Oxygen-Consumption Changes in Relaxation Response and Sleep, Blood-Lactate Changes of the Relaxation Response, Different Techniques Eliciting the Physiologic Changes of the Relaxation Response (table)

Figure 13.2. Sections of *The Relaxation Response*
(25th Anniversary Edition; 2000)

2 covers Western anatomy and physiology, vital functions, as well as specific medical conditions and their associated etiology (causes/sources). Here Benson identifies high blood pressure, or hypertension, as "the hidden epidemic" (4–7) and "a disease without symptoms" (29–36; see also Benson and Proctor 2010a, 15–17, 54–70; Benson and Proctor 2010b, 11–16). The third chapter provides detailed information on stress and indicators of beneficial and harmful physiological states. Chapter 4 emphasizes that individuals can influence their physiological responses to stress through various mental practices. He discusses the power of mind, the comparison between meditation and sleep, and the physiology of "different techniques for eliciting the physiologic changes of the relaxation response" (74–75). These include Transcendental Meditation, Zen and Yoga, Autogenic Training, progressive relaxation, hypnosis with suggested deep relaxation, and sentic cycles (emotional states with corresponding physiological changes). In chapter 5, Benson discusses premodern methods associated with various cultures and religious traditions that elicit the Relaxation Response. The methods in question are associated with the fourteenth-century *The Cloud of Unknowing*, Teresa of Ávila (1515–1582), the Eastern Orthodox Hesychasts, Jewish Kabbalah, Hindu classical Yoga, Buddhist Samatha-Vipassanā, Sufi prayer, and classical Daoist apophatic meditation, among others. For Benson, while such methods are culturally and religiously distinct, a commonly shared characteristic is to elicit the Relaxation Response: "We claim no innovation but simply a scientific validation of age-old wisdom" (129). In this chapter Benson also identifies the "four basic elements of meditation" (85–86). Chapter 6 covers some of the positive effects of Relaxation Response practice, including decreased blood pressure and decreased use of alcohol, tobacco, and illicit (not necessarily pharmaceutical) drugs. The seventh chapter provides more practical instruction on the Relaxation Response method and some testimonials and brief case studies of individuals who have benefited from the Relaxation Response. The final chapter is a brief conclusion that emphasizes the Relaxation Response as a universal human capacity and as a beneficial component of self-care, and specifically of stress management.

The Relaxation Response is a relatively simple and straightforward book, and its central theme is the Relaxation Response itself. On the most fundamental level, the Relaxation Response refers to a physiological state: "The Relaxation Response is a physical state of deep rest that changes the physical and emotional responses to stress. . . . [it is] the opposite of the fight or flight response" (www.relaxationresponse.org; see also Benson 2000, 53–54, 73, 111). In a certain sense, the Relaxation Response as physiological state is an alternative to the fight-or-flight response. Identified by Walter B. Cannon (1871–1945), the fight-or-flight response is an evolutionary capacity that involves the general discharge of the sympathetic nervous system during which an animal automatically or unconsciously fights or flees depending on the associated external stimulus (see Cannon 1915, 1932). Also described as acute stress response, this physiological reaction is thus a state of hyperarousal. Although the fight-or-flight response has an evolutionary purpose, namely, survival, Benson believes that it is an "emergency reaction" that has various inappropriate applications and harmful effects in the modern world. That is, humans still live in this existential mode, while actual threats to survival have diminished significantly, at least in most Western contexts. According to Benson, hypertension or high blood pressure, a contributing factor for heart attacks and strokes, "is related to stress through the inappropriate elicitation of the fight-or-flight response" (11; also xvi–xviii, 8–10, 47–54, 111–12, 138). In order to obtain optimal health, human beings must, in turn, learn to inhibit the fight-or-flight response, as unnecessary stress and elevated tension, and to elicit the Relaxation Response, as deep relaxation, as behavior modification and as therapeutic method. At a physiological level, the Relaxation Response is thus a wakeful hypometabolic or restful physiological state (65, 72). Especially when elicited through specific methods, the Relaxation Response has the following physiological characteristics: stimulation of hypothalamus, decreased (or relatively lower) sympathetic nervous system activity, decreased body metabolism, decreased respiratory rate, and decreased heart rate and blood pressure (54, 74–75, 111–18, 128).[28] The Relaxation Response thus counteracts stress.

Secondarily, the Relaxation Response refers to a specific method developed by Herbert Benson. This aspect of Benson's work is a bit more complicated. According to Benson, the Relaxation Response method is primarily a simplification and distillation of various tradition-specific practices, though it was originally inspired by Transcendental Meditation. Historically speaking, the Relaxation Response method derives from Transcendental Meditation (xv–xvi, xviii, 61–64, 111–18), though Benson believes that there are various examples of relevant methods (73–79, 80–110) and that the associated physiological state is universal (72, 74–75, 78–79, 82, 111–12, 117, 128, 140; see also Komjathy 2011a). As mentioned earlier, the TM method is a modern, relatively secularized form of meditation developed by Maharishi Mahesh. At the very least, it is a reconceptualized and decontextualized form of Hindu religious practice. Utilizing various *mantra*s from the Hindu tradition, the TM method is a *mantra*-based meditation practice that involves the repetition of a specific Sanskrit sound, a sound originally bestowed by Maharishi and eventually by certified TM teachers. While Benson readily acknowledges his debt to TM, he also rejects TM claims to superiority or uniqueness based on scientific research: "As the experiments progressed over several years, the concept developed that the various physiologic changes that accompanied Transcendental Meditation were part of an integrated response opposite the fight-or-flight response and that *they were in no way unique to Transcendental Meditation*" (72, italics in original). Moreover,

> It is important to remember that there is not a single method that is unique in eliciting the Relaxation Response. For example, Transcendental Meditation is one of the many techniques that incorporate these components. However, we believe that it is not necessary to use the specific method and specific *secret*, personal sound taught by Transcendental Meditation. *Tests at the Thorndike Memorial Laboratory of Harvard have shown that a similar technique used with any sound or phrase or prayer or mantra brings forth the same physiologic changes noted during Transcendental Meditation.* (128, italics in original)

In fact, Benson wrote *The Relaxation Response* as a response to claims of TM practitioners that TM was special and that the Relaxation Response was a repackaged version of TM (Komjathy 2011a).[29] That is, the title of the book has multiple levels of meaning. In addition to describing the physiological condition of the Relaxation Response as a response to Cannon's fight-or-flight response, the Relaxation Response method was an alternative to TM and other tradition-specific methods that can elicit the Relaxation Response. For Benson, the Relaxation Response method is "non-cultic" (129; also xix, 84–85, 126) and universally applicable regardless of one's religious commitments, or lack thereof. When asked about religious claims concerning the uniqueness of specific methods, Benson commented,

> How can you patent prayer? How can you patent communication between an individual and his or her conception of deity? This is universal. I've noticed that when people invoke the Relaxation Response with a particular technique, the effects are so profound that they often ascribe uniqueness to that technique or its system. There are traditions throughout the world and history that claim uniqueness. (Komjathy 2011a)

Within Benson's interpretations of religion, one thus finds both contextualist and perennialist perspectives (see 82–85, 109–10, 129). Benson is also unwilling to make a distinction between religiously-committed meditation and secularized meditation (Komjathy 2011a).

Coping with Stress and the Popular Imagination

Unlike many of the other works on contemplative practice in the present anthology, regarding which their modern influence is often negligible or nonexistent, Herbert Benson is still alive and active, and *The Relaxation Response* remains a contemporary work with wide circulation. We may, in turn, consider the influence of Benson himself, the text of *The Relaxation Response*, as well as the Benson-Henry Institute for Mind Body Medicine. By way of preface, we may also reflect on the degree to which we accept concepts like "stress as potential disease factor," "meditation as therapy," "experience as physiology," and "relaxation as happiness" not only as familiar but also as apparently self-evident givens. We may be thoroughly enculturated into a worldview indebted to individuals such as Selye and Cannon. As we have seen, each element of Benson's therapeutic meditation has a historical and cultural dimension, including identifiable influences. In addition to believing in stress and the importance of stress-management, we may also seek out meditation as a "therapy" within a larger allopathic medical system and use "scientific validation" as a constitutive element in determining which practice will be most attractive and efficacious. If all of this lines up, then we may have a personal recognition of the influence of Herbert Benson and Mind-Body Medicine. We may be sympathizers or adherents of Mind-Body Medicine, therapeutic meditation, and perhaps even the Relaxation Response itself.

There can be little debate that Herbert Benson has exerted tremendous influence on popular American culture, on therapeutic culture, and to a lesser extent on allopathic medicine, the latter of which remains generally conservative, dogmatic, and authoritarian. As will be discussed shortly, Benson's largest influence derives from his publications and also from the Benson-Henry Institute. However, Herbert Benson also occupies a central position in mainstream American culture as a lecturer and as one of the principal advocates and representatives of Mind-Body Medicine. He is a highly sought-after speaker and has given lectures throughout the world (see Benson 2000, xxii–xxvii; Benson 2011).

As mentioned, *The Relaxation Response* is Benson's most popular and influential work. It was the *New York Times* number 1 nonfiction bestseller, remains in print in its sixty-fourth printing, has sold five million copies, and has been translated into fourteen languages, including French, Italian, Korean, and Japanese (Harrington 2008, 219; Benson 2011). Although difficult to gauge in concrete terms, the sheer volume of sales and widespread distribution testify to the book's influence. In this respect, we should also remember that the Relaxation Response method was

Figure 13.3. Lockhart Building (Boston, MA)[30]
Source: Louis Komjathy

first developed and disseminated in the 1970s, but has remained influential in each subsequent decade to the present.

Finally, Benson was instrumental in founding the Mind/Body Medical Institute, now the Benson-Henry Institute for Mind Body Medicine (BHI) at Massachusetts General Hospital (MGH; Boston, Massachusetts). BHI offers a variety of programs, including training for healthcare professionals and stress-management courses for patients. As of the writing this chapter, BHI has offered hundreds of programs and trained tens of thousands of people in their stress-management system. BHI programs provide a window into perhaps the most significant influence of Herbert Benson: helping individuals to increase their ability to cope with the stress of modern life and increase their potential for wellness.

Beyond the Relaxation Response

A variety of interpretive issues related to Herbert Benson's therapeutic meditation have already been touched upon. These include the historical context and cultural influences related to

Benson's discovery of the "Relaxation Response." As discussed previously, we may locate it in the history of Mind-Body Medicine, 1960s countercultural movements—specifically the presence of Asian religious teachers in America—Transcendental Meditation, and what would eventually be categorized as "Baby Boomer spirituality" (see Roof 2001), as well as therapeutic meditation. It is, of course, somewhat problematic to present Mind-Body Medicine and therapeutic meditation as distinct from Herbert Benson, as he has been instrumental in their establishment and remains so in terms of their development. Nonetheless, we have seen that "stress," the scientific study of meditation, as well as physiological and eventually neuroscientific mappings of experience (i.e., consciousness or mind) have particular histories. I have, in turn, emphasized the ways in which Mind-Body Medicine functions like a religious tradition and a soteriological system. It has a particular worldview, set of practices, associated experiences, and projected outcomes, goals, and benefits. The practice of therapeutic meditation only makes sense from a particular perspective and within a specific worldview, namely, one in which allopathic medicine and science are privileged and in which individuals view meditation as technique (or set of techniques) and as "therapy." In this respect, it is quite legitimate, especially from a religiously-committed, contemplative, and/or comparative perspective, to question the corresponding construction of experience, parameters of interpretive authority, and relevance of scientific validation in contemplative practice. Other approaches are possible, and sociopolitical and cultural subtexts are involved.

By way of conclusion, and as a contribution to the present comparative anthology and to the emerging, interdisciplinary field of contemplative studies, I would like to highlight three other dimensions of *The Relaxation Response* that provide fertile ground for reflection: the place of method and conception of experience in contemplative practice, the actual comparative claims that Benson makes in *The Relaxation Response*, and the ethics and politics of appropriation. As mentioned, in Benson's therapeutic meditation, meditation becomes associated with the practice of methods, specifically methods that elicit the Relaxation Response. There is a corresponding emphasis on the physiological effects and characteristics of "relaxation." In this respect, we may recognize that contemplative practice need not and perhaps should not be reduced to technique. Contemplative practice includes specific views, orientations, and qualities. Benson himself moves in this direction when he broadens the types of practices that one can do. However, the repertoire is still somewhat restricted (it does not include art, for example), and every method must be characterized by repetition and passivity and must elicit the Relaxation Response. Along these lines, contemplative experience is primarily defined physiologically, and laboratory experimentation and technological measurement are required for validation. From an alternative perspective, one may consider the degree to which the "physiology of experience" actually correlates to lived and embodied being. Is contemplative practice and contemplative experience conducted in a laboratory or clinical setting really contemplative practice? What role do community, context, and place play in contemplative practice and contemplative experience? Here one thinks of Richard Davidson et al.'s neuroscientific experiments on Tibetan Buddhist monks. Is it simply a matter of having contemplatives "practice techniques" and measure "physiological effects," or does their residence and training in a community of dedicated adherents living in a high-mountain environ change such contemplative practice? Such questions direct one to consider tradition-specific views of contemplative practice as well as the larger soteriological system. That is, outside a modern context, the independent "practice of meditation" seems virtually nonexistent. As the other contributions of the present volume indicate, religiously-committed contemplative practice almost always involves, in some degree or another, community, diet, ethics, material culture, place, ritual, scripture study, and so forth. Herbert Benson and members of BHI recognize this as well: In the BHI stress-management program, there is emphasis on exercise, nutrition, and lifestyle (Benson and Stuart 2010).

Closely connected with the conception of meditation and experience are Benson's selection and interpretation of tradition-specific methods. In terms of meditation techniques strictly defined, *The Relaxation Response* discusses Buddhist Samatha-Vipassanā, Carmelite prayer, Daoist apophatic meditation, Eastern Orthodox prayer, Hindu classical Yoga, Jewish Kabbalah, Sufi prayer, and Zen Buddhist meditation. Scholars of these various traditions could, of course, take issue with Benson's characterizations. My primary interest, however, is in the selection itself and in Benson's claims that every meditation method is a "means to elicit the Relaxation Response." That is, from Benson's perspective, "meditation" apparently only refers to trophotropic (hypoaroused/hyperquiescent) methods, and these are defined from a therapeutic perspective as "stress-management strategies." In a manner paralleling problematic attempts to limit the category of "mystical experience" to trophotropic experiences (see Forman 1990; cf. Komjathy 2007, 2012), such a move excludes a wide variety of material that I would identify as "contemplative practices." These include alchemical, devotional, and visualization practices. Many of these methods, at least during specific moments of the practice, involve ergotropic states, that is, a high degree of arousal. This raises the question of the soteriological power or application of "stress." From a therapeutic perspective, stress is generally harmful, but can stress be used to propel practitioners into "higher states of consciousness"? One thinks of examples such as certain Zen Buddhist uses of *kōan*s to initiate *kenshō* or *satori* (awakening) experiences. In certain forms of contemplative practice, stress may be required. Benson himself recognizes this when he discusses Tibetan Tummo (*gTum-mo*; fierce woman/heat) practice as a form of "advanced meditation."[31] However, in the primary conception of meditation in Mind-Body Medicine, such methods will not help to relieve stress and develop relaxation; they are primarily examples of the power of the mind to influence the body.[32] In addition to being a potentially normative or quasi-sectarian view, such a perspective also utilizes a particular categorization of contemplative practice, namely, the trophotropic-ergotropic dyad. As discussed in the present volume, there are other ways of categorizing and interpreting contemplative practice and contemplative experience.

Finally and perhaps most challenging, the Relaxation Response method and therapeutic meditation draw our attention to the "ethics and politics of appropriation," specifically with respect to religious traditions. Almost every form of modern medicalized or secularized meditation derives from a religiously-committed contemplative practice, from a religious community and tradition. The resultant modification involves reconceptualization and decontextualization, or at least recontextualization. In the case of Herbert Benson's Relaxation Response method, this issue is extremely complex. As we have seen, the Relaxation Response method was originally adapted from Transcendental Meditation™ (TM™). On the one hand, one might be inclined, especially if one is a TM adherent or sympathizer, to view such a development as trademark or copyright infringement. However, Maharishi Mahesh himself reconceptualized and reconcontextualized Hindu *mantra*-practice and also engaged in spiritual entrepreneurship, especially evident in his attempts to collect celebrities and acquire wealth.[33] While Maharishi Mahesh was a birthright Hindu adherent, his TM system may be seen as a new religious movement (see Williamson 2010). That is, the Relaxation Response method derives from TM, which derives from Hindu *mantra*-practice, with the relation of the latter two deserving further research. Benson's Relaxation Response method might, in turn, represent a relatively innocuous example of appropriation, especially since it is explicitly secularized and medicalized and rejects claims of uniqueness, even with respect to the proposed method itself. However, this process of reconceptualization is located in a larger pattern of cultural exchange, wherein religious traditions (so-called "wisdom traditions") are often identified as "resources." One consequence is that religious adherents and communities are disempowered in the process. One also notices a corresponding pattern of domestication, wherein religiously-committed and tradition-based contemplative practice is purged of its corresponding soteriological and theological dimensions. It thus becomes domesticated according to dominant American values and concerns. While some might point out that "market forces" and the "law of supply and demand" lead to the appropriation and reconceptualization of tradition-derived methods, there are ethical and political dimensions. Moreover, more reflection is required on the motivations behind the appropriation and the reasons for the widespread popular appeal of reconceptualized practices such as the method described and advocated in *The Relaxation Response*.

Notes

I am grateful to Dr. Herbert Benson for his support of and contributions to the present chapter. Dr. Benson not only graciously granted interviews but also read and commented on the chapter. I am also grateful to Maureen Gilbert, Dr. Benson's administrative assistant, for her assistance with scheduling and supplying difficult-to-find materials.

1. When "Relaxation Response" appears without qualification, it refers to the corresponding physiological state, partially defined as the opposite of the "fight-or-flight response." When it refers to the related practice, I will speak of the "Relaxation Response method." The actual text will appear in italics as *The Relaxation Response*.

2. Unless otherwise indicated, biographical information comes from a telephone interview that I conducted on April 21, 2011 (Komjathy 2011a). When "Benson" occurs without documentation, it refers to Herbert Benson himself. For a comprehensive catalogue of Benson's publications, see Benson 2011. For an account of Benson's work in the context of Mind-Body Medicine, see Harrington 2008, 214–20.

3. Here it is important to note that the so-called white coat syndrome had not yet been identified. This is the phenomenon of patients exhibiting elevated blood pressure in a clinical setting but not in other contexts. It substantiates the connection between stress and hypertension.

4. Outside of *The Relaxation Response* and a few comments in his other general-audience books, Benson has only published two articles on TM. One discusses its possible therapeutic application to decrease drug abuse and the other addresses whether the movement is "science or cult" (see Benson 2011).

5. The findings of this research were not published, but it led to various subsequent publications (see Benson 2011). One also finds hints of influence in *The Relaxation Response* itself.

6. Benson emphasizes that his research has always been collaborative. In his own words, "The discovery of the Relaxation Response and the related research on the physiology of stress should not be solely associated with me" (Komjathy 2011a). Herbert Benson collaborated with many individuals on his academic and general audience works (see Benson 2011).

7. On his various professional positions, see Benson 2011.

8. Through an endowment from the Coors Foundation, the Herbert Benson Professorship (currently Mind-Body Medical Institute Professorship) in Medicine will be activated in Harvard Medical School upon Benson's retirement (Benson 2011; Komjathy 2011b).

9. Also known as János Hugo Bruno Selye, Hans Selye was of Austro-Hungarian origin and Hungarian ethnicity. He was born in Vienna in Austria-Hungary and grew up in Komárom, Hungary. He became a doctor of medicine and chemistry in Prague in 1929, went to Johns Hopkins University on a Rockefeller Foundation Scholarship in 1931, and then went to McGill University in Montreal, where he started researching the issue of stress in 1936. In 1945 he joined the Université de Montréal. See, for example, Szabo et al. 2012 and Selye's biography on the websites of the American Institute of Stress and Canadian Institute of Stress.

10. Walter Bradford Cannon was born in Prairie du Chien, Wisconsin. Cannon received his undergraduate degree in biology from Harvard College, after which he began medical school at Harvard in 1896. During this time, he started working in Henry Pickering Bowditch's (1840–1911) lab and in 1900 received his medical degree. After graduation, Cannon was hired by Harvard to instruct in the Department of Physiology. In 1906 Cannon became Higginson Professor and Chairman of the Department of Physiology at Harvard Medical School, a position he held until 1942. From 1914 to 1916 he was also President of the American Physiological Society. See Cannon's biography on the websites of the American Philosophical Society, which includes the Walter B. Cannon Papers, and of the American Physiological Society.

11. It is noteworthy that Benson devoted a substantial section of *The Relaxation Response* to discuss "stress," but that later publications almost presuppose familiarity in readers. One might, in turn, investigate the changing conceptions, including the shift toward "genetics."

12. Here we may note the widespread tendency to define meditation as a "relaxation method." However, there are forms of meditation, such as alchemy, visualization, and Zen *kōan*-based practice, which may involve a high degree of tension and/or physiological activity.

13. Herbert Benson has had very little involvement with the Mind and Life Institute. From his own perspective, "There is a strong emphasis on Vipassanā and Tibetan Buddhism there. While Vipassanā is an excellent technique, it is only one among many methods for eliciting the Relaxation Response" (Komjathy 2011b).

14. Some of these developments have also given rise to an increased respect for the source-traditions related to specific methods and to advanced practitioners of those methods and associated with the traditions. For example, there has been recent collaborative research between Tibetan Buddhist monks and neuroscientists (see Davidson and Harrington 2002; cf. Benson 1984, 29–82). One also finds the emergence of "neuro-phenomenology," or the attempt to involve first-person descriptions of contemplative practice with neuro-imagining techniques (see, e.g., Thompson 2010). While the latter may be read as another form of scientific validation, it points in opposite directions as well. As preliminary research confirms that advanced practitioners can accurately describe their experience (see, e.g., Brown and Engler 1984), it may rather point toward the irrelevance or decreased relevance of science. That is, it may move more in the direction of a postmodern and postcolonial approach to contemplative studies, in which "critical adherent perspectives" are included. On the most generous level, we might see the possibility of a fruitful conversation between contemplatives and neuroscientists as equally valid interpretive authorities. One would then have to consider alternative views on human psychology and consciousness.

15. One could, in turn, locate the emergence of therapeutic meditation in the larger American health and fitness movement.

16. Note that Anne Harrington (2008, 219–20) misidentifies this quotation as part of the original 1975 edition. That edition instead includes endorsements by the following individuals: David Ewing (*Harvard Business Review*; inside front dust jacket); Sidney Alexander (Lahey Clinic; same); Rabbi Mordecai L. Brill (Institute of Religion and Health; inside back dust jacket); as well as Noah Gordon (*The Journal of Human Stress*), Harvey Cox (Harvard Divinity School), and C. Paul Nay (Massachusetts Mutual Life), all on the back cover. The identities of these individuals also challenge some of Harrington's account.

17. In our conversation that explored this question, both Herbert Benson (reluctantly) and I agreed that the Relaxation Response method appears to be the beginning of "therapeutic meditation." Other forms

do not appear until about a decade later. The one exception may be Progressive Relaxation as created by Edmund Jacobson (1888–1983), PhD (Harvard; ca. 1912), MD (Northwestern University; 1915), an American physician who conducted most of his research at the Laboratory for Clinical Physiology in Chicago, Illinois. See Jacobson 1929, 1934. Having some connection to Biofeedback, Jacobson's Progressive Relaxation is often categorized as a "relaxation technique" or "mind-body relaxation."

18. A profitable study could be written on both the concept of "meditation" and the emergence of meditation as an imagined cross-cultural practice. For some important insights, see Baier 2009. As I have suggested in the introductory chapters of this volume, I see "meditation" as a viable comparative category, as long as we also understand that it approximates a wide variety of related, tradition-specific technical terms. See also the technical glossary in this volume.

19. This is partially true of Benson as well. As the years have progressed, Benson has recognized the importance of the "faith factor" and "support networks," has moved in the direction of more holistic and comprehensive "stress-management therapy," and has even spoken from his own perspective as an adherent of Judaism.

20. Relaxation Response from Transcendental Meditation, Mindfulness-Based Stress Reduction from Vipassanā, iRest from Yoga Nidra, and so forth. I have been unable to determine the status of Eugene Gendlin's Focusing method. If it was created independently, then it may be one of the only examples of therapeutic meditation not derived from a tradition-specific and religiously-committed form of contemplative practice. One may still wonder, however, at the wide range of possible influences, including the Religious Society of Friends (Quakers).

21. Benson's curriculum vitae also includes references to various articles related to the scientific validation of the Relaxation Response, specifically with respect to stress reduction and health benefits. For a brief discussion, see Andresen 2000, 26–30.

22. For Benson's attempt to address an evangelical audience and that community's reservations about "meditation," see Benson and Proctor 2010b.

23. Interestingly, Benson did not practice any form of meditation until almost twenty years after his initial experiments. Specifically, he began meditating in 1985. That is, he taught people the Relaxation Response method without actually personally practicing it. When I explored this fact with him, Benson responded, "I followed this approach because I did not want to lose my objectivity and neutrality. I was conducting scientific experiments. Moreover, the method is scientific, so correct practice leads to the corresponding physiological changes and medical benefits" (Komjathy 2011a).

24. Although *The Relaxation Response* can give the impression that community, place, and tradition are unimportant, Benson's actual work and subsequent publications as well as the existence of the Benson-Henry Institute indicate otherwise.

25. In this respect, one might also consider the ways in which the body, primarily as biological or physical entity, and/or the self, primarily as psychological agent, becomes sacred in contemporary secular materialist contexts. Here I do not mean views of the body and/or the self as a manifestation of the sacred or as a means through which to connect with the sacred, views that one finds in various religious traditions, but as (substitutes for) the sacred. We might refer to this as the "sacralization of self." That is, from a modern therapeutic perspective, the person, especially his or her "health" and *individual* life, becomes the primary concern and locus of meaning. See, for example, Vitz 1994; Heelas 1996; Harrington 2008; Goldman 2012.

26. That is, meditation or stress-management training now has a practical application in terms of corporate America, a way of life that is one of the primary sources of "stress" (see Benson 2000, 8–10, 41–46). Rather than a radically subversive or transformative influence, meditation may be appropriated into the larger capitalist system. This is a place where one might take issue with the conservative nature of allopathic medicine, including its intricate ties to the pharmaceutical companies, the US Food and Drug Administration (FDA), and the insurance industry. Also noteworthy here is the use of Richard Miller's iRest to treat soldiers with post-traumatic stress disorder (PTSD) from battlefield trauma as well as more

disturbing attempts to use meditation to create super-soldiers. An example of the latter is Warrior Mind Training (WMT) developed by Sarah Ernst and others, with the inaugural program conducted at the Marine Corps Air Station (San Diego, California) in 2005. See www.warriortraining.us. We might refer to the latter development as the "weaponization" or "military application" of meditation, and it is no coincidence that it is partially rooted in Orientalist constructions of "Japanese Samurai codes." See also Andresen 2000.

27. Although many of Benson's views and contributions may be familiar to contemporary readers of the present volume, we must keep in mind how radical the book was in its original 1975 printing and try to imagine that historical and cultural moment. A profitable study might, in turn, consider the relative importance, specific influence, and attractiveness of *The Relaxation Response* in each subsequent decade.

28. For a comparison of the physiology of the fight-or-flight response with that of the Relaxation Response, see Benson "Fight or Flight"; Neimark "Comparison."

29. We must again contextualize the original publication of *The Relaxation Response* (1975). At that time, Maharishi Mahesh and the TM movement were major players. Although TM has lost much of its cultural capital and cogency in the contemporary "spiritual marketplace" (see Roof 2001), it was nonetheless one of the original brands and products of Asian spirituality in the West. It also played and continues to play a major role in Baby Boomer spirituality, even after many sixty- and seventy-year-olds have "exited the cult."

30. As of the publication of the present volume, BHI is housed on the fourth floor of the Lockhart Building, which is located at 151 Merrimac Street in Boston, Massachusetts.

31. Benson 1984, 47–82; Benson 1996, 164–66; Benson 2000, xxxviii–xl. Interestingly, Tummo is not discussed in Benson and Proctor 2010a. See also Harrington 2008, 232–42.

32. As we have seen, Mind-Body Medicine is a psychosomatic therapeutic modality, emphasizing the ways in which one can consciously alter one's physiology, perhaps even genetics, and thus one's health. During my follow-up interview with Herbert Benson (Komjathy 2011b), I inquired about the alternative possibility, that is, the potential of corporeal modification to initiate transformations of consciousness (somatopsychic therapy?). Benson responded, "I don't know. We have not conducted research on this." In this respect, we might consider the "power of embodiment" as well as an integrated approach to human being.

33. This was one of the earliest attempts to develop "celebrity religion," that is, a system that appeals to and actively pursues celebrities. See Humes 2005; Williamson 2010. The Beatles famously studied with Maharishi Mahesh. One also thinks of the prominent hybrid spiritualist teacher Deepak Chopra (b. 1947), a former TM adherent. In terms of the contemporary period, the most conspicuous example of a celebrity-centered new religious movement is L. Ron Hubbard's (1911–1986) Church of Scientology. In this respect, the related phenomenon of "spiritual celebrities" (e.g., Deepak Chopra, the Dalai Lama, Wayne Dyer, Thich Nhat Hanh, Eckhart Tolle), with their associated cultural and economic capital, is also noteworthy.

Works Cited and Further Reading

Andresen, Jensine. 2000. "Meditation Meets Behavioral Meditation." In *Cognitive Models and Spiritual Maps*, edited by Jensine Andresen and Robert Forman, 17–73. Bowling Green: Imprint Academic.

Baier, Karl. 2009. *Meditation und Moderne*. 2 vols. Würzburg: Königshausen and Neumann.

Benson, Herbert. 1975. *The Relaxation Response*. New York: William Morrow.

———. 1979. *The Mind/Body Effect*. New York: Simon and Schuster.

———, with William Proctor. 1984. *Beyond the Relaxation Response*. New York: Times Books.

———, with Marg Stark. 1996. *Timeless Healing: The Power and Biology of Belief*. New York: Scribner.

———, with Miriam Z. Klipper. 2000. *The Relaxation Response: 25th Anniversary Edition*. New York: Avon.

———. 2011. "Curriculum Vitae." http://www.massgeneral.org/bhi/assets/pdfs/benson_cv.pdf. Accessed on January 1, 2011.

———. n.d. "Fight or Flight vs. Relaxation Response." www.relaxationresponse.org/FightOrFlight.htm. Accessed on January 1, 2011.

———. n.d. "Steps to Elicit the Relaxation Response." www.relaxationresponse.org/steps. Accessed on January 1, 2011.

Benson, Herbert, J. F. Beary, and M. P. Carol. 1974. "The Relaxation Response." *Psychiatry* 37: 37–46.

Benson, Herbert, and Aggie Casey. 2011. *Harvard Medical School Stress Management: Approaches for Preventing and Reducing Stress*. Cambridge: Harvard Medical School.

Benson, Herbert, J. A. Herd, W. H. Morse, and R. T. Kelleher. 1970. "Behaviorally Induced Hypertension in the Squirrel Monkey." *Circulation Research* 27.1, supplement 1: 21–26.

Benson, Herbert, and William Proctor. 2010a. *Relaxation Revolution*. New York: Scribner.

———. 2010b. "The Coming Relaxation Revolution: Introducing Evangelical Christians to the Science and Genetics of Mind Body Therapy." *Criswell Theological Review* 8.1: 3–28.

Benson, Herbert, and Eileen Stuart. 2010 (1992). *The Wellness Book: The Comprehensive Guide to Maintaining Health and Treating Stress-Related Illness*. New York and London: Scribner.

Benson-Henry Institute for Mind Body Medicine (BHI). n.d. "About." www.massgeneral.org/bhi/about. Accessed on January 1, 2011.

———. n.d. "Eliciting the Relaxation Response." www.massgeneral.org/bhi/basics/eliciting_rr.aspx. Accessed on January 1, 2011.

———. n.d. "Mind Body Medicine Education and Training." www.massgeneral.org/bhi/education. Accessed on January 1, 2011.

———. n.d. "Mind Body Treatments and Services." www.massgeneral.org/bhi/services. Accessed on January 1, 2011.

———. n.d. "Stress." www.massgeneral.org/bhi/basics/stress.aspx. Accessed on January 1, 2011.

———. n.d. "What Is Mind Body Medicine?" www.massgeneral.org/bhi/basics. Accessed on January 1, 2011.

———. n.d. "Stress Buster Tips for Stress Management." www.massgeneral.org/bhi/basics/managing/busters.aspx. Accessed on January 1, 2011.

Booth, Jeremy. 1977. "A Short History of Blood Pressure Measurement." *Proceedings of the Royal Society of Medicine* 70 (November 1977): 793–99.

Brown, Daniel, and Jack Engler. 1984. "A Rorschach Study of the Stages of Mindfulness Meditation." In *Meditation: Classic and Contemporary Perspectives*, edited by Roger Walsh and Deane Shapiro, 232–63. New York: Aldine.

Bull, Webster, and Martha Bull. 2011. *Something in the Ether: A Bicentennial History of Massachusetts General Hospital, 1811–2011*. Berkeley: Memoirs Unlimited.

Cannon, Walter Bradford. 1915. *Bodily Changes in Pain, Hunger, Fear, and Rage: An Account of Recent Researches into the Function of Emotional Excitement*. New York: Appleton-Century-Crofts.

———. 1929. *Bodily Changes in Pain, Hunger, Fear, and Rage: An Account of Recent Researches into the Function of Emotional Excitement*. 2nd ed. New York: Appleton-Century-Crofts.

———. 1932. *The Wisdom of the Body*. New York: Norton.

Dalai Lama, Herbert Benson, Robert Thurman, Howard Gardner, and Daniel Goleman. 1991. *MindScience: An East-West Dialogue*. Marblehead: Wisdom Publications.

Davidson, Richard, and Anne Harrington, eds. 2002. *Visions of Compassion: Western Scientists and Tibetan Buddhists Examine Human Nature*. Oxford and New York: Oxford University Press.

Dickinson, H. O., et al. 2006. "Lifestyle Interventions to Reduce Raised Blood Pressure: A Systematic Review of Randomized Controlled Trials." *Journal of Hypertension* 24.2: 215–33.

Engel, Klaus. 1997a. *Meditation: Volume 1 History and Present Time*. Berlin: Peter Lang.

———. 1997b. *Meditation: Volume 2 Empirical Research and Theory*. Berlin: Peter Lang.

Finland, Maxwell. 1982. *The Harvard Medical Unit at Boston City Hospital*. 3 vols. Boston: Harvard Medical School.

Forman, Robert K. C., ed. 1990. *The Problem of Pure Consciousness: Mysticism and Philosophy*. Oxford and New York: Oxford University Press.

Foucault, Michel. 1989 (1973). *The Birth of the Clinic: An Archaeology of Medical Perception*. Translated by A. M. Sheridan. London and New York: Routledge.

Gimello, Robert. 1978. "Mysticism and Meditation." In *Mysticism and Philosophical Analysis*, edited by Steven T. Katz, 170–99. Oxford and New York: Oxford University Press.

Goldman, Marion. 2012. *The American Soul Rush: Esalen and the Rise of Spiritual Privilege*. New York: New York University Press.

Good, Byron, et al., eds. 2010. *A Reader in Medical Anthropology: Theoretical Trajectories, Emergent Realities*. Malden: Wiley-Blackwell.

Gould, Stephen Jay. 1981. *The Mismeasure of Man*. New York: Norton.

Guyton, Arthur, and John Hall. 2006. *Textbook of Medical Physiology*. 11th ed. Philadelphia: Elsevier Saunders.

Harrington, Anne. 2008. *The Cure Within: A History of Mind-Body Medicine*. New York: Norton.

Harrington, Anne, and Arthur Zajonc, eds. 2006. *The Dalai Lama at MIT*. Cambridge: Harvard University Press.

Harvard Medical School (HMS). 2011. "HMS Affiliates." http://hms.harvard.edu/admissions/default.asp?page=affiliates. Accessed on January 1, 2011.

Heelas, Paul. 1996. *The New Age Movement: The Celebration of the Self and the Sacralization of Modernity*. Oxford: Blackwell.

Horowitz, Mardi, Nigel Field, and Catherine Classen. 1993. "Stress Response Syndromes and Their Treatment." In *Handbook of Stress*, 2nd ed., edited by Leo Goldberger and Shlomo Breznitz, 757–73. New York: Free Press.

Humes, Cynthia Ann. 2005. "Maharishi Mahesh Yogi: Beyond the TM Technique." In *Gurus in America*, edited by Thomas Forsthoefel and Cynthia Ann Humes, 55–79. Albany: State University of New York Press.

Iwamura, Jane. 2000. "The Oriental Monk in American Popular Culture." In *Religion and Popular Culture in America*, edited by Bruce David Forbes and Jeffrey H. Mahan, 25–43. Berkeley: University of California Press.

Jacobs, Gregg. 2001. "Clinical Applications of the Relaxation Response and Mind-Body Interventions." *Journal of Alternative and Complementary Medicine* 7.1: 93–101.

Jacobson, Edmund. 1929. *Progressive Relaxation*. Chicago: University of Chicago Press.

———. 1934. *You Must Relax*. Oxford: Whittlesey House.

———. 1974. *Progressive Relaxation: A Physiological and Clinical Investigation of Muscular States and Their Significance in Psychology and Medical Practice*. 3rd ed. Chicago: University of Chicago Press.

Kabat-Zinn, Jon. 1990. *Full Catastrophe Living*. New York: Delacorte Press.

Kabat-Zinn, Jon, L. Lipworth, and R. Burney. 1985. "The Clinical Use of Mindfulness Meditation for the Self-regulation of Pain." *Journal of Behavioral Medicine* 8: 163–90.

Katz, Steven, ed. 1978. *Mysticism and Philosophical Analysis*. Oxford and New York: Oxford University Press.

Kleinman, Arthur. 1981. *Patients and Healers in the Context of Culture*. Berkeley: University of California Press.

———. 1988. *The Illness Narratives: Suffering, Healing, and the Human Condition*. New York: Basic Books.

Komjathy, Louis. 2007. *Cultivating Perfection: Mysticism and Self-Transformation in Early Quanzhen Daoism*. Leiden: Brill.

———. 2011a. Telephone Interview with Herbert Benson. April 21, 2011.

———. 2011b. Follow-Up Telephone Interview with Herbert Benson. September 23, 2011.

———. 2012. "Mysticism." In *Encyclopedia of Global Religion*, edited by Mark Juergensmeyer and Wade Clark Roof, 855–61. Thousand Oaks: Sage.
Kuhn, Thomas. 1962. *The Structure of Scientific Revolutions*. Chicago: University of Chicago Press.
Levine, Herbert. 1992. "Profiles in Cardiology: Samuel A. Levine." *Clinical Cardiology* 15: 473–76.
Lopez, Donald, ed. 1995. *Curators of the Buddha: The Study of Buddhism under Colonialism*. Chicago: University of Chicago Press.
———. 1999. *Prisoners of Shangri-La: Tibetan Buddhism and the West*. Chicago: University of Chicago Press.
Luisi, Pier Luigi, ed. 2010. *Mind and Life: Discussions with the Dalai Lama on the Nature of Reality*. New York: Columbia University Press.
Lutz, Antoine, John Dunne, and Richard Davidson. 2007. "Meditation and the Neuroscience of Consciousness: An Introduction." In *The Cambridge Handbook of Consciousness*, edited by Philip Zelazo et al., 499–551. Cambridge and New York: Cambridge University Press.
McMahan, David. 2008. *The Making of Buddhist Modernism*. Oxford and New York: Oxford University Press.
McPhee, Stephen, and Gary Hammer. 2009. *Pathophysiology of Disease: An Introduction to Clinical Medicine*. 6th ed. New York: McGraw-Hill.
Murphy, Joseph, and Margaret Lloyd, eds. 2013. *Mayo Clinic Cardiology Concise Textbook*. 4th ed. London and New York: Mayo Clinic Scientific Press/Oxford University Press.
Murphy, Michael, and Steven Donovan. 1999. *The Physical and Psychological Effects of Meditation*. Sausalito: Institute of Noetic Sciences.
Neimark, Neil. n.d. "A Comparison between the Fight or Flight Response and the Relaxation Response." www.relaxationresponse.org/Neimark.htm. Accessed on January 1, 2011.
Ospina, Maria, et al. 2007. "Meditation Practices for Health: State of the Research." *Evidence Report/Technology Assessment* 155: 1–263.
Paine, Jeffrey. 2004. *Re-enchantment: Tibetan Buddhism Comes to the West*. New York: Norton.
Peterson, Gregory. 2003. "Demarcation and the Scientific Fallacy." *Zygon* 38.4: 751–61.
Popper, Karl. 1992 (1959). *The Logic of Scientific Discovery*. London and New York: Routledge.
Roof, Wade Clark. 2001. *Spiritual Marketplace: Baby Boomers and the Remaking of American Religion*. Princeton: Princeton University Press.
Selye, Hans. 1936. "A Syndrome Produced by Diverse Nocuous Agents." *Nature* 138: 32.
———. 1952. *The Story of the Adaptation Syndrome*. Montreal: Acta.
———. 1956. *The Stress of Life*. New York: McGraw-Hill.
———. 1993 (posthumous). "History of the Stress Concept." In *Handbook of Stress*, 2nd ed., edited by Leo Goldberger and Shlomo Breznitz, 7–17. New York: The Free Press.
Stenmark, Mikael. 2001. *Scientism: Science, Ethics and Religion*. Surrey: Ashgate.
Stoyva, Johann, and John Carlson. 1993. "A Coping/Rest Model of Relaxation and Stress Management." In *Handbook of Stress*, 2nd ed., edited by Leo Goldberger and Shlomo Breznitz, 724–56. New York: The Free Press.
Streett, R. Alan. 2010. "Interview with Dr. Herbert Benson and William Proctor." *Criswell Theological Review* 8.1: 29–33.
Szabo, Sandor, Yvette Tache, and Arpad Somogyi. 2012. "The Legacy of Hans Selye and the Origins of Stress Research: A Retrospective 75 Years after His Landmark Brief 'Letter' to the Editor of *Nature*." *Stress* 15.5 (September 2012): 472–78.
Taylor, Eugene. 2000. "The Connection between Mind and Body." *Harvard Medical Alumni Bulletin* (Winter): 40–47.
———. 2003. "A Perfect Correlation between Mind and Brain: William James's *Varieties* and the Contemporary Field of Mind/Body Medicine." *Journal of Speculative Philosophy* 17.1: 40–52.

Thompson, Evan. 2010. *Mind in Life: Biology, Phenomenology, and the Sciences of Mind.* Cambridge: Belknap Press.

Tweed, Thomas, and Stephen Prothero. 1998. *Asian Religions in America: A Documentary History.* Oxford and New York: Oxford University Press.

University of Alberta Evidence-Based Practice Center (UAEBPC). 2007. "Meditation Practices for Health: State of the Research." Agency for Healthcare Research and Quality, US Department of Health and Human Services, *Evidence Report/Technology Assessment* 155.

Viner, Russell. 1999. "Putting Stress in Life: Hans Selye and the Making of Stress Theory." *Social Studies of Science* 29.3: 391–410.

Vitz, Paul. 1994 (1977). *Psychology as Religion: The Cult of Self-Worship.* 2nd ed. Carlisle: Wm. B. Eerdmans.

Whorton, James. 2004. *Nature Cures: The History of Alternative Medicine in America.* Oxford and New York: Oxford University Press.

Williamson, Lola. 2010. *Transcendent in America: Hindu-Inspired Meditation Movements as New Religion.* New York: New York University Press.

*The Relaxation Response**

Herbert Benson (b. 1935), MD[1]

Selected and Annotated by Louis Komjathy

How are these anxieties and stresses affecting us? The presence of mental stress as a part of modern living has been the subject of a number of books, most of which concentrate on the psychology of stress.[2] We will consider stress from a somewhat different perspective, for our concern is not only the psychology but also the *physiology* of stress. We will explore what happens to you internally under stressful situations and how stress *physically* undermines your health. This will be done by examining the relation between your emotional reactions and what they may cost you in hypertension, heart attacks, strokes, and other diseases.[3] We will then point out what you can do about the effects of stress. We will show how, by your own personal adoption of a simple psychological technique, you can improve your physical and mental well-being. [Ch. 1, p. 4.]

---

*The present selection derives from the most recent edition of the text (2000), which consists of 179 pages, with 143 pages being actual writing. The selections presented here, which were chosen in consultation with Dr. Herbert Benson, basically parallel the original 1975 English edition. Readers will also benefit from consulting the following charts in *The Relaxation Response*: (1) The Stress of Adjusting to Change (39–40); (2) Physiologic Changes Associated with the Fight-or-Flight Response (49); (3) Physiologic Changes Associated with the Relaxation Response (54); and (4) Different Techniques Eliciting the Physiologic Changes of the Relaxation Response (74–75). Numbers in brackets indicate page numbers in the original publication, with the first appearance corresponding to the beginning of a new page. With the exception of note 20, which appears in the original text of *The Relaxation Response*, I have supplied all of the annotations. In keeping with religious studies and as a translation methodology of resistance (Lawrence Venuti), I adopt the principle of "defamiliarization" for annotations, that is, highlighting terms that should be strange but that have become commonplace. Hopefully, this will reveal certain cultural assumptions and influential conceptual frameworks. From the perspective of medical anthropology, we might consider the degree to which these are culturally and historically contingent, even if they have become normative. I am grateful to HarperCollins for permission to publish this selection. I wish to especially thank Peter London for his assistance. Excerpts from *The Relaxation Response*, by Herbert Benson, MD, with Miriam Z. Klipper. Copyright 1975 by William Morrow and Company, Inc. Reprinted by permission of HarperCollins Publishers.

1. An American cardiologist, Herbert Benson (MD, Harvard Medical School; 1961) is currently director emeritus of the Benson-Henry Institute for Mind Body Medicine (BHI; Boston, MA) and professor of medicine at Harvard Medical School (HMS).

2. As discussed in my introduction, "stress," at least as a concept and framework for understanding the human condition, was first developed by the Austrian-Canadian endocrinologist Hans Selye (1907–1982).

3. As an allopathic (Western biomedical) category, hypertension (HTN), or high blood pressure, is a chronic medical condition in which blood pressure in the arteries is elevated. A "heart attack," more technically referred to as myocardial infarction (MI) or acute myocardial infarction (AMI), with "infarction" being tissue death due to a local lack of oxygen, happens when blood stops flowing properly to part of the heart and the heart muscle is injured due to not receiving enough oxygen. A "stroke," more technically referred to as a cerebrovascular accident (CVA), is the rapid loss of brain function due to disturbance in the blood supply to the brain. See, for example, McPhee and Hammer 2009.

The Hidden Epidemic

We are in the midst of an epidemic,[4] one that is all too prevalent in the United States and other industrialized nations. The name of this epidemic is hypertension, the medical term for high blood pressure. Hypertension predisposes one to the diseases of atherosclerosis (hardening of the arteries), heart attacks, and strokes. These diseases [5] of the heart and brain account for more than 50 percent of the deaths each year in the United States. Therefore, it is not surprising that various degrees of hypertension are present in 15 to 33 percent of the adult population. Although this epidemic is not infectious in nature, it may be even more insidious, simply because its manifestations do not affect large numbers at the same time and because we are not generally aware that the disease is slowing developing within us. Throughout its course there are few, if any, symptoms. Yet each day we see it strike without warning, cutting short by decades the lives of our friends and loved ones. According to carefully compiled Government vital statistics, the diseases resulting from this epidemic account for an average of two deaths every minute in the United States alone. Put another way, that is nearly one million out of two million deaths a year. Translate this statistic into your own personal experience—the loss of a friend who leaves young children, the premature death of a father about to enjoy his retirement years.[5] You are a fortunate individual if you have not personally experienced the ravages of this epidemic.

High blood pressure, heart attacks, and strokes have markedly increased, not only afflicting a growing percentage of the population but steadily finding their way into younger age groups. The late Dr. Samuel A. Levine,[6] an eminent American cardiologist,[7] pointed out in 1963 that in families he had treated for many years, sons suffered [6] heart attacks at an average of thirteen years younger than the age at which the fathers experienced theirs. Today many cardiologists observe this same significant shift. Five to ten years ago it would have been a relatively rare event to witness a stroke or heart attack in a person in this thirties and it would have been astonishing if the patient were in his twenties. Now interns and house staff just starting in medicine consider heart attacks in men in their thirties commonplace.

---

4. In epidemiology (study of the patterns, causes, and effects of health and disease conditions), an epidemic, from Greek and literally meaning "upon people," occurs when new cases of a certain disease, in a given human population and during a given period, substantially exceed what is expected based on recent experience.

5. In a modern context, "retirement" generally refers to the point where a person permanently stops working. In the case of the United States, the "normal" or "full retirement age" is now sixty-seven, although it was previously sixty-five. At least at the present time, certain retirement benefits, so-called "social entitlement programs" but better understood in terms of a "social contract" and "social welfare," include Social Security payments and Medicare.

6. Samuel Albert Levine (1891–1966) was an influential Polish American cardiologist who received his MD from Harvard Medical School (HMS) in 1914. He worked for most of his career at Brigham and Women's Hospital (BWH; Boston, MA), HMS's second-largest teaching affiliate. See Levine 1992. The Levine scale (a numeric scoring system to characterize the intensity or the loudness of a heart murmur), Levine's sign (clenched fist held over the chest to describe ischemic chest pain), and Lown-Ganong-Levine (LGL) syndrome (a syndrome of pre-excitation of the ventricles due to an accessory pathway providing an abnormal electrical communication from the atria to the ventricles) are named after him. See, for example, Murphy and Lloyd 2013.

7. Cardiology is an allopathic medical specialization dealing with disorders of the heart. Allopathic physicians (MD) who specialize in this field of medicine are called cardiologists. Allopathic physicians who specialize in cardiac surgery are called cardiac surgeons.

There is no shortage of theories to explain the rapidly increasing prevalence of hypertension and the associated increase in the number of heart attacks and strokes, suffered mainly in the Western world. The traditional explanations have been (1) inappropriate diet, (2) lack of exercise, and (3) family disposition. Yet there is another factor, which has often been ignored: environmental stress. Although environmental stress is gaining recognition as an important factor in the development of these diseases, it is still poorly understood. All four factors play a role. What has yet to be adequately determined is the relative significance of each.

Doctors have recognized for years that stress is taking a toll. It is not difficult to understand the correlation between the highly competitive, time-pressured society in which we live and mental stress with its influence on heart disease. For example, a commonly heard warning is "Don't get upset, you'll get high blood pressure."[8] The problem has been how to quantify stress. In other words, [7] how do we objectively measure the effects of stress upon the body? Medicine has recently made inroads, moving from psychological speculation to hard, measurable physiologic data.

Our focus will be on the relation between stressful psychological events and their associated physiologic changes, as they affect your health. Traditionally, psychology and medicine have long been separated by their different methodologies of research. This dichotomy has kept most physicians from seeing the relation between the psychologically laden term "stress" (hinging as it does on personal behavior and environmental events) and the functioning of the body and related diseases. Although most doctors would agree that stress does affect health, they are not attuned to the psychological, nonmedical literature about stress. Concerned mainly with bodily signs and symptoms, the physician treats stress by prescribing medication and, when no specific diseases are present, by reassurance and counseling. More often than not he will dispense so-called tranquilizing drugs rather than delve into the psychological roots of the problem. On the other hand, most psychiatrists and psychologists[9] do not directly treat organic disease states. Their major concerns are emotions, thoughts, and personality. Psychiatrists may prescribe pills, but treatment is directed essentially to the psyche.[10] If bodily symptoms are apparent, the patient will most likely be referred to a medical doctor, [8] thus completing a circle with little interplay between the professions.

However, these traditional barriers are slowing crumbling. There is still a long way to go, and most physicians, because of the very paucity of concrete data, remain distrustful of psychosomatic or psychophysical diagnosis treatment.[11] Nevertheless, the specialty called psychosomatic medicine,

---

8. Blood pressure (BP), sometimes referred to as arterial blood pressure, is the pressure exerted by circulating blood upon the walls of blood vessels and is one of the principal vital signs in allopathic medicine. Blood pressure is measured by a device called a sphygmomanometer or blood pressure meter (also referred to as a sphygmometer), which is composed of an inflatable cuff to restrict blood flow and a mercury or mechanical manometer to measure the pressure. The device was invented by Samuel Siegfried Karl Ritter von Basch (1837–1905), an Austrian Jewish physician, in 1881. See Booth 1977.

9. In technical Western terms, a "psychiatrist" is an allopathic physician (MD) who specializes in psychiatry, that is, the diagnosis and treatment of mental disorders, often with pharmacological and pharmaceutical interventions. A psychologist is an individual who evaluates, diagnoses, treats, and studies behavior and mental processes. As a profession in the United States, psychology usually assumes a PhD.

10. As a Greek concept, psyche may designate emotion, intellect, life, mind, soul, spirit, and so forth. In more modern usages, psyche tends to refer to the totality of the human mind, whether conscious or unconscious activity. Psychology in turn endeavors to be the "scientific" or objective study of the psyche.

11. What today is generally referred to as "Mind-Body Medicine" (MBM), with some potential overlap with complementary alternative medicine (CAM).

which is the study and treatment of diseases caused or influenced by psychological events, is now a rapidly spreading field of medical research.

The Fight-or-Flight Response

The stressful consequences of living in our modern, Western society—constant insecurity in a job, inability to make deadlines because of the sheer weight of obligations, or the shift in social rules once binding and now inappropriate—will be described here in a manner that clearly explains how they lead to the ravaging diseases such as hypertension which are prevalent today and which are likely to become more widespread in the years ahead. We are all too familiar with the stresses we encounter. However, we are less knowledgeable about the consequences of these stresses, not only psychological but physiologic. Humans, like other animals, react in a predictable [9] way to acute and chronic stressful situations, which trigger an inborn response that has been part of our physiologic makeup for perhaps millions of years. This has been popularly labeled the "fight-or-flight" response.[12] When we are faced with situations that require adjustment of our behavior, an involuntary response increases our blood pressure, heart rate, rate of breathing, blood flow to the muscles, and metabolism, preparing us for conflict or escape.

This innate fight-or-flight reaction is well recognized in animals. A frightened cat standing with arched back and hair on end, ready to run or fight; an enraged dog with dilated pupils, snarling at its adversary; an African gazelle running from a predator; all are responding by activation of the fight-or-flight response. Because we tend to think of man in Cartesian terms,[13] as essentially a rational being, we have lost sight of his origins and of his Darwinian struggle for survival[14] where the successful use of the fight-or-flight response was a matter of life or death.

Man's ancestors with the most highly developed fight-or-flight reactions had an increased chance of surviving long enough to reproduce. Natural selection favored the continuation of the response. As progeny of ancestors who developed the response over millions of years, modern man almost certainly still possesses it.

In fact, the fight-or-flight response, with its bodily changes of increased blood pressure, rate of breathing, [10] muscle blood flow, metabolism, and heart rate, has been measured in man. Situations that demand that we adjust our behavior elicit this response. It is observed, for

---

12. As discussed in my introduction, the fight-or-flight response is a physiological "emergency state" discovered by Walter B. Cannon (1871–1945) around 1915. As the name suggests, it is a survival strategy characterized by hyperarousal and resulting in a spontaneous reaction either to fight or to flee, depending on the context-specific requirements.

13. René Descartes (1596–1650) was a French philosopher most well known for the famous maxim *cogito ergo sum* (Fr.: *Je pense, donc je suis*; "I think, therefore I am"). As expressed in the highly influential *Meditationes de prima philosophia* (Meditations on First Philosophy; dat. 1641), "Cartesian philosophy" is generally interpreted as a hyper-rationalist one, which is rooted in mind-body dualism. Today Cartesian views are challenged from various perspectives, especially those emphasizing embodiment and consciousness.

14. Charles Darwin (1809–1882) was a British naturalist best known for his contributions to evolutionary theory, specifically the notions of "natural selection" and "survival of the fittest" (via Herbert Spencer [1820–1903]). As expressed in his *On the Origins of Species* (dat. 1859), "Darwinian theory" is generally interpreted as a competitive and adversarial biological one. Today Darwinian views are qualified and sometimes challenged by ecological ones, which emphasize collaboration and symbiosis.

example, among athletes prior to a competitive event. But the response is not used as it was intended—that is, in preparation for running or fighting with an enemy. Today, it is often brought on by situations that require behavioral adjustments, and *when not used appropriately, which is most of the time, the fight-or-flight response repeatedly elicited may ultimately lead to the dire diseases of heart attack and stroke.*

If the continual need to adjust to new situations can bring on a detrimental fight-or-flight response, and if we live continuously with stressful events which trigger that response, it is natural to question whether we know how to check the dangerous results that inevitably follow. Take this line of reasoning one step further. If the fight-or-flight response resides within animals and humans, is there an innate physiologic response that is diametrically different? The answer is Yes. Each of us possesses a natural and innate protective mechanism against "overstress," which allows us to turn off harmful bodily effects, to counter the effects of the fight-or-flight response. This response against "overstress" brings on bodily changes that decrease heart rate, lower metabolism, decrease the rate of breathing, and bring the body back into what is probably a healthier balance. This is the Relaxation Response.

---

[11] This book will first explain the ways in which heart attacks and strokes develop within the body, often undetected, through the insidious mechanism of high blood pressure. We will show how high blood pressure is related to stress through the inappropriate elicitation of the fight-or-flight response.

Our main purpose, however, is to discuss the Relaxation Response, for it may have a profound influence on your ability to deal with difficult situations and on the prevention and treatment of high blood pressure and its related, widespread diseases including heart attacks and strokes. The Relaxation Response has always existed in the context of religious teachings. Its use has been most widespread in the Eastern cultures,[15] where it has been an essential part of daily existence. But its physiology has only recently been defined. Religious prayers and related mental techniques have measurable, definable physiologic effects on the body which will be explained. From the collective writings of the East and West, we have devised a simplified method of eliciting the Relaxation Response and we will explain its use in your daily life. You will learn that evoking the Relaxation Response is extremely simple if you follow a very short set of instructions which incorporate four essential elements: (1) a quiet environment; (2) a mental device such as a word or a phrase which should be repeated in a specific fashion over and over again; (3) the adoption of a passive attitude, which [12] is perhaps the most important of the elements; and (4) a comfortable position. Your appropriate practice of these four elements for ten to twenty minutes once or twice daily should markedly enhance your well-being. [Ch. 1, pp. 4–12.]

---

15. By "Eastern cultures," Herbert Benson presumably means those of South Asia and East Asia. In 1975, the date of the first publication of *The Relaxation Response*, Hinduism and Buddhism, including Japanese Zen, were fairly well known. By 2000, the time of the printing of the twenty-fifth anniversary edition, Tibetan Buddhism had also entered the popular American imagination, with the Fourteenth Dalai Lama winning the Nobel Peace Prize in 1989, later appearing in the Apple "think different" advertising campaign in the late 1990s, and his book *The Art of Happiness* (1998) becoming a *New York Times* bestseller. Two films also assisted the rise of Tibetan Buddhism, namely, *Kundun* (1997) and *Seven Years in Tibet* (1997).

A Disease with No Symptoms

Let's return to high blood pressure, or hypertension. High blood pressure may be dangerous. Not only does it increase development of atherosclerosis, but high blood pressure itself may cause vessels to burst. It also requires the heart to pump blood at high pressures, thus making the heart work harder. Pumping at high pressures places an excessive strain on the heart and the heart grows larger, as would any muscle that is worked excessively. A weight lifter's muscles increase in size because [30] he does the work of lifting barbells. So will heart muscle increase in size or bulk when doing the work of pumping harder. This results in what is called hypertensive heart disease, in which the heart is enlarged.[16]

Ordinarily, no symptoms are associated with high blood pressure for many years. You simply have the measurable finding of high blood pressure. The insidiousness of hypertension lies in its covert, seemingly harmless nature, which can end in permanent damage to the heart or brain or, at worst, in sudden death. Death of heart or brain tissue occurs either directly, through bursting vessels or an enlarging heart, or indirectly, through the development of atherosclerosis.

When atherosclerosis does develop, when high blood pressure actually brings about hardening of the arteries, the target is usually one or more of three organ systems: the heart, the brain, or the kidneys. The heart is the work organ. As previously noted, it must generate the increased blood pressure by pumping more forcefully and as a result the muscle fibers within the heart increase in size, enlarging the heart. The slow but steady process turns into a vicious cycle: as the heart enlarges to pump, it requires more blood flow through its own coronary arteries to maintain its own increased requirements. The enlarged heart is then more prone to have a heart attack, where heart muscle cells die because the nutrient demands of the heart are not met. Why did it not get sufficient [31] nutrients? At the same time that the heart, because of high blood pressure, enlarges and needs more blood flow to bring nutrients, the coronary arteries become progressively less able to carry larger quantities of blood, because of their inability to enlarge and also because of the increased development of atherosclerosis within these arteries.

High blood pressure affects the brain either directly, through high pressure that leads to bursting of blood vessels, a brain hemorrhage,[17] or indirectly, through the blockage of arteries by atherosclerosis. These events lead to temporary or permanent damage of brain functions called stroke or shock.

The third set of organs affected is the kidneys. Because of their normal role in blood pressure control, when they become diseased by high blood pressure, they make the high blood pressure worse. In the normal kidney, if blood pressure decreases to very low levels the kidneys secrete hormone substances that increase blood pressure.[18] The kidneys therefore act as sensors to maintain adequate blood pressure. If a minimal amount of atherosclerosis develops in the blood

---

16. Here the original text references a corresponding diagram (Figure 5; p. 23).
17. Here the original text references a corresponding diagram (Figure 6; p. 32).
18. A modern Western scientific category, hormones are a class of regulatory biochemicals produced in particular parts of organisms by specific cells, glands, and/or tissues and then transported by the bloodstream to other parts of the body, with the intent of influencing a variety of physiological and behavioral activities, such as the processes of digestion, metabolism, growth, reproduction, and mood control. Some important human hormones include epinephrine (also known as adrenalin), estrogen, insulin, testosterone, and so forth. See, for example, Guyton and Hall 2006.

vessels of the kidneys, it will decrease the amount of blood flow to these organs, and the kidneys will become shrunken.[19] The blocked kidney vessel leads to lower pressure within the kidney, and this organ responds in turn by secreting hormones that raise blood pressure throughout the body. We have a vicious cycle. The raising of [33] blood pressure actually leads to the development of more atherosclerosis; blood flow to the kidneys is further blocked by atherosclerosis, which leads to even higher blood pressure.

The solution is to stop the cycle before it begins. There is no mystique in the often repeated formula: the higher your blood pressure, the more likely you are to develop certain heart diseases, strokes, and kidney ailments. Science has not yet discovered why some people and not others are prone to have high blood pressure, or hypertension.

Hypertension is insidiously symptomless throughout its course. Though high blood pressure in some people may not have reached the point where it has become apparent by causing the diseases associated with it, doctors today are more apt to consider the physical findings of high blood pressure itself to be a disease state. Arbitrary limits have been drawn to dictate what is high blood pressure, what is normal, and what is in between high and normal, called borderline high blood pressure. High blood pressure is arbitrarily considered to be pressure greater than 159 millimeters of mercury[20] systolic or 94 diastolic.[21] Borderline high blood pressure is considered to be either between 140 and 159 systolic or between 90 [34] and 94 diastolic. Normal blood pressure is defined as lower than 140 systolic and 90 diastolic.[22]

At this point in medical knowledge we can identify the cause of only approximately 5 to 10 percent of the cases of high blood pressure; for 90 to 95 percent of the cases of hypertension we cannot. We know the cause when some of the body's mechanisms that control blood pressure are not functioning properly. As noted, the kidneys secrete potent substances within the bloodstream that will raise blood pressure, when they sense a lower blood pressure.

Indeed, one of the first ways hypertension was produced in animals[23] was through experiments performed in the nineteen-thirties by Dr. H. Goldblatt,[24] who discovered the relation between the kidneys and the elevation of blood pressure. In dogs, after removing one of the kidneys, he placed a clamp on the artery leading to the other. He thus decreased the blood pressure

---

19. The original text again refers to Figure 6 (p. 32).

20. Blood pressure is expressed in terms of millimeters of mercury. A column of mercury is raised a specific number of millimeters by a specific pressure. The higher the pressure, the higher the column raised.

21. During each heartbeat, blood pressure varies between a maximum (systolic) and a minimum (diastolic) pressure. The blood pressure in the circulation is principally due to the pumping action of the heart. Systole is understood as a force that drives blood out of the heart, while diastole is the period of time when the heart refills with blood after systole (contraction). See, for example, Guyton and Hall 2006.

22. The original text again refers to Figure 5 (p. 23).

23. Animal experimentation, also known as animal testing, is a widely used research methodology in scientific studies; it involves the use of "nonhuman" animals in experiments. Some commonly used animals include fish, mice, rats, "nonhuman" primates, and so forth. Such practices, including the related issues of animal welfare, freedom, and agency, deserve deep reflection in terms of ethics.

24. Harry Goldblatt (1891–1977), who received his MD from McGill University (Canada) in 1916, was a major twentieth-century researcher on the kidneys and high blood pressure, essential hypertension in particular. During his medical career, he worked at Case Western Reserve University (Cleveland, OH), Cedars of Lebanon Hospital (Los Angeles, CA), and finally Mount Sinai Hospital (Cleveland, OH). See the online *Encyclopedia of Cleveland History* (ech.case.edu) maintained by Case Western Reserve University and Western Reserve Historical Society.

of the remaining kidney. Secretion of kidney hormones followed, which resulted in permanent hypertension, or high blood pressure, in dogs. From that time on, much of the search for the cause of hypertension was drawn to malfunctions of the kidney. Certainly, in about 2 to 5 percent of cases of hypertension the cause may be found in a constricted artery going to the kidney. By removing the obstruction, we can cure the hypertension. But this accounts [35] for only a very small fraction of the millions of cases of hypertension seen in the United States today.

Very high blood pressure is also sometimes experienced during pregnancy, and this kind of hypertension can be cured. It can be controlled up to the time of delivery. When the mother delivers the baby, her blood pressure most often returns to normal levels. Tumors in the adrenal glands or in the brain can cause high blood pressure and are sometimes curable. Forms of hypertension linked to the thyroid gland can also be cured.[25] Surgery is often used to treat most of these types of hypertension.

But we still do not have an answer for 90 to 95 percent of the cases of hypertension called "essential hypertension." Essential hypertension is hypertension of unknown cause. "Stress" is a generally accepted explanation of hypertension, but there is skepticism among physicians about the role of stress. They are justifiably wary of such a cause-and-effect relation.

What is stress? How do you measure and quantify it? How is stress related to blood pressure? Because of the difficulties of measuring stress, relatively little research has been done on stress and high blood pressure. The reason is similar to the drunk's reason for looking for his cufflink at night under a lighted lamppost, when in fact he had lost the cufflink up the street. Asked why, he replied: "Because the light is better here." The kidneys are organs that have been well investigated, but stress, because of the difficulty of measuring it, has not been [36] studied well. Until recently the light in the above analogy was where the kidneys were; stress was with the cufflink. Though it is commonly assumed that people's feelings such as anger, fear, or anxiety play an important role in causing hypertension, our tools for gathering data in this area have been limited. Consequently, the subject has been inadequately studied. Yet situations leading to continuous behavioral adjustment, perhaps a better way to define what is stressful, may underlie the development of many of the causes of essential hypertension, the 90 to 95 percent of cases of high blood pressure which cannot be explained. [Ch. 2, pp. 29–36.]

Internal Signs of Stress

. . . Further research demonstrates that the chronic elicitation of the fight-or-flight response leads from transient elevations in blood pressure to a permanent state of hypertension. Drs. B. Folkow and E. H. Rubinstein, at the University of Goteborg in Sweden,[26] implanted wires in the brains

---

25. In mammals, the adrenal glands are endocrine glands that sit at the top of the kidneys; they are chiefly responsible for releasing hormones in response to stress. In vertebrate anatomy, the thyroid gland is one of the largest endocrine glands. Located in the neck, it controls how quickly the body uses energy and makes proteins. It also controls how sensitive the body is to other hormones. Guyton and Hall 2006, 931, 944.

26. Björn Folkow (1921–2012), MD, PhD, was professor of physiology at the University of Gothenburg (University of Goteborg; Gothenburg, Sweden). He was a member of the Royal Swedish Academy of Sciences and a foreign member of the Danish Academy of Sciences, the Russian Academy of Natural Sciences, and an honorary member of the American Physiological Society. See his obituary on the American Physiological Society website (www.the-aps.org). The article in question identifies Eduardo H. Rubinstein, MD, as affiliated with the Instituto de Investigaciones Medicas, Hospital Tornu in Buenos Aires, Argentina. It also appears that the research focused on cats rather than rats.

of rats in an area called the hypothalamus.[27] It is the hypothalamus that controls the evocation of the fight-or-flight response. The response could be evoked when the researchers passed an electric current through the wire. They then divided these rats into two groups, but stimulated the electrodes in only one group. Higher blood pressure developed in the rats stimulated to activate the fight-or-flight response. Those rats not subject to electrical stimulation maintained lower blood pressures.

When a single situation requiring behavioral adjustment occurs again and again, the fight-or-flight response is repeatedly activated. Ultimately, this repetition may lead to higher blood pressure on a permanent basis. It is our underlying theory that this is what happens in man in the development of permanent hypertension. The chronic arousal of the fight-or-flight response goes from the just transient elevation in blood pressure to permanent high blood pressure.

In the past, the fight-or-flight response had considerable evolutionary significance. Individuals with this response could survive more effectively, passing it on to their offspring. Though we chronically evoke the response, [52] modern society does not socially accept the fighting or running naturally associated with it. For example, you obviously do not run away from or hit your boss when he or she yells at you. Our innate reactions have not changed, but society has. The response is turned on, but we do not use it appropriately.

When the fight-or-flight response is evoked, a part of the *involuntary* nervous system called the sympathetic nervous system becomes highly active. If you want to lift your arm, you can willfully control the skeletal musculature of the *voluntary* nervous system to do so. The involuntary, or autonomic, nervous system deals with the everyday bodily functions that normally do not come into consciousness, such as the maintenance of heartbeat and blood pressure, regular breathing, the digestion of food. When the fight-or-flight response is evoked, it brings into play the sympathetic nervous system, which is part of the autonomic, or involuntary, nervous system. The sympathetic nervous system acts by secreting specific hormones: adrenalin or epinephrine and noradrenalin or norepinephrine. These hormones, epinephrine and its related substances, bring about physiologic changes of increased blood pressure, heart rate, and body metabolism.

The fight-or-flight response happens in an integrated fashion. It is integrated because it is controlled by a part of an area in the brain called the hypothalamus[28] and most, if not all, of the response occurs in a coordinated, simultaneous manner. Electrically stimulate [53] a specific area of the hypothalamus and there will be an outpouring of adrenalin or epinephrine and related hormones controlled by the sympathetic nervous system with the associated physiologic changes.

While the fight-or-flight response is associated with the overactivity of the sympathetic nervous system, there is another response that leads to a quieting of the same nervous system. Indeed, there is evidence that hypertensive subjects can lower their blood pressure by regularly eliciting this other response. This is the Relaxation Response, an opposite, involuntary response that causes a reduction in the activity of the sympathetic nervous system.[29] Since we cannot easily change the nature of modern life, perhaps better prevention and therapy of hypertension and other diseases related to the fight-or-flight response might be achieved by bringing forth the Relaxation Response. [Ch. 3, pp. 51–53.]

---

27. Here the original text references a corresponding diagram (Figure 8; p. 51).

28. The original text again refers to Figure 8 (p. 51).

29. Here the original text references a corresponding diagram (Figure 9; p. 54).

Age-Old Wisdom

The altered state of consciousness associated with the Relaxation Response has been routinely experienced in Eastern and Western cultures throughout all ages. Subjectively, the feelings associated with this altered state of consciousness have been described as ecstatic, clairvoyant, beautiful, and totally relaxing. Others have felt ease with the world, peace of mind, and a sense of well-being akin to that feeling experienced after a period of exercise but without the fatigue. Most describe their feelings as *pleasurable*. Despite the diversity of description, there appears to be a universal element of rising above the mundane senses, a feeling beyond that of common-day existence. Many authors have pointed out the similarities between Eastern and Western mysticism,[30] and have emphasized a universality of certain impulses in the human mind. Indeed, the subjective accounts of practitioners of different meditative backgrounds are similar to many experiences depicted in religious, historical, and philosophical writings. We will attempt to show that the Relaxation Response has been experienced throughout history. We will do so by extracting methods described in various literatures, primarily religious. Some of these methods are thousands of years old. Our chief purpose is to illustrate the age-old universality of this altered state of consciousness by citing certain elements that appear to be necessary to evoke this experience, or "response." No technique can claim uniqueness.[31] [Ch. 5, p. 82.]

Meditation: The Four Basic Elements

Most accounts of what we now call the Relaxation Response are subjective descriptions of deeply personal, unique experiences. However, there appear to be four basic elements underlying the elicitation of the Relaxation Response, regardless of the cultural source.

The first element is *a quiet environment*. One must "turn off" not only internal stimuli but also external distractions. A quiet room or a place of worship may be suitable. The nature mystics meditated outdoors.[32]

The second element is *an object to dwell upon*. This object may be a word or sound repetition; gazing at a symbol; concentrating on a particular feeling. For example, directing one's attention to the repetition of a syllable will help clear the mind. When distracting thoughts do occur, one can return to this repetition of the syllable to help eliminate other thoughts.

[86] The third element is *a passive attitude*. It is an emptying of all thoughts and distractions from one's mind. *A passive attitude appears to be the most essential factor in eliciting the Relaxation*

---

30. From a technical perspective, "mysticism" generally refers to mystical experience, or direct experiences of the sacred as understood by different individuals and communities. See Komjathy 2012.

31. This chapter includes a discussion of the various methods that elicit the Relaxation Response. As historical precedents, they thus add support for the Relaxation Response method. The practices in question are associated with the fourteenth-century *The Cloud of Unknowing*, Teresa of Ávila (1515–1582), the Eastern Orthodox Hesychasts, Jewish Kabbalah, Hindu classical Yoga, Buddhist Samatha-Vipassanā, Sufi prayer, and classical Daoist apophatic meditation, among others.

32. Presumably Benson is thinking of individuals such as the English Romantics William Wordsworth (1770–1850) and George Gordon Byron (1788–1824) as well as the American Transcendentalists Ralph Waldo Emerson (1803–1882), Henry David Thoreau (1817–1862), and Walt Whitman (1819–1892).

Response. Thoughts, imagery, and feelings may drift into one's awareness. One should not concentrate on these perceptions but allow them to pass on. A person should not be concerned with how well he or she is doing.

The fourth element is *a comfortable position*. One should be in a comfortable posture that will allow an individual to remain in the same position for at least twenty minutes. Usually a sitting position is recommended. We believe the sitting, kneeling, squatting, swaying postures assumed in various forms of prayer have evolved to keep the practitioner from falling asleep. The desired altered state of consciousness is not sleep,[33] but the same four elements will lead to sleep if the practitioner is lying down. [Ch. 5, pp. 85–86.]

Decreasing Blood Pressure

... Our hypothesis is that the Relaxation Response *decreases* and *counteracts* the increased sympathetic nervous system activity that accompanies the arousal of the fight-or-flight response. This sympathetic nervous system activity is reflected in the measures, reported in Chapter 4, of oxygen consumption, heart rate, respiratory rate, and blood pressure, which increase with the fight-or-flight response and decrease with the elicitation of the Relaxation Response.

This is one of the first studies in which the regular activation of the Relaxation Response has been tested in a group of hypertensive subjects, and it suggests a new approach to the therapy of hypertension, or high blood pressure. What we have presented are early results that are now being retested in other laboratories. Some of these other laboratories have already verified these findings.

[116] The risks of developing the atherosclerotic diseases, as pointed out in Chapter 2, are directly related to the level of blood pressure, and anything that lowers blood pressure without undue side effects is beneficial. Prescribed drugs that decrease blood pressure are therefore very effective therapy. Standard medical therapy means taking antihypertensive drugs, which often act by interrupting the activity of the sympathetic nervous system, thus lowering blood pressure. The pharmacologic method of lowering blood pressure is very effective and extremely important since, to again emphasize, lowered blood pressure leads to a lower risk of developing atherosclerosis and its related diseases such as heart attacks and strokes. The regular practice of the Relaxation Response is yet another way to lower blood pressure. Indications are that this response affects the same mechanisms and lowers blood pressure by the same means as some antihypertensive drugs. Both counteract the activity of the sympathetic nervous system. It is unlikely that the regular elicitation of the Relaxation Response by itself will prove to be adequate therapy for severe or moderate high blood pressure. Probably it would act to enhance the lowering of blood pressure along with antihypertensive drugs, and thus lead to the use of fewer drugs or a lesser dosage. In the case of mild hypertension, the regular evocation of the Relaxation Response may be of great value, since

---

33. In the scientific literature, much attention is given to the comparison between the physiology of "meditative states," "sleep states," and "dream states," with occasional concern for demonstrating that "meditation" is not comparable to "sleep." Here sleep is generally defined in scientific terms as a naturally recurring state characterized by altered consciousness (relative to waking), relatively inhibited sensory activity, and inhibition of nearly all voluntary muscles. It is distinguished from wakefulness by a decreased ability to react to stimuli, and it is more easily reversible than being in hibernation or a coma. Various additional distinctions, especially with respect to depth and types of sleep, are also utilized.

it has none of the pharmacologic side effects often present with drugs and might possibly supplant their use. *But no* [117] *matter how encouraging these initial results, no person should treat himself for high blood pressure by regularly eliciting the Relaxation Response. You should always do so under the care of your physician, who will routinely monitor your blood pressure to make sure it is adequately controlled.*

In brief, then, this initial controlled experiment shows that blood pressure can be lowered in hypertensive subjects through the use of the Relaxation Response. This experiment gives added weight to the concept that hypertension may be due in part to situations that require behavioral adjustment, since hypertension was alleviated by a behavioral technique, the regular use of the Relaxation Response. If high blood pressure can be alleviated by behavioral means alone, its cause may also lie in a behavioral mechanism.

By far the most appealing use of the Relaxation Response in relation to hypertension lies in its preventative aspects. To establish the preventative role of the Relaxation Response in hypertension, it is necessary to conduct large, expensive, and difficult investigations that often take many years to complete. We hope that such preventative studies may be started in the not-too-distant future.[34]

The Relaxation Response serves as a *natural* way to counteract increased sympathetic nervous system activity associated with the fight-or-flight response. This means that the Relaxation Response should be useful in alleviating other disease states where increased sympathetic nervous [118] system activity is a principal factor in the development of the disease or is an undesirable accompanying factor of that disease. For example, research is currently being carried out to test the usefulness of the Relaxation Response in alleviating various anxiety states. The usefulness of the Relaxation Response in treating the cardiac problem of dangerous, irregular heartbeats is also being tested. [Ch. 6, pp. 115–18.]

The case for the use of the Relaxation Response by healthy but harassed individuals is straightforward. It can act as a built-in method of counteracting the stresses of everyday living which bring forth the fight-or-flight response. We have also shown how the Relaxation Response may be used as a new approach to aid in the treatment and perhaps prevention of diseases such as hypertension. In this chapter, we will review the components necessary to evoke the Relaxation Response and present a specific technique that we have developed at Harvard's Thorndike Memorial Laboratory and Boston's [126] Beth Israel Hospital.[35] We again emphasize that, for those who may suffer from any disease state, the potential therapeutic use of the Relaxation Response should be practiced only under the care and supervision of a physician.

---

34. Here it is important to remember that *The Relaxation Response* was originally published in 1975, and much research has been conducted since then, including by Benson himself. See my introduction for an outline of his later research publications.

35. Established in 1923, the Thorndike Memorial Laboratory (TML) at Boston City Hospital (BCH) was the first clinical research laboratory in a municipal hospital in the United States. It became part of the Beth Israel Hospital in 1964. Located in Boston, Massachusetts, and established in 1996, Beth Israel Deaconess Medical Center (BIDMC) is the teaching hospital of Harvard Medical School (HMS). It came to be through the merger of the predecessor New England Deaconess Hospital, which was established in 1896 as part of the missionary charter of the Methodist Deaconesses to care for the city's residents, and Beth Israel Hospital, which was established in 1916 by the Boston Jewish community to meet the needs of the growing immigrant population. Today BIDMC consistently ranks in the top three recipients of biomedical research funding from the National Institutes of Health (NIH). See www.bidmc.org; Finland 1982, vol. 1; also Bull and Bull 2011.

How to Bring Forth the Relaxation Response

In Chapter 5 we reviewed the Eastern and Western religious, cultic, and lay practices that led to the Relaxation Response. From those age-old techniques we have extracted four basic components necessary to bring forth that response:

(1) A Quiet Environment

Ideally, you should choose a quiet, calm environment with as few distractions as possible. A quiet room is suitable, as is a place of worship. The quiet environment contributes to the effectiveness of the repeated word or phrase by making it easier to eliminate distracting thoughts.

(2) A Mental Device

To shift the mind from logical, externally oriented thought, there should be a constant stimulus: a sound, word, or phrase repeated silently or aloud; or fixed gazing [127] at an object. Since one of the major difficulties in the elicitation of the Relaxation Response is "mind wandering," the repetition of the word or phrase is a way to help break the train of distracting thoughts. Your eyes are usually closed if you are using a repeated sound or word; of course, your eyes are open if you are gazing. Attention to the normal rhythm of breathing is also useful and enhances the repetition of the sound or the word.

(3) A Passive Attitude

When distracting thoughts occur, they are to be disregarded and attention redirected to the repetition or gazing; *you should not worry about how well you are performing the technique*, because this may well prevent the Relaxation Response from occurring. Adopt a "let it happen" attitude. *The passive attitude is perhaps the most important element in eliciting the Relaxation Response. Distracting thoughts will occur. Do not worry about them. When these thoughts do present themselves and you become aware of them, simply return to the repetition of the mental device. These other thoughts do not mean you are performing the technique incorrectly. They are to be expected.*

(4) A Comfortable Position

A comfortable posture is important so that there is no undue muscular tension. Some methods call for a sitting position. A few practitioners use the cross-legged "lotus" [128] position of the Yogi.[36] If you are lying down, there is a tendency to fall asleep. As we have noted previously, the various postures of kneeling, swaying, or sitting in a cross-legged position are believed to have evolved to prevent falling asleep. You should be comfortable and relaxed.

---

36. Technically, a practitioner of *yoga*, with the latter term traditionally referring to Indian disciplines aimed at liberation (*mokṣa*) from *saṃsāra*, the apparently endless cycle of birth, death, and rebirth determined by karma, the universal law of moral cause and effect.

It is important to remember that there is not a single method that is unique in eliciting the Relaxation Response. For example, Transcendental Meditation[37] is one of the many techniques that incorporate these components. However, we believe it is not necessary to use the specific method and specific *secret*, personal sound taught by Transcendental Meditation. *Tests at the Thorndike Memorial Laboratory at Harvard have shown that a similar technique used with any sound or phrase or prayer or mantra brings forth the same physiologic changes noted during Transcendental Meditation*: decreased oxygen consumption; decreased carbon-dioxide elimination; decreased rate of breathing. In other words using the basic necessary components, any one of the age-old or the newly derived techniques produces the same physiologic results regardless of the mental device used. The following set of instructions, used to elicit the Relaxation Response, was developed by a group at Harvard's Thorndike Memorial Laboratory and was found to produce the same physiologic changes we had observed during the practice of Transcendental Meditation. This technique is now being [129] used to lower blood pressure in certain patients. A non-cultic technique, it is drawn with little embellishment from the four basic components found in the myriad of historical methods. We claim no innovation but simply a scientific validation of age-old wisdom. The technique is our current method of eliciting the Relaxation Response in our continuing studies at the Beth Israel Hospital of Boston.

1. Sit quietly in a comfortable position.

2. Close your eyes.

3. Deeply relax all your muscles, beginning at your feet and progressing up to your face. Keep them relaxed.

4. Breathe through your nose. Become aware of your breathing. As you breathe out, say the word, "ONE," silently to yourself. For example, breathe IN . . . OUT, "ONE"; IN . . . OUT, "ONE"; etc.[38] Breathe easily and naturally.

5. Continue for 10 to 20 minutes. You may open your eyes to check the time, but do not use an alarm. When you finish, sit quietly for several minutes, at first with your eyes closed and later with your eyes open. Do not stand up for a few minutes. [130]

6. Do not worry about whether you are successful in achieving a deep level of relaxation. Maintain a passive attitude and permit relaxation to occur at its own pace. When distracting thoughts occur, try to ignore them by not dwelling upon them and return to repeating "ONE." With practice, the response should come with little effort. Practice the technique once or twice daily, but not within two hours after any meal, since the digestive processes seem to interfere with the elicitation of the Relaxation Response.

---

37. As discussed in my introduction, Transcendental Meditation™ (TM™) is a form of modified Hindu *mantra* (sacred sound) practice developed and disseminated by Maharishi Mahesh (1918–2008).

38. As discussed in my introduction, Benson intended "one" here to simply refer to the number. However, it has received various metaphysical and theological interpretations. One in turn wonders about the potential effects of the associations. This dimension of the practice, the "faith factor," has been explored in Benson's later writings.

The subjective feelings that accompany the elicitation of the Relaxation Response vary among individuals. The majority of people feel a sense of calm and feel very relaxed. A small percentage of people immediately experience ecstatic feelings. Other descriptions that have been related to us involve feelings of pleasure, refreshment, and well-being. Still others have noted relatively little change on a subjective level. Regardless of the subjective feelings described by our subjects, we have found that the physiologic changes, such as decreased oxygen consumption, are taking place. [Ch. 7, pp. 125–30.]

Personal Experiences with the Relaxation Response

. . . One should not use the Relaxation Response in an effort to shield oneself or to withdraw from the pressures of the outside world which are necessary for everyday functioning. *The fight-or-flight response is often appropriate and should not be thought of as always harmful. It is a necessary part of our physiologic and psychological makeup, a useful reaction to many situations in our current world.* Modern society has forced us to evoke the fight-or-flight response repeatedly. We are not using it as we believe our ancestors used it. That is, we do not always run, nor do we fight when it is elicited. However, our body is being prepared for running or for fighting, and since this preparation is not always utilized, we believe anxieties, hypertension and its related diseases ensue. The Relaxation Response offers a natural balance to counteract the undesirable manifestations of the fight-or-flight response. We do not believe that you will become a passive and withdrawn person and less able to function and compete in our world because you regularly elicit the Relaxation Response. Rather, it has been our experience that people who regularly evoke the Relaxation Response claim they are more effective in dealing with situations that probably bring forth the fight-or-flight response. We believe that you will be able to cope better with difficult situations by regularly allowing your body to achieve a more balanced state through the physiologic effects of the Relaxation Response. You can expect this balanced state to last as long as you regularly bring forth the response. Within [139] several days after stopping its regular use, we believe, you will cease to benefit from its effects, *regardless* of the technique employed, be it prayer, Transcendental Meditation or the method proposed in this book. [Ch. 7, pp. 138–39.]

Throughout this book we have tried to show you that the Relaxation Response is a natural gift that anyone can turn on and use. By bridging the traditional gaps between psychology, physiology, medicine, and history, we have established that the Relaxation Response is an innate mechanism within us.

The Relaxation Response is a universal human capacity, and even though it has been evoked in religions both East and West for most of recorded history, you don't have to engage in any rites or esoteric practices to bring it forth. The experience of the Relaxation Response [141] has faded from our everyday life with the waning of religious practices and beliefs, but we can easily reclaim its benefits.

The people of the United States enjoy a standard of living and affluence beyond the experience of the majority of the world's people. But as individuals within this cornucopia, we are plagued by unhappiness. We seem never to be satisfied with what we have accomplished or what we possess. Perhaps it is ingrained in our present Western society that success and progress, no matter the price, are the name of the game. Go out, get as much as you can for yourself, don't be content with your present lot. The idealized work ethic reinforces the notion that monetary success and upward progression can be attained by a wide spectrum of the population. But even those who achieve these goals of monetary success and continued advancement are often not satisfied. They frequently find their lives thwarted by frustrating circumstances requiring behavioral adjustment. For those who do not advance in their careers or gain monetary security, behavioral adjustment is also necessary. Dissatisfaction, boredom, and unemployment should be looked upon as situations that require adjustment.

In most instances we cannot limit the situations that require behavioral adjustment. Because in our society we want more and we want it faster, this attitude does not leave time for relaxation or for appraising problems. When problems do develop, we look for a quick and easy [142] solution. Our answer, aided by extensive advertising, is often to take a pill. You have only to turn on the television set and look at the advertising to see how we are trained to deal with problems. If you have any tensions, pains, or insomnia, simply consume a tablet or capsule and your problems will disappear.

How can we thus deal with our anxieties and feelings of stress? Perhaps what we should do is modify our behavior by regularly evoking the Relaxation Response. If you view the Relaxation Response as a mechanism that effectively counters some of the harmful psychological and physiologic effects of our society, then the regular practice of the Relaxation Response may have an important place in your life. If you would regularly elicit this response, build it into your daily existence, the situations that activate your sympathetic nervous system could be counteracted by a process allowing your body to decrease its sympathetic nervous system activity. You would simply be using one innate body mechanism to counteract the effects of another.

Our Western society is oriented only in the direction of eliciting the fight-or-flight response. *Unlike the fight-or-flight response, which is repeatedly brought forth as a response to our difficult everyday situations and is elicited without conscious effort, the Relaxation Response can be evoked only if time is set aside and conscious effort is made.* Our society has given very little attention to the importance of relaxation. Perhaps our work ethic views a person who [143] takes time off as unproductive and lazy. At the same time, our society has eliminated many of the traditional methods of evoking the Relaxation Response. Prayer and meditation, as practiced by the ancients, have become part of our historical memory. We need the Relaxation Response even more today because our world is changing at an ever-increasing pace. Society should sanction the time for the Relaxation Response. Is it unreasonable to incorporate this inborn capacity into our daily lives by having a "Relaxation Response break" instead of a coffee break? You can choose any method of eliciting the response which best fits your own inclinations: a secular, a religious, or an Eastern technique. We could all greatly benefit by the incorporation of the Relaxation Response into our daily lives. At the present time, most of us are simply not making use of this remarkable innate, neglected asset. [Ch. 8, pp. 140–43.]

Chapter 14

Techniqueless Meditation

J. Krishnamurti's *This Light in Oneself*

Constance A. Jones

This Light in Oneself is a late twentieth-century anthology on "techniqueless meditation" or awareness beyond method. The text consists of transcriptions of various talks and addresses originally delivered in English by Jiddu Krishnamurti (1895–1986), an Indian philosopher and teacher who appealed to audiences in both East and West through his talks and publications that span over six decades. *This Light in Oneself* is a highly accessible text aimed at a diverse audience. It specifically emphasizes the need for freedom as an all-encompassing spiritual practice and existential approach beyond the disciplines of all traditions and techniques. As Krishnamurti expresses it, "Truth is a pathless land."

J. Krishnamurti, the Theosophical Society, and the Order of the Star in the East

Jiddu Krishnamurti was an iconoclastic thinker and spiritual adept whose teaching addresses the large questions of human existence. Originally brought to international prominence through his appointment as head of the Order of the Star in the East by the leadership of the Theosophical Society, he broke his relationship to this organization and became a teacher in his own right, without the benefit of any organization. Through his teaching and his personality, he influenced many world leaders in politics, science, religion, and philosophy and continues to inspire many who seek a fresh understanding of the human condition.

Born in Madanapalle, Andra Pradesh, in colonial India, Krishnamurti (lit., image of Krishna) grew up in an orthodox Brahmin family[1] steeped in the traditions of Hinduism and a sacred view of the world. His father, Jiddu Narayaniah, was a literate high-caste Brahmin and graduate of the University of Madras, who served in the Indian Civil Service as a junior civil servant and later as tax collector. Narayaniah's father had also been a civil servant in the

Madras Presidency, and his grandfather had served in the judicial department of the East India Company. Krishnamurti's mother, Sanjeevamma, was a devout and charitable woman known for her devotional nature, psychic gifts, and paranormal visions (Jayakar 1986, 16–17). Consistent with orthodox Hindu tradition, immediately after birth, Krishnamurti's horoscope was cast by an astrologer, who predicted that the child would become a great man, but only after encountering significant obstacles. According to orthodox Hindu observance, six days after the birth of a child, the important name-giving ceremony is held. Following tradition, the eighth child born to Narayaniah and Sanjeevamma was named "Krishnamurti" after the Lord Krishna,[2] himself an eighth child (Vernon 2002, 24–25).

At the age of six, Krishnamurti was initiated into the first stage of life of an orthodox Brahmin boy, the stage of chaste discipleship or *brahmacharya*. As part of the initiation ceremony, the Hindu priest placed the sacred thread over his right shoulder and whispered the sacred Gayatri *mantra* into his ear. A festival involving family and friends accompanied the initiation ceremony, and then the young boy was taken to a Hindu temple for prayers and then on to the nearest school to begin his educational career. All of these rituals are integral to the orthodox Brahmin tradition of Hinduism, and Krishnamurti's family strictly observed each rite (Jayakar 1986, 17–18).

The Jiddu family, as Brahmins, belonged to a high-caste minority, a significance that cannot be overstated. Brahmins represent a spiritual rather than a material elite and constitute, according to Hindu orthodoxy, the hereditary group that has arrived, through karma and reincarnation, at the last and highest stratum of spiritual evolution. They are considered purer in mind and body than the lower castes and, therefore, must obey strict prescriptions regarding marriage, eating, and physical contact in order to safeguard their purity. Brahmins must marry within their caste, must prepare and eat food only with Brahmins, and must not be in the physical proximity of lower-caste members, particularly out-castes, or Untouchables; to break any of these taboos causes ritual pollution. Non-Hindus, including Europeans, are considered out-castes, and the Jiddu family was required to "scrub" both the premises and the bodies of all family members when British visitors called at their residence in the course of Narayaniah's employment (Vernon 2002, 27–28). Throughout his childhood, Krishnamurti's life was circumscribed by the conventions of caste and, as with most young Brahmin boys, he was well schooled in the principles of religious and caste observance (Vernon 2000, 27–28).

As a child, Krishnamurti was physically delicate and suffered a number of recurring illnesses, including malaria. He took little interest in schoolwork and was often seen gazing off into the distance in a vague sort of reverie. He was a quiet and contemplative child, often lost in dreamy imaginings, which drew negative judgments from his teachers and peers. His mother seems to be the one person who appreciated his unusual behavior and saw his dreaminess as a type of gift (Vernon 2002, 28). He related that his happiest memories of childhood centered around his time with his mother, who would conduct Hindu worship (*puja*) in the family shrine, read to him from Indian scriptures, and teach him about karma and reincarnation. She regularly had visions of her daughter, Krishnamurti's sister, who had died years before and, eventually, in the presence of his mother, Krishnamurti also had visions of his sister. Later, after his mother's death, he also saw his mother's image in visions (Krishnamurti 1913–1915).

Up to the age of ten, when Krishnamurti's mother died, the family was intact, although they moved often because of the father's employment. Because Krishnamurti attended many different schools in various locations, his formal education was often interrupted. However, he received a consistent informal education throughout his first ten years, as both his father and his mother taught Krishnamurti about Theosophical ideas. His father attended conventions of the Theosophical Society in Madras and held meetings at the family home for the study of Theosophical ideas. Both parents respected Annie Besant (1847–1933), then prominent in the Theosophical Society, and taught him about the organization and its teaching.

In 1908, three years after the death of his mother, Krishnamurti's father took a position as assistant secretary in the Theosophical Society, a rapidly growing international spiritual movement, and moved with his four surviving sons to the International Headquarters of the Theosophical Society, at Adyar, outside Madras, India.

The Theosophical Society, founded in 1875 in New York City by Helena Petrovna Blavatsky (1831–1891), Henry Steel Olcott (1832–1907), and William Q. Judge (1851–1896), began as an organization dedicated to a synthesis of science, religion, and philosophy with the credo "There is no religion higher than truth." The founders sought to promote the study of insights from various world religions, investigate spiritualist and other occult phenomena, and foster the brotherhood of all humankind. Olcott became the first president (1875–1907), although the writings and teachings of Blavatsky became synonymous with the tenets of the society. The society accepted her self-description as a disciple of highly evolved beings, *mahatmas* (great souls), who had instructed her in esoteric truths that she referred to as the ancient wisdom, the secret doctrine, or Theosophy. She claimed to have contacted an occult brotherhood of these *mahatmas* in her travels in the Far East, particularly in Tibet. Their Perennial Philosophy became the basis of her writings (Blavatsky 1877, 1888; Murphet 1975; Campbell 1980).

Although the Theosophical Society has no official dogma, it sees itself as a body of truths that are the basis of all valid religions. Not a religion per se but rather a restatement of the essence of religion itself, the Theosophical Society affirms three objectives: (1) to form a nucleus of the Universal Brotherhood of Humanity without distinction of race, creed, sex, caste, or color; (2) to encourage the study of comparative religion, philosophy, and science; and (3) to investigate unexplained laws of nature and the powers latent in humans. The preamble to the bylaws refers to the hope of penetrating further than science had into "the esoteric philosophies of ancient times" (Campbell 1980, 28–29).

Blavatsky expounded a complex cosmological scheme and description of the human body and soul that includes multiple levels and hierarchies. Her cosmology delineates relationships among humanity, the angelic realms, and, ultimately, the divine. Theosophical ideas are largely drawn from the cosmological and psychological teachings of Hinduism and Buddhism and are portrayed in an amalgam of Hindu and Buddhist terminology, particularly the concepts of evolution, karma, and reincarnation (Jones and Ryan 2007, 444–45).

The first fifteen years of the movement saw trial alliances with other religious and psychic organizations in England, India, and the United States, none of which withstood the test of time. However, when Blavatsky and Olcott traveled to India and began to champion Indian aspirations for political unification and a revival of the Indian people's pride in the history, religion, and culture of their country, the organization attracted educated and influential British as well as Indians to their membership. Further, in 1880, they were welcomed in Ceylon as Western champions of Buddhism as they worked with Ceylonese Buddhists in their efforts to limit the influence of the most vituperative of Christian missionaries' propaganda. As Olcott stated, the Theosophical Society, which was committed to no particular religion, was "as loyally working with Indians to promote Hinduism as it had been with the Sinhalese Buddhists to revive Buddhism" (Olcott cited in Campbell 1980, 83–87). There then followed a widespread interest in Theosophical principles in America, Europe, and India. The synthesis of East and West, religion and science, as well as spiritual and educational understanding made Theosophy compelling to cosmopolitan, liberal people, regardless of nationality, who had been disappointed by the dogmatism of both religion and science and sought to unite the diverse peoples of the world in a peaceful brotherhood (Jones 2010).

Part of Theosophical teaching is the exploration of clairvoyant powers for discovering the hidden mysteries of nature and the esoteric powers of humanity. Founding Theosophists drew freely from their understanding of Western Esotericism, which includes a host of discrete but related movements from the dawn of Western civilization to the present. Esoteric movements can be aligned with and complementary to exoteric religions or bodies of knowledge: esoteric Islam is Sufism; esoteric Judaism is Kabbalah (Godwin 1994, xii). And esoteric movements can stand outside religious traditions, such as the occult sciences of astrology, alchemy, ritual magic, divination, spiritualism and psychism, as well as distinct movements such as Gnosticism, Pythagoreanism, Neo-Platonism, Hermeticism, and Rosicrucianism. Each movement assumes that an individual can comprehend symbol, myth, and ultimate reality only through a personal struggle for progressive illumination on successive levels (Faivre and Needleman 1995, xii). This personal struggle involves integrating the "profane" or outer world with an inner submission to a more conscious and transcendent reality that is contacted within the self (Faivre and Needleman 1995, xxvi). Theosophy combined these tenets of Western Esotericism with its understanding of Eastern thought, particularly Buddhist and Hindu ontologies, to form a worldview that includes a complex cosmology, an esoteric psychology, and an evolutionary scheme that encompasses eons. Esoteric tenets meshed well with Theosophical understanding of Eastern concepts of evolution, individual struggle, reincarnation, karma, initiation, and self-realization (De Purucker 1979).

It was this esoteric worldview, along with a heterogeneous milieu of Indians, Europeans, and Americans, into which the young Krishnamurti would be immersed in the next two decades of his life (Jones 2010).

The Theosophical Society at the time of Krishnamurti's youth was actively looking for a special incarnation of an advanced consciousness that could bring the world to a greater awareness of its potential. Drawing upon many religious traditions and prophecies, they sought a World Teacher who would destroy evil and restore righteousness on a global scale. The consciousness that was believed to be the same consciousness of the Lord Krishna of Hinduism, the Christ of Christianity, and the Lord Maitreya of Buddhism would incarnate into a contemporary person, conceived to be the "vehicle" of the World Teacher. As early as 1889 Blavatsky announced to members that the real purpose of establishing the Theosophical Society was to prepare humanity to receive the World Teacher. In 1896, five years after Blavatsky's death, Annie Besant reaffirmed this expectation (Lutyens 1975, 12–13). Charles Webster Leadbeater (1854–1934), a leading figure in the Theosophical Society who claimed to be clairvoyant and to be in regular contact with "ascended masters"[3] existing above the material plane on the astral plane, "discovered" Krishnamurti in 1909 in his early teen years and declared him as indeed the vehicle of the long-awaited World Teacher. Leadbeater, who said he could perceive energy fields through clairvoyance, offered as evidence of his discovery his own perception of Krishnamurti's personal aura, which Leadbeater claimed contained no trace of selfishness (Lutyens 1983, 1–3). Krishnamurti and his brother Nityananada (1898–1925) were then removed from their school and were instructed personally by Leadbeater and Leadbeater's occult master, Kuthumi,[4] who was believed by Theosophists to operate largely on the astral, not material, plane of existence, from which he contacted humans during their sleep.

Around the turn of the twentieth century the movement had begun to decline, but under the leadership of Annie Besant (1847–1933) many lodges in Europe, America, and India revived. Besant accepted Leadbeater's "discovery" of Krishnamurti as the World Teacher. In 1911, as president of the Theosophical Society, she created an organization called the Order of the Star in the East (OSE) devoted to realizing the World Teacher's mission, which the movement had anticipated since Blavatsky's time. Krishnamurti was immediately appointed head of the order and began to travel and address Theosophical audiences in this role, primarily in India, the United States, Great Britain, and Holland. Over the next decade he matured in his understanding of the order and the Theosophical Society (Lutyens 1975, 45–46).

Figure 14.1. J. Krishnamurti, circa 1924
Source: George Grantham Bain (photographer; 1865–1944),
George Grantham Bain Collection, Library of Congress

Over many months in 1922–1923, while residing at Ojai, California, Krishnamurti experienced a profound transformation. Begun as formal meditation, Krishnamurti's transformation, called "the process," contained moments of great beauty and clarity offset by periods of physical pain, even agony. He fell unconscious, conversed with nonphysical entities, and spoke from several personas. Krishnamurti's report of his transformation of consciousness is consistent with other reports of mystical nondualism, wherein personality dissolves into communion with all else. In his words, "I was in everything, or rather everything was in me, inanimate and animate, the mountain, the worm and all breathing things." Themes of his later teaching are found in his description of this transformation: "I have seen the Light. I have touched compassion which heals all sorrow and suffering; it is not for myself, but for the world.... I have drunk at the fountain of joy and eternal Beauty. I am God-intoxicated" (Lutyens 1990, 41–43).

After "the process" was complete (although sporadic incidents occurred even into the 1950s), he experienced a growing dissatisfaction with the authority structure of the Theosophical Society and its emphasis on occultism. At the death of his brother, which the occultists in the Theosophical Society did not foresee, his dissatisfaction became overwhelming, and he defined his stance relative to Theosophy as one of revolt. In his talks, dialogues, and writings, he began to emphasize the benefit of doubt and questioning, a direction antithetical to the Theosophical structure of that day. In revolt against all forms of spiritual authority, he disbanded the Order of the Star in the East in August of 1929 at the international meeting of the order in Ommen, Holland, declaring,

> I maintain that Truth is a pathless land, and you cannot approach it by any path whatsoever, by any religion, by any sect.... I do not want to belong to any organization of a spiritual kind.... If an organization be created for this purpose, it becomes a crutch, a weakness, a bondage, and must cripple the individual, and prevent him from growing, from establishing his uniqueness, which lies in his discovery for himself of that absolute, unconditioned Truth.... Because I am free, unconditioned, whole ... I desire those who seek to understand me, to be free, not to follow me, not to make out of me a cage.... You are all depending for your spirituality on someone else.... No man from outside can make you free.... You have been accustomed to being told how far you have advanced, what your spiritual status is. How childish! Who but yourself can tell you if you are incorruptible? ... For two years I have been thinking about this slowly, carefully, patiently, and I have now decided to disband the Order, as I happen to be its Head. You can form other organizations and expect someone else. With that I am not concerned, nor with creating new cages, new decorations for those cages. My only concern is to set men absolutely, unconditionally free. (Lutyens 1983, 15)

Later in 1929, at the age of thirty-four, Krishnamurti also resigned from the Theosophical Society. This year marked the onset of bleak economic times as the Great Depression (1929–1939) began and also signaled the beginning of decline in the society's membership. Having been buoyed by the influx of members that accrued due to the "discovery" of the World Teacher and Krishnamurti's charismatic appearances around the world, the society began to turn in another direction. The larger organization was in disarray, having suffered a series of disputes, scandals, defections, schisms, and lawsuits involving almost all of the leaders since and including Blavatsky.

After Krishnamurti's denunciation of the organization and its many offshoots, as well as any and all organizations, it became clear that the rigid structure and occult beliefs of the society had not been the major factor in its growth in the twentieth century. Rather, members had joined the Theosophical Society to be near the World Teacher, so that, with his denunciation, they felt comfortable resigning their membership as well. The society's leadership stood distant from the dissolution of the OSE, all the while maintaining that the OSE was only one of many offshoots of the original movement and that the parental organization would not be affected. In actuality, however, the central symbol of the organization had divorced himself from its fold and, further, had undermined the legitimacy of its organization as well as its central beliefs in the occult hierarchy of ascended masters. When addressing members of the society, Krishnamurti publicly labeled their lives "hypocritical," "deceitful," and "counterfeit" and any society based on religious hopes not only irrelevant but "pernicious." However, he was invited back regularly to speak to meetings of the Theosophical Society while Besant was in charge (Vernon 2002, 188–90).

And with this resignation, Krishnamurti began his second career, as a teacher in his own right, independent of any organization or tradition. Krishnamurti's intense involvement with the Theosophical Society and with the OSE until 1929 constitute a phase of his life that he repeatedly claimed he could not remember clearly. Even though Krishnamurti rejected the worldly acceptance of thousands of devotees attracted to him through the Theosophical and OSE organizations and signed over any shares in investments in these organizations, he nevertheless retained a united core of students, some quite wealthy, who were able to assure a continued lifestyle of comfort for him. Some individuals left the Theosophical Society in order to follow the teachings of Krishnamurti; others retained their membership in the society but held to their allegiance to Krishnamurti; still others came upon Krishnamurti's influence afresh, independent of his past, and became committed to the spread of his ideas. The effect was a significant entourage of committed individuals who were not members of any organization and did not join any "movement." The newly created foundations established in England, India, and the United States coordinated publication of Krishnamurti's writings and talks but, to this day, do not constitute organizations with regular memberships.

From 1929 until the outbreak of the Second World War (1939–1945), Krishnamurti traveled widely, consistently bringing to all audiences his usual themes of freedom, awareness, conditioning, love, and fear. Over these years his delivery became more polished, even as his message became more alarming. His notion of individual "revolutionary change" became more accented, and he refused to support one nationality or one identity over another in a time of accelerating global conflict—stances that led to suspicion and denigration in a time of war. As his appearances in front of public audiences grew more strained when he was questioned about his patriotism and nationalistic loyalties, he withdrew from public life and led a life of retreat and reflection until the end of the Second World War. He lived at his residence in the secluded Ojai Valley of southern California with a few associates.

Krishnamurti never formally married and was consistent in his negative evaluation of the institution, asserting that marriage restricts individual freedom, stultifies relationships, and sanctifies possessiveness, as it precludes the possibility of a genuine relationship with another. These views were in line with Krishnamurti's concern about the economic and social subjugation of women in India. Although against marriage, he was sensitive to lasting commitment in a relationship. Nor did he extoll the virtues of celibacy and asceticism, which he considered life-denying and artificially suppressive of natural drives. Not inconsistent with his teaching on sexuality and marriage, he carried on a committed relationship with Rosalind Rajagopal, the wife of his administrative and financial chief for over twenty years. Even though the Rajagopals did not divorce, their marriage was strained and both seemed to be supportive of the relationship between Rosalind and Krishnamurti. Even though three pregnancies occurred, the couple had no doubts that they would not reveal their relationship nor would they have a child together. Instead, Krishnamurti served as a doting father for Rosalind's only child, a girl named Radha, who was the only person to describe the relationship in print, only after the death of Krishnamurti (Sloss 1991). Even though Krishnamurti's relationship with Rosalind was not contrary to his teachings, he did essentially lead a double life over two decades without any public acknowledgment of his intimacy. The reasons for this secrecy have been the subject of much conjecture and even derision, but Krishnamurti's message and the general acceptance of his message seem to have been affected little (Vernon 2002, 199–204).

Figure 14.2. J. Krishnamurti, 1968
Source: Mark Edwards (photographer), Krishnamurti Foundation

From the end of the Second World War until his death in 1986, at the age of ninety, Krishnamurti continuously taught his insights to audiences worldwide, which grew progressively from an exclusive Theosophical orbit to include all sorts of individuals from a host of nations. He became a champion of freedom and inquiry and a relentless advocate of the discovery of "Truth" without the aid of any organization, religion, or belief system, allegiance to any of which he defined as participation in tyranny and self-hypnosis (Krishnamurti 1999, 17). His teaching emphasized the necessity of developing awareness of one's conditioning and one's bondage to thought, fear, and time. To realize the goal of making all of humanity absolutely, unconditionally free, he invited those who listened to him to observe their inner selves, including their motives and the functions of thought. With each audience, Krishnamurti inquired into the basic nature of humanity and discovered that real self-transformation involves an instantaneous awareness of the psyche and its workings. Accompanied by simplicity and humility, this awareness is believed to open a person to the reality of oneself. Transformation is seen as "freedom from the known," which is escape from the conditioning, beliefs, and emotions inculcated since infancy. The "known," he says, includes time, sorrow, and bondage. To be free, one must die to the "known" in order to discover for oneself Truth, which is limitless, unconditioned, and unapproachable by any path whatsoever (Krishnamurti 1969, 9–33).

Krishnamurti died in his beloved cottage in Ojai in 1986 from pancreatic cancer. Many of his admirers came to see him in his last months but were tactfully asked to leave. Only a few of his closest associates witnessed his last hours. Near the end, he called for a tape recorder to make a final statement, which he had to be assured would not be altered in any way. In short, he said,

> [F]or seventy years that super-energy—no—that immense energy, immense intelligence, has been using this body. I don't think people realize what tremendous energy and intelligence went through this body. . . . and now the body can't stand any more. You won't find another body like this, or that supreme intelligence, operating in a body for many hundred years. You won't see it again. When he goes, it goes. There is no consciousness left behind of *that* consciousness of *that* state. They'll all pretend or try to imagine they can get into touch with that. Perhaps they will somewhat if they live the teachings. But nobody has done it. Nobody. And so that's that. (Lutyens 1990, 204–6)

According to his wishes, he was cremated in nearby Ventura, California, with no ritual performed and no memorial set up in his honor (Vernon 2002, 242–44).

Life beyond Tradition, Systems, and Conditioning

The life and teaching of Krishnamurti, also referred to as "K" by his students and those close to him, are unique. He has been described as "the quintessential iconoclast of the twentieth century" (Sanat 1999, xi) and "the eminent thinker of our age" (Mehta 1987, 54). He brought a call to inquiry and an understanding that cannot be predicted from study of the influences in his life. Although several biographies point to a number of important influences, all of which have influenced his person, not one influence is represented totally in his teaching. He was born and raised in an orthodox Brahmin Hindu family, yet he does not identify himself as Brahmin, Hindu, or even Indian. Throughout his life he remained strictly vegetarian, did not consume any intoxicants, and practiced Hatha Yoga,[5] although he always said that the reasons for these practices were not to obey any authority or to align himself with any religion. Highly self-disciplined, he did not advise anyone else to follow these prescriptions. He was brought to prominence and educated by the Theosophical Society, yet he came to disavow the esoteric, especially clairvoyant, emphases of the society of his day. He conversed with scholars and teachers in a variety of religious and scientific traditions, yet he did not claim to follow or transmit any system or codified path. He had extraordinary experiences of illumination, yet he never advocated a search for the transcendent, psychic, or "divine"; to him, these realms, considered superhuman by most, are in fact to be found in the acute awareness found in everyday life.

Krishnamurti's relationship to the Theosophical Society remained a curious connection throughout his life, as it is today. The Theosophical Society, from which Krishnamurti emerged, is not a religious tradition but rather a pan-religious movement founded on the intention to incorporate the "highest teachings" of all religions in its quest for "Truth," undefined by nationality, tradition, or text. Krishnamurti came to define the Theosophical Society as limited in its perspective and authoritarian in its procedures; hence, his break from its umbrella and the imprimatur that brought him to prominence. In this break, he set his teachings apart as an inquiry into the human condition, independent of any allegiance or belief as to what constitutes an "authority" in spiritual or human questions. Even though he resigned from the Theosophical Society in 1929, many, if not most, of his stalwart followers remained in the movement, and the organization until today has continued to publish his work and to include his teachings in its workshops and conferences.

Krishnamurti's dedication to freedom and inquiry without the aid of any organization, religion, or belief system sets him outside the boundaries of any religious tradition. He was particularly disdainful of the effects of any identification of himself or another in terms of a religion, nation, or culture:

> When you call yourself an Indian or a Muslim or a Christian or a European, or anything else, you are being violent. Do you see why it is violent? Because you are separating yourself from the rest of mankind. When you separate yourself by belief, by nationality, by tradition, it breeds violence. So a man who is seeking to understand violence does not belong to any country, to any religion, to any political party or partial system; he is concerned with the total understanding of mankind. (Krishnamurti 1969, 51–52)

Krishnamurti applied this stricture to his own identity. When confronted by an educated Indian professional and told that his teaching was purely Advaita (Nondual) Vedanta, one of the major philosophical schools of Hinduism, Krishnamurti described himself in third person:

> Let us brush aside whether the speaker is an Indian brought up in this tradition, conditioned in this culture, and whether he is the summation of this ancient teaching. First of all he is not an Indian, that is to say, he does not belong to this nation or to the community of Brahmins, though he was born in it. He denies the very tradition with which you invest him. He denies that his teaching is the continuity

of the ancient teachings. He has not read any of the sacred books of India or of the West because they are unnecessary for a man who is aware of what is going on in the world—of the behaviour of human beings with their endless theories, with the accepted propaganda of two thousand or five thousand years which has become the tradition, the truth, the revelation. . . . Any acceptance of authority is the very denial of truth, as he has insisted that one must be outside all culture, tradition and social morality. . . . He totally denies the past, its teachers, its interpreters, its theories and its formulas. (Krishnamurti 1970a, 11–12)

Krishnamurti claims that he exists psychologically outside any tradition and that all individuals must also come to an awareness of the social and cultural conditioning that identification with any system entails. His rejection of the authority of any tradition or lineage and his insistence on the sole validity of an individual's observation of self removes Krishnamurti from the mantle of any readily identifiable tradition of spiritual or social practice. One cannot study the teachings of any established religion or philosophy and gain a complete orientation to Krishnamurti's teaching.

In terms of the associated "textual corpus," most of the publications that contain Krishnamurti's teaching are either recordings or transcriptions of his addresses, delivered in English, to audiences in various places. The talks invariably cover wide-ranging topics, so that any one talk might span the breadth of his teaching, from the function of thought to an analysis of global disharmony. Over the years, transcriptions have been parsed and organized into a number of anthologies that address specific topics, including meditation, education, religion, revolution, and change. One of these collections is the primary source excerpted here: *This Light in Oneself* (Shambhala, 1999). Another collection, *Meditations* (Shambhala, 2002), originally published in 1979, presents Krishnamurti's teaching on meditation even more succinctly.

In addition to transcribed talks, Krishnamurti also wrote in notebooks and journals, also in English, commenting to himself about the state of humanity, the challenges and perils of civilization, his communion with nature, observations of others around him, and his reflections on the nature of awareness. These journals and notebooks, referenced at the end of this introduction but not cited here, give an appreciation of his lifelong inquiry, the process of his attention to immediate surroundings, and how his musings reflect an ordered mind engaged with the present moment.

A number of biographies have been published. The most thorough accounts are written by those who knew him well, particularly Mary Lutyens (1908–1999) (1973, 1983, 1985, 1990), who grew up alongside Krishnamurti as the fourth and youngest daughter of Lady Emily Bulwer-Lutyens (1874–1964), one of Krishnamurti's closest friends and supporters, and Edwin Lutyens (1869–1944), architect and designer of New Delhi, capital of independent India; and Pupul Jayakar (1915–1997) (1986), who met Krishnamurti in India in the 1940s and served as his intellectual amanuensis, watching over him through a recurrence of the mysterious "process" in 1948 (Jayakar 1986, 122–35; Vernon 2002, 220). These accounts note the development of Krishnamurti's teaching as largely a function of the challenges and lessons met in his own life's trajectory. Krishnamurti conversed with many notables, including two Indian heads of state—the first prime minister of the new nation, Jawaharlal Nehru (1889–1964), and his daughter, Prime Minister Indira Gandhi (1917–1984). As will be discussed later, a number of literary figures, philosophers, commentators, and spiritual teachers cite his work as influential in their lives and work.

Meditation beyond Technique

Meditation is often defined as an effort in which rituals or specific techniques are used to move one beyond ordinary, scattered, and inharmonious states of body, mind, and emotions to a nonordinary state of stillness. As with many spiritual exercises, meditation can be understood as a means to an end, with the end conceived as a temporarily or permanently transformed consciousness. In this view, meditation is usually considered a process "set apart" from ordinary life—a process of preparation, of gathering together the whole of oneself, and of finding release from the mental disorganization that routinely accompanies random thoughts. However, some individuals do not view meditation as a process set apart but rather seek to integrate meditation into everyday life without the assistance of specific techniques, such as *mantras*, chanting, saying rosaries, or breathing exercises. Krishnamurti's view of meditation is even more radical, involving a transformation of each moment through inquiry, active attention, and awareness. As he summarizes, "Meditation is not a means to an end. It is both the means and the end" (1970a, 14). Moreover, "[O]ne must totally deny all postures, all breathing exercises, all activities of thought" (Krishnamurti 1999, 32). For Krishnamurti, true meditation is beyond technique and tradition (Krishnamurti 1999, 82); it is an all-pervading existential approach.

Krishnamurti teaches that, because all religions and soteriological systems (whether engaged in the goal of salvation, enlightenment, liberation, or self-realization) are the products of thought, they must be rejected. All beliefs—in deities, afterlife, or authority—tie individuals to the past, to the "known." To move beyond the known to the unknown is the challenge that Krishnamurti presents to all. Any promise derived from a system of thought can only be illusion, so Krishnamurti refused to delineate a cosmology, any soteriological system, or any tenets of belief. In this sense, his "path" is actually "no path," but his requirements are awareness, self-observation, inquiry, and mindfulness, without any reliance on "knowledge" or "discipline" derived from any authority.

Similar to Gautama the Buddha, Krishnamurti refused to refer to any deity or to any salvific claims for reward or punishment in an afterlife. Krishnamurti's view of the goal of human existence, then, must derive from the inferences we draw from his explanations. If we must categorize Krishnamurti's teaching in terms of world religious systems (an exercise he would disdain), it is most clearly aligned with Hindu, Buddhist, Jain, and Daoist (Taoist) systems of thought that view enlightenment and freedom in this life as the primary spiritual goal, in contrast to Western monotheistic emphases on salvation and an afterlife. His emphasis on the cause of suffering and the psychological bondage that results from attachment to personal image, identity, and thought is also consistent with Hindu, Buddhist, Jain, and Daoist notions of nonattachment. Krishnamurti concentrated on the human condition in the moment and refused to entertain conjecture about past and future, whether cast in terms of karmic debt, rewards and punishments, *maya* (illusion), or future bliss. He never referred to deities or angels, and, once dissociated from the Theosophical Society, he never again taught the reality of ascended masters, even though his first book was a record of his tutelage by ascended master Kuthumi, which Krishnamurti says were not his words but rather the words of the master who taught him (Krishnamurti 2009). Krishnamurti made occasional references to rebirth or reincarnation relative to his own life, and from these we may infer that he did not completely reject an Indian soteriology or cosmology, but he never included reincarnation as an element in his diagnosis of or remedy for the human condition. Instead, he emphasized revolutionary change in the moment and rejected evolutionary change—whether social, cultural, or spiritual—over time. In his appeal to immediate change and existence outside of psychological time, evolutionary change was not only not acceptable, it was also not possible.

Krishnamurti's call to self-examination is consistent with a number of spiritual teachings. His method of teaching, his refusal to address hypothetical and cosmological questions, and his rejection of any organization place him outside established traditions that incorporate belief systems, cosmologies, status hierarchies, and authority structures. When we attempt to infer from Krishnamurti's teaching some soteriological system, we see reflections of nature mysticism, the unity behind all diversity, and a call for individual responsibility. Our inferences evoke resonance with elements of Daoism, the *Upanishads*, nature mysticism, and forms of indigenous spirituality. What we do not see is any reflection of an established and authoritative social structure or system of thought—anything resembling a legitimizing institution. Rather, the moment of sincere self-observation is the only verification, the only legitimization, of his ideas that he would recognize.

Attempts, however cogent, to locate Krishnamurti by comparing his teaching to Advaita (Nondual) Vedanta Hinduism, the message and practice of Gautama the Buddha, or the esoteric practices of the Theosophical Society end in vain. He concentrated on the human condition in the moment and never referred to validating texts or intermediaries who could serve as conduits to the supernatural or an afterlife.

This Light in Oneself

This Light in Oneself: True Meditation, our primary text, was originally published in English in 1999 by Shambhala Publications[6] and Shambhala International. As the title indicates, the work emphasizes finding the Light within, which is an innate capacity for spiritual insight inherent in all beings. It also encourages readers (listeners) to practice "true meditation," that is, meditation beyond technique and as an all-encompassing existential approach. For Krishnamurti, true meditation involves continual inquiry based on awareness and attentiveness in each moment. Elsewhere he refers to this as "freedom from the known" and "choiceless awareness."

This Light in Oneself consists of transcriptions of a variety of talks and addresses to diverse audiences. It is ultimately intended for anyone interested in the pathless discovery of personal freedom. It consists of eighteen sections from seventeen associated talks and one journal entry. The sections are listed in figure 14.3, with asterisks (*) indicating selections contained in the present chapter. In "A New Consciousness," Krishnamurti emphasizes that our present culture and society are in dire need of a new way of being that may be brought about through a revolutionary, not evolutionary, process. According to Krishnamurti, we exist with an old consciousness, in which each person identifies with nationality, race, religion, gender, or whatever. Specifically, he explains how thought creates ideologies, belief systems, deities, and authority structures, and then, through thought, connects our personal selves with the very edifices that thought has created. Because we do not recognize our own participation in the creation of these entities through our own thought, we grant them external reality and attribute authority to them. In essence, we grant authority to the illusions that thought has created. We then begin to relate psychologically to these entities in regular patterns. In our conditioning to these patterns, we accept, conform to, and obey the authority that thought has created. We then further validate the illusions created

"A New Consciousness"* (*Krishnamurti's Journal*, 1973)	"To Live without the Action of Will"* (Brockwood Park, 1978)
"The Miracle of Attention"* (San Francisco, 1975)	"Harmony between the Known and Unknown" (Ojai, 1973)
"Living in Goodness" (Ojai, 1979)	"A Sacred Life" (Saanen, 1973)
"This Light in Oneself"* (Amsterdam, 1968)	"Observing from a Quiet Mind" (Saanen, 1976)
"To Inquire into Truth" (Ojai, 1982) (San Francisco, 1973)	"Enlightenment Is Not a Fixed Place"*
"The Beauty of Virtue" (Brockwood Park, 1973)	"The End of Searching" (Brockwood Park, 1979)
"The Summation of All Energy"* (Bombay, 1982)	"Pure Observation" (Saanen, 1983)
"The Eternally, Timelessly Sacred" (Madras, 1979)	Light Cannot Be Given By Another"* (Saanen, 1976)
"What Is Creation?"* (Brockwood Park, 1983)	"A Dimension Thought Cannot Touch" (Brockwood Park, 1972)

Figure 14.3. Sections of *This Light in Oneself*

by thought through justifying, legitimizing, and rationalizing these allegiances, which is yet more participation in thought (Krishnamurti 1999, 3).

> In order to understand the edifice created by thought, and thus to understand one's lack of freedom, there must be observation in the present moment, without interference from thought, authority, identification or conditioning. These psychological processes separate one part of self from another part of self and separate one person from another. (Krishnamurti 1999, 113)

Observation is seeing what is in the present moment, without involving any technique or any conceptualization of what is seen. (For example, when one sees a tree, one has a direct experience of the tree. If one then thinks, "That is a maple tree," one is no longer in the realm of the present but is in the realm of thought, knowledge, and the past.) Following a technique or method for meditation is a reliance on authority and an attempt to control and discipline thought. Using a technique or method for meditation is actually one fragment of thought trying to control another fragment of thought. A part of oneself, imbued with authority derived from thought, seeks to control another part of self that is fragmentary and scattered. However, both parts are oneself, and both parts depend upon thought for their existence. By seeking to control, suppress, or discipline thought through thought itself, one creates division in oneself and uses a great deal of energy to perpetuate this division (Krishnamurti 1999, 5).

Consciousness based on thought creates a reality and then proceeds to create an identification with what it perceives to be reality. As long as we operate through this identification, held in place through thought, we cannot be free. We need to enter a new consciousness in order to enter a place of freedom in ourselves, without psychological thought and without a self-image based on identification with what is "me" or "mine." Entering a new consciousness, in Krishnamurti's teaching, can occur only in the moment; it cannot be built in an incremental way over time, through thought.

Krishnamurti was adamant in his insistence that preparation and evolution cannot lead to a radical transformation of consciousness. Rather, he was convinced that divisions into "preparatory" and "actualized" as well as "means" and "ends" are fallacious and perpetuate the very divisions in consciousness that one needs to overcome. Instead of preparation and gradual achievement of a transformation (i.e., evolution of consciousness), one must enter a unitary state immediately, not through evolution but through revolution. One can live with a passion for transformation to such a degree that all divisions in consciousness cease and one becomes pure awareness, untainted by thought.

Krishnamurti's teaching on meditation rests firmly on an invitation to self-inquiry, not dependent upon any authority, teacher, or system. There is no prescribed path to self-inquiry and self-observation but rather an engagement with self in the moment through opening to an awareness that is unlimited and eternal. Identification with any position, belief system, or idea is set aside as fragmentary and contradictory when one enters meditation, which is a silence that contains a new intelligence, a new morality, and a wholeness (Krishnamurti 1999, 2).

In "The Miracle of Attention," Krishnamurti examines the problematic nature of thought. Participation in thought inevitably conditions us to live in the past, unable to experience the present moment and an expansion of awareness. We establish identities, separate ourselves from others, and define relationships through the constructions of thought. Always derived from and relating to the past, these cognitions constitute "knowledge." We are conditioned to live in the past as "secondhand people" as we accept the "knowledge" derived from our own past experience or from some authority, whether priest, scripture, or teacher. As secondhand people, we learn to revere "knowledge" presented to us through thought and become unable to perceive what is before us in the moment (Krishnamurti 1999, 111).

To Krishnamurti, one needs to see the truth of the situation—that the thinker is the thought, "[T]he controller is the controlled, the experiencer is the experienced. . . . They are not separate entities" (Krishnamurti 1999, 4). In Krishnamurti's teaching, meditation is not control of thought, reliance on external or internal authority, or disciplining of thought—all of which are common notions of meditation. Instead, meditation is a "transformation of the mind" (Krishnamurti 1999, 8), a revolution in the psyche, that has no division, no thought, and no identification. It is freedom and wholeness that accompanies a deep stillness and active attention.

Meditation is the state of attention in which the "me" is totally absent (Krishnamurti 1999, 73). Consequently, no trace of motive, will, or intention is present. The mind is free from fear, from the anxieties that accompany attachment to the image of "me" and free from the friction of a mind in conflict with itself. Life becomes a total movement, not fragmented and broken up into identities of "me" and "you" (Krishnamurti 1999, 68). With freedom from the known, the mind can confront the unknown. Without bondage to the past through thought, the mind can enter the present.

Thus, in "This Light in Oneself," Krishnamurti speaks about the importance of following the Light within. Because living in thought ties one to the past, freedom requires movement beyond thought, beyond even the revered "truths" of myth and tradition. As knowledge and thought eclipse the present, they serve as sources of psychological division as well as sorrow, pain, and anxiety. Change requires movement beyond knowledge and thought and apprehension of the immediate present independent of thought. The force of change comes only when one apprehends the condition of not-knowing in the present, without psychological dependence upon anyone. Seeing one's situation and facing the unknown alone constitute the only mechanism for change. Knowledge and time must be left behind, as must psychological dependence upon anyone. No one can see for another, so external authority is of no use. In Krishnamurti's words, "Be a light unto yourselves" (1999, 16–17).

Krishnamurti is stark in his assertion that no method, no person, and no system—however hallowed or ancient—can guide another to the freedom of an unconditioned mind. Repetition of words makes the mind "dull, stupid, mesmerized" and functions as imitation and self-hypnosis (Krishnamurti 1999, 17–18). Reliance on the authority of a person or system divides and distorts the mind. When one cannot rely on an authority, spiritual or otherwise, for one's realization, one must necessarily enter into an inquiry about human existence and the conditioning that accompanies human existence. Can this conditioning and its accompanying bondage be explored, appreciated, and transcended?

Real meditation lies beyond any procedures, beyond all effort, and beyond any consideration of "me." Only there can the mind be free from the known and free from psychological memory. Only there can meditation and order exist, so that the mind,

> which is not of thought, then becomes utterly quiet, silent—naturally, without any force, without any discipline. And in the light of that silence all action can take place, living daily from that silence. . . . in that silence there is quite a different movement, which is not of time, which is not of words, which is not measurable by thought, because it is always new. (Krishnamurti 1999, 22–23)

In "The Summation of All Energy," Krishnamurti emphasizes that moving beyond the limitations of thought opens one to the possibility of finding the "religious mind," a place of nonduality in which the divisions of observer/observed, seer/seen, and controller/controlled cease. Conventional meditation that relies on rituals, symbols, and discipline perpetuates the division and friction that accompanies thought and uses the energy of the mind and body to uphold these divisions. Freeing oneself of the need to hold these divisions in place opens a person to the possibility of contact with the summation of all energy, so that one can care, watch, and observe with full attention. In the undivided energy of full attention one participates in affection and compassion, hallmarks of the religious mind.

The full attention of meditation is not concentration, which is another form of division in the mind as one tries to exclude certain thoughts in order to concentrate on one thought. Concentration narrows one's attention and sets up a system of resistance in order to allow a single train of thought to the exclusion of another. Division, friction, choice, and conflict ensue. One part of the mind is set against another part of the mind. When Krishnamurti speaks of meditation, he points to the awareness that exists beyond duality and the choice, friction, and loss of energy that accompany duality. All of one's energy is available for observation. And, without the activity of thought and definitions of "me" and "not me," all of space is also available. One encounters a vast distance and limitless time, which is the pristine vitality of the brain. When one moves beyond the shackles of thought and its accompanying divisions, one meets freedom, outside the structures and "noises" of psychological memory. Here one encounters not relative but absolute silence in meditation (Krishnamurti 1999, 31–35). According to Krishnamurti,

> That state of mind can be understood only by yourself, by watching it and never trying to shape it, never taking sides, never opposing, never agreeing, never justifying, never condemning, never judging—which means watching without any choice. And out of this choiceless awareness perhaps the door will open and you will know what that dimension is in which there is no conflict and no time. (Krishnamurti 1960, 3:216)

Choiceless awareness is a particular attention that allows an undistorted perception of what is. Observation with this quality of attention reveals a situation in its simplest form, without any overlay of language or identification. When a situation is revealed in this way, the problematic nature of the situation resolves and one sees the truth, without distortion or avoidance. All of one's energy can go into observation rather than supporting an endangered identity or choosing between alternatives.

When the mind is not functioning through the screen of psychological memory, it is free to inquire into its limitations, to use all of its energy to observe. The mind is still, quiet, and undistorted. The mind participates in the sacred.

In "What Is Creation?" Krishnamurti, in posing the question of the nature of creation, approaches the possibility of moving beyond the world of manifestation in which everything that is created has both a beginning and an end. He inquires into the possibility of observing a reality beyond time that is neither created nor destroyed. "We are asking if there is something beyond all time" (Krishnamurti 1999, 49). When "innocent of time," one also experiences spaciousness. Unbound by time and space, one can have a "feeling of the complete wholeness and unity of life. . . . that can come only when there is love and compassion" (Krishnamurti 1999, 50). It is thus that one approaches infinity and the sacred nature of life.

Movement beyond time and space to apprehend the unity of life constitutes an inquiry that moves one beyond psychological memory and its inherent self-centered interest. Meditation is to come upon the origin of all of this, to apprehend the wholeness and unity of life, without distinction between observer and observed. As the famous Daoist text of the *Zhuangzi* (*Chuang-tzu*; Book of Master Zhuang) points out, "When there is no more separation between 'this' and 'that,' it is called the still-point of the Dao. At the still-point in the center of the circle one can see the infinite in all things" (Feng and English 1974, 29).

And so, "creation" takes on a new meaning when one exists without space, time, beginning, ending, or thought. In the absence of thought, creation becomes order and awareness becomes choiceless. One exists outside manifestation and, thus, outside the opposites that thought imposes on manifestation. The ordinary dualities of thinking (self/other, forcing/accepting, acting/seeing, doing/being, knowing/inquiring) cease to be operative. Just as love cannot have an opposite, one cannot observe the whole of existence while considering duality and choice (Krishnamurti 1999, 48–51).

Choice is not possible without thought; order is not possible with thought. One can move from the disorder of thought, time, and self-interest to the choiceless awareness of what exists. One leaves behind perception of the world as separate entities and the violence, conflict, jealousy, ambition, and aggressiveness that these distinctions entail. Seeing the world as a whole entails participation in love and compassion.

Krishnamurti deftly leads the reader through observation of the functions of thought and the personal identification that thought effects to a consideration of how personal transformation to choiceless awareness is the foundation for social and cultural change. His analysis of the order brought by choiceless awareness demonstrates how psychological change is the process for change in social and cultural dimensions (Sabzevary 2008).

In "To Live Without the Action of Will," Krishnamurti comments,

> Meditation is not something that *you* do. Meditation is a movement into the whole question of our living: how we live, how we behave, whether we have fears, anxieties, sorrows; whether we are everlastingly pursuing pleasure; and whether we have built images about ourselves and about others. (1999, 52–53)

When a person acts from identification (i.e., from having a sense of oneself), a duality is set up between observer and observed. I say to myself, "I am a meditator. I want to experience wholeness. Through my will, I can attain another state of consciousness." These thoughts and intentions set my identity apart from my actions. I assume that I can use the force of my intention to change my state of consciousness. However, when I observe myself, I see that I have created division and conflict within my own consciousness. One part of myself seeks to control another part of myself. I am divided and not whole.

Observation of this conversation in ourselves demonstrates that, because of thought, we are divided; thought creates divisions of authority, control, comparison, and evaluation. Thought, born from memory and what is known, also generates desire and an impetus to move beyond the present. Memory provides an image of self that we believe to be valid. We are wounded, hurt, grandiose, or whatever. Our attachment to this image of self is a source of anxiety, fear, and pain, as we seek to validate to ourselves and to others our notions of who we are. We seek deliverance from fear, anxiety, and suffering and call upon the action of will to take us from the present to a future in which these agonies will cease. Operating from the action of will divides us internally as we set intentions for searching, seeking, and desiring goals that will occur at some future time. We are fragmented and we are not living in the present moment. Yet we continue to divide our attention and energy in the pursuit of finding some wholeness, not in the present moment but in some future moment. And we continue to use thought to rationalize this division.

Meditation is movement out of division in oneself, into a wholeness that does not contain psychological identification, desire, or will. In meditation, one gains insight into the whole of oneself, which implies "having no motive, no remembrance, just instant perception of the nature of consciousness" (Krishnamurti 1999, 60). Meditation is also outside of the division that time creates; there is no tomorrow, psychologically (Krishnamurti 1999, 55). There is only the active attention of the present moment of awareness. Timeless, deathless, with no beginning and no end, meditation is a new consciousness that cannot evolve over time but must be found in an instant in a revolutionary process outside of time.

Krishnamurti equates the attention of the whole of oneself with the religious life. Compared to institutionalized religious perspectives, Krishnamurti defines the human condition as more abysmal and the human "enterprise" as more rigorous. However, in the end, he comes to a more comprehensive vision of human transformation and a more hopeful stance regarding human possibility. His greater estimation of human degradation, his grander projection for human development, and his insistence on self-observation as the only method for real transformation place him within the genre of esoteric religion (Schuon 1984, 33–41), all of whose members, like Krishnamurti, set themselves apart from institutionalized religions. Although Krishnamurti claims to have come upon his understanding without the aid of any teachers, spiritual mentors, religious traditions, or ancient lore, his insistence upon an individual search in which one must look within, learn from the observation, and be responsible for one's own transit through life joins him nevertheless with other esoteric forms of religion. Further, Krishnamurti is aligned with esotericism in his constant emphasis on ascertaining truth through observation of the obstacles in oneself that impede the quest for truth and through an assiduous discrimination between truth and knowledge. Esoteric religion, by its very nature, does not seek converts, nor does it measure its worth by membership numbers. It exists for the few, perhaps the one, who has sincerely looked and found that the world no longer enchants, that the organization and routinization of any truth will destroy its vitality, and that there is hope for real and radical transformation for individuals (Jones 1997, 3). From Krishnamurti's perspective,

> Any movement that is worthwhile, any action which has any deep significance, must begin with each one of us. I must change first; I must see what is the nature and structure of my relationship with the world—and in the very *seeing* is the doing; therefore I, as a human being living in the world, bring about a different quality, and that quality, it seems to me, is the quality of the religious mind. (Krishnamurti 1969, 119)

In "Enlightenment Is Not a Fixed Place," Krishnamurti emphasizes that meditation is an "absolute silence of the mind" (1999, 35). Unfettered by identification with what is "me" and "mine," without attachment to an image of self, and absent any motive to find pleasure, one can live without the psychological memory of a "me" that progresses, a "me" that achieves, and a "me" that suffers (Krishnamurti 1999, 34). One moves beyond the duality, division, and friction of psychological memory to enter a still and silent consciousness in which there is no control whatsoever. For Krishnamurti, rituals, symbols, postures, breathing exercises, and all systems invented by thought are not effective in bringing about the silence of meditation, because each of these factors implies division and control.

The attention of meditation is quiet but not passive. It is an awareness, a stillness, a "seeing" without conscious identification as a "seer." It is a listening with total attention, without identification of either "observer" or "observed," since identification invariably brings distortion of the truth of oneself. It is possible to be aware of one's conditioning, one's background, one's impulses, and the general disorder of one's mind without a desire to change, alter, or transform anything. The simple act of observing is what constitutes both the beginning and the end of meditation, both the first step and the last step (Krishnamurti 1999, 87). The irony of this situation is that real change is effected through *seeing* without distortion, simply seeing, rather than making any effort of will to transform.

Seeing oneself without distortion brings order. Once brought to awareness, the many elements of disorder—the contradictions, compulsions, opposing desires—of one's mind are transformed into order (Krishnamurti 1999, 89). For Krishnamurti, order in one's mind is the only entrée to meditation. Order in one's mind is virtue, even righteousness, and it accompanies learning. This order is not a blueprint imposed by society, culture, environment, or obedience. It comes only through the understanding and negation of disorder, through awareness of the many ways in which disorder allows contradictions, oppositions, and violence to exist unnoticed. "In understanding, in looking at disorder, being attentive, aware choicelessly of disorder, order comes naturally, easily, without any effort" (Krishnamurti 1999, 88–89).

In essence, order brings certainty, but this is a certainty not borne of thought and not describable. This certainty is intelligence that resides in being, not thinking—in attention, not thought. With awareness, one is free from the known and confronts the unknown. What has been said about this state of awareness in the past may be true, but it must be found again in each person, for oneself. Each one of us, individually, must learn independently what the truth is (Krishnamurti 1999, 91–93).

In "Light Cannot Be Given by Another," Krishnamurti observes that one must be free to be a "light to oneself" and that this light—this ability to apprehend the truth—cannot be given by any other person (Krishnamurti 1999, 111). When one discovers another state of consciousness and awareness, one discovers another intelligence. The heart enters the mind and the mind has a different quality. One discovers a state of consciousness that is limitless. But this discovery occurs only through "not knowing," through inquiry into what cannot be known through thought. This discovery and this awareness cannot be learned from another; each individual must discover it anew.

Similarly, to be aware of oneself without any choice in the present moment allows intelligence, the whole movement of the self, to flower. A radical transformation occurs "if there is no background, if there is no observer who is the background" (Krishnamurti 1999, 114). Identification of a distinct observer creates an intermediary between one's observation and truth and distorts perception through fear and desire. When the cognitive recognition of an observer is absent, one can observe without suppression or denial. In the very process of observing, change occurs. One becomes a light to oneself.

Only through self-observation can one be a light to oneself; when one is a light to oneself, one is a light to the world, because the world is not separate from oneself. In Krishnamurti's words, "You are the world" (Krishnamurti 1999, 112).

By way of summary,

> Love is not of the mind, it is not in the net of thought, it cannot be sought out, cultivated, cherished; it is there when the mind is silent and the heart is empty of the things of the mind. Love is meditation. Love is not a remembrance, an image sustained by thought as pleasure, nor the romantic image which sensuality builds; it is something that lies beyond all the senses and beyond the economic and social pressures of life. The immediate realization of this love, which has no root in yesterday, is meditation; for love is truth, and meditation is the discovery of the beauty of this truth. (KFAA)

Krishnamurti's teaching on meditation is an inquiry into the whole phenomenon of existence and how we can become free to participate in the sacred and limitless dimension of existence, which he also refers to as love. He begins with a diagnosis of how we are controlled and limited by thought and with a demonstration of how all inventions of thought, whether through religion, science, or self-reflection, chain us to the past, to time, and to the known. Then he asks if one can learn for oneself whether there is something unnamable, beyond time and not created by thought, which is not an illusion. He moves our deliberations from knowledge to inquiry, from thought to observation. He warns that our inquiry into the unperceivable and the unknowable must be ever new, residing in the present moment, without interference from the patterns of thought that bind us inexorably to the past. Our inquiry cannot depend upon authority, experiences, or knowledge, which are the very essence of thought. Instead, we must inquire into the possibility of finding a mind that is utterly quiet, without control, discipline, or effort. Can the mind, the whole organic structure, be completely still and utterly quiet, as well as empty of all contents, of all that it knows? Krishnamurti responds to his own question: only if the mind can observe its own limitation and, in that seeing, bring about the ending of the limitation. Through observing oneself without an image of oneself as observer, one enters a timeless, spaceless silence that is sacred and the ground of compassion and love.

Observing silently, when the observer is absent, brings an attention that includes a great deal of energy, whereas making an effort to be attentive wastes energy. In observing without an observer, the mind is empty and without illusion. The mind can inquire without a pattern from the past and can observe the biases of thought, brought over from years of conditioning to identities of race, gender, class, or religion. One can observe how division and fragmentation derive from these identities and keep the mind bound to the past. Exposed to the light of attention without effort, the mind can approach an intelligence and a perception that are only potentially ours in ordinary states of consciousness.

Meditation is inquiry that resides in stillness, silence, emptiness, and not-knowing so that the mind is capable of observing. When the mind and brain become extraordinarily quiet, there is no need for a discipline, a teacher, or a system. In fact, reliance on anything outside oneself will negate the possibility of an extraordinarily quiet mind. As Krishnamurti explains,

> And that is the only thing that is sacred—not the images, the rituals, the saviors, the gurus, the visions. Only that thing is sacred, which mind has come upon without asking because in itself it is totally empty. Only in that which has emptiness can a new thing take place. (Krishnamurti 1999, 133)

It is important to note that Krishnamurti's understanding of meditation, although described predominantly in intrapsychic terms, is the foundation of a teaching of biological as well as psychological transformation. He spoke early on of revolution, radical transformation and mutation, a change interpreted by most as being only psychological or spiritual. Later it became obvious that he was referring to biological and organic mutation as a fact, not only metaphor. His teaching emphasizes that proper undirected attention can bring about a mind that is free from the distortions of a conditioned brain and that a conditioned, patterned brain can change its physical structure. Brain cells can mutate, not incrementally over time, but in sudden transformations.

A number of recent developments in the biological and cognitive sciences support several of Krishnamurti's points: his insistence on revolutionary, not evolutionary, change; his teaching regarding mutation of brain cells; his imperative for dying to the known in order to free oneself from recursive patterns in the brain; the need for an attention that relates conscious and unconscious processes; and the perennial nature of change in the brain (Sanat 1999, 63–72).

Krishnamurti's insistence on mutation of the brain also serves as the foundation for a teaching of social and cultural transformation. As the conditioned brain demonstrates a closed-loop system of recursive and persistent patterning, mutations in the brain demonstrate freedom from these conceptual systems and a promise of significant change at the social level. Krishnamurti's teaching that "[y]ou are the world" is not only a figure of speech but declaration of a fact—that change in one part of the system is change in the system as a whole. Although the onus for transformation resides squarely with the individual in Krishnamurti's teaching, its effects extend to all, providing the possibility of love and compassion at group and global levels.

A Star in Both the East and the West: J. Krishnamurti's Legacy

The legacy of Krishnamurti lies in the innumerable lives affected by his teaching, only some of which are documented. Nonetheless, his influence, however unrecorded, has been significant. It is not uncommon to hear testimonials, such as "Reading Krishnamurti changed my life," "Krishnamurti gave me a new way to live," or "I read something of his each day." Unlike members of most new religious and spiritual movements, individuals who have been influenced by the ideas of Krishnamurti are not part of official membership numbers, because, in line with his teaching, no organization, no religion, and no movement has been established in his name for anyone to join. More accessible are the tangible traces of his legacy in several areas: his writings; audio and video recordings of his talks; conversations between Krishnamurti and academics, scientists, and youth; the foundations organized in his name; the schools functioning with his principles; and his influence on scholarship in a number of areas, particularly the dialogical process developed with David Bohm (1917–1992).

In a number of scholarly areas, Krishnamurti's teaching has been included in theoretical works on the intersections among psychology, sociology, and philosophy and in a growing number of doctoral dissertations. As an example, an educator, social activist, and philosopher cites Krishnamurti as important to the reintegration of philosophy and psychology, two areas of study only recently separated in the West (Mehta 1979, 1987). In this view, Krishnamurti's ideas fall at the nexus of perception and praxis, traditionally the respective purviews of the Indian

Figure 14.4. J. Krishnamurti Speaking at Brockwood Park School, Hampshire, England, 1972
Source: Mark Edwards (photographer), Krishnamurti Foundation

disciplines of Yoga and Tantra. This nexus constitutes an integral field that contains the secret of both self-transformation and world transformation (Mehta 1987, 162–64).

Another philosopher locates Krishnamurti in the long tradition of Perennial Philosophy and the current renaissance of Perennialism (Sanat 1999, 105). In this view, Krishnamurti's work integrates individual human transformation and global transformation in a nondual ontology and connects death to the life of the known with initiation into a new life—both goals of Perennialism (Sanat 1999, 100–5).

Another interpretation (Ravindra 1995) defines Krishnamurti as an extraordinary intelligence operating through an extremely sensitive body that is, in effect, a manifestation of a traditional Hindu image: "Two birds, inseparable companions, are perched on the same tree; one eats the sweet fruit and the other looks on without eating" (*Rig Veda* I.164.20). Ravindra notes that this dual nature of humanity, repeated in the influential Hindu texts of the *Upanishads* and the *Bhagavad Gita*, was central to Krishnamurti's teaching (Ravindra 1995, 30–31).

In terms of his writings and recordings, Krishnamurti's books remain in print and sell in new and used versions. Most publications derive from the transcriptions of his talks to audiences or dialogues with individuals. All of Krishnamurti's talks in the last decades of his life were video recorded, transcribed, and published under his name. As mentioned earlier, many collections of his ideas, organized by topic, have been republished. It is important to note that all of Krishnamurti's books remain in print, which is an indication of a sustained and perhaps growing appreciation of his teaching.

Consistent with the tenets of his thought, Krishnamurti did not create any religious group that one could join, nor did he leave any person, institution, or text that would serve as an authority for specifying a path to freedom. On an organizational level, Krishnamurti cooperated in the establishment of several foundations in those countries where his teachings received the most response and to which he regularly returned in his annual rounds of talks. The foundations are service organizations without membership rolls that facilitated his travel, arranged for his public appearances, and published transcripts of his talks and dialogues. Today the Krishnamurti Foundations in England (founded 1968), the United States (1969), and India (1971) and the Krishnamurti committees in other countries see to the publication of his writings, sponsor regular dialogue groups, and hold gatherings for study of the teachings. The foundations are not religious groups with specified memberships but are rather relatively noninstitutionalized organizations that coordinate dissemination of Krishnamurti's teaching.

Located in Ojai, California, the Krishnamurti Foundation America maintains a website (www.kfa.org; jkrishnamurti.org) that includes a directory of Krishnamurti organizations and schools now found in some forty countries around the world (Melton 2009, 995).

During his lifetime, Krishnamurti also founded schools for children and young adults in India, the United States, England, and Switzerland. These alternative schools continue today in their mission to provide a new definition and practice of education, free from the conditioning and authority structures prevalent in most educational institutions.

Krishnamurti also engaged in a variety of formal and public dialogues during his life. A number of publications record dialogues between Krishnamurti and scholars, philosophers, and educators: Allan Anderson (Krishnamurti 1991), Jacob Needleman (Krishnamurti 1973), and David Bohm (Krishnamurti and Bohm 1985), with the latter being especially noteworthy. In his later years, Krishnamurti joined with the physicist David Bohm in an exploration of the human condition through a series of taped and transcribed conversations. Both men recognized the limitations of traditional didactic teaching and sought a way in which truth and insight can be discovered within individuals and small groups. Krishnamurti and Bohm predicted that the actual structure of the human brain could change from increased awareness and open inquiry. They collaborated in an exploration of the limitations of thought and the possibility of accessing the "unlimited," the more and more subtle realms of reality. They posit that attention is the relation between the limited and the unlimited, so that through attention we can move into more and more subtle levels of the implicate (unmanifest) order of the universe. When the brain is quiet and the mind unoccupied, when there is silence, the brain can cease to be the initiator of action and to follow its own internal goals. Instead, the brain can then function as an antenna of sorts to pick up "more and more subtle levels of being" (Bohm 1996, 91–95). The more subtle levels of the implicate order are also the more general levels of reality, where the consciousness of one person differs little from the consciousness in another. It is this core unity that Krishnamurti refers to when he reminds us, "You are the world." In this research Krishnamurti and Bohm integrate physics and psychology into a call for transformation in the moment, outside of time and space, which is revolutionary change, not evolutionary incrementalism (Krishnamurti and Bohm 1985).

In addition to formal dialogues with scholars and audience members, Krishnamurti advocated the process of dialogue in small groups of individuals who sincerely seek to inquire into the human condition. The dialogical process, practiced today in all Krishnamurti Foundations, encourages individual inquiry without didactic formalism and authority structures as a means to find an attention that can relate us to more subtle levels of being and transformation of self and world. Dialogue in a group is an egalitarian journey toward discovery through exchange of ideas and observation of self with no expectation of an outcome. Dialogue sessions are always organized around questions and participants are encouraged to engage with others in a perpetual state of inquiry, so that initial questions generate further questions. Living with a question and interacting in a state of openness was to Krishnamurti the surest way to learning, transformation, and change. As exchange occurs, participants develop a deep state of listening, so that they are not formulating a response during another's verbal contribution but remain open to what the other is saying. Essential to development of the skill of listening is to set aside all assumptions one has about others, about the question at hand, and about oneself. If assumptions are operative, especially unconsciously, it is the assumptions that are looking at oneself and the assumptions that are hearing the other. To listen without assumptions not only allows the other's contribution to be understood more completely but also enables the hearer to observe how the other's comments affect oneself (Bohm 1996, 15–21, 69–72).

Ideally, the process of dialogue leads to an intense awareness that is not dependent upon psychological thought, because this awareness goes beyond the imagery and notions of habitual thought. In this place beyond the conditioned mind, through inquiry, one can discover a deeper layer of oneself; one can apprehend the source of thought, confusion, and contradiction in oneself. One can observe the very foundation of disorder in oneself and this discovery produces order in oneself. Revolutionary insight, necessary for real change in oneself, is possible. Moreover, mutual exchange with others at a deep level elicits a group awareness, a common consciousness. Egalitarian, mutual, and open participation in a group produces an impersonal fellowship, almost completely lacking in our society, that provides support and context for further observation (Bohm 1996, 84–95).

Dialogue allows the individual and the group to go beyond the inevitable limitations of thought to an unlimited ground of everything—which is our true being. It is here in the unlimited that we find silence, emptiness, acute awareness, sensitivity, and an awareness of the whole of existence—what Krishnamurti calls meditation.

Freedom from the Known

Meditation to Krishnamurti is not a practice but an instantaneous, immediate experience of moving beyond conditioning. He uses the word "revolutionary" to describe this phenomenon, as distinguished from our commonly held associations about "Eastern" meditation techniques as being evolutionary and incremental. In "revolutionary meditation," the limitations of thought cease and one enters a state of limitless space, infinity, in which all perception is enhanced. In this state one can understand the conditioned mind and the limitations of thought, because one stands outside these limitations. For Krishnamurti, meditation occurs; it is not achieved.

> Meditation is the awareness of fear, of the implications and the structure and the nature of pleasure, the understanding of oneself, and therefore the laying of the foundation of order, which is virtue, in which there is that quality of discipline, which is not

suppression, nor control, nor imitation. Such a mind then is in a state of meditation. (Krishnamurti 1972, 93)

Krishnamurti warned against meditation methods, emphasizing that anything practiced mechanically necessarily leads to mechanical results. He questioned whether one can come to an unconditioned state through any practice and whether anything spontaneous can be seen through something that is not spontaneous. Further, he was suspicious of meditation techniques because he observed that long-term meditation practice damages the mind, making it dull and rigid.[7] A mind made dull by a method cannot possibly be intelligent and free to observe (Krishnamurti 1972, 92).

In addition to the conditioning effect of meditation, Krishnamurti pointed out that when meditation practice is motivated by a searching mind or the desire to achieve anything—whether peace of mind or exalted states of consciousness—such a practice involves recognition, as one recognizes what one is searching for. "So, in the experience which comes through search in which recognition is involved, there is nothing new, it has already been known" (Krishnamurti 1972, 91). In this way, even visions of saints and saviors are conditioned, because they are recognized, known. There is nothing new in the experience of the vision. For Krishnamurti, real meditation must be a completely new and unanticipated experience with the unknown. Only in meeting the unknown is there freedom.

Further, when one asks "how" to meditate, the "how" implies a method and an "I" who experiences. Both the method and the identification of self as a meditator bring psychological space between the observer and the observed. When there is that space, there is division and fragmentation, both of which preclude the possibility of acute perception, which is real meditation (Krishnamurti 1972, 93–94). In addition, if a method is used to escape life or to find refuge from discomfort, practice can create an inner division. And if there is identification with the practice, meditation can become a tool for reinforcing, not transcending, illusion and for buttressing the ego. Thus, "If there is a meditator meditating, it is not meditation" (Krishnamurti 1978, 220).

Real meditation brings one into a sort of poverty in which one stands defenseless in the face of conventional needs—to be respectable, to do what one "should" do, to know oneself. The poverty of not knowing allows one to be poor inwardly and to cease the relentless drive to seek and to desire (Krishnamurti 1969, 60–61). Through an inner poverty, one can approach love, compassion, and experience of the sacred.

Krishnamurti's emphasis on "freedom from the known" points to a radical approach to living, in which rote learning, reliance on authority, and prescribed methods are harmful for, if not prohibitive of, awakening from one's state of conditioning. Critiquing all outward signs and trappings of "spirituality" and "wisdom," including the individual search for "enlightened masters" based on artificial and superficial criteria, Krishnamurti emphasizes,

> I hope you are listening to find out for yourself, for nobody, *nobody*, can teach you what meditation is, however long-bearded the gentleman may be, or whatever strange garments he may wear. Find out for yourself and stand by what you find out for yourself, and do not depend on anybody. (Krishnamurti 1999, 106; italics in original)

This involves a recognition of the limitations and potential dangers of attachment to teachers (including Krishnamurti), community, and tradition. Krishnamurti's teaching is a challenge to change; in his words, "Why don't you change?" Can adherence to a tradition, recitation of doctrinal statements, or repetition of techniques bring about a change in consciousness? Not in Krishnamurti's view.

Krishnamurti emphasized a nondualistic approach, emphasizing the ways in which oneself and the world are only conventionally distinct.

> In oneself lies the whole world, and if you know how to look and learn, then the door is there and the key is in your hand. Nobody on earth can give you either that key or the door to open, except yourself. (Krishnamurti 1981, 158)

Krishnamurti's famous statement "You are the world" is not metaphorical or poetic language. It is quite literal, meaning that only when individuals transform inside will the world reform. Similarly, virtue cannot be attained by a decision; it must be a real state of being. Krishnamurti asks that we consider the fact that each of us is actually the whole of humanity. We cannot appreciate this fact because we are the products of disorder, conflict, and the assumption that we are distinct individuals. Krishnamurti viewed all ideologies, whether religious or political, as forms of bondage and idiotic because they are the products of conceptual thinking that divides humanity. Thought itself causes division. If we can see that we share the consciousness of all humanity, we can touch a different quality of mind that is holistic, ordered, and integral. This mind that understands the truth of existence and the unity of humans will not harm itself or others. Aggression, violence, and brutality, both within and outside the self, will cease (Krishnamurti 1972).

Krishnamurti's view of the human condition is participatory and relational; it includes a "high anthropology." With these foci, his thought aligns with, if not presages, current thought in social constructionism (Gergen 2009)[8] and participatory studies (Ferrer and Sherman 2008; Lincoln et al. 2011). He shares with these paradigms the tenet that truth is not a fixed reality, independent of an observer, but rather a subjective-objective reality, which depends upon an observer to create the observed (see Gergen 2009). In Krishnamurti's words, "The observer *is* the observed" (1969, 96). Only through inquiry and finding out for oneself the relationship between observer and observed can one participate in Truth, which constitutes a "pathless land."

A participatory worldview is defined by relationship and holds social participation as a mutually enabling balance within and between people (Heron 1996). The participatory paradigm places human beings in relationship with a living world, identifying us as part of the whole rather than as separate creations of a transcendent god (Heron and Reason 1997). This way of being is the intersubjectivity essential to I-Thou relationships (Buber 1970) and a participatory ontology (Ferrer and Sherman 2008). As earlier recognized by Krishnamurti,

> Relationship, surely, is the mirror in which you discover yourself. Without relationship you are not; to be is to be related; to be related is existence. And you exist only in relationship; otherwise, you do not exist, existence has no meaning. (Krishnamurti 1949)

Krishnamurti's insights into meditation reveal the errors that we make in assuming that we have actual relationships with other humans. In reality, our images of others have relationships with others' images of us, while we, as humans, are not in relationship. Relationship based on images constitutes living in ideas, theories, and symbols, separated from real engagement with others (Krishnamurti 1969, 58). Such separation, division, and contradiction inevitably bring conflict, both within a person and among people, because thinking and acting with images and symbols constitutes "psychological thought" and the "psychological structure of society," both of which remove us from genuine awareness and genuine relationship with others (Krishnamurti 1969, 59–60).

Examination of relationship is consistent with the "relational turn" emerging in Western thought in several areas. De Quincey (2005, 2008, 2010) examines how "radical knowing" occurs when consciousness is understood through relationship. Spretnak (2011) describes relational "revelations" in a host of venues, from education and health to ecology and feminist studies. Ferrer and Sherman (2008) assess the "participatory turn" in spirituality, mysticism, and religious studies. These analyses of interrelatedness amplify Krishnamurti's insights and demonstrate his prescience in these areas before current scholarship "discovered," or rather "rediscovered," the intricate web that connects the cosmos.

Krishnamurti's insights move us from the world of thinking and identifying with our thoughts to the world of consciousness, beyond thought and beyond the content of thought. Since the seminal ideas of the American psychologist and philosopher William James (1842–1910) on the vagaries of consciousness (1929 [1902], 1996 [1911]), Western scholarship has expanded consideration of consciousness beyond phenomenology and into physics, biology, neurology, sociology, and anthropology. In each of these areas of inquiry, there is growing appreciation of the roles of intention, aim, and awareness, not simply as means of perception and thought but as actual mechanisms of change. Krishnamurti's collaboration with the American physicist David Bohm, discussed earlier, inquires into the ability of thought to be aware of itself, as the body is aware of its own movement through proprioception (Bohm 1994, 212–30), exactly as Krishnamurti specified. Bohm collaborated with Krishnamurti on mental proprioception, insight dialogue, and self-study. They analyzed how, through intention and being attentive, one can "be immediately aware of how thought produces a result outside ourselves" (Bohm 1994, 123). Study of mental proprioception is incorporated into many venues, including insight dialogue (Bohm 1985) and esoteric practices (Vaysse 1978).

Combs (2009) explores an integral understanding of the multifaceted nature of consciousness, including the perspectives of the Indian philosopher and guru Sri Aurobindo (1872–1950) (see Aurobindo 1972) and the Mother, the German-Swiss philosopher Jean Gebser (1905–1973) (see Feuerstein 1987), the American psychologist Ken Wilber (b. 1949) (see Wilber 2000, 2006), and the British writer and philosopher Aldous Huxley (1894–1963) (see Huxley 1962). Each of these contributions points to a participatory universe in which mechanisms of individual change involve intersubjectivity and critical inquiry. Consistent with Bohm's implicate order (2002) and Young's reflexive universe (1976), these analyses of integral consciousness support Krishnamurti's radical assertions of relationality and the participatory nature of transformation.

Krishnamurti's approach to meditation also aligns with the goals of humanistic psychology (Rogers 1980) and transpersonal psychology (Ferrer 2002), as all seek to rid us of unexamined assumptions about ourselves and conditioned processes of perception and cognition. Krishnamurti's approach is also aligned with the humanistic and transpersonal goals of development of being, reliance on direct experience, and unmediated awareness of what exists. However, Krishnamurti's approach to meditation contradicts any psychological system that encourages simple "thinking about" oneself in images or words or any religious or clinical worldview that promotes internal change through evolutionary or incremental advances in self-understanding. It also challenges "clinical" and "therapeutic applications" of meditation.

Krishnamurti's teaching about the possibilities of change is radically individualistic. He has no use for the structures of institutions and traditions that keep us in a place of ignorance regarding our true nature. In fact, conventional structures, whether cognitive or social, are part of our problem. From these structures, we accept conventional, thus secondary, definitions of who we are, individually and collectively, but we never learn, really learn, about ourselves firsthand. Through genetic conditioning, social programming, and continuous reinforcement, we identify ourselves as autonomous individuals, members of groups, and independent agents of action. All of this is a fiction, an illusion, according to Krishnamurti.

The aim and responsibility of human life is to rid ourselves of illusion, through careful examination of how the brain and mind operate. When the mind becomes completely attentive, not bound by the images of thought, then real awareness and real freedom occur. Relationships within the self and with others no longer depend upon images of self and images of others. One moves beyond self-hypnosis and illusion into meditation and into a clarity of mind that is "the only revolution" (Krishnamurti 1970a).

In summation, we have examined how Krishnamurti's teaching presages current inquiries into ontology and epistemology in a number of fields, including psychology, consciousness studies, and philosophical paradigms. Although few scholars in these fields credit him with inspiration for their ideas, Krishnamurti, when compared to current scholarship, is prescient in his analysis of truth, as both *summum bonum* and epistemology. He demonstrates that critical inquiry valorizes learning through personal experience and invalidates our complete dependence upon conceptual universes and linguistic thought. His approach aligns with several postmodern paradigmatic shifts in religious studies, human sciences, and philosophy. He shows how emic knowledge claims are valid, why we need a re-sacralization of life, how integralism is essential to human flourishing, and how intersubjectivity is involved in the cocreated nature of knowledge.

Krishnamurti addresses the problems of every human being, regardless of nationality, religion, class, age, or psychology. He looks into the cause of human suffering, social division, and conflict. The way out of these problems, he finds, is through critical self-examination in which the mind transforms itself completely and totally. This is the deep, psychological revolution—the only revolution—that can bring about real transformation in individuals, relationships, and society. We see that Krishnamurti's teaching, although completed almost a half century ago, remains in conversation with leading thinkers in many fields and his insights remain useful, if not essential, for our transformation. In terms of the comparative study of contemplative practice and contemplative experience, and perhaps a dynamic and lived form of contemplative being, Krishnamurti inspires us to investigate the limitations of any system, whether specific techniques, religious authorities, or "contemplative traditions." Krishnamurti suggests that "truth is a pathless land" and that true meditation involves "freedom from the known." This is the light in oneself.

Notes

1. The Brahmin, or priestly, caste is the highest of the four hereditary social classes in traditional Indian society. Traditionally speaking, although the associated history and lived phenomenon are complex, each caste is based on birth, which is karmic.

2. An important Hindu god, Krishna is generally regarded as the eighth incarnation of the god Vishnu and thus a key focus of devotion among Vaishnavites, or devotees of Vishnu.

3. Ascended masters are similar to the highly evolved beings, *mahatmas*, who Blavatsky claims taught her the mysteries of the universe.

4. The Theosophical hierarchy of etheric or quasi-corporal entities described by Blavatsky is complex. At the head of the hierarchy is the Lord of the World, perceivable only to a select few in exalted states of consciousness. Beneath the Lord of the World (described as male) is the Buddha and below him a trinity of Lords: the Mahachohan, the Manu, and the Maitreya. The Maitreya is the World Teacher who incarnates by descending into a human body at various times in history. Two of his incarnations known to us were Jesus and Krishna. Below the Lord Maitreya is a tier of other masters, including Kuthumi and El Morya. According to Blavatsky, this lowest rung on the etheric hierarchy contains entities who keep their ancient bodies and live in a remote region of Tibet, where she claims to have lived and studied (Lutyens 1975, 9–12; Vernon 2000, 12–13).

5. Hatha Yoga (Skt.: forceful union) is the practice of physical postures, breathing techniques, and movements undertaken to transform the human body to make it a worthy vehicle for self-realization. The union that is *yoga* is a yoke that unites body and mind, material and spirit, and masculine and feminine.

6. Shambhala is a popular press specializing in "spirituality" and "wisdom literature" founded by students of the Tibetan Buddhist teacher Chögyam Trungpa (1939–1987).

7. For an excellent discussion of Krishnamurti's criticism of meditation practices, see Linda E. Patrik's unpublished paper "Perilous Sitting," which was presented at the Birth Centenary of Krishnamurti, University of Miami, Ohio, May 1995.

8. Krishnamurti agrees that most human beings are characterized by high degrees of enculturation, social conditioning, and personal habituation. At the same time, in contrast to conventional social constructivist views, he holds that deconditioning is possible. There is a "higher" state of consciousness, pure consciousness, and a direct form of experiencing in which one is present to the immediacy of the moment. In his famous phrase, one may realize "freedom from the known."

Works Cited and Further Reading

Aurobindo, Sri. 1972. *The Synthesis of Yoga*. Pondicherry: All India Press.
Blavatsky, Helena Petrovna. 1877. *Isis Unveiled*. New York: J. W. Bouton.
———. 1888. *The Secret Doctrine: The Synthesis of Science, Religion and Philosophy*. London: Theosophical Publishing Company.
Bohm, David. 1985. *Unfolding Meaning: A Weekend of Dialogue*. London and New York: Routledge.
———. 1994. *Thought as a System*. London and New York: Routledge.
———. 1996. *On Dialogue*. London and New York: Routledge.
———. 2002. *Wholeness and the Implicate Order*. London and New York: Routledge.
Buber, Martin. 1970. *I and Thou*. Translated by Walter Kaufmann. New York: Simon & Schuster.
Campbell, Bruce F. 1980. *Ancient Wisdom Revived: A History of the Theosophical Movement*. Berkeley: University of California Press.
Combs, Allan. 2009. *Consciousness Explained Better: Towards an Integral Understanding of the Multifaceted Nature of Consciousness*. St. Paul: Paragon House.
De Purucker, Gottfried. 1979. *Fundamentals of the Esoteric Philosophy*. Edited by A. Trevor Barker. Pasadena: Theosophical University Press.
De Quincey, Christian. 2005. *Radical Knowing: Understanding Consciousness through Relationship*. Rochester: Park Street Press.
———. 2008. *Consciousness from Zombies to Angels: The Shadow and the Light of Knowing Who You Are*. Rochester: Park Street Press.
———. 2010. *Radical Nature: The Soul of Matter*. Rochester: Park Street Press.

Faivre, Antoine, and Jacob Needleman, eds. 1995. *Modern Esoteric Spirituality.* New York: Crossroad.
Feng, Gia-fu, and Jane English. 1974. *Chuang Tsu: Inner Chapters.* New York: Vintage.
Ferrer, Jorge. 2002. *Revisioning Transpersonal Theory: A Participatory Vision of Human Spirituality.* Albany: State University of New York Press.
Ferrer, Jorge N., and Jacob H. Sherman, eds. 2008. *The Participatory Turn: Spirituality, Mysticism, Religious Studies.* Albany: State University of New York Press.
Feuerstein, Georg. 1987. *Structures of Consciousness: The Genius of Jean Gebser.* Lower Lake: Integral Publishing.
Gergen, Kenneth. 2009. *An Invitation to Social Construction.* 2nd ed. Thousand Oaks: Sage.
Godwin, Joscelyn. 1994. *The Theosophical Enlightenment.* Albany: State University of New York Press.
Heron, John. 1996. *Co-operative Inquiry: Research into the Human Condition.* Thousand Oaks: Sage.
Heron, John, and Peter Reason. 1997. "A Participatory Inquiry Paradigm." *Qualitative Inquiry* 3: 274–94.
Holroyd, Stuart. 1980. *The Quest of the Quiet Mind: The Philosophy of Krishnamurti.* Wellingborough: Aquarian Press.
Huxley, Aldous. 1962. *The Perennial Philosophy.* Cleveland: World Publishing.
James, William. 1929 (1902). *The Varieties of Religious Experience.* New York: Modern Library.
———. 1996 (1911). *Some Problems of Philosophy: A Beginning of an Introduction to Philosophy.* Lincoln: University of Nebraska Press.
Jayakar, Pupul. 1986. *Krishnamurti: A Biography.* New York: Penguin.
Jones, Constance A. 1997. "J. Krishnamurti on the Religious Life." In *Spiritual Traditions: Essential Ways for Living,* edited by David Singh, n.p. Bangalore: United Theological College.
———. 2010. "Krishnamurti Foundations." In *Religions of the World: A Comprehensive Encyclopedia of Beliefs and Practices,* 2nd ed., edited by Gordon Melton and Martin Baumann, 4: 1661–63. 4 vols. Santa Barbara: ABC-Clio.
Jones, Constance A., and James D. Ryan. 2007. *Encyclopedia of Hinduism.* New York: Facts on File.
Krishnamurti, Jiddu. 1913–1915. *Autobiography.* (A 2,000 word unpublished manuscript written in 1913–1915). Adyar: Archives of the Theosophical Society.
———. 1949. "Fifth Talk at Rajghat: The Mirror of Relationship." www.jkrishnamurti.org/krishnamurti-teachings/view-text.php?tid=305&chid=4635&w=%20%22relationship%22. Accessed on June 1, 2014.
———. 1960. *Commentaries on Living, from the Notebooks of J. Krishnamurti.* Edited by D. Rajagopal. 3 vols. Wheaton: Theosophical Publishing House.
———. 1969. *Freedom from the Known.* New York: Harper and Row.
———. 1970a. *The Only Revolution.* New York: Harper and Row.
———. 1970b. *The Second Penguin Krishnamurti Reader.* Edited by Mary Lutyens. New York: Penguin.
———. 1972. *You Are the World.* Madras: Krishnamurti Foundation India.
———. 1973. *The Awakening of Intelligence.* San Francisco: Harper.
———. 1978. *The First and Last Freedom.* London: Victor Gollancz.
———. 1981. *Education and the Significance of Life.* San Francisco: Harper and Row.
———. 1991. *A Wholly Different Way of Living.* London: Victor Gollancz.
———. 1999. *This Light in Oneself: True Meditation.* Boston: Shambhala.
———. 2002 (1979). *Meditations.* Boston: Shambhala.
Krishnamurti, Jiddu (Alcyone). 2009. *At the Feet of the Master: Selected Writings of J. Krishnamurti.* Sacramento: Ancient Wisdom Publications.
Krishnamurti, Jiddu, and David Bohm. 1985. *The Ending of Time.* San Francisco: Harper.
———. 1986. *The Future of Humanity: A Conversation.* New York: Harper and Row.
Krishnamurti Foundation of America Archives (KFAA). wwwkfa.org/archives.php. Accessed on June 1, 2014.
Lincoln, Yvonna, Susan Lynham, and Egon Guba. 2011. "Paradigmatic Controversies, Contradictions, and Emerging Confluences, Revisited." In *The Sage Handbook of Qualitative Research,* 4th ed., edited by Norman Denzin and Yvonna Lincoln, 97–128. Thousand Oaks: Sage Publications.

Lutyens, Mary. 1975. *Krishnamurti: The Years of Awakening*. New York: Farrar, Straus and Giroux.

———. 1983. *Krishnamurti: The Years of Fulfillment*. New York: Farrar, Straus and Giroux.

———. 1985. *Krishnamurti: The Open Door*. New York: Farrar, Straus and Giroux.

———. 1990. *Krishnamurti: His Life and Death*. New York: St. Martin's.

Mehta, Rohit. 1979. *J. Krishnamurti and the Nameless Experience*. 3rd ed. Delhi: Motilal Banarsidass.

———. 1987. *The Secret of Self-Transformation: A Synthesis of Tantra and Yoga*. Delhi: Motilal Banarsidass.

Melton, J. Gordon 2009. *Melton's Encyclopedia of American Religions*. 8th ed. San Francisco: Gale.

Murphet, Howard 1975. *When Daylight Comes: A Biography of Helena Petrovna Blavatsky*. Wheaton: Theosophical Publishing House.

Ravindra, Ravi. 1995. *Krishnamurti: Two Birds on One Tree*. Wheaton: Theosophical Publishing House.

Rogers, Carl. 1980. *A Way of Being*. Boston: Houghton Mifflin.

Sabzevary, A. 2008. "Choiceless Awareness through Psychological Freedom in the Philosophy of Krishnamurti." PhD diss., California Institute of Integral Studies.

Sanat, Aryel. 1999. *The Inner Life of Krishnamurti*. Wheaton: Theosophical Publishing House.

Schuon, Frithjof. 1984. *The Transcendent Unity of Religions*. Wheaton: Theosophical Publishing House.

Sloss, Radha Rajagopal. 1991. *Lives in the Shadow with J. Krishnamurti*. Reading: Addison-Wesley.

Spretnak, Charlene. 2011. *Relational Reality: New Discoveries of Interrelatedness That Are Transforming the Modern World*. Topsham: Green Horizon.

Vaysse, Jean. 1978. *Toward Awakening: An Approach to the Teaching Left by Gurdjieff*. San Francisco: Far West.

Vernon, Roland. 2002. *Star in the East: Krishnamurti, the Invention of a Messiah*. Boulder: Sentient Publications.

Wilber, Ken. 2000. *Integral Psychology*. Boston: Shambhala.

———. 2006. *Integral Spirituality*. Boston: Shambhala.

Young, Arthur. 1976. *The Reflexive Universe: Evolution of Consciousness*. New York: Delacorte Press.

*This Light in Oneself: True Meditation**

J. Krishnamurti (1895–1986)

Selected and Annotated by Constance A. Jones

A New Consciousness[1]

A new consciousness and a totally new morality are necessary to bring about a radical change in the present culture and social structure. This is obvious, yet the Left and the Right and the revolutionary seem to disregard it. Any dogma, any formula, any ideology is part of the old consciousness; they are the fabrications of thought whose activity is fragmentations—the Left, the Right, the center. This activity will inevitably lead to bloodshed of the Right or of the Left or to totalitarianism. This is what is going on around us. One sees the necessity of social, economic, and moral change but the response is from the old consciousness, thought being the principal actor. The mess, the confusion, and the misery that human beings have got into are within the area of the old consciousness, and without changing that profoundly, every human activity [2]—political, economic, or religious—will only bring us to the destruction of each other and of the earth. This is so obvious to the sane.

One has to be a light to oneself; this light is the law. There is no other law. All the other laws are made by thought and so are fragmentary and contradictory. To be a light to oneself is not to follow the light of another, however reasonable, logical, historical, and however convincing. You cannot be a light to yourself if you are in the dark shadows of authority, of dogma, of conclusion. Morality is not put together by thought; it is not the outcome of environmental pressure, it is not of yesterday, of tradition. Morality is the child of love and love is not desire and pleasure. Sexual or sensory enjoyment is not love.

Freedom is to be a light to oneself; then it is not an abstraction, a thing conjured up by thought. Actual freedom is freedom from dependency, attachment, from the craving for experience. Freedom from the very structure of thought is to be a light to oneself. In this light all action takes place and thus is never contradictory. Contradiction exists only when that light is separate from action, when the actor is separate from action. The ideal, the principle, is the barren movement of thought and it cannot coexist with this light; one denies the other. Where the observer is, this

---

*These selections, which were chosen in consultation with Louis Komjathy, are used with permission from the Krishnamurti Foundation Trust (Brockwood Park, Hampshire, England; www.kfoundation.org) and Shambhala Publications. I am especially grateful to Jerome Blanche, Jonathan Green, Jaap Sluijter, and Duncan Toms for their assistance with and support for this chapter and the larger project. Edited by Roy McCoy of the Krishnamurti Foundation, the texts were originally published in *This Light in Oneself: True Meditation* (Shambhala, 1999), which is an English-language collection of a variety of previously unpublished talks given by J. Krishnamurti between 1968 and 1983 (see Krishnamurti 1999, 134). Numbers in brackets indicate page numbers in the original publication, with the first appearance corresponding to the beginning of a new page. J. Krishnamurti, *This Light in Oneself: True Meditation*, copyright 1996 by Krishnamurti Foundation Trust, Ltd. Reprinted by arrangement with The Permissions Company, Inc., on behalf of Shambhala Publications, Boston, Massachusetts. www.shambhala.com.

1. From Krishnamurti's journal (September 24, 1973).

light, this love, is not. The structure of the observer is put together by thought, which is never new, never free. There is no "how," no system, no practice. There is only the seeing that is the doing. You have to see, not through the eyes of another. This light, this law, is neither yours nor that of another. There is only light. This is love. [Pp. 1–2.]

The Miracle of Attention[2]

Can we put away all ideas, concepts, and theories and find out for ourselves if there is something sacred—not the word, because the word is not the thing, the description is not the described—to see if there is something real, not an imagination, not something illusory, fanciful, not a myth but a reality that can never be destroyed, a truth that is abiding?

To find that out, to come upon it, all authority of any kind, especially spiritual, must be totally set aside, because authority implies conformity, obedience, acceptance of a certain pattern. A mind must be capable of standing alone, of being a light to itself. Following another, belonging to a group, following methods of meditation laid down by an authority, by tradition, is totally irrelevant to one who investigates into the question of whether there is something eternal, [4] timeless, something that is not measurable by thought, that operates in our daily life. If it does not function as part of our daily life, then meditation is an escape and absolutely useless. All this implies that one must stand alone. There is a difference between isolation and aloneness, between loneliness and being able to stand by yourself clearly, unconfused, uncontaminated.

We are concerned with the whole of life, not one segment of it, one fragment of it, but the whole of what you do, what you think, what you feel, how you behave. As we are concerned with the whole of life, we cannot possibly take a fragment that is thought, and through thought resolve all of our problems. Thought may give authority to itself to bring all the other fragments together, but thought has created these fragments. We are conditioned to think in terms of progress, of gradual achievement. People believe in psychological evolution, but is there such a thing as the "me" psychologically achieving anything other than the projection of thought?

To find out if there is something that is not projected by thought, that is not an illusion, a myth, we must ask whether thought can be controlled, whether thought can be held in abeyance, whether thought can be suppressed, so that the mind is completely still. Control implies the controller and the controlled, doesn't it? Who is the controller? Is that not also created by thought, one of the fragments of thought, which has assumed authority as the controller? If you see the truth of that, then the controller is the controlled, the experiencer is the experienced, the thinker is the thought. They are not separate entities. If you understand that, then there is no necessity to control.

[5] If there is no controller because the controller is the controlled, then what happens? When there is a division between the controller and the controlled, there is conflict, there is a wastage of energy. When the controller is the controlled, there is no wastage of energy. Then there is the accumulation of all that energy that had been dissipated in suppression, in resistance, brought about through division as the controller and the controlled. When there is no division, you have

---

2. Public talk delivered at the Masonic Auditorium (1111 California Street) in San Francisco, California, on March 25, 1975.

all that energy to go beyond that which you thought must be controlled. In meditation it must be clearly understood that there is no control of thought, no disciplining of thought, because the one who disciplines thought is a fragment of thought, the one who controls thought is a fragment of thought. If you see the truth of that, then you have all the energy that has been dissipated through comparison, through control, through suppression, to go beyond what actually is.

We are asking whether the mind can be absolutely still, because that which is still has great energy. It is the summation of energy. Can the mind—which is chattering, always in movement; which is thought always looking back, remembering, accumulating knowledge, constantly changing—be completely still? Have you ever tried to find out if thought can be still? How are you going to find out how to bring about this stillness of thought? You see, thought is time and time is movement, time is measurement. In daily life you measure, you compare, both physically and psychologically. That is measurement, comparison means measurement. Can you live without comparison in daily life? Can you cease to compare altogether, not in meditation but in [6] daily life? You do compare when you are choosing from two materials, this cloth or that cloth, when you compare two cars, when you compare parts of knowledge, but psychologically, *inwardly* we compare ourselves with others. When that comparison ceases, as it must, then can we stand completely alone? That is what is implied when there is no comparison—which doesn't mean that you vegetate. So, in daily life, can you live without comparison? Do it once and you will find what is implied in that. Then you throw off a tremendous burden; and when you throw off a burden that is unnecessary you have energy.

Have you ever given attention to something totally? Are you giving attention to what the speaker is saying? Or are you listening with a comparative mind that has already acquired certain knowledge and is comparing what is being said to what you already know? Are you interpreting what is being said according to your own knowledge, your own tendency, your own prejudice? That is not attention, is it? If you give complete attention, with your body, with your nerves, with your eyes, with your ears, with your mind, with your whole being, there is no center from which you are attending, there is only attention. That attention is complete silence.

Please do listen to this. Nobody is going to tell you all these things, unfortunately, so please give your attention to what is being said, so that the very act of listening is a miracle of attention. In that attention there is no border, there is no frontier, and therefore there is no direction. There is only attention, and when there is that attention there is no me and you, there is no duality, there is no observer and the [7] observed. And this is not possible when the mind is moving in a particular direction.

We are educated and conditioned to move according to directions, from here to there. We have an idea, a belief, a concept, a formula that there is a reality, that there is bliss, that there is something beyond thought, and we fix that as a goal, as an ideal, a direction, and walk in that direction. When you walk in a direction there is no space. When you are concentrated and walk or think in a particular direction, you have no space in the mind. You have no space when your mind is crowded with attachments, with fears, with the pursuit of pleasures, with the desire for power, position. Then the mind is overcrowded, it has no space. Space is necessary, and where there is attention there is no direction, but rather space.

Now, meditation implies no movement at all. That means the mind is totally still, it is not moving in any direction. There is no movement, movement being time, movement being thought. If you see the truth of it—not the verbal description of it but the truth, which cannot be described—then there is that quiet, still mind. And it is necessary to have a quiet mind—but not in order to sleep longer, or to do your job better, or to get more money!

Most people's lives are empty, poor. Although they may have a great deal of knowledge their lives are poor, contradictory, not whole, unhappy. All that is poverty, and they waste their lives trying to become rich inwardly, cultivating various forms of virtue and all the rest of that silly nonsense. Not that virtue is not necessary; but virtue is order, and order can only be understood when you have gone into the [8] disorder in yourself. We do lead disorderly lives; that is a fact. Disorder is the contradiction, the confusion, the various assertive desires, saying one thing and doing another, having ideals, and the division between you and the ideals. All that is disorder, and when you are aware of it and give your whole attention to it, out of that attention comes order, which is virtue—a living thing, not a thing contrived, practiced, and made ugly.

Meditation in daily life is the transformation of the mind, a psychological revolution so that we live a daily life—not in theory, not as an ideal, but in every movement of that life—in which there is compassion, love, and the energy to transcend all the pettiness, the narrowness, the shallowness. When the mind is quiet—really still, not *made* still through desire, through will—then there is a totally different kind of movement that is not of time.

You know, to go into that would be absurd. It would be a verbal description and therefore not real. What is important is the art of meditation. One sense of the word "art" is to put everything in its right place, putting everything in our life, *in our daily life*, in the right place, so that there is no confusion. And when there is order, righteous behavior, and a mind that is completely quiet in our daily life, then the mind will find out for itself whether there is the immeasurable or not. Until you find that which is the highest form of holiness, life is dull, meaningless. And that is why right meditation is absolutely necessary, so that the mind is made young, fresh, innocent. *Innocent* means not able to be hurt. All that is implied in meditation that is not divorced from our daily living. In the very understanding of our daily living, [9] meditation is necessary. That is, to attend completely to what you are doing—when you talk to somebody, the way you walk, the way you think, what you think—to give your attention to that is part of meditation.

Meditation is not an escape. It is not something mysterious. Out of meditation comes a life that is holy, a life that is sacred. And therefore you treat all things as sacred. [Pp. 3–9.]

This Light in Oneself[3]

One can talk endlessly, piling words upon words, coming to various conclusions, but out of all the verbal confusion, if there is one clear action, that action is worth ten thousand words. Most of us are afraid to act, because we are confused, disorderly, contradictory and miserable. We hope, despite this confusion, this disarray, that some kind of clarity may come into being, a clarity that is not from another, a clarity that can never be clouded over, a clarity that is not given or induced or that can be taken away, a clarity that keeps itself without any effort of will, without any motive, a clarity that has no end and therefore no beginning.

---

3. Public talk delivered at the Congres Centrum (Weesperstraat 113) in Amsterdam, Netherlands, on May 19, 1968.

Most of us, if we are at all aware of our inward confusion, do desire this, we want such clarity. Let us see if we can come upon this clarity, so that your mind and your heart are [17] very clear, undisturbed, with no problems and no fear. It would be immensely worthwhile to see if one could be a light to oneself, a light that has no dependence on another and that is completely free. One can explore a problem intellectually, analytically, taking off layer after layer of confusion and disorder, taking many days, many years, perhaps a whole lifetime, and even then perhaps not find it. You can do that analytical process of cause and effect, or perhaps you can sidestep all that completely and come to it directly, without the intermediary of any authority of the intellect.

To do that requires meditation. That word, *meditation*, has become rather spoilt; like *love*, it has been besmirched. But it is a lovely word; it has a great deal of meaning. There is a great deal of beauty, not in the word itself but in the meaning behind the word. We are going to see for ourselves if we can come upon the state of mind that is always in meditation. To lay the foundation for that meditation one must understand what living is, living and dying. The understanding of life and the extraordinary meaning of death *is* meditation. It is not searching out some deep mystical experience, not a constant repetition of a series of words, however hallowed, however ancient. That only makes the mind quiet, but it also makes it rather dull, stupid, mesmerized. You might just as well take a tranquilizer, which is much easier. The repetition of words,[4] self-hypnosis, the following of a system or a method, is not meditation.

To experience implies a process of recognition. I had an experience yesterday, and it has given me either pleasure or pain. To be entirely with that experience one must recognize it. Recognition is of something that has already happened [18] before, and therefore experience is never new. Truth can never be experienced: that is the beauty of it, it is always new, it is never what happened yesterday. What happened yesterday, the incident of yesterday, must be completely forgotten or gone through, finished with, yesterday. To carry that over as an experience to be measured in terms of achievement, or to convey that extraordinary something to impress or convince others, seems utterly silly. One must be very cautious, guarded, about the word *experience*, because you can only remember an experience when it has already happened to you. That means there must be a center, a thinker, an observer who retains, holds the thing that is over. You cannot possibly experience truth. As long as there is a center of recollection as the "me," as the thinker, then truth is not. And when another says that he has an experience of the real, distrust him: don't accept his authority.

We all want to accept somebody who promises something, because we have no light in ourselves. But nobody can give you that light: no guru, no teacher, no savior, *no one*. We have accepted many authorities in the past, we have put our faith in others, and they have either exploited us or utterly failed. So one must distrust, deny all spiritual authority. Nobody can give us the light that never dies.

To follow another is to imitate. To follow implies not only denying one's own clarity, one's own investigation, one's integrity and honesty, but it also implies that in following, your motive is a reward. Truth is not a reward! If one is to understand truth, every form of reward and

---

4. Here Krishnamurti appears to be alluding to the use of *mantra*s (sacred sounds) in specific forms of Indian and specifically Hindu meditation. Given the date of the present talk, he may also be thinking of Maharishi Mahesh's (1918–2008) Transcendental Meditation (TM) movement, which gained in popularity in the 1950s and 1960s.

punishment must be totally set aside. Authority implies fear, and to discipline oneself for fear of not gaining what an exploiter says [19] in the name of truth or experience is to deny one's own clarity and honesty. If you say that you *must* meditate, that you must follow a certain path, a certain system, obviously you are conditioning yourself according to that system or method. Perhaps you will get what the method promises, but it will be nothing but ashes, for the motive is achievement, success; and at the root of that is fear.

Between yourself and myself there is no authority. The speaker has no authority whatsoever. He is not trying to convince you of anything or asking you to follow. When you follow somebody, you destroy that person. The disciple destroys the master and the master destroys the disciple. You can see this happening historically and in daily life: when the wife or the husband dominate each other they destroy each other. In that there is no freedom, there is no beauty, there is no love.

If we do not lay the right foundation, a foundation of order, of clear line and depth, then thought must inevitably become tortuous, deceptive, unreal, and therefore valueless. The laying of this foundation, this order, is the beginning of meditation. Our life, the daily life that we lead from the moment we are born until we die, through marriage, children, jobs, achievements, is a battlefield, not only within ourselves but also outwardly, in the family, in the office, in the group, in the community. Our life is a constant struggle. That is what we call living. Pain, fear, despair, anxiety, with enormous sorrow constantly our shadow, that is our life. Perhaps a small minority can observe this disorder without finding external excuses for this confusion, although there are external causes. Perhaps a small minority can observe the disorder, [20] know it, look at it not only at the conscious level but also at a deeper level, and neither accept nor deny that disorder, confusion, the frightening mess in ourselves and the world. It is always the small minority that bring about a vital change.

A great deal has been written about the unconscious mind, especially in the West. Extraordinary significance has been given to it. But it is as trivial, as shallow as the conscious mind. You can observe it yourself. If you observe you will see that what is called the unconscious is the residue of the race, of the culture, of the family, of your own motives and appetites. It is there, hidden. And the conscious mind is occupied with the daily routine of life, going to the office, sex, and so on. To give importance to the one or to the other seems utterly sterile. Both have very little meaning, except that the conscious mind has to have technological knowledge in order to earn a livelihood.

This constant battle, both within, at the deeper level, as well as at the superficial level, is the way of our life. It is a way of disorder, a way of disarray, contradiction, misery, and for a mind caught in that to try to meditate is meaningless, infantile. To meditate is to bring about order in this confusion; and not through effort, because every effort distorts the mind. To see truth the mind must be absolutely clear, without any distortion, without any compulsion, without any direction.

So the foundation must be laid. That is, there must be virtue. Order is virtue. This virtue has nothing whatever to do with the social morality that we accept. Society has imposed a certain morality on us, but society is the product of [21] every human being. Society with its morality says that you can be greedy; that you can kill another in the name of God, in the name of your country, in the name of an ideal; that you can be competitive, envious, within the law. Such morality is no morality at all. You must totally deny that morality within yourself in order to be virtuous. That is the beauty of virtue; virtue is not a habit, it is not something that you practice day after day. That is mechanical, a routine, without meaning, but to be virtuous means to know what disorder is, the disorder that is the contradiction within ourselves, the tyranny of various pleasures and desires and ambitions, greed, envy, fear. Those are the causes of disorder, within ourselves and outwardly. To be aware of that is to be in contact with disorder. And you can only be in contact with it when you don't deny it, when you don't find excuses for it, when you don't blame others for it.

Order isn't a thing that you establish—in the denial of disorder *there is* order. Virtue, which is order, comes out of knowing the whole nature and structure of disorder. This is fairly simple if we observe in ourselves how utterly disorderly and contradictory we are: we hate, and we think we love—that is the beginning of disorder, of duality; and virtue is not the outcome of duality. Virtue is a living thing, to be picked up daily; it is not the repetition of something that you called virtue yesterday. That is mechanical, worthless. So there must be order. And that is part of meditation.

Order means beauty; and there is so little beauty in our life. Beauty is not man-made; it is not in a picture, however modern or ancient; it is not in a building, in a statue, in a cloud, in a leaf, or on the water. Beauty is where there is [22] order—a mind that is not confused, that is absolutely orderly. And there can be order only where there is total self-denial, when the "me" has no importance whatsoever. The ending of the "me" is part of meditation; that is the *only* meditation.

You have lived in thought. You have given tremendous importance to thinking, but thinking is old, thinking is never new, thinking is the continuation of memory. If you have lived there, obviously there is some kind of continuity. And it is a continuity that is dead, over, finished. It is something old, but only that which ends can have something new. So dying is very important to understand. To die to everything that one knows. Have you ever tried it? To be free from the known, to be free from your memory, even for a few days; to be free from your pleasure, without any argument, without any fear; to die to your family, to your house, to your name; to become completely anonymous. It is only the person who is completely anonymous who is in a state of nonviolence, who has no violence. So die every day, not as an idea, but actually. Do do it sometime.

One has collected so much, not only books, houses, the bank account, but inwardly: the memories of insults, the memories of flattery, the memories of your own particular experiences, neurotic achievements which give you a position. To die to all that without argument, without discussion, without any fear, just to give it up; do it some time and you will see. To do it psychologically—not giving up your wife, your clothes, your husband, your children, or your house, but inwardly—is not to be attached to anything. In that there is great beauty. After all, that is love, isn't it? Love [23] is not attachment. When there is attachment there is fear. And fear inevitably becomes authoritarian, possessive, oppressive, dominating.

Meditation is the understanding of life, which is to bring about order. Order is virtue, which is light. This light is not to be lit by another, however experienced, however clever, however erudite, however spiritual. Nobody on earth or in heaven can light that, except yourself, in your own understanding and meditation.

To die to everything within oneself! For love is innocent and fresh, young and clear. Then, if one has established this order, this virtue, this beauty, this light in oneself, one can go beyond. This means that the mind, having laid order, which is not of thought, then becomes utterly quiet, silent—naturally, without any force, without any discipline. And in the light of that silence all action can take place, living daily from that silence.

And if one were lucky enough to have gone that far, then in that silence there is quite a different movement, which is not of time, which is not of words, which is not measurable by thought, because it is always new. It is that immeasurable something that man has everlastingly sought. But you have to come upon it, it cannot be given to you. It is not the word, not the symbol. Those are destructive. But for it to come, you must have complete order, beauty, love. Therefore you must die to every thing that you know psychologically, so that your mind is clear, not tortured, so that it sees things as they are, both outwardly and inwardly. [Pp. 16–23.]

The Summation of All Energy[5]

Thought is limited because knowledge is limited, and whatever action thought does, whatever it invents, must be limited. One must have a clear mind and a clear heart to understand what a religious mind is. To find out what a religious mind is, one must totally negate all the rituals and symbols invented by thought. If you deny, negate, that which is false, then you find what is true. You negate all the systems of meditation because you yourself see that these systems are invented by thought. They are put together by man. Because life is so shoddy, so uncertain, we want to have some deep satisfaction, some love, something that is stable, permanent, everlasting. We want something that is immutable, nonchanging, and we [32] think we will get it if we do certain things. Those things are invented by thought and thought in itself is contradictory, so any form of structure in meditation put together by thought is not meditation. This means a total denial, total negation of everything that man has invented psychologically. Not technologically, you can't deny that, but it is negation of all the things that man has created and written about in search of truth. Wanting to escape from our weariness, sorrow, and agony, we fall into that trap. So one must totally deny all postures, all breathing exercises, all activities of thought.

When all that is negated, then the question arises: Can thought come to an end? That is, thought as time, can time have a stop? Not the external time, but the time that is becoming—becoming enlightened, becoming nonviolent, a vain man trying to become humble. This whole pattern of becoming psychologically is time. Time is also thought. Can thought come to an end? Not through discipline, not through control, because who is that entity who disciplines? There is always in us this sense of duality: the controller and the controlled, the observer and the observed, the experiencer and the experienced, the thinker and the thought. There is always this divisive duality in us. Probably it is brought over from physical observation. There, there is duality: light and shade, dark and light, man, woman, and so on. We have probably brought that over into the field of the psyche. So is there a controller that is different from the controlled? Please go into this very carefully.

In classical, ordinary meditation, the gurus who propagate it are concerned with the controller and the controlled. They say to control your thoughts because thereby you will [33] end thought,

---

5. Public talk delivered at an unknown location in Bombay (Mumbai), India, on February 5, 1982.

or have only one thought. But we are inquiring into who the controller is. You might say, "It is the higher self," "It is the witness," "It is something that is not thought," but the controller *is* part of thought. Obviously. So the controller is the controlled. Thought has divided itself as the controller and that which it is going to control, but it is still the activity of thought. It is a strange phenomenon that thought invents gods and then it worships them. That is self worship.

So when one understands that the whole movement of the controller is the controlled, then there is no control at all. This is a dangerous thing to say to people who have not understood it. We are not advocating no control. We are saying that where there is the observation that the controller is the controlled, that the thinker is the thought, and if you remain with that whole truth, with that reality, without any further interference of thought, then you have a totally different kind of energy.

Meditation is the summation of all energy. Not the energy created by thought through friction, but the energy of a state of mind in which all conflict has completely ceased. The word *religion* probably means gathering together all your energy so that you can act diligently.[6] A religious mind acts diligently, that is, caring, watching, observing. In that observation there is affection, compassion.

Concentration is another invention of thought. In school you are told to concentrate on the book. You learn to concentrate, trying to exclude other thoughts, trying to prevent yourself from looking out of the window. In concentration there is resistance, narrowing down the enormous energy of [34] life to a certain point. Whereas in attention, which is a form of awareness in which there is no choice, a choiceless awareness, all your energy is there. When you have such attention there is no center from which you are attending, whereas in concentration there is always a center from which you are attending.

We ought also to talk together about space. The way we live in the modern world, one apartment on top of another, we have no space physically. There is no space outwardly, and inwardly we have no space at all because our brains are constantly chattering. Meditation is to understand or come upon the space that is not put together by thought, the space that is not space as the "me" and the "not me." That space is not invented space, the idea of space, but actual space; that is, vast distance, limitless distance, unhindered observation, perpetual movement without any barrier. That is vast space, and in that vast space there is no time, time as thought has stopped long ago, because of the observation that while thought has its own space, it has not that other vast space. When we want to learn a technique, thought as knowledge, time, needs space.

Memory is necessary at a certain level, but not at the psychological level. When there is always the awareness that cleanses the brain of any accumulation as memory, then the "me" progressing, the "me" achieving, the "me" in conflict, comes to an end because you have put your house in order. The brain has its own rhythm, but that rhythm has been distorted by our extravagance, by our ill-treating the brain through drugs, through faith, through belief, through drink, smoking. It has lost its pristine vitality.

[35] Meditation is the sense of total comprehension of the whole of life, and from that there is right action. Meditation is absolute silence of the mind. Not relative silence or the silence that

---

6. Under one interpretation, "religion" derives from the Latin *religio*, which may be related to *ligare* (lit., to bind or to connect).

thought has projected and structured, but the silence of order, which is freedom. Only in that total, complete, unadulterated silence is that which is truth, which is from everlasting to everlasting.

This is meditation. [Pp. 31–35.]

What Is Creation?[7]

What is the origin of all existence, from the minutest cell to the most complex brain? Was there a beginning at all, and is there an end to all this? What is creation? To probe into something totally unknown, not preconceived, and not be caught in any sentimental, romantic illusion, there must be a quality of brain that is completely free from all its conditioning, from all its programming, from every kind of influence, and therefore highly sensitive and tremendously active. Is that possible? Is it possible to have a mind, a brain, that is extraordinarily alive, not caught in any form of routine, not mechanical? Do we have a brain in which there is no fear, no self-interest, no self-centered activity? Otherwise it is living in its own shadow all the time, it is living in its own tribal, limited environment, like an animal tied to a stake.

[46] A brain must have space. Space is not only a distance between here and there, space implies being without a center. If you have a center and you move away from the center to the periphery, however far the periphery is, it is still limited. So, space indicates no center and no periphery, no boundary. Have we a brain that doesn't belong to anything, is not attached to anything—to experience, conclusions, hopes, ideals—so that it is really, completely free? If you are burdened, you can't walk very far. If the brain is crude, vulgar, self-centered, it cannot have measureless space. And space indicates—one is using the word very, very carefully—emptiness.

We are trying to find out if it is possible to live in this world without any fear, without any conflict, with a tremendous sense of compassion, which demands a great deal of intelligence. You cannot have compassion without intelligence. And that intelligence is not the activity of thought. One cannot be compassionate if one is attached to a particular ideology, to a particular narrow tribalism, or to any religious concept, for those limit. And compassion can only come—be there—when there is the ending of sorrow, which is the ending of self-centered movement.

So space indicates emptiness, nothingness. And because there is *not a thing* put there by thought, that space has tremendous energy. So the brain must have the quality of complete freedom and space. That is, one must be nothing. We are all something: analysts, psychotherapists, doctors. That is all right, but when we are therapists, biologists, technicians, those very identifications limit the wholeness of the brain.

[47] Only when there is freedom and space can we ask what meditation is. Only when one has laid the foundation of order in life can one ask what true meditation is. There cannot be order if there is fear. There cannot be order if there is any kind of conflict. Our inward house must be in complete order, so there is great stability, with no waffling around. There is great strength in that stability. If the house is not in order, your meditation has very little meaning. You can invent any kind of illusion, any kind of enlightenment, any kind of daily discipline, it will still be limited, illusory, because it is born out of disorder. This is all logical, sane, rational;

---

7. Public talk delivered at Brockwood Park in Bramdean, Hampshire, England, on September 4, 1983. This place eventually became the location of the Brockwood Park School, Krishnamurti Centre, and Krishnamurti Foundation Trust.

it is not something the speaker has invented for you to accept. May I use the words *undisciplined order*? Unless there is order that is not disciplined order, meditation becomes very shallow and meaningless.

What is order? Thought cannot create psychological order because thought itself is disorder, because thought is based on knowledge, which is based on experience. All knowledge is limited, and so thought is also limited, and when thought tries to create order it brings about disorder. Thought has created disorder through the conflict between "what is" and "what should be," the actual and the theoretical. But there is only the actual and not the theoretical. Thought looks at the actual from a limited point of view, and therefore its action must inevitably create disorder. Do we see this as a truth, as a law, or just as an idea? Suppose I am greedy, envious; that is what is; the opposite is not. But the opposite has been created by human beings, by thought, as a means of understanding "what is" and also as a means of escaping from "what is." But there is only "what is," and when you [48] perceive "what is" without its opposite, then that very perception brings order.

Our house must be in order, and this order cannot be brought about by thought. Thought creates its own discipline: do this, don't do that; follow this, don't follow that; be traditional, don't be traditional. Thought is the guide through which one hopes to bring about order, but thought itself is limited, therefore it is bound to create disorder. If I keep on repeating that I am British, or that I am French, or that I am a Hindu, or a Buddhist, that tribalism is very limited, that tribalism causes great havoc in the world. We don't go to the root of it to end tribalism; we try to create better wars. Order can come into being only when thought, which is necessary in certain areas, has no place in the psychological world. The world itself is in order when thought is absent.

It is necessary to have a brain that is absolutely quiet. The brain has its own rhythm, is endlessly active, chattering from one subject to another, from one thought to another, from one association to another, from one state to another. It is constantly occupied. One is not aware of it generally, but when one is aware without any choice, choicelessly aware of this movement, then that very awareness, that very attention, ends the chattering. Please do it, and you will see how simple it all is.

The brain must be free, have space and psychological silence. You and I are talking to each other. Thought is being employed because we are speaking a language. But to speak out of silence. . . . There must be freedom from the word. Then the brain is utterly quiet, though it has its own rhythm.

[49] Then what is creation, what is the beginning of all this? We are inquiring into the origin of all life, not only our life, but the life of every living thing: the whales in the depths, the dolphins, the little fish, the minute cells, vast nature, the beauty of a tiger. From the most minute cell to the most complex human—with all his inventions, with all his illusions, with his superstitions, with his quarrels, with his wars, with his arrogance, vulgarity, with his tremendous aspirations, and his great depressions—what is the origin of all this?

Now, meditation is to come upon this. It is not that *you* come upon it. In that silence, in that quietness, in that absolute tranquility, is there a beginning? And if there is a beginning, there must be an ending. That which has a cause must end. Wherever there is a cause, there must be an end. That is a law, that is natural. So is there a causation at all for the creation of man, the creation of all the way of life? Is there a beginning of all this? How are we going to find out?

What is creation? Not of the painter, nor the poet, nor the man who makes something out of marble; those are all things manifested. Is there something that is not manifested? Is there something that, because it is not manifested, has no beginning and no end? That which is manifested has a beginning, has an end. We are manifestations. Not of divine something or other, we are the result of thousands of years of so-called evolution, growth, development, and we also come to an end. That which is manifested can always be destroyed, but that which is not, has no time.

We are asking if there is something beyond all time. It has been the inquiry of philosophers, scientists, and religious [50] people to find that which is beyond the measure of man, which is beyond time. Because if one can discover that, or see that, that is immortality. That is beyond death. Man has sought this, in various ways, in different parts of the world, through different beliefs, because when one discovers, realizes that, then life has no beginning and no end. It is beyond all concepts, beyond all hope. It is something immense.

Now, to come back to earth. You see, we never look at life, our own life, as a tremendous movement with a great depth, a vastness. We have reduced our life to such a shoddy little affair. And life is really the most sacred thing in existence. To kill somebody is the most irreligious horror, or to get angry, to be violent with somebody.

We never see the world as a whole because we are so fragmented, so terribly limited, so petty. We never have the feeling of wholeness, where the things of the sea, the things of the earth, nature, the sky, the universe, are part of us. Not imagined—you can go off into some kind of fancy and imagine that you are the universe, and then you become cuckoo. But break down this small, self-centered interest, have nothing of that, and from there you can move infinitely.

And meditation is this, not sitting cross-legged, or standing on your head, or doing whatever one does, but having the feeling of the complete wholeness and unity of life. And that can come only when there is love and compassion.

One of our difficulties is that we have associated love with pleasure, with sex, and for most of us love also means jealousy, anxiety, possessiveness, attachment. That is what we call love. Is love attachment? Is love pleasure? Is love desire? Is love the opposite of hate? If it is the opposite of hate, [51] then it is not love. All opposites contain their own opposites. When I try to *become* courageous, that courage is born out of fear. Love cannot have an opposite. Love cannot be where there is jealousy, ambition, aggressiveness.

And where there is the quality of love, from that arises compassion. Where there is that compassion, there is intelligence—but it is not the intelligence of self-interest, or the intelligence of thought, or the intelligence of a great deal of knowledge. Compassion has nothing to do with knowledge.

Only with compassion is there that intelligence that gives humanity security, stability, a vast sense of strength. [Pp. 45–51.]

To Live Without the Action of Will[8]

Meditation is not something that *you* do. Meditation is a movement into the whole question of our living: how we live, how we behave, whether we have fears, anxieties, sorrows; whether we

---

8. Public talk delivered at Brockwood Park on September 3, 1978.

are everlastingly pursuing pleasure; and whether we have built images about ourselves and about others. That is all part of our life, and in the understanding of that life and the various issues involved in life, and actually being free from them, we inquire into meditation.

We must put complete order in our house. Our house is our self. That order is established, not according to a pattern, but when there is complete understanding of what disorder is, what confusion is, why we are in contradiction in ourselves, why there is this constant struggle between the [53] opposites, and so on. The very placing of things in their proper place is the beginning of meditation. If we have not done that—actually, not theoretically, in daily life, every movement of our lives—then meditation becomes another form of illusion, another form of prayer, another form of wanting something.

What is the movement of meditation? We must understand the importance of the senses. Most of us react or act according to the urges, demands, the insistence of our senses. Those senses never act as a whole; all our senses never function, operate, as a whole, holistically. If you observe yourself and watch your senses you will see that one or the other of the senses becomes dominant, one or the other of the senses takes a greater part in our daily living. So there is always imbalance in our senses.

What we are seeing now is part of meditation.

Is it possible for the senses to operate as a whole? Is it possible for you to look at the movement of the sea, the bright waters, the eternally restless waters, to watch those waters completely, with all your senses? Or to observe, to look at a tree, or a person, or a bird in flight, a sheet of water, the setting sun, or the rising moon, with all your senses fully awakened? If you do, then you discover—*for yourself, not from me*—that there is no center from which the senses are moving.

Are you doing this as we are talking?

Look at your girl, or your husband, or your wife, or a tree, with all the senses highly active. Then in that there is no limitation. You do it and you will find out for yourself. Most of us operate on partial or particular senses, we never move or live with all our senses fully awakened, flowering. [54] To give the senses their right place does not mean suppressing them, controlling them, running away from them. This is important because, if one wants to go into meditation very deeply, unless one is aware of the senses, they create different forms of neuroses, different forms of illusions; they dominate our emotions. When the senses are fully awakened, flowering, then the body becomes extraordinarily quiet. Have you noticed this? Most of us force our bodies to sit still, not to fidget, not to move about, but if all the senses are functioning healthily, normally, vitally, then the body relaxes and becomes very, very quiet. Do it as we are talking.

Is it possible to live life—daily, not just occasionally—without any form of control? That doesn't mean permissive activity, doing what one likes, rejecting tradition. Please consider seriously whether it is possible to live a life without any form of control, because when there is control there is the action of will. What is will? "I will do this; I must not do that"; isn't will the essence of desire? Please look at it; don't reject it or accept it, inquire into it. We are asking if it is possible to live a life in which there is not a shadow of control, in which there is not a shadow of the operation of will. Will is the very movement of desire. From perception, contact, sensation, arise desire and thought with its image.

Is it possible to live without the action of will? Most of us live a life of restraint, control, suppression, escape, but when you say, "I must control myself, my anger, my jealousy, my laziness, my indolence," who is the controller? Is the controller different from that which he controls? Or are they both the same? The controller is the controlled. The controller is the essence of desire, and he is trying to control his [55] activities, his thoughts, his wishes. Realizing all that, can one live a life that is not promiscuous, that is not just doing what one likes, but a life without any form of control? Very few people have gone into this question. I object to any system, any form of control, because the mind then is never free; it is always subjugating itself to a pattern, whether that pattern is established by another or by oneself.

Then, can time come to an end? Please see why this is important. Our brains are conditioned to time. Our brains are the result of a million years and more, immemorial centuries upon centuries, of conditioning. The brain has evolved, grown, flowered, but it is a very, very ancient brain. As it has evolved through time, it functions in time. The moment you say, "I will," it is in time. When you say, "I must do that," it is also in time. Everything that we do involves time and our brains are conditioned not only to chronological time, but also to psychological time. The brain has evolved through millennia and the very idea, the very question of whether it can end time is a paralyzing process. It is a shock to it.

Part of meditation is to find out for oneself whether time can stop. You can't do this by saying, "Time must stop"; it has no meaning. Is it possible for the brain to realize that it has no future? We live either in despair or in hope. Part of time is the destructive nature of hope: "I am miserable, unhappy, uncertain; I hope to be happy"; or faith, the invention of the priests throughout the world: "You suffer but have faith in God and everything will be all right." Faith in something involves time. Can you tolerate that there is no tomorrow, psychologically? It is part of meditation to find [56] out that psychologically there is no tomorrow. The hope for something, the pleasure of looking forward to it, is involved in time. Which doesn't mean that you discard hope, it means that you understand the movement of time. If you discard hope, then you become bitter, then you say, "Why should I live, what is the purpose of life?" And then all the nonsense begins of depression, agony, living without anything in the future.

We are asking whether thought as time can stop. Thought is important in its right place, but it has no importance whatsoever psychologically. Thought is the reaction of memory, it is born from memory. Memory is experience as knowledge stored up in the brain cells. You can watch your own brain, you don't have to become a specialist. The brain cells hold memory; it is a material process, there is nothing sacred, nothing holy about it. And thought had created everything that we have done: going to the moon and planting a silly flag up there; going to the depths of the sea and living there; all the complicated technology and its machinery. Thought has been responsible for all this. Thought has also been responsible for all wars. It is so obvious that you don't even have to question it. Your thoughts have divided the world into Britain, France, Russia, and so on. And thought has created the psychological structure of the "me." That "me" is not holy, something divine. It is just thought putting together the anxieties, the fears, the pleasures, the sorrows, the pains, the attachments, the fear of death. It has put together the "me," which is consciousness. Consciousness is what it contains; your consciousness is what you are: your anxieties, your fears, your struggles, your moods, your despairs, [57] pleasures, and so on. It is very simple. And that is the result of time. I have been hurt yesterday psychologically; you said something brutal to me and it has wounded me and is part of my consciousness. So consciousness is the result of time. When we ask if time can end, it implies the total emptying of this consciousness with its content. Whether you can do it or not is a different matter, but it implies that.

We are inquiring into time, and the immovable layers of consciousness—sensation, desire, the whole structure of it—to see whether that consciousness, which is a result of time, can empty itself completely, so that time ends psychologically. You are aware of your consciousness, aren't you? You know what you are, if you have gone into it sufficiently. If you have gone into it, you see that all the travail, all the struggle, all the misery, uncertainty, are part of you, part of consciousness. Your ambitions, your greed, your aggressiveness, your anger, your bitterness, are all part of this consciousness, which is the accumulation from a thousand yesterdays to today. And we are asking whether that consciousness, which is the result of time, psychological as well as physiological, can empty itself so that time comes to an end.

We are going to find out if it is possible. If you say it isn't possible, then you have closed the door. And if you say it is possible, you have also closed the door. But if you say, "Let's find out," then you are open to it, you are eager to find out.

If you are serious enough to go into it, the question now is whether it is possible to empty totally the whole content of our selves, the content of our consciousness, this consciousness which has been built through time. Is it not possible [58] to end one of the contents of your consciousness—your hurts, your psychological wounds? Most of us have been hurt psychologically, from childhood. That is part of your consciousness. Can you end that hurt completely, totally wipe it out without leaving a mark? You can, can't you? If you pay attention to the wound, then you know what has caused it: it is the image you have about yourself that has been wounded. You can end that image that is wounded if you go into it very deeply. Or if you are attached to somebody, your wife or your husband, or are attached to a belief, to a country, to a sect, to a group of people, to Jesus,[9] can you not completely logically, sanely, rationally end it? Because, you see, attachment implies jealously, anxiety, fear, pain; and, having pain, you become more and more and more attached. Seeing the nature of attachment is the flowering of intelligence. That intelligence sees how stupid it is to be attached, and it is finished.

So go into it. You have a particular psychological habit, say, always thinking in a certain direction. That is part of your consciousness. Can thought move away from that groove, from that rut? Of course it can. It is possible to empty the content completely. Now if you do it one thing at a time—your attachments, your hurts, your anxieties, and so on—it will take infinite time. So we are caught in time again. Is it possible to empty it instantly without involving time, as a whole, not in parts? When you do it part by part, you are still involved in time. If you really see the truth of it, then naturally you won't do it partially.

Consciousness is not mine; it is not my particular consciousness, it is the universal consciousness. My consciousness is like [59] your consciousness, or anybody else's consciousness: we both suffer, we both go through agonies, and so on. There may be a few who have flowered, are out of it, and gone beyond, but that is irrelevant.

---

9. Jesus of Nazareth (ca. 0–ca. 33 CE), the leader of a first-century Jewish messianic movement that eventually became the universalistic evangelical institution of Christianity. Identified as the "anointed one" (Heb.: *messiah*; Grk.: *kristos*), Jesus is generally considered by Christians to be the Son of God and thus is referred to as "Jesus Christ."

Is it possible to observe the thing in its entirety, wholly, and in the very observation of that totality, see the ending of it? Is it possible to observe your hurt or your anxiety or your guilt, totally? Suppose I feel guilty. Can I look at that guilt, see how it arose and what was the reason for it, see how I am dreading more of it, see the entire structure of guilt, and observe it wholly? Of course I can, but I can observe it wholly only when I am aware of the nature of being hurt. I can be aware of it if there is no direction or motive involved in that awareness.

I will go into it more. Suppose I am attached to something or somebody. Can't I observe the consequences of attachment, what is involved in attachment, how that attachment arose? Can't I observe the whole nature of it instantly? I am attached because I am lonely, I want comfort, I want to depend on somebody because I can't stand by myself, I need companionship, I need somebody to tell me, "You are doing very well, old boy." I need somebody to hold my hand; I am depressed and anxious. So I depend on somebody, and out of that dependence arises attachment, and from that attachment arise fear, jealousy, anxiety. Can't I observe the whole nature of it instantly? Of course I can if I am aware, if I am deeply interested to find out.

We are saying that, instead of doing it piecemeal, it is possible to see the whole nature and the structure and the movement of consciousness with all its content. The content [60] makes up consciousness, and to see it entirely is possible. And when you see the entirety of it, it disintegrates. To have a complete insight into the whole nature of consciousness implies having no motive, no remembrance, just instant perception of the nature of consciousness. And that very insight dissolves the problem.

Our whole technological development is based on measure; if we had no measurement, there could be no technological advance. Knowledge is movement in measure: I know, I shall know. It is all measurement, and that measurement has moved into the psychological field. If you watch yourself, you can see very easily how it works. We are always comparing psychologically. Now can you end comparison—which is also the ending of time? *Measure* means measuring myself against somebody and wanting to be like that, or not to be like that. The positive and the negative process of comparison are a part of measurement.

Is it possible to live a daily life without any kind of comparison? You do compare two materials, one color of corduroy against another. But psychologically, inwardly, can you be free of comparison completely, which means be free of measurement? Measurement is the movement of thought. So can thought come to an end? You see, most of us *try* to stop thinking, which is impossible. You may for a second say, "I have stopped thinking," but it is forced, it is compelled, it is a form of saying, "I have measured a second when I was not thinking." All those who went into this question deeply have asked if thought can come to an end. Thought is born from the known. Knowledge is the known, which is the past. Can that thought come to an end? Can there be freedom from [61] the known? We are always functioning from the known, and we have become extraordinarily capable and imitative, comparing. We have a constant endeavor to be something. So can thought come to an end?

We have talked about measurement, control, the importance of the senses and their right place. All this is part of meditation.

Can the brain, which is millions of years old, which is so heavily conditioned, so full of all that man has collected through centuries, the brain that is acting mechanically all the time, can that brain be free from the known, and can that brain never, never get old physically? Don't you ask sometimes whether this brain can lose its burden and be free and never deteriorate? That means never psychologically to register anything, never to register flattery, insult, impositions, pressures, but to keep the tape completely fresh. Then it is young. Innocence means a brain that has never been wounded. Innocence knows no misery, conflict, sorrow, pain. When they are all registered in the brain, it is always limited, old as it grows physically older. Whereas, if there is no recording whatsoever psychologically, then the brain becomes extraordinarily quiet, extraordinarily fresh. This is not a hope, this is not a reward. Either you do it and discover it, or you just accept words and say, "How marvelous that must be; I wish I could experience that." Because of insight, the brain cells undergo a change. They are no longer holding on to memories. The brain is no longer the house of vast collected antiquity.

Then, also, we must ask the question: Is there anything sacred in life? Is there anything that is holy, untouched by [62] thought? We have put what we call holy, sacred, in the churches as symbols—the Virgin Mary,[10] Christ on the cross. In India, they have their particular images, as do Buddhist countries, and those have become sacred: the name, the sculpture, the image, the symbol. But *is* there anything sacred in life? *Sacred* being that which is deathless, timeless, from eternity to eternity, that which has no beginning and no end. You can't find it out, nobody can find it out—it may come when you have discarded all the things that thought has made sacred. When the churches with their pictures, their music and their beliefs, their rituals, their dogmas, are all understood and discarded completely, when there is no priest, no guru,[11] no follower, then in that tremendous quality of silence there may come something that is not touched by thought, because that silence is not created by thought.

One has to go into the whole nature of silence. There is silence between two noises. There is silence between two thoughts. There is silence between two notes in music. There is silence after noise. There is silence when thought says, "I must be silent," and creates artificial silence, thinking it is real silence. There is silence when you sit quietly and force your mind to be silent. All those are artificial silences; they are not real, deep, uncultivated, unpremeditated silence. Silence can only come psychologically when there is no registration whatsoever. Then the mind, the brain itself, is utterly without movement. In that great depth of silence that is not induced, not cultivated, not practiced, there may come that extraordinary sense of something immeasurable, nameless.

The whole movement from the beginning to the end of this talk is part of meditation. [Pp. 52–62.]

Enlightenment Is Not a Fixed Place[12]

We ought to consider the relationship of religion to daily life, and whether there is, or is not, something unnameable, a timeless state of mind. One can call it enlightenment, a realization of the absolute truth. Can the human mind ever come upon something that is incorruptible, that

---

10. The Virgin Mary is an honorific name for Mary, the mother of Jesus of Nazareth. Expressed in foundational Christian faith statements such as the Apostles' Creed, Christians generally believe in the "virgin birth." Specifically, according to the standard account, Mary was a virgin when she became pregnant with Jesus, thus revealing God the Father. The Virgin Mary is a central object of devotion for many Christians.

11. "Guru" is a traditional Indian title of veneration meaning "teacher." In a modern American context, the term often came to be used in a pejorative way. As the present talk was delivered in 1978, one might reasonably assume the slowly emerging "guru scandals" that would plague various late 1970s and 1980s New Age movements. One might also recall Krishnamurti's experience of being identified as the "World Teacher" by the Theosophical Society.

12. Public talk delivered at the Masonic Auditorium in San Francisco on March 18, 1973.

is not put together by that human mind with its thought, something that must exist, which will give a perfume, a beauty, a loveliness to life?

Man, if you observe throughout history, has been seeking in so many different ways something beyond ordinary life, beyond this world. He has done everything possible—fasted, tortured himself, engaged in every form of neurotic behavior, [85] worshipped legends and their heroes, accepted the authority of others who said, "I know the way, follow me." Man, whether he is in the West or in the East, has always inquired into this question. The intellectuals, the philosophers, the psychologists, and the analysts see it as neurotic inquiry that has no value whatsoever. To them it is some form of hysteria, some form of make-believe, something to be totally avoided. Because they see around them absurdities in the name of religion, incredible behavior without reason, without any substance behind it, they prefer to deal with human beings who will conform to the pattern that is already established, or the pattern that they think is right. You must have observed all this in different ways.

But the intellect is only part of life. It has its normal place, but human beings throughout the world have given extraordinary importance to the intellect, the capacity to reason, to pursue something logically, to establish an activity based on reason and logic. Human beings are not merely intellectual entities, they are whole complex beings.

Man, you must have observed, wants to find something that is both rational and has depth, a full meaning, not invented by the intellect; and he has always, from ancient days, sought it out. Religion that is organized is a business affair, a vast machinery, to condition the human mind according to certain beliefs, dogmas, rituals, and superstitions. It is a very profitable business, and we accept it because our life is so empty. Life lacks beauty, so we want romantic, mystical legends. And we worship legends, the myths, but all the edifices man has built, physically as well as psychologically, have nothing whatsoever to do with reality.

[86] What is a mind that is free from all the human endeavor, that has really put aside everything that man has created in his search for this thing called reality? You know, this is one of the most difficult things to put into words. Words must be used but communication is not only verbal but nonverbal. That is, both you and the speaker must inquire at the same time, at the same level, with the same intensity. Then communion is possible between you and the speaker. We are trying to commune not only nonverbally but also verbally about this extraordinarily complex question, which needs clear, objective thinking, and also going beyond all thought.

Meditation is not for the immature. The immature can play with it as they do now, sitting cross-legged, breathing in a certain way, standing on their heads, taking drugs, in order to experience something original. Through drugs, through fasting, through any system, you can never find or come upon that which is eternal, timeless. There is no shortcut to all this. One has to work hard; one has to become very aware of what one is doing, what one is thinking, without any distortion. And all that requires great maturity, not of age but maturity of the mind to be capable of observation, seeing the false as the false, the true in the false, and truth as truth. That is maturity, whether in the political scene, in the business world, or in your relationship.

You have probably heard the word *meditation* or read something about it, or you may have followed some guru who tells you what to do. I wish you had never heard that word, then your mind would be fresh to inquire. Some people have been to India, but I don't know why they go there: truth isn't there; there is romance, but romance is not truth. [87] *Truth is where you are.*

It is not in some foreign country, it is where you are. Truth is what you are doing, how you are behaving. It is *there*, not in shaving your head or in all those stupid things that man has done.

Why should you meditate? The meaning of that word is to ponder, to think over, to look, to perceive, to see clearly. To see clearly, to observe without distortion, there must be an awareness of your background, of your conditioning. Just to be aware of it, not to change it, not to alter it, not to transform it or be free of it, but just to observe. In that observation to see clearly without distortion the whole content of consciousness is the beginning and the ending of meditation. The first step is the last step.

Why should one meditate and what is meditation? You know, if you looked out of your window in the morning and saw the extraordinary beauty of the morning light, distant mountains, and the light on the water, and if you observed without the word, without saying to yourself, "How beautiful that is," if you observed completely and were totally attentive in that observation, your mind must have been completely quiet. Otherwise you cannot observe, otherwise you cannot listen. So meditation is the quality of mind that is completely attentive and silent. It is only then that you can see the flower, the beauty of it, the color of it, the shape of it, and it is only then that the distance between you and the flower ceases. Not that you identify yourself with the flower, but the time element that exists between you and that, the distance, disappears. And you can only observe very clearly when there is nonverbal, nonpersonal but attentive observation [88] in which there is no center as the "me." That is meditation.

Now, to see whether you can observe nonverbally, without distortion, without the "me" as memory interfering, requires a great deal of inquiry. That implies that thought must not interfere in observation. That is to observe without the image in relationship with another, to observe another without the images you have built about the other. I do not know if you have tried it. The image is "you," the "you" that has accumulated various impressions, various reactions about another; that forms the image and so divides you from the other. And this division brings conflict. But when there is no image you can observe the other with a total sense of attention in which there is love, compassion, and therefore no conflict. That is observation without the observer. In the same way to observe a flower, everything about one, without division, for division implies conflict, and this division exists as long as thought becomes all important. And for most of us thought and the movement of thought, the activity of thought, is important.

And so the question arises: Can thought be controlled? Do you have to control thought so as not to let it interfere, but allow it to function in its proper place? Control implies suppression, direction, following a pattern, imitation, conformity. You have been trained to control from childhood, and in reaction to that the modern world says, "I won't control, I'll do anything I want." We are not talking about doing what one wants, that is absurd. And this whole system of control is also absurd. Control exists only when there is no understanding. When you see something very clearly, there [89] is no need for control. If my mind sees very clearly how thought interferes, how thought always separates, sees that the function of thought is always in the field of the known, then that very observation prevents all control of thought.

The word *discipline* means to learn, but not mechanically conforming, as it is accepted now. We are talking about a mind that is free from control and is capable of learning. Where there is learning there is no necessity at all for any kind of control. That is, as you are learning you are acting. A mind that is inquiring into the nature of meditation must always be learning, and learning brings its own order. Order is necessary in life. Order is virtue. Order in behavior is righteousness. Order is not the order that is imposed by society, by a culture, by environment, by compulsion or obedience. Order is not a blueprint; it comes into being when you understand disorder, not only outside you but in yourself. Through the negation of disorder is order. Therefore we must look at the disorder of our life, the contradictions in ourselves, the opposing desires, saying one thing and doing, thinking another. In understanding, in looking at disorder, being attentive, aware choicelessly of disorder, order comes naturally, easily, without any effort. And such order is necessary.

Meditation is a process of life in which relationship with each other is clear, without any conflict. Meditation is the understanding of fear, of pleasure. Meditation is the thing called love, and the freedom from death, the freedom to stand completely alone. That is one of the greatest things in life, because if you cannot stand alone inwardly, psychologically, you are not free. That aloneness is not isolation, a [90] withdrawal from the world. That aloneness comes into being when you totally negate, actually—not verbally but actually with your life—all the things that man has put together in his fear, in his pleasure, in his searching for something that is beyond the daily routine of life.

If you have gone that far, then you will see that it is only the mind that has no illusions, that is not following anybody and therefore is free of all sense of authority, that can open the door. It is only such a mind that can see if there is, or if there is not, a timeless quality.

It is important to understand the question of time, not daily chronological time, that is fairly simple and clear, but psychological time, the time of tomorrow—"I will be something," or "I will attain, I will succeed." Is the whole idea of progress, of time being from here to there, an invention of thought? There is obviously progress from the bullock cart to the jet, but is there psychological progress, the "me" becoming better, nobler, wiser? Can the "me," which is the past, the "me" that has accumulated so many things—the insults, flatteries, pain, knowledge, suffering—can that progress to a better state? To advance from here to the better, time is necessary. To become something, time is necessary. *But is there such a thing as becoming something?* Will you *become* something better—better in the sense of a better me, a more noble me with less conflict? That "me" is the entity that separates into the "me" and the "not me," the "we" and "they," the "me" as the American and the "me" as the Hindu, or the Russian, or whatever it is. So can the "me" ever become better? Or does the "me" have to cease completely and never think in terms of the better or of becoming [91] something more? When you admit the more, the better, you are denying the good.

Meditation is the total negation of the "me," so that the mind is never in conflict. A mind not in conflict is not in that state of peace that is just the interval between two conflicts, it is *totally* free from conflict. And that is part of meditation.

When you have understood psychological time, then the mind has space. Have you noticed how little space we have, both physically and inwardly? Living in large cities, in cupboards, in narrow spaces, we become more violent, because we need space physically. Have you noticed also how little space we have inwardly, psychologically? Our minds are crowded with imagination, with all the things that we have learned, with various forms of conditioning, influences, propaganda. We are full of all the things that man has thought about, invented, our own desires, pursuits and ambitions, fears, and so on, and therefore there is very little space. Meditation, if you go into it very deeply, is the negation of all this, so that, in that state of attention, there is vast space without boundary. Then the mind is silent.

You may have learned from others that you must go through a system of meditation, that you must practice so that the mind becomes silent, that you must attain silence in order to become enlightened. That is *called* meditation, but that kind of meditation is sheer nonsense because when you practice there is the entity that practices, becoming more and more mechanical, therefore limited, insensitive, dull. And why should you practice? Why should you allow another to come between you and your inquiry? Why should the priests, or your guru, or your book come between you and [92] what you want to find out? Is it fear? Is it that you want somebody to encourage you? Is it that you lean on somebody when you are yourself uncertain? And when you are uncertain and you lean on somebody for certainty you may be quite sure that you are choosing somebody who is equally uncertain. And therefore the person on whom you lean maintains that he is very certain. He says, "I know, I have achieved, I am the way, follow me." So beware of a man who says he knows.

Enlightenment is not a fixed place. There is no fixed place. *All one has to do is understand the chaos, the disorder in which we live.* In the understanding of that we have order and there comes clarity, there comes certainty. And that certainty is not the invention of thought. That certainty is intelligence. And when you have all this, when the mind sees all this very clearly, then the door opens. What lies beyond is not nameable. It cannot be described, and anyone who describes it has never seen it. It cannot be put into words because the word is not the thing, the description is not the described. All that one can do is to be totally attentive in relationship, to see that attention is not possible when there is image, to understand the whole nature of pleasure and fear, and to see that pleasure is not love, and desire is not love.

And you have to find out everything for yourself; nobody can tell you. Every religion has said, don't kill. To you those are just words, but if you are serious you have to find out what it means for yourself. What has been said in the past may be true, but that truth is not yours. You have to find out, you have to learn what it means never to kill. Then it is [93] your truth and it is a living truth. In the same way—not through another, not through practice of a system invented by another, not through the acceptance of a guru, a teacher, or a savior—you yourself in your freedom have to see what is truth, what is false, and find out for yourself completely how to live a life in which there is no strife whatsoever.

The whole of this is meditation. (Pp. 84–93.]

Light Cannot Be Given by Another[13]

One must be free to be completely a light to oneself. *A light to oneself!* This light cannot be given by another, nor can you light it at the candle of another. If you light it at the candle of another, it is just a candle, it can be blown out. The very investigation to find out what it means to be a

---

13. Public talk delivered outdoors in Saanen, Switzerland, on July 25, 1976.

light to oneself is part of meditation. We are going together to investigate what it means to be a light to oneself, and see how extraordinarily important it is to have this light.

Our conditioning is to accept authority—the authority of the priest, the authority of a book, the authority of a guru, the authority of someone who says he knows. In all spiritual matters, if one may use that word, *spiritual*, there must be [112] no authority whatsoever; otherwise you cannot be free to investigate, to find out for yourself what meditation means. To go into the question of meditation, you must be wholly, inwardly free from all authority, from all comparison, including the authority of the speaker, especially that of the speaker—that is, of me—because if you follow what he says it is finished. You must be aware of the importance of the authority of the doctor, the scientist, and understand the total unimportance of authority inwardly, whether it is the authority of another, or the authority of your own experience, knowledge, conclusions, prejudices. One's own experiences, one's own understanding, also become one's own authority: "I understand, therefore I am right." All those are forms of authority to be aware of. Otherwise you can never be a light to yourself. When you are a light to yourself you are a light to the world, because the world is you, and you are the world.

So there is no one to guide you, no one to tell you that you are progressing, no one to encourage you. You have to stand completely alone in meditation. And this light to yourself can only come when you investigate into yourself what you are. That is self-awareness, to know what you are. Not according to psychologists, not according to some philosophers, not according to the speaker, but to know, to be aware of your own nature, of your own thinking, feeling, to find out the whole structure of it. Self-knowing is extraordinarily important. Not the description given by another, but actually "what is," what you are; not what you think you are, or what you think you should be, but what actually is going on.

[113] Have you ever tried it? Do you know how difficult it is to be aware of what is actually taking place inside the skin, as it were? Because we observe through the knowledge of the past, and if you inquire with the knowledge that you have acquired as an experience, or have gathered from another, then you are examining yourself from the background of the past. Therefore you are not actually observing "what is." There must be freedom to observe, and then in that observation the whole structure and the nature of oneself begins to unroll. Very few people will tell you all this because they have self-interest, they want to form organizations, groups, the whole structure of that business. So please, if you don't mind, give your complete attention to what is being said.

To understand oneself there must be observation, and that observation can only take place *now*. And it is not the movement of the past observing the now. When I observe the now from my past conclusions, prejudices, hopes, fears, that is an observation of the present from the past. I think I am observing the now, but the observation of the now can take place only when there is no observer who is the past. Observation of the now is extraordinarily important. The movement of the past meeting the present must end there; that is the now. But if you allow it to go on, then the now becomes the future, or the past, but never the actual now. Observation can only take place in the very doing of it—when you are angry, when you are greedy, to observe it as it is. Which means not to condemn it, not to judge it, but to watch it and let it flower and disappear. Do you understand the beauty of it?

Traditionally we are educated to suppress, or to move in a certain direction. What we are saying is: observe your [114] anger, your greed, your sexual demands, whatever it is, and observe without the past so that the anger flowers and disappears, withers away. When you do that you will never be angry again. Have you ever done this? Do it some time and you will discover it for yourself. Allow observation in which there is no choice: just observe your greed, your envy, your jealousy, whatever it may be, and in the very observation of it, it flowers and undergoes a radical change. The very observation without the background brings about a change.

To be aware of oneself without any choice and to see what is actually happening in the now is to allow the whole movement of the self, the "me," to flower. And it undergoes a radical transformation, if there is no background, if there is no observer who is the background. In doing that, obviously, authority has no place. There is no intermediary between your observation and truth. In doing that, one becomes a light to oneself. Then you don't ask anybody at any time how to do something. In the very doing, which is the observing, there is the act, there is the change. Go at it!

So freedom to observe, and therefore no authority of any kind, is essential.

Then the search for experience, which we all want, must come to an end. I will show you why. Every day we have various kinds of experiences. The recording of it becomes a memory, and that memory distorts observation. If, for instance, you are a Christian, you have been conditioned for two thousand years in all your ideologies, beliefs, dogmas, rituals, the savior, and you want to experience that which you call—whatever it is. You will experience whatever it is because that is your conditioning. In India they have hundreds [115] of gods and they are conditioned to that and so they have visions of them, because they see according to their conditioning. When we are bored with all the physical experiences, we want some other kind of experience, the spiritual experience, to find out if there is a God, to have visions. You will have visions, experiences, according to your background, obviously, because your mind is conditioned that way. Be aware of that, and see what is implied in experiences.

What is implied in experiences? There must be an experiencer to experience. The experiencer is all that he craves for, all that he has been told, his conditioning. And he wants to experience something that he calls God, or nirvana, or whatever it is. So he will experience it. But the word *experience* implies recognition, and recognition implies that you already know. Therefore it is not something new. So a mind that demands experience is really living in the past, and therefore can never possibly understand something totally new, original. So there must be freedom from that urge for experience.

It is tremendously arduous to go into this kind of meditation, because we all want a rather easy, comfortable, happy, easygoing life. And so when something difficult comes, which demands your attention, your energy, you say, "Well that is not for me, I'll go another way."

Then, observe your fears, your pleasures, the sorrows, and all the complexities of daily living in relationship. Observe all that very carefully. To *observe* implies that there is no observer, therefore there is no question of suppressing, denying, accepting, but merely observing your fear. When there [116] is fear, it always distorts perception. When you are pursuing pleasure, that is a distorting factor. Or when there is sorrow, that is a burden. So the mind that is learning what meditation is must be free of this, and understand daily, everyday relationship. That is much more arduous, because our relationship with each other is based on our images of each other. As long as there is an image-maker, that image-maker prevents actual relationship with each other. It is essential to understand this before one can go very deeply into the subject of meditation, and that is why very few people meditate properly, rightly.

All systems of meditation, practicing a method day after day, assert that thought must be controlled, because thought is the disturbing factor for a still mind. Now when you look into it, who is the controller? You see the importance of controlling your thought, and you say, "I will try to control it," but all the time it slips away. You spend forty years controlling and every moment it is slipping away. So you have to ask who the controller is. And why is it so important to make such tremendous efforts to control? That means conflict between the thought that moves away and another thought that says, "I must control it." It is a battle all the time, a struggle, a conflict. So we must ask who is the controller. Is not the controller another thought? So one thought, which assumes dominance, says, "I must control the other thought." One fragment is trying to control another fragment.

What is important is to find out that there is only thinking, and not the thinker and the thought and so the thinker controlling thought. There is only thinking. We are concerned [117] then not with how to control thought, but with the whole process of thinking. Why should it stop? If there is only thinking, why should it stop? Thinking is a movement, isn't it? Thinking is a movement in time, from here to there. Can that time come to an end? That is the question, not how to stop thinking. In meditation, the gurus have laid emphasis on control, but where there is control there must be effort, there must be conflict, there must be suppression. And where there is suppression there are all kinds of neurotic behavior.

Is it possible to live without any control? That doesn't mean to do what you like, be completely permissive. In your daily life, psychologically, can you live without any control whatsoever? You can. We don't know a life in which there is no shadow of control. We all know only control. Control exists where there is comparison. I compare myself with you and I want to be like you, because you are more intelligent, more bright, more spiritual. I want to be like you, so I make an effort to be like you. If there is no comparison whatsoever psychologically, what takes place? I am what I am. I don't know what I am but I am that. There is no movement towards something which I think is more. When there is no comparison, what has taken place? Am I dull because I have compared myself with you who are clever, bright, or does the very word *dull* make me dull?

When you go to a museum you look at various pictures, you compare them, saying one is better than another. We are traditionally trained that way. In school, we say we must be better than another, and to beat the other. The whole movement of examinations is comparison, making effort. We are saying that when you understand the movement of [118] measurement, and when you see the unreality of it, psychologically, then you have "what is." You have exactly "what is." You can only meet "what is" when you have energy. That energy had been dissipated in comparison, but now you have that energy to observe "what is," to observe the now. Therefore "what is" undergoes a radical transformation.

So thought has divided itself as the controller and the controlled. But there is only thinking; there is no controller or the controlled, but only the act of thinking. Thinking is a movement in time as measure. Can that naturally, easily, without any control, come to an end? When I make an effort to bring it to an end, thinking is still in operation. I am deceiving myself by saying that the thinker is different from the thought. So there is only thinking. The thinker is the thought. There is no thinker if there is no thought. Can this thinking, which is a movement in time, come to an end? That is, can time have a stop?

Time is the past. There is no future time, the future is only the past meeting the present, modifying it and moving on. Time is a movement from the past, modified but still moving on.

That movement, which is the whole movement of knowledge, which is the whole movement of that which has been known, must stop. Unless you are free from that movement, there is no observation of the new. That movement must stop, but you can't stop it by will, which is to control. You can't stop it by desire, which is part of your sensation, thought, image. So how is this movement to come to an end, naturally, easily, happily, without your knowing?

Have you ever given up something that gives you great [119] pleasure—*at the moment*—dropped it instantly? Have you ever done it? You can do it with pain and sorrow, I am not talking of that, because you want to forget that, put it away. But something that gives you immense pleasure. Have you ever done it? To drop it instantly without any effort. Have you? The past is always our background. We live in the past—someone *has* hurt me, someone *has* told me—our whole life is spent in the past. The incident of now is transformed into memory, and memory becomes the past. So we live in the past. Can that movement of the past stop?

The past is a movement, modified through the present, to the future. That is the movement of time. The past is a movement, always going forward, meeting the present and moving. The now is nonmovement, because you don't *know* what the now is, you only *know* movement. You see, the immovable is the now. The now is the past meeting the present, and *ending* there. That is the now. So the movement of the past meets the now, which is immovable, and stops. So thought, which is a movement of the past, meets the present completely, and ends there. This has to be meditated over, thought over. You go into it.

The next thing is the mind, which is not only matter, the brain, it is also sensation and all the things that thought has put into that mind. It is consciousness, and in that consciousness there are all the various unconscious demands. Can that totality of consciousness be observed as a whole? Not fragment by fragment, because if we examine fragment by fragment it will be endless. It is only when there is an observation of the totality of consciousness that there is an ending of it, or the possibility of something else. So can this [120] totality of consciousness be observed as a whole? It can if you will do it. When you look at a map with the desire to go to a certain place, there is a direction. To observe the whole map is to have no direction. That is simple. See how simple it is, don't make it complex. So in the same way, to look at this whole consciousness is to have no direction, which means to have no motive. When you can observe anything totally, yourself or your consciousness, there is no motive and therefore no direction.

So to observe your consciousness wholly there must be no motive, no direction. Is that possible when you have been trained to do everything with a motive? Action with a motive is what we are trained to do, educated for. All our religions say, everything says, you must have a motive. But the moment you have a motive, which is either pleasure or pain, reward or punishment, that gives you a direction and therefore you can never see the whole. If you understand that, see that actually, then you have no motive. You don't ask, "How am I to get rid of my motive?" You can only see something totally when there is no direction, when there is no center from which a direction can take place. The center is the motive. If there is no motive, there is no center and therefore no direction. All this is part of meditation.

What then?

Now the mind is prepared to observe without any movement. Have you got it? Because you have understood authority and all the rest, you stand completely alone to be a light to yourself. Therefore there is no impingement; the mind, the brain is not registering. So the mind now is without a single movement. Therefore it is silent; not with an [121] imposed silence, not a cultivated silence, which has no meaning, but a silence that is not the result of stopping something, stopping noise. It is a natural outcome of daily living. And daily living has its beauty. Beauty is part of the nonmovement.

What is beauty? Is it the description? Is it the thing that you see, the proportions, the heights, the depths, the shadows, a painting or a sculpture by Michelangelo? What is beauty? Is it in the eye? Or is it out there? Or is it neither in your eye or out there? We say that a beautiful thing, beautiful architecture, a marvelous cathedral, or a lovely painting is out there. Or is it in the eye because it has been trained to observe, to see that what is ugly is not proportionate, has no depth, no style? Is beauty out there, or is it in the eye, or has it nothing to do with the eye or with the outside?

Beauty *is* when you are not. When you look, it is you who are looking, you who are judging, you who are saying, "That is a marvelous proportion," "That is so still, it has depth, it has such grandeur." It is all you looking, you giving it importance. But when you are not there, that is beauty. We want to express because that is self-fulfillment, but when that beauty is there, the expression of it may never take place. Beauty may be when you as a human being, with all your travail, your anxieties, pain, sorrow, are not there. Then there is beauty.

So the mind now is still, without a movement. Then what is there when movement stops?

Is compassion a movement? One thinks one is compassionate when one goes and does something for another, goes to some Indian village and helps the people. But all that is [122] various forms of sentimentality, affection, and so on. We are asking something much more important, which is, when there is no movement then what takes place, what is there? Is it compassion? Or is it beyond all that? That is, is there something that is totally original and therefore sacred? We don't know what is sacred. We think our images in a church, a temple, or a mosque are sacred, but the images are put together by thought. And thought is a material process, movement. When there is no movement, is there something totally original, totally untouched by humanity, untouched by all the movement of thought? That may be that which is original and therefore most holy.

This is real meditation. To start from the very beginning not knowing. Please, if you start with knowing, you end up in doubt. If you start with not knowing, you end up with absolute truth, which is certainty. I wonder if you capture this. We began by saying we must investigate into ourselves, and ourselves is the known, therefore empty the known. So from that emptiness all the rest of it flows naturally.

Where there is something most holy, which is the whole movement of meditation, then life has a totally different meaning. It is never superficial, *never*. If you have this, nothing matters. [Pp. 111–22.]

Part III

Reapproaching Contemplative Practice

Chapter 15

Comparative Reflections

Louis Komjathy

Sometimes a man stands up during supper . . .
because of a church that stands somewhere in the East.

—Rainer Maria Rilke

The looking itself is a trace of what we're looking for.

—Jalāl ad-Dīn Rūmī

Who can leap beyond the world's ties
And sit with me among white clouds.

—Hanshan (Cold Mountain)

We have now traversed the complex labyrinths of a wide variety of contemplative practices and contemplative traditions. We have learned how to sit in silence with the classical Daoist inner cultivation lineages and nineteenth-century British Quakers, to practice Hebrew letter permutations with sixteenth-century Lurianic Kabbalists in Jerusalem, to engage in *samatha* (calming) and *vipassanā* (insight) with the early Indian Buddhist community, to practice Sufi contemplation and visualization with twentieth-century Naqshbandi-Mujaddidi Sufis, to recite the Jesus Prayer with nineteenth-century Russian Orthodox monastics and pilgrims, to visualize the Pure Land with sixth-century Chinese Pure Land Buddhists, to purify consciousness and free spirit from materiality through Hindu classical Yoga in third-century India, to follow the model of Jesus Christ and Saint Dominic among thirteenth-century Spanish Dominicans, to practice Daoist internal alchemy among Chan Buddhist and Daoist monastics in eighteenth-century China, to enter relaxation and decrease stress in twentieth- and twenty-first-century America, and to forget technique, tradition, and teachers while listening to J. Krishnamurti's public talks in the modern world. In the process, we have seen the ways in which contemplative practices are located in specific religious traditions and soteriological systems.

In this chapter, I provide some reflections on the comparative study of contemplative practice and contemplative experience, contemplative literature, and contemplative traditions. Reengaging and developing themes and issues explored in the opening two introductory chapters, I specifically highlight interpretative issues and philosophical opportunities that emerge through comparative engagement with the texts contained in the present anthology. In keeping with a comparative religious studies methodology, I also attempt at times to defamiliarize the familiar (see Smith 1982, xiii; also Smith 2004, 383) and to familiarize the unfamiliar.

Conversations with Contemplatives

Many insights and challenges emerge from careful study of and reflection on contemplative literature. We may imagine this as a conversation, a conversation that has the potential to extend into additional conversations, cross-cultural, comparative, and interreligious. As David Tracy comments in *The Analogical Imagination*,

> Real conversation occurs only when the participants allow the question, the subject matter, to assume primacy. It occurs only when our usual fears about our own self-image die: whether that fear is expressed in either arrogance or scrupulosity matters little. That fear dies only because we are carried along, and sometimes away, by the subject matter itself into the rare event or happening named "thinking" and "understanding." For understanding *happens*; it *occurs* not as the pure result of personal achievement but in the back-and-forth movement of the conversation itself. (Tracy 1998, 101, italics in original)

The contributors to the present volume as well as engaged readers have participated and continue to participate in such a dialogic process. Contemplatives and contemplative traditions may inspire one to reflect more deeply on the nature of existence and the human condition, including the relative importance of a contemplative approach and religious commitments. We may learn to "think through" our sources (see, e.g., Hall and Ames 1987; Clooney 1996). Should we detach ourselves from physicality and the material world, including human relationship, or should we endeavor to become fully embodied and present in a participatory way? Is silence required for human sanity and flourishing? What is the relative significance of beauty and place for a sense of aliveness? Are spiritual companions and community necessary? Do we need sacred sites and pilgrimage as reminders? Are there things more important than health? Is there a place inside ourselves where we are always free and always well? To what extent does the known, the familiar, and the remembered orient us or limit us? Does contemplative practice support psychological well-being and spiritual connection, as well as provide a higher resilience to the challenges of human existence? Is contemplative practice a method to maintain sanity or an exercise in dying?

Engaging contemplatives and contemplative works as conversation partners for comparative religious studies, all of our authors have addressed particular interpretative and comparative issues in the final section of their introductions. In discussing classical Daoist apophatic meditation,

Harold Roth emphasizes the transformative effects and benefits of contemplative practice, with particular attention to the distinction between "states" and "traits." The former pertain to the inner experience of individual practitioners and tend to be ephemeral, while the latter pertain to more stable character qualities developed in interactions in the phenomenal world. In this respect, we might profitably recall the "introvertive" and "extrovertive" dimensions of contemplative practice. We might reflect on the degree to which contemplative practice results in radical transformations of personality and character and becomes embodied in the world.

Examining a parallel type of quietistic prayer in the Religious Society of Friends, which reveals interreligious similarity and intrareligious difference, Michael Birkel draws our attention to diverse conceptions of silence in contemplative traditions as well as the phenomenon of intertextuality and crosspollination. Specifically, Birkel emphasizes the ways in which a particular form of "Quaker prayer" is indebted to various earlier Catholic Quietists. We may consider the influences and contexts related to specific forms of contemplative practice. We may also reflect on the place of silence in the human condition.

In his chapter on Jewish Kabbalah, Shaul Magid provides reflection on the challenges and opportunities of translation, including the importance of the relationship between source-text and resultant translation. Magid draws particular attention to the relative appropriateness and viability of translating "untranslatable texts," as in the case of Kabbalistic texts based on Hebrew letter permutation. We might, in turn, wonder about the degree to which one must know specific languages in order to engage in contemplative practice. This is not just language strictly defined but also the complex informing worldviews, technical terms, and perhaps even direct experience with the associated method. Proficiency and fluency may be important considerations. In addition, if slightly more daring, one might reflect on the relative unsayability and incomprehensibility of the divine.

In her discussion of Southern Buddhist meditation, Sarah Shaw highlights the central importance of breath and breathing in contemplative practice. While breathing is always involved, specific approaches and communities utilize actual breath-observation and breath-regulation techniques. In a manner paralleling the body and posture, we may consider the place of breathing in contemplative practice, including the potential relationship between patterns of breathing and qualities of consciousness. We may consider the ways in which consciousness is affected by various patterns of embodiment.

Still another dimension of human being is explored in Arthur Buehler's study of Sufi contemplation. This is the place of light and energy in specific practices. Although rarely discussed in academic literature, there are traditions that view human personhood as an energetic system. We may reflect on various conceptions of self, including the possibility that certain practices activate unrecognized or hidden dimensions of being. Contemplative practice may result in transformed ontological conditions, awaken latent capacities, and alter our way of experiencing. It is possible that we are alienated from fundamental aspects of ourselves.

In his discussion of Eastern Orthodox prayer, John McGuckin emphasizes the way in which much contemplative practice is located within the larger parameters of tradition, including religious community, liturgical performance, and perhaps monastic commitment. Paralleling the place of elders in the classical Daoist inner cultivation lineages and the *shaykh* in Sufi contemplation, one key dimension of Hesychast prayer is the importance of a "spiritual father," that is, a teacher with deep experience and insight concerning the advocated practice. Interestingly, it appears that this guidance may continue after the teacher's death, which raises the question of the relationship among meditation, death, dying, and afterlife. McGuckin also emphasizes the place of pilgrimage, both literal and symbolic, in contemplative practice. We may consider contemplative practice as a kind of pilgrimage, a journey toward the sacred. We may also reflect on the degree to which this is an inward or outward undertaking.

Exploring Pure Land Buddhist visualization, Kenneth Tanaka suggests that creativity and imagination play a role in certain forms of contemplative practice, and that, perhaps like conscious alteration of breathing, visualization may also alter one's consciousness in important ways. Implicitly problematizing certain modern constructions of "Buddhist meditation," Tanaka also demonstrates that theistic devotion may be part of contemplative practice; "devotion," "meditation," and "prayer" may not be as distinct as often assumed. One may reflect on the extent to which contemplative practice is a form of remembrance and invocation. In addition, one's own "mind" may have the power to transform "reality." We may thus consider the various dimensions of consciousness and human psychology, including the problematic reduction of the former to "reason" and "intellect." Finally, given the centrality of Queen Vaidehī and her female attendants in the text, one wonders about the gendered dimensions of contemplative practice as well as the postmortem consequences of committed practice. Do particular methods connect one to and, following physical death, guarantee access into different sacred realms?

As visually complex as the *Guanjing* (Visualization Sutra) is, the *Yoga Sūtras* (Yoga Aphorisms) is equally sparse. In his discussion of this key text of Hindu classical Yoga, Edwin Bryant again draws our attention to the influence and importance of informing worldviews. In particular, we notice that Hindu classical Yoga has a distinctive view of consciousness, embodiment and the physical world, in which materiality is distraction and entanglement and one's "real self" is nonmaterial in nature. In this respect, one might reflect on the radical reconceptualization that occurs in so-called "American Yoga," with its influence from European gymnastic traditions and modern Western constructions of beauty, fitness, and body-image (see Michelis 2005; Singleton 2010; Syman 2010; also McMahan 2008). Finding some parallels with Roth's discussion, one also learns that Indian traditions suggest that certain forms of practice may transform consciousness in much more radical ways, including the potential attainment of "psychic abilities." We may thus consider contemplative practice as rooted in and an expression of a larger soteriological system. It may also be that ordinary life is actually the "altered state of consciousness" and "anomalous experience."

Addressing Dominican Catholic prayer, Paul Philibert inquires into the purpose of "contemplative literature," including whether such texts are actually intended to be "prayer manuals." In this respect, it is important to consider not only audience but also the contexts of composition and reception. Philibert's study also reveals often neglected aspects of contemplative practice, including art, material culture, reading, religious life, and sacred space. With some similarities to Pure Land visualization, this form of Dominican prayer also involves theistic devotion, but this time with kinesthetic and perhaps evangelistic dimensions. We may consider the ways in which specific methods are related to particular exemplars (e.g., Christ, Moses, St. Dominic) and potentially turn practitioners into someone else, at least to a certain degree. This includes specific values and commitments. It may be that contemplative techniques are complex systems of enculturation. In addition, a major purpose of contemplative practice may involve witnessing and embodied action in the form of social engagement.

With some parallels with the chapters by Roth, Buehler, and Bryant, my chapter on Daoist internal alchemy observes an alternative conception of self and the potential transformative effects

Figure 15.1. Cruciform Posture
Source: The *Novem modi orandi* (Nine Ways of Prayer) (Vatican Apostolic Library)

of dedicated and prolonged practice. I demonstrate that this form of contemplative practice utilizes an energetic view of personhood; from this Daoist perspective, there are hidden dimensions and capacities of human being. As internal alchemy also traditionally involves stage-based training under the guidance of a teacher, recalling Sufi contemplation and Eastern Orthodox prayer, it inspires us to consider the actual place of stages and sequence in contemplative practice. One may also come to see the body as consisting of nonspatial or semi-spatial dimensions, of "mystical (non)locations" that are portals into the sacred.

In my next chapter on Herbert Benson's Relaxation Response, I discuss the decontextualization and reconceptualization of contemplative practice in the modern world, specifically the emergence of modern therapeutic meditation in the context of Mind-Body Medicine. In the process, I suggest that, although often privileged as "scientific," modern therapeutic meditation also is located in a "religious tradition" and "soteriological system." Specifically, "health," "stress," and "science" have similar functions to more conventional "religious" concerns. We may, in turn, consider not only the rationales, purposes, and goals of particular methods but also the motivations and assumptions of different practitioners. We may wonder about the relative importance of wellness and self-care in modern (post)industrial and technological contexts.

Finally, Constance Jones provides important insights into the modern phenomenon of "trans-tradition" contemplative practice, with some connections to "unchurched spirituality."

Examining J. Krishnamurti's "techniqueless meditation," Jones, via Krishnamurti's radical model of psychological and spiritual freedom, challenges the privileging of method, religious authority, and tradition at the foundation of this volume. We may thus consider the contributions and limitations of community and tradition in contemplative practice. Perhaps there is a "light in oneself" and "truth is a pathless land."

Inspired by and going beyond our contributors' insights and reflections, one may also find oneself in additional conversations, conversations within, between, and beyond specific perspectives. One may confront the radical challenges and insights of a particular viewpoint, including the ways in which a given contemplative might respond to others. Each contribution highlights the importance of contemplative practice in human existence, especially with respect to existential, soteriological, and theological concerns.[1] At the same time, there are diverse methods, orientations, worldviews, experiences, and so forth. There are diverse claims, sometimes congruent, sometimes divergent. For example, elders of the classical Daoist inner cultivation lineages suggest that stillness is our innate nature, which is also the Dao in its own suchness, while Quaker Quietists understand silence as the condition for God's presence to emerge.[2] On some level, these are similar views, as both emphasize the importance of silence. However, the vocal ministry often inspired by Quaker silent worship stands in contrast to the classical Daoist commitment to abide in a condition beyond language and conception. One involves a mysticism of union and meditative absorption, while the other expresses a mysticism of communal participation. Interestingly, Jewish Kabbalists understand YHWH as *both* absolutely other and wholly present. Along a different track, Dominican Catholics emphasize salvation through Christ and the Church, while Pure Land Buddhists venerate Amitābha (Infinite Light) Buddha and his buddha-realm of Sukhāvatī. Both are forms of theistic devotion, but, if taken seriously, they confront us with a radical soteriological decision. This relational and dualistic theological viewpoint is challenged by the Southern Buddhist and Hindu classical Yoga emphasis on self-reliance. In the latter contemplative approaches, one must sit in one's own essential aloneness, in the purity and independence of isolated consciousness. There are degrees of self-power and other-power in different forms of contemplative practice. Interestingly, early Pure Land Buddhism utilizes both personal and communal meditation as well as *mantra*-based devotion, including the possibility that the consciousness that created the Pure Land and the Pure Land itself are nothing but one's own enlightened consciousness. This is just a sample of an almost endless variety of potential conversations that might be inspired by the present volume, and perhaps by a commitment to contemplative practice and contemplative ways of being.[3]

These and other reflections on the soteriological and theological dimensions of contemplative practice and religious adherence inform my conviction that the careful study of religion reveals mutually exclusive, equally convincing accounts of "reality." On a descriptive and comparative level, this is not problematic, but it often creates discomfort in individuals on a soteriological and theological level. As discussed in more detail later in this chapter, one may simply engage such perspectives in a cross-cultural and comparative way, through a method that just endeavors to understand. Here one thinks of Clifford Geertz's discussion of religion as a "symbol system" (Geertz 1973) or Mircea Eliade's treatment of the relationship between "myth and reality" (Eliade 1998). At the same time, various theological responses are viable. One of the most common involves Perennial Philosophy. This interpretative perspective claims that all religious doctrines are simply different attempts to describe the same reality; they are simply approximations of "Reality." Such a perspective might claim that contemplative practice ultimately has the same goals and the various forms of contemplative experience are fundamentally the same. As discussed in chapter 1 of the present volume, Perennial Philosophy utilizes an assumed monistic theology. While perhaps convincing for some on a theological level, this perspective simply does not hold up to critical scrutiny on evidential and interpretive grounds. Just as theologians may not avoid the Shoah ("Holocaust") in discussing the nature of "God" (see, e.g., Rubenstein 1992; Katz 2006), interpreters of contemplative practice and contemplative experience must consider the diversity and complexity of contemplative traditions, including as presented in this comparative sourcebook. In terms of Perennial Philosophy, such an account would have to use the materials in the present volume to make its case, which would ultimately prove unsupported and unconvincing. We must acknowledge that there are competing soteriological and theological claims, even if one finds these to be sources of discomfort and disturbance. As will be discussed later, exclusivism and inclusivism, let alone colonization and domestication, are not our only choices. One need not commit philosophical violence on others for the sake of "comfort" and "peace." The acceptance of diversity and plurality is equally viable. One might, in turn, engage in a larger, more constructive project rooted in religious pluralism, interreligious dialogue, and comparative theology.

Transformative Praxis

Before considering potentially more radical claims about "reality," we may ponder the insights into human existence that emerge through the study of contemplative practice, contemplative experience, contemplative traditions, and contemplative literature. Specifically, we may examine meditation and contemplative prayer as forms of transformative praxis (see Komjathy 2007; also Wilber et al. 1986; Murphy 1992). We may consider the descriptions of human potential and transformation found in the texts of the present volume and their associated traditions. In preparation for such inquiry, I would remind us that, as discussed in the opening chapters of the present volume, some potential characteristics of contemplative practice include attentiveness, awareness, interiority, presence, silence, transformation, and a deepened sense of meaning and purpose. Thus, as herein explored, "transformative praxis" has particular qualities and expressions.[4]

As discussed in chapter 2, the study of contemplative practice and contemplative experience may benefit from reflection on consciousness, embodiment, psychology, and so forth. In particular, I suggested that contemplative practice may result in specific types of psychosomatic and ontological transformations, what may be referred to as "psychologies of realization" (see also King 1999; Wilber 2000). These are the "benefits" and "effects" of contemplative practice. While related to different qualities of mind, personality characteristics, as well as values, it is also important to consider embodiment here (see Komjathy 2007), including behavior and movement patterns. That is, contemplative practice is not just about "mind." If one were slightly more daring and theologically inclined, one might utilize the concept of "anthropologies of realization," in the sense of claims about the fulfillment or transformation of human life and existence. In any case, "psychologies of realization" draw our attention to human potential and self-actualization. Our account may include insights derived from and applicable to humanistic, transpersonal, and contemplative psychology.

One largely shared dimension of contemplative practice involves virtue and ethics, that is, commitment to and development of specific values.[5] Various contemplative systems emphasize virtue and ethics as prerequisites and foundations for contemplative practice. Some examples include "morality" (Pali: *sīla*; Skt.: *śīla*), "precepts" (*sikkhāpada*), and "monastic discipline" (*vinaya*) in Buddhism; "virtue" (*de*) and "precepts" (*jie*) in Daoism; "moral restraints" (*yama*) and "ethical observances" (*niyama*) in Hinduism; "commandments" (*mitzvah*; pl. *mitzvot*) and "religious law" (*halakha*) in Judaism; and so forth. For example, beyond the fundamental Buddhist five precepts (no killing, no stealing, no sexual misconduct, no lying, and no intoxicants)[6] and the 227 rules (Pali: *patimokkha*; Skt.: *prātimokṣa*) for Theravāda monks, Buddhism identifies various "perfections" (*pāramitā*), or the culmination of particular qualities and virtues. In the case of certain Theravāda Buddhist expressions, there are "ten perfections," namely, generosity, morality, renunciation, wisdom, diligence, patience, honesty, determination, loving-kindness, and equanimity. Mahāyāna Buddhism tends to emphasize "six perfections": generosity, morality, patience, diligence, concentration (*dhyāna*), and wisdom (*prajñā*). In this respect, one also thinks of the "seven heavenly virtues" emphasized in certain forms of Christianity: chastity, temperance, charity, diligence, patience, kindness, and humility.[7] Of course, many more examples from various communities and traditions could be added. Here it is sufficient to reflect on the degree to which contemplative practice requires and supports ethical commitments. It is possible that contemplative practice inspires and stabilizes virtue.[8]

In terms of the present volume, the Daoist tradition identifies various benefits and transformative effects of committed and prolonged meditation. In his contribution, Harold Roth, following the cognitive psychologists B. Rael Cahn and John Polich, utilizes the distinction between "states" (transitory benefits and effects) and "traits" (enduring character changes). Some important Daoist states include concentration, detachment, emptiness, equanimity, refinement, serenity, stillness, and so forth. Related Daoist traits include effortlessness, flexibility, impartiality, perceptual acuity, resonance, simplicity, stability, suppleness, and so forth. Of course, here one may reasonably consider the degree to which these overlap and, at times, become indistinguishable. Along similar lines, Sufism, the contemplative and mystical strain of Islam discussed by Arthur Buehler, makes a distinction between "stages" (*maqaam*; pl.: *maqaamat*) and "states" (*haal*; pl.: *ahwal*).[9] "Stages," also referred to as "stations," indicate moments along the contemplative path (*tariqa*), often involving a set sequence of advancement. From a Sufi perspective, this dimension of practice is under the control of the contemplative or mystic. A representative Sufi approach follows seven stages: (1) repentance, (2) abstention, (3) asceticism, (4) poverty, (5) patience, (6) confidence, and (7) contentment. "States" indicate different spiritual conditions. "States" are believed to come from Allah and thus to be beyond the control of contemplatives and mystics, although religious praxis may prepare the way for them. Considered a form of grace, some common Sufi states include contraction, ecstasy, expansion, intimacy, intoxication, joy, loneliness, and so forth. Sometimes Sufi contemplative experience crosses such clear demarcations, as in the case of "dissolution of self" (*fanā*) and "abiding in Allah" (*baqā*). Nonetheless, the distinction brings attention to the source or trigger of particular types of experience and the associated interpretations. It also suggests that certain psychological conditions that are often defined negatively (for example, loneliness, suffering, and illness) may have a larger transformative effect and soteriological purpose. Some contemplatives and mystics may define them as "grace."

In the case of Hindu and Buddhist perspectives, partially explored by Edwin Bryant, Sarah Shaw, and Kenneth Tanaka, emphasis is sometimes placed on the development of *dhyāna*, pronounced *jhāna* in Pali. These terms may refer to concentrative meditation and/or associated meditative states, which are sometimes referred to as "attainments." According to the *Yoga Sūtras* (Yoga Aphorisms), correct practice eventually results in "concentration" (*dhyāna*) and "meditative absorption" (*samādhi*), to a state of psychological imperturbability. Similarly, the *Ānāpānasati Sutta* (Discourse on Mindfulness of Breathing) discusses four *jhāna*s. The associated states include the following: (1) initial and discursive thought, joy, happiness, and one-pointedness; (2) calmness, confidence, and tranquility; (3) composure, mindfulness, and clear comprehension; and (4) mindfulness and equanimity beyond discomfort or ease. In addition, in each case, the mind is free from the Five Hindrances—craving, ill-will, torpor, agitation, and doubt—and, in the final three stages, one no longer engages in discursive thought. Once again we encounter "consciousness" beyond discursive thought, reason, intellect, and so forth. These diverse qualities and characteristics also reveal community- and tradition-specific values. As discussed in more detail later in this chapter, different forms of contemplative practice may result in different forms of embodiment and being-in-the-world.[10]

On the more radical end of the spectrum, Hinduism, Buddhism, and Daoism sometimes identify "higher powers" that may emerge from dedicated and sustained practice. Related to the chapters by the previously mentioned contributors and to my own chapter on Daoist internal alchemy, Hinduism tends to refer to these capacities as *siddhi*, while Buddhism tends to use the category of *abhijñā* (Pali: *abhiññā*). These terms have been translated variously as "numinous abilities," "paranormal abilities," "psychic dispositions," and "supernatural powers."[11] The point is that, from such contemplative and religious perspectives, humans have latent capacities. In this respect, the Tantric and Yogic strains of Indian religions are especially relevant. One finds some parallels in Daoist alchemical systems, with Daoist discussions of "numinous abilities" (*shentong*; lit., spirit pervasion/divine connection) largely emerging under Buddhist influence. In any case, some typical numinous abilities include clairaudience, clairvoyance, dematerialization, multilocation, multivocality, precognition, rarefication, recollection of past lives, telepathy, and so forth. In addition, some religious traditions also identify less easily recognizable characteristics of advanced practitioners. For example, various Catholic Christian hagiographies highlight the abilities of certain saints to communicate with animals (see, e.g., Bell 1992; Waddell 1995).[12] This ability is also mentioned in the *Yoga Sūtras* (III.17) and in the *Rasskaz strannika* (Tale of a Pilgrim; chs. 2 and 4). Moreover, if one reads the latter text more literally, it appears that higher-level practitioners attain not only conscious postmortem existence but also the ability to provide spiritual direction to students after death. This parallels certain Daoist views, as expressed for example in Liu Huayang's mystical transmission, that teachers include "immortals," who may be both embodied and disembodied. Such claims fall under what in modern Western contexts is labeled "psi" or "paranormal phenomena." Often associated with "parapsychology" and dismissed as "pseudo-science," one may, nonetheless, consider the possibility of "extrasensory perception" and "psychokinesis" (see, e.g., Kripal 2006, 2010; Kakar and Kripal 2012).[13] While no doubt a major source of discomfort and radical subversiveness to some, these claims suggest that humans may have additional capacities, ones that are suppressed or delegitimized by dominant systems of enculturation and indoctrination. Such numinous abilities also bring the issue of subjective experience in relation to scientific quantification and validation, including interpretive authority, into high relief. In addition, we may reflect on the categories "natural/normal" and "supernatural/anomalous," and the ways in which these are understood in different communities. Is it possible that "normal" everyday consciousness is actually an "altered state of consciousness"?

In any case, the contemplative and religious maps of transformative praxis find some parallels in contemporary Western psychology, especially in humanistic and transpersonal psychology. The so-called third force, humanistic psychology partially developed as a response to the psychoanalytic approach of Sigmund Freud (1856–1939) and the behavioral approach of B. F. Skinner (1904–1990), including a tendency to "pathologize" the human condition. For present purposes, humanistic psychology, with its emphasis on human potential and self-actualization, and transpersonal psychology, with its emphasis on "spiritual" and "transcendent dimensions" of human existence, are relevant because they too provide maps of human aliveness and flourishing. Generally speaking, these psychological perspectives suggest that humans have various latent or unrecognized potentials and that fulfillment emerges through their actualization. For example, Abraham Maslow (1901–1970) identifies a "hierarchy of needs." From the most basic to the more advanced or higher, they include physiological (food, water, etc.), safety (body, shelter, etc.), belonging (family, friendship, etc.), esteem (achievement, respect, etc.), and self-actualization (Maslow 1999). According to Maslow, if an individual's foundational and fundamental needs are met, he or she may engage in a process of self-actualization, or the fulfillment of various potentialities. Some characteristics of self-actualizing and self-actualized people include acceptance, appreciation, creativity, discernment, fulfillment, humor, independence, joyfulness, positive regard, self-reliance, and sympathy (Maslow 1999). Interestingly, other features of such individuals include a commitment to satisfying relationships and situations as well as "unconditional positive regard" for others. As the perceptive reader may recognize, there are some noteworthy parallels with religious claims about spiritual realization. Such approaches suggest that one may overcome habituated tendencies, tendencies formed through social conditioning, familial obligations, and personal reactivity. In addition, one may have various "peak experiences" (Maslow 1964) and "optimal experiences" such as "flow" (Csikszentmihalyi 1990). That is, there are experiences that indicate and manifest self-actualization (see also Murphy 1992; Gendlin 1997).[14]

Each of these cartographies, or maps of transformation, suggests that there are moments or conditions in which one may feel fully alive. There is a conception of human fulfillment beyond enculturation and habituation. Almost every contemplative approach agrees that such ways of being involve deconditioning and some form of transformation, although it is possible that this is simply a different type of conditioning and enculturation (see ch. 1). While there are practice- and community-specific characteristics and values, contemplative traditions also provide larger insights into human possibility. They reveal both diverse capacities and shared humanity. They suggest that we may become "more"; we may cultivate and embody values and patterns of interaction that support human and perhaps transhuman flourishing. They also suggest that one may determine the depth of individuals' contemplative practice by observing their way of being and relating to others.

Another dimension of contemplative practice and contemplative experience centers on "stages," briefly introduced earlier. In terms of the present volume, though one might read Sufi contemplation and Eastern Orthodox prayer along these lines, the main stage-based practice is Daoist internal alchemy, which consists of eight stages according to the *Huiming jing* (Scripture on Wisdom and Life-Destiny). In terms of traditional Daoist models, one usually engages in a sequential training regimen (see Komjathy 2007, 2013a). That is, one must practice each method in order, with corresponding indications that the practice has been successful. This is often referred to as "signs of proof," "experiential confirmation," or "verification" (*zhengyan*).

If one interrupts or abandons the practice, and subsequently resumes it, one must start over from the beginning. That is, one must complete the process of psychosomatic transformation through a set process. It is also possible to read the *Guanjing* (Visualization Sutra) along similar lines, and we may recall a parallel conception in certain Sufi systems. However, some of the most developed stage-based models appear in Buddhist literature, wherein "stage" often corresponds to the Sanskrit technical term *bhūmi* (lit., ground). As described by the Indian Theravāda Buddhist commentator and scholar Buddhaghoṣa (5th c. CE) in his *Visuddhimagga* (Path of Purification), there are seven stages: (1) Purification of Conduct, (2) Purification of Mind, (3) Purification of View, (4) Purification by Overcoming Doubt, (5) Purification by Knowledge and Vision of What Is Path and Not Path, (6) Purification by Knowledge and Vision of the Course of Practice, and (7) Purification by Knowledge and Vision (Gunaratana 1985; Ñāṇamoli 1991; cf. Ehara et al. 1997; Kavanaugh and Rodriguez 1979).[15] The latter is the culmination of practice, with the goal of "liberation" (Pali: *nibbāna*; Skt.: *nirvāṇa*). Along similar lines, Daniel Brown (1986), drawing primarily on Indian contemplative traditions, has identified the following cross-cultural stages of meditation (see also Roth 1999, 136):[16]

I. Preliminary Ethical Practices

II. Preliminary Body and Mind Training

III. Concentration with Support

IV. Concentration without Support

V. Insight Practice

VI. Advanced Insight Practice

This is not the place to discuss the universal applicability of Brown's schema, especially considering the problematic privileging of "concentration" and "insight" (see ch. 1) and how much evidence would be required. Suffice it to say that Brown's research inspires one to consider the relative importance of sequence and the hierarchal ordering of practice and experience, including parallels that emerge through comparative analysis.

These various insights in turn require reflection on the degree to which "transformation," "stages," "extraordinary experience," and the like are emphasized in contemplative approaches. The implication of this discussion is that there are "higher" or more "advanced" forms of practice and states of consciousness. While I have suggested that this is the case in certain examples, other perspectives would challenge, or at least qualify, such concerns. For example, classical Daoism, the earliest form of Daoism explored by Harold Roth herein, emphasizes apophatic meditation, with an understanding that one's innate nature and the sacred (Dao) are characterized by stillness. Such practice simply involves returning to one's original condition of alignment with the Dao. "Transformation" is only apparently the case, and one either abides in a condition of pure being and direct experience (*ziran*) or not. Along similar lines, Chan (Zen) Buddhism, a Chinese school of Mahāyāna Buddhism that emphasizes meditation, often identifies "extraordinary experiences" as forms of distraction (see, e.g., Gimello 1978; Sharf 1995, 1998). While the tradition does recognize certain types of enlightenment experiences (Jpn.: *kenshō*; *satori*) as indicative of "spiritual progress," these are generally considered *by-products* of dedicated and prolonged practice. If one is overly concerned or attached to them, they may easily become sources of distraction and obstruction. A parallel example is found in certain systems of Daoist internal alchemy (see Komjathy 2007, 2013a), wherein "numinous abilities" and other types of experiences are simply identified as natural signs of successful training. They may confirm the efficacy of training, but they are ultimately irrelevant. Perhaps most radically, J. Krishnamurti, who is discussed by Constance Jones in this volume, challenges each and every system, including "contemplative ones." Any conception or concern may just as easily become a form of cognitive bondage as a source of freedom. This includes teachers, communities, traditions, and so forth. Applying Krishnamurti to the present discussion, hierarchical orderings, such as in the form of "levels," "stages," "progress," and so forth, may actually distort and limit consciousness.[17] Perhaps recalling the famous adage *tat tvam asi* (you are That) from the Hindu *Upanishads*, Krishnamurti encourages one to become realized in/to/through the present moment. From Krishnamurti's perspective, meditation is an all-pervading existential approach, which is "revolutionary," not evolutionary in nature. This recalls the Daoist emphasis on "innate nature" (*xing*); the Chan Buddhist concern for buddha-nature (Skt.: *tathāgatagarbha*); and perhaps even the view of certain Christian contemplatives and mystics, such as Meister Eckhart (1260–1328), about Christ as the Ground of one's being. In the language of Chan Buddhism, such perspectives might inspire one to consider, "What was the face before your birth?" This, perhaps, is a form of identity and a way of being free from conditioning and habituation, including that of contemplative systems. It is a conditionless or transpersonal "condition" in which one has disappeared into that which is beyond names and conceptions.[18] Such perspectives bring our attention to the diverse views, types, and purposes of contemplative practice and contemplative experience, including the degree to which "practice" or "experience" is emphasized and the possibility that practice must be central, regardless of whatever experiences occur.

Embodied being-in-the-world is the final dimension of transformative praxis that deserves consideration. While one might discuss actual physicality (e.g., posture) and somatic experience (see chs. 1 and 2), here I am more concerned with the ways in which contemplative practice is expressed as activity in the world. While some may assume that contemplative practice involves "navel gazing" and escapism, and others may assume that it inevitably leads to concern for others and the world at large, the situation is much more complex. In considering this dimension of contemplative practice, we may recall a number of previous points. First, drawing upon Walter Stace's (1960) distinction between "introvertive mysticism" and "extrovertive mysticism," albeit with a slightly different application (Roth 2000), we may consider the "inward" and "outward" dimensions of contemplative practice (see also Deikman 1982). Second, this topic relates to the various qualities and effects of contemplative practice, especially what might be considered "beneficial influences." That is, if contemplative practice makes us more fully human on some level, if it facilitates self-actualization, then how does this become expressed on communal, sociopolitical, and ecological levels? This is the "intersubjective" and "socially engaged" dimension of contemplative practice, and I would encourage us to avoid anthropocentrism in this respect. (I am not convinced that authentic contemplative practice could ultimately be anthropocentric.) As we have seen throughout the present volume, contemplative practice involves interiority, an inward orientation. At the same time, contemplatives inhabit various types of social space, and one may reasonably inquire about the degree to which introvertive transformation results in extrovertive expression and activity. We may investigate the potential influence that contemplative practice has on the associated community and larger society, specifically with respect to social engagement. Here we may recall my earlier discussion of "contemplative pedagogy" as transformative education (see ch. 1).

One prominent modern example of the extrovertive dimension of contemplative practice is Socially Engaged Buddhism (SEB) (see, e.g., Queen and King 1996; Queen 2000), sometimes simply referred to as "engaged Buddhism." With a deep root in Buddhist ethics and meditation, Socially Engaged Buddhists, perhaps expanding the meaning of the *bodhisattva* ideal, work to alleviate suffering in the world. Some major concerns include animal welfare, hunger, oppression, poverty, violence, and so forth. Along parallel lines, one thinks of the activities of certain Roman Catholic nuns who work among the poor and disenfranchised, perhaps as a way of identifying with Christ as model. Another profound example is the Religious Society of Friends, a form of Protestant Christianity deeply rooted in contemplative practice in the form of silent worship. This contemplative commitment is further expressed in the Quaker practice of spirit-directed (i.e., consensus-based) decision-making and common commitment to nonviolence, even to the point of pacifism. Such examples bring our attention to potential contemplative applications and approaches to human activity, including community and work. At the same time, they require reflection on the extent to which contemplatives and contemplative communities have a committed or explicit extrovertive expression. Here one thinks of ascetic or renunciant orientations, including the informing existential, soteriological, and theological views. These involve varying degrees of concern for the "mundane world." We also find intentional communities, such as monasteries, that involve some degree of withdrawal from the world and perhaps an implicit critique of the corruption that can and often does come from participating in ordinary society. It may be that grassroots, intentional communities are the form of social organization most conducive to contemplative practice. It may also be that contemplative practice is most fully expressed in such communities.

Such considerations also relate to the relationship among religion, peace, and violence, and they challenge simplistic claims about religion as the *sole* or *primary* source of discord and violence in the world. While religious adherents and communities no doubt have much to answer for in terms of violence (see, e.g., Wessinger 2000; Juergensmeyer 2003; Juergensmeyer et al. 2012; Lincoln 2006), the demonization of "religion" is rooted in simplistic analyses that fail to consider the complex relationship among ancestry, culture, nationalism, politics, religion, tribalism, and so forth. Just as religious views may contribute to psychological well-being or not, the "religion of the healthy-minded" and the "religion of the sick-minded," to use a slightly modified version of William James's terms (1999; cf. Freud 1989, 1990), so too religion may be a source of peace or violence in the world. In terms of our present discussion, it is possible that dedicated and prolonged contemplative practice results in deeper experiences of peace, both internally and externally. The "extrovertive dimension" of contemplative practice thus has some potential connections with peace studies; that is, contemplative practice may support peace and reconciliation. It might also be utilized as a stress-management technique and methodology for mediators, especially individuals who are stationed in difficult sociopolitical contexts. At the same time, one finds at least some examples wherein "contemplative traditions" have contributed to and perhaps even engaged in violence. Here I am thinking of the role that Zen Buddhists and Shinto adherents played in Japanese nationalism during World War II (see, e.g., Victoria 2006; Skya 2009). One could equally draw attention to the history of violence in the Tibetan Buddhist

Figure 15.2. United States Military Sniper[20]
Source: StockFreeImages.com

tradition (see, e.g., Samuel 1995; Lopez 1999; Dalton 2011) or the modern "weaponization of meditation" in the United States military.[19]

Many more examples could be given, but the point is that the potential connection between contemplative practice, violence, and military activity deserves further research. In this respect, one may reasonably wonder if authentic contemplative practice may be violent or if violence is a departure from contemplative practice. Perhaps contemplative practice may have a "military application" but ceases being "contemplative" at the moment that violence or killing occurs. That being said, I have no interest in "contemplative apologetics," and a deep and comprehensive approach to contemplative studies (see ch. 1) must be willing to investigate the entire phenomenon as objectively as possible.

Along similar lines, one also finds a disturbing pattern within the "therapeutic application" of meditation, namely, the use of meditation as a form of battlefield and triage medicine, such as in the treatment of post-traumatic stress disorder (PTSD). One example is use of Integrative Restoration (iRest), a modified form of Yoga Nidra developed by Richard C. Miller, PhD (b. 1948). Miller has collaborated with the Walter Reed Army Medical Center (Bethesda, MD) and the United States Department of Defense to study the efficacy of iRest. This protocol has been used with soldiers returning from Iraq and Afghanistan suffering from PTSD. Based on this work, in 2010 Eric Schoomaker, surgeon general of the United States Army, endorsed iRest as a complementary alternative medicine (CAM) for the treatment of chronic pain (see www.irest.us). While such programs are perhaps laudable for their work to alleviate human suffering, at least the suffering of certain human beings, it is also important to change the contexts that require violence and to challenge, perhaps oppose, certain human tendencies. Is it possible that the alleviation of PTSD through meditation supports, at least indirectly, violence and war in the world? Do we not need individuals with PTSD to remind us of the psychological consequences of killing and the horrors of war? One may inadvertently (uncontemplatively?) become complicit in the perpetuation of violence and injustice. Here I would draw attention to the ways in which contemplative practice is becoming reconceptualized and, in certain cases, domesticated. As I have suggested, certain forms of contemplative practice may be understood as "radical," "subversive," and a form of "resistance," especially to dominant values and systems. One might see contemplative practice, at least integrated, holistic, and uncompromised contemplative practice, as a form of resistance to certain industrial and modern tendencies (cf. Žižek 2001; see also Agamben 2013). Perhaps tradition-based contemplative practice inspires us to sit, *to refuse to move*, in specific communities and specific places informed by specific values. Perhaps it makes us more aware of and attentive to the importance of embodiment and place for human being and flourishing.

Such insights would, in turn, problematize the high degree of technological mediation at work in contemplative studies, especially in the form of neuroscience, "laboratories," and "scientific validation" (i.e., so-called "contemplative science"). Perhaps such approaches are antithetical to particular values and commitments of authentic contemplative practice. One might resist spiritual colonialism and socially acceptable domestications of contemplative practice *in the name of contemplative practice*. At the same time, we must confront a number of potentially troubling dimensions. This includes the ways in which contemplative practice might become yet another form of anesthetization and pacification, a substitute for mood-altering drugs and "antidepressants." Perhaps there are things that should generate anger and depression in us. Perhaps we need to acknowledge the potential importance of agitation and discomfort as well as the transformative effect of "stress." We also need to confront the possibility that, at least in the case of the United States, meditation may be a form of largely white, middle-class escapism. It may be a specific type of privilege and social injustice.

These points notwithstanding, we may understand integrated contemplative practice as a form of transformative praxis. On the most general level, it helps one to develop attentiveness, awareness, interiority, presence, silence, and a deepened sense of meaning and purpose. On a more specific level, different contemplative systems and religious traditions emphasize the cultivation and actualization of different qualities. These are the benefits and effects of committed and prolonged contemplative practice. This may manifest as a more conscious form of embodied being-in-the-world, one that includes various forms of social engagement. Careful study, deep engagement, and sustained reflection on the defining characteristics and transformative effects of contemplative practice may also reveal the importance of aesthetics, community, embodiment, and place in the human condition. It may be that deep contemplative practice not only requires such things but also awakens one to their importance. Perhaps they are the preconditions for human aliveness, flourishing, and transformation. Perhaps contemplative practice, in its fullest expression, is "ecological." Perhaps it enables one to hear the widespread and multilayered suffering in the world, not simply among human beings, and inspires one to work to alleviate it. It may result in a greater concern for life and sense of place. It may help one become both more sensitive and more resilient.

(En)countering Reality

If contemplative systems and religious traditions provide insights into the human condition, especially in terms of subjective experience as well as meaning and purpose, this is even more the case with respect to "reality." If taken seriously, the radical alterity and pluralism of these accounts contain challenges to various assumptions and views. In technical language, this aspect of contemplative practice relates to soteriology and theology, to claims about the ultimate purpose of human existence and about ultimate reality. It also may relate to "metaphysical" concerns, although once again degrees of immanence and transcendence come to the fore. As will be discussed momentarily, such considerations also relate to comparative theology and interreligious dialogue, or at least serious engagement with multiculturalism and religious pluralism.

We may begin by developing a methodology for engaging theological diversity. Even if one is an atheist or secular materialist, there can be little debate that concern for the "sacred" is a defining characteristic and central concern of religious adherents and communities. So, to fully understand contemplative practice, and religion by extension, we must consider the informing worldview, especially with respect to that which is defined as "divine" or "ultimately real." Here Clifford Geertz (1926–2006), an American anthropologist and advocate of "symbolic anthropology," is helpful.

> A religion is (1) a system of symbols which acts to (2) establish powerful, pervasive, and long-lasting moods and motivations in men [sic] by (3) formulating conceptions of a general order of existence and (4) clothing these conceptions with such an aura of factuality that (5) the moods and motivations seem uniquely realistic. (1973, 4)

According to Geertz, different religious traditions, which are basically cultural systems, involve different worldviews, different accounts of "reality." These not only create a sense of meaning but also establish psychological states characterized by belief and conviction. Through enculturation, religious adherents, and members of any given culture, come to believe in a certain type of world and universe. That is, Geertz's account is both anthropological and psychological. Such views also recall William James (1842–1910), an American philosopher and psychologist, who understands religion as rooted in "the feelings, acts, and experiences of individual men [sic] in their solitude, so far as they apprehend themselves to stand in relation to whatever they may consider the divine" (1999, 31). Although one might read James's description as quasi-theological (e.g., "whatever they may consider the divine"), it is more accurately psychological. While interested in various subjective experiences of the "sacred," James is quite careful to "bracket," in the language of a phenomenological approach to interpreting religion, truth-claims. From James's psychological perspective, it is enough that religious adherents believe that what they believe is true, and they should be studied as such. We need not concern ourselves with whether or not their accounts are actually true. Along similar lines, Mircea Eliade (1907–1986), a Romanian historian of religions and key figure in the establishment of religious studies as such, discusses the relationship between "myth" and "reality" (1998; see also Berger and Luckmann 1966). Religions include myths, and these myths are accounts of "reality." They also generate a distinct reality for the individuals who live in the associated mythology. Combining these various views, we may say that, at least on a descriptive, psychological, and perhaps even social level, different religious adherents inhabit different worlds. They have different values and concerns that inform their lives and create certain patterns of activity in the world. In addition, they actually lead to distinctive restructurings of the world and particular material environments (see, e.g., Heidegger 1977; Sartre 1991). However, in *The Sacred and the Profane*, Eliade apparently goes farther:

> Man [sic] becomes aware of the sacred because it manifests itself, shows itself, as something wholly different from the profane. To designate the *act of manifestation* of the sacred, we have proposed the term *hierophany*. . . . It could be said that the history of religions—from the most primitive to the most highly developed—is constituted by a great number hierophanies, by manifestations of sacred realities. (1987, 11; italics in original)

While it is possible to read this interpretation as parallel with the work *Myth and Reality*, I want to press it for the sake of argument. Under a more literal reading, Eliade appears to advocate a normative "polytheistic," or at least theologically pluralistic, definition of religion. Different religious traditions are based on "hierophanies" from different realities, and, by extension, they connect religious adherents to different sacreds. As will be discussed later, one may have different theological interpretations of such diversity, so here it is sufficient to consider that "reality" is plural, not singular; multiple, not unified. Of course, this requires further reflection on the relationship between individuality and collectivity, between unity and diversity. These may not be antithetical.

In terms of the present volume, contemplative literature includes competing claims about the nature of reality. Here we may recall my earlier discussion of the complex relationship among view, practice, and experience (see chs. 1 and 2). Contemplative practice is informed by and expresses particular worldviews, that is, "symbol systems" and "myths." At the same time, on a theological level, they may document and remember different "hierophanies," or manifestations of sacred *realities*:

> Buddhism (early): Not applicable (*nibbāna*) (consciousness)[21]
> Buddhism (later): Buddhas and bodhisattvas (Buddha-realms)
> Christianity: God/Christ (Heaven)
> Daoism: Dao and Daoist pantheon (energy and/or heavens)
> Hinduism: Brahman and Hindu pantheon (consciousness and/or heavens)
> Islam: Allah (Heaven)
> Judaism: YHWH (G-d) (World-to-Come)

Engagement with the various chapters reveals the defining characteristics of each of these accounts. Here we may simply consider a few comparative aspects. The Abrahamic traditions, at least conventionally speaking, believe in the same god (i.e., God). However, Christians, in contrast to Jews and Muslims, claim that God became incarnate in Jesus of Nazareth as Christ. This contradicts the fundamental theological position of Judaism and Islam: The nature of God is such that God cannot become physically embodied. Along similar lines, although perhaps in surprising ways, Hinduism generally defines the universe and human embodiment as samsaric in nature; Brahman is not manifest in the physical world. Just as *atman*, the eternal soul, is encased *inside* the body and *distinct from* the body, Brahman is transcendent. While it is possible to see some parallels with the Daoist concept of Dao, Daoists generally view the universe and physicality as manifestations of the Dao. Granted these are generalizations, but they may inspire various reflections. Is that which is identified as sacred in, beyond, or in and beyond the manifest universe? Is there a distinction between Nature and the sacred? Is the conception theistic or nontheistic? Is it encountered in relational or nonrelational ways? That is, is the conception dualistic or nondualistic? Regardless of whether such realities exist, the associated worldviews no doubt have actual consequences in terms of human experience, existential commitments, patterns of engagement, and ways of life.

On a more radical level, they point toward the emerging field of comparative theology (see, e.g., Tracy 2005; Clooney 2010; also Neville 1996; Ward 1998; Knitter 2002; Panikkar 2006). In this respect, we may consider both types of theological discourse and types of theology (Komjathy 2012, 2013b). Theological discourse may be descriptive, historical, normative, or comparative, although the discipline of theology (Christian theology) tends to be associated with adherent perspectives and normative truth-claims, including various approaches (e.g., feminist, liberationist, moral, systematic, etc.). These types are relatively straightforward: description, description with attention to historical context and cultural influence, truth-claims, and comparison. Comparative theological discourse also may be normative and constructive; that is, beyond simply comparing theological perspectives, one may attempt to generate theological positions based on comparison. In terms of types of theology, for comparative purposes, I would identify the following: animistic (gods/spirits in nature), atheistic (no gods), monistic (one impersonal reality [i.e., Reality]), monotheistic (one personal god [i.e., God]), panenhenic (Nature as sacred), pantheistic (sacred in the world), panentheistic (sacred in and beyond the world), and polytheistic (many personal gods). Depending on the informing worldview, these may or may not be contradictory or irreconcilable. In addition, while one may simply interpret these along descriptive, historical, and/or comparative lines, I would suggest that theological views are always normative on some level, even if avoided, ignored, or dismissed.

Various theological positions and responses are, in turn, viable. One of the most common would be a secular materialist one, in which theology is dismissed as "myth without reality." This, of course, is a theological position, although advocates may prefer the label of "a-theological" and emphasize different dimensions of religion. Another common response would involve a normative monistic position, especially in the form of Perennial Philosophy (see ch. 1). This position might claim that each account is simply a different interpretation of the same reality (i.e., Reality). However, for this view to be viable, it would have to utilize the materials in the present volume, which demonstrate that it is unsupported by evidence. Normative monists might, in turn, have two additional responses: (1) domesticate or dismiss the radical differences, or (2) accept religious difference but maintain their own theological position. Only the latter is viable, but it would be further challenged by other theological positions.

From my perspective, the comparative study of religion reveals mutually exclusive, equally convincing accounts of "reality." If one understands the informing worldviews, the "symbol systems" and "myths," if one learns to think through adherence, one finds that different adherents and communities live in different realities, even if this is only cognitively the case. Given the radical diversity and plurality of theological claims, one might, in turn, suggest that there are different manifestations of a singular reality. One finds such views in certain forms of Hinduism, such as in the claim that the various goddesses are expressions of the Goddess, or more technically that gods are simply expressions of Brahman in theistic forms. Alternatively, one might adopt a normative "polytheistic" or pluralist theological view: religious accounts are not simply different on a descriptive level, but they are actually about *different realities*. From this interpretive perspective, contemplative practice may lead to experiences of alternate realities, and such experiences have specific theological import and soteriological consequences.

The "encounter with reality" also relates to religious pluralism and interreligious dialogue (see, e.g., Tracy 1998; Panikkar 1999; Sherwin and Kasimow 1999; Hick 2005). Various responses are possible, which generally fall into the categories of exclusivism, relativism, inclusivism, and pluralism. Exclusivism privileges one particular view. Common exclusivist positions include religious fundamentalism and sectarianism as well as scientism and secular materialism. Relativism emphasizes that different perspectives are only relatively or conditionally true. They are determined by a given community, culture, historical context, and so forth. As relativism tends to be a form of secular materialism, common relativist positions include conventional social scientific interpretations of religion. Inclusivism tends to be rooted in and committed to a particular worldview but also recognizes other perspectives as offering important contributions. Inclusivism may be relatively weak or relatively strong, depending on its degree of commitment to one particular view and openness to other views. As inclusivism tends to be more universalistic and synthetic, and especially concerned with complementarity and harmony, common inclusivist positions include Christian ecumenism and much of what actually occurs in the name of "interreligious dialogue." Inclusivism tends to emphasize commonalities and areas of agreement. More technically defined, pluralism not only recognizes diversity and plurality but also represents a particular philosophical and theological response. In terms of the present volume and the preceding discussion, a pluralist position accepts and perhaps celebrates difference, including the radical challenges of otherness and dissimilarity. While exclusivism perhaps manifests in opposition and violence, in a drive toward subjugation and extermination of other, and while inclusivism perhaps manifests in collaboration and harmony but perhaps through domestication, homogenization, and convergence, pluralism views diversity and actual difference as beneficial. In place of the potential monoculture of exclusivism and inclusivism, pluralism accepts a world characterized by wildness, biodiversity, and symbiotic relationships. Concern for peace and violence thus need not require cognitive annihilation or transcendence of difference. It may, rather, require complete acceptance of difference. Authentic interreligious dialogue is one that, following David Tracy's recommendation, allows the conversation to assume primacy and becomes expressed in understanding. It is thus possible to be both committed and open (see Simmer-Brown 1999) and to accept that others have a similar degree of commitment, although to perhaps different values. While this may create discomfort, it also provides opportunities for dialogue and reflection.

Beyond exclusivist and insular responses to multiculturalism and religious pluralism, and beyond inclusivist tendencies toward domestication, we may adopt a pluralist approach. Regardless of one's theological commitments, that is, whether religion is simply about myth or about myth *and* reality, we may make space for radical difference, cognitive dissonance, and philosophical inquiry. We may consider the insights and challenges that come from careful study and sustained engagement with contemplative literature and contemplative traditions. Like a classroom in which the materials are discussed, this may be viewed as a form of interreligious dialogue. In terms of the present volume, we may wonder if there are actually "elders" and "lineages of inner cultivation." We may consider the importance and necessity of silence in human existence. We may ponder the possibility that some convictions and experiences are incommunicable and untranslatable. We may wonder if "awakening" is possible, including the potential requirement of renunciation or monasticism. We may inquire into hidden dimensions of the body, of a potential somatic experience of light and energy, and wonder about the importance of remembrance. We may reflect on the possibility that contemplative practice as preparation for dying and death as well as devotion is a prerequisite. We may consider the nature and characteristics of "purified consciousness," including the potential activation of "paranormal abilities." We may also begin to think of life as pilgrimage, with the corresponding requirement of correct orientation and reverence. We may inquire into the importance of aesthetics, community, and place, including the potential transformative effect of posture and location. We may wonder if walls, faced in meditation, are actually portals into something else. We may consider the meaning and purpose of stress, illness, and wellness in the human condition, including a way of life and livelihood rooted in the alleviation of suffering. And we may find that each and every system is a source of both restraint and freedom, even our most dearly held and fiercely rejected ones. We may, perhaps, engage in interreligious dialogue as existential commitment and lived contemplative practice.

Into the Labyrinth

The labyrinth may be viewed as a symbol for both contemplative practice and its academic study.[22] In the introductory chapters, the twelve specific chapters that are the core of this book, and these concluding comparative reflections, we have found ourselves in the labyrinth of contemplative studies. We have explored some of the defining characteristics and interpretive issues related to contemplative practice and contemplative experience.

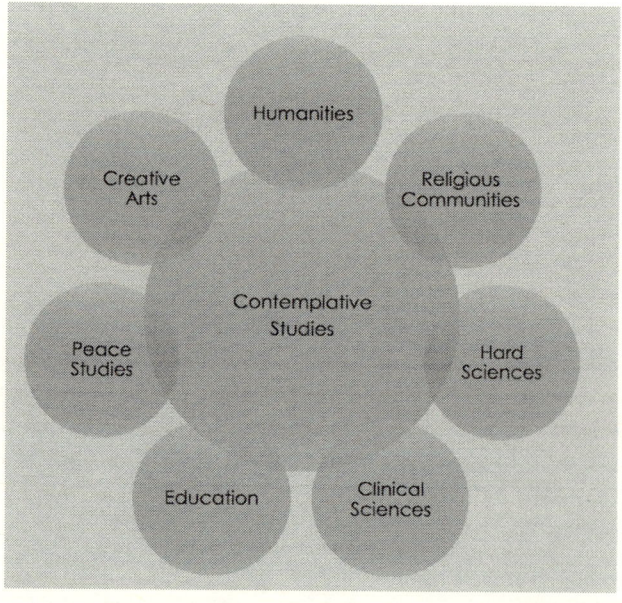

Figure 15.3. Contemplative Studies as Interdisciplinary Field

In the first introductory chapter on "contemplative practice," I discussed key issues in the emerging interdisciplinary field of contemplative studies, with an emphasis on actual interdisciplinarity as well as a comparative religious studies approach. In my conception of the field, the latter would be one particular expression of the broader area of the "humanities" or "liberal arts." Emphasis was placed on "contemplative practice" as a comparative category and contemplative studies as an emerging academic field, including "contemplative pedagogy," or teaching and learning informed by and perhaps as an expression of contemplative practice. With respect to the contemplative studies, I gave particular attention to a Contextualist approach as well as reflected on the contributions and limitations of empirical approaches, especially concerning the relative merits of neuroscience and neuroimaging technologies. Finally, I identified and discussed key issues in the study and practice of religiously-committed and tradition-based contemplative practice and contemplative experience.

The second introductory chapter examined "contemplative traditions," that is, the contemplative strains or dimensions of religious traditions. I in turn discussed the meaning and defining characteristics of "contemplative traditions." In particular, I provided some information on the entire spectrum of tradition-based contemplative practice in order to locate the works selected in this volume. Next, attention was given to the dimensions of contemplative practice, specifically the ways in which contemplative practice is located in larger religious and soteriological systems. Here I emphasized the multidimensional nature of religious practice, with contemplative practice being only one element. This was followed by a brief discussion of "contemplative experience," or types of experiences that occur within or are identified as important in the context of contemplative practice. I drew a distinction between contemplative experience, mystical experience, and religious experience. In addition, I discussed some of the types of experiences that are claimed to occur during committed and sustained practice. Next, I suggested that we may study contemplative practice through the lens of "psychologies of realization," that is, the types of psychologies utilized within contemplative traditions. In particular, I suggested that many contemplative traditions map human potential and more "advanced" ontological conditions. That is, committed and prolonged contemplative practice results in distinctive transformative effects. I then discussed "contemplative literature" and the contents of the present volume. Finally, attention was given to future prospects. While the previous chapter was more abstract and theoretical, this chapter was more concrete. I focused on specific examples of contemplative practice and contemplative experience and on contemplative traditions. Throughout this presentation, I drew upon the micro-studies of contemplative literature that form the center of this volume. These two introductory chapters thus were intended and may inspire one to consider contemplative studies, including contemplative practice, contemplative experience, contemplative pedagogy, and contemplative literature, in a more sophisticated and integrated way. We may explore key theoretical issues, relevant approaches, and interpretative frameworks for engaging in the academic study of meditation, contemplative prayer, and other cognate methods and disciplines.

We then moved into the specific chapters and texts, chapters 3 through 14. In sequential order, the topics and authors were as follows: (1) classical Daoist apophatic meditation by Harold Roth, (2) Quaker Christian silent prayer by Michael Birkel, (3) Lurianic Jewish Kabbalah by Shaul Magid, (4) Southern Buddhist meditation by Sarah Shaw, (5) Naqshbandi-Mujaddidi Sufi contemplation by Arthur Buehler, (6) Eastern Orthodox Christian prayer by John McGuckin, (7) Pure Land Buddhist visualization by Kenneth Tanaka, (8) Hindu classical Yoga by Edwin

Bryant, (9) Dominican Catholic prayer by Paul Philibert, (10) Wu-Liu Daoist internal alchemy by Louis Komjathy, (11) modern therapeutic meditation by Louis Komjathy, and (12) techniqueless meditation by Constance Jones. The volume thus contains a wide variety of texts from various traditions and historical periods. As mentioned in the introduction, each contributor also utilized a standardized format comprised of an introduction followed by an annotated translation and/or selection. Each introduction consisted of six sections: (1) biographical and historical background, (2) associated religious tradition and textual corpus, (3) religious and soteriological system, (4) textual survey of primary text, (5) legacy and influence, and (6) interpretive issues related to the comparative study of contemplative practice and contemplative experience. As conceived of by me, and as embraced, employed, and developed by each individual author, this template is one expression of a historical contextualist and comparative religious studies approach to contemplative studies, to the academic study of contemplative practice and contemplative experience. Particular attention was given to such important considerations as audience, authorship, context, date, genre, language, tradition, and so forth. These chapters thus provide a model for future research, especially in terms of religious studies informed by history, literary studies, and, at least in certain cases, philosophy and theology. As discussed in chapter 2, one can imagine many other studies, including tradition-specific monographs and other comparative volumes focusing on, for instance, practices specifically developed by and intended for women as well as more modern, "lived," and "living" forms of contemplative practice.

Moving still further into the labyrinth, contemplative practice and contemplative experience are diverse and multifaceted. We have explored this complexity through what I have labeled "contemplative literature," that is, literature that addresses contemplative practice in a detailed technical manner. We have found that there are diverse methods with distinctive informing worldviews as well as various goals and ideals. These are the larger religious systems, including soteriologies and theologies, in which religiously-committed and tradition-based contemplative practice occurs. While contemplative practice is often reduced to "technique" and sometimes to "physiology," we have seen that a more nuanced and comprehensive approach recognizes other dimensions as well. These include aesthetics, community, embodiment (e.g., posture), material culture, place, tradition, and worldview. Other relevant considerations include dietetics, ethics, ritual, scripture study, and so forth.

Traversing more inner circuits of the labyrinth, we have found that contemplatives, contemplative communities, contemplative literature, and contemplative traditions offer important insights into the human condition, including specific existential, soteriological, and theological claims and challenges. Taken seriously on their own terms, the texts of the present volume make certain claims about human potential and "self-actualization." Although diverse, they provide a glimpse into what I have referred to as "psychologies of realization." These include specific benefits and effects of committed and prolonged contemplative practice. Contemplative practice may lead to both more transitory states and more permanent traits. That is, one's subjective experience, personality, and way of being may be radically and profoundly altered through training. The texts of the present volume suggest that contemplative practice often leads to more beneficial psychological and ontological conditions, conditions that may further manifest in beneficial forms of embodied being-in-the-world and social engagement. In addition, different contemplative systems consist of distinctive soteriologies and theologies. They have different "myths" and "symbols systems," which imagine the world, universe, and ultimate reality in radically different ways. From my perspective, careful study of religion reveals mutually exclusive, equally convincing accounts of "reality." Religious adherents and communities, and members of any culture more generally, inhabit different worlds, at least cognitively speaking. In theological terms, one is confronted with diversity and plurality. It is possible that different contemplative practices derive from, orient one toward, and/or lead to the experience of different realities. That is, reality may be plural rather than singular, multiple rather than unified. A contemplative approach to being and living might thus manifest as a deeper commitment to comparative theology and interreligious dialogue, as an acceptance of multiculturalism and religious pluralism that is both committed *and* open.

By way of conclusion, we may return to the photograph of the labyrinth of Chartres Cathedral that graces the cover of the present volume. While many images could have been selected, and while some may be perplexed at the absence of a human figure in a recognizable meditation posture, this image may be considered both a literal and symbolic representation of contemplative practice. On a literal level, labyrinth walking is a contemplative practice (see, e.g., Kern 2000; Welch 2010).[23] One may literally traverse the labyrinth in Chartres Cathedral, and one can imagine the history of this practice, including its relationship to pilgrimage and sacred sites. At the same time, the labyrinth is located in a Roman Catholic cathedral utilizing French Gothic

Figure 15.4. Labyrinth (dat. 13th c.) in Chartres Cathedral, Chartres, France
Source: Jeff Saward, Labyrinthos

architecture and a cruciform design. Although the labyrinth is highlighted in the foreground, during Catholic Mass additional chairs or pews are placed over it. Gazing still further into the photograph, one sees the permanent pews for the Catholic congregation, the Catholic altar, the tabernacle, and, only faintly visible, the crucifix and stained glass rose window depicting the Virgin Mary and Jesus Christ as child. The latter window is both an entryway for light from without and a portal from within, especially into the Catholic imagination and projected sacred. From a traditional Catholic perspective, this is the light of God, or the sacred manifesting in the world for those with theistic reservations. As inspiration for deeper reflection on the context-specific and tradition-specific nature of contemplative practice, in whatever expression, the image brings our attention to other dimensions, such as aesthetics, community, material culture, place, ritual, spatiality, and so forth. We might further consider the actual materiality of the space, including its complex history, meaning, interpretation, purpose, and use.

On a more symbolic level, the labyrinth is an invitation to contemplative practice, a pilgrimage to the center. This center has been variously referred to as "emptiness," "ground," "light," "presence," "silence," and so forth. Different individuals and communities encounter, represent, and interpret it in distinctive ways. For some, it involves a path of theistic devotion, while others understand it as nonconceptual meditation aimed at transpersonal union. Some view it in terms of divine radiance, while others know it as the "darkness of unknowing." Some express it through icons, while others suggest that it is beyond image-based representations. Some have heard it as a hidden cantata, while others experience it as the silence that takes in everything. Recalling our earlier discussion, the labyrinth of contemplative practice includes attentiveness, awareness, interiority, presence, silence, transformation, and a deepened sense of meaning and purpose. It inspires one to consider the place of praxis, as well as adherence and commitment, in the human condition. It also opens one up to the possibility that contemplative practice may be as much about movement as stillness, as much about walking as sitting, as much about place as placelessness, as much about time as timelessness. One may, in turn, see the labyrinth as the path of engaged and prolonged practice. One may find that the labyrinth of contemplative practice leads into the center, the center that is, at the same time, a portal back into the world. Such a contemplative approach may bring us into the immediacy of the present, into the mysteriousness of being and aliveness.

Notes

The present chapter has benefited from the comments of Aaron Gross (University of San Diego), Beverly Lanzetta (Community of a New Monastic Way), and Kate Townsend (Daoist Foundation). My gratitude notwithstanding, all views and interpretations are my own.

1. Again, as comparative categories and as utilized in the present volume, soteriology refers to discourse on, study of, or theories about actualization, liberation, perfection, realization, salvation, or however an individual or community defines the ultimate purpose of human existence. Theology refers to discourse on the sacred, with the sacred being another comparative category for a given individual's or community's ultimate concern.

2. These generalizations are not meant to suggest that *all* adherents of the respective traditions would make such claims.

3. In this respect, one also thinks of the connection between contemplative practice and asceticism and monasticism in certain religious traditions. Some adherents and communities identify

certain prerequisites and requirements for contemplative practice, including temporary versus permanent renunciation and seclusion.

4. It is possible to argue that any form of praxis is transformative on some level, including forms of enculturation and social conditioning. See, for example, Bourdieu 1977; Mauss 1979. Cf. Murphy 1992; Komjathy 2007.

5. Such statements, of course, require further research, especially on the relative importance in different contemplative systems. Here one also thinks of the place of perception, emotionality, and physicality.

6. These precepts are actually much more complex. For example, "no lying" approximates a concern for "false speech," which includes defamation, duplicity, gossip, flattery, and so forth. "No stealing" approximates only taking what is offered. One reading of the latter is a Buddhist mendicant ethos. Such precepts draw attention to the importance of purity of thought, speech, and action, including "right livelihood."

7. Of course, "morality" has been widely criticized from various modern and postmodern perspectives. This includes in terms of issues of power, authority, and social function, specifically morality as social construct, means of political control, and socioeconomic oppression. Here one thinks of seminal figures such as Friedrich Nietzsche (1844–1900) and Michel Foucault (1926–1984). However, such perspectives are challenged by religious claims, of Daoism for example, that virtue is energetic in nature. That is, on a subjective level, the cultivation of virtue may result in a deeper sense of aliveness, connection, and support.

8. Here one also thinks of the relationship between diet and ethics. For example, is vegetarianism required for and an expression of deeper contemplative practice? If attentiveness and awareness are defining characteristics, one would assume that a more conscious form of eating would result. This, of course, relates to various bioregional and cultural contexts. Thus, it might be possible that some forms of hunting have contemplative and reverential characteristics. However, one wonders if any type of killing, the culmination of hunting conventionally conceived, could actually be "contemplative." It appears that nonviolence, both as commitment and expression, is an essential dimension of authentic contemplative practice. For an alternative perspective, see Ingold 2000, 2008.

9. Many of these technical terms are defined in the technical glossary at the end of the present volume.

10. These details problematize the emphasis on "wisdom" and "compassion" in popular presentations and contemporary appropriative agendas of meditation, and in secular and therapeutic approaches to contemplative studies. These are highly influenced by Tibetan Buddhist conceptions and concerns, especially as presented by the Dalai Lama.

11. From a comparative and cross-cultural perspective, one also thinks of the place of the "spiritual senses" in Christianity. See, for example, Gavrilyuk and Coakley 2012.

12. Contemplative systems and religious traditions emphasize exemplars. These are individuals who serve as models and ideals, especially with respect to religious attainment. They are people who have realized and come to embody specific values and commitments. Thus, one finds emphasis on "enlightened beings" (*buddha*; also *bodhisattva*) in Buddhism; "saints" (*hagios*) in Christianity; "sages" (*shengren*) and "immortals" (*xianren*) in Daoism; "realized beings" (*siddha*), "holy persons" (*sadhu*), and "renunciants" (*sannyasi*) in Hinduism; "prophets" (*nabi*), "teachers" (*sheikh*), and "scholars" (*ulama*) in Islam; "prophets" (*nevi*) and "teachers" (*rabbi*; also sages) in Judaism; and so forth. One often finds accounts and descriptions, as well as their revered qualities, in hagiographies or the equivalent literature. See, for example, Coan 1977; Hawley 1987. I am grateful to David Clough of the University of Chester for the references on "saints and animals."

13. Here one also thinks of the abilities of certain types of savants, such as in the case of some autistic individuals, as well as radical forms of empathy among some individuals with Down syndrome. Such examples perhaps demonstrate a cultural willingness to consider "extraordinariness" or "exceptionalism," but only if it accompanies a condition that falls under the categorization of "disorder" and "disability." On the latter, see Laing 1967. In terms of more "able-bodied persons," one also thinks of extreme sports. Viewed from a different perspective, such examples suggest that extraordinary abilities may be trained, as they are part of our shared humanity. Once again, we need to consider innate capacities in relation to conscious

cultivation. I am grateful to Aaron Gross (University of San Diego) for a conversation that inspired these reflections.

14. In the psychological, neuroscientific, and therapeutic literature, a variety of questionnaires, metrics, and inventories related to beneficial states and positive traits have also been utilized and developed. Some of these include the Cognitive and Affective Mindfulness Scale (CAMS), Mindful Attention Awareness Scale (MAAS), Profile of Mood States (POMS), Self-Compassion Scale (SCS), Spiritual Assessment Inventory (SAI), Spiritual Perspective Scale (SPS), Spiritual Well-Being Scale (SWBS), State-Trait Anxiety Inventory (STAI), and so forth. In this respect, one also thinks of the less popular, or more *popular*, Keirsey Temperament Sorter (KTS), Myers-Briggs Type Indicator (MBTI), Rorschach Test, and so forth.

15. Other interesting cartographies include "ten stages" according to the Mahāyāna Buddhist *Avataṃsaka Sūtra* (Flower Garland Sutra), *Laṅkāvatāra Sūtra* (Sutra on the Descent into Lanka), and *Śuraṅgama Sūtra* (Sutra on Indestructible [*Samādhi*]), as well as the Tibetan Buddhist *lamrim* (stages of the path) teachings, which are contained, for example, in the *Lam-rim chen-mo* (Great Treatise on the Stages of the Path of Enlightenment) by Tsong-kha-pa (1357–1419).

16. One important aspect of contemplative practice, related to both "states" and "stages," centers on dangers, difficulties, and obstacles. For example, one thinks of the Carmelite Catholic friar and mystic Juan de la Cruz's (John of the Cross; 1542–1591) discussion of the "dark night." See Kavanaugh 1988; FitzGerald 1996. This parallels a contemporary psychological concern with "spiritual emergencies." See Grof and Grof 1989. There is also the recent Dark Night Project initiated by Willoughby Britton of Brown University. In this respect, one may again reflect on the relative importance of teachers, community, training, and spiritual direction.

17. Here one may note the widespread marketing of "stage-based" and "advanced" practice among hybrid spiritualist teachers. It is important to consider the socioeconomic and psychological purposes of such constructions, including the ways in which they lead to fame, wealth, as well as power and authority for their representatives. This raises the question of the qualities and character of authentic spiritual teachers.

18. There is a fair amount of discussion on the "transpersonal dimensions" of spiritual realization, among both spiritual teachers and scholars. One might, in turn, reflect on the corresponding proliferation of the genre of "spiritual autobiography."

19. As briefly mentioned in my chapter on therapeutic meditation, there are various attempts to "weaponize" or "militarize" meditation. Meditative training is playing a role in the creation of so-called "super-soldiers." In keeping with the preceding discussion of "latent capacities," one might view such examples as the culmination of meditative training. Alternatively, one might highlight the desensitization and dehumanization that must occur for such a condition to be viable. One thinks of the informing ideologies, the high degree of enculturation, required to kill others in the name of "country," "freedom," "God," or whatever other fiction is involved. Although debatable, in my conception of contemplative practice, such expressions would not be "contemplative" because they lack essential characteristics.

20. This image brings our attention to the issue of perspective and location in perception. As is the case for the experience of military flyovers at various sporting events in the United States, one might reflect on the competing symbolisms, such as "protection" versus "threat."

21. A common misconception about ancient Buddhism is that it was atheistic, that is, that early Buddhists did not believe in deities. This clearly was not the case, although such historical facts may create discomfort among some Buddhist sympathizers. From a traditional Buddhist perspective, it is not that gods do not exist but rather that they are samsaric and cannot ultimately assist one on the path to liberation. In addition, theological concerns are a form of distraction. Thus, fundamental Buddhist "theology" might be better categorized as "a-theological."

22. Unlike a maze, a single-path (unicursal) labyrinth has only a single, nonbranching path, which leads to the center. A labyrinth in this sense has an unambiguous route to the center and back and is not difficult to navigate. With the right orientation and entry point, one finds the way to the center.

23. In terms of kinesthetic contemplative practice, one also thinks of the Stations of the Cross.

Works Cited and Further Reading

Agamben, Giorgio. 2013. *The Highest Poverty: Monastic Rules and Form-of-Life*. Translated by Adam Kotsko. Stanford: Stanford University Press.

Baudrillard, Jean, and Marc Guillaume. 2008. *Radical Alterity*. Translated by Ames Hodges. Cambridge: MIT Press.

Bell, David. 1992. *Wholly Animals: A Book of Beastly Tales*. Kalamazoo: Cistercian.

Berger, Peter, and Thomas Luckmann. 1966. *The Social Construction of Reality: A Treatise in the Sociology of Knowledge*. Garden City: Anchor Books.

Bourdieu, Pierre. 1977. *Outline of a Theory of Practice*. Translated by Richard Nice. Cambridge and New York: Cambridge University Press.

Brown, Daniel. 1986. "The Stages of Meditation in Cross-Cultural Perspective." In *Transformations of Consciousness*, edited by Ken Wilber et al., 219–83. Boston: Shambhala.

Cabezón, José. 2006. "The Discipline and Its Other." *Journal of the American Academy of Religion* 74.1: 21–38.

Cabezón, José, and Sheila Davaney, eds. 2004. *Identity and the Politics of Scholarship in the Study of Religion*. London and New York: Routledge.

Calais-Germain, Blandine. 2007. *Anatomy of Movement*. Rev. ed. Seattle: Eastland Press.

Carrette, Jeremy, and Richard King. 2004. *Selling Spirituality: The Silent Takeover of Religion*. London and New York: Routledge.

Clooney, Francis X. 1996. *Seeing through Texts: Doing Theology among the Śrīvaiṣṇavas of South India*. Albany: State University of New York Press.

———. 2010. *Comparative Theology: Deep Learning across Religious Borders*. West Sussex: Wiley-Blackwell.

Coan, Richard. 1977. *Hero, Artist, Sage, or Saint?* New York: Columbia University Press.

Coburn, Thomas, Fran Grace, Anne Klein, Louis Komjathy, Harold Roth, and Judith Simmer-Brown. 2011. "Contemplative Pedagogy: Frequently Asked Questions." *Teaching Theology and Religion* 14.2: 167–74.

Csikszentmihalyi, Mihaly. 1990. *Flow: The Psychology of Optimal Experience*. New York: Harper.

Csordas, Thomas J., ed. 1994. *Embodiment and Experience: The Existential Ground of Culture and Self*. Cambridge: Cambridge University Press.

Dalton, Jacob. 2011. *The Taming of the Demons: Violence and Liberation in Tibetan Buddhism*. New Haven: Yale University Press.

De Wit, Han. 1991. *Contemplative Psychology*. Translated by Marie Louise Baird. Pittsburgh: Duquesne University Press.

Deane-Drummond, Celia, and David Clough, eds. 2009. *Creaturely Theology: God, Humans and Other Animals*. Norwich: SCM Press.

Deikman, Arthur J. 1982. *The Observing Self: Mysticism and Psychotherapy*. Boston: Beacon Press.

Doob, Penelope Reed. 1992. *The Idea of the Labyrinth: From Classical Antiquity through the Middle Ages*. Ithaca: Cornell University Press.

Ehara, N. R. M., Soma Thera, and Kheminda Thera. 1977. *The Path of Freedom (Vimuttimagga)*. Kandy: Buddhist Publication Society.

Eliade, Mircea. 1987 (1959). *The Sacred and the Profane: The Nature of Religion*. New York: Harcourt Brace.

———. 1998 (1963). *Myth and Reality*. Prospect Heights: Waveland Press.

Feher, Michel, with Ramona Naddaff and Nadia Tazi, eds. 1989. *Fragments for a History of the Human Body*. 3 vols. New York: Zone Books.

Ferré, Robert. 2013. *Church Labyrinths*. San Antonio: Labyrinth Enterprises.

Ferrer, Jorge, and Jacob Sherman, eds. 2008. *The Participatory Turn: Spirituality, Mysticism, Religious Studies*. Albany: State University of New York Press.

Festinger, Leon. 1957. *A Theory of Cognitive Dissonance*. Stanford: Stanford University Press.

FitzGerald, Constance. 1996. "Impasse and Dark Night." In *Women's Spirituality*, edited by Joann Wolski Conn, 410–35. Mahwah: Paulist Press.

Foucault, Michel. 1972. *The Archaeology of Knowledge*. Translated by Rupert Swyer. New York: Pantheon Books.

Freire, Paulo. 1993 (1970). *Pedagogy of the Oppressed*. Translated by Myra Bergman Ramos. New York and London: Continuum.

Freud, Sigmund. 1989 (1927). *The Future of an Illusion*. Translated by James Strachey. New York: W. W. Norton.

———. 1990 (1913). *Totem and Taboo*. Translated by James Strachey. New York: W. W. Norton.

Gavrilyuk, Paul, and Sarah Coakley, eds. 2012. *The Spiritual Senses: Perceiving God in Western Christianity*. Cambridge and New York: Cambridge University Press.

Geertz, Clifford. 1973. *The Interpretation of Cultures*. New York: Basic Books.

Gendlin, Eugene. 1997 (1962). *Experiencing and the Creation of Meaning: A Philosophical and Psychological Approach to the Subjective*. Evanston: Northwestern University Press.

Gethin, R. M. L. 2001 (1992). *The Buddhist Path to Awakening*. Oxford: Oneworld.

Gimello, Robert. 1978. "Mysticism and Meditation." In *Mysticism and Philosophical Analysis*, edited by Steven T. Katz, 170–99. Oxford and New York: Oxford University Press.

Grof, Stanislav, and Christina Grof, eds. 1989. *Spiritual Emergency: When Personal Transformation Becomes a Crisis*. New York: Tarcher/Putnam.

Gunaratana, Mahathera H. 1985. *The Path of Serenity and Insight: An Explanation of the Buddhist Jhānas*. Delhi, Varanasi, Patna, Madras: Motilal Banarsidass.

Hall, Donald, and Roger Ames. 1987. *Thinking through Confucius*. Albany: State University of New York Press.

Hawley, John Stratton, ed. 1987. *Saints and Virtues*. Berkeley: University of California Press.

Heidegger, Martin. 1977. *The Question Concerning Technology*. Translated by William Lovitt. New York: Harper and Row.

Hick, John. 2005. *An Interpretation of Religion: Human Responses to the Transcendent*. 2nd ed. New Haven: Yale University Press.

Ingold, Tim. 2000. *The Perception of the Environment: Essays in Livelihood, Dwelling, and Skill*. London and New York: Routledge.

———. 2012. "Hunting and Gathering as Ways of Perceiving the Environment." In *Animals and the Human Imagination*, edited by Aaron Gross and Anne Vallely, 31–54. New York: Columbia University Press.

Iwamura, Jane. 2000. "The Oriental Monk in American Popular Culture." In *Religion and Popular Culture in America*, edited by Bruce David Forbes and Jeffrey H. Mahan, 25–43. Berkeley: University of California Press.

Jackson, Roger, and John Makransky, eds. 1999. *Buddhist Theology: Critical Reflections by Contemporary Buddhist Scholars*. London and New York: Routledge.

James, William. 1999 (1902). *The Varieties of Religious Experience*. New York: The Modern Library.

Juergensmeyer, Mark. 2003. *Terror in the Mind of God: The Global Rise of Religious Violence*. 3rd ed. Berkeley: University of California Press.

Juergensmeyer, Mark, Maro Kitts, and Michael Jerryson, eds. 2012. *The Oxford Handbook of Religion and Violence*. Oxford and New York: Oxford University Press.

Kakar, Sudhir, and Jeffrey Kripal, eds. 2012. *Seriously Strange: Thinking Anew about Psychical Experiences*. New York: Penguin.

Katz, Steven, ed. 2006. *The Impact of the Holocaust on Jewish Theology*. New York: New York University Press.

Kavanaugh, Kieran. 1988. *John of the Cross: Selected Writings*. Mahwah: Paulist Press.

Kavanaugh, Kieran, and Otillo Rodriguez. 1979. *Teresa of Avila: The Interior Castle*. Mahwah: Paulist Press.

Kern, Hermann. 2000 (1982). *Through the Labyrinth*. Edited by Robert Ferré and Jeff Saward. New York: Prestel.

King, Richard. 1999. *Orientalism and Religion: Postcolonial Theory, India and 'The Mystic East.'* London and New York: Routledge.
Knitter, Paul. 2002. *Introducing Theologies of Religions*. Maryknoll: Orbis Books.
Komjathy, Louis. 2007. *Cultivating Perfection: Mysticism and Self-Transformation in Early Quanzhen Daoism*. Leiden: Brill.
―――. 2012. "Mysticism." In *Encyclopedia of Global Religion*, edited by Mark Juergensmeyer and Wade Clark Roof, 855–61. Thousand Oaks: Sage.
―――. 2013a. *The Way of Complete Perfection: A Quanzhen Daoist Anthology*. Albany: State University of New York Press.
―――. 2013b. *The Daoist Tradition: An Introduction*. London and New York: Bloomsbury Academic.
―――. 2014. "THRS 394: Contemplative Traditions Syllabus." http://home.sandiego.edu/~komjathy. Accessed on June 1, 2014.
Kripal, Jeffrey. 2006. *The Serpent's Gift: Gnostic Reflections on the Study of Religion*. Chicago: University of Chicago Press.
―――. 2010. *Authors of the Impossible: The Paranormal and the Sacred*. Chicago: University of Chicago Press.
Kuhn, Thomas. 1996 (1962). *The Structure of Scientific Revolutions*. Chicago: University of Chicago Press.
Laing, R. D. 1967. *The Politics of Experience*. New York: Pantheon Books.
Lau, Kimberly. 2000. *New Age Capitalism: Making Money East of Eden*. Philadelphia: University of Pennsylvania Press.
Lincoln, Bruce. 2006. *Holy Terrors: Thinking about Religion after September 11*. 2nd ed. Chicago: University of Chicago Press.
Lopez, Donald S., Jr. 1999. *Prisoners of Shangri-La: Tibetan Buddhism and the West*. Chicago: University of Chicago Press.
Mander, Jerry. 1992. *In the Absence of the Sacred: The Failure of Technology and the Survival of the Indian Nations*. San Francisco: Sierra Club Books.
Maslow, Abraham H. 1964. *Religions, Values, and Peak Experiences*. New York: Viking.
―――. 1999 (1968). *Toward a Psychology of Being*. New York: John Wiley and Sons.
Mauss, Marcel. 1979. "Body Techniques." In *Sociology and Psychology*, translated by Ben Brewster, 95–123. London: Routledge and Kegan Paul.
McDannell, Colleen. 1995. *Material Christianity: Religion and Popular Culture in America*. New Haven: Yale University Press.
McMahan, David. 2008. *The Making of Buddhist Modernism*. Oxford and New York: Oxford University Press.
Michelis, Elizabeth. 2005. *A History of Modern Yoga: Patañjali and Western Esotericism*. London and New York: Continuum.
Milgram, Stanley. 2009 (1975). *Obedience to Authority: An Experimental View*. New York: HarperCollins.
Murphy, Michael. 1992. *The Future of the Body: Explorations into the Further Evolution of Human Nature*. New York: Penguin Putnam.
Ñāṇamoli, Bhikkhu. 1991. *The Path of Purification: Visuddhimagga: The Classic Manual of Buddhist Doctrine and Meditation*. 5th ed. Kandy: Buddhist Publication Society.
Neville, Robert Cummings. 1996. *The Truth of Broken Symbols*. Albany: State of New York University Press.
Panikkar, Raimon. 1999. *The Intra-Religious Dialogue*. Rev. ed. Mahwah: Paulist Press.
―――. 2006. *The Experience of God: Icons of Mystery*. Translated by Joseph Cunneen. Minneapolis: Augsburg Press.
Paper, Jordan. 2005. *The Deities Are Many: A Polytheistic Theology*. Albany: State University of New York Press.
Patterson, Charles. 2002. *Eternal Treblinka: Our Treatment of Animals and the Holocaust*. New York: Lantern Books.

Queen, Christopher, ed. 2000. *Engaged Buddhism in the West*. Somerville: Wisdom.
Queen, Christopher, and Sallie King, eds. 1996. *Engaged Buddhism: Buddhist Liberation Movements in Asia*. Albany: State University of New York Press.
Roth, Harold. 1999. *Original Tao: Inward Training (Nei-yeh) and the Foundations of Taoist Mysticism*. New York: Columbia University Press.
———. 2000. "Bimodal Mystical Experience in the 'Qiwu lun' Chapter of the *Zhuangzi*." *Journal of Chinese Religions* 28: 31–50.
———. 2008. "Against Cognitive Imperialism: A Call for a Non-Ethnocentric Approach to Cognitive Science and Religious Studies." *Religion East & West* 8 (October 2008): 1–26.
Rubenstein, Richard. 1992. *After Auschwitz: History, Theology, and Contemporary Judaism*. 2nd ed. Baltimore: Johns Hopkins University Press.
Said, Edward W. 1979. *Orientalism*. New York: Vintage Books.
Samuel, Geoffrey. 1995. *Civilized Shamans: Buddhism in Tibetan Societies*. Washington: Smithsonian.
Sartre, Jean-Paul. 1991. *Critique of Dialectical Reason*. Translated by Alan Sheridan-Smith. 2 vols. London: Verso.
Sharf, Robert. 1995. "Buddhist Modernism and the Rhetoric of Meditative Experience." *Numen* 42.3: 228–83.
———. 1998. "Experience." In *Critical Terms for Religious Studies*, edited by Mark C. Taylor, 94–116. Chicago: University of Chicago Press.
Sherwin, Byron, and Harold Kasimow, eds. 1999. *John Paul II and Interreligious Dialogue*. Maryknoll: Orbis Books.
Simmer-Brown, Judith. 1999. "Commitment and Openness: A Contemplative Approach to Pluralism." In *The Heart of Learning*, edited by Steven Glazer, 97–112. New York: Jeremy P. Tarcher.
Simmer-Brown, Judith, and Fran Grace, eds. 2011. *Meditation and the Classroom: Contemplative Pedagogy for Religious Studies*. Albany: State University of New York Press.
Singleton, Mark. 2010. *Yoga Body: The Origins of Modern Posture Practice*. Oxford and New York: Oxford University Press.
Skya, Walter. 2009. *Japan's Holy War: The Ideology of Radical Shinto Ultranationalism*. Durham: Duke University Press.
Smith, Jonathan Z. 1982. *Imagining Religion: From Babylon to Jonestown*. Chicago: University of Chicago Press.
———. 2004. *Relating Religion: Essays in the Study of Religion*. Chicago: University of Chicago Press.
Stace, Walter. 1960. *Mysticism and Philosophy*. London: Macmillan.
Syman, Stefanie. 2010. *The Subtle Body: The Story of Yoga in America*. New York: Farrar, Straus and Giroux.
Tracy, David. 1998. *The Analogical Imagination: Christian Theology and the Culture of Pluralism*. New York: Crossroad.
———. 2005 (1987). "Comparative Theology." In *The Encyclopedia of Religions*, edited by Lindsay Jones, vol. 13, 9125–34. Detroit: Macmillan Reference.
Turner, Frederick. 1983. *Beyond Geography: The Western Spirit against the Wilderness*. New York: Rutgers University Press.
Venuti, Lawrence. 2008. *The Translator's Invisibility: A History of Translation*. 2nd ed. London and New York: Routledge.
Victoria, Brian Daizen. 2006. *Zen at War*. 2nd ed. New York: Rowman & Littlefield.
Waddell, Helen. 1995. *Beasts and Saints*. London: Darton, Longman and Todd.
Ward, Keith. 1998. *Concepts of God: Images of the Divine in Five Religious Traditions*. London and New York: Oneworld.

Weinrich, Max. 1999 (1946). *Hitler's Professors: The Part of Scholarship in Germany's Crimes against the Jewish People*. New Haven: Yale University Press.
Welch, Sally. 2010. *Walking the Labyrinth: A Spiritual and Practical Guide*. Norwich: Canterbury Press Norwich.
Wessinger, Catherine. 2000. *How the Millennium Comes Violently: From Jonestown to Heaven's Gate*. New York: Seven Bridges Press.
Wilber, Ken. 2000. *Integral Psychology: Consciousness, Spirit, Psychology, Therapy*. Boston: Shambhala.
Wilber, Ken, Jack Engler, and Daniel Brown, eds. 1986. *Transformations of Consciousness*. Boston: Shambhala.
Zimbardo, Philip. 2007. *The Lucifer Effect: Understanding How Good People Turn Evil*. New York: Random House.
Žižek, Slavoj. 2001. "From Western Marxism to Western Buddhism." *Cabinet* 2 (Spring 2001): 33–35.

Appendix

Toward a Technical Glossary of Contemplative Studies

Louis Komjathy

abhijñā. Buddhist Sanskrit term (Pali: *abhiññā*) that refers to direct apprehension of *dhamma* (Skt.: *dharma*), in this case meaning "qualities," "states," and "phenomena," as well as more advanced "paranormal abilities" and "extrasensory perception." Literally means "knowing" or "knowledge." Some "higher cognitions" (*chalabhiññā*) include clairaudience, clairvoyance, dematerialization, recollection of past lives, telepathy, and so forth. *Abhijñā* has some parallels with the Indian Sanskrit term **siddhi**, which is most often utilized in Hinduism.

Absolute Unitary Being (AUB). Phrase coined by the neuroscientists Eugene d'Aquili (1940–1998; formerly of University of Pennsylvania Medical School) and Andrew Newberg (Thomas Jefferson University Hospital). Identified as an "advanced state" or "higher form of consciousness" characterized by an absolute sense of unity and pure, undifferentiated awareness. AUB is said to be absent of ego, subject/object dichotomies, language, sensation, and thought. In some sense parallels Robert K. C. Forman et al.'s **Pure Consciousness Events** and Abraham Maslow's **Being-cognition**.

active mode. Phrase coined by the clinical psychiatrist Arthur Deikman (University of California, San Francisco). A condition in which one acts in the world, often through manipulation of the environment. The musculoskeletal system is the primary form of engagement and participation. As located in Deikman's concept of "bimodal consciousness," contrasts with the **receptive mode**. More positively applied, one's physical engagement with the world.

altered state of consciousness (ASC). Phrase often associated with psychologist and parapsychologist Charles Tart (Institute of Transpersonal Psychology; Institute of Noetic Sciences) and his colleagues. A condition of mind that is significantly different from "ordinary" or "normal" consciousness. The latter is often defined scientifically as a normal waking beta-wave state. Often parallels **mystical experience**. Raises questions concerning normalcy.

anomalous experience. Extraordinary or uncommon experiences. Along with **altered states of consciousness**, often conflated with **mystical experience**. Actually includes hallucinatory experiences, synesthesia, lucid dreaming, out-of-body experiences (OBEs), psi-related experiences, alien abduction experiences, past-life experiences, possession, channeling, near-death experiences (NDEs), anomalous healing experiences, and so forth.

anthropology. In a technical sense, social scientific field focusing on the study of human culture. In a theological sense, study of the human with particular attention to larger parameters of being, especially in relation to the **sacred**.

āsana. Indian Sanskrit term for **posture**. Literally means "to sit down." The most famous traditional Indian meditative *āsana* is the full-lotus posture (*padmāsana*). Often associated with various forms of Hindu **yoga**. In classical Yoga, one of the so-called Eight Limbs (*aṣṭāṅga*): abstentions/moral restraints (*yama*), ethical observances (*niyama*), posture (*āsana*), breath control (***prāṇāyāma***), sensory withdrawal (*pratyāhāra*), concentration (*dhāraṇā*), meditation (***dhyāna***), and meditative absorption (***samādhi***). In a later expression of Hatha Yoga, there are eighty-four specific *āsana*s.

Being-cognition (B-cognition). Phrase coined by the humanistic psychologist Abraham Maslow (1908–1970) and especially developed in his work *Toward a Psychology of Being* (1962). Refers to a condition of open receptivity and pure being. In Being-cognition, a form of **self-actualization**, one simply accepts life as it is, especially through a holistic and receptive approach. Contrasted to **Deficiency-cognition** (D-cognition). Key B-values include aliveness, beauty, completion, goodness, integration, wholeness, self-sufficiency, simplicity, and so forth. Maslow's Being-cognition parallels Arthur Deikman's **receptive mode** and Erich Fromm's **being-mode**.

being-mode. Phrase coined by the humanistic psychologist Erich Fromm (1900–1980). Refers to a psychological condition rooted in love and concerned with shared experience and creative activity. Contrasted with the **having-mode**, which is rooted in craving, desire-fulfillment, and dissatisfaction; this condition focuses on material accumulation and is based in aggression and greed. Fromm's being-mode parallels Deikman's **receptive mode** and Abraham Maslow's **Being-cognition**. However, Deikman also envisions a lived, engaged, applied, and participatory expression through the **active mode**.

bhakti. Hindu Sanskrit term referring to devotion, specifically theistic devotion rooted in prayer, offerings, and worship. Examples include devotion to Shiva (Shaivism) and to Vishnu (Vaishnavism). May be used as a comparative category in the sense of devotionalism.

bhāvanā. Buddhist Pali term often translated as "meditation." More literally means "cultivation" and/or "development." Found in various Buddhist compound phrases, indicates the development of particular faculties or qualities, such as body (*kāya*), compassion (*karuṇā*), concentration (***samādhi***), loving-kindness (*mettā*), mind (*citta*), and wisdom (*paññā*; Skt.: *prajñā*).

bhūmi. Buddhist Sanskrit term that literally means "ground" or "foundation." Often translated as "**stage**." Technically speaking, stages through which a bodhisattva advances to become a Buddha. According to one expression, there are ten *bhūmi*s: joyous, stainless, luminous, radiant, difficult-to-cultivate, manifest, gone-afar, immovable, good intelligence, and cloud of doctrine.

Biofeedback. Process of gaining greater awareness of various physiological functions primarily through the utilization of instruments and technological measurements that provide information on the activity of those systems. One of the earliest forms of "technological meditation." As a therapeutic approach, widely utilized form of **therapeutic meditation**.

cartography. The act of mapping or the resultant maps. In the case of **contemplative studies**, involves developing comparative categories or types. As advocated in the present volume, includes devotional, **ergotropic**, **kinesthetic**, and **trophotropic** types, among others.

centering down. Quaker technical term that refers to the process of becoming silent and concentrated in preparation to hear God's divine guidance.

cognitive imperialism. Phrase coined by Harold Roth (Brown University), a scholar of classical Daoism and director of the Contemplative Studies Initiative at Brown University. Refers to an ethnocentric approach based in unquestioned assumptions and unexamined opinions, especially one's rooted Western European and Abrahamic views. By extension, the act of intellectual colonialism, or domesticating the radical challenges of alternative worldviews and accounts of "reality."

cognitive science. Interdisciplinary scientific study of mind and its processes, with particular emphasis on cognition (mental processes). There is some overlap with **neuroscience** and **consciousness studies**.

consciousness studies. Emerging interdisciplinary field dedicated to the study of consciousness. Includes philosophical, psychological, and neuroscientific approaches. Some glimpses may be gained by consulting the *Journal of Consciousness Studies*.

contemplatio. Latin word translated as "contemplation." In technical Roman Catholic Christian usage, **prayer** involving silent awareness of God's presence. Often contrasted with ***lectio divina*** (scripture study), ***meditatio*** (reflection on particular subjects), and *oratio* (silent or vocal prayer). Also located along a spectrum of practice, includes purgative, illuminative, and unitive states or ways.

contemplative experience. Experiences that occur within the parameters of **contemplative practice**, are associated with particular practices, and/or are deemed significant by contemplatives and their associated communities. May include more "mundane" or "ordinary" experiences such as emotional and mental agitation, pain, boredom, and so forth. More often associated with "uncommon" or "extraordinary" experiences such as ecstasy, meditative absorption, mystical union, and so forth.

contemplative pedagogy. Emerging approach to teaching and learning that incorporates **contemplative practice** and **contemplative experience**. May involve actual contemplative practice in the form of classroom exercises and extracurricular experiences. Alternatively, an educational approach informed by and/or expressed as contemplative practice.

contemplative practice. Comparative category with some rough equivalence to **meditation**. However, unlike "meditation," which sometimes implies seated **postures** and which is often reduced to Buddhist meditation, "contemplative practice" functions as a larger umbrella category. In terms of religious traditions, it encompasses meditation and **contemplative prayer**. Also may apply to "contemplative approaches" to art, dance, martial arts, music, painting, photography, **somatic disciplines**, theater, and so forth. Possible connective strands or family resemblances include attentiveness, awareness, interiority, presence, silence, transformation, and a deepened sense of meaning and purpose.

contemplative prayer. In a Christian context, usually **prayer** involving silent awareness of God's presence. The Christian equivalent to **meditation** as a comparative category.

contemplative psychology. **Psychology** informing, informed by, and utilized within **contemplative practice**. Subdiscipline of Western psychology associated with the Dutch psychologist Han de Wit (Shambhala International) and specifically expressed in his book *Contemplative*

Psychology (1991). On one level, indigenous or tradition-specific psychologies (theories of mind). On another level, a larger psychological modality informed by tradition-specific psychologies and by **contemplative practice** and **contemplative experience**.

contemplative reading. A way of reading texts, especially major religious works and spiritual classics, as a **contemplative practice**. Careful reading, reading that is considerate, reflective, and perhaps orientated toward something more. Contemplative reading is a way of approaching texts as more than texts. Reading texts as documentations of individual and communal lifeworlds, expressions of lived religiosity, as well as offerings and petitions to those who choose to engage in deep inquiry. Reading both informed by and informing contemplative practice. Contemplative reading has some parallels with ***lectio divina***.

contemplative science. Most often a designation for the neuroscientific study of **meditation**, including the use of a scientific methodology (e.g., evidence-based explanations, experimentation, and reproducibility) and technological interventionism, especially neuroimaging technology to measure brain activity ("consciousness"). May or may not involve critical **first-person discourse**, including in the form of **neurophenomenology**. First brought to prominence through B. Alan Wallace (Santa Barbara Institute for Consciousness Studies) in his book titled *Contemplative Science* (2007), but also represented in the work of various neuroscientific researchers of meditation (e.g., James Austin, Richard Davidson, Clifford Saron, Evan Thompson, Francisco Varela). Often involves a problematic privileging of Buddhist meditation ("Buddho-neuroscientific hegemony") and the conflation of **contemplative practice** with techniques and seated meditation. Sometimes used as a term of legitimation for **contemplation studies** to suggest that it is rooted in and validated by scientific evidence and quantification, with corresponding secular materialist assumptions. Brings issues of experiential confirmation, informing discourse community, praxis context, and interpretive authority into high relief.

contemplative studies. Emerging, interdisciplinary field dedicated to research and education on **contemplative practice** and **contemplative experience**, broadly and inclusively conceived. Often reduced to "**contemplative science**," the neuroscientific study of **meditation** and associated states of consciousness, or to "**contemplative pedagogy**," teaching and learning informed by and/or expressed as **contemplative practice**.

Contextualism. Methodological approach in which one gives particular attention to context. The latter may include biographical, cultural, and historical details. In the case of mysticism studies, especially associated with Steven Katz (Boston University), a scholar of Judaism and comparative mysticism, and his colleagues. Partially developed as a critique of **Perennial Philosophy**. As an approach to **contemplative studies**, involves locating contemplatives and contemplative texts in their associated communities and traditions.

dazuo. Literally, "to undertake sitting." A Chinese and Daoist technical term for seated **meditation**.

deautomatization. Phrase coined by the clinical psychiatrist Arthur Deikman (University of California, San Francisco). The process of inhibiting or undoing conditioned and habituated forms of psychological structuring and behavior patterns. Parallels traditional notions of deconditioning.

decontextualization. The process of removing something from its original context and associated tradition. Most often technically recontextualization. In terms of **contemplative practice**, the concept of decontextualization draws attention to source-culture and source-tradition, including informing worldviews and soteriological systems. In a modern context, decontextualization is most often done under the guise of hybrid spirituality, with associated tendencies of colonialization and domestication. Related to **reconceptualization**. Brings the issue of the ethics and politics of appropriation into high relief, including the consequences for the associated community and tradition.

Deficiency-cognition (D-cognition). Phrase coined by the humanistic psychologist Abraham Maslow (1908–1970) and especially developed in his work *Toward a Psychology of Being* (1962). Refers to a condition characterized by a sense of lack or scarcity. In Deficiency-cognition, one is in a constant state of dissatisfaction. Stands in contrast to **Being-cognition** and the conditions characterized by **self-actualization**.

dhikr (*zikr*). Islamic Arabic term meaning "remembrance (of Allah)." On a conventional level, Islamic devotional act usually involving the recitation—mostly silently—of the Names of Allah, ninety-nine in total, and of supplications taken from Qur'anic verses. Relates to *ṣalāt* (Islamic prayer) in general and Sufi contemplation (***muraqaba***) in particular.

dhyāna. A Hindu and Buddhist Sanskrit term meaning "concentration." May refer to concentrative meditation and/or associated meditative states.

embodiment. The condition of having a body or being embodied. In some sense, assumes a problematic distinction between mind and body. Nonetheless, brings attention to the relative importance of the body in **contemplative practice** and human existence. Also requires investigation of the specific conceptions of the body. May also refer to the ways in which particular commitments and traditions become embodied in practice and experience. Relates to **posture** in **contemplative practice** and **contemplative experience**.

emic. Insider perspectives. Often associated with the views of adherents, scholar-practitioners, and participant-observers. Emic approaches tend to overlap with **first-person discourse**.

epistemology. Discourse on, theories about, or the study of knowing. A major concern in the academic study of mysticism, including the evidential standing and philosophical import of **mystical experience**. Some possible ways of knowing include knowledge-about, knowledge-by-acquaintance, and knowledge-by-identity. The latter, a form of "mystical consciousness," has been especially advocated by Robert K. C. Forman (Forge Institute; formerly of Hunter College), a scholar of comparative mysticism and **consciousness studies**.

epistemology of enlightenment. Phrase coined by Richard King (University of Kent), a scholar of Indian philosophy and religion. Views of mind and soteriological systems that emphasize **human potential**, especially the possibility of deconditioning to attain an unmediated form of consciousness.

epistemology of limitation. Phrase coined by Richard King (University of Kent), a scholar of Indian philosophy and religion. Views of mind and soteriological systems that emphasize human limitation, especially the mediated nature of consciousness and cognition. Especially evident in Neo-Kantian and Constructivist views of mind.

ergotropic. A state of hyperarousal, characterized by higher levels of physiological and/or neurological activity. As a **cartography** of meditative and **mystical experience**, first advocated by Roland Fischer. The opposite of **trophotropic**.

ethics. In a technical sense, a branch of philosophy or a type of philosophical reflection that addresses questions about morality. More generally, designates both one's moral condition and views concerning virtue, especially virtuous conduct. Various contemplative systems emphasize virtue and ethics as prerequisites and foundations for **contemplative practice**. Some examples include "virtue" (*de*) and "precepts" (*jie*) in Daoism; "morality" (Pali: *sīla*; Skt.: *śīla*), "precepts" (*sikkhāpada*), and "monastic discipline" (*vinaya*) in Buddhism; "moral restraints" (*yama*) and "ethical observances" (*niyama*) in Hinduism; "commandments" (*mitzvah*; pl.: *mitzvot*) and "religious law" (*halakha*) in Judaism; and so forth. Often includes guidelines concerning thought, speech, and action, including livelihood and dietetics.

etic. Outsider perspectives. Often associated with the views of scholars and researchers. Perspectives that aim to be more "objective" and "neutral." Etic approaches tend to overlap with **third-person discourse**.

existentialism. In a technical sense, a movement within Western philosophy especially associated with Jean Paul Sartre (1905–1980) and Albert Camus (1913–1960). Places strong emphasis on human subjectivity and freedom. In a broader sense, of or relating to human existence, especially issues related to meaning and purpose. Often conflated with **theology**.

expectant waiting. Quaker technical term that refers to waiting to receive God's presence and guidance (divine leadings), usually at a Quaker Meeting.

felt sense. Phrase coined by the psychotherapist Eugene Gendlin (Focusing Institute; formerly of University of Chicago), and especially developed in his work *Experiencing and the Creation of Meaning* (1962). Unclear, preverbal sense of "something," as that something is experienced *in the body*. Although connected to emotion, more like an intuitive awareness. While more secular materialist and physiological, the concept of felt sense has some potential application to contemplative systems that develop energetic awareness and sensitivity.

first-person discourse. Subjective perspectives. In the case of **contemplative studies**, an approach or methodology advocated by Han de Wit (Shambhala International) in his book *Contemplative Psychology* (1991). Emphasizes the use of "critical subjectivity" and "critical first-person approaches," or approaches that utilize personal experience in a disciplined way. As a more inclusive and pluralistic approach, includes the possibility of "critical adherent discourse" and interreligious dialogue. The critical or disciplined first-person approach has some parallels with the concept of a "participatory approach" advocated by the psychologist Jorge Ferrer (California Institute of Integral Studies) and his colleagues. First-person discourse is often contrasted with **third-person discourse**.

flow. Term coined by the psychologist Mihaly Csikszentmihalyi (Claremont Graduate University; formerly of University of Chicago). As discussed in his book *Flow: The Psychology of Optimal Experience* (1990), a state of concentration or complete absorption with the activity at hand and the situation. It is a state in which people are so involved in an activity that nothing else seems to matter. Complete involvement or presence. Csikszentmihalyi's "flow" concept has some parallels with Abraham Maslow's notion of **peak experiences**.

having-mode. Phrase coined by the humanistic psychologist Erich Fromm (1900–1980). Refers to a psychological condition rooted in craving, desire-fulfillment, and dissatisfaction; this condition focuses on material accumulation and is based in aggression and greed. Contrasted with the **being-mode**, which is a psychological condition rooted in love and concerned with shared experience and creative activity. Fromm's having-mode parallels Abraham Maslow's **Deficiency-cognition**.

hesychia. Literally, "stillness" or "quiet." A Greek term used in Eastern Orthodox Christianity to refer to **contemplative prayer**, especially inner prayer and solitary practice utilizing the

Jesus Prayer. Often referred to as "inward prayer" or the "prayer of the heart." Related to Hesychasm, the Eastern Orthodox tradition of eremitic prayer.

hierophany. Term employed by the historian of religions Mircea Eliade (1907–1986; formerly of University of Chicago) to designate manifestations of sacred realities. Includes the claim that the history of religions centers first and foremost on distinct hierophanies. Read literally, seems to express a normative polytheistic or pluralistic **theology**.

hitbodedut. A Jewish Hebrew term for "mental seclusion." Often translated as "meditation." Jewish term for secluded, inward **prayer**. May include Kabbalistic forms of **contemplative practice**.

human potential. Humanistic and transpersonal psychological belief that human beings have untapped potentials that may be developed. These potentials may include "extraordinary" and "spiritual" capacities, such as those outlined in religious traditions (e.g., ***siddhi***). Human potential is connected to the associated process of **self-actualization** or becoming completely fulfilled and realized.

intersubjectivity. Literally, "between subjects." Often neglected aspect of **contemplative practice** and **contemplative experience**. Draws attention to teacher-student relationships, the importance of elders, and communal contexts.

jhāna. Buddhist Pali equivalent of the Sanskrit ***dhyāna*** (concentration). May refer to concentrative meditation and/or associated meditative states.

kavanah (*kavanot*). Jewish Hebrew term that literally means "intention" or "direction of the heart." Often described as a mindset or quality required for Jewish **prayer** and liturgical performance (*mitzvot*). In the case of Kabbalah, *kavanah* often refers to permutations of the divine name that aim to overcome the separation of forces in the Upper World. Potentially parallels conceptions of intentionality and "**mindfulness**" in other traditions.

kenshō. Japanese Zen Buddhist term derived from the Chinese Chan *jianxing*. Literally, "perceiving innate nature." Enlightenment experiences. Often described as sudden, spontaneous, and ephemeral. Interpreted variously as signs of successful training and/or as potential sources of distraction.

kinesthetic. Movement or physical activity. In terms of **contemplative pedagogy**, an approach to teaching and learning that incorporates movement. May involve actual courses in movement studies and **somatic disciplines**. In terms of **contemplative practice**, methods in which one engages in movement, such as dance, prostration, walking, and so forth. Usually contrasted with practices that utilize seated, standing, or lying down **postures**.

lectio divina. Latin phrase translated as "divine" or "holy reading." Scripture study. In technical Roman Catholic Christian usage, often contrasted with ***meditatio*** (reflection on particular subjects), *oratio* (silent or vocal prayer), and ***contemplatio*** (silent awareness of God's presence). Historically speaking, often associated with Saint Benedict of Nursia (ca. 480–547) and subsequently with the Order of Saint Benedict (Benedictines; OSB), a Roman Catholic religious order.

mandala. Indian Sanskrit term referring to sacred diagrams, which are usually geometrical and highly symbolic. In a broader comparative and cross-cultural sense, any sacred diagram utilized in religious practice.

mantra. Indian Sanskrit word meaning sacred sound or syllable. Often a component of Hindu and Buddhist meditation practice. In terms of Hinduism, one of the most common *mantras* is *aum* (*om*), which is sometimes claimed to be the mystical sound that created and underlies the universe. In the modern world, *mantra*s, loosely defined, are also used in practices such as Herbert Benson's Relaxation Response via Transcendental Meditation and Christian Centering Prayer. *Mantra* may be used as a comparative category to refer to specific sounds or phrases employed in meditation.

meditatio. Latin word translated as "meditation." In technical Roman Catholic Christian usage, **prayer** involving reflection on particular topics. Often contrasted with ***lectio divina*** (scripture study), *oratio* (silent or vocal prayer), and ***contemplatio*** (silent awareness of God's presence).

meditation. Comparative category with vague definitional parameters. Seated practices that apparently alter consciousness in identifiable ways. Often conflated with Buddhist meditation. There are diverse forms of meditation with diverse purposes and goals.

mindfulness. Technically speaking, an English approximation of the Buddhist technical terms ***sati*** (mindfulness) and/or ***vipassanā*** (insight). In a modern context, often used as an imprecise and vague referent for "meditation" and associated qualities, especially in clinical and pedagogical applications of **therapeutic meditation**, practices such as Mindfulness-Based Stress Reduction (MBSR). Also may be understood as a new religious movement (NRM).

minding the Light. Quaker technical term that refers to being attentive to the Inner Light. Traditionally refers to being guided by Christ as Friend and Light. In more modern contexts, becomes less theistic among some Friends.

mudrā. Indian Sanskrit term for sacred hand gestures and configurations. Often utilized in Hindu and Buddhist meditation practice. In the Hindu tradition, *mudrā*s often accompany *yoga* postures or Tantric ritual. A commonly used *mudrā* now well known in the West is the *Namaste* (homage to you) *mudrā*, in which the hands are joined at the level of the heart as a form of greeting. In terms of Buddhism, one finds the use of the *dhyāna* (concentration) *mudrā* (Pali: *jhāna muddā*), in which the hands rest in the lap, with the right hand placed on top of the left. As a standard *mudrā* used in Buddhist meditation, it sometimes involves touching the tips of the thumbs. *Mudrā* may be used as a comparative category to refer to hand configurations employed in meditation.

muraqaba. Islamic Arabic term that literally means "to keep watch." Refers to Sufi contemplation, including diverse practices such as "remembrance" (***dhikr***) and "visualization" (*rābiṭa*).

mystical experience. Experience of that which a given individual or community identifies as **sacred** or ultimately real. Includes diverse types of experiences and informing theologies. From a sophisticated and nuanced perspective, includes at least four key elements: the trigger (source), the actual experience (not reducible to physiology), its interpretation, and the context. The relationship between **meditation** and mysticism is complex, often varying depending on religious tradition. Some views include meditation as an induction technique for mystical experience, mystical experience as confirmation of meditative efficacy, and mystical experience as distraction. Requires reflection on the relative importance of practice and experience. There is some overlap between the categories **contemplative experience** and mystical experience, but the two should not be conflated.

neurophenomenology. Emerging neuroscientific approach especially associated with Francisco Varela (1946–2001; formerly of Centre National de Recherché Scientifique), Antoine Lutz (University of Wisconsin, Madison), and Evan Thompson (University of British Columbia). In terms of **contemplative studies** involves combining subjective descriptions of **contemplative practice** with neuroimaging (brain-mapping) technology. Preliminary research indicates that the subjective descriptions of **contemplative experience**, at least in the case of advanced contemplatives, are accurate and sophisticated with respect to consciousness as measurable by technology.

neuroscience. Technically, the scientific study of the nervous system. In a broad sense, the scientific study of the brain, mind, and consciousness. In terms of **contemplative studies**, often involves neuroimaging of brain states (brain-maps) through the use of complex technology. Earlier studies of **meditation** focused on physiological changes through electroencephalography (EEG) machines. More recent technology includes functional magnetic resonance imaging (fMRI), positron emission tomography (PET), and single photon emission computed tomography (SPECT). Sometimes referred to as "**contemplative science**," which primarily focuses on the neuroscientific study of Buddhist meditation. May result in the problematic phenomenon of neuroscientific reductionism, which often involves reducing **contemplative practice** to technique and **contemplative experience** to physiology (brain chemistry).

neurotheology. Contemporary neuroscientific study of the neural foundations of religious experience, spirituality, theology, and so forth. Particular emphasis is placed on the neural correlates and patterns of consciousness defined as "religious" or "spiritual." May be **reductionist** or nonreductionist.

ontology. Discourse on, theories about, and study of "being." Broadly conceived, related to existentialist, soteriological, and theological dimensions of existence. Often conflated with metaphysics or discourse on things "beyond the physical."

ontology of realization. Phrase coined by Louis Komjathy (University of San Diego), a scholar of Daoism and comparative religious studies. Views of self (being/personhood) and soteriological systems that emphasize human potential. Draws attention to the psychosomatic transformations and ontological shifts that occur in **contemplative practice** and religious training. Develops Richard King's notion of **epistemology of enlightenment** without privileging mind or knowing.

pāramitā. Buddhist Sanskrit technical term (Pali: *pāramī*) usually translated as "perfection." Specific meditative qualities or values. Virtues cultivated as a way of purification, of purifying *karma* and living an unobstructed life, while following the path toward enlightenment. In Mahāyāna (Greater Vehicle) Buddhism, the Six Perfections of Wisdom (*prajñā-pāramitā*) include charity (*dāna*), **ethics** (*śīla*), patience (*kṣānti*), effort (*vīrya*), concentration (***dhyāna***), and wisdom (*prajñā*).

pathology. Discourse on, theories about, or study of illness. Often used in a technical medical and psychiatric sense to refer to disease or the condition of being ill, especially with respect to etiology (origin) and categorization. Includes the tendency of pathologization, or excessively focusing on conditioning, habituation, illness, and so forth. Pathologization may also involve making something pathological, such as human nature or existence. In terms of **contemplative practice** and **contemplative experience**, may indicate potential dangers and pitfalls, including psychological breakdown. Also may draw attention to therapeutic dimensions or applications.

peak experiences. Phrase coined by the humanistic psychologist Abraham Maslow (1908–1970), and especially developed in his work *Religions, Values, and Peak Experiences* (1964). Specific transpersonal and ecstatic **states**, especially ones characterized by feelings of euphoria, harmony, interconnection, and so forth. Such experiences and the derivative insights tend to be described as having mystical, spiritual, or religious qualities. Maslow's concept of "peak experiences" has some parallels with Mihaly Csikszentmihalyi's **flow** concept.

Perennial Philosophy. Belief that *all* theological claims are simply approximate descriptions of a single, unitary transcendent reality (Truth). Assumes a normative monistic **theology**. Associated with Aldous Huxley (1894–1963), Huston Smith (b. 1919), and Frithjof Schuon (1907–1998), among others. Stands in contrast to **Contextualism**.

Perennial Psychology. Name coined by Robert K. C. Forman (Forge Institute; formerly of Hunter College), a scholar of comparative mysticism and **contemplative studies**, and his colleagues. Belief that all human beings contain the same underlying psychological constitution and spiritual potential. As contrasted with **Contextualism**, also referred to as Decontextualism, with the latter referring to deconditioned or unconditioned states. Has some parallels with Richard King's concept of **epistemology of enlightenment**.

postcolonialism. Approaches and commitments that attempt to overcome the legacies of European colonialism, Christian missionization, and Orientalism. In terms of **contemplative studies**, a postcolonialist and postmodern approach might include the perspectives of critical adherents and critical investigation of dominant cultural assumptions.

posture. Body configuration. On a basic level, there are four primary postures utilized in contemplative practice: sitting, standing, walking, and lying down (supine/prone). A central, but often overlooked dimension of **contemplative practice**, posture frequently embodies, literally and symbolically, the associated practice and tradition. Brought into high relief in **kinesthetic** contemplative practice and **somatic disciplines**.

prāṇāyāma. Sanskrit technical term used in various Indian traditions, including Hinduism and Buddhism, to refer to breath (*prāṇa*)-control or regulation techniques. *Prāṇa* may also refer to "subtle breath" or "energy," with some parallels to the Chinese concepts of *qi* and the Greek concept of *pneuma*.

prayer. Conventionally understood as human communication with divine and spiritual entities. Often reduced to petitionary forms. In a more comprehensive perspective, includes benediction, confession, contemplation, dedication, meditation, intercession, invocation, penitence, petition, supplication, thanksgiving (praise or adoration), and so forth. In terms of **contemplative practice**, **contemplative prayer** is roughly synonymous with **meditation** as a comparative category.

psi. Paranormal phenomena. In parapsychology (via Berthold P. Wiesner [1901–1972]), psi is the purported process of information or energy transference in extrasensory perception (ESP) or psychokinesis that is unexplained in terms of known physical or biological mechanisms. The term derives from the twenty-third letter of the Greek alphabet and relates to *psyche* (mind or soul) by extension. Some potential psi-related abilities and phenomena include clairaudience, clairvoyance, precognition, remote viewing, telepathy, telekinesis, and so forth. Related tradition-specific categories include *abhijñā* and *siddhi*.

psychology. Discourse on, theories about, or study of *psyche*. The latter concept is a Greek term that may designate emotion, intellect, life, mind, soul, spirit, and so forth. In a technical sense, the social scientific discipline that studies mind, especially with respect to emotion and human behavior. In a broad sense, views of consciousness and human emotional and behavior patterns. Often overlaps with **cognitive science**, **contemplative**

studies, **neuroscience**, theological anthropology, and so forth. Dominant forms of modern psychology include behavioral-cognitive, developmental, and psychoanalysis. In terms of **contemplative studies**, contemplative, humanistic, and transpersonal psychologies are most relevant. May include tradition-specific psychologies.

Pure Consciousness Event (PCE). Phrase coined by Robert K. C. Forman (Forge Institute; formerly of Hunter College), a scholar of comparative mysticism and **contemplative studies**, and his colleagues. Psychological condition or consciousness state characterized by contentless awareness. A direct and unmediated form of mystical consciousness beyond subject/object dichotomies. Identified by Forman and his colleagues as a "higher form of consciousness." As parallel to **trophotropic** types of experience, also problematically used as synonymous with the category of **mystical experienc**e.

qi (ch'i). Traditional Chinese and Daoist technical term best left untranslated. Variously rendered as "subtle breath" or "energy." Both physical respiration and a more subtle presence or vapor, which flows through the universe and self. As a potential bridge between "mind" and "body," challenges conventional views about materiality. Brings attention to the energetic dimensions of embodiment, existence, and experience. Pronounced *ki* in Japanese, *qi* has some parallels with the Indian Sanskrit notion of *prāṇa* and the Greek notion of *pneuma*.

receptive mode. Phrase coined by the clinical psychiatrist Arthur Deikman (University of California, San Francisco). A condition in which one abides in open receptivity. The sensory-perceptual system is the primary form of engagement and participation. As located in Deikman's concept of bimodal consciousness, contrasts with the **active mode**. Parallels Erich Fromm's **being-mode** and Abraham Maslow's **Being-cognition**.

reconceptualization. The process of redefining something in ways that deviate from its original framework, including associated concerns, values, views, and so forth. In terms of **contemplative practice**, the concept of reconceptualization draws attention to source-culture and source-tradition, including informing worldviews and soteriological systems. In a modern context, reconceptualization is most often done under the guise of hybrid spirituality, with associated tendencies of colonialization and domestication. Related to **decontextualization**. Brings the issue of the ethics and politics of appropriation into high relief, including the consequences for the associated community and tradition.

reductionism. The process or act of reducing something to something else. In the modern world, most prominent in the form of secular materialism or the belief that life is solely biological or material in nature. In terms of the study of consciousness and **contemplative experience**, often manifests as neuroscientific reductionism, or the belief that there is nothing beyond brain chemistry. Often includes attempts to define human experience and existence solely in terms of neurological activity. May involve the idea of human beings as "hard-wired" and religious beliefs as evolutionary adaptations, including the so-called "God delusion." Nonreductionist approaches to **contemplative studies** consider the entire spectrum and diverse dimensions of **contemplative practice** and **contemplative experience**, including existential, "paranormal," social, and theological ones.

religious experience. Any experience that occurs within religious communities or traditions, or experiences identified as religiously significant by individuals or communities. May include "ordinary" experiences such as ritual activity, **prayer**, **meditation**, scripture study, theological discourse, and so forth. These are activities that produce meaning and feelings of belonging in community members with regard to something defined as **sacred**. Religious experience is often conflated with **mystical experience**, but the latter is better understood as a subcategory of anomalous or religious experience.

sacred. Comparative category for that which is defined as ultimately real or significant by individuals or communities. In the case of religious traditions, requires identification of tradition-specific technical terms and defining characteristics. Also requires recognition of the diversity of theological perspectives and the fact that there are equally convincing, mutually exclusive accounts of "reality." Such multiperspectivism may suggest that "the sacred" is pluralistic rather than unitary in nature.

sādhanā. Indian Sanskrit term for "spiritual practice." More literally refers to "a means of accomplishing something." Used in various senses in different Indian religions, including in Hinduism and Buddhism. As a religious path, *sādhanā* may refer to spiritual exertion toward an intended goal, specifically liberation (*mokṣa* [*moksha*]).

ṣalāt (*ṣalāh*). Arabic term for Islamic **prayer**. One of the Five Pillars in Sunni Islam. To perform valid *ṣalāt*, Muslims must be in a state of ritual purity, which is mainly achieved by "ritual ablution" (*wuḍū'*) according to prescribed procedures. Often associated with "remembrance" (***dhikr***). Observant Muslims practice *ṣalāt* five times a day facing Mecca, Saudi Arabia. Consists of the repetition of a unit called a *rakat* (pl.: *rakaʿāt*) consisting of prescribed actions and words, including specific **postures** such prostrations (*sujūd/sajdah*). The number of obligatory (*fard*) *rakaʿāt* varies from two to four according to the time of day or other circumstances (such as Friday congregational worship). Utilizes various passages from the Qur'an, with the "Opening" chapter (*sura*), called "Sūrat al-Fātiḥah," being most important.

samādhi. Sanskrit technical term used in various Indian traditions, including Hinduism and Buddhism, to refer to a state of meditative concentration. Often translated as "meditative absorption," "one-pointedness," and "yogic stasis," and more problematically as "trance." In terms of the Eightfold Path, right effort (6), right mindfulness (7), and right concentration (8) are often categorized as *samādhi*.

samatha. Buddhist Pali technical term (Skt.: *śamatha*) that refers to "calm abiding." A form of Buddhist meditation wherein one calms the mind, specifically by stilling emotional and intellectual content and by becoming more psychologically stable.

sati. Buddhist Pali technical term that refers to "awareness" or "mindfulness." May refer to one of the seven factors of enlightenment as well as one element of the Noble Eightfold Path. As a form of Buddhist meditation, often involves awareness of various dimensions of human being during one's daily life. These include bodily functions, sensations, perceptions, thoughts, and so forth. In modern contexts, *sati* is often conflated with ***vipassanā*** (insight) meditation practice.

satori. Japanese Zen Buddhist term derived from the Chinese Chan *wu*. Literally, "awakening." Enlightenment. The state of spiritual freedom or liberation. Often used to designate ***kenshō*** experiences.

secularization. Technically the transformation of a society from close identification with religious values and institutions toward "nonreligious" (or irreligious) values and secular institutions. Also associated with the largely discredited "secularization thesis," with its assumed materialist and social constructivist view of "religion," which refers to the belief that as societies "progress," specifically through modernization and rationalization, religion loses its authority and will eventually disappear. In the case of **contemplative practice**, secularization is the process through which a given practice is extracted from its religious source-tradition, including associated worldview and soteriological system, and relocated in a secular materialist framework. Often involves colonialism and domestication. Examples include **therapeutic meditation** and various modern appropriative agendas. Often involves **decontextualization** and **reconceptualization**.

self-actualization. In humanistic and transpersonal **psychology**, the process of developing one's capacities and qualities, and the state of being fully functioning and fulfilled. Connected with **human potential**, or the belief that human beings have untapped potentials that may be developed. Self-actualization is generally characterized by such qualities as creativity, experimentation, fulfillment, joy, unconditional positive regard for others, vision, and so forth.

shikan-taza. Japanese Zen Buddhist term meaning "just sitting." Especially associated with Eihei Dōgen (1200–1253), the founder of the Japanese Sōtō (Chn.: Caodong) school. Related to the precursor Chan practice of "silent illumination" (Chn.: *mozhao*).

shouyi. Chinese Daoist technical term that literally means "guarding the One." Originally referred to classical Daoist apophatic meditation, or meditation that involves emptying the heart-mind and abiding in a state of stillness. It is contentless, nonconceptual, and nondualistic. As such, a major influence on the Zen Buddhist practice of **zazen** (Chn.: *zuochao*), especially in the form of "silent illumination" (Chn.: *mozhao*) and "just sitting" (Jpn.: **shikan-taza**). Later *shouyi* became a general Daoist category for "meditation," including a wide variety of methods.

siddhi. Indian Sanskrit term meaning "attainment" or "success." Numinous abilities. Sometimes translated as "psychic dispositions," "paranormal abilities," or "supernatural powers." Qualities and capacities developed through spiritual discipline. Often identified as "higher capacities." Different *siddhi*s are emphasized in Buddhism and Hinduism. Generally speaking, some include clairvoyance, clairaudience, imperviousness, multi- or translocation, multivocality, and so forth. *Siddhi* is basically parallel to the Buddhist Sanskrit term **abhijñā**.

silence. Key characteristic of **contemplative practice**. Often conceptualized as the absence of sound or voice but also understood as that which encompasses all sound. Within contemplative traditions, there are various conceptions of silence. In the modern world, the term is often utilized negatively to indicate unwillingness to speak out, especially about horrific psychological events and/or social injustice. From a contemplative and theological perspective, a method/state through which one gains deeper communion with the **sacred**.

somatic disciplines. Body- and movement-based practice. Traditionally includes practices such dance, martial arts, massage, ritual, and so forth. In the contemporary world, some prominent modern somatic disciplines include Alexander Technique, Applied Kinesiology, Authentic Movement, Autogenic Training, Feldenkrais Method, Pilates, Trager Approach, and so forth. Also brings attention to the embodied and physical dimensions of **contemplative practice**, including **posture**.

somatic mysticism. Phrase coined by Louis Komjathy (University of San Diego), a scholar of Daoism and comparative religious studies. On the most basic level, refers to the embodied dimensions of **mystical experience**. More strictly defined, mystical experience in which the **sacred** is experienced in/as/through the body, and in which the body itself is identified as sacred to some degree.

soteriology. Literally, "salvation-talk." Conventionally designates Christian soteriology, or salvation through Jesus Christ. As a comparative category, discourse on, theories about, or the study of actualization, freedom, liberation, perfection, realization, salvation, or however an individual or community defines the ultimate purpose of human existence. Connected to major goals of religious practice as well as **theology**. Like theology, soteriology must be considered in terms of tradition-specific terms and associated characteristics.

spiritual athleticism. Spiritual practices and existential approaches involving intense effort and/or extreme activities. Usually involves a sense of achievement, competition, extraordinary goals, and sometimes "superhuman feats."

spiritual capitalism. **Spirituality** as capitalism. Especially forms of "spirituality" that involve commodification, consumerism, profit-making, and self-promotion. In a modern context, key patterns include copyrighting and trademarking teachings, practices, organizations, and so forth.

spiritual colonialism. Appropriation and reconceptualization of tradition-specific views and practices done in the name of designer, hybrid "**spirituality**." As expressed in **Perennial Philosophy** and New Age spirituality, usually involves viewing religious traditions ("wisdom traditions") as "resources" for human development.

spiritual exhibitionism. Spiritual practices and existential approaches done in conspicuous ways and ways that aim to bring attention to oneself. Particularly related to concern for exposure, fame, recognition, and wealth. Often includes **spiritual athleticism**, or public demonstrations of "extraordinary powers" and performance of parlor tricks.

spiritual materialism. Phrase coined by Chögyam Trungpa (1939–1987), a famous Tibetan American Buddhist teacher, in his book *Cutting through Spiritual Materialism* (1973). Spiritual practices and existential approaches based in materialistic concerns, especially egoistic motivations.

spirituality. Literally "of or related to spirit." Conventionally speaking, "spirituality" refers to a problematic and inexact distinction between personal beliefs and (institutional) religion. In this sense, may refer to "unchurched spirituality" and/or unaffiliated religiosity but more often refers to designer, hybrid, and personal religious expressions. Often designated as "wisdom traditions" and organized into new religious movements (NRMs). Includes various forms of **cognitive imperialism**, **spiritual capitalism**, and **spiritual colonialism**. Conventionally speaking and in terms of received connotations, the category of "spirituality" has a complex history, with deep ties to Christianity. In Christian theological contexts, often used to distinguish affective approaches from theological or intellectual approaches. Today includes an emerging field of study referred to as Spirituality as an Academic Discipline, in which spirituality refers to the personal dimensions of lived religious adherence and practice. Has some parallel concerns with **contemplative studies**, especially **contemplative practice** and **contemplative experience**.

stages. Sequence or levels of practice. In the case of the Sufi Arabic *maqam* (pl.: *maqamat*), which is also translated as "stations," indicates moments along the contemplative path (*tariqa*), often involving a set sequence of advancement. From a Sufi perspective, this dimension of practice is under the control of the contemplative or mystic. A representative Sufi approach follows seven stages: (1) repentance, (2) abstention, (3) asceticism, (4) poverty, (5) patience, (6) confidence, and (7) contentment.

states. Types of experience or conditions of consciousness. In the case of the Sufi Arabic term *haal* (pl.: *ahwal*), indicates different spiritual conditions. Believed to come from Allah, and thus to be beyond the control of contemplatives and mystics, although religious praxis may prepare the way for them. A form of grace. Some common Sufi states include contraction, ecstasy, expansion, intimacy, intoxication, joy, loneliness, and so forth. Brings attention to the source or trigger of particular types of experience and the associated interpretations. Also problematizes the elevation of particular conditions and qualities, such as the overemphasis on (Buddhist-influenced) notions of wisdom and compassion in **contemplative studies**. In contemporary neuroscience, "states" are often used to refer to the inner experiences of individual practitioners and tend to be ephemeral. In certain respects, states relate to the introvertive dimensions of contemplative practice. They may be distinguished from **traits**.

theology. Literally, "god-talk." As a comparative category, discourse on, theories about, and the study of the **sacred**, with the sacred being another comparative category referring to the ultimate concern or reality as understood by a given individual or community. There are many types of theology, including "nontheistic" ones. Some types include animistic (gods or spirits in nature), atheistic (no gods), monistic (one impersonal reality [i.e., Reality]), monotheistic (one personal god [i.e., God]), panenhenic (Nature as sacred), pantheistic (sacred in the world), panentheistic (sacred in and beyond the world), and polytheistic (many personal gods). Conventionally speaking and in terms of received connotations, the category of theology has a complex history, with deep ties to Christianity. It is usually associated with adherent and normative discourse on "God." However, as a comparative category, theology relates to a wide variety of tradition-specific terms for the "sacred" and the corresponding characteristics.

therapeutic meditation (medicalized meditation). **Meditation** aimed at the restoration or maintenance of health and wellness, with "health" having diverse definitions. In the modern world, most "therapeutic meditation" utilizes decontextualized and reconceptualized practices, practices that have been appropriated from various religious traditions. Such practices are most often reconceptualized through a Western biomedical and scientific value-system, specifically as "stress-reduction" and "self-care" techniques. The most prominent forms include Mindfulness-Based Stress Reduction (MBSR), a modified form of Theravāda ***vipassanā*** developed by Jon Kabat-Zinn (b. 1944; University of Massachusetts Medical School), and the Relaxation Response, a modified form of Transcendental Meditation (TM) developed by Herbert Benson (b. 1935; Massachusetts General Hospital).

third-person discourse. Generally considered to be a form of observation in which one studies things without any personal investment. Aims to be a more "objective" or "neutral" perspective. Has some rough correspondence to **etic** perspectives and approaches. Often contrasted with **first-person discourse**.

traits. Technical term sometimes used in contemporary neuroscience to refer to more stable character qualities developed in interactions with the phenomenal world. In certain respects, traits relate to the extrovertive dimensions of contemplative practice. Related to long-term benefits and effects, especially positive alterations of character and qualities, traits may be distinguished from **states**.

trophotropic. A state of hypoarousal or hyperquiescence, characterized by lower levels of physiological and/or neurological activity. As a cartography of meditative and mystical experience, first advocated by Roland Fischer. The opposite of **ergotropic**.

typology. An interpretative framework based on types. In the case of **contemplative studies**, involves developing comparative categories. As advocated in the present volume, includes devotional, **ergotropic**, **kinesthetic**, and **trophotropic** types, among others.

ultimate concern. Phrase coined by the Protestant Christian theologian Paul Tillich (1886–1965). Refers to a concern that renders all other concerns only conditionally relevant or provisionally important. As a theological category, synonymous with that which is identified as **sacred** or ultimately real.

unconditional positive regard. A phrase developed by the humanistic psychologist Carl Rogers (1902–1987; formerly of the Center for Studies of the Person). Rooted in a person-centered approach to psychotherapy and **self-actualization**, unconditional positive regard is a form of interpersonal communication and interrelationship in which one maintains basic acceptance of and support for a person regardless of what the person says or does.

vipassanā. Buddhist Pali term (Skt.: *vipaśyanā*) that refers to "insight." Sometimes translated as "mindfulness," which better renders **sati**. A form of Buddhist meditation wherein one provisionally observes all phenomena with nondiscriminating awareness. Actually Buddhist meditation that aims to understand the true nature of (Buddhist) "reality." Includes application and confirmation of the foundational Buddhist worldview centering on such things as the "three characteristics of existence," namely, suffering (Pali: *dukkha*), impermanence (Pali: *anicca*), and no-self (Pali: *anattā*; Skt.: *anātman*).

visualization. Meditation practice involving visualizing or imagining particular things. Usually involves a high degree of visual content. Requires further investigation of the degree to which the associated practice involves imagination or actualization. Like devotional practices, visualization is often excluded from the categories of **meditation** and **contemplative practice**.

yoga. Indian Sanskrit technical term used in various Indian traditions, including Hinduism and Buddhism, derived from the root *yuj* (to yoke or to unite). Traditionally refers to disciplines, including **meditation**, aimed at spiritual liberation and/or divine union. Often defines the body and world as "samsaric." In a modern context, a hybrid spiritualist category that often refers to health and fitness routines emphasizing stretching and breathwork largely derived from Hatha Yoga and European gymnastic traditions fused with Western body-image and beauty ideals.

zazen. Japanese Zen Buddhist term derived from the Chinese Chan *zuochan*. Literally, "seated" or "sitting Zen." Historically speaking, *chan* is a Chinese transliteration of the Sanskrit term ***dhyāna*** (Pali: ***jhāna***), or concentration. In its more modern expression, *zazen* includes two primary forms: "silent illumination" (Chn.: *mozhao*), also known as "just sitting" (Jpn.: ***shikan-taza***), and *kōan* (Chn.: *gong'an*)-based meditation. The former is an emptiness-based meditation practice, while the latter utilizes enigmatic phrases and questions as meditation devices.

zhengyan. Chinese Daoist technical term for "experiential confirmation." Also translated as "signs of proof" and "verification." In Daoist internal alchemy (*neidan*) lineages, which often involve stage-based training, the efficacy of specific practices is confirmed by the appearance of specific benefits, qualities, and/or experiences. The latter may include **mystical experiences**. Draws attention to the potential transformative effects of **contemplative practice**.

About the Contributors

Michael Birkel (PhD, Study of Religion; Harvard University) is Professor of Religion at Earlham College in Richmond, Indiana (United States), where he has also served as director of the Newlin Center for Quaker Thought and Practice. His writings focus chiefly on Quaker spirituality and include *'A Near Sympathy': The Timeless Quaker Wisdom of John Woolman* (2003), *Silence and Witness: Quaker Spirituality* (2004), *Engaging Scripture: Encountering the Bible with Early Friends* (2005), *The Messenger That Goes Before: Reading Margaret Fell for Spiritual Nurture* (2008), and *Genius of the Transcendent: Mystical Writings of Jakob Boehme* (2010).

Edwin F. Bryant (PhD, Indic Languages and Cultures; Columbia University) is Professor of Hindu Religion and Philosophy at Rutgers University in New Jersey (United States). His primary areas of specialization are early Indian prehistory and history, Indian philosophy in general, and Yoga philosophies in particular, and the Krishna devotional traditions. His publications include *In Quest of the Origins of Vedic Culture* (2001), *Krishna: The Beautiful Legend of God* (2004), *The Yoga Sūtras of Patañjali* (2009), and several edited volumes. He is presently working on a set of translations of Yoga tales from the *Bhagavata Purana* and a series of edited volumes on themes from Indian philosophy.

Arthur F. Buehler (PhD, Study of Religion; Harvard University) is an independent scholar based in Amman, Jordan. His primary focus of research has been the Naqshbandi sufi lineage in India and Turkey. This investigation, including ten years of fieldwork, has resulted in numerous publications with special consideration given to contemplative practice. To date his major publications are *Sufi Heirs of the Prophet: The Indian Naqshbandiyya and the Rise of the Mediating Sufi Shaykh* (1998) and *Revealed Grace: The Juristic Sufism of Ahmad Sirhindi (1564–1624)* (2011), which is a partial translation of Ahmad Sirhindi's *Collected Letters*, the most detailed manual of contemplative practice in sufi literature. His *Recognizing Sufism: Transformative Practice in the Islamic Tradition* is forthcoming.

Constance A. Jones (PhD, Sociology; Emory University) is Professor of Transformative Inquiry at the California Institute of Integral Studies (CIIS) in San Francisco, California (United States) and chair of the Board of Directors of the Institute for the Study of American Religion in Santa Barbara, California, and Waco, Texas (United States). She is a sociologist of religion who researches Eastern and Western intellectual history (particularly the dissemination of Hindu and Buddhist beliefs and practices in the West), new religious movements, and Western esotericism. She has taught at a number of graduate programs and has received a number of awards, particularly a

Fulbright Fellowship to the Benares Hindu University and the Krishnamurti Research Center in Varanasi, India. She has published *The Legacy of G. I. Gurdjieff* (2005), *Encyclopedia of Hinduism* (2007), *Gurdjieff in Tiflis* (editor; 2008), *Melton's Encyclopedia of American Religions, Eighth Edition* (associate editor; 2009), and *Hinduism, Jainism, and Sikhism in America* (forthcoming).

Louis Komjathy (PhD, Religious Studies; Boston University) is Associate Professor of Theology and Religious Studies at the University of San Diego (United States). He is also founding co-chair (2004–2010) of the Daoist Studies Group of the American Academy of Religion, founding co-chair (2010–present) of the Contemplative Studies Group of the American Academy of Religion, founding codirector of the Center for Daoist Studies, and managing editor of the Contemplative Studies website. His primary area of specialization is Daoism, with particular interests in contemplative practice and mystical experience. In addition to various academic articles and book chapters, his major publications include *Title Index to Daoist Collections* (2002), *Cultivating Perfection: Mysticism and Self-Transformation in Early Quanzhen Daoism* (2007), *Handbooks for Daoist Practice* (2008), *The Way of Complete Perfection: A Quanzhen Daoist Anthology* (2013), *The Daoist Tradition: An Introduction* (2013), and *Daoism: A Guide for the Perplexed* (2014).

Shaul Magid (PhD, Judaic Studies; Brandeis University) is the Jay and Jeannie Schottenstein Professor of Jewish Studies and Professor of Religious Studies at Indiana University, Bloomington (United States). He is the author of *Hasidism on the Margin: Reconciliation, Antinomianism, and Messianism in Izbica and Radzin Hasidism* (2004), *From Metaphysics to Midrash: Myth, History, and the Interpretation of Scripture in Lurianic Kabbalah* (2008), *American Post-Judaism: Identity and Renewal in a Postethnic Society* (2013), and *Hasidism Incarnate: Hasidism, Christianity, and the Construction of Modern Judaism* (2014). *From Metaphysics to Midrash* was awarded the 2009 American Academy of Religion prize for best book in religion in the textual studies category.

John Anthony McGuckin (PhD, Patristics; Durham University) is the Nielsen Professor of Late Antique and Byzantine Christian History at Union Theological Seminary and Professor of Byzantine Christianity at Columbia University, both in New York City (United States). He is an archpriest of the Orthodox Church and an internationally renowned theologian of the Eastern Christian tradition. He has written extensively on the related areas of New Testament, Early Christian thought and culture, and Byzantine mysticism. He was elected a fellow of the Royal Society of Arts in 1986 and a fellow of the Royal Historical Society in 1996, was selected as the prestigious Luce Fellow in Church History in 2006, and was awarded the Order of St. Stephen the Great, the Cross of Moldavia and Bukovina, by the Romanian Orthodox Patriarch in 2008. Dr. McGuckin is the author of twenty-five books and over one hundred scholarly articles in international journals. Some of his publications include the following: *The Transfiguration of Christ in Scripture and Tradition* (1986), *St. Gregory of Nazianzus: An Intellectual Biography* (2000), *Standing in God's Holy Fire: The Spiritual Tradition of Byzantium* (2001), *The Book of Mystical Chapters* (2002), *The Orthodox Church: An Introduction to Its History, Theology, and Spiritual Culture* (2007), and the *Blackwell Encyclopedia of Eastern Orthodox Christianity* (2010).

Paul Philibert (S.T.D., Theology; Dominican Pontifical Faculty of Washington, D.C.; S.T.M., Order of Preachers) is retired Professor of Pastoral Theology who taught at Catholic University in Washington, D.C., Aquinas Institute of Theology in St. Louis (United States), and the University of Fribourg (Switzerland). He was a provincial superior in the Dominican Order and has served as a member of the order's Commission on Studies. He has published a number of translations, including of M. D. Chenu's *Aquinas and His Role in Theology* (2002) and of Yves Congar's *True and False Reform in the Church* (2011). His own books include *Stewards of God's Mysteries: Priestly Spirituality in a Changing Church* (2004), *The Priesthood of the Faithful: Key to a Living Church* (2005), and, with Thomas O'Meara, *Scanning the Signs of the Times: French Dominicans in the Twentieth Century* (2013).

Harold D. Roth (PhD, East Asian Studies; University of Toronto) is Professor of Religious Studies at Brown University in Providence, Rhode Island (United States). He also serves as the director of the Contemplative Studies Initiative at Brown University and as a steering committee member of the Contemplative Studies Group of the American Academy of Religion. He is a specialist in early Chinese religious thought, Daoism, the history of East Asian religions, the comparative study of mysticism, and a pioneer in the developing field of contemplative studies. His publications include six books: *The Textual History of the Huai-nan Tzu* (1992), *Original Tao: "Inward Training" (Nei-yeh) and the Foundations of Taoist Mysticism* (1999), *Daoist Identity: Cosmology, Lineage, and Ritual* (edited with Livia Kohn; 2002), *A Companion to Angus C. Graham's "Chuang Tzu": The Inner Chapters* (2003), *The Huainanzi: A Guide to the Theory and Practice of Government in Early Han China, by Liu An, King of Huainan* (with John S. Major, Sarah Queen, and Andrew S. Meyer, 2009); and an abridged version of the previous book titled *The Essential Huainanzi* (2012). He has also published over fifty articles on the early history and religious thought of the Daoist tradition, on the textual history and textual criticism of classical Chinese works, and on contemplative studies and contemplative pedagogy.

Sarah Shaw (PhD, English Literature; Manchester University) is a member of the Faculty of Oriental Studies, Oxford University, a member of Wolfson College, and a fellow of the Oxford Centre for Buddhist Studies (United Kingdom). Her main areas of study are Southern Buddhist narrative, meditation, and art. Her books and translations include *Buddhist Meditation: An Anthology of Texts* (2006), *The Jātakas: Birth Stories of the Bodhisatta* (2006), *An Introduction to Buddhist Meditation* (2009), *The Spirit of Buddhist Meditation* (2014), and, with Dr. Naomi Appleton, *The Ten Great Birth Stories of the Buddha* (2015).

Kenneth K. Tanaka (PhD, Buddhist Studies; University of California, Berkeley) is Professor of Buddhist Studies and Dean of Buddhist Education at Musashino University (Tokyo, Japan). He currently serves as president of two academic associations, the International Association of Shin Buddhist Studies and the Japanese Association for the Study of Buddhism and Psychology. His primary areas of specialization are Pure Land Buddhism and American Buddhism. Some of his major publications include the following: *The Dawn of Chinese Pure Land Buddhist Doctrine* (1990), *The Faces of Buddhism in America* (coedited with Charles Prebish; 1998), *Approaching the Land of Bliss: Religious Praxis in the Cult of Amitābha* (coedited with Richard Payne; 2003), *Pure Land Buddhism* (2004), and, in Japanese, *Amerika Bukkyō* (American Buddhism) (2010).

Index

1 Thessalonians 5:17, 174, 386, 388
"153 Practical and Theological Texts," 372, 393, 399
4'33", 41

A Guide to True Peace, 76, 79, 145–96, 707; text of, 171–96
A Plea for the Poor, 157
A Seeker of Unceasing Prayer. See *Iskatelia neprestannoi molitivy*
A Short and Very Easy Method of Prayer. See *Moyen court et très facile pour l'oraison*
A-di-da Phat, 422
abba, 58, 513
Abbey of Fontfroide, 528
Abbey of Gethsemani, 10
abbots, 382, 393, 506, 509, 537, 551
"Abbreviated Description of the Mode of Prayer," 386
abdomen, 102, 281, 286, 558, 564, 580
'Abdulkhaliq Ghujduwani. See Ghujduwani
'Abdullah Ansari Hirati. See Hirati
'Abdullah Shah, 307–8, 311–12, 314, 322, 328–29, 333
'Abdullatif (Shah), 308
'Abdulqadir al-Jilani. See Jilani
'Abdulrahman Saharanpuri. See Saharanpuri
Abhayagiri monastery, 286
Abhidhamma, 268, 276–77, 285
Abhidharma-kośabhāsyam, 285
abhiññā, 279, 713
Abhirati, 412
abilities. See capacities
ablution. See *mikveh*; *wuḍū'*
Abraham, 243, 248, 256, 263, 322, 337
Abrahamic traditions, 457, 463, 721
Abramović, Marina, 41

Absolute. See sacred
Absolute Unitary Being, 16, 70
absorption, 54, 114, 469, 471–72, 483, 491, 561, 579, 592, 710, 713. See also *samādhi*
abstention, 68, 404, 470, 491, 519, 572, 712. See also renunciation; *yama*
Abu Bakr, 313
Abu Hafs al-Suhrawardi. See Suhrawardi
Abu Sa'id, 308, 314
Abu'l-Hasan Zayd Faruqi. See Faruqi
Abu'l-Hasanat 'Abdulhayy, 307
Abu'l-Khayr 'Abdullah, 315
Abu'l-Khayr Rahmatullah Shah, 308
Abulafia Abraham, 201, 204–6, 208–18, 222–25, 241, 244, 247–48
abundance, 193, 253, 265, 273
abyss, 124, 193
academia, 4, 6, 9–11, 14, 33–37, 41, 44, 67, 73, 147, 164, 219, 223, 287, 322, 324–28, 458, 476, 505, 552, 570, 594–95, 606, 666, 724–25. See also pedagogy
acceptance, 35, 166, 183, 426, 651, 655, 678, 697, 711, 714, 722–23
accomplishment. See attainment
acquisitiveness, 68, 267, 297, 394, 423, 475–77, 491, 557, 651, 679, 682, 698
activating the Dharma Wheel, 564, 582–83
active mode, 70, 82
activity, 98, 107–9, 113, 128, 147, 152–53, 158, 165, 190, 267, 270–71, 277, 285, 289, 291, 309, 320–21, 329, 336, 344, 365, 413, 440, 470, 475, 488, 490, 503–8, 512–13, 528, 544–45, 595, 609, 632, 660, 662, 680, 711, 716, 721, 729. See also movement
actualization, 23–24, 70, 81, 564, 659, 707, 711–14, 716, 719, 726. See also potentiality

Adam, 154, 235, 249, 318, 334, 341, 347, 371, 375, 385
adaptation, 35, 336, 410, 461, 474–75, 506, 509, 527, 558, 601, 642
adherence, 10–12, 17, 22, 35, 53, 78, 189, 193, 202, 222, 547, 552–53, 565, 570, 600, 603, 605–6, 613, 617, 620–21, 623, 670, 673, 710, 717, 720–22, 727–28
adherents, 10–12, 17, 22, 25, 28, 33–34, 40, 42, 74–75, 78, 82
admonitions. *See* encouragement; precepts
Adonai, 258
adrenal glands, 636
adrenaline, 601, 637
Advaita Vedānta, 654, 657
advanced meditation. *See* levels; stages
adventure, 376
advice. *See* guidance; spiritual direction
Adyar, 647
aesthetics, 56, 59, 63, 155, 266, 270, 417, 504, 514, 531, 578, 667, 708–9, 719, 724, 726–28
affiliation, 20, 35, 311, 547, 565, 574
affinity, 166, 210, 342–43, 580, 585, 609, 657, 712
affliction. *See* suffering
Afghanistan, 323, 328, 718
Africa, 310, 509
afterlife, 66, 157, 196, 263, 555, 557–58, 571, 656–57, 708, 713. *See also* tradition-specific terms
agitation, 43, 71, 154, 159, 180, 183, 189, 193–94, 238, 250, 279, 299, 302–3, 353, 375, 464–65, 467, 469–70, 486, 527, 542, 544, 601–2, 610, 638, 640, 644, 650, 658, 671, 680, 711, 713, 717, 719
Ahai bar Josiah, 262
ahaṁkāra, 465–66
Ahavat Shalom Yeshiva, 214, 216
Ahmad Sirhindi. *See* Sirhindi
Ahmadi, 337
Ahrar. *See* 'Ubaydullah Ahrar
ahwāl, 68, 310
aisthesis noetikos, 380
Ajase complex, 425
Ajātśatru, 409, 416, 425, 437–39
Ajmer, 312
Akbar, 312–13
Akṣehir, 330

Akṣobhya, 412
Al-Azhar University, 315
Al-Futūḥāt al-Makkiyya, 310, 323–24
'Ala'uddin Simnani. *See* Simnani
alarm, 601, 642, 651
Albertus Magnus, 505, 510, 514, 531
Albi, 507
Albigensians, 505, 507–10, 520
Albotini, Judah, 213, 224
alchemical body, 558, 571, 578–92, 709
alchemy, 64, 199, 213, 547, 550, 554–56, 566, 568–71, 578, 615, 620, 622. *See also* external alchemy; internal alchemy
alcohol, 108, 171, 175, 404–5, 551, 559, 615, 654, 685
Alexander Technique, 53, 79
Alexander the Great, 480
'Ali Aqa mosque, 307
'Ali b. Abi Talib, 308
alignment, 97, 101, 103, 125, 127, 135, 138, 209, 267, 564, 715
Alimpii, 385
aliveness, 23, 70, 72, 571, 706, 714, 719, 728–29. *See also* being
Alkabetz, Shlomo, 198
Allah, 68, 309, 317, 319, 333, 338–40, 347, 350, 712, 721. *See also* God
allocentric pathway, 114
allopathic medicine, 21, 595, 598–600, 609–12, 617, 619, 623, 629, 631
almsgiving. *See* donations; generosity; support
aloneness. *See* independence; solitude
Alshekh, Moshe, 199
altar of the heart, 374
altars, 63, 257, 374, 504, 516–17, 519, 521–22, 532, 537, 580, 728
altered states of consciousness, 7, 23, 310, 321, 324–26, 329, 357, 638–39, 708, 713
alternative medicine. *See* complementary alternative medicine; medicine
alternative spirituality. *See* hybrid spirituality; spirituality
alterity, 11, 39, 74–75, 123, 129, 140, 477, 491, 671, 710, 720–23
altruism. *See* selflessness
Ambrose of Milan, 531
American Academy of Religion, 40, 327
American Council of Learned Sciences, 44

American Institute of Stress, 622
American Philosophical Society, 622
American Physiological Society, 622, 636
American Transcendentalists, 599, 638
American Yoga, 471, 474–75, 477, 480, 569, 708.
    See also appropriation; domestication; hybrid spirituality
Americanization, 424
Amida, 426, 431, 437
Amir Kulal, 312
Amita, 409, 431. See also Amitābha
Amit'a bul, 422
Amitābha, 65–66, 407–55, 580, 582, 710
Amitāyur-dhyāna-sūtra, 431, 437
Amitāyus. See Amitābha
Amituo, 409, 431, 437. See also Amitābha
Amituo jing, 412
Amnon Gross, 223
Amritsari, Muhammad Musa, 323, 325
Amsterdam, 680
Amvrosy, 368
amygdala, 28
An Apology for the True Christian Divinity, 149–51
An Ascetic Miscellany, 367
An Shigao, 285
Ānanda, 269, 292, 296, 416, 438–55
anarchic traditionalism, 218, 226
Andhra Pradesh, 307
angels, 215, 239, 251, 260, 262, 308–9, 335, 369, 507, 515, 520, 531, 537, 647, 656
Analects. See *Lunyu*
analytical thought. See discursive thought
ānāpāna-sati, 265–306
Ānāpānasati Sutta, 72, 76, 265–306, 707, 713; translation of, 296–306
anāsrava, 557, 564, 578
anātman, 36, 55, 267, 276–77, 284, 298, 411, 442–43, 451
Anatolia, 393
anatomy, 27, 29–30, 615. See also body
anattā. See *anātman*
Anderson, Allan, 668
Andra Pradesh, 645
Andresen, Jensine, 4, 6, 17–18
anesthetization, 631, 719
anga, 459, 470, 474
anger, 234, 239, 397, 438, 491, 533, 545, 557, 610, 636, 698–99, 719

Anglicans. See Church of England
Aṅguttaranikāya, 275
Anhui, 548, 551, 555, 562
anicca, 36, 55, 276–77, 283, 298–300, 442–43, 451
animal consciousness, 369
animal experimentation, 635
animal self, 333
animal welfare, 335, 717
animals, 24, 35, 42, 122, 125, 181, 242, 257, 316, 320, 335, 369, 403, 439, 446, 458, 477, 495, 582, 601, 615, 632–33, 635, 686–87, 713, 719, 729. See also specific animals
anitya. See *anicca*
Anle ji, 433
annihilation. See disappearance
annihilationism, 267, 433
annoyance. See agitation
Annual Monitor for 1844, 145–46
anomalous experience, 9, 23, 38, 64, 66, 152, 549, 654, 708, 713
anonymity, 58, 73, 145, 166, 171, 211, 226, 323, 359–60, 364, 366–67, 376, 383–84, 388, 408, 426, 503, 531, 567, 653, 683
Anonymous Essay on Devotion, 174
Anqing, 548, 551, 555, 562
Anthony, 386
anthropomorphism, 431
anthropologies of realization, 711
anthropology (field), 12–13, 43, 324, 600, 621, 720
anthropology (theology), 23, 43, 154, 165, 167, 249, 309, 311, 315–16, 333, 344, 369, 371–72, 374–75, 385, 396, 400, 410, 412, 423, 457, 463–68, 472, 477–78, 505, 515, 521, 553–58, 565, 569, 571–72, 578–92, 599–602, 609, 612, 623, 632, 647–48, 667, 671, 707–12, 726
anthropology of consciousness, 326
anthropocentrism, 23, 716, 719
antinomianism, 423
Antony of Padua, 513
anupassati, 283
Anurādhapura, 269, 286
Anuruddha, 296
anusmṛti, 416
Anwar Allah Faruqi. See Faruqi
anxiety, 196, 463, 467, 541, 610, 629, 636, 640, 659, 662, 688

apartheid, 327
aphorisms, 462, 468–69, 473, 483
apocalypticism, 219, 309
apologetics, 11, 25, 42, 71, 82, 376, 427, 718
apophasis, 90, 98, 105, 114, 208, 218–20, 222, 314, 340, 355, 375, 380–81, 396, 403, 462, 512, 522, 524, 542, 562, 580, 599, 664–65, 679–80, 697, 707, 710, 716, 723, 728
apophatic meditation, 4, 7–8, 36, 55, 58, 67, 77–78, 82, 89–143, 152–53, 156, 159, 166, 553, 558, 571–72, 591, 615, 638, 706–7, 715
apostasy, 392, 434, 570, 650
Apostles, 157, 373, 388, 390, 397–98, 508, 511, 519, 533, 535
apostolic, 504, 509
appetites. *See* desire
Apple Inc., 633
application, 75, 108, 223, 236, 272, 287, 290, 326–27, 416, 567, 597–98, 604, 609–10, 623–24, 715–19
Applied Kinesiology, 53, 79
appreciation. *See* gratitude
appropriation, 20, 34–35, 43, 53, 461, 471, 474–76, 571, 574, 597, 602, 605, 607, 612, 616, 619–21, 623, 642, 647, 708, 729. *See also* colonialism; domestication
Aquinas, Thomas, 57, 505, 510, 512, 520, 523–24, 531
Arabic, 54, 309–10, 315, 317, 324, 328, 336, 474
Aragón, 147
Aramaic, 367
Aranda, 505
Āraṇya, Harihārananda. *See* Harihārananda Āraṇya
Āraṇyaka, 478
Arca di San Domenico, 529, 541
archaeology, 96–97, 459, 478
archbishops, 361, 363, 367–68
archimandrite, 359, 361
architecture, 18, 56, 59, 63, 154–55, 214, 513, 516, 528, 532–45, 618, 667, 702, 709, 727–28. *See also* specific types
archivists, 363
Argentina, 593, 636
argumentation, 176, 269, 390, 425–28, 461, 472, 525, 542, 552, 585
arhat, 272–73, 280, 283, 297, 416, 433, 452
Ari. *See* Luria, Isaac

aristocracy, 361, 366, 377–79, 401, 422, 506–7, 520
Aristotle, 206, 463, 510
ark, 261, 531
arms. *See* limbs
army. *See* military
Aronson, Harvey, 291
arrogance, 160, 183, 235–36, 557, 687, 706
arrows, 522, 540
art, 4, 9, 11, 63, 79, 417, 425, 433, 444, 504, 514, 528, 536, 619, 680, 687, 708
artisans, 312, 345
asamprajñāta samādhi, 469–71, 479, 483–84
āsana, 470–72, 474–76, 480, 491–92
ascended masters, 648–51, 656, 674
ascent, 121, 189, 190, 215, 239–42, 247, 254, 264, 316, 318–20, 329, 335, 347, 355, 373–74, 376, 380, 582, 648
"Ascetic Discourse Sent at the Request of the Same Monks in India," 404
"Ascetic Discourses," 391
asceticism, 3, 13, 18, 22, 36–37, 39, 43, 68, 161, 187, 199, 201, 204–5, 210, 222, 224, 244, 260, 265–69, 296, 309, 317, 347, 370, 372, 378, 383, 391, 393, 457–59, 470–72, 476–77, 491–92, 498, 507–8, 518–19, 527, 534, 557, 560, 572, 651, 694, 712, 717, 728. *See also* specific practices
Ascona, 574
ashes, 142, 199, 525, 544, 553, 565, 682
ashram, 475
Ashtanga Vinyasa Yoga, 475
Asia Minor, 370
Asian religions, 218, 598–600, 602, 605, 619, 623, 633, 648. *See also* specific traditions
Aśoka, 272
aspirants, 75, 270, 275, 309–11, 315, 318–19, 322, 339, 342, 346–47, 354, 381–82, 388–89, 399, 412–16, 418, 420, 423, 429–31, 450, 452, 472, 527, 566
aspiration, 61, 174, 213–14, 339, 356, 380, 390, 396, 414, 417, 428, 440, 449, 451, 453–54, 566, 580, 585, 683, 687
āsrava, 557, 564, 578
assistance. *See* support
Association for Contemplative Mind in Higher Education, 10

Assyrian script, 240, 243
aṣṭāṅga, 457, 462, 470–72, 474, 491–93
astronomy, 92, 259–60, 262, 392, 496, 529
Athanasius of Alexandria, 384, 386
atheism. *See* secular materialism
atherosclerosis, 630, 634–35, 639
ātman, 459, 461, 465–67, 475, 477–78, 501, 721
atoms, 354–55
atonement, 4, 59, 150, 195, 385, 518, 528
attachment. *See* desire
attainment, 62, 64, 67, 69, 93, 176–77, 180, 188, 193, 267–68, 270–72, 278, 280, 283, 293, 296, 298, 309, 343, 369, 371, 389, 396, 416, 418, 420, 430, 432, 446, 476, 483, 486, 494, 496–98, 550, 554, 556, 560–61, 564, 579, 591, 659, 663, 670, 678, 681–82, 706, 708, 712–14, 730. *See also* benefits; goals; effects
attention, 3, 5–7, 9, 36–37, 54, 73, 75, 96–98, 101, 103, 105, 110, 112–14, 130, 134, 152, 162, 166, 172, 177–78, 180, 182, 184, 187, 189, 191, 205, 214, 236–37, 242, 244, 267, 270–71, 274, 276, 279, 281, 287, 299, 317, 322, 337–38, 340–41, 344, 348, 355, 366, 375, 381, 392–93, 395–96, 398, 400–3, 405, 440–42, 444, 471, 511, 515, 519, 521, 524–27, 535, 537, 539, 571–72, 583–84, 586, 595, 609, 638, 641, 650, 655–57, 659–60, 662–66, 668–69, 673, 678–81, 685, 687, 691, 695–97, 711, 719, 723, 728–29
attunement, 93, 132, 135, 293, 317, 544, 583
Aubin, Catherine, 514–15, 525–27
audience, 73, 75–76, 89, 145, 161, 197, 265, 284, 307, 315, 359, 361, 407, 420, 427, 457, 469, 503, 505, 547, 559, 561, 564–66, 569–70, 593, 601, 606, 622, 645, 651, 653, 655, 657–58, 667, 708, 726
Augustine of Hippo, 463, 528, 531
aum. See *om*
aura, 497, 648
Aurangabad, 328
aureole. *See* halo
Aurobindo, 672
austerity. *See* asceticism
Austin, James, 114
Austria, 601, 622, 629, 631
Authentic Movement, 53
authentication. *See* confirmation
authenticity, 23, 25, 36, 70, 93, 369, 480, 560, 730
authority, 11, 68, 81, 145, 210–11, 218, 226, 237, 271–73, 312, 315, 318, 384, 422, 427, 461, 475, 480, 506, 508, 528, 531, 598, 600, 603, 606, 610–11, 613, 617, 619, 622, 650–51, 653–60, 662, 665, 668–70, 673, 677–79, 681–82, 694, 696–99, 701, 709–10, 713, 729–30
Authors of the Impossible, 330
authorship, 73–76, 89, 120, 145, 171, 197, 234, 265, 268–69, 296, 307, 333, 359–61, 363–64, 388, 407, 437, 457–58, 483, 503, 531, 547, 578, 593, 629, 677, 726
autism, 729
autobiography, 11, 35, 163, 548, 573, 730
Autobiography of a Yogi, 479
autodidacticism, 36, 43, 607–9, 638–42
Autogenic Training, 53, 79, 609, 615
autonomic nervous system, 26–27, 637
autonomy. *See* independence
avaivartika, 412
Avalokiteśvara, 414, 418, 444, 446–55
Avataṃsaka Sūtra, 429, 550–51, 553–54, 579, 730
avatar. *See* incarnation
avidyā, 465
Avivi, Joseph, 201
avoidance, 160
Avon Books, 613
avyakta, 479
awakening, 247, 262, 265, 267–68, 271, 273, 276–78, 280, 297–98, 377, 395–96, 418, 431, 440, 449, 451, 453–54, 517, 529, 548, 553, 562, 566, 587–88, 620, 670, 689, 707, 719, 724
awareness, 3, 5–6, 9–10, 16, 23, 36–37, 44, 54, 69–70, 72–73, 95–96, 98–99, 103–4, 114, 121, 127, 131, 135, 153, 156, 180, 208, 279, 282, 287–89, 296–97, 321–24, 327, 336, 339–40, 348, 352–53, 369, 371, 375, 380–81, 463–64, 467, 469–70, 477, 479, 484, 487–88, 513, 517, 521–22, 524–25, 538–39, 541, 545, 571–72, 583, 595, 604, 639, 641–42, 645, 648, 651, 653–57, 659, 663–64, 668–69, 672–73, 681, 683, 685, 687, 691–92, 694–95, 698, 711, 719, 728–29
Āyurveda, 460
Azad Rasool, 323

Azikri, Eleazar, 224
'Azizan 'Ali Ramitani. *See* Ramitani

Ba Khin, U, 286
baalei teshuva, 226
Baby Boomer spirituality, 619, 624
Babylonia, 202
Babur, 312–13
Backhouse, William, 145–46, 149–51, 156–57, 164, 166–67, 171
Baghdad, 312, 316, 328, 341
Baha'uddin Naqshband, 312, 317, 322, 328, 336, 340
Bahir. See *Sefer Ha-Bahir*
Bain, George Grantham, 649
Baiyun guan, 551
Balaam, 245, 257–58
Balaklava, 366
Baldrian-Hussein, Farzeen, 550, 560
Bāmiyan, 409
Bangkok, 292–93
banyan tree, 267, 269, 273
baoyi, 55, 98, 128, 139, 579
Baptism (sacrament), 156, 158, 513, 516, 523
baqā', 319, 329, 344–45, 351, 354, 712
Baqibillah, Khwaja, 313, 338–39
Bar-Asher, Avishai, 213, 224–25
Barcelona, 234
Barclay, Robert, 149–51, 156
Barclay's Apology. See *An Apology for the True Christian Divinity*
Bardo Thodol, 66
barefeet, 508, 510, 520
Barger, A. Clifford, 595, 605
Barnabites. *See* Clerics Regular of St. Paul
barriers. *See* difficulties
Basilica of San Domenico, 528, 541
bast, 321
bathing, 81, 240, 242, 279, 438, 582, 586, 646
Battle of Badr, 312
Bausch, Philippina, 41
Bayazid II, 203
Baynes, Cary, 568, 570, 575
beards, 378, 565, 588, 670
bearing the cross, 151
Beat Generation, 602
Beatitudes, 540
Beauregard, Mario, 30–31

beauty, 99, 142, 196, 209, 309, 338, 342, 351, 370, 441, 474, 477, 497, 542, 638, 650, 665, 681–83, 687, 694–95, 702, 706, 708
becoming fully human, 70
Bedouelle, Guy, 511
begging. *See* mendicancy
behavior. *See* activity
behavior modification, 610, 615, 633, 637, 640, 644
behavioral psychology. *See* behaviorism
behaviorism, 22, 43, 595, 714
Beijing, 551, 555–56, 562
being, 40, 44, 70, 89, 106, 112–14, 333, 341, 346, 349, 356, 371, 374, 392, 400, 412, 425, 429, 477, 512–13, 522, 571, 590, 601–2, 619, 624, 645, 653–54, 656–57, 660–62, 664–71, 673, 679–81, 688, 698, 706–21, 723–24, 726, 728
Being-cognition, 23, 43, 70
being-mode, 23, 70
Beizong. *See* Quanzhen
Belamide, Paulino, 570
Belgium, 512
belief. *See* doctrine
belle de jour, 25
belle of the ball, 599
belonging. *See* commuity
ben David, Abraham, 243, 262
ben Shlomo Zalman, Elijah, 216
ben Yair, Pinhas, 234
ben-Asher, Abraham, 211
Benares, 291
benches. *See* furniture
Benedictines. *See* Order of Saint Benedict
benefits, 28, 33, 36, 43, 61–62, 65, 67–68, 82, 96, 100–3, 107, 138–43, 171, 174, 178, 183, 186, 189, 193, 211, 237, 253, 267, 280, 283, 330, 337, 339, 343, 347, 350, 371, 377, 390, 398, 401, 415, 420, 442, 447, 458, 472, 476, 491–92, 560–61, 572–73, 581, 589, 595, 605–7, 610–13, 615, 619, 623, 639, 643, 707, 711–12, 716, 718–19, 725–26. *See also* attainments; effects; goals
Benjamin, Walter, 227
Bengal, 323, 474, 478
Benson, Charles, 593–94
Benson, Hannah, 593
Benson, Herbert, 20, 42, 53, 62, 65, 593–624, 629, 709

Benson-Henry Institute for Mind Body Medicine, 20, 593, 597–98, 609–10, 612, 617–18, 620, 623, 629
Benson-Henry Protocol, 604, 606, 608–9
Berab, Jacob, 198
Berkeley, 424–25
Bernard of Clairvaux, 531
Besant, Annie, 647–49, 651
bespopovtsy, 384
Beth Israel Deaconess Hospital, 597, 640, 642
Beyond the Relaxation Response, 606
Bhagavad Gītā, 460–61, 467, 475–77, 479, 485, 499, 667
Bhagavān, 438
Bhagsu Mountain, 32
bhakti yoga, 59, 460–61, 475, 485. *See also* devotion
Bhaktivedanta, 475–76, 602
bhāṇaka, 275
Bhāsvatī, 474
bhāṣya, 473
bhāvanā, 54, 267, 273, 292
Bhoja Rāja, 458, 474
bhūmi, 715
Biale, David, 227
Bialik, Hayyim Nahman, 197, 219–21
Bible. *See* Christian Bible; Hebrew Bible
Biblioteca Apostolica Vaticana, 514, 525, 531, 709
biguan, 558–64, 591, 724
Bihar, 267, 474
Bikram Yoga©™, 20
Bilvavi Mishkan Evaneh, 226
Bimbisāra, 416, 437, 440
bimodal consciousness, 82
bimodal mystical experience, 112
Binyan Ariel, 201
Biofeedback, 44, 600, 609, 623
biology, 21, 24, 26, 32, 594–95, 601, 605–7, 612, 622–23, 632–33, 643–44, 651, 666
biomedicine. *See* allopathic medicine
birds, 125, 181, 444, 446, 449, 583, 667, 689
Birmingham, 163
Birth Stories. See Jātakas
Bīrunī al-, 474, 480
bishops, 360, 370, 376, 384, 506–8, 518
bittul, 205
Blagonravov, Veniamin, 363, 367
Blainey, Mark, 330

blasphemy, 176, 221
Blavatsky, Helena, 647–48, 650, 674
blessing, 162, 177, 181, 190, 192, 194–95, 254, 257, 273, 311, 322, 335, 337, 341–42, 348, 353, 373, 394, 396, 513, 518, 523, 525, 540
blimah, 219
blindness, 243, 248, 324, 373–74, 377, 401–3, 441
bliss. *See* joy
blood, 134, 219, 245, 259–60, 371, 514, 516, 523, 574, 601, 629, 631–32, 634–36, 677
blood pressure, 28, 595, 610, 611, 615–16, 621, 630–37, 639–40, 642
boats, 301, 416, 522, 562, 566, 591
Bodh Gaya, 267, 269, 291
bodhi, 265, 276, 588
Bodhi, Bikkhu, 275
bodhi tree. *See* banyan tree
bodhicitta, 440
Bodhidharma, 552, 558–59, 591
Bodhiruci, 434
bodhisattva, 56, 67, 269, 291, 302, 319, 409–10, 425, 437, 443, 453, 520, 717, 721. *See also* specific bodhisattvas
body, 20, 24, 32, 43, 64, 69–70, 81, 95–98, 102, 110, 114, 121, 125, 127, 131, 137–38, 142, 150, 180, 203–5, 208, 215, 220–22, 234, 238–39, 241, 247, 250, 253, 260–63, 266–67, 276, 278–82, 288, 298–300, 302–3, 307, 315–16, 324, 333–34, 338–39, 347–50, 354–56, 369, 375, 378, 380, 391, 395, 398, 400, 403, 431, 438, 448, 450, 458, 463–65, 467, 471, 474, 476–77, 479, 492, 495–97, 505, 507, 510–11, 513, 515–28, 531–45, 557–60, 565, 571–72, 574, 578–92, 593, 597, 600, 607, 612, 623–24, 631–33, 643–44, 646–47, 653, 656, 660, 667, 679, 689, 707–8, 715–16, 721
body-beyond-the-body. *See shenwai shen*
body-building, 475, 634
Bohm, David, 666, 668, 672
Böhme, Jakob, 149, 161, 163
Bologna, 79, 503–4, 513, 529, 541, 544
Bolsheviks, 360
Bombay (Mumbai), 684
bondage. *See* slavery
bonding with the *shaykh*, 321, 336, 342–43
bones, 138, 257, 397, 518, 561
bons hommes, 507

Book of Constitutions and Ordinations, 511–12, 524
Book of Creation. See *Sefer Yezeriah*
Book of Enoch, 247
Book of Illumination. See *Sefer Ha-Bahir*
Book of Master Lao. See *Laozi*
Book of Master Zhuang. See *Zhuangzi*
Book of Radiance. See *Zohar*
Book of Revelation, 151, 545
Book of Venerable Masters. See *Laozi*
books. *See* manuscripts; specific texts; texts
boons. *See* benefits; confirmation; verification
Boowa, Ajahn Maha, 286
boredom, 394, 398, 644
Bossuet, Jacques-Bénigne, 148–49
Boston, 593, 595–98, 618, 624, 640, 642
Bourgogne, 58
Bowditch, Henry Pickering, 622
bowing, 37, 235, 241, 337, 363, 393, 404, 438, 510, 515–18, 523, 527–28, 532, 543
bows, 522, 540
Boy Scouts of America, 424
Boyle, Leonard, 514–15, 525
Brahmā, 439
brahmacharya, 646
Brahmā-kings, 443
Brahman, 39, 459, 461, 478–79, 485, 721–22
Brāhmaṇa, 478
Brāhmaṇical period. *See* Vedic period
Brahmasūtrabhāṣya, 480
brahmavihāra, 269–70, 277–78, 280, 291, 298, 302
brahmins, 267–69, 271, 278, 474, 645–46, 654, 673
brain, 13, 26–31, 67, 595, 611, 629–30, 634, 636, 661, 666, 668, 673, 686, 692, 701
brain hemorrhage, 634
brain maps, 30, 604. *See also* neuroimaging
brain-imaging. *See* neuroimaging
brain-regions. *See* neuroregions
bread, 158, 376, 388, 396, 508, 524
breath, 7, 90, 97–98, 103, 109–10, 113, 253, 262, 265, 276, 279–84, 286, 290, 317, 321, 339–40, 350–52, 371, 400, 402, 470–71, 474, 491–92, 558, 560, 707. *See also* tradition-specific terms
breath control. *See* breathing; *prāṇāyāma*
breathing, 7, 55, 62, 90, 96, 98, 101–2, 104, 110, 126, 130, 182, 196, 206, 213, 221–22, 265–306, 317, 339, 350–52, 371, 374–75, 392–93, 400, 402, 405, 470–71, 474, 486, 491–93, 521, 580, 583–84, 595, 597, 601, 607–11, 616, 632–33, 637, 639, 641–42, 656, 663, 684, 694, 707–8
Breathing Mindfulness for Serious Beginners, 286
Breviary. *See* Divine Office; Liturgy of Hours
Brianchaninov, Ignatius, 366, 383
Bridal Chamber of the Word, 376
brides, 263, 376, 527
bridges, 513, 516, 558
Brigflatts Friends Meeting House, 155, 167
Brigham and Women's Hospital, 630
Brinton, Howard, 162, 165
Brit Menuha, 214, 236
Britton, Willoughby, 40, 730
Brockwood Park, 677, 686, 688
Brockwood Park School, 667
Brooke, Thomas Digby, 150
Brookline, 598
Brown University, 10, 34, 730
Brown, Daniel, 29–30, 69, 715
Buber, Martin, 220, 227
Buddha (person). *See* Śākyamuni; Siddhartha Gotama
Buddha of Infinite Life. *See* Amitābha
Buddha of Infinite Light. *See* Amitāyus
buddha-embryo. *See tathāgata-garbha*
buddha-mind, 415, 447
Buddha-nāma, 416
buddha-nature, 55–56, 520, 553, 716
buddha-realms, 413, 425–27, 440, 443, 449, 710, 721. *See also* specific buddha-realms
Buddha-Recollection Samādhi, 415, 431, 433–34, 446
Buddha-Visualization Samādhi, 420
Buddhadāsa, Bhikkhu, 282–83, 286, 300
Buddhaghoṣa, 57, 276, 278, 284–86, 293, 301, 715
buddhahood, 265, 301–2, 410, 416, 421, 428, 430–31, 447, 451, 550, 553–54, 556, 559, 579. *See also* awakening; enlightenment
buddhas (beings), 56, 268, 409–10, 415, 437, 440, 552, 562, 582, 721. *See also* specific buddhas
Buddhavacana, 272–73
buddhi, 465–66, 468, 479
Buddhism, 4–6, 8, 20, 24, 28–30, 34–37, 39, 44, 54–57, 65, 67, 75, 77–78, 112, 166, 222, 226,

265–306, 328–29, 407–55, 460–61, 475, 479, 491, 520, 529, 547–49, 551–55, 559, 579–81, 585–86, 588, 602–4, 615, 620, 633, 638, 647–48, 656, 687, 693, 707–8, 710, 712–13, 715, 721, 730. *See also* specific forms
Buddhist Academy, 426
Buddhist-Christian Studies, 10
Buddhist Churches of America, 424, 433
Buddho-Daoist syncretism, 552–56, 558, 562, 572, 579
budh, 265
Buehler, Arthur, 81
Bukhara, 312, 328, 336
Bukhari, Muhammad Badshah, 308
Bukkyō Dendō Kyōkai, 425
Buliang Yi, 136
bulls, 257
Bulwer-Lutyens, Emily, 655
Bunyan, John, 384
Bunyū Nanjō, 432
Buraq, 335
Burgundy, 506, 528
burial, 240, 263, 513, 529
Burma, 55–56, 80, 286
burning. *See* fire; warmth
burning bush, 524, 542
Business Magazine, 480
butterflies, 140–41
byproducts, 9, 38, 65, 68, 715
Byzantium, 345, 360, 368–69, 376, 382, 384, 393

Cage, John, 41
cages, 650
Cairo, 315
Caitanya Caritāmṛta, 478
Calabria, 199, 223
calendar, 63, 202, 242, 273–74, 280, 296, 370, 388, 438, 509–10, 516, 518–19, 528–29, 531, 534, 542, 606, 613
Caleruega, 505
California, 422, 424, 509, 624, 635, 650–53, 668, 678
California Institute of Integral Studies, 10
calling, 37, 196
Calling on the Name, 373, 379
Callistus II Xanthopoulos, 385–86, 393, 399–400
calming, 18, 55, 192, 276, 279, 283, 285–87, 293, 337, 339, 375, 390, 393, 398–99, 403, 433, 483–84, 492–93, 496, 501, 525, 545, 590, 637–38, 641, 658–59, 689, 695. See also *samatha*
calmness. *See* peace
Calvinism, 162
Camaldoli Hermitage, 10
Campbell, Joseph, 574
camels, 519, 535
Camino de Perfección, 79
Canada, 570, 601, 629, 635
Canadian Institute of Stress, 622
cancer, 653
Candid Missive. See *Otkrovennoe poslanie*
Candid Tale of a Pilgrim. See *Rasskaz strannika*
candles, 278, 389, 402, 508, 697
Candraprabha, 438
Cannon, Walter, 595, 601–2, 605–6, 615–17, 622, 632
canon, 166, 217, 271, 408, 411–13, 424, 432, 462, 476, 479, 507, 523, 555–56, 567, 606, 613, 655
canonization, 72, 408, 503, 505, 510, 513–14, 517, 525, 527, 538, 547, 555–56, 567
Cao Changhua, 549, 550, 556, 573
Caodong lineage, 18–19, 55, 558
capacities, 24, 65, 67–70, 72, 191, 270–71, 396, 399, 402–3, 410, 423, 426, 429–30, 494–95, 553, 558, 561, 581, 615, 632–33, 643–44, 647, 657, 707, 709, 713–14, 729–30
captivity. *See* imprisonment
Carcassonne, 507, 514
cardiology, 593–95, 597, 629–30
care for the poor, 146, 157, 164, 505, 509
carefree wandering. See *xiaoyao you*
carefulness. *See* attention
Carmelites. *See* Order of Carmelites
Carmilly-Weinberger, Moshe, 223
Caro, Joseph, 198
Carolingian Empire, 506
carpentry, 281, 381
Carthusian Order, 514
cartography, 6–9, 12, 27, 29, 33, 41, 56–57, 77–78, 221, 311, 315–16, 319, 324, 558, 572, 604, 619, 696, 701, 714, 725, 730
carts, 396, 401, 696
Case Western Reserve University, 635
Cassian, John, 150
caste, 267–69, 437–38, 491, 645–47, 673

Castilian, 514
casting off body and mind, 553
CAT. *See* computed axial tomography
cataphasis. *See* kataphasis
catechesis, 506
catechism, 275
Cathars. *See* Albigensians
catharsis, 208
cathedrals, 507, 509, 702, 727–28
Catherine of Siena, 505, 513
cats, 341–42, 560, 601, 632, 636
cattle, 458, 476, 478, 521
caution. *See* attention
caverns, 186, 270, 398, 550, 580
cavities, 580–81, 584
ceaseless prayer, 153, 162, 164, 190, 193, 359, 363, 371, 376, 388–405, 513, 527
Cedars of Lebanon Hospital, 635
celebrity. *See* fame
celebrity religion, 624
Celestial Cycle. *See* Macrocosmic Orbit; Microcosmic Orbit
Celestial Masters. *See* Tianshi
celibacy, 71, 328, 370, 414, 423, 471, 491–92, 551, 557, 559, 572, 583, 646, 651
cells (biology), 24, 634, 666, 686–87
cells (monastic). *See* rooms
cemeteries. *See* graves
center, 71, 95, 98, 111, 135, 140, 154, 162, 177, 187, 189, 196, 318, 343, 373, 580, 583, 661, 679, 681, 686, 689, 695, 701, 728, 730
Center for Contemplative Mind in Society, 10, 41, 44
Center for Corporate Health, 598, 612
Center for Daoist Studies, 574
Center for Mind and Brain, 31
Center for Mindfulness in Medicine, Health Care, and Society, 293, 604
Center for Training in Mind/Body Medicine, 598
centering down, 154, 156
Centering Prayer, 8, 33, 58, 80–81, 153, 166, 381
Central Asia, 313, 317, 329–30, 407–10, 413, 415, 437, 552. *See also* specific countries
central nervous system, 26
cerebral cortex, 26–28, 30
certification, 206
cessation. *See* calming; purification

cessation of outflow. *See* nondissipation
Ceylon, 647. *See also* Sri Lanka
chaff, 297
Chah, Achaan, 80
Chah, Ajahn, 286
chains, 312, 356, 518, 534, 665
chairs. *See* furniture
chakra, 316
challenges, 32, 65, 154, 174, 180–85, 369–70, 381, 390, 394, 400, 404–5, 477, 485, 488, 531, 544–45, 550, 572, 597, 644, 650, 655, 664, 719–24
chambers. *See* rooms
Chan Buddhism, 18–19, 55, 58, 64, 77–78, 89, 96, 111–12, 286, 330, 410, 421, 424, 426–27, 430, 547–48, 550–54, 556, 558–60, 562, 565–66, 568, 572, 574–75, 579, 581, 583, 585, 588–89, 591–92, 715–16
Chang'an, 420
change. *See* transformation
Changjiang, 92
chanhui, 59, 416
channeling. *See* mediumship
channels. *See* meridians
chanting. *See* recitation
chaos, 141, 185, 219, 697
chapels, 41, 44, 374, 389, 404, 516, 519, 541
chaplains, 424
chapter rooms. *See* rooms
character, 163, 204, 239, 268, 272, 278, 284, 288, 290, 292, 310, 334, 349, 353–54, 360, 369, 404, 429, 467–68, 485, 518, 525, 528, 631, 646, 650, 652, 670, 707, 711–14, 726, 730. *See also* virtue
characteristics. *See* qualities
chariot, 193, 239, 249
charism, 57, 379, 511, 528
charisma, 100, 226, 318, 330, 460, 650
charismatic generativity, 523
charity. *See* donations; generosity; support
charlatans, 318, 493
Charlemagne, 506
Chartres Cathedral, 727
chemotherapy, 519
ch'i. *See* qi
Ch'i-kung. *See* Qigong
Chicago, 478, 599, 623

Child of the Buddha, 561, 564–65, 587, 589
childhood, 173, 200, 223, 266, 360, 563, 565, 581, 588, 594, 646, 691
children, 91, 147, 161, 163, 176–77, 179, 184, 220, 235, 237, 262–63, 273, 375, 377, 385, 391, 421, 425, 428, 437–39, 443, 458, 476, 506, 518, 523, 527, 533, 538, 560–61, 588, 598, 630, 636, 645–46, 650, 652, 666, 668, 677, 682–83
China, 55, 90–91, 93, 109–10, 285–86, 345, 407–14, 419, 422, 424, 426–27, 431–33, 547–51, 566–67, 569, 605, 715
China Institute, 568
Chinese, 54–55, 314, 407–9, 415, 431, 437, 547, 556, 578–79
Chinese Buddhism, 55, 59, 89, 111–12, 407–55, 547–50, 552–55, 579, 715
Chinese medicine, 115, 581
Chinese religion, 89, 407, 547. *See also* specific traditions
Chishti, Fakhruddin, 308
Chishti, Ghulam Sadat, 308
Chishti, Muʻinuddin, 312
Chishti lineage, 308, 312, 328–29
Chitli Qabr, 308, 315, 328
Chittick, William, 323
Chodkiewicz, Michel, 323
choice, 57, 213, 216, 218, 221, 343, 417, 469, 492, 550, 607, 661–62, 664, 711
choiceless awareness, 23, 66, 657, 661–62, 664, 685, 687, 696, 699
Chongxuan, 112
Chongzhen Emperor, 550
Chopra, Deepak, 624
choreography, 522
Choudhury, Bikram, 20
Christ (Jesus), 9, 58, 63, 65, 146, 156–58, 161–62, 165, 171–72, 174–78, 189–91, 196, 359, 371–75, 377, 379, 382, 391–93, 395–96, 398, 400–5, 505, 511–25, 527–28, 531–45, 648, 691, 693, 708, 710, 716–17, 721, 728
Christ Within, 151, 158, 172. *See also* Inner Light; Inward Teacher
Christology, 151, 157–58, 161–62, 371–75, 512–13, 516–17, 522, 524, 716. *See also* Christ
Christian Bible, 80, 149, 151, 157, 163, 166, 173, 176, 180, 195, 274, 359, 361, 371, 374, 376–77, 388–89, 391–93, 397, 401, 408, 507, 515, 523, 531, 537, 544
Christianity, 4, 9, 25, 54–55, 57–58, 60, 72, 75, 77–80, 145–96, 205, 223–24, 244, 274, 309, 328, 359–405, 423, 503–545, 568, 647–48, 654, 699, 707–8, 710, 712, 716, 721. *See also* specific types
Chrysostom, John, 531
Chu (state), 96
Chuandao ji, 561
Chuang Chou. *See* Zhuangzi
Chuang-tzu. See *Zhuangzi*
Church Fathers, 359, 367, 370–73, 375–76, 385, 391–92, 394, 398–99, 402, 512, 518, 531
Church of England, 146
Church of Scientology, 624
Church of the Brethren, 167
churches (place), 146, 158, 364, 376, 379, 386, 388–89, 393, 396–97, 402, 507, 513, 516, 518–19, 525, 538, 541, 544–45, 693, 702, 705
churchgoers, 372
Chuzhen jie, 551
Cimin, 426
cinnabar, 556
ciphers, 371, 373, 462, 515
circle of contingent existence, 316, 321–22, 356–57
circles, 251, 311, 316, 319–20, 334, 339, 348, 351, 356–57, 592, 631, 661
circulation, 68, 78, 90, 93, 102, 104, 110, 133, 138, 197, 259, 360, 505, 557–62, 566–68, 580, 583–84, 601, 617, 631, 635
circumambulation, 433
circumcision, 248
Cistercians. *See* Order of Trappists
Citeaux, 428
citta, 69, 282–83, 465–70
citta-prasāda, 423
civil rights, 598
civil service exams, 549, 645–46
clairaudience, 24, 68, 497, 713
clairvoyance, 24, 67, 378, 441, 638, 648, 654, 713
clarity, 67, 106, 112, 132, 138–40, 240, 277, 357, 399, 454, 466–68, 486–87, 523, 592, 650, 673, 680–82, 697, 712–13
Clarke, J. J., 574

class. *See* economics
classical Daoism, 89–143, 553, 558, 572, 579, 706–7, 710, 715. *See also* inner cultivation lineages
classical Yoga, 59, 65–67, 69, 71, 77, 457–501, 609, 615, 620, 638, 708, 710, 712–13
classics. *See* spiritual classics
Classics of Western Spirituality (series), 80, 388
clay, 181, 318, 355
Claypole, Elizabeth, 154
Cleary, Thomas, 568, 570
cleaving, 205, 208–9, 211, 223–24, 243–45, 250, 253, 255, 257, 261
clergy. *See* priests
clerical marriage, 423, 506, 551
Clerics Regular of St. Paul, 148
Cleveland, 635
climate, 288, 404
clinical applications. *See* medicalization; therapeutic meditation
clinical science, 11–12, 33
closeness. *See* proximity
clothing, 56, 59, 63, 147, 158, 188, 194, 196, 239–41, 262–64, 279, 284, 302, 309, 311, 341, 388, 390, 504, 524–25, 528, 532–45, 565, 588, 649, 652, 670, 679, 683, 709, 718
clouds, 185, 196, 284, 394, 404, 448, 501, 532, 592, 680, 683, 705
Clough, David, 729
Cluny Abbey, 506
co-dependent origination. *See pratītya-samutpāda*
coalescing the immortal embryo, 564, 586–87
Coburn, Thomas, 40
Codex Bononiensis, 514
Codex Carcassonensis, 514
Codex Matritensis, 514
Codex Rossianus 3, 514–15, 531
cognitive dissonance, 723
cognitive science, 11, 26, 29
cognocentrism, 325–26
Cole, Peter, 221
Collected Letters. *See Maktubat*
collective unconscious, 569
Collomb and Balme, 514
Colombo, 269
colonialism, 14, 53, 74, 323, 509, 568–69, 645, 710–11. *See also* appropriation; domestication

color, 104, 132, 255, 278, 307, 314, 316–17, 348–49, 357, 439, 442–44, 447, 449, 468, 514, 531, 692, 707
Colorado, 570
Columbia University Press, 120
Combs, Allan, 672
comfort. *See* consolation
coming face to face with God, 312, 374
commandments. *See mitzvot*
commentaries, 108, 136, 202, 271, 281, 284–85, 411, 419–20, 426, 428, 432, 458, 462, 466–68, 471, 473–75, 480, 484, 556, 563, 565–66, 568–69, 575
commitments, 10–12, 17, 34–37, 42, 44, 53, 64, 72, 178, 187, 290, 297–98, 309, 311, 315, 336–37, 343, 352, 408, 411–13, 417, 421–22, 433, 449, 457, 471, 473, 476, 491, 511, 518, 534, 540, 548, 550–51, 559, 566, 581, 594, 597–99, 603, 605, 607, 632, 644, 647–48, 651, 654, 657, 673, 706–8, 711–12, 714, 717–24, 727–29
commodification, 457, 475–76, 602, 617, 620, 694, 698, 730
communal mysticism, 58
communication. *See* dialogue
Communion (sacrament). *See* Eucharist
communion (state), 65, 156, 185, 205, 211, 238–39, 364, 368, 508, 520, 540, 550, 655, 694, 713
community, 7, 12–13, 17–22, 32, 34–35, 38, 43, 53–55, 58, 60–67, 75, 79, 81, 93, 95, 128, 145, 149, 151, 153–54, 156, 166, 198–99, 202, 221, 237, 265, 267, 269–70, 272–74, 279, 284, 289, 296–305, 307–15, 336, 338, 343, 369, 380–81, 393, 408, 414, 416, 437, 475, 505, 507–9, 517–18, 526, 528, 535, 539, 542, 551, 565, 571–73, 595–96, 598, 600, 604–6, 611, 619–21, 623, 647, 650–51, 654, 669–70, 673, 682, 706–14, 716–17, 719–20, 722–24, 726–28, 730
Community of a New Monastic Way, 728
companionship. *See* friendship
comparative theology, 720–22, 727
comparison, 6, 12, 23, 25–26, 37, 69, 74, 78, 81–82, 167, 289, 324, 391, 571–72, 605–6, 619, 647, 673, 679, 692, 700, 705–35
compassion, 3, 30, 33, 36, 56, 72, 183, 192, 269–70, 277, 290–91, 297, 369, 410, 414–15,

418, 421, 423, 438–40, 447, 449, 453–54, 471, 486, 508–9, 517, 539, 541, 581, 586, 603, 605, 650, 661, 665–66, 670, 680, 685–86, 688, 695, 702, 729; as supposed *sine qua non* of contemplative practice, 72
competition, 132, 139, 428, 520, 552, 631, 633, 643, 682
compilation, 90–92, 104, 107–8, 145, 154, 167, 171, 239, 268, 272, 286, 360–61, 392, 419, 426, 437, 457, 461, 562, 630
complementary alternative medicine, 21, 599–600, 613, 631, 718
Complete Perfection. *See* Quanzhen
Compline, 393, 518, 534–35
compulsion. *See* conditioning; habituation; reactivity
compunction, 173, 517, 527, 533, 692
computed axial tomography, 603
computed tomography, 603
computers, 326, 465
concentration, 3, 5, 7, 9–10, 54, 69, 75, 90, 93, 98, 102–4, 112–14, 126–28, 153, 159, 179, 214, 239, 245, 255, 267, 282, 287–88, 291, 299–305, 321, 328, 336, 339, 341, 343, 346, 352, 380–81, 392, 398, 403, 415, 420, 430, 440–41, 442, 445–47, 454–55, 461, 463, 465, 468–72, 474–75, 479, 483–84, 486, 491, 493–94, 519, 521, 525, 542, 560, 572, 579, 607–9, 638–39, 641, 660, 679, 685, 712–13, 715
Conception Vessel, 557, 563–65, 582, 584–85
conditioning, 15, 23, 25, 70, 82, 95, 326, 527, 553, 569, 595, 597, 601, 603, 613, 617, 645–46, 651, 653–54, 657–60, 664–66, 668–70, 672–74, 677, 679, 682, 686, 691–92, 695–96, 698, 701, 708, 714, 716, 729. *See also* enculturation; habituation
conditions. *See* states
conferences, 10, 33–34
confession (prayer). *See* atonement
Confession (sacrament), 150, 153, 372, 393–94, 396, 517, 541, 544–45
confessionalism, 11
confidence, 68, 173–74, 176–77, 179, 275, 279–80, 285, 404, 450, 520, 527, 712–13
confinement. *See* imprisonment
confirmation, 21, 38, 65–66, 211, 217, 271, 289, 310, 315, 357, 381, 393–94, 446, 480, 531, 555, 561, 566, 600, 603, 611–13, 615, 617, 619, 622, 639, 642, 650–51, 657, 713–14, 716
conflict, 148, 151, 156, 309, 425, 461, 632, 651, 662, 671, 673, 678, 685–87, 693
Confucianism, 58–59, 78, 106, 109, 129, 548–49, 552, 560, 583
Confucius. *See* Kongzi
confusion, 4, 25, 133, 154, 250, 300, 302, 465, 495, 500, 669, 677, 680–82, 689
congregations, 146, 153, 377, 380, 382, 475, 527, 728
Congres Centrum, 680
Connecticut, 594
connecting the Governing and Conception Vessels, 564, 584–85
conscience, 57, 173
consciousness, 5–6, 13–17, 21, 23, 25, 30, 33, 37, 42–44, 65, 69–70, 73, 90, 97–98, 103, 113, 137, 159, 165, 265–66, 276, 290, 309, 324–27, 330, 365, 371–72, 374–75, 381, 425–31, 457, 462–68, 471–72, 474, 477, 479, 483, 498, 500, 525, 531, 553, 555, 558–59, 569, 571, 579, 588, 592, 599, 603, 609, 612, 619, 622, 632, 637–38, 648, 650, 653, 656–59, 662–63, 666–74, 677, 686, 690–92, 695, 701–2, 707–8, 710–11, 713, 715–16, 721, 724. *See also* mind; tradition-specific terms
Consciousness-Only. *See* Yogācāra
consciousness revolution, 325
consciousness studies, 9–10, 14, 17, 22–23, 26, 66, 69, 325, 673
consecration, 158, 368, 513, 517
consensus reality, 319, 329
conservation, 557–58, 561, 563, 578–81
conservatism, 35, 81, 204, 595, 597–99, 617, 623
Conservative Judaism, 594
consistency. *See* dedication
consolation, 152, 171, 174–75, 179–81, 185, 192, 194, 354, 377, 392, 394, 396, 398, 400–1, 403, 405, 453–54, 651, 711
constancy. *See* stability
Constantinople, 211, 361, 368, 370, 393, 399
constellations. *See* astronomy
constitution. *See* character
constraint. *See* restraint
Constructivism, 15–16, 70, 325
consumerism, 457, 475–77, 574, 620

consumption. *See* acquisitiveness
consumptive reading, 75
contemplata aliis tradere, 512, 527
contemplatio, 4, 54, 542
contemplation, 4, 54, 283, 307–57, 707
Contemplation Sutra. See *Guanjing*
contemplative approach, 3, 79, 706, 710, 716, 719, 724, 728
Contemplative Disciplines in Sufism, 329
contemplative epistemology, 25, 70
contemplative experience, 3, 9–11, 17, 22, 32, 38, 41, 53–54, 56, 64–69, 705–35. *See also* experience
contemplative literature, 3, 33, 40, 54, 60, 72–80, 705–6, 711, 721, 723, 725–26, *passim*; formalistic features of, 73. *See also* specific texts
contemplative pedagogy, 9–10, 34–35, 41, 717, 725
contemplative practice, 3–82, 705–35, *passim*; as remedy, 32, 36; defining characteristics of, 3–9, 40, 53; dimensions of, 4, 36, 60–64; globally distributed, 8; religiously-committed, 3, 10, 12–13, 17, 22, 36–37, 53–82; scientific study of, 5, 10, 20–21; secular, 4, 8, 20, 78; subversiveness of, 32; technical terms for, 54–55; tradition-based, 3, 10, 22, 32, 35–37, 43, 53–82; types of, 6–8. *See also* contemplative prayer; meditation; specific types; tradition-specific terms
Contemplative Practice Fellowships, 44
contemplative prayer, 4, 22, 24, 54, 57, 73, 81, 145, 147–49, 359, 711. *See also* contemplative practice; specific types
contemplative psychology, 22, 25–26, 70–71, 73, 94–95, 97–99, 101, 711
contemplative reading, 72, 75, 149
contemplative revival, 80
contemplative science, 12, 26, 31, 44, 719
contemplative studies, 3–44; approaches to, 12–33; as interdisciplinary field, 12–13; conferences on, 10; interpretive issues in, 33–40; organizations related to, 10, 32, 41; programs in, 10, 35, 41
Contemplative Studies Group, 40, 327
Contemplative Studies in Higher Education, 10
Contemplative Studies Initiative, 10
Contemplative Studies website, 41
Contemplative Teaching and Learning, 10
contemplative traditions, 3, 25, 35, 43, 53–82, 705–6, 711, 714, 717, 723, 725, 729, *passim*

Contemplative Traditions (course), 44, 48
contention. *See* competition
contentless, 7, 9, 16, 55, 62, 66, 81, 151–53, 465, 469, 553, 558–59, 591
contentment, 68, 180, 185, 191, 195–96, 267, 277, 310, 314, 336, 341, 377, 438, 491–92, 638, 643–44, 651, 702, 712, 714
context, 13–22, 32–33, 35, 53–54, 60–62, 64, 72, 74–75, 80, 95, *passim*
context of reception, 15
Contextualism, 3, 13–22, 74, 77, 725–26
contextualization, 17–21, 62, 74, 217, 325
Continental Quietists. *See* Quietism
Continuously-Moving Samādhi, 433
contraction. *See qabd*
control, 5, 24, 26, 28, 67, 104, 110–11, 126, 132, 136, 146, 173, 215, 312, 335, 378, 470–72, 484, 491–93, 497, 506, 536, 581, 595, 610–12, 634–37, 640, 658–60, 662–63, 670, 678–79, 684–85, 689–90, 692, 695, 700–1, 712
conversation. *See* dialogue
conversion, 44, 162, 173, 188–89, 361, 377–78, 392, 422, 434, 508, 510, 529, 559, 585, 603
conviction. *See* dedication
Conze, Edward, 430
Cook Ding, 100
cooling, 154, 429, 454
Coors Foundation, 621
Cordovero, Moshe, 198–203, 205, 211, 213–14, 216, 225, 237, 239, 244
corporatization, 598, 612, 617, 620, 623
corporeal soul. *See po*
corporeality. *See* body; physicality
corpses, 240, 271, 278, 289, 298, 529
Correct Principles of Celestial Immortality. See *Tianxian zhengli*
corruption. *See* defilements; delusion
cosmogony, 205
cosmology, 39, 60, 63, 90, 92–94, 104–5, 107–9, 111, 120–25, 198, 200–1, 205, 314–17, 322, 329, 333–34, 348, 392, 412, 428, 438–39, 443, 458, 590, 647–49, 656–57, 720
cosmos. *See* universe
cotton, 497
counterculture, 36, 72, 198, 218, 598–99, 619
counter-orthodoxy, 309
counting, 55, 284–85, 322, 339, 351–52, 385, 394–95, 420–21, 446, 454, 520, 535, 597, 607

Couplets of Reality. See *Mathnawi-yi ma'nawi*
courage, 181–82, 373, 688
court, 187, 422
covenant, 181, 246
covetousness. *See* acquisitiveness
Cracow, 237
cranes, 585
craving. *See* desire
creation, 200, 203, 206, 235, 316, 333, 353–55, 371, 400–1, 479, 499, 508, 513, 661, 686–87
creative arts, 11–12
creative writing, 11, 79
creativity, 24, 35, 39, 90, 92, 100, 165, 201–2, 211, 267, 269–72, 364, 372, 467, 499, 527, 708
Creator. *See* God
Credo, 510
cremation, 580, 653
Crime and Punishment, 360
Crimea, 366
criminalization, 567
Cripple Shu, 100
critical adherent discourse. *See* adherence; first-person discourse
critical first-person discourse. *See* first-person discourse
Croagh Patrick, 519
Cromwell, Oliver, 154
cross, 153, 157–58, 186, 371, 510–11, 516–25, 528, 538, 693, 709
cross-legged posture, 266, 280, 291, 293, 298, 317, 448, 564, 641, 688, 694
crosspollination, 42, 460, 547, 572, 585, 707
Crowe, Paul, 570
crown-point, 557–58, 564, 582, 584, 587
crowns, 182, 184, 186, 193, 209, 244, 247, 253–55, 447–48, 506
crucifix, 63, 516–17, 519, 521–22, 528, 709, 728
crucifixion, 157, 162, 185, 391, 516, 522, 538
cruciform, 515–16, 521, 538, 709
Crusades, 507–8
crutches, 650
crying. *See* tears
Csikszentmihalyi, Mihaly, 23, 70, 113
CT. *See* computed tomography
Cultivating the Energy of Life, 569, 578
cultivation, 95, 101, 104, 109, 141, 178, 267, 297–305, 310, 484, 486, 511, 550, 555, 560, 567, 579, 581, 585, 693, 712, 714, 719, 729–30
cultural capital, 20, 44
Cumbria, 167
cunxiang, 58
cupbearer, 342
cups. *See* vessels
cycles, 105, 113, 141, 143, 260, 277, 287, 296, 319, 428, 431, 452, 479, 557, 560, 580, 609, 615, 634–35

D'Aquili, Eugene, 70
Da'irat Machine Press, 321, 333
dais, 444–45
Dalai Lama (Fourteenth), 10, 32–33, 603, 624, 633, 729
Damascus, 198–200, 223, 310, 313, 315, 319
Dambulla Cave Temple, 270, 291
damnation, 147, 161, 234, 398, 453–54, 535, 545
dan (cinnabar), 556
dance, 4, 9, 11, 41, 59–60, 79, 81, 154, 438, 450, 609
Dandao jiupian, 556
dangers, 36, 43, 60, 68, 147, 184, 194, 365–66, 382, 416, 541, 544–45, 555, 561, 566, 572–73, 599, 601, 615, 632–34, 670, 685, 719, 730. *See also* difficulties
Daniil, 385
dantian, 558, 560–61, 574, 579–80, 584
Dao, 39, 55, 72, 89–90, 92–99, 103–7, 109, 112–13, 121–24, 126, 128–30, 132, 134, 136–37, 139, 141–43, 553–54, 559–60, 562, 564, 566, 579–81, 583, 585–86, 590, 592, 710, 715, 721–22
Daochuo, 411, 428–30, 433–34
Daode jing, 18, 89, 91, 109, 590. *See also Laozi*
Daoicized Buddhism, 553
Daoism, 4, 8, 16, 19–20, 25, 42, 54–55, 58, 64, 66–67, 75, 77, 89–143, 285, 434, 547–92, 615, 620, 638, 656–57, 661, 707, 712–16, 721, 729
Daoist Foundation, 581, 728
daojia, 93–94
daoshi, 585
daoshu, 110
Daoshu shier zhong, 567
Daoyin, 42, 110, 126, 567
Daozang jiyao, 551, 556, 562, 573
dark night, 42, 160, 730

Dark Night Project, 730
darkness, 94, 143, 182, 186, 196, 237–38, 245, 301, 393, 400, 403, 466, 523, 554, 636, 728
Darmstadt, 568
darśana, 475, 478
Darwin, Charles, 21, 601, 632
Das Buch Bahir, 219
Das Geheimnis der Goldenen Blüte, 568
Dato, Mordecai, 225
David, 181, 184, 193, 246, 531, 533, 539
Davidson, Richard, 30, 33, 603, 619
Day of Atonement, 385
Day of Judgment, 340, 344, 398
Dazhidu lun, 426
dazuo, 54
de (inner power), 72, 95, 100–1, 103, 107, 109, 121, 125–26, 129, 134, 137, 139, 712
De eruditione praedicatorum, 510
De Quincey, Christian, 672
De Wit, Han, 25, 43, 70–71
deacons, 366, 389, 518
dead ashes, 142, 553, 565
death, 55, 66, 141, 143, 148, 153, 157, 162, 180, 186, 190, 194, 200, 216, 234, 237, 240, 249–50, 257, 259–60, 262–63, 266, 268–69, 271–72, 278, 285, 291, 297–98, 308, 335, 365, 377–78, 381, 386, 396, 403, 412, 418, 420, 425, 441, 444, 446–48, 450–53, 463, 467, 495, 504, 514, 516, 521–22, 535, 550, 554–55, 557–58, 560, 563, 566–67, 571, 573, 581, 584, 592, 594–95, 630, 632, 634, 646–48, 650, 653, 663, 667, 681–83, 688, 690, 693, 696, 706, 708, 713, 724
death by a kiss, 250
death penalty, 272
deautomatization, 23, 82
debate. *See* argumentation
Deccan, 307, 321, 328, 333
deceased teachers, 20, 66, 240, 310, 317, 339, 342, 365, 377, 381, 397, 399, 401, 403, 548, 559, 648–49, 708, 713
deception, 133, 151–52, 178, 182, 194, 471, 651–52, 682, 700
decomposition, 259–60, 278
deconditioning, 16, 23, 42, 381, 467, 527, 650–51, 656, 660, 674, 691, 714, 716
deconstruction, 477
Decontextualism, 42

decontextualization, 7, 34, 53, 474–76, 604–5, 616, 620, 642, 708–9, 718–19. *See also* reconceptualization
decorations, 438–39, 443–44, 447, 514, 650
dedication, 4, 54, 65, 75, 79, 126, 151, 178–79, 186, 191–92, 236, 245, 297–98, 311, 330, 346, 365–66, 390–92, 395–96, 400, 402, 422, 449, 455, 467, 471, 473, 477, 488, 491, 513, 518, 527, 531–45, 550, 558, 565–66, 579, 581, 583, 586–87, 610, 612, 648, 652, 654, 670, 685, 694, 709–13, 715, 717, 725–26
deep slumber of prophecy, 250
deer, 585
Deer Park, 267
defamiliarization, 39, 629, 706
deficiencies, 21, 24, 43, 70, 77–78, 182–83, 241, 336, 351, 383, 525, 560, 569, 570, 580, 603
Deficiency-cognition, 23, 70
defilements, 71, 133, 136, 154, 171, 175, 183, 186, 195, 200, 238–40, 243, 246, 252, 267, 276, 297–98, 339, 356, 368, 396, 401, 415, 429, 440–41, 453–55, 464–65, 472, 491, 506–7, 513, 541, 554, 557, 579, 646, 664, 717
deification, 371–72, 375, 384–85, 517
Deikman, Arthur, 23, 43, 70, 82
deities. *See* specific deities
deity yoga, 8, 56, 446, 505, 515–16, 527
Deleanu, Florin, 293
Delhi, 308, 313, 315, 323, 328, 338
Dell, William, 149, 167
delusion, 36, 43, 64, 138, 154, 193, 297, 382, 402, 446, 453–55, 465–67, 477, 483, 488, 491, 554, 557, 560, 579, 651, 656, 659, 664, 673
democratization, 381
demonization, 717
demons, 68, 203, 226, 260, 272, 440, 573
Deng Huiji, 555, 562, 567
denial. *See* asceticism; detachment
Denmark, 505
densification, 479
Denver, 570
depression. *See* sadness
Descartes, René, 463, 632
descent, 92, 94, 112, 190, 199, 208, 235, 242, 245, 249, 253, 258–60, 308, 313, 318–19, 328–29, 365, 371, 374–75, 377–78, 388, 582, 639, 646, 648
Desikachar, T. K. V., 575

desire, 25, 58, 71, 98, 101, 104, 122, 132–37, 152, 154, 160, 165, 172, 175, 178–79, 181, 183–88, 190–91, 193–95, 204–5, 219, 236, 259, 277, 283–84, 297, 301–2, 304, 312, 339, 351, 378, 391–92, 394–96, 398, 403, 405, 416–17, 421, 423, 428–30, 441, 445, 449, 454, 458, 464, 467, 471–72, 476–77, 484, 486, 489, 511, 520, 523, 527, 535, 539, 557, 561, 644, 651, 656, 658–59, 662–64, 669–70, 677, 679–80, 683, 689–90, 692, 696–97, 699, 713

Desert Fathers and Mothers, 58, 359, 367, 370, 374, 384, 392

deserts, 282, 309, 342, 370, 542

despair. *See* sadness

detachment, 101, 129, 147, 182, 193, 196, 237, 283, 297, 299–300, 305, 385, 395, 397, 403, 461, 463–64, 466, 470–72, 479, 484–86, 492, 498, 557, 596, 608–9, 638–39, 641–43, 651, 670, 683, 693, 712

determination, 180–81, 186, 265, 273, 279, 336, 341–42, 353, 355–56, 373, 382, 391, 395, 400, 402, 413, 422, 430, 455, 467, 471, 477, 484, 518, 527, 548, 550, 558, 565, 579, 583, 586, 648, 663, 670, 685, 694, 709, 712

deva, 439, 444, 447, 450, 454–55

Devadatta, 416, 437, 439

Devanagri script, 321

devekut, 205, 208–9, 211, 223–24, 243–44, 250, 253, 256–57, 261

development. *See* actualization; evolution; potentiality

developmental psychology, 22

devotion, 4, 7–8, 37, 59, 65, 68, 73, 77–78, 149, 172, 188, 193, 203–4, 216, 224, 236, 244, 246, 287, 309, 341, 359–60, 365, 370, 389, 407, 410, 412–13, 421, 424, 427, 438–39, 444, 460–61, 475–76, 484–85, 488, 491–92, 505, 507, 509–11, 513, 516, 518–20, 526–27, 531–45, 550, 620, 673, 694, 708, 710, 724, 728

devil, 184, 544–45

dhamma. See *dharma*

Dhammapada, 278, 293

Dhammasāmi, 288

Dharamsala, 32

dhāraṇā, 470–71, 478, 491, 493–94

dhāraṇī, 450

dharma (phenomena), 283, 298, 300–5, 318, 427, 441, 450, 453–54

dharma (teachings), 372, 277–78, 285, 289, 292, 413–14, 418, 421, 438, 444, 446, 448–51, 453, 559, 585

Dharma Wheel, 557, 559, 563–64, 582–85

Dharma-body. *See dharmakāya*

dharma-megha, 473, 501

Dharmākara, 409–10, 412–13, 421, 437, 445, 452

dharmakāya, 421

dharmatā, 428–30

dhikr, 8, 60, 309, 315, 321–23, 335–36, 337–41, 343, 345–46, 349, 354

dhyāna, 54–55, 266, 271, 276–77, 279, 281–82, 287, 289, 291, 298, 302, 471, 478, 489, 491, 493–94, 552, 564, 712–13

dhyāna yoga, 460–61

dialogical process, 666, 668, 706

dialogue, 35, 74, 81, 191, 196, 210, 275, 289, 377, 390, 401, 416, 520, 522, 524–25, 527, 531, 537, 617, 650, 662, 666–69, 672, 706–11, 713, 723

Diamond Sūtra, 427

diamond-body, 579

diamonds, 56, 427, 441, 443–45, 447, 579

diaries, 200, 214, 225

diasporas, 198, 218, 246

Diego d'Azevedo, 505, 507, 528

dietetics, 18, 22, 63, 110, 177, 242, 247, 256, 266, 272, 274, 337, 354, 357, 376–77, 383, 390, 396–97, 401, 404, 438, 471, 508, 524–25, 542, 550, 556–57, 580, 594, 610–11, 620, 631, 642, 646, 714, 726, 729

difficulties, 64, 160, 173–74, 176, 178, 180–85, 189, 191, 210, 248, 287–88, 290, 317–18, 337, 343, 351, 369–70, 381, 390, 394, 400, 404, 413, 441, 448, 472, 477, 485, 488–89, 496, 501, 518, 531, 544–45, 550, 555, 566, 572–73, 597, 633, 636, 641, 644, 646, 650, 655, 663–64, 673, 679, 681, 684, 689, 699, 716, 730

digestion, 601, 634, 637, 642

Dīghanikāya, 275

Dihlawi, Nasiruddin Qadiri, 308

diligence. *See* dedication

Dilun, 419

Dimitry of Rostov, 377

directing *shaykh*s, 322

"Directions to Hesychasts," 385, 393, 399
disappearance, 153, 161–62, 165, 185, 188–90, 193, 195, 205, 245, 250–51, 319, 334, 342, 344–45, 351, 353–54, 430, 439, 489, 555, 558–59, 561–62, 564, 583, 590, 592, 650, 653, 712, 716
disappearing into emptiness, 564, 592
discernment, 72, 75, 156, 252, 262, 279, 317, 386, 400, 402, 451, 468, 485, 489–91, 498, 500–1, 541
disciples. *See* students
discipline (commitment), 34, 43, 151, 153, 204, 311, 313, 416, 457, 461–62, 470, 488, 518, 527, 541, 645, 654, 669, 679, 682, 684, 695
discipline (corporeal). *See* flagellation
discourse community, 15, 22, 34
Discourse on Confirmation of Golden Immortality. See *Jinxian zhenglun*
"Discourse on Faith," 386
Discourse on Mindfulness of Body. See *Kāyagatāsati Sutta*
Discourse on Mindfulness of Breathing. See *Ānāpānasati Sutta*
Discourse on the Foundations of Mindfulness. See *Satipatthāna Sutta*
discourse records. See *yulu*
Discourse Records from the Shared Lineage of Immortals and Buddhas. See *Xianfo hezong yulu*
discrimination, 7, 37, 56, 135, 210, 252, 465–66, 470, 489, 498, 501, 553, 631, 647, 654, 658, 662–63, 665, 671, 678–79, 692, 702
discursive thought, 5–6, 153, 195, 266, 279, 285, 309, 326, 713
disease. *See* sickness
disengagement, 28, 82, 131, 178, 181–82, 184, 187, 189, 196, 471, 491, 493, 512, 557, 596, 608–9, 638–39, 641–43, 656, 670, 683, 696
disgust. *See* repulsion
disorientation, 64, 71, 178, 250, 344, 353, 382–83, 465–66, 477, 495, 512, 557, 566, 573, 644, 680, 706
disposition. *See* character
disputation. *See* argumentation
dissemination. *See* circulation; transmission
dissipation, 179, 182, 555, 557, 564, 571, 578–81, 658, 678–79. *See also* disappearance
dissolution. *See* disappearance

distance. *See* proximity
distraction, 65, 98, 152–53, 156, 160, 178–79, 193, 284–85, 288, 341, 354, 375, 380, 441, 468–70, 472, 486, 493–94, 525, 561, 573, 596, 638, 641, 708, 715–16, 730
disturbance. *See* agitation
diversity, 14, 16, 34, 77–78, 271, 657, 705–6, 711, 720–23, 726–27
divination, 127, 245, 252, 646
divine abiding. See *brahmavihāra*
divine emanations. See *sephirot*
divine energy. See *fayḍ*; *tawajjuh*
divine knowledge. *See* gnosis
divine leadings. *See* calling; spiritual direction
divine love, 57, 147, 162, 189, 405, 511
Divine Office, 63, 510, 516, 528, 531, 542. *See also* Liturgy of Hours
divine presence, 66, 81, 152–53, 156, 158, 161–62, 172, 175, 177–78, 180, 184–85, 190, 193, 195, 235–36, 246, 333–34, 336, 339–40, 369, 371–73, 375, 378, 380–81, 385, 392, 400, 403, 513, 537, 542, 710
divine reading. See *lectio divina*
divine rupture, 198, 200, 203, 216
divinity. *See* sacred
divinization, 6, 39, 247, 561
Dobrotolyubié, 369–70, 383, 391–92
doctors. *See* physicians
doctrine, 17–18, 62, 68, 72, 149, 271, 287, 367, 373, 419, 424, 428, 528, 559, 606–8, 647–48, 653, 656–57, 671, 677, 691, 693–94. *See also* worldview
Dōgen. *See* Eihei Dōgen
dogma. *See* doctrine; worldview
dogmatism, 11, 19, 25, 35, 42, 71, 82, 373, 600, 617, 647–48
dogs, 601, 632, 635–36
dokusan, 55
domestication, 7, 14, 37, 42, 53, 74, 571, 621, 623, 710–11, 719, 722–23. *See also* appropriation; colonialism
Domingo de Guzmán, 9, 13, 58, 503–8, 513, 515–29, 531–45, 708
Dominican prayer, 9, 57–59, 63, 65, 72, 77, 503–545, 708
Dominican Prayer Book, 523
Dominican Publications, 529
Dominicans. *See* Order of Preachers

donations, 187, 275, 309, 364, 378, 390, 523–24, 534, 550, 566, 594, 598, 621, 651. *See also* generosity; support
Donglin si, 411
dongtian, 550
Donkey Taming Pictures, 320
donkeys, 320
doors, 128, 172, 244, 353, 381–82, 394, 516, 581, 661, 671, 691, 697, 709, 724, 728
Dorrien, Gary, 165
Dostoevsky, Fyodor, 360, 382
doubt, 186, 297, 397, 427, 442, 486, 555, 557, 573, 650–51, 702, 713, 715
dove, 196
Down syndrome, 729
Dragon Gate lineage. *See* Longmen lineage
drama. *See* theater
dream-teachings, 66, 377, 381, 386, 399–401, 548
dreams, 140, 143, 210, 237–38, 241–42, 250, 252–53, 260, 377, 381, 386, 396, 399–401, 486, 548, 639, 649
drinking. *See* alcohol
dropping away of body and mind, 115
drowning, 353, 538
dṛṣṭi, 427, 433
drugs. *See* specific types
drunkenness. *See* intoxication
dry method, 277
dual cultivation, 555, 565, 579–80
dualism, 4, 7, 32, 37–39, 104, 113–14, 257, 312, 374, 463, 464, 467, 473, 501, 507–8, 512, 553, 631–32, 661–62, 667, 671, 678, 683–84, 710. *See also* objectivity; subjectivity
Duc Vien Temple, 422
dukkha, 36, 55, 276–77, 298, 442–43, 451
dullness, 160, 189, 394, 400, 660, 670, 680–81, 697, 700, 713
Dunhuang, 108, 425
Dunne, John, 30
duration, 57, 62, 179, 260–61, 280, 288, 292, 337, 339–40, 351, 354, 370–71, 374, 377, 385, 393–95, 397, 400–2, 420, 433, 449–51, 517, 519, 535, 541, 548, 586, 591, 608–10, 612, 633, 639, 642, 670, 709
dust, 134, 257, 277, 448, 467–68, 533, 589
duty. *See* commitments
dyads, 8, 612
Dyer, Wayne, 624

dying, 67, 107, 186, 188–89, 191, 195, 418, 420, 450–53, 550, 556, 666–67, 681, 683–84, 706, 708, 724
Dzogchen, 56

Early Dominicans, 510, 529
Early Middle Chinese, 579
ears, 125–27, 132, 137–38, 239, 402, 679
ease, 108, 110, 114, 128, 392, 400, 586, 608–9, 633, 638–39, 641–42, 644, 684, 696, 701, 712–13
East Asia, 90, 102, 410, 412, 419, 424, 432, 437, 633. *See also* specific countries
East India Company, 646
East Mountain lineage, 112
East-West dialogue, 603
East-West Schism, 368, 508
Easter, 388, 519
Eastern Orthodoxy, 4, 57, 63, 359–405, 508, 615, 638, 707, 713–14
Eastern Park, 296
Eastern religions (misnomer). *See* Asian religions; specific traditions
eating. *See* dietetics
Eckhart von Hochheim, 167, 505, 529, 716
eclecticism, 226, 600
ecology, 632, 672, 716, 719. *See also* conservation; interdependence; place; world
economics, 34, 41, 62, 328, 423, 506–7, 524, 550, 594, 597–98, 610, 612, 617, 620–21, 624, 643, 650–51, 665, 673, 680, 683, 694, 698, 730
ecstasy, 8, 64, 319, 337, 346–47, 350, 352, 355, 357, 531, 538, 571, 638, 643, 650
ecumenism, 58, 80, 380–81, 604–6, 616, 621, 641–42, 647–48, 723
edification, 516, 520, 525
editions. *See* texts
education, 10, 12, 34–35, 41, 82, 147–49, 154, 264, 275, 399, 423, 506–7, 509–10, 519, 549, 593, 598, 610, 645–47, 666–68, 672, 679, 698, 717, 723. *See also* learning; teaching
Edwards, Mark, 652, 667
EEG. *See* electroencephalography
effects, 3, 21, 28, 31, 37, 39, 54, 60, 62, 65, 67–68, 75, 81, 91, 95, 100–3, 107, 174, 178, 183, 253, 267, 271, 289, 298, 310, 330, 336–37, 339–40, 342–43, 346–47, 350,

effects *(continued)*
 365–66, 372, 381, 390–91, 395, 397, 400, 415, 447, 470, 472–73, 491–92, 498, 515, 521–22, 560–61, 572–73, 583, 595, 599, 604, 606–7, 610–12, 615, 617, 629, 631, 633, 636, 639–41, 643–44, 707–9, 711–13, 716, 718–19, 724–26. *See also* attainments; benefits; goals

efficacy. *See* benefits; confirmation; effects; verification

effluence, 253–55, 262

effort, 67, 159–61, 178, 180–84, 189, 191–93, 195, 243, 245–46, 265, 267, 271, 279, 287–88, 301, 304, 322, 330, 336–37, 342, 352–53, 355, 411, 413, 430, 467, 471, 484–85, 488, 491–92, 507, 518, 521, 527, 550, 581, 583, 586, 642, 648, 660, 663–64, 671, 680, 682, 684, 688, 692, 694, 700, 712

effortlessness. *See* ease

effulgences, 341–42, 345, 347–48, 350, 352, 354, 466

egalitarianism, 147, 151, 420, 423, 598, 647, 657, 665, 669

ego-self. *See nafs*

egocentric pathway, 114

egotism, 23, 43, 68, 100, 105, 172, 183, 186–88, 193, 210, 312, 316, 318, 322, 330, 335, 349, 416, 430, 463, 465, 469, 472, 484, 489, 497, 499, 583, 648, 659–62, 678

Egypt, 199–200, 203, 211, 216, 263, 315, 370, 393, 397

eight beatitudes, 540

eight extraordinary meridians, 557, 559–60, 584

Eight Gates. *See Shemoneh Shearim*

eight limbs. *See aṣṭāṅga*

eight precepts, 438, 453

eight principles, 321

eight *samādhi*s, 452

eight stages, 547, 557, 563–64, 578–92

eight steps, 607, 609

Eightfold Path, 267, 291, 297–98

Eighteenth Vow, 421, 445

Eihei Dōgen, 18–19, 80, 115–16, 558

Einstein, Albert, 318

ekaggatā, 277

El Castillo Interior, 79

elders, 36, 64, 66, 89–91, 95, 106, 120, 128, 146, 153, 296, 307, 321, 335, 352, 359–61, 363, 365–67, 377, 381, 390–96, 414, 440, 505, 518, 531, 560, 663, 707, 710, 723. *See also* teachers

Eleazar of Garmiza, 247

Eleazar of Worms, 247

electricity, 637

electroencephalography, 5, 28, 603

electrodes, 637

elephants, 495

Eliade, Mircea, 32, 40, 479, 574, 710, 720–21

Elijah, 234, 256, 261, 263, 522, 538–39

Elijah da Vidas, 201, 210, 236–37

Elijah del Medigo, 217, 225

elitism, 36, 43, 79, 273, 381, 423, 518, 598–99, 646–47, 651, 682

elixir fields. *See dantian*

elixirs, 550, 556–57, 563, 584

emaciation, 439

emanation, 198, 207, 255, 268, 316, 334, 342, 345, 350, 588

embodiment, 9, 20, 23, 36, 37, 61, 64, 70, 72, 74, 99, 129, 134, 208, 235, 342, 369, 463–64, 467, 471, 477, 485, 512, 527, 532–45, 548, 571, 574, 578, 583, 586, 607, 612, 619, 624, 632, 653, 667, 706–8, 711, 713–14, 716, 719, 721, 726, 729

embryo, 55, 553, 555, 557–58, 561, 563, 580–81, 586–87

embryo of immortality. *See xiantai*

emergency state, 601–2, 611, 615, 632

emic, 34, 552

Emmaus, 524

Emory University, 10

emotions, 25, 29, 71, 95, 98, 122, 137, 152, 156, 172, 175–76, 182, 192, 277, 282, 289, 299–300, 302, 311, 369, 396–97, 401, 404, 429, 464, 470, 511, 516–18, 524, 531, 573, 579, 601, 615, 629, 631, 634, 636, 638–39, 643, 653, 656, 659, 678, 688–89, 729

empathy. *See* compassion

Emperor Wu, 92, 109

emperors. *See* politics; specific emperors

empiricism, 21–22, 725

employment. *See* work

emptiness, 9, 37, 55–56, 89–90, 94–95, 97, 99–101, 103–4, 106, 110, 112, 121, 127, 130, 134–35, 137, 142, 152, 161, 179, 185–86, 190,

196, 200, 203, 255, 266, 320, 352–53, 356, 374, 396, 410, 418, 426–27, 433, 441–43, 479, 487, 552–53, 555, 558, 560, 562, 564, 572, 580, 590–92, 665, 669, 680, 686, 712, 728. *See also* tradition-specific terms
empty vessel. *See* vessels
emptying, 16, 18, 90, 95–96, 98, 104, 112, 114, 130, 152, 241, 527, 558, 594, 638, 690–91
enchantment, 218, 327, 660, 663, 681
enclothment, 262
encouragement, 135, 160, 277–78, 281–82, 287, 290, 293, 337, 379, 391, 393, 395, 398, 414, 416, 440, 444, 450, 508, 510, 516, 519, 531, 538, 570, 610, 640, 647, 669, 672, 697–98
enculturation, 16, 35, 72, 617, 674, 708, 713, 720, 729–30. *See also* conditioning; habituation
End of the Dharma. *See mofa*; *mappō*
end times. *See* apocalypticism; eschatology
endocrine glands, 601, 636
endocrinology, 601, 629
endowed chairs, 35, 621
enemies. *See* difficulties
energeia, 371–73, 385
energetics, 72, 103, 105, 110
energy, 26, 90, 93, 97, 102–3, 109, 111, 115, 187, 257, 296, 315, 317–18, 321–22, 324–25, 335–36, 339, 343, 345–46, 354–55, 372–73, 522, 525, 528, 566, 571, 580, 636, 648, 653, 660, 678–79, 684, 709. *See also* tradition-specific terms
England. *See* Great Britain
Engler, Jack, 29–30
English, 145, 220, 292, 323, 364, 375–76, 379, 424–25, 514, 556, 567–69, 578, 613, 645, 655, *passim*
English Commonwealth. *See* Great Britain
English Romantics, 638
English Sacramentary, 527
engraving, 246, 249, 345
enlightened masters, 670
enlightenment, 19, 26, 30, 37, 64, 71, 106–7, 128–29, 136–37, 140, 158, 173, 186, 194, 245, 252–53, 255, 265–68, 272–73, 276, 278–80, 291, 335, 345, 350, 365, 384, 391, 398, 401, 408, 410–13, 416, 418, 421, 425, 427, 429–31, 440, 450–51, 453–55, 465, 468, 474, 486, 490, 493, 524, 548, 552–57, 559, 561, 565–66, 579, 581, 584, 586, 588, 591–92, 648, 654, 656, 663, 684, 686, 693, 697, 710, 715
enstasy, 8, 78, 82
entanglements, 191, 403, 463–65, 467, 557, 561, 708
entering into God, 371
entering silence, 564, 591
entheogens, 23
enthusiasm, 234, 267, 284, 375, 379, 382, 393, 395–96, 400, 402, 485, 520, 531
entification, 315–16, 318–19, 329
environment. *See* context; place; world
epics (genre), 460, 472, 478
epidemics, 611, 615, 630
epinephrine, 601, 634, 637
epistemologies of enlightenment, 69
epistemologies of limitation, 69
epistemologies of possibility, 70
epistemology, 13, 15–16, 39, 113, 327, 461–62, 635, 673
Epistle to the Romans, 162, 373
Epistula ad totius Catholicae Ecclesiae Episcopos de quibusdam rationibus christianae meditationis, 81
equality. *See* egalitarianism
equanimity, 67, 72, 101, 137, 153, 161–62, 208, 210, 214, 224, 244–45, 253, 265, 267, 269, 279, 290, 298–305, 427, 486, 712–13
equilibrium. *See* homeostasis
Eranos Society, 574
eremiticism, 368
Erez Israel, 198–99, 213
ergotropic, 7–8, 17, 40
Ernst, Carl, 328–29
Ernst, Sarah, 624
eroticism, 219–22. *See also* sexuality
errors. *See* mistakes
eruption, 221
escapism, 19, 24, 43, 378, 430, 451, 632, 643, 653, 670, 678, 680, 687, 689, 716, 719
eschatology, 157, 309, 340, 411
Eskildsen, Stephen, 573
esotericism. *See* secrecy; Western Esotericism
Esposito, Monica, 573
Essential Instructions on the Golden Elixir. *See Jindan yaojue*
eternalism, 267, 433

eternity, 161, 171, 243–44, 247, 349, 355, 465, 470, 477, 479, 485, 487–88, 492, 659, 663, 665, 678, 686, 693–94
ethereal soul. See *hun*
ethics, 18–20, 22, 35–37, 39, 58, 62–63, 67, 69, 146, 151, 157, 198, 205, 214, 265, 267, 277, 310, 323, 372, 408, 414, 452, 461, 470–71, 551, 559, 566, 579, 583, 611, 619–21, 635, 648, 651–52, 677, 682, 711–12, 715, 717, 726, 729. *See also* virtue; tradition-specific terms
ethnicity, 89, 145, 197, 265, 307, 313, 359, 407, 424, 457, 503, 547, 593, 645, 647, 654, 657, 665, 682, 717, 719
ethnocentrism, 32, 325, 475, 568
ethnography, 13, 292, 322–23, 325, 568, 621
etic, 34
Etz Ha-Daat Tov, 225
Etz Hayyim, 201, 207, 216
Eucharist, 158, 372, 510, 516, 518, 531
euphoria, 64
Eurocentrism. *See* ethnocentrism
Europe, 380, 463–64, 475, 504, 506–10, 525, 543, 556, 568–69, 574, 645–49, 654, 708. *See also* specific countries
Eusebius, 519, 535
evaṃ me sutaṃ, 269, 273
evangelical Christianity, 81, 163, 166, 623
evangelism, 11, 368, 504–9, 524–26, 585, 708
Eve, 154, 375
Everard, John, 149
evolution, 19, 24, 26, 69–71, 467, 615, 637, 643, 646–48, 656–57, 659, 666, 668, 672, 678, 688, 716
Examen, 6, 57–58
examination. *See* inquiry
examination of conscience. *See* Examen
exceptionalism. *See* elitism; extraordinariness
excitement. *See* enthusiasm
exclusivism, 79, 327, 598, 602, 616, 711, 723
exegesis. *See* commentaries; interpretation
exemplars, 93, 100, 106, 108, 110, 113, 129, 151, 211, 272, 321, 326, 372, 403, 410, 413, 434, 457, 472, 479, 496, 503–5, 508, 515–16, 531–45, 585, 650–52, 708, 717, 726, 729. *See also* specific people; tradition-specific terms
exercise, 610–11, 620, 631, 638
Exercitia spiritualia, 6, 57, 384

exhalation, 96–97, 105, 189, 281, 287, 291, 298–300, 371, 400, 402, 486, 582–83, 597, 607, 642. *See also* breathing
exhaustion. *See* tiredness
exile, 19, 150, 199, 203, 213, 263, 376, 438, 518
existentialism, 22–24, 26, 36, 40–41, 65, 70–71, 81, 202, 239, 242, 277, 309, 311, 339, 350–51, 379, 458, 470–71, 476–77, 512, 526, 572, 594–95, 601, 605, 610–11, 615, 623, 629, 640, 643, 645, 653–54, 656–57, 660, 662, 665, 666–71, 679–81, 688, 698, 706–21, 723–24, 726, 728
exorcism, 545
exoticism, 508, 604–5
expansion. *See bast*
expectant waiting, 156, 158, 172
expectation, 160, 288, 607–8, 641, 669
experience, 9–10, 15–17, 22, 26, 30–31, 34, 38–40, 44, 54–55, 61–62, 64–65, 70, 75, 81, 93, 96, 99–100, 113, 163, 174, 240, 267, 282, 288, 309, 311–12, 319, 324, 326, 337, 354, 357, 360, 364–65, 374, 379, 381, 383, 390–91, 394–96, 400–1, 415, 423, 462–68, 472, 484, 489, 491–92, 496, 516–17, 519, 522, 528, 531, 548, 553, 561, 564, 571, 573, 594, 599–602, 611–13, 617, 619, 622, 630, 638, 643, 650, 656, 658–59, 665, 669–70, 672–73, 677–78, 681, 686–88, 698–99, 707, 710, 712–16, 720–24, 728, 730. *See also* specific types; subjectivity
experiencing, 14–15, 44, 65, 707
experimental research. *See* quantification; science
experimentation, 31–32, 41, 44, 146, 214, 310, 595–96, 598–99, 603, 619, 623, 635, 640
Explanation of Yoga. *See Yogavārttika*
exposure. *See* vulnerability
external alchemy. *See waidan*
extraordinariness, 23–24, 38, 64, 68, 194, 319–20, 327, 366, 383, 427, 434, 472, 512, 523, 544, 553, 561, 584, 599, 602, 616, 638, 642, 647–48, 654, 670, 681, 708, 713, 715, 729
extraordinary experience. *See* anomalous experience
extrasensory perception. *See* paranormal abilities
extremism. *See* fanaticism
extrovertive, 82, 93, 112–13, 128–29, 152, 157–58, 163, 175, 177, 320, 329, 352, 365, 400, 513, 524–25, 643, 707–8, 716–17
eyebrows, 365, 379, 439, 446–47

eyes, 104, 125–27, 132, 137–38, 241, 251, 288, 319, 335–36, 341, 347, 349, 374, 379, 392–93, 400, 415, 440–42, 446, 452, 495, 519, 521, 535, 537, 574, 607–8, 642, 679, 702
eyn sof, 205, 208, 243–44, 253–55, 258
Ezekial, 190, 213, 521
Ezra of Gerona, 240

face before birth, 553, 583
faces, 56, 59, 96, 162, 200, 236–37, 241, 246, 248, 266, 272, 312, 339, 342–44, 347, 353, 374, 378, 403, 405, 417, 447, 459, 504, 517, 520, 524–25, 533, 543–44, 553, 561, 583, 605, 632, 642, 649, 652, 670, 716, 724
facing the wall. See *biguan*
faith, 152, 158, 173–74, 178, 180–81, 188–89, 193, 246, 279, 287, 309, 314–15, 336, 350, 369, 380, 400, 405, 411, 423, 430–31, 449–50, 453, 485, 507, 513, 515, 596, 606–7, 681, 682, 690. See also worldview
faith factor, 42, 605, 607, 609, 613, 623, 642
Fakhruddin Chishti. See Chishti
fallenness, 154, 186, 191, 203, 371, 375, 385
falun. See Dharma Wheel
Falun gong, 567
fame. See reputation
familiarization, 39, 706
family, 23, 318, 337, 377–78, 382, 396, 423, 455, 505, 549, 560, 593–94, 598, 610, 630–31, 646, 682–83, 714
Family of the Dao. See *daojia*
family resemblance, 4, 6
Fa'an, 411
fanā, 319, 329, 334, 344–45, 354–56, 712
fanaticism, 172, 379, 508
Fanjeaux, 526
fannao, 557, 579
fantasies, 159, 402
fanzhao, 565, 574
Faqirullah Shikarpuri. See Shikarpuri
Farangi Mahal, 307
farmers, 499, 507
farms, 377, 507
Farrar, Straus and Giroux, 483
Faruqi, Abu'l-Hasan Zayd, 315
Faruqi, Anwar Allah (Shah), 308

fasting, 205, 213, 237, 242, 260–61, 266, 309, 339, 508, 519, 694
fasting of the heart-mind. See *xinzhai*
fate, 397, 554, 571
Father (God), 171, 174–75, 179
fatigue. See tiredness
faults. See deficiencies
fayd, 315–18, 324, 335–36, 339, 341–42, 345, 347–48, 350, 352, 354
fear, 194, 235–37, 266, 271, 277, 310, 312, 336, 398, 464, 524, 636, 651, 653, 659, 662, 664, 669, 679–83, 690, 692, 696, 699, 706
fearlessness, 277, 404, 659
feast days. See calendar
Feast of Weeks, 388
Fedorov, Paisii, 360, 363–65, 371, 383–84
feelings. See emotions
Feldenkrais Method, 53, 79
Fell, Margaret, 79
fellowship. See belonging; friendship
felt sense, 66, 357
female alchemy. See *nüdan*
femininity, 79, 103, 123, 129, 227, 259, 674
feminism, 79, 672, 722
Fénelon, François, 145, 147–50, 153, 156–58, 163–64, 166–67
Feniger, Siegmund, 286
ferial days, 534
Ferrer, Jorge, 40, 80, 327, 672
fetters, 98, 101, 141, 143, 280, 293, 297, 403, 663
fetus, 561, 563–64, 580, 587–89
Fetzer Institute, 10, 604
fields, 143, 181, 208, 258, 297, 309, 343, 499, 514, 558, 560–61, 574, 623, 648, 682, 684, 692, 695, 718
fieldwork, 13, 32, 292, 568, 605
fikr, 343
fight-or-flight response, 26, 595, 601–2, 605, 611, 613, 615–16, 621, 623, 632–33, 636–37, 639–40, 643–44
fighting. See violence
fingers, 251, 348, 381, 447, 450
fire, 177, 179, 185, 194–95, 220, 241, 249, 256, 340, 382, 393, 400, 402, 405, 430, 443, 453, 458, 466–68, 477, 524, 542, 544, 557, 580–81, 584, 586, 591
firing times. See *huohou*

first-person discourse, 9, 11, 15, 25, 32–35, 40–41, 70, 81
First Buddhist Council, 268–69
Fischer, Roland, 8, 40–41
fish, 416, 418, 687
Fisher, Mary, 79
fishermen, 423
Fitzwilliam Museum, 96
five abstentions, 71
five aggregates, 36
five elements, 497
five essentials, 419
five faculties, 276, 297
five fetters, 297
five grave offenses, 416, 420–21, 433, 451, 454
five hindrances, 713
five kinds of suffering, 441
five *kośa*s, 478
Five Phases, 103, 105, 110, 135, 141, 580
Five Pillars, 309, 311
five *prāṇa*s, 497
five precepts, 451, 453, 471, 491, 559, 583, 712
five realms, 447
five vows. *See* five precepts
flagellation, 150–51, 161, 187, 515–16, 518–19, 527, 534, 694
flesh. *See* body
flies, 525, 544
Florence, 528
Florensky, Pavel, 363
Florilegium, 369, 382, 392
flour, 438
flourishing, 32, 35, 42, 75, 92, 100, 138, 353, 673, 706, 714, 719
flow, 23, 113, 208–9, 241, 244, 250, 261, 317, 346, 375, 390, 494, 511, 551, 557, 558, 632, 702, 714
Flow Yoga, 574
Flower Garland Sutra. *See Avataṃsaka Sūtra*; *Huayan jing*
flowers, 278–79, 284, 293, 296, 442–44, 450, 454, 561, 588
flowing cognition, 93, 100–1, 106, 112, 114, 129, 140
fluids. *See* vital substances
flying, 130, 335, 438–39, 450, 455, 497
fMRI. *See* functional Magnetic Resonance Imaging
focus. *See* concentration

Focusing, 20, 606, 623
Folkow, Björn, 636
food. *See* dietetics
Food and Drug Administration, 623
"For the Encouragement of Monks in India," 404
forbearance. *See* patience
foresters, 377, 397
forests, 63, 208, 280, 286, 298, 366, 377, 397, 402, 411, 443, 478, 525
forgetting, 16, 42, 114, 178, 182, 192, 196, 288, 337, 350, 354–55, 397, 430, 539, 559, 565, 584, 586, 592, 651, 681, 701
forgiveness, 57, 153, 263, 339, 389, 439, 535, 604
formalism, 526
Forman, Robert K. C., 16–18, 42, 70, 326
formlessness, 95, 124, 279, 287, 330, 339, 348, 402, 425, 430, 580, 586–87
Fort, Andrew, 40, 80
forty-eight vows, 409, 412, 421, 445, 452
forty objects of meditation, 278, 285
fossilization, 475
Foucault, Michel, 729
foundations, 39, 62, 89–90, 92–93, 95, 97, 141–42, 199, 204, 209, 219, 234, 257, 260, 263, 267, 272, 276, 280, 289, 309, 326, 338, 367, 369, 408, 468, 506, 531, 552, 557–60, 568, 572, 575, 583, 662, 666, 669, 681–82, 686, 712
fountains, 188, 192, 255, 257, 650
four aspirations, 337
four assemblies, 277
four difficulties, 550
four elements, 259, 278, 285, 299, 333–35, 350, 355, 468, 490, 497
four essential components, 607, 615, 633, 638–39, 641
four foundations of mindfulness, 276, 280–84, 289, 297–300, 304
four great sights, 265–66
four *jhāna*s, 267, 279, 713
four *marga*s, 461
Four Noble Truths, 267, 442, 452
four postures, 338, 394, 422
four stages of enlightenment, 293, 440, 452
four stages of visualization, 415
four virtues, 583
four *yoga*s, 461
Fourteenth Dalai Lama. *See* Dalai Lama

fourth bhūmi stage, 420
Fox, George, 151, 154, 163–64
Fox, Victoria, 483
foxing, 55
Fra Angelico, 504, 528
France, 58, 148, 505, 507, 509–10, 514, 526, 531, 600, 613, 617, 632, 687, 690, 727
Frances, Mordecai, 200
Francis de Sales, 150, 160–62, 167
Francis of Assisi, 506, 513
Franciscans. *See* Order of Friars Minor
Franfurt am Main, 568
Franny and Zoey, 379–80
free and easy wandering. *See xiaoyao you*
freedom, 26, 70, 154, 160, 162, 191, 193–94, 196, 222, 265–67, 277, 283, 304, 380, 398, 400, 464, 477, 486, 490, 524, 528, 594, 635, 650–51, 653–62, 665–66, 668–70, 673, 677–78, 681–82, 686–87, 689, 694–97, 699, 701–2, 706, 710, 716, 724, 730
freedom from the known, 66, 653, 656–57, 659, 666–67, 669–70, 673, 683, 692, 702, 710
French, 514, 526
French, Reginald Michael (R. M.), 378
French Revolution, 509
frequency, 339–40, 363, 371, 374, 377, 385, 391, 393–95, 397, 400, 420
Frère Roger, 58
Freud, Sigmund, 42, 70, 425, 714
friars, 503, 509–10, 513, 516–17, 523, 525, 528, 531, 540–41
Friars Preachers. *See* Order of Preachers
Friary of San Marco, 528
Fricchione, Gregory, 598
friendship, 156, 181, 271, 273, 288, 311, 317–18, 336, 342, 345–46, 348, 353–54, 382, 401–3, 455, 486, 495, 505, 514, 524–25, 527, 542, 544–45, 550, 566, 630, 647, 651, 653, 655, 667, 706
Fromm, Erich, 23, 70
Frommann, Immanuel, 224
frontal lobe, 29
fruit, 68, 154, 163, 165, 179, 193, 202, 280, 283–84, 293, 298–99, 309, 347, 391, 438, 443, 470, 479, 485, 489, 491, 501, 512, 542, 566, 594, 667. *See also* benefits; confirmation; effects; verification
Fry, Elizabeth, 164

fulfillment, 23, 26, 70–71, 75, 158, 162, 211, 237, 254, 261, 284, 298–99, 351, 372, 374, 377, 389, 412–13, 443, 476–77, 501, 540, 598, 702, 711, 714
Fulk of Toulouse, 509
Full Catastrophe Living, 606
full-lotus posture. *See* lotus-posture; *padmāsana*
functional Magnetic Resonance Imaging, 30–31, 114, 603
fundamentalism, 42, 309, 723
funding. *See* economics
Fung Loy Kok, 570
fuqi, 58
furnace, 195, 580
furniture, 154–55, 158, 293, 381, 385, 450, 600, 609, 667, 727–28
"Further Texts," 393, 399

Gabriel (angel), 251, 308–9
Gabriel's Hadith, 308–9, 311, 314
Gagnon, Bernard, 266, 270
Gal Vihara, 266, 291
Galata Mevlevihanesi, 59
Galilee, 524
Galileo, 325
Galleria Nazionale dell'Umbria, 504
gambling, 154
Gandhi, Indira, 655
Ganges, 413, 446–47
gangsters, 288
Gansu, 425
ganying, 107
Gao Shuangjing, 555
Gaon of Vilna, 216
Garden of Eden, 154, 250, 260
Garden of Gethsemane, 519
gardens, 154, 250, 260, 290, 394, 396, 519
Garonne River, 522, 538
Gate of Life, 574, 578, 581
gates, 129, 132–33, 176, 197, 210, 234, 259, 276, 394, 405, 578, 580–81
Gates of Heaven, 129, 132
Gates of Holiness. *See Shaarei Kedusha*
gathered (sense of meeting), 66, 156
Gayatri *mantra*, 646
Gaza, 370
gaze, 152, 235, 242–43, 245, 248, 257–59, 441, 521, 533, 542, 574, 641

gazelle, 632
Ge Hong, 140
Geertz, Clifford, 39–40, 710, 720
Gehenna, 234
gelassenheit, 161
Gelug, 286
gender, 79, 114, 227, 574, 657, 665, 673, 708
gender equity, 598
Gendlin, Eugene, 20, 606, 623
genealogy. *See* lineage
General Adaptation Syndrome, 601
generativity, 523, 527
generosity, 67, 157, 175, 183, 187, 265, 267, 271, 273, 277, 285, 309, 352, 356, 378, 390, 396, 505, 509, 523–24, 539, 550, 586, 594, 646, 651, 712
Genesis, 220
genetics, 606–7, 612, 622, 624, 631, 673
genre, 73, 89, 102, 145, 197, 265, 272, 275, 307, 359–60, 363–64, 376, 378, 407, 412–13, 459, 468–69, 503, 505, 515, 547, 593, 645, 726. *See also* specific genres
gentry, 361
genuflection, 510–11, 519–20, 527–28, 535–36
Gerard de Frachet, 513
Gerizim, 158
German, 220, 227, 567–69, 578
Germany, 237, 529, 531, 568
gestures. *See* body; posture
Gethin, Rupert Mark Lovell (R. M. L.), 274, 291
Gethsemani Encounter (conference), 10
geyi, 112
Ghazali al-, 239
ghosts, 120, 127–28, 245, 439
Ghujduwani, 'Abdulkhaliq, 312, 317, 321, 352
Ghulam 'Ali Shah, 308, 313–15, 328
Ghulam Sadat Chishti. *See* Chishti
gifts, 68, 173–74, 187, 369, 398, 523–24, 540, 542, 643, 646
Gikatilla, Joseph, 236, 258
Gilbert, Dorothy Lloyd, 149–50
Gilbert, Maureen, 621
Gimello, Robert, 65, 68
Gītā. See *Bhagavad Gītā*
glands, 601, 634. *See also* specific glands
globalization, 313, 323–24, 474–76, 506, 602, 604, 613, 617, 647–48

gnosis, 157, 198, 241, 251, 256–57, 305, 310, 333–34, 336, 341, 348, 351, 355, 368–69, 376, 459–61, 475, 495, 544
Gnosticism, 648
goals, 61–62, 67, 81, 96, 142, 152–53, 297, 309, 315, 333, 336–37, 339, 342–43, 346–47, 350–51, 381, 412–13, 415, 426, 431, 468–71, 484–85, 490, 561, 597–99, 604–5, 607, 611, 619, 647, 656, 668–70, 679–80, 709, 711, 726. *See also* attainments; benefits; effects
God, 39, 54, 57, 147, 152–54, 157, 159–60, 164–65, 171–74, 176–77, 179–81, 183, 185, 187–89, 192–93, 195–96, 198, 203–5, 211, 217, 220, 234–36, 238–40, 244–46, 253, 256, 258–59, 261–62, 309, 311, 315–16, 318–23, 333–36, 343, 345–49, 354, 356–57, 368, 371–76, 378, 380–82, 385, 389–91, 393–95, 398, 507, 510–11, 520, 523, 531–32, 537, 539, 542, 594, 606, 650, 682, 690, 699, 710–11, 721, 728, 730
God delusion, 31
God Helmet, 30–32
God of Abraham, 243, 256
God of Nahor, 243
God-intoxicated, 650
Godhead, 203, 208, 235, 374, 475
gods. *See* specific gods
Godself, 198, 200, 203, 253
Goenka, S. N., 36, 80, 286–87
Gogol, Nikolai, 360
going native, 605
Goldblatt, Harry, 635
goldsmith, 293
Goldstein, Joseph, 80
Gombrich, Richard, 292
gong'an, 56
gongguo ge, 58–59
good and evil, 151, 159, 172, 175, 188, 195, 200, 217, 237–38, 249, 257–58, 309, 337, 389, 507
good deeds. *See* activity
Good Friday, 510, 520
Good Friday Experiment, 32, 44
Gorky, Maxim, 378
Gospel of John, 158, 167, 172, 175, 179, 371
gospels, 80, 146, 158, 164, 172, 191, 367, 372, 382, 519, 524–25, 533, 535, 543

Gospodi Isusi Christe, sine Bozhe, pomilui me, 384, 392
Gough, James, 149
Governing Vessel, 557, 563–65, 582, 584–85
government. *See* politics
grace, 57, 68, 81, 153–54, 156, 162, 172, 176, 181–82, 189, 190, 195, 317, 352–53, 356, 371–72, 374–75, 378, 384–85, 396, 403, 405, 423, 469, 512–13, 516–17, 520–24, 539–40, 542, 712
Grace, Fran, 40
grades. *See* levels
Gradual School, 553
grafting, 513, 523
Graham, Angus Charles (A. C.), 109
Grantham Bain Collection, 649
gratitude, 4, 57, 152, 310, 336, 371, 395, 398, 400, 403, 454–55, 527, 531, 542–43
graves, 66, 240, 262, 271, 398, 513
Great Britain, 145–46, 163–64, 167, 286, 292, 323, 480, 510, 568, 574, 632, 645, 647, 649, 651, 667–68, 677, 686–87, 690
Great Calming and Contemplation. *See Mohe zhiguan*
Great Depression, 650
Great Prayer of Intercession, 520
Great Peace. *See taiping*
Great Purity. *See* Taiqing
Greater Celestial Cycle, *See* Macrocosmic Orbit
greed. *See* acquisitiveness
Greece, 360–61, 381, 384, 392, 457, 463, 480
Greek, 54, 234, 361, 367–68, 370, 375, 384, 392, 632
Greek East, 508, 531
Gregorian Chant, 58
Gregory VII, 506–7
Gregory IX, 510, 513
Gregory of Nyssa, 384
Gregory of Sinai, 369, 385–86, 393, 399–401, 405
Gregory the Great, 531
Grellet, Stephen, 163
Grenkov, Amvrosii, 363, 365
Gries, Zeev, 218
Grisha, 360
Grof, Stanislav, 23, 70, 326
Gross, Aaron, 728, 730
grotto-heavens. *See dongtian*

ground, 152, 181, 343–44, 382, 414, 418, 426, 441–42, 444, 527, 533, 579, 665, 669, 715, 728
Grubb, Sarah Lynes, 149
Gu Yutao, 550
guan (observation), 409, 431–32, 437
Guan wuliang shoufo jing. *See Guanjing*
Guan Zhong, 90, 120
Guangcheng, 115
Guanjing, 66–67, 72, 76, 79, 407–55, 708, 715
Guanzi, 71, 89–91, 98, 102, 104, 108–9, 120. *See also Neiye; Xinshu shang*
guarding the One. *See shouyi*
Guenin-Lelle, Dianne, 148
guesthouses, 359, 364, 376, 390, 393, 403, 536
Guía espiritual, 148, 150, 167, 180, 183, 187, 190, 194
guidance, 25, 237, 268–70, 288, 290, 296–305, 307, 315, 318, 322–24, 335, 337, 343–44, 347, 359, 365, 369, 376–83, 386, 389–98, 407–8, 411, 416–18, 441, 462–63, 469, 504–5, 515–25, 527, 531–45, 548, 556, 560, 565–66, 571–72, 579, 607–10, 631, 633, 641–42, 645, 653–54, 656, 660, 707–10, 713
Guide for the Perplexed. *See Moreh Nevukhim*
guidelines, 19, 104, 107, 152, 343, 468, 574, 612
guides to prayer, 72, 708. *See also* contemplative literature; specific texts
guigen, 94
guilds, 312, 507
guilt. *See* compunction
guna, 467–68, 472, 479, 484, 489–90, 491, 500–1
Guo Xiang, 92, 108
Guodian, 91
Gurney, Joseph John, 164
guru, 476, 605, 665, 672, 681, 684, 693–94, 697–98
gushen, 105, 111
Guyon, Jeanne Marie, 79, 145, 147–49, 151, 153, 156–57, 163, 166–67, 180
Gyatso, Tenzin. *See* Dalai Lama
gymnastics, 110, 475, 480, 708

Ha-Gadol, Eliezer, 264
haal, 68, 712
Habiburrahman Saharanpuri. *See* Saharanpuri
habituation, 16, 23, 43, 71, 82, 122, 184, 187, 326, 375, 381, 395, 467, 527, 553, 560, 674, 682, 714, 716. *See also* conditioning; enculturation

habitus, 222
Hadith, 307–9, 312, 315, 318, 337–38, 347, 353, 355
hagiography, 314, 472, 510, 713, 729
hair, 309, 338, 342, 350, 423, 446–47, 458, 565, 588, 632, 695
Hajj, 309
halakha, 198–99, 202–4, 223, 712
halakim, 210
halal, 357
halls, 56, 59, 274, 345, 433
hallucinations. *See* visions
halo, 446–48, 504, 532–43, 709
hamakom, 235
hamitboded, 237
Hampshire, 667, 677, 686, 688
Han (state), 92
Han dynasty, 92, 96, 109, 556
Han Feizi, 91
handmaiden, 533, 537
hands, 56, 59, 96–97, 127, 138, 171, 177, 240, 243, 252, 266, 311, 317, 370, 376, 417, 438, 447, 450–51, 459, 504, 520–23, 525, 538–40, 543, 564, 671, 586–91
Hanh, Thich Nhat, 19, 529, 602, 624
Hanhagot, 225
happiness. *See* joy
haqiqa, 311, 314, 333, 348
Harappa culture, 459, 478
Harappan seal, 459
Hare Krishnas. *See* International Society for Krishna Consciousness
Hariharānanda Āraṇya, 474, 479
harm, 138, 566, 595, 615, 633, 643, 680, 683, 691, 701
harmony, 42, 100, 104–5, 134, 335–37, 378, 517, 580–81, 583, 643, 655, 723
HarperCollins, 613, 629
Harrington, Anne, 600, 604–5, 622
Harris, J. Rendel, 149, 163–64
Harvard Medical School, 593, 595, 597–98, 601, 603, 605, 621–22, 629–30
Harvard University, 20, 593, 598, 603, 605, 616, 622–23, 640, 642
harvest, 191, 527
Harvey, Peter, 290
hasid, 211, 254

Hasidei Ashkenaz, 237
Hasidism, 199, 201, 208–9, 216, 223–24, 226, 244
Hatha Yoga, 654, 674
Haṭha-yoga-pradīpikā, 475, 480
hatred, 267, 277, 297, 356, 423, 492, 683, 713
having mode, 23, 70
Hawaii, 433
hawk, 438
Hayyat, Judah, 247
head, 116, 129, 152, 158, 174–76, 199, 205, 235, 249, 256, 279, 302, 317, 335, 349, 351, 360, 393, 405, 439–40, 447, 497, 505–6, 510, 521, 524, 532, 540, 542, 558–59, 565, 582, 586, 589, 645, 649–50, 688, 694–95
healing, 57, 186, 216, 258, 283, 311, 317, 377, 397, 438, 509, 520, 522, 524, 594, 597, 599–600, 604, 606–9, 612, 636, 650
Healing and the Mind, 604
health, 21, 28, 42, 67, 110, 283, 289, 311, 474–75, 477, 558, 567, 597–600, 602, 604–5, 607, 609, 611–12, 615, 623–24, 629, 631, 640, 672, 689, 706, 709; as (substitute) sacred, 474–75, 611
health and fitness movements, 474, 567, 569, 599, 622, 708
healthcare, 593, 597–98, 610, 618
hearing. *See* listening
heart, 57, 71, 152, 154, 157–59, 162, 171–77, 180, 182–84, 186, 192–93, 196, 234, 236, 240, 252, 263, 267, 309, 316–17, 321–22, 330, 334, 337–43, 345–48, 351, 356–57, 359–60, 363, 365–66, 369, 371, 373–75, 377–80, 390–94, 396–98, 400–4, 430, 449, 496, 512, 515, 517, 520, 522, 524–25, 535, 557–58, 564–65, 574, 579, 581, 594, 601, 629–30, 634, 664–65, 681, 684
heart attacks, 615, 629–31, 633, 639
heart disease, 594–95, 631, 635
heart rate, 28, 595, 611, 616, 632–33, 639
heart-mind. *See xin*
heartbeat, 335, 365, 374, 400, 402, 601, 610, 637, 640
heat. *See* warmth
Hebrew, 54, 60, 197, 203–4, 206, 208, 213, 215, 218–19, 222, 226–27, 234, 236–37, 241, 254–55, 258, 264, 707
Hebrew Bible. *See* Tanakh

hegemony, 11, 200
Hegesippus, 519
hegumen, 360, 371
hell. *See* damnation
Henan, 427
henosis, 372
Henry, John William II, 597
Herbert Benson Professorship, 621
herbology, 498
hereditary *shaykh*s, 322
heresy, 68, 147–49, 154, 251, 257–58, 505–7, 509–10
Hermeticism, 648
hermitage, 377, 390–91, 394, 397–99, 555, 591
Heshang gong, 128
Hesychasm, 57, 244, 359–405, 615, 638
hesychia, 54, 224, 244, 369, 380
Hesychius of Sinai, 397
heterodoxy, 461, 479
Hidayat al-talibin, 314
hierarchy, 152, 175, 551, 647–48, 651, 657, 674, 715–16. *See also* elitism; extraordinariness
hierarchy of needs, 43, 714
hieromonk, 360, 366, 370
hierophany, 32, 721
Higashi Honganji Buddhist Temple, 433
Higashi Honganji Mission of Hawaii, 433
high blood pressure. *See* hypertension
higher education. *See* academia
Highest Clarity. *See* Shangqing
Hilary of Poitiers, 531
Hildegard of Bingen, 81
Hillel, Yaakov Moshe, 197, 206, 216, 218
Hīnayāna (misnomer). *See* Southern Buddhism; Theravāda
Hindi, 321
hindrances. *See* defilements; delusion; difficulties
Hindu nationalism. *See* Hindutva
Hinduism, 6, 8, 10, 20, 25, 28, 37, 39, 54–55, 58–59, 65–67, 69, 75, 77, 82, 112, 222, 316, 321, 329, 438–39, 457–501, 599, 602, 616, 620, 633, 638, 645–48, 654, 656–57, 673, 681, 687, 696, 708, 710, 712–13, 716, 721–22
Hindutva, 475, 480
hippocampus, 28
Hirati, Abdullah Ansari, 329
hishtavut, 208, 210

hisō-hizoku, 423
Historia Ecclesiastica, 535
Historic Peace Churches, 167
historicism, 12–14, 16–17, 62, 74, 167, 216, 222, 269, 428, 600, 605, 617, 643, 726–28
history of science, 600
hitbodedut, 54, 208–9, 223, 238
hitbonenut, 209
holiness, 174, 186, 195, 234, 246, 277, 297, 311, 379, 383, 398, 505, 507–8, 513, 523, 538, 541, 680
holism, 37, 357, 505, 514, 521, 528, 599–600, 656, 659, 671, 678, 685, 688, 719
Holland, 649–50
Holmes, Oliver Wendell Sr., 605
Holocaust. *See* Shoah
holy. *See* sacred
Holy Fathers. *See* Church Fathers
Holy Land, 198, 518
Holy of Holies, 385, 540
holy reading. *See lectio divina*
Holy Spirit, 152, 157, 161, 163, 172–74, 176–79, 182, 191–92, 195, 202, 208–10, 213–14, 224, 234–35, 238, 245–46, 251–52, 368–69, 371–73, 379, 385, 388–89, 403, 516, 521, 523–25, 532, 540–41, 544
Holy Trinity Monastery, 363
Homayun, Shamim, 320
home, 63, 136, 178, 200, 262, 376, 536
homelessness, 396. *See also* mendicancy
homeostasis, 26, 284, 479, 602, 643
homoousion, 374
Hompa Hongwanji of Hawaii, 433
Hōnen, 411, 422–23, 432–33
honesty, 71, 265, 267, 348, 414, 471, 491, 559, 583, 681, 712
Hong Kong, 570
Hongdu, 548
Honorius III, 509
Hooton, Elizabeth, 79
hope, 174, 310, 336, 524, 663, 688
hormones, 601–2, 612, 634–37
horse training, 593
horses, 335, 405, 522, 593
Hoshanah Raba, 202
hospitals, 164, 361, 597, 605, 611. *See also* specific hospitals

Hot Yoga. *See* Bikram Yoga©™
householders. *See* laypeople
houses, 63, 154–55, 167, 193, 198, 200, 214, 239, 242, 262, 389, 426, 533, 541, 647, 683, 685–87, 689, 693
Houshmand, Zara, 32, 34
Hsüan-hsüeh. *See* Xuanxue
Huai River, 92
Huaigan, 428, 434
Huainan (state), 92, 106, 114
Huainanzi, 89, 94, 102–4, 106, 107–10, 113, 120; translation of, 124–25, 132–35, 137–38, 141–43
huandan, 550
Huang-Lao boshu, 115
Huangdi neijing suwen, 103
Huayan Buddhism, 551–54, 575, 579
Huayan jing, 550–51, 559, 579
Hubbard, L. Ron, 624
Hudaybiya, 311
Huiguan, 411
huiming, 547–48, 555, 578–81, 585
Huiming jing, 64, 66, 69, 76, 547–92, 708–9, 714; translation of, 578–92
Huineng, 112, 426
Huiri, 426–27
Huiyuan. *See* Jingying Huiyuan; Lushan Huiyuan
human potential. *See* potentiality
humanistic psychology, 13, 22–23, 26, 42–43, 70, 672, 711, 714
humanities, 11–12, 326–27, 725
Humbert of Romans, 503–4, 510, 516–17
humility, 161, 171–72, 176–77, 180–81, 183, 186, 214, 234–37, 245, 339, 352–53, 373, 378, 394, 403–4, 516–18, 527, 532, 538, 653, 684, 706, 712
humor, 106, 714
hun, 128, 143, 558
Hungary, 510, 622
hunger, 186, 195, 337, 397, 416, 439, 496, 540, 594, 717
hungry ghosts, 439
hunting, 24, 729
huohou, 581
husbandmen, 175, 181
huts. *See* hermitage
Huxley, Aldous, 14, 672
Huyun, 64, 549, 551, 562

Huzhou, 550
Huzi, 100
hybrid spirituality, 19, 35, 53, 61, 222, 461, 471, 474–75, 568–69, 574, 598–600, 619, 624, 647–48, 666, 708–10, 730
hybridization, 572
Hyderabad, 307–8, 321, 328, 333
hyerarousal. *See* ergotropic
hymns, 198, 376, 478, 520, 525
hyperquiescence. *See* trophotropic
hypertension, 28, 595, 610–11, 615, 621, 629–33, 635–37, 639–40, 643
hypnosis, 240, 600, 609, 615, 653, 660, 673, 681
hypoarousal. *See* trophotropic
hypocrisy, 338, 349, 651
hypothalamus, 28, 616, 637

Iberia, 203
Ibn al-'Arabi, 60, 310, 315, 319, 323–24
Ibn Arabi Society, 323
Ibn Daud, Abraham, 262
Ibn Zamra, David, 200, 216
ice, 430, 441
I-ching. See *Yijing*
iconoclasm, 81, 645, 653
iconography, 266, 409, 417, 504, 514, 521, 525, 565, 709, 728
icons, 369, 378, 403, 409, 525, 528, 638, 693, 709, 728
ideals. *See* exemplars; models
Idel, Moshe, 209, 211, 214, 223–24
identification, 56, 446, 477, 505, 511, 513–25, 531–45
identity. *See* adherence; being; existentialism; personhood; specific dimensions; subjectivity
idiocy, 176, 252, 397, 566, 671
idleness. *See* laxity; seclusion
idolatry, 243, 518
idols, 243
Iggeret Ha-Kodesh, 261
Iggeret Ha-Levanon, 225
Iggeret Ramban, 256
Ignacio de Loyola, 57, 384, 509
Ignatios. *See* Ignatius of Xanthopoulos
Ignatius of Loyola. *See* Ignacio de Loyola
Ignatius of Xanthopoulos, 385–86, 393, 399–400
ignorance, 130, 200, 297, 312, 319, 325, 344, 397, 423, 430, 453, 463–67, 470, 472, 477,

479, 483, 486, 488, 490–91, 523, 557, 560, 583, 630, 651, 673
ihsan, 309, 314, 336
IHWH. *See* YHWH
illiteracy, 175, 178, 274, 360, 507
illness. *See* sickness
illumination. *See* enlightenment; light
illustrations, 514–15, 532–45, 558, 563–64, 566, 575, 578–92, 629, 634–35, 637
imagery, 73, 151, 153, 159, 190, 248, 285, 289, 315, 374, 378, 409, 414–15, 417, 426, 427–28, 431, 433, 449, 465, 467, 490, 493–94, 525, 532–45, 608, 639, 662, 665, 669, 671–72, 689, 702, 708, 728
imagination, 7, 24, 154, 171–72, 178, 180, 187, 239, 253–54, 338, 375, 388, 392–93, 396, 400, 402–3, 414–15, 442, 444, 464, 483–84, 653, 678, 696, 708, 728
iman, 309, 314
imitation of Christ, 149, 511, 515–25, 527, 531–45
immanence, 39, 339, 385, 425, 553, 720, 722
immediacy, 23, 69–70, 152, 191, 498, 651–52, 654–61, 663, 665, 668, 672, 674, 678, 680–81, 686, 695, 698–99, 701, 715–16, 728
immigration, 199–200, 203, 223, 422, 593, 599, 602, 619, 640
immortal embryo. *See xiantai*
immortality, 20, 66, 194, 247, 477, 547, 549–50, 556–60, 571, 580, 584, 592, 663, 688
immortals, 548–49, 554, 561, 571, 648, 713
impartiality, 100–1, 712
impatience. *See* agitation
Imperatorskoe Pravoslavnoe Palestinskoe Obshchestvo, 382–83
impermanence, 36, 55, 276–77, 298–300, 442–43, 451
imperviousness. *See* protection
implements. *See* paraphernalia
implicate order, 668, 672
impoverishment. *See* poverty
impregnation, 240
imprints. *See* traces
imprisonment, 148, 164, 374–75, 402, 416, 437–40, 463–64, 466–67, 519, 661
impurities. *See* defilements
in-breath. *See* inhalation
Inagaki Hisao, 425, 433, 437

incantations, 450, 589
incarnate mindfulness, 512, 526–28
incarnation, 39, 371–73, 384, 458, 512, 516–17, 648, 674–75, 721
incense, 522, 541, 567
inclusivism, 79, 166, 410, 560, 566, 605–6, 621, 641–42, 647–48, 711, 723
incomprehensibility. *See* apophasis
incubation, 563–64, 586
indescribablity. *See* apophasis
independence, 275, 425, 441, 472, 477, 488, 498, 538, 564, 650, 653–54, 656–60, 666, 669–71, 673, 677–78, 681, 696–97, 699, 701, 710, 715–16, 720
indeterminacy of translation, 34
India, 39, 57, 113, 265–67, 291, 307–8, 310, 312–13, 316, 321, 328, 333, 338, 342, 408–10, 412, 415, 428, 437, 457–63, 473–77, 480, 509, 552, 570, 574, 605, 641, 645–49, 651, 654–55, 655, 666–68, 673, 681, 684, 693–94, 708, 713, 715
indifference. *See* detachment; equanimity; impartiality
indigenous peoples, 157
indigenous religions, 58, 60, 78, 410, 657
indoctrination, 11, 30, 35, 72, 595, 713, 717–19, 730
Indonesia, 310
Indra, 439
"Indra's Jeweled Net," 579
Indus River, 478
Indus Valley Civilization. *See* Harappa culture
industrialization, 476, 569, 602, 610–11, 630, 709, 719
ineffability. *See* apophasis
inertia. *See tamas*
inferior parietal lobule, 28
inferior temporal lobe, 28
infinitude. *See* eternity
inflammation, 395, 531
ingestion, 58, 557
inhalation, 96–97, 105, 121, 279, 281, 287, 291, 298–300, 339, 371, 400, 402, 486, 582–83, 597, 607, 642. *See also* breathing
inheritance, 24, 92, 154, 201–2, 506, 540
initiation, 62, 79, 218, 308, 311, 314, 321–22, 366, 646, 648, 667
injury. *See* harm

innate nature, 55, 72, 89, 95, 110, 121–22, 132, 134, 141, 483, 548, 553, 555, 561, 565, 579–81, 583, 643, 673, 710, 715–16
inner cultivation lineages, 58, 67, 71, 79, 89–143, 558, 707, 710, 723
inner landscape, 574
inner life. *See* interiority
Inner Light, 151, 157–58, 172. *See also* Christ Within; Inward Teacher
inner observation. See *neiguan*
inner power. See *de*
inner teacher, 318
innocence, 176, 196, 371, 382, 661, 680, 683, 693
Innocent III, 506–7, 509
Innocent XI, 148
innovation. *See* adaptation
inquiry, 25, 59, 75, 166, 253, 287, 302, 304, 324, 327, 340, 401, 478, 513, 653, 655, 657, 659–61, 665, 668–69, 671–73, 685, 688–89, 691, 694, 697–98, 702, 706, 711, 723
Inquisition, 154
insanity, 38, 573
insiders. *See* adherents; emic; first-person discourse
insight, 69, 267, 271, 276–77, 279, 284, 286–87, 289, 293, 355, 376, 415, 429, 477, 490, 493, 501, 579, 591, 647, 653, 657, 663, 668, 672–73, 692–93, 707, 710–11, 715, 719, 723–24
insight into the non-arising of *dharma*s, 418–19, 441, 447, 450–51, 454
Insight into Truth. *See Tattvavaiśāradī*
insight meditation. *See vipassanā*
inspection. *See* observation
inspiration, 44, 149, 393–94, 515, 538–39, 555, 712, 719
Institute of Buddhist Studies, 424
institutional religion. *See* religion
institutions, 20, 35, 93, 146, 323, 422, 433, 551, 597, 645, 650–51, 653–54, 657, 663, 666, 673, 691, 699
instruction. *See* guidance; teaching
"Instructions for the Cook." *See* "Tenzo kyōkun"
instrumentalism, 604, 656
insurance industry, 623
integral psychology, 327
Integral Yoga Institute, 475
integralism, 24, 327, 512, 672–73, 719
integration, 25, 37, 71, 81, 128, 236, 505, 556, 558, 565, 571, 580, 588, 656, 671, 681, 719
Integrative Restoration, 20, 606, 623, 718

intellect, 71, 95, 122, 152, 206, 251, 256–57, 261, 318, 360, 369, 429, 465–66, 468–69, 472, 498, 500, 512, 523, 527, 667, 681, 694, 708, 713
intellectual history, 568–69, 574
intensity. *See* effort
intention, 160, 181, 215, 235, 240, 245, 253–54, 267, 309, 341, 350, 517, 524, 572, 581, 583, 654, 659, 662
intercession, 4, 373, 521–23, 537. *See also* mediation
interdependence, 410, 552, 579, 671
interdisciplinarity, 3, 12–13, 17, 22, 41, 69, 73–74
interior prayer. *See* contemplative prayer
interior temple, 374
interiority, 4, 6–7, 25, 32, 37, 54, 58, 114, 134, 146–47, 151, 153–54, 156–57, 162–63, 165–66, 171, 175–82, 185, 187–89, 192–93, 221, 274, 310, 318, 321, 337–38, 346, 350, 355–57, 359, 365, 367, 370, 372, 374, 376–77, 379, 382, 385, 390, 392–94, 396, 398, 400–2, 405, 468, 483, 486–87, 494, 512, 520–21, 524, 526, 560, 571, 574, 581, 586, 645, 653, 657, 659, 670, 672, 679, 681, 683, 685–86, 696, 707–8, 711, 716, 719, 728. *See also* enstatic; introvertive
intermediary. *See* mediation
interment. *See* burial
internal alchemy. See *neidan*
International Mevlana Foundation, 59
International Society for Krishna Consciousness, 59, 475
internet, 166, 323
interpretation, 12–13, 15–16, 18, 30–31, 33–40, 44, 54, 61, 72, 74, 77–78, 108, 113, 167, 200–1, 287, 324–25, 360, 376, 398–99, 401–2, 425–31, 455, 462, 473–74, 514–15, 523, 552, 562, 579, 600, 603, 606, 611–13, 617–20, 622, 655, 705–35
interreligious dialogue, 25, 42, 74, 167, 706, 720, 723–24, 727
intersubjectivity, 35, 64, 81, 327, 471, 491, 505, 512, 611, 650–51, 671–73, 706, 716
intertextuality, 145, 147–49, 363, 366, 376, 707
interventionism, 32
interviews, 42, 55, 621, 624
intimacy, 68, 222, 310, 318–19, 321, 338, 340, 342–44, 346–47, 350–51, 353–57, 376, 401, 511, 520, 652

intoxication, 175, 194, 267, 329, 378, 404, 636, 650
Introduction to the Devout Life, 160
introvertive, 82, 93, 112–13, 128–29, 152, 157, 163, 177, 320, 513, 707–8, 716
intuition, 277, 488, 496
invented tradition, 548
inventories, 730
investigation. *See* inquiry
invincibility. *See* protection
invisibility, 495
invocation, 4, 7, 21, 373, 376, 389, 392, 396, 400, 405, 438, 453, 513, 708
inward prayer. *See* contemplative prayer
Inward Teacher, 158, 172–73, 178. *See also* Christ Within; Inner Light
Inward Training. *See Neiye*
Iqbal Academy, 321
Iran, 202, 310
Iraq, 202, 312, 316, 328, 341, 718
Ireland, 519, 525, 529
iRest. *See* Integrative Restoration
Irkutsk, 360, 363, 377
iron chain, 518, 534
Irshad Husayn, 314
Isaac, 256, 263
Isaac Nineveh, 391
Isaac of Acre, 208, 210, 213–14, 224, 236, 238, 243–44
Isaac the Blind, 204, 206, 243
Isaac the Syrian, 391
Isaiah, 176, 183, 194, 389
Isaiah the Solitary, 392
Isidore of Seville, 531
Isipatana, 291
Iskatelia neprestannoi molitivy, 361, 363–64, 366–67, 383
ISKCON. *See* International Society for Krishna Consciousness
Islam, 4, 8, 37, 54, 58–60, 68, 75, 77, 81, 205, 307–57, 409, 478, 648, 654, 707, 712, 721
Islamic law. *See shari'a*
Islamization, 310
Israel, 198, 216, 218, 220, 236, 245–46, 257, 383, 386, 518, 522
Israelites, 204
Isserles, Moshe, 217
Istanbul, 59, 313, 323, 328, 361, 368, 370, 393, 474

Īśvara, 469–71, 479, 485, 488, 491–92
Īśvarakṛṣṇa, 464
Italian, 514
Italy, 79, 200, 203, 214, 216–17, 223, 392, 503–4, 509–10, 513–14, 528, 531, 541, 593, 613, 617
itinerancy, 503, 508–9, 524–25, 544–45
Iyengar, Bellur Krishnamachar Sundararaja (B. K. S.), 475
Iyengar Yoga, 475

Jacob, 181, 256, 263
Jacobson, Edmund, 623
Jahanbabadi, Kalimullah, 313
Jahangir, 313
Jainism, 39, 58, 60, 81, 268, 460–61, 465, 471, 475, 479, 491, 656
Jalal ad-Din Rumi. *See* Rumi
Jambu River, 443–44, 446–47
Jambudvīpa, 439
James, William, 40, 42, 164, 325, 594, 605, 672, 717, 720
Janney, Samuel McPherson, 163
Janson, James, 145–46, 149–51, 156–57, 164, 166–67, 171
jāpa, 475
Japan, 18–19, 55–56, 286, 408, 410–11, 419, 422–25, 432–33, 552, 602, 613, 617, 633, 717
Japanese Samurai codes, 624
Jarrett, Bede, 511
Jātakas, 266, 291
Jayakar, Pupul, 655
Jazirat al-Rawda, 200
Jellenik, Adolph, 206
Jeongto, 410
Jericho, 373
Jerusalem, 158, 196, 197, 206, 216, 223, 226, 361, 377–78, 383, 386, 540
Jesuits. *See* Society of Jesus
Jesus Christ, the Bearer of the Water of Life: A Christian Reflection on the New Age, 81
Jesus of Nazareth, 157–58, 173–74, 186, 367, 373–74, 382, 386, 388, 403, 508, 518, 520, 537, 540, 674, 691, 721. *See also* Christ
Jesus Prayer, 57, 63, 73, 359–405, 518, 533, 707
jewels, 263, 439–41, 474, 487, 491, 579
Jewish law. *See halakha; torah*
Jewish Renewal, 226
jhāna. *See dhyāna*

jiafu zuo, 564
Jiangsu, 437, 567
Jiangxi, 411, 548–51, 555
Jianye, 437
Jiazai, 428, 434
jihad, 312
Jilani, 'Abdulqadir al-, 312, 328
Jileguo, 433
Jindan yaojue, 549, 556
Jin'gai mountains, 550, 573
Jin'gai xindeng, 573
jing (scripture), 555
jing (vital essence), 99, 101, 103–5, 109, 111, 120–21, 125–26, 133, 138, 143, 555, 557–58, 561, 571, 574, 578–79, 581
jingshen, 104, 133–35, 143
Jingtu, 6, 56, 59, 65, 78, 407–55, 552, 580, 582, 708, 710, 712–13. *See also* Jōdo
Jingtu lun, 429, 433
Jingtu shiyi lun, 426–27, 429
Jingying Huiyuan, 411, 419–20, 432
jingzuo, 58, 560
Jinhua zongzhi, 549, 567–68
jinn, 335
Jinxian zhenglun, 555, 561, 563, 567, 584
Jiujiang, 411, 549
Jīvaka, 438
Jixia Academy, 90
Jizang, 419
jñāna, 459, 461
jñāna yoga, 460–61, 475
Jōdo, 407, 410–11, 422–24, 433
Jodo Mission of Hawaii, 433
Jōdo Shinshū, 411, 423–24, 432–33
Jodo-shu North America Buddhist Mission, 433
Jogye Order, 56
jōgyō zanmai, 433
John Hopkins University, 622
John of Damascus, 531
John of Karpathos, 404
John of the Cross. *See* Juan de la Cruz
John W. Henry and Company, 597
Jois, Pattabhi, 475
Jonah, 252
Jones, Rufus, 164–65
Jordan of Saxony, 517
Jōshū, 56
Joshua, 263

journals, 151, 156, 370, 655, 678
journey, 160, 162, 318–19, 346, 382, 401, 403, 405, 448, 469, 505, 515, 524–25, 531, 536, 544–45, 567, 669, 705, 708
Journey to the Holy Land, 385
joy, 135, 162, 174, 184–86, 190, 192, 195–96, 217, 235, 237, 240, 250, 266, 269, 279, 282, 287, 298–99, 301–5, 341, 351, 365, 372, 392, 394–96, 398, 401, 403, 413, 441, 451–52, 454–55, 484, 486, 488, 492, 524, 535, 537, 579, 617, 638, 643, 646, 650, 679, 713
Juan de la Cruz, 42, 58, 148, 160, 730
Judah the Pious, 214, 237
Judaism, 39, 54, 58, 60, 74, 77, 80, 158, 197–264, 385, 388, 518, 524, 593–94, 606, 620, 623, 631, 638, 640, 648, 707, 710, 712, 721
Judea, 524
Judge, William, 647
judgment, 142, 188, 210, 235–36, 465, 511, 541, 646, 662, 702
jugular vein, 341
Junayd, 316, 341–42
Jung, Carl, 326, 568–69, 574–75
junzi, 93
Jurchens, 548
jurists. *See* ulama
just sitting. *See* shikan taza
justice. *See* social justice
"Jūundō-shiki," 19

Kaaba, 309
Kabat-Zinn, Jon, 20–21, 293, 604–6
Kabbalah, 60, 197–264, 615, 620, 638, 648, 707, 710
kabbalah ma'asit, 241
kabbalah shimushit, 241
Kabbalat ha-Ari, 201
Kagyu, 286
kaivalya, 59, 461, 469, 472–73, 498–501
Kālayaśas, 407–9, 413, 437
Kalimullah Jahanabadi. *See* Jahanbabadi
Kallistos. *See* Callistus II Xanthopoulos
Kamakura period, 19, 422, 432
kamma. *See* karma
kammaṭṭhāna, 278
Kant, Immanuel, 70
Kaplan, Aryeh, 218, 226, 234
Kapleau, Philip, 80

kardia, 374
karma, 19, 39, 268, 277, 410–11, 414, 416, 434, 439–40, 444–46, 448, 450–55, 461, 470, 472, 475, 485, 489, 495, 499, 501, 561, 565, 611, 641, 646–48, 656, 673
karma yoga, 460–61, 475, 499
karmāśaya, 471
karmic materiality. See *prakṛti*
Karo, Joseph, 203
Karpathos, 404
kashf, 357
kashrut, 247, 594
kasiṇa, 278, 289
Kāśyapa, 552, 588. See also Mahākassapa
kataphasis, 512
Katha Upaniṣad, 459
Kattika, 280, 296
Katz, Steven, 15
Kausokalybites, Maximos, 392
kavanah, 205, 217
Kavka, Martin, 221–22
kavod, 373
Kāyagatāsati Sutta, 275
Kazakhstan, 328
Kazan, 360, 363–64, 371, 378, 388
Keating, Thomas, 19, 33, 58, 153
Kelly, Thomas, 166
kenosis, 527
Kenoyer, J. M., 459
kenshō, 620, 715
Kephalaia Praktika Kai Theologika. See "153 Practical and Theological Texts"
Kepler, Johannes, 325
kernels, 312
Ketavim Hadashim shel R. Hayyim Vital, 197
Keyserling, Hermann Alexander Graf, 568
Khalid al-Kurdi. See Kurdi
Khidr, 317, 352
Khin, Ba, 80
Khitrovo, V. N., 383
Khundian Sharif, 314
Khwaja Muhammad Ma'sum, 313, 342
Khyber Pakhtunkhwa, 323
kidneys, 133–34, 136, 557–58, 574, 578–80, 634–36
Kiev, 368, 385
Kiev Caves Lavra, 366
killing. See violence

kindness, 131, 209, 244, 262, 271, 291, 336, 378, 415, 447, 452, 470, 583, 594, 712
kinesthetic. See movement
King, Richard, 69
King James Bible, 150, 171, 274
kingdom of heaven, 163, 171, 177–78, 186, 194, 196, 372, 385, 398, 400, 403, 524, 540
kings. See politics; royalty; specific kings
kīrtan, 8, 475
kissing, 197, 220–21, 249–50, 524, 543
Klein, Anne, 40
kleśa, 472, 557, 579
Klipper, Miriam, 606, 629
kloyzim, 202
knapsack, 359, 376–77, 379, 388, 397
kneeling, 385, 405, 440, 451, 513, 515, 518–20, 525, 527, 533, 535–36, 609, 639, 641
knots, 128, 191, 385, 394
knowing, 24, 25, 70, 98, 125, 129–30, 142, 157, 483, 488, 491–92, 659, 665, 679, 683–84, 697, 701–2, 715. See also epistemology
knowledge of God. See gnosis
kōan, 56, 620, 622
Kois, Margaret, 596
Kokand, 313
Kolzow, Andrew, 529
Komjathy, Louis, 39, 44, 70, 109
Komudī, 280, 296
Kongtong, 115
Kongzi, 91, 99, 130–31
Konya, 312
Kook, Abraham Isaac, 224
Korea, 55, 286, 408, 410, 419, 421–24, 613, 617
Kornfield, Jack, 80
kośa, 478
Kosawa Heisaku, 425
kosher. See *kashrut*
koujue, 566
Kozelsk, 363, 366
Kozlov, Mikhail, 359, 361, 363–67, 383–84, 388
Kripal, Jeffrey, 40, 80, 330
Krishnamāchārya, 474–75
Krishnamurti, Jiddu, 53, 64, 66, 81, 602, 645–74, 677, 709–10, 716
Krishnamurti Foundation, 651–52, 667–68, 677
kriyā yoga, 470, 472, 479, 488
Kṛṣṇa, 460, 475, 646, 648, 673–74
kṣatriya, 438

Kuan-tzu. See Guanzi
Kuanglu, 549, 551
Kubrawi lineage, 317
Kugle, Scott, 329
Kuhn, Thomas, 325
Kumārajīva, 112, 432
Kundalinī Yoga, 59
Kundun, 633
Kunlun. *See* Mount Kunlun
Kuo Hsiang. See Guo Xiang
Kurdi, Khalid al-, 313
Kushinagar, 291
Kuthumi, 649, 656, 674
Kwok, Jenny, 289, 293
Kyoto, 424
Kyrie Iesou Christe, Yie tou Theou, eleison me, 384, 392

La Ciencia Tomista, 514
La Combe, François, 148
la illaha illa Allah, 309, 317, 338, 350–53
labor. *See* work
laboratories, 34, 310, 605, 611, 619, 622, 639, 719
Laboratory for Clinical Physiology, 623
labyrinth walking, 727
labyrinths, 705, 724–28, 730
Lacordaire, Henri-Dominique, 511
Lahore, 321, 323
laity. *See* laypeople
lakes, 418
lakṣaṇa, 565, 586
Lam-rim chen-mo, 57, 730
lamps, 179, 301, 467, 491, 573, 636
Land of Utmost Bliss. *See* Sukhāvatī
Landau, Ezekiel, 226
landowners, 313, 361, 389–90
language, 7, 29, 60, 72–73, 75–76, 89, 106, 110, 114, 121–23, 145, 147, 156, 166, 168, 172, 176, 197, 203, 208–9, 212, 217–20, 226, 236–38, 254–55, 258, 265, 287, 307, 311, 317, 319, 321–24, 338, 340, 348–49, 351, 353, 359, 366, 371–73, 375, 380, 384, 392, 407, 409, 457–58, 470, 476, 479, 485, 487–88, 495, 503, 507, 519, 524, 543, 547, 556, 566, 593, 596, 599, 607, 609, 616, 633, 638, 641–42, 645, 660–61, 671–73, 677–80, 684, 687, 707, 710, 713, 726. *See also* specific languages

Laṅkāvatāra Sūtra, 730
Lanshakov, Iakov, 385
Lanzetta, Beverly, 728
Lao Dan, 91
Lao-tzu. See Laozi
Laow, Ajahn Maha, 292
Laozi (person), 91
Laozi (text), 76, 89–91, 93–94, 98–100, 102–11, 113, 120; translation of, 122–23, 127–29, 139–40
Laozi xiang'er zhu, 108
Larson, Gerald James, 464
larynx, 394
lashing. *See* flagellation
Lateran IV, 506
latifa, 316, 333, 344
Latin, 54, 292, 368, 507, 514, 519, 569
Latin West, 508, 531
laughter, 135, 524, 527, 542
laxity, 147, 193, 240, 350, 393, 395, 400, 467, 486, 507, 644, 689, 713
laying the foundations, 560
laypeople, 62, 79–80, 154, 267, 271, 274–75, 280, 286, 289, 292–93, 296, 359, 361, 364, 366, 369, 376, 380–81, 407, 410, 413, 419, 423–24, 434, 454–55, 506–7, 510, 551–53, 560, 566, 606, 611
Leadbeater, Charles Webster, 648–49
learning, 9, 128, 204, 241, 268, 292, 311, 366, 381, 392, 405, 423, 460, 469, 505, 659, 663–65, 667, 669–70, 673, 695–96, 725
lectio divina, 4, 58, 75, 166, 370, 523
lectures. *See* public talks
ledgers of merit and demerit. See *gongguo ge*
Legge, James, 568
legitimation. *See* confirmation
legs. *See* limbs
leifa, 550
"Lekha Dodi," 198
Lengyan jing, 551, 553, 559, 579, 586, 589
Lengyan zhou, 589
Lent, 519
Leo the Great, 531
lepers, 520, 535
Lesser Celestial Cycle. *See* Microcosmic Orbit
lethargy, 160, 467, 573
letter permutation, 60, 197, 201, 206, 208–9, 211, 213, 215, 217, 219, 223, 225, 234–35, 241–42, 254–55, 264, 707

letters (genre), 154, 313–14, 319, 323, 363, 367
levels, 13, 29–31, 69–70, 237, 242, 251, 253, 259, 261, 270–71, 290, 296–97, 310, 319, 323, 342, 369–70, 374–75, 377, 381, 383, 409, 412, 415–16, 418, 420, 428, 449–54, 470, 551, 554, 561, 572, 579, 599, 620, 622, 644, 647–48, 674, 695, 712, 715–16, 725, 730. *See also* stages
Levine, Samuel, 630
levitation, 250, 403, 497, 538
li (patterns/principle), 104, 107, 115, 131
Li Hanxu, 563
Li Niwan, 550
Li Xiren, 550
Li Zhenyuan, 549, 567
liberal arts, 11, 35, 725
liberation, 26, 59, 66, 71, 81, 267, 272, 276, 278, 282–84, 290, 292, 298–300, 305, 400, 410–11, 442, 453, 457, 461–62, 464–65, 468, 472–74, 477, 485, 490, 493, 498, 501, 507, 584, 589, 591–92, 641, 656, 715, 730
libraries, 109, 360, 361–62, 365, 367, 370, 382–83, 392, 503, 507, 514, 525, 531
Library of Congress, 649
life management skills, 598
life-destiny. See *ming*
light, 137, 151–52, 154, 158, 172, 178, 180–81, 191, 193–94, 196, 200, 203, 208, 237–38, 245, 252–57, 278, 342–43, 345–52, 355–57, 365, 372, 375, 384, 390–92, 395, 398, 401–3, 439–40, 442–44, 446–48, 450–53, 465–68, 495–97, 523, 561, 565, 584, 586, 589, 591–92, 636, 645, 648, 650, 657, 660, 664, 673, 677–78, 680–81, 683, 695, 697–99, 701, 707, 710, 724, 728
Light of the Jewel of Yoga. See *Yogamaṇiprabhā*
Light on Haṭha Yoga. See *Haṭha-yoga-pradīpikā*
limbic system, 28
limbs, 97, 125, 127, 139, 249, 261, 341, 351, 459, 474, 521–23, 538, 560, 586, 637
lineage, 55, 58–59, 62, 90, 92–94, 106, 110, 179, 223, 273, 275, 307–8, 312, 318, 325, 328, 330, 337, 352, 363, 393, 424, 433, 474–76, 547–51, 553, 555–57, 566, 569–70, 572, 581, 595–96, 600, 602–3, 605–6, 646–47, 655, 707
Linji lineage, 56
lips, 374–75, 392, 515

listening, 131, 172–73, 178, 187, 220, 251, 269, 273–75, 280, 292, 296–305, 354–55, 361, 380, 389, 392–94, 396–97, 400, 402, 440, 444, 453–55, 496–97, 520–21, 524, 537, 542, 544, 653, 657, 664, 667, 669, 679, 706, 719, 728
litanies, 322, 330, 337, 393
Litany of the Saints, 518
literacy, 75, 175, 292, 397, 574
literary criticism, 360
literature, 9, 11, 79. *See also* texts
liturgy, 37, 63, 146, 153, 158, 199, 202, 242, 271, 367–68, 372, 380–81, 384, 388, 393, 505–6, 508–10, 516–18, 520, 524–25, 527–28, 534, 537, 541, 707. *See also* ritual
Liturgy of Hours, 63, 542. *See also* Divine Office
Liu An, 92, 106, 114, 120
Liu Huayang, 64, 66, 547–48, 550–52, 555–67, 571–74, 578, 713
Liu Yiming, 567
Liu-Song dynasty, 437
lived religion, 3, 10, 35, 64, 74–75, 94, 419, 424, 726
livelihood, 11, 267, 377, 385, 396, 423, 594, 644, 682, 724, 729. *See also* work
location. *See* place
locatedness, 11, 13–22, 34–35, 63
Lockhart Building, 618, 624
logic. *See* rationality
logos, 369, 375
Logos (Christ), 172, 189–91, 195, 371–75, 398, 512
Lokottaravāda, 412
Lombardy, 504
London, Peter, 629
loneliness, 68, 180, 185, 196, 573, 678, 680, 692, 712
longevity, 110, 550, 555, 584–85
Longgang, 550
longing, 68, 300, 302–3, 340, 354–55, 389–90, 395, 397, 543, 705
Longmen Grottoes, 427
Longmen lineage, 547–51, 555, 562, 567–68, 573–74, 578
Loori, John Daido, 41, 80
Lord. *See* God
Lord Jesus Christ, Son of God, have mercy on me, 371, 373, 380, 384, 392, 393–94, 400, 518, 533

Lord of the World, 674
Lord of Yoga. See Īśvara
Lord's Prayer, 395
Los Angeles, 635
lost practices, 82. See also reconstructed practices
lostness. See disorientation
lotus flower, 279–80, 296–97, 414, 418, 420, 428, 439–40, 443–48, 451–55, 588–89
lotus-posture, 288, 293, 298, 441, 459, 471, 478, 492, 564–65, 586, 609, 641
Lotus Sūtra, 419
Louis XIV, 148
love, 43, 57–58, 81, 160, 162, 165, 172, 174–77, 179, 181, 193–96, 220–21, 250, 310–12, 318, 322, 333, 336, 341–45, 350, 353, 375, 378, 396, 398, 400–3, 515–16, 520, 527, 533, 604, 630, 651, 661, 665–66, 670, 677–78, 680–83, 688, 695–97
Love of the Beautiful. See *Philokalia*
Lover of Beauty. See *Philokalia*
loving-kindness. See *mettā*
Lü Dongbin, 554
Lu K'uan Yü, 574
lu-registers, 561
lucidity. See clarity; *sattva*
Lucknow, 307
Lüezhu jinglun nianfo famen wangsheng jingtu ji, 426
Luk, Charles, 574
Luke 18:13, 384–85, 392, 533
Lukka, Irina, 383
Lumbinī, 291
"Lun zhengyan," 561
Lunyu, 59
Luoyang, 427
Luria, Isaac, 197–202, 210, 213–14, 216–17, 219, 225, 244
Lurianic Kabbalah, 60, 77, 197–264, 707
Lushan, 411, 549
Lushan Huiyuan, 411
Lüshi chunqiu, 92, 98–99
Luther, Martin, 423, 508
Lutyens, Edwin, 655
Lutyens, Mary, 655
Lutz, Antoine, 30
lying, 267, 414, 559
lying down, 194, 268, 338, 393, 422, 609, 639, 641

Ma'arekhet Ha-Elohut, 246–47
Macarius of Egypt, 149
macrocosm. See universe
Macrocosmic Orbit, 560
Madanapalle, 645
Mādhyamaka, 419, 427
Madras, 646–47
Madrid, 314
Māgadha, 437
magistrates, 377
Magnetic Encephalography, 114
Mahābhārata, 460–62, 478, 480
Mahācunda, 296
Mahākaccana, 292, 296
Mahākappina, 296
Mahākassapa, 296
Mahākoṭṭhita, 296
Mahāmaudgalyāyana, 416, 438–39, 455
Mahāmudrā, 69, 286
Mahāpirit, 274, 292
Maharishi Mahesh, 21, 28, 480, 599, 602–3, 616, 620, 624, 642, 681
Mahāsamaya Sutta, 292
Mahāsaṃghika, 412
Mahāsthāmaprāpta, 414, 418, 444, 446, 448–55
Mahāsudassana Sutta, 272
mahatma, 647, 674
Mahāvastu, 416, 432
Mahāvihāra, 286
Mahāvīra, 268
Mahāyāna, 55, 67, 112, 269, 319, 407–55, 552–53, 559–60, 565, 571, 579, 712, 715, 730
Mahmud Effendi, 323
Mahmud Ustaosmanoğlu, 313
Mahmut II, 313
Maimonides, Moses, 206, 217, 240, 248
Main, John, 80
Maitreya, 427–28, 431, 648, 674
Maitrī Upaniṣad, 459–60, 462, 478
majjhimā paṭipadā, 267, 271, 430
Majjhimanikāya, 275
Major Trends in Jewish Mysticism, 14, 216, 223
Makarii, 366
Makarios of Corinth, 370, 383–84, 392
Maktubat, 313–14, 319, 323–24, 329–30, 339, 349
malaria, 646
mammals, 24, 636
mana, 465–66

Manahij al-sayr, 315
Manchus, 548
mandala, 278, 417
Mandonnet, Pierre, 511
Manichaeism, 507, 513
manifesting the Transformation Body, 564, 590
Mañjuśrī, 437
Mansur 'Ali Khan, 308
mantra, 6–7, 20–21, 37, 57–58, 82, 113, 309, 317, 338, 350–53, 359, 384, 392, 416, 420–21, 453–54, 475–76, 479, 485, 498, 513, 596–97, 599, 602, 607–9, 616, 620, 633, 638, 641–42, 646, 656, 681, 710. *See also* language; sound
manuscripts, 91, 94, 201, 206, 211, 214, 216–17, 224–25, 234, 285, 330, 361, 363–67, 369–71, 376–77, 383, 388, 474, 503–4, 514–15, 525–26, 531, 562, 567
mappō, 411, 422
maps. *See* cartography
maqaam, 68, 310–11, 314, 318–19, 329–30, 335–36, 343, 346–49, 357, 712
Marine Corps Air Station, 624
marks, 278, 298, 377, 443, 445–47, 467, 471, 565, 586, 691
marriage, 147, 377, 423, 527, 551, 646, 651–52, 682, 691
marrow, 173, 537, 544
Marsh Chapel Experiment. *See* Good Friday Experiment
Martha, 191
martial arts, 23, 53, 79, 324
martyrs, 312
Mary, 191, 533, 693, 728
Maslow, Abraham, 22–23, 43, 70, 714
Masonic Auditorium, 678, 693
Mass, 37, 510, 521, 524, 527, 531, 537–38, 728
Massachusetts, 593, 597, 603, 618
Massachusetts General Hospital, 20, 593, 597, 618
Massachusetts Institute of Technology, 603
Master General, 503, 510, 516
Master Kong. *See* Kongzi
Master Lai, 100
Master Lao. *See* Laozi
Master Zhuang. *See* Zhuangzi
masters. *See* elders; teachers
mastery. *See* attainment; levels; power; progress
material culture, 56, 59, 63, 96–97, 154–55, 202, 266, 270, 376–78, 385, 417, 432–33, 459, 503–4, 508, 513–14, 516, 528, 532–45, 561, 566, 618, 620, 649, 652, 667, 708, 718, 726–28. *See also* specific types
material world. *See* world
materialism, 7, 326, 458, 476–77, 512, 708. *See also* secular materialism
materialistic religiosity, 458
Mathnawi-yi ma'nawi, 314, 330, 345
Matins, 393
Matt, Daniel, 219
maturation, 564
Mawangdui, 91, 94
mawlana, 308
Maximes des saints, 148
Maxims of the Saints. *See Maximes des saints*
May, Gerald, 160
MBSR. *See* Mindfulness-Based Stress Reduction
McGill University, 622, 635
meaning. *See* existentialism
measurement, 5, 7, 21, 391, 597, 599–601, 603, 613, 619, 631–34, 636, 639, 678–81, 684, 688, 692, 700, 713
meat. *See* slaughtered animal flesh
Mecca, 309, 328
Meccan Revelations. *See Al-Futūḥāt al-Makkiyya*
Mediaeval Studies, 514, 531
mediating *shaykh*, 322
mediation, 26, 32, 208, 311, 315, 322, 343, 373, 523, 657, 664, 681, 717, 719
medical anthropology, 600, 629
medical offices, 595
medicalization, 7, 20, 33, 36, 595, 597–98, 600, 604–5, 607, 616–17, 619–21, 642, 672, 718–19, 729
medicalized meditation. *See* therapeutic meditation
medication. *See* pharmaceutical drugs
medicine, 183, 284, 311, 361, 377, 397, 458, 460, 593–601, 604, 613, 622, 630–31, 635, 643, 718–19. *See also* healing; specific types
meditatio, 4, 521, 542
meditation, 4–6, 8, 16, 22, 24, 26, 28, 35, 37, 39–40, 54, 60, 65, 73, 77, 162, 194, 206, 209, 218, 222, 265–66, 328, 343, 379, 421, 423, 431, 433, 445–46, 460–61, 467, 470–71, 476, 491, 493–94, 548–49, 552, 571, 579, 600–6, 655–57, 662–63, 665–66, 669–70, 673–74, 678–702, 707–11, 725, 727; as independent tradition, 37, 60–61, 602, 605–6, 619, 623; as

meditation *(continued)*
  medicine, 593, 597, 600–6, 617, 623–24; as new religious movement, 602, 605; as relaxation method, 593, 596, 600–6, 638; as scientific, 602–3; as supposed Asian/Eastern discipline, 57; as technique, 604–5; weaponization of, 624, 718. *See also* contemplative practice; specific types
Meditation and Kabbalah, 218, 226
Meditation and the Bible, 218
Meditation and the Classroom, 10
Meditation as Medicine, 604
meditation hall, 56, 274
meditation manuals, 72, 314, 462, 478, 558. *See also* contemplative literature; specific texts
meditation room. *See* rooms
Meditationes de prima philosophia, 464, 632
Meditations (Krishnamurti), 655
Meditations on First Philosophy. See Meditationes de prima philosophia
meditative absorption. *See* absorption
meditative mind, 30, 73, 415, 447
mediumship, 7, 513, 548
meeting for worship. *See* silent worship
meeting house, 154–55, 167
meetings (Quaker), 146
MEG. *See* Magnetic Encephalography
Meghiya, 271, 284
Meier, Fritz, 330
Meiji period, 423
Meister Eckhart. *See* Eckhart von Hochheim
melancholy. *See* sadness
melete, 521
melting, 401–2
membership, 650–51, 663, 666, 668, 673, 698. *See also* affiliation; adherence
memorization, 292, 308, 393, 462, 521, 563
memory, 25, 29, 266, 268, 271, 278, 292, 296, 375, 393, 400, 403, 439, 462, 464, 479, 483, 485, 487, 489, 495, 499–500, 514, 608, 644, 646, 651, 659, 661–63, 665, 677, 679, 681, 683, 685, 690, 692–93, 695, 699, 701, 706, 713, 724
Menahem Azaria da Fano, 203
mendicancy, 275, 297, 364, 373, 503, 506, 508–10, 523–25, 544–45, 729
Meninger, William, 33, 58
Mennonites, 167
menstruation, 558, 579, 610
mentors. *See* teachers
merchants, 396, 409, 416
mercuric sulfide, 556
mercury, 635
mercy, 174, 253, 371, 375, 388, 392–93, 395–96, 401, 438, 517, 522–23, 533, 535, 539–40
meridians, 557, 559–61, 565, 571, 584–85
merit, 297, 391, 398, 410, 413, 430, 437, 440, 448–50, 455
merit transference, 449, 451–52
Merton, Thomas, 80
Mesmer, Franz Anton, 600
Mesmerism, 600
mesmerized. *See* enchantment; hypnosis
messiah, 198–200, 203, 217, 246
messianism, 199–202, 214, 224, 328
metabolism, 21, 26, 595, 611, 616, 632–34
metaphor, 16, 32, 98–99, 101, 105, 111, 221, 270, 275, 288, 426, 430, 501, 579, 666, 671. *See also* specific metaphors
metaphysics, 23, 60, 113, 199, 201, 203, 214, 216, 219, 223, 376, 385, 425, 429, 460–61, 463, 465–67, 472–73, 479, 484, 487, 500, 590, 642, 694, 720
methodologies of the subjective, 327
methods. *See* techniques
Metropolitan Museum of Art, 417, 432
mettā, 55, 265, 269–70, 277, 284, 287, 290, 297, 712
Mevlana. *See* Jalal ad-Din Rumi
Mevlevi lineage, 59, 312
Mevlevi Lodge. *See* Galata Mevlevihanesi
Mevo Shearim, 224
Mexico, 509
mianbi. See biguan
Miaowu, 555
mice, 342
Michael (angel), 251
microcosm, 92, 330, 334–35
Microcosmic Orbit, 555, 557–60, 563–64, 582, 584–85
Middle East, 330. *See also* specific countries
middle way. *See majjhimā paṭipadā*
Middletown, 594
Midnight Office, 393
Midrash, 202, 204, 206, 220
Midrash Raba, 202

Migāra, 296
migraines, 44
mikro-schema, 364, 383
mikveh, 240, 242, 257
military, 93, 218, 423–24, 506–7, 623–24, 717–19, 730
Miller, Richard, 20, 606, 623, 718
Mīmāṁsā, 461, 479
Min Yide, 573
mind, 5, 16, 26, 32, 43–44, 66, 69, 71, 73, 93, 95, 98, 103–4, 114, 121, 125, 130–32, 142, 154, 174, 180, 209, 267, 265, 276, 282, 286, 289, 293, 299–300, 347, 352, 374, 377, 380, 392–93, 396, 398, 400, 431, 447, 463–68, 470–72, 476–77, 479, 486–87, 492, 494, 500–1, 525, 537, 553, 558, 593, 597, 605, 615, 619–20, 631–32, 656, 659–60, 663–64, 666, 671, 673, 679–82, 693, 695, 701–2, 708, 711, 715. See also consciousness; tradition-specific terms
Mind and Life Institute, 10, 603, 622
mind of God, 521
mind wandering, 641
mind-body. See psychosomatic
Mind/Body Medical Institute, 20, 593, 597, 603, 613, 618
Mind-Body Medicine, 8, 21, 62, 326, 593, 597, 600–6, 609–13, 617–19, 621, 631, 709
mind-seal, 591
mind-to-mind transmission, 553, 588
mindfulness, 5, 7, 9, 29, 55, 114, 152–53, 166, 265, 276, 287, 296, 298, 300, 444, 446, 449, 454–55, 517, 525–27, 529, 599, 604–5, 656, 713; as new religious movement, 605. See also *sati*; *vipassanā*
Mindfulness-Based Stress Reduction, 8, 20, 293, 604, 623
mindfulness of body, 281
mindfulness of breathing. See *ānāpāna-sati*
mindfulness of *dhamma*s, 283–84
mindfulness of feeling, 282
mindfulness of mind, 282–83
minding the Light, 156
ming (life-destiny), 127, 547–48, 555, 557, 565, 578–81, 585
Ming dynasty, 548–51, 566
mingmen. See Gate of Life
minimalism. See simplicity

ministers, 146, 156, 158, 163, 438–39, 513
ministry, 149, 156, 163, 504–5, 507–9, 512–13, 524–26, 528, 536, 544–45, 710. See also guidance; spiritual direction
Mir Dard, 308
Mir Nu'man, 314
miracles, 202, 220, 222, 379, 416, 515, 518, 522, 538, 600, 659, 678, 679
Miracula beati Dominici, 540
mirrors, 98–99, 106, 111, 128, 247–48, 319, 341, 345, 440–41, 445, 466–68, 472, 516, 671
Mirza Jan-i Janan, 308, 328–29
misfortune, 100, 107, 134, 137, 404–5, 448, 561
Mishkan Ha-Edut, 259–60
Mishna, 239–40, 262
Miskin Shah, 308
misogi, 81
missionaries, 173, 364, 368, 407–8, 413, 433, 441, 475, 505, 509, 511, 524–25, 528, 544–45, 552, 568–69, 647, 649
mistakes, 160, 176, 366, 381–82, 463, 498, 517, 566, 580, 583, 671. See also challenges; dangers; difficulties
mitdabek, 209
mitzvot, 200, 202–3, 205, 208–9, 240, 245, 261, 389, 533, 712
models, 93, 151, 272, 321, 326, 372, 378, 382, 392–393, 403, 410, 413, 434, 457, 472, 479, 496, 503–5, 508, 515–16, 531–45, 585, 600, 650–52, 664, 679–80, 682, 686, 694, 696, 708, 717, 726, 729
Modena, Leon, 217, 226
modernity, 37, 61, 78, 211, 216, 220, 322, 474–76, 612, 619, 629, 637, 640, 643, 709, 719
mofa, 411, 433
Moggallāna, 292, 296
Mohe zhiguan, 286
Mohenjo-daro, 459, 478
Moism, 106, 129
mokṣa, 59, 66, 457, 460–61, 472, 475, 477, 641
Moldavia, 370, 386
Moldavian Monastery, 361
Molinos, Miguel, 145, 147–49, 151, 153–54, 156–57, 160, 162–64, 166–67
monasteries, 287, 328, 360–61, 368, 382–83, 433, 503, 506–8, 510, 514, 528, 551, 565, 717. See also specific monasteries
Monastery of Saint Agnes, 79

Monastery of Saint John the Forerunner, 393
Monastery of Saint Mamas, 393
monastic manuals, 551. *See also* specific texts
monasticism, 3, 13, 20, 22, 32–34, 36–37, 55, 57–58, 62, 64, 159, 205, 265, 267–69, 275, 279, 287, 238, 359–60, 361, 363, 365–66, 368–70, 376–77, 381–83, 392–93, 408, 410, 416, 421, 503, 506, 509, 513–14, 519, 528, 538–39, 547–51, 553, 557, 559–60, 568, 707, 712, 724, 728
monastics, 32–33, 36, 43, 265, 267–69, 271, 273–75, 284, 289, 292, 296–305, 363–65, 373, 376–79, 381, 390, 392–93, 407–8, 411, 413, 419, 421–25, 432–34, 437, 451–52, 506, 508–9, 512, 523, 528, 547–52, 555, 559, 562, 565, 573, 585–86, 588, 622, 712
Mongols, 368
monism, 14, 35, 37, 74, 112, 378, 475, 711, 722
monkey keeper, 100, 112, 140
monkeys, 140, 595
monotheism, 14, 475, 656. *See also* God
Montreal, 622
moon, 124–25, 242, 280, 296–97, 442–43, 496, 574, 591–92, 689–90
morality. *See* ethics
Moreh Nevukhim, 206, 217, 240, 248
Morgenstern, Yizhak Meir, 226
mortification. *See* asceticism
Moscow, 360–61, 363, 365–66, 368, 383, 392
Moscow University, 366
Moses, 204, 248–49, 251, 255, 261, 322, 337, 352–53, 388, 517, 522, 524, 542, 708
Moshe de León, 259–60
mosques, 307, 311, 702
mosquitos, 244
mothers, 122–23, 184, 636, 646, 672. *See also* family; parents
motivation, 73, 79, 194, 361, 379, 393, 453, 468, 490, 499, 505, 548, 602, 621, 653, 680–82, 692, 701, 709
Mount Athos, 360–61, 363–64, 369–70, 376, 383, 388, 392–93
Mount Kunlun, 580
Mount Sinai, 388
Mount Sinai Hospital, 635
Mount Sumeru, 439–40, 445–46
Mount Wangwu, 550
Mount Zion, 196

mountains, 63, 115–16, 121, 124, 134, 142, 158, 196, 241, 250, 353, 370, 380, 423, 439, 519, 549–50, 560, 565–66, 580, 592, 619, 650, 705
"Mountains and Waters Sutra." *See* "Sansui-kyō"
movement, 7, 70, 81, 143, 192, 206, 222, 238, 351, 374, 380, 385, 400–1, 492, 510, 521, 524–25, 528, 535–36, 560, 580, 607–9, 659–60, 662, 664, 672, 679–80, 688, 693, 701–2, 706, 708, 711, 719, 728, 730
movement awareness, 4, 9, 53, 609
movement studies, 4, 9
Moy Lin-shin, 570
Moyen court et très facile pour l'oraison, 148, 150–51, 167, 174–75, 177, 180, 182–83, 187–90, 193–94
Moyers, Bill, 604
mozhao, 9, 18, 55, 558, 560
Mu, 56
mud, 105, 140, 404, 497
mudrā, 81, 266, 291, 417, 504, 521, 564
Mughal Empire, 313, 321, 323
Muhaddith, 307
Muhaddith of the Deccan. *See* 'Abdullah Shah
Muhammad, 307–9, 311–12, 321–22, 328, 335–38, 340, 347–48, 350–51, 353, 355
Muhammad Badshah Bukhari. *See* Bukhari
Muhammad ibn 'Abdulwahhab, 328
Muhammad Irshad Husayn, 314
Muhammad Ma'sum, 308
Muhammad Musa Amritsari. *See* Amritsari
Muhammad Parsa, 317
Muhammad Zubayr Sirhindi-Mujaddidi. *See* Sirhindi-Mujaddidi
Muhammadan reality, 315–16, 348–49
Mu'inuddin Chishti. *See* Chishti
mujaddid, 328–29, 333, 336, 339, 353, 356
Mujaddidi lineage. *See* Naqshbandi-Mujaddidi lineage
Mujaddidi Wayfaring. *See Suluk-i Mujaddidiyya*
mukabeleh, 312
Muktananda, 475
Müller, Max, 432
multiculturalism, 11, 720, 723, 727, *passim*
multidisciplinarity, 17
multilingualism, 495
multilocation, 24, 67, 439, 455, 559, 561, 590, 713

multiperspectivalism, 12
multivocality, 24, 713
Mun, Ajahn, 286
mundane world. *See* world
muraqaba, 54, 307–57
Murphy, Michael, 19, 23–24, 43
muscles, 5, 137–38, 339, 518, 607, 611, 632, 634, 637, 639, 641–42
mushahada, 309, 336
music, 4, 9, 11, 79, 81, 96, 130, 238, 267, 290, 312, 370, 381, 438, 442, 444, 507, 510, 542
muslim, 310. *See also* Islam
mustikos, 385
Muzaffar Husayn, 308
myocardial infarction. *See* heart attack
Myozen, 18
mysterious female. *See xuanpin*
mysteriousness, 94, 99, 122, 158, 166, 171, 196, 374, 391, 396, 399, 404, 517, 524, 526, 544, 583, 648, 680, 728
mystic powers. *See siddhi*
mystical being, 44
mystical body, 505, 517, 528, 558, 571, 709
mystical experience, 9, 14–15, 17, 37–38, 41, 44, 54, 60, 64–67, 72, 82, 112, 165, 204–5, 209, 213, 245, 365–66, 399, 416–18, 444, 548, 579, 592, 594, 620, 647, 650, 670, 681, 713, 725
mystical experiencing, 44
mystical literature, 72, 220
mysticism, 7, 9, 11, 13–14, 26, 35, 37, 58, 60, 65, 96, 112, 147, 161, 163, 167, 198, 201, 204–5, 221, 223, 307, 309–10, 327, 365, 372, 374, 379–81, 385, 392, 459, 505, 529, 571, 638, 647, 657, 672, 710, 712, 716
myth, 16, 94, 109, 204, 412–13, 425, 462, 648, 660, 678, 694, 710, 720–23, 726
Myth and Reality, 721

Na Mo Bu Dha Ya, 287
nāḍa yoga, 461
nāḍi, 496–97
nafs, 312, 317–20, 322, 330, 333–35, 337, 344–45, 349, 352–56
nāga, 455
Nāgārjuna, 433
Nahman of Bratslav, 208
Nahmanides, Moshe, 214, 220, 234, 236, 250–51, 255

Nahor, 243
naïveté, 13–14, 16, 365
Najmuddin Kubra, 316
Najmuddin Razi, 316
Nakamura Hajime, 431
nakedness, 161, 185, 196, 243, 392, 588
nāma, 289, 299
names, 94, 122–23, 136, 140, 167, 178, 181, 184, 209, 211, 215, 217, 220, 236–38, 242–44, 255, 311–12, 315, 319, 321, 334, 338, 340, 348–49, 353–54, 359, 366, 367, 373–74, 379, 385, 392, 395–96, 409, 411, 416, 419–24, 430, 453–55, 470, 485, 511, 520, 554, 561, 573, 580, 590, 630, 646, 666–67, 682–83, 693–94, 697, 716, 730. *See also* language
namo Amituofo, 416, 420–21, 453–54
namu Amida Butsu, 453
Ñāṇamoli, Bhikkhu, 275
Nanchang, 548–49, 555
Nanhua zhenjing, 89. *See also Zhuangzi*
Nanjing, 437
Nanu Majdhub, 308
Nanzong, 550
Naqshbandi lineage, 308, 311–12, 317–18, 322, 328, 336, 338, 346, 707
Naqshbandi-Mujaddidi lineage, 307–57
Naqshbandi-Qadiri lineage, 308, 311
Naqshbandiyya-Khalidiyya lineage, 313
Nara, 433
Narayaniah, Jiddu, 645–46
Naro-Fominsk, 366
Naropa University, 10
Nasiruddin Qadiri Dihlawi. *See* Dihlawi
Nasruddin, 320, 330
nationalism, 475, 568, 648, 651, 654, 657, 673, 682, 717–19, 730
Native American religions, 58, 78
natural selection, 632
naturalness, 67, 100, 375, 397, 403, 642–43, 651, 713
Nature, 19, 64, 94, 108–9, 152, 601, 632, 638, 648, 655, 688, 722
navel, 102, 136, 317, 350–51, 496, 558, 561, 564, 574, 580, 584
navel gazing, 716
NDE. *See* near death experiences
Neamt, 361, 384
near death experiences, 66

Near East, 309. *See also* specific countries
nearness. *See* proximity
Needham, Joseph, 574
Needleman, Jacob, 668
nefesh, 252–53, 256–57, 259–61
Nehru, Jawaharlal, 655
neidan, 8, 32, 38, 58–59, 64, 66, 68–69, 111, 115, 547–92, 708–9, 714, 716
neiguan, 58
Neiye, 72, 89–90, 95, 97, 99, 102–7, 109, 115, 120; translation of, 120–22, 125–27, 138–39
nembutsu, 411, 414, 422–23, 453–54
Neoplatonism, 198, 206, 222, 254, 648
Nepal, 291, 410, 432
nerves, 350
nervous system (human), 26–27, 601–2, 637. *See also* specific division
neshama, 253, 255, 259, 262
neshima, 253
Nestorian Christianity, 421
Netherlands, 649–50, 680
netherworld, 200
nets, 442–44, 665
neuroimaging, 3, 13, 17, 26, 28, 30–31, 33, 114, 603–4, 622, 725
neurophenomenology, 33, 622
neuroregions, 26–29, 43–44, 603–4
neuroscience, 3, 9–14, 17, 21–22, 26–33, 42, 55, 60, 69, 97, 113–14, 603, 619, 622, 719, 725, 730
neuroscientific reductionism. *See* reductionism
neurotheology, 44
neurotransmitters, 601, 612
neutrality, 55, 599, 603, 623
nevuah, 208, 210
New Age. *See* hybrid spirituality
new being, 191, 513
new consciousness, 518, 568, 657, 659, 663, 677
New Delhi, 655
New Directions for Community Colleges, 10
New Directions for Teaching and Learning, 10
New Hebrew, 222
new religious movements, 60, 605–6, 611, 619–20, 624, 666
New Revised Standard Version, 515
New Testament, 163, 371, 385, 386, 531
New York, 426, 593–94, 647
New York Times, 593, 613, 617, 633

Nguyen, Cuong Tu, 422
nian (recollection), 416
nianfo, 411, 414, 453–54
nibbāna. See *nirvāṇa*
Nicephorus the Monk, 386, 392, 394, 399, 401
Nicholson, James Michael, 570, 575
Nietzsche, Friedrich, 219, 729
nikāya, 275
Nikiphoros the Monk. *See* Nicephorus the Monk
Nikodemos of the Holy Mountain, 370, 383–84, 392
Nikon, 368
Nile, 200
nimbus. *See* halo
nine apertures, 104, 131, 138
nine cemetery contemplations, 66
Nine Essays on the Way of the Elixir. See *Dandao jiupian*
nine grades of rebirth, 409, 415–16, 418, 420, 430, 432, 449–54
Nine Palaces, 559
Nine Practices, 108, 132
nine steps of relaxation, 607–8
nine ways of praying, 503, 513–28, 531–45
Nine Ways of Praying of Saint Dominic. See *Novem modi orandi sancti Dominici*
Ninveh, 252
nirbīja samādhi, 469–70, 479, 488
nirodha, 469, 472, 494
nirvāṇa, 112, 277, 292, 297, 410, 562, 591, 699, 715, 721
Nirvāṇa Sūtra, 419
nirvicāra-samādhi, 487
nirvitarka-samāpatti, 487
Nityananada, 648, 650
niyama, 470–72, 491–92, 712
no-self. See *anātman*
Nobel Peace Prize, 633
nobility. *See* aristocracy
nonaction. See *wuwei*
Nonbeing, 110–11, 143, 580, 590
nonconceptual, 7, 9, 55, 469, 487, 553, 558–59, 591, 728
nondenominational. *See* nonsectarian
nondissipation, 557, 560–61, 564, 578–81
nondualism, 39, 55, 70, 95, 257, 266, 334, 374, 492, 553, 650, 654, 660–62, 667, 671, 722
nonretrogression, 412–13, 415, 428, 450

nonreturners, 280, 297, 440
nonsectarian, 20, 43, 53, 61, 78. *See also* ecumenism
nonviolence, 71, 146, 167, 414, 440, 449, 471, 491, 559, 583, 683–84, 717, 729
Normae S. Congregationis pro doctrina fidei de modo procedendi in diudicandis praesumptis apparitionibus ac revelationibus, 68
normalcy, 67, 713
normativity, 14, 68, 71, 74, 77, 204, 206, 217–18, 620, 629, 720–23
North Point Press, 483
North Star, 104
Northern School (Chan Buddhism), 553
Northern School (Daoism). *See* Beizong
Northwestern University, 623
nothingness. *See* emptiness
nous, 369, 375, 385, 400
novelette, 376
Novem modi orandi, 9, 13, 58, 63, 72, 76, 79, 503–545, 708–9; translation of, 531–45
Novem modi orandi sancti Dominici. *See Novem modi orandi*
novitiate, 452, 521, 535
nüdan, 58, 79, 574
nullification. *See* disappearance
Numata Center for Buddhist Translation and Research, 425, 437
numerology, 207–8, 215, 446, 492
numinosity, 67, 94–95, 110, 127, 129, 133, 548, 565, 580, 585, 587–88, 590–92, 713, 716
numinous abilities. *See* paranormal abilities
nuns, 8, 30–31, 38, 79, 292, 365, 452, 503, 509–10, 514, 526, 538, 551, 717. *See also* monastics
nutrition. *See* dietetics
Nüyu, 114, 136
Nyanaponika Thera, 286
Nyāya, 461, 479
Nyāya Sūtras, 462
Nyingma, 286

oaths. *See* commitments
obedience. *See* surrender
obeisance. *See* bowing; reverence
object mode, 23
objectification, 11, 33
objectives. *See* goals

objectivity, 22, 33, 41, 55, 81, 113, 325, 425–31, 599, 603, 623, 631, 718
objects, 7, 59, 135, 172, 178–79, 182, 250, 278–79, 285, 289, 292, 414–15, 418, 431, 442, 444–45, 463, 465–66, 468–72, 479, 483–84, 486–88, 492–93, 500, 516, 539, 603, 607, 609, 633, 638, 641
obligations. *See* commitments
observances. *See niyama*
observation, 34, 58, 122, 180, 182, 184, 191, 281–89, 339, 341–42, 344, 352, 392, 403, 413, 415, 431, 451, 464–66, 490, 513, 542, 560, 590, 595, 609, 653–56, 658–59, 660–61, 664–65, 669–70, 682, 684–85, 689, 692, 694–95, 698–99, 701, 707–8
obstacles. *See* difficulties
obstruction. *See* difficulties
occipital lobe, 29
Ocean of Qi, 580–81
oceans, 189, 192, 310, 423, 446, 580, 592, 688–90
Odessa, 377
Oedipus complex, 425
offerings, 75, 182, 273, 413, 438, 458, 511, 516, 522–23, 540–41, 550, 646
officials. *See* ministers
Ohio, 635
oil, 396, 467, 471, 493, 508
Ojai, 650–53, 668
Olam Ha-Bah, 235, 236, 243, 721
Olcott, Henry Steel, 647–48
Old Believers, 361, 364, 368–69, 383
Old Castile, 505
Old Ritualists. *See* Old Believers
Old Testament. *See* Hebrew Bible
Olympus, 370
om, 470, 479, 485
Ommen, 650
omnipresence, 405
omnipotence, 498
omniscience, 469, 472, 479, 485, 495–96, 498, 561
On Becoming a Person, 23
"On Commandments and Doctrines," 393, 399
"On Experiential Confirmation." *See* "Lun zhengyan"
"On Faith," 393, 399
"On Guarding the Intellect," 392

On Our Own Terms, 604
"On Prayer," 393, 399
"On Stillness," 385, 393, 399
On the Formation of Preachers. See *De eruditione praedicatorum*
On the Origins of Species, 632
"On the Signs of Grace and Delusion," 393, 399
"On Watchfulness and Holiness," 397
"On Watchfulness and the Guarding of the Heart," 392, 394, 399
once-returners, 280, 297
one (number), 20, 42, 597, 607, 642
One (sacred), 55, 98, 111, 113, 128, 139, 142, 319, 339, 348, 353, 357, 579–80, 592
one-pointedness, 113, 266, 277, 279, 441, 445, 492–94, 713
ontologies of realization, 70
ontology, 39, 65, 72
openness. See receptivity
oppression, 35, 146, 148, 151, 194, 368, 437–39, 540, 567, 653, 683, 713, 717, 723
optimal experience, 23, 113, 602, 615, 714
Optino Hermitage, 360–61, 363, 365–67, 384
'Or Neerav, 205
orality, 91, 102, 268–69, 273, 275, 314, 407–8, 413–14, 432, 437, 462, 473, 510, 566
orans. See *orante*
orante, 521–22
oratio, 4
order, 101, 104, 107–9, 122, 125–26, 134, 220, 222, 254–55, 257, 310, 337, 386, 399–401, 403, 443, 445, 448, 550, 655, 660, 662, 664, 669, 680, 682–87, 689, 696–97
Order of Carmelites, 8, 30–31, 42, 57–58, 79, 160, 620, 730
Order of Cistercians of the Strict Observance. See Order of Trappists
Order of Friars Minor, 504, 509, 513
Order of Preachers, 13, 57–58, 79, 161, 503–45, 708, 710
Order of Saint Benedict, 58, 528
Order of the Brothers of Our Lady of Mount Carmel. See Order of Carmelites
Order of the Star in the East, 645, 649–51
Order of Trappists, 58, 507, 528, 531
ordinary people. See conditioning; enculturation; habituation

ordination, 62, 147–48, 153, 199, 277, 364, 366, 424, 506, 518, 549, 551–52, 572–73, 611
organ-meridian system, 558, 571, 581, 584
organs, 115, 131, 134–35, 137, 142, 249, 260–61, 341, 374, 558, 571, 581, 584, 634–35
Orientalism, 57, 309, 327–28, 569, 603–5, 624, 647, 674, 694
Orientalism and Religion, 69
orientation, 63, 69, 189, 379, 438–39, 441, 505, 511, 571, 619, 655, 706, 710, 716, 724, 727, 730
origin. See source
original face, 561, 583
original nature. See innate nature
original sin, 154
Orkhot Hayyim, 264
ornaments. See decorations
orphans, 237
Orthodox Judaism, 198, 218, 594. See also Judaism
Orthodox Unity. See Zhengyi
orthodoxy, 68, 211, 214, 309, 430, 461, 475–76, 479, 509, 528, 531, 550–51, 645–46, 654
orthography, 168, 171
orthopraxy, 310, 458
Orthros, 393
Oscar-Berman, Marlene, 27
Osho. See Rajneesh
Osma, 505
Osman Nuri Topbaş, 313
other-power, 421, 423–24, 710
otherness. See alterity
Otkrovennoe poslanie, 363, 367, 383
Otkrovennyi ilisa, 363, 367
Otkrovennyi rasskaz strannika dukhovnomu svoemu ottsu. See *Rasskaz strannika*
Ottoman Empire, 198, 200
"Our Father." See Lord's Prayer
out-breath. See exhalation
out-of-body experience, 497
outcastes, 646
outcomes. See benefits; effects; goals
outflow. See dissipation
outsiders. See etic; third-person discourse
Overmyer, Daniel, 570
Ox Head (school), 112
oxen, 141. See also cattle
Oxford Buddhist Vihāra, 292

Oxford Centre for Buddhist Studies, 293
Oxford University Press, 424
Oxherding Pictures, 330, 592
Ozar ha-Kavod, 244

pacification, 719
pacifism, 717
pada, 468–69, 483, 488, 493, 498
padmāsana, 293, 298, 441, 459, 471, 478, 492, 564–65, 586, 609, 641
Pafnutii Borovski Monastery, 363, 366
Pahnke, Walter, 44
pain. *See* suffering
painter, 190
Pakistan, 314, 321, 459
Pala di Perugia, 504
palaces, 265–66, 272, 296, 313, 345, 352, 396, 398, 429, 438–40, 443, 445, 450, 558–59, 561, 565, 580
Palamas, Gregory, 369
Palencia, 505
Palestine, 197–98, 215, 220, 239, 370
Pāli, 54, 265, 291–92, 408
Pāli Canon. *See Tipiṭaka*
palliative care, 604
Pamiat'o molitvennoi, 363, 366
pāna, 281
Pāṇini, 458
paññā. *See prajñā*
Panteleimon Monastery. *See* Saint Panteleimon Monastery
papacy, 148, 505–9, 528
papal bulls, 509
Paphlagonia, 393
Paquette, Vincent, 30–31
paradigms, 24, 43, 271, 325–26, 475, 476, 595, 599, 613, 623, 671, 673
paradise, 174, 413, 430, 540, 580
Parākramabāhu I, 291
Paramahansa Yogānanda, 479, 602
pāramī. *See pāramitā*
pāramitā, 67, 265, 443, 712
paranormal abilities, 23–24, 67–68, 82, 100, 123, 250–52, 279, 293, 296, 366, 401–3, 416–17, 438, 441, 449, 452–53, 467, 483, 492–99, 522, 538, 544, 561, 590, 646–48, 654, 708, 713, 724. *See also* specific abilities

paraphernalia, 56, 59, 63, 240–41, 297, 376, 380, 532–45, 561, 709, 718
parasympathetic nervous system, 24, 26–27, 602
Pardes Rimonim, 198, 237
parents, 177, 179, 234, 296, 318, 391, 414, 416, 421, 425, 428, 437–40, 452, 527, 549–50, 581, 593–95, 630, 645–47, 652
Parfenii, 385
parietal lobe, 29
parinibbana, 291
Paris, 509
parishes. *See* congregations
participant-observation, 13, 34, 74, 568
participatory approach, 671–72, 706, 710
parzufim, 200
Pas, Julian, 433
passivity. *See* quietism; receptivity
Passover, 244
pastoral psychology, 25. *See also* spiritual direction
Patañjali, 457–60, 461, 468–73, 477, 483
path, 68, 148, 163, 175, 177, 180, 184, 186, 188, 192, 238, 272, 274, 276–77, 283, 286, 290, 310–12, 314–15, 319–20, 322, 324, 333, 336–37, 342–45, 347, 349, 357, 369, 377, 380–82, 398, 411, 426, 428, 442, 460–61, 474, 485, 497, 513, 519, 524–25, 544, 578, 582–85, 589, 645, 650, 653–54, 656, 659, 668, 682, 697, 715, 728, 730
path of dissipation, 578
Path of Freedom. *See Vimuttimagga*
Path to Purification. *See Visuddhimagga*
pathless land, 645, 650, 653, 656–57, 671, 673, 710
pathologization, 36, 42, 44, 70, 714
pathology, 22–24, 164, 594, 714, 718–19. *See also* sickness
patience, 67–68, 152, 172, 178, 180–81, 183–86, 192, 265, 290, 310, 336, 375, 393, 396–97, 650, 712
patients, 597–98, 606, 610–11, 618, 621, 642
patriarchs, 111–12, 131, 181, 246, 249, 256, 263, 368, 393, 399, 411, 426, 552, 562, 582
patriarchy, 35, 79
Patristics, 368, 384, 507
Pattabhi Jois. *See* Jois
Paul of Tarsus, 162, 173–74, 190–91, 194, 371, 373, 391, 397, 463, 531, 540

Paulist Press, 80, 384, 388
Pavāraṇā, 280, 296
pavilions, 442, 444
PCE. *See* Pure Consciousness Event
peace, 55, 67, 71, 101, 105–6, 132, 134, 138, 140, 151–52, 159, 161–62, 174, 177–78, 182, 184, 186, 188–96, 236, 245, 253, 266–67, 277, 287, 320, 337, 353, 366, 369, 378, 386, 395–96, 398, 400–1, 438, 467–68, 471, 543, 638, 647, 711–13, 717, 723
peace studies, 12, 34, 717
peak experiences, 23, 714
pearl of great price, 162, 190, 196, 368
pearls, 142, 162, 190, 196, 368, 443–45, 584
peasants, 359, 361, 368, 378, 388, 394, 396–97
pedagogy. *See* contemplative pedagogy; education; learning; teaching
pedagogy of faith, 518
pedigree. *See* lineage
Pelikan, Jaroslav, 371
penance (practice). *See* repentance
Penance (sacrament). *See* Confession
penetration, 111, 127, 129, 132, 134, 142, 177–78, 220, 222, 227, 258, 316, 397, 403, 429, 469, 484, 487–88, 524, 526, 531, 535, 586
Penglai, 561
Penington, Isaac, 161
Penn, William, 163
Pennington, M. Basil, 58
Pentateuch. *See* Torah
Pentecost, 161, 199, 388
Pentkovsky, Alexsei, 361, 367, 383–84
Perault, William, 531
perception, 5, 7, 16–17, 25, 29, 71, 90, 95–96, 98–99, 100–1, 103–4, 113, 131, 134, 142, 172, 178, 248, 250, 266, 274, 277–78, 286, 312, 355, 400, 441–42, 446–47, 464, 467, 483–84, 488, 492, 495, 500, 523, 557, 638–39, 659, 661–64, 666, 669–70, 672, 687, 689, 692, 699, 712–13, 715, 729–30
Perennial Philosophy, 14, 16, 74, 617, 638, 641–42, 647, 667, 710–11, 722
Perennial Psychology, 42
perfection, 81, 111, 113, 137, 153, 157–58, 162, 166, 175–76, 183, 185–86, 194–96, 263, 265, 309, 311, 314, 322, 333–34, 336–37, 342–43, 347, 353, 390–91, 439, 492, 497, 580, 583, 591, 712

Perfection of Wisdom. *See* *Prajñā-pāramitā*
performance arts, 11, 37, 81
perfume, 438, 452, 694
perineum, 557, 579, 582, 584
Period of Disunion (China), 407, 437, 556
Period of the Last Dharma. *See* *mofa*; *mappō*
peripheral nervous system, 26
persecution. *See* oppression
perseverance. *See* determination
Persia, 202
Persian, 307, 315, 321, 323–24
Persinger, Michael, 30
personal experience. *See* experience; subjectivity
personality. *See* character
personhood, 5, 21–22, 36, 43, 64, 95, 99, 105, 123, 128, 130, 134, 151, 154, 160, 165, 186, 197, 205, 252–53, 259, 267, 293, 297, 307, 311–12, 315–16, 333, 369, 371–72, 374–75, 385, 396, 400, 410, 412, 423, 457, 463–68, 472, 477–78, 521, 553–58, 565, 569, 571–72, 578–92, 599–602, 609, 612, 623, 647, 648, 651, 654, 657, 662, 667, 671, 707–12, 726; as (substitute) sacred, 474–75, 568–69, 623, 632. *See also* tradition-specific terms
Perugia, 504, 528
Perugia Altarpiece. *See* *Pala di Perugia*
pervasion, 95, 99, 105–6, 113, 122, 128, 131, 139, 466–67, 561, 650, 713
Pesach, 244
PET. *See* Positron Emission Tomography
Peter, 191, 508, 518
petition, 4, 7, 37, 57, 75, 322, 330, 337, 371, 373, 389–90, 393, 405, 438–39, 453, 513, 531, 708
phallocentrism, 227
Pharisees, 202, 373
pharmaceutical drugs, 595, 600, 609, 611, 615, 623, 631, 639–40, 644, 681, 719
phenomena. *See* *dharma*; objects; world
phenomenal world. *See* world
phenomenology, 11, 17, 22, 325, 672, 720
philanthropy, 147
Philokalia, 359, 361, 365–66, 367, 369–70, 372, 374–75, 377–79, 382–86, 391–94, 396–401, 403–4
"philosophical Daoism" (misnomer), 93–94, 554
philosophy, 11, 13–14, 17, 19, 23, 26, 33, 35, 60, 108, 250, 268–69, 324, 327, 372, 457,

459, 463, 472, 473, 478, 594, 605, 632, 645, 647–48, 654, 666, 688, 698, 706, 720
philosophy of religion, 13
philosophy of religious practice, 13
photography, 4, 41, 79, 596, 618, 649, 652, 667
phylacteries. *See tefillin*
physical fitness, 475
physicality, 7, 20, 32, 64, 95, 121, 142, 192, 238, 247, 259, 311, 316–17, 324, 333–34, 342, 349–51, 354, 356, 374–75, 398, 463–65, 468, 474, 477, 505, 507–8, 510, 511, 513, 515–28, 558–59, 579, 623, 646, 666, 679, 685, 706, 708, 716, 721–22, 729
physicians, 175, 311, 438, 595, 600, 610–11, 613, 630–31, 640
Physicians of the Heart, 329
physiology, 5, 7–8, 10, 21, 26–28, 32–33, 60, 65, 67, 131, 134, 324, 560, 571, 593–605, 607, 612–13, 615–17, 619–20, 624, 629, 631–33, 637, 642–44, 691, 726
piety, 150, 156, 166, 193, 199–201, 204, 210, 223, 240, 250, 257, 371, 378, 505–8, 519, 527, 533, 545, 549
Pilate, Pontius, 534
Pilates, 53, 79
pilgrimage, 198, 309, 346, 359–64, 370–71, 376–78, 382–83, 388, 519, 522, 541, 705–6, 708, 724, 727–28
Pilgrim's Progress, 384
Pilgrims' Booklets, 362, 382–83
pillars, 99, 196, 255, 309, 311, 314, 352, 518
Pious Thoughts Concerning the Knowledge and Love of God, 150, 167, 172
Pisano, Nicola, 529, 541
pitfalls. *See* dangers
pivots, 132, 562, 583
place, 19, 32–33, 35, 55–56, 59–60, 62–63, 81, 214, 240, 243, 278, 280, 288, 291, 296–98, 323, 353, 359–60, 376, 379, 394, 402, 413, 415, 425, 437–40, 491–92, 499, 503, 516, 522, 524–25, 532–45, 550, 552, 564–65, 574, 579, 583, 593, 595, 597, 607–8, 611, 618–20, 623, 633, 638, 641, 649, 651–53, 658, 660, 663, 667, 683, 685, 693, 695, 702, 706, 708–9, 719, 724, 726–28. *See also* specific places
placebo, 606, 613
plague, 198, 200, 223, 537
planetary cultre, 568

platform, 440, 442
Platform Sūtra, 426
Plato, 272, 463, 508, 512
plough, 175, 181
pluralism, 11, 14, 16, 77, 462, 705–6, 711, 720–23, 727
pneuma, 121, 385, 560, 580
po, 128, 143, 558
poetry, 90, 102, 104, 108, 220, 222, 563, 579, 582–84, 586, 588, 590–92, 687
Poland, 200, 203, 217, 237, 510, 593, 630
polemics. *See* argumentation
polestar, 496
polishing, 183–85, 341, 345
politics, 19–20, 33, 35, 41, 43, 89–90, 92–92, 94, 99–100, 107–9, 116, 123, 132, 139, 146–48, 157, 265, 271, 312, 323, 328, 368, 416, 437–38, 475, 506, 508, 520, 548–49, 567, 570, 574, 595, 598, 603, 617, 619–21, 645–47, 650, 677, 694, 709, 716–19, 730
pollution. *See* defilements
Polonnawura, 266, 291
polytheism, 14, 278, 417, 439, 458, 571, 685, 699, 721–23, 730
ponds, 414, 418, 443–44, 449–50, 452–54
Pontifical University of Saint Thomas, 526
Poonyathiro, Boonman, 286, 288
Pope, Russell, 149–50
popes. *See* papacy
popovtsy, 368
popular culture, 14, 75, 552, 568–69, 598–601, 621, 729
popular imagination, 14, 568, 600, 617, 633, 729
popularization, 548, 568, 572, 612, 621
pores, 446, 448
Porta Coeli, 514
portability, 289
Portugal, 203
positive thinking, 600, 609, 615
Positron Emission Tomography, 30, 114
possession, 7, 126, 129, 159, 162, 175, 184, 193, 376, 388, 444, 448, 490–91, 497, 522, 573
postcolonialism, 11, 70, 622
posterior superior parietal lobule, 28
postliteracy, 75
postulants, 364, 383
postmodernism, 11, 326–27, 622, 673, 729
postmortem existence. *See* afterlife

post-traumatic stress disorder, 623, 718–19
postural yoga, 475–77, 480, 708
posture, 6, 37, 58, 62–63, 80–81, 96–98, 101, 113, 205, 215, 266, 270, 280, 287–88, 291, 293, 298, 317, 338, 350, 374, 380, 385, 394, 422, 441, 459, 470–71, 474–75, 491–92, 504–5, 510–11, 513, 515–25, 532–45, 557, 564, 571, 586, 588, 590–91, 607–9, 633, 639, 641–42, 656, 663, 684, 688, 694, 707, 709, 716, 724, 726–27. *See also* specific postures
potentiality, 19, 23, 35, 43, 54, 63, 69–70, 154, 157, 165, 469, 564, 612, 648, 653, 668, 673, 707, 711–14, 725–26. *See also* actualization
poverty, 68, 146, 157, 161, 164, 175, 235, 257, 310, 336, 378, 386, 390, 396, 505, 508, 510, 523, 540, 559, 594, 670, 680, 717
power, 11, 20, 24, 34–36, 44, 56, 68, 162, 174, 177, 181, 192, 194, 252, 254, 258, 273, 334, 337, 346, 373–74, 390–91, 416–17, 421, 430, 441, 445, 449, 453, 458, 472, 489, 491–92, 496–98, 506, 508, 512, 520, 522–23, 544, 595, 600, 604, 609, 611–12, 615, 617, 620, 622, 647–48, 650–51, 654, 679, 708, 713, 729–30
power of suggestion, 600, 609
practice. *See* praxis; specific practices
practice of negation and affirmation, 314, 317, 321–22, 330, 338, 350–54
Prague, 226, 622
Prairie du Chien, 622
praise. *See* recognition
prajñā, 112, 267, 274, 553, 712
Prajñā-pāramitā literature, 553
prakṛti, 66, 460–61, 463–65, 467–69, 472, 474, 477, 479, 484–85, 487, 490, 499
prāṇa, 324, 464, 497
praṇāmāsana, 438
praṇava, 470
prāṇāyāma, 470–72, 474, 491–93, 707
praṇidhāna, 412
pratītya-samutpāda, 411
pratyāhāra, 470, 472, 491, 493
pratyutpanna-samādhi, 415, 432
praxis, 24, 38–40, 43, 61, 65, 70, 711–19, 728–29. *See also* specific practices.
pray without ceasing, 174, 190, 359, 371, 376, 388–90, 392, 394, 397
prayer, 4, 6, 8, 20, 37, 39, 57–58, 60, 73, 77, 145, 148, 151–52, 171, 174, 177, 236, 238, 245, 252, 254–55, 309, 322, 336, 359, 363, 365–66, 368–70, 373–74, 377, 379, 385, 388–90, 439, 503, 505, 511, 513, 522, 526, 531, 548, 596, 607, 633, 639, 642–43, 656, 689, 707–8, 711. *See also* contemplative prayer; specific types
prayer beads, 385, 394
prayer of the heart, 176, 359, 365, 369–71, 374, 384, 392, 394, 399, 401–3
prayer rope, 380, 385, 394, 396, 405
prayer shawl. *See tallit*
preaching, 199, 296, 389–90, 437, 505, 507–9, 511–13, 517, 521, 523–27, 535, 540, 544–45
precepts, 37, 190, 202, 211, 267, 278, 296–97, 389, 408, 413–14, 421, 429, 438, 440, 449, 451–52, 471, 551, 559, 712, 729
precognition, 495, 713
preconditions. *See* preparation
predestined affinities. *See yuanfen*
predictability, 597, 603
prediction. *See* prophecy
Predosterezhenie Iisusovu molitvu, 366
prefrontal cortex, 28
pregnancy, 564, 636, 652
prelest, 382
Prémontré, 509
Premonstratensian Canons, 509
preparation, 62, 69, 173, 194, 197, 204–5, 213–14, 225, 234, 238–40, 242, 244, 271, 278, 311, 343, 346, 391, 402, 404, 417, 457, 470, 488, 509, 520, 527, 531, 550, 557, 572, 583, 643, 659, 701, 712, 719, 724, 729
prerequisites. *See* preparation
presbyter, 397
presence, 3–4, 6, 37, 66, 94, 129, 159, 191, 333–37, 342–44, 346, 354–55, 357, 454, 463, 498, 512, 515, 522, 532, 559, 561, 585, 588, 650–51, 654–63, 665, 668, 672, 674, 678, 680, 687, 695, 698, 701, 706, 710–11, 715–16, 719, 728. *See also* divine presence
Presence of God. *See* divine presence
present moment. *See* immediacy
presentist fallacy, 79
pride, 159–60, 173, 177, 183–84, 365, 404, 647
Prier avec son corps, 515, 526
priests, 36, 43, 63, 146, 148, 153, 158, 360–61, 363, 365–68, 372–73, 378, 380, 382, 385, 389–90, 401, 423, 505–7, 509, 518, 523, 531,

537, 541, 544, 551, 585, 611, 646, 659, 690, 693, 697–99
primitive Christianity, 174–75
Prince Ji, 550, 556
printing. *See* publication
priories, 505, 509–10, 513–14, 524, 529, 537, 543–44
prison. *See* imprisonment
prison camps, 519
Pritzker Zohar, 219
problems. *See* difficulties
process, 5, 15, 23–24, 29–30, 64, 66, 70, 82, 92, 94, 98, 102–3, 105, 114, 120, 123, 151, 158, 160, 176, 195, 202–3, 209, 214, 217, 238, 245, 249, 254, 259, 273, 275, 287, 289–90, 292, 310, 312, 317, 319, 328–29, 335, 338–39, 343, 345, 357, 364, 375, 415, 418, 430, 457, 463, 465, 467–68, 471, 497, 503, 505, 510, 550, 554–58, 560–61, 563–64, 566, 572, 580, 601, 611, 634, 642, 644, 650, 655–58, 662–64, 666, 668, 672, 681, 690, 692, 696, 700, 702, 706, 714–15
Proctor, William, 606
productivity, 598, 612, 643, 680
Profession of Faith. See *Shahada*
professionalization, 611
prohibition. *See* proscription
prognostication. *See* divination
progress, 180, 186, 191–92, 265, 267, 271, 290, 296, 321, 338–40, 346–47, 369, 374, 379, 386, 394, 399, 411, 426, 440, 486, 493, 512, 520, 523, 527, 558, 561, 566, 644, 647–48, 659, 663, 678, 696, 698, 712, 714–16. *See also* attainment; stages
Progressive Relaxation, 609, 615, 623
pronunciation, 340
proof. *See* confirmation; verification
prophecy, 157, 176, 192, 197, 199, 201–2, 204–5, 208–11, 213–14, 224–25, 235, 237–38, 240, 245–48, 250–52, 259–61, 309–10, 313, 315, 317–19, 322, 337, 353, 419, 447, 450–51, 512, 520–21, 533, 537, 540–42, 646, 648, 650, 707
prophetic expandability, 512
prophets, 157, 176, 190, 192–94, 204, 209–10, 234–238, 246–52, 259–60, 307–12, 315, 317–18, 321–22, 326, 334, 336–38, 347, 352, 520–22, 533, 537, 540–42, 544, 729. *See also* specific prophets

proprioception, 672
proscription, 206, 217, 345, 389, 538, 646
proselytization, 11, 323. *See also* evangelism
prosperity. *See* abundance
protection, 243, 273, 276, 377, 401, 405, 416, 497, 535, 633, 706, 730
Protestant Christianity, 58, 146, 149–50, 161, 163, 166–67, 171, 176, 371, 423, 508–9, 717. *See also* specific denominations
prostration, 363, 365, 389, 417, 439, 510–11, 513, 515, 517–18, 525, 527–28, 533, 548–49
Prouille, 510, 526
provenance, 73
Provence, 204
providence. *See* grace
proximity, 141, 191, 196, 221, 235, 237–38, 309–11, 318–19, 338, 340, 342–43, 345–47, 349–51, 353–57, 374, 381, 389, 395, 401, 403, 440–41, 465, 479, 518, 520, 685–86. *See also* intimacy
pṛthagjana, 420
Pryce, Elaine, 150, 164
psalms, 242, 245, 373, 393, 510, 515, 518, 521, 525, 531, 533
pseudography, 367
pseudonymity, 73
psi phenomena, 330
psyche, 43, 97, 104, 121, 369, 569, 631, 653, 659, 684
psychedelic drugs, 23, 598, 615, 621
psychiatry, 597, 631
psychic dispositions. *See* paranormal abilities
psychoanalysis, 22, 43, 70, 289, 425, 600, 714
Psychodiagnostik, 29
psychologies of realization, 25, 54, 65, 69–72, 711, 725–26
psychologization, 7, 568–69, 718–19
psychology, 7, 9, 10–11, 13–14, 17, 19, 22–26, 28–30, 35, 39, 42–44, 54, 64, 66, 165, 310–12, 324–27, 415, 425, 463–8, 470, 525, 568–69, 574–75, 594, 605, 610, 622–23, 631–32, 643–44, 648, 656–60, 663, 666, 668–70, 672–73, 679–80, 682–83, 685, 687, 691, 701–2, 706–14, 717–20, 730. *See also* specific types
Psychology Club, 568
psychosis, 23, 68

psychosomatic, 24, 37, 69, 95, 128, 463, 471, 475, 477, 518, 526–28, 547, 554, 556–57, 571, 579, 593, 597–606, 609, 612, 623–24, 631, 711, 715
psychotherapy. *See* psychoanalysis
PTSD. *See* post-traumatic stress disorder
pu (uncarved block), 105, 111, 132, 140–41, 143
public talks, 73, 164, 617, 650, 657, 667–68, 677–704
publication, 145–47, 149–50, 171, 197, 201, 206, 211, 216–18, 222, 226, 287, 321, 364–65, 368, 370, 376, 378, 388, 392, 424, 432, 514, 529, 549, 555, 562, 566, 567–68, 579, 593, 601, 606, 613, 645, 651, 667. *See also* specific publications; specific publishers
punishment, 211–12, 257, 271, 518, 527, 534, 656, 682, 701
Punjab, 313–14, 322–23, 333
Puṇṇa Mantāṇiputta, 292
Purāṇa, 460, 480
Pure Abodes, 297
Pure Consciousness Event, 16, 42, 66, 70
Pure Land (buddha-realm), 407, 410–11. *See also* Sukhāvatī
Pure Land (school). *See* Jingtu
Pure Land Sutra. See *Sukhāvatī-vyūha Sūtra*
pure spirit. See *puruṣa*
purgation, 151, 184
purification, 59, 69, 73, 81, 101, 105, 135, 151, 161–62, 171, 183–85, 195, 214, 236, 240, 242, 252, 257, 267, 271, 277, 283–85, 290, 296, 302, 317, 330, 335–36, 339, 343, 345–46, 349–51, 353–54, 371, 377, 396, 427, 431, 455, 457, 471–72, 477, 486, 488, 492, 496, 501, 554, 557, 561, 579, 583, 599, 685, 715, 724
Puritanism, 146, 149
purity, 73, 137, 139, 157, 162, 174–75, 179, 182–83, 189, 194, 196, 234, 240, 245, 263, 338, 345, 375, 391, 398, 401, 425, 440, 463–65, 468, 470, 477, 479, 488, 491, 498, 541, 572, 583, 591–92, 646, 650, 710, 712, 729
Purity of Heart and Contemplation Symposium (conference), 10
Pūrna, 438
purpose. *See* existentialism
puruṣa, 66, 457, 463–70, 472, 474, 477, 479, 483–84, 487, 490, 492, 496, 498, 500–1
Pythagoreanism, 648

Qabalah. *See* Kabbalah
qabd, 321
Qadiri lineage, 308, 312–13, 322, 328
Qi (state), 90, 102, 114
qi (subtle breath), 90, 92–94, 97, 99, 101–3, 107, 109–11, 120–21, 123, 125–28, 130, 134–38, 142, 324, 550, 555, 557–61, 571, 574, 579–81, 587–88
Qigong, 42, 547, 567, 571, 609
qihai. *See* Ocean of Qi
Qin (state), 90–92, 114
Qing dynasty, 548–51, 562, 566–67
Qingdao, 568
qingjing, 132, 137–38
Qingjing jing, 109, 132
Qingxu, 550
Qiu Chuji, 551
quadrant system of consciousness, 327
Quaker Strongholds, 163
Quakerism à la Mode, 150
Quakers. *See* Religious Society of Friends
qualities, 25, 53, 56–57, 65, 70, 72, 95, 99, 101, 103, 129, 134, 137, 146, 172, 274, 420, 431, 443, 445–46, 462, 467–68, 518, 527, 561, 565, 586, 596, 604, 607, 615, 619, 663–64, 669–71, 686, 707, 711, 713–14, 716, 719, 721, 729–30. *See also* specific qualities
quantification, 5, 7, 10, 26, 28, 44, 595–97, 599–601, 603, 613, 619, 631, 636, 713
Quanzhen, 108, 132, 547, 550–51, 554–55, 562, 567–68, 574–75, 578
Queen Vaidehī. *See* Vaidehī
quenching the Spirit, 149, 156, 398
querents. *See* aspirants
quest, 205, 209
quiet. *See* silence; stillness
quiet sitting. See *jingzuo*
quietism (approach), 7, 58, 151–58, 560, 707, 710. *See also* apophatic meditation; silence; stillness
Quietism (movement), 79, 145, 147–50, 153, 156–57, 163–64, 166–67, 707, 710
Quine, Willard Van Orman (W. V.), 34
Qunawi, Sadruddin, 324
Qur'an, 308, 313, 315, 318, 322, 333, 335, 337, 345, 349, 352, 354–55, 408

rabbinate, 200
Rabbinic Judaism. *See* Judaism

race. *See* ethnicity
radiance. *See* light
radical empiricism, 325, 672
radicalness, 199, 204, 268, 477, 506, 599, 623–24, 650–51, 656, 659, 670, 673, 677, 708, 710–11, 713, 719, 722
Rāhula, 285
Rahula, Walpola, 287–88
rain, 280, 284, 297, 404, 439
rain retreat, 280, 296–97
Rāja Yoga, 478, 480
Rajagopal, Desikacharya (D.), 652
Rajagopal, Rosalind, 652
Rājagṛha, 437
rajas, 467–69, 479, 490
rājās, 265, 267
Rajasthan, 312
Rajneesh, 81
Ramadan, 309, 337
RAMAK. *See* Cordovero, Moshe
Rāmānanda Sarasvatī, 474, 480
Ramitani, 'Azizan 'Ali, 339
ranks. *See* hierarchy; levels
rapture, 523, 540
rarefication, 496–97, 561, 713
Rasskaz strannika, 63, 66, 73, 76, 359–405, 707, 713; translation of 388–405
rationality, 152, 172–73, 177, 310, 324, 326, 330, 360, 369, 375, 390, 427, 479–80, 604, 632, 686, 694, 708, 713
Ratnaprabhā, 480
rats, 601, 636–37
Ratzinger, Joseph, 81
Ravad, 262
Ravindra, Ravi, 667
reactivity, 23, 71, 629, 632, 643, 689, 714
reading, 72, 75, 180, 197, 221–22, 236, 269, 324–25, 361, 364, 370, 376, 378–79, 389, 392–94, 397–98, 400, 403, 405, 446, 512, 515, 523–24, 537, 542–43, 545, 566–67, 620, 657, 708, 726
reality, 14, 35, 38–39, 72, 81, 140, 311, 314–16, 322, 325, 327, 333, 335, 337, 348, 421, 425–31, 441, 459–60, 463–64, 512, 523, 554, 592, 647–48, 653, 657, 659, 668, 671, 678–79, 685, 694, 708, 710–11, 720–24, 726–27
realization, 19, 56, 70, 81, 93, 95, 111, 122, 342, 349, 357, 412–13, 437, 454, 457, 465, 468, 470, 472, 486, 553, 561, 565, 580, 590–92, 648, 650, 653, 656, 688, 690, 693, 711–12, 714, 716, 730
reaping, 181, 191, 566
reason. *See* rationality
rebirth. *See* reincarnation
Recanati, Menahem, 249
Recanati 'al Ha-Torah, 249
receptive mode, 23, 70
receptivity, 66, 113–14, 129, 147–48, 153, 166, 173, 175, 186, 189, 223, 244, 287, 393, 516, 538, 540, 572, 583, 596, 604, 607–9, 619, 633, 638, 641–43, 664, 669–70, 723, 727
recitation, 37, 58, 63, 215, 220, 238–40, 242, 245–46, 268–69, 272–73, 275, 277, 283–85, 287, 289, 292, 296, 317, 322, 337, 365, 375, 380–81, 384, 395, 397, 411, 413–14, 416–24, 429–31, 433, 439–40, 449–50, 453, 470, 475, 479, 509, 516, 518, 531, 533, 539, 542, 656, 670
recognition, 100, 237, 245, 404, 487, 516, 545, 552, 589, 599, 617, 664, 670, 679, 681, 683, 699, 714, 722
recognizability, 100
recollection (practice). *See* remembrance
recollection (state). *See* memory
Recollection of a Life of Prayer. See *Pamiat'o molitvennoi*
reconceptualization, 7, 34–35, 53, 60, 74, 78, 82, 474–76, 547, 551–56, 558–59, 571, 585, 597, 602, 604–5, 607, 612–13, 616, 620–21, 642, 647, 708–9, 718–19. *See also* decontextualization
reconciliation, 368, 373, 377, 384, 717
reconditioning, 16, 24
reconstructed practices, 17, 60, 78, 82
recontextualization, 620
recorded sayings. See *yulu*
recordings, 655, 666–67
redactions. *See* manuscripts; publication; texts
redemption. *See* salvation
reductionism, 11, 17, 21–22, 31–32, 41, 78, 595, 723
refectories, 364, 376, 383
refinement, 184, 195, 375, 403, 471, 527, 547, 554–58, 560–61, 579–81, 607, 712
reflection, 4, 11, 24, 32–33, 53, 55, 57–59, 109, 149, 167, 182, 310, 440, 444, 466, 468, 472, 484, 501, 512, 515, 525, 537, 542, 595, 619, 621, 635, 650–51, 655, 657, 665, 705–35

reform, 368, 506–7
Reform Judaism, 606
refuge. *See* sanctuary
refugee camps, 519
regret. *See* compunction
regulation, 24, 471, 492, 581, 601, 658–59, 662, 665, 670–71, 678, 707
"Regulations for the Auxiliary Cloud Hall." *See* "Jūundō-shiki"
reincarnation, 24, 68, 265, 267–68, 271, 277, 280, 285, 297, 409–10, 412, 415–16, 418–19, 421–23, 429–32, 434, 439, 442, 444–46, 448, 450–54, 463, 465, 470, 479, 489, 492, 495, 555, 559, 571–72, 580, 590, 646–48, 656, 713, 723
reinvention, 550
relationship, 16, 64, 70, 200, 215, 289, 317, 324, 342, 367, 381, 393, 425, 448, 512, 645, 651–52, 659, 663, 671–73, 694–97, 699, 706, 714
relativism, 327, 723
relaxation, 5, 24, 26, 28, 65, 102, 107, 380, 492, 525, 570–71, 573, 593–644, 689; as supposed *sine qua non* of contemplative practice, 605
Relaxation Response (practice), 8–9, 20–21, 26, 28, 53, 62, 65, 67, 82, 593–644, 709
relaxation response (state), 20–21, 593–96, 599, 602, 607, 610, 615–16, 621–22, 633, 637–38, 640, 642–44
Relaxation Response Resiliency Program, 598
Relaxation Revolution, 606
reliability. *See* stability
relics, 541, 580
religion, 6, 11, 14, 17, 34–35, 40, 43, 61–63, 77, 93, 108, 309, 314, 326, 379, 570–73, 596, 598–600, 602, 604–5, 611, 615–16, 617, 619–21, 633, 638, 641–43, 645, 647–48, 653–54, 656–57, 663, 665, 684–85, 693–94, 697, 706, 709, 717, 720–22, 725, *passim*
religion, study of. *See* religious studies
religious adherence. *See* adherence
"religious Daoism" (misnomer), 93–94, 554
religious experience, 9, 31, 54
religious orders, 57, 148, 503–5, 509. *See also* specific orders
religious pluralism. *See* pluralism
religious practice. *See* praxis
Religious Society of Friends, 8, 58, 66, 79, 145–96, 623, 707, 710, 717

religious studies, 3, 5–6, 9–13, 17–18, 22, 26, 34, 44, 53, 64, 66–67, 70, 72–75, 78, 81, 167, 324, 326–27, 477, 594, 605–6, 629, 672–73, 705–11, 720
remembered wellness, 606–7
remembrance (practice), 8, 60, 285, 287, 309, 315, 321, 323, 334–36, 337–41, 343, 345–46, 349, 354, 374, 401, 414, 446, 449, 455, 521, 584, 606, 708, 724. *See also* tradition-specific terms
remembrance (state). *See* memory
remorse. *See* compunction
remote viewing, 495
renewal, 58, 184, 246, 379, 380, 424, 506, 509, 550, 647–48
renewer. *See mujaddid*
renunciants (Hinduism). *See sannyasi*
renunciation, 147, 152, 153, 161, 185–86, 191, 265–66, 268, 297, 386, 389, 396, 398, 401, 410, 451, 457–60, 470–72, 475–76, 484, 491–92, 508, 516, 560, 572, 643, 650–51, 656, 683, 693, 696, 712, 717, 724, 729
Renshou si, 549, 555, 562
repentance, 68, 236, 239, 310–11, 336, 339–40, 347, 373, 383, 416, 439, 453, 516, 518–19, 527, 533–34, 544, 712
repetition, 274–75, 289, 321–22, 338–39, 350, 352, 371, 380, 393, 402, 454, 485, 513, 521, 585, 596, 599, 604, 607–8, 616, 619, 633, 637–38, 641, 656, 660, 670–71, 681, 683
representativeness, 42, 53, 74, 77
reproducibility, 597, 603
reputation, 198, 423, 589, 670, 679, 730. *See also* recognition
requirements. *See* commitments
research. *See* specific approaches
Reshit Hokhma, 201, 210, 225, 237
resignation, 157, 159, 161–62, 164, 182, 184, 186–89, 192, 651
resiliency, 67, 598, 706, 719
resistance, 21, 33, 146, 176, 182, 218, 318, 325, 368, 597, 601, 629, 650, 660, 678, 685, 719
resolution. *See* determination
respiration. *See* breathing
responsibility. *See* commitments
responsiveness. *See* sensitivity
rest, 21, 178, 192–95, 536, 602, 615–16

restraint, 154, 178, 234, 438–39, 470, 477, 491–92, 494, 724
results. *See* benefits; effects
resurrection, 180, 234–35, 251, 373, 388, 398, 521–22, 538
retirement, 152, 172, 177–80, 621, 630. *See also* seclusion
retreat, 109, 182, 185, 273–74, 280, 284, 292, 296–97, 337, 519, 550, 591
returning to the Source. *See guigen*
Revata, 296
revelation, 68, 156–57, 163, 173, 202, 246, 249–51, 268, 336, 357, 396, 401, 403–4, 454, 512, 524–25, 537, 541, 544, 555, 589, 655, 672
reverence, 43, 126, 152, 177, 182, 235, 241, 297, 318, 386, 392, 438–40, 444, 452, 516–17, 521, 523, 526, 532, 535, 537–39, 541, 543, 548, 724, 729
reverting the radiance. *See fanzhao*
revitalization. *See* renewal
revival. *See* renewal
revolution, 650–51, 656–57, 659, 663, 666, 668–69, 673, 677, 680, 716. *See also* radicalness
revolutionary meditation, 669
Ṛg Veda, 458
rheumatic fever, 594
rheumatism, 397
Rhineland, 237
Rice University, 10
Rinzai lineage, 55–56, 80
rite of profession, 518
ritual, 4, 22, 33, 36–37, 39, 58–60, 63, 91, 130, 146, 158, 199, 202–4, 208, 223, 271, 273–74, 292, 309, 311, 315, 322, 336, 367–68, 381, 393, 395–96, 458–59, 476, 479, 510, 517, 519, 526–27, 534, 547, 561, 611, 620, 643, 646, 653, 656, 660, 663, 665, 693–94, 699, 707, 726, 728
ritual bathing. *See mikveh*; *wuḍūʾ*
Rituale Professionis Ritus, 518
rivers, 92, 139, 142, 285, 328, 538. *See also* specific rivers
roads, 32, 177, 193, 353, 364–65, 369, 374, 377–78, 380, 401, 404, 524–25, 531, 536, 544, 553, 582–83
Roberts, Thomas, 326
robes. *See* clothing
Rockefeller Foundation Scholarship, 622

Roebuck, Valerie, 269, 293
Roesler, Ulrike, 293
Rogers, Carl, 22–23, 70
Rohr, Richard, 80
Roman Catholicism, 4, 9, 17, 37, 57–58, 63, 65, 68, 79–81, 147–50, 153–54, 162–63, 166, 292, 325, 368, 371, 381, 385, 392, 503–545, 707–8, 710, 713, 717, 727–28, 730
Roman Empire, 367, 368, 506
Roman Missal, 526–27
Romania, 361, 381
Rome, 503, 506, 508–9, 514, 526, 528, 538
rooms, 247, 339, 374–75, 400, 439, 518, 524, 528, 535, 542, 565, 574, 638, 641
roots, 163, 278, 298, 309, 489, 579, 631, 682
Rosicrucianism, 648
Rorschach, Hermann, 29
Rorschach test, 28–30, 36
rosary, 338, 380, 385, 394–96, 405, 656
Rosenberg, Larry, 80
Rosenzweig, Franz, 197, 220, 227
Roth, Harold, 10–11, 34, 40–41, 44, 55
Rothko, Mark, 41
Rothko Chapel, 10, 41
Royal Society, 147
royalty, 90, 148, 209, 265, 271, 368, 398, 411, 437–39, 506–7, 533, 550, 556
Rozhdestvenskii, Nikon, 360, 363, 382
ruah, 253–54, 259–60
ruah ha-kodesh, 208, 210–11, 224
Rubinstein, Eduardo, 636
rudder, 192
Rujing, 19
Rule of Benedict, 528
Rule of Saint Augustine, 509–10, 528
"Rules for Zazen." *See* "Zazen-gi"
Rumi, Jalal ad-Din, 60, 81, 312, 314, 323, 330, 345
rumination, 5, 72, 192, 521, 657
rūpa, 289, 299
Rupandehi, 291
Russia, 73, 359–70, 376–82, 385–86, 397, 690, 696
Russian, 359, 376, 378, 384, 392
Russian Orthodoxy, 359–405, 707
Russian Revolution, 360–61

Saanen, 697

Sabbath, 537. *See also* Shabbat
sabīja samādhi, 469
sacralization of self, 623
sacramental embodiment, 512, 517
sacraments, 146, 150, 153, 156, 166, 368, 371–72, 375, 380–81, 508, 510, 512–13, 516, 517, 527–28, 541, 544. *See also* specific sacraments
sacred, 7, 13–15, 31, 36–37, 39, 42–43, 63–64, 66–67, 69, 72, 81, 94, 107, 146, 165, 200, 205, 208, 220, 234–35, 268, 311, 315–16, 329, 369, 371, 376, 390, 428, 431, 459, 461, 469, 510, 523–24, 553–54, 581, 594, 606, 611, 623, 647–48, 654, 661, 665, 670, 673, 678, 680–81, 688, 690, 693, 702, 707–9, 715, 720–24, 726, 728. *See also* theology; tradition-specific terms
Sacred Books of the East, 424
Sacred Congregation for the Doctrine of the Faith, 81
sacred realms, 240, 256, 297, 315–16, 327, 431, 440, 561, 571, 580, 589, 647, 708, 721. *See also* tradition-specific terms
sacred sites. *See* place
sacrifice, 182, 186, 189, 193, 257, 271, 312, 371, 365, 458–59, 476, 516, 519, 521–23, 541
sacristans, 377, 541, 544–45
sacristy, 538, 541
Sad Madyan, 329
Saddhatissa, 286
sādhana, 469–72, 488–93
sadness, 19, 180, 183, 196, 237, 239–40, 250, 323, 379, 381, 397, 405, 439, 470, 486, 524, 573, 594–95, 610, 644, 687, 690, 692–93, 702, 719
Sadruddin Qunawi. *See* Qunawi
Sa'dullah Husayni, 308
Safed, 197–203, 209, 216, 223, 225
Safed school, 197
safety, 43, 184, 610, 714
Safrin, Netanel, 216–18, 225
sage-kings, 93, 100–1, 107
sages, 93, 98, 100–1, 107, 113, 120, 123, 128–29, 133, 135–36, 138, 140, 202, 204, 239–40, 246, 249–51, 256–57, 260, 326, 480, 579, 581
Sahā, 412–14, 418, 428
Saharanpuri, 'Abdulrahman, 308
Saharanpuri, Habiburrahman, 308
sails, 192, 222
Saint Benedict's Monastery, 33

Saint Catherine's Monastery, 393, 397
Saint Dominic. *See* Domingo de Guzmán
Saint George Monastery, 366
Saint Ignatius. *See* Ignacio de Loyola
Saint Michael the Archangel Monastery, 363, 383
Saint Nicholas Chapel, 528
Saint Panteleimon Monastery, 360–61, 363–64, 370–71, 376, 383, 388
Saint Patrick, 519
Saint Petersburg, 366, 401
Saint Petersburg Trinity-Sergiev Lavra, 366
Saint Sava Monastery, 366
Saint Simon Monastery, 363, 366
Saint Teresa. *See* Teresa of Ávila
sainthood. *See* canonization
saints, 162, 326, 373, 384, 393, 503, 505, 510, 514, 518, 522, 529, 531, 670, 713, 729. *See also* specific saints
Śaiva, 460
Śaiśnāga dynasty, 437
sajjhāya, 269
Śakra, 439, 443–44, 447
Śakta, 460, 496
Śakyāmuni, 37, 265, 284, 291, 407–9, 414, 416–19, 431–32, 437–55, 552, 554–55, 588–89, 674. *See also* Siddhartha Gotama
Salat, 4, 37, 309, 322, 336–38
Salinger, J. D., 379–80
saliva. *See* vital substances
Salonika, 198, 203
Saltmarsh, John, 149
salvation, 26, 63, 71, 81, 146–47, 154, 157–58, 165, 171–72, 174–76, 186, 199–200, 203, 217, 246, 268, 309, 311–12, 371–73, 377–78, 384, 391–92, 398, 410–11, 418, 422–23, 427, 430, 448, 507–8, 511–12, 517, 519, 522, 524–25, 531, 539, 600, 648, 656, 665, 670, 681, 691, 697, 710
Salzberg, Sharon, 80
samā, 60
samādhi, 54, 65, 112, 267, 274, 279, 286, 291, 301, 315–16, 432, 440, 442, 450, 454–55, 469–74, 479, 483–89, 491–94, 496, 498, 501, 549, 554, 560–62, 564, 579, 581, 713
samāna prāṇa, 497
Samantabhadra, 437
samāpatti samādhi, 470, 487
Samaritan, 158

Samarqand, 328
samatha, 55, 78, 265–306, 615, 620, 638, 715
Samatha Foundation of North America, 293
Samatha Trust, 293
samgītikāras, 273
Sāṁkhya, 460–61, 464, 467, 472, 478–80
Sāṁkhya-Kārikā, 464–65
samprajñāta samādhi, 469–70, 483–85, 487
saṁsāra, 39, 43, 66, 71, 267, 277, 413, 428, 431, 447–48, 465–66, 475–77, 479, 591, 641, 721, 730
saṁskāra, 471–72, 479, 483–84, 487–88, 494–95, 499, 501
Samurai, 423, 624
saṁyama, 472, 493–94, 495–98
Saṁyuttanikāya, 275–76
San Diego, 624
San Francisco, 424, 678, 693
San Jose, 422
San Sisto, 503, 538
sanbao, 558, 571
sanctification, 176, 193, 261, 378, 516–17, 519
sanctity. *See* holiness
sanctuary, 184, 191–92, 333, 356, 373, 375, 402, 541, 670
saṅgha, 269–70, 272–73, 280, 414, 416, 437, 444, 453
Sanhedrin, 199
sanity, 164, 677, 686, 691, 706
Sanjeevamma, 646
sanjiao, 548
Śaṅkara, 461, 474, 478
Sanlun, 419
sannyasi, 457–60, 474, 480
Sanqing, 561
Sanskrit, 54, 268, 285, 291, 407, 412, 431–32, 437, 457–58, 470, 478–80, 483, 485, 553, 574, 579, 616, 715
"Sansui-kyō," 19, 115
Santa Barbara Institute for Consciousness Studies, 10, 31, 286, 603
Sarajevo, 368
Sāriputta, 292, 296
śarīra, 580
Sarnath, 293
Saron, Clifford, 31
Sarug, Israel, 203–4
Satan, 318, 341, 344, 354, 507

satchel. *See* knapsack
Satchidananda, 475
sati, 55, 265–306
satipaṭṭhāna, 280
Satipatthāna Sutta, 66, 272, 275–76, 281
satisfaction. *See* contentment
satori, 620, 715
sattva, 466–71, 479, 490, 495
satta-visuddhi, 69
Saudi Arabia, 328
Saul, 245
savants, 729
Sāvatthī, 296–97
savitarka-samāpatti, 487
Saward, Jeff, 727
Sayadaw, Mahasi, 80, 286
Sayyid, 328
scale of stress impact, 610
scandals, 650, 652, 693
Scandinavia, 510
scarcity. *See* deficiencies
Schilbrack, Kevin, 40, 80
Schillebeeckx, Edward, 512
Schiller, Hannah. *See* Benson
schizophrenia, 44
Schmitt, Jean-Claude, 514
scholar-practitioners, 75, 78, 166, 223, 288–89, 292, 323–25, 379–82, 526–28, 574, 623
scholarship. *See* academia; study; learning
scholasticism, 216, 308, 363, 366, 376, 391, 419, 475, 510, 521
Scholem, Gershom, 14, 197, 201, 216, 219–23, 225–27
School of Wisdom, 568
schools, 55, 76, 89, 111–12, 147, 150, 163, 165, 197, 203, 211, 214–16, 223, 253, 269, 277, 281, 284–89, 311, 323, 341, 360, 366, 369, 380, 407–12, 422–24, 457–58, 460, 507, 550–54, 560, 566, 568, 581, 593–95, 646, 666–68, 685, 700, 723
Schoomaker, Eric, 718
Schuon, Frithjof, 14
Schwartz, Itamar, 226
science, 5, 10, 12, 17, 21, 25–26, 28, 32–34, 41, 43–44, 62, 67, 147, 177, 310, 323, 326, 474, 480, 509, 569, 595–97, 599–603, 605, 611–13, 616–17, 619, 622–23, 635, 639, 645, 647, 654, 665–66, 709, 713, 719. *See also* specific fields

scientific evidence. *See* benefits; confirmation; effects; verification
scientific reductionism. *See* reductionism
scientism, 44, 600, 723
Scientology. *See* Church of Scientology
Scots College, 150
scribes, 199, 224, 360, 409, 507
scripture. *See* literature; specific texts; texts
Scripture on the Dao and Inner Power. See *Daode jing*
Scripture on Wisdom and Life-Destiny. See *Huiming jing*
scripture study, 36–37, 39, 63, 75. *See also* contemplative reading; *lectio divina*
se-zither player, 96
sea. *See* ocean
sealing the body, 557, 564, 578–81
seasons, 104, 135, 141, 181–2, 185, 191, 296, 377, 394, 519
seated. *See* sitting
seclusion, 20, 54, 108, 116, 152, 214, 224, 244, 252, 259, 270, 305, 368, 377, 395, 397–98, 401, 535, 549–50, 560, 565, 591, 701, 729
second Islamic millennium, 328–29, 333, 336, 339, 353, 356
Second Vatican Council, 81
secondhand people, 659
second-person discourse, 35. *See also* intersubjectivity
secrecy, 173, 177, 183, 199, 202, 204, 219, 222–23, 225, 241–43, 245–46, 249–52, 261–64, 287, 310, 338, 343–44, 354, 357, 373, 375, 377, 381, 392, 399, 438, 462, 468, 471–72, 474, 480, 484, 494–95, 512, 522, 525, 537, 539, 541, 548, 553, 557–58, 562, 566–68, 571–72, 579–80, 583, 586, 588–89, 616, 642–43, 647–48, 652, 654
Secret of the Golden Flower. See *Jinhua zongzhi*
secret voice, 173, 178
sectarianism, 11, 19, 42, 269, 330, 368, 472, 476, 508, 559, 570, 580, 585, 598–99, 602, 616, 620, 638, 642, 723
secular materialism, 7, 11–12, 17, 20–21, 31–32, 35, 37, 41, 53, 64, 67, 326, 595, 600, 611–12, 623, 720–23, 730f
secularization, 4, 7, 9, 20, 53, 61, 64, 79, 218–20, 475–76, 600, 604–5, 607, 616–17, 620–21, 642–43, 729

security. *See* safety
seeds, 284, 312, 343, 485, 487, 494, 498, 580–81
seekers. *See* aspirants
Sefer Ha-Bahir, 204, 219, 243
Sefer Haredim, 224
Sefer Hasidim, 214, 237
Sefer Hizyonot, 200, 225
Sefer Meirat Eynaim, 243
Sefer Recanati, 249
Sefer Yezeriah, 206, 242
Sekida, Kazuki, 80
selection practice, 74, 77
Selenginsk, 363–64
self. *See* personhood
self-activating prayer. *See* spontaneity
self-actualization. *See* actualization
self-care, 20, 597, 600, 607–10, 613, 615, 640, 709
self-cultivation. *See* cultivation
self-flagellation. *See* flagellation
self-mortification. *See* asceticism
self-power, 423–24, 710
self-realization. *See* realization
Self-Realization Fellowship, 59
self-regulation. *See* regulation
self-reliance. *See* independence
self-transformation. *See* transformation
selflessness, 100–1, 114, 140, 210, 277, 410, 475, 550, 648, 659, 717
Seljuq dynasty, 330
Selye, Hans, 601–2, 606, 617, 622, 629
sema, 59–60, 81
semen, 256–57, 557–58, 579
sending out the transcendent spirit, 560, 563–64, 587–89
Sengji, 411
Sengzhao, 112
sensations, 156, 178, 180, 182, 250, 269, 282, 341, 346, 348, 353, 355, 365–66, 375, 377–78, 395–96, 398, 400–4, 520, 611–12, 638–39, 643, 689, 691, 701
senses, 7, 29, 71, 81, 115, 128, 131, 141, 159, 178, 180, 182, 187, 190, 195, 220, 249–51, 263, 265, 267, 275, 286, 299, 301–2, 304, 341, 352–53, 355, 366, 374–75, 380, 385, 458, 465–66, 470–71, 474, 477, 483–84, 486, 488, 490–94, 496, 497–98, 523, 557, 638, 677, 689, 713. *See also* specific senses

sensitivity, 72, 99, 107, 140, 156, 345, 348, 357, 369, 380, 397, 587, 667–69, 686, 712, 719
separation, 19, 66, 238–39, 240–41, 248, 259, 311, 319–20, 470, 485, 581, 658–661, 665, 670–71, 678
sephirot, 200, 203–5, 207–9, 223, 235, 242, 244, 248–49, 253–55, 258–59, 261–62
sepia photogravure, 360
sequence. *See* stages
Seraphim of Sarov, 386
Serbia, 381
serenity. *See* peace
Sergiyev Posad, 363
Sermon at Deer Park, 267, 270, 291
Sermon on the Mount, 540
sermons, 265, 296, 363–64, 389, 391, 408
Seroy, Jeff, 483
serpents, 458
service. *See* generosity; social engagement
servitude, 335, 342, 353–55, 361, 390, 403, 532
seṣa, 458
sesshin, 55
setting, 73
seven factors of awakening, 276, 280, 283–84, 287, 289, 297–98, 300, 304–5
seven heavenly virtues, 712
seven heavens, 353
seven realities, 333
Seven Sages of the Bamboo Grove, 108
seven stages of insight, 490
seven stages of purification, 69, 715
Seven Years in Tibet, 633
sexuality, 159, 186, 190, 195, 205, 256–57, 259, 265, 267–68, 378, 381, 405, 414, 458, 471, 559, 565, 578, 583, 650–51, 677, 682, 688, 698
Shaanxi, 411
Shaar Ha-Gamul, 250
Shaar Ha-Gilgulim, 223
Shaar Ha-Kavvanot, 252, 256
Shaar Kevod Ha-Shem, 262
Shaarei Kedusha, 60, 76, 197–264, 707; translation of, 234–64
Shaarei Orah, 258
Shaarei Zedek, 224
Shabbat, 198–200, 262
shadows, 142, 177, 315, 319, 334–35, 341, 348–49, 353–54, 677, 686, 689, 702

Shah Piran, 308
Shahada, 317–18, 350, 353
Shaivism, 59, 77
shaktipat, 324
shamanism, 33, 326, 571
Shamatha Project, 31, 603
Shambhala Guide to Sufism, 328–29
Shambhala International, 657
Shambhala Publications, 568–69, 657, 674, 677
shame. *See* compunction
Shamen bujing wangzhe lun, 411
Shamim Homayun. *See* Homayun, Shamim
Shandao, 411, 419, 421–23, 429, 432–34
Shandong, 568
Shangqing, 58, 111, 131
Shanxi, 550
Shapira, Kalonymous Kalman, 224
Shapiro, Deane, 6
shared humanity, 74, 714–15, 729
shari'a, 311–14, 336–37, 340–41, 343, 347, 354–56
shariat. See *shari'a*
Shattari lineage, 308
Shavuot, 199, 202, 388
shaykh, 307–8, 311–12, 314, 316–18, 321–25, 333, 335, 337–38, 340, 342–48, 350, 354, 357, 707
Shear, Jonathan, 16
shearim, 210
sheep, 175
sheikh. See *shaykh*
shekinah, 235–38, 245, 250–51, 256, 261, 373
Shelun, 419
Shema, 242
Shemoneh Shearim, 201, 203, 216
shen (spirit), 95, 99, 101, 104–6, 109, 111, 122, 126, 132, 135–36, 138, 141, 143, 550, 557–58, 560, 563–64, 571, 581, 584, 587
Sheng Yen, 80
shengren, 93, 110
shenwai shen, 555, 557–59, 561, 564, 580, 588
shepherd, 175–76
Shi jingtu qunyi lun, 434
shikan taza, 9, 18–19, 55, 78, 558
Shikarpuri, Faqirullah, 316, 329
shimush, 241–42
Shin Buddhism. *See* Jōdo Shinshū
shinjin, 423

Shinran, 411–12, 422–23, 432–33
Shinto, 19, 58, 60, 81
shipwreck, 522, 538
shiur koma, 246
Shoah, 711
Shobogenzo, 19
shock, 634, 690
shouyi, 55, 58, 98, 101, 111, 115, 127, 579
shrines, 375, 513, 529, 541, 646
Shuanglin si, 548, 551
Shulhan Arukh, 198–99, 203, 217
shvirat ha-kelim, 203
Siberia, 360, 366, 377, 383
sickness, 21, 42, 137, 200, 260, 263, 266, 283, 311, 317, 378, 397, 401, 403, 405, 438, 463, 467, 477, 518–19, 524, 573, 594, 597, 600–2, 610–11, 615, 629–35, 637, 639, 643, 646, 653, 712, 718–19, 724
siddha, 496
Siddha Yoga, 324, 475
Siddha Yoga Dham Associates, 475
Siddhartha Gotama, 265–71, 279, 284, 291, 296–305, 407–8, 437, 581, 656–57
siddhi, 24, 67–68, 441, 452–53, 467, 472, 493–99, 561, 590, 646, 713
siddhi yoga, 461
sight, 17, 29, 131, 204, 279, 285, 288, 355, 374, 379, 415, 441, 443, 455, 489–90, 496, 715
sign of the cross, 390, 396, 452, 544
signs. *See* benefits; confirmation; effects; transformation; verification
Sikhism, 58, 60
śīla, 69, 267, 712
silence, 4, 6, 9, 16, 25, 32, 37, 54, 62, 66, 101, 114, 146, 152, 154, 156–59, 162, 166–67, 172, 177–82, 187, 189–90, 195, 274, 296–97, 323, 338–39, 342, 352, 354, 374–75, 379–81, 383, 385, 393, 395, 398, 402–3, 461, 469, 511–12, 535, 561, 564, 572, 588, 591–92, 607–9, 633, 638, 641–42, 659–61, 663–65, 668–69, 679, 681, 683–6, 687, 693, 695, 697, 700–1, 705–7, 710–11, 719, 723, 728
silent illumination. *See mozhao*
silent prayer, 145–96, 707. *See also* contemplative prayer
silent worship, 58, 66, 149, 153, 154, 156, 167, 172, 710, 717
Silk Road, 409

Sima Chengzhen, 111, 131
Sima Tan, 94
Simmer-Brown, Judith, 40
Simnani, 'Ala'uddin, 317, 319, 329
simony, 506
simplification, 548, 555, 572–73, 597, 607, 612, 616, 633
simplicity, 101, 105, 132, 141, 146–47, 151–52, 162, 166, 171, 173, 176, 180, 195–96, 379–80, 390, 394, 396, 399, 422, 462, 508, 612, 653, 687, 712
sin, 154, 166, 172–73, 175–76, 183, 187, 191, 195, 211, 235–37, 239, 245–46, 249, 257, 259, 311, 341, 350, 371–73, 385, 388, 393, 396, 398, 400, 403–4, 423, 511, 513, 516–17, 522, 528, 533–34, 544, 611
Sinai. *See* Mount Sinai
Sinai Peninsula, 393, 397
sincerity, 157, 171, 181, 205, 236, 340, 342, 348, 353, 416, 420, 423, 430, 449
Sindh, 459
Sindhu River, 478
sine qua non, 72, 204, 605
sinews, 137
singing, 58, 376, 438, 510, 515, 531
Sinification, 552–54
Single Photon Emission Computed Tomography, 30
single-state fallacy, 326
Sirhind, 313, 328, 333, 342
Sirhindi, Ahmad, 308, 310, 313–16, 318–19, 323–24, 328–30, 333, 336, 339, 341–43, 348–49, 353, 356
Sirhindi-Mujaddidi, Muhammad Zubayr, 308
Sisaket, 292
Sister Cecilia, 79, 503, 538, 540
Sister Leonida, 365
sitting, 6, 37, 54, 79, 96–98, 113, 199, 205, 241, 256, 266, 280, 288–89, 296, 298, 338–39, 354, 393–94, 421–22, 448, 459, 471, 515, 523, 542–43, 558, 571–72, 607–9, 639, 641–42, 688, 693–94, 705, 719, 728
sitting-in-forgetfulness. *See zuowang*
Śiva, 475
Sivananda, 474
Sivananda Yoga Vedanta Centre, 475
six conditions, 352
Six Dynasties (China), 427

six forms of mindfulness, 449
six hallmarks, 365
six perfections, 67, 443, 712. See also *pāramitā*
six phases, 582–83
six schools of Indian philosophy, 457–58, 461–63, 475, 478–79
six steps of relaxation, 607
sixteen contemplations. *See* sixteen visualizations
sixteen objects, 414–15, 418
sixteen stages, 281–83, 285, 290
sixteen visualizations, 409, 414, 418, 425, 441–54
Sixtus II, 538
skepticism. *See* doubt
Skilling, Peter, 269, 273, 291
skillful means. See *upāya*
skills, 65, 112, 141, 271, 290, 396–97, 507
skin, 138, 263, 448
Skinner, B. F., 595, 714
skull, 496
sky, 104, 120, 356, 442, 444, 449, 452, 497, 582, 592, 688
slaughtered animal flesh, 471, 519, 551, 559
Slavia Orthodoxa, 360, 380, 382
slavery, 147, 157, 163, 193, 398, 518, 653, 660–61, 671, 716
Slavonic, 361, 370, 382, 384, 388, 392
Slavonic Library, 362, 383
Slavs, 368
sleep, 143, 180, 210, 238, 241–42, 268, 336, 390, 392–95, 399, 405, 442, 467, 483–84, 486, 513, 519, 535–36, 595, 609–11, 615, 639, 641, 644, 649, 680
sleep derivation, 205
Sloss, Radha Rajagopal, 652
Smart, Ninian, 40
smiling, 440, 588
Smith, Hannah Whittall, 163
Smith, Huston, 14, 326
Smith, J. Z., 40
Smith, T. Allan, 384, 388
Smyrna, 393
snow, 241
sobriety, 551, 559, 572, 583, 654
social constructivism, 671, 674
social engagement, 10, 25, 33, 146–47, 151, 157, 164, 503–8, 512, 519, 544–45, 594, 598, 647, 655, 662, 666, 669, 682, 708, 716–19, 726

social justice, 34, 157, 265, 272, 521, 540, 598, 619–21, 647, 718–19
social location. *See* locatedness
social organization, 7, 17–18, 93–94, 146, 151, 366, 368, 509–10, 597, 645, 647, 649–51, 657, 666, 668, 698, 717
social sciences, 326, 672, 723. *See also* specific fields
social support, 600, 610, 623
socialization. *See* enculturation
Socially Engaged Buddhism, 717
society, 19, 23, 34, 43, 146, 312, 361, 368, 378, 471, 476, 512, 602, 610, 629–30, 637, 640, 643–44, 682, 696, 716–20
Society of Jesus, 6, 8, 57, 80, 156, 325, 384–85, 509
Society of Saint-Sulpice, 148
socius, 524–25
Socrates, 272
Sod Ha-Kedusha, 261
Sogen, Omori, 80
solidarity, 517, 519, 523
solitude, 59, 62, 116, 136, 182, 208–9, 237–39, 241, 251, 273–75, 289, 321, 368, 385, 393–94, 396–98, 401, 461, 464–65, 472, 492, 498, 542, 544, 565, 591, 678, 701, 705, 710, 720
Solomon, 246, 256
soma, 498
Soma Thera, 293
somatic disciplines, 23, 53, 79, 572
somatic nervous system, 26
Son (Christ). *See* Christ
Son Buddhism, 56, 286
Soṇa, 267
Song dynasty, 554, 556
"Song of Cultivating Immortality." *See* "Wu zhenren xiuxian ge"
Song of the Lord. See *Bhagavad Gītā*
soteriology, 6, 17, 19, 21–22, 26, 35–37, 39, 42–43, 53–55, 59–61, 63, 65, 67, 71, 74, 78, 81, 93, 96, 157, 271, 277–78, 291–92, 309, 312, 371, 415, 420, 430, 461, 463–68, 471, 474–78, 559–61, 572, 574, 599, 601, 605–6, 611, 619–21, 648, 656, 706, 708–11, 717, 720, 723, 725–26, 728. *See also* tradition-specific terms
Sōtō lineage, 4, 9, 18, 55, 66, 80, 115, 558

soul, 128, 143, 147, 153, 159, 162, 172–74, 176–81, 183–85, 187, 189–90, 205–6, 222, 238, 240–41, 245, 249–50, 252–53, 255–57, 259–61, 264, 354–55, 369, 372, 374–75, 377, 379, 385, 389, 394, 396, 398, 400, 403, 457, 465–67, 479, 485, 501, 507, 511, 517, 524, 526, 531, 535, 555, 558, 647, 721. *See also* tradition-specific terms
sound, 7, 17, 21, 62, 132, 153, 324, 339, 345, 350, 443, 449, 452, 476, 479, 596, 599, 607, 609, 616, 633, 638, 641–42, 728
source, 93, 94–95, 109, 124, 138, 190, 192, 196, 244, 249–50, 252, 254, 259, 310, 315, 334, 346–47, 357, 392, 393, 465–66, 470, 537, 562, 582, 590, 632, 669, 686–87, 702, 707, 712
source-traditions, 603–4, 622
South Africa, 327
South America, 594. *See also* specific countries
South Asia, 458, 602, 604, 633. *See also* specific countries
Southeast Asia, 273–74, 283, 287, 292, 408. *See also* specific countries
Southern Buddhism, 6, 265–306, 602, 707, 710, 712–13. *See also* Theravāda
Southern School (Chan Buddhism), 553
Southern School (Daoism). *See* Nanzong
Soviet Union, 379
sowing, 181
Spain, 58, 147–48, 201, 213, 234, 503–7, 509–10
sparks, 200, 203, 239
spatiality, 7, 56, 59, 80–81, 114, 154–55, 417, 532, 661, 679, 685–86, 708–9, 716, 727–28
SPECT. *See* Single Photon Emission Computed Tomography
speculation, 403, 657
speech, 133, 235–37, 239–40, 246, 251, 254, 261, 267, 271, 279, 337–38, 354, 374, 376, 390, 394, 414, 483, 515, 518, 520, 523, 537, 541–42, 679–80, 689, 713, 729
spells. *See* incantations
Spencer, Carole, 166
Spencer, Herbert, 632
sphygmomanometer, 631
spine, 397, 560
spirit, 95, 99, 104–6, 126, 132, 135–36, 138, 141, 143, 173–74, 179, 181, 186, 190, 253–54, 310, 330, 341, 348, 355, 390, 398, 401, 521, 550, 558–60, 563–64, 571, 579, 581, 584, 587–88, 591, 650, 717
spirit-writing, 548, 556
spiritual aridity, 151, 158, 160, 174, 179, 180–82, 193
spiritual athleticism, 36, 520, 572, 670
spiritual capitalism, 19, 68, 78, 457, 568, 574, 599, 617, 620–21, 624, 694, 698, 730
spiritual celebrities, 602, 624, 633, 730
spiritual charisma, 330
spiritual classics, 58, 379, 457, 476, 593, 606, 613
spiritual colonialism, 19, 53, 68, 78, 569, 571, 574, 708, 719
spiritual direction, 25, 36, 55, 63–64, 66, 153–54, 156–57, 160–61, 166, 172, 183–84, 187, 192, 195, 269–70, 288, 296–305, 307, 310, 315, 317–18, 322, 343, 347, 359, 364, 370, 377, 379–83, 389–98, 416, 441, 469, 504–5, 512, 515–25, 527, 531–45, 548, 556, 560, 565–66, 569, 571–73, 579, 607–10, 645, 653–54, 656, 707–10, 713, 730
spiritual dryness. *See* spiritual aridity
spiritual exercises, 505. *See also* contemplative practice; specific practices; techniques
Spiritual Exercises. See Exercitia spiritualia
spiritual exhibitionism, 36, 572
spiritual father. *See starets*
spiritual guide. *See shaykh*
Spiritual Guide. See Guía espiritual
Spiritual Homilies, 149
spiritual marketplace, 624, 730
spiritual materialism, 36, 68, 730
spiritual seeking, 598–99
spiritual senses, 81, 263, 374, 400
spirituality, 19, 23, 53, 61, 64, 70, 151, 161–62, 165–66, 311, 360–61, 364, 368, 370–71, 379, 381, 392, 414, 505, 508–9, 511, 525–26, 598, 619, 647–48, 654, 666, 670, 672, 674, 678, 698, 708–10
spirituality as an academic discipline, 13
spontaneity, 93, 99–101, 107, 110, 194, 266, 339, 346, 350, 396, 401, 669–70
sports, 23, 609, 633, 729–30
spouses, 205, 256, 292, 527, 682–83, 689, 691
Spretnak, Charlene, 676
śrāvaka, 449

Sri Lanka, 56, 266, 269–70, 278, 285–86, 288, 291–92, 408, 647–48
śrūti, 268
stability, 100–3, 111, 113–14, 125–26, 128, 132, 135, 184–85, 189, 267, 277, 284, 297, 337, 343–44, 352, 382, 401, 422, 465, 477, 486, 496, 500, 565, 579, 587, 643, 664, 671, 686, 688, 697, 702, 712–13
Stace, Walter, 112–13, 716
stages, 4, 29–31, 38, 57–58, 68–69, 193, 210–11, 237, 265, 271–273, 276–78, 280–90, 296–97, 310–11, 314, 318–19, 329–30, 335–37, 343, 346–49, 357, 374–75, 381, 386, 389, 398–401, 412–15, 418, 420, 440, 450, 452, 467–69, 471, 483–84, 490, 493–94, 527, 547, 550, 554, 560–61, 563–64, 572, 578–92, 593, 596, 601, 607–9, 633, 638–39, 641–42, 647, 695, 709, 712, 714–16, 730. *See also* levels
standardization. *See* systematization
standing, 235, 268, 338, 354, 375, 380, 385, 394, 399, 422, 446, 454, 513, 515, 520–24, 527, 532, 537–41, 608–9, 642, 678, 688, 694, 701
starets, 63, 66, 73, 359–61, 364–67, 369–70, 372, 377, 379, 381–83, 390–96, 399–400, 405, 707
Stark, Marg, 606
starvation. *See* hunger; poverty
stasis, 380
states, 7–8, 10, 16, 21, 23, 25, 37, 55, 65–71, 97, 99, 101, 111–12, 129–30, 136–38, 146–47, 152, 180, 182–84, 187, 195, 210, 223, 235–36, 238, 240, 243, 245–46, 249, 261, 263, 266–67, 273, 279, 282, 284, 290, 301–2, 310, 312, 315, 317, 319, 321, 324, 329, 339, 342, 344, 346, 348, 352, 355, 357, 365, 369, 380, 385, 395, 402, 405, 432, 442, 463, 465–66, 469–70, 471–72, 479, 483–85, 487, 489, 493–94, 501, 527, 540, 562, 569, 571–73, 579, 595, 601–2, 607, 610–12, 615, 631, 636, 638–40, 643, 653, 656, 659, 661, 669–71, 681, 685, 693, 697, 707, 712–13, 715–16, 720, 725–26, 730. *See also* specific states
stations. *See* stages
Stations of the Cross, 730
statuary, 96, 266, 291, 427, 683
stealing. *See* thievery
Steindl-Rast, David, 80
Stephen, Caroline, 163–64

steps. *See* stages
Stewart, Harold, 437
Stewart, Tony, 330
sticks, 518, 534
still, small voice, 172
stilling. *See* calming
stillness, 37, 54–55, 65, 89–90, 94–95, 97, 99–101, 103, 106, 110–14, 121–22, 125, 127, 132–34, 136–38, 140, 142–43, 146–47, 152, 154, 157, 172, 177, 180, 182, 185, 191, 194, 196, 224, 277, 281–83, 287, 298, 301–5, 320, 337, 339, 351, 369, 374–75, 380, 393–94, 398, 415, 427, 433, 463, 465, 467–72, 479, 484, 487–88, 522, 525, 542, 558, 560–61, 565, 572, 607–8, 633, 637–38, 641, 643, 646, 656, 659–61, 664–65, 668, 678–81, 683, 687, 689, 695, 700, 702, 705, 710, 712–13, 715, 728
stools. *See* furniture
storehouse, 499, 580
stories, 100, 140, 202, 266, 271–72, 283, 301, 360, 373, 377, 434, 503–4, 507, 515–16, 522, 531, 541, 544, 588, 591, 600
storms, 162, 192, 196
Stoudios, 393
stream-enterers, 280, 297, 452
stress, 21, 28, 67, 595, 597, 600–2, 607, 609–11, 613, 615, 617–23, 629, 631–33, 636, 640, 644, 709, 719, 724
stress management, 20, 67, 597–98, 600, 602, 607–10, 613, 615, 617–18, 620, 623, 640, 717
stress reduction, 602, 606, 623
Stress Reduction Clinic, 604
stretching, 474
strokes, 615, 629–31, 633–35, 639
struggle. *See* difficulties
students, 90, 93–95, 148, 199, 243, 268, 270, 296, 307–9, 314, 337, 367, 390, 392, 475, 508, 524–25, 553, 566, 605, 646, 651, 653, 682
study, 200, 202, 204, 216, 236, 241, 249, 256, 261, 268, 277, 280, 292, 310, 366, 370, 393–94, 460, 472, 488, 491–92, 505, 509, 511, 523–24, 526–27, 549, 583, 620, 631–32, 646, 653, 668, 672, 719, 723, 726
subject-object distinctions. *See* dualism
subjectivity, 9, 11, 17, 26, 33, 35, 38, 40, 66, 71, 75, 81, 113, 269, 325, 425–31, 470, 479, 553,

subjectivity *(continued)*
  599, 601, 619, 622–23, 638, 643, 673, 706, 713, 720, 726, 729
submission. *See* surrender
subtext, 74–75, 324–25, 368, 570, 598, 603, 619
subtle body, 263, 307, 309, 315–16, 324, 347–49, 496–97, 555, 557, 561, 565, 571–72, 578–92, 648–49
subtle centers, 307, 309, 314–18, 320–22, 325, 330, 333–36, 338, 340–41, 347–50, 355–57, 558, 561
subtle physiology, 496–97, 557, 560–61
subtle tortoise channel, 496
subversiveness, 32, 148, 567, 623, 711, 713, 719
success. *See* attainment
suchness, 100, 277, 454, 561, 684, 687, 698, 710, 715
Sudden School, 553
ṣūf, 309
suffering, 25, 36, 43, 55, 71–72, 151, 157, 161, 180–81, 183, 186, 192, 194, 265, 289, 297, 371, 377, 395, 400, 404, 410–11, 417, 439, 441–44, 448, 451, 454, 463, 465, 470, 477, 486, 488–91, 517, 519, 521, 531–34, 541, 566, 594, 601, 603–4, 610–11, 623, 629–31, 644, 650, 653, 656, 660, 662, 673, 677, 680, 682, 684, 686–87, 689, 691, 693, 699, 702, 712, 717–19, 724
Sufi Heirs of the Prophet, 322, 324–25, 329
sufi lodges, 323, 328
Sufi Meditation and Contemplation, 329
Sufism, 54, 59–60, 68, 81, 166, 198, 205, 208, 224, 244, 307–57, 615, 620, 638, 648, 707, 709, 712, 714–15
suhbat, 317–18, 342
Suhrawardī, Abu Hafs al-, 312
Suhrawardī lineage, 312
suicide, 284, 379, 595
Sukhāvatī, 407, 410–14, 416–18, 420, 425–31, 433, 437, 440–55, 580, 582, 710
Sukhāvatī-vyūha Sūtra, 411–13, 421, 429, 445
Sukkot, 202
Sulam ha-Aliyah, 224–25
sulphur, 545
Sulpicians. *See* Society of Saint-Sulpice
suluk, 333
Suluk-i Mujaddidiyya, 75, 307–57, 707; translation of, 333–57

Sumedho, Ajahn, 286
Summa de vitiis et virtutibus, 531
Summa Theologiae, 512, 520
sun, 189, 191, 196, 248, 392, 414, 418, 420, 441–43, 454, 496, 574, 591, 689
Sun Tingbi, 555, 562, 566, 573
śūnyatā, 112, 410–11, 418, 441–42, 552–53
super-soldiers, 624, 730
supernatural powers. *See* paranormal abilities
supplication, 4, 177, 255, 353, 539, 541
support, 7, 69, 109, 114, 141, 174, 184, 237, 246, 267, 273–74, 277, 280–81, 287, 361, 379, 393–94, 486, 509, 434, 539, 550, 566, 597, 621, 650–51, 653, 668, 715, 729
Śūraṅgama Sūtra, 551, 554, 579, 730
śūraṃgama-samādhi, 415
surgery, 595, 600, 609, 611, 636
surrender, 153, 157, 161–62, 178, 186, 188–91, 193, 235, 245, 309–10, 314, 318, 335, 341, 361, 402, 430, 471, 492, 511, 516–18, 520, 527, 532, 538, 648, 670
survival, 615, 632, 637, 714
survival of the fittest, 21, 601, 632
sustenance, 43
sūtra, 265, 268–69, 271–72, 274–75, 284, 287, 296, 407, 437, 457, 461–62, 473, 555, 585
Sutra on Visualizing the Buddha of Infinite Life. See Guanjing
sutta. *See sūtra*
Sutta-piṭaka, 268, 271, 275
Suzuki, Daisetsu Teitaro (D. T.), 426, 602
Suzuki, Shunryu, 80, 602
Śvetāśvatara Upaniṣad, 459
sweat. *See* vital substances
Sweden, 636
sweeping, 193
Switzerland, 568, 574, 668, 697
sword, 173, 438–39
SYDA. *See* Siddha Yoga Dham Associates
symbol systems, 39, 710, 720–22, 724, 726
symbolism, 61, 63, 73, 374, 376, 428, 431, 478, 521–22, 525, 566, 568, 579, 648, 651, 660, 663, 693, 727–28, 730
Symeon the New Theologian, 369, 372, 374, 386, 392–93, 399–400
Symeon the Studite, 393
sympathetic engagement, 78. *See also* dialogue; thinking through

sympathetic joy, 269, 290, 297–98
sympathetic nervous system, 21, 26–27, 602, 615–16, 637, 639–40, 644
sympathizers, 145, 218, 329, 552, 569, 603, 617, 620, 730
sympathy. *See* compassion
synagogues, 524, 537, 606
syncretism, 25, 226, 409, 428, 548–49, 552, 555–56, 558–59, 562, 568, 572, 579, 582, 647, 723. *See also* crosspollination
Syncretists (Daoism), 92, 107
Syria, 198, 310, 313, 315, 319, 370, 374
systematization, 103, 198–99, 202–3, 276, 281, 291, 310–11, 329, 354, 411, 413, 457–58, 460, 462, 465, 471, 507, 509–10, 550–51, 555–56, 573, 597–98, 607–9
systems, 26, 53, 56, 63

tabarruk, 311
Tabernacle, 261, 518, 728
tablets, 190, 345
taboo of subjectivity, 11, 325
T'ai-chi ch'üan. *See* Taiji quan
Taiji quan, 42, 609
Taima Mandala, 417, 425, 432–33
Taimadera Temple, 433
taiping, 109
Taiping jing, 109
Taiqing, 140, 143
Taishō Canon, 424, 431–32
Taittirīya Upaniṣad, 478
Taiwan, 421
Taiyi jinhua zongzhi. See *Jinhua zongzhi*
Taizé Community, 58, 380
Taizé Prayer, 58
Takakusu Junjirō, 424, 431
Tale of a Pilgrim. See Rasskaz strannika
Taliban, 328, 409
talking. *See* speech
tallit, 239, 241
Talmud, 202, 204, 246, 256, 261
tamas, 467–69, 471, 479, 490, 495
Tambov, 360, 363
Tanakh, 198–99, 204, 220, 372–73, 531
Tang dynasty, 420, 426, 554, 564, 586
Tanjing, 112
Tanluan, 411, 428–29, 434
Tantra, 6, 38, 56, 59, 460, 475, 496, 570, 667, 713

Tantric Buddhism. *See* Vajrayāna
tantric yoga, 461
Tao. *See* Dao
Tao-te ching. *See Daode jing*
Taoism. *See* Daoism
Taoist Tai Chi Society, 570
Taoist Yoga (misnomer), 569, 574. *See also* Daoyin
tariqa, 68, 311–12, 314, 333, 337, 341
Tart, Charles, 23, 326, 330
tasawwuf, 310, 328
tat tvam asi, 716
Tatars, 368
Tathāgata, 413, 439, 441, 445, 449, 561, 566, 581, 586, 589
tathāgata-garbha, 55, 553, 559, 561, 581, 716. *See also* buddha-nature; buddhahood
tathatā, 428
Tattvavaiśāradī, 474
Tauler, Johannes, 148–50, 152, 161, 163, 167
tawajjuh, 321–22, 324, 335–36, 339, 342–43, 345–46, 354–55
tawhid, 353
tax collectors, 373, 385
teachers, 19–20, 30, 62–66, 81, 90, 93–95, 199, 210, 237, 241–42, 245, 251, 268, 270, 287, 296, 307–8, 310–11, 314, 321–22, 335, 370, 376, 381, 396, 414, 416, 420, 440, 452, 462, 474–76, 485, 505, 513, 524–25, 531–32, 548–50, 553, 560, 562, 566, 569, 571–73, 599, 605, 645–46, 648, 651, 654, 659, 663, 670, 674, 681–82, 684, 693–94, 697–98, 707, 709, 713, 716, 730. *See also* elders
teaching, 9, 30, 64, 93, 156, 158, 173, 183, 199, 203, 239, 265, 268–69, 271–72, 274–75, 280, 284–85, 288, 290, 296–305, 318, 323, 350, 353, 374, 381, 390–98, 408, 413, 433, 441, 455, 462–63, 469, 503–5, 509–12, 524–25, 536–37, 541, 550, 560, 565–66, 579, 581, 589, 598, 607–9, 633, 647, 650–55, 657, 666–68, 673, 725
tears, 205, 398, 400, 417, 439, 513, 517, 524, 527, 531, 533, 535, 538, 542
technical terms, 3–4, 40, 54–55, 93, *passim*. *See also* specific terms
techniqueless meditation, 53, 645–702, 710
techniques, 22, 24, 31–34, 36, 54, 60, 62, 65, 72, 78, 80, 98–99, 101, 149, 156, 176–77, 184, 187, 197, 201–2, 204–5, 213–14, 217–18,

techniques *(continued)*
221–23, 225, 239, 271, 287, 289–90, 310, 314, 317–18, 330–31, 336–37, 341–42, 346–47, 369, 374, 380–81, 394–95, 400, 402, 413–15, 418, 431, 442, 454, 459–63, 470, 474–76, 483, 505, 547, 549–50, 557–59, 563–65, 571–72, 578–92, 596, 600, 602–5, 607–12, 615–17, 619–20, 622, 629, 633, 638–43, 645, 656–58, 660, 669–71, 673, 678, 681–82, 685, 688, 694, 700, 707–10, 715, 726
techniques of the heart-mind. *See xinshu*
techniques of the Way. *See daoshu*
technological meditation, 44, 600, 602–3, 718–19
technology, 5, 7, 13, 26, 28, 30–32, 44, 476, 569, 595, 599–603, 610, 613, 619, 631, 635, 682, 692, 709, 718–19, 725. *See also* specific types
tefillin, 240–41
tehom, 203
teleology, 209
telepathy, 68, 403, 439, 495, 713
teleportation, 67
telescopes, 325
Temirtau, 328
temperament. *See* character
Temple (Jerusalem), 158, 196, 199–200, 210, 240, 374, 385, 540
temples, 177–78, 182, 273–74, 280, 286–87, 292, 424, 433, 515, 548–49, 702. *See also* specific temples
temporal lobe, 29–30
temporal lobe epilepsy, 44
temptation, 159–61, 182, 184, 195, 400, 402, 405, 541, 545
ten doubts, 427
ten evil deeds, 454
ten good deeds, 414, 416, 420, 440
ten perfections, 712. *See also pāramitā*
ten stages, 336, 730
Tendai, 19, 422, 424, 433
tension, 5, 267, 519, 527, 611, 615, 622, 641, 644
tents, 395–96
"Tenzo kyōkun," 19
Teresa of Ávila, 8, 38, 58, 79, 160, 163, 615, 620, 638
terminology. *See* technical terms

testimony, 146, 151, 158, 186, 359, 483, 503, 510, 513–14, 517, 525, 531, 538, 544, 615, 622, 666, 708
Testimony of the Darlington Monthly Meeting, 146
Tetragrammaton. *See* YHWH
texts, 12, 14, 17, 40, 60, 72, 73, 75, 89, 120, 145, 171, 197, 234, 241, 265, 269, 274, 296, 307, 324, 326, 333, 359–60, 363–67, 376–78, 388, 392–93, 396–97, 407–9, 411, 457, 488, 491, 503, 507, 515, 523–25, 537, 542, 543, 547–49, 553–56, 561, 596, 606, 629, 638, 645–46, 654–55, 659, 677, 683, 697–98, 707, 711, *passim*
"Texts on Prayer," 393, 399
Thailand, 80, 274, 286, 288, 292–93
thanksgiving. *See* gratitude
The Alms Bowl, 229
The Analogical Imagination, 706
The Art of Happiness, 633
The Artist is Present, 41
The Beattles, 624
The Breakout Principle, 606
The Cloud of Unknowing, 58, 615, 638
The Experience of Meditation, 16, 42
The Future of the Body, 23–24
The Heart of Buddhist Meditation, 286
The Heart of Learning, 10
The Imitation of Christ, 149
The Interior Castle. *See El Castillo Interior*
The Mind/Body Effect, 606
The Pilgrim Continues His Way, 364, 376
The Pilgrim's Tale, 384
The Relaxation Response, 21, 76, 593–644, 709; text of, 629–44
The Sacred and the Profane, 721
"The Seal of the Naqshbandi-Mujaddidi Masters," 322
The Secret of the Golden Flower, 567–68, 578
The Spiritual Training of the Inner Person, 386
The Tale of a Pilgrim. *See Rasskaz strannika*
The Three Pure Land Sutras, 425
The Unselfishness of God and How I Discovered It, 163
The Varieties of Religious Experience, 594
The Way of a Pilgrim, 364, 376, 388. *See also Rasskaz strannika*

The Way of Perfection. See Camino de Perfección
The Way of True Peace and Unity, 167
The Wellness Book, 606
theater, 4, 9, 37, 79
theism, 37, 39, 62, 74, 78. *See also* specific gods; specific types
themes, 73
theodicy, 205
theology, 6, 11, 13–14, 17, 22–23, 25, 32, 35, 37–39, 41, 43–44, 60, 63, 65–66, 68, 71, 81, 94, 147, 149–50, 154, 158, 165–66, 174, 328, 361, 368, 371, 374–76, 384, 399, 425, 458, 462, 469, 476, 505, 508–10, 514, 516, 525–26, 528, 553–54, 568, 594, 606, 611, 621, 642, 647, 656, 710–11, 717, 720–24, 726, 728, 730. *See also* sacred; tradition-specific terms
theology of the body, 44
Theophan the Recluse, 360–61, 370, 384
Theory and Practice of Buddhist Meditation (course), 34
theosis, 372
Theosophical Society, 645, 647–51, 653–54, 656–57, 674
Theosophy (movement), 645, 647–51
theosophy (view), 205–6, 208, 210, 241–42, 247, 254, 647–49, 674
Theotokos, 364
therapeutic meditation, 7, 8–9, 20, 33, 53, 61, 67, 79, 289, 293, 593–644, 672, 709, 718–19, 729–30. *See also* specific types
therapy, 5, 617, 619, 639
Theravāda, 20, 55–57, 69, 78, 269–70, 286, 288, 408, 410, 424, 433, 440, 712, 715. *See also* Southern Buddhism
theurgy, 208, 214, 255
thievery, 175, 240, 267, 377–78, 453, 471, 491, 559, 594
things. *See* objects
thinking. *See* thought
thinking through, 39, 706
third-person discourse, 9, 11, 32–34, 41, 81, 269
thirst, 174, 177, 341, 496, 535, 539–40
thirteen visualizations, 409, 441–49
thirty-seven factors of awakening, 280, 298
thirty-six contemplations, 333
This Light in Oneself, 76, 645–702, 709; text of, 677–702

Thomas à Kempis, 149, 163
Thompson, Evan, 33, 40
Thorndike Memorial Laboratory, 20, 616, 640, 642
thought, 25, 29, 95–96, 100, 125, 127, 152, 154, 177–78, 180, 192, 215, 236, 238, 242, 250, 255, 258, 263, 271, 279, 284, 337, 339, 341, 350, 369, 375, 380, 393, 396, 398, 402, 404, 463–65, 467–69, 479, 487, 491, 495, 518, 541, 590, 638, 641, 653, 656–59, 662, 671–72, 677–79, 683–84, 700, 706, 710, 716, 729
threads, 462, 467
threat. *See* dangers
Three Bodies. *See trikāya*
three characteristics of existence, 36, 55, 276–79, 298, 442–43, 451
three dimensions of Islam, 311, 314
three effects of interior prayer, 401
three elements, 467–68, 489–90, 495
three fetters, 297
three fires, 581
three forms of consciousness, 375
three *guṇa*s, 467
three hand positions, 521
Three Islands, 561
three keys, 369
three kinds of faith, 449
three kinds of transcendent knowledge, 452
"Three Methods of Prayer," 374, 386, 392–93, 399
three modes of intimacy with God, 333
three motivations, 361
three objectives, 647
Three Passes, 560
three poisons, 423, 491
three practices, 336
three pure acts, 414, 417, 440
Three Pure Land Sutras, 407, 411–13, 425, 432, 437
Three Purities. *See* Sanqing
Three Realms, 440, 561
Three Refuges, 273, 287, 414, 440, 444, 453
three signs of purification, 350
three stages, 236–37, 527, 560, 563, 601
Three Teachings. *See sanjiao*
three transformations, 495
Three Treasures, 115, 414, 558, 571
three types of perfections, 333

three ways of knowing, 488
three walking postures, 525, 544
"Three Ways of Prayer." See "Three Methods of Prayer"
three *yoga*s, 475
three-legged stool, 600, 609, 613
throat, 395, 402, 496
throne, 179, 196, 246, 253–55, 259, 261, 316, 333–34, 347, 349, 356–57, 403, 414, 418, 438, 445
thunder, 397, 550
thunder magic. See *leifa*
thyroid gland, 636
Tianshi, 108, 132, 551
Tiantai Buddhism, 286, 419, 422, 551–52, 554, 579
Tiantai mountains, 550
Tianxian jie, 551
Tianxian zhengli, 556, 573
Tibet, 286, 408, 410, 432, 605, 647, 674
Tibet House, 603
Tibetan Book of the Dead. See *Bardo Thodol*
Tibetan Buddhism, 6, 10, 30, 32–34, 36, 55–57, 69, 72, 286, 408, 410, 433, 599, 602–3, 619–20, 622, 633, 674, 717, 729–30
Tikkun Hazot, 199, 202
Tillich, Paul, 40
time, 62, 134, 322, 334, 339, 350, 356, 370, 388, 428, 431, 472, 485, 487, 491–92, 494, 499, 550, 581, 583, 592, 653, 656–57, 659–60, 663, 665, 678, 680, 684, 688, 690–91, 693, 695–96, 700–1, 728
timeframe, 57, 59, 153, 179, 242, 264, 280, 288, 296, 330, 337, 339, 347, 350–51, 354, 357, 370, 390, 393–94, 401–2, 438, 449–51, 509, 517, 519, 534–35, 548, 586, 591, 608–10, 612, 633, 639, 642, 670, 709
Timeless Healing, 606, 611
Timur (Tamerlane), 312
Timurid kingdom, 313
Tịnh Độ, 410
Tipiṭaka, 268–69, 272, 275, 285, 291–92, 408
tiredness, 192, 246, 395, 536, 601, 638
TM™. *See* Transcendental Meditation™
Tobolsk, 374, 377, 401, 403
Tolle, Eckhart, 624
Tolstoy, Lev, 360, 378
Tomer Devorah, 205, 225

tongue, 337–39, 347, 352, 395, 403, 557–58
Torah, 199, 202–3, 207, 211, 220, 225, 234, 236, 240–41, 243, 246, 249, 254–56, 261–62, 388
Toronto, 570
torso, 560, 565, 578, 582, 584
tortoises, 496, 585
Toulouse, 507–9, 522, 526, 538
tourism, 198
Toward a Psychology of Being, 23
towers, 414, 418
Townsend, Kate, 581, 728
traces, 143, 344, 590, 691, 705
Tractate Kallah, 236
Tracy, David, 706, 723
tradition, 3, 6, 12, 14, 16–17, 22, 24–25, 34–35, 37, 43, 53–54, 60–64, 67, 70, 73–78, 80–81, 93–94, 128, 211, 219, 221–22, 267, 269, 284, 368, 408, 462, 471, 476–77, 485, 527, 531, 548, 559, 572–73, 581, 595–97, 600, 602–6, 611, 619–21, 623, 638, 645, 651, 653–54, 656–57, 659–60, 663, 670, 673, 677, 681, 687, 689, 705–13, 716, 719, 725–26, 728–29
traditional medicine, 21
Traditional Modes of Contemplation and Action (conference), 10
traditionalization, 78, 480, 548
Trager Approach, 53, 79
training, 36–37, 61–62, 64, 81–82, 94–95, 98, 114, 136, 147, 245, 272, 287, 296–305, 313, 316, 318, 322–23, 381, 386, 394–95, 402, 413, 470, 488, 507, 548–49, 553–55, 557, 561–64, 573, 595, 598, 607–11, 618, 700–1, 709, 714, 729–30
trains, 315, 383, 596, 661
traits, 99, 101, 138–43, 214, 239, 349, 353–54, 707, 712, 726, 730
trance, 520
tranquility. *See* stillness
transcendence, 39, 339, 385, 425, 428, 431, 469, 471, 508, 547, 553, 571, 594, 638, 647–48, 651, 654, 671, 720–21
Transcendental Meditation™, 8–10, 20–21, 28, 33, 59, 80, 82, 480, 595–96, 599, 602–3, 606–7, 609, 615–16, 619–22, 624, 642–43, 681
transcription, 217, 224, 268–69, 296, 360, 370, 407–9, 507, 549, 645, 653, 655 657, 666–68, 677

transformation, 3, 6, 23–24, 37, 43, 54, 65, 69, 75, 81, 89, 93–96, 99, 112–14, 136–38, 141, 143, 157, 160, 184–85, 188, 191, 194–96, 310–12, 317–18, 323, 327, 330, 348, 356–57, 372, 384, 412, 423, 443–44, 462–63, 467, 494–95, 499–500, 506, 512–13, 517, 521, 524, 527, 554–57, 561, 566, 571–73, 579–80, 589, 591, 610, 624, 644, 650–51, 653, 655–56, 659, 662–64, 666–73, 677, 680, 682, 693, 695, 699, 701, 707, 708–9, 711–19, 724–26, 728–29
Transformation Body, 559, 564, 590
transgression, 211, 451, 453–54
translation, 14, 34, 77, 112, 120, 149–50, 167, 197, 212, 218–23, 234, 296, 323–25, 330, 333, 364, 370, 376, 378–79, 384, 388, 407, 409, 411, 413, 424–25, 431–32, 437, 474, 483, 514, 526, 529, 531, 567–70, 578, 613, 617, 629, 707
translocation. *See* multilocation
transmigration. *See* reincarnation
transmission, 65, 91, 94, 100, 102, 251, 255, 268–69, 272, 275, 285, 292, 307–8, 314, 317, 321–22, 324, 335, 346, 354, 360, 367, 376, 378, 403, 407–9, 411, 413, 432–33, 441, 454–55, 462, 473, 476, 510, 512, 527, 541, 548–50, 552–53, 556–57, 559–62, 566, 568, 579, 581, 586, 589, 598–99, 605, 617, 647, 650, 653–54, 656, 668, 674, 713
transmutation. *See* alchemy; refinement
transpersonal psychology, 13, 22–24, 26, 35, 42–43, 70, 326, 672, 711, 714
Trappists. *See* Order of Trappists
travel, 198, 297, 317, 337, 359, 364–66, 376–78, 390, 396–97, 401, 451, 497, 518, 524–26, 531, 535–37, 544–45, 567, 649, 651, 668, 705
travelogue, 73, 359, 376
Trāyastriṃśa, 443
treasure, 190, 196
Treasury of the True Dharma-Eye. See *Shobogenzo*
Treaty of Verdun, 506
Tree of Life. See *Etz Hayyim*
trees, 267–68, 280, 298, 309, 343–44, 403, 414, 418, 442–44, 446, 449–50, 521, 658, 667, 689
Treis Odai Proseuches. *See* "Three Methods of Prayer"
trials. *See* challenges; difficulties
Trieste, 593
trigger, 32, 44, 69, 595, 597, 608, 632, 712

trikāya, 434, 445, 447, 559, 590
Trinity, 174, 371, 372–74, 508, 516, 532
Trinity Lavra of Saint Sergius, 363
Trinity Sunday, 388
Tripitaka Translation Series, 424–25, 437
Triple Gem. *See* Three Refuges
Trisagion prayers, 395
Troepol'skii, Arsenii, 360, 363, 366–67, 383–84
trophotropic, 7–8, 17, 21, 28, 36, 40, 65, 73, 78
Trostyanskiy, Sergey, 388
Trungpa, Chögyam, 68, 81, 602, 674
trust, 158, 310, 336–37, 352, 377, 411, 442, 513, 527, 535, 599, 613
truthfulness. *See* honesty
Tsong-kha-pa, 57, 730
Tugwell, Simon, 510–11, 514–15, 525, 529, 531
Tummo, 620, 624
Tuolanshan, 96
Turfan, 409
Turkey, 59, 310, 312, 314, 323, 330, 361, 368, 370, 393
Turner, Charles, 326
turning the Dharma Wheel, 559, 585
Tuṣita, 427–28, 430–31
Tweedie, Irena, 329
twenty-five *tattva*s, 464
twenty-six contemplations, 354
twenty-three contemplations, 322
two categories of practice, 414
two meditations, 266
two steps of relaxation, 596, 604, 607, 619
two truths, 426, 428–30
two-handed handclasp, 311
types. *See* cartography; typology
typology, 6–9, 33, 77–78
Tysiacha let russkogo palomnichestva, 383
Tyumen Oblast, 401
tzu-jan. See *ziran*

'Ubaydullah Ahrar, 312
udāna prāṇa, 497
Ukraine, 208, 361, 370, 392
ulama, 311–12, 318
ultimate concern, 39, 63. *See also* sacred
Ultimate Pure Being, 16
ultimate reality. *See* reality; sacred
'Umdat al-suluk, 314
uncarved block. See *pu*

unchurched spirituality, 53, 78. *See also* hybrid spirituality; spirituality
unconditional positive regard, 23, 70, 714
understanding, 110, 153, 159, 165, 172, 176, 209, 212, 221, 244, 254, 260, 289, 341, 354–55, 369, 371, 373, 375, 398, 429–30, 451, 453, 459, 461, 467, 490, 511, 518–19, 523, 566, 569, 595, 597, 654, 669, 672, 680–1, 683, 687, 689, 696, 698, 706, 710, 713
Undifferentiated Essence, 315–16, 322, 329, 336, 341, 347–51, 354, 356
UNESCO World Heritage Sites, 291, 478
Unheimlichkeit, 220
unification. *See* union
unio mystica, 209, 223–24
union, 7, 37, 55, 66, 82, 98, 99–100, 105, 112–13, 128, 130–31, 141, 143, 147, 153, 158, 162, 174, 185, 189, 194–96, 209, 216, 254, 257, 277, 279, 284, 301, 319, 321–22, 351, 371–74, 385, 391, 398, 446, 461, 516, 523, 558, 558–60, 564, 571, 579–81, 590, 592, 594, 647, 650, 710, 712, 728
United States, 28, 30, 75, 164, 286, 433, 474, 478, 480, 568, 593, 598, 602, 605, 613, 630, 636, 647–49, 651, 668, 718–19
United States Department of Defense, 718
United States military, 424, 623–24, 718
unity, 42, 209, 219, 253, 256, 322, 338–39, 353, 355, 357, 374, 393, 516, 580, 592, 594, 647, 657, 659, 668, 671, 688
Universal Brotherhood of Humanity, 647–48
universal salvation, 411, 427
universalism, 19, 166, 491, 596, 599, 604, 606, 615–16, 621, 638, 641–43, 647–48, 673, 714–15, 723
universe, 92, 95, 102–6, 208, 315–17, 334, 347, 410, 425, 443, 496, 522, 558, 565, 571, 647, 668, 688, 720–21, 726. *See also* cosmology
Université de Montréal, 622
universities. *See* academia; specific universities
University of British Columbia, 570
University of Goteborg, 636
University of Helsinki, 362, 383
University of Madras, 645
University of Massachusetts Medical School, 293, 604
University of Michigan, 10

University of Redlands, 10
University of San Diego, 40, 80, 728
University of Virginia, 10
University of Wisconsin, 603
unknowability. *See* apophasis
unlearning. *See* deconditioning
unmediated. *See* immediacy
unsayability. *See* apophasis
unveiling, 351, 355, 357, 390
Upaniṣadic period, 460–61
Upaniṣads, 459–61, 477–79, 485, 657, 667, 716
upanissaya, 273
Upatissa, 57, 281, 285–86
upāya, 424
uposatha, 273, 296–97
Ur-Yoga, 462
Urdu, 307, 315, 321, 333
usnīsa, 565
Uttar Pradesh, 291, 307
Uyghurs, 409, 431
Uzbekistan, 312–13, 323, 328, 336

Vācaspati Miśra, 473–74
Vaidehī, 79, 409, 414, 416–19, 431–32, 438–55, 708
Vaiśeṣika, 461, 479
Vaiśeṣikha Sūtras, 463
Vaiṣṇava, 59, 77, 460, 673
Vajirañāṇa, P. Mahāthera, 278
Vajrayāna, 56
Valencia, 147, 514
Valiant Sixty, 79
validation. *See* confirmation; verification
Valiuddin, Mir, 329
valley spirit. *See gushen*
valleys, 140, 196, 560
values, 34, 41, 72. *See also* commitments; specific values
Varanasi, 291
Varela, Francisco, 33, 603
Vasili, 388
Vasilisk, 366, 383
Vassa, 280
Vasubandhu, 285, 429, 434
Vatican, 81
Vatican Library. *See* Biblioteca Apostolica Vaticana
Vedānta, 460–61, 463, 470, 473–74, 478–79, 654

Vedanta Society, 59, 474
Vedānta Sūtras, 462–63, 473, 478, 480
Vedas, 438, 457–59, 478, 480, 498
Vedic period, 457–60, 476–79
Vedic science, 599, 602
Vedic Yoga, 475
vegetarianism, 471, 551, 559, 654, 729
veils, 197, 220–21, 335, 342, 345, 351, 445
veins, 350
Velichovsky, Paisy, 361, 365, 370, 383–84, 392
veneration. *See* reverence
venia, 517, 525–26
Venice, 225, 370
Ventura, 653
Venuti, Lawrence, 629
verification, 21, 33, 37, 39, 62, 65–66, 177, 381, 393–94, 531, 555, 561, 566, 600, 603, 611–13, 615, 617, 619, 622, 639, 642, 650–51, 657, 713–14, 716
vernacular, 208, 279
verse. *See* poetry
vertebrates, 24
Vespers, 393
vessels, 105, 111, 175, 191–92, 200, 203, 210, 239, 256, 261, 342, 557, 559, 648
vestments. *See* clothing
vexations, 160, 183, 557
vibhūti, 469, 472, 493–98
Vicaire, Marie-Humbert (M. H.), 510–11, 525–26
vices. *See* defilements
Vietnam, 55, 408, 410, 422, 424, 602
view. *See* perception; worldview
viewpoint, 73
vigil, 199, 202, 513
vigilance. *See* dedication
vigor. *See* effort; vitality
Vijñāna, 472, 480, 500
Vijñānabhikṣu, 466, 473–74
villages, 389, 394, 402, 580
Vimalakīrti Sūtra, 112, 425, 553
Vimuttimagga, 56, 276, 281, 286
Vinaya, 267–68, 281, 407–8, 414, 452, 712
Viniyoga, 475
violence, 35, 196, 328, 378, 404, 414, 416, 423, 438–39, 471, 476, 491, 535, 553, 559, 623–24, 632–33, 654, 662, 664, 671, 677, 682–83, 688, 697, 711, 717–19, 723, 729–30

Vipassanā (movement), 8, 36, 55, 80, 286, 605, 609, 615
vipassanā (practice), 6, 8, 10, 20, 28, 36, 55–56, 60, 69, 78, 80, 265–306, 431, 599, 602, 604, 620, 622–23, 638, 715
vipaśyanā. *See vipassanā*
Viradhamma, Ajahn, 286
Virginia, 163
virtual reality, 75
virtue, 67, 131, 162, 172–75, 187–88, 190, 194, 265, 277, 309, 313, 336, 391, 413–14, 417, 438, 440, 452–53, 471, 486, 489, 501, 531, 559, 572, 583, 648, 651, 664, 669, 671, 680, 682–83, 696, 711–12, 729. *See also* ethics
Visākhā, 296
Vishnu-devananda, 475
visibility, 100, 177
visions, 17, 204, 210, 238, 240, 246–48, 250–53, 310, 317, 324, 357, 365, 377, 396, 400, 402–3, 414–16, 418, 432, 439–40, 444, 446, 450, 496, 548, 561, 610, 646, 665, 670, 699, 715
Visions of Compassion, 32–33
visitations, 377, 381, 394, 416, 437, 439–40, 444, 450, 561
Viṣṇu, 458, 673
Viṣṇu Purāṇa, 462
visualization, 6–7, 56, 58–59, 65–66, 73–74, 78, 111, 206, 213, 215, 219, 222, 249, 272, 307–57, 407–55, 608–9, 612, 620, 622, 707–8
Visualization Sutra. *See Guanjing*
visualizing the *shaykh*, 321, 339, 343–45, 347–48, 352
Visuddhimagga, 57, 69, 276, 286, 715
vita apostolica, 508
vita contemplativa, 512
Vitae Fratrum, 513
Vital, Hayyim, 197–227, 234
Vital, Moshe, 201
Vital, Samuel, 201, 203
vital energy. *See qi*
vital essence. *See jing*
vital signs, 631
vital substances, 557–58, 561, 571, 601
vitality, 67, 139, 180, 182, 350, 517, 558, 579–80, 661, 663, 685
viva voce, 510
Vivaraṇa, 474

Vivekānanda, 474, 478, 480, 602
vocal ministry, 156, 710
vocality, 62, 173, 178, 208, 218, 242–43, 247, 250, 254–55, 338–39, 352, 363–65, 371, 375, 390, 396, 402, 405, 413–14, 513, 515, 518, 532–35, 537–39, 542, 596–97, 599, 602, 609, 641
vocation. *See* calling
void. *See* emptiness
volcano, 221, 227
volition, 157, 161, 165, 179, 186, 188, 190, 193, 221, 253, 271, 356, 378, 390, 404, 531, 659, 662–63, 680, 688–89
von Basch, Samuel Siegfried Karl Ritter, 631
Von der wahren Gelassenheit, 161
voracious reading, 75
vows. *See* commitments
vṛtti, 466–67, 469–70
Vulgate Bible, 150, 171, 515
vulnerability, 517, 521, 525, 670
Vulture Peak, 437–39, 455
Vyāsa, 462, 473, 480, 493, 496, 499
Vysha Monastery, 363
Vyshenskaia Hermitage, 360–61

Wabash Center, 40, 80
Wahhabism, 309, 328
waidan, 556–57
waiting. *See* patience
wakefulness, 199, 247, 250, 262, 377, 401
walking, 130, 175–76, 180, 354, 394, 396–97, 401–2, 404, 422, 448, 525, 544–45, 609, 679–80, 727–28, 730
wall-gazing. *See biguan*
Wallace, B. Alan, 31–33, 286, 293, 603
Wallis, Glenn, 285, 293
Walsh, Roger, 23
Walter Reed Army Medical Center, 718
Wancheng, 555, 562
wandering, 176, 178, 186, 266, 365, 378, 385–86, 388–89, 396–97, 494, 580, 641
Wang Bi, 91, 108
Wang Changyue, 550–51, 573
Wang Tai, 100
war, 178, 182, 184, 194, 196, 312, 368, 393, 395, 458, 476, 519, 522, 682, 687, 717–19
warmth, 236, 351, 365–66, 372, 377, 396–97, 400–2, 586, 594, 620

Warring States (period), 100
Warrior Mind Training, 624
warriors. *See* caste; military; violence
Watanabe Kaigyoku, 431
watchfulness. *See* attention; observation
watchmen, 377
water, 99, 105, 111, 124, 140, 177, 190, 249–50, 254–55, 257, 259, 278–79, 282, 301, 317, 346, 414, 418, 441–44, 449, 468, 493, 497, 508, 535, 557, 592, 683, 689, 695, 714
Waterwheel, 557, 582
Watts, Alan, 602
way, 177, 180, 391
Way. *See* Dao
Way of Heaven, 135
way of immortality, 550
Way of Tranquility and Adaptation, 100
Way of Wisdom and Life-Destiny, 548, 566, 589
wayfarers, 310, 316, 335, 337–38, 340–41, 345–47, 350, 357
wayfaring, 307, 315, 318–20, 324, 333, 335–36, 343, 347, 355, 357
wealth, 20, 235, 378, 423, 458, 506, 508, 557, 594, 612, 620, 643, 651, 680, 683, 730
weaponization, 624, 718, 730
weather, 404
websites, 166, 323, 597, 668
weeping. *See* tears
weightlessness, 403
Weimo, 549
Weismann, Itzchak, 329
wellness, 21, 23, 34, 70, 237, 272, 283–84, 289, 471, 475–76, 517, 599–600, 602–3, 606, 609–11, 618, 629, 638, 643, 706, 709, 724
wellspring. *See* source
Wesleyan University, 594
Western Esotericism, 480, 568, 574, 648
Western Pure Land. *See* Sukhāvatī
Western religions (misnomer). *See* specific traditions
Westport, 519
wet method, 277
What the Buddha Taught, 288
wheels, 396, 443, 582–83
whip, 518–19
whirling, 60
Whirling Dervishes. *See* Mevlevi lineage
White Cloud Monastery, 551
white coat syndrome, 621

Whittier, John Greenleaf, 163
Wilber, Ken, 16, 19, 23, 70, 326–27, 330, 672
Wilcher, Marilyn, 598
wilderness, 544
Wilhelm, Helmut, 574
Wilhelm, Richard, 567–70, 574–75, 578
will. *See* volition
William Morrow, 593, 613, 629
wind, 192, 222, 453
windows, 191
wine, 508. *See also* alcohol
wired for God, 606
Wisconsin, 622
wisdom, 3, 36, 53, 56, 67, 90, 98, 107, 112, 121, 133, 143, 173, 176–77, 183, 194–95, 235–37, 241, 255, 265–67, 271, 284, 286, 290, 300–2, 304, 315, 334, 366, 376, 380, 382, 390–91, 398–99, 404, 410, 418, 427, 430, 437–38, 448, 453, 467, 487–89, 501, 521, 523, 537, 548, 553, 555, 557, 578–81, 585, 592, 615, 638, 642, 647, 670, 712, 729
wisdom poetry, 90, 102, 106
wisdom traditions, 16, 19, 327, 621, 674
withdrawal. *See* disengagement
withered wood, 142, 553, 565
witnessing. *See muraqaba*; testimony
Wolfson, Elliot, 235, 261
womb, 448, 553, 565, 581
womb of Buddhahood. *See tathāgata-garbha*
women, 30, 35, 58, 79, 114, 136, 146–48, 268–69, 271, 289, 292, 296, 378, 381, 404–5, 409, 416–19, 438–55, 503, 505, 509–10, 513–14, 526, 532, 541, 551, 558, 569, 574, 579, 651, 708, 726. *See also* specific women
Wong, Eva, 569–70, 574–75, 578
Wonhyo, 421–23
wood, 142, 297, 395, 553, 565
wood-block printing, 566
Woodbrooke, 163
wooden stick, 518, 534
woods. *See* forests
woodworking, 281, 381
wool, 309, 385, 394
Woolman, John, 156–57
Word (Christ). *See* Logos
work, 175, 267, 343, 345, 377, 382, 390, 393–94, 396, 403, 507, 511, 586, 594, 598, 610, 612, 632, 644, 680, 682, 717. *See also* livelihood

workshops, 610, 654
world, 25, 66, 105, 135, 172, 178–79, 192, 203–4, 217, 239, 241, 250, 283–84, 289, 316, 318, 330, 334–35, 340, 344, 349, 351, 354, 369, 371, 400, 403, 410, 412, 460, 463–67, 474, 476, 483–84, 487, 488, 500, 507, 544, 592, 638, 644, 655, 661, 663–64, 669, 694, 698, 706–8, 713, 717, 720–21, 726, 728
World-Honored One. *See* Buddha
world of action, 259
world of command, 315–19, 330, 333–35, 347–49, 356–57
world of creation, 259, 316, 319–20, 333–34, 347, 356
world of formation, 259
world of sovereignty, 315, 338, 347
world religions, 58, 76, 78
World to Come. *See Olam Ha-Bah*
World Teacher, 648–51, 674, 693
World War I, 568
World War II, 651, 653, 717
World's Parliament of Religions, 478, 599
worldview, 10, 16–17, 20, 22, 34, 36, 38–40, 53–54, 61, 67, 69, 74, 79–80, 90, 113, 222, 267, 271, 293, 427, 458, 461, 474–78, 551, 552, 565, 571–72, 599, 603, 606–8, 611–12, 617, 619, 644, 647–48, 656, 672, 707–8, 710, 715–16, 720–23, 726, 730. *See also* doctrine
worms, 234, 650
Worobec, Christine, 383
worship, 4, 146, 153, 158, 171–72, 190, 309, 318, 337, 341, 351, 370, 374, 427, 438–39, 444, 450–51, 455, 470, 472, 476, 508, 519–20, 638, 641, 646, 685, 694
Wu Lizhai, 549
Wu Shouxu, 550, 556, 567, 573
Wu Shouyang, 64, 66, 548–51, 554–56, 567, 573–74, 578
Wu Taiyi, 550
Wu Xide, 549
"Wu zhenren xiuxian ge," 556, 573
Wu-Liu lineage, 547–51, 554–56, 559–60, 562, 567–68, 572, 575, 578
Wu-Liu xianzong, 555–56, 562, 567, 578
wudū', 309, 336–38
Wuliang shoufo, 409, 437. *See also* Amitābha
Wuliang shoufo jing, 412
Wuliangshou jing youpotishe yuansheng, 434

wulou, 557, 578
wuwei, 95, 99, 101, 104, 107–8, 110, 113, 128, 132–33
wuxing, 103, 105, 110, 580
wuyao, 419
Wynne, Alexander, 271

Xi'an, 411
Xianfo hezong yulu, 556, 573
Xiang Xiu, 108
Xiangji si, 411
xianren. *See* immortals
xiantai, 553, 555, 557–61, 563–64, 580, 586–87
xiaoyao you, 96, 100
xin (heart-mind), 71–72, 93, 95, 121, 125, 130–32, 142, 553, 557, 563–65, 579, 592
xing (innate nature), 89, 95, 110, 121–22, 132, 134, 141, 556, 561, 565, 573, 579–81
xingming, 556, 565, 579–81
Xingming fajue mingzhi, 567
Xingming guizhi, 567
Xinjiang, 323, 329, 409
xinshu, 90, 94–95, 132
Xinshu shang, 89–90, 98, 102, 104, 106–7, 109, 120; translation of, 131–32, 136
Xinshu xia, 100
xinzhai, 55, 58, 98, 101, 111, 114, 130, 553
Xipai, 563
Xisheng jing, 111
xuanpin, 105, 111
Xuanxue, 91–92, 108
Xunzi, 91
Xuzhou Museum, 96

Yadin, Azzan, 219
yakṣa, 455
Yam Shel Hokhma, 226
yama, 470–71, 491, 712
Yāma Heaven, 445–46
Yamada Meiji, 409
Yan Hui, 99, 106, 130–31
yang-spirit. *See yangshen*
yangshen, 66, 555, 557–59, 564, 580, 588–89
Yangsheng, 42, 110, 567
yantra, 287
Yearley, Lee, 112–13
Yellow Emperor, 115

Yellow River, 92
YHWH, 39, 204, 240–41, 244, 250, 255, 258, 372, 710, 721
Yijing, 568
Yin Xi, 111
Yin Yoga, 574
yin-yang, 103, 107, 110, 120, 123–24, 135, 137, 141
Yinfu jing, 109, 135
yinshi, 93, 100–1, 106, 112, 114, 129, 140
yoga (discipline), 6, 55, 59, 457–501, 569–70, 574, 641, 667, 674, 688, 694, 713. *See also* American Yoga; classical Yoga
"Yoga and Meditation East and West," 574
Yoga Aphorisms. *See Yoga Sūtras*
Yoga Journal, 480
Yoga Nidra, 20, 623, 718
Yoga school, 457–58, 461–63, 468, 473. *See also* classical Yoga
Yoga Sūtras, 59, 65–67, 71, 73, 76, 457–501, 708, 713; translation of, 483–501
Yogācāra, 293, 419, 434, 480, 500
Yogalehrbuch, 285
Yogamaṇiprabhā, 474
Yogānanda. *See* Paramahansa Yogānanda
Yogavārttika, 474
yogī, 459–61, 469, 471–72, 477–80, 485, 490–91, 493, 495, 498–99, 641
yogic stasis. *See samādhi*
Yom Kippur, 385
Yonkers, 593
Your Maximum Mind, 606
yuanfen, 565
Yuktidīpikā, 467
yulu, 111, 553, 566
Yunnan, 549

zaddik, 211, 246–47, 260, 262
Zaikonospasskii Monastery, 366
Zangwai daoshu, 548, 551, 556, 562, 573, 578
Zawwar Husayn, 314
zazen, 8, 36–37, 55, 60, 80, 552, 599, 603, 609, 615, 620
"Zazen-gi," 18, 80
zeal. *See* enthusiasm
zealotry. *See* fanaticism
Zen Buddhism, 4, 9, 18–19, 30, 36–37, 41, 55–56, 66, 77–78, 80, 115, 210, 286, 410,

424, 426, 430, 433, 597, 599, 602–3, 607, 615, 620, 633, 717
zendō, 55
zeruf otiot, 234
Zhang Jingxu, 549
Zhang Lu, 108
Zhang-Li-Cao, 550
Zhanran Huizhenzi, 567
Zhao Bichen, 567
Zhao Zhensong, 550
Zhao Zhixin, 550, 556
Zhejiang, 550, 562
zhengyan, 555, 561, 714
Zhengyi, 551
zhenren, 93, 110, 143
zhiren, 93, 110
Zhiyi, 286, 419
Zhong-Lü, 554
Zhongji jie, 551
Zhongjie an, 555, 562
Zhongli Quan, 554
zhoutian, 557, 560

Zhu Changchun, 550
Zhu Youjian, 550
Zhuang Zhou. *See* Zhuangzi
Zhuangzi (person), 92, 96, 106, 140–41
Zhuangzi (text), 18, 56, 76, 89, 91, 93–94, 97–100, 102–3, 106–13, 116, 120, 553; translation of, 123–24, 129–31, 136, 140–41, 574, 661
zikr. See *dhikr*
zimzum, 200, 203
Zionism, 226
ziran, 99–101, 110, 123, 128, 715
Zohar, 200–1, 204, 206, 210–11, 216, 219, 223, 225, 240, 244, 250, 259
Zosima, 383
Zuishang yisheng huiming jing. See *Huiming jing*
Zujajat al-masabih, 307
zuochan, 55, 552, 456, 558–59
zuowang, 55, 58, 97–99, 101, 111, 131, 553
Zuowang lun, 111
Zurich, 568
Zwei Abhandlungen über die Naqšbandiyya, 330